The Four Imams and their Schools

ABŪ ḤANĪFA | MĀLIK | AL-SHĀFIʿĪ | AḤMAD

سير الأئمة الأربعة المأثورة

The Four Imams and their Schools

ABŪ ḤANĪFA | MĀLIK | AL-SHĀFIʿĪ | AḤMAD

by

Gibril Fouad Haddad

Foreword by
Sayyid Yusuf Hashim al-Rifaʿi

INSTITUTE FOR SPIRITUAL & CULTURAL ADVANCEMENT

THE FOUR IMAMS AND THEIR SCHOOLS
Abu Hanifa, Malik, al-Shafi'i, Ahmad

Cover design by author. Cover photo: Depiction of the Kaaba surrounded by the tents of the Four Sunni Schools of Law from *Dalā'il al-Khayrāt* (a compilation of blessings on the Prophet Muhammad for each day of the week) by Muhammad b. Sulaymān al-Jazūlī (d. 870/1465). Manuscript Arca Artium RB 231 from mid-18th-c. Kashmir. Source: Virtual Hill Museum & Manuscript Library https://www.vhmml.org/

Text design by Abdallateef Whiteman.

Reprint: Institute for Spiritual & Cultural Advancement, Fenton, MI (USA)
First edition: Muslim Academic Trust, UK

Published in the US by Institute for Spiritual & Cultural Advancement
17195 Silver Parkway #401, Fenton, MI 48430 USA
Tel: (810) 593-1222
Email: info@sufilive.com
Web: http://www.sufilive.com
Purchase online at: http://www.isn1.net

ISBN: 978-1-930409-19-4

Cataloging-in-Publication Data

Haddad, Gibril Fouad, 1960-

The Four Imams and Their Schools: Abu Hanifa, Malik, al-Shafi'i, Ahmad.
Foreword by Sayyid Yusuf Sayyid Hashim al-Rifa'i (1932-2018).
560 p. + xxiv p. 23 cm.
1. Islamic law -- History. 2. Sunnites -- Biographies. 3. Islam -- Doctrines. I. Author. II. Title.

وصلَّى الله على النبيِّ الأُمِّيِّ سيِّدنا محمَّدٍ وآله وصحبه وسلَّم

الإهداء

إلى أُمّي الكريمة وإلى أستاذي إمام الوقت مولانا

الشيخ محمد ناظم عادل الحقَّاني القبرصي

حفظه الله تعالى ونفعنا به والمسلمين آمين

وإلى أرواح أئمَّة السلف الصالح ومقلِّديهم إلى يوم الدين.

This book is humbly dedicated to my dear Mother and to my Teacher, the Imām of our time, Mawlānā al-Shaykh Muḥammad Nāẓim 'Ādil al-Ḥaqqānī al-Qubruṣī as well as the pious Imāms of the Salaf and those who imitate them until the Day of Resurrection.

يَـٰٓأَيُّهَا ٱلَّذِينَ ءَامَنُوٓا۟ أَطِيعُوا۟ ٱللَّهَ وَأَطِيعُوا۟ ٱلرَّسُولَ وَأُو۟لِى ٱلْأَمْرِ مِنكُمْ ۖ

﴾O you who believe! Obey Allāh, and obey the Messenger and those of you who are in authority﴿ (4:59).

فَسْـَٔلُوٓا۟ أَهْلَ ٱلذِّكْرِ إِن كُنتُمْ لَا تَعْلَمُونَ

﴾Question the People of the Remembrance if you know not﴿ (16:43, 21:7).

قُلْ هَلْ يَسْتَوِى ٱلَّذِينَ يَعْلَمُونَ وَٱلَّذِينَ لَا يَعْلَمُونَ ۗ إِنَّمَا يَتَذَكَّرُ أُو۟لُوا۟ ٱلْأَلْبَـٰبِ

﴾Are those who know equal with those who know not? But only people of understanding will pay heed﴿ (39:9).

عَنْ جَابِرٍ ﷺ قَالَ رَسُولُ اللهِ صَلَّى اللَّهُ عَلَيْهِ وَسَلَّمَ أَلَا سَأَلُوا إِذْ لَمْ يَعْلَمُوا فَإِنَّمَا شِفَاءُ الْعِيِّ السُّؤَالُ د جه مي حم

Ḥadīth of the Prophet ﷺ: "Could they not ask if they knew not? The only cure for ignorance is to ask!"[1]

"If the Companions made ablution to the wrists I swear I would have done the same, even as I read the verse of ablution as stating ﴿**to the elbows**﴾ (5:6)."

(Ibrāhīm al-Nakha'ī)

وَمَالِكٌ وَسَائِرُ الأَئِمَّــــةِ كَذَا أَبُو الْقَاسِمِ هُدَاةُ الأُمَّةِ

فَوَاجِبٌ تَقْلِيدُ حِبْرٍ مِنْهُمُ كَذَا حَكَى الْقَوْمُ بِلَفْظٍ يُفْهَمُ

(جوهرة التوحيد)

"Mālik and the rest of the Imāms [of *fiqh*], similarly Abū al-Qāsim [al-Junayd and the rest of the Imāms of *taṣawwuf*] are the guides of this Umma. Therefore the imitation (*taqlīd*) of one of those authorities [in each of the two fields] is obligatory. This was stated by the [learned] Folk in unmistakable terms."

(Al-Laqānī, *Jawharat al-Tawḥīd*)

[1] Narrated from Jābir by Abū Dāwūd, Ibn Mājah, al-Dārimī, and Aḥmad.

SELECTIVE TEACHER–STUDENT LINEAGE OF THE EARLY IMĀMS OF SUNNA ﷺ

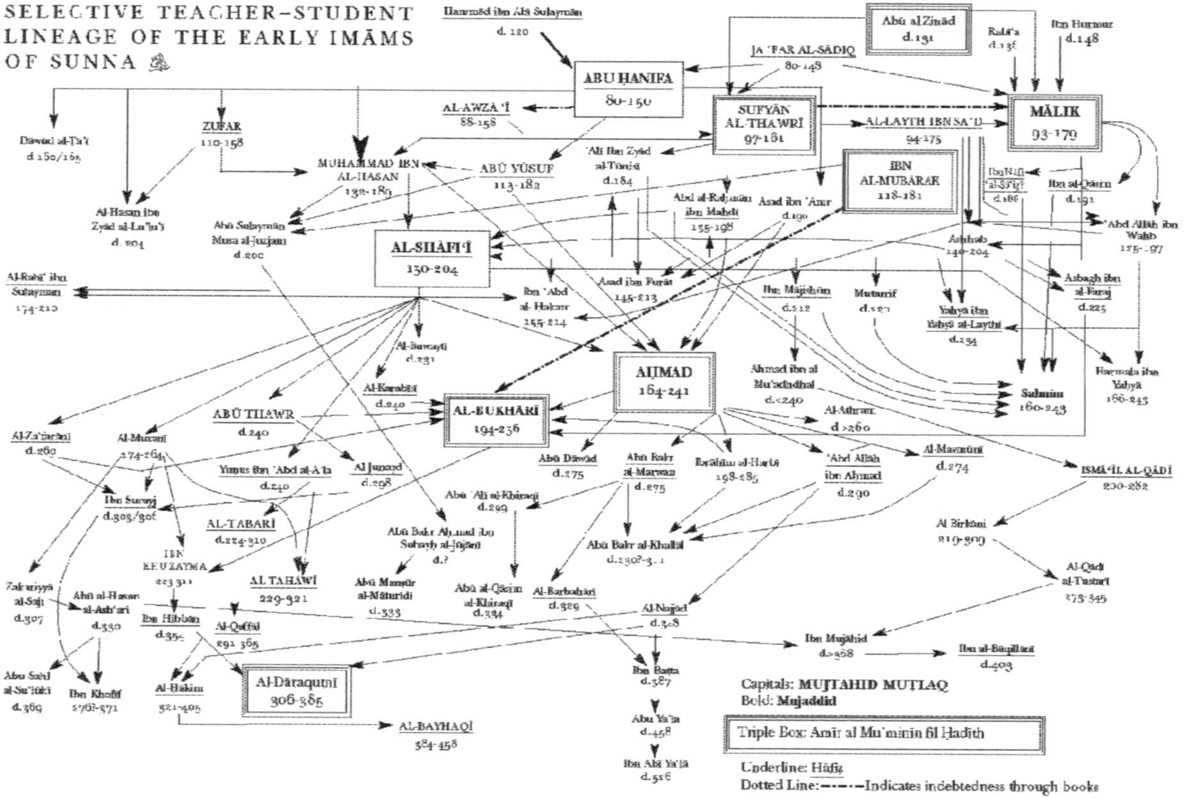

CONTENTS

Dedication III
Epigraphs V
Teacher-Student Lineage of the Early Imāms VIII
Contents IX

AUTHOR'S PREFATORY NOTES

Chains of transmission – Main sources – Dates – Websites XV
Abbreviations XIX
Commendation by Sayyid Yūsuf Hāshim al-Rifā'ī:
English Translation XXII
Arabic Text XXIV

PREFACE 1

ABŪ ḤANĪFA AL-NU'MĀN ﷺ
The Prophet's ﷺ Allusion to Imām Abū Ḥanīfa 7
Abū Ḥanīfa is the Only *Tābi'ī* Among the Four Imāms 8
His Authorities and Disciples in Ḥadīth 9
His Trustworthy Rank in Ḥadīth Narration 10
His *Musnad* 10
Abū Ḥanīfa's Major Early Colleagues 10-26
Abū Yūsuf–Muḥammad–Zufar–Dāwūd al-Ṭā'ī–Al-Ṭaḥāwī
Abū Ḥanīfa Innovated the Sub-Headings of *Fiqh* 26
Sufyān al-Thawrī's Awe before Abū Ḥanīfa 28
Ibn Jurayj's Praise of Abū Ḥanīfa 28
Ibn al-Mubārak's Praise and Vindication of Abū Ḥanīfa 28
Ibn 'Ā'isha's Vindication of Abū Ḥanīfa 29

Imām Mālik's Praise of Abū Ḥanīfa 29-30
Yaḥyā ibn Sa'īd al-Qaṭṭān's *Taqlīd* of Abū Ḥanīfa 30
Al-Shāfi'ī's Praise of Abū Ḥanīfa's Leadership in *Fiqh* 30
Al-Faḍl ibn Dukayn's Praise of Abū Ḥanīfa 31
Al-Dhahabī's Praise of Abū Ḥanīfa 31
Abū Ḥanīfa on Imitation (*Taqlīd*) 31-32
His Scrupulous Godwariness and Generosity 32
Trials of the Imām 33
His Incessant Worship and Nickname of "Pillar" 33-34
Some Positions of Abū Ḥanīfa 34-40
His Inference of the Time of *'Aṣr* from the Parable of the Communities 31
On Facing the Prophet's ﷺ Grave During *Du'ā'* 33
His Supposed Objection to *Tawassul* (Using Intermediaries) 34
The Cancellation of Ablution by Laughter 36
Abū Ḥanīfa's Definition of Sunnism 41
His Praise of Ja'far al-Ṣādiq 41
His Definition of Belief (*Īmān*) 41-42
The Sunnī *Irjā'* of Abū Ḥanīfa and His School 42-44
"*Īmān* neither increases nor decreases" 44-45
The Differentiation between *Islām* and *Īmān* 45-47
Ibn Ḥajar's Commentary on al-Bukhārī's Chapter-Title and Narration of the Ḥadīth of *Īmān* and *Islām* 48-51
Abū Ḥanīfa on the Prophet's ﷺ Parents in Paradise 51-64
His Precedence in Dialectic Theology (*Kalām*) 65
Encounters with the *Khawārij* 66
Encounter with the *Qadariyya* 67
The Early Ḥanafī Imāms Entered *Kalām* Disputations 67
Abū Ḥanīfa's Works in *Kalām* 67-76
The Letter to 'Uthmān al-Battī 69-74
The Aim of those who Deny the Existence of Sunni *Kalām* 76-77
The First *Mutakallim* is 'Alī ibn Abī Ṭālib ﷺ 77
The Involvement of the *Mujtahid* Imāms in *Kalām* 77-78
Imām Abū Manṣūr al-Māturīdī 79-84
Some of Abū Ḥanīfa's Great Contemporaries 84-114
Al-Ḥasan al-Baṣrī–Ja'far al-Ṣādiq–Al-Awzā'ī–Sufyān al-Thawrī–Ibn al-Mubārak

The Use of Weak Ḥadīths in Issues of Morals 114-116
Abū Ḥanīfa's Foresight 116-117
Sayings of Abū Ḥanīfa 117-119
Insignificance of this World in Comparison to the Hereafter 117
Ḥadīth Without *Fiqh* 118
Respect with the *Salaf* 118
God-Fearing Scrupulousness in Giving Fatwā 118
Life-Stories of the Learned and Pious 118
Who are the *Awliyā*? 118
Thirst for Leadership 119
Forbearance 119
Understanding Priorities 119
His Sense of Humour 119

MĀLIK IBN ANAS ﷺ

The Prophet's ﷺ Prediction of Imām Mālik 121-23
Abū Ḥanīfa's Praise of Mālik 123
Mālik's Reliance on Abū Ḥanīfa 123
The *Muwaṭṭa'* 124
Mālik's Authorities in the *Muwaṭṭa'* 125
Mālik's Severity in Verifying Ḥadīth Transmittors 125-26
The Unreliability of the Righteous 126-134
Ad Sensum (*riwāya bil-ma'nā*) vs. *ad Litteram* (*bil-lafẓ*) 134-139
Mālik's Alleged Criticism of Ibn Isḥāq 140-142
The *Muwaṭṭa'* is All *Ṣaḥīḥ* Except for Four Narrations 143-145
The Narrators of the *Muwaṭṭa'* from Mālik 145-146
Major Disciples of Mālik 146-153
Ibn Nāfi'–Ibn al-Qāsim–Ibn Wahb–Ashhab–Ibn al-Mājishūn–Asad ibn al-Furāt–Ibn 'Abd al-Ḥakam–Muṭarrif–Aṣbagh–Suḥnūn
The "Practice of Madīna" 154-155
The Seven Jurists of Madīna 155
The "Epistle on the *'Amal* of the People of Madīna" 156-157
The Spurious "Epistle to al-Rashīd" 158
Sadl of the Hands in *Ṣalāt* 158
Mālik's Standing as an Imām of the Sunna 158-159
His Trial at the Hand of al-Manṣūr 159-160

His Self-Imposed Seclusion 160
His Manners and Ethics 161
His Gravitas (*Hayba*) 162
His Preference for *'Arḍ* in Ḥadīth Transmission 162
His Staunch Defense of *Madhhab* Differences 162-166
Sayings of Mālik 166-182
Pious Simple Living 166
Regress in History 166
Istiwā' 167
"Descent" of Allāh Most High 153
A Weak Report Attributing Location to Allāh Most High 169-170
On Those Who Attribute Organs to Allāh Most High 170
Religious Disputation 170-171
On Wisdom being *Fiqh* and a Light 171
Naiveness a Virtue of Paradise 171-175
The Precedence of Meanings Over Wordings 175
On the Sunna Being the Ark of Salvation 175
On the *Rāfiḍī Shī'a* 175
To Say "I Do Not Know" Is Part of Knowledge 176
On Praiseworthy *Kalām* 176
Belief Increases and Consists in Speech and Deeds 176-177
On *Tabarruk* (Seeking Blessings Through Relics) 177
On Shaving the Moustache Being an Innovation 177
On the Necessity of the Turban for Learned Muslims 178-179
The Inappropriateness of Asking One's Age 179
On the Priority of *Fiqh* over *Taṣawwuf* 179
On the Necessity of Combining *Fiqh* with *Taṣawwuf* 179-181
On the Vision of Allāh ﷻ in the Hereafter 181
On *Tawassul* (Using An Intermediary) 181-182
Mālikī Fatwā Textbooks and Terminology 182-183
Mālik's Biographers 183

AL-SHĀFI'Ī ﵀

Al-Shāfi'ī is from the House of the Prophet ﷺ 185-186
Prophetic Ḥadīths Alluding to Imām al-Shāfi'ī 186-188
Al-Shāfi'ī's Early Years 189
His Early Prowess 189-190

Studies with Mālik and Muḥammad al-Shaybānī 190
The Yemeni *Fitna* and Hārūn al-Rashīd 190-191
His Defense of Mālik 191-192
His Study of the Ḥanafī *Madhhab* 192
His Move Away from Mālik's *Madhhab* 193
His Preference of al-Layth to Mālik 193
The Epistle (*al-Risāla*) 193
Ibn Mahdī 193-195
His *Taqlīd* of the Companions and Successors 195
Dates of His Trips to Baghdād and Move to Egypt 195
Al-Shāfi'ī Reconciled the Schools of Ḥadīth and *Fiqh* 196
Most Ḥadīth Masters Follow the Shāfi'ī School 196
Ibn Ḥanbal and Yaḥyā al-Qaṭṭān's Praise of al-Shāfi'ī 196-197
The Superiority of *Fiqh* over Ḥadīth 197-205
  Ḥadīth Misguides Those Devoid of *Fiqh* 198-200
  The Imāms of Ḥadīth Defer to the Imāms of *Fiqh* 200
  Knowledge is not Memorization but a Light 201
  The Ḥadīth of the Jurists is Preferable to That of the Non-Jurists 201-202
  Knowing the Ḥadīth is Different From Practicing It 202
  Understanding the Ḥadīth is Superior to Knowing It 202-23
  Most Ḥadīth Scholars Do Not Possess Intelligence of the Ḥadīth 204
  Not Every Sound Hadīth Forms Evidence 204-205
Al-Shāfi'ī's *Tawassul* Through Abū Ḥanīfa at His Grave 205-206
His *Tabarruk* With Aḥmad ibn Ḥanbal's Shirt 206
Al-Shāfi'ī's "Old" and "New" Schools 206-214
  Al-Buwayṭī–Al-Muzanī–Al-Rabī'–Al-Za'farānī–Al-Karabīsī–
  Abū Thawr–Yūnus ibn 'Abd al-A'lā
The *Basmala* in the Shāfi'ī School 214
Touch Nullifies Ablution in the Shāfi'ī School 215
Al-Shāfi'ī's Unique Mastery of the Arabic Language 216
Interpretation (*Ta'wīl*) *vs.* Committal of Meaning (*Tafwīḍ*) 216-217
Al-Ḥumaydī's *'Aqīda* 217-219
Al-Shāfi'ī and Dialectic Theology (*Kalām*) 220
Definition of the Principles of the Religion (*Uṣūl al-Dīn*) 220
His Acknowledgment of Sunnī *Kalām* 220-222
Al-Shāfi'ī Possessed Full Mastery of *Kalām* 222-224
The Uncreatedness of the Qur'ān 224

Three Books Falsely Attributed to the Imām 224
"If the Ḥadīth is Authentic, that is my *Madhhab*" 225-226
The Ḥanafī position on *taqlīd* 226
The Ḥanbalī position on *taqlīd* 227-229
Al-Shāfi'ī and *Taṣawwuf* 229-230
Al-Shāfi'ī's Division of *Bid'a* into "Good" and "Bad" 231-233
His Emphasis on Love of the Prophet ﷺ and His Family 233-234
Aphorisms of al-Shāfi'ī 235-243
On the Masters of ḥadīth 235
Learn *fiqh* before you lead others 235
'Actions count only according to intentions' 235
Early signs of merit in children 235
The two most emphasized sunna prayers 235-237
Disbelief coexists with disbelief 238
Islām is *īmān*... 237
... But *īmān* increases and decreases 237
Wise study is better than *dhikr* and *nafl* 238-239
Poverty and servanthood are prerequisites to learning 240
Reason is experience 240
Irremediable matters 240
Self-discipline 240-241
Never swear oaths 241
Choosing one's residence carefully 241
Choosing one's companions carefully 241
The perils of wealth 242
Self-knowledge inures against calumny 242
Prayer behind innovators 242-243
Every book is flawed except the Qur'ān 243
Accepting the Ḥadīth is not optional 243
His Assiduous Recitation of the Qur'ān 243-244
His External Appearance 244-245
Later Figures Connected to the Shāfi'ī School 245-299
Dāwūd al-Ẓāhirī–Al-Junayd–Ibn Surayj–Al-Ṭabarī–
Ibn Khuzayma–Ibn Ḥibbān–Al-Qaffāl–Al-Dāraquṭnī–
Al-Ḥākim–Al-Bayhaqī–Qāḍī Ḥusayn
Biographies of al-Shāfi'ī 299-300

AḤMAD IBN ḤANBAL ﷺ
Imām Aḥmad's Foremost Teachers in Ḥadīth 301-302
His Teachers in *Fiqh*: al-Shāfi'ī and the Ḥanafī Imāms 302-303
His Foremost Leadership in Ḥadīth Memorization 303
An Authority in Ḥadīth Rather than *Fiqh*? 303-305
His Flight from Authorship in Jurisprudence 305
His Godfearing Modesty and Self-Deprecation 306
His Stringent Criterion for *Ijtihād* 306
The Danger of Misusing Ḥadīth 306
Advice to Would-Be Writers 306-307
The Admiration of His Contemporaries for Him 307
His Insistence on Written Records in Ḥadīth Narration 307
Works Related from the Imām 308-310
The Persecution (*al-Miḥna*) 310-313
His *Taraḥḥum* of Abū Ḥanīfa Under the Whip 313
His Respect for Difference of Opinion 313-314
Some of the Imām's Contemporaries and Colleagues 314-357
Bishr al-Ḥāfī–Ibn al-Madīnī–Ibn Sallām–Ibn Abī Shayba–Ibn Rāhūyāh–Al-Bukhārī–Are the two *Ṣaḥīḥs* 100% *ṣaḥīḥ*?–Al-Athram–Al-Marwazī–Abū Dāwūd–Al-Tustarī–Al-Ḥarbī–'Abd Allāh ibn Aḥmad ibn Ḥanbal
Later Figures Connected to the Ḥanbalī School 358-363
Al-Khallāl–Al-Barbahārī–Al-Najjād–Ibn Baṭṭa–Ibn Abī Ya'lā and his father
Imām Aḥmad and *Kalām* Theology 363-365
Ibn 'Asākir's *Fatwā* on *Kalām* 365-366
Ibn al-Subkī's *Fatwā* on *Kalām* 366
Al-Shāṭibī's *Fatwā* on *Kalām* 366
Al-Qushayrī's *Fatwā* on *Kalām* 366-368
Abū Zahra's and Other *Fatwās* on *Kalām* 368-370
Aḥmad's Positions in *Kalām*: On *Istiwā'* 370
On Allāh Not Possessing a Limit (*Ḥadd*) 370-374
Examples of Aḥmad's *Ta'wīl* in the Attributes 374-378
Aḥmad Ibn Ḥanbal's *'Aqīda* and Pseudo-Ḥanbalī *'Aqīda* 379
A contemporary example of this difference 380-383

Aḥmad and al-Ḥārith al-Muḥāsibī 383-386
Imām Aḥmad's *Taṣawwuf* and Fond Love of Ṣūfīs 386-389
Aḥmad Recommended *Tawassul* in Every *Du'ā'* 389
Aḥmad Practiced *Tabarruk* or Blessing from Relics 390-392
His Marriages 392
His Turban and Dress 392-393
A Reply to Ibn Abī al-Dunyā 393
On *Tahajjud* for the Student of Knowledge 393-394
His Prohibition of Cursing Yazīd ibn Mu'āwiya 394-395
On the Term *Ummat Muḥammad* ﷺ 395
On Obligatory Imitation (*Taqlīd*) in the Religion 395-398
Those Who Are Imitated in Islām (*al-Muqalladūn*) 398-403
Those Who Wrote Imām Aḥmad's Biography 403
From the *Reliance of the Traveller* 403-404
His Meeting with the Prophet ﷺ in Dream 404
A *Ṣiddīq* 404
Major Figures of the Late *Madhhab* 405-408
Salient Fatwās of Imām Aḥmad and his School 408-412
- Desirability of visiting the Prophet ﷺ in Madīna 408
- Desirability of seeking blessing from the Prophet ﷺ and the saints 408-409
- *Takbīr* upon terminating recitation of the Qur'ān 409
- Obligatoriness of praying *Ẓuhr* after *Jumu'a* 409
- Desirability of pronouncing intention before all acts of worship 410
- *Tarāwīḥ* prayer is twenty *rak'as* 410
- Instructing the dead following burial 410-411
- Reciting the Qur'ān over the graves 411-412

APPENDICES

The Controversy over the Pronunciation of the Qur'ān 413
The Titles *Shaykh al-Islām, Muḥaddith, 'Ālim, Amīr al-Mu'minīn fil-Ḥadīth,* and *Ahl al-Ḥadīth* 427
A Concise Sunni Glossary of *Fiqh,* Ḥadīth, *Kalām,* and *Taṣawwuf* 446

INDICES

Chains of Transmission for the Citations in This Book

After rendering glory, praise, and thanks to Allāh together with blessings and fragrant greetings of peace upon the Imām of the Godwary People of God: The weak slave who hopes for the forgiveness of his Lord, the author, Gibrīl Fouād Ḥaddād, was honored with added connection and lineage in faith, in the form of unbroken narrative links, to the eminent works cited in this book beginning with its main sources cited below. I narrate these works by permission (*ijāza*) from the Inheritors of the Prophet ﷺ blessed with the lights of both communal and special Friendship as well as the nobility of narration and Ḥadīth Science. These Teachers include the blessed recipient and chronicler of the *asānīd* of the senior Masters of transmission East and West in our time, Shaykh Muḥammad ibn al-Sayyid Ibrāhīm al-Ya'qūbī; the chronicler of the Damascene heritage, Shaykh Muḥammad Muṭī' al-Ḥāfiẓ; the vast recipient of the senior Masters East and West, Shaykh Muḥammad Taysīr al-Makhzūmī; Shaykh Ḥusayn Aḥmad 'Usayrān al-Ṣaydāwī – all of the above among the Shaykhs of Syro-Palestine; then the late Shaykh al-Islām of *Ahl al-Sunna* in the two Sanctuaries, Shaykh Muḥammad ibn al-Sayyid 'Alawī al-Mālikī; and the noble spokesman of *Ahl al-Sunna* and the People of *Taṣawwuf*, Shaykh Yūsuf ibn al-Sayyid Hāshim al-Rifā'ī.

Main Sources

The main sources used for this work are the encyclopedia of *ṭabaqāt* or synchronic biographies *Ḥilyat al-Awliyā' wa-Ṭabaqāt al-Aṣfiyā'* ("Adornment of the Saints and Biographical Layers of the Pure") by the Ḥadīth Master and Ṣūfī historian of Aṣbahān **Abū Nu'aym**; *Tahdhīb al-Asmā' wal-Lughāt* ("Emendation of the Names and Terms") by the arch-Saint and Master of Damascus, Muḥyī al-Dīn Yaḥyā ibn Sharaf **al-Nawawī**; *Siyar A'lām al-Nubalā'* ("Lives of the Eminent Nobility") and *Tadhkirat al-Ḥuffāẓ* ("Memorial of the Ḥadīth Masters") both peerless works of synchronic biography by the foremost Damascene Master of Ḥadīth and its sciences, Shams al-Dīn **al-Dhahabī**; his student, Qāḍī al-Quḍāt, Shaykh al-Islām Tāj al-Dīn **Ibn**

al-Subkī's masterpiece of Ḥadīth science, history, synchronic biography, heresiography, and literature, *Ṭabaqāt al-Shāfi'iyya al-Kubrā* ("Major Biographical Layers of the Shāfi'īs"); the Mālikī Ḥadīth Master **Ibn 'Abd al-Barr**'s *al-Intiqā' fī Faḍā'il al-A'immat al-Thalāthat al-Fuqahā'* ("Merits of the Three Jurist Imāms"); the paramount historian and Master of the Ḥadīth sciences **al-Khaṭīb** al-Baghdādī's *Tārīkh Baghdād* ("History of Baghdād"); and the works of the absolute Imām in Ḥadīth, immaculate Shaykh al-Islām, and *Ḥāfiẓ* par excellence, **Ibn Ḥajar** al-'Asqalānī.

Dates and Websites

Dates in the text and footnotes are usually Hijrī while publication dates in the bibliography are usually Gregorian. Not all the material on the websites cited in this book is necessarily endorsed or approved by the author.

Abbreviations

'Abd al-Razzāq = His *Muṣannaf* in Ḥabīb al-Raḥmān al-A'ẓamī's 11-volume edition.
Abū Dāwūd = His *Sunan.*
Abū Ya'lā = His *Musnad.*
Aḥmad = His *Musnad* in Shu'ayb al-Arna'ūṭ's 50-volume edition.
Al-Bazzār = His *Musnad.*
Bidāya = Ibn Kathīr's *al-Bidāya wal-Nihāya* in the Dār al-Ma'ārif edition.
Al-Bukhārī = His *Ṣaḥīḥ.*
Al-Dārimī = His *Sunan* in al-Ghamrī's 10-vol. edition *Fatḥ al-Mannān.*
Al-Dhahabī's *Siyar* = His *Siyar A'lām al-Nubalā'* in the 19-volume Dār al-Fikr edition unless otherwise stated.
Fatḥ, Fatḥ al-Bārī = By Ibn Ḥajar in the 13-volume 'Abd al-Bāqī edition.
Al-Ḥākim = His *Mustadrak* in the original 4-volume Hyderabad edition.
Al-Haythamī = His *Majma' al-Zawā'id* in the 10-volume edition.
Ibn Abī Shayba = His *Muṣannaf* in Kamāl al-Ḥūt's 7-volume edition.
Ibn 'Asākir = His *Tārīkh Dimashq* in the 70-volume Dār al-Fikr edition.
Ibn Ḥibbān = His *Ṣaḥīḥ* in al-Arna'ūṭ's 18-volume Risāla edition.
Ibn Mājah = His *Sunan.*
Ibn Sa'd = His *Ṭabaqāt al-Kubrā* in the 8-volume Dār Ṣādir edition.
Iṣāba = Ibn Ḥajar's *al-Iṣāba fī Tamyīz al-Ṣaḥāba* in the 8-volume edition.
Kanz = Al-Hindī's *Kanz al-'Ummāl.*
Muslim = His *Ṣaḥīḥ.*
Al-Nasā'ī = His ("Minor") *Sunan* (*al-Mujtabā*).
Al-Tirmidhī = His *Sunan.*

الرموز

ت	سنن الترمذي
حب	صحيح ابن حبان
حل	حلية الأولياء لأبي نعيم
جه	سنن ابن ماجه
حم	مسند أحمد
خ	صحيح البخاري
خت	التاريخ الكبير للبخاري
خط	تاريخ الخطيب
د	سنن أبي داود
ز	مسند البزار
ش	مصنف ابن أبي شيبة
ض	الأحاديث المختارة للضياء المقدسي
ط	مسند أبي داود الطيالسي
طأ	الموطأ
طب طس طص	المعجم الكبير والأوسط والصغير للطبراني
ع	مسند أبي يعلى
عد	الكامل في الضعفاء ابن عدي
عق	مصنف عبد الرزاق
ق	ما اتفق عليه الشيخان
قط	سنن الدارقطني
كنز	كنز العمال للمتقي الهندي
ك	مستدرك الحاكم
م	صحيح مسلم
مج	مجمع الزوائد للهيثمي
مي	سنن الدارمي
ن	سنن النسائي الصغرى (المجتبى)
هب	شعب الإيمان للبيهقي
هق	السنن الكبرى للبيهقي

Commendation by al-Sayyid Yūsuf Hāshim al-Rifāʿī

Founder and principal, al-Imān Sharīʿa School, Kuwait
World spiritual leader of the Rifāʿī Ṣūfī path founded by his ancestor
President, World Union of Islamic Propagation and Information
Author of books on contemporary issues, law, and history
Former State Minister of the State of Kuwait

IN THE NAME OF ALLĀH ALL-BENEFICENT MOST MERCIFUL

We praise and thank Him and we greet his noble Messenger and his Family and Companions! To proceed:

The dear brother, teacher, accomplished researcher and writer, Gibrīl Ḥaddād, who was born in Lebanon, emigrated to the United States where he accepted Islām, and presently resides in Damascus, who follows the Shāfiʿī *Madhhab* and the Naqshbandī *Ṭarīqa*, has asked me to write a few lines on this book of his entitled *The Lives and Works of the Four Imāms.* I welcomed his request and gladly responded as the author has taken great care to clarify the following topics in his book:

1 – The importance and precedence of **the *Fiqh* and comprehension of the noble Ḥadīth** over and above its mere transmission, narration, and memorization.

2 – The highlighting of simple living and **sufism in the life of Imām Aḥmad ibn Ḥanbal** – Allāh be well-pleased with him – together with his love and profound respect for the great Ṣūfī Friends of God in his time and those of their disciples and students that attended his gatherings.

3 – He demonstrated, without leaving any room for doubt, the difference and distinction between what is meant by the forbidden type of theology (*kalām*) in the terminology of the early Ulema of *Ahl al-Sunna wal-Jamāʿa* – namely the discourse of the *Muʿtazila*, the *Qadariyya*, the *Jabriyya*, and their likes – and what is meant by **the Sunni science of *kalām* which is intimately synonymous with the science of monotheism** (*ʿilm al-tawḥīd*) and that of the fundamental principles of the Religion (*uṣūl al-dīn*). None of the foremost references among the books of *Ahl al-Sunna wal-Jamāʿa* is devoid of this [latter type of Sunnī *Kalām*], beginning with the Imāms of our righteous Predecessors among the *Ahl al-Ḥadīth*, the Ashʿarīs, and the Māturīdīs.

4 – The highlighting and affirmation of the **tolerance, generosity of spirit, and acceptance of divergent opinion** that characterized our Predecessors among the Four Imāms – Allāh Most High be well-pleased with them. Such ethics must be our model and the standard followed by the contemporary generations of Muslim missionaries and students of the noble Knowledge.

5 – Drawing attention to the **division of innovation** (*bid'a*) **given by Imām al-Shāfi'ī between good and bad** (*ḥasana wa-sayyi'a*), a division followed after him by the Scholars of his School such as al-'Izz ibn 'Abd al-Salām, al-Nawawī, Ibn Ḥajar al-'Asqalānī, then the remainder of the Ulema of the other Schools who accepted this division except for the odd man out.

There is no doubt that these important matters which the author addressed – may Allāh Most High reward him amply – are among the imperative needs and the basic fundamentals of our time and the time to come. This is especially true for both immigrant and new Muslims in the West who lack the reliable and trustworthy references in such Law-related issues. For we now witness much arrogance from semi-Ulema militant in summoning people to "free and rid themselves" of the Schools of the *Salaf* and discard their consummate Jurisprudence, which this mercy-bearing Muslim *Umma* has long since endorsed, generation after generation!

I ask Allāh Most High that He cause this effort to benefit all and grant its author and publisher thanks and reward. May Allāh grant the author success – since he excels in both Arabic and English – in translating it and publishing it in Arabic so that its usefulness will be complete and reach all Muslims East and West. Allāh hears supplication and is able over all things! And may Allāh send blessings and greetings of peace upon our Master Muḥammad and his Family and Companions.

Written by the mortal hand of
Yūsuf ibn al-Sayyid Hāshim ibn al-Sayyid Aḥmad al-Rifā'ī al-Ḥusaynī

Allāh Most High forgive him!
Mizza, Damascus
26 Jumādā al-Ākhira 1423
3 September 2002

تقريظ

فضيلة الشيخ السيد يوسف بن السيد هاشم الرفاعي

بسم الله الرحمن الرحيم

نحمده ونصلّي ونسلّم على رسوله الكريم وآله وصحبه

وبعد: -

فقد رغب إليَّ الأخ الكريم الأستاذ البحّاثة المحقق المصنّف جبريل حداد اللبناني ولادة، الأمريكي مهجراً وإسلاماً، الشامي الدمشقي إقامة، الشافعي مذهباً، النقشبندي خرقةً، أن أكتب له سطوراً قليلة بحق كتابه هذا الموسوم (سِيَر الأئمّة الأربعة المأثورة) فاستجبت لذلك مرحِّباً ومسروراً. حيث أن المصنّف حرص في كتابه هذا على توضيح ما يلي:

١- أهمية وأولية (فقه ومفهوم الحديث الشريف) على مجرّد نقله وروايته وتحمّله المحض؛

٢- إبراز جانب الزهد والتصوّف في حياة الإمام أحمد بن حنبل رضي الله تعالى عنه، ومودّته وإجلاله لكبار من الأولياء الصوفية في زمانه ولمن كان يحضر مجلسه من مريديهم وتلاميذهم؛

٣- أبرز وأوضح جلياً الفرق والتباين بين المقصود بعلم الكلام المنهي عنه عند المتقدمين من أهل السنّة والجماعة (وهو كلام المعتزلة والقدرية والجبرية وأمثالهم) وبين (علم الكلام السّنّي) المرادف والملتصق (بعلم التوحيد) و(علم أصول الدين) الذي لا يخلو منه أمهات مراجع كتب أهل السنّة والجماعة ابتداءً بأئمّة السلف الصالح من أهل الحديث والأشاعرة والماتريديّة؛

٤- إبراز وإثبات السماحة وسعة الصدر وتقبل رأي المخالف الذي كان عليه سلفنا من الأئمّة الأربعة رضوان الله تعالى عليهم، مما يجب أن يكون أسوة وقدوة للأجيال المعاصرين من الدعاة وطلبة العلم الشريف؛

٥- لفت النظر إلى تقسيم البدعة لدى الإمام الشافعي إلى (حسنة وسيئة) وتبعه عليه رجال مذهبه كالعز بن عبد السلام والنووي وابن حجر العسقلاني ومن ثم شاركهم في ذلك بقية رجال المذاهب الثلاثة المعتمدة إلا من قل وانفرد.

ولا شك أن هذه الأمور الهامة التي تطرق إليها المصنف، جزاه الله تعالى خيراً، من ضروريات وأساسيات زماننا هذا وما بعده، خصوصاً للذين يعيشون من المسلمين في المهجر والمسلمين الجدد في الغرب، الذين يفتقدون المصادر المعتمدة الموثوقة في هذا المجال من العلوم الشرعية في زمان كثر فيه تطاول أنصاف العلماء وزاد فيه خوضهم في الدعوة للتحرر والانفلات والانسلاخ من مذاهب السلف وفقههم العتيد الذي ارتضته الأمة المسلمة المرحومة خلفاً عن سلف.

أسأل الله تعالى أن ينفع بهذا الجهد المشكور المأجور مؤلّفه وناشره وأن يوفّق الله تعالى المؤلف الذي يجيد اللغتين (العربية والانجليزية) لترجمته ونشره بالعربية لتكمل فائدته ويعم نفعه المسلمين جميعاً في المشرق والمغرب، إنّه تعالى سميع الدعاء وعلى كل شيء قدير.

وصلّى الله تعالى على سيّدنا محمّد وآله وصحبه وسلّم.

وكتبه بيده الفانية

يوسف بن السيد هاشم بن السيد أحمد الرفاعي الحسيني

عفى الله تعالى عنه

في مزّة دمشق، ٢٦ جمادى الآخرة ١٤٢٣، الموافق ٣-٩-٢٠٠٢

بِسْمِ ٱللَّهِ ٱلرَّحْمَٰنِ ٱلرَّحِيمِ

﴾In the Name of Allāh All-Beneficent Most Merciful﴿

Praise, glory, and thanks belong to Allāh Most High Whose blessings cannot be encompassed! Blessings and salutations of peace upon His Beloved Messenger and greatest Mercy, our Master Muḥammad ﷺ, and upon his Family and Companions! Of the immense kindness of our Lord – after Faith – is the love and following of those He has greatly favored with the Inheritance of the Holy Prophet ﷺ: the learning that saves here and hereafter. Allāh extols them in His Book:

إِنَّمَا يَخْشَى ٱللَّهَ مِنْ عِبَادِهِ ٱلْعُلَمَٰٓؤُا۟

﴾**The erudite alone among His bondsmen fear Allāh**﴿ (35:28),

وَٱلرَّٰسِخُونَ فِى ٱلْعِلْمِ يَقُولُونَ ءَامَنَّا بِهِۦ كُلٌّ مِّنْ عِندِ
رَبِّنَا ۗ وَمَا يَذَّكَّرُ إِلَّآ أُو۟لُوا۟ ٱلْأَلْبَٰبِ

﴾**And those who are of sound instruction say: We believe therein; the whole is from our Lord; but only men of understanding really heed**﴿ (3:7),

وَإِذَا قِيلَ ٱنشُزُوا۟ فَٱنشُزُوا۟ يَرْفَعِ ٱللَّهُ ٱلَّذِينَ ءَامَنُوا۟
مِنكُمْ وَٱلَّذِينَ أُوتُوا۟ ٱلْعِلْمَ دَرَجَٰتٍ ۚ وَٱللَّهُ بِمَا تَعْمَلُونَ خَبِيرٌ

﴾**Allāh will exalt those who believe among you, and those who have knowledge, to high ranks; Allāh is informed of what you do**﴿ (58:11).

At the forefront of those Divinely-supported guiding stars and arks of safety are the men and women Allāh Most High chose as Companions for His perfected Beloved, followed, in his own words ﷺ, by those who kept company with them, then the next generation. Among them rose figures of exceptional learning, piety, and intelligence who codified the Science of Life and Death every human being needs: correct belief, pristine worship, and upright living, known as a whole by the word Religion. This corpus of living knowledge both derives from and elucidates the Qur'ān; the Sunna of the Prophet ﷺ

is its second foundation; all as transmitted and explained by his *Ṣaḥāba* to the *Tābiʿīn.* Thus rose the *Madhāhib* or "Paths" – the noble Schools of Law.

By the Divine will, four of these Schools have crossed the centuries as the Muslims' *qibla* of apprenticeship in the way of pleasing their Lord, just as the four walls of the magnificent Kaʿba form the *qibla* of their adoration of Him and the four Rightly-Guided Caliphs – Allāh be pleased with them! – were the *qibla* of their loyalty as the citizens of His kingdom on earth.

The reward of the founders of the four *Madhāhib* is incalculable. By throwing open the gates of salvation and clearing its ways they gave birth to us – as does every teacher of the *Dīn* – in the "world without end." This book is a drop in the ocean of thanks owed our spiritual parents – as Imām al-Nawawī called them. Through it the readers may learn more about our magnificent Predecessors. May it renew our spiritual and intellectual lineage with them, with the Last Prophet ﷺ, and with the All-Cherishing, Most Generous God.

May Allāh forgive the mistakes of this book and garland with its acceptance the names of His Friends in the hearts of His English-speaking seekers.

وَٱلَّذِينَ جَآءُو مِنۢ بَعۡدِهِمۡ يَقُولُونَ رَبَّنَا ٱغۡفِرۡ لَنَا
وَلِإِخۡوَٰنِنَا ٱلَّذِينَ سَبَقُونَا بِٱلۡإِيمَٰنِ وَلَا تَجۡعَلۡ فِي قُلُوبِنَا
غِلّٗا لِّلَّذِينَ ءَامَنُواْ رَبَّنَآ إِنَّكَ رَءُوفٞ رَّحِيمٌ

﴿**And those who came into the faith after them say: Our Lord! Forgive us and our brethren who were before us in the faith, and place not in our hearts any rancour toward those who believe. Our Lord! You are Full of Pity, Merciful**﴾ (59:10).

Damascus, 27 Dhūl-Qiʿda 1423 / 30 January 2003

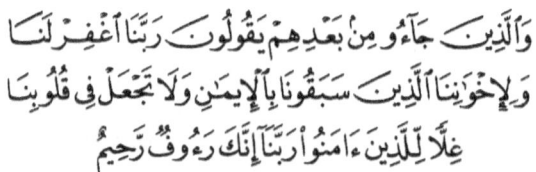

The Four Imāms and their Schools

ABŪ ḤANĪFA | MĀLIK | AL-SHĀFI'Ī | AḤMAD

ABŪ ḤANĪFA AL-NUʿMĀN [2]

Allāh Be Well-Pleased with Him

AL-NUʿMĀN IBN THĀBIT ibn Kāwūs ibn Hurmuz ibn Marzubān al-Taymī, al-Imām Abū Ḥanīfa (80-150), called "the True *Faqīh*" by Mālik, "the Imām" by Abū Dāwūd, *Faqīh al-Milla* by al-Dhahabī, and "the Imām, one of those who have reached the sky" by Ibn Ḥajar, the first of the four *mujtahid* Imāms whose School survived to our time and acquired the greatest following among the Sunnī Schools, is known in the Community as "The Greatest Imām" (*al-Imām al-aʿẓam*). Abū Muʿāwiya al-Ḍarīr – the trustworthy ḥadīth Master Muḥammad ibn Khāzim al-Taymī al-Saʿdī al-Kūfī (d. 195) – said: "Love of Abū Ḥanīfa is part of the Sunna."

The Prophet's Allusion to Abū Ḥanīfa

Imām al-Kawtharī said that the Imām is generally considered an Iraqi of Persian origin.[3] Al-Qārī[4] said Abū Ḥanīfa – said to be a descendent of Sāsān, the Persian king – is foretold by the Prophet in the ḥadīth: "Were belief (*al-īmān*) to be found at the Pleiades, a man from those people (pointing to Salmān al-Fārisī) would go there to obtain it."[5] Another version states: "Were knowledge (*al-ʿilm*) hanging at the Pleiades, people – or: a man – from Persia would go there to obtain it."[6] Hence Abū Hurayra used to pay special attention to the Persians and say to them: "Draw near, Banū Farrūkh! For if knowledge were hanging at the Pleiades, there would be, among you, one/

---

[2] Main sources: al-Khaṭīb, *Tārīkh Baghdād* (13:324-356); al-Dhahabī, *Manāqib Abī Ḥanīfa* (p. 22-36) and *Tadhkirat al-Ḥuffāẓ* (1:168); Ibn Ḥajar, *Tahdhīb al-Tahdhīb* (10:450); Ibn Kathīr, *Bidāya* (10:114); al-Suyūṭī, *Tabyīḍ al-Ṣaḥīfa* (p. 94-95); al-Haytamī, *al-Khayrāt al-Ḥisān*; al-Ṣāliḥī, *ʿUqūd al-Jumān*.

[3] Al-Kawtharī, *Iḥqāq al-Ḥaqq* (p. 39).

[4] In *Sharḥ ʿAyn al-ʿIlm* (1874 ed. 1:36).

[5] Narrated from Abū Hurayra by al-Bukhārī, Muslim, and al-Tirmidhī.

[6] Narrated from Abū Hurayra by Aḥmad with good chains through Shahr ibn Ḥawshab cf. al-Haythamī (10:64) and al-Dhahabī, *Tadhkirat al-Ḥuffāẓ* (3:972) and *Siyar* (Risāla ed. 10:210, 14:11); Ibn al-Ghiṭrīf (d. 377) in his *Juzʾ* (p. 99 §57); Abū Nuʿaym in the *Ḥilya* (1985 ed. 6:64); Ibn Ḥibbān (16:299 §7309); al-Bayhaqī in *Shuʿab al-Īmān* (4:342 §5330); and in *Aḥādīth al-Shāmūkhī* (d. 443) (p. 23 §3). Ibn Ḥazm in *al-Iḥkām*

those who would take it."[7] Another version states "the Religion" (*al-dīn*).[8]

عَنْ أَبِي هُرَيْرَةَ رَضِيَ اللَّهُ عَنْهُ قَالَ كُنَّا جُلُوسًا عِنْدَ النَّبِيِّ صَلَّى اللَّهُ عَلَيْهِ
وَسَلَّمَ فَأُنْزِلَتْ عَلَيْهِ سُورَةُ الْجُمُعَةِ وَآخَرِينَ مِنْهُمْ لَمَّا يَلْحَقُوا بِهِمْ قَالَ قُلْتُ مَنْ
هُمْ يَا رَسُولَ اللَّهِ فَلَمْ يُرَاجِعْهُ حَتَّى سَأَلَ ثَلَاثًا وَفِينَا سَلْمَانُ الْفَارِسِيُّ وَضَعَ
رَسُولُ اللَّهِ صَلَّى اللَّهُ عَلَيْهِ وَسَلَّمَ يَدَهُ عَلَى سَلْمَانَ ثُمَّ قَالَ لَوْ كَانَ الْإِيمَانُ
عِنْدَ الثُّرَيَّا لَنَالَهُ رِجَالٌ أَوْ رَجُلٌ مِنْ هَؤُلَاءِ ق وَعَنْ أَبِي هُرَيْرَةَ رَضِيَ اللَّهُ عَنْهُ
قَالَ قَالَ رَسُولُ اللَّهِ صَلَّى اللَّهُ عَلَيْهِ وَسَلَّمَ لَوْ كَانَ الدِّينُ عِنْدَ الثُّرَيَّا لَذَهَبَ
بِهِ رَجُلٌ مِنْ فَارِسَ أَوْ قَالَ مِنْ أَبْنَاءِ فَارِسَ حَتَّى يَتَنَاوَلَهُ م وَعَنْ شَهْرِ بْنِ
حَوْشَبٍ عَنْ أَبِي هُرَيْرَةَ رَضِيَ اللَّهُ عَنْهُ قَالَ سَمِعْتُهُ يَقُولُ قَالَ رَسُولُ اللَّهِ
صَلَّى اللَّهُ عَلَيْهِ وَسَلَّمَ لَوْ كَانَ الْعِلْمُ بِالثُّرَيَّا لَتَنَاوَلَهُ أُنَاسٌ مِنْ أَبْنَاءِ فَارِسَ

حم حل حب هب

Abū Ḥanīfa is the Only *Tābiʿī* among the Four Imāms

He is the first of the four *mujtahid* Imāms and the only Successor (*tābiʿī*) among them, having definitely seen the Companion Anas ibn Mālik ﷺ (d. 91) in Baṣra but – according to Walī al-Dīn al-ʿIrāqī, al-Sakhāwī, and al-Qārī – without reporting from him,[9] probably also ʿAbd Allāh ibn Abī Awfā in Kūfa according to Ibn Ḥajar as reported by

---

6:288) declared this wording "*ṣaḥīḥ* without the slightest doubt" but his purpose is to discredit the narration predicting Mālik. Aḥmad al-Ghumārī's claim that this wording is forged – cf. ʿAbd Allāh al-Ghumārī's *Bidaʿ al-Tafāsīr* (p. 179-181) – is incorrect.

[7] Narrated by Abū Khaythama in *al-ʿIlm* (p. 21 §82) with a chain of *Ṣaḥīḥayn* narrators.

[8] Narrated from Abū Hurayra by Muslim and from Ibn Masʿūd by al-Ṭabarānī in *al-Kabīr* (10:204 §10470).

[9] Al-Khaṭīb in his *Tārīkh* (4:207) narrated from al-Dāraquṭnī the latter's denial that

al-Qārī in *Sharḥ Musnad Abī Ḥanīfa*, and possibly also Sahl ibn Saʻd al-Sāʻidī in Madīna, Abū al-Ṭufayl ʻĀmir ibn Wāthila in Makka, ʻAbd Allāh ibn Unays, ʻAbd Allāh ibn al-Ḥārith ibn Jaz' al-Zabīdī, and ʻĀ'isha bint ʻAjrad.[10]

It is narrated that Abū Ḥanīfa's father carried his infant son to ʻAlī ؓ and that the latter supplicated for him and his progeny. Ismāʻīl ibn Ḥammād ibn Abī Ḥanīfa said: "We have hope that Allāh ﷻ answered the supplication of ʻAlī ibn Abī Ṭālib."[11]

His Authorities and Disciples in Ḥadīth

Ibn Ḥajar in his *Tahdhīb* and others said that Abū Ḥanīfa narrated ḥadīth from ʻAṭā' ibn Abī Rabāḥ, al-Ḥasan al-Baṣrī, ʻĀṣim ibn Abī al-Nujūd, ʻAlqama ibn Marthad, Ḥammād ibn Abī Sulaymān (d. 120), al-Ḥakam ibn ʻUtayba, Salama ibn Kuhayl, Abū Jaʻfar Muḥammad ibn ʻAlī, ʻAlī ibn al-Aqmar, Ziyād ibn ʻAlāqa, Saʻīd ibn Masrūq al-Thawrī, ʻAdī ibn Thābit al-Anṣārī, ʻAṭiyya ibn Saʻīd al-ʻAwfī, Abū Sufyān al-Saʻdī, ʻAbd al-Karīm Abū Umayya, Yaḥyā ibn Saʻīd al-Anṣārī, and Hishām ibn ʻUrwa among others ؓ.

From him narrated: his son Ḥammād, Ibrāhīm ibn Ṭahmān, Ḥamza ibn Ḥabīb al-Zayyāt, Zufar ibn al-Hudhayl, Abū Yūsuf al-Qāḍī, Abū Yaḥyā al-Ḥammānī, ʻĪsā ibn Yūnus, Wakīʻ, Yazīd ibn Zurayʻ, Asad ibn ʻAmr al-Bajalī, Ḥakkām ibn Yaʻlā ibn Salm al-Rāzī, Khārija ibn Muṣʻab, ʻAbd al-Majīd ibn Abī Rawād, ʻAlī ibn Mus-hir, Muḥammad ibn Bishr al-ʻAbdī, ʻAbd al-Razzāq, Muḥammad ibn al-Ḥasan al-Shaybānī, Muṣʻab ibn al-Miqdām, Yaḥyā ibn Yamān, Abū ʻIṣma Nūḥ ibn Abī Maryam, Abū ʻAbd al-Raḥmān al-Muqrī, Abū Nuʻaym al-Faḍl ibn Dukayn, Abū ʻĀṣim, and others ؓ.

Abū Ḥanīfa had ever seen Anas ibn Mālik. Al-Suyūṭī asserted the sighting in *Tabyīḍ al-Ṣaḥīfa* (p. 5). Yūsuf (ibn Ḥasan) ibn ʻAbd al-Hādī al-Ḥanbalī, known as Ibn al-Mibrad (840-909) wrote a large volume (still unpublished) on the merits of Abū Ḥanīfa titled *Tanwīr al-Ṣaḥīfa bi-Manāqib al-Imām Abī Ḥanīfa* in which he said: "Among those who show fanaticism against Abū Ḥanīfa is al-Dāraquṭnī." This is quoted in Ibn ʻĀbidīn's *Ḥashiyat Radd al-Muḥtār* (1:37). ʻAbd al-Fattāḥ Abū Ghudda in his commentary of al-Lacknawī's *al-Rafʻ wal-Takmīl* (p. 70 n. 1) also said: "Al-Dāraquṭnī's fanaticism against Abū Ḥanīfa is well-known" and he gives several sources listing the scholars who said the same.

[10] See al-Ṣafadī's *al-Wāfī bil-Wafayāt* (5:406) and al-Lacknawī's *Sanad al-Anām Sharḥ Musnad al-Imām* and *Iqāmat al-Ḥujja* (p. 83-89) in addition to the references cited in this entry.

[11] Narrated by al-Khaṭīb in *Tārīkh Baghdād* (13:326).

His Trustworthy Rank in Ḥadīth Narration

Muḥammad ibn Sa'd al-'Awfī said: I heard Ibn Ma'īn say: "Abū Ḥanīfa was trustworthy (*thiqa*), he did not narrate any ḥadīth except what he had memorized, nor did he narrate what he had not memorized." Ṣāliḥ ibn Muḥammad al-Asadī reported the same from Ibn Ma'īn.[12]

His *Musnad*

Abū Ḥanīfa narrated an amount of ḥadīths with his chains back to the Prophet ﷺ. His narrations were collected by various ḥadīth Masters to form about seventeen parts, each titled *Musnad Abī Ḥanīfa,* the whole exceeding in size the *Musnad* and *Sunan* of Imām al-Shāfi'ī. The chains of these *Masānīd* were collected by al-Ṣāliḥī in his *'Uqūd al-Jumān.* Commentaries were given by al-Qārī (in *Sharḥ Musnad Abī Ḥanīfa*) and al-Zabīdī (in *'Uqūd al-Jawāhir al-Munīfa*) among others, the most complete study probably being the four-volume *al-Mawāhib al-Laṭīfa 'alā Musnad Abī Ḥanīfa* by the ḥadīth Master Muḥammad 'Ābid al-Sindī.

Abū Ḥanīfa's Major Early Colleagues

The two foremost colleagues of the Imām, known as "the Two Companions" (*al-ṣāḥibān*) or "the Two Shaykhs" (*al-shaykhān*) in the Ḥanafī compendiums, are the major Jurists Abū Yūsuf and Muḥammad, respectively Abū Yūsuf Ya'qūb ibn Ibrāhīm ibn Ḥabīb al-Anṣārī, a descendant of the Companion Abū Dujāna, and Abū 'Abd Allāh Muḥammad ibn al-Ḥasan al-Shaybānī. The latter also studied under Abū Yūsuf then al-Shāfi'ī studied under him. Third in order of importance, although older than both of them, came Zufar ibn al-Hudhayl. All of them died in Baghdād. There were many more besides them.

ABŪ YŪSUF[13]

The Qāḍī, the Imām, the erudite Jurist of the Iraqis, Ya'qūb ibn Ibrāhīm ibn Ḥabīb ibn Khunays ibn Sa'd ibn Ḥabta [= Sa'd ibn 'Awf

[12] Ibn Ḥajar, *Tahdhīb al-Tahdhīb* (10:449-452 §817). We refuted at length the weak claim that some declared Abū Ḥanīfa weak in Ḥadīth in the last volume of the *Encyclopedia of Islamic Doctrine.*

[13] Main sources: al-Dhahabī, *Tadhkirat al-Ḥuffāẓ* (1:292-294) and Ibn 'Abd al-Barr, *al-Intiqā'* (p. 329-331).

ibn Baḥīr or Bujayr ﷺ] al-Bajalī al-Anṣārī al-Kūfī —ﷺ (113-182) is no. 42 in the sixth biographical layer of the ḥadīth Masters just before Abū Mu'āwiya Muḥammad ibn Khāzim al-Kūfī al-Ḍarīr (d. 195) in al-Dhahabī's *Tadhkirat al-Ḥuffāẓ*. His ancestor Sa'd ibn Ḥabta – Ḥabta being his mother's name – fought hard at the battle of the Trench despite his young age so that the Prophet ﷺ asked him his name and said: "Allāh make your grandfather happy! Come near!" Then he wiped his head and supplicated for him.[14]

Abū Yūsuf took ḥadīth from Hishām ibn 'Urwa, Abū Isḥāq al-Shaybānī, 'Aṭā' ibn al-Sā'ib, and their layer. From him took Muḥammad ibn al-Ḥasan al-Shaybānī, Aḥmad ibn Ḥanbal, Bishr ibn al-Walīd al-Kindī, Yaḥyā ibn Ma'īn – who praised him and recommended him –, 'Alī ibn al-Ja'd, 'Alī ibn Muslim al-Ṭūsī, 'Amr ibn Abī 'Amr, and others. He began the pursuit of knowledge early. Al-Ṭabarī narrates that Abū Yūsuf was first a student of Muḥammad ibn 'Abd al-Raḥmān ibn Abī Laylā, then Abū Ḥanīfa. His father was poor, so Abū Ḥanīfa supported Abū Yūsuf regularly. The latter narrates:

> My father died when I was little and my mother placed me with a bleacher. I used to pass by Abū Ḥanīfa's circle and sit there. My mother would follow me, take me by the hand, away from the gathering, and return me to the bleacher's shop. Then I would escape again and, against her wishes, sit with Abū Ḥanīfa. One day she had had enough and went to him, shouting, "This boy is an orphan with nothing to his name except what I feed him from my spinning, and you are spoiling him and causing my ruin!" Abū Ḥanīfa said, "Woman, be quiet! He is right here, learning the Science, and he shall be feasting on flour and honey pastries with pistachio butter (*fālūdhaj*) in dishes of turquoise (*fayrūzaj*)!" She replied, "You are an old man who has lost his senses!" Later, when I became a judge, I was with [Hārūn] al-Rashīd one day when they brought flour and honey pastry in a dish of turquoise and Hārūn said to me, "Eat from this!" Seeing this, I smiled. When he pressed me to say why, I told him what Abū Ḥanīfa had said. He replied, "Truly, knowledge raises one's

[14] Narrated by Ibn 'Abd al-Barr in *al-Intiqā'* (p. 330) and *al-Istī'āb* (2:584=2:51) and al-Suhaylī in *al-Rawḍ al-Unuf* (3:247), the latter without the words "Allāh make your grandfather happy."

state both in life and in the hereafter. Allāh have mercy on Abū Ḥanīfa! He used to see with the eyes of the mind what cannot be seen with the eyes of the head."[15]

Abū Yūsuf prayed two hundred daily supererogatory *rak'as* even after he became the head judge of Iraq, an office he held under three caliphs: al-Mahdī, al-Hādī, and al-Rashīd, the last of whom held him in the highest esteem.

'Alī ibn Ḥarmala said that after every prayer Abū Yūsuf would say: "O Allāh! Forgive me and Abū Ḥanīfa." Among his sayings: "**Whoever pursues the rarities of ḥadīth will lie**, whoever pursues wealth through alchemy will be poor, and whoever studies the Religion through [non-Sunni] *kalām* will become a heretic." Several Imāms spoke in similar terms. Al-Awzā'ī said: "Whoever holds on to the rare and unusual positions of the Scholars has left Islām."[16] Al-Thawrī said: "Whoever pursues the rare and the unusual has gathered up all evil." Something similar is related from 'Abd al-Raḥmān ibn Mahdī.[17] Sulaymān al-Taymī said: "If you take the dispensation (*rukhṣa*) or error (*zalla*) of every *'Ālim*, you will become the gathering point of every evil."[18]

The writer of these lines narrates by permission (*ijāza*) from al-Sayyid Muḥammad ibn al-Sayyid Ibrāhīm al-Ya'qūbī, from the late Muftī of Shām al-Sayyid Abū al-Yusr 'Ābidīn, from his grandfather the *Amīn al-Fatwā* of Shām al-Sayyid 'Abd al-Ghanī 'Ābidīn (d. 1307), from the *Muḥaddith* and *Musnid* of Shām al-Shaykh 'Abd al-Raḥmān ibn Muḥammad al-Kuzbarī al-Shāfi'ī the grandson, (1184-1262), from Shaykh Muṣṭafā ibn Muḥammad al-Raḥmatī al-Ḥanafī al-Dimashqī al-Madanī al-Ayyūbī al-Anṣārī (1135-1205), from the *'Ārif* al-Shaykh 'Abd al-Ghanī al-Nābulusī (d. 1143) – who granted the request of Shaykh Muṣṭafā's father for an *ijāza* to his young son[19] – from Najm al-Dīn Muḥammad ibn Muḥammad al-Ghazzī (d. 1061), from his father Badr al-Dīn Muḥammad al-Ghazzī al-'Āmirī al-Dimashqī (d. 984),

[15] In Ibn Kathīr, *Bidāya* (10:180). Al-Kawtharī doubted its authenticity.

[16] Cited by al-Dhahabī, *Siyar* (1997 ed. 7:99).

[17] See p. 427 (epigraph)

[18] Narrated by Ibn al-Ja'd in his *Musnad* (p. 200), Ibn 'Abd al-Barr in *Jāmi' Bayān al-'Ilm* (2:927 §1766-1767) cf. Ibn Ḥazm, *Iḥkām* (6:883), and 'Aẓīm Ābādī, *'Awn al-Ma'būd* (13:187).

[19] Cf. Muḥammad Jamīl al-Shaṭṭī, *A'yān Dimashq* (p. 276-277).

from Shaykh al-Islām al-Qāḍī Zakariyyā ibn Muḥammad al-Anṣārī (d. 926), from the *Ḥāfiẓ* Ibn Ḥajar al-'Asqalānī (d. 852), from Abū al-'Abbās Shihāb al-Dīn Aḥmad ibn 'Umar ibn 'Alī ibn 'Abd al-Ṣamad al-Baghdādī al-Jawharī (725-809) – Ibn 'Imād said he would sway with emotion during ḥadīth audition yet possessed gravitas – from the *Ḥāfiẓ* Abū 'Abd Allāh Shams al-Dīn Muḥammad ibn Aḥmad ibn 'Uthmān al-Dhahabī (d. 748), from Aḥmad ibn Isḥāq al-Abarqūhī, from Mubārak ibn Abī al-Jawād, from Aḥmad ibn Abī Ghālib, from 'Abd al-'Azīz ibn 'Alī, from Abū Ṭāhir al-Mukhliṣ, from Muḥammad ibn Hārūn al-Ḥaḍramī, from Isḥāq ibn Abī Isrā'īl, from Abū Yūsuf al-Qāḍī, from Abū Ḥanīfa, from 'Alqama ibn Marthad, from Sulaymān ibn Burayda, from his father, that Mā'iz ibn Mālik came to the Messenger of Allāh ﷺ and confessed to committing adultery. The Prophet ﷺ turned him away but he came back and confessed to adultery again. The Prophet ﷺ turned him away again but he came back a third time and confessed to adultery again. The Prophet ﷺ turned him away a third time. When he came back confessing for the fourth time, the Prophet ﷺ asked his people about him: "Is he at all insane in your opinion?" They said no. He ordered his execution. He was stoned in a place where rocks were scarce. His death was too slow, so he hurried to a place where rocks were abundant. People followed him and stoned him until they killed him. They mentioned this to the Messenger of Allāh ﷺ and asked permission to bury him and pray over him, which he gave them. He said: **"He repented with a repentence such that if swarms of people** (*fi'āmun min al-nās*) **had repented thus, it would have been accepted from them."**[20] Al-Dhahabī said of his chain: "This is a high [=short], connected chain (*hādhā isnādun 'ālin muttaṣil*)." Shaykh Muḥammad al-Ya'qūbī said the same of his chain to the *Ḥāfiẓ* Ibn Ḥajar.

MUḤAMMAD [21]

Abū 'Abd Allāh Muḥammad ibn al-Ḥasan ibn Farqad al-Ḥarastānī al-Wāsiṭī al-Shaybānī *mawlāhum* al-Kūfī ﵀ (132-189), the godly

[20] Narrated from Burayda by Abū Yūsuf in *al-Āthār* (p. 157) and al-Dhahabī in the *Tadhkira* (1:294). The ḥadīth of Mā'iz ibn Mālik is among the *mutawātir* narrations.

[21] Main sources: al-Dhahabī, *Tārīkh al-Islām* (Years 181-190: p. 358-362 §312), al-Shīrāzī, *Ṭabaqāt al-Fuqahā'* (p. 135), al-Nawawī, *Tahdhīb* (1:81-82), al-Khaṭīb, *Tārīkh Baghdād* (2:173-181), Ibn Khallikān, *Wafayāt* (4:184), Ibn 'Imād, *Shadharāt al-Dhahab* (1:322-324), and Abū al-Wafā' al-Afghānī, *Ṭabaqāt al-Ḥanafiyya* (p. 42).

Mujtahid Imām, Faqīh, and Muftī of the Irāqis became, with Abū Yūsuf – his second teacher, whom he succeeded as head judge for Hārūn al-Rashīd – the spokesman of the School of their teacher Abū Ḥanīfa so that they are known as "the Two Colleagues" (*al-ṣāḥibān*). When his father first brought him to Abū Ḥanīfa to school him, the latter said: "Shave his head and let him wear old clothes lest he cause a problem [to people because of his attractiveness]." Also among his teachers: Mis'ar, Mālik ibn Mighwal, Sufyān al-Thawrī, al-Awzā'ī, and Mālik ibn Anas. He said he spent three years with the latter and heard seven hundred ḥadīths from him. His narration of the *Muwaṭṭa'* is one of the Motherbooks.

Muḥammad ibn al-Ḥasan said: "My father left me thirty thousand dirhams. I spent fifteen thousand on [learning Arabic] grammar and poetry, and fifteen thousand on ḥadīth and *fiqh*."

Al-Shāfi'ī studied under him and praised him lavishly. He said that the first time he saw Muḥammad ibn al-Ḥasan the latter was surrounded by a circle of people, replying to their questions. "I looked at him," al-Shāfi'ī said, and noticed he was among the most handsome of people. His forehead looked like ivory. His clothes were elegant. I asked him a question and he replied promoting his School, fast as an arrow." He also said:

> "I never asked anyone a difficult question but that their face showed displeasure, except Muḥammad ibn al-Ḥasan."
>
> "From Muḥammad ibn al-Ḥasan I took two camel-loads of learning." "I spent sixty dinars buying his books."
>
> "I never saw a big-bodied man with a lighter spirit."
>
> "I could say that the Qur'ān was revealed in the tongue of Muḥammad ibn al-Ḥasan because of his immense eloquence."

Abū 'Ubayd al-Qāsim ibn Sallām said: "I never saw more learned in the Book of Allāh than him!"

Imām Aḥmad was asked: "From where do you know all those minutiae?" He replied: "From the books of Muḥammad ibn al-Ḥasan."

Al-Ṭaḥāwī narrated from Yūnus ibn 'Abd al-A'lā, from al-Shāfi'ī, that whenever Muḥammad ibn al-Ḥasan sat to debate *fiqh* or other, he would order for a referee to sit in the middle and adjudicate on each matter.

In ḥadīth al-Shāfi'ī narrated from him, al-Dāraquṭnī defended his reliability, Aḥmad preferred Abū Yūsuf and did not narrate anything from him, al-Nasā'ī considered him weak, as did Ibn Ma'īn, al-Jūzjānī, and Ibn Ḥibbān, all from the perspective of meticulous memorization (*ḍabṭ*) since they praised him unanimously for his intelligence and integrity (*'adl*).

Among Muḥammad ibn al-Ḥasan's works: *al-Āthār*, in print with an extensive commentary by the late jurist and linguist Abū al-Wafā' al-Afghānī; *al-Jāmi' al-Ṣaghīr* which Yaḥyā ibn Ma'īn said he wrote in full under his dictation; and *al-Siyar al-Kabīr* which is among the books al-Shāfi'ī bought and studied, then refuted. Muḥammad ibn al-Ḥasan said of *al-Ḥiyal*: "This book is not one of ours [*i.e.* one of the books of our School] but was cast into them." Aḥmad ibn Abī 'Imrān said: "It was actually authored by Ismā'īl ibn Ḥammād ibn Abī Ḥanīfa."

Abū Ḥāzim al-Qāḍī said that he heard Bakr al-'Ammī say: "Ibn Samā'a and 'Īsā ibn Abān took the beauty of [their] *Ṣalāt* from none other than Muḥammad ibn al-Ḥasan." His devotion (*wird*) in every day and night was recitation of one eighth of the Qur'ān.

The owner of the house in which he died narrates that he saw him weeping on his death-bed. "Do you weep with [all your] learning?" He replied: "What if Allāh ﷻ makes me stand before Him and asks, 'Muḥammad! What brought you forth to Me? Jihād in My way? Or the pursuit of My good pleasure?' What can I reply?" The Qāḍī Aḥmad ibn Abī Rajā' said that he heard his father – Maḥmūyah, who was considered one of the *Abdāl* – say: "I dreamt of Muḥammad ibn al-Ḥasan [after his death] and asked him what had happened to him. He said: 'I was forgiven.' 'Through what?' 'I was told: We did not place all this learning in you except to forgive you.'"

ZUFAR

Abū al-Hudhayl Zufar ibn al-Hudhayl ibn Zufar ibn al-Hudhayl ibn Qays al-'Anbarī al-Tamīmī al-Baṣrī ﵀ (110-158) the pious *Mujtahid* Imām and trustworthy ḥadīth Master of noble birth, was "extremely scrupulous, sharp in his analogies, scarce in his writing, memorizing everything he writes" (Wakī'), "trustworthy and reliable" (Yaḥyā ibn Ma'īn), "a man of wisdom, religion, understanding, and scrupulous Godwariness" (Ibn 'Abd al-Barr), "the Godly *Mujtahid Faqīh*... one of the oceans of *Fiqh* and the truly wise men of the time" (al-Dhahabī).

He took ḥadīth from Sulaymān ibn Mahrān al-A'mash, Yaḥyā ibn Sa'īd al-Anṣārī, Muḥammad ibn Isḥāq the author of the *Maghāzī*, Ayyūb al-Sakhtiyānī (or Sikhtyānī), Sa'īd ibn Abī 'Arūba, and many others. Among those who narrated it from him: Ibn al-Mubārak, Muḥammad ibn al-Ḥasan, Wakī' ibn al-Jarrāḥ, Sufyān ibn 'Uyayna, al-Faḍl ibn Dukayn, al-Ḥasan ibn Ziyād al-Lu'lu'ī, and others including Imām Abū 'Āṣim al-Nabīl al-Ḍaḥḥāk ibn Makhlad (122-212), the grandfather of Imām Ibn Abī 'Āṣim (206-287).

Zufar was entirely devoted to ḥadīth and was one of its experts. One day a question arose which neither he nor his colleagues were able to solve. He went to Abū Ḥanīfa who gave him an answer. Zufar said: "From where did you get this?" Abū Ḥanīfa replied: "Because of such-and-such a ḥadīth and its analogy from such-and-such perspective." Abū Ḥanīfa continued: "But if the question were such-and-such, what would be its answer?" Zufar became more perplexed than he had been for the first question. Abū Ḥanīfa gave him the reply then quizzed him and replied for him a third time. Zufar went back to his colleagues and quizzed them in the same manner. They were even more perplexed than him. When he gave them all the replies they said: "From where did you get all this?" He said from Abū Ḥanīfa. "With these three questions," Zufar narrates, "I became the leader of my circle." Then he went to study with Abū Ḥanīfa for over twenty years and was one of those who wrote books in his *Madhhab.*

Zufar's fatwa is followed in seventeen matters in the Ḥanafī *Madhhab* over that of the Imām and his two companions. There are several recensions of these fatwas, as in Abū Zayd al-Dabbūsī's *Ta'sīs al-Naẓar*, al-Nasafī's poem on *khilāf* and its commentaries, and other works.

In al-Baṣra Zufar reached the point where people would leave 'Uthmān ibn Muslim al-Battī's circle to come study under him. When the Baṣrians expressed admiration at Zufar's *fiqh* he said: "If only you had seen Muḥammad ibn al-Ḥasan!" Another time he said: "Abū Yūsuf is the most knowledgeable of those that came before." Even more would he say, "This is the position of Abū Ḥanīfa" until the Baṣrians became far more amenable to the Imām and his *fiqh*, after having having borne hostility toward him before.

Al-Ḥusayn ibn al-Walīd said: "He [Zufar] was the strongest of the Imām's companions and the sharpest in his analysis." Ibn 'Abd al-Barr said in *al-Intiqā'* that Zufar succeeded Abū Ḥanīfa at the head of his study circle, then Abū Yūsuf, then Muḥammad ibn al-Ḥasan.

'Abd al-Raḥmān ibn Mālik ibn Mighwal narrated that a man asked Abū Ḥanīfa: "Last night I drank fermented juice (*nabīdh*) and am not sure whether I divorced my wife or not." He replied: "She is your wife until you become sure that you divorced her." He went to Sufyān al-Thawrī and asked him the same question. He replied: "Go and declare that you have brought her back (*rāji'hā*). If you did not divorce her, it is of no consequence." Then he asked Sharīk ibn 'Abd Allāh who replied: "Divorce her, then bring her back." Then he asked Zufar who said: "Did you ask anyone else before me?" He said yes and named all of the above. Zufar endorsed Abū Ḥanīfa's reply and praised Sufyān's but laughed at Sharīk's then said: "This is like a man who passed by water splashing, some of which reached his garment, whereupon Abū Ḥanīfa said: 'Your garment is clean and prayer complete until you become sure about the water [being dirty],' while Sufyān said: 'Wash it, and if it were clean in the first place it is only cleaner now,' but Sharīk said [in effect]: 'Go piss on it then wash it!'"

Muḥammad ibn al-Ḥasan said: "I saw Zufar debate Abū Yūsuf. The latter would overcome him with narrations from Abū Ḥanīfa and reports but when it came to analogy Zufar would win." Al-Faḍl ibn Dukayn said: "Zufar would sit squarely and lean against a pillar, wearing a big white *qalansuwa* while Abū Yūsuf would shift a lot during debate, so that Zufar would say to him at times: 'Where are you running off to? Pick any "door" [*i.e.* chapter] you wish!'" Ḥammād and Muḥammad ibn 'Amāra said: "I saw Abū Ḥanīfa one day with Abū Yūsuf on his left and Zufar on his right, debating each other and flatly refuting each other question after question, from morning to *ẓuhr*, while Abū Ḥanīfa refereed. When the call to prayer was raised, Abū Ḥanīfa slapped his hand on Zufar's thigh and said: 'Do not seek leadership in a country where Abū Yūsuf can be found!'"

Abū Ḥanīfa said: "Our companions here are thirty-six. Twenty-eight are fit for judgeship, six are fit for giving fatwa, and two – pointing to Abū Yūsuf and Zufar – are fit for keeping the judges and muftis in line!"

Shaddād ibn Ḥakīm asked Asad ibn 'Amr: "Who possessed more *fiqh*, Abū Yūsuf or Zufar?" He replied: "Zufar was more Godfearing (*awra'*)." Shaddād said: "I am asking you about *fiqh*." Asad replied:

"Shaddād! With fear of God a man rises." Abū Muṭīʿ al-Balkhī reportedly called Zufar "a *Ḥujja* [Great Proof] among people" but, as for Abū Yūsuf, "the world dazzled him a little bit." Al-Kawtharī comments: "This is the lot of those who become judges: people gossip about them. Yet the common welfare is not achieved except through upright judges. Ibn al-Wardī was right when he said: *Truly, all people are enemies to the holders of judgeship – and I mean the upright ones!*"

Wakīʿ would go to Zufar mornings and to Abū Yūsuf evenings then focussed on Zufar since he had more time.

Among Zufar's sayings: "Whoever sits [to teach] before his time is brought low." No doubt, he took this from the Imām, who said something very similar.

Al-Khaṭīb in his *Tārīkh Baghdād* also listed the following among the Companions of Abū Ḥanīfa as reported by Ismāʿīl ibn Ḥammād: Asad ibn ʿAmr al-Bajalī, ʿĀfiyat al-Awdī, Dāwūd al-Ṭāʾī, al-Qāsim ibn Maʿn al-Masʿūdī, ʿAlī ibn Mus-hir, Yaḥyā ibn Zakariyyā ibn Abī Zāʾida, Ḥibbān and Mindal, both sons of ʿAlī al-ʿAnazī. None of them reached the level of Zufar and the Two Companions.

Abū ʿAlī al-Ḥasan ibn Ziyād al-Luʾluʾī al-Kūfī al-Anṣārī (d. 204), one of the major pious and learned Imāms of *fiqh*, also took *fiqh* from Abū Ḥanīfa as well as from Zufar and Abū Yūsuf.[22]

DĀWŪD AL-ṬĀʾĪ

Abū Sulaymān Dāwūd ibn Nuṣayr al-Kūfī al-Ṭāʾī (d. 160 or 165) narrated ḥadīth from a number of the *Tābiʿīn* and took *fiqh* from Abū Ḥanīfa who predicted that he would devote himself entirely to worship. Ibn Ziyād al-Luʾluʾī reported, "Zufar and Dāwūd al-Ṭāʾī al-Kūfī at first were colleagues, then Dāwūd left *fiqh* for asceticism while Zufar combined the two."

Ibn al-Jawzī in *Ṣifat al-Ṣafwa* narrates that Abū Ḥanīfa said to Dāwūd: "Abū Sulaymān! As for the instrument, we have mastered it." Dawūd said: "What is left?" Abū Ḥanīfa said: "What is left is to put it into practice!" Dāwūd said: "When I heard this, my soul stirred me to seclusion and solitariness, but I told it: Sit with them for a year and do not raise a peep during that time." During that year, he said, "A question would

---

[22] Cf. al-Kawtharī's monograph *al-Imtāʿ bi-Sīrat al-Imāmayn al-Ḥasan ibn Ziyād wa-Ṣāḥibihi Muḥammad ibn Shujāʿ* and the end of *Taʾnīb al-Khaṭīb*.

come up which made me crave to answer it more than someone parched craves water, but I would not answer." After one year, he went into seclusion.

Among Dāwūd's sayings: "Fear Allāh and keep piety with your parents; fast from the world and make death your breakfast; run away from people as you would from a lion, without disparaging them nor leaving their congregation." "Be satisfied with a little from the world together with safety in Religion, just as worldly people are satisfied with the world together with corruption in their Religion." "Despair is the natural end of our deeds, but our hearts drag us to hope." "Beware! Lest Allāh find you where He forbade you to be; beware lest He not find you where He ordered you to be; be ashamed of His nearness to you and His power over you!" To a student who wished to learn archery: "Archery is fine but your days are counted; look well how you spend them."

Abū Bakr Muḥammad ibn Abī Dāwūd said he heard Shīdūyah ask Dāwūd: "What do you think of a man who enters upon those ['Abbāsī] princes and commands them good and forbids them from evil?" Dāwūd said: "I fear he will be lashed." He said: "What if he endures it?" Dāwūd replied: "I fear the sword for him." He said: "What if he endures it?" Dāwūd replied: "I fear for him the deeply-hidden disease – vanity (*al-'ujb*)."

Muḥammad ibn 'Uthmān al-Ṣayrafī said that Dāwūd only came out of his house upon hearing the *iqāma* then, when the Imām gave *salām*, jumped up and returned to his house. His daily diet was bread, salt, and water. One time he ate dates out of craving, after which he swore never to touch dates again. One time his maidservant cooked him a dish but he said: "Take it to So-and-so's orphans. If I eat it, it will end up in the midden, but if they eat it, it will be stored up in the Divine presence."

At a funeral one day, Dāwūd was heard to say: "Whoever fears the Divine threat, all that seems far looms near to him; whoever harbors endless hopes, his deeds are feeble; everything that is going to take place is actually near! Know, my brother, that everything that keeps you away from your Lord is a misfortune for you. Know that the dwellers of the graves are happy for what they sent forth and regret their useless occupations, while the dwellers of the world fight and compete with one another precisely over what the grave-dwellers regret."

Visitors once said to one another, upon seeing him sitting on the dusty ground: "This is an ascetic (*zāhid*)." He said: "The ascetic is one who first evaluates then leaves!" When Sufyān al-Thawrī visited him with Abū Khālid al-Aḥmar the latter was miffed that Dāwūd did not so much as look at Sufyān, but Sufyān told him: "He is unconcerned by affection; did you not see his eyes? They see other than what we fiddle with." To another visitor who offered to have the cobwebs in his ceiling swept Dāwūd said: "Do you not know that he [ﷺ] detested superfluous gazes?" After that he refused visitors and communicated from behind his door.

Dāwūd inherited from his parents or his freedwoman twenty pieces of gold which sufficed him for twenty years, after which he would sell the wood of his roof for sustenance until he lived in the last sheltered corner of his house. Ḥammād [ibn Salama] and/or Abū Yūsuf said to him: "Dāwūd! You are satisfied with so little of this world!" He replied: "Do you know who is satisfied with much less? Those who are happy with all this world in exchange for the hereafter!" To al-Ḥārith ibn Idrīs who asked him for counsel Dāwūd replied: "The soldiers of death await you."

Dāwūd's frequent prayer: "*Allāhumma!* Your care has piled cares upon me and barred my way to sleep. My desire to see You has tied me up and barred me from pleasures. I am in Your jail – O Generous One – under arrest!" Then he would repeat a verse of the Qur'ān over and over. His neighbor, overhearing, said: "It would seem to me as if all the pleasures of this world were summed up in that verse." Abū Nu'aym [al-Faḍl ibn Dukayn] said he saw an ant crawl on Dāwūd's face lengthwise and widthwise while Dāwūd did not even feel it because of his anxiety and sorrow. Abū Dāwūd al-Ṭayālisī said he was present at Dāwūd's deathbed and he never witnessed a harder agony. Ḥāfṣ ibn 'Umar al-Ju'fī said the reason for his final illness was that Dāwūd read a verse that mentioned hellfire that affected him deeply. He repeated it all night long until morning then gave up the ghost, his head resting on a clay brick.

Ibn al-Jawzī said the report that "Dāwūd al-Ṭā'ī was a silk-maker" is probably about Dāwūd ibn Abī al-Hind al-Baṣrī rather than al-Ṭā'ī, who did not have a profession. That report states that for forty years, he left his house with his luncheon which he gave away as alms, then he would go home and eat dinner with his family and they never knew that he was fasting.

AL-ṬAḤĀWĪ [23]

Abū Ja'far Aḥmad ibn Muḥammad ibn Salāma ibn Salama ibn 'Abd al-Malik al-Azdī al-Ḥajrī al-Miṣrī al-Ṭāḥāwī ﷺ (229-321), the humble, self-effaced, scrupulous, peerless *Faqīh*, absolute *Mujtahid*, and unrivalled Imām and Master of the *Madhhab* in ḥadīth and its sciences, was "matched by none of those who followed" (Ibn Yūnus, al-Ṣafadī, al-Suyūṭī), "unanimously agreed upon in his trustworthiness" (al-'Aynī, al-Sam'ānī, al-Dhahabī, al-Suyūṭī), "the Master in all the Schools of *Fiqh*" (Ibn 'Abd al-Barr), "one of the established trustworthy giants among the ḥadīth Masters" (Ibn Kathīr), who shared the same *Shuyūkh* in ḥadīth as Muslim, al-Nasā'ī, Abū Dāwūd, and Ibn Mājah, and "whose *Sharḥ Ma'ānī al-Āthār* definitely surpasses the *Sunan* in excellence" (al-Kawtharī)![24]

A student of his maternal uncle al-Muzanī, Abū Ja'far first followed the Shāfi'ī School until al-Muzanī's death in 264, after which he focused on three Cairene ḥadīth Masters of superlative Religion and *Fiqh*, all of them Ḥanafīs: the Qāḍī of Shām, Kūfa, and Karkh (Baghdād) Abū Khāzim 'Abd al-Ḥamīd ibn 'Abd al-'Azīz al-Sakūnī al-Baṣrī (d. 292), the saintly Qāḍī of all Egypt Abū Bakrah Bakkār ibn Qutayba al-Baṣrī (d. 270), and his successor the Qāḍī of all Egypt Abū Ja'far Aḥmad ibn Abī 'Imrān Mūsā ibn 'Īsā al-Baghdādī (d. 280) whom al-Ṭaḥāwī frequented for twenty years and who was probably the decisive reason behind his switching to the Ḥanafī School. After this, al-Ṭaḥāwī said he dreamt of al-Muzanī complaining to him: "Abū Ja'far robbed me of you, Abū Ja'far!" However, the claim that the reason for his adoption of the Ḥanafī School was that "he had seen his uncle and teacher turning to the works of Ḥanafī Scholars to resolve many thorny issues of *fiqh* etc." is most likely untrue since al-Muzanī's *Mukhtaṣar* and his other works are replete with refutations of the Ḥanafī School.

Ibn Ḥajar discussed the categories of ḥadīth Mastership (*ḥifẓ*) in his biographical note on Ibn Rāfi' al-Salāmī (d. 774) and said, "In truth, Ibn Rāfi' is closer to the definition of *ḥifẓ* by the standards of *Ahl al-ḥadīth* than Ibn Kathīr. Ibn Rāfi' focussed on short-chained narrations, short treatises, dates of death, and ḥadīth auditions more

[23] Main sources: al-Arna'ūṭ, introduction to his edition of al-Ṭaḥāwī's *Sharḥ Mushkil al-Āthār*, and al-Kawtharī, *al-Ḥāwī fī Sīrat al-Imām al-Ṭaḥāwī*.

[24] This claim, even if untrue, indicates the high rank of al-Ṭaḥāwī and his work.

than Ibn Kathīr. The latter is closer to the definition of *ḥifẓ* by the standards of the *Fuqahā'*, because of his great familiarity with the juristic and Qur'anic commentary texts, than Ibn Rāfi'. The two of them would make up an accomplished *Ḥāfiẓ* but few are those that attained such a level after the early period, such as Ibn Khuzayma, al-Ṭaḥāwī, Ibn Ḥibbān, al-Bayhaqī, and, in the latter period, our Shaykh, al-'Irāqī."[25]

WORKS OF AL-ṬAḤĀWĪ

- *Aḥkām al-Qur'ān*, his *Tafsīr*, partly extant and now published in Turkey.
- *Akhbār Abī Ḥanīfa*, also known as his *Manāqib*.
- *Bayān I'tiqād Ahl al-Sunna wal-Jamā'a 'alā Madhhab Fuqahā' al-Milla Abī Ḥanīfa wa-Abī Yūsuf al-Anṣārī wa-Muḥammad ibn al-Ḥasan* ("Exposition of the Creed of the People of the Sunna and the Congregation According to the Teachings of the Jurists of the Community, Abū Ḥanīfa and his Companions"), known as the *'Aqīda Ṭaḥāwiyya*. This is one of the most reliable concise early texts of Sunni doctrine.[26] Among its tenets is the creed that the Companions, the *'Itra*, and the Twelve Imāms, – Allāh be well-pleased with them all – put together are below the level of a single Prophet:

  §98. *We do not prefer any of the saintly men among the Community over any of the Prophets but, rather, we say that any one of the Prophets is better than all the awliyā' put together.*

  The *Ṭaḥāwiyya* received many commentaries. Among the most reliable are Akmal al-Dīn al-Bābartī's and 'Abd al-Ghanī al-Ghunaymī al-Maydānī's Māturīdī commentaries. Al-Kawtharī said:

  "The *'Aqīda Taḥāwiyya* received several commentaries, among them Najm al-Dīn Abū Shujā' Bakbars al-Nāṣirī al-Baghdādī's – one of Sharaf al-Dīn al-Dimyāṭī's Shaykhs – that of Sirāj al-Dīn 'Umar ibn Isḥāq al-Ghaznawī al-Miṣrī, that of Maḥmūd ibn Aḥmad ibn Mas'ūd al-Qūnawī, that of Sharḥ al-Ṣadr 'Alī ibn

[25] Ibn Ḥajar, *Inbā' al-Ghumr* (1:62).

[26] Cf. therevival.co.uk/articles/aqeeda_tahawi.htm, and recently translated into English by Shaykh Hamza Yusuf.

Muḥammad al-Adhra'ī and others. A commentary came out, authored by an unknown [Ibn Abī al-'Izz] spuriously affiliated with the Ḥanafī school, but whose handiwork proclaims his ignorance of this discipline and the fact that he is an anthropomorphist who has lost his compass."[27]

- *Ikhtilāf al-Fuqahā'*, an unfinished masterpiece of *fiqh* erudition unfortunately lost, but its abridgment by Abū Bakr al-Rāzī al-Jaṣṣāṣ (d. 370) is preserved in full and was published in India and Damascus.
- *Mukhtaṣar al-Ṭaḥāwī* in Ḥanafī *Fiqh*, praised by the *Muḥaddith* 'Abd al-'Azīz al-Dihlawī in *Bustān al-Muḥaddithīn* as a proof of al-Ṭaḥāwī's status of *Mujtahid muṭlaq* and his free range of positions, some conforming to the *Madhhab*, some given precedence over those of the *Madhhab*. This work received many commentaries, the most important one being Abū Bakr al-Rāzī al-Jaṣṣāṣ's.
- *Al-Nakhl*, a book on date palms.
- *Naqd Kitāb al-Mudallisīn*, a critique and refutation of al-Karābīsī's work in which the latter unwisely gave arguments to the enemies of ḥadīth. This work is lost.
- *Sharḥ Ma'ānī al-Āthār*, his earliest work, in which he focussed to a large extent on the jurisprudence of the Ḥanafī Imāms in his discussion of all the issues he brought up. This work is a didactic manual of tremendous use for students of jurisprudence and differences. It served as the foundation for the *Mushkil* where he focussed on ḥadīth and gave greater leeway to his *Ijtihād*. Among the commentaries the *Ma'ānī* received: the *Ḥāfiẓ* 'Abd al-Qādir al-Qurashī's [Ibn al-Turkmānī's student] *al-Ḥāwī fī Takhrīj Aḥādīth al- Ṭāḥāwī* and al-Badr al-'Aynī's three commentaries:

[27] Al-Kawtharī, *al-Ḥāwī fī Sīrat al-Imām al-Ṭaḥāwī* (p. 38-39). Muḥammad ibn 'Alā' al-Dīn 'Alī ibn Muḥammad ibn Muḥammad ibn Abī al-'Izz, Ṣadr al-Dīn al-Dimashqī al-Ṣāliḥī (d. 792) is unknown in the Ḥanafī biographical sources but is mentioned in other sources due to the affair that led to his eleven-month imprisonment from 784 to 785. Ibn 'Imād al-Ḥanbalī (d. 1089) devoted 5 lines to him in his ten-volume *Shadharāt al-Dhahab* (6:326) in which he mentions that Ibn Abī al-'Izz was the Ḥanafī judge for Damascus, then for Cairo for one month, after which he excused himself and came back to Damascus. There, he was accused of disrespecting the Prophet ﷺ and remained incarcerated until a new governor gave him amnesty. The story is told by Ibn Ḥajar in the chapter for the year 784 in his *Inbā' al-Ghumr* (1:258-260).

Nakhb al-Afkār fī Sharḥ Ma'ānī al-Āthār, Mabānī al-Akhbār fī Sharḥ Ma'ānī al-Āthār, and *Naghm al-Akhyār fī Rijāl Ma'ānī al-Āthār.*

- *Sharḥ Mushkil al-Āthār,* a large, late work, his *magnum opus,* published in sixteen volumes by Shaykh Shu'ayb al-Arna'ūṭ who describes the Imām's method as gathering two authentic but apparently contradictory ḥadīths in each chapter – without specific topical order or organization – and discussing the various ways in which the purported contradiction is resolved according to the principles of lexical usage, *tafsīr,* jurisprudence and *qiyās,* with special consideration for the principles in use in the Ḥanafī *Madhhab,* and – almost overcoming all other aspects – ḥadīth science. If the two ḥadīths are not of comparable strength then the stronger one is put forward and the weaker one superseded. The full title of this work is *Bayān Mushkil Aḥādīth Rasūlillāhi* ﷺ *wa-Istikhrāji mā fīhi min al-Aḥkāmi wa-Nafī al-Taḍāddi 'anhā* ("Exposition of the Problematic Ḥadīths of the Messenger of Allāh ﷺ, Extraction of the Rulings Contained Therein, and Refutation of the Notion that They Show Contradiction"). The original inspiration for this genre in Islām was pioneered by Imām al-Shāfi'ī in his much smaller *Ikhtilāf al-Ḥadīth,* followed by others such as Ibn Qutayba's masterful *Ta'wīl Mukhtalif al-Ḥadīth* ("The Explanation of Conflicting Narrations"), Ibn Mahdī al-Ṭabarī's *Ta'wīl al-Aḥādīth al-Mushkalāt al-Wāridāt fil-Ṣifāt,* and Ibn Fūrāk's *Mushkil al-Ḥadīth.* These should not be confused with the works dealing exclusively with lexical difficulties such as Ibn Sallām's *Gharīb al-Ḥadīth,* Thābit ibn Qāsim al-Andalusī al-Saraqasṭī al-Sharīṭī's (d. 314) *al-Dalā'il fī Gharīb al-Ḥadīth,* Ibrāhīm al-Ḥarbī's *Gharīb al-Ḥadīth,* al-Khaṭṭābī's *Gharīb al-Ḥadīth,* Ibn al-Athīr's *al-Nihāya fī Gharīb al-Ḥadīth wal-Athar,* Ibn al-Jawzī's *Gharīb al-Ḥadīth,* and al-Zamakhsharī's *al-Fā'iq.*

Al-Ṭaḥāwī narrates in the *Mushkil* the famous ḥadīth in which the Prophet ﷺ rested or received revelation with his head in 'Alī's ؓ lap until sunset, after which – since 'Alī had not prayed *'Aṣr* – the Prophet ﷺ raised his hand and supplicated until the sun moved back up from the West.[28] Al-Ṭaḥāwī mentioned that the

[28] Narrated from Asmā' bint 'Umays by al-Ṭabarānī in *al-Kabīr* (24:144-151 §382, 390-391 cf. Ibn Abī 'Āṣim, *al-Sunna* 2:598 §1323) and al-Ṭaḥāwī in *Sharḥ Mushkil al-Āthār* (3:92-95 §1067-1068) through two 'Alawī chains cf. al-Haythamī (8:297); also

ḥadīth Master Aḥmad ibn Ṣāliḥ (d. 248) considered it a duty for every *'Ālim* to memorize this ḥadīth as it provides one of the proofs of Prophethood. Yet Ibn Taymiyya summarily dismissed al-Ṭaḥāwī's expertise in ḥadīth because of this narration which he declared forged in his *Minhāj al-Sunna al-Nabawiyya* as did Ibn al-Jawzī before him. Al-Qāḍī 'Iyāḍ considered it authentic and Ibn Ḥajar rejected the claim of forgery, authenticating a similar ḥadīth from Jābir: "The Prophet ﷺ commanded the sun which lagged back for an hour during the day."[29] In any case, the Ulema concur that al-Ṭaḥāwī was a major ḥadīth Master regardless of his ruling on this ḥadīth.

- *Al-Shurūṭ al-Awsaṭ, al-Kabīr,* and *al-Ṣaghīr,* in which al-Ṭaḥāwī shows his unsurpassed mastery of the science of *shurūṭ* or Correct Transactions.
- *Sunan al-Shāfi'ī,* narrated from his uncle al-Muzanī from the Imām. This monograph of al-Shāfi'ī's narrations comes to us from al-Ṭaḥāwī through three of his students: Abū al-Qāsim Maymūn ibn Ḥamza al-Mu'addal; Muḥammad ibn al-Muẓaffar ibn Mūsā al-Bazzār the ḥadīth Master; and Abū Bakr Muḥammad ibn Ibrāhīm ibn 'Alī ibn 'Āṣim al-Muqri'. The work known as the *Musnad* of al-Shāfi'ī is different and was compiled by the trustworthy ḥadīth Master Abū al-'Abbās al-Aṣamm (247-346) from his hearing al-Rabī' ibn Sulaymān al-Murādī's narrations from the Imām in *al-Umm.*[30]
- *Tafsīr Mutashābih al-Akhbār,* mentioned by Ibn Taymiyya in *Minhāj al-Sunna al-Nabawiyya.*

Ibn Mandah and Ibn Shāhīn; al-Ḥusayn by al-Dūlābī in *al-Dhurriyyat al-Ṭāhira* (p. 91 §164); from Abū Hurayra by Ibn Mardūyah with a fair chain per al-Suyūṭī in the *Durar* (p104 §99); and from 'Alī; deemed *ṣaḥīḥ* by al-Suyūṭī after al-Qāḍī 'Iyāḍ in *al-Shifā* (p. 347-348 §684) cf. *Fayḍ al-Qadīr* (§7889), Ibn al-Ḥadhdhā' al-Ḥaskānī (d. >470), Ibn Burhān al-Dīn al-Ḥalabī, Ibn al-Zamalkānī, and others while Ibn al-Jawzī, Ibn Taymiyya, al-Mizzī, al-Dhahabī in the *Mīzān* and *Tartīb al-Mawḍū'āt,* and al-Qārī in *al-Maṣnū'* declared it forged; cf. Ibn Kathīr, *Bidāya* (5:80-90), al-Nabhānī, *Ḥujjat Allāh* (p. 398).

[29] Narrated from Jābir by al-Ṭabarānī in *al-Awsaṭ* with a fair chain; cf. *Fatḥ* (6:221) and al-Haythamī (8:296). The editor of the *Mushkil* cites all the negative rulings but does not mention this. Further, his edition of the *Mushkil* is missing the words of al-Ṭaḥāwī cited by 'Iyāḍ verbatim (cf. Ibn al-Zamalkānī, *'Ujālat al-Rākib* p. 44): "These two ḥadīths [from Asmā' bint 'Umays] are firmly established as authentic and their narrators are trustworthy (*fa-hādhāni al-ḥadīthāni thābitāni wa-ruwātuhumā thiqāt*)!"

[30] Cf. al-Dhahabī, *Siyar* (10:397).

- *Al-Taswiya bayna Ḥaddathanā wa-Akhbaranā*, showing that the two terms can be identical in ḥadīth terminology.

Al-Ṭaḥāwī once said: "None imitates except a fanatic or a dolt" (*lā yuqallidu illā 'aṣabiyyun aw ghabī*). The meaning of this phrase is not absolute but applies only if three conditions are met: one is actually qualified and capable of discerning the stronger position without the shadow of a doubt and has reached certainty of its superiority yet follows the weaker position out of loyalty to his School.[31]

The author narrates by *ijāza* from Shaykh Muḥammad Muṭī' al-Ḥāfiẓ al-Dimashqī with his chain through Shaykh Ismā'īl al-'Ajlūnī the compiler of *Kashf al-Khafā'*, through Shaykh al-Islām Zakariyyā al-Anṣārī, through Shaykh Muḥyī al-Dīn Ibn 'Arabī, from Ibn 'Asākir with a strong chain through al-Ṭaḥāwī, from Yūnus ibn 'Abd al-A'lā al-Ṣadafī, from 'Abd Allāh ibn Wahb ibn Muslim, from 'Abd Allāh ibn 'Umar ibn Ḥafṣ, from 'Abd al-Raḥmān ibn Qāsim, from his father al-Qāsim ibn Muḥammad, from his grand-aunt 'Ā'isha ﷺ the Mother of the Believers who said: "I saw someone the Day of the Trench with the exact appearance of Diḥya ibn Khalīfa al-Kalbī, mounted, speaking with the Messenger of Allāh ﷺ in private, wearing a turban with its extremity hanging on his back. I asked the Messenger of Allāh ﷺ about him and he said: 'This is Gibrīl ﷺ, he ordered me to go out to [fight] the Banū Qurayẓa.'"[32]

Abū Ḥanīfa Innovated the Sub-Headings of *Fiqh*

Al-Suyūṭī said that Abū Ḥanīfa was the first in Islam to organize the writing of *fiqh* under sub-headings embracing the whole of the Law, beginning with purity (*ṭahāra*) followed by prayer (*ṣalāt*), an order which was retained by all subsequent Scholars such as Mālik, al-Shāfi'ī, Abū Dāwūd, al-Bukhārī, Muslim, al-Tirmidhī, and others.[33]

[31] This does not apply to every single imitator of a School. It would have been preferable that the editor of *Sharḥ Mushkil al-Āthār* clarify this distinction, but he is satisfied with quoting al-Ṭaḥāwī's statement four times or more in his introduction without once clarifying it. Imām Zufar, for example, generally imitated Abū Ḥanīfa's positions after his death because he declared his inability to reach absolute certainty of the superiority of his finding when it contradicted that of the Imām in view of his knowledge of the latter's perspicuity. Cf. al-Nawawī, Ibn 'Ābidīn, and Ibn Rajab below (p. 227).

[32] Narrated by Ibn 'Asākir (5:367-368).

[33] Cf. also *I'lā' al-Sunan, Muqaddima, Abū Ḥanīfa wa-Aṣḥābuh* (p. 78).

All these and their followers are indebted to him and give him a share of their reward because he was the first to open that road for them, according to the ḥadīth of the Prophet ﷺ:

> He who starts something good in Islām has its reward and the reward of those who practice it until the Day of Judgement, without lessening in the least the reward of those who practice it. The one who starts something bad in Islām will incur its punishment and the punishment of all those who practice it until the Day of Judgement without lessening their punishment in the least.[34]

عَنْ الْمُنْذِرِ بْنِ جَرِيرٍ عَنْ أَبِيهِ قَالَ كُنَّا عِنْدَ رَسُولِ اللَّهِ صَلَّى اللَّهُ عَلَيْهِ وَسَلَّمَ
فِي صَدْرِ النَّهَارِ قَالَ فَجَاءَهُ قَوْمٌ حُفَاةٌ عُرَاةٌ مُجْتَابِي النِّمَارِ أَوِ الْعَبَاءِ مُتَقَلِّدِي
السُّيُوفِ عَامَّتُهُمْ مِنْ مُضَرَ بَلْ كُلُّهُمْ مِنْ مُضَرَ فَتَمَعَّرَ وَجْهُ رَسُولِ اللَّهِ صَلَّى
اللَّهُ عَلَيْهِ وَسَلَّمَ لِمَا رَأَى بِهِمْ مِنْ الْفَاقَةِ فَدَخَلَ ثُمَّ خَرَجَ فَأَمَرَ بِلَالًا فَأَذَّنَ وَأَقَامَ
فَصَلَّى ثُمَّ خَطَبَ فَقَالَ يَا أَيُّهَا النَّاسُ اتَّقُوا رَبَّكُمُ الَّذِي خَلَقَكُمْ مِنْ نَفْسٍ
وَاحِدَةٍ إِلَى آخِرِ الْآيَةِ إِنَّ اللَّهَ كَانَ عَلَيْكُمْ رَقِيبًا وَالْآيَةَ الَّتِي فِي الْحَشْرِ اتَّقُوا
اللَّهَ وَلْتَنْظُرْ نَفْسٌ مَا قَدَّمَتْ لِغَدٍ وَاتَّقُوا اللَّهَ تَصَدَّقَ رَجُلٌ مِنْ دِينَارِهِ مِنْ دِرْهَمِهِ
مِنْ ثَوْبِهِ مِنْ صَاعِ بُرِّهِ مِنْ صَاعِ تَمْرِهِ حَتَّى قَالَ وَلَوْ بِشِقِّ تَمْرَةٍ قَالَ فَجَاءَ رَجُلٌ
مِنْ الْأَنْصَارِ بِصُرَّةٍ كَادَتْ كَفُّهُ تَعْجِزُ عَنْهَا بَلْ قَدْ عَجَزَتْ قَالَ ثُمَّ تَتَابَعَ النَّاسُ
حَتَّى رَأَيْتُ كَوْمَيْنِ مِنْ طَعَامٍ وَثِيَابٍ حَتَّى رَأَيْتُ وَجْهَ رَسُولِ اللَّهِ صَلَّى اللَّهُ
عَلَيْهِ وَسَلَّمَ يَتَهَلَّلُ كَأَنَّهُ مُذْهَبَةٌ فَقَالَ رَسُولُ اللَّهِ صَلَّى اللَّهُ عَلَيْهِ وَسَلَّمَ مَنْ سَنَّ
فِي الْإِسْلَامِ سُنَّةً حَسَنَةً فَلَهُ أَجْرُهَا وَأَجْرُ مَنْ عَمِلَ بِهَا بَعْدَهُ مِنْ غَيْرِ أَنْ يَنْقُصَ

[34] Narrated from Jarīr ibn 'Abd Allāh by Muslim.

مِنْ أُجُورِهِمْ شَيْءٌ وَمَنْ سَنَّ فِي الْإِسْلَامِ سُنَّةً سَيِّئَةً كَانَ عَلَيْهِ وِزْرُهَا وَوِزْرُ
مَنْ عَمِلَ بِهَا مِنْ بَعْدِهِ مِنْ غَيْرِ أَنْ يَنْقُصَ مِنْ أَوْزَارِهِمْ شَيْءٌ م ت ن جه حم

Sufyān al-Thawrī's Awe before Abū Ḥanīfa

Although he had felt acrimony toward Abū Ḥanīfa at first, Sufyān al-Thawrī later said: "We were in front of Abū Ḥanīfa like small birds in front of the falcon." He stood up for him when Abū Ḥanīfa visited him after his brother's death, saying: "This man holds a high rank in knowledge, and if I did not stand up for his science I would stand up for his age, and if not for his age then for his Godwariness (*wara'*), and if not for his Godwariness then for his jurisprudence (*fiqh*)."

Ibn Jurayj's Praise of Abū Ḥanīfa

Rawḥ ibn 'Ubāda said: "I was with Ibn Jurayj in the year 150 when the news of Abū Ḥanīfa's death reached him. He winced and pain seized him; he said: 'Knowledge has departed.' Ibn Jurayj died that same year."[35]

Ibn al-Mubārak's Praise and Vindication of Abū Ḥanīfa

Ibn al-Mubārak praised Abū Ḥanīfa and called him a Sign of Allāh. Both al-Thawrī and Ibn al-Mubārak said: "Abū Ḥanīfa was in his time the most knowledgeable of all people on earth." Abū Wahb Muḥammad ibn Muzāḥim said that he heard Ibn al-Mubārak say: "The most knowledgeable of human beings in *fiqh* (*afqah al-nās*) is Abū Ḥanīfa. I have never seen anyone like him in *fiqh*."

Ibn Ḥajar also related that Ibn al-Mubārak said: "If Allāh had not rescued me with Abū Ḥanīfa and Sufyān [al-Thawrī] I would have been like the rest of the common people." Al-Dhahabī relates it as: "I would have been an innovator."[36]

Like every Friend of Allāh, Abū Ḥanīfa had his enemies. 'Abdān said that he heard Ibn al-Mubārak say: "If you hear them mention Abū Ḥanīfa derogatively then they are mentioning me derogatively. In truth I fear for them Divine displeasure." Ḥāmid ibn Ādam al-Marwazī

[35] Ibn Ḥajar, *Tahdhīb al-Tahdhīb* (10:449-452 §817).

[36] Ibn Ḥajar, *Tahdhīb* (10:449-452 §817) and al-Dhahabī's *Manāqib Abī Ḥanīfa.*

said: I heard Ibn al-Mubārak say: "I never saw anyone more fearful of Allāh than Abū Ḥanīfa, even on trial under the whip and through money and property."

Ibn al-Mubārak relates his visit to al-Awzā'ī in Beirut and the latter's question about Abū Ḥanīfa:

> "Khurāsānī! Who is that innovator who came out in al-Kūfa, known as Abū Ḥanīfa?" I went back home and pored over the books of Abū Ḥanīfa, extracting from them several outstanding discussions, which took me three days. The third day, I came back – he was the *mu'adhdhin* as well as the imām of their mosque [in Beirut] – with the book [of excerpts] in my hand. He asked, "What book is this?" I handed it to him. He read one of its discussions at random. He kept on reading as he was standing – after raising the *adhān* – until he read the first part of the book. Then he placed the book in his sleeve, raised the *iqāma*, prayed, and brought out the book again. He said, "Khurāsānī! Who is al-Nu'mān ibn Thābit?" I said, "A shaykh I met in Iraq." He said, "This is a grand master (*hādhā nabīlun min al-ashyākh*). Go to him and take as much as you can from him!" I said, "This is the Abū Ḥanīfa you forbade me to see."[37]

Ibn 'Ā'isha's Vindication of Abū Ḥanīfa

Ibn Abī Dāwūd said on the authority of Naṣr ibn 'Alī that he heard Ibn Dāwūd al-Khuraybī say: "Among the people there are plenty of enviers and ignorant ones concerning Abū Ḥanīfa." Aḥmad ibn 'Abda the Qāḍī of Rayy said that his father said: "We were with [Abū 'Abd al-Raḥmān 'Ubayd Allāh ibn Muḥammad ibn Ḥafṣ] Ibn 'Ā'isha [al-'Ayshī al-Taymī al-Baṣrī] (d. 228) when he mentioned a fatwa of Abū Ḥanīfa, then he said: 'Truly, if you had seen him you would have wanted him. Truly, his similitude and yours is as in the saying:

Curse them much or not, I care little to blame you;
But fill – if you can! – the space they left vacant.' "

Imām Mālik's Praise of Abū Ḥanīfa

Al-Layth ibn Sa'd said to Imām Mālik: "I see you sweating." Mālik

[37] Narrated by al-Khaṭīb in *Tārīkh Baghdād* (13:338).

replied: "I sweated with Abū Ḥanīfa. Verily he is a true *faqīh*, O Egyptian!"[38]

Shaykh al-Islām Zakariyyā al-Anṣārī in *Sharḥ al-Bukhārī* and Ibn Khallikān in *Wafayāt al-A'yān* – both Shāfi'īs – count al-Layth among the Ḥanafīs as do the Ḥanafī books of *Ṭabaqāt*.

Yaḥyā ibn Sa'īd al-Qaṭṭān's *Taqlīd* of Abū Ḥanīfa

Ibn Ḥajar narrates in his notice on Abū Ḥanīfa in *Tahdhīb al-Tahdhīb* that Aḥmad ibn 'Alī ibn Sa'īd al-Qāḍī said that he heard Yaḥyā ibn Ma'īn say that he heard Yaḥyā ibn Sa'īd al-Qaṭṭān [Aḥmad ibn Ḥanbal's shaykh] say: "This is no lie on our part, by Allāh! We have not heard better than Abū Ḥanīfa's opinion, and we have followed most of his sayings."[39]

Al-Shāfi'ī's Praise of Abū Ḥanīfa's Leadership in *Fiqh*

Al-Shāfi'ī referred to Abū Ḥanīfa's pioneering in *fiqh* in his famous saying: "People are all the dependents of Abū Ḥanīfa in *fiqh*, Ibn Isḥāq in history, Mālik in ḥadīth, and Muqātil in *tafsīr*."[40] Others who are credited with being the first to compile books in Islām are the *Qadarī* Sa'īd ibn Abī 'Arūba [Ibn Mahrān], al-Awzā'ī, and Ibn Jurayj who said: "No one consigned [Islamic] knowledge into books before me."[41]

Al-Khaṭīb goes on to name also al-Rabī' ibn Ṣubayḥ, Shu'ba ibn al-Ḥajjāj, Ḥammād ibn Salama (all three in Baṣra), Ma'mar ibn Rāshid in Yemen, Sufyān al-Thawrī in Kūfa, Mālik ibn Anas in Madīna, then

[38] Narrated by al-Qāḍī 'Iyāḍ in *Tartīb al-Madārik* (1:152) cf. al-Kawtharī in *Ta'nīb al-Khaṭīb* (orig. ed. p. 7).

[39] About Yaḥyā al-Qaṭṭān, Imām Nawawī relates on the authority of Isḥāq al-Shāhidī: "I would see Yaḥyā al-Qaṭṭān – Allāh the Exalted have mercy on him! – pray the midafternoon prayer, then sit with his back against the base of the minaret of his mosque. Then 'Alī ibn al-Madīnī, al-Shādhakūnī, 'Amr ibn 'Alī, Aḥmad ibn Ḥanbal, Yaḥyā ibn Ma'īn, and others would stand before him and ask him questions about ḥadīth standing on their feet until it was time for the sunset prayer. He would not say to a single one of them: 'Sit' nor would they sit, out of awe and reverence." Al-Nawawī, *al-Tarkhīṣ fil-Ikrām bil-Qiyām li-Dhawī al-Faḍl wal-Maziyya min Ahl al-Islām 'alā Jihat al-Birr wal-Tawqīr wal-Iḥtirām lā 'alā Jihat al-Riyā' wal-I'ẓām* ("The Permissibility of Dignifying, by Standing up, Those Who Possess Excellence and Distinction among the People of Islām in the Spirit of Piousness, Reverence, and Respect, not in the Spirit of Display and Pomp") (p. 58).

[40] Cf. Ibn Ḥajar, *Tahdhīb al-Tahdhīb* (10:449-452 §817).

[41] Cf. al-Khaṭīb, *al-Jāmi' li-Akhlāq al-Rāwī* (2:424).

Sufyān ibn 'Uyayna in Makka, Hushaym ibn Bashīr in Wāsiṭ, Jarīr ibn 'Abd al-Ḥamīd in Rayy, 'Abd Allāh ibn al-Mubārak in Khurāsān, Wakī' ibn al-Jarrāḥ, Yaḥyā ibn Zakariyyā ibn Abī Zā'ida, Muḥammad ibn Fuḍayl ibn Ghazwān (all three in Kūfa), 'Abd Allāh ibn Wahb in Egypt, al-Walīd ibn Muslim in Damascus, then 'Abd al-Razzāq ibn Hammām, Abū Qurra Mūsā ibn Ṭāriq (both in Yemen), and Rawḥ ibn 'Ubāda in Baṣra.

Al-Dāraquṭnī said: "The first to have compiled a *Musnad* and updated it was Nu'aym ibn Ḥammād."[42]

Al-Faḍl ibn Dukayn's Praise of Abū Ḥanīfa

Al-Khaṭīb narrated from Abū Ḥanīfa's student Abū Nu'aym al-Faḍl ibn Dukayn[43] that the latter said: "Muslims should make *du'a* to Allāh on behalf of Abū Ḥanīfa in their prayers, because the *Sunan* and the *fiqh* were preserved for them through him." He also said: "Abū Ḥanīfa dived for the meaning of matters so that he reached their outermost limits."

Al-Dhahabī's Praise of Abū Ḥanīfa

Al-Shāfi'ī said: "Knowledge revolves around three men: Mālik, al-Layth, and Ibn 'Uyayna." Al-Dhahabī commented: "And it revolves also around al-Awzā'ī, al-Thawrī, Ma'mar, Abū Ḥanīfa, Shu'ba, and the two Ḥammāds [ibn Zayd and ibn Salama]."[44] Al-Dhahabī wrote one volume on the life of each of the other three great Imāms and said: "The account of Abū Ḥanīfa's life requires two volumes."

Abū Ḥanīfa on Imitation *(Taqlīd)*

Like Mālik, al-Shāfi'ī, and Aḥmad, Abū Ḥanīfa advocated imitation of the Companions and said: "As for the Companions of the Messenger of Allāh ﷺ, I follow the position of whomever I wish among them nor do I differ from the position of all of them. I only need investigate the

[42] *Ibid.* (2:443 §1956).

[43] This is not the ḥadīth Master Abū Nu'aym al-Aṣbahānī but the ḥadīth Master al-Faḍl ibn Dukayn 'Amr ibn Ḥammād al-Taymī al-Kūfī (130-219), one of the *Umarā' al-Mu'minīn fīl-Ḥadīth*, the Shaykh of al-Bukhārī, Aḥmad, Ibn Ma'īn, and others. Al-Khaṭīb, *op. cit.* (2:270 §1611) narrates that al-Faḍl was narrating ḥadīth when one of the students said: "Abū Nu'aym! I have run out of blank pages!" Al-Faḍl ignored him. When he repeated his remark al-Faḍl said: "Go write in the ear of a goose, you flea-hunter!" See also p. 302.

[44] Al-Dhahabī, *Siyar* (7:412).

positions of those who come after them – the *Tābiʿīn* and subsequent generations."[45] Al-Ṣāghānī said on the authority of Ibn Maʿīn that he heard ʿUbayd ibn Abī Qurra say that he heard Yaḥyā ibn al-Ḍarīs say that he saw Sufyān [al-Thawrī] being asked by a man: "What do you have against Abū Ḥanīfa?" He said: "And what is wrong with Abū Ḥanīfa? I heard him say: 'I take [rulings] from the Book of Allāh ﷻ and if I do not find what I am looking for, then I take from the Sunna of the Messenger of Allāh ﷺ, and if I do not find it there, then from any of the sayings that I like from the Companions, nor do I prefer someone else's saying over theirs, until the matter ends with Ibrāhīm [al-Nakhaʿī], al-Shaʿbī [Abū Ḥanīfa's first teacher], Ibn Sīrīn, and ʿAṭā': these are a folk who exerted their reasoning (*ijtihād*) and I exert mine as they did theirs.'"[46] Sufyān had criticized Abū Ḥanīfa, a junior *Tābiʿī*, for placing his own opinion at the same level as that of the senior *Tābiʿīn*. Another example of similar brilliance is the superiority of al-Awzāʿī (d. 158) over his *Tābiʿī* Shaykh Makḥūl (d. 113).[47]

His Scrupulous Godwariness and Generosity

Ibn Abī Khaythama narrated from Sulaymān ibn Abī Shaykh: "Abū Ḥanīfa was extremely scrupulous (*wariʿ*) and generous (*sakhī*)."[48] The biographies all report that he was particularly generous to his students and supported those of them who were in need, most notably Abū Yūsuf.

Ismāʿīl ibn Ḥammād ibn Abī Ḥanīfa said that his father (Ḥammād) said: When my father died we asked al-Ḥasan ibn ʿAmāra to undertake his ritual washing. After he did he said: "May Allāh have mercy on you and forgive you, Abū Ḥanīfa! You did not eat except at night for thirty years, and your right side did not lay down at night for forty years. You have exhausted whoever comes after you!"[49]

The author of *Nuzhat al-Majālis* mentioned that one time Abū Ḥanīfa received some merchandise. Merchants came to him looking to buy it for a certain amount. Abū Ḥanīfa said: "Wait until the sun rises." In the morning, other merchants came to him looking to buy it

[45] Cited by Ibn ʿAbd al-Barr in his *Jāmiʿ Bayān al-ʿIlm* (2:908).

[46] Ibn Ḥajar, *Tahdhīb al-Tahdhīb* (10:449-452 §817).

[47] As related and emphatically endorsed by al-Dhahabī in the *Siyar* (Fikr ed. 7:89).

[48] Ibn Ḥajar, *Tahdhīb al-Tahdhīb* (10:449-452 §817).

[49] *Ibid.*

for a higher amount than the former merchants. He said: "I have made the intention to sell it to the others."

Trials of the Imām

'Alī ibn Ma'bad said on the authority of 'Ubayd Allāh ibn 'Amr al-Rāqī: "Ibn Hubayra told Abū Ḥanīfa to undertake the judgeship of Kūfa and he refused, so he had him lashed 110 times – ten times a day for eleven days – but still he refused. When he saw this he let him go."[50]

Shaykh Wahbī Ghāwjī mentioned in his biography of Abū Ḥanīfa that the Imam underwent four *fitnas*. The first and second were with the *Khawārij*, the third with the governor Ibn Hubayra in 130, and the fourth with Abū Ja'far al-Manṣūr who imprisoned and tortured him then released him under house arrest until his death in Baghdad.[51]

His Incessant Worship and Nickname of "Pillar"

Ibrāhīm ibn Rustum al-Marwazī said: "Four are the Imāms that recited the entire Qur'ān in a single *rak'a*: 'Uthmān ibn 'Affān, Tamīm al-Dārī, Sa'īd ibn Jubayr, and Abū Ḥanīfa." Among those who completed a *khatma* in every twenty-four hours were Mujāhid the great Qur'ānic commentator, 'Alī ibn 'Abd Allāh al-Bāriqī al-Azdī, Sa'd ibn Ibrāhīm ibn 'Abd al-Raḥmān ibn 'Awf al-Zuhrī, Ḥabīb ibn Abī Thābit the *Tābi'ī*, the Ṣūfī Shaykh Ibn Khafīf al-Shīrāzī, and others. Like the two Imāms al-Bukhārī and al-Shāfi'ī, Abū Ḥanīfa reportedly made sixty complete recitations (*khatma*) of Qur'ān every Ramaḍān – one in the day and one in the night – besides his teaching and other duties.

Al-Nawawī in *al-Tibyān fī Ādāb Ḥamalat al-Qur'ān* cites among those who completed three or four *khatmas* every day and/or night were Sulaym ibn 'Itr the Qāḍī of Cairo under Mu'āwiya – as narrated respectively by Ibn Abī Dāwūd and Abū 'Umar al-Kindī – and Abū al-Mughīra Manṣūr ibn Zādhān al-Wāsiṭī (d. 131), while Ibn al-Kātib Abū 'Alī al-Ḥusayn or al-Ḥasan ibn Aḥmad (d.>340) is reported to have completed eight *katmas* in every twenty-four hours, four in the day and four at night, "and this is the most that was ever reported."[52]

50 *Ibid.* and al-Muwaffaq, *Manāqib Abī Ḥanīfa* (2:12).

51 Cf. *Intiqā'* (p. 243, 255, 324-325) and Ibn al-Bazzāzī's *Manāqib Abī Ḥanīfa* (2:19) unless he died in prison, poisoned cf. al-Muwaffaq's *Manāqib* (2:174), in a state of *sajda* as narrated by al-Muwaffaq (2:185) from Abū Ḥayyān al-Ziyādī. Allāh knows best.

52 Al-Nawawī, *al-Tibyān* (1992 ed. p. 45-49=1993 ed. p. 54-61).

Ibn al-Mubārak said: "Abū Ḥanīfa for a long time prayed all five prayers with a single ablution." It is also reported that he prayed the dawn prayer with the same ablution as the night prayer for over forty years, as did Mālik, Sulaymān ibn Ṭarkhān al-Taymī and others.

Al-Suyūṭī relates in *Tabyīḍ al-Ṣaḥīfa* that Mis'ar ibn Kidām came to observe Abū Ḥanīfa and saw him all day long in the mosque, teaching relentlessly, answering every question from both the scholars and the common people, not stopping except to pray, then standing at home in prayer when people were asleep, hardly ever eating or sleeping, and yet the most handsome and gracious of people, always alert and never tired, day after day for a long time, so that in the end he said: "I became convinced that this was not an ordinary matter, but friendship with Allāh (*wilāya*)."

Abū 'Āṣim al-Nabīl said that Abū Ḥanīfa's nickname was "the Pillar" (*al-watad*) because he spent so much time standing in prayer. He would pray at night at such length that his neighbors would invoke Allāh for mercy on his behalf and when he died, the funeral prayer was performed six times over him due to the huge crowds in Baghdād.[53]

Imām al-Nawawī in his introduction to *al-Majmū'* cited from Imām Abū Ḥanīfa the saying: "One must arm oneself, in the pursuit of *fiqh*, with strong focus (*jam' al-hamm*), and, in the severing of [harmful] ties, with small means to meet one's needs – without increase."

Some Positions of Abū Ḥanīfa

HIS INFERENCE OF THE TIME OF *'ASR* FROM THE PARABLE OF THE COMMUNITIES

An example of Abū Ḥanīfa's perspicuity in inferring legal rulings from source-texts is his reading of the following ḥadīth:

> The Prophet ﷺ said: "Your life in comparison to the lifetime of past nations is like the period between the time of the mid-afternoon prayer and sunset. Your example and the example of the Jews and Christians is that of a man who employed laborers and said to them: 'Who will work for me until mid-day for one *qīrāṭ*[54] each?' The Jews worked until mid-day for one *qīrāṭ* each. Then the man said: 'Who will work for me from mid-day until the *'aṣr* prayer for one *qīrāṭ* each?' The Christians worked from mid-day until the

[53] Ibn Kathīr, *Bidāya* (10:123).

[54] A unit of measure, part of a dinar.

'aṣr prayer for one *qīrāṭ* each. Then the man said: 'Who will work for me from the *'aṣr* prayer until the *maghrib* prayer for two *qīrāṭs* each?' And that, in truth, is all of you. Truly you have double the wages. The Jews and Christians became angry and said: 'We did more labor but took less wages!' Allāh said: 'Have I wronged you in any of your rights?' They replied no. Then He said: 'This is My Blessing which I give to whom I wish.'"[55]

عَنْ ابْنِ عُمَرَ رَضِيَ اللَّهُ عَنْهُمَا عَنْ النَّبِيِّ صَلَّى اللَّهُ عَلَيْهِ وَسَلَّمَ قَالَ مَثَلُكُمْ
وَمَثَلُ أَهْلِ الْكِتَابَيْنِ كَمَثَلِ رَجُلٍ اسْتَأْجَرَ أُجَرَاءَ فَقَالَ مَنْ يَعْمَلُ لِي مِنْ غُدْوَةٍ
إِلَى نِصْفِ النَّهَارِ عَلَى قِيرَاطٍ فَعَمِلَتْ الْيَهُودُ ثُمَّ قَالَ مَنْ يَعْمَلُ لِي مِنْ نِصْفِ
النَّهَارِ إِلَى صَلَاةِ الْعَصْرِ عَلَى قِيرَاطٍ فَعَمِلَتْ النَّصَارَى ثُمَّ قَالَ مَنْ يَعْمَلُ لِي
مِنْ الْعَصْرِ إِلَى أَنْ تَغِيبَ الشَّمْسُ عَلَى قِيرَاطَيْنِ فَأَنْتُمْ هُمْ فَغَضِبَتْ الْيَهُودُ
وَالنَّصَارَى فَقَالُوا مَا لَنَا أَكْثَرَ عَمَلًا وَأَقَلَّ عَطَاءً قَالَ هَلْ نَقَصْتُكُمْ مِنْ حَقِّكُمْ
قَالُوا لَا قَالَ فَذَلِكَ فَضْلِي أُوتِيهِ مَنْ أَشَاءُ خ ت حم

It was deduced from the phrase "We did more labor" that the time of mid-day to *'aṣr* must always be longer than that between *aṣr* and *maghrib*. This is confirmed by the following reports:

- The Prophet ﷺ hastened to pray *ẓuhr* and delayed praying *'aṣr*.[56]

عَنْ أُمِّ سَلَمَةَ رَضِيَ اللهُ عَنْهَا أَنَّهَا قَالَتْ كَانَ رَسُولُ اللهِ صَلَّى اللَّهُ عَلَيْهِ
وَسَلَّمَ أَشَدَّ تَعْجِيلًا لِلظُّهْرِ مِنْكُمْ وَأَنْتُمْ أَشَدُّ تَعْجِيلًا لِلْعَصْرِ مِنْهُ ت حم وَعَنْ
عَلِيِّ بْنِ شَيْبَانَ رَضِيَ اللهُ عَنْهُ قَالَ قَدِمْنَا عَلَى رَسُولِ اللهِ صَلَّى اللَّهُ عَلَيْهِ
وَسَلَّمَ الْمَدِينَةَ فَكَانَ يُؤَخِّرُ الْعَصْرَ مَا دَامَتِ الشَّمْسُ بَيْضَاءَ نَقِيَّةً د

[55] Narrated from Ibn 'Umar by al-Bukhārī, al-Tirmidhī, and Aḥmad.

[56] Narrated from Umm Salama ؓ by al-Tirmidhī and Aḥmad with sound chains per *I'lā' al-Sunan* (2:42 §490) cf. a similar report from 'Alī ibn Shaybān by Abū Dāwūd.

- The Prophet ﷺ said: "Allāh have mercy on someone who prays four *rak'as* before *'aṣr.*"[57]

عَنْ ابْنِ عُمَرَ رَضِيَ اللهُ عَنْهُمَا قَالَ قَالَ رَسُولُ اللهِ صَلَّى اللهُ عَلَيْهِ وَسَلَّمَ
رَحِمَ اللَّهُ امْرَأً صَلَّى قَبْلَ الْعَصْرِ أَرْبَعًا د ت وحسّنه

- 'Alī ؓ delayed praying 'aṣr until shortly before the sun changed and reprimanded the *mu'adhdhin* who was hurrying him with the words: "He is trying to teach us the Sunna!"[58]
- Ibrāhīm al-Nakha'ī said: "Those that came before you used to hasten more than you to pray *ẓuhr* and delay more than you in praying *'aṣr.*"[59] Al-Tahānawī said: "Those that came before you" are the Companions.
- Ibn Mas'ūd also delayed praying *'aṣr.*[60]

Sufyān al-Thawrī and Abū Ḥanīfa therefore lengthened the time between *Ẓuhr* and *'Aṣr* by (1) considering that the time for *'Aṣr* began when the shadow of an object reached two lengths and (2) preferably delaying the latter prayer for as long as the sun did not begin to redden – up to one hour before *Maghrib.* An added benefit of Abū Ḥanīfa's position is the increase of permitted time for *nawāfil,* as they are not permitted after *'Aṣr.* That the earlier time (one-length shadow) is both the beginning of *'Aṣr* time and the preferred time is the fatwa of the companions of the Imām – Imāms Muḥammad ibn al-Ḥasan and Abū Yūsuf, in line with the other Three Schools, on the basis of other sound evidence to that effect.

57 Narrated from Ibn 'Umar by Abū Dāwūd and al-Tirmidhī who graded it *ḥasan gharīb.*

58 Narrated from Ziyād ibn 'Abd al-Raḥmān al-Nakha'ī by al-Ḥākim (1:192) who said it is *ṣaḥīḥ,* and al-Dhahabī concurred as claimed in *I'lā' al-Sunan* (2:43-44 §493) but Ziyād is unknown. Al-Dāraquṭnī in his *Sunan* (1:251) names him Ziyād ibn 'Abd Allāh al-Nakha'ī – another unknown. And Allāh knows best.

59 Narrated by 'Abd al-Razzāq with a sound chain according to al-Tahānawī in *I'lā' al-Sunan* (2:44 §494).

60 Narrated from 'Abd al-Raḥmān ibn Yazīd by 'Abd al-Razzāq (1:551 §2089) and Ibn Abī Shayba (§22701) with sound chains according to *I'lā' al-Sunan* (2:45 §496).

The summation of the Ḥanafī position is as follows:

The top Scholars of the late Ḥanafī school have deemed the Imām's position to be more sound, as expressed by Kamāl ibn al-Humām in *Fatḥ al-Qadīr*, Ibn Nujaym in his *Baḥr al-Rā'iq* (and in a separate treatise he wrote just on the topic), as well as Ibn 'Ābidīn himself in his *Radd al-Muḥtār* (*al-Ḥāshiya*), where he objected to al-Ḥaskafī quoting that the fatwa is on the position of the Two Companions. Ibn 'Ābidīn's student, al-Maydānī, approvingly quotes his teacher's position in his *Lubāb fī Sharḥ al-Kitāb*. Among the late Ḥanafī ḥadīth Masters – besides Ibn al-Humām – who chose the Imām's position was Imām Badr al-Dīn al-'Aynī and Mullā 'Alī al-Qārī, as well as most of the great Ḥanafī ḥadīth commentators and *Fuqahā'* of the Indo-Pakistani sub-continent, except Imām al-Lacknawī. As Ibn 'Ābidīn mentions in his *Ḥāshiya* and Imām Ashraf 'Alī al-Tahānawī in his *Imdād al-Fatāwā*, the principle (*aṣl*) is to clear one's obligations with certainty. Given the difference of the Imām in this issue [whose proofs are well discussed in *I'lā' al-Sunan, Awjaz al-Masālik, Badhl al-Majhūd*, and other works, as well as *Fatḥ al-Qadīr*], it is religiously more precautionary to follow Imām Abū Ḥanīfa's position. Of course, if it means missing a congregation or causing *fitna*, then it would be superior to act on the position on the Two Companions. [61]

ON FACING THE PROPHET'S ﷺ GRAVE DURING DU'Ā'

The position is held by some of the Ḥanafī Masters such as Abū al-Layth al-Samarqandī and those that followed him such as al-Kirmānī and al-Sarrūjī as well as al-Kumushkhānawī in *Jāmi' al-Manāsik*, his commentary on Raḥmat Allāh al-Sindī's *Jamī' al-Manāsik*, that Abū Ḥanīfa forbade the facing of the Noble Grave during supplication. However, al-Qārī in *al-Maslak al-Mutaqassiṭ* – his large commentary on the same work by al-Sindī – said that [1] Ibn al-Humām said that it is belied by Abū Ḥanīfa's own narration in his *Musnad* from Ibn 'Umar that it is part of the Sunna to face the Noble Grave and turn one's back to the *Qibla*; [2] Ibn al-Humām also said, "This [narration of Ibn 'Umar] is the sound position (*al-ṣaḥīḥ*) in the *madhhab* of Abū Ḥanīfa, and Abū al-Layth's claim that his *madhhab* is the contrary is untenable

[61] Shaykh Farāz Rabbānī, private communication.

because the Messenger of Allāh ﷺ is alive, and whoever comes to someone who is alive faces him"; [3] al-Qārī added that this is confirmed by al-Fayrūzābādī's narration from Ibn al-Mubārak that Abū Ḥanīfa observed al-Sakhtiyānī do the same during the latter's visitation.[62] Allāh knows best.

HIS SUPPOSED OBJECTION TO *TAWASSUL* (USING INTERMEDIARIES)

Imām Abū Ḥanīfa nowhere objected to *tawassul* but only – as narrated from Abū Yūsuf in *Kitāb al-Āthār* – to the use of specific wordings in supplication, namely, "by the right You owe to So-and-so" (*bi-ḥaqqi fulāni 'alayk*) and "by the joints of power and glory in Your Throne" (*bi-ma'āqid al-'izz min 'arshik*).[63] The reason for this is that, on the one hand, Allāh owes no one any right whatsoever except what He Himself condescends to state on His part as in the verse ﴿**To help believers is incumbent upon Us (*ḥaqqun 'alaynā*)**﴾ (30:47). On the other hand, "by the right owed so-and-so" is an oath and is therefore a formula restricted to Allāh ﷻ Himself on pain of *shirk*. Imām Abū Ḥanīfa said: "Let one not swear any oath except by Allāh alone, with a pure affirmation of *tawḥīd* and sincerity."[64] A third reason is that the expression "the joints of power and glory in Your Throne" is a lone-narrator report and is therefore not retained nor put into practice, in accordance with the rule for any such reports that might suggest anthropomorphism.

Those that claim[65] that the Imām objected to *tawassul* altogether are unable to adduce anything to support such a claim other than the above caveat, which is not against *tawassul* but against a specific, prohibitive wording in *tawassul*. A proof of this is that it is permissible in the Ḥanafī School to say "by the sanctity/honor of so-and-so in Your presence" (*bi-ḥurmati/bi-jāhi fulān*). This is stated in the *Fatāwā Bazzāziyya* (6:351 in the margin of the *Fatāwā Hindiyya*) and is also the position of Abū al-Layth al-Samarqandī and Ibn 'Ābidīn.

[62] Al-Qārī, *al-Maslak al-Mutaqassiṭ* (p. 282), Ibn al-Humām, *Fatḥ al-Qadīr* (3:180).

[63] Cf. al-Zabīdī, *Itḥāf* (2:285), Ibn Abī al-'Izz, *Sharḥ al-'Aqīda al-Ṭaḥāwiyya* (1988 9th ed. p. 237), *Durr* (2:630), *Fatāwā Hindiyya* (5:280), al-Qudūrī, *Sharḥ Mukhtaṣar al-Karkhī*, chapter on detested matters.

[64] Cf. al-Kāsānī, *Badā'i' al-Ṣanā'i'* (3:8).

[65] Cf. Ibn Taymiyya, *Majmū' al-Fatāwā* (1:202-203) and his imitators.

Even so, there is authentic evidence in [1] the ḥadīth of Fāṭima bint Asad,[66] [2] the ḥadīth "O Allāh, I ask You by the right of those who ask You (*bi-ḥaqqi al-sā'ilīna 'alayk*),"[67] [3] the ḥadīth: "O Allāh, I ask You by

[66] Narrated from Anas by al-Ṭabarānī in *al-Kabīr* (24:351) and *al-Awsaṭ* (1:152) and Abū Nu'aym in his *Ḥilya* (1985 ed. 3:121) with a chain containing Rawḥ ibn Ṣalāḥ concerning whom there is difference of opinion among the authorities. He is unknown according to Ibn al-Jawzī in *al-'Ilal al-Mutanāhiya* (1:260-270), Ibn 'Adī in *al-Kāmil* (3:146 §667), and al-Dāraquṭnī in *al-Mu'talif wal-Mukhtalif* (3:1377); Ibn Mākūlā in *al-Ikmāl* (5:15) declared him weak while al-Ḥākim asserted he was trustworthy and highly dependable (*thiqa ma'mūn*) – as mentioned by Ibn Ḥajar in *Lisān al-Mīzān* (2:465 §1876), Ibn Ḥibbān included him in *al-Thiqāt* (8:244), and al-Fasawī considered him trustworthy (cf. Mamdūḥ, *Raf'* p. 148). Al-Haythamī (9:257) said: "Al-Ṭabarānī narrated it in *al-Kabīr* and *al-Awsaṭ*, its chain contains Rawḥ ibn Ṣalāḥ whom Ibn Ḥibbān and al-Ḥākim declared trustworthy although there is some weakness in him, and the rest of its sub-narrators are the men of sound ḥadīth." I was unable to find Abū Ḥātim's declaration of Rawḥ as trustworthy cited by Shaykh Muḥammad ibn 'Alawī, cf. *Mafāhīm* (10th ed. p. 145 n. 1). Nor does Shaykh Maḥmūd Mamdūḥ in his discussion of this ḥadīth in *Raf' al-Mināra li-Takhrīj Aḥādīth al-Tawassul wal-Ziyāra* (p. 147-155) mention such a grading on the part of Abū Ḥātim although he considers Rawḥ "truthful" (*ṣadūq*) and not "weak" (*ḍa'īf*), according to the rules of ḥadīth science when no reason is given with regard to a narrator's purported discreditation (*jarḥ mubham ghayr mufassar*). Mamdūḥ (p. 149-150) noted that although Albānī in his *Silsila Ḍa'īfa* (1:32-33) claims it is a case of explicated discreditation (*jarḥ mufassar*) yet he himself declares identically formulated discreditation cases as unexplained and therefore unacceptable in two different contexts! Al-Mālikī adds that the ḥadīth is also narrated from Ibn 'Abbās by Ibn 'Abd al-Barr – without specifying where – and from Jābir by Ibn Abī Shayba, but without the *du'ā*. Imām al-Kawtharī said of this ḥadīth in his *Maqālāt* (p. 410): "It provides textual evidence whereby there is no difference between the living and the dead in the context of using a means (*tawassul*), and this is explicit *tawassul* through the Prophets, while the ḥadīth of the Prophet ﷺ from Abū Sa'īd al-Khudrī [see next note] constitutes *tawassul* through the generality of the Muslims, both the living and the dead."

[67] A *ḥasan* ḥadīth of the Prophet ﷺ according to Shaykh Maḥmūd Mamdūḥ in his monograph *Mubāḥathat al-Sā'irīn bi-Ḥadīth Allāhumma Innī As'aluka bi-Ḥaqqi al-Sā'ilīn* narrated from Abū Sa'īd al-Khudrī by Aḥmad with a fair chain according to Ḥamza al-Zayn (10:68 §11099) – a weak chain according to al-Arna'ūṭ (17:247-248 §11156) who considers it, like Abū Ḥātim in *al-'Ilal* (2:184), more likely a *mawqūf* saying of Abū Sa'īd himself; Ibn Mājah with a chain he declared weak, Ibn al-Sunnī in *'Amal al-Yawm wal-Layla* (p. 40 §83-84), al-Bayhaqī in *al-Da'awāt al-Kabīr* (p. 47=1:47 §65), Ibn Khuzayma in *al-Tawḥīd* (p. 17-18=1:41) [and his *Ṣaḥīḥ* per al-Būṣīrī, *Zawā'id* (1:98-99)], al-Ṭabarānī in *al-Du'ā'* (p. 149=2:990), Ibn Ja'd in his *Musnad* (p. 299), al-Baghawī in *al-Ja'diyyāt* (§2118-2119) and – *mawqūf* – by Ibn Abī Shayba (6:25=10:211-212) and Ibn Abī Ḥātim, *'Ilal* (2:184). Al-'Irāqī in *Takhrīj Aḥādīth al-Iḥyā'* (1:291) graded it *ḥasan* as a *marfū'* ḥadīth as did the ḥadīth Masters al-Dimyāṭī in *al-Muttajir al-Rābiḥ fī Thawāb al-'Amal al-Ṣāliḥ* (p. 471-472), Ibn Ḥajar in *Amālī al-Adhkār* (1:272-273) and al-Mundhirī's

the joints of power in the Throne,"[68] and [4] the ḥadīth: "Do you know the right owed to Allāh by His slaves and the right owed by Allāh to his slaves?"[69] to support the permissibility of such a wording. If the above objection is authentically reported from Abū Ḥanīfa then either he did not deem these ḥadīths authentic by his standards, or they did not reach him. An illustration of this is that Abū Yūsuf permitted the formula "By the joints of power...".[70] Further, the opposite is also reported from Abū Ḥanīfa, namely, that he permitted *tawassul* using those very expressions. Ibn 'Ābidīn said: "In the *Tatārkhāniyya*: The *Āthār* also report what shows permissibility." Then he cites – from al-Qārī's *Sharḥ al-Niqāya*, al-Munāwī quoting Ibn 'Abd al-Salām (cf. the very first of his *Fatāwā* in the printed Risāla edition), and al-Subkī – further explanations that it is permitted, then he cites the fatwa by Ibn Amīr al-Ḥajj in the thirteenth chapter of *Sharḥ al-Munya* that permissibility is not limited to *tawassul* through the Prophet ﷺ but extends to the *Ṣāliḥīn*.[71]

THE CANCELLATION OF ABLUTION BY LAUGHTER

Among the noted positions of the Imām Abū Ḥanīfa and his School is that laughter during prayer – other *than* the Janāza prayer – invalidates one's ritual purity and he must repeat both the ablution and the prayer. This is based on the Prophetic narration, "Whoever laughs [during prayer], let him renew both his ablution and his prayer."[72]

Shaykh the ḥadīth Master Abū al-Ḥasan al-Maqdisī in *al-Targhīb* (1994 ed. 2:367 §2422=1997 ed. 2:304-305) and as indicated by Ibn Qudāma, *Mughnī* (1985 Dār al-Fikr ed. 1:271). Mamdūḥ in his monograph rejected the weakening of this ḥadīth by Nāṣir Albānī and Ḥammād al-Anṣārī.

[68] Narrated from [1] the Companion Qayla bint Makhrama by al-Ṭabarānī in *al-Kabīr* (25:12) with a fair chain according to al-Haythamī (10:124-125); [2] Ibn Mas'ūd by al-Bayhaqī in *al-Da'awāt al-Kabīr* (2:157 §392) – Ibn al-Jawzī in *al-Mawḍū'āt* (2:142) claimed that it was forged as cited by al-Zayla'ī in *Naṣb al-Rāya* (4:272-273) but this ruling was rejected by al-Suyūṭī in *al-La'āli'* (2:68); [3] *maqṭū'* from Wuhayb by Abū Nu'aym in the *Ḥilya* (1985 ed. 8:158-159); [4] Abū Hurayra by Ibn 'Asākir with a very weak chain cf. Ibn 'Arrāq, *Tanzīh al-Sharī'a* (1:228); and [5] Abū Bakr in *al-Tadwīn* and *al-Firdaws*.

[69] Narrated from Mu'ādh in the *Sunan* and Aḥmad except al-Nasā'ī.

[70] Cf. al-Kāsānī, *Badā'i' al-Ṣanā'i'* (5:126).

[71] Ibn 'Ābidīn, *Ḥāshiya* (6:396-397).

[72] A weak *mursal* narration from Abū al-'Āliya by al-Ṭabarānī, al-Dāraquṭnī in his *Sunan* (1:167-171) and al-Bayhaqī in the *Sunan* (1:147) and *Khilāfiyyāt* cf. Muḥammad ibn al-Ḥasan, *Āthār al-Sunan* (1:421); al-Haythamī (2:82); al-Tahānawī, *I'lā' al-Sunan*

Abū Ḥanīfa's Definition of Sunnism

Abū Ḥanīfa gave one of the pithiest definitions of Sunnism in Islam: "The doctrine of *Ahl al-Sunna wal-Jamā'a* consists in preferring the Two Shaykhs (*tafḍīl al-shaykhayn*) [Abū Bakr and 'Umar], loving the Two Sons-in-law (*ḥubb al-khatanayn*) ['Alī and 'Uthmān], and [deeming lawful the] wiping on leather socks [in ablution] (*al-masḥ 'alāl-khuffayn*)."[73] The middle part of his statement is elucidated by al-Awzā'ī's saying: "Love of 'Alī and 'Uthmān together – Allāh be well-pleased with them! – is not found except in the heart of a Believer."[74] Abū Ḥanīfa also said: "I did not wipe on the two *khuffs* until it became for me as clear as the sun [in its proofs]."

His Praise of Ja'far al-Ṣādiq

Both Mālik – in the *Muwaṭṭa'* – and Abū Ḥanīfa – in his *Musnads* – narrated from Ja'far ibn Muḥammad al-Ṣādiq. Abū Ḥanīfa said: "I never saw one greater in *fiqh* than Ja'far ibn Muḥammad."[75]

His Definition of Belief (*Īmān*)

Both al-Māturīdī and al-Ṭaḥāwī followed Abū Ḥanīfa and his companions in the position that belief (*al-īmān*) consists in "conviction in the heart and affirmation by the tongue," without adding, as do Mālik, al-Shāfi'ī, Aḥmad ibn Ḥanbal and their schools, "practice with the limbs." Al-Māturīdī, as also related from Abū Ḥanīfa, went so far as to

---

(1:158-162=1:95-104); al-Zayla'ī, *Naṣb al-Rāya* (1:29-52=1:47-75); Ibn al-Turkmānī, *al-Jawhar al-Naqī* (1:42); and, especially, al-Lacknawī's comprehensive *al-Ḥashāsa* [or *al-Sahsaha*] *bi-Naqḍ Wuḍū' al-Qahqaha*.

[73] Narrated by Ibn 'Abd al-Barr in *al-Intiqā'* through several different chains. Cf. Abū Ḥanīfa in *Lisān al-Aḥkām*. Also related from Sufyān al-Thawrī by al-Lālikā'ī in *I'tiqād Ahl al-Sunna* (1:152) despite al-Ghumārī in *al-Burhān* (p. 82) who cites from Ibn Abī Khaythama through 'Abd al-Razzāq a report that Sufyān al-Thawrī preferred 'Alī to Abū Bakr and 'Umar. This is not the position reported from the *Salaf*. Al-Qārī said in *Sharḥ al-Fiqh al-Akbar* (p. 140): "It is patent that to prefer 'Alī to the Two Shaykhs contravenes the doctrine of *Ahl al-Sunna wal-Jamā'a* according to what the totality of the *Salaf* follow." See the positions of *Ahl al-Sunna* on the preferability of Abū Bakr over the other three and that of 'Uthmān over 'Alī or vice-versa in our biography of our Master 'Alī ؓ.

[74] Cited by al-Dhahabī in *Siyar A'lām al-Nubalā'* (1997 ed. 7:95).

[75] Narrated from al-Ḥasan ibn Ziyād al-Lu'lu'ī by Ibn 'Adī with his chain in *al-Kāmil fīl-Ḍu'afā'* (2:132), al-Mizzī, *Tahdhīb al-Kamāl* (5:79), al-Dhahabī with his chain from Ibn 'Uqda, *Siyar* (Risāla ed. 6:257) cf. *Tadhkira* (1:166), Ibn Tughrīburdā, *al-Nujūm al-Zāhira* (2:9), and Ibn Abī Awfā, *Ṭabaqāt al-Ḥanafiyya* (1:486).

declare that the foundation of belief consisted only in conviction in the heart, the tongue's affirmation being a supplementary integral or pillar (*rukn zā'id*).[76]

This position was a pivot of disagreement among the Imāms of the *Salaf.* Imām al-Bukhārī took issue with Imām Abū Ḥanīfa over it and devoted pages of his *Ṣaḥīḥ* trying to refute him. This is the context of al-Bukhārī's famous statement: "I met more than one thousand men from the Ḥijāz, Iraq, Syria, Egypt, Khurāsān," and so on until he said: "I never saw a single one of them differ on the following: 'Religion consists in words and deeds, and the Qur'ān is the Speech of Allāḥ'" The first half of the statement is directed against the *Murji'a* and the doctrine of Imām Abū Ḥanīfa that deeds are the complement and not the essence of *īmān.* One of the most explicit proofs in support of the latter is the Prophetic ḥadīth: "*Islām* is public affirmation while *īmān* is in the heart."[77]

عَنْ أَنَسٍ رَضِيَ اللهُ عَنْهُ قَالَ كَانَ رَسُولُ اللَّهِ صَلَّى اللَّهُ عَلَيْهِ وَسَلَّمَ يَقُولُ
الْإِسْلَامُ عَلَانِيَةٌ وَالْإِيمَانُ فِي الْقَلْبِ قَالَ ثُمَّ يُشِيرُ بِيَدِهِ إِلَى صَدْرِهِ ثَلَاثَ مَرَّاتٍ
قَالَ ثُمَّ يَقُولُ التَّقْوَى هَاهُنَا التَّقْوَى هَاهُنَا حم ش ع ز ورجاله رجال الصحيح مج

The Sunnī *Irjā'* of Abū Ḥanīfa and His School

Because of their stated position that deeds are not part of the essence of belief, Abū Ḥanīfa, his Shaykh Ḥammād ibn Abī Sulaymān, and his School are known as Murji'a in the Sunni sense as brilliantly expounded by the Imām himself in his *Risāla ilā 'Uthmān al-Battī.* Ibn Ḥajar said:

Irjā' has the sense of "delaying" and carries two meanings among

[76] Al-Ṭaḥāwī, *'Aqīda* §62: "Belief consists in affirmation by the tongue and acceptance by the heart." See Ibn Abī al-'Izz, *Sharḥ al-'Aqīda al-Ṭaḥāwiyya* (4th ed. p. 373-374, 9th ed. p. 332). See also *Risālat Abī Ḥanīfa ilā 'Uthmān al-Battī* in 'Abd al-Fattāḥ Abū Ghudda, *Namādhij min Rasā'il al-A'immat al-Salaf* (p. 21-28).

[77] Narrated from Anas by Aḥmad, Ibn Abī Shayba, Abū Ya'lā, and al-Bazzār with a chain of *Ṣaḥīḥ* narrators according to al-Haythamī cf. al-Munāwī, *Fayḍ al-Qaḍīr.*

> the Scholars: some mean by it the delaying in declaring one's position in the case of the two warring factions after 'Uthmān's time [i.e. neither following nor rejecting either one]; and some mean by it the delaying in declaring that whoever commits grave sins and abandons obligations enters the Fire, on the basis that in their view belief consists in assertion and conviction and that quitting deeds [i.e. ceasing from obeying commands and prohibitions] does not harm it.[78]

The Sunni *Murji'a* belong to the latter category with the important provision that they do not hold that quitting deeds does not harm belief in the sense of threatening to destroy it: on the contrary, they hold that quitting deeds does harm the quitter since "Acts of disobedience harm their author, contrary to the belief of certain factions."[79] Al-Mizzī relates in his *Tahdhīb al-Kamāl* from Abū al-Salṭ al-Harawī this clarification whereby a Sunnī *Murji'* is thus called not because he considers that "quitting deeds does not harm belief" but only because he professes hope (*yarjū*) of salvation for great sinners, as opposed to the *Khawārij* who declare sinners disbelievers, and the *Mu'tazila* who disbelieve in the Prophet's ﷺ intercession for great sinners. In this sense Abū Ḥanīfa and the Māturīdī school of doctrine hold what all other Schools of *Ahl al-Sunna* hold. As for the *Murji'a* who rely on faith alone exclusively of deeds, they belong to the heretical sects, and the attribution of Abū Ḥanīfa to such a belief is calumny and fabrication. Al-Kawtharī said:

> Al-Maqbalī counted it among the "mistakes of the learned" to define the [non-Sunni] *Murji'* as one who holds that unrepentent grave sinners are under the Divine discretion (*taḥt al-mashī'a*) and refer to this kind the ḥadīths blaming the *Murji'a*. Rather, the [non-Sunni] *Murji'a* are those who said there is no threat of punishment for those who pray (*Ahl al-Ṣalāt*), so they delay them from the threat of punishment to begin with. As for their being under the Divine discretion, this is literally explicit in the Book and the Sunna and known through mass-transmission. He mentioned this in *al-Abḥāth*. So the *Irjā'* of Abū Ḥanīfa is the

[78] In *Hadī al-Sārī* (2:179).

[79] Al-Qārī, *Sharḥ al-Fiqh al-Akbar* (p. 67, 103).

unadulterated Sunna creed and to libel him with the innovative sense of *Irjā'* is unadulterated calumny.[80]

Al-Dhahabī said: "The disapproved *Murji'a* are those who accepted Abū Bakr and 'Umar as Caliphs but withheld taking a position concerning 'Uthmān and 'Alī."[81] It is obvious that the Ḥanafī Imāms do not enter into such a definition. Imām Abū Ḥanīfa said in his *Fiqh al-Akbar*:

> The best of mankind after the Prophets, peace be upon them all, are Abū Bakr al-Ṣiddīq, then 'Umar ibn al-Khaṭṭāb, then 'Uthmān ibn 'Affān Dhūl-Nūrayn, then 'Alī ibn Abī Ṭālib al-Murtaḍā, Allāh be well pleased with all of them; they are men worshipping their Lord, steadfast upon truth and on the side of truth. **We follow loyally all of them** (*natawallāhum jamī'an*). Nor do we mention any of the Prophet's ﷺ Companions except in good terms.[82]

"*Īmān* neither increases nor decreases"

The difference with Abū Ḥanīfa which al-Bukhārī and Ibn Ḥibbān were picking upon resides, among others, in Abū Ḥanīfa's view that *īmān* – belief – stands for one's Islam and vice-versa and therefore neither increases nor decreases once acquired. It is a fundamental tenet of the Māturīdī School with which al-Bukhārī differed and which is illustrated by the latter's chapter-titles like "*Ṣalāt* is part of belief," "Belief increases and decreases" etc. in his *Ṣaḥīḥ* as al-Zayla'ī pointed out.[83] The vast majority of Ḥanafīs and the entire Māturīdī School of doctrine hold the opposite view, as illustrated by al-Qārī's naming two

80 Al-Kawtharī as cited in Abū Ghudda, *Namādhij min Rasā'il A'immat al-Salaf* (p. 22).

81 In *Tārīkh al-Islām* (3:358f.).

82 In 'Alī al-Qārī, *Sharḥ al-Fiqh al-Akbar* (1984 ed. p. 96-101).

83 In *Naṣb al-Rāya* (1:355-356): "No student of the Science adorned himself with a better garment than fairness and distance from fanaticism.... Al-Bukhārī is very much pursuing an agenda in what he cites from the Sunna against Abū Ḥanīfa, for he will mention a ḥadīth and then insinuate something about him, as follows: "The Messenger of Allāh ﷺ said such-and-such, while some people said such-and-such" By "some people" he means Abū Ḥanīfa, so he casts him in the ugliest light possible, as someone who dissents from the ḥadīth of the Prophet ﷺ! Al-Bukhārī also says in the beginning of his book: "Chapter whereby *Ṣalāt* is part of Belief," then he proceeds with the narrations of that chapter, and his purpose in that is to refute Abū Ḥanīfa's position that deeds are

chapter-titles of his *Sharḥ al-Fiqh al-Akbar*: "Belief neither increases nor decreases," and another chapter is entitled: "The believers are equal in belief but differ in deeds," and another: "The grave sin [such as not performing *Ṣalāt*] does not expel one from belief." All the above is also the sound doctrine of *Ahl al-Sunna*, as opposed to some Khārijī extremists – past and present – who declare anyone who commits a major sin to be a disbeliever in need of repeating his *shahāda* or be killed – and the latter contradicts the view of Imam Aḥmad, who insisted that no Muslim should be called a disbeliever for any sin.[84]

The Differentiation between *Islām* and *Īmān*

Imām Abū Ḥanīfa stipulated that a Muslim should never add *in shā Allāh* when saying "I am a *Mu'min*" as it would connote doubt over his Islamic belief. This is clear from the Imām's debate with the *Qadariyya* and his epistle to al-Battī. It is also the position of Imām Mālik.[85] Al-Shāfi'ī, Aḥmad, and the Ash'arī School preferred that one add *inshā' Allāh* to this affirmation even though al-Shāfi'ī shared Abū Ḥanīfa's opinion that "*Islām*" and "*Īmān*" were one and the same (as did al-Bukhārī although the latter differed radically with Abū Ḥanīfa on the consequences). Aḥmad said: "If a man is asked: 'Are you a *mu'min*?' Let him say: 'I am a *mu'min*, if Allāh wills.' Or let him say: 'I hope that I am a *mu'min*.' Or: 'I believe in Allāh, His angels, His Books, and His Messengers.'"[86] Abū Bakr al-Marwazī said: "Abū 'Abd Allāh [Aḥmad ibn Ḥanbal] was asked: 'Should we say that we are *mu'minūn*?' He

---

not part of belief although many *fuqahā'* do not realize this. And I swear by Allāh, and again – by Allāh! – that if al-Bukhārī had found one ḥadīth [to the effect that *Ṣalāt* really is part of Belief] which met his criterion or came close to it, then his book would certainly not have been devoid of it, nor that of Muslim!"

[84] In Ibn Abī Ya'lā, *Ṭabaqāt al-Ḥanābila* (1:329). For further elaborations on these distinctions see the works of al-Kawtharī, al-Ījī's *Mawāqif*, Abū Ghudda's notes on Ibn 'Abd al-Barr's *Intiqā'* and al-Lacknawī's *al-Raf' wal-Takmīl*, and al-Tahānawī in *Abū Ḥanīfa wa-Aṣḥābuhu al-Muḥaddithūn* (p. 52-53 introduction to *I'lā' al-Sunan*).

[85] Sīdī Muṣṭafā Baṣīr: "One may say he is a real believer on the evidence of the verse ﴾**Those are they who are in truth believers**﴿ (8:4) for possessing five traits: their hearts tremble at the mention of Allāh; His signs increase them in faith; they rely on Him; they pray; and they spend of what Allāh has granted them. And Mālik – Allāh have mercy on him – used to say: 'I am a believer, and praise belongs to Allāh.'" Cf. al-Qāḍī 'Iyāḍ, *Tartīb al-Madārik* (2:42).

[86] Narrated from al-Iṣṭakhrī by Ibn Abī Ya'lā in *Ṭabaqāt al-Ḥanābila* (1:25).

replied: 'No, but we should say that we are *muslimūn.*'"[87] Abū Muḥammad Rizq Allāh al-Tamīmī said: "He [Aḥmad] used to say: '*Īmān* is definitely other than *islām.*'"[88]

This is also the Ash'arī position as forwarded by Ibn Khafīf, Ibn al-Bāqillānī, and al-Qushayrī. Ibn Khafīf said in *al-'Aqīda al-Ṣaḥīḥa*: "Belief (*al-īmān*) is different from submission (*al-islām*).... Belief, declaring the absolute Oneness of Allāh, and knowledge of Allāh have an outward appearance (*ẓāhir*) as well as a reality (*ḥaqīqa*). Every believer (*mu'min*) is a Muslim but not every Muslim is a believer."[89] Ibn al-Bāqillānī said in *al-Tamhīd*: "*Īmān* is one of the characteristics (*khiṣāl*) of *islām*. Every *īmān* is *islām* but not vice-versa."[90] Al-Qushayrī wrote in his *Risāla*:

> Abū al-'Abbās al-Sayyārī said: "His bestowal is of two kinds: generosity (*karāma*) and entrapment (*istidrāj*). Whatever He causes to abide in you is Generosity. Whatever He removes from you is entrapment. Therefore say: 'I am a Believer if Allāh wills' (*anā mu'minun in shā' Allāh*)." ... Abū Bakr al-Wāsiṭī said: "Whoever says, 'I am a believer in Allāh really' (*anā mu'minun billāhi ḥaqqan*), will be told, 'reality indicates direct view, eyesight, and encompassment. Whosoever has none of this, his claim to that effect is invalid.'" He means by this the position of *Ahl al-Sunna* that the real believer is he who has been definitely decreed to enter Paradise. Whoever is unaware of this – which is part of secret Divine wisdom – his claim that he is a real believer is invalid.[91]

Ibn al-Subkī mentioned as one of the proofs of the Ash'arī position the ḥadīth of the Prophet ﷺ that "A man assuredly does the deeds of the people of Paradise as far as the people can see but he is in fact one of the people of Hellfire; and another man assuredly does the deeds of the people of Hellfire as far as the people can see but he is in fact one of the people of Paradise."[92] "The addition *as far as the people can*

[87] *Ibid.* (2:14).

[88] *Ibid.* (2:302).

[89] Ibn Khafīf, *al-'Aqīda al-Ṣaḥīḥa* (§70) in our *Ash'arī School*.

[90] Ibn al-Bāqillānī, *Tamhīd al-Awā'il* (p. 390).

[91] See also Ibn 'Abd al-Salām's short treatise, *Ma'nā al-Īmān wal-Islām*, *Ṭabaqāt al-Ḥanābila* (1:25, 2:14, 2:302), and Shaykh Muḥyī al-Dīn Ibn 'Arabī's epistle *al-Mu'min wal-Muslim wal-Muḥsin*.

[92] Narrated from Sahl ibn Sa'd al-Sa'idī by al-Bukhārī and Muslim.

see there is of huge import, immense benefit [as a proof] for Ash'arīs, and greatly useful for *Ahl al-Sunna wal-Jamā'a* in relation to the question of 'I am a *mu'min* if Allāh wills.' Let whoever can understand what it signals understand."[93]

The ḥadīth of Ḥāritha (or Ḥārith) supports the Ḥanafī position – Abū Ḥanīfa mentions it in *al-Fiqh al-Akbar* – but it is weak. Ḥāritha was asked by the Prophet ﷺ: "How are you this morning, Ḥāritha?" He replied: "This morning I am a real believer." The Prophet ﷺ said: "Take care of what you say: what is the reality of your belief?" He said: "I have turned myself away from this world until its rocks and its gold became the same for me by keeping awake at night and by keeping myself thirsty by day; and I can almost see the Throne of my Lord in full sight; and I can almost see the people of the Garden of Paradise visiting each other; and I can almost see the people of the Fire wailing to each other in it." The Prophet ﷺ said: "Ḥāritha! You do know: therefore cleave to it!" (*'arafta falzam*). Some versions add: "This is a believer, Allāh has illumined his heart" (*mu'minun nawwara Allāhu qalbah*).[94]

عَنْ زُبَيْدِ بْنِ الْحَرِثِ – لم تلق الصحابة – قَالَ قَالَ رَسُولُ اللهِ صَلَّى اللهُ عَلَيْهِ
وَسَلَّمَ كَيْفَ أَصْبَحْتَ يَا حَارِثَ بْنَ مَالِك قَالَ أَصْبَحْتُ مُؤْمِناً حَقّاً قَالَ
إِنَّ لِكُلِّ قَوْلٍ حَقِيقَةً فَمَا حَقِيقَةُ ذَلِكَ قَالَ أَصْبَحْتُ عَزَفْتُ نَفْسِي عَنِ الدُّنْيَا
وَأَسْهَرْتُ لَيْلِي وَأَظْمَأْتُ نَهَارِي وَكَأَنِّي أَنْظُرُ إِلَى عَرْشِ رَبِّي قَدْ أَبْرَزَ لِلْحِسَاب
وَكَأَنِّي أَنْظُرُ إِلَى أَهْلِ الْجَنَّةِ يَتَزَاوَرُونَ فِي الْجَنَّةِ وَكَأَنِّي أَسْمَعُ عَوَاءَ أَهْلِ النَّارِ
قَالَ فَقَالَ لَهُ عَبْدٌ نَوَّرَ الإِيمَانُ فِي قَلْبِهِ إِنْ عَرَفْتَ فَالْزَمْ ش طب القضاعي عبد بن
حميد عق ز هب وفي الزهد ميزان وقالا منكر وقال الحافظ في الإصابة معضل

93 Ibn al-Subkī, *Ṭabaqāt al-Shāfi'iyya al-Kubrā* (4:39).

94 Narrated from al-Ḥārith ibn Mālik al-Anṣārī – some chains have "al-Ḥāritha ibn al-Na'mān al-Anṣārī" – by al-Ṭabarānī in *al-Kabīr* (3:266 §3367), al-Quḍā'ī in *Musnad al-Shihāb* (2:127 §1028), 'Abd ibn Ḥumayd in his *Musnad* (p. 165 §445), al-Bazzār, Abū Nu'aym in the *Ḥilya* (1985 ed. 1:242), al-Haythamī (1:57 "Chapter on the Reality of

Ibn Ḥajar's Commentary on al-Bukhārī's Chapter-Title and Narration of the Ḥadīth of *Īmān* and *Islām*

Al-Bukhārī's Words "CHAPTER: GIBRĪL'S QUESTION ON ĪMĀN, ISLĀM, ETC."

We have seen that al-Bukhārī considers *īmān* and *islam* expressions of a single meaning.[95] Since Gibrīl's question about *īmān* and *islam* and the answer he received appeared, of necessity, to differentiate between them – the former signifying truthfulness in specific matters, the latter, the display of specific matters – he [al-Bukhārī] attempted to cancel out the distinction by interpreting it figuratively (*bil-ta'wīl*), according to his preconception.

Al-Bukhārī's Words "AND THE [Prophet's ﷺ] DECLARATION [to Gibrīl]"

That is: "together with the declaration that conviction (*al-i'tiqād*), together with deeds, make up Religion."

Al-Bukhārī's Words "AND HOW HE EXPOUNDED [īmān to 'Abd al-Qays's delegation]"

That is: "together with what he expounded to the delegation to the effect that *īmān* is *islām* itself," since he explained *īmān* in the narration to the delegation in the same terms in which he explained *islām* here.[96]

Belief and its Perfection" *Bāb ḥaqīqat al-īmān wa-kamālih*), al-'Askarī in *al-Amthāl*, Ibn al-Mubārak in *al-Zuhd*, 'Abd al-Razzāq through two chains, Ibn Mandah, al-'Uqaylī in *al-Ḍu'afā'* (2:290 §864, 4:455 §2085), al-Bayhaqī with three chains in the *Shu'ab* (7:362-363) and *al-Zuhd* (p. 355), al-Dhahabī in his *Mīzān* (4:469 *munkar*) from Ibn al-Najjār, Ibn Aṣram in *al-Istiqāma*, Ibn Sa'īd, and Ibn Abī Shayba (6:170 §30425 *mu'ḍal*). Abū Ḥanīfa mentions it in *al-Fiqh al-Akbar* and Ibn Kathīr in his *Tafsīr* for the verse (8:4). Ibn Ḥajar in his *Iṣāba* (1:597 §1480) lists its many chains and says that this is a ḥadīth *mu'ḍal* – with a chain missing at least two sub-narrators) and *mawṣūl* – identical with *muttaṣil*, *i.e.* linked back to a Companion through a Successor. Ibn 'Aṭā' Allāh explains this ḥadīth at length in *Laṭā'if al-Minan* (1:176-186).

[95] Cf. *Fatḥ al-Bārī*, beginning of the book of *Īmān* (1959 ed. 1:45-55) and the chapter previous to this (1:111). Al-Za'farānī reported that al-Shāfi'ī in his commentary on the ḥadīth "Free her, for she is a believer," said: "Islām is *īmān*." In al-Bayhaqī, *Manāqib al-Shāfi'ī* (1:395).

[96] The Prophet ﷺ imposed upon the delegation of the tribe of 'Abd al-Qays belief in Allāh alone and said: "Do you know what belief in Allāh alone is?" They replied: "Allāh and His Messenger know best." He said: "The testimony that there is no god but Allāh, and that Muḥammad is the Messenger of Allāh; the accomplishment of prayer; the remittance of the purification-tax; the fasting of Ramaḍān; and that you give one fifth of the spoils." Narrated from Ibn 'Abbās as part of a longer ḥadīth by al-Bukhārī in

Al-Bukhārī's Words "AND THE SAYING OF ALLĀH"

That is: "together with the verse's indication that *islām* itself is the Religion, and the indication of Abū Sufyān's relation that *īmān* is the Religion.[97] All this requires that *islām* and *īmān* be one and the same." This is the substance of al-Bukhārī's words.

[*The Difference Between* Islām *and* Īmān]

Abū 'Awāna al-Isfarāyīnī reports in his *Ṣaḥīḥ* from al-Shāfi'ī's companion al-Muzanī the categorical opinion that they are the expressions of a single meaning, and that he heard it from al-Shāfi'ī; Abū 'Awāna also reports from Imām Aḥmad the categorical opinion that they are two different meanings. Each position has mutually contradictory proofs. Al-Khaṭṭābī said: "Two great Imāms have compiled texts on this question with much evidence supporting each position, and they hold opposite opinions.[98] The truth is that there is a general

---

the book of *Īmān* (§53, *Fatḥ al-Bārī* 1959 ed.) and Muslim.

97 There are two relations of Abū Sufyān to that effect, both narrated by al-Bukhārī at the end of the first book of his *Ṣaḥīḥ* (Book of the Beginning of Revelation):

(1) "Heraclius summoned the Roman authorities to his villa (*daskara*) in Ḥimṣ, ordered the gates locked, then looked at them and said: 'Romans! Do you want to reap success, do what is right, and ensure that your empire will endure? Follow this Prophet.' At this, they fled like wild asses and made for the gates, but found them locked. When Heraclius saw their loathing of what he had proposed to them he despaired of their belief (*īmān*). 'Bring them back to me,' he ordered; then he addressed them again: 'I said this just now only to test the strength of your attachment to your religion (*dīn*), of which I am satisfied.' At this they prostrated to him and they were happy again. That was the last we heard of Heraclius." Narrated as part of a longer ḥadīth by al-Bukhārī and Muslim.

(2) Heraclius asked me [Abū Sufyān] about the Prophet's ﷺ followers: "Are their numbers increasing or decreasing?" I said they are increasing. He said: "Does any of them recant out of discontent with his religion after entering it?" I said no [...] Then Heraclius said to the translator: "Say to him [Abū Sufyān]: "I asked you whether their numbers were increasing or decreasing and you said the former; and indeed such is the case with belief (*īmān*) until it is complete. I asked you if any of them reneged out of discontent with their religion (*dīn*) after entering it and you said no; and indeed such is belief (*īmān*) when its elation (*bashāsha*) pervades the heart." Narrated both as part of a longer ḥadīth by al-Bukhārī and Muslim, and as an independent ḥadīth by al-Bukhārī.

98 See also Ibn Rajab's discussion in the beginning of his *Jāmi' al-'Ulūm wal-Ḥikam*.

understanding and a particular understanding for each of the two. Every *mu'min* is a Muslim, but not every Muslim is a *mu'min*." This is the gist of what he said. It presupposes that Islām is not applied, as a word, to belief and performance together, as opposed to *īmān*, which supposedly applies to both of them. This is refuted by the saying of Allāh: ﴾**And I have chosen for you as religion Islām**﴿ (5:3) for Islām entails both performance and belief, since an unbelieving performer does not have an acceptable religion.[99] This is the argument used by al-Muzanī and Abū Muḥammad al-Baghawī.

Al-Baghawī said concerning the ḥadīth of Gibrīl: "The Prophet ﷺ used *islām* here as a word for visible performance of deeds, and *īmān* as a word for the hidden aspect of belief. This is not because performance is not part of *īmān*, nor because confirmation (*al-taṣdīq*) is not part of *islām*, but only as the itemization of a unified whole whose heading is the Religion (*al-dīn*). This is why the Prophet ﷺ said: 'He came to teach you your religion,' and Allāh ﷻ said: ﴾**And I have chosen for you as religion Islām**﴿ (5:3), ﴾**And whoso seeks as religion other than the Surrender (to Allāh) it will not be accepted from him**﴿ (3:85). For religion does not deserve Divine pleasure and acceptance except if confirmation is part of it." This is the end of al-Baghawī's words.

[*The Complementariness of Islām and Īmān*]

What emerges from the sum of the proof-texts is that *islām* and *īmān* each have a proper legal sense (*ḥaqīqa shar'iyya*) as well as a proper lexical sense (*ḥaqīqa lughawiyya*). However, each term presupposes the other to complete its own meaning (*kullun minhumā mustalzimun lil-ākhar bi-ma'nā al-takmīl*). For just as the performer of an action is not a perfect *muslim* unless he believes, so is the believer not a perfect *mu'min* unless he performs. Whenever the word *īmān* is used in the place of *islām* or vice versa, and whenever one is used in the sense of both, it is a metaphorical usage (*'alā sabīl al-majāz*). The actual sense becomes clear through the context. If they occur together in the

99 Al-Khaṭṭābī is correct in that he is paraphrasing the Qur'ān, ﴾ **Say: You believe not, but rather say 'We submit' for *īmān* has not yet penetrated your hearts**﴿ (49:14) and is confirmed by the ḥadīth of the Prophet ﷺ from Anas in Aḥmad, "Islām is proclaimed while *īmān* is in the heart" cited by Ibn Kathīr in his *Tafsīr* in explanation of the verse ﴾**but Allāh has endeared the faith (*al-īmān*) to you and has beautified it in your heart**﴿ (49:7) nor is it necessarily true that al-Khaṭṭābī's statement presupposes what Ibn Ḥajar said.

course of a question, they are construed in the literal sense; if they do not occur together or if it is not in the course of question, then they may be construed either literally or metaphorically depending on whatever is mentioned along with them.

Al-Ismāʿīlī said that the above explanation was that of *Ahl al-Sunna wal-Jamāʿa*: "They said that the meaning of *īmān* and *islām* differs only when they are mentioned together. If one is mentioned alone, the other enters into its definition." Likewise, what Muḥammad ibn Naṣr related – and Ibn ʿAbd al-Barr followed him – saying that the majority equated the two regardless of what is mentioned in the ḥadīth of ʿAbd al-Qays, and what al-Lālikāʾī and Ibn al-Samʿānī said to the effect that *Ahl al-Sunna wal-Jamāʿa* differentiated between the two on the basis of the content of the ḥadīth of Gibrīl. Allāh is the Grantor of all success![100]

Abū Ḥanīfa on the Prophet's ﷺ Parents in Paradise

Mullā ʿAlī al-Qārī (d. 1014) claimed in *Sharḥ al-Fiqh al-Akbar, Muʿtaqad Abī Ḥanīfa*, and *Sharḥ al-Shifā'* that Imām Abū Ḥanīfa said, "The parents of the Prophet ﷺ died as disbelievers" and that this was the Māturīdī position. He was refuted harshly by his student the *Faqīh* and Friend of Allāh, Imām ʿAbd al-Qādir ibn Muḥammad ibn Aḥmad al-Ṭabarī (d. 1022), during the latter's lessons in the Makkan Sanctuary.[101] Al-Qārī died in Makka shortly after those lectures from a bad fall – Allāh have mercy on him and forgive him. Shaykh Ibrāhīm al-Ḥalabī, the Ḥanafī *faqīh*, held the same view as Mullā ʿAlī al-Qārī as does al-ʿAẓīm Ābādī in *ʿAwn al-Maʿbūd.*

Both Shaykh Wahbī Sulayman Ghāwjī al-Albānī in his 1998 edition of al-Qārī's *Sharḥ al-Fiqh al-Akbar* entitled *Minaḥ al-Rawḍ al-Azhar* (p. 18-19) and in his *Arkān al-Īmān* (1974, 2nd ed. 1999 p. 208-209) and Ḥasan ʿAlī al-Saqqāf in his epistle *Ilqām al-Ḥajar lil-Mutaṭāwil ʿalā al-Ashāʿirati min al-Bashar* (p. 77 n.5) reiterated the erroneous claim – first made by the Egyptian Shaykh Muṣṭafā al-Ḥammāmī the imām of al-Zaynabī Mosque in Cairo in his book *al-Nahḍat al-Iṣlāḥiyya* and, after him, by the Turkish researcher Khalīl Ibrāhīm Qūtlāy in his book *al-*

[100] *Fatḥ al-Bārī* (1959 ed. 1:115-125 §50).

[101] ʿAbd al-Qādir al-Ṭabarī is mentioned in *Khulāṣat al-Athar* (2:456-457), al-Ziriklī's *al-Aʿlām* (4:44), and the Ḥanafī compendium *Ṭarb al-Amāthil* (p. 513 §255) although he was Shāfiʿī.

Imām al-Qārī wa-Atharuhu fil-Ḥadīth – that al-Qārī in *Sharḥ al-Shifā'* changed the opinion he had voiced in the *Sharḥ al-Fiqh al-Akbar* which he wrote three years before his death.

Shaykh Ghāwjī cited Qūtlāy's report from al-Qārī, allegedly from *Sharḥ al-Shifā'* (1:601) as saying:

> As for Abū Ṭālib, the report of his conversion to Islām is inauthentic. As for the conversion of his [the Prophet's] parents, there are various positions concerning it, the most correct being that they did convert to Islām as agreed upon by the foremost authorities of the Community, as shown by al-Suyūṭī in the three epistles he authored. (*Wa-Abū Ṭālib lam yaṣiḥḥa islāmuhu, wa-ammā islāmu abawayhi fa-fīhi aqwāl, wal-aṣaḥḥu islāmuhumā 'alā mā ittafaqa 'alayhi al-ajillatu min al-umma, kamā bayyanahu al-Suyūṭī fī Rasā'ilihi al-thalāth al-mu'allafa.*)

However, the original Istanbul edition actually states (1:601), as does the later Cairo edition (1312/1894 ed. 3:60-62):

> As for Abū Ṭālib, the report of his conversion to Islam is inauthentic. Al-Tilimsānī's statement – 'The conversion of his mother to Islām was narrated with a sound chain and the conversion of both his parents was narrated' – is rejected back to him. I have clarified this issue in a monograph [*sc. Mu'taqad*] I wrote in refutation of al-Suyūṭī's three epistles. (*Wa-Abū Ṭālib lam yaṣiḥḥa islāmuhu, wa-ammā qawlu al-Tilimsānī 'wa-ruwiya islāmu ummihi bi-isnādin saḥīḥin, wa-ruwiya islāmu abawayh' fa-mardūdun 'alayhi kamā bayyantu hādhihi al-mas'alata fī risālatin mustaqillatin raddan 'alā al-Suyūṭī fī Rasā'ilihi al-thalāth.*)

Another misquotation of the Istanbul edition of *Sharḥ al-Shifā'* (1:648) states:

> As for what they mentioned of his ﷺ bringing his two parents back to life, the soundest view is that this took place, as held by the trustworthy vast majority (*al-jumhūr al-thiqāt*) and as stated by al-Suyūṭī in his three epistles. (*Wa-ammā mā dhakarū min iḥyā'ihi 'alayhi al-ṣalātū wal-salām abawayhi fal-aṣaḥḥu annahu waqa'a, 'alā mā 'alayhi al-jumhūru al-thiqāt, kamā qāla al-Suyūṭī fil-rasā'il al-thalāth.*)

However, the original Istanbul edition actually states (1:648-649), as does the later Cairo edition (1312/1894 ed. 3:99):

> As for what was mentioned about him ﷺ resuscitating his two parents and their belief in him – per the narration of al-Ṭabarānī and others from 'Ā'isha – the ḥadīth Masters agree that it is weak, as explicitly stated by al-Suyūṭī.[102] Ibn Diḥya even said it is forged[103] and contradicts the Qur'ān and Sunna. I have expounded this in a monograph examining this issue in detail, in refutation of the learned al-Suyūṭī in the three epistles he composed and exposing the weakness of his proofs. (*Wa-ammā mā dhakarū 'anhu* ﷺ *min iḥyā'i abawayhi wa-īmānihimā bih, 'alā mā rawāhu al-Ṭabarānī wa-ghayruhu 'an 'Ā'isha, fattafaqa al-ḥuffāẓu 'alā ḍa'fihi, kamā ṣarraḥa bihi al-Suyūṭī. Qāla Ibn Diḥya huwa mawḍū'un mukhālifun lil-kitābi wal-sunna. Wa-qad bayyantuhu fī risālatin mustaqillatin li-taḥaqquqi hādhihi al-mas'alati raddan 'alā al-'allāmat al-Suyūṭī fī rasā'ilihi al-thalāth al-mu'allafa wa-bayānan li-dalā'ilihi al-muḍa''afa.*)[104]

On the established position of the majority of *Ahl al-Sunna* and the totality of the Ash'arī School that the parents of the Prophet ﷺ are saved, see:

- Al-Suyūṭī's fatwas in *Majmū' Tis' Rasā'il* and *al-Ḥāwī lil-Fatāwā* such as *Masālik al-Ḥunafā', al-Durūj al-Munīfa, al-Ta'ẓīm wal-Minna,* and other works.[105]
- Al-Sha'rānī in the relevant chapters *of al-Yawāqīt wal-Jawāhir* and *al-Mīzān al-Kubrā.*
- Al-Haytamī in his *Fatāwā Ḥadīthiyya* and his marginalia on *Mughnī al-Muḥtāj.*
- Al-Qasṭallānī in *al-Mawāhib al-Lāduniyya* and al-Zarqānī in its commentary.

[102] This is contradicted by al-Sayyid Aḥmad Zaynī Daḥlān in his *Sīra* (1:60).

[103] As did al-'Aẓīm Ābādī in his *'Awn al-Ma'būd* and al-Ghumārī in *al-Fawā'id al-Maqṣūda* (p. 98) cf. al-Saqqāf, *Ilqām* (p. 75-76).

[104] I brought these two radical tamperings of al-Qārī's text and meaning to the attention of Shaykh al-Ghāwjī in his home in Damascus to his shock, as he had relied on Khalīl Qūtlāy's report of al-Qārī's words although it seems – and Allāh knows best – that the origin of this grave error lies at the door of Shaykh Muṣṭafā al-Ḥammāmī.

[105] See our extensive translations in the *Encyclopedia of Islamic Doctrine* (2:143-159).

- Ibn al-Humām in *al-Musāyara* and Ibn Abī Sharīf in its commentary.
- Sayyid Muḥammad ibn 'Abd al-Rasūl al-Barzanjī, *Sadād al-Dīn wa-Sidād al-Dayn fī Najāt al-Abawayn al-Sharīfayn*, a refutation of al-Qārī.
- Al-Ṭaḥṭāwī and Ibn 'Ābidīn in their respective commentaries on *al-Durr al-Mukhtār*.[106]
- Imām al-Bājūrī in *Sharḥ Jawharat al-Tawḥīd*.
- Imām al-Jazūlī in *Dalā'il al-Khayrāt* in which he said: "Allāh send blessings upon the best of those who made sublime

وَصَلَّى اللهُ عَلَى أَفْضَلِ مَنْ طَابَ مِنْهُ النَّجَارُ،

their origin." This is the same meaning as the Prophet's ﷺ attribute of

كَرِيمُ الطَّرَفَيْنِ ﷺ

Karīm al-Ṭarafayn – "Noble on both sides of his parents."

- The erudite Scholar Muḥammad Mar'ashī Sājiqlī Zādah (d. 1150) in his epistle *al-Faraḥ wal-Surūr fī Wāliday al-Rasūl* ﷺ.
- Muḥammad ibn 'Umar al-Bālī al-Madanī al-Ḥanafī (fl. 1285), *Subul al-Salām fī Ḥukmi Ābā'i Sayyid al-Anām* ﷺ.
- The ḥadīth Master Murtaḍā al-Zabīdī in his epistle *al-Intiṣār li-Wāliday al-Nabī al-Mukhtār* ﷺ.
- Shaykh 'Abd Allāh al-Būsnawī al-Rūmī (d. 1054) in his epistle *Maṭāli' al-Nūr al-Sanī al-Munabbi' 'an Ṭahārati Nasab al-Nabī al-'Arabī* ﷺ, cited in full in the fourth volume of al-Nabhānī's *Jawāhir al-Biḥār*.
- Imām al-Kawtharī in his introduction to Imām Abū Ḥanīfa's *al-'Ālim wal-Muta'allim*.
- Qāḍī Yūsuf al-Nabhānī in *Ḥujjat Allāh 'alā al-'Ālamīn*.

[106] Cf. Ibn 'Ābidīn, *Ḥāshiya* (1386/1966 ed. 3:183 after *Bāb Nikāḥ al-Kāfir* and 4:231).

- Al-Dirdīr in his *Mawlid.*
- 'Amrāwī and Murād, *Wā'iẓun Ghayru Mutta'iẓ.* ("A Heedless Admonisher"), a refutation of Abū Bakr al-Jazā'irī.
- Shaykh Wahbī Sulaymān al-Ghāwjī's *Arkān al-Īmān* and his commentary on al-Qārī's *Sharḥ al-Fiqh al-Akbar.*
- Ḥasan 'Alī al-Saqqāf in his epistle *Ilqām al-Ḥajar lil-Mutaṭāwil 'alā al-Ashā'irati min al-Bashar* (p. 65-78) in defense of Imām al-Bājūrī against the aspersions of a "Salafī" writer.

It is related that Ibn 'Ābidīn at first wrote a chapter in his *Ḥāshiya* on the meaning of "The death of the Prophet's ﷺ father and mother as disbelievers." As he was researching his chapter, a *majdhūb* who was well known for his intense piety (perhaps al-Ghawwāṣṣ) suddenly stopped praying behind him at the Ta'dīl mosque in Damascus. Asked why, he said: "Do you not say that one of the preconditions of *Ṣalāt* is purity? So how can I pray behind him [Ibn 'Ābidīn] when I see him immersed up to his ears in filth?" News of this reached Ibn 'Ābidīn, who was a scrupulous man and held the righteous in the highest esteem. He examined his conscience and searched for what could have earned such a disgrace. He became certain that the reason was this particular chapter he was in the process of writing. He tore up the papers and changed the chapter to read "The revival of the Prophet's ﷺ father and mother as believers" and this is the way the chapter stands in the *Ḥāshiya* today. The *Majdhūb* saw the cleanliness return and he resumed praying behind the Imām, but he never found out the reason why.[107]

Al-Haytamī in *al-Fatāwā al-Ḥadīthiyya* said that the reliable manuscripts of *al-Fiqh al-Akbar* do not contain the statement "The parents of the Prophet ﷺ died as disbelievers" and that therefore it should not be attributed to Imām Abū Ḥanīfa. This is also held by al-Zabīdī, al-Kawtharī, Muṣṭafā Sayf al-Ḥammāmī in his book *al-Nahḍat al-Iṣlāḥiyya*, and our teacher Shaykh Wahbī Ghāwjī. Al-Haytamī also states that their salvation is asserted by Shaykh Muḥyī al-Dīn Ibn 'Arabī, on the basis of narrations in the two *Ṣaḥīḥs* on *iṣṭifā'* and on the best of centuries.

[107] Narrated to the author by Dr. Sāmir al-Naṣṣ as he heard it from his teacher Imām Abūl-Yusr 'Ābidīn, the grand-nephew of Ibn 'Ābidīn.

Al-Dhahabī in *al-'Ulūw* attributes *al-Fiqh al-Akbar* to Abū Ḥanīfa's student, Abū Muṭī' al-Ḥakam ibn 'Abd Allāh al-Balkhī, as mentioned by Shaykh Shu'ayb al-Arna'ūṭ in his edition of *Aqāwīl al-Thiqāt* (p. 63). This is true, strictly speaking, only of the version known as *al-Fiqh al-Absaṭ*. As for the actual *Fiqh al-Akbar*, its chain of transmission goes up to the Imām not through Abū Muṭī' but through Ḥammād, Abū Ḥanīfa's son.[108]

Imām al-Kawtharī in his introduction to Imām Abū Ḥanīfa's *al-'Ālim wal-Muta'allim* (Azhariyya 2001 reprint p. 7-8) said:

> Some of the manuscripts [of *al-Fiqh al-Akbar*] state: "And the two parents of the Prophet ﷺ died in a state of primordial nature (*mātā 'alā al-fiṭra*)." The word *al-fiṭra* can easily be corrupted to read *al-kufr* in *kūfī* calligraphy and in most others. "They did not die in a state of disbelief" (*mā mātā 'alā al-kufr*) seems to show that the Greatest Imām wished to refute those who narrate the ḥadīth "My father and your father are both in the Fire" in support of the sense that the Prophet's two parents are in the Fire. For the ascription of a human being to Hellfire is impermissible except with an iron-clad proof (*dalīl yaqīnī*); and such a subject is not a practical issue in which a conjectural proof (*dalīl ẓannī*) might suffice.
>
> The ḥadīth Master Muḥammad al-Murtaḍā al-Zabīdī – the commentator of the *Iḥyā'* and author of the Arabic Dictionary [*Tāj al-'Arūs*] – said in his treatise *al-Intiṣār li-Wāliday al-Nabī al-Mukhtār*, which I saw written in his own handwriting at the house of our Shaykh Aḥmad ibn Muṣṭafā al-'Umarī al-Ḥalabī the learned and venerable Muftī of al-'Askar – I paraphrase – that when the copyist saw a repetition of *mā* in the phrase "They did not die" (*mā mātā*), he mistook one of them for a diplology so he suppressed it, after which his erroneous version became widespread, and that one of the proofs for this is the context of the passage: if Abū Ṭālib and the two parents came under the same description, all three would have been mentioned in one and the same clause instead of being split up into two separate ones, since the ruling at hand supposedly did not differ among them.

[108] Cf. note 139.

> This is an excellent point made by the *ḥāfiẓ* al-Zabīdī. However, he apparently did not see the copy which had the actual script *mā mātā* but only reported that script from those who had seen it. By the grace of Allāh, I myself did see the script *mā mātā* in two old manuscripts held in Dār al-Kutub al-Miṣriyya, and a friend of mine saw the two scripts *mā mātā* and *'alā al-fiṭra* in two old manuscripts in the said Maktabat Shaykh al-Islām. 'Alī al-Qārī, on the other hand, based his *Sharḥ* on the faulty manuscript and spoke inappropriately – Allāh forgive him![109]

Shaykh Wahbī Ghāwjī – Allāh save and keep him – also said in his edition of the Imām's *al-Fiqh al-Akbar* (adduced in full in his biography, *Abū Ḥanīfa al-Nu'mān: Imām al-A'immati al-Fuqahā'*), in a footnote appended to the sentence "And the two parents of the Messenger of Allāh ﷺ died in a state of *fiṭra*": "What I saw in a good manuscript copy in Maktabat Shaykh al-Islām 'Ārif Ḥikmat [in Madīna] was the wording, 'did not die in a state of disbelief' (*mā mātā 'alā al-kufr*).[110]

Dr. 'Ināyatullāh Iblāgh al-Afghānī in the 1987 2nd edition of his published doctoral thesis titled *al-Imām al-A'ẓam Abū Ḥanīfa al-Mutakallim* ("The Greatest Imām, Abū Ḥanīfa, the Theologian"), said:

> Regarding the text [of *al-Fiqh al-Akbar*] we find among some of the manuscripts certain variants. For example, we find in some of them: "and the two parents of the Prophet ﷺ died according to Pristine Disposition" (*mātā 'alā al-fiṭra*). In some others, it is: "did not die as disbelievers" (*mā mātā 'alā al-kufr*) while in others yet, we find: "died as disbelievers" (*mātā 'alā al-kufr*).
>
> The erudite scholar al-Kawtharī noted that the word *fiṭra* can be easily altered to read *kufr* in Kufic Arabic calligraphy. It is highly probable, therefore, that the copy with "died according to Pristine Disposition" was changed to "died disbelievers." The original reading implies that the Greatest Imām was arguing against those who adduce the ḥadīth: "My father and your father

[109] Al-Kawtharī, introduction to Abū Ḥanīfa's *al-'Ālim wal-Muta'allim* (Azhariyya 2001 reprint p. 7-8) cf. Ghāwjī, *Abū Ḥanīfa* (p. 258).

[110] Ghāwjī, *Abū Ḥanīfa* (6th ed. p. 315-316 n. 3 and p. 257). Maktabat Shaykh al-Islām 'Ārif Ḥikmat (Compendium §226 or §234 ms. 161).

are both in Hellfire."[111] The way to respond to their [allegation] is [to show] that holding that the woman is also in Hellfire cannot be affirmed except with a definite proof (*dalīl qaṭ'ī*) and this is not a practical (*'amalī*) matter in order for an indefinite proof (*dalīl ẓannī*) to suffice for it. Consequently, what might be held regarding the parents of the Messenger of Allāh ﷺ being in Hellfire, is not based on a definitive proof.

Moreover, we find more evidence in what was mentioned by the [Ḥanafī Ash'arī] ḥadīth Master Muḥammad Murtaḍā al-Zabīdī – the commentator of the *Iḥyā'* and author of the *Qāmūs* – in his booklet *al-Intiṣār li-Wāliday al-Nabī al-Mukhtār* ("Defence of the Parents of the Chosen Prophet"). He said that when the copier (*nāsikh*) saw the double occurrence of *mā* in the words *mā mātā*, he thought that one of them was superfluous [i.e. by diplology] and removed it. Then it so happened that this incorrect copy became widespread.

Another evidence to this [interpolation] is the context of the report (*siyāq al-khabar*), because if Abū Ṭālib [the Prophet's uncle] and his [the Prophet's] parents had all been in one state, he [Abū Ḥanīfa] could have combined them in one sentence ("and the parents and uncle of the Prophet ﷺ died disbelievers") as opposed to the two given ("and the parents of the Prophet ﷺ died disbelievers and Abū Ṭālib, the uncle of the Prophet ﷺ died a disbeliever") if there were really no difference between them in that verdict. This is a good analysis from al-Ḥāfiẓ al-Zabīdī. Finally, 'Allāma al-Kawtharī mentioned that he saw the copy that contains *mā mātā* in two manuscripts in Dār al-Kutub al-Miṣriyya. I went back to view them and found them as al-Kawtharī had mentioned.

Furthermore, 'Allāma al-Kawtharī mentioned in his editions of the treatises (*rasā'il*) of Abū Ḥanīfa kept in Dār al-Kutub al-Miṣriyya, number 24205, that "There exists manuscripts of [*al-Fiqh al-Akbar*] in Maktabat al-Fātiḥ in al-Āstāna [present-day Istanbul].

As for the evidence of the ḥadīth in *Ṣaḥīḥ Muslim* whereby the Prophet ﷺ said, upon being asked by a man about the fate of his

[111] Narrated by Muslim and al-Bazzār cf. *Kashf al-Astār* (1:65). Shaykh 'Abd Allāh al-Ghumārī included it in his *al-Fawā'id al-Maqṣūda fī Bayān al-Aḥādīth al-Shādhdha al-Mardūda* (p. 93)!

father: "Your father is in the Fire" then, as the man was walking away, the Prophet ﷺ called him back and added "Both my father and your father are in the Fire":

(i) Muslim cites three different wordings for this ḥadīth, each with a different chain. Only one out of the three contains the words "My father" and its chain contains (a) Thābit al-Bunānī from whom Ayyūb al-Sakhtyānī did not narrate – as mentioned by al-Dhahabī in his *Mīzān* – and whom Ibn 'Adī mentioned in his compendium of weak narrators because of some denounced narrations imputed not to him, but by weak narrators from him; and (b) Ḥammād ibn Salama because of whose memory lapses al-Bukhārī did not retain his narrations, as mentioned by Ibn Ḥajar in his introduction to *Fatḥ al-Bārī* and by other Imāms of ḥadīth such as al-Bayhaqī and Ibn Rajab.[112]

(ii) Furthermore, the Prophet's ﷺ words "My father" do not necessarily mean his actual father 'Abd Allāh ibn 'Abd al-Muṭṭalib but can refer to any of his uncles or forefathers – such as his uncles Abū Lahab or Abū Ṭālib or his grandfather 'Abd al-Muṭṭalib – as pointed out by al-Suyūṭī. Al-Jazīrī in *al-Fiqh 'alā al-Madhāhib al-Arba'a*[113] explains it to refer to his uncle Abū Lahab. His calling his uncle "father" is similar to what Imām al-Rāzī and others said about the Prophet Ibrāhīm ﷺ calling his uncle Āzar "my father."[114] It is a characteristic of the awesome eloquence of the Prophet ﷺ that he spoke with the most clarity and elegance any human being ever used, but the array of meanings encompassed by his words is beyond confinement. An example of this expressive power of the Prophet ﷺ is his answer to the Arabian nomad who asked him and his friends at the time of Badr, "From where do you hail?" The Prophet ﷺ answered: "We hail from the water." Then he walked away while the nomad kept asking: "Which water? The water of Iraq?"[115] It was also said that the Prophet ﷺ used double-entendre (*tawriya*) so as to soothe the feelings of the questioner with regard to his father.[116]

[112] Cf. Ibn Ḥajar, *Taqrīb* and al-Arna'ūṭ and Ma'rūf, *Taḥrīr al-Taqrīb* (2:318-319 §1499).

[113] Book of *nikāḥ*, chapter on the marriage of non-Muslims.

[114] Cf. al-Alūsī, *Rūḥ al-Ma'ānī* (7:194-196).

[115] Narrated by Ibn Hishām (3:163).

[116] Cf. al-Saqqāf, *Ilqām* (p. 74).

The proof that the Arabs called their grandfathers "father" is in the Prophet's ﷺ calling al-Ḥasan "this son of mine"[117] and in the poetic lines the Prophet ﷺ himself recited during battle in *Ṣaḥīḥ al-Bukhārī:*

I am the Prophet, this is no lie:
I am the son of 'Abd al-Muṭṭalib.

The line "This son of mine shall achieve great matters" upon the noble birth of the Prophet ﷺ is also reported from 'Abd al-Muṭṭalib in the books of Sira, and Ādam ﷺ is addressed with the words: "This is your son Dāwūd" as narrated in Ṣaḥīḥ al-Bukhārī. The "righteous father" of the two orphans in Sūrat al-Kahf was a seventh-generation ancestor according to the commentaries. Arabs generally claimed sonship to whichever of their ancestors they prided themselves in, usually the most famous figure. Inversely, derision was expressed by attributing sonship with a non-famous figure, as the unbelievers did by calling the Prophet ﷺ "Ibn Abī Kabsha."

The proof that "father" was used for one's uncle is in the verse ﴿**We shall worship your God, the God of your fathers, Ibrāhīm and Ismā'īl and Isḥāq**﴾ (2:133).[118] Another proof is found in the narration of Baḥīrā in which the monk Baḥīrā asks to know who the Prophet's ﷺ father is, whereupon Abū Ṭālib said: "He is my son," to which the monk replied: "It cannot be because his father is not alive."[119] Also, in the cognomen Umm 'Abd Allāh given by the Prophet ﷺ to 'Ā'isha after her nephew – the son of her sister – 'Abd Allāh ibn al-Zubayr. [120]

[117] Cf. [1] the words spoken by the Prophet ﷺ from the pulpit with al-Ḥasan by his side: "Verily, this son of mine – al-Ḥasan – is a leader among men (*sayyid*), and Allāh may put him in a position to reconcile two great factions of the Muslims." Narrated from Abū Bakra by al-Bukhārī with four chains, al-Tirmidhī (*ḥasan ṣaḥīḥ*), al-Nasā'ī, Abū Dāwūd, and Aḥmad with four chains. [2] The narration of the long prostration during which al-Ḥasan would jump on the Prophet's ﷺ shoulders after which the latter said: "My son was riding me and I hated to rush him until he was finished" Narrated by Aḥmad with a sound chain as per al-Arna'ūṭ (25:419-420 §16033), al-Nasā'ī, Ibn Abī 'Āṣim in *al-Āḥād wal-Mathānī* (§934), Ibn Abī Shayba (12:100-101), al-Ṭabarānī in *al-Kabīr* (§7107), and al-Ḥākim (3:626-627, 3:165-166 *ṣaḥīḥ*).

[118] Cf. al-Bayḍāwī, *Tafsīr* (4:384).

[119] Narrated by Ibn Hishām, *Sīra* (1:322), Ibn Sa'd (1:155), al-Ṭabarī, *Tārīkh* (1:519), al-Taymī's *Dalā'il al-Nubuwwa* (p. 231), and Ibn al-Jawzī in *Ṣifat al-Ṣafwa* (1:69).

[120] Cf. Ibn Ḥajar, *al-Iṣāba*, entry on 'Ā'isha.

(iii) Regardless of all the foregoing, a golden rule of "respectful unspeakableness" applies with the Divine statements about the Prophet ﷺ such as that "his being a mere mortal man," "a human being like the others," that "if he lied against his Lord he would be destroyed," that "he did not know what Belief was nor the Book" etc. Just because Allāh said something of His Beloved in the Qur'ān or just because the Prophet ﷺ said something of himself in the ḥadīth does not automatically entitle every person to say it! Thus, it is impermissible and pure impiety for us to repeat the words of the Prophet ﷺ concerning his father in the ḥadīth of Muslim since he himself said: "Do not harm the living by insulting the dead,"[121] and Allāh ﷻ said: ﴾**Those who annoy Allāh and the Prophet, Allāh curses them in this life and in the hereafter**﴿ (33:57). Hence, when the Qāḍī Abū Bakr ibn al-'Arabī was asked about a person who would repeat such a statement about the two Prophetic parents, he replied: "Such a man is cursed."[122]

(iv) Further, to discuss the two Noble Parents of the Prophet ﷺ is in direct violation of the injunction of the Prophet ﷺ himself as established by the following ḥadīths:

> A man from the *Anṣār* insulted the memory of al-'Abbās's father who lived in the Time of Ignorance, whereupon al-'Abbās slapped him. The man's people came and said: "By Allāh, we shall slap him just as he slapped him," and they girded their weapons. News of this reached the Prophet ﷺ who ascended the pulpit and said: "People! Who among the dwellers of the earth is deemed most honorable in the presence of Allāh?" They said, "You." He continued: "Al-'Abbās is part of me and I am part of him. < Do not insult our dead, thereby harming our living."> The people then came to the Prophet ﷺ and said: "Messenger of Allāh! We seek refuge in Allāh from your anger. Ask forgiveness for us."[123]

[121] Cf. note 123.

[122] Cf. al-Suhaylī, *Rawḍ* (1:298-299) and al-Suyūṭī, *Masālik al-Ḥunafā'* in his *Ḥāwī*.

[123] Narrated from Ibn 'Abbās by Aḥmad and al-Nasā'ī with a sound chain per al-'Irāqī in *Takhrīj Aḥādīth al-Iḥyā'*. The bracketed segment is also narrated from al-Mughīra ibn Shu'ba by al-Tirmidhī, Aḥmad, and al-Quḍā'ī in *Musnad al-Shihāb* (2:81 §925).

عَنِ ابْنِ عَبَّاسٍ رَضِيَ اللهُ عَنْهُمَا أَنَّ رَجُلًا وَقَعَ فِي أَبٍ كَانَ لَهُ فِي الْجَاهِلِيَّةِ فَلَطَمَهُ الْعَبَّاسُ فَجَاءَ قَوْمُهُ فَقَالُوا لَيَلْطِمَنَّهُ كَمَا لَطَمَهُ فَلَبِسُوا السِّلَاحَ فَبَلَغَ ذَلِكَ النَّبِيَّ صَلَّى اللَّهُ عَلَيْهِ وَسَلَّمَ فَصَعِدَ الْمِنْبَرَ فَقَالَ أَيُّهَا النَّاسُ أَيُّ أَهْلِ الْأَرْضِ تَعْلَمُونَ أَكْرَمُ عَلَى اللهِ عَزَّ وَجَلَّ فَقَالُوا أَنْتَ فَقَالَ إِنَّ الْعَبَّاسَ مِنِّي وَأَنَا مِنْهُ لَا تَسُبُّوا مَوْتَانَا فَتُؤْذُوا أَحْيَاءَنَا فَجَاءَ الْقَوْمُ فَقَالُوا يَا رَسُولَ اللَّهِ نَعُوذُ بِاللَّهِ مِنْ غَضَبِكَ اسْتَغْفِرْ لَنَا ن حم وصحح الحافظ العراقي إسناده

> The daughter of Abū Lahab – Durra ﵂ or Subay'a ﵂ – came to the Messenger of Allāh ﷺ and said, "Messenger of Allāh! The people are calling me the daughter of the Fuel of Hellfire!" The Messenger of Allāh ﷺ stood up angry and said on the pulpit: "What is the matter with the people that harm me in my relatives? Whoever harms my relatives harms me, and whoever harms me has harmed Allāh!"[124]

The Holy Prophet ﷺ emphasized respect for his own ancestry. When Ḥassān ibn Thābit asked permission to lampoon the pagans in satirical poetry, the Prophet ﷺ replied: "What about my [shared] lineage [with them]?" Ḥassān said: "I will withdraw you from them the way a hair is withdrawn from the dough!" (al-Bukhārī). Then the Prophet ﷺ instructed him to go to Abū Bakr to study the Prophet's ﷺ lineage in detail (al-Ṭabarānī), so that he could lampoon the pagans as he had instructed the Muslim poets to do (Muslim).

(v) Finally, the author has not met any of the pious Ulema of Syro-Palestine, the Ḥijāz, Yemen, North Africa, and the rest of the world who did not hold the most profound respect for the two parents of the

[124] Narrated from Ibn 'Umar, Abū Hurayra, and 'Ammār ibn Yāsir by Ibn Abī 'Āṣim in *al-Āḥād wal-Mathānī* (5:470 §3165), Ibn Isḥāq, al-Ṭabarānī, Abū Nu'aym, and Ibn Mandah, cf. Ibn Ḥajar, *Iṣāba* (7:634-635) and al-Muḥibb al-Ṭabarī in the beginning of his *Dhakhā'ir al-'Uqbā*.

Holy Prophet 🌺, many of them mentioning "Allāh be well-pleased with them" (🌺) after their names, while some Ulema actually include them in the invocation of blessings and peace after mention of the Prophet 🌺. There is also, in Aleppo, a long-standing mosque by the name of "*Jāmi' Āmina bint Wahb* 🌺."

The rightly-guided Caliph, 'Umar ibn 'Abd al-'Azīz 🌺, once faced a Muslim administrator whom he heard say that the father of the Prophet 🌺 was a *kāfir*. 'Umar said: "Shall I cut off his tongue? Shall I cut off his hand? Shall I cut off his leg?" Then he ordered that the man be ostracized.[125]

Also in affirmation of the salvation of the two Noble Parents and in refutation of al-Qārī is the book by Imām al-Barzanjī (d. 1103), *Sadād al-Dīn*, perhaps the most complete reference-work on the topic. Al-Barzanjī writes (p. 108-109) the same as al-Haytamī, but in reference to *al-Fiqh al-Absaṭ*. He cites (p. 80) the report of 'Umar ibn 'Abd al-'Azīz adduced above.

Al-Shawkānī (d. 1250) in *al-Badr al-Ṭāli'* defended al-Qārī whom he characterized as a *mujtahid* persecuted for his independent views – an unmistakable reference to himself. The only school that still defends al-Qārī's hapless stand on the question today is the "Salafī"/Wahhābī school in the person of Mashhūr Salmān who recirculated al-Qārī's *Mu'taqad*, and Abū Bakr al-Jazā'irī.[126]

As for the ḥadīth "Your mother is in the Fire [...] My mother is with your mother," it is very weak and, moreover, contains an indication that the Prophet's 🌺 intercession may serve to bring them out of the Fire: "Whatever I ask my Lord about the two of them [the Prophet's 🌺 parents], I hope that He will give me. I shall stand, on that day, at the praiseworthy Station."[127]

As for the ultimate salvation of Abū Ṭālib from the Fire, Shaykh

---

[125] Narrated by Ibn 'Asākir (45:222) and cited by al-Suyūṭī in *Tanzīh al-Anbiyā' 'an Tasfīh al-Aghbiyā'* in his *Ḥāwī lil-Fatāwā*.

[126] On this man see al-Sayyid Yūsuf al-Rifā'ī's *Advice to Najd*, Murād and 'Amrāwī's *Wā'iẓ ghayr Mutta'iẓ*, and our monograph *Albānī and His Friends*.

[127] Narrated from Ibn Mas'ūd by Aḥmad, al-Ṭabarī in his *Tafsīr*, al-Ḥākim (2:365= 1990 ed. 2:396), al-Dārimī (book of *Riqāq*), Abū al-Shaykh in *al-'Aẓama*, and Ibn al-Mundhir, all with very weak chains because of 'Uthmān ibn 'Umayr who is disclaimed as a narrator (*munkar al-ḥadīth*) cf. Shaykh Aḥmad Shākir in his edition of the *Musnad* (4:31-32 §3787), al-Haythamī (10:361-362), and al-Dhahabī's rejection of al-Ḥākim's grading of authentic.

'Abd al-Hādī Kharsa said its strongest proof is in the words of the Prophet ﷺ that he interceded for him to be in a shallow level of Hellfire [in al-Bukhārī and Muslim] whereas Allāh ﷻ said of the unbelievers, ﴾**The mediation of no mediators will avail them then**﴿ (74:48). However, it can be answered that the verse is excepted by the fact that the first, general intercession of the Prophet ﷺ for mankind at the universal Station (*al-Maqām*), on the Day of Judgment, includes the disbelievers. So does his ulterior intercession for the lessening of their eternal punishment in the Fire.

It is also related that some of the Ash'arī Imāms such as al-Qurṭubī, al-Subkī, and al-Sha'rānī said that Abū Ṭālib was saved, according to Sayyid Aḥmad Zaynī Daḥlān in his luminous treatise *Asnā al-Maṭālib fī Najāt Abī Ṭālib* (Cairo: Muḥammad Effendī Muṣṭafā, 1305/1886) who cites Imām al-Suhaymī and the Ḥanafī Mufti of Makka Shaykh Aḥmad ibn 'Abd Allāh al-Mirghānī to that effect. They mention, among other evidence, the narration from al-'Abbās ؓ by Ibn Sa'd in his *Ṭabaqāt* (1:118):

> 'Affān ibn Muslim told us: Ḥammād ibn Salama told us: From Thābit [ibn Aslam al-Bunānī]: From Isḥāq ibn 'Abd Allāh ibn al-Ḥārith [ibn Nawfal] who said: al-'Abbās said: "I said: 'Messenger of Allāh, do you hope anything for Abū Ṭālib?' He replied: 'I hope for everything good [*i.e.* for him] from my Lord.'"

The above narrators are all trustworthy and their transmission is sound, except that the meaning of the ḥadīth is unspecific. Further, al-Qurṭubī in his *Tafsīr* (for verses 6:26 and 9:53) and Ibn al-Subkī in *Ṭabaqāt al-Shāfi'iyya al-Kubrā* (1:91-94) hold different positions from those ascribed to them above and 'Alī himself said that Abū Bakr is the only Companion to have both parents – Abū Quḥāfa and Umm al-Khayr – enter Islām.[128] And Allāh knows best.

[128] Narrated from 'Ā'isha by Mālik in his *Muwaṭṭa'*, Ibn Sa'd (3:194-195), al-Bayhaqī in *al-Sunan al-Kubrā* (6:169-170 §11728, 6:178 §11784, 6:257 §12267), 'Abd al-Razzāq (9:101), al-Ṭaḥāwī in *Sharḥ Ma'ānī al-Āthār* (4:88), *Istī'āb* (4:1807), *Naṣb* (4:122), Ibn al-Jawzī in *Ṣifat al-Ṣafwa* (1:265), al-Nawawī in *Tahdhīb al-Asmā'* (2:574, 2:630), al-Lālikā'ī in *Karāmāt al-Awliyā'* (p. 117), al-Mizzī in *Tahdhīb al-Kamāl* (35:380), and Muḥibb al-Dīn al-Ṭabarī in *al-Riyāḍ al-Naḍira* (2:122-123 §576).

His Precedence in Dialectic Theology *(Kalām)*

Abū Ḥanīfa is the earliest Imām of *kalām* among the *Salaf*, preceding by a century and a half the two Imāms of Sunni doctrine, Abū al-Ḥasan al-Ash'arī and Abū Manṣūr al-Māturīdī. He is the first formulator of the principles of *Tawḥīd* among the Four Imāms in opposition to the non-Sunnī sects. 'Abd al-Qāhir al-Baghdādī stated:

> The first of the scholars of *kalām* among the jurists and foremost chiefs of the schools of Law are Abū Ḥanīfa and al-Shāfi'ī. Abū Ḥanīfa wrote a book against the Qadarīs entitled *al-Fiqh al-Akbar* and a treatise in support of the position of *Ahl al-Sunna* whereby capacity or acting-power (*al-istiṭā'a*) is, or coincides with deed (*al-fi'l*) [...]. While al-Shāfi'ī authored two books in *kalām*: one on the sound explanation of prophethood in refutation of Brahmanism,[129] the other a refutation of the people of vain passions [*i.e.* innovators].[130]

It is established that Abū Ḥanīfa – in his own words – specialized in *kalām* before he began to accompany his teacher Ḥammād ibn Abī Sulaymān and turned to *fiqh*: "I used to investigate *kalām* until I reached a level of expertise in it for which I became a reference."[131] This is confirmed by Muwaffaq al-Dīn ibn Aḥmad al-Makkī al-Khwārizmī (d. 568) in his *Manāqib Abī Ḥanīfa*: "Abū Ḥanīfa did not cease to ply *kalām*, debating the scholars, until he became an expert in *kalām*;"[132] "Abū Ḥanīfa used to preside over a gathering of knowledge in *kalām*."[133] Abū Ḥanīfa further said:

[129] As cited by Abū Manṣūr al-Baghdādī in *Uṣūl al-Dīn* (p. 308) and his commendation of the Shāfi'ī school over the Ḥanafī entitled *Naqd Abī 'Abd Allāh al-Jurjānī fī Tarjīḥ Madhhab Abī Ḥanīfa*, cited by Ibn al-Subkī in his *Ṭabaqāt al-Wusṭā* (in *Ṭabaqāt al-Shāfi'iyya al-Kubrā* 5:146).

[130] In *Uṣūl al-Dīn* (p. 308).

[131] Narrated from Zufar by al-Khaṭīb in *Tārīkh Baghdād* (13:333) with his chain: Abū Ḥanīfa > Zufar > al-Ḥasan ibn Ziyād > al-Walīd ibn Ḥammād >Ja'far ibn Muḥammad ibn Ḥāzim > Ibrāhīm al-Nakha'ī > al-Ḥarīrī > al-Khallāl >al-Khaṭīb.

[132] Narrated from Abū Ḥafṣ al-Ṣaghīr by al-Muwaffaq in *al-Manāqib* (1:63) as cited by al-Kawtharī in his introduction to al-Bayāḍī's *Ishārāt al-Marām* (p. 4). Al-Khwārizmī's book was printed together with Muḥammad ibn Muḥammad al-Kardarī al-Bazzāzī work bearing the same title. Cf. Ḥajjī Khalīfa, *Kashf al-Ẓunūn* (2:1838); al-Kawtharī, *Ta'nīb al-Khaṭīb* (1998 ed. p. 20).

[133] Narrated from al-Zaranjārī by al-Muwaffaq in *al-Manāqib* (1:63.).

I was granted to debate [the Scholars] in *kalām*. I did this for a period of time in which I would enter *kalām* disputations and confront others by means of it. At that time most disputers and debaters were in al-Baṣra, and I went to al-Baṣra over twenty times, sometimes remaining there for a year or more. I challenged various parties of the *Khawārij* such as the *Ibāḍiyya*, the *Safariyya*, and others, as well as various parties of the *Ḥashwiyya*.[134]

Encounters with the *Khawārij*

Ibn 'Abd al-Barr in *al-Intiqā'* and al-Qārī in his biography of the Imām entitled *al-Thimār al-Janiyya* narrate that after the Khārijīs entered Kūfa with al-Ḍaḥḥāk ibn Qays al-Shaybānī at their head, one day, a number of them invaded the Imām's house and, catching hold of him said, "Say, you repent of *kufr*." The Imām said, "I repent of all manners of *kufr*." The Khārijīs maintain that by committing a sin a man becomes a *kāfir*, which amounts to saying that sin and *kufr* are identical. Somebody later on went to the Khārijīs and told them that the Imām's answer was a double-entendre and that what he meant was that he repented of their own *kufr*. The Khārijīs came back to the Imām and seized him. "Is it on the basis of firm knowledge or merely suspicion that you act?" inquired the Imām. "Only suspicion," replied the Khārijīs. "In that case," said the Imam, "﴾**Verily, sometimes doubting is a sin**﴿ (49:12), therefore repent of *kufr*." They said: "You, also, repent of *kufr*." He replied: "I repent of all manners of *kufr*."[135]

In another version the report goes: "Repent. – Of what should I repent? – Repent!! – Of what should I repent??" (*Tub! – Mimmā atūb? Tub!! – Mimmā atūb??*) Al-Ḍaḥḥāk then said: "Of your assent to the arbitration [between Mu'āwiya and 'Alī]!" Abū Ḥanīfa said: "Will you debate with me?" He replied yes. The Imām said, "What if we disagree? Who will decide between us?" He said So-and-so. The Imām said: "So you accept him as a judge?" He replied yes. The Imām said: "Then you have accepted arbitration!" Al-Ḍaḥḥāk remained speechless. This was in 127.

[134] Narrated from al-Ḥārith by al-Muwaffaq in *al-Manāqib* (1:59).

[135] As cited in al-Ghāwjī, *Abū Ḥanīfa al-Nu'mān* (p. 264-265).

Encounter with the *Qadariyya*

Ibn 'Abd al-Barr narrates with his chain to the Imām in *al-Intiqā'* that seventy of the Qadariyya came to Kūfa and approached him intending to debate him. "In what will you debate me?" he asked. They said: "In *qadar*!" He replied: "*Qadar* is like the sun. The more you look into it, the more dazzled and perplexed you become." Among the questions they put to him: "Abū Ḥanīfa, are you a *mu'min*?" He said yes. They continued: "Are you a *mu'min* in the sight of Allāh?" He said: "Are you asking me of my knowledge and my resolve or of the knowledge of Allāh and His resolve?" They said: "Of your knowledge, of course! We are not asking you about the knowledge of Allāh." He replied: "In my knowledge, I know that I am a *mu'min*. I do not presume anything of Allāh in His knowledge."

The Early Ḥanafī Imāms Entered *Kalām* Disputations

Al-Muwaffaq also narrated from Ḥafīẓ al-Dīn Muḥammad ibn Muḥammad al-Kardarī (d. 827) – the author of the *Fatāwā Bazzāziyya* – that Jamāl al-Dīn Abū Ya'lā Aḥmad ibn Mas'ūd al-Aṣfahānī narrated from Khālid ibn Zayd al-'Umarī: "Abū Ḥanīfa, Abū Yūsuf, Muḥammad [ibn al-Ḥasan], Zufar, and Ḥammād ibn Abī Ḥanīfa were a group that entered into *kalām* disputations at the same time as they were Imāms of knowledge."[136]

It is due to this foremost rank in *kalām* on the part of the early Ḥanafī Imāms that al-Ṭaḥāwī entitled his statement of doctrine *Bayān I'tiqād Ahl al-Sunna wal-Jamā'a 'alā Madhhab Fuqahā' al-Milla Abī Ḥanīfa wa-Abī Yūsuf al-Anṣārī wa-Muḥammad ibn al-Ḥasan* ("Exposition of the Doctrine of the Jurists of the Muslim World, Abū Ḥanīfa, Abū Yūsuf, and Muḥammad ibn al-Ḥasan").

Abū Ḥanīfa's Works in *Kalām*

Among the works of the Imām in *kalām*:[137]

- *Al-Fiqh al-Akbar* ("The Supreme Wisdom"), authentically narrated from the Imām by his son Ḥammād. The Ash'arī Shaykh Abū

[136] Narrated in *al-Manāqib* (1:38).

[137] The full chains of transmission for all these works are given in al-Muwaffaq's *Manāqib* and al-Kawtharī's *Ta'nīb al-Khaṭīb* as well as (in part) his introduction to al-Bayāḍī's *Ishārāt al-Marām* (p. 6).

al-Muẓaffar al-Isfarāyīnī[138] said in his book *al-Tabṣīr fil-Dīn*: "*Al-Fiqh al-Akbar* was narrated to us by trustworthy people through a reliable way and a sound chain of transmission from Naṣīr ibn Yaḥyā [up to] Abū Ḥanīfa."[139] This work received at least fifteen commentaries, among them those of al-Qārī, al-Maghnīsāwī, and al-Bayāḍī, all three of them in print. In it the Imām said:

"Allāh is One not in the sense of a number but in the sense that He has no partner whatsoever.... He is 'something' unlike any other thing, and the meaning of 'something' here is to affirm Him without body (*jism*), nor indivisible substance (*jawhar*), nor accident (*'araḍ*); and He has no limit (*ḥadd*)."

"Whatever Allāh ﷻ mentioned in the Qur'ān about the 'Face,' 'Hand,' and 'Essence,' these are His Attributes without asking how. [*I*.e. their proof-text (*aṣl*) is known while their description (*waṣf*) is unknown to us (al-Maghnīsāwī).] Let it not be said that His Hand is [but] His Power (*qudra*) or Bounty (*ni'ma*) because doing so is a nullification of the Attribute [which the Qur'ān affirms (al-Maghnīsāwī)] and is the position of the Qadarīs and Mu'tazilīs. His Hand is an Attribute without asking how!" [Al-Qārī comments: "That is, without knowledge of any modality, exactly as we are incapable of having knowledge of the true nature (*kunh*) of the rest of His Attributes, not to mention the true nature of His Essence."]

Imam Abū Ḥanīfa's caveat does not contradict the Māturīdī position that the Attributes of corporality are not corporal (as in al-Ṭaḥāwī's *'Aqīda*) but are among the *mutashābihāt* (as in al-

[138] Imām Abū al-Muẓaffar Ṭāhir ibn Muḥammad al-Isfarāyīnī al-Shāfi'ī al-Ash'arī, known as Shahafūr (d. 471), author of *Tāj al-Tarājim fī Tafsīr al-Qur'ān lil-A'ājim* cf. Ḥajjī Khalīfa, *Kashf al-Ẓunūn* (1:268, 1:442). In his book *al-Tabṣīr fil-Dīn wa-Tamyīz al-Firqat al-Nājiya min Firaq al-Hālikīn* he defines *Ahl al-Sunna wal-Jamā'a* as the Ash'arīs.

[139] In *al-Tabṣīr* (p. 113) as cited by al-Kawtharī in his introduction to al-Bayāḍī's *Ishārāt al-Marām* (p. 5). The complete chain is 'Alī ibn Aḥmad al-Fārisī < Naṣīr [not Nuṣayr nor Naṣr] ibn Yaḥyā [al-Balkhī (d. 268)] < Abū Muqātil <'Iṣām ibn Yūsuf [ibn Maymūn al-Balkhī (d. 210 or 215)] < Ḥammād ibn Abī Ḥanīfa < Abū Ḥanīfa. (*Ibid*. p. 6.) Shaykh Wahbī Sulaymān Ghāwjī said in his edition of al-Qārī's *Sharḥ al-Fiqh al-Akbar* (p. 13) that he saw in Maktabat Shaykh al-Islām 'Ārif Ḥikmat in Madīna (Compendium §226 or §234) a manuscript of the *Fiqh al-Akbar* with the same chain.

Pazdawī's *Uṣūl* and its *Sharḥ* by al-Bukhārī). These guidelines – avoidance of figurative interpretation, avoidance of corporal explanation, and affirmation that *Yad* and such expressions are among the *Mutashābihāt* – are also within the Ash'arīs' method. The latter allow the option of interpretation if it coincides with the bases of the Arabic language and the general purport of *'Aqīda*, as does Imām al-Māturīdī in *Kitāb al-Tawḥīd.* And Allāh knows best.

[In al-Maghnīsāwī only:] "And Muḥammad ﷺ is His Beloved (*ḥabībuh*)."

- *Al-Waṣiyya* ("The Testament"), a brief treatise dictated by Abū Ḥānīfa on his death-bed according to the Sunna, in which he states: "The meeting (*liqā'*) of Allāh Most High with the dwellers of Paradise is by visual sight without modality, nor simile, nor direction" and "We affirm that Allāh established Himself over the Throne without his having need for it and without settlement on it as He is the Preserver of the Throne and other than the Throne. If He stood in need for it, He would have been unable to bring the world into being or dispose of it, just as created beings [are unable]. And if He became in need of sitting down and settling, then, before creating the Throne, where was Allāh ﷻ? Rather, He is greatly and immensely transcendent beyond all such notions."[140]

- *Risālat Abī Ḥanīfa ilā 'Uthmān al-Battī*, a brief letter to the *Mujtahid* of Baṣra Abū 'Amr 'Uthmān ibn Muslim al-Battī (d. 143) also narrated through Naṣīr ibn Yaḥyā – from Abū 'Abd Allāh Muḥammad ibn Samā'a al-Tamīmī, from Abū Yūsuf, from Abū Ḥanīfa, in which the Imām explains the principle of his School whereby *īmān* has two, not three pillars, namely: conviction in the heart and affirmation by the tongue, in refutation of those who imputed him with the label of *Murji'*. Following is the text of the *Risāla*:

From Abū Ḥanīfa to 'Uthmān al-Battī: *Salāmun 'alayk*! Truly I

[140] Printed [1] together with al-Nasafī's *Matn al-Manār fī Uṣūl al-Fiqh* (Cairo: al-Maṭba'at al-Maḥmūdiyya, 1326) and [2] edited by al-Kawtharī and reprinted by al-Maktaba al-Azhariyya lil-Turāth (Cairo, 2001) together with *al-'Ālim wal-Muta'allim*, *al-Fiqh al-Absaṭ*, *al-Fiqh al-Akbar*, and *Risālat Abī Ḥanīfa ilā Uthmān al-Battī*.

render praise and glory before you to Allāh beside Whom there is no God. To proceed: I advise you to fear Allāh and obey Him. He suffices as a reckoner and requiter.

I received your letter. I understood what it contained in the way of your *naṣīḥa* and your holding us dear. You said that what impelled you to write it was your ardent concern for goodness and sincere good faith. This is precisely how we viewed it.

You mentioned that you had heard I belong to the *Murji'a* and that I say: [a grave sinner is but] a misguided believer (*mu'minun ḍāll*). You said that you found this hard to bear. I do swear! There is no excuse in anything that removes one far from Allāh nor any guidance in the innovations invented by the people. We are commanded nothing other than what the Qur'ān brought, what Muḥammad ﷺ called us to, and what his Companions practiced until the people split into factions. Anything else is newfangled innovation. Therefore, understand this letter of mine to you. Beware of your own preconceived opinion lest the devil come to you. May Allāh make us and you immune through obedience of Him! We ask success of Him for us and for you through His Mercy.

Let me remind you that the people were polytheists before Allāh ﷻ sent Muḥammad ﷺ. He sent Muḥammad who called them to Islām. He summoned them to witness that there is no God but Allāh alone without partner, and to confirm what he had brought on the part of Allāh ﷻ.

Whoever entered Islām at that time was a believer (*mu'min*) exempt from polytheism. His property, honor, and blood were sacred. He owned all the rights and sacred status owned by the Muslims. Whoever did not do this when called to do it was a disbeliever devoid of belief. His property and blood were licit. Nothing was accepted from him except one of two things: either to enter Islām or be killed, except for what Allāh ﷻ mentioned about the remittance of the *jizya* by the People of the Book.

Then the categorical obligations (*farā'iḍ*) descended, after that, on the people of confirmation (*ahl al-taṣdīq*). Applying those obligations was a practice done together with belief. This is why Allāh ﷻ says, ﴾**those who believe and do good works**﴿ and ﴾**whoso believes in Allāh and does right**﴿. There are other similar verses in the Qur'ān. Therefore, whoever falls short of practice does not fall short of confirmation but has realized confirmation without practice.

If the one who fell short of practice necessarily fell short of confirmation he would then exit from the name of belief and its sanctity by virtue of falling short of practice just as those who fell short of confirmation came out of the name of belief, its sanctity, and the rights that come with it, returning to their previous state of polytheism. Another way by which the difference between the two is known is that people do not differ in confirmation nor do they excel one another in it while they may excel one another in practice, and their categorical obligations differ.

So the Religion of the [angelic] inhabitants of the heaven and that of the [human] Messengers is one. Thus did Allāh ﷻ say, ⟨**He has ordained for you that religion which He commended unto Noah, and that which We inspire in you (Muḥammad), and that which We commended unto Ibrāhīm and Mūsā and 'Īsā, saying: Establish the religion, and be not divided therein**⟩ (42:13).

Therefore, know that the guidance that consists in confirming Allāh and His Messengers is not like the guidance that consists in the deeds He has made obligatory. What is the difficulty in this for you? Consequently you call someone a *mu'min* while he is ignorant of the categorical obligations of which he has no idea; but you have to call him a *mu'min* because of his confirmation, just as Allāh ﷻ has named him in His Book, though he may be called ignorant in whatever obligations he does not know. Only, he has to learn what he does not know. Now: is the one who is misguided away from the knowledge of Allāh ﷻ and the knowledge of His Messenger the same as the one who is misguided away from what the people have learnt after they became believers? Allāh ﷻ said, concerning His teaching the categorical obligations, ⟨**Allāh expounds unto you, so that you err not** (*an taḍillū*)⟩ (4:176); and He said, ⟨**so that if the one errs** (*an taḍilla*) **the other will remember**] (2:282); and He said, ⟨**He said: I did it then, when I was of those who are astray** (*min al-ḍāllīn*)⟩ (26:20), meaning, one of the ignorant.

The overwhelming proof is from the Book of Allāh ﷻ. The Sunna confirms this too clearly and plainly to allow any ambiguity for such as you. Do you not say, "A believer who does wrong (*mu'min ẓālim*)," or "a believer who sins" (*mu'min mudhnib*), or "a believer who commits mistakes" (*mu'min mukhṭi'*), or "a disobedient believer" (*mu'min 'āṣin*), or "a believer who rebels" (*mu'min jā'ir*)? Can he be, in what he did wrong and committed mistakes, guided just as he is guided in belief? Or is he astray from the right for erring?

As for the saying of the sons of Ya'qūb ﷺ to their father, ﴾**Lo! you are in your old aberration (*fī ḍalālika al-qadīm*)**﴿ (12:95): do you think that they meant, "You are in your old disbelief (*kufrika*)"? Allāh forbid that you should understand this when you are so well-versed in the Qur'ān.

Know that if the matter were indeed as you have written to us, namely, that people gave confirmation before the categorical obligations, then the categorical obligations came, then the people of confirmation should have deserved the name of confirmation through the deeds at the time they were made responsible for them! But you did not explain to me what they were following, what religion they were, and what status you consider them to have before that point. For they do not deserve that name except through deeds at the time they were made responsible for them.

If you claim that they are believers (*mu'minūn*) to whom apply all the rulings of the Muslims and their sacred status, you have said the truth and this is correct as I have written to you above. However, if you say that they are disbelievers (*kuffār*), you have committed innovation and contravened the Prophet ﷺ and the Qur'ān! And if you say, as the obdurate innovators say, that he is neither a disbeliever nor a believer, then know that this claim is an innovation and contravenes the Prophet ﷺ and his Companions.

'Alī ﷺ was named the Commander of the Believers (*Amīr al-Mu'minīn*) and so was 'Umar ﷺ. Did they mean by such a name that they were the Commanders of those who obey all the categorical obligations? 'Alī named those of Syro-Palestine who fought him, "Believers." He named them thus in his letter expounding his case. Were they well-guided when he was fighting them? The Companions of the Messenger of Allāh ﷺ fought among themselves. The two factions were not both well-guided. Then what is the name of the rebel faction in your view? By Allāh! I do not know, among the people of the one *qibla*, a sin greater than manslaughter, especially that of the Companions of

Muḥammad ﷺ! What, then, is the name of each of the two factions in your view? They cannot both be well-guided simultaneously.

If you say that they were both well-guided (*muhtadiyān*) at one and the same time, you have committed innovation. If you say that they are both misguided (*ḍāllān*) at one and the same time, you have committed innovation. And if you say that one of them is well-guided, then what is the other? If you reply " Allāh knows best", you have replied correctly. Understand well what I have just written!

Know, also, that I say: The People of the *Qibla* are all *mu'minūn*. I do not declare them to be out of *īmān* if they lost something of the categorical obligations. Whoever obeys Allāh Most High in all of the categorical obligations together with *īmān*, such is among the dwellers of Paradise in our view, and whoever leaves *īmān* and deeds, such is a disbeliever and among the dwellers of the Fire. As for he who obtains *īmān* but loses something of the categorical obligations, he is a sinful *mu'min*, and Allāh Most High does what He wishes with him. If He wishes, he punishes him, and if He wishes, He forgives him. If He punishes him for losing something, He punishes him for a sin, and if He forgives him, He forgives him his sin.

I say, concerning the past disagreements of the Companions of the Messenger of Allāh ﷺ among themselves: Allāh knows best. Surely, you hold no other opinion concerning the people of the *Qibla*, because this is what the Companions of the Messenger of Allāh ﷺ enjoined and this is what those who conveyed the Sunna and the *Fiqh* enjoined. Your brother 'Aṭā' ibn Abī Rabāḥ[141] said – as we detailed this issue to him – that this was what the Companions of the Messenger of Allāh ﷺ prescribed. Sālim [ibn 'Ajlān Abū Muḥammad al-Umawī al-Afṭas (d. 132)] said that Sa'īd ibn Jubayr said this was what the Companions of Muḥammad ﷺ prescribed. Your brother Nāfi' [Mawlā Ibn 'Umar] said this was what 'Abd Allāh ibn 'Umar prescribed – Allāh be well-pleased with both of them! 'Abd al-Karīm [ibn Mālik al-Jazarī al-Khaḍramī (d. 127)] also said, on the authority

[141] A Nubian *Tābi'ī* (d. 114). The Imām said he never saw better than him.

of Ṭāwūs [ibn Kaysān al-Yamānī (d. 106)], on the authority of Ibn 'Abbās – Allāh be well-pleased with both of them! – that this is what Ibn 'Abbās prescribed. I have heard that when 'Alī ibn Abī Ṭālib ☙ wrote the famous case (*al-qaḍiyya*), he named both parties *mu'minīn* at one and the same time.

This is also what 'Umar ibn 'Abd al-'Azīz said, as narrated from him by those of your brothers who met him according to what I heard about you. Then he said: "Put together a book on this for me," after which he taught it to his son and ordered them to teach it. Teach it to those that sit with you – may Allāh have mercy on you! – for he held a place of high esteem among the Muslims. Know that the best of what you taught and will ever teach people is the Sunna. But you must know who those qualified are and ought to learn it!

As for what you mentioned concerning the name of *Murji'a*: what is the sin of those who speak justly and fairly and whom the innovators have labeled thus? Rather, they [the *Murji'a*] are the people of justice and the people of the Sunna! But this name is only what ill-wishers have named them. I swear that it brings no dishonor at all to a just and fair person to whom you call the people and they respond to you, if the ill-wishers call them *Murji'a*! If they do such a thing then this name is an innovation. Does this in any way disgrace what you took from the people of justice?

If I did not fear to be lengthy and prolong this explanation I would have detailed for you further the matters about which I have just written. If you find anything obscure or if the people of innovation instil some doubt in you, let me know, and I will reply to you concerning it if Allāh wills. I want for you – as for my own soul – every good, and Allāh is our reliance!

Do not be long in replying to me with your salaam and whatever you need. Allāh grant us a blessed return and a good life! The greeting of Allāh upon you, the mercy of Allāh, and His blessings! Glory and praise belong to Allāh! And may Allāh send blessings upon our Master Muḥammad and upon his House and all his Companions.[142]

---

[142] *Risālat Abī Ḥanīfata ilā 'Uthmān al-Battī* in *Namādhij min Rasā'il al-A'immat al-Salaf wa-Adabihim al-'Ilmī* (p. 21-28), ed. 'Abd al-Fattāḥ Abū Ghudda (Aleppo: Maktab al-Maṭbū'āt al-Islāmiyya, 1996).

- *Al-'Ālim wal-Muta'allim* ("The Teacher and the Apprentice"), placed by Abū al-Muẓaffar al-Isfarāyīnī "among the overwhelming proofs against atheists and innovators,"[143] narrated through two chains, both of them through Abū Ḥanīfa's student Abū Muqātil Ḥafṣ ibn Salm al-Fazārī al-Samarqandī but actually attributed by some to Abū Muqātil, who is – in either case – mostly discarded.[144]

- *Al-Fiqh al-Absaṭ* ("The Greatest Wisdom"), the same work as the *Fiqh al-Akbar* but in catechetic form narrated from the Imām exclusively by Abū Muṭī' al-Ḥakam ibn 'Abd Allāh ibn Muslim al-Balkhī al-Khurāsānī through Abū 'Abd Allāh al-Ḥusayn ibn 'Alī al-Alma'ī al-Kāshgharī (d. >484), both of them discarded as narrators. In this version the Imām is related to state:

  [1] "Whoever says, 'I do not know whether my Lord is in the heaven or on earth' commits disbelief (*qad kafar*), as does whoever says, 'He is on the Throne and I do not know whether the Throne is in the heaven or on earth.'" Imām Abū al-Layth al-Samarqandī (d. 373) i*n his Sharḥ al-Fiqh al-Absaṭ* (misattributed to al-Māturīdī) and Imām al-Bayāḍī in *Ishārāt al-Marām* all said: "He is a disbeliever because he attributes a place to Allāh Most High."[145]

  [2] "**﴾The Hand of Allāh is above their hands﴿** (48:10), not like the hand of creatures, and it is not a limb (*laysat bi-jāriḥa*)."

  [3] "If someone says, 'Where is Allāh?' The answer for him is that Allāh existed when there was no 'where,' no creation, nothing! And He is the Creator of everything!" This is confirmed as the true position of the Imām by al-Ṭaḥāwī's article in his *Exposition of the Doctrine of Ahl al-Sunna wal-Jamā'a* that "This is the religion of the Muslims. Anyone that does not guard himself against negation [of the Divine Attributes] or likening [Allāh to something else],

[143] In *al-Tabṣīr* (p. 113) as cited by al-Kawtharī in his introduction to al-Bayāḍī's *Ishārāt* (p. 5).

[144] Cf. al-Ḥākim, *al-Madkhal ilā al-Ṣaḥīḥ* (p. 130 §42), al-Dhahabī, *Mīzān* ('Ilmiyya 2:219), Ibn Ḥajar, *Lisān* (2:322-323), Ibn al-Jawzī, *al-Ḍu'afā' wal-Matrūkīn* (1:221), and al-Khalīlī, *Irshād* (3:975).

[145] Abū al-Layth al-Samarqandī, *Sharḥ al-Fiqh al-Absaṭ* (p. 25) cf. Ghāwjī, *Abū Ḥanīfa* (p. 260).

has gone astray and missed transcendence. For our Lord – Glorified and Exalted! – is only described in terms of oneness and absolute singularity. No creation is in any way whatsoever like Him. He is beyond having limits placed on Him, or having boundaries, or having parts, limbs, and organs! Nor is He contained by the six directions as all created things are."

Certain versions of the *Fiqh al-Absaṭ* have undergone identifiable interpolations such as that narrated by the anthropomorphist al-Harawī al-Anṣārī in his book *al-Fārūq fil-Ṣifāt* as pointed out by al-Kawtharī.[146]

The above documentation shows that the pious *Salaf* did not wholly condemn involvement in *kalām* as a blameworthy activity but only, as Imām Abū Zahra pointed out, its specific use by the innovators – particularly their main sect, the *Mu'tazila* – who diverged from the doctrines of *Ahl al-Sunna.*[147] Those whom the *Salaf* meant in their condemnations of *kalām* were the likes of Dāwūd al-Jawāribī,[148] Ibn Karrām,[149] and other leaders of sects such as those described in heresiographies such al-Ash'arī's *Maqālāt al-Islāmiyyīn,* al-Baghdādī's *al-Farq bayn al-Firaq,* Ibn Ḥazm's *al-Fiṣal fil-Milal,* and al-Shahrastānī's *al-Milal wal-Niḥal.*

The Aim of those who Deny the Existence of Sunni *Kalām*

As for those who, today, insist on claiming that the *Salaf* rejected all of *kalām* in unqualified terms, their aim in such a misrepresentation is threefold:

- First, to empower themselves to cast the label of *bid'a* against those who do not agree with their anthropomorphist leanings,

146 In his introduction to al-Bayāḍī's *Ishārāt al-Marām* (p. 6 n. 1) as well as his edition of the *Fiqh al-Absaṭ* together with *al-'Ālim wal-Muta'allim* and other doctrinal texts of the Imām.

147 "Whenever you hear Abū Yūsuf or Muḥammad or al-Shāfi'ī or Ibn Ḥanbal and others [among the early Imāms] revile the science of *kalām* and those who take knowledge by following the methods of the *mutakallimūn,* know that they only meant the *Mu'tazila* by their criticism, and their methods." Abū Zahra, *Abū Ḥanīfa* (p. 133).

148 "He described the God that he worshipped as possessing all the human organs except the pudenda and the beard." Al-Shahrastānī, *al-Milal wal-Niḥal* (1:105, 1:187).

149 He used to say: "Allāh is firmly seated on the Throne and He is in person (*dhātan*) on the upper side of it." Al-Shahrastānī, *al-Milal wal-Niḥal* (1:108).

in calculated ignorance of the strong proofs adduced by the Ash'arī and Māturīdī Scholars of *kalām* against the heresies of the *Ḥashwiyya* and *Mujassima.*

- Second, to instill literalism into the hearts of uneducated Muslims and degree-bearing Muslims uneducated in the Religious sciences, as well as fear of learning the foundations of belief from the mouth of the great scholars who elucidated the texts of the Qur'ān and Sunna, on the specious grounds that "all that people need is the Qur'ān and Sunna."
- Third, to promote the idea that all the Sunni Imāms of the *Khalaf* – the majority of whom are Ash'arīs – are in fact *Jahmī*-like innovators as opposed to two or three controversial figures that happened to revive anthropomorphist doctrines.

The First *Mutakallim* is 'Alī ibn Abī Ṭālib ﷺ

The truth is that all four of the Four Imāms practiced or supported *kalām*, in one form or another, precisely to refute *kalām*-based innovations. In so doing they actually imitated the major Companions who had debated the Khawārij and defeated them both in disputation and on the field. Imām al-Ghazzālī said: "The first to initiate (*sanna*) the invitation of innovators back to the fold of truth through disputation is 'Alī ibn Abī Ṭālib ﷺ who sent Ibn 'Abbās ﷺ to the *Khawārij* to speak to them."[150]

The Involvement of the *Mujtahid* Imāms in *Kalām*

The following are authentic examples illustrating the involvement of the Imāms in *kalām* after Abū Ḥanīfa:

- It is established that Imām al-Shāfi'ī entered *kalām* disputations with Ḥafṣ al-Fard[151] over the issue of the creation of the Qur'ān until he declared Ḥafṣ a disbeliever, and he used to nickname him "Ḥafṣ the Isolated" (Ḥafṣ al-Munfarid). Ḥafṣ had tried unsuccessfully to make 'Abd Allāh ibn 'Abd al-Ḥākim and Yūsuf ibn 'Amr ibn Yazīd debate him before al-Shāfi'ī accepted – and

[150] Al-Ghazzālī, *Iḥyā' 'Ulūm al-Dīn* (1:96).

[151] Abū 'Amr al-Baṣrī Ḥafṣ al-Fard, also known as Abū Yaḥyā, he came to Baṣra as a Mu'tazilī then turned against them and joined the Jabriyya as stated by Ibn al-Nadīm in *al-Fihrist* (p. 255).

defeated him.[152] Al-Bayhaqī said: "And how could he [al-Shāfi'ī] possibly consider the *kalām* of *Ahl al-Sunna wal-Jamā'a* reprehensible when he himself practiced it, debated those he debated, and exposed the fallacies of those who had cast doubt into the minds of some of his students?"[153] Al-Shāfi'ī also debated the Mu'tazilī Ibrāhīm ibn Ismā'īl ibn 'Ulayya – the student of Abū Bakr al-Aṣamm – and the Jahmī Bishr al-Marīsī at whose house he once resided when he first came to Baghdad.[154]

- Imām Mālik compiled a refutation of the Qadariyya for the benefit of his student Ibn Wahb.[155]
- Imām al-Awzā'ī debated and defeated the Qadarī Ghaylān ibn Muslim al-Dimashqī upon the request of the Caliph Hishām ibn 'Abd al-Malik ibn Marwān, after which Hishām had Ghaylān executed.[156]
- Imām Aḥmad's disputations with Abū 'Īsā Muḥammad ibn 'Īsā Barghūth and his condemnations of the Jahmiyya and Mu'tazila over the issue of the creation of the Qur'ān and the Divine Attributes are recorded in a number of the books of his School, as well as his numerous statements of doctrine – narrated by Ibn Abī Ya'lā in his *Ṭabaqāt al-Ḥanābila* – which are, with Abū Ḥanīfa's works, among the early manifestos of Sunnī *kalām*.[157]
- Imām al-Bukhārī compiled a refutation of the Qadariyya and other sects entitled *Khalq Af'āl al-'Ibād*, and was expelled from Naysābūr by the Ḥanbalīs because of what they perceived as an unacceptable stand in *kalām*.

[152] Ibn 'Asākir, *Tabyīn Kadhib al-Muftarī* (1404 ed. p. 338-340) and al-Bayhaqī, *Manāqib al-Shāfi'ī* (1:455). See also al-Lālikā'ī, *Uṣūl Ahl al-Sunna* (2:252-253).

[153] Al-Bayhaqī, *Manāqib al-Shāfi'ī* (1:454-455).

[154] Cf. al-Bayhaqī, *Manāqib al-Shāfi'ī* (1:229, 1:407, 1:464), Ibn Taymiyya, *Muqaddima fil-Tafsīr* (Risāla ed. p. 69), and al-Lacknawī, *al-Fawā'id al-Bahiyya* (p. 94).

[155] Narrated by al-Qāḍī 'Iyāḍ in *Tartīb al-Madārik* (1:204). Al-Dhahabī declared its chain of transmission sound (*ṣaḥīḥ*) in *Siyar A'lām al-Nubalā'* (Arna'ūṭ ed. 8:88).

[156] Cited by Shīth ibn Ibrāhīm (d. 598) in *Ḥazz al-Ghalāṣim* (p. 112) cf. al-Rāzī, *I'tiqādāt Firaq al-Muslimīn* (1:40), al-Yāfi'ī, *Marham al-'Ilal* (1992 ed. p. 133) and Ibn Taymiyya, *Bayān Talbīs al-Jahmiyya* (1:275= *al-Ta'sīs fī Radd Asās al-Taqdīs*).

[157] It is ironic that the spurious work entitled *al-Radd 'alā al-Zanādiqa* and attributed to Imām Aḥmad by anti-Ash'arīs today, is a work of the worst sort of *kalām* cf. p. 309.

Imām Abū Manṣūr al-Māturīdī[158]

The foremost exponent of the doctrine of Abū Ḥanīfa is Muḥammad ibn Muḥammad ibn Maḥmūd Abū Manṣūr al-Samarqandī al-Māturīdī al-Ḥanafī (d. 333) of Māturīd in Samarqand, *Shaykh al-Islām*. With Abū al-Ḥasan al-Ash'arī he is the foremost Imām of the *mutakallimūn* of *Ahl al-Sunna*. Known in his time as the Imām of Guidance (*Imām al-Hudā*), Abū Manṣūr studied under Abū Naṣr al-'Ayādī and Abū Bakr Aḥmad al-Jūzjānī. Among his senior students were 'Alī ibn Sa'īd Abū al-Ḥasan al-Rustughfānī,[159] Abū Muḥammad 'Abd al-Karīm ibn Mūsā ibn 'Īsā al-Pazdawī, and Abū al-Qāsim Isḥāq ibn Muḥammad al-Ḥākim al-Samarqandī. He excelled in refuting the *Mu'tazila* in Transoxiana while his contemporary Abū al-Ḥasan al-Ash'arī did the same in Baṣra and Baghdād. Their two Schools went on to encompass the massive majority of the Sunnī Muslim Ulema up to our day. He died in Samarqand where he lived most of his life. The founder of the Egyptian Salafiyya Munīriyya Press, Munīr 'Abduh Aghā wrote: "There is not much [doctrinal] difference between Ash'arīs and Māturīdīs hence both groups are now called *Ahl al-Sunna wal-Jamā'a*."[160]

Imām 'Abd al-Qāhir al-Baghdādī (d. 429) defined *Ahl al-Sunna wal-Jamā'a* as "the Scholars of the four Schools and their followers, the Scholars of ḥadīth, the Scholars of Arabic grammar, the Scholars of *tafsīr*, the Ṣūfīs, the people making *jihād*, and the general masses of the Muslims." Imām Abū al-Muẓaffar al-Isfarāyīnī, in his book *al-Tabṣīr fīl-Dīn wa-Tamyīz al-Firqat al-Nājiya min Firaq al-Hālikīn* ("Enlightenment in the Religion and the Differentiation between the Saved Group and the Sects of those who are Destroyed"), defines *Ahl al-Sunna wal-Jamā'a* as the Ash'arīs. Al-Ījī (d. 756) said: "The Saved Group which is excepted from the Prophet's ḥadīth 'All of them are

[158] Main sources for this section: al-Lacknawī, *al-Fawā'id al-Bahiyya fī Tarājim al-Ḥanafiyya* (p. 319-320 §412); Ibn Abī al-Wafā', *al-Jawāhir al-Muḍiyya fī Ṭabaqāt al-Ḥanafiyya* (p. 130, 310, 362-363); al-Kawtharī, introduction to al-Bayāḍī's *Ishārāt al-Marām*.

[159] He narrated from Imām Abū Ḥanīfa the saying: *kullu mujtahidin muṣībun wal-ḥaqqu 'inda Allāhi wāḥid* which means "Every scholar who strives [towards truth] is correct [whatever his finding], even if the truth in the Divine presence is one." Accordingly, al-Rustughfānī differed with al-Māturīdī who considered that the *mujtahid* is wrong in his *ijtihād* if his finding differs from the truth. Ibn Abī al-Wafā', *Ṭabaqāt al-Ḥanafiyya* (p. 310, 362-363).

[160] In *Namūdhaj min al-A'māl al-Khayriyya* (p. 134).

in the Fire except one: Those that adhere to what I and my Companions follow' – are the Ash'arīs, the *Salaf* among the scholars of ḥadīth, and [generally speaking] *Ahl al-Sunna wal-Jamā'a*."[161] The later Ḥanbalī Ṣufī al-Saffarīnī (d. 1188) offers a similar definition in his *Lawā'iḥ al-Anwār*: "*Ahl al-Sunna* consist of three groups: the textualists (al-Athariyya), whose Imām is Aḥmad ibn Ḥanbal, the Ash'arīs, whose Imām is Abū al-Ḥasan al-Ash'arī, and the Māturīdīs, whose Imām is Abū Manṣūr al-Māturīdī ... and they are all one sect, the saved sect, and they are *Ahl al-Ḥadīth*."[162] More restrictive is the definition given by al-Haytamī, al-Bayḍāwī, and al-Saharanfūrī: "When we use the term *Ahl al-Sunna wal-Jamā'a*, what is meant are the Ash'arīs and the Māturīdīs." Similarly, Imām Ibn 'Abd al-Salām said: "Agreement has formed in subscribing to al-Ash'arī's doctrine among the Shāfi'īs, the Mālikīs, the Ḥanafīs, and the elite of the Ḥanbalīs."[163] Imām 'Abd Allāh ibn 'Alawī al-Ḥaddād (d. 1132) said:

> If you look with a sound understanding into those passage relating to the sciences of faith in the Book, the Sunna, and the sayings of the *Salaf*... you will know for certain that the truth is with the party called 'Ash'arī,' named after the Shaykh Abū al-Ḥasan al-Ash'arī, Allāh have mercy on him, who systematized the foundations of the creed of the people of the truth and recorded its earliest versions, these being the beliefs which the Companions and the best among the Successors agreed upon ... The Māturīdīs are the same as the Ash'arīs in the above regard. [164]]

Al-Māturīdī surpasses Imām al-Ṭaḥāwī as a transmitter and commentator of Imām Abū Ḥanīfa's legacy in *kalām*.

Among al-Māturīdī's works:

- *Bayān Awhām al-Mu'tazila;*
- *Al-Jadal fī Uṣūl al-Fiqh;*
- *Ma'ākhidh al-Sharā'i'*;
- *Al-Maqālāt;*

[161] Al-Ījī, *al-Mawāqif* (p. 429).
[162] Al-Saffārīnī, *Lawā'iḥ al-Anwār* (1:141-142, 1:260, 2:15, 2:138-139).
[163] In Ibn al-Subkī, *Ṭabaqāt al-Shāfi'iyya al-Kubrā* (3:365, 3:373).
[164] Al-Ḥaddād, *Book of Assistance* (p. 40-41), chapter entitled "On Doctrine."

- *Radd Awā'il al-Adilla*, a refutation of the Mu'tazilī al-Ka'bī's book entitled *Awā'il al-Adilla*;
- *Radd al-Imāma*, a refutation of the Shī'ī conception of the office of *Imām;*
- *Radd al-Tahdhīb fil-Jadal*, another refutation of al-Ka'bī;[165]
- *Radd al-Uṣūl al-Khamsa*, a refutation of Abū Muḥammad al-Bāhilī's exposition of the so-called "Five Principles" of the *Mu'tazila*;
- *Radd Wa'īd al-Fussāq*, a refutation of the Mu'tazilī and Khārijī doctrine that all grave sinners among the Muslims are doomed to eternal Hellfire (their "Third principle");
- *Al-Radd 'alā Uṣūl al-Qarāmiṭa*;
- *Ta'wīlāt al-Qur'ān* ("Book of the Interpretations of the Qur'ān"), of which Ibn Abī al-Wafā' said: "No book rivals it; indeed, no book even comes near it among those who preceded him in this discipline."[166] Ḥajjī Khalīfa cites it as *Ta'wīlāt Ahl al-Sunna* and quotes as follows al-Māturīdī's definition of the difference between "explanation" (*tafsīr*) and "interpretation" (*ta'wīl*):

  "*Tafsīr* is the categorical conclusion (*al-qaṭ'*) that the meaning of the term in question is this, and the testimony before Allāh Almighty that this is what He meant by the term in question; while *ta'wīl* is the preferment (*tarjīḥ*) of one of several possibilities without categorical conclusion nor testimony."[167]

- *Al-Tawḥīd* on the doctrine of Ahl al-Sunna. In it he states the following:

  The Muslims differ concerning the place of Allāh ﷻ. Some have claimed that Allāh is described as being "established over the Throne" (*'alāl-'arshi mustawin*), and the Throne for them is a dais (*sarīr*) carried by the angels and surrounded by them [as in the verses]: ﴾**And eight will uphold the Throne of their Lord that day, above them**﴿ (69:17) and ﴾**And you see the angels thronging round the Throne**﴿ (39:75) and ﴾**Those who bear**

[165] Cf. Ḥajjī Khalīfa, *Kashf al-Ẓunūn* (1:518).

[166] Ibn Abī al-Wafā', *al-Jawāhir al-Muḍiyya* (p. 130).

[167] In Ḥajjī Khalīfa, *Kashf al-Ẓunūn* (1:334-335).

the Throne, and all who are round about it﴿ (40:7). They adduced as a proof for that position His saying: ﴾**The Merciful established Himself over the Throne**﴿ (20:5) and the fact that people raise their hands toward the heaven in their supplications and whatever graces they are hoping for. They also say that He moved there after not being there at first, on the basis of the verse ﴾**Then He established Himself over the Throne**﴿ (57:4).

Others say that He is in every place because He said ﴾**There is no secret conference of three but He is their fourth, nor of five but He is their sixth, nor of less than that or more but He is with them wheresoever they may be**﴿ (58:7), and ﴾**We are nearer to him than his jugular vein**﴿ (50:16) and ﴾**And We are nearer unto him than you are, but you see not**﴿ (56:85) and ﴾**And He it is Who in the heaven is God, and in the earth God**﴿ (43:84). This group consider that to say that He is in one place at the exclusion of another necessitates a limit for Him, and that every limited object comes short of whatever is greater than it, which would constitute a disgraceful defect. Further, they consider that to be in one place necessitates need for that place together with the necessity of boundaries [...] Others deny the ascription of place to Allāh, whether one place or every place, except in the metaphorical senses that He preserves them and causes them to exist.

Shaykh Abū Manṣūr [al-Māturīdī] – may Allāh have mercy on him – says: The sum of all this is that the predication of all things to Him and His predication – may He be exalted! – to them is along the lines of His description in terms of exaltation (*'ulūw*) and loftiness (*rif'a*), and in terms of extolment (*ta'ẓīm*) and majesty (*jalāl*), as in His saying: ﴾**the Sovereignty of the heavens and the earth**﴿ (2:107, 3:189, 5:17-18, 5:40 etc.) ﴾**Lord of the heavens and the earth**﴿ (13:16, 17:102, 18:14, 19:65, etc.), "God of all creation" (*ilāh al-khalq*), ﴾**Lord of the worlds**﴿ (1:2, 5:28, 6:45, 6:162, 7:54, etc.), "above everything" (*fawqa kulli shay'*) and so forth. As for the predication of specific objects to Him, it is along the lines of His specific attribution with generosity (*al-karāma*), high rank (*al-manzila*), and immense favor (*al-tafḍīl*) for what is essentially meant to refer to Him, as in His sayings ﴾**Lo! Allāh is with those who keep their duty unto Him**﴿

(16:128), ﴾**And the places of worship are only for Allāh**﴿ (72:18), ﴾**The she-camel of Allāh**﴿ (7:73, 11:64, 91:13), 'The House of Allāh' (*bayt Allāh*), and other similar instances. None of these examples is understood in the same way as the predication of created objects to one another[...]

Abū Manṣūr – may Allāh have mercy on him! – further says: The foundation of this issue is that Allāh Almighty was when there was no place, then locations were raised while He remains exactly as He ever was. Therefore, He is as He ever was and He ever was as He is now. Exalted is He beyond any change or transition or movement or cessation! For all these are portents of contingency (*ḥudth*) by which the contingent nature of the world can be known, and the proofs of its eventual passing away[...]

Furthermore [concerning the claim that Allāh is on the Throne], there is not, in the context of spatial elevation, any particular merit to sitting or standing, nor exaltation, nor any quality of magnificence and splendor. For example, someone standing higher than roofs or mountains does not deservedly acquire loftiness over someone who is below him spatially when their essence is identical. Therefore, it is not permissible to interpret the verse [20:5] in that sense, when it is actually pointing to magnificence and majesty. For He has said ﴾**Verily, it is your Lord Who created the heavens and the earth**﴿ (7:54, 10:3, 21:56) thereby pointing to the extolment of the Throne, which is something created of light, or a substance [or jewel] the reality of which is beyond the knowledge of creatures. It was narrated that the Prophet ﷺ – describing the sun – said: "Gibrīl brings it, in his hand, some of the light of the Throne with which he clothes it just as one of you wears his clothes, and so every day that it rises"; he also mentioned that the moon receives a handful of the light of the Throne.[168] Therefore, the predication of *istiwā'* to the Throne is along two lines: first, its extolment in the

[168] Something similar is narrated – without naming the angel – as part of a very long ḥadīth from Ibn 'Abbās by Abū al-Shaykh with a very weak chain in *al-'Aẓama* (4:1163-1179). Another ḥadīth states: "The Messenger of Allāh ﷺ told me that the sun, the moon, and the stars were created from the light of the Throne." Narrated from Anas by Abū al-Shaykh in *al-'Aẓama* (4:1140). See also al-Suyūṭī's *Ḥabā'ik* and *Hay'a*.

light of all that He said concerning His authority in Lordship and over creatures; second, its specific mention as the greatest and loftiest of all objects in creation, in keeping with the customary predication of magnificent matters to magnificent objects, just as it is said: "So-and-so has achieved sovereignty over such-and-such a country, and has established himself over such-and-such a region." This is not to restrict the meaning of this sovereignty literally, but only to say that it is well-known that whoever owns sovereignty over this, then whatever lies below it is meant *a fortiori*.[169]

Elsewhere al-Māturīdī says: "To suggest a place for Allāh is idolatry."[170]

Most of the Ḥanafī School follows al-Māturīdī in doctrine, but he achieved lesser fame than al-Ash'arī because the latter entered into countless debates to defeat the opponents of *Ahl al-Sunna* while al-Māturīdī, as Imām al-Kawtharī said, "lived in an environment in which innovators had no power." The absence of notices on Imām Abū Manṣūr al-Māturīdī in both al-Dhahabī's *Siyar* and his *Tārīkh al-Islām* is a major omission in those masterpieces of biographical history.

Some of Abū Ḥanīfa's Great Contemporaries

AL-ḤASAN AL-BAṢRĪ

Al-Ḥasan ibn Abī al-Ḥasan Yasār Abū Sa'īd al-Baṣrī (d. 110), al-Faqīh, the great Imām of Baṣra, was the leader of the ascetics and scholars of the *Tābi'īn*. He was the son of a freedwoman of Umm Salama the Mother of the Believers and a freedman of Zayd ibn Thābit, the stepson of the Prophet. Umm Salama nursed him. His mother took him as a child to 'Umar who supplicated for him with the words: "O Allāh! Make him wise in the Religion and beloved to people." He became known for his strict and encompassing embodiment of the Sunna of the Prophet, famous for his immense knowledge, piety and simple living (*zuhd*), fearless remonstrances of the authorities, and power of attraction both in discourse and appearance. One of the early formal Ṣūfīs in both the general and the literal sense, he

[169] Al-Māturīdī, *Kitāb al-Tawḥīd* (p. 72).

[170] Quoted in Abū Ḥanīfa, *Kitāb al-Fiqh al-Akbar bi-Sharḥ al-Qārī* (Cairo: Dār al-Kutub al-'Arabiyya al-Kubrā, 1327/1909) p. 16; cf. al-Māturīdī, *Sharḥ al-Fiqh al-Akbar* in *Majmū'at Rasā'il* (Hyderabad: Dā'irat al- Ma'ārif al-Niẓāmiyya, 1903).

wore all his life a cloak of wool (*ṣūf*). He was the reason for which Ḥabīb al-ʿAjamī abandoned trading and entered the path of asceticism and perpetual worship.[171]

Al-Ḥasan was considered by the *Salaf* to be one of the "Substitute-Saints" (*al-Abdāl*).[172] Anas 🙵 narrated that the Prophet 🙵 said: "The earth will never lack forty men similar to the Friend of the Merciful [Ibrāhīm 🙵], and through them people receive rain and are given help. None of them dies except Allāh substitutes another in his place." Qatāda said: "We do not doubt that al-Ḥasan is one of them."[173]

Al-Ḥasan is one of the great ḥadīth Masters and narrators of the *Tābiʿīn*, responsible for transmitting over 1,400 narrations in the Nine Books alone. The ḥadīth Masters have concluded that he did not narrate anything directly from Abū Hurayra.[174] Imāms Aḥmad and al-Tirmidhī narrated from Qatāda, from al-Ḥasan, from Abū Hurayra, that the Prophet 🙵 said: "If you were to dangle a man from a rope down to the lowest earth, he would find Allāh!" The correct grading of this lone-narrator ḥadīth is weak, hence al-Tirmidhī only said that it was *gharīb* without adding *ḥasan* nor *ṣaḥīḥ*.[175]

---

[171] Cf. chapter on Ḥabīb al-ʿAjamī in Ibn al-Mulaqqin's *Ṭabaqāt al-Awliyā'*.

[172] On the *Abdāl* ḥadīths see our *Forty Ḥadīths on the Excellence of Syro-Palestine*.

[173] Narrated from Anas by al-Ṭabarānī in *al-Awsaṭ* with a fair chain and from Ibn Masʿūd with a chain containing two unknown narrators cf. al-Haythamī (10:63).

[174] As stated by Ibn Ḥajar in *Tahdhīb al-Tahdhīb* (2:231), al-Dhahabī in *Mīzān al-Iʿtidāl* (1:527), and Ibn Abī Ḥātim in *al-Marāsīl* (p. 43). See also al-Ḥākim's chapter on the *mudallisūn* in *Maʿrifat Anwāʿ ʿUlūm al-Ḥadīth*. Cf. Al-Tirmidhī: "Al-Ḥasan did not narrate anything from Abū Hurayra according to Ayyūb [al-Sikhtiyānī], Yūnus ibn ʿUbayd, and ʿAlī ibn Zayd." Al-Tirmidhī, *Sunan*, book of *Zuhd*, remarks on the ḥadīth, "Who shall take from me these words and then put them into practice or teach whoever will put them into practice? Guard yourself from all prohibited matters, and you shall be the most worshipful of people; be content with whatever Allāh has allotted you and you shall be the richest of people; treat your neighbour with utmost kindness and you shall be a Believer; love for people whatever you love for yourself and you shall be a Muslim; do not laugh much for much laughter extinguishes the heart." Narrated from Abū Hurayra by al-Tirmidhī (*gharīb*) and Aḥmad in his *Musnad* with a chain containing Abū Ṭāriq, who is unknown.

[175] The same ḥadīth also reached us through Qatāda, from al-Ḥasan, from al-Aḥnaf ibn Qays, from Ibn ʿAbbās cf. al-Ṭabarānī in *al-Awsaṭ* (4:248-249 §4107) and Ibn al-Jawzī, *al-ʿIlal al-Mutanāhiya* (1:28-29) and through yet another chain from Aḥmad ibn ʿAbd al-Jabbār, from Abū Muʿāwiya, from al-Aʿmash, from Abū Naṣr, from Abū Dharr; cf. al-Bayhaqī in Ibn al-Jawzī's *ʿIlal* (1:26) but al-Dhahabī in the *Mīzān* ('Ilmiyya ed. 7:434) pointed out that Abū Naṣr is completely unknown.

The Masters disagree about al-Ḥasan's narration from 'Alī ibn Abī Ṭālib.[176] Al-Tirmidhī said in his *Sunan*: "He did meet 'Alī, but we do not know if he narrated from him." Imām Aḥmad considered that he did narrate from 'Alī[177] and it is related that he said: "'Alī told me..." Al-Suyūṭī in *Ta'yīd al-Ḥaqīqat al-'Aliyya* and Shaykh Aḥmad al-Ghumārī in *al-Burhān al-Jalī* both cite narrative chains of transmission supporting al-Ḥasan's direct narration from 'Alī. 'Abd al-Razzāq even narrates that 'Alī ﷺ once followed al-Ḥasan's recommendation in a judicial case![178] However, al-Ḥasan was merely fifteen at the time of 'Alī's *bay'a* in Madīna, after which 'Alī moved to al-Kūfa and al-Ḥasan stayed in Madīna. Al-Bazzār in his *Musnad* – at the end of the section devoted to the narrations of Sa'īd ibn al-Musayyab from Abū Hurayra – listed the Companions from whom al-Ḥasan narrated and those from whom he did not narrate.[179]

The ḥadīth Master Abū Nu'aym al-Aṣfahānī mentions in his biographies of Ṣūfīs entitled *Ḥilyat al-Awliyā'* ("The Adornment of the Saints") that it is al-Ḥasan's student 'Abd al-Wāḥid ibn Zayd (d. 177) who was the first person to build a Ṣūfī *khānqa* or guest-house and school at Abadān on the present-day border of Iran with Iraq.[180] It was on the basis of al-Ḥasan and his students' fame as Ṣūfīs that it was claimed, "*Taṣawwuf*'s place of origin is Baṣra."[181] More accurately, Baṣra is chief among the places of renown for the formal development of the schools of self-discipline, asceticism, and self-purification which became known as *taṣawwuf*, but whose principles are none other than the Qur'ān and the Sunna.[182]

[176] "Al-Ḥasan did not hear anything directly from 'Alī... nor from Abū Hurayra." Narrated from Yaḥyā ibn Ma'īn by al-Dhahabī in the *Siyar* (Arna'ūṭ ed. 4:566). Cf. Walī al-Dīn al-'Irāqī, *Tuḥfat al-Taḥṣīl* (p. 67-68) and Ibn Ḥajar, *Ta'rīf Ahl al-Taqdīs* (p. 56 §40) and *Tahdhīb* (2:231), also al-Sakhāwī, *Maqāṣid*, in the entry *khirqa*.

[177] Ibn Abī Ya'lā, *Ṭabaqāt al-Ḥanābila* (1:192): "My father (al-Qāḍī Abū Ya'lā) narrated to us *qirā'atan*: 'Īsā ibn Muḥammad ibn 'Alī narrated to us: I heard 'Abd Allāh ibn Muḥammad (Imām Abū al-Qāsim al-Baghawī) say: I heard Abū 'Abd Allāh Aḥmad ibn Muḥammad ibn Ḥanbal say: 'Al-Ḥasan did narrate (*qad rawā*) from 'Alī ibn Abī Ṭālib.'"

[178] As narrated by 'Abd al-Razzāq (7:412) cf. al-Qal'ajī, *Mawsū'at Fiqh al-Ḥasan al-Baṣrī* (1:21).

[179] This list was reproduced by al-Zayla'ī in *Naṣb al-Rāya*, first section (*Ṭahāra*).

[180] Abū Nu'aym, *Ḥilyat al-Awliyā'* (6:155).

[181] Ibn Taymiyya in his essay *al-Ṣūfiyya wal-Fuqarā'* in *Majmū' al-Fatāwā* (11:16).

[182] See the section on *taṣawwuf* in the *Encyclopedia of Islamic Doctrine* (2:5-18).

Al-Ḥasan used to swear by Allāh that the true believer could not feel other than sadness in this world.[183] He would say: "Our salt has disappeared; what good is left in us?"[184] in his commentary of the ḥadīth reported from the Prophet ﷺ: "The likeness of my Companions is like salt in food. Food is not good without it."[185] He also said:

> We laugh and yet – who knows? – perhaps Allāh has looked at some of our works and said, "I will not accept anything from you." Woe to you, son of Ādam! Can you fight Allāh? Whoever disobeys Allāh is fighting Him. By Allāh! I have met seventy veterans of Badr. Most of their garments were wool. Had you seen them you would have said they are crazy, and had they seen the best among you they would have said: "Those people will have no part in the Hereafter." Had they seen the worst among you they would have said: "Those people do not believe in the Day of Reckoning." I have seen people for whom this world was cheaper than the dust under their feet! I have seen people the like of whom would come home at night, not finding more than his own portion of food, and yet say: "I shall not put all of this into my belly. I shall certainly give some away for the sake of Allāh." Then he would give away some of his food in charity, even if he were more in need of it than its recipient.[186]

183 Narrated from Shumayṭ, 'Abbād ibn Hishām, Ḥazm ibn Abī Ḥazm, and others by Abū Nu'aym in the *Ḥilya* (2:133).

184 In *Nasīm al-Riyāḍ* (3:469).

185 *Mathalu aṣḥābī ka-mathali al-milḥi fīl-ṭa'ām.* Narrated from Anas by al-Bazzār, Abū Ya'lā (5:151 §2762) with a weak chain according to Shaykh Ḥusayn al-Asad because of Suwayd ibn Sa'īd (*layyin* in the *Taqrīb*, see also al-Dhahabī's *Mughnī*), Ismā'īl ibn Muslim al-Makkī [*ḍa'īf*] – cf. al-Haythamī (10:18) – and the vague narrative mode (*'an'ana*) of al-Ḥasan al-Baṣrī. Al-Bazzār said, as in Ibn Ḥajar's *Mukhtaṣar Zawā'id Musnad al-Bazzār* (2:365 §2021): "We know no one that narrates it from al-Ḥasan except Ismā'īl, although he is not a strong memorizer." Also narrated by Ibn al-Mubārak in *al-Zuhd* (p. 200), al-Quḍā'ī in *Musnad al-Shihāb* (2:275 §838), al-Baghawī in *Sharḥ al-Sunna* (14:73 §3863) and Ibn 'Abd al-Barr in *al-Istī'āb* (8:15-16) all with chains containing Ismā'īl. Also narrated from al-Ḥasan by al-Azdī in his *Jāmi'* (after 'Abd al-Razzāq's *Muṣannaf* 11:221) and 'Abd Allāh ibn Aḥmad ibn Ḥanbal in *Faḍā'il al-Ṣaḥāba* (1:58, 2:907), both with a weak *mursal* chain missing a link between Ma'mar and al-Ḥasan. Ibn Ḥajar cited it in *al-Maṭālib al-'Āliya* (§4207) and al-'Ajlūnī in *Kashf al-Khafā'* (2:257) while al-Nabhānī included it in *al-Arba'īn min Amthāl Afṣaḥ al-'Ālamīn* (p. 50 §26).

186 Narrated from 'Alqama ibn Marthad by Abū Nu'aym in the *Ḥilya* (1985 ed. 2:134).

Imām al-Ghazzālī relates al-Ḥasan's words on the personal struggle against one's lusts (*jihād al-nafs*) in the section of his *Iḥyā'* entitled *Kitāb Riyāḍat al-Nafs wa-Tahdhīb al-Akhlāq wa-Mu'ālajat Amrāḍ al-Qalb* ("Book of the Training of the Ego, Disciplining of Manners, and Remedies for the Heart's Diseases") that al-Ḥasan al-Baṣrī said:

> Two thoughts roam over the soul, one from Allāh, one from the enemy. Allāh shows mercy on a servant who settles at the thought that comes from Him. He embraces the thought that comes from Allāh, while he fights against the one from his enemy. To illustrate the heart's mutual attraction betwen these two powers the Prophet said: "The heart of the believer lies between two fingers of the Merciful"[187][...] The fingers stand

[187] Narrated from 'Abd Allāh ibn 'Amr by Muslim, from Anas by al-Tirmidhī (*ḥasan ṣaḥīḥ*), and from al-Nawwās ibn Sam'ān by Aḥmad, al-Nasā'ī, Ibn Mājah, Ibn Ḥibbān, al-Ḥākim, and others, all with sound chains. Al-Ḥākim declared the ḥadīth sound. The continuation of the ḥadīth states that the Prophet ﷺ used to say: "O Transformer of hearts! Make firm our hearts in Your Religion," and that he also said: "And the balance is in the hand of the Merciful; He elevates a people while he abases others, and so until the Day of Resurrection." Ibn 'Abd al-Salām said: "The meaning is that Allāh exerts His custody over [the heart] with His power and determination as He wills, changing it from disbelief to belief and from obedience to disobedience or the reverse. It is like His saying: ﴾**Blessed is He in Whose hand is the dominion**﴿ (67:1) and ﴾**O Prophet! Say unto those captives who are in your hands**﴿ (8:70). It is understood that the captives were not left in the physical hands of the Muslims but that they were subdued and conquered by them. The same applies to the expressions: "Specific and non-specific matters are in the hand of so-and-so," and "The slaves and the animals are in the hand of so-and-so." It is understood that all these mean that they are in his control (*istīlā'*) and disposal and not in his physical hand. Similarly the saying of Allāh: ﴾**Or he agrees to forgo it in whose hand is the marriage tie**﴿ (2:237). The marriage tie is not in his physical hand, but the hand is only an expression of his empowerment and his ability to dispose of the matter. For one to say: "I believe in this matter what the *Salaf* believed" is a lie. How does he believe what he has no idea about, and the meaning of which he does not know? Nor is speaking about the meaning a reprehensible innovation, but rather an obligatory excellent innovation (*bid'a ḥasana wājiba*), whenever something dubious appears. The only reason the *Salaf* kept away from such discourse is that in their time no one construed the words of Allāh and those of His Prophet to mean what it is not permissible to construe them to mean. If any such dubiousness had appeared in their time they would have shown it to be a lie and rejected it strenuously! Thus did the Companions and the *Salaf* refute the Qadariyya when the latter brought out their innovation, although they did not use to address such matters before the Qadariyya appeared on the scene. Nor did they reply to the individuals who mentioned them. Nor did any of the Companions relate any of it from the Prophet ﷺ since there was no need

for upheaval and hesitation in the heart [...] If man follows the dictates of anger and appetite, the dominion of Satan appears in him through idle passions (*hawā*) and his heart becomes the nesting-place and container of *shayṭān*, who feeds on *hawā*. If he does battle with his passions and does not let them dominate his ego (*nafs*), imitating in this the character of the angels, at that time his heart becomes the resting-place of angels and they alight upon it.

An illustration of al-Ḥasan al-Baṣrī's extreme Godwariness and scrupulousness (*wara'*) is given by his following statement, also quoted by al-Ghazzālī: "Forgetfulness and hope are two mighty blessings upon the progeny of Ādam; but for them, the Muslims would not walk in the streets."[188]

Al-Ḥasan interpreted the verse ﴿**Nay, both His hands are spread wide, and He bestows as He wills**﴾ (5:64) to refer to Divine kindness and goodness.[189] Similarly, like the lexicographer al-Naḍr ibn Shumayl (b. 122), he interpreted the *qadam* of Allāh ﷻ to mean "those whom Allāh has sent forth" (*qaddamahum*) in the ḥadīth of the Prophet ﷺ:

Hellfire will keep asking: "Is there more?" until the Lord of Might places His *qadam* (lit. "foot") in it. Then it will say: "Enough! Enough!" (*qaṭṭ qaṭṭ*) and gather up all its parts together. There will still remain room in Paradise until Allāh originates a creation which He will place in the remainder of Paradise.[190]

Imām al-Khaṭṭābī said:

The meaning of *qadam* here is possibly a reference to those whom Allāh has created of old or 'sent forth' for the Fire to complete the number of its inhabitants. Everything that is 'sent forth' is a *qadam*, in the same way that the verbal noun of demolishing (*hadama*) is a *hadm* or ruin, and that of seizing (*qabaḍa*) is *qabḍ* or seizure. Likewise Allāh said: ﴿**They have a sure founda-**

---

for it. And Allāh knows best." Al-'Izz ibn 'Abd al-Salām, *Fatāwā* (p. 55-57) and *al-Fatāwā al-Mawṣiliyya* (p. 45-47).

188 In al-Ghazzālī, trans. T.J. Winter, *The Remembrance of Death* (p. 18).

189 Narrated by Ibn al-Jawzī in *Daf' Shubah al-Tashbīh* (Saqqāf ed. p. 115).

190 Narrated from Anas by al-Bukhārī and Muslim.

> **tion** (*qadam ṣidq*) **with their Lord**﴾ (10:2) with reference to the good works which they have sent forth. This explanation has been transmitted to us from al-Ḥasan al-Baṣrī. It is supported by the Prophet's ﷺ saying in the aforementioned ḥadīth: "As for Paradise, Allāh will create for it a special creation." Both meanings (*i.e.* respectively pertaining to the Fire and Paradise) are in agreement with the sense that Paradise and hellfire will be provided with an additional number of dwellers to complete their respective numbers, at which point they will be full.[191]

Ibn Ḥibbān said: "The Arabs use *qadam* to mean 'repository.' Exalted is Allāh beyond placing His 'foot' in the fire or any other such meaning!"[192]

Concerning the ḥadīth of the Prophet ﷺ: "More people shall enter Paradise through the intercession of a certain man from my Community than there are people in the tribes of Rabī'a and Muḍar," al-Ḥasan said: "That is Uways al-Qaranī."[193] On the verse ﴾**If you love Allāh, follow me, and Allāh will love you**﴾ (3:31) al-Ḥasan said: "Whoever knows his Lord loves Him and whoever knows the world does without it."[194] Al-Qurṭubī relates, in his commentary on the verse ﴾**A multi-colored drink issues from their bellies, in it there is healing for people**﴾ (16:69), that al-Ḥasan disliked to use medicine other than made with honey or milk.

About the memorizers of Qur'ān al-Ḥasan said:

> The reciters of Qur'ān are three types. The first type take the Qur'ān as a merchandise by which to earn their bread; the second type uphold its letters and lose its laws, aggrandizing themselves over the people of their country, and seeking gain through it from the rulers. There are many memorizers of Qur'ān that belong to that type. May Allāh not increase them. Finally, the third type have sought the healing of the Qur'ān and placed it on the sickness of their hearts, fleeing with it to their

[191] Al-Khaṭṭābī, *Ma'ālim al-Sunan* (Ḥimṣ ed. 5:95). Cf. Ibn al-Jawzī, *Daf' Shubah al-Tashbīh* (Saqqāf ed. p. 15) and al-Bayhaqī, *al-Asmā' wal-Ṣifāt* (Kawtharī ed. p. 352).

[192] Ibn Ḥibbān, *Ṣaḥīḥ* (1:502). The Arabic word used for "repository" is *mawḍi'*.

[193] Narrated by Aḥmad in *al-Zuhd* (Beirut: al-'Ilmiyya, 1993 p. 416, 414).

[194] In al-Qārī's commentary on the *Iḥyā'* entitled *Sharḥ 'Ayn al-'Ilm* (2:354-355).

places of prayer, wrapping themselves in it. Those have felt fear and put on the garment of sadness. Those are the ones for whose sake Allāh sends rain and victory over the enemies. By Allāh! That kind of memorizer of Qur'ān is more rare than the purest gold (literally "red sulphur").[195]

Ibn al-Jawzī wrote a 100-page book on al-Ḥasan's life and manners entitled *Adab al-Shaykh al-Ḥasan ibn Abī al-Ḥasan al-Baṣrī.* In his chapter on al-Ḥasan in his anthology of Muslim saints entitled "The Portrait of Purity" (*Ṣifat al-Ṣafwa*), he mentions a report that al-Ḥasan left behind a white cloak (*jubba*) made of wool which he had worn exclusively of any other for the past twenty years, winter and summer, and that when he died it was in a state of immaculate beauty, cleanness, and quality.

Among al-Ḥasan's sayings: "Those who feel the least necessity for the wise person of knowledge are usually his immediate family."[196] "If you are of a coarse character, then acquire gentleness (*taḥallam*); and if you are not learned, then learn (*ta'allam*); a person seldom imitates a certain group without becoming one of them."[197] "Have you ever seen a *faqīh*? The *faqīh* is he who has renounced the world, longs for the hereafter, possesses insight in his Religion, and worships his Lord without cease."[198] Ibn Mufliḥ al-Ḥanbalī mentions that al-Ḥasan categorized the act of kissing the Muslim Scholar's hand as "obedience to Allāh" (*ṭā'a*).[199]

Imām al-Suyūṭī recounted in one of his fatwas entitled *al-Minḥa fīl-Sibḥa* ("The Profit in *Dhikr*-Beads") the story of 'Ikrima, who asked his teacher 'Umar al-Mālikī about *dhikr*-beads. The latter replied that he had also asked his teacher al-Ḥasan al-Baṣrī about it, who replied: "Something we have used at the beginning of the road we are not

[195] In al-Qāsim ibn Sallām, *Faḍā'il al-Qur'ān* (p. 60 §4).

[196] Narrated from Mūsā ibn Murdī by al-Khaṭīb in *al-Jāmi'* (2:471 §1993).

[197] Al-Najm al-Rāzī relates it from al-'Askarī on the authority of Ḥumayd al-Ṭawīl as stated by al-'Ajlūnī in *Kashf al-Khafā* (§2436).

[198] As cited by al-'Aynī in *'Umdat al-Qārī*, Book of *'Ilm*, in his commentary on the ḥadīth: "He for whom Allāh desires immense good, He grants him understanding in the Religion" cf. Ibn al-Jawzī, *Manāqib al-Ḥasan al-Baṣrī* (p. 16). See also Imām Mālik's definition of wisdom and al-Shāfi'ī's, al-Tustarī's, and Ibn Ḥibbān's definitions of knowledge. For the superior merit of *'ilm* and the Ulema see Ibn 'Abd al-Barr's *Jāmi' Bayān al-'Ilm wa-Faḍlih* and Imām al-Baghawī's *Sharḥ al-Sunna* (1:272-282).

[199] Ibn Mufliḥ al-Ḥanbalī, *al-Ādāb al-Shar'iyya* (2:271).

desirous to leave at the end. I love to remember Allāh with my heart, my hand, and my tongue." Al-Suyūṭī comments: "And how should it be otherwise, when the *dhikr*-beads remind one of Allāh Most High, and a person seldom sees *dhikr*-beads except he remembers Allāh, which is among the greatest of its benefits."[200] Abū Hurayra possessed a thread with two thousand knots and would not sleep until he had used it all for *dhikr*.[201] He said: "Verily, I make glorification (*tasbīḥ*) of Allāh Almighty every day according to my ransom (*qadar diyyatī*), twelve thousand times."[202]

In the book he devoted to the sayings and deeds of the Ṣūfīs, *Rawḍat al-Muḥibbīn wa-Nuzhat al-Mushtāqīn* ("The Garden of the Lovers and Excursion of the Passionate"), Ibn al-Qayyim relates that a group of women went out on the day of *'Īd* and went about looking at people. They were asked: "Who is the most handsome person you have seen today?" They replied: "It is a Shaykh wearing a black turban." They meant al-Ḥasan al-Baṣrī.[203]

Imām Ibn Jahbal al-Kilābī wrote:

> Whenever al-Ḥasan al-Baṣrī ﵁ spoke on the science of *tawḥīd*, he would begin by taking out of his gathering all those that were not fit to hear. May Allāh have mercy on the *Salaf*! They did not speak about doctrine except with the *Ahl al-Sunna* among them

[200] Al-Suyūṭī, *al-Ḥāwī lil-Fatāwī*. Cf. section on *dhikr*-beads in al-Shawkānī's *Nayl al-Awṭār* (2:316-317) and Zakariyyā al-Kandihlawī's *Ḥayāt al-Ṣaḥāba*. Albānī's astounding claim that whoever carries *dhikr*-beads in his hand to remember Allāh is misguided and innovating was refuted in Maḥmūd Mamdūḥ's *Wuṣūl al-Tahānī bi-Ithbāt Sunniyyat al-Sibḥa wal-Radd 'alā al-Albānī* ("The Alighting of Mutual Benefit and the Confirmation that *Dhikr*-Beads are a Sunna in Refutation of Albānī"). Another refutation was published by Ḥāmid Mirzā Khān al-Firghānī al-Namnakānī in the seventh of his *al-Masā'il al-Tis'* (Madīna: Maktabat al-Īmān, 1985) p. 44-48. Another Wahhābī, Bakr Abū Zayd, acknowledges that Imām Ibn Ḥajar al-'Asqalānī was never seen without his *dhikr*-beads in hand, then exclaims that this proves nothing!

[201] Narrated by Abū Nu'aym in the *Ḥilya* (1:383) and al-Dhahabī in the *Siyar* (Risāla ed. 2:623) and *Tadhkira* (1:35).

[202] Narrated by Abū Nu'aym in the *Ḥilya* (1:383), al-Bayhaqī in the *Sunan* (8:79), Ibn Ḥazm in *al-Muḥallā* (10:396), Ibn al-Jawzī in *Ṣifat al-Ṣafwa* (1:691), al-Dhahabī in the *Siyar* (Risāla ed. 2:610) and *Tadhkirat al-Ḥuffāẓ* (1:35), Ibn Rajab in *Jāmi' al-'Ulūm wal-Ḥikam*, and Ibn Ḥajar in the *Iṣāba* (7:442) where he said that Ibn Sa'd narrates it with a sound chain in his *Ṭabaqāt*.

[203] Ibn al-Qayyim, *Rawḍat al-Muḥibbīn* (p. 225).

– for the Sunna is the basis of the verifying authorities – and they withheld any such discourse from newcomers. They said: "Newcomers see things for the first time and are barely starting on their way. They have no prior experience and no firm foothold in these matters – even if they are seventy years old. Sahl [ibn 'Abd Allāh al-Tustarī] said – Allāh be well-pleased with him: "Do not acquaint newcomers with the secrets before they become firmly settled in their belief that the God is One and that the subject of monotheism is Unique, Everlasting, and transcends modality and place. Thoughts cannot encompass Him nor can hearts conceive of Him in terms of 'how'."[204]

One of the most remarkable ḥadīths al-Bukhārī narrates in his *Ṣaḥīḥ* is from al-Ḥasan al-Baṣrī, from Anas, from the Prophet ﷺ who related that after Allāh allows him to intercede for the dwellers of the Fire, Allāh shall say: "By My Power, by My Majesty, by My Supremacy, and by My Greatness! I shall take out of the Fire whoever said: *lā ilāha illa'llāh.*"[205]

JA'FAR AL-ṢĀDIQ[206]

Abū 'Abd Allāh Ja'far al-Ṣādiq ibn Muḥammad ibn 'Alī ibn al-Shahīd Abī 'Abd Allāh al-Ḥusayn ibn Amīr al-Mu'minīn 'Alī ibn Abī Ṭālib al-Qurashī al-Hāshimī al-'Alawī al-Nabawī al-Madanī (80-148) the Imām of Madīna, Shaykh of the Banū Hāshim, and direct descendant of the Prophet ﷺ from 'Alī and Fāṭima. His mother was Umm Farwa bint al-Qāsim ibn Muḥammad ibn Abī Bakr the daughter of Asmā' bint 'Abd al-Raḥmān ibn Abī Bakr, hence he used to say: "Abū Bakr al-Ṣiddīq is my father twice."

He saw some of the Companions such as Anas and Sahl ibn Sa'd. He narrated from his father Abū Ja'far Muḥammad al-Bāqir (mostly *mursal* reports), 'Ubayd Allāh ibn Abī Rāfi', 'Urwa ibn al-Zubayr, 'Aṭā' ibn Abī Rabāḥ, al-Qāsim ibn Muḥammad, Nāfi' al-'Umarī, Muḥammad ibn al-Munkadir, al-Zuhrī, and others. From him narrated his son Mūsā al-Kāẓim, Yaḥyā ibn Sa'īd al-Anṣārī, Yazīd ibn 'Abd Allāh

[204] Ibn Jahbal, *al-Radd 'alā Ibn Taymiyya* (Refutation of Ibn Taymiyya) §15 (forthcoming *in shā' Allāh*).

[205] Al-Bukhārī, *Ṣaḥīḥ*, book of *Tawḥīd*.

[206] Main sources: al-Dhahabī, *Siyar* (6:438-447 §948), Abū Nu'aym, *Ḥilya* (3:193).

ibn al-Hād, Abū Ḥanīfa, Abān ibn Taghlib, Ibn Jurayj, Mu'āwiya ibn 'Ammār al-Duhnī, Ibn Isḥāq, the two Sufyāns, Shu'ba, Mālik, 'Abd al-'Azīz al-Darāwardī, Muslim ibn Khālid al-Zanjī, Yaḥyā al-Qaṭṭān, Abū 'Āṣim al-Nabīl, and others.

Al-Darāwardī said Mālik did not openly narrate from Ja'far until the Banū 'Abbās began to hold sway.

Ja'far was a trustworthy source of ḥadīth according to the vast majority of the authorities including al-Shāfi'ī, Ibn Ma'īn, Abū Ḥātim, Ibn 'Adī, and Ḥafṣ ibn Ghiyāth. The latter told the Baṣrians: "If you were in al-Kūfa the shoes would rain on you" for rejecting the narrations of Ja'far. Al-Dhahabī said of Yaḥyā ibn Sa'īd al-Qaṭṭān's weakening of Ja'far: "This is one of his grave slips."

'Amr ibn Abī al-Miqdām said: "If you saw Ja'far ibn Muḥammad you would know that he is a Prophetic descendent. I saw him standing at the Jamra, saying: 'Ask me, ask me!'" From Ṣāliḥ ibn Abī al-Aswad: "He would say, 'Ask me before you no longer have me! For no one after me will narrate to you the like of my narrations.'" (He inherited this trait of authoritative learning from his grandfather 'Alī ﷺ who, alone among the Companions, used to say the same.[207] 'Umar ﷺ said: "I seek refuge in Allāh from a problem which Abū al-Ḥasan cannot solve," and "Were it not for 'Alī, 'Umar would have perished" (*lawlā 'Alī la-halaka 'Umar*).[208] Similarly 'Ā'isha ﷺ said: "'Alī is the most knowledgeable one about the Sunna among those who remain," and Ibn 'Abbās: "If a trustworthy source tells us of a *fatwā* of 'Alī, we do not seek any further concerning it."[209]) At the same time, Ja'far said humbly: "We do not – by Allāh! – know everything they think we know. Surely, others have more knowledge than we."

Abū Ḥanīfa said: "I felt awe before Ja'far which I did not feel before Abū Ja'far [al-Manṣūr the Caliph]."

Ja'far would feed people to the point he had nothing left for his own dependents. He once said: "Allāh prohibited usury so that people would not deprive one another of right behavior."

Ja'far al-Ṣādiq intensely detested the *Rāfiḍa*, whom he knew to

[207] Narrated from Sa'īd ibn al-Musayyab by Ibn 'Abd al-Barr in *al-Istī'āb* (3:40-41), Ibn 'Asākir in *Tārīkh Dimashq* (42:399), and al-Suyūṭī in *Tārīkh al-Khulafā'*.

[208] Narrated by Ibn Abī Khaythama cf. al-Ghumārī in *al-Burhān al-Jalī* (p. 71).

[209] All three reports are narrated by Ibn Sa'd (2:339), Ibn 'Abd al-Barr in *al-Istī'āb* (3:39-40), and al-Suyūṭī in *Tārīkh al-Khulafā'*.

object to his ancestor Abū Bakr and his successor. Ibn 'Uyayna and Ibn Abī 'Umar al-'Adanī narrated from Ja'far, from his father: "In the time of the Prophet ﷺ, the family of Abū Bakr were called the family of the Messenger of Allāh ﷺ." When Mu'āwiya ibn Ḥudayj mentioned that his neighbor claimed Ja'far said he repudiated Abū Bakr and 'Umar, Ja'far retorted: "May Allāh repudiate your neighbour! By Allāh, I hope that my parentage with Abū Bakr benefits me." In another narration he says: "What man curses his own grandfather? May the intercession of Muḥammad ﷺ not include me if I do not consider Abū Bakr and 'Umar my leaders! I repudiate whoever repudiates them." Al-Dhahabī stated that the latter statement is *mutawātir* from Ja'far then invoked curses upon anyone who claimed that Ja'far spoke such words hypocritically or meant otherwise. In another narration he said: "Whoever claims that I am infallible and that obedience is due to me, I repudiate them; I also repudiate whoever claims that I repudiate Abū Bakr and 'Umar." In yet another narration he said to a questioner about Abū Bakr and 'Umar: "You are asking about two men who tasted from the fruits of Paradise."

Maslama ibn Ja'far al-Aḥmasī asked Ja'far, "Is it true you hold that whoever speaks a triple divorce in ignorance is held to have divorced only once?" He replied: "This is not our position! Rather, whoever speaks a triple divorce, it is as he said."

Among Ja'far's sayings:

> "Whoever invokes blessings upon Muḥammad ﷺ and upon the people of his House one hundred times, Allāh ﷻ fulfills one hundred of his needs."
>
> "There is no provision better than fear of Allāh; there is nothing better than silence; there is no worse enemy than ignorance; and there is no more devastating disease than lying."
>
> "The Jurisprudents are the trustees of the Prophet-Messengers. When you see the Jurisprudents resort to the Sultans, condemn them!"
>
> "One's good deed does not become complete without three things: hastening it, belittling it, and hiding it."

Asked by an irritated al-Manṣur: "Why did Allāh create flies?" Ja'far replied: "To humble tyrants."

About al-Manṣūr's avarice: "Praise and glory to Allāh who has deprived him of the *dunyā* which he has tried to purchase with his *ākhira*."

"If you hear something unpleasant from your brother do not take offense. If what he said is true, it is a punishment hastened; if not true, it is a good deed you earned without doing anything."

"Mūsā ﷺ said: 'My Lord! I ask You that no one mention me except in a good way.' He replied: 'I have not done this even for Myself.'"

To Sufyān al-Thawrī: "Give abundant thanks and praise to Allāh upon receiving His favors for He said ﴿**If you give thanks, I will give you more**﴾ (14:7) and seek forgiveness abundantly when sustenance is blocked, for He said ﴿**Seek pardon of your Lord! Lo! He was ever Forgiving. He will let loose the sky for you in plenteous rain, And will help you with wealth and sons, and will assign unto you Gardens and will assign unto you rivers**﴾ (71:10-12). And if a contrary matter concerns you on the part of the sultan or other, say abundantly *Lā ḥawla walā quwwata illā billāh,* for it is the key of deliverance and one of the treasures of Paradise."

In commentary of the verse ﴿**Therein lie portents for the *mutawassimīn***﴾ (15:75) he said, "Those who possess insight (*al-mutafarrisīn*)."

Al-Dhahabī narrates with his chain to al-Faḍl ibn al-Rabī', from his father:

Al-Manṣūr summoned me and said: "Ja'far ibn Muḥammad questions my rule! May Allāh kill me if I do not have him killed!" I went to him and said, "Come to the Commander of the Believers at once." He washed and got dressed – I believe he mentioned they were new clothes – and I preceded him, asking permission for him to enter. He said: "Let him in and Allāh kill me if I do not have him killed!" When he saw him coming in he stood up and received him, saying: "Welcome to him of the clean slate, innocent of corruption and treachery! Welcome to my brother and paternal cousin!" He sat him next to him on the dais and faced him squarely, enquiring of his good health. Then he said: "Ask me anything you need!" Ja'far replied: "The people of Makka and Madīna – their payment has been delayed, so give orders that they be paid." He said, "I will." Then he said: "Woman! Bring me the gift!" She brought him a glass oil-flask containing *ghāliya* perfume.[210] Ja'far took

[210] A mix of scented oil made of musk, amber, and aloes (*'ūd*) used by the Prophet ﷺ.

it and left. I followed him and said: "Son of the Messenger of Allāh! I brought you and was sure he would kill you, and you saw what happened. I saw you moving your lips as you were coming in. What were you saying?" Ja'far replied: "I said:

O Allāh! Guard me with Your sight that never sleeps!
Cover me with Your unfailing protection!
Save me with Your power over me!
Do not cause me to perish while I have You as my hope!
My Lord, how many favors have You lavished on me for which I thanked you little!
With how many tests have You tried me for which I have shown little endurance!
You for Whose favors I have little thanked, yet You did not deprive me!
You at Whose trials I showed little endurance, yet You did not fail me!
You Who saw me persisting in sins, yet You did not expose me!
You Whose favors can never be counted!
You Whose goodness is never interrupted!
Help me in my Religion with my worldly matters!
Help me in my Hereafter with Godwariness!
Guard me in all that I do not perceive!
Do not leave me to my soul in its vagaries!
You Whom sins in nothing harm and Whom forgiveness diminishes not!
Forgive me that which harms You not!
Give me that which diminishes You not!
All-Giver! I ask you quick deliverance, patient endurance, safety from all trials, and gratefulness for safety!

اللهم احرُسْني بِعَيْنِك التي لا تنام واكْنُفْني برُكْنِك الذي لا يُرام واحفَظني بقُدْرَتِك عَلَيَّ ولا تُهْلِكْني وأنت رَجائي. رَبِّ كَمْ مِنْ نِعْمَةٍ أَنْعَمْتَ بِهَا عَلَيَّ قَلَّ لَكَ عِندها شُكري! وَكَمْ مِن بَلِيَّةٍ اِبْتَلَيْتَني بها قَلَّ لها عِندَك صَبْرِي! فَيَا مَنْ قَلَّ ثَمَّ نِعْمَتِهِ شُكْرِي فَلَمْ يَحْرِمْني! وَيَا مَنْ قَلَّ ثَمَّ بَلِيَّتِهِ صبري فَلَم يَخْذُلْنِي! وَيا مَنْ رَآنِي عَلَى المَعَاصِي فَلَمْ يَفْضَحْنِي! وَيَا ذَا النِّعَمِ الَّتي لا

تُحْصَى أَبَداً ! وَيَا ذَا المَعْروفِ الَّذي لا يَنْقَطِعُ أَبَداً ! أَعِنِّي عَلَى دِيني بِدُنْيَا ! وَعَلى آخِرَتي بِتَقْوَى ! وَاحْفَظْنِي فِيمَا غِبْتُ عَنْهُ ! وَلا تَكِلْني إلى نَفْسِي فِيمَا خَطَرَتْ ! يَا مَنْ لا تَضُرُّهُ الذُّنوبُ وَلا تَنْقُصُهُ المَغفِرة ! اغفِرْ لي مَا لا يَضُرُّكَ وَأَعْطِنِي ما لا يَنْقُصُكَ ! يا وَهَّابُ أسألك فَرَجاً قريباً وصبراً جميلاً والعافيَةَ من جميع البلايا وشُكْرَ العَافِيَةِ.

The ḥadīth Master Ibn Shāhīn al-Ḥanbalī (d. 385) said: "Two righteous men have been tried because of evil people: Ja'far ibn Muḥammad and Aḥmad ibn Ḥanbal."[211] Similarly Ibn al-Ṣalāḥ (d. 643) said: "Two Imāms have been afflicted because of their followers although they are innocent of them: Aḥmad ibn Ḥanbal was tried with the anthropomorphists (*al-mujassima*), and Ja'far al-Ṣādiq with the [Shī'ī] Rejectionists (*al-Rāfiḍa*)."[212] Among the forgeries attributed by the latter to Imām Ja'far is his supposed condoning of temporary marriage (*mut'a*). Al-Bayhaqī cites Ja'far as calling *mut'a* "pure fornication" (*'ayn al-zinā*).[213]

AL-AWZĀ'Ī [214]

'Abd al-Raḥmān ibn 'Amr ibn Yuḥmad Abū 'Amr al-Awzā'ī ﵀ (88-158), *Shaykh al-Islām*, the saintly, wise Scholar of the People of Shām, was one of the *mujtahid* Imāms of the *Salaf* along with the Four Imāms, Sufyān al-Thawrī, al-Ṭabarī, and others, the first – with Ibn Jurayj and Abū Ḥanīfa – to compile the Sunna of the Prophet ﷺ and the Companions under *fiqh* subheadings. Born orphaned and poor in Ba'labak and raised in al-Kark in the Biqā' valley, he came to live in the area known as – and populated by – the *Awzā'* or "variegated tribes" in Damascus then moved to Beirut where he remained garrisoned until his death, his fame having spread to the entire Islamic world of his

[211] Narrated by Ibn 'Asākir in *Tabyīn Kadhib al-Muftarī* (p. 164-165).

[212] Cited by Ibn al-Subkī in his *Qā'ida fil-Jarḥ wal-Ta'dīl* (p. 43) cf. his *Ṭabaqāt al-Shāfi'iyya al-Kubrā* (2:17).

[213] Cited by Ibn Ḥajar, *Fatḥ* (9:173) and al-Shawkānī, *Nayl al-Awṭār* (6:271).

[214] Main source: al-Dhahabī, *Siyar* (7:86-104 §1049).

time. One of those who combined assiduous worship with Science and the affirmation of truth, he is considered a Proof in himself (*ḥujja*) as a narrator, known for his superlative understanding of the Law, great erudition, and piety. Al-Shāfi'ī said: "I never saw a man whose *fiqh* resembled his *ḥadīth* more than al-Awzā'ī."[215]

He narrated from a host of *Tābi'īn*, among them 'Aṭā' ibn Abī Rabāḥ, Abū Ja'far Muḥammad al-Bāqir, 'Amr ibn Shu'ayb, Makḥūl – whom he surpassed in knowledge –, Qatāda, Rabī'a ibn Yazīd al-Qaṣīr, Bilāl ibn Sa'd, al-Zuhrī, Yaḥyā ibn Abī Kathīr – his first Shaykh,– 'Abd al-Raḥmān ibn al-Qāsim, 'Aṭā' al-Khurāsānī, 'Ikrima, 'Alqama, Ibn al-Munkadir, al-Walīd ibn Hishām, Muḥammad ibn Sīrīn, Nāfi' Mawlā Ibn 'Umar – Ibn 'Umar's freedman – and many others. From him narrated his two Shaykhs al-Zuhrī and Yaḥyā ibn Abī Kathīr, Shu'ba, al-Thawrī, Mālik, Sa'īd ibn 'Abd al-'Azīz, Ismā'īl ibn 'Ayyāsh, Baqiyya, Yaḥyā al-Qaṭṭān, and many others.

Al-'Abbās ibn al-Walīd said:

> I never saw my father admire anything in the world as much as he admired al-Awzā'ī. He used to exclaim about him: "Glory to You! You do what You wish. My son! Kings are powerless to discipline themselves and their own children the way that al-Awzā'ī disciplined himself. I never in my life heard him say an excellent word except the listener was bound to observe that it applied to him. Nor did I ever see him laugh without restraint. Whenever he addressed the subject of our return to our Maker, I would say to myself: I wonder, is there one heart in this gathering that is not weeping?"

Al-Hiql said: "Al-Awzā'ī gave replies covering about seventy thousand issues." 'Abd al-Raḥmān ibn Mahdī said: "The People (*al-nās*) in their time were four: Ḥammād ibn Zayd in al-Baṣra, al-Thawrī in al-Kūfa, Mālik in al-Ḥijāz, and al-Awzā'ī in al-Shām."[216] Ismā'īl ibn 'Ayyāsh said: "I heard people say, in the year 140, that in our day the wise scholar of the *Umma* was al-Awzā'ī." When the latter came to Makka, Sufyān al-Thawrī walked ahead of him shouting: "Open the way for the Shaykh!" Mālik compared the two saying: "One of them [Sufyān] is more knowledgeable than the other, but is not fit to be the

[215] A reference to al-Awzā'ī's faithful application of his knowledge in his life.

[216] This is a notable example of the use of *al-nās* to mean the major Ulema of the *Sunna*, as in the titles of the ḥadīth Masters recensed by al-Khaṭīb in his *Sharaf Aṣḥāb al-Ḥadīth*.

Imām [*i.e.* the Caliph], while the other [al-Awzā'ī] is." This was also the opinion of al-Fazārī, 'Alī ibn Bakkār, and Ibn al-Mubārak.

He was fearless in telling the truth to princes. After massacring the Banū Umayya, the harsh King 'Abd Allāh ibn 'Alī – al-Saffāḥ's uncle – summoned him and asked him in front of his court: "What is your opinion of what we have done?" Al-Awzā'ī related: "I thought to myself and decided to tell him the truth, bracing for certain death. I narrated to him the ḥadīth: 'Actions count only according to intentions.'[217] He said: 'What do you say about our killing the people of that dynasty?' I narrated to him the ḥadīth: 'Killing a Muslim is forbidden except in three cases: adultery after marriage, apostasy after Islām, and unlawful manslaughter.'[218] He continued: 'Tell me about the caliphate, is it not our inheritance as stipulated by the Prophet ﷺ?' I replied: 'Had this been the case, 'Alī ؓ would have never left anyone come before him.' He said: 'But what do we say about the treasure of the Banū Umayya?' I replied: 'If it were licit for them, it is illicit for you, and if it were illicit for them, it is even more illicit for you!'"

Al-Awzā'ī did not rise from his place of morning prayer until sunrise, and the sun did not pass the zenith except he was seen standing in prayer. Al-Walīd ibn Mazyad said: "No one surpassed him in intensity of worship." Among his sayings:

- Marwān al-Tātarī said that al-Awzā'ī said: "Whoever stands in prayer at length at night, Allāh shall make the station of the Day of Resurrection easy for him."
- Al-Walīd ibn Muslim and 'Abd Allāh ibn al-Mubārak related that al-Awzā'ī said: "This science was noble, men would transmit it to one another, but when it spread to books, those other than its rightful custodians became involved with it."[219]
- "Whoever holds on to the rare and unusual positions of the Scholars has left Islām." Similar statements are reported from

[217] Narrated from 'Umar in the Nine Books except Mālik and al-Dārimī. See al-Shāfi'ī and Abū Dāwūd's remarks on this foundational ḥadīth (p. 235 and 344).

[218] Narrated from Ibn Mas'ūd by al-Bukhārī, Muslim, and in the Four *Sunan*; from 'Uthmān by al-Tirmidhī (*ḥasan*), al-Nasā'ī, Ibn Mājah, Aḥmad, al-Ḥākim (4:350), al-Shāfi'ī in his *Musnad*, al-Bazzār in his *Musnad*; and from 'Ā'isha by Abū Dāwūd. See al-Bayhaqī's *Kitāb al-Murtadd* in *Ma'rifat al-Sunan* (12:237-258).

[219] This statement refers to the books which are passed on for circulation as in mod-

Sufyān al-Thawrī, Abū Yūsuf, Ibn Mahdī, Sulaymān al-Taymī, Aḥmad, and Ibn 'Abd al-Salām. This advice is of the utmost importance today for those who cling to newfangled fatwas permitting bank interest, removing the *ḥijāb*, handshake between the sexes, combining prayers without excuse, and other charged issues such as suicide warfare or the targeting of civilians.[220]

- "The Book stands in greater need of the Sunna than the Sunna does of the Book." Ibn 'Abd al-Barr said: "That is because the Sunna expounds the meaning of the Book."[221]
- Al-Walīd ibn Mazyad said that al-Awzā'ī, asked to define humility (*khushū'*) in prayer, replied: "Downcast gaze, lowering the wing of submission, and softness of heart which is sorrow and dread." He also said: "I saw al-Awzā'ī, he was like a blind man because of his humility."
- Al-Walīd heard al-Awzā'ī define the naïve (*al-ablah*) as "he who is in blind ignorance of evil but acutely discerning of goodness."[222]
- "Whoever remembers death much, a little suffices him for livelihood; whoever realizes that his utterances are counted as deeds, his speech becomes spare."
- "The distraction of the learned is better than the wisdom of the ignorant." This is similar to their saying, "The good deeds of the righteous are the sins of the Friends of Allāh" (*ḥasanāt al-abrār sayyi'āt al-muqarrabīn*).

---

ern times, not to those used by the early narrators as mnemonic records when narrating. It is established that early ḥadīth narrators did not narrate except from record. 'Abd Allāh ibn Aḥmad ibn Ḥanbal said: "I never saw my father narrate except from a book, save less than a hundred ḥadīths." *Siyar* (9:457). The best sources on the proof-texts for writing among the Companions and early generations are Ibn 'Abd al-Barr's chapter *Dhikr al-Rukhṣa fī Kitāb al-'Ilm* in his *Jāmi' Bayān al-'Ilm* (1:298-338), al-Bayhaqī's similarly entitled chapter in *al-Madkhal* (p. 411-424), and al-Khaṭīb al-Baghdādī's book *Taqyīd al-'Ilm* ("The Fettering of Knowledge"). See also al-Ḥakīm al-Tirmidhī's chapter entitled "Writing is the means to fetter knowledge and preserve it from oblivion" in his *Nawādir al-Uṣūl* (p. 39-41).

[220] See http://webpages.marshall.edu/~laher1/terrorism.html for foundational Islamic texts on the latter issue.

[221] Narrated by al-Dārimī and others and cited by Ibn 'Abd al-Barr in *Jāmi' Bayān al-'Ilm* (2:1193-1194 §2351) and al-Shāṭibī in *al-Muwāfaqāt* (Salafiyya ed. 1343 4:10).

[222] On the praise of naïveness in the Prophetic ḥadīths see p. 171-174.

- "If the caliphate had been a stipulation (*waṣiyya*) [to 'Alī] by the Messenger of Allāh ﷺ, 'Alī would have never permitted the two arbiters."
- "We used to joke and laugh, but when people begin to follow us, I do not see how we can even smile."
- "If we accepted what the people gave us every time, we [Scholars] would lose all merit before them."
- 'Abd Allāh ibn Aḥmad narrated from al-Ḥasan ibn 'Abd al-'Azīz from 'Amr ibn Abī Salama al-Tinnīsī that al-Awzā'ī said: "I saw myself as if carried up by two angels who camped me in front of the Lord of Power and Might. He said to me: 'Are you my servant 'Abd al-Raḥmān who commands good deeds?' I replied: 'By Your Power and Might! You know best.' Then they descended again and brought me back to where I first was."

Among al-Awzā'ī's notable rulings is that the thigh is part of a man's legal nakedness in the mosque, but not in the bath.[223]

A report from al-Awzā'ī states: "We would say, at a time when the *Tābi'īn* were plenty, that Allāh ﷻ is above His Throne (*fawqa al-'arsh*)" but its chain is weak.[224] As for the report that he said: "He is over the

[223] The rulings of the Four Schools agree that the definition of "nakedness" (*'awra*) for a man is all that is above the knees and below the navel front and back whether in public or private. Among the proofs for this is the Prophet's ﷺ saying: "The [man's] thigh is nakedness." Narrated from Jarhad al-Aslamī, 'Alī, and Muḥammad ibn Jaḥsh – all with sound chains according to al-Arna'ūṭ – by Mālik, Abū Dāwūd, Ibn Mājah, Aḥmad, al-Ḥākim (4:180-181), Abū Ya'lā (§331), al-Ṭaḥāwī in *Sharḥ Mushkil al-Āthār* (4:401-406 §1697, §1699, §1700, §1704), al-Baghawī in *Sharḥ al-Sunna* (9:21-22), Ibn Ḥibbān (4:609-611), and others. Al-Ṭaḥāwī said in *Sharḥ Ma'ānī al-Āthār* (1:474): "Mass-narrated, sound reports from the Prophet ﷺ have reached us that the thigh is nakedness." Al-Kattānī cited it in *Naẓm al-Mutanāthir.*

[224] Narrated by al-Bayhaqī in *al-Asmā'* (Kawtharī ed. p. 408; Ḥāshidī ed. 2:304 §865) with a chain containing Muḥammad ibn Kathīr ibn Abī 'Aṭā' al-Miṣṣīṣī who is weak as declared by most of the Imāms of ḥadīth in Ibn Abī Ḥātim, *al-Jarḥ wal-Ta'dīl* (8:69) and confirmed by al-Arna'ūṭ and Ma'rūf in *Taḥrīr al-Taqrīb* (3:310-311 §6251). Note the false claims of Ibn Taymiyya in his *Fatwā Ḥamawiyya* (p. 299-300=*Majmū' al-Fatāwā* 5:39=*Rasā'il* 1:431) and his student Ibn al-Qayyim in his *Ṣawā'iq al-Mursala* (2:211) and *Ijtimā' al-Juyūsh* (p. 31) respectively that its chain is sound and all its narrators trustworthy, a claim perpetuated by Albānī in his *Mukhtaṣar al-'Ulūw* (p. 137-138) and al-Tuwayjirī in his edition of the *Ḥamawiyya.*

Throne just as He described Himself,"[225] it is narrated from al-Tha'ālibī with indefinite missing links between the two. Al-Tha'ālibī is himself a problematic source.

Muḥammad ibn 'Abd al-Raḥmān al-Sulamī said: "I saw al-Awzā'ī; he was of above-average build, slim, somewhat swarthy, and he used henna." He used to wear a round turban without a hanging extremity (*'adhaba*). Al-Dhahabī said: "In addition to his brilliance in the science and his foremost rank in works, he was also a master in the art of writing letters." Four communities attended his funeral in Beirut: the Muslims carried his bier, followed by the Jews, the [Diophysite] Christians, and the [Monophysite] Copts. Yazīd ibn Madh'ūr said: "I saw al-Awzā'ī in my sleep and asked him: 'Show me a level by which to draw near to Allāh.' He replied: 'I did not see a level higher than that of the wise Ulema, and, after it, that of the grief-stricken (*al-maḥzūnīn*).'"

SUFYĀN AL-THAWRĪ[226]

Sufyān ibn Sa'īd ibn Masrūq Abū 'Abd Allāh al-Thawrī al-Muḍarī al-Kūfī ﵁ (97-161), the Godfearing, wise, grief-stricken, *Mujtahid* Imām, was "Commander of the Believers in Ḥadīth" – the highest level in ḥadīth Mastership –, "Shaykh al-Islām, the Imām of ḥadīth Masters, the leader of the practicing Ulema in his time, the author of the *Jāmi'*" (al-Dhahabī). His father was a junior *Tābi'ī* Muḥaddith and he thus began his scholarly career at home. Abū Isḥāq al-Sabī'ī recited when he saw Sufyān coming: ﴾**And We gave him wisdom when a child**﴿ (19:12). His *Shuyūkh* numbered 600. Ibn al-Jawzī claimed that his students numbered over 20,000 but al-Dhahabī said: "This is preposterous; they hardly reached 1,000. I know none of the ḥadīth Masters from whom more narrated than Mālik, and those number 1,400 – including the liars and the unknown!"

Among the praises related about him:

- "I wrote from 1,100 Shaykhs, but from none better than Sufyān." (Ibn al-Mubārak)
- "I never saw better than Sufyān." (Yūnus ibn 'Ubayd – he had

[225] Narrated from al-Tha'ālibī by al-Dhahabī in *al-'Ulūw* (p. 393 §696).

[226] Main source: al-Dhahabī, *Siyar* (Fikr ed. 7:174-211 §1083), in which he helped himself with Ibn al-Jawzī's *Manāqib Sufyān al-Thawrī*.

seen Sa'īd ibn Jubayr, Ibrāhīm al-Nakha'ī, 'Aṭā', and Mujāhid.)

- "If 'Alqama and al-Aswad were present they would stand in need of Sufyān." (Abū Ḥanīfa)
- "I never saw one resemble the *Tābi'īn* more than Sufyān al-Thawrī." (Ibn Abī Dhi'b)
- "I never saw stronger in ḥadīth memorization than al-Thawrī, nor more ascetic than Shu'ba, nor more intelligent than Mālik, nor of better counsel to the *Umma* than Ibn al-Mubārak [...] Sufyān is the most knowledgeable of them." "I could not look at Sufyān directly, he was too intimidating and full of majesty." (Ibn Mahdī)
- "I never saw anyone more informed of the *ḥalāl* and the *ḥarām* than Sufyān al-Thawrī" (Ibn 'Uyayna).
- "This is the most expert (*afqah*) of people on earth." (Zā'ida)
- "I never saw anyone like Sufyān al-Thawrī."(Ibn Wahb) Ibn Wahb narrates that he saw Sufyān prostrate after *Maghrib* and not raise his head until the call for *'Ishā'*.
- "By Allāh! Sufyān was more knowledgeable than Abū Ḥanīfa." (Fuḍayl ibn 'Iyāḍ) "He is above Mālik in all things." (Yaḥyā ibn Sa'īd al-Qaṭṭān) "If these two concur on something – al-Thawrī and Abū Ḥanīfa – then this is a strong position." (Ibn al-Mubārak)
- "Al-Thawrī for us was the Imām of all the people [...] Sufyān in his time was like Abū Bakr and 'Umar in theirs." (Bishr al-Ḥāfī)
- "If I had been asked to choose someone to lead this *Umma* [as a Caliph] I would have chosen Sufyān al-Thawrī." (Al-Awzā'ī)
- "I never saw a man who follows the Sunna more rigorously or in whose body I would love to be more than Sufyān al-Thawrī." (Al-Shāfi'ī)
- "Do you know who is the Imām? The Imām in my view is Sufyān al-Thawrī. No-one comes before him in my heart!" (Aḥmad to Abū Bakr al-Marwadhī)
- "Sufyān is the *'Ālim* of the *Umma* and its Worshipper." (Al-Muthannā ibn al-Ṣabbāḥ)
- "Truly, if I see a person accompany Sufyān, that person becomes great in my view." (Abū Bakr ibn 'Ayyāsh)

Sufyān spoke precious words on money matters. He was once asked a question while he was buying something. He replied: "Leave me, my heart is with my dirham right now." He said: "I much prefer to leave behind ten thousand dirhams over which Allāh takes account of me, rather than stand in need of people." He also said: "In the past, money was disliked; but today it is the shield of the believer." To a man who told him: "Abū 'Abd Allāh! You hold dinars in your hand?!" He replied: "Be quiet! Were it not for them, the kings would use us to wipe themselves (*la-tamandala binā al-mulūk*)!" He also said: "The *'Ālim* is the cure in the Religion and money its disease. If the *'Ālim* drags the disease to himself, when can he heal others?"[227]

Long before the *Iḥyā'*, Sufyān warned against the mere thirst for knowledge at the expense of the training of the ego. He possessed a photographic memory – "I never forgot anything I had memorized" – but, more importantly, "I never memorized a single ḥadīth except I practiced it, at least once." "He said: "Adorn knowledge and the ḥadīths with yourselves, not vice versa." He also said: "The ugliest of people is he who pursues the world through the work of the hereafter." Abū Dāwūd al-Ṭayālisī said he heard Sufyān say: "I do not fear anything that might enter me into the Fire more than the ḥadīths." He also said: "Would that I had recited the Qur'an and stopped there." He also said: "Whoever increases in knowledge increases in pain; if I knew nothing it would be easier for my predicament." He also said: "If ḥadīth were a good it would have vanished just as goodness has vanished... Pursuing the study of ḥadīth is not part of the preparation for death, but a disease that preoccupies people!" Al-Dhahabī comments:

> By Allāh, he has spoken the truth! [...] Today, in our time, the quest for knowledge and ḥadīths no longer means for the ḥadīth Scholar the obligation of living up to it, which is the goal of ḥadīths. He is right in what he said because pursuing the study of ḥadīths is other than the ḥadīth itself.[228]

Al-Dhahabī also said:
Love of ḥadīth in itself and its practice for the sake of Allāh is

[227] Al-Dhahabī, *Tadhkirat al-Ḥuffāẓ* (1:204).

[228] Al-Dhahabī as cited in al-Sakhāwī, *al-Jawāhir wal-Durar fī Tarjamat Shaykh al-Islām Ibn Ḥajar (al-'Asqalānī)*, ed. Ḥāmid 'Abd al-Majīd and Ṭaha al-Zaynī (Cairo: Wizārat al-Awqāf, 1986) p. 21-22.

> required and part of one's provision for the Return; but love of its narration, its shortest chains, excessive focus on knowing and understanding it – that is what is blamed and feared on the part of Sufyān, al-Qaṭṭān, and the people of [spiritual] observance, for much of this is a curse on the *muḥaddith.*[229]

Yet when he was asked: "Until when will you study ḥadīth?" he replied: "And what greater goodness is there for me but ḥadīth, so that I might turn to it?" Al-Ashja'ī said: "I heard from al-Thawrī 30,000 ḥadīths." Sufyān also said: "There is no need better than [the study of] ḥadīth if the intention is correct." He also said: "If a man were to try and lie in [narrating] ḥadīth, even inside his own house, Allāh would cause someone to overpower him." To a man who said to him: "Narrate to us just as you heard," he replied: "No, by Allāh! This is impossible. These are only the meanings." "If I tell you that I am narrating to you just as I heard, do not believe me." "Were we to narrate to you exactly in the way we heard, we would not narrate to you a single ḥadīth." Ibn Mahdī said: "We would be with Sufyān as if he had been summoned for his last reckoning. We did not dare speak a word to him. Then we would mention a ḥadīth and all this fear would be dispelled and nothing remain except *ḥaddathanā ḥaddathanā.*" Qabīṣa said: "If you saw Sufyān you would think he is a monk but when he started narrating you could not recognise him."

On the chain of transmission: "The *isnād* is the weapon of the believer. Whoever has no weapon, with what is he fighting?" Something similar is related from al-Zuhrī, Ibn al-Mubārak, Ibn 'Uyayna, Muslim, Ḥammād ibn Zayd, and many others.[230]

Sufyān called the kissing of the hands of the Ulema a Sunna. On *Taṣawwuf* he said: "Among the best of people is the Ṣūfī learned in *Fiqh*"[231]; "I found the reform of my heart between Makka and Madīna, among a community of strangers who wore wool and ample coats"; "Simple living (*zuhd*) does not consist in eating chaff and wearing coarse cloth, but in keeping hopes short and searching out the coming of death"; "I never saw rarer *zuhd* than the renouncing of

[229] *Siyar.* There is more in al-Dhahabī's *Tadhkirat al-Ḥuffāẓ.*

[230] Cf. Ibn Rajab, *Sharḥ 'Ilal al-Tirmidhī* (1:56-62).

[231] Narrated by al-Harawī al-Anṣārī in his *Ṭabaqāt al-Ṣūfiyya*, Ibn al-Jawzī in *Ṣifat al-Ṣafwa*, and Ibn al-Qayyim in *Madārij al-Sālikīn* (2:330).

leadership. You might see a man renounce food, money, and dress, but when it comes to leadership, he maneuvers and battles."

Sufyān also said: "A man must force his child to learn because he is responsible for him." To a boy in the first row of prayer he said: "Have you reached puberty?" If not, he would make him stand in a back row.

Asked why he abandoned soldiery (*al-ghazū*), Sufyān replied: "Because they do not observe the categorical obligations (*innahum yuḍayyi'ūna al-farā'iḍ*)." Imām al-Nawawī in *al-Tibyān fī Ādāb Ḥamalat al-Qur'ān* mentions that 'Abd al-Ḥamīd al-Ḥimmānī asked Sufyān al-Thawrī about a man who battles: is it more beloved to Sufyān, or that he recite the Qur'ān? He answered: "That he recite the Qur'ān, because the Prophet ﷺ said: 'The best of you is the one who has learnt the Qur'ān and teaches it.'"[232]

To Shu'ayb ibn Ḥarb he said: "What you wrote will not benefit you until:

– you consider correct the wiping of the two *khuffs* [in *wuḍū'*];
– the softening of *Bismillāh al-Raḥmān al-Raḥmān al-Raḥīm* in prayer becomes dearer to you than its recitation out loud;
– you believe in *qadar*;
– you pray behind every righteous and unrighteous imām;
– you hold that jihād continues until the Day of Resurrection;
– you endure patiently under the flag of the sultan whether just or unjust."

Shu'ayb said: "Every single *Ṣalāt*?" He replied: "No, only *Jumu'a* and the two *'Īds*, otherwise, you are free to choose and not to pray except behind one you trust and know he is from *Ahl al-Sunna*. When you stand before Allāh, if He asks you about this, tell him, 'My Lord! Sufyān ibn Sa'īd told me this.' Then leave me with my Lord." Al-Dhahabī said: "This is firmly established as authentic from Sufyān."[233]

He used to give precedence to 'Alī over 'Uthmān, which al-Dhahabī calls "slight Shī'ism." Yet he narrates that Sufyān said: "Love

[232] Narrated from 'Uthmān ibn 'Affān ﷺ by al-Bukhārī, al-Tirmidhī, Abū Dāwūd, Ibn Mājah, and Aḥmad.

[233] *Tadhkira* (1:207).

of both 'Uthmān and 'Alī are not found together except in the heart of the noblest men." He also narrates that Sufyān said: "Whoever says that 'Alī was more deserving of the Caliphate than Abū Bakr and 'Umar has declared that Abū Bakr, 'Umar, 'Alī, the *Muhājirūn*, and the *Anṣār* were all wrong. I am not sure whether such a person's acts of worship rise to the heaven." "Whoever places anybody before Abū Bakr and 'Umar has made light of twelve thousand Companions of the Messenger of Allāh ﷺ with whom the Messenger of Allāh was well-pleased when he died!" Asked about a man who died insulting Abū Bakr he said: "Such a man is a disbeliever in Allāh Most High." "Do we pray over him?" "No, and fie to him!" "But he says *lā ilāha illā Allāh*?" He replied: "Do not touch him with your hands. Raise him up on a slab of wood until you bring him down into his grave."

In his *Tafsīr* Sufyān said: "﴾**We lead them on**﴿ (7:182, 68:44) means We lavish blessings on them but prevent them from giving thanks." He also said: "He is not a wise person (*faqīh*) who does not consider difficulties a blessing and fortune a trial." Sufyān once spent the night in the house of Ibn Mahdī and started weeping. To his questioners he replied: "I care less for my sins than for this dust, but I fear deprivation of faith before dying." 'Aṭā' al-Khaffāf said he never met Sufyān except he saw him weeping. When he asked him why, Sufyān replied, "Because I am afraid of being written among the wretched in the Mother of the Book." He also said: "Whoever is content with the world, fear of the next life is removed from his heart." Yet Qabīṣa said he found Sufyān so inclined to joking that he lagged behind him whenever he could – to avoid his jokes – and 'Īsā ibn Muḥammad relates that Sufyān sometimes laughed to the point of lying down and stretching his legs. Al-Mu'āfā used to rebuke him, saying: "What is this, Sufyān? This is not the manner of the Ulema!" And Sufyān would accept it from him.

Sufyān was the farthest of people from kings and princes. He would not eat at their tables nor return their salaams; instead he would avoid them and ignore them until they showed humility and repentence. Al-Qārī relates that Sufyān said: "I may meet the rich man I despise (for his immorality) and if he says to me: How are you this morning? my heart will immediately lean towards him; what about those who eat their dainty dishes and tread their costly carpets? O Allāh! Do not let me owe a depraved man a favor for which my heart will look kindly upon him."[234] Muḥammad ibn 'Abd al-Wahhāb said: "I never saw princes and rich men sit more meekly than in the gathering of Sufyān al-Thawrī." In our own time this was also observed from the Moroccan ḥadīth Master Muḥammad ibn Ja'far al-Kattānī. Sufyān also said: "Those kings left the hereafter to you, so leave the world to them!"

Yaḥyā ibn 'Abd al-Malik ibn Abī Ghaniyya said: "I never saw anyone with a sterner face (*aṣfaqa wajhan*) for the sake of Allāh." Sufyān said: "If a man's neighbors all praise him, then he is an evil man because he might have seen them do something wrong but he says nothing and meets them with a smile; or he is a flatterer."

Among his sayings: "Safety lies in not being known." "I never met anyone except they warned me against fame." "I fear Allāh has abandoned this *Umma* by having people need me. I wish I could live among people who do not know me." "The less people you know, the less slander you commit." "Having many brothers is part of folly in one's Religion."

Qabīṣa said that no one sat with Sufyān except they remembered death. Yūsuf ibn Asbaṭ narrates that he once handed Sufyān the ablution-pot in the evening and left him holding it pensively. At dawn, he had not moved and said: "I am still thinking about the next life." He would reach states of anxiety about the Day of Judgment in which he urinated blood. He said: "I may see something against which I ought to speak out but I do not, then I urinate blood." He also said: "I felt the fear of God to a point I wondered how I could still be alive, then I would say to myself: I have a fixed term of life, but I wish it were made lighter for me. My fear is such that I fear losing my mind." "I ask Allāh to take away some of my fear of Him." Ibn Mahdī said: "Night after night I would catch sight of Sufyān sitting up and calling out: 'The Fire! The Fire! I cannot sleep nor feel pleasure anymore because I think of the Fire.'"[235] Abū Nu'aym said that Sufyān would be useless for days whenever this state overtook him.

Sufyān's garb was coarse and ragged and he ate dried meat and eggs. He said to Mu'ammal: "I do not tell you not to eat good things. Dress well and eat good things." Aḥmad ibn Yūnus said: "I once ate fruit at Sufyān's house, he said: 'This was brought to us as a present.'"

[234] Cited by al-'Ajlūnī in *Kashf al-Khafā'*, ḥadīth *Idhā ra'ayta al-qāri'a yalūdhu...*

[235] Also in the *Ḥilya* (7:60) and *Tārīkh Baghdād* (9:157).

'Abd al-Razzāq said: "Sufyān once ate dates with butter, then he rose and prayed until noon."

Abū al-Layth al-Samarqandī (d. 373) narrates in his *Tanbīh al-Ghāfilīn* by way of Sa'īd ibn 'Umayr al-Anṣārī who fought in the battle of Badr that the Messenger of Allāh ﷺ said: "Whoever invokes blessings upon me from my Community sincerely from his heart once, Allāh ﷻ sends ten blessings upon him and raises him ten degrees." Abū al-Layth continues:

I heard my father narrate that it happened that, while Sufyān al-Thawrī was circumambulating the Ka'ba, he saw a man who did not raise a foot nor lower a foot without making *ṣalāt* for the Prophet ﷺ. Sufyān said he told him: "O man! You have left saying *subḥān Allāh* and *lā ilāha illāllāh* and have proceeded with the *ṣalāt* on the Prophet ﷺ! Do you have any explanation regarding this?"

The young man asked: "Who are you, may Allāh pardon you?" "I am Sufyān al-Thawrī."

The young man said: "Had it not been that you are one of the Strangers among the people of your own time (i.e. one of *Ahl al-Sunna*), I would not have told you of my condition, nor revealed to you my secret.

"I went out with my father on pilgrimage to the Holy House of Allāh, until I reached one of the resting-stations. My father became sick and I nursed him. One night, when I was at his bedside, he died and his face turned dark. So I said, 'We belong to Allāh and to Him we return!' Then I pulled the covers over his face, after which sleep overcame me and I slept.

"I saw a man next to me with a face such as I had never seen a more handsome one, nor clothes cleaner than his, nor a scent finer than his. He kept approaching until he came close to my father and removed the covers from his face, whereupon the face of my father became full of light.

"Then the man started to go back, so I held onto his clothes and said: 'O servant of Allāh! Who are you, with whom Allāh has graced us in this foreign land?' He said:

'Do you not you know me? I am Muḥammad ibn 'Abd Allāh, who brought the Qur'ān! Your father transgressed against himself, but he used to invoke *ṣalāt* on me frequently, and when he was affected with whatever affected him he called on me for help *(isthaghātha bī)*, and I am a prompt helper of one who makes much *ṣalāt* on me *(wa-anā ghayyāthun li-man akthara al-ṣalāta 'alayy).'*

"Then I woke up and saw that the face of my father was bright."[236]

This report illustrates the acceptability of asking the Prophet ﷺ for help even after his life not on the basis of the dream – for dreams are not retained by the *Sharī'a* for the derivation of legal rulings – but on the basis of the account of the dream being part of the teaching of Islam and *taqwā* by one of the luminaries of the Community. The acceptability of this narration to the author, the narrator, and the Community indicates that they viewed its contents as being valid.

Aḥmad ibn Yūnus said: "I heard Sufyān al-Thawrī countless times say, '*Allāhumma sallim sallim, Allāhumma sallimnā, warzuqnā al-'āfiyata fīl-dunyā wal-ākhira.*'" 'Abd al-Razzāq said he heard Sufyān say to Wuhayb: "By the Lord of this [human] frame, I do love death!"

When Ibn Mahdī took care of Sufyān in his last illness, he asked him about the permissibility of leaving the congregational prayer to that end. Sufyān said: "Serving a Muslim in need for one hour is better than congregational prayer." Ibn Mahdī said: "From whom did you hear this?" Sufyān replied: "'Āṣim ibn 'Ubayd Allāh narrated to me from 'Abd Allāh ibn 'Āmir ibn Rabī'a, from his father [the Companion 'Āmir ibn Rabī'a al-'Anzī]: 'I would prefer serving one man among the Muslims who is in need for a single day, to sixty years of congregational prayers in which I never missed the opening *Takbīra*!'" Sufyān became afflicted with chronic diarrhea. The night of his death, Ibn Mahdī relates, he made his ablution sixty times. When he felt the end was near he left his bed and put his cheek on the ground, saying, "Abū 'Abd al-Raḥmān! How hard it is to die!" He then said: "Recite Yā Sīn over me, for I was told it makes it easier for the sick man." Ibn Mahdī said: "I recited and did not finish before he expired."

Muṣ'ab ibn al-Miqdām said he dreamt of the Prophet ﷺ holding Sufyān by the hand and thanking him. Ibrāhīm ibn A'yan also dreamt of him and asked him: "What happened to you?" Sufyān replied: "I am with the ﴾**Noble and righteous**﴿ (80:16)." Ibn al-Qayyim in *al-Rūḥ* reports that Ibn 'Uyayna said: "I saw Sufyān al-Thawrī in sleep [after his

236 Al-Samarqandī, *Tanbīh al-Ghāfilīn*, ed. Shaykh Aḥmad Salām (Beirut: Dār al-Kutub al-'Ilmiyya, c.1986) p. 319-320.

death] and said, 'Give me your final command!' He said, 'Make little of the knowledge of men.'" Qubayṣa ibn 'Uqda said, "I saw Sufyān al-Thawrī in sleep after his death and I said, 'What has Allāh done with you?' He said, 'I looked at my Lord face to face, and He said to me:

> *My pleasure is with you, Ibn Sa'īd!*
> *You stood (in worship) when night fell,*
> *Sad with tears and firm of heart.*
> *Behold! Choose which castle you wish,*
> *And visit me; for I am not far from you!"*

Sufyān ibn 'Uyayna also said: "I saw Sufyān al-Thawrī after his death, flying in the Garden from palm tree to tree and from tree to palm tree, saying, ❮**For the like of this let the workers work**❯ (37:61) but the narration in the *Siyar* has ❮**Praise be to Allāh, Who has fulfilled His promise unto us**❯ (39:74). He was asked, 'By means of what were you brought into the Garden?' He said, 'Godwariness, godwariness (*wara'*)!'"

Of his moving words: "Weeping is ten parts, one for Allāh, and nine for other than Allāh. If the part that is for Allāh comes once a year, that is plenty." Ibn Mahdī said: "I could hardly hear Sufyān's recitation because of his weeping."

Ibn al-Mubārak visited al-Firyābī and said: "Bring out the ḥadīth of al-Thawrī for me." Then he started weeping until his beard became wet and said: "Allāh have mercy on him! I do not think I shall ever see the like of him again."

IBN AL-MUBĀRAK

'Abd Allāh ibn al-Mubārak ibn Wāḍiḥ Abū 'Abd al-Raḥmān al-Ḥanẓalī *Mawlāhum* al-Turkī (118-181), Shaykh al-Islām, *Amīr al-Mu'minīn fīl-Ḥadīth*, was one of the foremost, major pious Imāms and ḥadīth Masters of the *Salaf*. Al-Bukhārī began his career by memorizing his compilations.

In addition to his highly respected scholarly exertions he traded and practiced jihād. It is claimed that he wrote to his friend Fuḍayl ibn 'Iyāḍ:

> *O worshipper in the Two Sanctuaries, if you could only behold us!*
> *You would see that you, in your devotions, are only playing.*
> *If you are one whose cheek is tinged with his tears,*
> *Then our chests are dyed with our blood!*

However, the Prophet ﷺ said: "Even if one strikes the unbelievers and idolaters with his sword until it breaks and he is completely dyed with their blood, the Rememberers of Allāh are a degree above him!"[237] And Ibn al-Mubārak himself, in his book *al-Zuhd*, gives precedence to the *jihād* of *dhikr.*

Al-Tirmidhī said in his *Sunan*: "Most of the people of knowledge follow what was narrated from 'Umar, 'Alī, and other than the two of them from the Companions of the Prophet ﷺ that the *Tarāwīḥ* consist of twenty *rak'as* and this is the position of al-Thawrī, Ibn al-Mubārak, and al-Shāfi'ī"[238] *i.e.* contrary to the forty-one *rak'as* preferred by the *Salaf* of Madīna as well as Isḥāq ibn Rāhūyah, following Ubay ibn Ka'b.

'Alī ibn al-Ḥasan ibn Shaqīq said that Ibn al-Mubārak "never gave fatwā except upon the strength and on the basis of transmitted reports."[239] He further said: "I was with 'Abd Allāh ibn al-Mubārak in the mosque on a cold winter night and we rose to leave. When we reached the door he reminded me of a ḥadīth and I reminded him of another. We did not stop rehearsing to each other until the *mu'adhdhin* came and raised the morning *adhān.*"[240]

Among his sayings:

- "The *isnād* is an integral part of the Religion, otherwise anyone can say anything."[241]
- "Let your reliance be upon transmitted reports, and use, for personal opinion, only whatever the ḥadīth expounds to you."[242]
- "If Allāh had not rescued me with Abū Ḥanīfa and Sufyān [al-Thawrī] I would have been like the rest of the common people."[243]
- "If I were to slander anyone, I would slander my parents, for they are the most deserving of my good deeds."
- "The only one that can carry the title *Shaykh al-Islām* is Abū Bakr

[237] Narrated from Abū Sa'īd al-Khudrī by al-Tirmidhī (*gharīb*) and Aḥmad.

[238] See, for al-Shāfi'ī, al-Bayhaqī's *Ma'rifat al-Sunan wal-Āthār* (4:40).

[239] 'Alī ibn al-Ḥusayn ibn Shaqīq as cited by Ibn Abī Ḥātim in his introduction to *al-Jarḥ wal-Ta'dīl* (p. 262).

[240] In al-Khaṭīb, *al-Jāmi'* (2:402-416 §1875-1877, §1880-1889, §1899, §1904).

[241] Narrated by Muslim, *Ṣaḥīḥ*, introduction, and al-Khaṭīb in his *Tārīkh* (6:166).

[242] Narrated from 'Abdān ibn 'Uthmān by Ibn 'Abd al-Barr in *Jāmi' Bayān al-'Ilm* (2:1050 §2023, 2:1070 §2073) with a sound chain according to al-Zuhayrī.

[243] Narrated by Ibn Ḥajar in *Tahdhīb al-Tahdhīb* (10:449-452 §817).

al-Ṣiddīq, who preserved the *zakāt* and fought against the apostates."[244]

- "Whoever is given a portion of love and he has not been given an equivalent amount of awe, has been cheated."[245]
- "I do not say the Qur'ān is the Creator nor that it is created. Rather, it is the Speech of Allāh, inseparable from Him."[246]
- In praise of the utmost high status of the Prophetic Companions he said: "The dust in the nostrils of Mu'āwiya's horse is better than 'Umar ibn 'Abd al-'Azīz."[247]
- "It is incumbent upon a wise person not to make light of three things: Ulema, Sultans, and brothers. Whoever makes light of the Ulema, his hereafter is lost; whoever makes light of the Sultan, his worldly life is lost; and whoever makes light of his brothers, his dignity is lost."[248]
- "It may be a small action becomes great by its intention; and it may be a great action becomes small by its intention."[249]
- "One may narrate from [a weak narrator] to a certain extent or those ḥadīths pertaining to good conduct (*adab*), admonition (*maw'iẓa*), and simple living (*zuhd*)."[250]

THE USE OF WEAK ḤADĪTHS IN ISSUES OF MORALS

Ibn al-Mubārak's conditional rule for narrating weak ḥadīths is in conformity with the unanimous view of the *Salaf* who permitted their use in *faḍā'il al-a'māl* as opposed to *'aqīda* or the rulings pertaining to *ḥalāl and ḥarām.* This is stated or practiced by Sufyān al-Thawrī, Ibn 'Uyayna, 'Alī ibn al-Madīnī, Yaḥyā ibn Ma'īn, Aḥmad, 'Abd al-Raḥmān ibn Mahdī, Ibn Abī Ḥātim, al-Bukhārī in other than the *Ṣaḥīḥ*, al-Tirmidhī, and others.[251]

244 In al-Sakhāwī, introduction to his *al-Jawāhir wal-Durar.*

245 Cited by Ibn al-Qayyim in *Rawḍat al-Muḥibbīn.*

246 Narrated by al-Bayhaqī, *Asmā' wal-Ṣifāt* (Kawtharī ed. p. 264-265; Ḥāshidī ed. 2:14-17).

247 Shaykh Aḥmad Sirhindī stated in his *Maktūbāt* that al-Haytamī related it in *al-Sawā'iq al-Muḥriqa* from Ibn al-Mubārak.

248 Narrated by al-Sulamī with his chain in *Ṭabaqāt al-Ṣūfiyya* as cited by al-Dhahabī.

249 Cited by al-Dhahabī, *Siyar* (Risāla ed. 8: 400).

250 Narrated by Ibn Abī Ḥātim in *Muqaddimat al-Jarḥ wal-Ta'dīl* (2:30) and cited by Ibn Rajab in *Sharḥ 'Ilal al-Tirmidhī* (1:73).

251 Cf. al-Khaṭīb, *Kifāya* (p. 162-163=133-134), Ibn Abī Ḥātim, *Muqaddimat al-Jarḥ*

This rule was mentioned by Ibn al-Ṣalāḥ and others in *Ma'rifat 'Ulūm al-Ḥadīth* and its commentaries.[252] It is the Consensus of the Ulema according to al-Bayhaqī, Ibn 'Abd al-Barr, al-Nawawī, Ibn Taymiyya, al-Qārī, and 'Alawī ibn 'Abbās al-Mālikī in *al-Manhal al-Laṭīf fī 'Ulūm al-Ḥadīth,* provided certain conditions are met.[253] Ibn Daqīq al-'Īd, al-'Irāqī, and Ibn Ḥajar list three conditions: that the ḥadīth not be very weak;[254] that it match a principle already established in the Law; and that one not positively hold that the Prophet ﷺ said or did it while al-Nawawī simply states: "As long as it is not forged."[255]

The dissent reported from Imām Muslim, Ibn Ḥazm, Ibn al-'Arabī, and al-Shawkānī is inaccurate. The correct position of Imām Muslim in the introduction to his *Ṣaḥīḥ* is that he forbade the use of forgers and other abandoned narrators, not of truthful weak ones, in conformity with the position of Aḥmad and the rest of the *Salaf.*[256] Muslim also says: "The sound reports from the trustworthy (*thiqāt*) narrators and those whose reliability is convincing are more than that we should be forced to transmit reports from those who are not trustworthy and whose reliability is not convincing." The difference is clear between saying we are not forced to use weak narrators and saying that one absolutely cannot transmit from them. A proof of this is his use of the weak narration from 'Ā'isha: "Treat people according to their ranks" and the fact that his strictness in narrators drops a notch in the ḥadīths of *raqā'iq* or *faḍā'il al-a'māl* in the *Ṣaḥīḥ,* as in the case of

(2:30-38), Ibn Rajab, *Sharḥ 'Ilal al-Tirmidhī* (1:73), Ibn Ḥajar, end of *al-Nukat 'alā Ibn al-Ṣalāḥ* (2:887-888), al-Suyūṭī, *Tadrīb*, al-Lacknawī, *al-Ajwiba al-Fāḍila*, etc.

[252] Ibn al-Ṣalāḥ, *'Ulūm al-Ḥadīth* (p. 93=1984 ed. p. 103).

[253] Al-Bayhaqī, *Dalā'il al-Nubuwwa* (1:33-34); Ibn 'Abd al-Barr, *Tamhīd* (1:127); al-Nawawī, *Majmū'* (5:63), *Irshād Ṭullāb al-Ḥaqā'iq* (p. 107-108), *Sharḥ Ṣaḥīḥ Muslim* (introduction), and *Adhkār* (introduction p. 5) cf. Ibn 'Allān, *Futūḥāt al-Rabbāniyya* (1:84); Ibn Taymiyya, *Sharḥ al-'Umda* (1:171), *Majmū' al-Fatāwā* (18:26, 18:65-66), *Miswaddat Āl Taymiyya* (p. 233, 246, 461); al-Qārī, *Sharḥ al-Shifā'* (2:91) and *Mirqāt* (2:381); 'Itr, *Manhaj al-Naqd* (p. 291-296) and *Uṣūl al-Jarḥ wal-Ta'dīl* (p. 140-143).

[254] Yet al-Sakhāwī in *al-Qawl al-Badī'* (p. 432) says of a certain ḥadīth: "In sum, it is a very weak ḥadīth (*ḍa'īf jiddan*) that is written in meritorious deeds (*yuktabu fī faḍā'il al-a'māl*), but as for its being forged, no, it is not [forged]." Al-Kawtharī voices a dissenting view in his *Maqālāt* (p. 139-140=p. 45).

[255] *Irshād* (p. 107-108) cf. al-Sakhāwī, *al-Qawl al-Badī'*, al-Suyūṭī, *Tadrīb* (p. 196).

[256] Cf. al-Nawawī, *Sharḥ Ṣaḥīḥ Muslim* (introduction), Ibn al-Qayyim, *I'lām al-Muwaqqi'īn* (1:31), al-Sakhāwī, *al-Qawl al-Badī'* (p. 474), and 'Itr, notes on Ibn Rajab's *Sharḥ 'Ilal al-Tirmidhī* (1:75-76).

Shaddād ibn Sa'īd Abū Ṭalhā al-Rāsibī, al-Walīd ibn Abī Walīd, or Ya'qūb ibn Isḥāq al-Ḥaḍramī.[257]

The correct position of Ibn al-'Arabī is as he states himself regarding a certain weak ḥadīth: "Its chain is unknown, but it is preferable to put it into practice [...]"[258]

Al-Shawkānī acts similarly with regard to the ḥadīths of the timings of cupping in *Nayl al-Awṭār.*

As for Ibn Ḥazm's statement against the use of weak narrations in absolute terms:[259] he elsewhere states in preference for the use of weak ḥadīth over the use of juridical opinion (*ra'y*), as does Ibn al-'Arabī.[260]

Abū Ḥanīfa's Foresight[261]

Abū Ḥanīfa was known for his keen foresight (*firāsa*). He said to Dāwūd al-Ṭā'ī: "You are going to devote yourself entirely to worship." He said to Abū Yūsuf: "You will have much to do with the world." We already mentioned the story of his prediction of Abū Yūsuf's princely future. He also foresaw Mālik's merit among the Scholars of al-Madīna.[262]

Ibn Ḥabīb narrates in his *'Uqalā' al-Majānīn* that Sufyān al-Thawrī, Mis'ar [ibn Kidām al-Hilālī al-Kūfī (d. 153)], Abū Ḥanīfa, and Sharīk ibn 'Abd Allāh al-Nakha'ī (d. 177) were arrested and taken to al-Manṣūr [who wanted to force one of them to be chief judge]. Abū Ḥanīfa said: "I will use a ruse to save myself, Sufyān will escape on the way, Mis'ar will act the madman, and Sharīk will fall." On the way, Sufyān said to his guard: "I need the privy." The guard waited behind a certain wall but Sufyān hailed a passing barge, telling them: "The man behind the wall wants to kill me!" They hid him and took him. The guard came back without him and his chief beat him up. The remaining three entered to see al-

257 The erroneous claim of a handful of authors such as al-Qāsimī in *Qawā'id al-Taḥdīth* (p. 94) or 'Ajāj al-Khaṭīb in *Uṣūl al-Ḥadīth* (p. 231) that Ibn al-'Arabī and Ibn Ma'īn were opposed to the use of weak ḥadīths in absolute terms, stems from good faith in Ibn Sayyid al-Nās, al-'Irāqī, al-Sakhāwī, and al-Suyūṭī's claims to that effect.

258 Ibn al-'Arabī, *'Āriḍat al-Aḥwadhī* (10:205) cf. *Fatḥ al-Bārī* (10:606) as cited by Muḥammad 'Awwāma in his marginalia on *al-Qawl al-Badī'* (p. 472).

259 Ibn Ḥazm, *al-Fiṣal fil-Milal wal-Niḥal* (2:83=2:69).

260 Cf. Ibn Ḥazm, *al-Iḥkām* (6:225-226) and Ibn al-'Arabī, *al-Maḥṣūl* (p. 98) and *Marāqī al-Zulaf* as cited in Ibn 'Arrāq, *Tanzīh al-Sharī'a* (2:209-210).

261 This section mostly from al-Ṣāliḥī's *'Uqūd al-Jumān* (p. 248-250).

262 Cf. p. 123.

Manṣūr. Mis'ar walked up to him, shook his hand, and said: "How are you, Commander of the Believers after me? How are your female slaves? How are your beasts of burden? You will make me chief judge, yes??" A man standing next to the Caliph said: "This is a madman!" Al-Manṣūr replied: "You are right. Take him out!" They let him go. Abū Ḥanīfa was summoned next. He came forward and said: "Commander of the Believers, I am al-Nu'mān ibn Thābit the son of the slave silkmaker in al-Kūfa. The people of al-Kūfa will never accept that the son of a slave silkmaker be judge over them!" He said: "You spoke truly." Sharīk began to speak but the Caliph said: "Shut up! No one remains but you, so give your pledge!" Sharīk said: "Commander of the Believers, I have memory lapses." He said: "Chew resin gum!"[263] Sharīk said: "I joke too much." The Caliph said: "We will make honey pastries for you to eat before you sit in your chair to judge!" Sharīk said: "I will judge whoever comes and goes!" The Caliph said: "Judge, be it myself and my own son!" Sharīk said: "Then I will." Sharīk is famous for his statement to Thābit the ascetic: "Whoever prays much at night, his face becomes beautiful by day,"[264] often mistaken for a Prophetic ḥadīth.

It is related that Abū Ḥanīfa said: "Most of the cases in which faith (*al-īmān*) is removed from a person is at the time of death and its cause is the commission of injustice."[265]

Like al-Shāfi'ī after him, Abū Ḥanīfa practiced physiognomy. He said: "If you see a man with a long head, know he is a fool"; "If you see a person who is both tall and intelligent, hold on to him for they are rare!"

Sayings of Abū Ḥanīfa

INSIGNIFICANCE OF THIS WORLD IN COMPARISON TO THE HEREAFTER

From al-Ḥasan ibn Ziyād al-Lu'lu'ī: "Whoever prizes his own soul, the whole world counts for little to him, including its hardships. Whoever seeks to be safe from the punishment of the hereafter, let him care little with the punishment of the world."

[263] The mountain shrub *lubān* or olibanum (=frankincense) resembles the mastic tree and strengthens memory.

[264] Cf. al-Ḥākim, *al-Madkhal ilā Ma'rifati Kitāb al-Iklīl* (p. 107-108 §170-171).

[265] Narrated in *al-Tadhkirat al-Mu'aẓẓamiyya*?

ḤADĪTH WITHOUT *FIQH*

From Rajā' al-Harawī: "Whoever learns ḥadīth without *fiqh* is like the pharmacist that assembles medicaments without knowing which applies to what until the physician comes. Thus remains the student of ḥadīth, he does not know the application of his ḥadīth until the *Faqīh* comes."

RESPECT FOR THE *SALAF*

To Abū Yūsuf who asked him which of 'Alqama or al-Aswad was greater, he replied: "By Allāh! I do not mention them except to make supplication and *istighfār* for them because of their rank. How could I prefer one to the other?"

GOD-FEARING SCRUPULOUSNESS IN GIVING FATWĀ

From Abū Yūsuf: "Whoever gives a response in the Religion and does not think that Allāh will take him to account for it, such a person takes his Religion and his own soul lightly."

Yazīd ibn al-Kumayt narrated that a man debated with Abū Ḥanīfa and said to him: "Fear Allāh!" whereupon Abū Ḥanīfa became stern, his face paled, and he looked down then said: "My brother! May Allāh reward you with goodness. How much do people stand in need of one who reminds them of Allāh when they become pleased with the learning that emanates from them, and when they should seek only Allāh with their works! Know that I never spoke a word of knowledge except in full consciousness that Allāh Most High would take me to account for my answer. I have no firmer purpose than to be safe!"

LIFE-STORIES OF THE LEARNED AND PIOUS

"Stories about the Ulema and their merits are dearer to me than much of jurisprudence because they are the manners and ethics of the Folk."[266]

WHO ARE THE *AWLIYĀ'*?

Al-Faḍl ibn Dukayn cited Abū Ḥanīfa as saying: "If the people of learning are not the friends of Allāh, then Allāh has no friends!"[267]

[266] Cited by Ibn 'Abd al-Barr, *Jāmi' Bayān al-'Ilm* (1:117), al-Qāḍī 'Iyāḍ, *Tartīb al-Madārik* (1:23), al-Sakhāwī, *I'lān* (p. 20), and al-Maqarrī, *Azhār al-Riyāḍ* (1:21-22).

[267] Cited by Imām al-Nawawī in *al-Tibyān fī Ādāb Ḥamalat al-Qur'ān.*

THIRST FOR LEADERSHIP

From Ibn al-Mubārak: "Whoever pursues leadership before his time remains humiliated forever after that."

FORBEARANCE

To Bukayr ibn Ma'rūf who told Abū Ḥanīfa: "People criticize you and you reply to no one?" He replied: "It is but the favor of Allāh, He gives it to whomever He wishes." 'Abd al-Ḥamīd al-Ḥimmānī said that he was with Abū Ḥanīfa when a man came in and said: "Sufyān al-Thawrī criticizes you." Abū Ḥanīfa said: "Allāh have mercy on Sufyān! Even if he had died in the time of Ibrāhīm al-Nakha'ī, the Muslims would have missed him sorely."[268]

UNDERSTANDING PRIORITIES

From Ibrāhīm ibn Suwayd: "Battle (*al-ghazwa*) in the way of Allāh after performing the pilgrimage of Islām is better than fifty pilgrimages."

His Sense of Humor

The author of *'Uqūd al-Jumān* mentions that Abū Ḥanīfa had a Rāfiḍī neighbor who had named his two mules *Abū Bakr* and *'Umar* out of spite for the Two Shaykhs, and he used to give less fodder to the second mule. One time this person was nowhere to be seen and Abū Ḥanīfa enquired about him. "He was trampled to death by one of his mules," came the reply. Abū Ḥanīfa said, "No doubt the one he named 'Umar?" They said yes.[269]

[268] Cf. Abū al-Mu'ayyad Muwaffaq Aḥmad al-Makkī in his *Manāqib* (1:155, 2:13).

[269] Al-Ṣāliḥī, *'Uqūd al-Jumān* (p. 247-248) cf. al-Ṣufūrī, *Nuzhat al-Majālis* (2:164).

MĀLIK IBN ANAS[270]

Allāh Be Well-Pleased with Him

MĀLIK IBN ANAS ibn Mālik ibn 'Amr, al-Imām, Abū 'Abd Allāh al-Ḥimyarī al-Aṣbaḥī al-Madanī (93-179), was the Shaykh of Islām, Proof of the Community, Imām of the Abode of Emigration, and Knowledgeable Scholar of Madīna predicted by the Prophet. The second of the four major *mujtahid* Imāms, whose school filled North Africa, al-Andalus, much of Egypt, and some of al-Shām, Yemen, Sudan, Iraq, and Khurāsān. Al-Qurṭubī in his *Tafsīr* on the verse ﴾**Allāh knows that which every female bears and that which the wombs absorb and that which they grow. And everything with Him is measured**﴿ (13:8) mentioned that Imām Mālik's mother gave birth to him after two years of pregnancy – some said three. This phenomenon was also reported of al-Ḍaḥḥāk, Muḥammad ibn 'Ajlān, and Haram ibn Ḥayyān.

The Prophet's Prediction of Imām Mālik

The Prophet said: "Very soon will people beat the flanks of camels in search of knowledge and they shall find no one more expert than the knowledgeable scholar of Madīna."[271] Another narration states:

[270] Main sources: Abū Nu'aym, *Ḥilya* (6:345-392 §386); al-Dhahabī, *Siyar* (7:382-437 §1180); M. Fu'ād 'Abd al-Bāqī, Introduction to Mālik's *Muwaṭṭa'*; Ibn 'Abd al-Barr, *Intiqā'* (p. 33-114); Ibn 'Asākir, *Kashf al-Mughaṭṭā*; Qāḍī 'Iyāḍ, *Tartīb*.

[271] Narrated from Abū Hurayra by Aḥmad, al-Tirmidhī who said it is *ḥasan* – in some manuscripts *ḥasan ṣaḥīḥ* – al-Ḥākim (1:90-91) with three chains, declaring it *ṣaḥīḥ* by Muslim's criterion, al-Bayhaqī in *al-Sunan al-Kubrā* (1:386) and *Ma'rifat al-Sunan* (1:87), Ibn Ḥibbān (9:52-53 §3736), al-Khaṭīb with four chains in *Tārīkh Baghdād* (5:306-307, 6:376-377, 13:17), and al-Nasā'ī without the words "very soon" in *al-Sunan al-Kubrā* (2:489 §4291). Ibn 'Abd al-Barr said in *al-Intiqā'* (p. 50-51) that its chain consists entirely of Imāms in the Religion. Al-Dhahabī said in the *Siyar* (7:388): "This is a ḥadīth whose chain is neat and content strange," while al-Arna'ūṭ declares the chain weak in Aḥmad's *Musnad* (13:358-360 §7980), after declaring the same chain sound and "meeting Muslim's criterion" in three places of his edition of al-Ṭaḥāwī's *Sharḥ Mushkil al-Āthār* (10:186-188 §4016-4018)! His grading of *ḍa'īf* is based on the fact that Ibn Jurayj – who alone relates it – "did not state having heard this narration directly from his source, and he practices this concealment (*tadlīs*) only when his source is weak, and here he uses indecisive transmission terminology (*'an'ana*) [from] Abū al-Zubayr. The latter is also a

"The people – or the students of knowledge – shall set forth from East and West without finding a *'ālim* other than the *'ālim* of the people in Madīna."[272]

عَنْ أَبِي هُرَيْرَةَ ﷺ رِوَايَةً يُوشِكُ أَنْ يَضْرِبَ النَّاسُ أَكْبَادَ الْإِبِلِ يَطْلُبُونَ الْعِلْمَ

فَلَا يَجِدُونَ أَحَدًا أَعْلَمَ مِنْ عَالِمِ الْمَدِينَةِ ت حسّنه حم ن في الكبرى حب خط ك

صححه على شرط مسلم وأقره الذهبي هق وفي المعرفة

Al-Tirmidhī, al-Qāḍī 'Iyāḍ, Ibn 'Abd al-Barr, al-Dhahabī and others relate from Sufyān ibn 'Uyayna, 'Abd al-Razzāq, Ibn Mahdī, Ibn Ma'īn, Dhu'ayb ibn 'Imāma, Ibn al-Madīnī, and others that they considered that Scholar to be Mālik ibn Anas. Ibn Ḥazm went to his usual extremes by claiming that "whoever asserts that Mālik was meant by the Prophet ﷺ [in this narration] lied against him and should find his abode in Hellfire"![273]

---

mudallis who uses indecisive transmission terminology here." However, Ibn Jurayj is related to use both decisive and indecisive transmission terminology for the same ḥadīth, such as the ḥadīth of Jābir that "The Prophet ﷺ circumambulated the House during the Farewell Pilgrimage mounted and would touch the Black Stone corner with his camel-prod so that people would see him prominently and ask him questions, because they had come to him in droves." In the two chains of the latter ḥadīth narrated by Aḥmad. Ibn Jurayj says "*akhbaranī Abū al-Zubayr*" while in the chain retained by Muslim he simply says "*'an Abī al-Zubayr.*" This is one example among several. This shows that Muslim considered Ibn Jurayj's transmission from Abū al-Zubayr as direct whether the term used was decisive or indecisive. Muslim retained at least two chains where Ibn Jurayj narrates exclusively "from" (*'an*) Abū al-Zubayr Muḥammad ibn Muslim al-Azdī, "from" (*'an*) Jābir: [1] "The Prophet ﷺ slaughtered a cow on behalf of 'Ā'isha on the Day of Sacrifice." [2] "The Prophet ﷺ prohibited the sale of surplus water." Furthermore, one of al-Ṭaḥāwī's narrations of the ḥadīth of the *'ālim* of Madīna has decisive transmission terminology between Ibn Jurayj and Abū al-Zubayr. Shaykh Shu'ayb authenticates this in his edition of al-Ṭaḥāwī, but in his edition of the *Musnad* he declares it "a copyist's lapse or else a lapse on the part of al-Ṭaḥāwī's shaykh, who is not known." Shākir declared the chain sound in his edition of the *Musnad* (8:99-100 §7976). Al-Mizzī in *Tuḥfat al-Ashrāf* (9:445) considered it a *mawqūf* report from Abū Hurayra and Ibn Qudāma in Ibn al-Ḥanbalī's *Muntakhab* relates the same opinion from Aḥmad. If this is correct, Abū Hurayra was apparently referring to himself. Allāh knows best.

[272] Narrated from Abū Mūsā al-Ash'arī by Ibn 'Abd al-Barr in *al-Intiqā'* (p. 51-52).

[273] Cf. Ibn Ḥazm, *al-Risāla al-Bāhira* (p. 50-57 §33-48).

It is also related from Ibn 'Uyayna that he later considered it to be 'Abd Allāh ibn 'Abd al-'Azīz al-'Umarī,[274] saying: "The *'ālim* is none other than he who fears Allāh, and we know no one that feared Allāh more than al-'Umarī."[275] Al-Dhahabī said of the latter: "He possessed knowledge and good *fiqh*, spoke the truth fearlessly, ordered good, and remained aloof from society. He used to press Mālik in private to renounce the world and seclude himself." Al-Ṭaḥāwī also considered the ḥadīth to refer to al-'Umarī.[276]

Abū Ḥanīfa's Praise of Mālik

It is narrated that Abū Ḥanīfa recommended Mālik – whom he met when he went on pilgrimage – among the scholars of Madīna: "If there is any excellence in them it lies in the fair-haired, blue-eyed youth." Another narration states: "I saw great knowledge spread in it [Madīna], and if any single person possesses it all it is the fair-skinned youth." [277]

Mālik's Reliance on Abū Ḥanīfa

Mālik counted Abū Ḥanīfa among his teachers as established by the report narrated by al-Qāḍī 'Iyāḍ whereby al-Layth ibn Sa'd said:

I met Mālik in al-Madīna and said to him: "I see you wiping the sweat off your brow?" He replied: "I sweated with Abū Ḥanīfa. He is assuredly a *faqīh*, O Egyptian!" Later I met Abū Ḥanīfa and said to him: "What a compliment that man [Mālik] paid you!" He replied: "By Allāh! I never saw anyone faster in giving a truthful answer and thorough study."[278]

Mālik relied upon Abū Ḥanīfa's jurisprudence as related by al-Shāfi'ī's Shaykh and Aḥmad ibn Ḥanbal's Grandshaykh, 'Abd al-'Azīz

[274] This is not al-Qāsim ibn Muḥammad contrary to 'Ā'isha Bewley's misidentification in her translation of Ibn Taymiyya's *Risāla Madaniyya, The Madinan Way* (p. 27).

[275] Narrated by Ibn Ḥibbān (9:54).

[276] In *Sharḥ Mushkil al-Āthār* (10:188-190).

[277] Both reports narrated by al-Gharnāṭī al-Mālikī in *Intiṣār al-Faqīr al-Sālik lil-Imām al-Kabīr Mālik* (p. 139) as cited by Abū Ghudda in *al-Intiqā'* (p. 43).

[278] Narrated by al-Qāḍī 'Iyāḍ in *Tartīb al-Madārik* (1:152).

ibn Muḥammad al-Darāwardī: "Mālik ibn Anas used to look into Abū Ḥanīfa's books and benefit from them."[279]

The *Muwaṭṭa'*

Mālik compiled *al-Muwaṭṭa'* ("The Approved"), formed of the sound narrations of the Prophet ﷺ from the people of the Ḥijāz together with the sayings of the Companions, the Successors, and those after them. It was hailed by al-Shāfi'ī as the soundest book on earth after the Qur'ān, the nearest book on earth to the Qur'ān, the most correct book on earth after the Qur'ān, and the most beneficial book on earth after the Qur'ān, according to four separate narrations. This was before al-Bukhārī and Muslim produced their compilations.

Ibn 'Abd al-Barr said that Mālik was the first to compile a book formed exclusively of sound narrations. Abū Bakr ibn al-'Arabī said: "The *Muwaṭṭa'* is the first foundation and the core, while al-Bukhārī's book is the second foundation in this respect. Upon these two all the rest have built, such as Muslim and al-Tirmidhī." Shāh Walī Allāh said something similar and added that it is the principal authority of all four Schools of Law, which stand in relation to it like the commentary stands in relation to the main text. Mālik composed it in the course of forty years, having started with ten thousand narrations until he reduced them to their present number of under 2,000.

Mālik said: "I showed my book to seventy jurists of Madīna, and every single one of them gave me his approval (*kulluhum wāṭa'anī 'alayh*), so I named it 'The Approved'." Imām al-Bukhārī said that the soundest of all chains of transmission was "Mālik, from Nāfi', from Ibn 'Umar." Ibn al-Ṣalāḥ lists it among the few chains the Scholars of ḥadīth call "the Golden Chain" and there are eighty narrations with this chain in the *Muwaṭṭa'*.

The *Muwaṭṭa'* was transmitted in different versions by Mālik's students, notably Yaḥyā ibn Yaḥyā al-Laythī (d. 232) and Muḥammad ibn al-Ḥasan al-Shaybānī (d. 189). Yaḥyā's version contains 1781 ḥadīths. Of these, 898 are sayings of Companions (613) and Successors (285), while 883 are sayings of the Prophet ﷺ, including 600 which go back to him without interruption (*musnad*), 222 without a Companion narrator (*mursal*), and 61 without *isnāds*, nearly all of which are found

[279] Cited with its chain to Ibn Abī al-'Awwām by Abū Ghudda in *al-Intiqā'* (p. 43).

elsewhere with full *isnāds*. Al-Shaybānī's version of the *Muwaṭṭa'* contains 429 ḥadīths from the Prophet ﷺ and 750 from others, including Companions (628)and Successors (112), with the remainder from later figures.

Mālik's Authorities in the *Muwaṭṭa'*

Among those Mālik narrated from in the *Muwaṭṭa'* are Ayyūb al-Sikhtyānī, Ja'far ibn Muḥammad (al-Ṣādiq), Zayd ibn Aslam, 'Aṭā' al-Khurāsānī, al-Zuhrī, Ibn al-Munkadir, Nāfi' the freedman of Ibn 'Umar, 'Alqama, and others. Among those who narrated from Mālik: Ibn Jurayj, Ḥammād ibn Abī Ḥanīfa,[280] al-Awzā'ī, Sufyān al-Thawrī, Shu'ba, Ibn al-Mubārak, Muḥammad ibn al-Ḥasan, 'Abd al-Raḥmān ibn Mahdī, Wakī', Yaḥyā al-Qaṭṭān, al-Shāfi'ī, Ibn Wahb, Abū Dāwūd al-Ṭayālisī, 'Abd al-Razzāq, and many others – over a thousand Shaykhs according to al-Dāraquṭnī. Al-'Alā'ī said the reason for this high number was Mālik's early fame, long life, and pivotal location.[281] Ibn 'Abd al-Barr said it is incorrect that al-Zuhrī narrated from Mālik. Rather, he narrated from his uncle Abū Suhayl Nāfi' ibn Mālik.

Mālik's Severity in Verifying Ḥadīth Transmittors

Sufyān ibn 'Uyayna said: "May Allāh have mercy on Mālik – how severe his examination of ḥadīth narrators was!"[282] Ma'n and others related that Mālik said: "There are four types of narrators one does not take from: an outright scoffer, even if he is the greatest narrator; an innovator who invites people to his innovation; someone who lies about people, even if I do not charge him with mendacity in ḥadīth; and a righteous, honorable worshipper if he does not memorise what he narrates."

Ibn Abī Uways said: "I heard my maternal uncle Mālik ibn Anas say: 'Verily this learning is Religion. Therefore look well from whom you take your Religion.[283] I have encountered seventy of those who say

[280] The claim that Abū Ḥanīfa himself narrated from Mālik, based on two narrations of uncertain chains of transmission, was questioned by Ibn Ḥajar, as cited by Abū Ghudda in his notes on Ibn 'Abd al-Barr's *al-Intiqā'* (p. 42).

[281] Al-'Alā'ī, *Bughyat al-Multamis* (p. 65).

[282] Narrated from 'Alī ibn al-Madīnī by Ibn 'Abd al-Barr in *al-Intiqā'* (p. 52).

[283] Narrated *maqṭū'* from Ibn Sīrīn by al-Tirmidhī at the end of his *Shamā'il*, Muslim, *Muqaddima*, and al-Nawawī, *Tibyān*, the last third of the chapter on the etiquette of the teacher.

Qāla Rasūlullāh ﷺ by those very columns – pointing to the mosque of the Messenger ﷺ – but I did not take anything from them. Yet, if any one of them had been placed in charge of the state treasury-house he would have been worthy of trust for it. But they were not qualified for the Science. Then Ibn Shihāb [al-Zuhrī] came and we crowded his door.'" Muṭarrif ibn 'Abd Allāh related that Mālik said: "I encountered in this city [Madīna] Shaykhs who were people of merit and righteousness. They narrated ḥadīths but I did not hear a thing from any of them because they did not [accurately] know what they were narrating."

The Unreliability of the Righteous

Mālik's phrase "a righteous, honorable worshipper who does not memorise what he narrates" refers to the two conditions *sine qua non* of the trustworthy narrator, who must possess not only moral uprightness (*'adāla*) but also thorough accuracy in transmission (*ḍabṭ*).

Masrūq related the example of an upright but inaccurate admonisher (*qāṣṣ*) who spoke to the people of Kinda and said, "There will be smoke on the Day of Resurrection which will deprive the hypocrites of their hearing and sight, but the believers will only suffer something like a cold (*zukām*)." When news of this reached Ibn Mas'ūd he became angry and sat up, saying: "People! Whoever knows something, let him say it; but whoever does not know, let him say, 'Allāh knows best!' It is an integral part of knowledge, when one does not know something, to say, 'Allāh knows best!' Allāh ﷻ said to His Prophet ﷺ: ﴿ **Say: No reward do I ask of you for this (Qur'ān), nor am I a pretender** ﴾ (38:86)!" Then Ibn Mas'ūd proceeded to explain that all the latter-day phenomena, including the great smoke, pre-date the Day of Resurrection.[284]

عَنْ مَسْرُوقٍ قَالَ بَيْنَمَا رَجُلٌ يُحَدِّثُ فِي كِنْدَةَ فَقَالَ يَجِيءُ دُخَانٌ يَوْمَ الْقِيَامَةِ
فَيَأْخُذُ بِأَسْمَاعِ الْمُنَافِقِينَ وَأَبْصَارِهِمْ يَأْخُذُ الْمُؤْمِنَ كَهَيْئَةِ الزُّكَامِ فَفَزِعْنَا فَأَتَيْتُ
ابْنَ مَسْعُودٍ وَكَانَ مُتَّكِئًا فَغَضِبَ فَجَلَسَ فَقَالَ مَنْ عَلِمَ فَلْيَقُلْ وَمَنْ لَمْ يَعْلَمْ
فَلْيَقُلِ اللَّهُ أَعْلَمُ فَإِنَّ مِنَ الْعِلْمِ أَنْ يَقُولَ لِمَا لَا يَعْلَمُ لَا أَعْلَمُ فَإِنَّ اللَّهَ قَالَ لِنَبِيِّهِ ﷺ قُلْ مَا

[284] Narrated by al-Bukhārī, Muslim, al-Tirmidhī, and Aḥmad.

أَسْأَلُكُمْ عَلَيْهِ مِنْ أَجْرٍ وَمَا أَنَا مِنَ الْمُتَكَلِّفِينَ وَإِنَّ قُرَيْشًا أَبْطَئُوا عَنِ الْإِسْلَامِ فَدَعَا
عَلَيْهِمُ النَّبِيُّ صَلَّى اللَّهُ عَلَيْهِ وَسَلَّمَ فَقَالَ اللَّهُمَّ أَعِنِّي عَلَيْهِمْ بِسَبْعٍ كَسَبْعِ
يُوسُفَ فَأَخَذَتْهُمْ سَنَةٌ حَتَّى هَلَكُوا فِيهَا وَأَكَلُوا الْمَيْتَةَ وَالْعِظَامَ وَيَرَى الرَّجُلُ
مَا بَيْنَ السَّمَاءِ وَالْأَرْضِ كَهَيْئَةِ الدُّخَانِ فَجَاءَهُ أَبُو سُفْيَانَ فَقَالَ يَا مُحَمَّدُ
جِئْتَ تَأْمُرُنَا بِصِلَةِ الرَّحِمِ وَإِنَّ قَوْمَكَ قَدْ هَلَكُوا فَادْعُ اللَّهَ فَقَرَأَ فَارْتَقِبْ يَوْمَ
تَأْتِي السَّمَاءُ بِدُخَانٍ مُبِينٍ إِلَى قَوْلِهِ عَائِدُونَ أَفَيُكْشَفُ عَنْهُمْ عَذَابُ الْآخِرَةِ
إِذَا جَاءَ ثُمَّ عَادُوا إِلَى كُفْرِهِمْ فَذَلِكَ قَوْلُهُ تَعَالَى يَوْمَ نَبْطِشُ الْبَطْشَةَ الْكُبْرَى
يَوْمَ بَدْرٍ وَلِزَامًا يَوْمَ بَدْرٍ ﴿الٓمٓ غُلِبَتِ الرُّومُ﴾ إِلَى ﴿سَيَغْلِبُونَ﴾ وَالرُّومُ
قَدْ مَضَى ق ت حم

This is precisely why the Prophet ﷺ said: "Let no one speak publicly except a ruler, his authorised agent, or a fraud (*mukhtāl*)."[285] Two other versions in Aḥmad state: "or a self-promoter" (*murā'in*), "an affected person" (*mutakallif*). When news of this reached Ka'b al-Aḥbār, he was never seen speaking in public gatherings again.[286] That is, in *khuṭba* or fatwā.[287]

عَنْ عَوْفِ بْنِ مَالِكٍ الْأَشْجَعِيِّ رَضِيَ اللهُ عَنْهُ قَالَ سَمِعْتُ رَسُولَ اللَّهِ
صَلَّى اللَّهُ عَلَيْهِ وَسَلَّمَ يَقُولُ لَا يَقُصُّ إِلَّا أَمِيرٌ أَوْ مَأْمُورٌ أَوْ مُخْتَالٌ د مي حم وفي
رواية عنده أَوْ مُرَاءٍ وفي رواية أخرى أَوْ مُتَكَلِّفٍ وفي رواية أخرى عنده قَالَ فَبَلَغَ ذَلِكَ
كَعْبًا - كعب الأحبار - فَمَا رُئِيَ يَقُصُّ بَعْدُ يعني في الخطبة أو الفتوى كما أفاد الخطابي في
معالم السنن وغريب الحديث

285 Narrated from 'Awf ibn Mālik by Abū Dāwūd, Ibn Mājah, al-Dārimī, and Aḥmad.
286 Narrated by Aḥmad (29:587 §18050 *ḥasan li-ghayrih*).
287 Cf. al-Khaṭṭābī, *Ma'ālim al-Sunan* (4:188) and *Gharīb al-Ḥadīth* (1:615).

Thus, the Prophet ﷺ warned all Muslim public speakers to question their own motives. When 'Imrān ibn Ḥuṣayn saw a *qāṣṣ* he exclaimed, "We belong to Allāh and to Him do we return! I heard the Messenger of Allāh ﷺ say, 'Recite the Qur'ān and ask Allāh with it before a people appear that will ask people with it!'"[288]

عَنْ الْحَسَنِ الْبَصْرِيِّ قَالَ مَرَّ عِمْرَانُ بْنُ حُصَيْنٍ بِرَجُلٍ يَقُصُّ فَقَالَ عِمْرَانُ إِنَّا لِلَّهِ وَإِنَّا إِلَيْهِ رَاجِعُونَ سَمِعْتُ رَسُولَ اللَّهِ صَلَّى اللَّهُ عَلَيْهِ وَسَلَّمَ يَقُولُ اقْرَءُوا الْقُرْآنَ وَسَلُوا اللَّهَ تَبَارَكَ وَتَعَالَى بِهِ مِنْ قَبْلِ أَنْ يَجِيءَ قَوْمٌ يَسْأَلُونَ النَّاسَ بِهِ ت وحسّنه حم

Al-Ḥārith ibn Mu'āwiya asked 'Umar permission to speak in gatherings to which 'Umar assented reluctantly: "As you like!" Al-Ḥārith said, "I will only decide what you say!" 'Umar said: "I fear for you that you will speak in gatherings and begin to feel superior to them. Then you will continue to speak in public until you imagine yourself as high above them as the Pleiades. Then Allāh will lower you accordingly below their feet the Day of Resurrection!"[289]

عَنِ الْحَارِثِ بْنِ مُعَاوِيَةَ الْكِنْدِيِّ أَنَّهُ رَكِبَ إِلَى عُمَرَ بْنِ الْخَطَّابِ ﷺ يَسْأَلُهُ عَنْ ثَلَاثِ خِلَالٍ إِلى أن قال وَعَنِ الْقَصَصِ فَإِنَّهُمْ أَرَادُونِي عَلَى الْقَصَصِ فَقَالَ مَا شِئْتَ كَأَنَّهُ كَرِهَ أَنْ يَمْنَعَهُ قَالَ إِنَّمَا أَرَدْتُ أَنْ أَنْتَهِيَ إِلَى قَوْلِكَ قَالَ أَخْشَى عَلَيْكَ أَنْ تَقُصَّ فَتَرْتَفِعَ عَلَيْهِمْ فِي نَفْسِكَ ثُمَّ تَقُصَّ فَتَرْتَفِعَ حَتَّى يُخَيَّلَ إِلَيْكَ أَنَّكَ فَوْقَهُمْ بِمَنْزِلَةِ الثُّرَيَّا فَيَضَعَكَ اللَّهُ تَحْتَ أَقْدَامِهِمْ يَوْمَ الْقِيَامَةِ بِقَدْرِ ذَلِكَ حم

288 Narrated by al-Tirmidhī (*ḥasan*) and Aḥmad.

289 Narrated by Aḥmad.

For all his dislike of public admonishers, 'Umar gave permission to Tamīm al-Dārī to stand and address public gatherings. Al-Sā'ib ibn Yazīd said this was unprecedented in the time of the Prophet ﷺ and Abū Bakr, and calls Tamīm the first *qāṣṣ* in Islām.[290] 'Umar also gave unlimited permission to Abū Hurayra to narrate from the Prophet ﷺ at his own discretion.

عَنِ السَّائِبِ بْنِ يَزِيدَ أَنَّهُ لَمْ يَكُنْ يُقَصُّ عَلَى عَهْدِ رَسُولِ اللَّهِ صَلَّى اللَّهُ عَلَيْهِ وَسَلَّمَ وَلَا أَبِي بَكْرٍ وَكَانَ أَوَّلَ مَنْ قَصَّ تَمِيمٌ الدَّارِيُّ اسْتَأْذَنَ عُمَرَ بْنَ الْخَطَّابِ أَنْ يَقُصَّ عَلَى النَّاسِ قَائِمًا فَأَذِنَ لَهُ عُمَرُ حم

The following reports – all in Aḥmad's *Musnad* with good chains – illustrate the behavior 'Umar feared. As the *Tābi'ī* 'Ubayd ibn 'Umayr al-Marwazī was addressing a Madīnan gathering in the presence of Ibn 'Umar, he said that the Prophet ﷺ had said: "The similitude of the hypocrite is as a sheep between two sheepfolds (*rabīḍayn*). When it comes to this one they butt it and when it comes to that one they butt it." Ibn 'Umar intervened and said: "The Prophet ﷺ did not say this. What he said is: 'As a sheep between two flocks (*ghanamayn*).'" The Shaykh was miffed and became angry. Ibn 'Umar said: "Truly! Had I not heard it, I would not have corrected what you said."

عَنْ أَبِي جَعْفَرٍ مُحَمَّدِ بْنِ عَلِيٍّ قَالَ بَيْنَمَا عُبَيْدُ بْنُ عُمَيْرٍ يَقُصُّ وَعِنْدَهُ عَبْدُ اللَّهِ بْنُ عُمَرَ فَقَالَ عُبَيْدُ بْنُ عُمَيْرٍ قَالَ رَسُولُ اللَّهِ صَلَّى اللَّهُ عَلَيْهِ وَسَلَّمَ مَثَلُ الْمُنَافِقِ كَشَاةٍ مِنْ بَيْنِ رَبِيضَيْنِ إِذَا أَتَتْ هَؤُلَاءِ نَطَحَتْهَا وَإِذَا أَتَتْ هَؤُلَاءِ نَطَحَتْهَا فَقَالَ ابْنُ عُمَرَ لَيْسَ كَذَلِكَ قَالَ رَسُولُ اللَّهِ صَلَّى اللَّهُ عَلَيْهِ وَسَلَّمَ إِنَّمَا قَالَ رَسُولُ اللَّهِ صَلَّى اللَّهُ عَلَيْهِ وَسَلَّمَ كَشَاةٍ بَيْنَ غَنَمَيْنِ قَالَ فَاحْتَفَظَ الشَّيْخُ وَغَضِبَ فَلَمَّا رَأَى ذَلِكَ عَبْدُ اللَّهِ قَالَ أَمَا إِنِّي لَوْ لَمْ أَسْمَعْهُ لَمْ أَرُدَّ ذَلِكَ عَلَيْكَ حم

[290] Narrated by Aḥmad.

Another version from Muḥammad al-Bāqir states that ʿUbayd had said "a sheep between two flocks (*ghanamayn*)" and Ibn ʿUmar intervened and said the correct version was "a sheep between two sheepfolds (*rabīḍayn*)." When ʿAbd Allāh ibn Ṣafwān remarked to Ibn ʿUmar that the two were one in meaning, he replied: "Thus did I hear it." A third authentic version adds that he said: "Woe to you! Do not lie about the Messenger of Allāh!"

عَنْ أَبِي جَعْفَرٍ مُحَمَّدٍ الْبَاقِرِ رَضِيَ اللَّهُ عَنْهُ قَالَ كَانَ عَبْدُ اللَّهِ بْنُ عُمَرَ إِذَا سَمِعَ مِنْ نَبِيِّ اللَّهِ صَلَّى اللَّهُ عَلَيْهِ وَسَلَّمَ شَيْئًا أَوْ شَهِدَ مَعَهُ مَشْهَدًا لَمْ يُقَصِّرْ دُونَهُ أَوْ يَعْدُوهُ قَالَ فَبَيْنَمَا هُوَ جَالِسٌ وَعُبَيْدُ بْنُ عُمَيْرٍ يَقُصُّ عَلَى أَهْلِ مَكَّةَ إِذْ قَالَ عُبَيْدُ بْنُ عُمَيْرٍ مَثَلُ الْمُنَافِقِ كَمَثَلِ الشَّاةِ بَيْنَ الْغَنَمَيْنِ إِنْ أَقْبَلَتْ إِلَى هَذِهِ الْغَنَمِ نَطَحَتْهَا وَإِنْ أَقْبَلَتْ إِلَى هَذِهِ نَطَحَتْهَا فَقَالَ عَبْدُ اللَّهِ بْنُ عُمَرَ لَيْسَ هَكَذَا فَغَضِبَ عُبَيْدُ بْنُ عُمَيْرٍ وَفِي الْمَجْلِسِ عَبْدُ اللَّهِ بْنُ صَفْوَانَ فَقَالَ يَا أَبَا عَبْدِ الرَّحْمَنِ كَيْفَ قَالَ رَحِمَكَ اللَّهُ فَقَالَ قَالَ مَثَلُ الْمُنَافِقِ مَثَلُ الشَّاةِ بَيْنَ الرَّبِيضَيْنِ إِنْ أَقْبَلَتْ إِلَى ذَا الرَّبِيضِ نَطَحَتْهَا وَإِنْ أَقْبَلَتْ إِلَى ذَا الرَّبِيضِ نَطَحَتْهَا فَقَالَ لَهُ رَحِمَكَ اللَّهُ هُمَا وَاحِدٌ قَالَ كَذَا سَمِعْتُ حم وفي رواية عنده عَنْ يَعْفُرَ بْنِ رُوذِيٍّ سَمِعْتُ عُبَيْدَ بْنَ عُمَيْرٍ وَهُوَ يَقُصُّ يَقُولُ يَقُولُ رَسُولُ اللَّهِ صَلَّى اللَّهُ عَلَيْهِ وَسَلَّمَ مَثَلُ الْمُنَافِقِ كَمَثَلِ الشَّاةِ الرَّابِضَةِ بَيْنَ الْغَنَمِ فَقَالَ ابْنُ عُمَرَ وَيْلَكُمْ لَا تَكْذِبُوا عَلَى رَسُولِ اللَّهِ صَلَّى اللَّهُ عَلَيْهِ وَسَلَّمَ إِنَّمَا قَالَ رَسُولُ اللَّهِ ﷺ مَثَلُ الْمُنَافِقِ كَمَثَلِ الشَّاةِ الْعَائِرَةِ بَيْنَ الْغَنَمَيْنِ حم

Another *Tābiʿī* story-teller, Abū Tamīma al-Hujaymī al-Baṣrī, confessed to flatly refusing to obey Ibn ʿUmar until the latter invoked the express command of the Prophet ﷺ. Abū Tamīma said: "I would sit and tell stories (*kuntu aquṣṣu*) after the *fajr* prayer [in Madīna] then pray [before sunrise], which Ibn 'Umar forbade me to do. I refused to obey him. This happened three times. Then he forbade me again, saying: 'I prayed behind the Messenger of Allāh ﷺ, and I prayed with Abū Bakr, 'Umar, and 'Uthmān and none of them would pray [after *fajr*] until the sun had risen!'"[291]

عَن أَبِي تَمِيمَةَ الْهُجَيْمِيِّ قَالَ لَمَّا بَعَثْنَا الرَّكْبَ قَالَ أَبُو دَاوُدَ يَعْنِي إِلَى
الْمَدِينَةِ قَالَ كُنْتُ أَقُصُّ بَعْدَ صَلَاةِ الصُّبْحِ فَأَسْجُدُ فَنَهَانِي ابْنُ عُمَرَ
فَلَمْ أَنْتَهِ ثَلَاثَ مِرَارٍ ثُمَّ عَادَ فَقَالَ إِنِّي صَلَّيْتُ خَلْفَ رَسُولِ اللَّهِ صَلَّى
اللَّهُ عَلَيْهِ وَسَلَّمَ وَمَعَ أَبِي بَكْرٍ وَعُمَرَ وَعُثْمَانَ رَضِيَ اللَّهُ عَنْهُمْ فَلَمْ
يَسْجُدُوا حَتَّى تَطْلُعَ الشَّمْسُ د

The twin pre-conditions of moral uprightness and accuracy elucidates the paradox current among ḥadīth scholars whereby "No one lies more than the righteous."[292] This is the reason – and Allāh knows best – that Mālik did not narrate anything from his teacher Ibn Hurmuz although, as al-Qāḍī 'Iyāḍ relates in *Tartīb al-Madārik*, he sat with him every morning for thirteen to sixteen years. In this respect it is important to remember that the early Muslims – including the Companions such as Ibn 'Umar in the report already mentioned – also used the expression "to lie" (*kadhaba*) to mean "to speak inaccurately."

One of the reasons for the "lies of the righteous" is also good faith. The righteous do not doubt the Muslim's attribution of a saying to his Prophet ﷺ, and so they accept it without suspicion. This is an Adamic quality as illustrated by the verse ﴾**And he** [Satan] **swore unto them** [Adam and Eve] **saying: Lo! I am a sincere adviser unto you**﴿ (7:21), whereupon Ādam believed him without suspecting that Satan might lie and perjure himself. It is also a Ṣiddīqī quality. Abū Umāma al-Bāhilī said: "Truly, the most trusting of people are the most truthful

[291] Narrated by Abū Dāwūd.

[292] Cf. Ibn Rajab's *Sharḥ 'Ilal al-Tirmidhī* towards the end, and other books of *muṣṭalaḥ*. See Dr. Nūr al-Dīn 'Itr's *Uṣūl al-Jarḥ wal-Ta'dīl* (p. 108-109).

among them in speech, and the most distrustful of people are the most untruthful among them in speech."[293] Dr. Nūr al-Dīn 'Itr said: "The manner of the righteous who narrate everything indiscriminately stems from purity of heart and good opinion. The Scholars have said about such narrators: 'Lies run off their tongue without their intending it.'"[294] According to this view, there is a fundamental difference between the latter and those who deliberately forge lies or narrate forgeries passing for ḥadīth and who are condemned by the Prophet's ﷺ saying: "Whoever lies about me wilfully, let him take right now his seat in the Fire!"[295]

Hence, the *Salaf* disapproved of ḥadīth narration by unschooled story-tellers (*al-quṣṣāṣ*) and pious Shaykhs (*al-ṣāliḥīn*) who are unaware or oblivious of the strict rule of the Ulema that "suspicion is required in two activities: that of the ḥadīth narrator and that of the qāḍī." Al-Shāfi'ī said: "If Mālik had the slightest doubt about a ḥadīth, he discarded the entire ḥadīth." Yaḥyā ibn Sa'īd al-Qaṭṭān said: "We did not see, concerning the *ṣāliḥīn*, anyone lie more than they do in ḥadīth. That is: lies run off their tongue without their intending it." 'Āṣim said: "Do not sit with the *quṣṣāṣ*."[296]

Aḥmad disapproved of them, yet when he heard one publicly lambasting his persecutor, the Mu'tazilī Ibn Abī Du'ād, Aḥmad said: "How useful they [the *quṣṣāṣ*] are for the general public!"[297]

Similarly, the free hand of the great *Fiqh*-imbued Ṣūfī Shaykhs in story-telling is based upon the priority of motivating hearts and pushing people to repent and change. Their record of success in this respect needs no illustration here. At the same time, the *Salaf* applied the name of *dhikr* not to gatherings of admonition but rather to those of learning which they rightly considered superior since the knowledgeable Believer is seventy levels above the unlearned. Ibn Sīrīn said:

[293] Narrated by Abū al-Ḥasan al-Qazwīnī in his *Amālī* cf. al-Suyūṭī, *al-Jāmi' al-Ṣaghīr* (§2202 *ḍa'īf*), *Kanz* (§6854).

[294] *E.g.* Muslim, introduction to his *Ṣaḥīḥ*.

[295] A mass-narrated (*mutawātir*) ḥadīth from many Companions in al-Bukhārī and Muslim. One version narrated from Ibn 'Abbās by Aḥmad with three chains, al-Tirmidhī (*ḥasan*), and – with a sound chain – Ibn Abī Shayba begins with the words: "Avoid relating my words except what you know for sure."

[296] Both in Abū Zahra, *Ibn Ḥanbal* (p. 216).

[297] Narrated from al-Khallāl by al-Dhahabī in the *Siyar* (9:429).

I entered the mosque and saw Sumayr ibn ʿAbd al-Raḥmān telling stories (*yaquṣṣu*) and Ḥumayd ibn ʿAbd al-Raḥmān teaching in another corner of the mosque. After I sat and began wondering which gathering to join, I dozed off and heard a voice in my sleep, saying, "If you wish, I can show you Gibrāʾīl's place in Ḥumayd's circle."[298]

عَنْ ابْنِ سِيرِينَ قَالَ دَخَلْتُ الْمَسْجِدَ فَإِذَا سُمَيْرُ بْنُ عَبْدِ الرَّحْمَنِ يَقُصُّ وَحُمَيْدُ بْنُ عَبْدِ الرَّحْمَنِ يَذْكُرُ الْعِلْمَ فِي نَاحِيَةِ الْمَسْجِدِ فَمَيَّلْتُ إِلَى أَيِّهِمَا أَجْلِسُ فَنَعَسْتُ فَأَتَانِي آتٍ فَقَالَ مَيَّلْتَ إِلَى أَيِّهِمَا تَجْلِسُ إِنْ شِئْتَ أَرَيْتُكَ مَكَانَ جِبْرَائِيلَ مِنْ حُمَيْدِ بْنِ عَبْدِ الرَّحْمَنِ مي

This is similar to the ḥadīth of the Prophet's ﷺ preference of the circle of knowledge to the circle of *duʿā'*.[299]

ʿAṭā' al-Khurāsānī said, "The gatherings of *dhikr* are the gatherings where the lawful and the prohibited things are taught – how to pray, fast, marry, divorce, sell, buy [...]"[300]

قال أبو هزان قلت لعطاء مَا مَجْلِسُ الذِّكْرِ قال مَجْلِسُ الْحَلَالِ وَالْحَرَامِ وَكَيْفَ تُصَلِّي وَكَيْفَ تَصُومُ وَكَيْفَ تَنْكِحُ وَكَيْفَ تُطَلِّقُ وَتَبِيعُ وَتَشْتَرِي وفي

الباب عن يزيد بن سمرة عن عطاء حل سير صفة الصفوة

[298] Narrated by al-Dārimī.

[299] See n. 621.

[300] Narrated by Abū Nuʿaym in the *Ḥilya* (3:313 and 5:195), al-Dhahabī in the *Siyar* (Risāla ed. 6:142), and Ibn al-Jawzī in *Ṣifat al-Ṣafwa* (4:151). "Perhaps ʿAṭā' intended to inform people that teaching and learning Sharīʿa are also a form of *dhikr*, but in any case it is clear from the Prophet's ﷺ explicit words [...] that 'sessions of *dhikr*' cannot be limited to teaching and learning Sacred Law alone but primarily mean gatherings of Muslims to invoke Allah in *dhikr*." Shaykh Nuḥ Keller, *Ṭarīqa Notes*.

The Scholars devoted books to the subject of the *Quṣṣāṣ* such as al-Khaṭīb's *al-Quṣṣāṣ*, Ibn al-Jawzī's *al-Quṣṣāṣ wal-Mudhakkirīn*, Ibn Taymiyya's *Aḥādīth al-Quṣṣāṣ*, al-'Irāqī's *al-Bā'ith 'alā al-Khalāṣ min Ḥawādīth al-Quṣṣāṣ* ("The Stimulant of Deliverance from the Tales of Story-Tellers"), and al-Suyūṭī's *Taḥdhīr al-Khawāṣṣ min Akādhīb al-Quṣṣāṣ* ("Warning the Elect Against the Lies of Story-tellers").

Ad Sensum (riwāya bil-ma'nā) vs. ad Litteram (bil-lafẓ)

The Ḥanafī ḥadīth Master Murtaḍā al-Zabīdī began his great commentary on the *Iḥyā'* with an explanation that al-Ghazzālī's method of ḥadīth citation by conveying the general meaning without ascertaining the exact wording, had a basis in the practice of the Companions and *Salaf*:

> The verification of the wording of narrations was not an obligation for al-Ghazzālī – Allāh have mercy on him! He would convey the general meaning, conscious of the different significations of the words and their mutual conflict with one another avoiding what would constitute interpolation or arbitrary rendering of one term with another.
>
> A number of the Companions have permitted the conveyance of Prophetic ḥadīths in their meanings (*riwāya bil-ma'nā*) rather than their very wordings (*riwāya bil-alfāẓ*). Among them were 'Alī, Ibn 'Abbās, Anas ibn Mālik, Abū al-Dardā', Wāthila ibn al-Asqa', and Abū Hurayra ﷺ.[301] Also, a greater number of the Successors, among them the Imām of Imāms al-Ḥasan al-Baṣrī, al-Sha'bī, 'Amr ibn Dīnār, Ibrāhīm al-Nakha'ī, Mujāhid, and 'Ikrima. Ibn Sīrīn said: "I would hear a ḥadīth from ten different people, the meaning remaining one

[301] Al-Khaṭīb in *al-Jāmi' li-Akhlāq al-Rāwī* (2:24, 2:26-28) mentions Ibn Mas'ūd, Abū al-Dardā', Anas, 'Ā'isha, 'Amr ibn Dīnār, 'Āmir al-Sha'bī, Ibrāhīm al-Nakha'ī, Ibn Abī Nujayḥ, 'Amr ibn Murra, Ja'far ibn Muḥammad ibn 'Alī, Sufyān ibn 'Uyayna, and Yaḥyā ibn Sa'īd al-Qaṭṭān as allowing the narration of Prophetic ḥadīth other than in its precise original wording. He narrates examples from Ibn Mas'ūd (§1113), Abū al-Dardā' (§1114-1115), and Anas (§1116-1117) to that effect. He also narrates the prohibition of narrating Prophetic ḥadīths other than in their precise original wording from Wakī' (2:24 §11108), Mālik (2:25 §1110-1111). Al-Khaṭīb documents this subject at length in *al-Kifāya* (p. 203-211).

but the wordings differing."[302] Similarly, the Companions' wordings in their narrations from the Prophet ﷺ have differed one from another. Some of them, for example, will narrate a complete version; others will narrate the gist of the meaning; others will narrate an abridged version; others yet replace certain words with their synonyms, deeming that they have considerable leeway as long as they do not contradict the original meaning. None of them intends a lie, and all of them aim for truthfulness and the report of what he has heard: that is why they have leeway. They used to say: "Mendacity is only when one deliberately intends to lie."[303]

'Imrān ibn Muslim [al-Qaṣīr] narrated that a man said to al-Ḥasan [al-Baṣrī]: "O Abū Sa'īd! When you narrate a ḥadīth you put it in better and more eloquent terms than when one of us narrates it." He replied: "There is no harm in that as long as you have fully expressed its meaning."[304] Al-Naḍr ibn Shumayl (d. 208) said: "Hushaym (d. 183) used to make a lot of mistakes in Arabic, so I adorned his narrations for you with a fine garment" – meaning, he arabised it, since al-Naḍr was a grammarian (*naḥwī*).[305] Sufyān [al-Thawrī] used to say: "When you see a man show strictness in the wordings of ḥadīth, know that he is advertising himself." He narrated that a certain man began to question Yaḥyā ibn Sa'īd al-Qaṭṭān (d. 198) about a specific wording inside a ḥadīth. Yaḥyā said to him: "*Yā Fulān*! There is not in the whole world anything more sublime than the Book of Allāh, yet He has permitted that its words be recited in seven different dialects. So do not be so strict!"[306]

[302] Also narrated from Abū al-Aḥwaṣ Muḥammad ibn al-Haytham by al-Khaṭīb in *al-Jāmi' li-Akhlāq al-Rāwī* (2:21 §1099).

[303] See on this chapter, al-Khaṭīb, *Kifāya* (1986 ed. p. 239-247=Madīna ed. p. 204-211).

[304] Narrated by al-Khaṭīb, *Kifāya* (1986 ed. p. 243=Madīna ed. p. 207) and *Jāmi'* (2:22 §1101-1102). Cf. al-Shāfi'ī – without naming al-Ḥasan or al-Zuhrī – in *al-Risāla* (p. 275).

[305] Ismā'īl ibn Umayya said: "We used to correct Nāfi' [Ibn 'Umar's freedman] if he made mistakes of language [in his narrations] but he would refuse and say: 'Nothing but exactly what I heard.'" Cited by al-Dhahabī in the *Siyar* (5:567).

[306] Cf. al-Shāfi'ī, *al-Risāla* (p. 274).

In the ḥadīth Master al-Suyūṭī's commentary on [al-Nawawī's] *al-Taqrīb wal-Taysīr*, in the fourth part of the twenty-sixth heading,[307] the gist of what he said is as follows:

If a narrator is not an expert in the wordings and in what shifts their meanings to something else, there is no permission for him to narrate what he heard in terms of meaning only. There is no disagreement concerning this. He must relate the exact wording he has heard. If he is an expert in the matter, [opinions have differed:] a large group of the experts of ḥadīth, *fiqh*, and *uṣūl* said that it is not permitted for him to narrate in other than the exact same words. This is the position of Ibn Sīrīn, Tha'lab, and Abū Bakr al-Rāzī [al-Jaṣṣāṣ] the Ḥanafī scholar.[308] It is also narrated as Ibn 'Umar's position [as illustrated in the reports of 'Ubayd ibn 'Umayr al-Marwazī quoted above].

At any rate, the vast majority of the *Salaf* and *Khalaf* from the various groups, among them the Four Imāms, permit narration in terms of meaning in all the above cases provided one adduces the meaning.[309] This dispensation is witnessed to by the practice of the Companions and *Salaf*, and shown by their narrating a single report in different wordings. There is a ḥadīth of the Prophet ﷺ relevant to the issue narrated by Ibn Mandah in *Ma'rifat al-Ṣaḥāba* and al-Ṭabarānī in *al-Kabīr* from

[307] Al-Suyūṭī, *Tadrīb al-Rāwī fī Sharḥ Taqrīb al-Nawāwī* (1:532-539).

[308] Cf. al-Khaṭīb in *al-Kifāya* (1986 ed. p. 242=Madīna ed. p. 207) who also names Ibrāhīm ibn Maysara, al-Qāsim ibn Muḥammad, Rajā' ibn Ḥaywa, and Ibn Ṭāwūs.

[309] Al-Suyūṭī, *Tadrīb al-Rāwī* (1:532-533, cf. *Taqrīb* p. 77-78). Al-Nawawī continues in his *Taqrīb* (p. 78=*Tadrīb* 1:538): "This holds true in other than ḥadīth compilations (*muṣannafāt*). The alteration of a ḥadīth compilation is impermissible, even if in the same sense. Also, it is imperative for the one who narrates in terms of meaning to say, at the conclusion of his narration: 'or something near it' – *aw kamā qāl, aw naḥwahu, aw shibhahu* – or other such expressions." Al-Suyūṭī adduces proofs that this was the practice of Ibn Mas'ūd, Abū al-Dardā', and Anas ibn Mālik. Further proofs to this effect are adduced by al-Tirmidhī in his book *al-'Ilal al-Kabīr* and its commentary by Ibn Rajab entitled *Sharḥ 'Ilal al-Tirmidhī* (1:145-152), al-Khaṭīb in *al-Kifāya* (1986 ed. p. 232-247=Madīna ed. p. 198-211), and al-Qāḍī 'Iyāḍ in *al-Ilmā'* (p. 174-178). See also Ibn Ḥajar's discussion and its commentary by al-Qārī in his commentary on Ibn Ḥajar's *Sharḥ al-Nukhba* entitled *Sharḥ Sharḥ Nukhbat al-Fikar fī Muṣṭalaḥāt Ahl al-Athar* ("Commentary on Ibn Ḥajar's Commentary on his own book 'Chosen Thoughts on the Terminology of Ḥadīth Scholars'" p. 497-502).

'Abd Allāh ibn Sulaymān ibn Aktham[310] al-Laythī [='Abd Allāh ibn Sulaym ibn Ukayma][311] who said: "I said: 'Messenger of Allāh! Verily, when I hear a ḥadīth from you I am unable to narrate it again just as I heard it from you.'" That is, he adds or omits something. The Prophet ﷺ replied: "As long as you do not make licit the illicit or make illicit the licit, and as long as you adduce the meaning, there is no harm in that."[312] When

[310] This is a misspelling in al-Zabīdī's text.

[311] As stated by Ibn Ḥajar in *al-Iṣāba* and *Taʿjīl al-Manfaʿa*. Al-Ḥusaynī erred in *al-Ikmāl* (p. 565 §1211) when he identified the Ibn Ukayma cited in Aḥmad as 'Abd Allāh ibn Sulaym ibn Ukayma, as the Ibn Ukayma of the *Sunan*, the *Muwaṭṭa'*, and Aḥmad is named by al-Tirmidhī in the *Sunan* – and others – as 'Umara or 'Ammār ibn Ukayma al-Laythī. Muslim (3:1566), Ibn Ḥibbān (5:158, 13:238-239), Abū Ya'lā (12:348), and Ibn 'Abd al-Barr in *al-Tamhīd* (17:237) further identify him as 'Amr ibn Muslim ibn 'Ammār ibn Ukayma al-Laythī, all agreeing that he is not a Companion, but a Successor who narrated from both Abū Hurayra and Sa'īd ibn al-Musayyab. As for 'Abd Allāh ibn Sulaym(an) ibn Ukayma – al-Ṭabarānī's narrator – he is unknown.

[312] Narrated from 'Abd Allāh ibn Sulaymān ibn Ukayma by al-Ṭabarānī in *al-Kabīr* (7:100 §6491, 117) and Ibn Qāni' (d. 351) in *Muʿjam al-Ṣaḥāba* (3:17), both with a chain containing two unknown narrators – Ya'qūb ibn 'Abd Allāh ibn Sulaym(an) ibn Ukayma and his father 'Abd Allāh ibn Sulaym(an) – as stated by al-Haythamī (1:154), cf. al-Sakhāwī, *Fatḥ al-Mughīth* (3:145). Also narrated by al-Jawraqānī (d. 543) in *al-Abāṭīl* (1:90-97) where he said: "This ḥadīth is null and void (*bāṭil*), and there is confusion (*iḍṭirāb*) in its chain." Still, al-Khaṭīb adduced it through two similar chains in his discussion of the permissibility of narration in terms of meaning in *al-Kifāya* (1986 ed. p. 234 = Madīna ed. p. 198), as well as al-Qārī in *Sharḥ Sharḥ Nukhbat al-Fikar* (p. 498). Also narrated from Salama ibn al-Akwa' by Ibn 'Asākir as stated by Ibn Ḥamza al-Ḥusaynī in *al-Bayān wal-Taʿrīf* (2:77-78). Ibn Ḥajar narrates it in *al-Iṣāba* (3:166 §3436, 6:341 §8532) and says: "Ibn al-Jawzī included it among the forgeries, blaming al-Walīd ibn Salama for it, but it is not as he claimed. For Ibn Mandah narrated it [in *Maʿrifat al-Ṣaḥāba*] through another way from 'Umar ibn Ibrāhīm, from Muḥammad ibn Isḥāq ibn Ukayma, from his father, from his grandfather, in similar terms. However, 'Umar is a contemporary of al-Walīd. Ibn Mandah narrated it through another way from 'Umar ibn Ibrāhīm, saying: 'from Muḥammad ibn Isḥāq ibn 'Abd Allāh ibn Sulaym.' He added 'Abd Allāh in his genealogy. Then he cited it under 'Abd Allāh's entry with this chain. It was also narrated by Abū al-Qāsim ibn Mandah in his book *al-Waṣiyya* through two chains going back to al-Walīd ibn Salama, 'from Isḥāq ibn Ya'qūb ibn 'Abd Allāh ibn Ukayma, from his father, from his grandfather.' There are other discrepancies [...] Abū Mūsā [al-Aṣbahānī] in *al-Dhayl* [*li-Maʿrifat al-Ṣaḥāba* by Ibn Mandah] and Ibn Mardūyah also narrated it in *Kitāb al-ʿIlm*, both through 'Abdān al-Marwazī [...] I believe some reshuffling took place and that the correct chain is: Muḥammad ibn Isḥāq, from 'Abd Allāh ibn Sulaym ibn Ukayma, from his father, from his grandfather." In *Taʿjīl al-Manfaʿa* (p. 531 §1440) Ibn Ḥajar declares Ibn Mandah's

this was mentioned to al-Ḥasan he said: "Were it not for this, we would never narrate anything."[313]

Al-Shāfiʿī[314] adduced as his proof [for the same position] the ḥadīth "The Qurʾān was revealed in seven dialects."[315]

Al-Bayhaqī narrated from Makḥūl that he and Abū al-Azhar went to see Wāthila [or Wāʾila] ibn al-Asqaʿ and said to him: "Narrate to us a ḥadīth of the Prophet ﷺ in which there is no omission, no addition, and nothing forgotten." He replied: "Has any of you ever recited anything from the Qurʾān?" They said: "Yes, but we have not memorised it very well. We sometimes add 'and' or the letter *alif*, or omit something." He said: "If you cannot memorise the Qurʾān which is written down before you without adding and omitting something from it, then how about narrations which we heard from the Prophet ﷺ, some of them only once? Suffice yourself, whenever we narrate them to you, with the general meaning!"[316] He narrated something similar from Jābir ibn ʿAbd

chains "flimsy" (*wāhiya*). Thus he considers the ḥadīth weak, but not forged. Its content is confirmed by two other ḥadīths of the Prophet ﷺ adduced by al-Khaṭīb, the first: "As long as one adduces the meaning, let him narrate it," and the second: "I did not mean to prohibit that [one should not narrate verbatim], but only that whoever falsely claims that I said something which I did not say, and his purpose is to shame me and smear Islām – or: to smear me and shame Islām." Narrated respectively from Ibn Masʿūd and an unnamed Companion by al-Khaṭīb in *al-Kifāya* (1986 ed. p. 234-235 = Madīna ed. p. 198). Abū Hurayra said "The Prophet ﷺ was asked about a man who narrates something he said while interchanging the position of clauses or words, and the Prophet ﷺ replied: 'There is no harm in it as long as he adduces the meaning.'" Narrated by al-Ḥakīm al-Tirmidhī in *Nawādir al-Uṣūl* (p. 389). So the mass-transmitted ḥadīth narrated in unconditional terms from Salama ibn al-Akwaʿ by al-Bukhārī in his *Ṣaḥīḥ* (book of *ʿIlm*): "Whoever says that I said something which I did not say, let him prepare himself for his seat in the Fire" must be understood in terms of those other ḥadīths. This is confirmed by the comments of the Companions and Successors related by al-Zabīdī and the practice of the *Salaf* as demonstrated by al-Ḥakīm al-Tirmidhī (p. 389-390, *Aṣl* §268) as quoted in full by al-Qāsimī in *Qawāʿid al-Taḥdīth* (p. 223-224), and Allāh knows best.

[313] Narrated by al-Khaṭīb: *Jāmiʿ* (2:21-22 §1100), *Kifāya* (Madīna ed. p. 207).

[314] In *al-Risāla* (p. 274).

[315] Narrated from ʿUmar and Ibn ʿAbbās by al-Bukhārī, Muslim, and Aḥmad, and also from Ubayy ibn Kaʿb in the *Sunan*.

[316] Narrated by al-Khaṭīb in *al-Jāmiʿ* (2:20-21 §1098) and *al-Kifāya* (1986 ed. p. 239= Madīna ed. p. 204). Al-Khaṭīb also narrates something identical from Qutayba. In al-

Allāh in *al-Madkhal*: "Ḥudhayfa said to us: 'We are Bedouin Arabs, we may cite a saying without its proper order.'" He also narrated from Shu'ayb ibn al-Ḥajjāb: "I visited al-Ḥasan together with 'Abdān. We said to him: 'Abū Sa'īd! Someone may narrate a ḥadīth in which he adds or from which he omits something.' He said: 'Lying is only when someone deliberately intends this.'"[317] [...] [He narrated something similar from Ibrāhīm al-Nakha'ī,[318] al-Sha'bī,[319] al-Zuhrī,[320] Sufyān,[321] 'Amr ibn Dīnār,[322] and Wakī'.[323]][324]

The Imāms of ḥadīth are unanimous in accepting the "narration in meaning" only on condition that the narrator masters the Arabic language and his narration does not present an aberration or anomaly (*shudhūdh*), among other conditions.[325] Al-Zabīdī's documentation of the majority position that it is permissible to narrate the ḥadīths of the Prophet ﷺ in their meanings rather than their wordings is also the position of Ibn al-Ṣalāḥ in his *Muqaddima*, but the latter avers that the dispensation no longer applies at a time when the ḥadīths are available to all in published books.[326] Shaykh Nūr al-Dīn 'Itr adopts the latter position: "The last word on this subject is to prohibit ḥadīth narration in the sense of meaning only, because the narrations have all been compiled in the manuals of ḥadīth, eliminating the need for such a dispensation."[327]

Ḥakīm al-Tirmidhī's version in *Nawādir al-Uṣūl* (p. 389) Makḥūl asks: "Has any of you stood in prayer at length at night?"

317 Narrated by al-Khaṭīb in *al-Kifāya* (1986 ed. p. 244 = Madīna ed. p. 208).

318 See n. 301.

319 See n. 301.

320 Al-Khaṭīb, *al-Jāmi'* (2:22 §1103).

321 Al-Khaṭīb, *al-Jāmi'* (2:23 §1104-1106).

322 See n. 301.

323 Also Ḥammād ibn Zayd as narrated in al-Khaṭīb, *al-Jāmi'* (2:23-24 §1107). However, the reports indicate that Wakī', like Mālik, forbade *al-riwāya bil-lafẓ* and insisted on the precise original wording, cf. n. 301.

324 Al-Zabīdī, *Itḥāf al-Sādat al-Muttaqīn* (1:48-49).

325 'Itr, *Manhaj al-Naqd* (p. 227-230).

326 Ibn al-Ṣalāḥ, *'Ulūm al-Ḥadīth* (p. 214).

327 Nūr al-Dīn 'Itr, ed, Ibn Ḥajar, *Sharḥ al-Nukhba=Nuzhat al-Naẓar fī Tawḍīḥ Nukhbat al-Fikar* (p. 95 n. 1). Cf. al-Qāsimī's *Qawā'id al-Taḥdīth* (p. 223-225) and Ṭāhir al-Jazā'irī's *Tawjīh al-Naẓar* (p. 298-312).

Mālik's Alleged Criticism of Ibn Isḥāq[328]

A narration which al-Dhahabī said was fabricated by Sulaymān al-Shādhakūnī states that when Mālik was supposedly asked "why he had called Ibn Isḥāq a liar," he said, – supposedly – "because Hishām ibn 'Urwa told me!" When the latter was asked, he said – supposedly: "Because he [Ibn Isḥāq] narrated from my wife Fāṭima bint al-Mundhir, with whom I began to cohabit when she was nine years old, and not one man has seen her until she went back to Allāh Most High!" Al-Dhahabī comments: "And how can Hishām ibn 'Urwa be sure? Perhaps he [Ibn Isḥāq] heard from her in the mosque, or when he was a boy, or he went in to her house and she narrated to him from behind a curtain, even if so, what then? [...]. The man never said he had seen her! Are we to rely solely upon such evidence to declare as a liar one of the learned people of knowledge? This is unacceptable. Further, Muḥammad ibn Sūqa [one of al-Bukhārī and Muslim's narrators] narrated from her[...]. In addition, she was thirteen years older than Hishām and probably was not given to him until she was in her mid-twenties!"[329] In the *Siyar*, al-Dhahabī says: "Ibn Isḥāq is beyond doubt truthful in his narration from Fāṭima bint al-Mundhir[...]. And Hishām is truthful in swearing that Ibn Isḥāq never saw her. So then, he did not see her, nor did the man claim he ever did. He only mentioned that he narrated from her. I myself have heard ḥadīth from many women whom I never saw. Similarly, many of the *Tabi'īn* narrated from 'Ā'isha and never saw her face[...] and she could have written to him also[...]. But Qāḍī Abū Yūsuf told the truth when he said: 'Whoever pursues rare narrations will be known as a liar,' and this is among the greatest faults of Ibn Isḥāq, for he narrates from just anyone, without scruples – Allāh forgive him!" Then he adds: "And it is possible that she was one of Ibn Isḥāq's nursing-aunts, so he could go in and see her, and Hishām never knew of this."

When Ya'qūb ibn Shayba asked Ibn al-Madīnī about Mālik's condemnation of Ibn Isḥāq, he replied: "Mālik neither sat with him nor knew him! What did Ibn Isḥāq narrate in al-Madīna?" Ya'qūb said: "What about Hishām ibn 'Urwa's condemnation?" He replied: "What Hishām said is no proof [...]. Authenticity shows too plainly in his [Ibn

[328] See *Jawāb al-Ḥāfiẓ al-Mundhirī* and Abū Ghudda's marginalia (p. 73-79).

[329] Al-Dhahabī, *Mizān* (3:470-471).

Isḥāq's] narrations." Ibn al-Qayyim avers that Hishām ibn 'Urwa's story amounts to zero evidence in the weakening of Ibn Isḥāq and considers him trustworthy. Al-Bukhārī narrated that Sufyān al-Thawrī was asked why the Scholars of Madīna did not narrate from Ibn Isḥāq. He replied: "I sat with him for seventy-odd years and never heard any of the people of Madīna accuse him of anything." (Ibn Sa'd said that Ibn Isḥāq went out of Madīna early in his career. He died in Baghdād.)

Al-Mundhirī said in his *Jawāb 'an As'ilatin fil-Jarḥ wal-Ta'dīl* that the reason some did not rely upon Ibn Isḥāq's narration despite their considering him truthful was probably because of his alleged Shī'ism or Qadarism. Duḥaym said that Mālik's criticism had nothing to do with ḥadīth but only with the fact that Ibn Isḥāq had been accused of being a Qadarī innovator. Ibn Isḥāq was actually flogged on those grounds one time. Yet Muḥammad ibn 'Abd Allāh ibn Numayr said: "People accused Ibn Isḥāq of *qadar*, but he was the farthest of people from it!"

Some might question that Mālik's only source is Hishām ibn 'Urwa, because he himself reportedly declared Hishām also a liar, as narrated from Muḥammad ibn Fulayḥ by al-Khaṭīb in his *Tārīkh*! That is, in daily conversation, not in ḥadīth, since Mālik narrates from Hishām. Al-Khaṭīb said this report was odd and its chain weak while Mālik's statement about Ibn Isḥāq was widespread.

Al-Dhahabī said that Ibn Isḥāq preceded Mālik in compiling ḥadīth works in Madīna. As for Mālik calling him "one of the *Dajjāls*," this took place when someone told Mālik that Ibn Isḥāq had boasted of being the farrier (*bayṭār*) of Mālik's knowledge, which irked Mālik although the boast disparages neither Mālik nor his knowledge but amounts to saying that Ibn Isḥāq knew more. Al-Ṣan'ānī saw in this enough reason to dismiss Mālik's disparagement of Ibn Isḥāq altogether, as criticism caused by anger is simply not relied upon. There is further reason to believe that Mālik did not hold the opinion reported from him about Ibn Isḥāq. Al-Bukhārī said that Ibrāhīm ibn al-Mundhir said that Ismā'īl ibn Abī Uways was among the staunchest he had seen in following Mālik, yet he possessed all the narrations of Ibn Isḥāq in the *Sīra* and narrated them.[330]

[330] Cf. al-Dhahabī, *Siyar* (Dar al-Fikr ed. 7:34).

As for *Sīra,* Mālik recommended Mūsā ibn 'Uqba while Mālik's student, Imām al-Shāfi'ī, differed and recommended Ibn Isḥāq's. Mālik may have so highly recommended Mūsā only because he wished not to narrate the *Sīra* from Ibn Isḥāq, as diagnosed by al-Dhahabī who said: "Al-Shāfi'ī categorically preferred Ibn Isḥāq for the *Sīra.*" Ibn Isḥāq narrated from Abān ibn 'Uthmān ibn 'Affān (d. 105), a very early *Sīra* author whose folios were lost. Another early *Sīra* authority, 'Āṣim ibn 'Umar ibn Qatāda ibn al-Nu'mān al-Anṣārī (d. 120 or 129), whose *Maghāzī* and *Manāqib al-Ṣaḥāba* are one of Ibn Isḥāq's principal sources, said of his student: "There shall not cease to be knowledge among the people as long as Muḥammad ibn Isḥāq lives." Al-Zuhrī praised him lavishly and even placed him above Mālik, saying: "There shall continue to be vast *'Ilm* in Madīna as long as this one [Ibn Isḥāq] is there." Another time al-Zuhrī said, "in all the Ḥijāz."

Imām Aḥmad said of Ibn Isḥāq: "*Ḥasan* in his *ḥadīth*" while al-Tirmidhī declared his ḥadīth *ṣaḥīḥ* and al-'Ijlī said: "*Thiqa*" (trustworthy) as did Ibn Ma'īn and others. Shu'ba and Sufyān al-Thawrī titled him "*Amīr al-Mu'minīn fil-Ḥadīth,*" the highest possible accreditation in Ḥadīth Mastership given to only thirty scholars in the history of Islām to our time! Ibn 'Adī said he researched Ibn Isḥāq's narrations in depth and could not find a single one which he might categorically declare weak. He probably meant the narrations that come to us only through Ibn Isḥāq, which number 1,000 according to al-Bukhārī. Muslim retained seven of them in his *Ṣaḥīḥ* as secondary corroborations (*mutāba'āt*).

Al-Dhahabī said in *Mīzān al-I'tidāl* that Ibn Isḥāq was one of the notable Imāms and that he was fair (*ḥasan*) and acceptable in his narrations, truthful, "except that he included too many rejected, broken-chained things and falsely attributed poetry in his *Sīra*" and except in what only he narrates, for it contains condemned things and he is not entirely reliable in his memory. In the *Siyar,* chapter on Ibn Isḥāq, he writes: "We do not claim infallibility from rare mistakes for the Imāms of narrator-criticism, nor from uttering harsh words against those with whom they had experienced something that caused enmity and hatred. It is a well-known fact that much of their mutual bickering is futile and to be dismissed."

The *Muwaṭṭa'* is All *Ṣaḥīḥ* Except for Four Narrations

Al-Suyūṭī said: "There is no *mursal* narration in the *Muwaṭṭa'* which does not have one or more strengthening proofs (*'āḍid aw 'awāḍid*)." Ibn 'Abd al-Barr composed a book in which he listed all the narrations of the *Muwaṭṭa'* that are either *mursal, munqaṭi',* or *mu'ḍal,* and he provided complete sound chains for all of them except four:

- "In truth I do not forget, but I am made to forget so that I shall start a Sunna." This is the second ḥadīth in the book of *Sahū* and is one of the "unattributed conveyances" (*balāghāt*) of Mālik for which he was criticised, although Ibn 'Abd al-Barr said in *al-Tamhīd*: "Its meaning is true in the principles (*uṣūl*)."[331]

عَنْ مَالِكٍ أَنَّهُ بَلَغَهُ أَنَّ رَسُولَ اللَّهِ صَلَّى اللَّهُ عَلَيْهِ وَسَلَّمَ قَالَ إِنِّي لأَنْسَى أَوْ أُنَسَّى لِأَسُنَّ طا

- "The Prophet ﷺ was shown the lifespans of people before his time, or whatever Allāh willed of it, and seemed alarmed that the lifespans of his Community were too brief to reach the amount of deeds reached by previous communities who lived long. Whereupon Allāh gave him the Most Precious Night (*laylat al-qadr*), which is better than a thousand months." This is the fifteenth ḥadīth in the book of *I'tikāf*.[332]

عَنْ مَالِكٍ أَنَّهُ سَمِعَ مَنْ يَثِقُ بِهِ مِنْ أَهْلِ الْعِلْمِ يَقُولُ إِنَّ رَسُولَ اللَّهِ صَلَّى اللَّهُ عَلَيْهِ وَسَلَّمَ أُرِيَ أَعْمَارَ النَّاسِ قَبْلَهُ أَوْ مَا شَاءَ اللَّهُ مِنْ ذَلِكَ فَكَأَنَّهُ تَقَاصَرَ أَعْمَارُ أُمَّتِهِ أَنْ لَا يَبْلُغُوا مِنَ الْعَمَلِ مِثْلَ الَّذِي بَلَغَ غَيْرُهُمْ فِي طُولِ الْعُمْرِ فَأَعْطَاهُ اللَّهُ لَيْلَةَ الْقَدْرِ خَيْرٌ مِنْ أَلْفِ شَهْرٍ طا هب وفي فضائل الأوقات

[331] Cf. *Fatḥ* (3:101), al-Zarqānī, *Sharḥ al-Muwaṭṭa'* (1:282, 1:294, and 2:292), and *Tamhīd* (24:375). Al-Khaṭṭābī cites it in his *Iṣlāḥ Ghalaṭ al-Muḥaddithīn* (p. 62).

[332] Also related from Mālik by al-Bayhaqī, *Shu'ab* (3:323), *Faḍā'il al-Awqāt* (p. 208).

- Mu'ādh ibn Jabal said: "The last instruction I received from the Messenger of Allāh ﷺ when I put my foot in the stirrup was: 'Beautify your manners for the people, Mu'ādh ibn Jabal!'" This is the first ḥadīth of the book of *Ḥusn al-Khuluq* and Ibn Sa'd and al-Bayhaqī's chain for it shows that Mālik narrated it from Abū Sa'īd Yaḥyā ibn Sa'īd al-Anṣārī, *munqaṭi'* from Mu'ādh. Ibn 'Abd al-Barr and al-Suyūṭī said that this narration, also, was authentically related from the Prophet ﷺ in meaning but from Abū Dharr (in al-Tirmidhī, al-Dārimī, and Aḥmad).[333]

عَنْ مَالِك أَنَّ مُعَاذَ بْنَ جَبَلٍ قَالَ آخِرُ مَا أَوْصَانِي بِهِ رَسُولُ اللَّهِ صَلَّى اللَّهُ عَلَيْهِ وَسَلَّمَ حِينَ وَضَعْتُ رِجْلِي فِي الْغَرْزِ أَنْ قَالَ أَحْسِنْ خُلُقَكَ لِلنَّاسِ يَا مُعَاذُ بْنَ جَبَلٍ طأ وقد سمعه الإمام عن يحيى بن سعيد أبي سعيد الأنصاري رواه ابن سعد هب وقال الحفاظ معناه صحيح كما جاء عَنْ أَبِي ذَرٍّ قَالَ قَالَ لِي رَسُولُ اللَّهِ ﷺ اتَّقِ اللَّهِ حَيْثُمَا كُنْتَ وَأَتْبِعِ السَّيِّئَةَ الْحَسَنَةَ تَمْحُهَا وَخَالِقِ النَّاسَ بِخُلُقٍ حَسَنٍ ت مي حم قَالَ الترمذي وَفِي الْبَاب عَنْ أَبِي هُرَيْرَةَ وقَالَ حَسَنٌ صَحِيحٌ ثم أسنده عَنْ مُعَاذٍ عَنْ النَّبِيِّ ﷺ نَحْوَهُ وقَالَ قال مَحْمُودٌ يعني ابن غيلان العدوي وَالصَّحِيحُ حَدِيثُ أَبِي ذَرٍّ

- "If clouds appear towards the sea then go northwards, that is the mark of heavyish rain." This is the fifth ḥadīth of the book of *Istisqā'* and is narrated by al-Ṭabarānī and Abū al-Shaykh with a full *marfū'* chain from 'Ā'isha in *al-'Aẓama*, both through al-Wāqidī.[334]

[333] Ibn Sa'd (3:585) and al-Bayhaqī, *Shu'ab* (6:245 §8029). Ibn 'Abd al-Barr, *al-Taqaṣṣī* (p. 249) as cited by 'Itr in his notes on Ibn Ḥajar, *Sharḥ al-Nukhba* (p. 80) cf. *Tamhīd* (24:300).

[334] Narrated from 'Ā'isha by al-Ṭabarānī in *al-Awsaṭ* (7:371) and Abū al-Shaykh in *al-'Aẓama* (4:1248), both with a very weak chain because of al-Wāqidī cf. al-Haythamī (2:217), and *mursal* by al-Shāfi'ī in *al-Umm* with another very weak chain cf. Ibn 'Abd al-Barr, *Tamhīd* (24:377).

عَنْ مَالِكٍ أَنَّهُ بَلَغَهُ أَنَّ رَسُولَ اللَّهِ صَلَّى اللَّهُ عَلَيْهِ وَسَلَّمَ كَانَ يَقُولُ إِذَا أَنْشَأَتْ
بَحْرِيَّةً ثُمَّ تَشَاءَمَتْ فَتِلْكَ عَيْنٌ غُدَيْقَةٌ طاً فهذه الأحاديث الأربعة من بلاغات مالك في الموطأ

التي قيل عنها إنها لا يوجد لها سند مرفوع إلا هذا الأخير رواه اطبراني وأبو الشيخ مسندا عن عائشة

والشافعي مرسلا عن التابعي إسحاق بن عبدالله والطريقان ضعيفان جدا

Among the ḥadīth Masters, al-'Irāqī and his student Ibn Ḥajar agreed with Ibn 'Abd al-Barr – and the near-totality of the authorities – that the above four ḥadīths have no *ṣaḥīḥ* chain. Shaykh Muḥammad al-Shinqīṭī mentioned in his *Dalīl al-Sālik ilā Muwaṭṭa' al-Imām Mālik* (p. 14) that Shaykh Ṣāliḥ al-Fulānī al-'Umarī al-Madanī said: "Ibn al-Ṣalāḥ provided complete chains for the four ḥadīths in question in an independent treatise which I have in my possession, written in his own hand." Shaykh Aḥmad Shākir said: "But al-Shinqīṭī did not mention what these chains were, so the Scholars cannot rule on the question."[335]

The Narrators of the *Muwaṭṭa'* from Mālik

Al-Zarqānī counted as sixty-nine the number of those who narrated the *Muwaṭṭa'* directly from Mālik, geographically spread as follows:

- Seventeen in al-Madīna, among them its learned Scholar and trustworthy ḥadīth Master Abū Muṣ'ab Aḥmad ibn Abī Bakr ibn al-Ḥārith al-Zuhrī (152-242), whose version received a recent edition;
- Two in Makka, among them al-Shāfi'ī;
- Ten in Egypt, among them the scrupulous, Godfearing Imām 'Abd Allāh ibn Wahb ibn Muslim al-Fihrī – the only student of his Mālik ever called a *Faqīh*, he narrated 100,000 ḥadīths[336]; 'Abd Allāh ibn Yūsuf al-Tinnīsī al-Dimashqī, whose narration al-Bukhārī chose; Ibn al-Qāsim al-'Utaqī whose daily *wird* included two *khatmas* of the glorious Qur'ān;[337] and Dhūl-Nūn al-Miṣrī;

[335] But see the epistle published by Shaykh 'Abd Allāh ibn Muḥammad al-Siddīq al-Ghumārī, *Risāla fī Waṣl al-Balāghāt al-Arba'a fil-Muwaṭṭa'*, recently republished by Abū Ghudda father and son within their *Khams Rasā'il fī 'Ulūm al-Ḥadīth* (p. 179-212).

[336] As stated by Ibn 'Abd al-Barr in *al-Intiqā'* (p. 94).

[337] As narrated by al-Dhahabī in the *Siyar* (9:15) chapter on Imām Asad ibn al-Furāt.

- Twenty-seven in Iraq, among them 'Abd al-Raḥmān ibn Mahdī, whose narration Aḥmad ibn Ḥanbal chose, Yaḥyā ibn Yaḥyā al-Tamīmī al-Ḥanẓalī al-Naysābūrī, whose narration Muslim chose, and Abū Ḥanīfa's student Muḥammad ibn al-Ḥasan al-Shaybānī, whose version greatly differs from the others and also contains other than what is narrated from Mālik, so that it became known as *Muwaṭṭa' Muḥammad*;
- Two from al-Qayrawān;
- Two from Tunis;
- Seven from al-Shām;
- Thirteen in al-Andalus, among them the jurist Yaḥyā ibn Yaḥyā al-Laythī "the Sage of Andalus" – thus nicknamed by Mālik himself – whose version is the most commonly used today and is the version meant by the term "*Mālik's Muwaṭṭa'*." He is mainly responsible for the spread of the Mālikī School in al-Andalus and its replacing al-Awzā'ī's.

Major Disciples of Mālik[338]

The principal pillars of the Mālikī School after its Imām are Ibn al-Qāsim, Ashhab, Ibn 'Abd al-Ḥakam, and Suḥnūn, in addition to many more major jurisprudent disciples. Among them:

IBN NĀFI' AL-ṢĀ'IGH

Abū Muḥammad 'Abd Allāh ibn Nāfi' Mawlā Banū Makhzūm ﷺ (d. 186), a peer of Ashhab, he narrated from Mālik and was the Muftī of al-Madīna after him by the Imām's own appointment. He is famed as the principle repository of Mālik's juridical opinion although weak in ḥadīth and illiterate: "I accompanied Mālik for forty years but wrote nothing from him; everything for me was through memorization." He taught Suḥnūn and the major disciples of the Imām. He and Ibn al-Mājishūn are called "the Two Peers" (*al-qarīnān*).

IBN AL-QĀSIM

Abū 'Abd Allāh 'Abd al-Raḥmān ibn al-Qāsim ibn Khālid ibn Junāda al-'Utaqī ﷺ (d. 191) was the Godfearing trustworthy ḥadīth Master and compiler of the *Mudawwana* – a principal source of Mālikī

[338] Cf. Ibn Farḥūn, *al-Dībāj al-Mudhahhab fī Ma'rifati A'yān 'Ulamā' al-Madhhab*.

Fiqh, "of the senior Egyptians and their Jurist, a pious man who narrated little and was precise and meticulous" (al-Dāraquṭnī). He accompanied Mālik for twenty years and narrated from him, al-Layth, Ibn al-Mājishūn, Muslim ibn Khālid al-Zanjī, and others. From him narrated Aṣbagh, Suḥnūn, Yaḥyā ibn Yaḥyā al-Andalusī, Muḥammad ibn 'Abd al-Ḥakam, and others. Mālik compared him to a pouch filled with musk and said: "Ibn al-Qāsim is a *Faqīh*," instructing him to disseminate the Science. Ibn Wahb gave him exclusive precedence in the knowledge of Mālik's Jurisprudence as did Ashhab and Yaḥyā ibn Yaḥyā. Qāḍī 'Abd al-Wahhāb[339] and the entire School therefore give precedence to the narration of the *Mudawwana* or "Record" by Suḥnūn – his close student – from Ibn al-Qāsim from Mālik. Among Ibn al-Qāsim's sayings: "There is no goodness in proximity to those in the government" and "Beware the slavery of the free: having too many brothers." His daily devotion (*wird*) was two *khatma*s of the Qur'ān.

IBN WAHB

Abū Muḥammad 'Abd Allāh ibn Wahb ibn Muslim al-Qurashī *Mawlāhum* ﵁ (125-197) narrated from four hundred authorities and took *fiqh* from Mālik over a period of thirty years, al-Layth, and others. From him narrated Aṣbagh, Suḥnūn, Aḥmad ibn Ṣāliḥ, Ibn 'Abd al-Ḥakam, Abū Muṣ'ab al-Zuhrī, and others including al-Shāfi'ī's companion the Egyptian *Ḥāfiẓ* Ḥarmala ibn Yaḥyā al-Tujībī who narrated from him one hundred thousand ḥadīths.[340] Mālik would write him: "To 'Abd Allāh ibn Wahb the Faqīh of Egypt," "To Abū Muḥammad the Muftī," and he did not write to anyone else in such terms. Aṣbagh said: "Ibn Wahb is the most knowledgeable of the disciples of Mālik in the *Sunan* and transmitted reports, except that he also narrated from the weak authorities. He was nicknamed 'the Encyclopedia' (*dīwān al-'ilm*). There is no one who was not rebuked by Mālik at some point except Ibn Wahb whom he used to venerate and love." He said of him: "Ibn Wahb is a '*Ālim*." He compiled a great *Jāmi'*, a major *Muwaṭṭa'*, a minor one, a thirty-volume compilation of Mālik's responses, and other works in *Fiqh*. When the Caliph wrote to appoint him to the chief Judgeship of Egypt he

339 Ibn Ḥazm reportedly said: "If the Mālikīs had only 'Abd al-Wahhāb [ibn 'Alī ibn Naṣr al-Baghdādī] and al-Bājī, it would suffice them."

340 Cf. al-Dhahabī, *Tadhkirat al-Ḥuffāẓ* (2:486).

took to his house saying: "The Ulema will be raised with the Prophets and the Judges with the Sultans!" He said: "I obliged myself to fast one day each time I committed slander but found this too easy; then I obliged myself to give away a dirham in charity each time I committed slander but found this too difficult; so I gave up slandering." One day, after he heard the ḥadīths on the afflictions of the hereafter read back to him from his *Jāmiʿ* he fainted and was carried to his house where he died shortly after.

ASHHAB

Abū ʿUmar Miskīn ibn ʿAbd al-ʿAzīz ibn Dāwūd al-Qaysī al-ʿĀmirī al-Jaʿdī, nicknamed Ashhab (140-204), was a pious, Godfearing, meticulous and trustworthy narrator and the chief Mālikī Jurisprudent in Egypt after Ibn al-Qāsim. He narrated from Mālik, al-Layth, al-Fuḍayl ibn ʿIyāḍ, and others. From him narrated Suḥnūn, Ibn ʿAbd al-Ḥakam, and others. Ibn ʿAbd al-Barr said that among Mālik's students in Egypt, only al-Ashhab and Ibn al-Ḥakam met al-Shāfiʿī. The latter said: "I saw no-one more knowledgeable in the Law (*afqah*) than Ashhab." They died at an interval of eighteen days, al-Shāfiʿī first.

IBN AL-MĀJISHŪN

Abū Marwān ʿAbd al-Malik ibn ʿAbd al-ʿAzīz ibn ʿAbd Allāh ibn Abī Salama al-Mājishūn (d. 212) the sea of knowledge, a Jurisprudent and Muftī of Madīna, a contemporary of Mālik more than his actual student, he studied mostly under his father, then with Mālik and others. Whenever al-Shāfiʿī rehearsed *Fiqh* with him, people would not understand them because they spoke the desert Arabic of Hudhayl and Kalb. Suḥnūn and Ibn Ḥabīb praised him lavishly and preferred him to most of Mālik's companions. They studied under him as well as Aḥmad ibn al-Muʿadhdhal (d. <240) the teacher of the absolute *Mujtahid* Ismāʿīl al-Qāḍī (200-282). The latter reported that Ibn al-Mājishūn excelled in the interpretation of dreams.

The Master of eloquence and *Fiqh* Ibn al-Muʿadhdhal was asked: "How does your eloquence compare to that of your teacher ʿAbd al-Malik?" He replied: "If the tongue of ʿAbd al-Malik were tied in knots it would still be more vigorous than my tongue at its best."

Mājishūn or "red-faced" was the nickname of ʿAbd al-Malik's granduncle Abū Yūsuf Yaʿqūb ibn Abī Salama, given to him by Sukayna bint al-Ḥusayn ibn ʿAlī ibn Abī Ṭālib ﷺ. Ibn al-Mājishūn's father, ʿAbd al-ʿAzīz, is related to have said, when asked about the Jahmiyya:

> To proceed: I have understood the following from what the Jahmiyya and those that disagreed with them have said concerning the Attribute of the Lord of Might. His magnificence is beyond description or estimation; tongues will sooner dry up than account for His nature (*ṣifa*); minds are at an end before they begin to know His power; His magnificence has turned back the minds to their point of departure, ❴**weakened and made dim**❵ (67:4). For they were ordered only to examine and reflect upon what He created with perfect measure; and "how" is asked only of what used not to be and then was. As for He Who never changes, never ceases to exist, has always existed without beginning, and like unto Whom there is nothing and no one: no one knows "how" He is except He. <How could He be known as He is Who has no beginning, does not die, and does not turn to dust? How can the attribute of anything of His possess a limit (*ḥadd*) or an endpoint (*muntahā*) that anyone might get to know or the extent of which he might define?[341] Yet He is the manifest Truth, truer than Whom there is none, and nothing stands more manifest than He.> The proof that minds are powerless to ascertain His nature (*ṣifa*) is that they are powerless to ascertain the nature of the smallest one of his creatures. You can hardly see it move or disappear due to its smallness while its hearing and sight are completely imperceptible, <not to speak of what goes on in its mind, which is even far more removed and hidden from you than what can be observed of its hearing and sight.>"[342]

---

[341] This negation of limit for Allāh ﷻ is the creed of the *Salaf* (cf. p. 370-374). The anthropomorphists try to annull this axiom with the claim that "He has limits which He knows" although the *Salaf* never said such a thing but the contrary. In other words, Ibn al-Mājishūn says, "How can the attribute of anything of His possess a limit or an endpoint that He or anyone might know or the extent of which He or anyone might define?" Nor does an infinite sequence of numbers have a limit although numbers are created. We do not say that "They have limits which Allāh ﷻ knows" but rather that "Allāh ﷻ knows they have no limit." And Allāh knows best.

[342] Part of a longer report narrated by al-Dhahabī it in the *Siyar* (Risāla ed. 7:311-312). He incorrectly declares it *ṣaḥīḥ* from Ibn Mājishūn in his *ʿUlūw* (Saqqāf ed. p. 402-404=Riyadh ed. p. 141-142=Madīna ed. p. 105-106=*Mukhtaṣar* p. 144-145) without

ASAD IBN AL-FURĀT

Abū 'Abd Allāh Asad ibn al-Furāt ibn Sinān Mawlā Banī Sulaym al-Ḥarrānī al-Maghribī ﷺ (145-213), the Qāḍī, was originally from Naysābūr but born in Diyār Bakr in present-day Turkey. He, al-Buhlūl ibn Rāshid, and Suḥnūn took *fiqh* principally from the great North African teacher Abū al-Ḥasan 'Alī ibn Ziyād al-Tūnisī al-'Absī (d. 183) who narrated from al-Layth and Sufyān al-Thawrī before taking from Mālik the *Muwaṭṭa'* as did Asad later on, then again from Muḥammad ibn al-Ḥasan. He also took *fiqh* from the latter, Abū Yūsuf, and Asad ibn 'Amr al-Bajalī and is therefore numbered among the Ḥanafīs in their biographies although he seems to have settled on the School of Mālik. His record of Ibn al-Qāsim's responses to Ḥanafī questions is the original *Mudawwana*, known as *al-Asadiyya*,[343] but when Suḥnūn reviewed and corrected it with Ibn al-Qāsim, Asad refused to alter it. Ibn al-Qāsim was hurt and supplicated: "Allāh! do not grant blessing to the *Asadiyya*." Suḥnūn's own 36,000-question *Mudawwana*, is by far the one most relied upon in the School. Asad was killed in Sicily, at the head of a Muslim detachment.

IBN 'ABD AL-ḤAKAM

Abū Muḥammad 'Abd Allāh ibn 'Abd al-Ḥakam ibn A'yun ibn al-Layth ﷺ (155-214) the pious, trustworthy Master, was an accomplished Jurisprudent in the *Fiqh* of Mālik, and a friend of al-Shāfi'ī who died in his house. He narrated from Mālik, al-Layth, 'Abd al-Razzāq, the paramount Master al-Qa'nabī – whom Mālik once called "the best of the people of the earth" – and others. including al-Shāfi'ī whose books he copied in their entirety. From him narrated Ibn Ḥabīb, al-Rabī' ibn Sulaymān, and others. He succeeded Ashhab in

---

providing the chain but does provide it in the *Siyar*: through 'Umar ibn Muḥammad ibn 'Īsā al-Jawharī who is known to have narrated at least one forgery (cf. *Mīzān*), from al-Athram, from 'Abd Allāh ibn Ṣāliḥ al-Juhanī who is at best of fair narrations subject to confirmation [cf. al-Dhahabī, *Mīzān* (2:440-445 §4383). Al-Arna'ūṭ said of him in *Taḥrīr al-Taqrīb* (2:222 §3388): "Truthful (*ṣadūq*), his memorization leaves something to be desired, of fair narrations in follow-ups (*al-mutāba'āt*)."] Also partly narrated by al-Lālikā'ī (2:502-503) with a broken chain through Abū Ḥātim al-Rāzī, and cited by Ibn Baṭṭa in the Turkish ms. of his *Ibāna*. Al-Dhahabī omits the bracketed segments from the *'Ulūw* and *Siyar*. Also cited by his teacher Ibn Taymiyya in his *Fatwā Ḥamawiyya* (p. 311-321) = *Majmū' al-Fatāwā* (5:42-46).

[343] Cf. al-Bardha'ī's description of it to Abū Zur'a in his *Su'ālāt* (p. 533-534).

Egypt and authored, among other works, *al-Mukhtaṣar al-Kabīr, al-Awsaṭ,* and *al-Ṣaghīr,* three-sized abridgments of Ashhab's works, the smallest focusing on the *Muwaṭṭa',* containing respectively eighteen thousand questions, four thousand questions, and 1,200 questions.

MUṬARRIF

Abū Muṣ'ab Muṭarrif ibn 'Abd Allāh ibn Muṭarrif al-Yasārī al-Hilālī (d. 220) was the trustworthy Scholar and maternal nephew of Mālik. He accompanied him for seventeen years for *fiqh* and ḥadīth. Aḥmad said that the ḥadīth Masters gave him precedence over the disciples of the Imām.

AṢBAGH

Abū 'Abd Allāh Aṣbagh ibn al-Faraj ibn Sa'īd al-Miṣrī (>150-225), the trustworthy ḥadīth Master, narrated from al-Darāwardī and others. Having entered Madīna after the death of Mālik he took *fiqh* from Ibn al-Qāsim, Ibn Wahb, and Ashhab who recommended him as his successor. He was the scribe and principal disciple of Ibn Wahb , who once said: "If it were not an innovation, Aṣbagh, we would crown you with a diadem the way kings crown their knights." He taught Ibn Waḍḍāḥ al-Qurṭubī and Ibn Ḥabīb among others. Ibn al-Mājishūn said: "Egypt never produced the like of Aṣbagh." Ibn Ma'īn said: "Aṣbagh was among the most informed of all creation in the juridical sayings of Mālik. He knows them question by question, when he said them, and who differed with him." He authored a book on principles, a commentary on the difficult words of the *Muwaṭṭa',* a compilation of his lessons with Ibn al-Qāsim in twenty-two volumes, and other works.

YAḤYĀ IBN YAḤYĀ AL-LAYTHĪ

Abū Muḥammad Yaḥyā ibn Yaḥyā ibn Kathīr al-Laythī al-Andalusī (d. 234), famed for his gravitas and wisdom, narrated from al-Layth and Mālik, from whom he took the *Muwaṭṭa'* the very year of his death, having first heard it from the pious Jurisprudent of al-Andalus, Ziyād ibn 'Abd al-Raḥmān, nicknamed Shabṭūn (d. 193). He then took *fiqh* from Ibn al-Qāsim, also hearing Ibn Wahb and others. He related that when he bade Mālik farewell the latter said: "Practice sincere faithfulnes (*naṣīḥa*) with Allāh, His Book, and the leaders of the Muslims and their common public." Yaḥyā said: "Al-Layth gave me the same counsel."

SUḤNŪN

Abū Sa'īd 'Abd al-Salām ibn Sa'īd ibn Ḥabīb ibn Ḥassān al-Tannūkhī, nicknamed Suḥnūn or Saḥnūn ﷺ (160-240), was a pious, ascetic, scrupulous, perspicuous Imām and Qāḍī of immense learning and photographic memory, "the Master of the Scholars of the Maghrib" (Yūnus ibn 'Abd al-A'lā), "rather, the Master of the Scholars East and West" (Ḥamdīs), "ninety-nine times – by Allāh! – better informed than Asad [ibn al-Furāt]" (Ashhab).

Originally from Ḥimṣ in Syro-Palestine, he is one of the greatest Imāms of the School of Mālik and its principal pillar with Ibn al-Qāsim and Ashhab whom he both surpassed, according to 'Isā ibn Miskīn. He missed meeting Mālik only because of his poverty, taking *fiqh* from all his early and major disciples including Ibn al-Mājishūn, Ibn Nāfi' al-Ṣā'igh, and Muṭarrif. Ibn al-Qāsim said: "No one like Suḥnūn ever came to us from North Africa." Ibn Waḍḍāḥ said: "Suḥnūn could narrate twenty-nine readings. I never met the like of him in *Fiqh* in the East."

Suḥnūn said: "I memorised these books until they became in my breast like the Mother of the Qur'ān." He compiled the *Mudawwana* that became the chief reference work of the people of Qayrawān and the entire School, which spread in massive numbers thanks to his first-rate students. Al-Dhahabī said: "It is said that the number of his students reached nine hundred."[344] Ibn 'Ajlān al-Andalusī said: "None was granted a greater blessing, after the Companions of the Messenger of Allāh ﷺ, than that granted to Suḥnūn in his disciples. They were Imāms in every country." Ibn Ḥārith said: "Suḥnūn was the one with the best disciples; the wisest disciples; and the best informed disciples. These were his own attributes to begin with, and he educated his followers with them – Allāh grant them mercy!" As a judge he wore *dhikr*-beads around his neck and used the back of his hand liberally to discipline transgressors on the spot. He took no income from the Sultan but from the *jizya* of *Ahl al-Kitāb*. He would banish from the marketplace any merchant caught cheating. Among his sayings:

- "When Allāh loves one of His servants, He empowers over him someone to harm him." This is the mark of many of the Friends of Allāh.

[344] Yet he did not include him in *Tadkhirat al-Ḥuffāẓ*!

- To his son: "Greet people, for this plants affection in their hearts. Greet your enemy and be lenient with him. The head of belief in Allāh is leniency with people."
- "Leaving the prohibited is better than all the types of worship of Allāh Most High; and leaving the permitted is better than taking it to spend it in the way of Allāh."
- "Leaving a tenth of a coin of what Allāh forbade is better than seventy thousand pilgrimages followed by seventy thousand *'Umras*, all of them accepted; better than seventy thousand horses completely equipped and armed in the way of Allāh; better than seventy thousand camels slaughtered at the Ka'ba as offerings; and better than emancipating seventy thousand believers from the descendants of the Prophet Ismā'īl ﷺ."
- "Whoever does not put his knowledge into practice, such knowledge will not benefit him but will harm him."
- "Better beg for food rather than earn it through *'ilm*!"
- To Ibn al-Qaṣṣār on his death-bed: "Do you not firmly believe in the Messengers, Resurrection, Judgment, Paradise and Hell, and that the best of this *Umma* is Abū Bakr, then 'Umar, and that the Qur'ān is the uncreated Speech of Allāh, and that Allāh will be seen on the Day of Resurrection, and that He ﴾**established Himself on the Throne**﴿ (20:5, 40:7), and that one must not take up arms against the leaders of the Muslims even if they transgress? Then die in peace."
- To those who blamed him for assuming judgeship after teaching for so long: "I have been giving judgments for forty years! Is giving fatwā anything other than giving judgment? (*hal al-futyā illā al-qaḍā'?*)."
- "Those who hasten most in responding with fatwas are those with the least knowledge." "I never saw anyone sell his hereafter for someone else's *dunyā* more than muftīs." "I memorise questions that comprise eighty different responses from eighty different authorities; how can I be quick in giving a response?" "Correct swift response is a worse *fitna* than the *fitna* of wealth."[345]

[345] *I.e.* because one becomes proud of oneself and/or will err. The last five paragraphs are from al-Dhahabī's *Siyar* (10:70-74 §1980).

The "Practice of Madīna"

Imām Mālik is the connection of the Community to the knowledge of the Sunna as it was preserved by the authorities of the Prophet's ﷺ city, al-Madīna al-Munawwara. Like the rest of the Four Imāms he advocated imitation of the Companions, but he focussed on those of Madīna because he considered them the closest of all Muslims in accurately representing the practice of the Prophet ﷺ. This reference-point of Mālik's jurisprudence is called "the practice of Madīna" (*'amal al-Madīna*) and is observed time and again in his phrase: "This is what I have found (or seen) the people of knowledge practicing." Al-Darāwardī said: "When Mālik says: 'This is what I have observed the people of our country agree upon and this is what is agreed upon among us' he means [principally] Rabī'a ibn Abī 'Abd al-Raḥmān and ['Abd Allāh ibn Yazīd] Ibn Hurmuz." [346] "It is said that Mālik took the bulk of the *Muwaṭṭa'* from Rabī'a."[347]

Shaykh Ḥamza Yūsuf Hanson has explained the concept of the Practice of Madīna thus:

> Madīna is the city in which the Islamic legal system and the Islamic social order were fully implemented. For that reason, Mālik is an inheritor of a social expression of the totality of the Islamic teaching. Thus the *Muwaṭṭa'* records what he would consider a city in Submission. For that reason he would say: "If I find an isolated Ḥadīth, not *mutawātir*, with one or two chains from the *Ṣaḥāba*, and I find 1,000 of the people of knowledge from the *Tābi'īn* in Madīna[348] doing something else, their actions override the solitary transmission of that Ḥadīth." *I.e.*, the fact that they are not

[346] Narrated by Ibn 'Abd al-Barr in *Jāmi' Bayān al-'Ilm* (2:1082 §2108).

[347] Ibn Taymiyya, *The Madīnan Way* (p. 18).

[348] Imām Mālik's words were, "I prefer a thousand [conveying] from a thousand to one [conveying] from one." 'Iyāḍ, *Tartīb al-Madārik* (1:66). There is no mention of any "1,000 of the people of knowledge from the *Tābi'īn*." Al-Nasā'ī in his *Tasmiyat Fuqahā' al-Amṣār* names exactly seventeen *Tābi'īn* jurists in Madīna and there is hardly a sound ḥadīth contradicted by the unanimous practice of the latter, much less one hundred or one thousand. Otherwise, the practice of Madīna in the time of Mālik would have been obligatory for the entire *Umma*, which was never the case. The totality of the people of knowledge, both Companions and Successors, worldwide up to the last *Tābi'ī* alive (Khalaf ibn Khalīfa) – including the narrator-Companions – recorded in al-Dhahabī's *Siyar A'lām al-Nubalā'* do not reach 1,300.

following that Ḥadīth and that they were people who lived in the presence of the *Ṣaḥāba* – and that practice would have been done in the presence of the *Ṣaḥāba*, among whom were men like Ibn 'Umar and 'Umar ibn al-Khaṭṭāb and women like 'Ā'isha ﷺ – and that these people knew better what the final Islamic decision was on the matter. Imām Mālik for that reason would consider the action of "the people of Madīna" – but when he says that, he really does not mean everybody, he means the people of knowledge in the city, and the city was filled with people of knowledge. Imām Mālik felt that *the action was a Ḥadīth*, only it had achieved the status of *mutawātir* because of its agreement in the city of Madīna – even if he did not have an actual verbal transmission of that matter. For example, there is a sound Ḥadīth that the Prophet ﷺ told people not to fast on [Jumu'a]. But in the *Muwaṭṭa'*, Imām Mālik knew that Ḥadīth and said: "I found the people of knowledge in this city fasting." They considered it to be a virtuous day to fast. His point was that they were doing that action in the presence of the *Ṣaḥāba*, and none of the *Ṣaḥāba* said you cannot fast on [Jumu'a]. Therefore, Imām Mālik is saying that the fact that they transmitted this as a virtuous day to fast, and it was not rejected because of that Ḥadīth, he considered isolated transmissions of the Ḥadīth to be weaker than the transmission of *'amal*, "action."[349]

THE SEVEN JURISTS OF MADĪNA

Imām Abū Manṣūr al-Baghdādī relates in *Naqd Abī 'Abd Allāh al-Jurjānī* that Mālik said that when the Seven Jurists of Madīna concur on a ruling, they constitute a Consensus in Islām which becomes binding upon all and forbidden to contravene.[350] These seven are: Sa'īd ibn al-Musayyab, al-Qāsim ibn Muḥammad ibn Abī Bakr, 'Urwa ibn al-Zubayr, Khārija ibn Zayd, Abū Salama ibn 'Abd al-Raḥmān, 'Ubayd Allāh ibn 'Utba, and Sulaymān ibn Yasār. Ibn al-Mubārak names Sālim ibn 'Abd Allāh ibn 'Umar instead of Abū Salama while Abū al-Zinād mentions Abū Bakr ibn 'Abd al-Raḥmān ibn al-Ḥārith instead of either. Some name Muḥammad ibn 'Amr ibn Ḥazm.[351]

349 Adapted from a 1998 interview cf. http://www.witness-pioneer.org

350 In Ibn al-Subkī, *Ṭabaqāt al-Shāfi'iyya al-Wusṭā*, as cited in the 1992 ed. of his *Ṭabaqāt al-Shāfi'iyya al-Kubrā* (5:147).

351 Cf. al-Nawawī, *al-Taqrīb* (p. 98).

The "Letter on the *'Amal* of the People of Madīna"

Among the authentically related works of Imām Mālik is a brief letter to Imām al-Layth ibn Sa'd ﷺ on the *'amal* of Madīna in which Mālik says:

> Allāh ﷻ said in his Book, ﴾**And the first to lead the way, of the Emigrants and the Helpers, and those who followed them in goodness: Allāh is well-pleased with them and they are well pleased with Him, and He has made ready for them Gardens underneath which rivers flow, wherein they will abide for ever. That is the supreme triumph**﴿ (9:100). And He said: ﴾**Therefore give good tidings (O Muḥammad) to my bondmen Who hear advice and follow the best thereof. Such are those whom Allāh guides, and such are men of understanding**﴿ (39:17-18).
>
> People are all dependent on the practice of Madīna. Emigration took place there. The Qur'ān was revealed there. There, the licit was declared licit and the illicit illicit. The Messenger of Allāh ﷺ was physically present among them. They witnessed the revelation and the descent of the Qur'ān. He commanded them and they obeyed him. He instituted the Sunna for them and they followed him until Allāh Most High took him back and chose for him His presence ﷺ!
>
> Then, after him, those that followed him most closely in his *Umma* rose up and took leadership after him. Whatever took place among them of which they knew [the applicable ruling] they applied it. Whatever they did not know about, they enquired about it; then they followed what they considered the strongest path according to their striving and the recentness of their bond. If someone contravened another, or brought up a stronger and more deserving course of action, the former was abandoned in favour of the latter. Then came the Successors after the Companions. They trod that path and followed those *Sunan*.
>
> Therefore, since the matter is so evident in al-Madīna, I do not deem it fit for anyone to do otherwise, because of that inheritance the Madīnans have received and which it is not allowed for anyone else to claim. If the people of other regions said: "This is the practice which is in our countries, and this is the practice

which our earlier generations have received and applied," they would not be on a parity of trust. They could not rightfully claim this as the people of Madīna can.[352]

Al-Layth replied with a brilliant letter on *ikhtilāf* in which he reminded Mālik that the Companions had differed among themselves, then the *Tābi'īn* with the Companions and among themselves, and so forth until Ibn Shihāb and Rabī'a ibn 'Abd al-Raḥmān (Rabī'at al-Ra'ī) in Madīna, who may give divergent answers to the same question and with whom many of the Madīnans themselves differed, including Mālik. Al-Layth then listed many of the great Companions praised by the Prophet ﷺ and trusted by him and by the Rightly-Guided Caliphs who had emigrated from Madīna: **in Syro-Palestine**, 'Ubayda ibn al-Jarrāḥ, Khālid ibn al-Walīd, Yazīd ibn Abī Sufyān, 'Amr ibn al-'Āṣ, Mu'ādh ibn Jabal, Shuraḥbīl ibn Ḥasana, Abū al-Dardā', Bilāl ibn Rabāḥ; **in Egypt**, Abū Dharr, al-Zubayr ibn al-'Awwām, Sa'd ibn Abī Waqqāṣ;[353] **in Ḥimṣ** alone, seventy veterans of Badr; **in Iraq**, Ibn Mas'ūd, Ḥudhayfa ibn al-Yamān, 'Imrān ibn al-Ḥuṣayn, and 'Alī ibn Abī Ṭālib. Al-Layth then gave several examples in which the fatwa of the non-Madīnans showed more conformity to the first generations than the practice of Madīna. Among those examples are the non-joining of prayers in case of rain, unlike the fatwa of Madīna; the non-receiving of testimony with less than two male witnesses or one male and two women, unlike the fatwa of Madīna which allowed one male witness; the disallowing of early payment of the full dowry, unlike the fatwa of Madīna which allowed it even before death or divorce; the strict performance of *khuṭba* before the prayer for rain (*istisqā'*), unlike the fatwa of Madīna which put the prayer first, followed by the *khuṭba*.[354]

Al-Layth's reply evidently influenced Mālik in his defense of *madhhab* differences (see below).

[352] *Risālat Mālik ilāl-Layth fī Faḍli 'Ilmi Ahl al-Madīnati wa-Tarjīḥihi 'alā 'Ilmi Ghayrihim* in *Namādhij min Rasā'il al-A'immat al-Salaf wa-Adabihim al-'Ilmī* (p. 29-32), ed. 'Abd al-Fattāḥ Abū Ghudda (Aleppo: Maktab al-Maṭbū'āt al-Islāmiyya, 1996).

[353] See al-Suyūṭī, *Durr al-Saḥāba fīman Dakhala Miṣr min al-Ṣaḥāba* ("Those of the Companions that Entered Egypt"), documenting 350 names, seven of them women.

[354] *Risālat al-Layth ilā Mālik ibn Anas* in *Namādhij min Rasā'il al-A'immat al-Salaf* (p. 33-41). See the 500-page study by 'Abd al-Salām 'Allūsh, *Taqrīb al-Madārik bi-Sharḥ Risālatay al-Layth ibn Sa'd wa-Mālik* (Beirut: al-Maktab al-Islāmī, 1995).

The Spurious "Letter to al-Rashīd"

Al-Dhahabī's opinion is that the letter to al-Rashīd attributed to Mālik is a forgery due to the unheard-of ḥadīths found in it.

Sadl of the Hands in *Ṣalāt*

The fatwā of Imām Mālik and the "current" (*mashhūr*) position of the later Mālikī School concerning the position of the hands during the obligatory prayer is that they hang loose by the sides (*sadl*). This is related from Mālik by Ibn al-Qāsim in the *Mudawwana.* A divergent Mālikī fatwā deems it Sunna that the hands be grasped (*qabḍ*), right hand on top of left hand, or left wrist, or left forearm. This is related from Mālik from Muṭarrif and Ibn al-Mājishūn in the *Wāḍiḥa* and is the position of al-Lakhmī, Ibn 'Abd al-Barr, Ibn al-'Arabī, Ibn Rushd in the *Muqaddimāt,* 'Iyāḍ who considers it the *Jumhūr* position in his *Ikmāl,* and others, in line with the totality of the *Madhāhib* including the three Schools, Sufyān, Isḥāq ibn Rāhūyah, Abū Thawr, Dāwūd ibn 'Alī, and al-Ṭabarī. A third fatwā of Imām Mālik – from the *qarīnayn* (Ibn Nāfi' and Ibn al-Mājishūn) – stipulates neutrality (*ibāḥa*) between the two cases.[355] All but the Shāfi'īs (and Aḥmad according to one narration) prefer the male worshipper's hands to be on or below the navel in *qabḍ.*

Sadl is an example of the pre-eminence of Madinan practice over non-mass-transmitted Prophetic and Companion-reports and is nowadays a symbol of Sunnī *Madhhabism* over the free-thinking interpretations of the texts that pass, among some, for following the *Salaf.*

Mālik's Standing as an Imām of the Sunna

Imām Mālik was keenly aware of his mission as both the transmitter and the elucidator of the Sunna. This is characteristic of his students' praise of him, beginning with al-Shāfi'ī's famous sayings: "No one constitutes as great a favour to me in the Religion of Allāh as Mālik"; "When the Scholars of knowledge are mentioned, Mālik is the guiding star"; and "Mālik and Ibn 'Uyayna are the peers [in ḥadīth transmission], and were it not for Mālik and Ibn 'Uyayna the knowledge of the Ḥijāz would have disappeared." 'Abd Allāh ibn Wahb said

[355] Cf. http://www. cincimasjid.com/articles/lsh_sadl-yadain.htm by Lumumba Shakūr; and Muḥammad Riyāḍ, *Uṣūl al-Fatwā wal-Qaḍā' fil-Madhhab al-Mālikī* (p. 436).

incessantly: "Every memoriser of ḥadīth that does not have an Imām in *fiqh* is misguided (*ḍāll*), and if Allāh had not rescued us with Mālik and al-Layth (ibn Sa'd), I would have been misguided."[356]

Abū Muṣ'ab recounts the following story:

> I went in to see Mālik ibn Anas. He said to me: "Look under my place of prayer or prayer-mat and see what is there." I looked and found a certain writing. He said: "Read it." It contained the account of a dream which one of his brothers had seen and which concerned him. Mālik recited it [from memory]: "I saw the Prophet ﷺ in my sleep. He was in his mosque and the people were gathered around him, and he said: 'I have hidden for you under my pulpit (*minbar*) something good – or: knowledge – and I have ordered Mālik to distribute it to the people.'" Then Mālik wept, so I got up and left.[357]

His Trial at the Hands of al-Manṣūr

The caliph Abū Ja'far al-Manṣūr – although himself reputed as a jurist and *muḥaddith* – had forbidden Mālik to narrate the ḥadīth: "The divorce of the coerced does not take effect" (*laysa 'alā mustakrahin / li mukrahin ṭalāq*)[358] due to its political application to the coerced pledge (*bay'a*) to the caliph then in effect. A spy then came to Mālik and asked him about divorce, whereupon Mālik narrated the ḥadīth

[356] Ibn Abī Zayd, *al-Jāmi' fil-Sunan* (p. 118-119)and Ibn 'Abd al-Barr, *al-Intiqā'* (p. 60-61). See Shaykh 'Abd al-Fattāḥ Abū Ghudda's comments on this statement in his notes on al-Lacknawī's *al-Raf' wal-Takmīl* (2nd ed. p. 368-369, 3rd ed. p. 90-91).

[357] Ibn al-Jawzī, *Ṣifat al-Ṣafwa* (1/2:120), chapter titled "Layer 6 of the People of Madīna." The account is also in Abū Nu'aym's *Ḥilya*, 'Iyāḍ's *Tartīb*, al-Dhahabī's *Siyar*, and al-Harawī al-Anṣārī's *Dhamm al-Kalām* (4:132).

[358] Narrated *mawqūf* from Ibn 'Abbās by Ibn Abī Shayba (1:238b, 5:48), 'Abd al-Razzāq in his (6:407), al-Bayhaqī's *Sunan* (7:357), al-Bukhārī in his *Ṣaḥīḥ* without a chain, and others. Al-Manṣūr ruled 136-158. He is the one that slew the descendents of the Prophet ﷺ, Muḥammad and Ibrāhīm, the sons of 'Abd Allāh ibn Ḥasan ibn al-Ḥasan ibn 'Alī ibn Abī Ṭālib in the year 145 together with a large number of the People of the Prophet's ﷺ House. Al-Suyūṭī says he was the first to introduce dissension between the House of 'Abbās and the House of 'Alī who had been as one previously. He also harmed or imprisoned a number of major scholars such as 'Abd al-Ḥamīd ibn Ja'far, Ibn 'Ajlān, and Abū Ḥanīfa whom he whipped for refusing a judgeship. The year he jailed Sufyān al-Thawrī and 'Abbād ibn Kathīr he died. Al-Suyūṭī, *Tārīkh al-Khulafā'* (p. 279-280).

in front of everyone. Ja'far ibn Sulaymān (d. 175), the governor of Madīna and cousin of al-Manṣūr, had Mālik seized, lashed, and racked until his shoulder was dislocated and he passed out. When he came to, he said: "He [al-Manṣūr] is absolved of my lashing." When asked why he had absolved him, Mālik replied: "I feared to meet the Prophet ﷺ after being the cause for the perdition of one of his relatives."[359]

Ibrāhīm ibn Ḥammād said he saw Mālik being helped up and walking away, carrying one of his arms with the other hand. Then they shaved his face and he was mounted on a camel and paraded. He was ordered to deprecate himself aloud, whereupon he said: "Whoever knows me, knows me; whoever does not know me, my name is Mālik ibn Anas, and I say: The divorce of the coerced is null and void!" When news of this reached Ja'far, he said: "Let him go." After this episode Mālik's stature reached the skies.

His Self-Imposed Seclusion

Abū Muṣ'ab said: "Mālik did not pray in congregation for twenty-five years. He was asked: 'What is preventing you?' He said: 'Lest I see something reprehensible and be obliged to change it.'"[360] Another narration from Abū Muṣ'ab states: "After Mālik left the [Prophet's] Mosque he used to pray in his house with a congregation that followed him, and he prayed the *Jumu'a* prayer alone in his house."[361] Ibn Sa'd narrates from al-Wāqidī: "Mālik used to come to the Mosque and pray the prayers and the *Jumu'a*, as well as the funeral prayers. He used to visit the sick and sit in the Mosque where his companions would come and see him. Then he quit sitting there and instead would pray and leave, and he quit attending the funeral prayers. Then he quit everything, neither attending the prayers nor the *Jumu'a* in the mosque. Nor would he visit anyone who was sick or other than that. The people bore with it, for they were extremely fond of him and respected him extremely. This lasted until he died. Asked about it, he would say: 'Not everyone can mention his excuse.'"[362]

359 Al-Manṣūr was the great-grandson of Ibn 'Abbās, the Prophet's ﷺ cousin.
360 Al-Dhahabī, *Siyar* (7:395).
361 Al-Dhahabī, *Siyar* (7:424).
362 Ibn Sa'd (5:468-469).

His Manners and Ethics

Imām Mālik held the ḥadīths of the Prophet ﷺ in such reverence that he never narrated anything nor gave a *fatwā* unless in a state of ritual purity. Ismāʿīl ibn Abī Uways said: "I asked my uncle – Mālik – about something. He bade me sit, made ablution, sat on the couch, and said: *lā ḥawla wa-lā quwwata illā billāh*. He did not give a *fatwā* without saying it first." Al-Haytham said: "I heard Mālik being asked forty eight questions, to thirty-two of which he replied: 'I do not know.'" Abū Muṣʿab reported that Mālik said: "I did not begin to give *fatwās* until seventy scholars first witnessed to my competence to do it."

Mālik's ethics, together with the states of awe and emotion which were observed on him by his entourage, were no doubt partly inherited from great Shaykhs of his such as Jaʿfar al-Ṣādiq, Ibn Hurmuz, and Ibn Shihāb al-Zuhrī. He would visit his teacher Ibn Hurmuz (d. 148) every day from morning to night for a period of about eight years and recounts: "I would come to Ibn Hurmuz, whereupon he would order the servant to close the door and let down the curtain, then he would start speaking of the beginning of this *Umma*, and tears would stream down his beard."

The Mālikī Shaykh Ibn Qunfudh al-Qusanṭīnī (d. 810) wrote:

> It was the practice of the Pious Predecessors and the Imāms of the past that whenever the Prophet ﷺ was mentioned in their presence they were overwhelmed by reverence, humbleness, stillness, and dignity. Jaʿfar ibn Muḥammad ibn ʿAlī ibn al-Ḥusayn ibn ʿAlī ibn Abī Ṭālib ؓ would turn pale whenever he heard the Prophet ﷺ mentioned. Imām Mālik ؓ would not mention a ḥadīth except in a state of ritual purity. ʿAbd al-Raḥmān ibn al-Qāsim ibn Muḥammad ibn Abī Bakr al-Ṣiddīq would turn red and stammer whenever he heard the Prophet ﷺ mentioned. As for ʿĀmir ibn ʿAbd Allāh ibn al-Zubayr ibn al-ʿAwwām al-Asadī, he would weep until his eyes had no tears left in them. When any ḥadīths were mentioned in their presence they would lower their voices. Mālik said: "The Prophet's ﷺ sanctity (*ḥurma*) is in death as his sanctity in life."[363]

---

[363] Abū al-ʿAbbās Aḥmad ibn al-Khaṭīb, known as Ibn Qunfudh al-Qusanṭīnī al-Mālikī, *Wasīlat al-Islām bil-Nabī ʿalayhi al-Ṣalātu wal-Salām* (p. 145-146). Al-Dhahabī cites a report in his chapter on al-Awzāʿī in the *Siyar* (7:94) whereby the latter was like a blind man due to his humility (*khushūʿ*).

His Gravitas *(Hayba)*

Qutayba said: "When we went to see Mālik, he would come out to us adorned, wearing *kuḥl* on his eyes, perfumed, wearing his best clothes, sit at the head of the circle, call for palm-leaf fans, and give each one of us a fan." Al-Wāqidī said: "Mālik's circle was a circle of dignity and courtesy. He was a man of majestic countenance and nobility. There was no part of self-display, vain talk, or loud speech in his circle. His reader would read for all, and no one looked into his own book, nor asked questions, out of awe before Mālik and out of respect for him."

His Preference for *'Arḍ* in Ḥadīth Transmission

It is known that Mālik's way in the transmission of ḥadīth, like Ibn al-Musayyab, 'Urwa, al-Qāsim, Sālim, Nāfi', al-Zuhrī, and others, was *'arḍ* ("reading by the student") and not *samā'* ("audition from the Shaykh"). In both cases the student states, by convention, "So-and-so narrated to us" (*ḥaddathanā fulān*), although a small minority of ḥadīth Scholars used *akhbaranā* for *'arḍ* and reserved *ḥaddathanā* for *samā'*.

When the Caliph al-Mahdī sent his sons Hārūn and Mūsā to learn from Mālik, the latter would not read to them but told them: "The people of Madīna read before the Scholar just like children read to the teacher, and if they make a mistake, he corrects them!" Similarly when Hārūn al-Rashīd with his own two sons requested Mālik to read for them, he replied: "I stopped reading for anybody a long time ago." When Hārūn requested the people to leave so that he could read freely before Mālik, the latter also refused and said: "If the common people are forbidden to attend because of the elite, the latter will not profit!" When Hārūn attended Mālik's gathering together with the people, sitting on a high chair, Mālik asked him to come down in an indirect way, whereupon Hārūn came down and sat on the ground in front of Mālik.

His Staunch Defense of *Madhhab* Differences

Even in Mālik's time there were those who forwarded the idea of a unified *madhhab* and the ostensive removal of all differences between the Sunni Schools of Law. Three successive Caliphs tried to impose the *Muwaṭṭa'* and Mālik's School upon the entire Islamic world of their time, but Imām Mālik refused to allow it every time this was suggested to him. His arguments against the idea of unifying the *Madhāhib* provide fundamental lessons on the mercy of differences among the Community of Muslims.

Abū Ja'far al-Manṣūr said to Mālik: "I want to unify this knowledge. I shall write to the leaders of the armies and to the rulers so that they make it law, and whoever contravenes it shall be put to death." Mālik replied:

> Commander of the Believers, there is another way. Truly, the Prophet ﷺ was present in this Community, he used to send out troops or set forth in person, and he did not conquer many lands until Allāh ﷻ took back his soul. Then Abū Bakr ؓ arose and he also did not conquer many lands. Then 'Umar ؓ arose after the two of them and many lands were conquered at his hands. As a result, he faced the great necessity of sending out the Companions of Muḥammad ﷺ as teachers and people did not cease to take from them, notable scholars from notable scholars until our time. If you now go and change them from what they know to what they do not know they shall deem it disbelief (*kufr*). Rather, confirm the people of each land with regard to whatever knowledge is there, and take this knowledge to yourself.

Al-Manṣūr said: "How far you went! Just compile this knowledge for al-Mahdī!"[364]

In another narration al-Manṣūr said to Mālik after hearing his answers to certain questions he put to him: "I have resolved to give the order that your writings be copied and disseminated to every Muslim region on earth, so that they be put in practice exclusively of any other rulings. They will leave aside innovations and keep only this knowledge. For I consider that the source of knowledge is the narrative tradition of Madīna and the knowledge of its scholars." Mālik replied: "Commander of the Believers, do not! For people have already heard different positions, heard ḥadīths, and related narra-

[364] Narrated from 'Utba ibn Ḥammād al-Qāri' al-Dimashqī by Ibn Abī Ḥātim in his introduction to *al-Jarḥ wal-Ta'dīl* (p. 29). Al-Mahdī was al-Manṣūr's successor and ruled from 158 unil his death in 169. Mūsā ibn al-Mahdī, Abū Muḥammad al-Hādī ruled 169-170; al-Rashīd Hārūn Abū Ja'far ibn al-Mahdī ruled 170-193.

tions. Every group have taken whatever came to them and put it into practice, conforming to it while other people differed. To take them away from what they have been professing will cause a disaster. Therefore, leave people with whatever school they follow and whatever the people of each country chose for themselves." Al-Manṣūr said: "I swear by my life that I would have commanded it if you had let me!"[365]

Al-Manṣūr's son, the caliph al-Mahdī, tried again: "O Abū 'Abd Allāh, make a book which I will make law for the *Umma*!" Mālik replied: "As for this region of the world – meaning the Maghreb – you need not task yourself;[366] as for al-Shām, al-Awzā'ī is there. As for the people of Iraq, they are the people of Iraq!"[367]

Al-Mahdī's brother, the Caliph al-Rashīd, tried again: "Abū 'Abd Allāh, let us copy these books and distribute them far and wide so as to make the *Umma* follow them!" Mālik replied: "Commander of the Believers! **The difference of the Ulema are a mercy from Allāh ﷻ to this Community.**[368] Each follows whatever is considered correct by him and each is well-guided and each seeks Allāh."[369] Another version states that he said: "The Companions differed in the Branches (*al-furū'*) and split into factions (*tafarraqū*), and each one of them was correct in himself."[370]

[365] Narrated from al-Wāqidī by Ibn Sa'd in the supplemental volume of his *Ṭabaqāt* (p. 440) and from al-Zubayr ibn Bakkār by Ibn 'Abd al-Barr in *al-Intiqā'* (p. 81). Al-Dhahabī said of al-Wāqidī in his *Siyar* (al-Arna'ūṭ ed. 7:142): "Although there is no disagreement over his weakness, yet he speaks truthfully and is of great standing." Ibn Sayyid al-Nās states something similar in the introduction to his *'Uyūn al-Athar*.

[366] He said this because most of Mālik's students had gone to the Maghreb.

[367] Narrated by al-Qāḍī 'Iyāḍ in *Tartīb al-Madārik* (1:193) and al-Dhahabī in the *Siyar* (al-Arna'ūṭ ed. 8:78).

[368] On this fundamental principle see Dr. Sa'ūd ibn 'Abd Allāh al-Funaysān's *Ḥadīth Ikhtilāf Ummatī Raḥma Riwāya wa-Dirāya* (Riyāḍ: Maktabat al-Rushd, 1999) and our *Sunna Notes II: The Excellent Innovation*.

[369] Narrated by al-Khaṭīb in *al-Ruwāt 'an Mālik* as cited by al-'Ajlūnī in *Kashf al-Khafā'* (1:65 §153). Ibn al-Athīr attributes to Mālik the saying "The differences among the Companions of Muḥammad ﷺ are a mercy for the servants of Allāh" in the introduction to his *Jāmi' al-Uṣūl fī Aḥādīth al-Rasūl* as stated by Ibn al-Mulaqqin in his *Tuḥfat al-Muḥtāj ilā Adillat al-Minhāj* and Ibn al-Subkī in *Ṭabaqāt al-Shāfi'iyya*.

[370] Narrated from from 'Abd Allāh ibn 'Abd al-Ḥakam by Abū Nu'aym in the *Ḥilya* (1985 ed. 6:322) and thus cited by Ibn Taymiyya in *Majmū' al-Fatāwā* (30:79) and *al-Fatāwā al-Kubrā* (5:18), although al-Dhahabī in the *Siyar* (7:414) said: "Its chain of transmission is fair, but the narrator may have erred in naming Hārūn." 'Iyāḍ in *Tartīb*

Another narration states that one or more of the three caliphs said to Mālik: "Work with me, for I have resolved to make the *Muwaṭṭa'* law for the people in the same way 'Uthmān made the Qur'ān law for them." Mālik replied: "There is no way for you to do this, the reason being that the Companions of the Prophet ﷺ scattered East and West after his time and narrated from him; consequently, the people of every region possess knowledge."[371]

Shaykh Muḥammad 'Awwāma pointed out that the above narrations all share two common aspects: Mālik's endorsement of the differences of the Companions and the subsequent differences of the Community on the same lines after them as well as his refusal to subsume all the Sunni schools into a single *madhhab*. He noted the model of *adab* they provide:

> Of the high ethics of the Ulema is to leave people to follow whatever they are following as long as there is a lawful justification for it, without bringing confusion into the state they are in. Consider the saying of Imām Mālik narrated by Ibn Abī Ḥātim: "If you now go and change them from what they know to what they do not know they shall deem it disbelief!" He said this although the caliph wanted to change them to what Mālik himself had narrated and compiled in his *Muwaṭṭa'*. That is: to what was, in his view, preferable and more correct! Nor did this excessive rigor on the part of the common people upset Mālik. Nor did he consider it misguidance. Nor did he express the necessity of opposing them for it and forcing them to abandon that position. Nor did he accuse them of fanaticism (*ta'aṣṣub*) nor of blind imitation (*al-taqlīd al-a'mā*) nor any other similar type of name-calling which has lately jarred our ears through the endless carping of certain writers.[372]

al-Madārik (1:214) names al-Mahdī for a similar account.

[371] Narrated by Abū Nu'aym in the *Ḥilya* (1985 ed. 6:331) where the caliph is identified as al-Ma'mūn. 'Iyāḍ in *Tartīb al-Madārik* (1:209) said: "Mālik did not reach the days of al-Ma'mūn, he died before them, and the mention of al-Ma'mūn here is an error." He goes on to identify the caliph as al-Rashīd.

[372] 'Awwāma, *Adab al-Ikhtilāf* (p. 39-40). He means "Salafis" but his remarks also apply to " 'Abd al-Qādir Murābiṭ" and his sect.

Mālik's respect for scholarly differences in the examples cited above also elucidates his two statements about the juristic differences among the Companions: "It is not as some people said – that there is wide leeway (*fīhi tawsi'a*). That is not so. Rather, there is either wrong or right." "There is wrong and there is right, so it must be investigated."[373]

Ibn al-Ṣalāḥ cited these two statements then said:

> There is no leeway in the sense that there is no leeway to just pick and choose without stopping to consider the most correct position (*al-rājiḥ*), while there is leeway in the sense that there is room for *ijtihād* among their positions, nor can we declare one of their positions definitely correct exclusively of the rest or preclude *ijtihād* that leads to its opposite.[374]

Imām Aḥmad squarely disagreed with Mālik and, like Abū Ḥanīfa, deemed it impermissible to question the correctness of a Companion's fatwā.[375] Even Mālik leans to this position in his saying, "Each Companion was correct in himself."

Sayings of Mālik

ON PIOUS SIMPLE LIVING

- From Ibn Wahb: "The saying has reached me[376] that none renounces the world and guards himself except he ends up speaking wisdom."
- "None attains his goal in this Science until he is sorely tried with poverty and yet puts this Science first, before everything else!"[377]

ON REGRESSION IN HISTORY

- From Ibn Wahb: "Knowledge diminishes and does not increase. Knowledge has diminished incessantly after the Prophets and the Books." This report shows that in Mālik's understanding the

[373] Both in Ibn 'Abd al-Barr, *Jāmi' Bayān al-'Ilm* (2:906-907, 2:922).

[374] Ibn al-Ṣalāḥ, *Adab al-Muftī wal-Mustaftī* (p. 126).

[375] Cf. n. 1050.

[376] This is a phrase that denotes attribution to the Prophet ﷺ in Mālik's terminology and this saying is indeed confirmed by authentic Prophetic reports, cf. note 640.

[377] Cited by al-Nawawī in his introduction to his *Majmū'* (1:64).

name *'ilm* is applied only to knowledge of Allāh Most High and knowledge that benefits in the hereafter, not merely in this life.

ON THE VERSE OF *ISTIWĀ'*

- From Ja'far ibn 'Abd Allāh: "We were with Mālik when a man came and asked him: 'Abū 'Abd Allāh! ﴾**The Merciful established Himself over the Throne**﴿ (20:5). How is He established?' Nothing affected Mālik so much as that man's question. He looked at the ground and started prodding it with a twig he held in his hand until he was completely soaked in sweat. Then he lifted his head and said: 'The "how" of it is inconceivable; the 'establishment' part of it is not unknown; belief in it is obligatory; asking about it is an innovation; and I believe that you are a man of innovation.' Then he gave an order and the man was led out."[378]
- From Ibn Wahb: "We were with Mālik when a man asked him: 'Abū 'Abd Allāh! ﴾**The Merciful established Himself over the Throne**﴿ (20:5). How is His establishment?' Mālik lowered his head and began to sweat profusely. Then he lifted up his head and said: '﴾**The Merciful established Himself over the Throne**﴿ just as He described Himself. One cannot ask "how"; "how" does not apply to Him. And you are an evil man, a man of innovation. Take him out!' The man was led out."[379]
- From Yaḥyā ibn Yaḥyā al-Tamīmī and Mālik's Shaykh Rabī'a ibn Abī 'Abd al-Raḥmān: "We were with Mālik when a man came and asked him: 'Abū 'Abd Allāh! ﴾**The Merciful established Himself over the Throne**﴿ (20:5). How is He established?' Mālik lowered his head and remained thus until he was completely soaked in sweat. Then he said: 'The establishment is not unknown; the "how" is inconceivable; belief in it is obligatory; asking about it is an innovation; and I do not think that you are anything but an innovator.' Then he ordered that the man be led out."[380]

[378] Al-Dhahabī, *Siyar* (7:415).

[379] Narrated by al-Bayhaqī with a sound chain, *al-Asmā' wal-Ṣifāt* (2:304-305 §866), al-Dhahabī, *Siyar* (7:416), and Ibn Ḥajar, *Fatḥ* (1959 ed. 13:406-407; 1989 ed. 13:501).

[380] Narrated by al-Bayhaqī with a sound chain, *al-Asmā' wal-Ṣifāt* (2:305-306 §867), al-Baghawī in *Sharḥ al-Sunna* (1:171), al-Lālikā'ī in *Sharḥ Uṣūl al-I'tiqād* (2:398), Ibn Abī Zayd al-Qayrawānī in *al-Jāmi' fil-Sunan* (p. 123), Abū Nu'aym in the *Ḥilya* (6:325-326),

Shaykh al-Islām Taqī al-Dīn al-Subkī pointed out that the inconceivability of the modality of *istiwā'* proved that it precluded the meaning of sitting.[381]

ON THE "DESCENT" OF ALLĀH ﷻ

❖ From Muṭarrif ibn 'Abd Allāh – al-Bukhārī's Shaykh – and Ḥabīb ibn Abī Ḥabīb on the ḥadīth of descent ("Our Lord ﷻ descends [*yanzilu*] every night to the nearest heaven in the last third of the night and says: Who is supplicating Me so that I may answer him? Who is asking forgiveness from Me so that I may forgive him?"):[382] "It is our Blessed and Exalted Lord's command which descends <every pre-dawn [*kulla saḥar*]>[383]; as for Him, He is eternally the same, He does not move or go to and fro."[384] Ibn Rushd in *Sharḥ*

cf. Ibn 'Abd al-Barr in *al-Tamhīd* (7:151) and Ibn Ḥajar, *Fatḥ* (13:407). Note that the wording that says: "The 'how' is unknown" (*al-kayfu majhūl*) is falsely attributed to Imām Mālik, although also cited from Rabī'a with a sound chain by al-Bayhaqī in *al-Asmā' wal-Ṣifāt* (2:306 §868) and without a chain by Ibn al-'Arabī in *'Āriḍat al-Aḥwadhī* (2:235), but is an aberrant narration (*riwāya shādhdha*). Yet it is predictably the preferred wording of Ibn Taymiyya in *Dar' Ta'āruḍ al-'Aql wal-Naql* (1:278) and *Fatāwā* (17:373), as he infers from it support for his positions although he reports it as "The 'how' is inconceivable" in his *Ḥamawiyya* (p. 307).

381 In *al-Sayf al-Ṣaqīl* (p. 128).

382 Narrated from Abū Hurayra by al-Bukhārī, Muslim, Mālik, Abū Dāwūd, al-Tirmidhī, Aḥmad, and al-Dārimī. It is narrated from twenty-three Companions and therefore *mutawātir* as indicated by al-Kattānī in *Naẓm al-Mutanāthir.* One of al-Baghawī's wordings in *Sharḥ al-Sunna* (4:66) has: "He comes down" (*yatanazzalu*).

383 The bracketed words are only in al-Qāḍī 'Iyāḍ's wording in the *Tartīb* (2:44).

384 Narrated from Muṭarrif by Ibn 'Abd al-Barr in *al-Tamhīd* (7:143) with a weak chain because of Jāmi' ibn Sawāda as per al-Dāraquṭnī in Ibn Ḥajar's *Lisān* (2:93). Also narrated from Ṣāliḥ ibn Ayyūb from Ḥabīb ibn Abī Ḥabīb – who is very weak – by al-Dhahabī in *Siyar A'lām al-Nubalā'* (8:418). The latter reported in his *Mīzān* (1:452) from Ibn 'Adī's *Kāmil* (2"818) the opinion that all of Ibn Abī Ḥabīb's narrations are forged but this is an extreme statement in light of three factors: (a) 'Iyāḍ questions the weakening of Ḥabīb in the *Madārik* (3:167); (b) Ibn 'Abd al-Barr in *al-Tamhīd* (24:177) mentioned Ḥabīb as merely weak, adding: "His reports from Mālik are full of mistakes and condemned matters"; (c) Ṣāliḥ ibn Ayyūb said: "I mentioned this report to Yaḥyā ibn Bukayr and he said: "Excellent, by Allāh! and I did not hear it from Mālik." Narrated by al-Dhahabī who describes Ibn Bukayr in *Tadhkirat al-Ḥuffāẓ* (2:420) as "the *muḥaddith* of Egypt, the Imām and trustworthy ḥadīth Master [...] one of the vessels of knowledge together with truthfulness and complete reliability [...] Where is the like of Ibn Bukayr in his leadership in the Religion, his insight in fatwā, and the abundance of

al-'Utbiyya – a commentary on an early work of Mālikī *fiqh* by Muḥammad ibn Aḥmad ibn 'Abd al-'Azīz al-'Utbī al-Qurṭubī (d. 255) – stated that Mālik's position is that "The Throne is not a location of settledness for Allāh (*mawḍi' istiqrār Allāh*)."[385]

A WEAK REPORT ATTRIBUTING LOCATION TO ALLĀH ﷻ

❖ The report attributing to Imām Mālik the words: "Allāh is in the heaven and His knowledge is in every place" is a rejected (*munkar*) anomalous (*shādhdh*) report of questionable authenticity narrated through Aḥmad ibn Ḥanbal from Surayj ibn al-Nu'mān al-Lu'lu'ī[386] from 'Abd Allāh ibn Nāfi' al-Ṣā'igh from Mālik.[387] Imām Aḥmad himself declared 'Abd Allāh ibn Nāfi' al-Ṣā'igh weak (*ḍa'īf*), Abū Zur'a frowned at his name and declared him "disclaimed" (*munkar*), al-Bukhārī questioned his memorization, and Ibn 'Adī stated that he transmitted oddities (*gharā'ib*) from Mālik.[388] As for the content of the report, Abū Ghudda noted in his commentary on Ibn 'Abd al-Barr's *al-Intiqā'* that it is contradicted by what is firmly established in mass-transmitted narrations from Mālik and by al-Ṣā'igh's other report from Mālik omitting the above words.[389]

---

his learning?" (d) Ibn 'Abd al-Barr in *al-Tamhīd* (7:143) also narrates this report from Ḥabīb, then goes on to narrate it from Muṭarrif, adding: "It is possible that the matter be as Mālik said, and Allāh knows best." It is established that Jāmi' did narrate from Muṭarrif; cf. al-Mizzī in *Tahdhīb al-Kamāl* (28:71).

385 As quoted in *Fatḥ al-Bārī* (1959 ed. 7:124 §3592).

386 Misspelt Shurayḥ in al-Saqqāf's edition of *al-'Ulūw* (p. 396 §340) and al-Mahdī's edition of *al-Sharī'a* (p. 293 §663-664). Shurayḥ ibn al-Nu'mān al-Ṣā'idī al-Kūfī is a *Tābi'ī* who died before al-Ṣā'igh was born.

387 In Ibn 'Abd al-Barr's *al-Intiqā'* (p. 71), al-Dhahabī's *Mukhtaṣar al-'Ulūw* (p. 247), and al-Ājurrī's *al-Sharī'a* (p. 293 §663-664).

388 Al-Dhahabī, *Mīzān* (2:513-514 §4647); al-'Uqaylī, *al-Ḍu'afā'* (2:311), Ibn 'Adī, *al-Kāmil* (4:242 §1070=4:1556); Abū Ḥātim, *al-Jarḥ wal-Ta'dīl* (5:183); Ibn Ḥajar, *Tahdhīb al-Tahdhīb* (6:46-47 §99), cf. Ibn Farḥūn, *Dībāj* (p. 213). Dr. Nūr al-Dīn 'Itr, however, states in his margins on al-Dhahabī's *al-Mughnī fil-Ḍu'afā'* (1:513 §3396) that al-Ṣā'igh is very reliable when narrating from Mālik and that Ibn Ḥajar declared him trustworthy (*thiqa*) in *al-Taqrīb*. The latter grading was actually downgraded to "truthful" (*ṣadūq*) by al-Arna'ūṭ in *al-Taḥrīr* (2:277 §3659). Albānī in his notes in *Mukhtaṣar al-'Ulūw* (p. 140) criticized al-Kawtharī for citing al-Ṣā'igh as weak in his introduction to al-Bayhaqī's *al-Asmā' wal-Ṣifāt* (p.), but he himself cites him as weak in *al-Silsila al-Ḍa'īfa* (2:231-232) cf. al-Saqqāf in his edition of *al-'Ulūw* (p. 397 n. 708)!

389 In Ibn 'Abd al-Barr, *al-Intiqā'* (p. 71 n. 3 and p. 73).

The report is made further dubious by the fact that Mālik was well-known to condemn any statements about the Essence and Attributes of Allāh ﷻ other than sound reports,[390] particularly statements suggesting anthropomorphism.[391] He was known to order that the verses and ḥadīths of the Attributes be passed on exactly as they came,[392] going so far as to forbid that ḥadīths such as "Allāh created Adam in his/His image" be narrated lest people be confused by them.[393] His strong affirmation of Transcendence (*tanzīh*) is also famous, as illustrated by his characterization of the modality of *istiwā'* as rationally inconceivable[394] – thus precluding any anthropomorphic notions – and his verdict of death against anyone that points to his own hand or eye while referring to the corresponding Divine Attributes.

ON THOSE WHO ATTRIBUTE ORGANS TO ALLĀH ﷻ

- From Ibn Wahb: "I heard Mālik say: 'Whoever recites ﴾**the Hand of Allāh**﴿ (3:73, 5:64, 48:10, 57:29) and indicates his hand, or recites ﴾**the Eye of Allāh**﴿ (cf. 20:39, 11:37, 23:27, 52:48, 54:14) and indicates that organ of his: let it be cut off to discipline him over Divine Sacredness and Transcendence above what he has compared Him to, and above his own comparison to Him. Both his life and the limb he compared to Allāh are cut off.'"[395]

ON DISPUTATION IN THE RELIGION

- From Ma'n: "Disputation (*al-jidāl*) in the Religion fosters self-display, does away with the light of the heart and hardens it, and produces aimless wandering."
- From Abū Muṣ'ab: "I detest talking about Religion just as the people of our country [al-Madīna] detest and prohibit it, in the

[390] See below, n. 396.

[391] For example Mālik said: "Allāh is neither ascribed a limit nor likened with anything" (*lā yuḥaddad wa-lā yushabbah*). Ibn al-'Arabī, *Aḥkām al-Qur'ān* (4:1740).

[392] As mentioned by al-Tirmidhī in his *Sunan* (Book of *zakāt*, ḥadīth "Verily, Allāh accepts the *zakāt* and takes it with His right Hand [...]"), Ibn al-Jawzī in his *Daf' Shubah al-Tashbīh* (p. 195-196), al-Dhahabī in *Siyar A'lām al-Nubalā'* (al-Arna'ūṭ ed. 8:105), Ibn Abī Zayd al-Qayrawānī, *al-Jāmi'* (p. 124), and others.

[393] Al-'Uqaylī, *al-Ḍu'afā'* (2:251 §806). Cf. al-Dhahabī, *Mīzān al-I'tidāl* (3:645 §7938) and al-Bājī, *al-Muntaqā* (1:357).

[394] See above, n. 378-381.

[395] In Ibn al-'Arabī al-Mālikī, *Aḥkām al-Qur'ān* (4:1740).

sense of Jahm's doctrine, *qadar*, and the like. I do not like to speak except about what relates to practice. When it comes to talking about the Religion, I prefer to keep silent about it."[396] Al-Shāṭibī cited this statement then commented: "The Congregation of the Muslims follow Imām Mālik's position, except if one is obliged to speak. One must not remain silent if his purpose is to refute falsehood and guide people away from it, or if one fears the spread of misguidance or some similar danger."[397]

ON WISDOM AND KNOWLEDGE BEING *FIQH* AND LIGHT

❖ From Ibn al-Qāsim: "I heard Zayd ibn Aslam say: ﴾**And unto each of them We gave judgment (*ḥukm*) and knowledge**﴿ (21:79) that wisdom (*al-ḥikma*) is intellect (*al-'aql*]. What comes to my heart is that wisdom is superlative understanding (*al-fiqh*) in the Religion of Allāh. What clearly shows this is that you may see someone quite reasonable and clear-sighted in worldly matters, and someone else weak in worldly matters but knowledgeable and judicious in the matter of his Religion. Allāh gave him this but deprived the former of it. This wisdom, therefore, is superlative understanding in the Religion of Allāh (*al-fiqhu fī dīnillāh*)."[398]

NAÏVETY A VIRTUE OF THE PEOPLE OF PARADISE

Related to Mālik's words are the Prophet's ﷺ ḥadīths: "O Allāh! Do not make any loss of ours be in our Religion, nor make the world our greatest concern, nor make it the sum total of our knowledge!"[399]

عَنْ ابْنِ عُمَرَ ﵄ قَالَ قَلَّمَا كَانَ رَسُولُ اللَّهِ ﷺ يَقُومُ مِنْ مَجْلِسٍ حَتَّى
يَدْعُوَ بِهَؤُلَاءِ الدَّعَوَاتِ لِأَصْحَابِهِ اللَّهُمَّ اقْسِمْ لَنَا مِنْ خَشْيَتِكَ مَا يَحُولُ
بَيْنَنَا وَبَيْنَ مَعَاصِيكَ وَمِنْ طَاعَتِكَ مَا تُبَلِّغُنَا بِهِ جَنَّتَكَ وَمِنَ الْيَقِينِ مَا

396 Narrated by al-Lālikā'ī in *Sharḥ I'tiqād Ahl al-Sunna* (1:148) and cited by al-Shāṭibī in *al-Muwāfaqāt* (2:332).

397 Al-Shāṭibī, *al-Muwāfaqāt* (2:332). See also p. 365f. and footnote 1115 *infra.*

398 Cf. al-Ṭabarī, *Tafsīr* (verse 21:79) and al-Mahdawī, *Taḥṣīl*; cf. Ḥamīd Laḥmar in *al-Imām Mālik Mufassiran* (p. 279). See also al-Ḥasan al-Baṣrī's definition of the *faqīh* (p. 81), and al-Shāfi'ī, al-Tustarī, and Ibn Ḥibbān on knowledge (p. 218, 317, 245).

399 Narrated from Ibn 'Umar by al-Tirmidhī (*ḥasan gharīb*) and al-Ḥākim (1:528 *ṣaḥīḥ*).

تُهَوِّنُ بِهِ عَلَيْنَا مُصِيبَاتِ الدُّنْيَا وَمَتِّعْنَا بِأَسْمَاعِنَا وَأَبْصَارِنَا وَقُوَّتِنَا مَا
أَحْيَيْتَنَا وَاجْعَلْهُ الْوَارِثَ مِنَّا وَاجْعَلْ ثَأْرَنَا عَلَى مَنْ ظَلَمَنَا وَانْصُرْنَا عَلَى
مَنْ عَادَانَا وَلَا تَجْعَلْ مُصِيبَتَنَا فِي دِينِنَا وَلَا تَجْعَلِ الدُّنْيَا أَكْبَرَ هَمِّنَا وَلَا
مَبْلَغَ عِلْمِنَا وَلَا تُسَلِّطْ عَلَيْنَا مَنْ لَا يَرْحَمُنَا ت قال حسن غريب ك صححه

"Most of the people of *Paradise* are the naïve (*al-bulh*)"[400];

عَنْ أَنَسٍ رَضِيَ اللهُ عَنْهُ قَالَ قَالَ رَسُولُ اللهِ صَلَّى اللهُ عَلَيْهِ وَسَلَّمَ إِنَّ
أَكْثَرَ أَهْلِ الْجَنَّةِ الْبُلْهُ ز مسند الشهاب عد تهذيب الكمال

"Forbidden to the Fire is every gentle, lenient, easy-going person who is near to the people."[401]

عَنِ ابْنِ مَسْعُودٍ رَضِيَ اللهُ عَنْهُ أَنَّ رَسُولَ اللهِ ﷺ قَالَ حُرِّمَ عَلَى النَّارِ
كُلُّ هَيِّنٍ لَيِّنٍ سَهْلٍ قَرِيبٍ مِنَ النَّاسِ

حم حب طب هب وفي الباب عن جابر ع طس طص هب وأبي هريرة طس حل هب

[400] Narrated from Anas by al-Bazzār (§1983) who graded it weak and al-Quḍā'ī in *Musnad al-Shihāb* (2:110 §989-990) while al-Qurṭubī declared it *ṣaḥīḥ* in his *Tafsīr* (verses 26:83-89) and *Tadhkira* (2:228); this was questioned by al-'Irāqī in *al-Mughnī 'an Ḥaml al-Asfār*, who quoted Ibn 'Adī's rejection of the ḥadīth in *al-Kāmil* (3:313 §773): "disclaimed as narrated through this chain" (*hādhā al-ḥadīth bi-hādhā al-isnād munkarun*). He did not mean the content of the ḥadīth as its veracity is confirmed by the next one. The best grading for the chain of Anas's narration is that of "soft" (*layyin*) in al-Fattanī's *Tadhkirat al-Mawḍū'āt* (p. 29) and al-'Ajlūnī's *Kashf al-Khafā'* (1:164, 1:286) because of Salama ibn Rawḥ. See also al-Mizzī's *Tahdhīb* (26:113 §5465), al-Suyūṭī's *al-Durar al-Muntathira* (p. 93 §68), al-Sakhāwī's *al-Maqāṣid al-Ḥasana* (p. 74), and al-Zarkashī's *al-Tadhkira* (p. 170). The ḥadīth is also narrated with a weak chain from Jābir as stated by Ibn 'Adī (1:191 §31), Ibn al-Jawzī in *al-'Ilal al-Mutanāhiya* (2:934-935 §1558-1559), and Ibn Ḥajar in *Lisān al-Mīzān* (1:240 §755).

[401] Narrated from [1] Ibn Mas'ūd by Aḥmad, Ibn Ḥibbān (2:215-216), al-Ṭabarānī in *al-Kabīr* (10:231 §10562), and al-Bayhaqī, *Shu'ab* (7:535 §11251); [2] Jābir by Abū Ya'lā (3:379 §1853), al-Ṭabarānī in *al-Awsaṭ* (1:256 §837) and *al-Ṣaghīr* (1:72 §89), and

"Paradise says: None enters me except the weak and wretched among the people and their simple-minded [*ghirratuhum*]"[402];

عَنْ أَبِي هُرَيْرَةَ رَضِيَ اللهُ عَنْهُ قَالَ رَسُولُ اللَّهِ صَلَّى اللَّهُ عَلَيْهِ وَسَلَّمَ تَحَاجَّتِ الْجَنَّةُ وَالنَّارُ فَقَالَتِ النَّارُ أُوثِرْتُ بِالْمُتَكَبِّرِينَ وَالْمُتَجَبِّرِينَ وَقَالَتِ الْجَنَّةُ فَمَا لِي لَا يَدْخُلُنِي إِلَّا ضُعَفَاءُ النَّاسِ وَسَقَطُهُمْ وَغِرَّتُهُمْ

الحديث م حم

"The believer is guileless and noble [*al-mu'minu ghirrun karīm*] while the wicked man is perfidious and miserly [*wal-fājiru khibbun la'īm*]"[403];

عَنْ أَبِي هُرَيْرَةَ رَضِيَ اللهُ عَنْهُ قَالَ قَالَ رَسُولُ اللَّهِ صَلَّى اللَّهُ عَلَيْهِ وَسَلَّمَ الْمُؤْمِنُ غِرٌّ كَرِيمٌ وَالْفَاجِرُ خِبٌّ لَئِيمٌ ت د حم

"The believer is easy and lenient [*hayyinun layyinun*] to the point you will think him a fool [*aḥmaq*] in his leniency."[404]

عَنْ أَبِي هُرَيْرَةَ رَضِيَ اللهُ عَنْهُ قَالَ قَالَ رَسُولُ اللَّهِ صَلَّى اللَّهُ عَلَيْهِ وَسَلَّمَ الْمُؤْمِنُ هَيِّنٌ لَيِّنٌ تَخَالُهُ مِنَ اللِّينِ أَحْمَقَ هب قال تفرد به يزيد بن عياض وليس بالقوي

وروي من وجه آخر صحيح مرسلا

al-Bayhaqī, *Shu'ab* (6:272 §8126); [3] Abū Hurayra by al-Ṭabarānī in *al-Awsaṭ* (6:38 §5725), Abū Nu'aym, *Ḥilya* (2:356), and al-Bayhaqī, *Shu'ab* (6:271 §8124).

402 Narrated from Abū Hurayra by Muslim and Aḥmad.

403 Narrated from Abū Hurayra by al-Tirmidhī (*gharīb*), Abū Dāwūd, Aḥmad, al-Ḥākim (1:43), and 'Abd al-Razzāq, a fair narration as indicated by al-Dhahabī in his *Talkhīṣ* and stated by Ibn Ḥajar in *al-Ajwiba 'alā al-Qazwīnī* [with al-Qārī's *Mirqāt* 1994 ed. 1:546-549] and al-Suyūṭī as quoted in *'Awn al-Ma'būd*.

404 Narrated from Abū Hurayra by al-Bayhaqī in the *Shu'ab* (6:272 §8127) cf. al-

The *ghirr* and *bulh* are those who were ignorant of evil ways in the world but knowledgeable in their Religion,[405] or those whose hearts were guileless towards people,[406] or those who lacked skill in worldly ways,[407] or those like old women, Bedouins, and their like, who remained staunch in their Religion.[408] Ibn al-Athīr cites some of these narrations under the entries *b-l-h* and *gh-r-r* in *al-Nihāya* as well as Muḥammad ibn Abī Bakr al-Rāzī in *Mukhtār al-Siḥāḥ*.

- From Ibn Wahb: "In the verse ﴾**and he shall instruct them in the Book and in wisdom**﴿ (2:129, 62:2), 'wisdom' is the Sunna. In the verses ﴾**And We gave him wisdom when a child**﴿ (19:12), ﴾**He said: I have come unto you with wisdom**﴿ (43:63), ﴾**And He will teach him the Scripture and wisdom**﴿ (3:48), ﴾**And bear in mind that which is recited in your houses of the revelations of Allāh and wisdom**﴿ (33:34), 'wisdom' is obedience of Allāh, observance of Him, superlative understanding in the Religion, and deeds in conformity with it."
- Ibn Wahb said: "I also heard Mālik say: 'Wisdom and knowledge are a light by which Allāh guides whomever He pleases; it does not consist in knowing many things.'"[409] Another version states: "Knowledge does not consist in narrating much. Knowledge is but a light which Allāh places in the heart."[410] This is similar to the statements of Ibrāhīm al-Khawwāṣ: "Knowledge does not consist in narrating much. Only he is learned who follows up on knowl-

Qārī, *al-Mirqāt* (1994 ed. 8:813). Al-Bayhaqī said it is *mursal ṣaḥīḥ*.

405 As explained by Abū 'Uthmān al-Maghribī and al-Awzā'ī in *Kashf al-Khafā'* and *Siyar A'lām al-Nubalā'* (1997 ed. 7:92), also al-Munāwī in *Fayḍ al-Qadīr* (2:79).

406 As stated by Ibn Qutayba in *Ta'wīl Mukhtalif al-Ḥadīth* (1995 ed. p. 270= p. 297).

407 Cf. al-Nawawī, *Sharḥ Ṣaḥīḥ Muslim* and al-Suyūṭī, *al-Dībāj* (6:191 §2847).

408 As stated by al-Qārī in *al-Asrār al-Marfū'a* (p. 125-127 §53). The "Salafī" editor of the latter, M.L. al- Ṣabbāgh, rejected the ḥadīth as *munkar* and exclaimed: "Islām was never for one day a Religion that supports naïvety or the simple-minded!" This is refuted by the narrations of Muslim and the *Sunan* cited above.

409 In al-Khaṭīb, *al-Jāmi' li-Akhlāq al-Rāwī* (2:174 §1526), Abū Nu'aym, *Ḥilya* (1985 ed. 6:319), Ibn 'Abd al-Barr, *Jāmi' Bayān al-'Ilm* (1:83-84), al-Qāḍī 'Iyāḍ, *Tartīb al-Madārik* (2:62), al-Shāṭibī, *al-Muwāfaqāt* (4:97-98), al-Ghazzālī, *Iḥyā'* (1:27), and al-Dhahabī, *Siyar* (Risāla ed. 8:107).

410 Cited by Ibn al-Jawzī in *Ṣifat al-Ṣafwa* (2:179) and Ibn Kathīr in his *Tafsīr* (3:555).

edge and puts it into practice, obeying the *Sunan*, even if he knows little";[411] and 'Abd Allāh ibn 'Utba: "Knowledge does not consist in narrating much. Knowledge is fear of Allāh [*al-khashya*]."[412]

- From Ibn Wahb: "A ruling is one of two kinds [*al-ḥukmu ḥukmān*]: a ruling brought by the Book of Allāh and one stipulated by the Sunna." Mālik also said: "And the opinion of a mujtahid for it may be that he shall be granted success." He also mentioned the pretender and disparaged him.[413]

ON THE PRECEDENCE OF MEANINGS OVER WORDINGS

- "It is with meanings that worship has been imposed upon us, not with wordings" (*Bil-ma'ānī-stu'bidnā lā bil-alfāẓ*).[414]

ON THE SUNNA BEING THE ARK OF SALVATION

- From Ibn Wahb: "The Sunna is the ark of Nūḥ ﷺ. Whoever boards it is saved, and whoever remains away from it perishes."[415]

ON THE RĀFIḌĪ SHĪ'A

- From Abū 'Urwa al-Zubayrī: We were with Mālik ibn Anas when they mentioned a man who found fault with the Companions of the Messenger of Allāh ﷺ. When he heard this, Mālik recited the verse ﴿**Muḥammad is the Messenger of Allāh and those with him are hard against the disbelievers and merciful among themselves. You (O Muḥammad) see them bowing and falling prostrate (in worship), seeking bounty from Allāh and (His) acceptance. The mark of them is on their foreheads from the traces of prostration. Such is their likeness in the Torah and their likeness in the Gospel like as sown corn that sends forth its shoot and strengthens it and rises firm upon its stalk, delighting the sowers that He may enrage the disbelievers with (the sight of) them**﴾ (48:29) then Mālik said

411 Narrated by al-Bayhaqī in *Shu'ab al-Īmān* (2:294 §1823).

412 Narrated by Ibn Abī 'Āṣim in *al-Zuhd* (p. 158), Aḥmad in *al-Wara'* (p. 80), and Abū Nu'aym in the *Ḥilya* (1985 ed. 1:131).

413 Narrated from Ibn Wahb by Ibn 'Abd al-Barr in *al-Tamhīd* (4:266).

414 I found no source for this statement penned by Zakariyyā the Calligrapher but retained it in the hope such a source be found.

415 Narrated from Ibn Wahb by al-Khaṭīb in *Tārīkh Baghdād* (7:336) and al-Suyūṭī in *Miftāḥ al-Janna* (p. 162 §391).

(after the mention of the *kuffār* in the verse): "Whoever among the people has become one who harbors spite towards any of the Companions of the Prophet ﷺ, this verse has hit him."[416]

TO SAY "I DO NOT KNOW" IS PART OF KNOWLEDGE

- From Muḥammad ibn Maslama al-Makhzūmī: "The shield of the *'ālim* is: 'I do not know.' If he neglects it, he will receive a mortal blow."[417]
- From Khālid ibn Khidāsh: "I traveled all the way from Iraq to see Mālik about forty questions. He did not answer me except on five. Then he said: 'Ibn 'Ijlān used to say: "If the *'ālim* bypasses 'I do not know,' he will receive a mortal blow." Something similar is related from Ibn 'Abbās. This is also related from Ibn 'Umar, Ibn Mas'ūd, al-Sha'bī, and al-Qāsim.[418]
- From al-Haytham ibn Jamīl: "I saw Mālik ibn Anas being asked forty-eight questions, and he replied to thirty-two of them: 'I do not know.'"
- From Ibn Wahb: "I heard 'Abd Allāh ibn Yazīd ibn Hurmuz say: 'The *'Ālim* must instill in those who sit with him the phrase "I do not know" until it becomes a foundational principle (*aṣl*) before them and they seek refuge in it from danger.'"

ON PRAISEWORTHY *KALĀM*

- From Ibn Wahb: "Ibn Hurmuz was proficient in dialectic theology (*baṣīran bil-kalām*) and he used to refute the people of vain disputation (*ahl al-ahwā'*). He was one of the most knowledgeable people in the differences of the scholars in those disputations."[419] Mālik spent thirteen to sixteen years at the feet of Ibn Hurmuz.

BELIEF INCREASES AND CONSISTS IN SPEECH AND DEEDS

- From Ibn al-Qāsim: "Mālik used to say: 'Belief increases.' He would stop short of saying that it decreases."

[416] Narrated by Abū Nu'aym in the *Ḥilya* (6:327) and al-Khallāl in *al-Sunna* (2:478) cf. 'Iyāḍ, *al-Shifā* (Fikr ed. 1:54).

[417] Ibn 'Abd al-Barr, *al-Intiqā'* (p. 74-75) for this and the next three reports.

[418] As related from al-Athram by Ibn Abī Ya'lā, *Ṭabaqāt al-Ḥanābila* (1:70-71).

[419] Narrated by Ibn 'Asākir in *Tabyīn Kadhib al-Muftarī* (al-Kawtharī ed. p. 352).

- From Ibn Wahb: "Asked about faith (*al-īmān*), Mālik defined it as 'speech and works' (*qawlun wa-'amal*). I asked: Does it increase and decrease? He replied: 'Allāh ﷻ mentioned in more than one verse in the Qur'ān that *īmān* increases.' I asked: But does it decrease? He said: 'Leave alone talk about its decrease once and for all.' I said: Can we say that some [type of] *īmān* is better than another? He said yes."[420]

ON *TABARRUK* (SEEKING BLESSINGS THROUGH RELICS)

- From Ibn Abī al-Zubayr: "I saw 'Aṭā' ibn Abī Rabāḥ enter the [Prophet's] Mosque, then take hold of the pommel of the Pulpit, after which he faced the *Qibla* [to pray]."
- When one of the Caliphs manifested his intention to replace the wooden pulpit of the Prophet ﷺ with a pulpit of silver and jewels, Mālik said: "I do not consider good that people be deprived of the Prophet's ﷺ relics." (*Lā arā an yuḥrama al-nāsu āthāra rasūlillāh!*)

ON SHAVING THE MOUSTACHE BEING AN INNOVATION

- In the *Muwaṭṭa'*: "Shaving the moustache is an innovation." It is elsewhere related that Mālik himself was tall, heavy-set, imposing of stature, very fair, with white hair and beard but bald, with a thick beard and blue eyes; he "detested and condemned" shaving of the moustache, disliked inordinate length for the beard [421] and he always wore beautiful clothes, especially white. Both clipping (*qaṣṣ*) and removal (*iḥfā'*) of the moustache are Sunna according to all – including al-Ṭabarī – except Mālik, who considered clipping the moustache sunna but removing it a *bid'a*.

420 Ibn 'Abd al-Barr, *al-Intiqā'* (p. 69).

421 Cf. Ibrāhīm al-Nakha'ī in al-Ghazzālī's *Iḥyā'* (1:143): "I am surprised to see a reasonable man wearing an inordinately long beard instead of trimming it to medium length... It is said the longer the beard, the less the intelligence." More importantly, the Prophet ﷺ forbade the two self-displays (*al-shuhratayn*): excessive shortness and excessive length in garments. Narrated from Abū Hurayra and Zayd ibn Thābit by al-Bayhaqī in *Shu'ab al-Īmān* (5:169 §6231) and al-Suyūṭī, *al-Jāmi' al-Ṣaghīr* (§9403).

ON THE NECESSITY OF THE TURBAN FOR LEARNED MUSLIMS

- From 'Abd al-'Azīz al-Uwaysī al-Madanī: "The turbans should not be neglected. I wore the turban before I had a hair on my face. I saw over thirty men wearing the turban in Rabī'a's circle. 'Abd al-'Azīz ibn al-Muṭṭalib told me: 'One day I entered this mosque without a turban and my father condemned me in a manner I hate to remember, saying: 'You dare enter the mosque bare-headed?!'[422] Turbans and sandals are the practice of the ancient Arabs, hardly ever seen among non-Arabs."[423]
- From Ibn Abī Zayd: "The turban was worn from the beginning of Islām and it did not cease to be worn until our time. I did not see any among the People of Excellence who did not wear the turban, such as Yaḥyā ibn Sa'īd, Rabī'a, and Ibn Hurmuz. I would see in Rabī'a's circle more than thirty men wearing turbans and I was one of them; Rabī'a did not put it down until the Pleiades rose and he used to say: 'I swear that I find it increases intelligence.' Gibrīl ﷺ was seen in the image of [the Companion] Diḥya [ibn Khalifa] al-Kalbī wearing a turban with its extremity hanging between his shoulder-blades."[424] Ashhab said: "When Mālik wore the turban he passed it under his chin (*taḥannak*) and let its extremity (*'adhaba*) hang behind his back, and he wore musk and other scents."[425]

[422] Baring the head in Islām is the sign of a man of low condition unless it is done out of humility. "He was asked about people that gather in a mosque, making *dhikr* and reading Qur'ān, praying to Allāh and taking their turbans off their heads and crying, while their intention is not pride nor self-display but seeking to draw closer to Allāh[...]" Ibn Taymiyya, *Majmū' al-Fatāwā* (22:523). Ibn al-Subkī mentions "Shaykh 'Alī al-Ḥajjār, the Bare-Headed, the saintly man[...]" and quotes Ibn Daqīq al-'Īd as saying: "What is carried on top of the head should not be put down" in *Ṭabaqāt al-Shāfi'iyya al-Kubrā* (9:213, 9:231). "According to the Ḥanafī school [among] the disliked acts (*al-makrūhāt*) in prayer are: [...] *I'tijār,* which is to tie a scarf around the head and leave the center bare[...] [or] praying bareheaded out of laziness. As for praying bareheaded out of humbleness and submission, it is permitted (*jā'iz*) and not disliked." Al-Jazīrī, *al-Fiqh 'alā al-Madhāhib al-Arba'a, Kitāb al-Ṣalāt* (p. 280-281). Note that the ruling merely said "permitted," not "desirable" as misreported in *Fiqh al-Sunna*!

[423] Al-Khaṭīb, *al-Jāmi' li-Akhlāq al-Rāwī* (1:605-606 §900).

[424] Ibn Abī Zayd, *al-Jāmi' fil-Sunan* (1982 ed. p. 228-229).

[425] On the *taḥannuk* Sunna of wearing the turban see p. 392. For documentation on the wearing of the turban by the Companions and Successors see the chapters thus

- From Muṭarrif: "I asked permission from my mother to go and write [= pursue the scholarly life] and she said: 'First, wear the garb of Scholars then you can go and write.' She then took me and dressed me in short-hemmed (*mushammara*) garments, placed a tall headcover (*al-ṭawīla*) on my head and tied a turban around it then said: 'Now go and write.'"[426]

THE INAPPROPRIATENESS OF ASKING ONE'S AGE

- 'Abd al-'Azīz al-Uwaysī al-Madanī also reported from Mālik that he detested that a man be asked his age for the questioner might often underestimate him as being too young or too old according to his whim. To the question: "What is your age?" Mālik replied: "Get to the point." Similarly, al-Buwayṭī reported that al-Shāfi'ī said: "It is not chivalrous (*murū'a*) for a man to reveal his age."[427]

ON THE PRIORITY OF *FIQH* OVER *TAṢAWWUF*

- A man asked Mālik about something in the inward science (*'ilm al-bāṭin*) whereupon the latter became angry and said: "Truly none knows the inward science except those who know the outward science! When he knows the outward science and puts it into practice, Allāh shall open for him the inward science – and that will not take place except by the opening of his heart and its enlightenment."[428]

ON THE NECESSITY OF COMBINING *FIQH* WITH *TAṢAWWUF*

- Reported from Mālik without a chain: "He who practices *taṣawwuf* without learning Sacred Law corrupts his faith (*tazandaqa*), while he

---

entitled in Ibn Abī Shayba's *Muṣannaf* and al-Bayhaqī's *Shu'ab al-Īmān* as well as our bilingual monograph titled *The Turban in Islām.*

[426] Al-Khaṭīb, *Jāmi'* (1:605 §899); al-Rāmahurmuzī, *al-Muḥaddith al-Fāṣil* (p. 80). The *ṭawīla* ("tall") is a conic headcover that was also worn by Imām Abū Ḥanīfa as narrated by Ibn 'Abd al-Barr in *al-Intiqā'* (p. 326) and described there by Shaykh 'Abd al-Fattāḥ Abū Ghudda after Ḥusayn al-'Ubaydī's *al-Malābis al-'Arabiyya al-Islāmiyya fil-'Aṣr al-'Abbāsī* (p. 589).

[427] Both reports in al-Sakhāwī's *I'lān* (p. 11-12). See also Ibn Abī Zayd's *Jāmi'* for the report on Mālik.

[428] Cited without chain by al-Qāḍī 'Iyāḍ, *Tartīb al-Madārik* (2:41).

who learns Sacred Law without practicing *Taṣawwuf* corrupts himself (*tafassaqa*). Only he who combines the two proves true (*taḥaqqaqa*)."[429] Shaykh Aḥmad Zarrūq said: "Islām necessitates deeds, and there is no self-purification (*taṣawwuf*) without knowledge of the Law (*fiqh*), as the external Divine rulings are not known except by knowledge of the Law; and there is no knowledge of the Law without self-purification, as there is no deed without sincerity in self-application, and there is neither without belief. Hence, the Law requires all of them by definition, just as the body and the soul necessitate each other, as one cannot exist or be complete in the world except in conjunction with the other. That is the meaning of Imām Mālik's saying: "He who enters *taṣawwuf* without learning [...]"[430]

Certain opponents of *taṣawwuf* adduce two weak-chained reports – originating in a man from the city of Naṣībīn who has been graded *munkar al-ḥadīth* – to claim that Imām Mālik derided group *dhikr*.

> i) Al-Tinnīsī said: We were sitting with Mālik with his companions around him. A man from the people of Naṣībīn said, "We have some people who go by the name of Ṣūfīs. They eat a lot then they start [chanting] poems (*qaṣā'id*), after which they stand up and start dancing." Mālik asked, "Are they boys (*ṣibyān*)?" He said no. Mālik asked, "Are they insane?" He said, "No, they are old men (*mashāyikh*) and other than that, and they are mature and sane (*'uqalā'*)." Mālik said, "I never heard that any of the people of Islām do this." The man said to him, "Indeed, they do! They eat, then they stand up and start dancing intensively (*dawā'ib*), and some of them slap their heads, and some their faces." Mālik started laughing then went into his house. His companions said to the man, "You were, O man, ill luck (*mash'ūm*) for our friend [Mālik]. We have been sitting with him thirty-odd years and never saw him laugh except today."[431]

429 Cited without chain of transmission by al-Qārī (d. 1014) in *Sharḥ 'Ayn al-'Ilm* (1989 ed. 1:33) and *Mirqāt al-Mafātīḥ* (1892 ed. 1:256), Aḥmad Zarrūq (d. 899) in the Fourth of his *Qawā'id al-Taṣawwuf* (Cairo, 1310), 'Alī al-'Adawī (d. 1190) in his commentary on Ibn Abī Zayd's *Risāla* (Beirut?: Dār Iḥyā' al-Kutub al-'Arabiyya, n.d. 2:195), Ibn 'Ajība (d. 1224) in *Īqāẓ al-Himam fī Sharḥ al-Ḥikam* (Cairo: Ḥalabī, 1392/1972 p. 5-6) and al-Tatā'ī in his commentary on Ibn Rushd's *Muqaddima*.

430 Aḥmad Zarrūq, *op. cit.*

431 Narrated without chain by al-Qāḍī 'Iyāḍ in *Tartīb al-Madārik* (2:53-54).

ii) 'Abd al-Mālik ibn Ziyād al-Naṣībī said: "We were with Mālik when I mentioned to him Ṣūfīs in our city. I said to him that they wear fancy Yemenite clothes, and do such and such. He replied, 'Woe to you! Are they Muslims?' He then laughed until he lay on his back. Some of his companions said to me, 'What is this? We have not seen more trouble (*fitna*) caused to the Shaykh than you, for we never saw him laugh!'"[432]

Neither of the above reports shows disapproval of group *dhikr* but only that some people who passed for Ṣūfīs in his time apparently committed certain excesses or breaches of the *Sharī'a*. Nor is it clear from the reports that Imām Mālik did other than tolerate them, and Allāh knows best.

ON THE VISION OF ALLĀH ﷻ IN THE HEREAFTER

❖ Ibn 'Abd al-Barr in *al-Intiqā'* and others relate that Mālik and al-Shāfi'ī adduced as proof of the believers' vision of Allāh ﷻ in the hereafter the verses ﴿**That day will faces be resplendent, looking toward their Lord**﴾ (75:22-23) and ﴿**Nay! Verily, from their Lord, that day, shall they [the transgressors] be veiled**﴾ (83:15).[433]

ON *TAWASSUL* (USING AN INTERMEDIARY)

❖ Al-Qāḍī 'Iyāḍ narrates in *al-Shifā* and *Tartīb al-Madārik* from Ibn Ḥumayd that the Caliph Abū Ja'far al-Manṣūr asked Mālik whether it is preferable to face the Prophet ﷺ or the *Qibla* when supplicating. Mālik answered: "Why should you not face him when he is your means (*wasīla*) to Allāh and that of your father Ādam on the Day of Resurrection?"[434] This report is also narrated

432 Narrated by al-Khallāl in *al-Ḥathth 'alā al-Tijāra wal-Ṣinā'a wal-'Amal* (ed. Abū Ghudda, §97) with a weak chain because of 'Abd al-Mālik ibn Ziyād al-Nāṣibī who is "disclaimed in his narrations and untrustworthy" (*munkar al-ḥadīth, ghayr thiqa*) according to al-Azdī as per Ibn al-Jawzī in *al-Ḍu'afā' wal-Matrūkīn* (1:149) while Ibn Ḥibbān in his *Thiqāt* (8:390) said he reports oddities from Mālik.

433 Cf. Ibn 'Abd al-Barr, *al-Intiqā'* (p. 73, 145-136). Both Pickthall's and Yūsuf 'Alī's translations parenthetically annul the meaning of the vision of Allāh, respectively: 'Nay, but surely on that day they will be covered from (the mercy of) their Lord)' and 'Verily, from (the Light of) their Lord, that Day, will they be veiled'. But Palmer has: 'Nay, verily, from their Lord on that day are they veiled'.

434 'Iyāḍ, *al-Shifā* (p. 520-521) and *Tartīb al-Madārik* (2:101).

by Abū al-Ḥasan ['Alī ibn al-Ḥasan ibn Muḥammad ibn al-'Abbās] Ibn Fihr al-Mālikī al-Miṣrī *(fl.* 440) in his *Faḍā'il Mālik* while al-Zarqānī in his commentary on *al-Mawāhib al-Lāduniyya* said al-Qāḍī 'Iyāḍ narrated it in *al-Shifā* from Mālik "with a good, or rather sound chain" as did al-Khafājī in his commentary on the *Shifā'*.[435] Ibn Qunfudh positively attributes it to Mālik[436] while the ḥadīth Master Ibn Jamā'a said: "The report is related by the two ḥadīth Masters Ibn Bashkuwāl and al-Qāḍī 'Iyāḍ in *al-Shifā*, and no attention is paid to the words of those who claim that it is forged purely on the basis of their idle desires."[437]

Mālikī Fatwā Textbooks and Terminology[438]

The principal eighteen sources of fatwā in the Mālikī School are Mālik's *Muwaṭṭa'*; Ibn al-Qāsim's *Mudawwana*; al-'Utbī's *'Utbiyya*, also known as the *Mustakhraja*; *Uṣūl al-Futyā fil-Fiqh* by Muḥammad ibn al-Ḥārith al-Khushanī (d. 361); *al-Tafrī'* by 'Ubayd Allāh ibn al-Ḥusayn, known as Ibn al-Jallāb al-Baṣrī (*d.* 378); *al-Nawādir wal-Ziyādāt* and *al-Risāla al-Fiqhiyya* by Ibn Abī Zayd (d. 386); *al-Kāfī fī Fiqh Ahl al-Madīna* by Ibn 'Abd al-Barr (d. 463); *al-Muqaddimāt al-Mumahhidāt* and *al-Bayān wal-Taḥṣīl limā fil-Mustakhraja min al-Tawjīh wal-Ta'līl* by Ibn Rushd (d. 520); *al-Qawānīn al-Fiqhiyya* by Ibn Juzayy (d. 771); Ḍiyā' al-Dīn al-Janadī's (d. 776) *Mukhtaṣar al-Shaykh Khalīl ibn Isḥāq* (an abridgment of Khalīl's abridgment of Abū 'Umar ibn al-Ḥājib's abridgment of al-Bardha'ī's abridgment of Ibn Abī Zayd's abridgment of the

[435] Al-Nabhānī, *Shawāhid al-Ḥaqq* (p. 186-188); al-Khafājī, *Nasīm al-Riyāḍ* (3:398).

[436] In *Wasīlat al-Islām* (p. 145-146).

[437] In *Hidāyat al-Sālik* (3:1381), in reference to Ibn Taymiyya's claims in his *Fatāwā* (27:166, 28:26). The report is also stated without attribution to Mālik by al-Buhūtī, *Kashshāf al-Qinā'* (2:516-517) and al-Shirwānī, *Ḥawāshī Tuḥfat al-Muḥtāj* (2:164) while 'Iyāḍ's chain was graded "weak or forged" by Sulaymān ibn 'Abd Allāh ibn Muḥammad ibn 'Abd al-Wahhāb in his book *Taysīr al-'Azīz al-Ḥamīd fī Sharḥ Kitāb al-Tawḥīd* (p. 312); cf. al-Shawkānī in *Nayl al-Awṭār*, following in this Ibn Taymiyya and his student Ibn 'Abd al-Hādī in *al-Ṣārim al-Munkī* (p. 244), although al-Zarqānī in *Sharḥ al-Mawāhib* rejects this claim as "stemming either from ignorance or arrogance" and states that the books of the Mālikīs are replete with the stipulation that *du'ā'* be made while facing the grave; cf. al-Qābisī, Abū Bakr ibn 'Abd al-Raḥmān, Khalīl's *Mansak*, al-'Abdarī, *al-Tāj wal-Iklīl* (3:400), al-Ḥaṭṭāb, *Mawāhib al-Jalīl* (3:400), and others.

[438] Cf. Muḥammad Riyāḍ, *Uṣūl al-Fatwā wal-Qaḍā' fil-Madhhab al-Mālikī* (p. 272-274, 470-471, 583-587).

Mudawwana!); *al-Dhakhīra* by al-Qarāfī (d. 684); *Tabṣirat al-Ḥukkām fī Uṣūl al-Aqḍiya wa-Manāhij al-Ḥukkām* by Burhān al-Dīn Ibrāhīm ibn 'Alī ibn Farḥūn (d. 799); *Tuḥfat al-Ḥukkām fī Nukat al-'Uqūd wal-Aḥkām* by Abū Bakr ibn Muḥammad ibn 'Āṣim al-Andalusī (d. 829); *Lāmiyyat al-Zaqqāq* by 'Alī ibn al-Qāsim al-Tujībī (d. 912); *al-Murshid al-Mu'īn 'alā al-Ḍarūrī min 'Ulūm al-Dīn* by 'Abd al-Wāḥid ibn 'Āshir al-Anṣārī al-Fāsī (d. 1040); and *al-Majmū'* and its commentary by Muḥammad ibn Muḥammad al-Amīr al-Kabīr (d. 1232). The terminology used to indicate the reliability of the fatwā in descending order of strength is as follows:

"Agreed upon" (*muttafaqun 'alayh*);
"Predominant" (*rājiḥ*) as opposed to "weak" (*al-qawl al-ḍa'īf*);
"Current" (*mashhūr*) as opposed to "odd" (*shādhdh*);
"On a par with its opposite" (*musāwī li-muqābilih*);
"In conformity with practice" (*mā jarā bihil-'amal*).

Mālikī terminology also includes "definite position of Mālik" (*al-madhhab*); "variant sayings of Mālik" (*al-riwāyāt*); "variances among the Masters" (*al-ṭuruq, al-aqwāl*); "rulings by subsequent Mālikī Mujtahids" (*al-awjuh*); of final, required applicability (*wājib al-taṭbīq*) among the predominant or current or practiced positions (*al-qawl al-mu'tamad*); "restricted concurrence" among the Mālikīs (*ittifāq*) as opposed to "general concurrence" of the Umma (*ijmā'*); "position of the vast majority" (*lafẓ al-jumhūr*), whether among the Mālikīs (in which case the *jumhūr* is also the *mashhūr* but not vice-versa) or among the Schools as a whole; "imitation" without citing proof nor method (*taqlīd = ittibā' = iqtidā'*); "conclusive endeavor" from the Jurisprudent to extract a presumptive ruling to which he feels nothing more can be added (*ijtihād*).

Mālik's Biographers

Al-Qāḍī 'Iyāḍ numbered those who wrote a biography of Mālik as thirty-three and listed their names. These are also found in al-Dhahabī's *Siyar*. The latter added: "Abū Nu'aym also wrote a long chapter on Mālik in his *Ḥilya*." Al-Suyūṭī also wrote a monograph on Mālik's *Manāqib*.

AL-SHAFI'Ī[439]

Allāh Be Well-Pleased with Him

MUḤAMMAD IBN IDRĪS ibn al-'Abbās ibn 'Uthmān ibn Shāfi' ibn al-Sā'ib ibn 'Ubayd ibn 'Abd Yazīd ibn Hāshim ibn al-Muṭṭalib ibn 'Abd Manāf ibn Quṣay, al-Imām al-Shāfi'ī, Abū 'Abd Allāh al-Shāfi'ī al-Ḥijāzī al-Makkī al-Azdī al-Qurashī al-Hāshimī al-Muṭṭalibī (150-204) the offspring of the House of the Prophet, was the peerless one of the great *mujtahid* Imāms and Jurisprudent *par excellence*, the scrupulously pious ascetic and Friend of Allāh, praised by Aḥmad ibn Ḥanbal as "like the sun over the world and good health for people – do these two have replacements or successors?"[440] He laid down the foundations of *fiqh* in his *Risāla*, which he said he revised and re-read eighty times, then said: "Only the Book of Allāh is perfect and free from error."

Al-Shāfi'ī is from the House of the Prophet

He is the cousin of the Prophet descending from al-Muṭṭalib who is the brother of Hāshim, 'Abd al-Muṭṭalib's father. Both his great-great-grandfather, Shāfi', and the latter's father, al-Ṣā'ib, were Companions of the Prophet, as were al-Ṣā'ib ibn 'Ubayd's uncles – 'Ubayd ibn 'Abd Yazīd's brothers – 'Ujayr and Rukāna, the man who wrestled with the Prophet.[441] Al-Ṣā'ib's mother, al-Shifā' bint al-Arqam ibn Hāshim ibn 'Abd Manāf, is the daughter of Khālida bint Asad ibn Hāshim, sister of Fāṭima bint Asad, the mother of 'Alī ibn Abī Ṭālib, whom the Prophet called his second mother.[442]

Someone praised the Banū Hāshim in front of the Prophet, whereupon the latter interlaced the fingers of his two hands and said:

439 Main sources: al-Shāfi'ī, *Dīwān*; Abū Nu'aym, *Ḥilya* (9:71-172 §442); al-Nawawī, *Tahdhīb al-Asmā' wal-Lughāt* (1:44-67 §2); al-Dhahabī, *Siyar* (8:377-423 §1539, 10:79, 10:649); Ibn al-Subkī, *Ṭabaqāt al-Shāfi'iyya al-Kubrā* (2:133-134, 3:299-301); Ibn Ḥajar, *Tawālī al-Ta'nīs* (p. 3-157); Ibn 'Abd al-Barr, *al-Intiqā'* (p. 115-182).

440 Narrated by Ibn 'Abd al-Barr in *al-Intiqā'* (p. 125).

441 Narrated by Abū Dāwūd and al-Tirmidhī with a very weak chain.

442 Cf. Ibn Ḥajar, *Tawālī al-Ta'nīs* (p. 34-39), *al-Iṣāba* (3:23, 3:310, 4:104; on

"We and they are but one and the same" and "The Banū Hāshim and the Banū 'Abd al-Muṭṭalib are but one and the same."[443]

Al-Nawawī listed three peculiar merits of al-Shāfi'ī: his sharing the Prophet's ﷺ lineage at the level of their common ancestor 'Abd Manāf; his birth in the Holy Land of Palestine and upbringing in Makka; and his education at the hands of superlative scholars together with his own superlative intelligence and knowledge of the Arabic language.

Prophetic Ḥadīths Predicting al-Shāfi'ī

Ibn Ḥajar added two more merits to al-Nawawī's list: the ḥadīth of the Prophet ﷺ, "O Allāh! Guide Quraysh, for the science of the Scholar that comes from them will encompass the earth. O Allāh! You have let the first of them taste bitterness, so let the latter of them taste reward."[444]

Aḥmad also narrates with two chains the prohibition of cursing the Quraysh and the Prophet's ﷺ statement to Qatāda ibn al-Nu'mān al-Ẓafarī: "You might see among them men with deeds next to which you

Rukāna: 2:497, 2:542, 6:336, 6:655, 7:718); For the ḥadīth on Fāṭima bint Asad see our biography of *Sayyidinā* 'Alī ﷺ, forthcoming *in shā Allāh.*

443 Both narrated from 'Uthmān by al-Bukhārī in his *Ṣaḥīḥ*.

444 Narrated from Abū Hurayra by Ibn Abī 'Āṣim in *al-Sunna* (2:637-638), al-Khaṭīb in *Tārīkh Baghdād* (2:60-61), and al-Bayhaqī in *Manāqib al-Shāfi'ī* (1:27) and *Ma'rifat al-Sunan* (1:207 §417); from Ibn Mas'ūd by al-Ṭayālisī (p. 39), Ibn Abī 'Āṣim in *al-Sunna* (2:637-638, 641), al-Shāshī in his *Musnad* (2:169), Abū Nu'aym in the *Ḥilya* (1985 ed. 6:285, 9:65), and al-Bayhaqī in *Manāqib al-Shāfi'ī* (1:26) and *Ma'rifat al-Sunan* (1:206 §413-414) through al-Naḍr ibn Ḥumayd al-Asadī al-Kindī who al-Bukhārī and Abū Ḥātim said is discarded; cf. al-Dhahabī, *Siyar* (Risāla ed. 10:82) and *Mīzān*; from Ibn 'Abbās by Abū Nu'aym in the *Ḥilya* (1985 ed. 9:65), al-Bayhaqī in *Manāqib al-Shāfi'ī* (1:24-25), and al-Quḍā'ī; from 'Alī by al-Bayhaqī in *Manāqib al-Shāfi'ī* (1:24) and *Ma'rifat al-Sunan* (1:207 §415); and from all four Companions by Ibn Ḥajar in *Tawālī al-Ta'nīs* (p. 42-44) all with weak chains which, al-Bayhaqī and Ibn Ḥajar said, if collated, make the ḥadīth strong. Ibn Ḥazm declared it *ṣaḥīḥ* in *al-Iḥkām* (6:286) but his evident intention was to detract from the Mālikī School. Both Ibn Ḥazm and Ibn Ḥajar took al-Naḍr to be Abū Qaḥdham ibn Ma'bad al-Baṣrī who is of stronger status than Ibn Ḥumayd; al-Bayhaqī names both in his chain to Ibn Mas'ūd in the *Ma'rifa* without deciding which is the correct link. The second sentence is narrated alone from Ibn 'Abbās by al-Tirmidhī who said it is *ḥasan ṣaḥīḥ gharīb*, and by Aḥmad with a good chain according to Ibn Ḥajar in *Tawālī al-Ta'nīs* (p. 44), sound according to Shākir in his edition of the *Musnad* (2:553 §2170), and fair per al-Aḥdab in *Zawā'id Tārīkh Baghdād* (1:490).

will despise your own deeds and envy them whenever you see them. If I did not fear Quraysh's tyranny I would disclose to them all the good

عَن ابْن عَبَّاس ﵄ قَالَ قَالَ رَسُولُ اللَّه ﷺ اللَّهُمَّ اهْدِ قُرَيْشاً فَإِنَّ عِلْمَ الْعَالِمِ مِنْهُمْ يَسَعُ طِبَاقَ الأَرْضِ اللَّهُمَّ أَذَقْتَ أَوَّلَهَا نَكَالاً فَأَذِقْ آخِرَهَا نَوَالاً حل هق في مناقب الشافعي ومعرفة السنن والآثار وَعَنْ عَلِيٍّ ﵁ مَرْفُوعاً لا تَؤُمُّوا قُرَيْشاً وَأْتَمُّوا بِهَا وَلا تَقَدَّمُوا عَلَى قُرَيْشٍ وَقَدِّمُوهَا وَلا تُعَلِّمُوا قُرَيْشاً وَتَعَلَّمُوا مِنْهَا فَإِنَّ أَمَانَةَ الأَمِينِ مِنْ قُرَيْشٍ تَعْدِلُ أَمَانَةَ اثْنَيْنِ مِنْ غَيْرِهِمْ وَإِنَّ عِلْمَ عَالِمِ قُرَيْشٍ يَسَعُ طِبَاقَ الأَرْضِ هق في المناقب وَعَنْ عَبْدِ اللهِ بْنِ مَسْعُودٍ ﵁ قَالَ قَالَ رَسُولُ اللَّهِ ﷺ لا تَسُبُّوا قُرَيْشاً فَإِنَّ عَالِمَهَا يَمْلأُ الأَرْضَ عِلْماً اللَّهُمَّ إِنَّكَ أَذَقْتَ أَوَّلَهَا عَذَاباً وَوَبَالاً فَأَذِقْ آخِرَهَا نَوَالاً ط ابن أبي عاصم في السنة مسند الشاشي حل هق في المناقب ومعرفة السنن إسناده ضعيف جدا وَعَنْ أَبِي هُرَيْرَةَ ﵁ عَنْ رَسُولِ اللَّهِ ﷺ أَنَّهُ قَالَ اللَّهُمَّ اهْدِ قُرَيْشاً فَإِنَّ عَالِمَهَا يَمْلأُ طِبَاقَ الأَرْضِ عِلْماً اللَّهُمَّ كَمَا أَذَقْتَهُمْ عَذَاباً فَأَذِقْهُمْ نَوَالاً دَعَا بِهَا ثَلاثَ مَرَّاتٍ ابن أبي عاصم في السنة خط هق في المناقب ومعرفة السنن قال الحافظ في توالي التأنيس أسانيدها ضعيفة وبمجموعها يقوى وَعَنْ مُحَمَّدِ بْنِ إِبْرَاهِيمَ مرسلاً أَنَّ قَتَادَةَ بْنَ النُّعْمَانِ الظَّفَرِيَّ وَقَعَ بِقُرَيْشٍ فَكَأَنَّهُ نَالَ مِنْهُمْ فَقَالَ رَسُولُ اللَّهِ ﷺ يَا قَتَادَةُ لا تَسُبَّنَّ قُرَيْشاً فَلَعَلَّكَ أَنْ تَرَى مِنْهُمْ رِجَالاً تَزْدَرِي عَمَلَكَ مَعَ أَعْمَالِهِمْ وَفِعْلَكَ مَعَ أَفْعَالِهِمْ وَتَغْبِطُهُمْ إِذَا رَأَيْتَهُمْ لَوْلا أَنْ تَطْغَى قُرَيْشٌ لأَخْبَرْتُهُمْ بِالَّذِي لَهُمْ عِنْدَ اللَّهِ عَزَّ وَجَلَّ حم ورواه مسنداً

Allāh has in store for them."

Another ḥadīth of the Prophet ﷺ says: "Truly Allāh ﷻ shall send forth for this Community, at the onset of every hundred years, some-

عَنْ أَبِي هُرَيْرَةَ رَضِيَ اللهُ عَنْهُ فِيمَا أَعْلَمُ عَنْ رَسُولِ اللهِ صَلَّى اللهُ عَلَيْهِ وَسَلَّمَ قَالَ إِنَّ اللَّهَ يَبْعَثُ لِهَذِهِ الأُمَّةِ عَلَى رَأْسِ كُلِّ مِائَةِ سَنَةٍ مَنْ يُجَدِّدُ لَهَا دِينَهَا د ابن عبد البر في الإنتقاء ك هق في معرفة السنن وصححه الحفاظ ويروى أيضاً بلفظ مَنْ يُجَدِّدُ لَهَا أَمْرَ دِينِهَا هق في المناقب ترتيب المدارك الانتقاء لابن عبد البر البداية طبقات الشافعية الكبرى وغيرها من المراجع المعتبرة انظر بحث الشيخ عبد الفتاح في تتمة تحقيق الانتقاء

one/those who will renew for it <the status of >its Religion."[445]

The scholars agreed, among them Abū Qilāba (d. 276) and Imām Aḥmad, that the "Quraysh" narration signified al-Shāfi'ī,[446] and the "Renewer" narration signified 'Umar ibn 'Abd al-'Azīz and then al-Shāfi'ī.[447]

Al-Bayhaqī also mentioned another great merit, the superlative praise of Yemen and Yemenis by the Prophet ﷺ in numerous sayings of his, as al-Shāfi'ī is from Yemen on his mother's side.

445 A sound ḥadīth by agreement of the ḥadīth Masters cf. al-Suyūṭī in *Mirqāt al-Su'ūd ilā Sunan Abī Dāwūd* as cited by al-'Aẓīm Ābādī in *'Awn al-Ma'būd* (4:182) who also cited the authentication of al-Zayn al-'Irāqī as *ṣaḥīḥ*, narrated "with a strong chain" as stated by Ibn Ḥajar in *Tawālī al-Ta'nīs* (p. 49) from Abū Hurayra by Abū Dāwūd in his *Sunan*, al-Ḥākim (4:522), Ibn 'Adī in the introduction to *al-Kāmil* (1:152), al-Khaṭīb in *Tārīkh Baghdād* (2:61), al-Sakhāwī in *al-Maqāṣid al-Ḥasana* (p. 121-122), al-'Ajlūnī in *Kashf al-Khafā'* (1:243) – both declaring its chain sound and its narrators trustworthy –, al-Munāwī in *Fayḍ al-Qadīr* (2:281), al-Bayhaqī in *Manāqib al-Shāfi'ī* (1:53) and *Ma'rifat al-Sunan*, and Ibn 'Abd al-Barr in *al-Intiqā'* (p. 126). Shaykh 'Abd al-Fattāḥ Abū Ghudda documented it at length at the conclusion of his edition of the latter (p. 341-350) to show that some versions add the word "status" (*amr*).

446 As narrated by al-Rāzī in *Manāqib al-Shāfi'ī* (p. 126), al-Bayhaqī in *Ma'rifat al-Sunan* (1:207 §417) and *Manāqib al-Shāfi'ī* (1:54), Abū Nu'aym in the *Ḥilya* (9:65), al-Khaṭīb in *Tārīkh Baghdād* (2:60-61), al-Mizzī in *Tahdhīb al-Kamāl* (3:22 §1162) and Ibn Ḥajar's *Tawālī al-Ta'nīs* (p. 45).

447 As narrated in al-Bayhaqī's *Manāqib al-Shāfi'ī* (1:54), Ibn Ḥajar's *Tawālī al-Ta'nīs* (p. 47-49), al-'Ajlūnī's *Kashf al-Khafā'*, and elsewhere.

Moreoever, al-Bayhaqī said, most of al-Shāfiʿī's knowledge is taken from the people of Makka and Madīna – and Makka and Madīna are Yemeni.

Al-Shāfiʿī's Early Years

He was born in the village of Ghazza by the town of ʿAsqalān in 150 – the year of Imām Abū Ḥanīfa's death – shortly after his father's death in Shām. His mother took him at the age of two to the Ḥijāz, where he grew up among her Azdī Yemeni relatives. Later, fearing the waste of his *sharīf* lineage, she moved him to Makka. Al-Shāfiʿī was early a skillful archer, then he took to learning language and poetry until he devoted himself to *fiqh*, beginning with ḥadīth. His mother could not afford to buy him paper and he would write his lessons on bones, particularly shoulder-bones. He memorised the Qur'ān at age seven, then Mālik's *Muwaṭṭa'* at age ten, at which time his teacher would deputise him to teach in his absence. He received permission to give fatwa at age fifteen.[448]

His Early Prowess

Abū Manṣūr al-Baghdādī in *Manāqib al-Shāfiʿī* and *Naqd Abī ʿAbd Allāh al-Jurjānī fī Tarjīḥ Madhhab Abī Ḥanīfa* relates the following example of the Imām's perspicuity at an early age:

> Al-Shāfiʿī was sitting at Mālik's feet one day when a man came in and said: "I sell turtle-doves, and one of my customers returned one of them to me today, saying that it does not coo, so I swore to him on pain of divorce that my turtle-dove coos all the time!" Mālik said: "You have divorced your wife and are not to approach her." Al-Shāfiʿī was fourteen at the time. He said to the man: "Which happens more, your turtle-dove's cooing or its silence?" The man said: "Its cooing." Al-Shāfiʿī said: "Your marriage is valid and there is no penalty for you." Whereupon Mālik frowned at him saying: "Boy, how do you know this?" Al-Shāfiʿī replied: "Because you narrated to me from al-Zuhrī, from Abū Salama ibn ʿAbd al-Raḥmān, from Umm Salama, that Fāṭima bint Qays said: 'Messenger of Allāh! Abū Jahm and Muʿāwiya

448 Narrated by Ibn Abī Ḥātim, *Manāqib al-Shāfiʿī wa-Ādābuh* (p. 39).

have both proposed to me.' The Prophet ﷺ replied: 'Mu'āwiya is penniless and as for Abū Jahm he does not put down his staff from his shoulder.'[449] That is, most of the time – Arabs assert the more frequent of two actions [exclusively of the other] because of its constancy. Since this man's turtledove coos more than it is silent, I can declare it constant in its cooing." Mālik was pleased at his reasoning.[450]

The scholars said that Allāh ﷻ accelerated the intelligence of al-Shāfi'ī and al-Nawawī because he gave them a short lifespan. Al-Ḥumaydī narrated that the *Faqīh* of Makka, Imām Muslim ibn Khālid al-Zanjī (100-180), said to al-Shāfi'ī: "Give fatwā, Abū 'Abd Allāh! It is time you gave fatwā," at which time al-Shāfi'ī was fifteen years old. Abū 'Ubayd al-Qāsim ibn Sallām said: "If the intelligence of an entire nation was brought together he would have encompassed it."

Studies with Mālik and Muḥammad al-Shaybānī

In 163, at age thirteen, al-Shāfi'ī went to see Mālik in Madīna, who was impressed by his memory and intelligence. Among his most prominent teachers were Mālik and Muḥammad ibn al-Ḥasan al-Shaybānī although he later took position against both of them in *fiqh*. He said, "Mālik is my teacher," and "I always held Muḥammad ibn al-Ḥasan in the highest esteem and spent sixty dinars buying all his books."

The Yemeni *Fitna* and Hārūn al-Rashīd

Some of the Qurashīs recommended al-Shāfi'ī to the new governor of Yemen, a Muṭṭalibī, and he went back to Yemen as his aide. He held a judgeship in Najrān during which his fame reached the stars for his sense of fairness and his acceptance on the part of the people. This did not last. The governor, al-Shāfi'ī, and a number of 'Alawīs were

449 Narrated by al-Bukhārī and Muslim. *I.e.* he is a wife-batterer or he travels much. Al-Fayrūzābādī in *Ṭabaqāt al-Shāfi'iyyīn* (published as *Ṭabaqāt al-Fuqahā'*, Baghdad: al-Maktabat al-'Arabiyya, 1356/1937-8) cites al-Ṭabarī's (whom he considers Shāfi'ī) citation of al-Shafi'ī explanation as *kathīr al-safar* ("constantly traveling") but Muslim's variant narration and Aḥmad's state verbatim that the Prophet ﷺ said: "As for Abū Jahm, the man beats women" (*ḍarrābun lil-nisā'*). Al-Tirmidhī has something similar.

450 In Ibn al-Subkī, *Ṭabaqāt al-Shāfi'iyya al-Kubrā* (5:147-148).

summoned to Baghdād in chains, all of them accused of being 'Alawī agitators by the agent of the Caliph Hārūn al-Rashīd in Yemen. They were executed one after another. When al-Shāfi'ī was introduced before the Caliph, he said:

> Commander of the Believers! What do you say about a man [*i.e.* a 'Abbāsī] who has two paternal cousins [*i.e.* a Muṭṭalibī and a 'Alawī], one of whom [the Muṭṭalibī] deems him his intimate family, places him in his own lineage, affirms that his property is taboo to him except by his permission, that his daughter is unmarriageable to him except by his betrothal, and that he considers him to own the same rights over him as he would over himself. The other [the 'Alawī], however, claims that the man is beneath him, that he is higher than him in lineage, that he is his slave, his daughter his bondswoman, that she belongs to him without his permission, and that his property is his booty. Which of them should you rightly patronise, Commander of the Believers? You are that man and here are your two paternal cousins!

Hārūn asked al-Shāfi'ī to repeat to him his parable three times until he understood what he meant. Then he spared his life but ordered him detained.

Certain chroniclers mention a report that begins with the words of the Caliph al-Ma'mūn, "I tested al-Shāfi'ī in everything, and I found him accomplished in all of it [...]" but al-Sakhāwī showed that the two never met.[451]

His Defense of Mālik

Al-Shāfi'ī formed the project of asking Imām Muḥammad al-Shaybānī to intercede for him at the time he was being detained in Baghdād. However, when he witnessed him disparaging al-Madīna and its scholars one day, he rose and said, "Mādīna is the sacred precinct of the Prophet ﷺ, its people his Companions and relatives-in-law, those that came after them the Successors and elite of this *Umma.* And if, by 'the people of Madīna,' you meant one man, Mālik ibn Anas, then say his name and leave the rest alone!" Al-Shaybānī replied, "I meant Mālik

[451] Cf. al-Sakhāwī, *al-I'lān wal-Tawbīkh* (p. 11).

ibn Anas." Al-Shāfi'ī said, "Mālik is one man, and there were in Madīna jurists other than him," then he proceeded to refute al-Shaybānī's published critique of the Madīnans point by point. When the caliph heard of the incident, he said, "And why should Muḥammad ibn al-Ḥasan be irked that a man from Banū 'Abd Manāf silence him?" Then he had five thousand dinars dispatched to al-Shāfi'ī and released him. Al-Shāfi'ī used a full fifty dinars to pay the barber for a cupping and he gave the rest to those Meccans and Qurashīs that were present, retaining only one hundred dinars for himself.[452]

His Study of the Ḥanafī *Madhhab*

Al-Shāfi'ī took the opportunity of being in Baghdād to study under Muḥammad ibn al-Ḥasan until he "became thoroughly familiar with their positions," meaning the disciples of Imām Abū Ḥanīfa. The story of persuading Imām Muḥammad to change his position to his over an issue in robbery (*ghaṣb*) is told by the Shāfi'ī chroniclers while the Ḥanafīs favour the story of al-Muzanī's frequent perusal of Ḥanafī books being the cause of al-Ṭaḥawī's switch to their School.[453]

Al-Shāfi'ī said: "From Muḥammad ibn al-Ḥasan I wrote one [a variant states "two"] camel-load[s]" and "I never saw anyone whose face did not show distaste when asked a difficult question except Muḥammad ibn al-Ḥasan."[454] He never met Abū Yūsuf but narrates from him through Muḥammad in *al-Umm* and the *Musnad*.[455]

It is related that Imām al-Shāfi'ī prayed one time after shaving with hair all over his clothes, at a time when he considered hair impure. Asked about it he replied: "When we cannot avoid something (*ḥaythu ubtulīnā*), we follow the ruling of the Iraqis [*i.e.* the Schools of Abū Ḥanīfa and Sufyān] in the matter."[456] Al-Bayhaqī in the *Manāqib* relates that al-Shāfi'ī's final position is that hair is pure.

452 Al-Bayhaqī, *Manāqib* (1:106-116).

453 Cf. al-Bayhaqī, *Manāqib al-Shāfi'ī* (1:109-110), Abū Nu'aym, *Ḥilya* (9:74-77), al-Rāzī, *Manāqib al-Shāfi'ī* (p. 105-106), Ibn Abī Ḥātim, *Ādāb al-Shāfi'ī* (p. 160-163), al-Khalīlī, *Irshād* (1:431); cf. al-Kawtharī, *al-Ḥāwī min Sīrat al-Ṭaḥāwī* (p. 17). Imām al-Ḥaramayn goes overboard in his *Mughīth al-Khalq* in arguing for the superiority of al-Shāfi'ī to Abū Ḥanīfa and Mālik as does al-Kawtharī in his rebuttal *Iḥqāq al-Ḥaqq*.

454 Both reports narrated by Ibn 'Abd al-Barr in *al-Intiqā'* (p. 119) and others.

455 The report that al-Shāfi'ī debated Abū Yūsuf is a forgery cf. al-Kawtharī as cited by Abū Ghudda in his marginalia on Ibn 'Abd al-Barr's *Intiqā'* (p. 107).

456 Cited by al-Bānī in *'Umdat al-Taḥqīq fil-Taqlīd wal-Talfīq* (p. 93) cf. 'Awwāma, *Adab al-Ikhtilāf* (p. 77).

His Move Away from Mālik's *Madhhab*

Al-Ḥākim narrated from 'Abd Allāh ibn 'Abd al-Ḥakam: "Al-Shāfi'ī never ceased to speak according to Mālik's position and he would say: 'We do not differ from him other than the way colleagues would,' until some young men spoke unbecomingly at length behind his back, whereupon al-Shāfi'ī resolved to put his differences with Mālik in writing. Otherwise, his whole life he would say, whenever asked something: 'This is what the Teacher said' – *hādhā qawl al-ustādh* – meaning Mālik."[457]

His Preference of al-Layth to Mālik

Al-Shāfi'ī said: "Al-Layth [ibn Sa'd] is stronger in *fiqh* (*afqah*) than Mālik but his School perished for lack of students."[458] This was also the view of Ibn al-Mubārak, Sa'īd ibn Abī Ayyūb, and Yaḥyā ibn Bukayr while al-Darāwardī put al-Layth even above Rabī'at al-Ra'ī. Al-Layth recited the *Basmala* out loud and gave *Salām* to the front in *Ṣalāt*.

The Epistle *(al-Risāla)*

Mūsā ibn 'Abd al-Raḥmān ibn Mahdī narrated that the reason al-Shāfi'ī wrote his masterpiece of juridical principles entitled "The Epistle" (*al-Risāla*) was that 'Abd al-Raḥmān ibn Mahdī wrote to him to ask for his help after being criticised in al-Baṣra for not renewing his ablution following his cupping. Ibn Mahdī read it and said: "This is the speech of a young man granted understanding." Al-Muzanī said: "I have been looking into al-Shāfi'ī's *Risāla* for fifty years, and I do not recall a single time I looked at it without learning some new benefit." There are two versions of the *Risāla*, "the Old," excerpted in the books of *Manāqib* and elsewhere, and the final version in print.

IBN MAHDĪ [459]

Abū Sa'īd 'Abd al-Raḥmān ibn Mahdī ibn Ḥassān al-'Anbarī al-Baṣrī (135-198) was one of the major early Imāms of ḥadīth, Sufyān

457 Ibn Ḥajar, *Tawālī al-Ta'nīs* (p. 153-154).

458 Narrated by al-Mizzī, *Tahdhīb al-Kamāl* (24:270); cf. al-Dhahabī, *Siyar* (Fikr ed. 7:452=Risāla ed. 8:156) and *'Ibar* (1:267), Ibn Kathīr, *Bidāya* (10:166), Ibn Ḥajar, *Tahdhīb al-Tahdhīb* (8:415), and Ibn 'Imād, *Shadharāt al-Dhahab* (1:285-286).

459 Sources: al-Khaṭīb, *Jāmi'* (2:382-383 §1835, 1837-838), Ibn Farḥūn, *Dībāj* (p. 238).

al-Thawrī's devoted student, 'Alī ibn al-Madīnī's Shaykh, and a Mālikī according to the latter. Al-Shāfi'ī said: "I know not his peer in the entire world." He heard Mālik, the two Sufyāns, the two Ḥammāds, Shu'ba, Ibn al-Mājishūn, and Sharīk. From him narrated Ibn Wahb, Aḥmad, Ibn Ma'īn, Ibn al-Madīnī, Ibn Sallām, Ibn Abī Shayba, and others. Whenever he read out the ḥadīth, Ibn Mahdī would order all his students to be silent, reciting ﴿**O you who believe! Lift not up your voices above the voice of the Prophet**﴾ (49:2).[460]

Asked how he could tell the authentic ḥadīth from the inauthentic Ibn Mahdī replied: "As the physician knows the madman." Challenged about his dismissal of a man's narration he replied: "Have you seen the man who brings a coin to the jeweller, asking him to examine a certain coin? If the jeweller says to him, 'It is counterfeit' and he challenges his opinion the jeweller will reply: 'Stick to my job for twenty years as I have done so that you will know what I know.'" Another time he said: "The knowledge of ḥadīth is inspiration (*ilhām*)." This elucidates the narration of the Prophet ﷺ: "If you hear a ḥadīth reported from me which your hearts recognise, at which your hair and skin become tender, and you feel that it is near to you: know that I am nearer to it than you. And if you hear a ḥadīth being reported from me of which your hearts disapprove, from which your hair and skin recoil, and you feel that it is far from you: know that I am even farther from it than you."[461]

عَنْ أَبِي حُمَيْدٍ - عبد الرحمن بن سعد الساعدي - وَأَبِي أُسَيْدٍ - مالك ابن ربيعة الساعدي - رضي الله عنهما أَنَّ النَّبِيَّ صَلَّى اللَّهُ عَلَيْهِ وَسَلَّمَ قَالَ إِذَا سَمِعْتُمُ الْحَدِيثَ عَنِّي تَعْرِفُهُ قُلُوبُكُمْ وَتَلِينُ لَهُ أَشْعَارُكُمْ وَأَبْشَارُكُمْ وَتَرَوْنَ أَنَّهُ مِنْكُمْ قَرِيبٌ فَأَنَا أَوْلَاكُمْ بِهِ وَإِذَا سَمِعْتُمُ الْحَدِيثَ عَنِّي تُنْكِرُهُ قُلُوبُكُمْ وَتَنْفِرُ مِنْهُ أَشْعَارُكُمْ وَأَبْشَارُكُمْ وَتَرَوْنَ أَنَّهُ مِنْكُمْ بَعِيدٌ فَأَنَا أَبْعَدُكُمْ مِنْهُ حم ز حب وإسناده صحيح مج

[460] 'Iyāḍ, *al-Shifā* (Fikr ed. 1:43).

[461] Narrated from Abū Ḥumayd al-Anṣārī and Abū Usayd al-Sā'idī by Aḥmad (al-Arna'ūṭ ed. 25:456 §16058 *isnād ṣaḥīḥ 'alā sharṭ Muslim*), al-Bazzār (*Mukhtaṣar al-Zawā'id* §187), Ibn Ḥibbān (1:263 §63) and others with a sound chain of *Ṣaḥīḥ* narra-

Certain proponents of the Madīnan School incorrectly cite Ibn Mahdī as saying, "The Sunna of the people of Madīna is more excellent than ḥadīth." The correct form of this statement is "Some of the Sunna of the people of Madīna is better than the ḥadīth" – meaning, said Ibn ʿAbd al-Barr, better than the ḥadīth we have with us in Iraq.⁴⁶²

His *Taqlīd* of the Companions and Successors

Like Abū Ḥanīfa, Mālik, and Aḥmad, al-Shāfiʿī advocated the imitation of the Companions. Ibn al-Qayyim said: "There is an obligatory imitation (*taqlīd wājib*), a forbidden imitation, and a permitted imitation [...]. The obligatory one is the imitation of those who know better than us, as when a person has not obtained knowledge of a proof from the Qurʾān or the Sunna concerning something. Such an imitation has been reported from Imām al-Shāfiʿī in many places, where he would say: 'I said this in *taqlīd* of ʿUmar ؓ' or 'I said that in *taqlīd* of ʿUthmān ؓ' or 'I said that in *taqlīd* of ʿAṭāʾ.' As al-Shāfiʿī said concerning the Companions: 'Their opinion for us is better than our opinion to ourselves.'"⁴⁶³ He also said, in reply to the question of which Companion should be followed if there is variance among their opinions on a single issue: "One of them can be followed if I do not find a Qurʾanic proof, nor a Sunna, nor Consensus, nor anything tantamount to the above, or inferable by analogy."⁴⁶⁴

Dates of His Trips to Baghdād and Move to Egypt

Al-Shāfiʿī travelled to Baghdād three times: first as a student, in 184, with the group of Yemeni descendants of ʿAlī ؓ, then as a recognised Imām in *fiqh* in 195, returning to Makka two years later, then in 198 for a few months, after which he went to Egypt where he remained until his death.⁴⁶⁵ When he entered Egypt he was patronised by the ascetic friend of the poor and descendant of the Prophet ﷺ, al-Sayyida Nafīsa, who ordered his bier brought into her house when he died so that she could recite the funeral prayer over him, and carried the bier.⁴⁶⁶

---

tors cf. al-Haythamī (1:150) and Ibn Kathīr in his *Tafsīr* (1:473, 2:264).

⁴⁶² In Ibn ʿAbd al-Barr, *al-Tamhīd* (1:79, 1:81). See these reports in *Tārīkh Baghdād*.

⁴⁶³ Ibn al-Qayyim, *Iʿlām al-Muwaqqiʿīn ʿan Rabb al-ʿĀlamīn* (2:186-187). See below, section entitled "Those who are imitated in Islām" (p. 398).

⁴⁶⁴ Al-Shāfiʿī, *al-Risāla* (§1805).

⁴⁶⁵ Ibn ʿAbd al-Barr, *al-Intiqāʾ* (p. 117) with al-Kawtharī's comments.

⁴⁶⁶ Ibn Kathīr, *Bidāya* (Turāth ed. 10:286=Maʿārif ed. 10:262) and Ibn ʿImād,

Al-Shāfi'ī Reconciled the Schools of Ḥadīth and *Fiqh*

Al-Shāfi'ī is the paradigm of ḥadīth-informed jurisprudence among the *Salaf*, gathering under one roof the superlative insight of Abū Ḥanīfa and Mālik's legal opinion (*ra'ī*) on the one hand and, on the other, the extensive knowledge of narrators and the evidence they transmitted which characterised al-Bukhārī and Aḥmad. The latter said: "We did not cease to curse the people of legal opinion and they would curse us, until al-Shāfi'ī came and reconciled our differences."[467] Ibn 'Abd al-Salām said that there is not a single ḥadīth that did not reach al-Shāfi'ī in one form or another, whether *musnad*, *mursal*, or *munqaṭi'*.[468]

Most Ḥadīth Masters Follow the Shāfi'ī School

Most of the Ḥadīth Masters documented in al-Dhahabī's *Tadhkirat al-Ḥuffāẓ* and its continuations by al-Ḥusaynī, Ibn Fahd, and al-Suyūṭī, follow the *madhhab* of Imām al-Shāfi'ī.

Ibn Ḥanbal and Yaḥyā al-Qaṭṭān's Praise of al-Shāfi'ī

Aḥmad ibn Ḥanbal said: "Not one of the Scholars of ḥadīth touches an inkwell or a pen without owing a huge debt to al-Shāfi'ī." Aḥmad's shaykh, Yaḥyā ibn Sa'īd al-Qaṭṭān, said: "I supplicate Allāh ﷻ for al-Shāfi'ī even inside my prayer," while Aḥmad himself said he supplicated for al-Shāfi'ī for forty years.[469]

Shadharāt (2:21). Cf. al-Dhahabī, *Siyar* (8:426-427 §1544). This is al-Sayyida al-Mukarrama Nafīsa bint al-Ḥasan ibn Zayd ibn al-Ḥasan ibn 'Alī ibn Abī Ṭālib al-Qurashiyya al-Hāshimiyya al-'Alawiyya al-Ḥasaniyya (d. 208) the wife of Isḥāq the son of Imām Ja'far ibn Muḥammad al-Ṣādiq ؉.

[467] Narrated by al-Qāḍī 'Iyāḍ in *Tartīb al-Madārik* (1:91 and 3:181). 'Iyāḍ explained: "He meant that al-Shāfi'ī held fast to the transmitted evidence and to putting it into practice, at the same time showing them that they needed legal opinion, that the rulings of the Religion were built upon it, that it consisted in analogy according to its principles and methods, being inferred out of them. He showed them the method of its inference and the dependence upon its postulates and contingencies. Thus the ḥadīth scholars understood that sound legal opinion is a branch of the principle, and the scholars of legal opinion understood that there can be no branch without principle coming first, and that it is impossible not to put the *sunan* and sound reports first."

[468] Cf. Ibn Kathīr, *Bidāya* (Ma'ārif ed. 10:276).

[469] Cited by Ibn Kathīr in the *Bidāya* (Maṭba'at al-Sa'āda 1st ed. 10:253=2nd ed. 10:286).

When Aḥmad first asked Isḥāq ibn Rāhūyah to "Come and see a man the like of whom your eyes have not yet seen" – meaning al-Shāfi'ī – Isḥāq faulted Aḥmad for attending the *fiqh* sessions of their peer in age and leaving the ḥadīth sessions of the older Sufyān ibn 'Uyayna. Aḥmad replied: "Woe to you! If you miss a ḥadīth with a shorter chain it will not harm you to find it elsewhere with a longer chain. But if you do not have the reasoning of this man [al-Shāfi'ī], I fear you will never be able to find it elsewhere!" Isḥāq asked al-Shāfi'ī a few questions, after which he turned to a friend from Merv and said to him in Persian: "*Mardak rā kamālī nīst* – the manling lacks finish." Al-Shāfi'ī, perceiving the slight, turned to Isḥāq and, in a rapid-fire succession of proofs, defeated him. After this incident Isḥāq would say: "I consider it my greatest blessing when I fully understand al-Shāfi'ī's discourse" while the latter expressed disapproval of Isḥāq's title as the jurisprudent of Khurāsān.[470]

When Yaḥyā ibn Ma'īn expressed shock at the fact that Aḥmad ibn Ḥanbal was seen standing at the foot of al-Shāfi'ī, holding his stirrup as the latter sat mounted, Aḥmad retorted: "If you want to learn jurisprudence, come and hold his other stirrup."[471] Aḥmad forbade Ibn Ma'īn from criticizing al-Shāfi'ī, saying: "Your eyes have never seen the like of al-Shāfi'ī" and "You understand nothing, Abū Zakariyyā, of the meanings of al-Shāfi'ī's words! And whoever fails to understand something, opposes it."[472] He told Ibn Rāhūyah something similar.

The Superiority of *Fiqh* over Ḥadīth

﴾**He gives wisdom to whomever He will, and whoever receives wisdom receives immense good**﴿ (2:269). "He for whom Allāh desires immense good, He grants him superlative understanding in the Religion (*yufaqqihhu/yufqihhu fīl-dīn*)."[473] "It may be that one carries understanding without being a person of understanding; it may be that one carries understanding to someone who possesses more understanding than he."[474]

470 Al-Bayhaqī, *Manāqib al-Shāfi'ī* (1:213), al-Sakhāwī in the introduction to his *al-Jawāhir wal-Durar*, Ibn 'Abd al-Barr, *al-Intiqā'* (p. 124-125), and others.

471 Narrated by Ibn 'Abd al-Barr in *al-Intiqā'* (p. 126).

472 Cited by Ibn 'Abd al-Barr in *al-Intiqā'* (p. 178).

473 Ḥadīth of the Prophet ﷺ narrated from Mu'āwiya by al-Bukhārī and Muslim.

474 See n. 718.

Imām al-Shāfi'ī apparently took from Imām Abū Ḥanīfa his famous statement, "You [the Scholars of ḥadīth] are the pharmacists but we [the Jurists] are the physicians."[475] This is also reported from al-A'mash and Abū Sulaymān Ibn Zubar[476] and was probably proverbial. Mullā 'Alī al-Qārī commented: "The early scholars said that the ḥadīth scholar without knowledge of *fiqh* is like a seller of drugs who is no physician: he has them but he does not know what to do with them; and the *fiqh* scholar without knowledge of ḥadīth is like a physician without drugs: he knows what constitutes a remedy, but does not have it available."[477]

Imām Aḥmad is related by his students Abū Ṭālib and Ḥumayd ibn Zanjūyah to have said: "I never saw anyone adhere more to ḥadīth than al-Shāfi'ī. No one preceded him in writing down ḥadīth in a book." The meaning of this is that al-Shāfi'ī possessed the intelligence of ḥadīth after which Aḥmad sought, as evidenced by the latter's statement: "How rare is *fiqh* among those who know ḥadīth!" This is a reference to the ḥadīth: "It may be one carries understanding (*fiqh*) – that is, memorises the proof-texts of *fiqh* – without being a person of understanding (*faqīh*)."[478] The *Salaf* and *Khalaf* elucidated this rule in many famous statements showing that, for all the exalted status of the *Muḥaddith*, the *Faqīh* excels him.

ḤADĪTH MISGUIDES THOSE DEVOID OF *FIQH*

- Cautioning against the danger of misusing ḥadīth to the point of committing sin, Imām Aḥmad narrated from Muḥammad ibn Yaḥyā al-Qaṭṭān (d. 233) that the latter said: "If one were to follow every dispensation *(rukhṣa)* that is in the ḥadīth, he would become a transgressor (*fāsiq*)."[479]
- Ibn Abī Zayd al-Mālikī reports Sufyān ibn 'Uyayna as saying:

475 Cited from al-Rabī' by al-Dhahabī in the *Siyar* (Risāla ed. 10:23).

476 Narrated by Ibn Ḥibbān in *al-Thiqāt* (8:467-468) and al-Khaṭīb in *Naṣīḥat Ahl al-Ḥadīth* (p. 45) cf. al-Zayla'ī, *Naṣb al-Rāya* (introduction), al-Dhahabī, *Tadhkirat al-Ḥuffāẓ* (3:997) and *Siyar* (Risāla ed. 16:441), and al-Ṣāliḥī, *'Uqūd al-Jumān* (p. 322).

477 Al-Qārī, *Mu'taqad Abī Ḥanīfata al-Imām fī Abaway al-Rasūl 'Alayhi al-Ṣalāt wal-Salām* (p. 42).

478 A nearly mass-narrated (*mashhūr*) sound ḥadīth of the Prophet ﷺ reported from several Companions by al-Tirmidhī, Abū Dāwūd, Ibn Mājah, and Aḥmad. See n. 718.

479 Aḥmad, *al-'Ilal* (1:219).

"Ḥadīth is a pitfall (*maḍilla*) except for the *fuqahā'*," and Mālik's companion 'Abd Allāh ibn Wahb very frequently said: "Ḥadīth is a pitfall except for the Ulema. Every memoriser of ḥadīth who does not have an Imām in *fiqh* is misguided (*ḍāll*), and if Allāh had not rescued us with Mālik and al-Layth [ibn Sa'd], we would have been misguided."[480] Ibn Abī Zayd comments: "He [Sufyān] means that non-jurists might take something in its external meaning when, in fact, it is interpreted in the light of another ḥadīth or some evidence which remains hidden to him; or it may in fact consist in discarded evidence because of some other [abrogating] evidence. None can meet the responsibility of knowing this except those who have deepened their learning and obtained *fiqh*." Imām al-Haytamī said something similar.[481] Ibn Wahb is also reported to have said: "I met three hundred and sixty learned people of knowledge but without Mālik and al-Layth I would have strayed."[482] Another versions states: "Were it not for Mālik ibn Anas and al-Layth ibn Sa'd I would have perished; I used to think everything that is [authentically] related from the Prophet ﷺ must be put into practice."[483] Another version says, "I gathered many ḥadīths and they drove me to confusion. I would consult Mālik and al-Layth and they would say to me, 'take this and leave this.'"[484] Ibn Wahb had compiled 120,000 narrations according to Aḥmad ibn Ṣāliḥ.[485] Hence, Ibn 'Uqda replied to a man who had asked him about a certain narration: "Keep such ḥadīths to a minimum for, truly, they are unsuitable except for those who know their interpretation. Yaḥyā ibn Sulayman narrated from Ibn Wahb that he heard

480 Ibn Abī Ḥātim in the introduction of *al-Jarḥ wal-Ta'dīl* (p. 22-23); Ibn Abī Zayd, *al-Jāmi' fil-Sunan* (p. 118-119); Ibn 'Abd al-Barr, *al-Intiqā'* (p. 60-61); al-Dhahabī. See Shaykh 'Abd al-Fattah Abū Ghudda's comments on this statement in his notes on al-Lacknawī's *al-Raf' wal-Takmīl* (2nd ed. p. 368-369, 3rd ed. p. 90-91).

481 In *al-Fatāwā al-Ḥadīthiyya* (p. 283).

482 Narrated by Ibn Ḥibbān in the introduction to *al-Majrūḥīn* (1:42). He then narrates from Ibn Wahb a similar statement where he adds the names of 'Amr ibn al-Ḥārith and Ibn Mājishūn.

483 Narrated by Ibn 'Asākir and al-Bayhaqī cf. Ibn Rajab, *Sharḥ al-'Ilal* (1:413) and 'Awwāma, *Athar al-Ḥadīth al-Sharīf fī Ikhtilāf al-A'immat al Fuqahā'* (p. 76).

484 Narrated by Qāḍī 'Iyāḍ. in *Tartīb al-Madārik* (2:427).

485 In Ibn al-Subkī, *Ṭabaqāt al-Shāfi'iyya al-Kubrā* (2:128).

Mālik say: 'Many of these ḥadīths are [a cause for] misguidance; some ḥadīths were narrated by me and I wish that for each of them I had been flogged with a stick twice. I certainly no longer narrate them!'"[486] By his phrase, "Many of these ḥadīths are misguidance," Mālik means adducing them in the wrong place and meaning, because the Sunna is wisdom and wisdom is to place each thing in its right context.[487]

- Ibn al-Mubārak said: "If Allāh had not rescued me with Abū Ḥanīfa and Sufyān [al-Thawrī] I would have been like the rest of the common people." Al-Dhahabī relates it as: "I would have been an innovator."[488]

THE IMĀMS OF ḤADĪTH DEFER TO THE IMĀMS OF *FIQH*

- Imām Aḥmad's teacher, Yaḥyā ibn Sa'īd al-Qaṭṭān (d. 198), despite his foremost status as the Master of ḥadīth Masters and expert in narrator-recommendation and discreditation (*al-jarḥ wal-ta'dīl*), would not venture to extract legal rulings from the evidence but followed in this the fiqh of Abū Ḥanīfa as he explicitly declared: "We do not belie Allāh. We never heard better than the legal opinion (*ra'ī*) of Abū Ḥanīfa and we followed most of his positions."[489] Similarly, Muḥammad ibn 'Abd Allāh ibn 'Abd al-Ḥakam said: "If it were not for al-Shāfi'ī I would not have known how to reply to anyone. Because of him I know what I know."[490] As for Muḥammad ibn Yaḥyā al-Dhuhlī (d. 258) of Khurāsān, whom Abū Zur'a ranked above Imām Muslim and who is considered an *Amīr al-Mu'minīn fil-Ḥadīth* ("Commander of the Faithful in the Science of Ḥadīth"), he never considered himself a non-*muqallid* but said: "I have made Aḥmad ibn Ḥanbal an Imām in all that stands between me and my Lord."[491] Mis'ar ibn Kidām said the same with regard to Imām Abū Ḥanīfa.[492]

486 Narrated by al-Khaṭīb, *al-Faqīh wal-Mutafaqqih* (2:80).

487 Shaykh Ismā'īl al-Anṣārī as quoted by 'Awwāma, *Athar* (p. 77).

488 Ibn Ḥajar, *Tahdhīb* (10:449-452 §817) and al-Dhahabī's *Manāqib Abī Ḥanīfa.*

489 Narrated by al-Dhahabī, *Tadhkira* (1:307) and Ibn Ḥajar, *Tahdhīb* (10:450).

490 Narrated by Ibn 'Abd al-Barr in *al-Intiqā'* (p. 124).

491 Narrated by al-Dhahabī in the *Siyar* (10:205). On the title *Amīr al-Mu'minīn fil-Ḥadīth* see p. 427 below.

492 Cf. Ibn Abī al-Wafā, last page of the Karachi edition of *al-Jawāhir al-Muḍiyya.*

KNOWLEDGE IS NOT MEMORIZATION BUT A LIGHT

Fiqh is the context of many statements of the Imāms on knowledge consisting in wisdom, benefit, deeds, and light rather than learning and memorization. Mālik: "Wisdom and knowledge are a light by which Allāh guides whomever He pleases; it does not consist in knowing many things."[493] Al-Shāfiʿī': "Knowledge is what benefits. Knowledge is not what one has memorised."[494] Al-Dhahabī: "[Knowledge (*al-ʿilm*) is] not the profusion of narration, but a light which Allāh casts into the heart. Its condition is followership (*ittibāʿ*) and the flight away from egotism (*hawā*) and innovation."[495] Al-Khaṭīb in his brief *Iqtiḍā' al-ʿIlm al-ʿAmal* ("Learning Necessitates Deeds") narrates many statements to this effect from Ibn Masʿūd, Abū Hurayra, Abū al-Dardā', Abū Qilāba, al-Zuhrī, al-Tustarī, Ibn ʿUyayna, and others of the Salaf. This Islamic understanding of knowledge elucidates al-Ḥasan al-Baṣrī's report that the Prophet ﷺ said: "The energy of the Ulema is help and care while the energy of fools is to quote" (*himmat al-ʿulamā' al-riʿāya wa-himmat al-sufahā' al-riwāya*)[496] and the statement of the ʿAbbāsī Caliph ʿAbd Allāh ibn al-Muʿtazz (249-296): "The learning of the hypocrite consists in his discourse while the learning of the Believer consists in his deed."[497]

THE ḤADĪTH OF THE JURISTS IS PREFERABLE TO THAT OF THE NON-JURISTS

- Wakīʿ preferred long-chained narrations through the *fuqahā'* to short-chained ones through non-*fuqahā'* and said: "The ḥadīth current among the jurists is better than the one current among ḥadīth scholars."[498] This is a foundational rule in the Ḥanafī School which, like Yaḥyā al-Qaṭṭān, Wakīʿ followed.[499]

493 In Ibn ʿAbd al-Barr, *Jāmiʿ Bayān al-ʿIlm* (1:83-84), al-Qāḍī ʿIyāḍ, *Tartīb al-Madārik* (2:62), al-Shāṭibī, *al-Muwāfaqāt* (4:97-98).

494 Narrated from al-Khallāl by al-Bayhaqī in *Manāqib al-Shāfiʿī* (2:149). "The knowledge that benefits is that whose rays expand in the breast and whose veil is lifted in the heart." Ibn ʿAṭā' Allāh, *Ḥikam* (§213).

495 *Siyar* (10:642).

496 Narrated *mursal* from al-Ḥasan by Ibn ʿAsākir and al-Khaṭīb in *al-Jāmiʿ li-Akhlāq al-Rāwī* (1983 ed. 1:88 §27) cf. *al-Jāmiʿ al-Ṣaghīr* (§9598) and *Kanz* (§29337).

497 Narrated by al-Khaṭīb in *Iqtiḍā' al-ʿIlm al-ʿAmal* (p. 38).

498 Cited by al-Dhahabī in the *Siyar* (al-Arna'ūṭ ed. 9:158, 12:328-329).

499 Cf. al-Dhahabī, *Tadhkira* (1:307) and Ibn Ḥajar, *Tahdhīb al-Tahdhīb* (11:126-127).

- Al-A'mash also said: "The ḥadīth that jurists circulate among themselves is better than that which ḥadīth narrators circulate among themselves."[500]
- Ibn Rajab said Abū Dāwūd in his *Sunan* was more concerned with the jurisprudence of the ḥadīth than with its chains of transmission.[501] This is also the case with al-Bukhārī's *Ṣaḥīḥ* while Muslim, Ibn Mājah, and al-Nasā'ī focussed on the benefits of its transmission chains and text variants – Muslim being the most thorough and reliable in these regards. Al-Tirmidhī gave equal weight to the *fiqh* of the ḥadīth and the study of its transmission although Abū Dāwūd is somewhat stricter in ḥadīth authentication while al-Nasā'ī surpasses them both.[502]

KNOWING THE ḤADĪTH IS DIFFERENT FROM PRACTICING IT

- Sufyān al-Thawrī used to say to the ḥadīth scholars: "Come forward, O weak ones!"[503] He also said: "If ḥadīth were a good thing it would have vanished just as all goodness has vanished," and "Pursuing the study of ḥadīth is not part of the preparation for death, but a disease that preoccupies people." Al-Dhahabī commented: "He said this verbatim. He is right in what he said because pursuing the study of ḥadīth is other than the ḥadīth itself."[504]

UNDERSTANDING THE ḤADĪTH IS SUPERIOR TO KNOWING IT

- Isḥāq ibn Rāhūyah said: "I would sit in Iraq with Aḥmad ibn Ḥanbal, Yaḥyā ibn Ma'īn, and our companions, rehearsing the narrations from one, two, three routes of transmission [...] But when I said: What is its intent? What is its explanation? What is its *fiqh*? they would all remain mute except Aḥmad ibn Ḥanbal."[505]
- Sufyān said: "The explanation (*tafsīr*) of the ḥadīth is better than the ḥadīth."[506] Another wording states: "The explanation of the

[500] In al-Sakhāwī, *al-Jawāhir wal-Durar* (p. 21).
[501] Ibn Rajab, *Sharḥ 'Ilal al-Tirmidhī* (1:411).
[502] Cf. al-Kawtharī's notes on al-Ḥāzimī's *Shurūṭ al-A'immat al-Khamsa* (p. 72-73).
[503] Cited from Zayd ibn Abī al-Zarqā' by al-Dhahabī, *Siyar* (al-Arna'ūṭ ed. 7:275).
[504] In al-Sakhāwī, *al-Jawāhir wal-Durar* (p. 20-23).
[505] Narrated by Ibn Abī Ḥātim in the introduction to *al-Jarḥ wal-Ta'dīl* (p. 293), Ibn al-Jawzī in *Manāqib Aḥmad* (p. 63), and al-Dhahabī in *Tārīkh al-Islām* (ch. on Aḥmad).
[506] Narrated by al-Harawī al-Anṣārī in *Dhamm al-Kalām* (4:139 §907).

ḥadīth is better than its audition."[507] Abū ʿAlī al-Naysābūrī said: "We consider understanding superior to memorization."[508] Ibn Mahdī regretted not having written, after every ḥadīth he had recorded, its explanation.[509]

- The perspicuity and *fiqh* of Abū Thawr among the ḥadīth Masters is famous. A woman stood by a gathering of scholars of ḥadīth comprising Yaḥyā ibn Maʿīn, Abū Khaythama, Khalaf ibn Sālim, and others. She heard them saying: "The Prophet ﷺ said," and "So-and-so narrated," and "No one other than So-and-so narrated," etc. She asked them: "Can a woman in her menses wash the dead?" for that was her occupation. No one in the entire gathering could answer her and they began to look at one another. Abū Thawr arrived, and they referred her to him. She asked him the same question and he said: "Yes, she can wash the dead, as in the ḥadīth of al-Qāsim from ʿĀʾisha: 'Your menses are not in your hand,'[510] and her narration that she would scrub the Prophet's ﷺ hair at a time she was menstruating.[511] If the head of the living can be washed [by a woman in her menses], then *a fortiori* the dead!" Hearing this, the ḥadīth scholars said: "Right! So-and-so narrated it, and So-and-so told us, and we know it from such-and-such a chain," and they plunged back into the narrations and chains of transmission. The woman said: "Where have you all been up to now?"[512]
- Ibn ʿAbd al-Barr cites Imām Aḥmad as saying: "From where does Yaḥyā ibn Maʿīn know al-Shāfiʿī? He does not know al-Shāfiʿī nor has any idea what al-Shāfiʿī says!"[513] Ibn Rāhūyah similarly conceded defeat before al-Shāfiʿī's *fiqh* although himself reputed for *fiqh*.[514]

[507] In Ibn ʿAbd al-Barr, *Jāmiʿ Bayān al-ʿIlm* (2:175).

[508] In al-Dhahabī, *Tadhkirat al-Ḥuffāẓ* (2:776).

[509] In Ibn Rajab, *Sharḥ ʿIlal al-Tirmidhī* (1:41).

[510] In Muslim and the Four *Sunan*.

[511] In al-Bukhārī and Muslim.

[512] Ibn al-Subkī, *Ṭabaqāt al-Shāfiʿiyya*, al-Sakhāwī, introduction to *al-Jawāhir wal-Durar*, and al-Haytamī, *Fatāwā Ḥadīthiyya* (p. 283) cf. report from Aḥmad by Ibn Rajab, *Dhayl Ṭabaqāt al-Ḥanābila* (1:131); al-ʿUlaymī, *al-Manhaj al-Aḥmad* (2:208).

[513] Ibn ʿAbd al-Barr, *Jāmiʿ Bayān al-ʿIlm* (2:160).

[514] Cf. p. 324.

MOST ḤADĪTH SCHOLARS DO NOT POSSESS UNDERSTANDING OF THE ḤADĪTH

- 'Abd al-Razzāq al-Ṣan'ānī, Sufyān's contemporary, was the teacher of the pillars of ḥadīth memorization – Aḥmad, Ibn Rāhūyah, Ibn Ma'īn, and Muḥammad ibn Yaḥyā al-Dhuhlī. Yet when Muḥammad ibn Yazīd al-Mustamlī asked Aḥmad: "Did he ['Abd al-Razzāq] possess *fiqh*?" Aḥmad replied: "How rare is *fiqh* among those who know ḥadīth!"[515]
- Anas ibn Sīrīn said: "I came to Kūfa and found in it 4,000 persons pursuing ḥadīth and 400 persons who had obtained *fiqh*."[516]
- Ḥujjat al-Islām Imām al-Ghazzālī in *al-Mustaṣfā* and Imām Ibn Qudāma in *Rawḍat al-Nāẓir* both said that a *'Ālim* may be an Imām in a particular science and an uneducated common person in another.
- Ibn 'Abd al-Salām said: "Most ḥadīth scholars are ignorant in *fiqh*."[517] A majority of 90% according to Anas ibn Sīrīn – among the Salaf!
- Al-Dhahabī said: "The majority of the ḥadīth scholars have no understanding, no diligence in the actual knowledge of ḥadīth, and no fear of Allāh regarding it."[518] All of the authorities al-Dhahabī listed as "those who are imitated in Islām" are Jurisprudents and not merely ḥadīth masters.[519]
- Al-Sakhāwī in his biography of Ibn Ḥajar entitled *al-Jawāhir wal-Durar* states that al-Fāriqī said: "One who knows chains of ḥadīth but not the legal rulings derived from them cannot be counted among the Scholars of the Law." Al-Fāriqī's student Ibn Abī 'Aṣrūn (d. 585) also followed this view in his book *al-Intiṣār*.[520]

NOT EVERY SOUND ḤADĪTH FORMS EVIDENCE

- Ibrāhīm al-Nakha'ī said: "I hear a ḥadīth then I look to see what part of it applies. I apply it and leave the rest."[521] Shaykh

[515] Narrated by Abū Ya'lā in *Ṭabaqāt al-Ḥanābila* (1:329) cf. Abū Ghudda's introduction to Muḥammad's *Muwaṭṭa'* and his essay *al-Isnād min al-Dīn* (p. 68).

[516] Narrated by al-Rāmahurmuzī in *al-Muḥaddith al-Fāṣil* (p. 560).

[517] Ibn 'Abd al-Salām, *al-Fatāwā al-Mawṣiliyya* (p. 132-134).

[518] In al-Sakhāwī, *al-Jawāhir wal-Durar* (p. 18).

[519] See p. 398, "Those who are imitated in Islām".

[520] Al-Sakhāwī, *al-Jawāhir wal-Durar* (p. 20-23).

[521] Narrated from Ibn Abī Khaythama by Abū Nu'aym in the *Ḥilya* (4:225) and Ibn

Muḥammad 'Awwāma said: "Meaning, what is recognised by the authorities is retained while anything odd (*gharīb*), anomalous (*shādhdh*), or condemned (*munkar*) is put aside." Yazīd ibn Abī Ḥabīb said: "When you hear a ḥadīth, proclaim it; if it is recognised [keep it], otherwise, leave it."[522]

- Ibn Abī Laylā said: "A man does not understand ḥadīth until he knows what to take from it and what to leave."[523]
- 'Abd al-Raḥmān ibn Mahdī, the Commander of the Believers in Ḥadīth, said: "It is impermissible for someone to be an Imām [i.e. to be imitated] until he knows what is sound and what is unsound and until he does not take everything [sound] as evidence, and until he knows the correct way to infer knowledge [in the Religion]."[524]
- Al-Shāfi'ī narrated that Mālik ibn Anas was told: "Ibn 'Uyayna narrates from al-Zuhrī things you do not have!" He replied: "Why, should I narrate every single ḥadīth I have heard? Only if I wanted to misguide people!"[525]

Shaykh 'Abd al-Fattāḥ Abū Ghudda mentioned some of the above examples and commented: "If the likes of Yaḥyā al-Qaṭṭān, Wakī' ibn al-Jarrāḥ, 'Abd al-Razzāq, Yaḥyā ibn Ma'īn, and those comparable with them, did not dare enter into *ijtihād* and *fiqh*, then how rash are the claimants to *ijtihād* in our time! On top of it, they call the *Salaf* ignorant without the least shame or modesty! Allāh is our refuge from failure."[526]

His *Tawassul* Through Abū Ḥanīfa at His Grave

Al-Khaṭīb narrates in *Tārīkh Baghdād* that the truthful (*ṣadūq*) *qāḍī* al-Ḥusayn ibn 'Alī al-Ṣaymarī narrated to them, that the trustworthy

---

Rajab in *Sharḥ 'Ilal al-Tirmidhī* (1:413).

[522] In Ibn Rajab, *Sharḥ 'Ilal al-Tirmidhī* (1:413).

[523] In Ibn 'Abd al-Barr, *Jāmi' Bayān al-'Ilm* (2:130).

[524] Narrated by Abū Nu'aym in the *Ḥilya* (9:3).

[525] Narrated by al-Khaṭīb in *al-Jāmi' li-Akhlāq al-Rāwī* (2:109).

[526] Abū Ghudda, *al-Isnād min al-Dīn* (p. 68). He means by his remarks al-Albānī and others. Abū Ghudda's student, Muḥammad 'Awwāma, listed several examples of this rule of the *Salaf* in his *Athar al-Ḥadīth al-Sharīf fī Ikhtilāf al-A'immat al-Fuqahā'* ("The Effect the Noble Ḥadīth Had on the Differences of the Imāms of Jurisprudence").

(*thiqa*) Imām 'Umar ibn Ibrāhīm [ibn Aḥmad] al-Muqrī told him, that the trustworthy Shaykh Makram ibn Aḥmad told them, that 'Umar ibn Isḥāq ibn Ibrāhīm told them, that the trustworthy Shaykh 'Alī ibn Maymūn told them: "I heard al-Shāfi'ī say: 'I swear[527] I seek the blessing of Abū Ḥanīfa (*innī la'atabarraku bi-Abī Ḥanīfa*) and come to his grave every day' – meaning as a visitor. 'Whenever I have a certain need I pray two *rak'as* then I come to his grave and ask Allāh ﷻ for my need at his grave, and before little it is fulfilled.'"[528] If authentic, this is a strong rebuttal of those who claim that none among the Salaf visited the graves of the *awliyā'* for the mere purpose of making *du'ā* there, such as al-Shawkānī in *al-Durr al-Naḍīḍ*, although he declares it permissible to make *du'ā* once there.

His *Tabarruk* With Aḥmad ibn Ḥanbal's Shirt

It is also related that Imām al-Shāfi'ī sought blessing from drinking the washing-water of Imām Aḥmad's shirt. While in Egypt, al-Shāfi'ī sent his disciple al-Rabī' with a letter to Aḥmad warning him of his impending trial at the hands of the authorities and advising him not to yield to them. When he read the letter, Aḥmad wept and took off one of his two shirts, giving it to al-Rabī' as a gift. When the latter returned to Egypt and recounted the meeting, al-Shāfi'i told him: "I do not begrudge you the shirt; but just soak it and give me the water so that I may obtain blessings through it (*li-atabarraka bihi*)."[529]

Al-Shāfi'ī's "Old" and "New" Schools

Two schools of jurisprudence or *madhāhib* are actually attributed to al-Shāfi'ī, embracing all his positions and legal opinions (*fatāwa*). These two schools are known in the terminology of jurists as "The Old" (*al-qadīm*) and "The New" (*al-jadīd*), corresponding respectively to his

[527] Better translated as "I certainly do seek..." in light of the saying also reported from al-Shāfi'ī: "I never swore by Allāh – neither truthfully nor deceptively."

[528] Narrated by al-Khaṭīb in *Tārīkh Baghdād* (1:123) cf. al-Kawtharī in his *Maqālāt* (p. 453) and by Ibn Abī al-Wafā' in *Ṭabaqāt al-Ḥanafiyya* (p. 519) through al-Ghaznawī. Al-Haytamī cites it in the thirty-fifth chapter of his book on Imām Abū Ḥanīfa entitled *al-Khayrāt al-Ḥisān*.

[529] Narrated from al-Rabī' through two chains by Ibn 'Asākir (5:311-312) and Ibn al-Subkī in *Ṭabaqāt al-Shāfi'iyya al-Kubrā* (2:36); cf. al-Munāwī in *Ṭabaqāt al-Ṣūfiyya al-Kubrā* (1:518) and al-'Irāqī in *Fatḥ al-Muta'āl*, the latter adding: "Ibn Taymiyya also related it." Al-Dhahabī deems this report inauthentic in the *Siyar* (10:396).

stays in Iraq and Egypt. The most prominent transmitters of the New among al-Shāfi'ī's students are al-Buwayṭī, al-Muzanī, and al-Rabī' in *al-Umm* ("The Motherbook"). The most prominent transmitters of the Old are al-Za'farānī, Aḥmad ibn Ḥanbal, al-Karābīsī, and Abū Thawr in *Kitāb al-Ḥujja* ("Book of the Proof"). What is presently known as "the Shāfi'ī position" refers to the New except in approximately twenty-two questions, in which Shāfi'ī scholars and muftis have retained the positions of the Old.[530]

AL-BUWAYṬĪ

Yūsuf ibn Yaḥyā Abū Ya'qūb al-Miṣrī ﷺ (d. 231) was the examplary, pious, ascetic Imām of *fiqh* and of perpetual *dhikr* and worship. Al-Shāfi'ī named him the most knowledgeable person in his School – over al-Muzanī – and foretold his death with the words: "You will die wearing iron." He died in 231 in jail, bound in chains in Iraq for refusing to say that the Qur'ān was created. He said: "Allāh created everything with 'Be!' (*kun*). If it is created, then creatures are created by creatures." Allāh have mercy on him.[531]

AL-MUZANĪ

Yaḥyā ibn Ismā'īl ibn 'Amr ibn Muslim, Abū Ibrāhīm al-Muzanī al-Miṣrī (175-264), "the erudite Imām, the Jurist of this Community, and the standard-bearer of ascetics" (al-Dhahabī), was al-Shāfi'ī's student and the principal early authority of his School. He taught Ibn Khuzayma, Ibn Abī Ḥātim, and Ibn Jarīr al-Ṭabarī as well as his maternal nephew Abū Ja'far al-Ṭaḥāwī. Al-Shāfi'ī called al-Muzanī the standard-bearer of his School. This was consolidated through the high fame of his abridgment (*mukhtaṣar*) of al-Shāfi'ī's *al-Umm* which in turn was elaborated and refined by subsequent generations of jurists. With the *Mukhtaṣar* he authored *al-Jāmi' al-Kabīr, al-Ṣaghīr, al-Manthūr, al-Masā'il al-Mu'tabara, al-Targhīb fil-'Ilm, al-Wathā'iq,* and other works. In the *Mukhtaṣar* he differed with al-Shāfi'ī on a number of questions but among his greater concerns was the refutation of the Ḥanafīs.

When the Ḥanafī *qāḍī* Bakkār ibn Qutayba took up judgeship in Egypt and met al-Muzanī, one of his companions asked the latter: "The ḥadīths mention both the prohibition of fruit mash (*taḥrīm al-*

530 Cf. al-Mas'ūdī, *al-Mu'tamad min Qadīmi Qawl al-Shāfi'ī.*

531 Cf. al-Dhahabī, *Siyar* (10:67-69 §1978).

nabīdh) and its permissibility (*taḥlīlih*); why did you [Shāfi'īs] give precedence to its prohibition?" Al-Muzanī replied: "No one ever declared it prohibited in *Jāhiliyya*; then it was declared *ḥalāl* for us, and agreement formed over its permissibility; then it was declared *ḥarām*. This, therefore, gives pre-eminence to the narrations of *taḥrīm*." Bakkār approved of this reply. Al-Dhahabī comments: "Furthermore, the ḥadīths of *taḥrīm* are many and sound, which is not the case with the ḥadīths of permission (*ibāḥa*)." Bakkār was succeeded by Aḥmad ibn Abī 'Imrān who became al-Ṭaḥāwī's teacher and the probable reason he adopted the Ḥanafī School after al-Muzanī died.

Al-Muzanī said: "I devoted myself to washing the dead so that my heart would soften, and it became my practice." He washed al-Shāfi'ī when the latter died, and used to say: "I am only one of al-Shāfi'ī's merits."[532]

AL-RABĪ'

Abū Muḥammad al-Rabī' ibn Sulaymān ibn 'Abd al-Jabbār al-Murādī al-Miṣrī 🕮 (174-270) was the Imām, *Muḥaddith*, chief Jurisprudent of his time, first *mu'adhdhin* and teacher of the *Mu'adhdhinīn* in the mosque of al-Fusṭāṭ. He narrated from 'Abd Allāh ibn Wahb, al-Baghawī, al-Shāfi'ī, al-Tinnīsī, and from him narrated Abū Dāwūd, Ibn Mājah, al-Nasā'ī, Abū Zur'a, Abū Ḥātim, al-Ṭaḥāwī, al-Faḍl ibn Dukayn, and countless others.

About two hundred students took the Shāfi'ī School from al-Rabī'. Ibn al-Subkī related that the Shāfi'ī Scholars considered his narration from al-Shāfi'ī sounder from the viewpoint of transmission while they considered al-Muzanī's sounder from the viewpoint of *fiqh*, although both were established Masters.

Al-Shāfi'ī said to al-Rabī': "How I love you!" and another time: "Rabī'! If I could spoon feed you the Science I would spoon feed it to you." Al-Qaffāl al-Shāshī in his *Fatāwā* relates that al-Rabī' was slow in his understanding, and that al-Shāfi'ī once repeated an explanation forty times for him in a gathering, yet he did not understand it, then got up and left in embarrassment. Later, al-Shāfi'ī called him in private and resumed explaining it to him until he understood. This shows the accuracy of Ibn Rāhūyah's statement about understanding al-Shāfi'ī's discourse.

[532] Cf. al-Khalīlī, *al-Irshād* (1:429-431) and al-Dhahabī, *Siyar* (10:335-338 §2145).

Al-Rabī' said: "One time al-Shāfi'ī invited people to a feast. After the people ate, al-Buwayṭī said to me: 'Sit and eat.' I replied: 'Who has authorised us [students] to eat?' Whereupon al-Shāfi'ī, hearing me, said: '*Subḥan Allāh!* You [al-Rabī'] have permission to take all I own.' Another time he saw me write down an account of a certain expense so he said: 'Do not waste your paper for trivial matters. I am not asking any account of you.' I said: 'But Umm Abī al-Ḥasan [al-Rabī''s wife] sometimes asks me to get her something, so I buy it for her without asking you first.' Al-Shāfi'ī replied: 'Sleepy-head! (*yā ṭawīl al-ruqād*) You have permission to take all I own.'"

Al-Rabī' and al-Muzanī taught the Baṣran ḥadīth Master Zakariyyā ibn Yaḥyā al-Sājī, who then taught the great Imām Abū al-Ḥasan al-Ash'arī.

AL-ZA'FARĀNĪ

Abū 'Alī al-Ḥasan ibn Muḥammad ibn al-Ṣabbāḥ al-Baghdādī al-Bazzār al-Za'farānī ﵀ (d. 260) the ḥadīth Master, philologian, and Jurist, formerly a Ḥanafī, was one of al-Bukhārī's Shaykhs together with other companions of al-Shāfi'ī such as 'Abd Allāh ibn al-Zubayr al-Ḥumaydī, Abū Thawr, and al-Karābīsī. He took ḥadīth from Ibn 'Uyayna. He was famous for his knowledge of Arabic and his eloquence. Al-Bayhaqī narrated with his chain from 'Abd Allāh ibn Aḥmad ibn Ḥanbal that Imām Aḥmad said: "When al-Shāfi'ī came to us [in Baghdād] I took Isḥāq ibn Rāhūyah by the hand and we went to al-Za'farānī, saying, 'This man came and we need to hear from him these books. You are more eloquent (*afṣaḥ*) than us, so you can read them for us before him. So he read them, and the transmission was, for al-Za'farānī, of the *qirā'atan* type and, for us, of the *'arḍan* type."[533]

Al-Za'farānī said: "I asked al-Shāfi'ī about reciting the Qur'ān at the graveside and he said: *la ba'sa bihi*–There is no harm in it."[534] This is also the position of Isḥāq ibn Rāhūyah, Aḥmad, and Muḥammad ibn al-Ḥasan al-Shaybānī as well as the Mālikī School according to al-Qurṭubī.[535]

533 Narrated by al-Bayhaqī, *Manāqib* (1:226).

534 Al-Khallāl narrates it in *al-Amr bil-Ma'rūf* (p. 123 §243), al-Suyūṭī in *Sharḥ al-Ṣudūr* (p. 311), and Ibn Qayyim al-Jawziyya in *Kitāb al-Rūḥ* (Madanī ed. p. 18).

535 Al-Qurṭubī said: "As for reciting over the grave our companions are categorical that it is lawful, and others say the same." Al-Suyūṭī mentioned it in his *Sharḥ al-Ṣudūr* (p.

AL-KARĀBĪSĪ

Al-Ḥusayn ibn ʿAlī ibn Yazīd, Abū ʿAlī al-Karābīsī ﵀ (d. 245 or 248) the trustworthy ḥadīth Master, a scholar of Ḥanafī then Shāfiʿī *fiqh* and *kalām*, "one of the oceans of the Science" according to al-Dhahabī, was one of al-Shāfiʿī's major disciples in Iraq whom al-Ṣayrafī recommended, together with Abū Thawr, to his students. He also took ḥadīth from ʿAlī ibn al-Madīnī, al-Shādhakūnī, and others.

Al-Karābīsī is related to say: "When a ḥadīth Scholar narrates a report, both outward and inner knowledge of this report become obligatory, just as dictated by mass-narrated reports." At the same time, he held that "The slip of one scholar of knowledge demolishes Islām, whereas the slips of a thousand ignoramuses do not." Accordingly he was strict in his refusal of any ruling at variance with the letter of the Law in patent legal matters, such as the acceptance of the testimony of a single witness provided he swears an oath.[536]

Al-Karābīsī was severely taken to task by Abū Thawr, Muḥammad ibn ʿAqīl al-Firyābī, Ḥubaysh, and Aḥmad for his book *Kitāb al-Mudallisīn* in which he unwittingly provided arguments for the enemies of the Sunna, such as the disparagement of al-Aʿmash.[537] This book was refuted by Imām al-Ṭaḥāwī in a five-volume work, unfortunately lost.

Al-Karābīsī narrated that al-Shāfiʿī said: "After the Prophet ﷺ people were in difficulty and did not find anyone under the sky better than Abū Bakr. Thus they used him as the one who carried the responsibility of the people."

When he heard that Imām Aḥmad had declared as an innovation his statement that the pronunciation of the Qur'ān was created, al-Karābīsī said: "One's pronunciation means something other than the thing pronounced" (*talaffuẓuka yaʿnī ghayra al-malfūẓ*). Then he said of Aḥmad: "What shall we do with this boy? If we say 'created' he says *bidʿa*, and if we say 'not created' he says *bidʿa*!" The Ḥanbalīs were angered and declared him unacceptable as a narrator. Al-Dhahabī

---

311). See below for the position of Imām Aḥmad and his School (p. 411-412).

[536] For example, Muʿāwiya's acceptance of Umm Salama's single testimony on behalf of her cousin, or Zurāra's of Abū Miljaz's single testimony, or Shurayḥ's of Abū Qays's single testimony.

[537] See Ibn Rajab at the very end of his book *Sharḥ ʿIlal al-Tirmidhī* (2:806-807).

commented: "There is no doubt that what al-Karābīsī innovated and explained in the question of the pronunciation is the truth. But Imām Aḥmad refused it to preclude the extension of the question to the Qur'ān itself, since one cannot distinguish the pronunciation from the pronounced – which is the Speech of Allāh ﷻ – except in the mind."[538] Similarly, Ibn ʿAbd al-Barr stated that al-Karabīsī was only stating the position of most of his generation over the issue of pronunciation, such as Ibn Kullāb, Abū Thawr, and Dāwūd al-Ẓāhirī (as well as al-Bukhārī and Muslim).[539]

ABŪ THAWR

Abū ʿAbd Allāh Ibrāhīm ibn Khālid al-Kalbī al-Baghdādī, nicknamed Abū Thawr ؓ (d. 240), was a major Scholar, the *mujtahid* Imām and ḥadīth Master of Iraq, a student of al-Shāfiʿī and Sufyān ibn ʿUyayna, from whom narrated Abū Dāwūd, Ibn Mājah, al-Baghawī, and others, and one of the foremost compilers of al-Shāfiʿī's jurisprudence.

The Ḥanbalī Ibn Abī Yaʿlā narrated in his *Ṭabaqāt al-Ḥanābila* that ʿAbd al-Wahhāb al-Warrāq (d. 251) said: "Abū Thawr is a Jahmī! When he was asked of the ḥadīth whereby 'Allāh created Ādam in his/His image' (*ʿalā ṣūratihi*)[540] he said: 'it means only in Ādam's image, not in the image of the Merciful.' I do not treat him in any other way than Aḥmad ibn Ḥanbal did: he deserted Abū Thawr and whoever said what he said." Ibn Abī Yaʿlā elsewhere narrates from Ibrāhīm ibn Abbān al-Mawṣilī that a man told Aḥmad: "I heard Abū Thawr say that Allāh created Ādam in Ādam's own form." Aḥmad remained silent a long time, then supposedly struck his hand upon his face and said: "This is evil speech. This is Jahm's speech. This man is a Jahmī, avoid him!"[541]

Al-Warrāq's and al-Mawṣilī's reports from Aḥmad attacking Abū Thawr are representative of the general unreliability of Ibn Abī Yaʿlā's *Ṭabaqāt al-Ḥanābila* in reporting Imām Aḥmad's positions in *ʿaqīda*

538 Cf. *Siyar* (10:81-82 §1988) and *Ṭabaqāt al-Shāfiʿiyya al-Kubrā* (2:117-126 §25).

539 Ibn ʿAbd al-Barr, *al-Intiqā'* (p. 165).

540 Narrated from Abū Hurayra by al-Bukhārī and Muslim. See Ibn Khuzayma's *Kitāb al-Tawḥīd* (p. 37-41) and al-Qurṭubī's *al-Asnā* (2:93-94). See explanation immediately below and also p. 262.

541 In Ibn Abī Yaʿlā, *Ṭabaqāt al-Ḥanābila* (1:93 and 1:212).

and *fiqh* without bias, school-partisanship, or error. What is authentically retained from Aḥmad concerning Abū Thawr is that Aḥmad recommended him while generally disapproving of the compilation of *fiqh* books out of scrupulous Godwariness.

Al-Dhahabī narrates the following reports in the chapter on Abū Thawr in his *Siyar*:

- Abū Bakr al-A'yān said: "I asked Aḥmad ibn Ḥanbal about Abū Thawr and he said: 'I have known him to adhere to the Sunna for fifty years. I consider him cut in the same cloth as Sufyān al-Thawrī!'"
- 'Abd al-Raḥmān ibn Khāqān said: "I asked Aḥmad ibn Ḥanbal about Abū Thawr and he said: 'I have heard nothing but good about him, except that I don't like the talk with which they [i.e. jurists] end up in their books.'"
- Aḥmad was asked about a question [in jurisprudence] and he said: "Ask someone else. Ask the jurists. Ask Abū Thawr."

Al-Dhahabī concludes his biographical notice with the words: "He [Abū Thawr] is without question a proof of the highest reliability" (*huwa ḥujjatun bilā taraddud*).[542] This shows that he rejected the authenticity of the reports of Aḥmad's condemnation of him, especially in the light of the reports on Abū Thawr's brilliance in *fiqh*.

Apart from school partisanship, a strong motive for Ibn Abī Ya'lā's citation of the attacks on Abū Thawr is the anthropomorphist bent in Ibn Abī Ya'lā's own interpretation of the ḥadīth of Ādam's creation. This is somewhat corroborated by Ibn al-Jawzī's reference to Abū Ya'lā as a *mushabbih* in the opening page of his *Daf' Shubah al-Tashbīh*.

As for the ḥadīth of the creation of Ādam ﷺ, *Ahl al-Sunna* concur that different meanings are possible as stated in al-Qurṭubī's *Tafsīr* and his *al-Asnā fī Sharḥ Asmā' Allāh al-Ḥusnā*, al-Nawawī's *Sharḥ Ṣaḥīḥ Muslim*, al-Munāwī's *Fayḍ al-Qadīr*, and elsewhere:

a) The meaning whereby "Allāh created Ādam in his image [directly]" – *i.e.* in his finished form without making him pass through the stages of embryonic formation; further, Ādam was

[542] Cf. *Siyar* (10:77 §1984). See also *Ṭabaqāt al-Shāfi'iyya al-Kubrā* (2:76-77 §15).

created in Paradise in the same form in which he died on earth, without change.[543] This meaning is confirmed by the narration of Imām Aḥmad in his *Musnad* with a fair chain from Abū Hurayra that the Prophet ﷺ said: "The people of Paradise shall enter Paradise naked, beardless, fair, long-haired, kohl-eyed, aged thirty-three, in the form of Ādam, sixty cubits by seven cubits."

b) The meaning whereby "Allāh created Ādam in the image of the Merciful"[544] – i.e. by sharing with him some of His Attributes, in their relative and not their full sense, such as life, hearing, sight, knowledge, and so forth. The predication of image to the Merciful therefore signifies possession, dignity, and bestowal as in the attribute of possession in the verse [the she-camel of Allāh] (90:13), not body part or appearance. This was clarified by al-Rāghib al-Iṣfahānī in *Mufradāt Alfāẓ al-Qur'ān*, al-Nawawī, and al-Haytamī.[545]

c) A third possible meaning is derived from a variant version of this ḥadīth: "When one of you fights, let him avoid [striking] the face [of the enemy], for Allāh created Ādam in his [that man's] likeness."[546]

Ibn Qutayba in *Mukhtalif al-Ḥadīth* investigates the different meanings then, after purportedly adopting a non-interpretive position (*bilā kayf*), speaks of the Merciful "possessing a form unlike all other forms" (*ṣūra lā kal-ṣuwar*), to which al-Māzarī responds: "This is like the anthropomorphists' words, 'a body unlike all other bodies' (*jismun lā kal-ajsām*)!"[547]

Al-Bayhaqī, following Abū Thawr, gave precedence to the first meaning according to the demands of sound doctrine and the greater soundness of the narrations which do not mention the Merciful.[548] This is also the interpretation followed by Ibn Khuzayma

543 Cf. al-Qurṭubī, *al-Asnā* (2:93-95).

544 The narration in this wording is weak by agreement of the Imāms of ḥadīth as stated by al-Māzarī in *al-Muʿlim bi-Fawā'id Muslim* (3:171).

545 Al-Nawawī in *Sharḥ Ṣaḥīḥ Muslim* (16:166) and al-Haytamī in his *Fatāwā Ḥadīthiyya* (p. 290-293).

546 Narrated from Abū Hurayra by al-Bukhārī and Muslim.

547 Al-Māzarī, *al-Muʿlim* (3:172) as cited in *Sharḥ Ṣaḥīḥ Muslim* (16:166).

548 In *al-Asmā' wal-Ṣifāt* (al-Ḥāshidī ed. 2:60-65; al-Kawtharī ed. p. 289-291).

in *Kitāb al-Tawḥīd.* Imām Mālik actually forbade his students from narrating this ḥadīth so as not to spread confusion among people.[549]

YŪNUS IBN 'ABD AL-A'LĀ

Abū Mūsā Yūnus ibn 'Abd al-A'lā al-Ṣadafī al-Miṣrī ﷺ (d. 264), the Imām and trustworthy ḥadīth Master, Shaykh al-Islām, and *Faqīh* whom al-Shāfi'ī praised, saying there was no-one more intelligent than him, he was among al-Ṭaḥāwī's and al-Ṭabarī's teachers.[550]

The *Basmala* in the Shāfi'ī School

A notable position of Imām al-Shāfi'ī and his School is the obligatory recitation of the *Basmala* – ﴿ IN THE NAME OF ALLĀH, THE ALL-BENEFICENT, THE MOST MERCIFUL ﴾ (1:1) as the first verse of Sūrat al-Fātiḥa and of every Sūra of the Qur'ān except the ninth, al-Tawba. This position was analyzed by Shaykh al-Islām Zayn al-Dīn al-'Irāqī among others.[551] One of its proofs is that "The Prophet ﷺ would not know that a particular Sūra had ended until he heard the *Basmala* being recited to him."[552]

There is also Consensus that the *Basmala* should be written in the *Muṣḥaf* at the top of each Sūra except the ninth – Sūrat al-Tawba, also entitled Barā'a – together with the Consensus that nothing that is not part of the Qur'ān should be written into the *Muṣḥaf.* The only divergence is that al-Shāfi'ī, Aḥmad, Isḥāq ibn Rāhūyah and others said the *Basmala* is part of each Sūra except al-Tawba; while the Ḥanafīs, Aḥmad in another narration, and Dāwūd al-Ẓāhirī said they are an independent verse at the top of each Sūra but not part of it.[553] An array of proofs for the view that it is part of each Sūra is presented in the book *Ḥawla Tafsīr Sūrat al-Fātiḥa* (p. 33-43) by the late ḥadīth Master of Aleppo, al-Sayyid 'Abd Allāh Sirāj al-Dīn.[554]

549 Cf. al-'Uqaylī, *al-Ḍu'afā'* (2:251 §806).

550 Al-Dhahabī, *Siyar* (Risāla ed. 12:348).

551 In his book *Ṭarḥ al-Tathrīb* (4:189-190).

552 Narrated from Ibn 'Abbās by Abū Dāwūd with a sound chain, al-Ḥākim, al-Bazzār, al-Ṭabarānī, and al-Bayhaqī in *Ma'rifat al-Sunan.*

553 Cf. Dr. Nūr al-Dīn 'Itr's *Fī Tafsīr al-Qur'ān wa-Uslūbihi al-Mu'jiz 'Ilmiyyan wa-Bayāniyyan,* 3rd ed. (Damascus: Maṭba'at al-Ṣabāḥ, 1999), p. 11.

554 One of the best reviews of this issue also is al-Qurṭubī's *Tafsīr Sūrat al-Fātiḥa.*

Touch Nullifies Ablution in the Shāfi'ī School

Al-Shāfi'ī took the verse ﴾**Or if you have touched women**﴿ (4:43) literally, and considered that contact between the sexes, even accidental or unintentional, nullified ablution. This is also the position of Ibn Mas'ūd (as mentioned by al-Shāfi'ī), Ibn 'Umar, al-Sha'bī, al-Nakha'ī, al-Zuhrī, and al-Awzā'ī, which is confirmed by Ibn 'Umar's report: "Whoever kisses or touches his wife with his hand must renew his *wuḍū'*." It is authentic and related in numerous places including the *Muwaṭṭa'*. They all read the above verse literally, without interpreting "touch" to mean "sexual intercourse" as do the Ḥanafīs, or "touch with pleasure" as do the Mālikīs.

The reasoning of the Shāfi'īs is strong on many levels. Among them:

- Al-Shāfi'ī's expertise in the Makkan dialect – the main dialect of the Qur'ān – and his foremost strength in the Arabic language;
- The rule of *mughāyara* or non-redundancy in the Qur'ān: Allāh ﷻ first mentions the state of major ritual impurity resulting from sexual intercourse as a cause for the necessity of *ghusl* then acts that cause ritual impurity remediable with *tayammum*, among them, natural need and touching a [*non-maḥram*] woman. Hence, *lams* cannot mean sexual intercourse since the term *junuban* was already mentioned in the verse to cover this meaning. Thus, the Scholars said, *lams* must refer to a lesser act that is not on the level of sexual relations as this would be redundant: ﴾**O you who believe! Draw not near unto prayer when you are drunken, till you know that which you utter, nor when you are polluted, save when journeying upon the road, till you have bathed. And if you are ill, or on a journey, or one of you comes from the privy, or you have touched women, and you have no water, than go to high clean soil and rub your faces and your hands therewith. Lo! Allāh is Benign, Forgiving**﴿ (4:43).

Since the Shāfi'ī ruling on *lams* is also the most precautionary one of the Four Schools, they recommended it as the way of scrupulousness (*wara'*) and to preclude difference (*khilāf*).

Al-Shāfi'ī's Unique Mastery of the Arabic Language

Al-Shāfi'ī was known for his peculiar strength in Arabic language, poetry, and philology. He is the only Qurayshī of the Four Imams and the only one of the Four to be raised in Makka, the cradle of the chief Qur'anic dialect. His *Dīwān* of poetry is among the masterpieces of Arabic literature.

Al-Bayhaqī narrated:

> [From al-Rabī']: Al-Shāfi'ī was an Arab to his soul and an Arab in his speech. If you had seen him and seen the beauty of his expression and eloquence you would have been awestruck. If he had authored his books in the way that he used to speak, no one would have been able to read them.[555]

> [From Ibn Hishām:] I was al-Shāfi'ī's close companion for a long time and I never heard him use anything other than a word which, carefully considered, one would not find (in its context) a better word in the entire Arabic language. [...] Al-Shāfi'ī's discourse, in relation to language, is a proof in itself.

> [From al-Ḥasan ibn Muḥammad al-Za'farānī:] A group of bedouins used to frequent al-Shāfi'ī's gathering with us and sit in a corner. One day I asked their leader: "You are not interested in scholarship; why do you sit with us?" They said: "We come to hear al-Shāfi'ī's language."[556]

> [From al-Muzanī:] Al-Shāfi'ī asked Ibrāhīm ibn 'Ulayya after they finished listening to a girl singing Arabic poetry: "Does this bring joy to your soul?" He said no. Al-Shāfi'ī said: "You have no feelings!" (*mā laka ḥiss*).[557]

Interpretation *(Ta'wīl) vs.* Committal of Meaning *(Tafwīḍ)*

Al-Shāfi'ī trod the path of the noble *Salaf* in avoiding any interpretation of the verses and narrations pertaining to the Divine Attributes. Like his teacher Mālik, he practiced "committal of the meaning"

555 Narrated by al-Bayhaqī, *Manāqib* (1:19).
556 *Ibid.* (2:42-46).
557 *Ibid.* (2:210).

(*tafwīḍ al-maʿnā*) to a higher authority, as in his saying: "I believe in what comes from Allāh in the meaning meant (*murād*) by Allāh ﷻ and I believe in what comes from the Messenger of Allāh in the meaning meant by the Messenger of Allāh ﷺ."[558]

عن الإمام الشافعي رضي الله عنه آمَنْتُ بِاللَّهِ وَبِمَا جَاءَ عَنِ اللَّهِ عَلَى مُرَادِ اللَّهِ وَآمَنْتُ بِرَسُولِ اللَّهِ وَبِمَا جَاءَ عَنْ رَسُولِ اللَّهِ عَلَى مُرَادِ رَسُولِ اللَّهِ ذكره ابن قدامة في

لمعة الاعتقاد وذم التأويل والمواهبي في العين والأثر

Asked about the Attributes he said: "It is forbidden for minds to represent Allāh ﷻ. It is forbidden for the imagination to conceive limits for Him (*tuḥiddah*). It is forbidden for speculation to presume anything about Him. It is forbidden for souls to think about His Essence. It is forbidden for consciences to deepen reflection about Him. It is forbidden for thoughts to grasp other than what He described Himself with, as conveyed by His Prophet ﷺ!"[559]

At the same time, rare instances of interpretation are recorded from him. Al-Bayhaqī relates that al-Muzanī reported from al-Shāfiʿī the following commentary on the verse ﴾**To Allāh belong the East and the West, and wheresoever you turn, there is the face (*wajh*) of Allāh**﴿ (2:115): "It means – and Allāh knows best – thither is the bearing (*wajh*) towards which Allāh has directed you." Al-Bayhaqī continues: "The ḥadīth Master Abū ʿAbd Allāh [al-Ḥākim] and the ḥadīth Master al-Qāḍī Abū Bakr ibn al-ʿArabī have related to us from Mujāhid that he said regarding this verse: "It means the direction of prayer to Allāh (*qibla*), therefore wheresoever you are, East and West, do not turn your faces except towards it."

Al-Ḥumaydī's *ʿAqīda*

Among the senior colleagues of al-Shāfiʿī was the major Imām and ḥadīth Master al-Ḥumaydī – Abū Bakr ʿAbd Allāh ibn al-Zubayr ibn

558 Cited by Ibn Qudāma in *Lamʿat al-Iʿtiqād* (Ryadh ed. p. 10=Damascus ed. p. 9=ʿUthaymīn ed. p. 36) and *Dhamm al-Taʾwīl* (1994 ed. p. 9 = 1981 ed. p. 11 and 1994 ed. p. 42 = 1986 ed. p. 44), al-Mawāhibī in *al-ʿAyn wal-Athar* (Damascus: al-Maʾmūn ed.) p. 62, and Ibn Taymiyya in *al-Risāla al-Madaniyya* (p. 121), *al-ʿAqīda al-Aṣfahāniyya* (p. 86), and *Majmūʿ al-Fatāwā* (4:2 and 6:354).

559 Narrated from al-Rabīʿ ibn Sulaymān by Ibn Qudāma in *Dhamm* (p. 20-21 §34).

ʿĪsā (d. 219). The foremost student of Ibn ʿUyayna, he accompanied al-Shāfiʿī in the last ten years of his life, from the time he settled in Baghdād to his death in Cairo and would have succeeded him there were it not for Ibn ʿAbd al-Ḥakam. He once said: "By Allāh! For me to charge against those who reject the ḥadīth of the Messenger of Allāh ﷺ is dearer than to charge against the Turks." He authored a brief, straightforward statement of Sunni doctrine[560] in which he said:

The Sunna in our understanding consists of

[1] belief in the foreordained Divine decree (*al-qadar*), the good and the bad, the sweet and the bitter, and to know with certainty (*an yaʿlam*) that whatever befell one was never to not befall him; that whatever did not befall him was never to befall him; and that all this was caused to pass (*qaḍāʾ*) by Allāh Most Glorious.

[2] [Knowledge] that belief consists of word and deed, that it increases and decreases, that no word benefits except with deeds, nor any word and deeds except with intention, nor any word, deeds, and intention except according to the Sunna.

[3] Invoking mercy upon all the Companions of Muḥammad ﷺ for Allāh ﷻ said: ﴾**And those who came into the faith after them say: Our Lord! Forgive us and our brethren who were before us in the faith**﴿ (59:10). Thus we were not ordered except to ask for their forgiveness. Therefore, whoever insults them or disparages them or any of them follows other than the Sunna and has no right to the fifth of the spoils (*fay'*). More than one authority narrated to us that Mālik ibn Anas said: "Allāh Most High divided the spoils by saying: ﴾**And (it is) for the poor fugitives who have been driven out from their homes and their belongings, who seek bounty from Allāh and help Allāh and His messenger. They are the loyal ones. Those who entered the city and the faith before them love these who flee unto them for refuge, and find in their breasts no need for that which has been given them, but prefer (the fugitives) above themselves though poverty become**

[560] Published by Ḥabīb al-Raḥmān al-Aʿẓamī at the end of his edition of al-Ḥumaydī's *Musnad* and again recently at Ryadh's Maktabat al-Rushd.

their lot. And whoso is saved from his own avarice, such are they who are successful. And those who came (into the faith) after them say: Our Lord Forgive us and our brethren...﴿ (59:8-10). Whoever does not say is excluded from those who were given the right to the fifth."

[4] [Belief] that the Qur'ān is the word of Allāh. I heard Sufyān [ibn 'Uyayna] say: "The Qur'ān is the word of Allāh, and whoever says that is is created is an innovator. We never heard anyone say such a thing." I also heard Sufyān say: "Belief consists of word and deed, it increases and decreases." His brother Ibrāhīm ibn 'Uyayna then said to him: "Abū Muḥammad, do not say that it decreases." He became angry and said: "Be quiet, boy! Yes, it decreases to the point where there remains nothing of it."

[5] Affirming [the reality of] the vision [of Allāh Most High] after death and

[6] all that the Qur'ān and the ḥadīth said, such as ﴾**The Jews say: the hand of Allāh is fettered. Their own hands are fettered**﴿ (5:64), ﴾**and the heavens are rolled in His right hand**] (39:67) and similar texts in the Qur'ān and the ḥadīth. We add nothing to them nor do we explain them. Rather, we stop exactly where the Qur'ān and the Sunna stopped. You must say: ﴾**The Merciful established Himself over the Throne**﴿ (20:5). Whoever claims other than this is a Jahmī nullifier (*mu'aṭṭil*).

[7] We do not say, as the *Khawārij* said, that anyone that commits a grave sin (*kabīra*) has committed apostasy. Nor do we declare anyone a disbeliever for any sin committed. Disbelief (*kufr*) is only in leaving the five [pillars] mentioned by the Prophet ﷺ: "Islām is built upon five [pillars]: the testimony that there is no God but Allāh and that Muḥammad is the Messenger of Allāh, the observance of the prayer, the payment of the poor-tax, the fast of Ramaḍān, and the pilgrimage to the House."[561]

[561] Narrated from Ibn 'Umar by al-Bukhārī, Muslim, al-Tirmidhī, al-Nasā'ī, and Aḥmad.

Al-Shāfiʿī and Dialectic Theology *(Kalām)*

Al-Zaʿfarānī said: "Al-Shāfiʿī was the most eloquent of men, yet, if theology was probed in his gathering, he would say, 'We are not people of *kalām.*'"[562] His hatred of *kalām* was due to his extreme caution against errors which bear heavy consequences as they induce one into false beliefs. Among his sayings concerning this: "My ruling concerning the practitioners of *kalām* is that they be flogged, then seated upon a camel and paraded among the clans and the tribes while a herald proclaims: 'This is the reward of those who abandon the Book and the Sunna to take up *kalām*!'"[563] "It is better for a scholar of knowledge to give a *fatwā* after which he is said to be wrong than to theologise and then be said to be a heretic (*zindīq*). I hate nothing more than theology and theologians." Al-Dhahabī commented: "This indicates that the position of Abū 'Abd Allāh concerning error in the tenets of faith (*al-uṣūl*) is that it is not the same as error in the course of scholarly exertion in the branches." The reason is that in belief and doctrine neither *ijtihād* nor *ikhtilāf* are permitted. In this respect al-Shāfiʿī said: "It cannot be asked 'Why?' concerning the Principles, nor 'How?'"

Definition of the Principles of the Religion *(Uṣūl al-Dīn)*

Yūnus ibn 'Abd al-Aʿlā narrated that al-Shāfiʿī defined the Principles as "Qur'ān, Sunna, analogy (*al-qiyās*), and Consensus (*al-ijmāʿ*)"; he defined the latter to mean "The adherence of the Congregation (*jamāʿa*) of the Muslims to the conclusions of a given ruling pertaining to what is permitted and what is forbidden after the passing of the Prophet ﷺ."

His Acknowledgment of Sunnī *Kalām*

Yet al-Shāfiʿī acknowledged a Sunni type of *kalām* in defense of the Sunna and never closed the door on the qualified use of *kalām* as shown by his statement, "Every *mutakallim* according to the Qur'ān and Sunna possesses diligence, while every other type is delirious!"[564]

[562] In al-Harawī al-Anṣārī's *Dhamm al-Kalām* (4:309 §1169).

[563] Narrated from al-Zaʿfarānī, Abū Thawr, and al-Karābīsī by Ibn 'Abd al-Barr in *al-Intiqā'* (p. 133-134).

[564] Narrated from al-Karābīsī by al-Bayhaqī, *Manāqib* (1:470), *Siyar* (Risāla ed. 10:20).

Al-Bayhaqī detected in this statement a clear acknowledgment of the difference between Sunnī and non-Sunnī *kalām*.[565] Al-Shāfi'ī also said:

> Mālik was asked about *kalām* and monotheism (*tawḥīd*) and he said: "It is inconceivable that the Prophet ﷺ taught his Community hygiene and did not teach them about Oneness. And Oneness is exactly what the Prophet ﷺ said: 'I was ordered to fight people until they say *There is no God but Allāh*.'[566] So, whatever makes blood and property untouchable – that is the reality of Oneness (*ḥaqīqat al-tawḥīd*)."[567]

Al-Ḥalīmī similarly said: "In this ḥadīth there is explicit proof that that declaration (*lā ilāha illallāh*) suffices to save oneself from all the different kinds of disbelief in Allāh Almighty."[568] Further, the Prophet ﷺ heard a call [to prayer] coming from a valley saying: "I bear witness that there is no God but Allāh and that Muḥammad is the Messenger of Allāh" whereupon he said: "And I bear witness to the same, and I bear witness that no one bears witness to the same without clearing himself of *shirk* (associating a partner to Allāh)."[569] These are

[565] Cf. al-Bayhaqī, *Manāqib al-Shāfi'ī* (1:470).

[566] A mass-narrated (*mutawātir*) ḥadīth of the Prophet ﷺ narrated by al-Bukhārī, Muslim, and others from nineteen Companions cf. al-Kattānī in *Naẓm al-Mutanāthir.*

[567] Narrated from al-Muzanī by al-Sulamī cf. *Siyar* (Risāla ed. 10:26).

[568] In al-Bayhaqī, *al-Asmā' wal-Ṣifāt* (Kawtharī ed. p. 96; Ḥāshidī ed. 1:235). Al-Ḥusayn ibn al-Ḥasan ibn Muḥammad ibn Ḥalīm, Abū 'Abd Allāh al-Qāḍī al-Bukhārī al-Shāfi'ī al-Ḥalīmī (d. 403) is "the qāḍī, erudite Scholar, and foremost leader of the scholars of ḥadīth and *kalām* in Transoxiana" and one of the ḥadīth Masters. He authored important works and is an authority in the Shāfi'ī school and among early Ash'arīs. Al-Ḥākim took ḥadīth from him and al-Bayhaqī transmitted some of his scholarship in his *Asmā' wal-Ṣifāt* and *Shu'ab al-Īmān* where he quotes him as saying: "The beating of the hand-drum (*al-duff*) is not allowed except for women as it is originally one of their practices, and the Messenger of Allāh ﷺ cursed the men who imitate women." [In al-Bayhaqī, *Shu'ab al-Īmān* (4:283). The ḥadīth is narrated from Ibn 'Abbās by al-Bukhārī, al-Tirmidhī (*ḥasan ṣaḥīḥ*), Abū Dāwūd, Ibn Mājah, and Aḥmad.] Al-Bājūrī reports that al-Ḥalīmī, like the Mu'tazila, considered the angels to be superior to the Prophets except our Master the Prophet Muḥammad ﷺ. Cf. al-Dhahabī, *Siyar* (13:141-143 §3752) and *Tadhkirat al-Ḥuffāẓ* (3:1078); al-Bājūrī, *Sharḥ Jawharat al-Tawḥīd* (p. 293).

[569] Aḥmad and al-Ṭabarānī in *al-Awsaṭ* relate it with a sound chain, as stated by al-Haythamī in *Majma' al-Zawā'id.*

proofs against those who, in later times, innovated obligatory subdivisions for *tawḥīd* or legislated that their own understanding of the Divine Attributes was a precondition for the declaration of Oneness.

As for al-Shāfi'ī's saying reported from Abū Thawr, "Whoever clothes himself in *kalām* shall never succeed," al-Bayhaqī said: "**He only means** – and Allāh knows best – **the *kalām* of the people of vain lusts who abandon the Book and the Sunna and depend solely on reason (*'aql*), readjusting the Book to it**; and when the Sunna is brought up to them, further exposing their inconsistencies, they cast aspersions on its narrators and turn away from it. As for the People of the Sunna, their *madhhab* in the Foundations is based on the Book and the Sunna; whoever of them had recourse to reason did so only to disprove the *madhhab* of those who claimed that proofs were invalid rationally." Al-Bayhaqī further stated that al-Shāfi'ī also desired for his students to avoid the perils that became rife in the caliphal inquisition periods.

Al-Shāfi'ī Possessed Full Mastery of *Kalām*

Ibn Abī Ḥātim narrated from al-Rabī' that al-Shāfi'ī said: "If I wished, I could produce a book against each one of those who deviated, but dialectic theology is none of my business, and I would not like to be attributed any part in it."[570] Similar to the above is his advice to his student al-Muzanī: "Take proofs from creation about the Creator, and do not burden yourself with the knowledge of what your mind did not reach." Al-Muzanī said: "I debated a certain man who asked me questions that almost caused me to doubt in my Religion. I came to al-Shāfi'ī and recounted to him the whole matter. He said to me: 'Where are you?' I replied, 'In the mosque!' He said: '[Nay!] You are in Tārān [a whirlpool in the Red Sea] and its waves are crashing down on you! This is a favourite issue of atheists and its answer is such-and-such. It would be better for someone to be tried with all the harms that Allāh has created rather than be tried with *kalām*!'" Al-Bayhaqī cited this report and commented: "This shows al-Shāfi'ī's excellent knowledge of the issue and the obligation of exposing the distortions of atheists whenever needed. By *kalām*, he meant the

570 Al-Dhahabī said: "This breath of fresh air is mass-narrated from the Imām." Note that al-Shāfi'ī also spoke of his wish not to have a single letter out of all his works attributed to him, regardless of topic.

atheism of the atheists and the innovations of the innovators, and Allāh knows best."[571]

Al-Bayhaqī relates with a sound chain an anecdote whereby Ibn Khuzayma was won over to the position of the Muʿtazilī orator Abū ʿAbd al-Raḥmān on a question related to the pre-eternity of the Speech of Allāh ﷻ. When he realised his mistake he admitted, before his companions, to his lack of training in *kalām* with the words: "If a perfumer cannot properly practice shoemaking or carpentry, will you blame a *faqīh* and ḥadīth scholar if he does not excel in *kalām*? For my teacher [al-Muzanī] told me more than once: 'Al-Shāfiʿī forbade *kalām* for us.'" When news of this reached Ibn Abī Ḥātim in Ray, he said: "What does Abū Bakr [Ibn Khuzayma] want with *kalām*? It is preferable for both us and him not to meddle with what we did not learn."[572] Commenting on al-Muzanī's words al-Bayhaqī said: "Al-Muzanī was an ascetic, scrupulously Godwary person who used to avoid the company of princes. He kept himself away from *kalām* lest he be forced to appear before them as he saw had happened to al-Buwayṭī and his likes among *Ahl al-Sunna* in the days of al-Muʿtaṣim and al-Wāthiq."[573]

Al-Bayhaqī also said:

> And how could he possibly consider the *kalām* of *Ahl al-Sunna wal-Jamāʿa* reprehensible when he [al-Shāfiʿī] himself practiced it, debated those he debated, and exposed the fallacies of those who had cast doubt into the minds of some of his students?[574] [...] In this there is an indication that involvement in *kalām* is undesirable, according to those of our Imāms who stipulated it, only for the reason we have shown and because the reprehensible type of *kalām* is only that of the people of innovation, which contravenes the Book and the Sunna. As for the *kalām* that agrees with the Book and the Sunna, and is expounded rationally and wisely, then such *kalām* is praiseworthy and

571 Al-Bayhaqī, *Manāqib al-Shāfiʿī* (1:458).

572 Al-Bayhaqī, *al-Asmā' wal-Ṣifāt* (Kawtharī ed. p. 267-269; Ḥāshidī ed. 2:21-23). The account is related in full by al-Dhahabī in the *Siyar* after al-Ḥākim's *Tārīkh Naysābūr.*

573 Al-Bayhaqī, *Manāqib* (1:467) cf. Ibn ʿAsākir, *Tabyīn* (Kawtharī ed. p. 351).

574 Al-Bayhaqī, *Manāqib al-Shāfiʿī* (1:454-455).

desirable whenever needed. Al-Shāfi'ī used it and so did others of our Imāms – Allāh be well-pleased with them! – when needed, as we have mentioned.[575]

The Uncreatedness of the Qur'ān

Al-Shāfi'ī said: "The Qur'ān is the Speech of Allāh, uncreated."[576] To Ḥafṣ al-Fard who had said that the Qur'ān was created, al-Shāfi'ī said: "You have disbelieved in Allāh Most High (*kafarta billāhi al-'aẓīm*)!" Then he said to his companions: "It is better for someone to meet Allāh with sins the like of the mountains of Tihāma rather than to meet Him with one iota of what that man and his friends believe!"[577]

Three Books Falsely Attributed to the Imām

The books attributed to Imām al-Shāfi'ī under the titles *'Aqīdat al-Shāfi'ī*, *Waṣiyyat al-Shāfi'ī*, and *al-Fiqh al-Akbar* are forgeries. The *'Aqīda* is narrated through Abū al-'Izz Aḥmad ibn 'Ubayd Allāh ibn Kādish al-'Ukbarī and his Shaykh Abū Ṭālib Muḥammad ibn 'Alī ibn al-Fatḥ al-'Ishārī. Ibn Kādish was declared a liar by Ibn al-Najjār, admitted forging a ḥadīth before his student Ibn 'Asākir as related by Ibn Ḥajar,[578] and was said to be sloppy (*mukhliṭ*) in his narrations as related by Ibn Kathīr,[579] while al-'Ishārī narrated the spurious *'Aqīda* without knowing that it was a forgery.[580] The *Waṣiyya* is narrated through Abū al-Ḥasan 'Alī ibn Aḥmad ibn Yūsuf al-Hakkārī (d. 486), also accused of forgery,[581] and al-Dhahabī explicitly declared it inauthentic.[582] As for the *Fiqh al-Akbar*, a look at its style will reveal a *kalām* terminology that was not in use until centuries after al-Shāfi'ī's time. The continued presence of these books on market shelves is a sad exercise in irresponsibility on the part of certain book publishers and sellers.[583]

575 Al-Bayhaqī, *Manāqib al-Shāfi'ī* (1:463-467).

576 Narrated from Abū Sa'īd al-Miṣrī by al-Bayhaqī in *Manāqib al-Shāfi'ī* (1:407).

577 Narrated through Ibn Khuzayma from al-Rabī'; and from Ibn al-Jārūd by al-Bayhaqī in *Manāqib al-Shāfi'ī* (1:407 and 1:454).

578 Ibn Ḥajar, *Lisān al-Mīzān* (1:218 §677).

579 Ibn Kathīr, *Bidāya* (Year 526).

580 Ibn Ḥajar, *Lisān al-Mīzān* (5:301 §1019).

581 Ibn Ḥajar, *Lisān al-Mīzān* (4:195 §519) and al-Dhahabī, *Mīzān* (3:112).

582 *Siyar* (8:412).

583 Most notably the director of Beirut's al-Maktab al-Islāmī and al-Albānī's publisher, Zuhayr Shāwīsh, who recently re-published the pseudo-*Waṣiyya*.

"If the Ḥadīth is Authentic, that is my *Madhhab*"

One of the most misunderstood statements of Imām al-Shāfi'ī is his famous phrase: "When the authenticity of the ḥadīth is established, that is my *madhhab.*" The Ulema of the School explained, contrary to the populist approaches of "Salafīs," that this principle addresses the jurists who are capable of sifting the abrogating and sound ḥadīths from the abrogated and unsound ones as well as extracting the rulings from their collective evidence according to the principles of the Law and those of the Arabic language.[584] Al-Nawawī said:

> What Imām al-Shāfi'ī said does not mean that everyone who sees a *ṣaḥīḥ* ḥadīth should say "This is the *madhhab* of al-Shāfi'ī," applying the purely external or apparent meaning of his statement. What he said most certainly applies only to such a person as has the rank of *ijtihād* in the *madhhab.* It is a condition for such a person that he be firmly convinced that either Imām al-Shāfi'ī was unaware of this ḥadīth or he was unaware of its authenticity. And this is possible only after having researched all the books of al-Shāfi'ī and other similar books of the companions of al-Shāfi'ī, those who took knowledge from him and others similar to them.
>
> This is indeed a difficult condition to fulfill. Few are those who measure up to this standard in our times.[585] What we have explained has been made conditional because Imām al-Shāfi'ī had abandoned acting purely on the external meaning of many ḥadīths, which he declared and knew. However, he established proofs for criticism of the ḥadīth or its abrogation or specific circumstances or interpretation and so forth. Shaykh Abū 'Amr [Ibn al-Ṣalāḥ] said: "It is no trivial matter to act according to the literal meaning of what Imām al-Shāfi'ī said. For it is impermissible for every *faqīh* – let alone an ordinary person (*'āmmī*) – to act independently with what he takes to be a proof from the ḥadīth...

[584] See, in particular, Shaykh al-Islām Taqī al-Dīn al-Subkī's *Ma'nā Qawl al-Imām al-Muṭṭalibī Idhā Ṣaḥḥa al-Ḥadīthu Fahuwa Madhhabī*; Ibn al-Ṣalāḥ's *Adab al-Muftī wal-Mustaftī*; and the first volume of al-Nawawī's *al-Majmū'*.

[585] *I.e.* al-Nawawī's times, *a fortiori* ours. Among those who lived in al-Nawawī's century were al-Fakhr al-Rāzī, Ibn al-Ṣalāḥ, al-Mundhirī, Ibn 'Abd al-Salām, al-Qurṭubī, Ibn al-Qaṭṭān, al- Ḍiyā' al-Maqdisī, Ibn Qudāma, and Ibn Daqīq al-'Īd!

Therefore, any Shāfi'ī that finds a ḥadīth that contradicts his School must examine whether he is absolutely accomplished in all the disciplines of *ijtihād*, or in that particular topic, or specific question. [If he is,] then he has the right to apply it independently. If he is not, but finds that contravening the ḥadīth bears too heavily upon him – after having researched it and found no justification for contravening it – then he may apply it if another independent Imām other than al-Shāfi'ī applies it. This is a good reason for him to leave the *madhhab* of his Imām in such a case."[586]

THE ḤANAFĪ POSITION ON *TAQLĪD*

Similarly, Ibn 'Ābidīn said:

Deep knowledge of the evidence (*ma'rifat al-dalīl*) is only possible for someone at the level of *ijtihād* (*mujtahid*), for it hinges on knowing for sure that the evidence is free of that which opposes it, which in turn hinges on complete awareness of all the proofs (*istiqrā' al-adillati kullihā*), which is only possible for a *mujtahid*. As for merely knowing that a given *mujtahid* took a given ruling from a given set of evidences, it is of little consequence [...]. **Anyone who is not an "absolute *Mujtahid*" (*al-mujtahid al-muṭlaq*) is obligated to practice *taqlīd*** even if he is a *mujtahid* in certain issues of *fiqh* or certain sciences such as inheritance laws – if we take the position that *ijtihād* can be parcelled, which is the truth. In such a case, he imitates someone else in all that in which he is helpless. It was also said [*i.e.* this is a weak position] that "the *'Ālim* is obligated to practice *taqlīd* only on condition that the correctness of the *Mujtahid*'s proof/basis (*mustanad*) is clear to him, otherwise, *taqlīd* is impermissible for him." The first position is that of the massive majority (*al-jumhūr*). The second is that of some of the *Mu'tazila* [...]. [This] shows that **knowledge of the proof is incumbent only upon the absolute *Mujtahid*** and it is not incumbent upon anyone else, not even someone who is *mujtahid* inside the *Madhhab*.[587]

586 Al-Nawawī, *al-Majmū' Sharḥ al-Muhadhdhab* (1:64), citing Ibn al-Ṣalāḥ's *Fatāwā wa-Masā'il* (1:54, 1:58-59). Cf. al-Tahānawī, *I'lā' al-Sunan* (2:290-291).

587 *Sharḥ 'Uqūd Rasm al-Muftī*, in *Rasā'il Ibn 'Ābidīn* (1:30); thanks to Shaykh Farāz Rabbānī.

THE ḤANBALĪ POSITION ON *TAQLĪD*

Ibn Rajab said in his brief epistle treatise *al-Radd ʿalā Man Ittabaʿa Ghayr al-Madhāhib al-Arbaʿa* ("Refutation of Those Who Follow Other than the Four Schools"):

> If it is asked, "What do you say about Imām Aḥmad and other Imāms who prohibit imitating them and recording their sayings, and Imām Aḥmad's statement: Do not write my words, nor the words of So-and-so and So-and-so; instead, learn as we learned? This is frequently found in their statements." It is answered: There is no doubt that Imām Aḥmad used to prohibit [pursuing] the opinions of Scholars and being preoccupied with memorising and writing them. He would order people to busy themselves with the Qur'ān and Sunna: memorising, understanding, writing, and studying them; writing the accounts of the Companions and their Successors – not the words of those after them – and knowing the sound and the weak, and that which is put to use from that which is cast out as an odd statement. There is no doubt that this is one of the things that require preoccupation with learning first, before anything else. Whoever knows this and reaches the farthest limits in it, to which Imām Aḥmad pointed, his knowledge will have become close to the knowledge of Imām Aḥmad. Such a person is not bound [by the requirement of *taqlīd*] and is not meant by the present discourse [*i.e.* Ibn Rajab's fatwa that one is obligated to follow one of the Four Schools]. We are only concerned with curbing those who have not reached such an end nor elevated themselves to such a summit nor understood, of this learning, more than a tiny trickle – and this is the case for the majority of the people of our time! Indeed, this has always been the case for the majority of the people for ages, in spite of the claim of many of them to have reached the farthest ends and the highest summits, when most have not even risen to the most elementary steps!

Similarly, the Ḥanbalī Imām al-Saffārīnī's summary of his School's position on *taqlīd* can be paraphrased thus:

People who are unqualified to make *ijtihād* are required to make *taqlīd* of one of the four *Madhhabs*: Ḥanafī, Mālikī, Shāfi'ī, or Ḥanbalī. These *Madhhabs* have been verified, refined, preserved and transmitted involving such great numbers that even the most basic student of a given *Madhhab* can differentiate between what is and what is not part of the *Madhhab*, and can even differentiate between well-known and rare opinions. The only *Madhhabs* that can be followed today are these four, because no other *Madhhabs* meet the same conditions of *tawātur*, being verified, and being preserved. This is important because, without these three things taking place, how can we be certain of what the Imām of the *Madhhab* really said? [Adhering to a specific *Madhhab*:] Today, the predominant opinion is that one needs to stick to a specific *Madhhab*. [Moving to another one:] The best known position is that if we say that it is obligatory to stick to a specific *Madhhab*, it is permissible to move to another *Madhhab* on a particular issue. There are three basic opinions here:

1. It is unconditionally unlawful to follow another *Madhhab* on a particular issue;
2. It is unconditionally lawful to follow another *Madhhab* on a particular issue;
3. It is permissible if one acts according to what is entailed by the *Madhhab* that he follows for that particular issue. [This is the most correct opinion.]

[Seeking dispensations:] It is not permissible for laymen (*'awāmm*) to seek out dispensations, and doing so is moral corruption (*fisq*). The conditions for doing this are three:

1. That the person not combine between the *Madhhabs* in such a way that contradicts scholarly consensus, such as marrying without a dowry, without the bride's guardian, and without witnesses since there is no *mujtahid* scholar who has given this as his opinion.
2. That the person believe the merit (*faḍl*) of the one he is following, even if it is based on transmitted (and not first hand) evidence.
3. That the person not seek out the easiest from among the *Madhhabs* [without excuse].

[Making *taqlīd* of the inferior:] It is permissible to follow another School on a particular issue when the other School is superior or equal. It is also permissible when the other School is inferior according to the majority of Ḥanbalīs, the Ḥanafīs, the Mālikīs, and most Shāfi'īs.[588]

Al-Shāfi'ī and *Taṣawwuf*

Al-Shāfi'ī recommended *taṣawwuf* on condition that knowledge accompany it. He declared in his *Dīwān*:

Faqīhan wa-ṣufiyyan fakun laysa wāḥidan
fa'innī wa-ḥaqqillāhi iyyāka anṣaḥu
Fadhālika qāsin lam yadhuq qalbuhu tuqan
wahādhā jahūlun kayfa dhūl-jahli yaṣluḥu

Be both a jurisprudent and a ṣūfī – never just one of the two.
Truly, by the Divine Right, I am advising you sincerely!
For the former is hardened, his heart tastes no Godwariness,
While the latter is ignorant – of what use is the ignorant?[589]

This is similar to Imām Sufyān al-Thawrī's statement that "Among the best of people is the Ṣūfī learned in jurisprudence."[590]

Among al-Shāfi'ī's sayings on Sufism and Ṣūfīs:

- "I accompanied the Ṣūfīs for ten years and benefited but two words from them: their statement that time is a sword: if you do not cut it, it cuts you; and their statement that deprivation is immunity."[591] Some versions have "three words" and add "their statement that if you do not keep your ego busy with truth it will keep you busy with falsehood."

[588] Ḥanbalī section thanks to Shaykh Mūsā Furber. On the – similar – Mālikī position see http://www.masud.co.uk/ISLAM/misc/mhfatwa.htm for the fatwās of al-Qarāfī, Muḥammad 'Illīsh, and others.

[589] Al-Shāfi'ī, *Dīwān* (p. 177 §45).

[590] Narrated by al-Harawī al-Anṣārī in his *Ṭabaqāt al-Ṣūfiyya*.

[591] Narrated from Muḥammad ibn Muḥammad ibn Idrīs al-Shāfi'ī by al-Bayhaqī in *Manāqib al-Shāfi'ī* (2:208) cf. Ibn al-Qayyim in *Madārij al-Sālikīn* (3:128) and *al-Jawāb al-Kāfī* (p. 208-209) and al-Suyūṭī in *Ta'yīd al-Ḥaqīqat al-'Aliyya* (p. 15).

- "If a rational man does not become a Ṣūfī he does not reach noon but that he is a dolt!"[592] Abū Nu'aym narrates this from Muḥammad ibn 'Abd al-Raḥmān ibn al-Faḍl, from Abū al-Ḥasan [Aḥmad ibn Muḥammad ibn al-Ḥārith] ibn al-Qattāt [al-Miṣrī], from the *thiqa* Muḥammad ibn Abī Yaḥyā, from the *thiqa* Imām Yūnus ibn 'Abd al-A'lā, from the Imām.
- A contrary version of the latter saying reads: "A rational man does not become a Ṣūfī except he reaches noon a dolt!"[593] Al-Bayhaqī narrates this from al-Ḥākim, from Abū Muḥammad Ja'far ibn Muḥammad ibn al-Ḥārith, from al-Ḥasan ibn Muḥammad ibn al-Ḍaḥḥāk (Ibn Baḥr), both of unknown reliability. This is the preferred version of Sufi-detractors.
- Imām al-Nawawī in his *Bustān al-'Ārifīn fil-Zuhd wal-Taṣawwuf* ("The Garden of the Knowers in Asceticism and *Taṣawwuf*") narrated with his chain from al-Shāfi'ī the saying: "Only the sincere one (*al-mukhliṣ*) can recognise self-display (*al-riyā'*)." Al-Nawawī comments: "This means that it is impossible to know the reality of self-display and see its hidden shades except for one who resolutely seeks (*arāda*) sincerity. Such a one strives for a long time, searching, meditating, examining at length within himself until he knows, or knows something of what self-display is. This does not happen for everyone. Indeed, this happens only with special ones (*al-khawāṣṣ*). However, for a given individual to claim that he knows what self-display is, this is real ignorance on his part."[594]
- In Makka al-Shāfi'ī was the student of al-Fuḍayl ibn 'Iyāḍ. He is said to have taken *taṣawwuf* from the ascetic shepherd Shaybān al-Rā'ī. Little is known of the latter and there is no report of the two having ever met but there is a narration that Shaybān went on pilgrimage on foot with Sufyān al-Thawrī who witnessed him tame a lion and tweak its ear[595] – Allāh have mercy on them and be well-pleased with them!

[592] Narrated from Yūnus ibn 'Abd al-A'lā by Abū Nu'aym, *Ḥilya* (1985 ed. 9:142).

[593] Narrated by al-Bayhaqī, *Manāqib* (2:207) cf. Ibn al-Jawzī, *Ṣifat al-Ṣafwa* (1:25) and *Talbīs Iblīs* (1985 ed. p. 447) and Ibn Taymiyya in his *Istiqāma* (p. 414).

[594] Al-Nawawī, *Bustān al-'Ārifīn* (p. 53-54).

[595] In Abū Nu'aym, *Ḥilya* (1985 ed. 7:68-69) and al-Dhahabī, *Siyar* (7:203-203=al-Arna'ūṭ ed. 7:268). Another rare narration reports other miraculous gifts of his (*karāmāt*) in Abū Nu'aym, *Ḥilya* (1985 ed. 8:317 §434=1997 ed. 8:354 §425).

Al-Shāfiʿī's Division of *Bidʿa* into "Good" and "Bad"

A major contribution of al-Shāfiʿī in the foundations of the Law is his division of innovated matters (*al-muḥdathāt*) into good and bad depending on whether they conform with or violate the guidelines of the Religion. One famous illustration of this distinction is in the words of ʿUmar ﷺ about the *tarāwīḥ* or congregational supererogatory night prayers in the month of Ramadan: "What a fine innovation this is!"[596] Ḥarmala narrated that al-Shāfiʿī said: "Therefore, whatever innovation conforms to the Sunna is approved (*maḥmūd*), and whatever opposes it is abominable (*madhmūm*)."[597] This is an essential, indispensable criterion for the determination of true *bidʿa* as clarified by later authorities:

> "Everything innovated in contravention of the Lawgiver's command and the latter's specific and general proof" (Imām al-Haytamī).[598]

> "All that did not exist in the first three centuries and for which there is no basis among the Four Principles of Islām" (Imām al-*Lacknawī*) i.e. Qur'ān, Sunna, *Ijmāʿ*, and *Qiyās*.[599]

Thus it is not enough for something merely to be novel to be a *bidʿa*; it must also contradict the Religion.

Al-Rabīʿ narrated that al-Shāfiʿī said:

> Whatever is innovated and contradicts something in the Book or a Sunna or a Companion report (*athar*) or a point of Consensus (*ijmāʿ*): that innovation is misguidance (*fa-hādhihi al-bidʿa ḍalāla*). However, whatever good was innovated without contradicting any one of the above: that is an innovation which is not

596 Narrated by Mālik in *al-Muwaṭṭaʾ* and al-Bukhārī in his *Ṣaḥīḥ*.

597 Narrated by Abū Nuʿaym with his chain through Abū Bakr al-Ājurrī in *Ḥilyat al-Awliyāʾ* (9:121 §13315) and by al-Bayhaqī in his *Madkhal* (§253) and *Manāqib al-Shāfiʿī* (1:469) with a sound chain, as stated by Ibn Taymiyya in his *Darʾ Taʿāruḍ al-ʿAql wal-Naql* (p. 171).

598 Al-Haytamī, *al-Tabyīn fī Sharḥ al-Arbaʿīn* (p. 32).

599 Cf. al-Lacknawī, *Iqāmat al-Ḥujja* (p. 12).

blameworthy (*fahādhihi muḥdathatun ghayru madhmūma*). 'Umar said, concerning the [*tarāwīḥ*] prayers of Ramaḍān: "What a fine *bid'a* this is!" meaning that it was innovated without having existed before and, even so, there was nothing in it that contradicted the above.[600]

If, indeed, "only the *bid'a* that contradicts the Sunna is blameworthy"[601] it follows that there must be a kind of praiseworthy *bid'a* as 'Umar showed ﷺ.

Al-Bayhaqī commented:

Of this kind also is the confrontation of the people of innovation – when they show them and bring up their false positions – and their refutation and confutation of their pseudo-proofs. Even if such is an innovation, nevertheless, it is a praiseworthy one and does not contradict what was mentioned previously. The Prophet ﷺ was asked about *qadar* and he gave a reply concerning it. So did the Companions when they were asked about it, as we narrated from them. The only difference is that they contented themselves, at the time, with the Prophet's ﷺ reply, then with its report, while the innovators in our time do not content themselves with the report nor do they even accept it. Therefore, it is necessary to refute their falsehoods, when they bring them up, with whatever constitutes a proof in their eyes. And success is from Allāh.[602]

This is a clear-cut defense of the necessity and the Sunna character of *kalām* in the defense against innovators on the part of Imām al-Bayhaqī. Something similar is reported from Ibn al-Ṣalāḥ, al-Nawawī, Ibn al-Subkī, Ibn 'Ābidīn, and other great Imāms.

Consequently, the Ulema of the *Madhhab* divided innovation (*al-bid'a*) into good and bad, notably Shaykh al-Islām, Imām Ibn 'Abd al-Salām in his *Qawā'id al-Kubrā* or "Major Axioms of Jurisprudence."

600 Narrated from al-Rabī' by al-Bayhaqī, *Manāqib al-Shāfi'ī* (1:469) cf. *Siyar* (8:408).
601 Ibn al-'Arabī, *'Āriḍat al-Aḥwadhī* (10:147).
602 Al-Bayhaqī, *Manāqib al-Shāfi'ī* (1:469).

Agreement formed in the Four Schools around this division, as illustrated by the endorsement of some major later authorities in each school. Among the Ḥanafīs: Ibn 'Ābidīn, al-Turkmānī, and al-Tahānawī;[603] among the Mālikīs: al-Ṭurṭūshī, al-Qarāfī, Ibn al-Ḥājj, and al-Zarqānī;[604] consensus among the Shāfi'īs;[605] and reluctant acceptance among the later Ḥanbalīs, who altered al-Shāfi'ī and Ibn 'Abd al-Salām's terminology to read "lexical innovation" (*bid'a lughawiyya*) and "legal innovation" (*bid'a shar'iyya*), respectively matching al-Shāfi'ī's "approved" and "abominable."[606]

His Emphasis on Love of the Prophet ﷺ and His Family

Al-Muzanī said: "I never saw any of the Scholars make something obligatory on behalf of the Prophet ﷺ as much as al-Shāfi'ī in his books, and this was due to his high remembrance of the Prophet ﷺ. He said in the Old School: 'Supplication ends with the invocation of blessings on the Prophet ﷺ, and its end is but by means of it.'" Al-Karābīsī said: "I heard al-Shāfi'ī say that he disliked for someone to say 'the Messenger' (*al-Rasūl*), but that he should say 'The Messenger of Allāh' (*Rasūlullāh*) out of reverence (*ta'ẓīm*) for him."[607]

Abū Ḥātim al-Rāzī narrated from Ḥarmala that al-Shāfi'ī said: "The Caliphs (*al-khulafā'*) are five: Abū Bakr, 'Umar, 'Uthmān, 'Alī, and 'Umar ibn 'Abd al-'Azīz." This signified the Rightly-Guided Caliphs. In his *Dīwān* he named them "leaders of their people, by whose guidance one obtains guidance," and wrote of the Family of the Prophet ﷺ:

603 Ibn 'Ābidīn, *Ḥāshiya* (1:376); al-Turkmānī, *al-Luma' fil-Ḥawādith wal-Bida'* (Stuttgart, 1:37); al-Tahānawī, *Kashshāf Iṣṭilāḥat al-Funūn* (Beirut, 1966, 1:133-135).

604 Al-Ṭurṭūshī, *Kitāb al-Ḥawādith wal-Bida'* (p. 158-159); Ibn al-Ḥājj, *Madkhal al-Shar' al-Sharīf* (Cairo, 1336/1918 2:115).

605 Abū Shāma, *al-Bā'ith 'alā Inkār al-Bida' wal-Ḥawādith* (Riyad: Dār al-Rāya, 1990 p. 93, Cairo ed. p. 12); al-'Izz ibn 'Abd al-Salām, as mentioned by the following; al-Nawawī, *al-Adhkār* (Beirut: al-Thaqāfiyya, p. 237), and *Tahdhīb al-Asmā' wal-Lughāt* (3:22); Ibn Ḥajar, *Fatḥ al-Bārī* (13:253-254); al-Suyūṭī, introduction to *Ḥusn al-Maqṣid fī 'Amal al-Mawlid* in *al-Ḥāwī lil-Fatāwī*. Etc. Note that "consensus" (*ijmā'*) is more inclusive than "agreement" (*ittifāq*), and binding.

606 Ibn Rajab, *al-Jāmi' fil-'Ulūm wal-Ḥikam* (2:50-53), and Ibn Taymiyya's section on *bid'a* in his *Iqtiḍā' al-Ṣirāṭ al-Mustaqīm Mukhālafat Aṣḥāb al-Jaḥīm*. This is also the position of Ibn Kathīr in his commentary of the verse: ﴿**The Originator of the heavens and the earth!**﴾ (2:117) in his *Tafsīr*. He followed Ibn Taymiyya in this.

607 Narrated by al-Bayhaqī in *Manāqib al-Shāfi'ī* (1:425) and al-Harawī al-Anṣārī in *Dhamm al-Kalām* (4:188).

The Family of the Prophet are my intermediary to him! (wasīlatī)
Through them I hope to be given my record with the right hand.

and

Family of the Messenger of Allāh! To love you is an obligation
Which Allāh ordained and revealed in the Qur'ān.
It is enough proof of your immense glory that
Who invokes not blessings upon you [in *Tashahhud*], *his prayer is invalid.*

The Qur'ānic commentator and ḥadīth Master Ibn Kathīr (d. 774) said:

I heard my Shaykh, the erudite Imām and ḥadīth Master Abū al-Ḥajjāj al-Mizzī say – Allāh immerse him in His immense mercy! – that the first to speak on the subject [of the superiority of the evidentiary miracles (*mu'jizāt*) of the Prophet ﷺ over those of all previous Prophets] was the Imām Abū 'Abd Allāh Muḥammad ibn Idrīs al-Shāfi'ī ﷺ. The Ḥadīth Master Abū Bakr al-Bayhaqī – Allāh have mercy on him! – narrated in his book *Dalā'il al-Nubuwwa* from his Shaykh Abū 'Abd Allāh al-Ḥākim: Abū Aḥmad ibn Abī al-Ḥasan told me: 'Abd al-Raḥmān ibn Abī Ḥātim al-Rāzī told us: From his father who said that 'Amr ibn Sawwād [ibn al-Aswad ibn 'Amr al-'Āmirī al-Baṣrī (d. 245)] said that al-Shāfi'ī said: "All that Allāh gave to the Prophets he also gave to Muḥammad ﷺ." 'Amr said: "He gave 'Īsā ﷺ [the power] to resurrect the dead." He replied: "He gave Muḥammad ﷺ the tree-stump beside which he used to address the people, and when a pulpit was built for him [and he moved away], the stump began to moan until its voice was heard:[608]

[608] Narrated from Sahl ibn Sa'd by al-Bukhārī and Muslim; from Jābir and Ibn 'Umar by al-Bukhārī and Aḥmad; from Burayda and from Abū Sa'īd al-Khudrī by al-Dārimī; from Ibn 'Abbās by al-Dārimī, Aḥmad, and Ibn Mājah; from Anas by al-Tirmidhī (*ḥasan ṣaḥīḥ gharīb*), Aḥmad, and Ibn Mājah; from Umm Salama by al-Bayhaqī in *Dalā'il al-Nubuwwa*; from Ubay ibn Ka'b by al-Shāfi'ī, Aḥmad, al-Dārimī, Ibn Mājah, Abū Ya'lā, and Sa'īd ibn Manṣūr. This ḥadīth was declared mass-narrated (*mutawātir*) by 'Iyāḍ in *al-Shifā* (chapter on the miracles of the Prophet ﷺ), Tāj al-Dīn al-Subkī in *Sharḥ Mukhtaṣar Ibn al-Ḥājib*, al-Suyūṭī in *al-Azhār al-Mutanāthira*, and al-Kattānī in *Naẓm al-Mutanāthir* while 'Abd al-Ra'ūf al-Munāwī in his commentary on al-'Irāqī entitled *Sharḥ Alfiyyat al-Siyar* said it is mass-narrated in meaning (*mutawātir al-*

this is a greater miracle than that." These were his very words.[609]

Aphorisms of al-Shāfiʿī

ON THE ḤADĪTH MASTERS

"When I see a man among the Masters of ḥadīth it is as if I saw the Prophet ﷺ alive." [610]

LEARN *FIQH* BEFORE YOU LEAD OTHERS

"Learn *fiqh* before you reach leadership for when this happens, there is no way to study it any more." [611] This is reminiscent of ʿUmar's similar advice: "Learn *fiqh* before you are given leadership." [612]

'ACTIONS COUNT ONLY ACCORDING TO INTENTIONS'

"The ḥadīth, 'Actions count only according to intentions,' pertains to seventy different sub-headings of jurisprudence." [613]

EARLY SIGNS OF MERIT IN CHILDREN

"If modesty and awe are found in a young boy, expect his success."

THE TWO MOST EMPHASIZED SUNNA PRAYERS

"Whoever leaves either the Sunna of *fajr* or *Salāt al-Witr* [once] is in a worse state than if he had left all the supererogatory prayers."[614] Muʿādh ibn al-Muthannā (d. 288), declared trustworthy by al-Dhahabī, related something similar from Imām Aḥmad: "Whoever abandons the *witr* prayer deliberately is an evil-doer who is abandoning a Sunna of the Prophet ﷺ, and he is no longer considered an upright person." [615]

---

maʿnā) as indicated by al-Bayhaqī in *Dalāʾil al-Nubuwwa* and Ibn Ḥajar in *Fatḥ al-Bārī*. Cf. ʿAbd Allāh al-Ghumārī, *al-Ibtihāj* (p. 167-168).

609 Ibn Kathīr, *al-Bidāya wal-Nihāya* (Turāth ed. 6:289=Maʿārif ed. 6:258).

610 Narrated from Yūnus ibn ʿAbd al-Aʿlā by al-Khaṭīb, *Sharaf Aṣḥāb al-Ḥadīth* (p. 46).

611 Narrated from Aḥmad ibn Ṣāliḥ by al-Khaṭīb in *Naṣīḥat Ahl al-Ḥadīth* (p. 21).

612 Narrated by al-Khaṭīb in *Naṣīḥat Ahl al-Ḥadīth* (p. 24).

613 Narrated from al-Rabīʿ ibn Sulaymān by al-Khaṭīb in *al-Jāmiʿ* (2:442-443 §1955).

614 Narrated from al-Rabīʿ in *al-Umm* (1:142).

615 Ibn Abī Yaʿlā, *Ṭabaqāt al-Ḥanābila* (1:339 §489), al-Dhahabī, *Siyar* (11:69 §2477).

The order of emphasis for Sunna prayers in the Shāfi'ī School according to the *Muqaddima Ḥaḍramiyya* is as follows:

- the two *'Īd* prayers,
- then the sun-eclipse prayer (*kusūf*),
- then the moon-eclipse prayer (*khusūf*),
- then the prayer for rain (*istisqā'*),
- then the *witr* from a minimum of one to a maximum of eleven *rak'ats*, always odd, and which Imām al-Haytamī said also counts as *tahajjud* if prayed after rising from sleep,
- then the Sunna of *fajr*,
- then the two pre-*farḍ* Sunna *rak'as* of *ẓuhr* or *Jumu'a*,
- then the two post-*farḍ* ones after them,
- then the two post-*farḍ* Sunna *rak'as* of *maghrib* and *'ishā'*,
- then the twenty *rak'as* of *Tarāwīḥ* with *taslīm* after each two (and if done after each four then the prayer is invalid), its time being the same as that for *witr*,
- then the *Ḍuḥā* numbering from two to eight between post-sunrise *irtifā'* and pre-noon *istiwā'* but preferably in the midsection of that period, with *taslīm* preferably after each two (but valid otherwise),
- then the two *rak'as* of *iḥrām*, *ṭawāf*, and *taḥiyya*, the latter optionally in conjunction (*i.e.* with a shared *niyya*) with other prayers, even *farḍ*, and *iḥrām* coming last of the three in preference, acording to al-Haytamī,
- then the two *rak'as* after *wuḍū'*.

Imām al-Haytamī said in his commentary on the *Muqaddima Ḥaḍramiyya* entitled *al-Minhāj al-Qawīm* that it is permissible to pray the pre-*farḍ* Sunna after the *farḍ* if missed before. The *Muqaddima* continues: It is desirable (*mustaḥabb*) to add to the above:

- two *rak'as* before and after *ẓuhr* and *Jumu'a*,
- four *rak'as* before *'aṣr*,
- two *rak'as* before *maghrib*, before *'ishā'*, and before travel – in one's house,
- two *rak'as* in the mosque after travel,
- the prayers of *istikhāra*, need (*ḥāja*), and *tasbīḥ*, to which Imām

al-Haytamī added the *awwābīn* prayer of twenty *rak'as* [eight minimum] between *maghrib* and *'ishā'*.

(In the Ḥanafī School the *Witr* and *'Īd* prayers come before the entirety of *Sunna* prayers and nearest of all prayers to the *Farḍ*, in a category of their own, followed by the Sunna of *fajr*, then the four pre-*farḍ* Sunna *rak'as* of *ẓuhr*, then the rest of the twelve "emphasised Sunna" *rak'as*: two after *ẓuhr*, two after *maghrib*, two after *'ishā'*, while the *Tarāwīḥ* are a collective emphasised Sunna or *sunnatun mu'akkadatun kifāya*. Then follow the desirable devotions or *mustaḥabbāt*: four *rak'as* after *ẓuhr* (either by making the two confirmed sunna *rak'as* four or separately); four or two *rak'as* before *'aṣr*, six *rak'as* after *maghrib* (commonly known as *ṣalāt al-awwābīn* although this name applies rather to the *ḍuḥā* prayer) ideally in sets of two (the confirmed sunna can be included as part of the six if one chooses); two *rak'as* before *'ishā* and four *rak'as* after (one may include the confirmed sunnas in this).)

ISLĀM IS *ĪMĀN*...

Al-Za'farānī reported that al-Shāfi'ī in his commentary on the ḥadīth "Free her, for she is a believer"[616] said: "Islām is *īmān*."[617]

... BUT *ĪMĀN* INCREASES AND DECREASES

Al-Bayhaqī narrated in his *I'tiqād*, *Manāqib al-Shāfi'ī*, and elsewhere that al-Shāfi'ī said: "*Īmān* consists in word and deed and it can increase and decrease."

[616] On this ḥadīth the watchful Muslim ought to keep strictly to the commentaries of the Sunni Imāms al-Bayhaqī [cf. p. 263], al-Qushayrī [in his *Bayān al-I'tiqād* at the beginning of his *Risāla*], al-Nawawī in *Sharḥ Ṣaḥīḥ Muslim* [cf. our biography of him], Ibn Ḥajar, and al-Qārī in his commentary on the ḥadīth in *al-Mirqāt Sharḥ al-Mishkāt* (orig. ed. 3:492) [cited in full in our biography of Imām al-Nawawī], and ignore the rest, especially the slurs of the people of innovation and anthropomorphism. Ibn Ḥajar said: "Al-Kirmānī [Shams al-Dīn Muḥammad ibn Yūsuf ibn 'Alī d. 668] said [in *al-Kawākib al-Darārī Sharḥ Ṣaḥīḥ al-Bukhārī*]: 'The literal meaning of "the one who is in the heaven" is not meant, for Allāh is transcendent beyond place. However, since the direction of elevation is nobler than any other direction, Allāh predicated it to Himself to indicate the loftiness of His Essence and Attributes.' Others addressed in similar terms the expressions that came down concerning aboveness (*fawqiyya*)." *Fatḥ al-Bārī* (1959 ed. 13:412).

[617] In al-Bayhaqī, *Manāqib al-Shāfi'ī* (1:395). On the contextual difference of the two terms see our translation of Ibn Khafīf's *'Aqīda* §70 and appended footnote.

DISBELIEF COEXISTS WITH DISBELIEF

"Belief cannot coexist with disbelief, while disbelief can coexist with disbelief." Abū Isḥāq al-Isfarāyīnī comments: "If, together with belief, one holds a view such as that the world is without beginning, or other such position which contradicts belief, then belief is altogether annulled in that person; while disbelief, such as to assert the Trinity, if together with it one holds that Satan challenges the Merciful and wins battles over Him, as Manicheans believe, then his *shirk* in the Trinity is not annulled but compounded by his Manichean *shirk*." Ibn al-Subkī commented: "One can infer from this that belief neither increases nor decreases, while disbelief can increase or decrease. Ponder this."[618]

WISE STUDY IS BETTER THAN *DHIKR* AND *NAFL*

"The study of ḥadīth is better than supererogatory prayer and the pursuit of knowledge is better than supererogatory prayer."[619] Ibn al-Jawzī said something similar.[620] The Prophet ﷺ is related to have said, upon entering the Mosque and seeing two circles, one of *du'ā'*, the other of teaching and knowledge: "They both have immense goodness but these teach *fiqh* and I was but sent as a teacher (*innamā bu'ithtu mu'alliman*)." Then he sat with the second group. In some versions he adds: "These are better and have what is needed!"[621]

[618] Ibn al-Subkī meant "belief" (*īmān*) here in the sense of "Islām." It is established that belief can increase, just as Allāh said in His Book (8:2, 33:22). The majority of the scholars hold that belief increases and decreases, but not in the sense of the confirmation of one's faith (*al-taṣdīq*). In the latter sense, the *mutakallimūn* – notably Abū Ḥanīfa and the Māturīdī School – said that belief neither increases nor decreases. Cf. Ibn Khafīf, *al-'Aqīda al-Ṣaḥīḥa* §70 and note, cf. Ibn Ḥajar's discussion and his list of the various positions. *Fatḥ* (1959 ed. 1:45) and above, ch. on Abū Ḥānīfa.

[619] Narrated by Ibn 'Abd al-Barr in *al-Intiqā'* (p. 138) and others.

[620] In *Ṣayd al-Khāṭir* (p. 195).

[621] Narrated from 'Abd Allāh ibn 'Amr ibn al-'Āṣ by al-Dārimī (3:64-66 §365), Ibn Mājah, Ibn al-Mubārak in *al-Zuhd* (p. 488-489 §1388), through him al-Ṭayālisī in his *Musnad* (p. 298 §2251), al-Ḥārith in his (1:185 §40), both through Ibn al-Mubārak, al-Khaṭīb with four chains in *al-Faqīh wal-Mutafaqqih* (1:88-90 §30-32, §34=1:10-11), al-Bayhaqī in *al-Madkhal ilā al-Sunan al-Kubrā* (1:38 §462=p. 306), and Shaykh Muḥammad YāSīn al-Fādānī al-Makkī in *al-'Ujāla fil-Aḥādith al-Musalsala*, through al-Dārimī, all through the pious African Qāḍī 'Abd al-Raḥmān ibn Ziyād ibn An'um al-Afrīqī who is weak but acceptable in narrations pertaining to morals, while al-

عَنْ عَبْدِ اللَّهِ بْنِ عَمْرٍو رَضِيَ اللهُ عَنْهُمَا أَنَّ رَسُولَ اللَّهِ صَلَّى اللَّهُ عَلَيْهِ وَسَلَّمَ مَرَّ بِمَجْلِسَيْنِ فِي مَسْجِدِهِ فَقَالَ كِلَاهُمَا عَلَى خَيْرٍ وَأَحَدُهُمَا أَفْضَلُ مِنْ صَاحِبِهِ أَمَّا هَؤُلَاءِ فَيَدْعُونَ اللَّهَ وَيَرْغَبُونَ إِلَيْهِ فَإِنْ شَاءَ أَعْطَاهُمْ وَإِنْ شَاءَ مَنَعَهُمْ وَأَمَّا هَؤُلَاءِ فَيَتَعَلَّمُونَ الْفِقْهَ أَوِ الْعِلْمَ وَيُعَلِّمُونَ الْجَاهِلَ فَهُمْ أَفْضَلُ وَإِنَّمَا بُعِثْتُ مُعَلِّمًا قَالَ ثُمَّ جَلَسَ فِيهِمْ مي جه ابن المبارك في الزهد ط الحارث في المسند خط في الفقيه والمتفقه هق في المدخل جميعهم عن القاضي الجليل عبدالرحمن بن زياد بن أنعم الأفريقي وهو ضعيف

Ibn ʿAbd al-Barr in *Jāmiʿ Bayān al-ʿIlm wa-Faḍlih* listed the many ḥadīths of the Prophet ﷺ on the superior merit of knowledge. However, al-Shāfiʿī by this saying meant the essence and purpose of knowledge, not knowledge for its own sake which leads to Satanic pride. The latter is widely available while true knowledge is the knowledge that leads to Godwariness. This is confirmed by al-Shāfiʿī's saying: "Knowledge is what benefits. Knowledge is not what one has memorised."[622] He declaimed:

I complained to Wakīʿ of my poor memory.
He told me to quit sins once and for all.
He told me knowledge is a light:
His light Allāh grants not to those who sin.[623]

These are correctives for those content to parrot the definition of knowledge in Islām merely as "knowledge of the proof" (*maʿrifat al-dalīl*).

Bukhārī considered him reliable. In addition, all but Ibn Mājah's chain contain ʿAbd Allāh ibn Rāfiʿ al-Tannūkhī, who is also weak. Ibn Mājah's chain is through Dāwūd ibn al-Zibriqān who is discarded, from Bakr ibn Khunays who is weak. Cf. al-Būṣīrī, *Miṣbāḥ* (1:32), *Mīzān*, *Mughnī*, *Kāmil*, and *Taqrīb*.

[622] Cf. note 494 above.

[623] Al-Shāfiʿī, *Dīwān* (p. 54).

POVERTY AND SERVANTHOOD ARE PREREQUISITES TO LEARNING

- "The pursuit of knowledge is out of the question except for one who is bankrupt." He was asked: "Not even for the sufficient one who has his need (*al-ghanī al-makfī*)?" He replied: "Not even for the sufficient one who has his need."[624]
- "None that pursues this Science through wealth and self-importance shall succeed. But he who pursues it with humility, poverty, and serving the Ulema, shall succeed."
- "Knowledge will never be attained except through bearing with humiliation."

REASON IS EXPERIENCE

- "Intellect (*al-'aql*) consists of experience (*al-tajriba*)."
- "The wise person is not the one who, faced with a choice between good and evil, chooses good, but the one who, faced with a choice of two evils, chooses the lesser evil."

IRREMEDIABLE MATTERS

- "There are three things about which a physician is powerless: idiocy, plague, and senility."
- "Protection against an evil neighbour is useless."

SELF-DISCIPLINE

- "Disciplining the human being is harder than disciplining a beast."
- "Whoever does not become chaste shall remain foolish; whoever is accused of committing sins shall remain fearful and lowly; whoever abstains is safe; he whose appetites run amok, his worries grow; and whoever marries much will not be safe from scandals.
- "Satiation weighs down the body, hardens the heart, does away with sagacity, brings on sleep, and weakens one from worship."

[624] In al-Nawawī's introduction to his *Majmū'* (1:64).

This is similar to the definition of *taṣawwuf* as "hunger" (*al-jūʿ*) given by some of the early masters, who acquired hunger as a permanent attribute and were called "hungerers" (*jūʿiyyūn*). Notable examples are the Ṣūfī masters Sahl ibn ʿAbd Allāh al-Tustarī – who reached a state such that he broke his fast once only every twenty-five days – and al-Qāsim ibn ʿUthmān al-ʿAbdī al-Dimashqī al-Jūʿī (d. 248) "the Imām, exemplar, *walī*, the *muḥaddith*, the Shaykh of the Ṣūfīs and the friend of Aḥmad ibn al-Ḥawārī" (al-Dhahabī). ʿAbd Allāh ibn ʿUmar said: "I never ate to satiation since I entered Islām."[625]

NEVER SWEAR OATHS

- "I never swore by Allāh – neither truthfully nor deceptively." This is based on the Prophet's ﷺ prohibition of swearing oaths to Abū Bakr al-Ṣiddīq in the ḥadīth of the dream-interpretation related from Ibn ʿAbbās in the two *Ṣaḥīḥs* and *Sunan*: "Do not swear (*lā tuqsim*)!" Al-Tustarī said: "The truthful and trustful Saints (al-Ṣiddīqūn) never swear by Allāh ﷻ, nor commit back-biting, nor does backbiting take place around them, nor do they eat to satiation. If they promise, they are true to their word, and they never speak in jest."

CHOOSING ONE'S RESIDENCE CAREFULLY

- "No one should reside in a region where there is neither a knowledgeable person of Religion nor a physician."

CHOOSING ONE'S COMPANIONS CAREFULLY

- "The companionship of one who does not fear Allāh ﷻ causes disgrace."
- "One must take care to pursue the company of those who are faithful and truthful, just as one takes care to entrust his property only to those who are trustworthy and reliable."
- "The causes of inferiority in men are: talking too much, advertising secrets, and trusting each and everyone."
- "The anger of noble folk shows in their deeds. while the anger of lowly folk shows in their tongues."

625 Narrated by Abū Nuʿaym, *Ḥilya* (1:371 §1031).

THE PERILS OF WEALTH

- "The worst wrongdoer against his own soul is he who, after he acquires wealth and status, disdains his relatives, shuns his acquaintances, scorns the people of nobility, and swaggers before the people of merit."
- "When someone is granted ease after poverty, his ego runs to do four things: he disowns the patron who helped him, takes a concubine over and above his wife, destroys his house, and builds another one."

SELF-KNOWLEDGE INURES AGAINST CALUMNY

- "Whoever knows himself, calumnies will never harm him."
- "Whoever witnesses his own weakness has been granted uprightness" (*man shahida al-ḍaʿfa min nafsihi nāla al-istiqāma*).[626]
- "High hopes have cut off men's necks the way a mirage betrays the one who sees it and leaves behind whoever trusts it."
- "It is a wonder that the human being occupies himself with something the disposal of which belongs to someone else."
- "Whoever is overcome by the love of this world and its lusts shall be forced into subjugation by its people, and whoever is satisfied with little shall be free of this subjection."[627]

PRAYER BEHIND INNOVATORS

- Al-Buwayṭī asked: "Should I pray behind the *Rāfiḍī*?" Al-Shāfiʿī *said:* "Do not pray behind the *Rāfiḍī*, nor behind the *Qadarī*, nor behind the *Murji'*." Al-Buwayṭī said: "Define them for us." He replied: "Whoever says 'Belief consists only in speech' is a *Murji'*, and whoever says 'Abū Bakr and 'Umar are not [true] Imāms' is a *Rāfiḍī*, and whoever attributes destiny to himself is a *Qadarī*." The status of the prayer behind innovators depends on the kind of *bidʿa* they practice. If it is a *bidʿa mukaffira* or innovation that constitutes *kufr* such as, for example, believing that there will be a new Prophet after the Prophet Muḥammad ﷺ, the prayer behind them is invalid and must be repeated. (Nor are their remains washed nor prayed upon.) If it is only a *bidʿa mufassiqa*

[626] In al-Nawawī, *Tahdhīb al-Asmā'* (1:75-76).

[627] All sayings narrated by Ibn 'Abd al-Barr in *al-Intiqā'* (p. 138, 157-159).

or innovation that constitutes moral corruption (such as, for example, believing that "the knowledge of the Four Imāms is purely speculative"), the prayer behind people of such belief is abominable but valid. If there is dispute among the Ulema whether the innovation is actually a *bid'a mukaffira* then the prayer behind that *imām* is forbidden (*ḥarām*) but if it takes place it is valid, although it is desirable (*mustaḥabb*) to repeat it within the period of that prayer. This is the case of the prayer behind those who hold anthropomorphist beliefs. Although the preferable (*rājiḥ*) opinion is that they are not apostates, there is a difference of opinion among the Ulema in relation to their anthropomorphic creed. Since this difference is over *'aqīda*, it follows that the prayer behind them is prohibited but valid.[628] And Allāh knows best.

EVERY BOOK IS FLAWED EXCEPT THE QUR'ĀN

- "If a book were double-checked seventy times, a mistake could still be found in it. Allāh will not have any faultless book except His Book." Al-Muzanī related this and also said: "I read back *al-Risāla* to the Imām al-Shāfi'ī eighty times. Every single time he would correct a mistake in it. In the end he said: "Enough! Allāh will not have any faultless book except His Book."[629]

ACCEPTING THE ḤADĪTH IS NOT OPTIONAL

- After al-Shāfi'ī narrated a ḥadīth to a man who asked him about a certain matter the latter said: "Do you also say the same?" whereupon al-Shāfi'ī jumped, his color changed, and he said: "Woe to you! What earth would carry me, what heaven would shade me if I narrated from the Messenger of Allāh ﷺ something that I did not adhere to? Yes, I adhere to it heart and soul! Yes, I adhere to it heart and soul!"[630]

His Assiduous Recitation of the Qur'ān

Al-Shāfi'ī is the first in Islām to have authored a book on the merits of

[628] Cf. Khalīl, *Mukhtaṣar, Ṣalat al-Jamā'a* under the words *"ka-ḥarūriyya"*.

[629] Narrated by al-Khaṭīb in *Mūḍiḥ Awhām al-Jam' wal-Tafrīq* (1:6).

[630] Narrated by al-Ḥākim as cited by Ibn al-Qayyim in *I'lām al-Muwaqqi'īn* (2:286).

the Qur'ān, titled *Faḍā'il al-Qur'ān*,[631] followed by al-Qāsim ibn Sallām.

Like Abū Ḥanīfa, al-Bukhārī, and others, he is related to have recited the entire Qur'ān each day at prayer, and twice a day in the month of Ramaḍān. Al-Karābīsī said: "I spent eighty nights in the same house with al-Shāfi'ī. He used to pray for about one third of the night. I never saw him recite more than fifty verses – meaning in a single *rak'a* – and he never passed by a verse of mercy but that he asked Allāh for mercy for himself and for the believing men and women, nor did he pass by a verse of punishment without seeking refuge in Allāh and asking Him for salvation for himself and for the believing men and women."

He once told his students: "*Fiqh* has distracted you from the Book of Allāh. After night prayer I open it in front of me and it remains so until morning."

His External Appearance

Yūnus ibn 'Abd al-A'lā described al-Shāfi'ī as "of medium height, with a bright forehead, soft skin, tending to swarthiness, with a sparse side-beard (*khafīf al-'āriḍayn*)." Al-Muzanī said: "I never saw one more handsome of face than al-Shāfi'ī. If he grasped his beard it would not exceed his fist." Ibn Rāhūyah described him in Makka as wearing bright white clothes with an intensely black beard. Al-Za'farānī said that when he was in Baghdād in the year 195 he dyed his beard with henna.

Al-Rabī' said: "He was thrifty in his dress and wore thin clothes of linen and Baghdādī cotton. He sometimes wore a headcover (*qalansuwa*) that was not very tall but he wore the turban and the *khuff* very often. Not one day passed without his giving charity and he used to give charity at night, especially in Ramaḍān, searching out the poor and the destitute. He spent on his family the way wealthy merchants and the nobility spend. He was the most generous of people to sit with." Al-Rabī' also said: "Mālik's companions boast that his gathering comprised about sixty turban-wearers (*mu'ammam*). By Allāh! I have counted three hundred turbaned men in al-Shāfi'ī's gathering, excluding those I could not see."

[631] As stated by al-Kattānī in *al-Risāla al-Mustaṭrafa* (p. 59).

Al-Za'farānī said: "Al-Shāfi'ī used to wear a large turban, as if he were a desert Arab. In his hand he held a large staff (*hirāwa*)."[632] In the introduction of his great compendium of Shāfi'ī *fiqh* titled *al-Majmū'* al-Nawawī mentions that al-Shāfi'ī used a walking stick. One day he was asked: "Why do you carry a stick when you are neither old nor an invalid?" He replied: "To remind myself that I am only a traveller in this world." Yet, Imām al-Shāfi'ī was chronically ill for most of his life and afflicted with permanent bleeding caused by hemorroids, by which the Almighty Creator ﷻ caused his death early. Whenever he sat to teach, a pail was placed under his seat and blood dripped into it. Allāh be pleased with him and grant him the greatest mercy!

Al-Shāfi'ī was buried in al-Qarāfa in Cairo. Ibn al-Kīzānī, an Egyptian poet notorious for his anthropomorphist belief, died in 562 and was buried near Imām al-Shāfi'ī. Later, the pious Shaykh al-Khabūshānī (510-587) ordered Ibn al-Kīzānī's remains dug up and buried elsewhere, saying: "The *Ṣiddīq* and the *Zindīq* are not buried together." The Ḥanbalīs of the area waged a campaign of intimidation against him but he defeated them.[633]

Later Figures Connected to the Shāfi'ī School

DĀWŪD AL-ẒĀHIRĪ[634]

Dāwūd ibn 'Alī ibn Dāwūd ibn Khalaf al-Iṣbahānī al-Ẓāhirī (d. 275) was the first literalist. Al-Khaṭīb said of him: "He was a scrupulously Godwary and devoted Imām." He began by following al-Shāfi'ī in *fiqh* and was the first to write his biography (*Manāqib al-Shāfi'ī*). Then he left him, negated the validity of analogy (*qiyās*) – one of the legislative sources of the Religion – and published books in which he deviated from the *Salaf* and innovated his own method, due to which the Scholars deserted him. He considered the Qur'ān to be created (*muḥdath*). Al-Qāḍī 'Iyāḍ reported that some early Māliki Ulema considered his entire School an innovation of miguidance (*bid'a*).[635] Despite this he is considered truthful in his narrations. The most

[632] In al-Harawī al-Anṣārī's *Dhamm al-Kalām* (4:309 §1169).

[633] *Ṭabaqāt al-Shāfi'iyya al-Kubrā* (6:90, 7:15-16), *Siyar* (20:454, 21:205).

[634] *Mīzān* ('Ilmiyya ed. 3:27) and *Siyar* (14:469); *Lisān* (2:422-424).

[635] Cf. al-Shāṭibī, *al-Muwāfaqāt* (3:154).

famous of those who adhered to his School is Ibn Ḥazm al-Andalusī. Others are the Ṣūfī master Abū al-Ḥasan Ruwaym ibn Aḥmad al-Baghdādī (d. 303), possibly the Ṣūfī ḥadīth Master Ibn Abī 'Āṣim (d. 287), Khālid ibn Aḥmad al-Ẓāhirī, the School's main representative in Bukhārā from which he contrived Imām al-Bukhārī's expulsion, and Abū 'Āmir Muḥammad ibn Sa'dūn al-'Abdarī (d. 524), one of Ibn 'Asākir's teachers, described by him as an ill-mannered anthropomorphist. Shaykh Muḥyī al-Dīn Ibn 'Arabī is said to have followed the Ẓāhirī School but he himself denied it, as quoted by Ibn 'Imād in *Shadharāt al-Dhahab* (5:20) from Ibn 'Arabī's two poems *al-Rā'iyya* and *al-Nūniyya.*

AL-JUNAYD[636]

Al-Junayd ibn Muḥammad ibn al-Junayd, Abū al-Qāsim al-Nahāwandī al-Baghdādī al-Qawārīrī al-Khazzāz al-Shāfi'ī ﵁ (d. 298) was the Imām of the World in his time, the Shaykh of the Ṣūfīs and "Diadem of the Knowers." He accompanied his maternal uncle Sarī al-Saqaṭī, al-Ḥārith al-Muḥāsibī, and others. Abū Sahl al-Ṣu'lūkī narrates that as a boy al-Junayd heard his uncle being asked about thankfulness (*shukr*), whereupon he said: "It is to not use His favours for the purpose of disobeying Him." He took *fiqh* from Abū Thawr – in whose circle he would give fatwas at twenty years of age – and, it was also said, from Sufyān al-Thawrī. He once said: "Allāh did not bring out a single science on earth accessible to people without giving me a share in its knowledge." He used to go to the market every day, open his shop, and commence praying four hundred *rak'as* until closing time. In *fiqh* he followed al-Shāfi'ī's disciple, Abū Thawr.

Among his sayings about the Ṣūfī Path: "Whoever does not memorise the Qur'ān and write ḥadīth is not fit to be followed in this matter. For our Science is controlled by the Book and the Sunna." To Ibn Kullāb who was asking him about *taṣawwuf* he replied: "Our *madhhab* is the singling out of the pre-eternal from the contingent, the desertion of human brotherhood and homes, and obliviousness to past and future." Ibn Kullāb said: "This kind of speech cannot be debated." Ibn

[636] Al-Qushayrī, *Risāla* (p. 148-150); al-Khaṭīb, *Tārīkh Baghdād* (7:241); Ibn 'Imād, *Shadharāt al-Dhahab* (2:228-230); al-Dhahabī, *Siyar* (11:153-155 §2555); Ibn al-Subkī, *Ṭabaqāt al-Shāfi'iyya al-Kubrā* (2:260-275 §60).

Surayj would say, whenever he defeated his adversaries in debate: "This is some of the blessing from my sittings with al-Junayd." Al-Qushayrī relates from al-Junayd the following definitions of *taṣawwuf*:

- "Not the profusion of prayer and fasting, but wholeness of the breast and selflessness."[637]
- *"Taṣawwuf* means that Allāh causes you to die to your self then gives you life in Him."
- "It means that you be solely with Allāh with no attachments."
- "It is a war in which there is no peace."
- "It is the upholding of every high manner and the repudiation of every low one."
- "It is supplication together with inward concentration, ecstasy together with attentive hearing, and action combined with compliance [with the Sunna]."
- "It is the removal of minor impurity" (*raf' al-ḥadath*).

When his uncle asked him to speak from the pulpit he deprecated himself, but then saw the Prophet ﷺ in his dream reiterating the order. Ibn Kullāb once asked al-Junayd to dictate for him a comprehensive definition of *tawḥīd* he had just heard him say. He replied: "If I were reading from a record I would dictate it to you." The Mu'tazilī al-Ka'bī said: "My eyes did not see his like. Writers came to hear him for his linguistic mastery, philosophers for the sharpness of his speech, poets for his eloquence, and *kalām* scholars for the contents of his speech." Al-Khuldī said: "We never saw, among our Shaykhs, anyone in whom learning (*'ilm*) and actual state (*ḥāl*) came together save al-Junayd. If you saw his *ḥāl* you would think that it took precedence over his *'ilm*, and if he spoke you would think that his *'ilm* took precedence over his *ḥāl*."

Like the Sunni Imāms of his generation, al-Junayd hated theological disputations about Allāh and His Attributes: "The least [peril] that lies within *kalām* is the elimination of the awe of Allāh from the heart. And when the heart is left devoid of the awe of Allāh, it becomes devoid of belief."

At one time a young Christian asked him: "What is the meaning of

637 In al-Qushayrī, *Kitāb al-Samā'* in *al-Rasā'il al-Qushayriyya* (Sidon and Beirut: al-Maktabat al-'Aṣriyya, 1970), p. 60.

the ḥadīth of the Prophet ﷺ: 'Beware the vision (*firāsa*) of the believer for he sees with the light of Allāh'?"[638] Al-Junayd remained immersed

[638] A sound (*ṣaḥīḥ*) ḥadīth narrated through Yaḥyā ibn Ma'īn from Abū Umāma al-Bāhilī by al-Ṭabarānī in *al-Mu'jam al-Kabīr* (8:121) and *Musnad al-Shāmiyyīn* (2:407) with a fair (*ḥasan*) chain according to al-Haythamī (10:268 chapter on *firāsa*); Ibn 'Abd al-Barr in *Jāmi' Bayān al-'Ilm* (1:677 §1197) with a fair chain according to al-Zuhayrī; al-Ḥakīm al-Tirmidhī in *Nawādir al-Uṣūl*; Ibn 'Adī in *al-Kāmil* (4:1523, 6:2401); Abū Nu'aym in *Ḥilyat al-Awliyā'* (6:118) and *al-Arba'īn 'alā Madhhab al-Mutaḥaqqiqīn min al-Ṣūfiyya* (p. 104); al-Khaṭīb in *al-Tārīkh* (5:99); al-Bayhaqī in *al-Zuhd al-Kabīr* (p. 159-160 §358); al-Suyūṭī who declared it fair (*ḥasan*) in *al-La'āli' al-Maṣnū'a* (2:329-330) as did al-Shawkānī in *al-Fawā'id al-Majmū'a* (p. 243-244); and through the trustworthy ḥadīth Master Muḥammad ibn 'Awf al-Himṣī by al-Quḍā'ī in *Musnad al-Shihāb* (1:387=1:476). The slight defect (*'illa*) of Abū Umāma's chain revolves around al-Bukhārī's shaykh, the narrator 'Abd Allāh ibn Ṣāliḥ al-Juhanī. [Cf. al-Dhahabī, *Mīzān* (2:440-445 §4383). Al-Arna'ūṭ said of him in *Taḥrīr al-Taqrīb* (2:222 §3388): "Truthful (*ṣadūq*), his memorization is somewhat lacking, but of fair narrations in follow-ups (*al-mutāba'āt*)."] However, Shaykh Maḥmūd Mamdūḥ in his monograph *Bishārat al-Mu'min bi-Taṣḥīḥ Ḥadīth Ittaqū Firāsat al-Mu'min* presents a convincing argument that the ḥadīth should be graded *ṣaḥīḥ*, as it is established that 'Abd Allāh ibn Ṣāliḥ narrated it to Yaḥyā ibn Ma'īn and Muḥammad ibn 'Awf from his written record, and Ibn Ḥajar said of him in *al-Taqrīb* (p. 308 §3388) "He is confirmed when narrating from his book" (*thabtun fī kitābih*) and again in his introduction to *Fatḥ al-Bārī* entitled *Hadī al-Sārī* (p. 414): "Whatever comes from him through the narration of the major experts such as Yaḥyā ibn Ma'īn, al-Bukhārī, Abū Zur'a, and Abū Ḥātim, is from his sound narrations (*min ṣaḥīḥi ḥadīthih*)." The ḥadīth is also narrated from Abū Sa'īd al-Khudrī by al-Tirmidhī (*gharīb*); al-Bukhārī in his *Tārīkh* (7:354); al-Ṭabarī and Ibn Kathīr in their *Tafsīrs* (14:31-32 and 2:556); Abū Nu'aym in *al-Ḥilya* (10:281-282); al-'Uqaylī in *al-Ḍu'afā'* (4:129); Abū al-Shaykh in *al-Amthāl* (p. 78); al-Sulamī in *Ṭabaqāt al-Ṣūfiyya* (p. 156) and *al-Arba'īn*; al-Khaṭīb in *Tārīkh Baghdād* (3:191, 7:242); al-Qushayrī in his *Risāla* (2:480); al-Quḍā'ī in *Musnad al-Shihāb* (1:387); al-Mālīnī in *al-Arba'īn fī Shuyūkh al-Ṣūfiyya* (p. 91), and Ibn al-Subkī in *Ṭabaqāt al-Shāfi'iyya al-Kubrā* (2:268), all with weak chains because of 'Aṭiyya ibn Sa'd al-'Awfī who concealed his sources. Also narrated with very weak chains from Thawbān, Ibn 'Umar, and Abū Hurayra by al-Ṭabarī, Abū al-Shaykh, Abū Nu'aym, Ibn Abī Ḥātim, and Ibn Kathīr in their commentaries of the verse ﴾**Therein lie portents for those who read the signs**﴿ (15:75); and from other Companions with very weak chains. Among the incorrect rulings on the grade of this ḥadīth are those given by Ibn al-Jawzī and the philologist al-Ṣāghānī who included it among the forgeries in their respective *Mawḍū'āt* (3:147 and p. 27). Al-Sakhāwī in *al-Maqāṣid al-Ḥasana* (§23) rejects the grading of *mawḍū'*, but considers its chains all weak as does al-Aḥdab in *Zawā'id Tārīkh Baghdād* (4:340-343 §687). In confirmation of the general authenticity of this narration the scholars cited another narration whereby the Prophet ﷺ said: "Allāh has servants who know [the truth about people] through reading the signs" (*tawassum*). Narrated from Anas by al-Bazzār as cited in *Zawā'id Musnad al-Bazzār* (4:243), al-Ṭabarānī in *al-Awsaṭ* (§2956), al-Ṭabarī, al-Qurṭubī, and Ibn Kathīr

in thought then lifted his head and said: "Submit, for the time has come for you to accept Islām." The young man embraced Islām on the spot.[639] Al-Junayd defined the Knower (*al-'ārif*) as "He who addresses your secret although you are silent."

Ibn al-Jawzī cites another example of Junayd's *kashf* in his *Ṣifat al-Ṣafwa*:

> Abū 'Amr ibn 'Alwān relates: I went out one day to the market of al-Ruḥba for something I needed. I saw a funeral procession and I followed it to pray with the others. I stood among the people until they buried the dead man. My eyes unwittingly fell on a woman who was unveiled. I lingered looking at her. Then I held back and began to beg forgiveness of Allāh ﷻ. On my way home an old woman told me: "My master, why is your face all darkened?" I took a mirror and behold! my face had turned dark. I examined my conscience and searched: Where did calamity befall me? I remembered the look I cast. Then I sat alone somewhere, fervently asking for Divine forgiveness. I decided to live austerely for forty days.[640] [During that time] the thought came

in their *Tafsīrs* (14:32, 10:43, and 2:556), al-Quḍā'ī in *Musnad al-Shihāb* (2:170), and both Abū Nu'aym and Ibn al-Sunnī in their *al-Ṭibb al-Nabawī* as stated by al-'Ajlūnī in *Kashf al-Khafā'* (1:42 §3632) and al-Ghumāri in *Fatḥ al-Wahhāb* (2:170), all with fair chains according to Ibn Ḥajar in *Mukhtaṣar al-Zawā'id* (2:506 §2302), al-Haythamī (10:268), and al-Sakhāwī in *al-Maqāṣid al-Ḥasana* (p. 20). Al-Dhahabī in his *Mīzān* (1:334) declares it "disclaimed" (*munkar*) not because the ḥadīth itself is weak but only because no one narrates it other than Bakr ibn al-Ḥasan – Abū Bishr ibn al-Muzalliq – whose actual grading is "truthful" (*ṣadūq*) as stated by al-Dhahabī, while others declared him "trustworthy" (*thiqa*). Shaykh Mamdūḥ in the same monogaph (p. 35-38) faulted as incorrect 'Abd al-Raḥmān al-Mu'allimī al-Yamānī's grading of this ḥadīth as weak in his notes on al-Shawkānī's *Fawā'id* (p. 245).

639 Al-Qushayrī, *Risāla* cf. Ibn Kathīr, *Bidāya* (11:114); Ibn Khallikān, *Wafayāt* (1:374).

640 Cf. ḥadīth of the Prophet ﷺ: "None dedicates to Allāh forty days/mornings but that He causes the wellsprings of wisdom to break forth from his heart to his tongue." Narrated by Ibn Abī Shayba (7:80), al-Quḍā'ī in *Musnad al-Shihāb* (1:285), Aḥmad, Hannād, and Ibn al-Mubārak, all three in their *Zuhd*, al-Daylamī in *Musnad al-Firdaws* (3:564), Abū Nu'aym in the *Ḥilya* (5:189, 10:70) and others through so many chains both from Companions – Ibn 'Abbās, Abū Ayyūb al-Anṣārī, Abū Mūsā al-Ash'arī, 'Alī, Abū Dharr, and Anas – and *mursal* – from Makḥūl and Ṣafwān ibn Sulaym – that it reaches the grade of *ḥasan ṣaḥīḥ* according to al-Ghumārī in *al-Mudāwī li-'Ilal al-Jāmi' al-Ṣaghīr wa-Sharḥay al-Munāwī* (6:108-111) although al-Sakhāwī

to my heart: "Visit your Shaykh, al-Junayd." I travelled to Baghdād. When I reached the room where he lived I knocked at the door. I heard him say from inside: "Come in, Abū 'Amr! You sin in al-Ruḥba and we ask forgiveness for you here in Baghdād!"[641]

About the Ṣūfīs al-Junayd said:

- "They are the members of a single household that none but they can enter."
- "The Ṣūfī is like the earth: every kind of abomination is thrown upon it, but naught but every kind of goodness grows from it."
- "If you see a Ṣūfī caring for his outer appearance, then know that his inward being is corrupt."
- "The Ṣūfī is like the earth: both the righteous and the sinners walk upon it. He is like the clouds: they give shade to all things. He is like the raindrop: it waters all things."

Ibn Qayyim al-Jawziyya related from al-Sulamī that al-Junayd said: "The truthful seeker (*al-murīd al-ṣādiq*) has no need for the scholars of knowledge" and "When Allāh desires great goodness for the seeker, He makes him flock to the Ṣūfīs and prevents him from accompanying those who read books (*al-qurrā'*)."[642] This does not refer to an abandonment of knowledge but to the pursuit of practice over memorization. As he said: "The way to Allāh ﷻ is closed except to those who follow the footsteps of the Prophet ﷺ and adhere to his Sunna. Allāh ﷻ said, ﴾**Verily in the messenger of Allāh you have a good example for him who looks unto Allāh and the last Day, and remembers Allāh much**﴿ (33:21)."[643] This is confirmed by his saying reported by al-

declared it weak in his *Maqāṣid* (§1054). Its meaning refers to (1) observing congregational prayer from its very start as well as (in Imām Zayd's narration in his *Musnad*) (2) fasting and (3) consuming only licit sustenance. Cf. *Sharḥ Sunan Ibn Mājah* (1:58), *Fayḍ al-Qadīr* (4:273, 6:43-44), and *Kashf al-Khafā* (2:292-293). For four more similar ḥadīths see *al-Mudāwī* (6:295-298). A fourth meaning is Godwary simple living as illustrated by Mālik's statement: "None renounces the world and guards himself except he will speak wisdom." Narrated from Ibn Wahb by al-Dhahabī in the *Siyar* (Risāla ed. 8:109).

641 In Ibn al-Jawzī, *Ṣifat al-Ṣafwa* 1(2):271, chapter on al-Junayd (§296).

642 Ibn Qayyim al-Jawziyya, *Madārij al-Sālikīn* (2:366).

643 Narrated by Abū Nu'aym in the *Ḥilya* (10:257), al-Khaṭīb in *al-Faqīh wal-*

Dhahabī: "We did not take *taṣawwuf* from what So-and-So said and what So-and-So-said, but from hunger, abandonment of the world, and severance of comforts." Al-Junayd also said: "Among the marks of the wrath of Allāh against a servant is that He makes him busy with that which is of no concern to him."[644]

Ibn al-Qayyim in *al-Fawā'id* and *Zād al-Ma'ād* asserts the superiority of the struggle against the ego (*jihād al-nafs*) over all struggles, and cites al-Junayd:

> Allāh ﷻ said: ﴿**Those who have striven for Our sake, We guide them to Our ways**﴾ (29:96). He has thereby made guidance dependent on *jihād.* Therefore, the most perfect of people are those of them who struggle the most for His sake, and the most obligatory of *jihāds* (*afraḍ al-jihād*) are the *jihād* against the ego, the *jihād* against desires, the *jihād* against the devil, and the *jihād* against the lower world. Whoever struggles against these four, Allāh will guide them to the ways of His good pleasure which lead to His Paradise, and whoever leaves *jihād,* then he leaves guidance in proportion to his leaving *jihād.* Al-Junayd said: "[The verse means] Those who have striven against their desires and repented for Our sake, We shall guide them to the ways of sincerity. And one cannot struggle against his enemy outwardly except by struggling against these enemies inwardly. Then whoever is given victory over them will be victorious over his enemy. Whoever is defeated by them, his enemy defeats him."[645]

Ibn 'Ābidīn related in his fatwā on the permissibility of *dhikr* gatherings:

> The Imām of the two groups [*Ṣūfis* and *Fuqahā'*], our Master al-Junayd, was told: "Certain people indulge in ecstatic behavior (*wajd*), swaying with their bodies." He replied: "Leave them to their happiness with Allāh! They are the ones whose affections

---

Mutafaqqih (1:150), al-Sulamī in *Ṭabaqāt al-Ṣūfiyya* (p. 159), al-Qushayrī in *al-Risāla* (1:117), Ibn al-Jawzī in *Talbīs Iblīs* (p. 19) and *Ṣifat al-Ṣafwa* (2:418), and al-Suyūṭī in *Miftāḥ al-Janna* (p. 148 §333, p. 155 §357).

644 In Ibn al-Jawzī, *Ṣifat al-Ṣafwa,* chapter on al-Junayd.

645 Ibn Qayyim al-Jawziyya, *al-Fawā'id,* ed. Muḥammad 'Alī Quṭb (al-Iskandariyya: Dār al-Da'wa, 1992) p. 50 and *Zād al-Ma'ād* (Risāla ed. 3:5-10).

have been smashed by the Path and whose breasts have been torn apart by effort – and they are unable to bear it. There is no blame on them if they breathe awhile as a remedy for their intense state. If you tasted what they taste, you would excuse their exuberance."[646]

In *Kitāb al-Fanā'* ("Book of the Annihilation of the Self") al-Junayd states:

> As for the select and the select of the select, who become alien through the strangeness of their conditions – presence for them is loss, and enjoyment of the witnessing is struggle. They have been effaced from every trace and every signification that they find in themselves or that they witness on their own. The Real has subjugated them, effaced them, annihilated them from their own attributes, so that it is the Real that works through them, on them, and for them in everything they experience. It is the Real which confirms such exigencies in and upon them through the form of its completion and perfection.[647]

Al-Junayd went on pilgrimage on foot thirty times. On his deathbed he recited the Qur'ān incessantly. Al-Jarīrī related that he told him: "Abū al-Qāsim! Put yourself at ease." He replied: "Abū Muḥammad! Do you know anyone that is more in need of Qur'ān at this time, when my record is being folded up?" He finished one *khatma* then started again until he recited seventy verses of Sūrat al-Baqara, then he died. Ibn 'Imād al-Ḥanbalī said: "If we were to speak of his merits we could fill volumes."

Ja'far al-Khuldī said: "I saw al-Junayd in my sleep [after he died] and said to him, 'What did Allāh do with you?' He replied: 'All those subtle allusions were swept away, and all those lofty expressions vanished. Nothing was of use to me except a few genuflections I prayed before the dawn.'"

IBN SURAYJ

Al-Qāḍī Abū al-'Abbās Aḥmad ibn 'Umar ibn Surayj al-Shirāzī al-

[646] Seventh treatise in Ibn 'Ābidīn's *Rasā'il*, titled *Shifā' al-'Alīl wa-Ball al-Ghalīl fī Ḥukm al-Waṣiyya bil-Khatamāt wal-Tahālīl* (1:172-173).

[647] Translation communicated to the author by Dr. Michael Sells.

Miṣrī ﷺ (d. 303 or 306) the ḥadīth Master and *Faqīh* was known as the Swooping Falcon (*al-Bāz al-Ashhab*) – a nickname later famed for Shaykh 'Abd al-Qādir al-Gīlānī. Ibn al-Subkī also calls him "the Fierce Lion Against the Dissenters of the *Madhhab* of al-Shāfi'ī." The nickname "the Little Shafi'i" was given to him by Abū Ḥafṣ al-Muṭawwi'ī, a praise probably deserved by no one after him more than Imām al-Bayhaqī.

Ibn Surayj is listed by al-Dhahabī in the *Siyar* among "Those Who Are Imitated in Islām" in the generation of *Imām al-A'imma* Ibn Khuzayma and Imām al-Ṭabarī. In the previous generations al-Dhahabī lists the more senior Shāfi'ī authorities such as Abū Thawr (d. 240), al-Buwayṭī (d. 231), and al-Muzanī (d. 264). It is true that Ibn Surayj was said to be preferred to all of the above, including al-Muzanī! This is reported by Abū Isḥāq al-Shirāzī and all the authors of *Ṭabaqāt al-Shāfi'iyya* such as Ibn al-Subkī, al-Isnawī, Ibn Kathīr, Ibn al-Qāḍī Shuhba, and others. Abū Ḥāmid al-Isfarāyīnī – considered one of the *Mujaddids* for the fourth century – proclaimed himself Ibn Surayj's imitator but only "in the externals of *fiqh*, not the delicate matters" (*al-raqā'iq*).

Abū al-Ḥasan al-Shayrajī al-Farḍī said that Ibn Surayj's works in the *Madhhab* amounted to 400, although many of them were in ḥadīth and *zuhd*. Ibn al-Subkī said: "We only saw a few of them," indicating that most of those works were lost.

Ibn Surayj was the peerless admonisher (*wā'iẓ*) of his time and apparently was also a fierce debater. To Abū Bakr Muḥammad ibn Dāwūd al-Dīnawarī who once said to him: "Allow me to swallow!" – *i.e.* let me catch my breath – Ibn Surayj replied: "I'll let you swallow the whole Tigris!" *i.e.* the main river of Baghdād after the Euphrates, both famed for their sweet water. Another time: "Give me some time!" Ibn Surayj: "I give you from now to the Hour of Judgment!" He refuted the books of Muḥammad ibn al-Ḥasan al-Shaybānī against al-Shāfi'ī.

Ibn Surayj was Qāḍī of Shīrāz and he took ḥadīth from al-Za'farānī, Abū Dāwūd al-Sijistānī, and others; and *fiqh* from Abū al-Qāsim al-Anmāṭī, al-Muzanī, and others. Al-Dāraquṭnī and others narrated from him. He went to Cairo and lived there for a long time, and hence is called al-Miṣrī, but he died in Baghdād at age 87. His grave is in the West side there and was visited for its blessing (*tabarruk*) in the time of Ibn Khallikān. His son 'Umar taught the Iraqis in the rulings on *ṭahāra* organised by his father and he authored an abridgment of his *Fiqh* entitled *Tadhkirat al-'Ālim wal-Muta'allim.*

Among Ibn Surayj's famous students is Muḥammad Ibn Khafīf ibn Asfakshad, Abū 'Abd Allāh al-Shīrāzī al-Ḍabbī al-Shāfi'ī (276?-371) the centenarian Ṣūfī disciple of Abū al-Ḥasan al-Ash'arī of whom al-Dhahabī said: "He is at the same time one of the most knowledgeable Shaykhs in the external sciences (*'ulūm al-ẓāhir*)." Ibn Khafīf reported from Ibn Surayj that the proof that love of Allāh was a categorical obligation (*farḍ*) was in the verse: ﴾**Say: If your fathers, and your sons, and your brethren, and your wives, and your tribe, and the wealth you have acquired, and merchandise for which you fear that there will be no sale, and dwellings you desire are dearer to you than Allāh and His messenger and striving in His way: then wait till Allāh brings His command to pass. Allāh guides not wrongdoing folk**﴿ (9:24), for punishment is not threatened except for a categorical obligation.

Ibn al-Subkī in *Ṭabaqāt al-Kubrā* and Ibn 'Imād in *Shadharāt al-Dhahab* report that Ibn Surayj was unanimously considered the *Mujaddid* of his century and he is thus listed by al-Suyūṭī (along with Abū al-Ḥasan al-Ash'arī) in his *Tuḥfat al-Mujtahidīn bi-Asmā' al-Mujaddidīn* ("The Gem of the Striving Scholars: the Names of the Renewers of the Religion") for the third century.

Ibn al-Subkī said that his Shaykh al-Dhahabī considered the word *man* [the Arabic personal pronoun translatable as "one who" or "those who"] in the ḥadīth of the Renewer (*Mujaddid*) to refer to the plural. Thus, the *Mujaddids* for the Third century, for example, were Ibn Surayj in *Fiqh*, al-Ash'arī in *Uṣūl al-Dīn*, and al-Nasā'ī in ḥadīth, while in the Sixth they were 'Abd al-Ghanī [Abū Muḥammad Taqī al-Dīn ibn 'Abd al-Wāḥid ibn 'Alī al-Jammā'īlī al-Maqdisī the Ḥanbalī (d. 600)] in ḥadīth and Fakhr al-Dīn al-Rāzī in *Kalām.*

Among Ibn Surayj's sayings: "I never saw a student of *fiqh* work in *kalām* and succeed: he lost *fiqh* yet he will not attain true knowledge of *kalām!*" Imām Fakhr al-Dīn al-Rāzī's father, Ḍiyā' al-Dīn al-Khaṭīb said in his book *Ghāyat al-Marām*: "Abū al-'Abbās was the most brilliant of al-Shāfi'ī's Schoolmen in *Kalām* just as he was their most brilliant one in *fiqh.*" Among Ibn Surayj's famous works is *al-Furūq fī Furū' al-Shāfi'iyya* ("The Variations in the Jurisprudence of the Shafi'īs"), questions and answers on al-Muzanī's *Mukhtaṣar* of al-Shāfi'ī's *al-Umm.*

AL-ṬABARĪ[648]

Muḥammad ibn Jarīr ibn Yazīd ibn Kathīr, Abū Ja'far al-Ṭabarī (224-310) was one of the major *mujtahid* Imāms and the founder of a School of Law – the Jarīrī *madhhab* – which remained for 150 years after his death, then faded. He is the author of a massive commentary on the Qur'ān; an equally large universal history; a biographical history entitled *Tārīkh al-Rijāl*; an encyclopedia of jurisprudence entitled *al-Basīṭ* and a medium-sized work entitled *Laṭīf al-Qawl fī Aḥkām Sharā'i' al-Islām*, which he abridged into a smaller work; a book on the dialects and sciences of the Qur'ān entitled *al-Qirā'āt wal-Tanzīl wal-'Adad*; the unfinished book of *Faḍā'il* on the immense merits of the Companions; *al-Manāsik* on the rites of Pilgrimage; *al-Musnad* ("Narrations with Uninterrupted Chains"); the unfinished *Tahdhīb al-Āthār* ("Classification of Transmitted Reports"); *Tabṣīr Ulī al-Nahī* ("Admonishment for the Wise") for the people of Ṭabaristān; *Ma'ālim al-Hudā* ("Sign-Posts of Guidance"); the monument of erudition *Ikhtilāf 'Ulamā' al-Amṣār fī Aḥkām Sharā'i' al-Islām*, known as *Ikhtilāf al-Fuqahā'* ("Differences of the Jurists"); and *Tartīb al-'Ulamā'* ("Taxonomy of the Scholars of Knowledge"). Al-Dhahabī praises the latter book and mentions that al-Ṭabarī begins it with the rules of conduct for the purification of the self and the sayings of the Ṣūfīs. As for the book *Ṣarīḥ al-Sunna* ("The Explicit Sunna"), its chains of transmission contains too many unknowns and weak links for it to be authentically attributed to him.

In one of his classes al-Ṭabarī asked: "What is the status of one who says Abū Bakr and 'Umar are not two Imāms of guidance?" Ibn al-A'lam replied: "He is an innovator." Al-Ṭabarī said: "An innovator? Just an innovator? Such a person should be put to death! Whoever claims that Abū Bakr and 'Umar are not two Imāms of guidance should definitely be put to death!"[649]

Al-Ṭabarī limited his *Tafsīr* of the Qur'ān and his great history to thirty volumes each out of compassion for his students, as he originally intended to write three hundred volumes respectively. Al-Khaṭīb heard the linguist 'Alī ibn 'Ubayd Allāh al-Lughawī say: "Muḥammad ibn Jarīr spent forty years writing forty pages a day." Abū Ḥāmid al-

648 Main source: al-Dhahabī, *Siyar* (11:291-301 §2696).

649 In Ibn Ḥajar, *Lisān al-Mīzān* (5:101).

Isfarāyīnī the *faqīh* said: "If a man travelled all the way to China to obtain the *Tafsīr* of Muḥammad ibn Jarīr it would not be too much." This alludes to the ḥadīth narrated from the Prophet ﷺ: "Seek knowledge even as far as China."[650] Ḥusaynak ibn 'Alī al-Naysābūrī said the first question Ibn Khuzayma asked him was: "Did you write anything from Muḥammad ibn Jarīr?" Ḥusaynak said no, for "he would not show himself, and the Ḥanbalīs forbade people from going in to see him." Ibn Khuzayma said: "You did poorly. To write from him alone would have been better for you than all those from whom you wrote." Ibn Khuzayma himself had read al-Ṭabarī's *Tafsīr* in seven months, after which he said: "I know not, on the face of the earth, anyone more knowledgeable than Abū Ja'far [al-Ṭabarī], and the Ḥanbalīs were

[650] Narrated from Anas by al-Bayhaqī in *Shu'ab al-Īmān* (4:290) and *al-Madkhal*, Ibn 'Abd al-Barr in *Jāmi' Bayān al-'Ilm*, and al-Khaṭīb through three chains at the opening of *al-Riḥla fī Ṭalab al-Ḥadīth* (p. 71-76 §1-3) where Dr. Nūr al-Dīn 'Itr declares it weak (*ḍa'īf*), all through Abū 'Ātika al-Baṣrī who is very weak. Also narrated from Ibn 'Umar, Ibn 'Abbās, Ibn Mas'ūd, Jābir, and Abū Sa'īd al-Khudrī, all through very weak chains. The ḥadīth Master al-Mizzī said it has so many chains that it deserves a grade of fair (*ḥasan*), as quoted by al-Sakhāwī in *al-Maqāṣid al-Ḥasana*. Al-'Irāqī in his *Mughnī 'an Ḥaml al-Asfār* similarly stated that some Scholars declared it sound (*ṣaḥīḥ*) for that reason, even if al-Ḥākim and al-Dhahabī correctly said no sound chain is known for it. Ibn 'Abd al-Barr's "Salafī" editor Abū al-Ashbal al-Zuhayrī declares the ḥadīth *ḥasan* in *Jāmi' Bayān al-'Ilm* (1:23ff.) but all the above fair gradings actually apply to the wording: "Seeking knowledge is an obligation upon every Muslim." The first to declare the "China" ḥadīth forged seems to be Ibn al-Qaysarānī (d. 507) in his *Ma'rifat al-Tadhkira* (p. 101 §118) although al-Sakhāwī reports from Ibn Ḥibbān the verdict *bāṭil lā aṣla lahu*. This grading was kept by Ibn al-Jawzī in his *Mawḍū'āt* but rejected, among others, by al-Suyūṭī in *al-La'āli'* (1:193), al-Mizzī, al-Dhahabī in *Talkhīṣ al-Wāhiyāt*, al-Bājūrī's student Shams al-Dīn al-Qāwuqjī (d. 1305) in his book *al-Lu'lu' al-Marṣū'* (p. 40 §49), and notably by the Indian *muḥaddiths* Muḥammad Ṭāhir al-Fattanī (d. 986) in his *Tadhkirat al-Mawḍū'āt* (p. 17) in which he declares it *ḥasan*, and Murtaḍā al-Zabīdī in his monograph *al-'Iqd al-Thamīn fī Ḥadīth Uṭlubū al-'Ilma wa-law bil-Ṣīn*. Al-Munāwī, like Ibn 'Abd al-Barr before him, gave an excellent explanation of the ḥadīth in his *Fayḍ al-Qadīr* (1:542). See also its discussion in al-'Ajlūnī's *Kashf al-Khafā'* under the ḥadīth: "Seeking knowledge is an obligation upon every Muslim," itself a fair (*ḥasan*) narration in Ibn Mājah because of its many chains as stated by al-Mizzī, although al-Nawawī in his *Fatāwā* (p. 258) declared it weak while Dr. Muḥammad 'Ajāj al-Khaṭīb in his notes on al-Khaṭīb's *Jāmi'* (2:462-463) declared it "sound due to its witness-chains" (*ṣaḥīḥ li-ghayrih*) as did al-Suyūṭī and Aḥmad al-Ghumārī in his monograph *al-Mus-him fī Ṭuruqi Ḥadīthi Ṭalabu al-'Ilmi Farīḍatun 'alā Kulli Muslim* Cf. al-Sindī's *Ḥāshyat Sunan Ibn Mājah* (1:99), al-Munāwī's *Fayd. al-Qadīr* (4:267), al-Sakhāwī's *al-Maqāṣid al-Ḥasana* (p. 275-277), and Abū Ghudda, *Khams Rasā'il (fī 'Ulūm al-Ḥadīth)* 245).

unjust towards him."[651]

The Caliph al-Muktafī requested al-Ṭabarī to write a certain book for him. When it was finished, a gift was produced for him but he refused to take it. He was told: "You must ask for your need, whatever it is." He replied: "I ask the Commander of the Faithful to forbid street begging on the day of *Jumu'a.*" This was done as he requested.[652]

In his book *Ikhtilāf al-Fuqahā'* al-Ṭabarī mentions the differences of opinion between Mālik, al-Awzā'ī, Sufyān al-Thawrī, al-Shāfi'ī, Abū Ḥanīfa, Abū Yūsuf, Muḥammad ibn al-Ḥasan, and Abū Thawr. He mentions some of the jurists among the Companions, the Successors, and their Followers until the second century. When he was asked for the reason why he did not mention Imām Aḥmad ibn Ḥanbal in his book he replied that Aḥmad was not a Jurist (*faqīh*) but a ḥadīth Scholar (*muḥaddith*). The Ḥanbalīs disapproved of this and reportedly roused the people against him, preventing visitors and students from visiting him in the daytime, so he died and was buried in his house. Al-Ṭabarī's reply is neither new nor unique of its kind as several of those who wrote about the differences among jurists did not mention Aḥmad ﵁.

Was al-Ṭabarī a Shāfi'ī? He took Shāfi'ī *fiqh* from Yūnus ibn 'Abd al-A'lā among others. Abū Muḥammad al-Farghānī – one of the major narrators of al-Ṭabarī's books – states: "Hārūn ibn 'Abd al-'Azīz related to me: Abū Ja'far al-Ṭabarī said to me: 'I have given rulings according to the *fiqh* of al-Shāfi'ī for ten years in Baghdād, and Ibn Bashshār al-Aḥwal (the teacher of Ibn Surayj) took it from me.' When al-Ṭabarī's learning increased, his striving and research led him to produce everything from among the categories of knowledge in his books, and there remained nothing that he did not give Muslims advice about."

651 Narrated by Ibn al-Athīr in *al-Kāmil fil-Tārīkh* (Dār Ṣādir ed. 8:134-136) [year 310]; al-Khaṭīb in *Tārīkh Baghdād* (2:164); Ibn Kathīr in *al-Bidāya* (11:166); and al-Dhahabī in the *Siyar* (11:294, 297 §2696).

652 The Prophet ﷺ said: "Whoever begs people for money so that he can accumulate it is asking for a hot coal. Therefore let one [who begs] take little, and consider it much." Narrated from Abū Hurayra by Muslim and Aḥmad. And: "One of you keeps begging until when he meets Allāh Most High, there is not a piece of flesh left on his face." Narrated from Ibn 'Umar by al-Bukhārī and Muslim. See the *Reliance of the Traveller* (p. 774, r39.0) for the legal ruling on begging.

The authors of the books of synchronical layers (*Ṭabaqāt*) are unanimous that he is a *mujtahid muṭlaq* (capable of independent legal reasoning), but they differ whether he is also at the same time a follower of the Shāfi'ī school like Abū Thawr, who is considered both a *mujtahid muṭlaq* and a follower of al-Shāfi'ī.[653] Al-Isnawī and al-Sharqāwī did not mention him in their biographies of the Shāfi'īs, while [Abū Isḥāq] al-Shīrāzī says in the introduction to his "Biographical-Layers [of the Jurists]" that he is not counted among the Shāfi'īs. Aḥmad ibn Qāsim al-'Abbādī said, "He is among our scholars" in the *Ṭabaqāt al-Shāfi'iyyīn.* Al-Rāfi'ī in *al-Muḥarrar* says: "Due to his dissents, Ibn Jarīr is no longer considered of those in our *madhhab,* although he is counted among the layers of the companions of al-Shāfi'ī." Al-Nawawī mentions this in *Tahdhīb al-Asmā' wal-Lughāt.* This distinction is often overlooked by the chroniclers who are interested in enlarging the numbers of their Imām's followers and including prestigious names among them, as with Ibn Abī Ya'lā's inclusion of Abū 'Ubayd Ibn Sallām and al-Bukhārī in *Ṭabaqāt al-Ḥanābila* and Ibn al-Subkī's inclusion of the latter in *Ṭabaqāt al-Shāfi'iyya.*

An incident was related to have taken place between al-Ṭabarī and some Ḥanbalīs in Baghdād over the explanation of the verse of the Exalted Station [17:79], whereby al-Ṭabarī reportedly recited:

subḥāna man laysa lahu anīsun wa-mā lahu fī 'arshihi jalīsu

Glory to Him Who has no comrade
nor companion sitting with Him on His Throne!

Upon hearing this, the account goes, the irate Ḥanbalīs pelted al-Ṭabarī with their inkwells and he sought shelter in his house.[654] The report seems dubious in light of al-Ṭabarī's lengthy defense, in his *Tafsīr,* of Mujāhid's narration of the Prophet's ﷺ seating on the Throne "with Allāh!" Al-Ṭabarī went to great length to show that

[653] Imām al-Suyūṭī also described himself as both a *mujtahid muṭlaq* and a follower of the Shāfi'ī school in his book *al-Radd 'alā Man Akhlada ilāl-Arḍ wa-Jahila annal-Ijtihāda fī Kulli 'Aṣrin Farḍ* ("The Refutation of Those Who Cling to the Earth and Ignore That Scholarly Striving is a Religious Obligation in Every Age").

[654] Al-Suyūṭī, *Taḥdhīr al-Khawāṣṣ min Akādhīb al-Quṣṣāṣ* cf. Frederik Kern in the introduction to his edition of al-Ṭabarī's *Ikhtilāf al-Fuqahā'* (Cairo, 1902).

Mujāhid's report is authentic from the perspectives both of transmission and reason as we mention in Part Four of this book. Furthermore, al-Suyūṭī's report is not found anywhere else. What is well-established is that the Ḥanbalīs persecuted al-Ṭabarī for failing to mention Imām Aḥmad in his book as we showed. Another reason mentioned by al-Dhahabī, was the antagonism between al-Ṭabarī and the Ḥanbalī Abū Bakr ibn Abī Dāwūd, who falsely accused him of being a *Rāfiḍī*.

IBN KHUZAYMA[655]

Muḥammad ibn Isḥāq ibn Khuzayma, Abū Bakr al-Sulamī al-Naysābūrī al-Shāfi'ī ⚛ (223-311) was "the Imām of Imāms (*Imām al-A'imma*), major ḥadīth Master, polymath, ocean of science, Ka'ba of the scholars, who wore the diadem of the Godwary and donned the garment of the friends of Allāh." He took *fiqh* from two of al-Shāfi'ī's closest students, al-Muzanī and al-Rabī' ibn Sulaymān al-Murādī, as a result of which he kept a staunch allegiance to al-Shāfi'ī. He once rebuked someone who had brought up the Ḥanbalī School with the words: "Is Aḥmad ibn Ḥanbal anything but one of al-Shāfi'ī's young pupils?" Among his Shaykhs in ḥadīth were al-Sa'dī, al-Baghawī, Abū Qudāma, al-Wāsiṭī, and many others. Among his students were al-Bukhārī, Muslim, Ibn Ḥibbān, Abū Sahl al-Ṣu'lūkī, and innumerable others. He was said to have reached the level of *mujtahid muṭlaq*. He declared having asked for knowledge that profits upon drinking water from Zamzam, in accordance with the Prophet's ⚛ ḥadīth: "Zamzam water makes true whatever it is drunk for"[656] Ibn Surayj said of him: "He brings out the anecdotes from the Prophet's ḥadīth with a chisel."

Ibn Khuzayma's *magnum opus* is his *Ṣaḥīḥ*, unfortunately lost for the

[655] Sources: al-Dhahabī, *Siyar* (11:358-368 §2735, 8:402); Ibn al-Subkī, *Ṭabaqāt al-Shāfi'iyya al-Kubrā* (3:109-119 §120); Ibn Kathīr, *al-Bidāya wal-Nihāya* (11:170).

[656] Narrated from Jābir by Aḥmad, Ibn Mājah, Ibn Abī Shayba, al-Khaṭīb in *Tārīkh Baghdād* (3:179, 10:166) and al-Bayhaqī with a good chain as stated by al-'Ajlūnī (*ḥasan li-ghayrih*) in *Kashf al-Khafā*; from Ibn 'Abbās by al-Ḥākim (1:473=1990 ed. 1:646) and al-Dāraquṭnī in his *Sunan* (2:289 §238); from 'Abd Allāh ibn 'Amr by al-Bayhaqī in *al-Sunan al-Kubrā* (5:148); and from Mu'āwiya by al-Fākihī in *Akhbār Makka*. Al-Būṣīrī in *Zawā'id ibn Mājah* and al-Nawawī declared its chain weak but a number of other ḥadīth Masters said it is a fair (*ḥasan*) narration due to the number of its chains and definitely *ṣaḥīḥ* as a *mursal* narration, among them Ibn al-Qayyim and Ibn Ḥajar as reported by al-

most part, and the extant part – in print – amounts to a third of the original work. His criterion for soundness, like Ibn Ḥibbān's in his *Ṣaḥīḥ* and (to a weaker extent) al-Ḥākim in his *Mustadrak*, is to regroup both the *ḥasan* and the *ṣaḥīḥ* under the latter appellation, unlike the stricter criteria followed by the Two Masters, al-Bukhārī and Muslim, in their like-named compilations. The claim that Ibn Khuzayma's *Ṣaḥīḥ* emulates Muslim's in reliability is, therefore, an exaggeration.

Ibn Khuzayma was humble, modest, generous, and scrupulously Godwary. He once went out into the streets and marketplaces of Naysābūr and invited everybody he saw to his gardens for a feast where all kinds of food were served to them. Despite this great wealth he was heard to say: "I do not remember ever owning more than two shirts." He once corrected the Emir Ismā'īl ibn Aḥmad on the chain of a ḥadīth, after which the Emir's scholars confided to him that they had known it to be mistaken for twenty years but had never dared correct him. Ibn Khuzayma said: "It is unlawful for me to hear a ḥadīth of the Prophet ﷺ narrated with a mistake without my correcting it." His student Abū 'Amr ibn Ismā'īl reported that Ibn Khuzayma refrained from taking anything handed to him with the left hand, and he always prayed two *rak'as* before sitting to write something. Sa'īd ibn Ismā'īl al-Ḥayrī said: "Truly Allāh repels affliction from the people of Naysābūr because Abū Bakr Muḥammad ibn Isḥāq is in it."

In his notice on al-Ṭabarī in the *Siyar* al-Dhahabī cites al-Khaṭīb's narration of the following incident:

Muḥammad ibn Jarīr al-Ṭabarī, Muḥammad ibn Isḥāq ibn Khuzayma, Muḥammad ibn Naṣr al-Marwazī, and Muḥammad ibn Hārūn al-Rūyānī were travelling together in Egypt and ran out of food. They remained hungry for several days. One night in the house

---

Suyūṭī in *al-Durar al-Muntathira* (p. 243-244 §383) and al-Munāwī (5:404), while al-Mundhirī, al-Dimyāṭī (in al-Suyūṭī's *Tadrīb al-Rāwī* [Faryābī ed. 1:158='Abd al-Laṭīf ed. 1:145=1:80] and *Ziyādāt al-Jāmi' al-Ṣaghīr*), and al-Suyūṭī (in al-Sindī's edition of Ibn Mājah, cf. *al-Durar*) declared the ḥadīth *ṣaḥīḥ*. Al-Sindī added: "The people of knowledge have experienced its veracity." See also al-Shawkānī, *Nayl al-Awṭār*, book of *Manāsik*, chapter on Zamzam water. Ibn Ḥajar in *Talkhīṣ al-Ḥabīr* (2:268) cites al-Dīnawarī's narration: "We were with Sufyān ibn 'Uyayna when a man came and asked him: 'Abū Muḥammad! Is the ḥadīth you told us about Zamzam water true?' He replied yes. The man said: 'I just drank it for the purpose that you narrate to me a hundred ḥadīths.' Ibn 'Uyayna said to him: 'Sit' and he narrated to him a hundred ḥadīths."

in which they had taken up residence, they drew lots to decide which of them would have to go out and beg for food on behalf of the others. The lot fell on Ibn Khuzayma. He said: "Give me a moment so that I can make the Deliberation Prayer (*ṣalāt al-istikhāra*). He started praying and they sat waiting by the candle-light, whereupon someone knocked at the door. They opened it to find the envoy of the governor of Egypt. He said: "Which of you is Muḥammad ibn Naṣr?" They pointed him out, and the envoy handed him a packet containing fifty dinars. Then he said: "Which is Muḥammad ibn Jarīr?" And so forth until he gave each fifty dinars. Then he said: "The governor slept at midday and saw in his dream the Muḥammads (*al-Maḥāmid*) starving, so he sends you these packets, and he makes you swear an oath that when they finish, send one of you to him [for more]."

Among Ibn Khuzayma's *fiqh* positions in which he contravened the Shāfi'ī School:

- "Congregation is a condition for the validity of [*farḍ*] prayer"; but this is the position of the Ḥanbalīs alone among the Four Sunnī Schools.
- "Raising the hands (in every integral of prayer in which one stands) is one of the pillars of prayer the omission of which invalidates it." The *Madhhab* stipulates this is is not a pillar but a Sunna.
- "Whoever prays the congregational prayer alone behind a row must repeat it;" but the *Madhhab* considers his prayer valid, only recommending to gently pull back, after *iḥrām*, someone from the preceding row.

Ibn Khuzayma's acknowledgement of his lack of training in *kalām*, which we cited in the section on al-Muzanī ("If a perfumer cannot properly practice shoemaking or carpentry, will you blame a *faqīh* and ḥadīth Scholar if he does not excel in *kalām*?"), illustrates the following advice by al-Shawkānī:

> We saw many of our contemporaries that were involved in the pursuit of knowledge showing impartiality and fairness in questions related to the Law, sticking to the evidence. But when they heard a question in a particular science of which they had no knowledge, such as logic, *kalām*, or astronomy (*al-hay'a*) and the

like, their disposition made them run away and they made others run away as well. All this while they have no idea what the question is nor do they understand it at all! It would be far more appropriate for them to be quiet, acknowledge their shortcoming, and keep back at whatever point Allāh kept them back. Let them answer steadfastly, whenever asked about it: "I do not know."[657]

Al-Ḥākim counted Ibn Khuzayma's works as over a hundred and forty titles. His *Kitāb al-Tawḥīd* ("Doctrine of Oneness") is largely an anthropomorphist manifesto first published in the sixties by a "Salafī" amateur in ḥadīth science and lavishly cited by "Salafīs" for its literalism in interpreting the Attributes. It was renamed *Kitāb al-Shirk* ("Book of Polytheism") by al-Fakhr al-Rāzī.[658] Al-Bayhaqī related that Ibn Khuzayma repented of writing it while al-Dhahabī pointed out that it also contains figurative interpretations, for example his explanation of "the image of Allāh" (*al-ṣūra*) as meaning "the image given to Ādam by Allāh" in the ḥadīth: "If you fight your brother, avoid striking the face, for Allāh created Ādam in His image."[659]

Al-Dhahabī said Ibn Khuzayma was "one of the extremists (*Ghulāt*) in the literal affirmation [of the Divine Attributes]."[660] An example of this extremism is the statement reported by al-Ḥākim and al-Dhahabī in the *Siyar*: "Whoever does not definitely confirm that Allāh ﷻ is established over His Throne above His seven heavens is a disbeliever whose blood is licit, and his property is to be divided among the Muslims!" Al-Dhahabī comments: "Ibn Khuzayma's speech, although true [!], is too blunt." Another version states: "Whoever does not definitely confirm that Allāh is established over His Throne above His seven heavens, separate (*bā'in*) from His creation, he is a disbeliever who must be summoned to repent, otherwise his head should be cut off and he must be dumped on a garbage-heap so that his stench will not disturb Muslims and non-Muslim citizens."[661] The evidence to which Ibn Khuzayma alludes does not support his terms but only says:

657 Al-Shawkānī, *Adab al-Ṭalab* (p. 124) cited in the preface to *al-Badr al-Ṭāli'* (p. 12).

658 In *al-Tafsīr al-Kabīr* (14:27 §151).

659 Narrated from Abū Hurayra by Muslim; also al-Bukhārī without the words "your brother." Cf. Ibn Khuzayma, *al-Tawḥīd* (p. 37-41) and section on Abū Thawr *supra*.

660 In *al-'Ulūw* (p. 500).

661 Narrated by al-Harawī in *Dhamm al-Kalām* (4:377 §1245) and al-Dhahabī in his

﴾**The Merciful established Himself over the Throne**﴿ (20:5) without the rephrasing in the passive and additions laden on his phrase, as al-Dhahabī remarked concerning a similar claim by 'Uthmān ibn Sa'īd al-Dārimī:

> In his book *al-Naqd* he ['Uthmān ibn Sa'īd al-Dārimī] said: "The Muslims all agree that Allāh is above His Throne, above His heavens." I say the clearest thing on this topic is the saying of Allāh: ﴾**The Merciful established Himself over the Throne**﴿ (20:5). Therefore, let it pass as it came, just as we learned to do from the school of *Salaf*![662]

In *al-Tawḥīd* Ibn Khuzayma also cites, as his proof for establishing that Allāh has a foot and other limbs, the verse: ﴾**Have they feet wherewith they walk or have they hands wherewith they hold, or have they eyes wherewith they see, or have they ears wherewith they hear?**﴿ (7:195) This proof contradicts rather than confirms the sound position of the *Salaf* as expressed by al-Muqri' and narrated by Abū Dāwūd in his *Sunan* whereby ﴾**Allāh is All-Hearing, All-Seeing**﴿ (4:58) means "He can hear and see" – without any mention of bodily appendages that pertain to those faculties. Al-Kawtharī pointed out that Ibn Khuzayma's understanding of this point is identical to that of the anthropomorphists of Ṭabaristan and Isfahān who said: "If He does not have eyes, nor ears, nor hand, nor foot, then what we are worshipping is a watermelon!" and they claim, in support of their views, that Allāh in the Qur'ān has derided those who lacked limbs by saying: ﴾**Have they feet wherewith they walk?**﴿:[663]

> Ibn al-Jawzī said of Ibn Khuzayma's interpretation of this verse: Truly I wonder at that man who, with all his skill in the science of transmission of ḥadīth, says such a thing and asserts for Allāh

'Ulūw (p. 500) cf. *Mukhtaṣar al-'Ulūw* (p. 225-226) with a sound chain from al-Ḥākim, from Muḥammad ibn Ṣāliḥ ibn Hāni', from Ibn Khuzayma. Al-Saqqāf claimed "Muḥammad ibn Ṣāliḥ ibn Hāni' is of unknown status for us (*majhūl 'indanā*) so this chain is unestablished" but al-Ḥākim himself declared him "trustworthy and trusted" *thiqa ma'mūn* cf. Ibn Ḥajar, *Lisān* (5:239) while Ibn Kathīr in his *Bidāya* (11:225) said *thiqa zāhid*! See also Ibn al-Subkī, *Ṭabaqāt al-Shāfi'iyya al-Kubrā* (3:174).

662 Al-Dhahabī, *Siyar* (10:643).

663 Quoted by al-Kawtharī in his *Maqālāt* (p. 361) from al-Saksakī's *al-Burhān fī Ma'rifat 'Aqā'id Ahl al-Adyān* ("The Demonstration Concerning the Knowledge of the Doctrines of the Adherents of Various Religions").

what he vilifies the idols for not having, such as a hand that strikes and a foot that walks! He should have asserted the ear also! If he had been granted understanding, he would not have spoken thus, and he would have understood that Allāh reviled the idols by contrasting them with those who worship them. The meaning is: You yourselves have hands and feet, how then do you worship what lacks them both?[664]

Al-Ḥākim in his *Tārīkh Naysābūr*, al-Bayhaqī in *al-Asmā'*, and Ibn Ḥajar in *Fatḥ al-Bārī* reported that Ibn Khuzayma regretted authoring *al-Tawḥīd* and "went back to the way of the *Salaf*."[665]

IBN ḤIBBĀN[666]

Muḥammad ibn Ḥibbān ibn Aḥmad ibn Ḥibbān, Abū Ḥātim al-Tamīmī al-Sijistānī al-Samarqandī al-Bustī Al-Shāfi'ī (d. 354) was the meticulous, erudite Imām, jurist philologist, astronomer, physician, *mutakallim*, admonisher, trustworthy ḥadīth Master, and expert in narrator discreditation and commendation (*al-jarḥ wal-ta'dīl*). He was of Arab ancestry and Afghan birth. He took *fiqh* and ḥadīth from Ibn Khuzayma, and travelled over all the territories of the Sunni world of his time in pursuit of the ḥadīths of the Prophet, taking knowledge from over two thousand Shaykhs in the countries of present-day Central Asia, Iran, Iraq, Turkey, Syro-Palestine, and Egypt. Al-Dhahabī recounts the above then exclaims: "Thus let all high energies be!" Of these two thousand Shaykhs, twenty-one are retained in Ibn Ḥibbān's masterpiece, the *Ṣaḥīḥ*, each one of them a foremost, trustworthy ḥadīth Master and authority in ḥadīth and its sciences. Among them are Ibn Khuzayma and Abū Ya'lā al-Mawṣilī the compiler of the *Musnad*.

The following story illustrates Ibn Ḥibbān's unflagging energy. As he was pouring questions on Ibn Khuzayma on a road trip they were making with other scholars, the latter exclaimed: "You dolt! Give me a break and stop badgering me!" Whereupon Ibn Ḥibbān began to write Ibn Khuzayma's words. When someone asked him why he was

664 Ibn al-Jawzī, *Daf' Shubah al-Tashbīh* (p. 172-174).

665 Al-Bayhaqī, *Asmā'* (Kawtharī ed. p. 269=Ḥāshidī ed. 2:23), Ibn Ḥajar, *Fatḥ* (13:492).

666 Sources: al-Dhahabī, *Tadhkirat al-Ḥuffāẓ* (3:920), *Siyar* (12:246-253 §3268); Ibn al-Subkī, *Ṭabaqāt al-Shāfi'iyya al-Kubrā* (3:131-135 §125); al-Arna'ūṭ, Introduction to Ibn Ḥibbān's *Ṣaḥīḥ*.

writing this, Ibn Ḥibbān replied: "I write everything he says."

Ibn Ḥibbān held judgeships in Nasā, Samarqand, and elsewhere, where he experienced the hostility of some Ḥanafī shaykhs who did not welcome him in their communities. Ibn Ḥibbān retaliated by turning against their Imām and writing book after book against Abū Ḥanīfa ﵁: the "Defects of His Merits," (*ʿIlal Manāqib Abī Ḥanīfa*), the "Defamations" (*Mathālib Abī Ḥanīfa*), and the "Defects of What is Transmitted Through Him" (*ʿIlal Mā Ustunida ilā Abī Ḥanīfa*), in ten volumes each. These books have been rightly forgotten. Ibn al-Ṣalāḥ commented in his *Ṭabaqāt al-Shāfiʿiyya*: "Ibn Ḥibbān went too far."

Among Ibn Ḥibbān's books recommended by al-Khaṭīb for ḥadīth students:

- *Al-ʿArḍ ʿalā al-Muḥaddith* in 2 volumes
- *Al-Asāmī wal-Kunā* in 8 volumes
- *Al-Asāmī al-Shādhdha* in 3 volumes
- *Al-Ashriba* in 3 volumes
- *Awwal Man Naẓara fil-Rijāl wa-Faḥaṣa ʿanhum* in one volume
- *Al-Ḍuʿafāʾ* in 10 volumes
- *Ikhtilāf al-Ḥadīth* in 5 volumes
- *Al-Ikhwa wal-Akhawāt* in 3 volumes
- *ʿIlal Ḥadīth Ibn ʿUyayna* in thirteen volumes
- *ʿIlal al-Musnad* in thirty volumes
- *Kitāb al-ʿIlal li-Ismāʿīl al-Qāḍī* in fourteen volumes
- *Kitāb Yaḥyā wa-ʿAbd al-Raḥmān fil-Rijāl* in 5 volumes
- *Madhāhib al-Muḥaddithīn* in 2 volumes.
- *Man Ḥaddatha Thumma Rajaʿa ʿanh* in 2 volumes
- *Man lā Yuḥtajju bi-Ḥadīthihi wa-lā Yasquṭ*
- *Man Nazala min al-Ṣaḥāba Sāʾir al-Buldān* in 5 volumes
- *Man Rawā ʿan Rajulin lam Yarah* in one volume
- *Man Yuʿraf bi-Ismin Dūna Ismi Abīh* in 2 volumes
- *Man Yuʿraf bil-Laqab wal-ʿIlal al-Mutafarriqa* in thirty volumes
- *Manāqib al-Shāfiʿī*
- *Al-Mudallisīn* in 5 volumes
- *Shuʿab al-Īmān,* based on the Prophetic ḥadīth: "Faith (*īmān*) has seventy-odd branches."[667] Ibn Ḥibbān relates that he decided to draw their exact list and began by counting all the acts of obedience but found that they exceeded that number by far; then he

[667] See n. 783.

limited himself to the acts described by the Prophet ﷺ in the Sunna as being part of faith but fell short; then he limited himself to the book of Allāh and again fell short. Finally, he joined together the Book and the Sunna, eliminating repetitions, and came up with exactly seventy-nine orders and prohibitions related to Faith. He said: "I understood at that time that what was meant was what I found in the Book and the Sunna."

- *Su'ālātuhu Yaḥyā* in 2 volumes
- *Al-Ṭabaqāt* in 10 volumes
- *Tafsīr Gharīb al-Ḥadīth* in 5 volumes
- *Al-Tārīkh* in 10 volumes
- *Al-Thiqāt* in 10 volumes. A frequent mistake of those who write about ḥadīth without having benefited from a thorough grounding in its sciences is to belittle Ibn Ḥibbān's strictness in narrator-commendation (*ta'dīl*) because of the known fact that whenever a narrator's reliability was unknown he included him in his *Thiqāt.* The truth is that his method is not as simplistic as this since his narrator-commendation entries in the *Thiqāt* belong to one of two categories:

1. A narrator concerning whom there is a difference of opinion among the authorities of commendation and discreditation, but is established by Ibn Ḥibbān to be trustworthy. In this respect Ibn Ḥibbān's opinion may be as strict as any of the scholars in the field.
2. A narrator who is *mastūr* or *majhūl al-ḥāl* – meaning that neither commendation nor discreditation is available concerning him – but is established by Ibn Ḥibbān to narrate from and transmit to a trustworthy narrator, and thereby classified by him as trustworthy. In this respect only can Ibn Ḥibbān's method be termed lenient.[668]

Ibn Ḥibbān considered weak any ḥadīth Master that does not know the *fiqh* of the ḥadīths he narrates, as stated by Ibn Rajab in his *Sharḥ 'Ilal al-Tirmidhī* (*al-riwāya bil-ma'nā*).

[668] Cf. Mamdūḥ, *Raf' al-Mināra* (p. 151). See also Ibn Ḥajar and al-Suyūṭī's rejection of the claim that Ibn Ḥibbān was overly lenient in his grading of ḥadīth respectively in al-Sakhāwī's *Fatḥ al-Mughīth* (1:36) and al-Suyūṭī's *Tadrīb al-Rāwī* (Rīyad ed. 1:36) as quoted by al-Arna'ūṭ in his introduction to Ibn Ḥibbān (1:38).

Ibn Ḥibbān narrowly escaped death at the hand of the authorities for having said: "Prophethood is knowledge and deeds." Al-Dhahabī excused him by comparing the sense of the phrase to the Prophet's ﷺ ḥadīth: "The Pilgrimage is 'Arafa":[669] just as the whole pilgrimage does not consist in standing at 'Arafa, similarly, prophethood does not consist in knowledge and deeds, but they are found in it to perfection and completion. As for the philosophers' claim that Prophethood is acquired through learning and practice, then that is undeniably disbelief and heresy, but it is not what Ibn Ḥibbān meant. He provoked anger and suspicion another time among the anthropomorphists by declaring in the introduction of his work *al-Thiqāt* that "Allāh has no limit (*ḥadd*)." This caused his expulsion from Khurāsān and Sijistān, where the trend of attributing limit to Allāh ﷻ was dominant.[670] When the Ḥanbalī Ṣūfī Ismā'īl al-Harawī al-Anṣārī asked the opinion of his shaykh Yaḥyā ibn 'Ammār[671] – both were anthropomorphists – about Ibn Ḥibbān as a narrator, Ibn 'Ammār said: "He was very learned but had little religion. He came to us and denied that Allāh had a limit, so

[669] Narrated from 'Abd al-Raḥmān ibn Ya'mar by al-Tirmidhī (*ḥasan ṣaḥīḥ*), Abū Dāwūd, al-Nasā'ī, Ibn Mājah, Aḥmad, and al-Dārimī.

[670] This trend survives in our time in the words of those who say "Allāh has limits which only He knows of" in conformity with Ibn Taymiyya's claims – without a single chain of transmission – in his *Majmū' al-Fatāwā* (5:184, 5:376-377) that "it is established that Ibn al-Mubārak said': "Allāh is above his heavens, over His Throne, with a limit no one knows except Himself" (*Allāhu fawqa samāwātihi 'alā 'arshihi bi-ḥaddin lā ya'lamuhu ghayruhu*) and that "it is also established from Aḥmad, Isḥāq, and others of the Imāms." None of the narrations from Ibn al-Mubārak, Aḥmad, and Isḥāq provided by al-Dhahabī in *al-'Ulūw* and *Siyar A'lām al-Nubalā'* corroborates any of the above, but all show that they only said: "Allāh is above his heavens, over His Throne," some adding, "distinct/separate (*bā'in*) from His creation." Ibn Taymiyya further mentions (5:376) Ibn Baṭṭa's narration whereby Ḥammād ibn Zayd ascribed place to Allāh ﷻ. When asked: "Our Lord descends to the nearest heaven – does it mean He removes Himself from one place to another place? (*yataḥawwalu min makān ilā makān?*)" Ḥammād said: "He Himself is in His place, and He comes near His creation in any manner He likes (*huwa fī makānihi yaqrabu min khalqihi kayfa shā'*)." The question and its answer cannot be authentically established to have taken place since Ibn Baṭṭa's reliability was questioned and the doctrine of attributing place to Allāh ﷻ is unheard of among the *Salaf*.

[671] Of Yaḥyā, al-Dhahabī himself said in the *Siyar* (13:310 §3932): "His zeal against innovators and the *Jahmiyya* pushed him to trespass against the way of the *Salaf*"; while al-Harawī was repeatedly jailed then expelled from Herat for inciting violence against students of the Ash'arī school whom he considered disbelievers.

we expelled him from Sijistān." The ḥadīth Master al-'Alā'ī comments: "Wonder of wonders! By Allāh! Who is more deserving of being expelled and declared a Godless innovator?" while Ibn al-Subkī says: "Just look at the ignorance of this critic of ḥadīth Scholars! I truly wonder who deserves blame more: the one who asserts limits for His Lord or the one who denies them?"[672] Al-Dhahabī awkwardly places Yaḥyā ibn 'Ammār and Ibn Ḥibbān on the same level, on the grounds that nowhere in the Qur'ān and Sunna is it said that Allāh has no limits – yet acknowledging that limits are the characteristics of creatures, and that Allāh is exalted above being qualified by limit. He also invokes the strange concept that the limitless is the necessary characteristic of the non-existent:

> I say Ibn Ḥibbān's denial of a limit for Allāh and the other's assertion of limits are both a kind of meddlesome discourse, and it would have been better for both parties to say nothing. For there is no text for either the denying or the asserting[673] while there is nothing like unto Allāh whatsoever. Therefore, whoever asserts limit to Allāh is told: "You have given limits to Allāh by your view without proof from a text, and he who has limits is [necessarily] created – exalted is Allāh beyond this!" while the one who asserts limit says to the other: "You have reduced your Lord to a non-existent thing, for there is no limit to the non-existent." Therefore, whoever affirms Transcendence for

[672] Narrated in al-Dhahabī, *Tadhkirat al-Ḥuffāẓ* (3:921), *Siyar* (Risāla ed. 16:96), and *Mīzān* (6:99); Ibn al-Subkī, *Ṭabaqāt al-Shāfi'iyya al-Kubrā* (3:132) and his stand-alone, edited *Qā'ida fil-Jarḥ wal-Ta'dīl* (p. 31-33) [in *Ṭabaqāt al-Shāfi'iyya al-Kubrā* (3:13)]; and Ibn Ḥajar, *Lisān* (5:113).

[673] Imām al-Kawtharī said in his *Maqālāt* (p. 350-353): "In *al-Ta'sīs fi Radd Asās al-Taqdīs* ("The Laying of the Foundation: Refutation of [al-Rāzī's] *Asās al-Taqdīs*" = *Talbīs al-Jahmiyya* 1:118) Ibn Taymiyya says: 'It is well-known that the Book, the Sunna, and the Consensus nowhere say anything to the effect that bodies are all created, nor that Allāh Himself is not a body! None of the Imāms of the Muslims ever said such a thing. Therefore if I also choose not to say it, it does not expel me from the Religion nor from the Law.' Indeed the above is complete impudence. What did he do with all the verses declaring Allāh to be far removed from having anything like unto Him? Does he expect that every absurdity that every idiot can come up with be addressed with a specific text? Is it not enough that Allāh ﷻ said ﴾**Nothing whatsoever is like unto Him**﴿ (42:11)? Does he consider it permissible for someone to say: Allāh eats this, chews this, and tastes that, just because no text mentions the opposite??"

Allāh and keeps silent, he is safe and has followed the road of the *Salaf*.[674]

Ibn Ḥajar rejects al-Dhahabī's reasoning as fallacious:

> Al-Dhahabī's words, "the one who asserts limit says to the other: 'You have reduced your Lord to a non-existent thing, for there is no limit to the non-existent'" are untrue. We do not grant that to deny limit to Allāh is tantamount to reducing Him to the non-existent after the certitude of His existence. The truth is that Ibn Ḥibbān was right.[675]

This is confirmed by one of the authorities invoked by "Salafīs" in matters of doctrine by the name of Ibn Abī al-ʿIzz:

> The *Salaf* all agree that human beings have no knowledge of any limit for Allāh and that they do not give any of His Attributes any limits. Abū Dāwūd al-Ṭayālisī said: "Sufyān, Shuʿba, Ḥammād ibn Zayd, Ḥammād ibn Salama, Sharīk, and Abū ʿAwāna did not attribute any limits [to Allāh], nor any likeness, nor any simile."[676]

The above is a confirmation from a purportedly "Salafī" source that the statements suggesting anthropomorphism attributed to the two Ḥammāds are inauthentic.

Among Ibn Ḥibbān's notable remarks in his *Ṣaḥīḥ*:

- His definition of "knowledge" to mean "knowledge of the Sunna" in the Prophet's ﷺ ḥadīth "Time shall grow short and knowledge decrease,"[677] in view of the increase of every other type of knowledge in modern times.
- His reference to the superiority of accompanying one's wife on her obligatory pilgrimage to the supererogatory jihād according to the ḥadīth whereby a man said to the Prophet ﷺ: "I enlisted for

674 Al-Dhahabī, *Mīzān al-Iʿtidāl* (3:507).

675 Ibn Ḥajar, *Lisān al-Mīzān* (5:114).

676 Ibn Abī al-ʿIzz, *Sharḥ al-ʿAqīda al-Ṭaḥāwiyya* (1391/1971 ed. p. 239).

677 Narrated from Abū Hurayra by al-Bukhārī, Muslim, Abū Dāwūd, and Ibn Mājah: "Time shall grow short, knowledge decrease, dissensions appear, avarice confront the people, and massacres abound." He was asked: "Messenger of Allāh, what is the latter?" He replied: "Killing, killing!" See the discussion of this ḥadīth in al-ʿIrāqī's *Ṭarḥ al-Tathrīb* (4:26-29).

such-and-such a campaign and my wife is going out on pilgrimage." He replied: "Go and make pilgrimage with your wife."[678]

- His reference to the desirability of placing one's fingers in the ears upon making *talbiya* before the *Ka'ba*, according to the ḥadīth: "I can almost see Mūsā placing his two fingers in his ears, and lauding his Lord with a loud voice."[679]

AL-QAFFĀL AL-SHĀSHI[680]

Muḥammad ibn 'Alī ibn Ismā'īl, Abū Bakr al-Qaffāl al-Shāshī al-Shāfi'ī al-Marwazī of Tashkent ﷺ (291-365), the grammarian, philologist, and meticulous Imām of notably high chains of transmission, a companion of al-Ash'arī and like him a former Mu'tazilī, became an Imām of jurisprudence and its principles, a ḥadīth Scholar, the Imām of the Shāfi'īs in Transoxiana, and the author of important works in the School according to al-Fayrūzābādī. His most prominent student is the Shāfi'ī reference nicknamed "The High Authority of the Community" (*Ḥabr al-Umma*), al-Qāḍī Ḥusayn. Al-Qaffāl took ḥadīth from Ibn Khuzayma, al-Ṭabarī, al-Baghawī, and others. From him, learned among others, al-Ḥākim, Ibn Mandah, al-Sulamī, and al-Ḥalīmī who said: "Our Shaykh, al-Qaffāl, was the best informed of the Scholars of his time I have met." Among his books were *Dalā'il al-Nubuwwa, Maḥāsin al-Sharī'a, Adab al-Qaḍā'*, and a commentary on al-Shāfi'ī's *Risāla*. Al-Dhahabī said: "Among his rare positions quoted in [al-Nawawī's] *Rawḍat al-Ṭālibīn* [1:401] is that the sick person is allowed to join two prayers together."

AL-DĀRAQUṬNI[681]

'Alī ibn 'Umar ibn Aḥmad ibn Mahdī, Abū al-Ḥasan al-Dāraquṭnī al-Baghdādī al-Muqri' al-Shāfi'ī ﷺ (306-385), *Amīr al-Mu'minīn* in ḥadīth – the highest level of a ḥadīth Master[682] – was a major, trustworthy ḥadīth Master of the Shāfi'ī school named "the Imām,

[678] Narrated from Ibn 'Abbās by al-Bukhārī.

[679] Narrated from Ibn 'Abbās by Muslim, Ibn Mājah, and Aḥmad.

[680] Main sources: Abū Isḥāq al-Shīrāzī, *Ṭabaqāt al-Fuqahā'* (1:209), Ibn 'Asākir, *Tabyīn* (p. 183); al-Dhahabī, *Siyar* (12:373-374).

[681] Sources: al-Dhahabī, *Siyar* (12:483-492 §3530); Ibn al-Jawzī, *Ṣifat al-Ṣafwa* (2:471).

[682] On this title see p. 427.

superexcellent ḥadīth Master, Shaykh al-Islām, emblem of the giants of knowledge, one of the oceans of the Science and the Imāms of the world" by al-Dhahabī. He narrated and transmitted ḥadīth from and to countless major scholars of the science. He excelled in the knowledge of the defects of narrators and ḥadīth narrations, the canonical readings of the Qur'ān, *fiqh* and the differences of opinion among the jurists, the Arabic language, and the historical disciplines.

Al-Dāraquṭnī once sat in Ismā'īl al-Saffār's gathering and began to copy a volume he had with him at the same time as Ismā'īl was dictating his own volume of ḥadīth. A man said to al-Dāraquṭnī: "Your audition [of Ismā'īl's narration] is invalid while you are copying [something else]." Al-Dāraquṭnī said: "My audition is different from yours. How much have you memorised from what he has narrated so far?" The man said: "Nothing." Al-Dāraquṭnī said: "He has narrated eighteen ḥadīths so far." Then he began to list their complete chains and narrated them one by one.

Rajā' ibn Muḥammad al-Mu'addil said to him: "Have you ever met anyone of your level?" He replied: ﴿**Therefore justify not yourselves**﴾ (53:32). I insisted, whereupon he said: "I never saw anyone who gathered together what I have gathered." Ibn Abī al-Fawāris asked him one day about a certain ḥadīth and he answered him. Then he said to him: "Abū al-Fatḥ! There is not, between the East and the West, anyone who knows this other than myself."

Someone asked Abū Dharr al-Harawī: "You are from Herat; why do you follow Mālik's School and al-Ash'arī's doctrine?" He replied: "I was walking with al-Dāraquṭnī when I saw the latter greet the qāḍī Abū Bakr [Ibn al-Bāqillānī], kissing his face and his eyes. After they parted I asked him who this was. He replied: 'This is the Imām of Muslims and the defender of the Religion, Abū Bakr ibn al-Ṭayyib.' I began to frequent him ever since."[683]

Ibn al-Jawzī relates that al-Dāraquṭnī said: "We used to seek blessings from Abū al-Fatḥ al-Qawāsī's grave."

Al-Mu'addil also narrated the following: "We were at al-Dāraquṭnī's house one day, listening to someone who was reading ḥadīth while al-Dāraquṭnī was praying some supererogatory prayers. A ḥadīth came

[683] Narrated from Abū al-Walīd al-Bājī's *Firaq al-Fuqahā'* by al-Dhahabī in *Tadhkirat al-Ḥuffāẓ* (3:1104-1105). Ibn 'Asākir narrates something similar in *Tabyīn Kadhib al-Muftarī*.

up that mentioned Nuṣayr ibn Dhu'lūq. The reader pronounced 'Bashīr' whereupon al-Dāraquṭnī said *subḥān Allāh.* Then the reader said 'Bushayr' and al-Dāraquṭnī said *subḥān Allāh.* Then the reader said 'Yusayr.' At that time al-Dāraquṭnī recited: ﴾**Nūn. By the Pen and that which they write**﴿ (68:1)."

Al-Dāraquṭnī was once asked to arbitrate between two groups in Baghdād who differed whether 'Uthmān was preferable to 'Alī or vice-versa. He relates: "At first I withheld from taking any position and considered reserve best. But I then reached the conclusion that Religion dictated other than silence. So I said: 'Uthmān is better than 'Alī with the agreement of the assembly of the Companions. This is the position of *Ahl al-Sunna,* and it is the first knot of the *Rāfiḍa* one cuts loose." Al-Dhahabī comments:

> To prefer 'Alī [to 'Uthmān] is neither *Rafḍ* nor a *bid'a,* for several of the Companions and Successors did.[684] Both 'Uthmān and 'Alī possess great merits and precedence and are among the foremost martyrs. However, the vast majority of the Community agree to give precedence to 'Uthmān,[685] and this is our position also; and better than both of them without doubt are Abū Bakr and 'Umar. Whoever differs with this is a hardened Shī'ī. Whoever disrespects the Two Shaykhs [Abū Bakr and 'Umar] while accepting the validity of their imāmate is a disgusting *Rāfiḍī.* As for those who both insult them and reject the validity of their imāmate, they are extremist *Rāfiḍīs* – may Allāh lead them to perdition!"[686]

[684] Cf. al-Haytamī, *Fatāwā Ḥadīthiyya* (p. 155) and Ibn Ḥazm's *al-Fiṣal* and *al-Muḥallā* as quoted in al-Ghumārī's *al-Burhān* (p. 85-88). To prefer 'Alī is not necessarily *Rafḍ* nor a *bid'a* but is the paving-ground of *Rafḍ* and *bid'a.* It has been argued that a Sunna can be over-emphasized until it becomes the mark of innovation – such as wearing the robe (*thawb*) to mid-calf or touching toes in *Ṣalāt* – at which point that Sunna has to be suspended so as to preclude resemblance (*tashabbuh*) with innovators.

[685] As in Abū Ḥanīfa's *al-Fiqh al-Akbar* and al-Ṭaḥāwī's *'Aqīda.*

[686] Al-Qārī said in *Sharḥ al-Shifā'* (2:92): "Al-Nawawī said that cursing the Companions is one of the most depraved acts (*min akbar al-fawāhish*), while the author ['Iyāḍ] counts it among the major sins (*kabā'ir*). Such offense is punished with corporal punishment according to the vast majority, while according to some of the Mālikīs and Ḥanafīs the offender is executed. In some of the books of the latter, it is stated that to insult the two Shaykhs (Abū Bakr and 'Umar) constitutes disbelief (*kufr*)." Al-Nawawī said in *Sharḥ Ṣaḥīḥ Muslim*: "Know that to insult the Companions is prohibited and

Al-Dāraquṭnī was one of the greatest experts on the defects of ḥadīth that ever lived. He authored a large work on the topic entitled *al-'Ilal* as well as a major compilation of 5,687 ḥadīths entitled *al-Sunan*. The latter differs from its namesakes among ḥadīth collections in that he did not intend it as a source of evidence and practice (*lil-iḥtijāj wal-'amal*) – as did the authors of the Four Books of *Sunan*, al-Dārimī, Sa'īd ibn Manṣūr, and others – but as a critique of some jurists and a source of reference for the defects (*'ilal*) of the *Sunan* works. Yet he named it *Sunan* rather than *'Ilal* because he organised it according to *fiqh* headings, as opposed to ḥadīth headings, which he reserved for his *'Ilal*. This explains why al-Dāraquṭnī's *Sunan* contains such a high proportion of weak and even forged ḥadīths. Hence, Shaykh 'Abd al-Fattāḥ Abū Ghudda stated that its proper title should be *al-Sunan al-Ma'lūla* or *Gharā'ib al-Sunan*.[687]

In his *Kitāb al-Tatabbu'* al-Dāraquṭnī argues for the weakness of certain ḥadīths in al-Bukhārī and Muslim[688] while he compiled another manual listing about eighty ḥadīths in which Mālik in his *Muwaṭṭa'* contravened the rest of the Masters in his chain or in his wording.

Al-Dāraquṭnī recommended visiting the graves of Prophets and the Friends of Allāh for the sake of obtaining blessing and intercession and narrated in his *Sunan* the Prophet's ﷺ ḥadīth: "Whoever visits my grave, my intercession will be guaranteed for him."[689]

---

constitutes one of the grave prohibited indecencies (*al-fawāḥish al-muḥarramāt*) whether with regard to those of them involved in a dissension or other than them, because they entered those conflicts on the conviction of their *ijtihād* and interpretation."

687 See Abū Ghudda, *al-Sunna al-Nabawiyya wa-Bayān Madlūlihā al-Shar'ī wal-Ta'rīf bi Ḥāl Sunan al-Dāraquṭnī* (p. 22-40).

688 See the biographical section on al-Bukhārī for more on this topic.

689 Narrated from Ibn 'Umar by al-Dāraquṭnī in his *Sunan* (2:278 §194), al-Ṭayālisī (2:12), al-Dūlābī in *al-Kunā wal-Asmā'* (2:64), al-Khaṭīb in *Talkhīṣ al-Mutashābih fil-Rasm* (1:581), Ibn al-Dubaythī in *al-Dhayl 'alā al-Tārīkh* (2:170), Ibn Abī al-Dunyā in *Kitāb al-Qubūr*, al-Bayhaqī in *Shu'ab al-Īmān* (3:490), al-Ḥakīm al-Tirmidhī in *Nawādir al-Uṣūl* (p. 148), al-Haythamī (4:2), al-Subkī in *Shifā' al-Siqām* (p. 12-14), Abū al-Shaykh, Ibn 'Adī in *al-Kāmil* (6:235, 6:351), al-'Uqaylī in *al-Ḍu'afā'* (4:170), al-Bazzār with a very weak chain containing 'Abd Allāh ibn Ibrāhīm al-Ghifārī [cf. Ibn Ḥajar's *Mukhtaṣar* (1:481 §822)] with the wording **(1)** "Whoever visits my grave, my intercession shall take place for him" (*ḥallat lahu shafā'atī*), and Ibn Ḥajar who indicated its grade of *ḥasan* in *Talkhīṣ al-Ḥabīr* (2:266) as it is strengthened by other ḥadīths which both he and al-Haythamī mention, such as: **(2)** "Whoever visits me without any avowed purpose other than to visit me, it is

عَنِ ابْنِ عُمَرَ رَضِيَ اللهُ عَنْهُمَا قَالَ قَالَ رَسُولُ اللهِ صَلَّى اللهُ عَلَيْهِ وآلِهِ وَسَلَّمَ مَنْ زَارَ قَبْرِي وَجَبَتْ لَهُ شَفَاعَتِي قط ط خط في تلخيص المتشابه الدولابي في الكنى هق في الشعب وممن صححه ابن السكن وعبد الحق والسبكي وممن حسّنه ضياء الدين المقدسي في فضائل الأعمال والحافظ في التلخيص الحبير والسخاوي في القول البديع والسمهودي والغساني وابن حجر الهيتمي واللكنوي والشيخ عبد الفتاح أبو غدة وتلميذه محمود ممدوح وليّن أسانيده الذهبي وقال تقوي بعضها البعض وممن ضعّفه البيهقي وابن خزيمة والسيوطي ووضّعه بعض المتأخرين كابن تيمية وأتباعه والله تعالى أعلم

---

incumbent upon me to be his intercessor on the Day of Resurrection." Narrated by al-Ṭabarānī in *al-Awsaṭ* and *al-Kabīr* with a chain containing Maslama ibn Sālim and by Ibn al-Sakan in his *Sunan al-Ṣiḥāḥ* as stated by al-Shirbīnī in *Mughnī al-Muḥtāj* (1:512). **(3)** "Whoever makes pilgrimage then visits me after my death it is as if he visited me in my life." Narrated by al-Ṭabarānī in *al-Kabīr* (12:406), al-Dāraquṭnī (2:278), and al-Bayhaqī in *al-Sunan al-Kubrā* (5:246 §10054-10055) all through Ḥafṣ ibn Abī Dāwūd al-Qārī, whom only Aḥmad declared passable (*ṣāliḥ*). Mamdūḥ said (p. 337-340) it is more *ḍaʿīf* than other weak ḥadīths in this chapter. **(4)** "Whoever visits my grave after my death is as those who visited me in my life." Narrated by al-Ṭabarānī in *al-Kabīr* (12:406) and *al-Awsaṭ* (1:94) with a chain containing ʿĀ'isha bint Yūnus, whose status is uncertain, and from Ḥāṭib by al-Dāraquṭnī (2:278); cf. al-Maqdisī, *Faḍā'il al-Aʿmāl* (p. 108) with another chain which al-Dhahabī said was one of the best chains in that chapter. Mamdūḥ said (p. 330-334) it is *ḍaʿīf* but not *mawḍūʿ*, contrary to the claims of Ibn Taymiyya and his imitators. **(5)** "Whoever makes pilgrimage and does not visit me, has been rude to me." Narrated by al-Dāraquṭnī in his *Sunan*. Al-Lacknawī said: "It is not forged as Ibn al-Jawzī and Ibn Taymiyya said; rather, a number of Scholars considered its chain fair, and a number considered it weak." Mamdūḥ (p. 344-346) considers it forged. Al-ʿUqaylī in *al-Ḍuʿafā'* (4:170) declared the chains of Ibn ʿUmar's narration "soft" (*layyina*) as did al-Dhahabī, the latter adding – as did al-Bayhaqī and al-Fattanī in *Tadhkirat al-Mawḍūʿāt* – that they strengthened each other as none contains any liar or forger, as stated by al-Suyūṭī in *al-Durar al-Muntathira*, al-Munāwī, and al-ʿAjlūnī in *Kashf al-Khafā* (2:328-329). The narration **(6)** "Whoever visits me in al-Madīna anticipating reward (*muḥtasiban*), I shall be for him a witness and an intercessor on the Day of Resurrection," narrated from Anas by al-Bayhaqī in *Shuʿab al-Īmān* (3:489-490), al-Jurjānī in *Tārīkh Jurjān* (p. 220, 433), Ibn Abī al-Dunyā, Ibn ʿAsākir, al-Janadī, and others, through Abū al-Muthannā Sulaymān ibn Yazīd al-Madanī al-Kaʿbī who was declared weak by al-Dāraquṭnī, Abū Ḥātim, and Ibn Ḥibbān while al-Tirmidhī considered his narrations fair; cf. Ibn Ḥajar, *Lisān* (7:481) and *Tahdhīb* (12:242). It was declared fair by al-Suyūṭī in *al-Jāmiʿ al-Ṣaghīr* (§8716) and "fair or rather sound through its corroborators" by al-Ghumārī in *al-Mudāwī* (6:290) in confir-

This is a fair (*ḥasan*) narration as concluded by Imām Abū al-Ḥasanāt al-Lacknawī,[690] his editor ʿAbd al-Fattāḥ Abū Ghudda, and Maḥmūd Mamdūḥ,[691] although some early scholars declared it sound (*ṣaḥīḥ*) such as Ibn al-Sakan in *al-Sunan al-Ṣiḥāḥ* and ʿAbd al-Ḥaqq al-Ishbīlī in *al-Aḥkām*, followed by *Shaykh al-Islām* al-Taqī al-Subkī in *Shifāʾ al-Siqām* in view of the totality of the chains.[692] Other ḥadīth scholars who considered it authentic are the ḥadīth Master Ḍiyāʾ al-Dīn al-Maqdisī,[693] Ibn Ḥajar's student the ḥadīth Master al-Sakhāwī,[694] the ḥadīth Master of Madīna al-Samhūdī[695] and Imām Ibn Ḥajar al-Haytamī in *al-Jawhar al-Munaẓẓam fī Ziyārat al-Qabr al-Mukarram.* Al-Ghassāni (d. 682) did not include it in his recension of al-Dāraquṭnī's weak narrations entitled *Takhrīj al-Aḥādīth al-Ḍiʿāf min Sunan al-Dāraquṭnī.*[696] Some late scholars, beginning with Ibn Taymiyya, are undecided whether to grade this ḥadīth weak or forged.

Imām al-Lacknawī said about this ḥadīth:

> There are some who declared it weak [e.g. al-Bayhaqī, Ibn Khuzayma, and al-Suyūṭī], and others who asserted that all the ḥadīths on visiting the Prophet ﷺ are forged, such as Ibn Taymiyya and his followers, but both positions are false for those who were given right understanding, for verification of the case dictates that the ḥadīth is *ḥasan*, as Taqī al-Dīn al-Subkī has expounded in his book *Shifāʾ al-Siqām.*"[697]

Among those who fall into the category of "Ibn Taymiyya and his followers":

- Muḥammad (ibn Aḥmad) ibn ʿAbd al-Hādī (705-744) who wrote *al-Ṣārim al-Munkī* in violent refutation of al-Subkī's book on visita-

mation of al-Subkī in *Shifāʾ al-Siqām.*

690 In *Ẓafar al-Amānī* (p. 422) and *al-Ajwibat al-Fāḍila* (p. 155).

691 In his *Rafʿ al-Mināra* (p. 280 and p. 318).

692 As related by Ibn Ḥajar in *Talkhīṣ al-Ḥabīr* (2:267). Cf. al-Shawkānī in *Nayl al-Awṭār* (5:95) and al-Sindī in his notes on Ibn Mājah.

693 Ḍiyāʾ al-Dīn al-Maqdisī, *Faḍāʾil al-Aʿmāl* (p. 108).

694 In *al-Qawl al-Badīʿ* (p. 160).

695 In *Saʿādat al-Dārayn* (1:77).

696 Published at Riyadh: Dār ʿĀlam al-Kutub, 1991.

697 Al-Lacknawī, *Ẓafar al-Amānī* (p. 422).

tion but contradicted his own position in another book of his: he makes much ado about the reliability of 'Abd Allāh ibn 'Umar al-'Umarī in *al-Ṣārim al-Munkī*, but relies upon him in another book, *al-Tanqīḥ*![698] Mamdūḥ refuted his weakening of this ḥadīth in great detail[699] and stated that *al-Ṣārim al-Munkī* is at the root of all subsequent generalizations in weakening the ḥadīths that concern the desirability of visitation.[700]

- The late 'Abd al-'Azīz ibn Bāz who reiterated Ibn Taymiyya's imprudent verdict: "The ḥadīths that concern visiting the grave of the Prophet ﷺ are all weak, indeed forged";[701]
- The late Nāṣir al-Albānī,[702] who claimed that the visit to the Prophet ﷺ ranks among the innovations,[703] although he himself was the Innovator of our time.
- A certain Nāṣir al-Jadya', who in 1993 obtained his Ph.D. with First Honors from the University of Muḥammad ibn Sa'ūd after writing a 600-page book entitled *al-Tabarruk* in which he perpetuates the same aberrant claim.[704]

Imām al-Sakhāwī said:

> The emphasis and encouragement on visiting his noble grave is mentioned in numerous ḥadīths, and it would suffice to show this if there was only the ḥadīth whereby the truthful and God-confirmed Prophet promises that his intercession among other things becomes guaranteed for whoever visits him, and the Imāms are in complete agreement from the time directly after his passing until our own time that this [i.e. visiting him] is among the best acts of drawing near to Allāh.[705]

698 Ibn 'Abd al-Hādī, *Tanqīḥ* (1:122) cf. Mamdūḥ, *Raf' al-Mināra* (p. 12).

699 In *Raf' al-Mināra* (p. 280-318).

700 In *Raf' al-Mināra* (p. 9).

701 In his annotations on Ibn Ḥajar's *Fatḥ al-Bārī* (1989 ed. 3:387), echoing the exact words used by Ibn Taymiyya in his *Minhāj* (1986 ed. 2:441) and *Fatāwā* (27:119).

702 In his *Irwā' al-Ghalīl* (4:337-338) in which he imitated Ibn 'Abd al-Hādī.

703 In *Talkhīṣ Aḥkām al-Janā'iz* (p. 110) and elsewhere in his writings.

704 Nāṣir al-Jadya', *al-Tabarruk* (p. 322). Note that all these books are presently available in print, but not *Shifā' al-Siqām*!

705 Al-Sakhāwī, *al-Qawl al-Badī'* (p. 160). He contradicts himself in *al-Maqāṣid al-Ḥasana* (p. 413) where he adopts al-Dhahabī's opinion that "the chains of the ḥadīth of visitation are all 'soft' (*layyina*) but strengthen each other because none of them contains any liar."

There is no contest among the jurists of the Four Schools as to the probative force of the narration of Ibn 'Umar, as it is adduced time and again by the jurists to support the strong desirability of visiting the Prophet ﷺ in Madīna, especially, among Ḥanbalī sources alone, Ibn Qudāma's *Mughnī, Muqni'*, and *Kāfī*; Ibn Mufliḥ's *Mubdi'*; al-Buhūtī's *Kashshāf al-Qinā'*, Ibn Dawyān's *Manār al-Sabīl*, etc.[706]

See also the additional sound texts illustrating the visit to the Prophet ﷺ, among them that of the Companion Bilāl ibn Rabāḥ al-Ḥabashī ﷺ who came all the way from Damascus with the expressed intention of visiting the Prophet ﷺ to greet him and, upon arrival, rubbed his face against the Prophet's grave in tears before proceeding to raise the *adhān* upon the request of the two grandsons of the Prophet ﷺ, upon them peace.[707] See also the Companions' practice of seeking the Prophet ﷺ as a means for their needs by visiting his grave, such as Bilāl ibn al-Ḥārith al-Muzanī, Abū Ayyūb al-Anṣāri, 'Ā'isha, and Fāṭima ﷺ, all as cited in the sections on *Tawassul* and Visitation in the *Encyclopedia of Islamic Doctrine According to Ahl al-Sunna wal-Jamā'a*.[708] And Allāh knows best.

AL-ḤĀKIM

Al-Ḥākim is Muḥammad ibn 'Abd Allāh ibn Muḥammad ibn Ḥamdūyah, Abū 'Abd Allāh al-Ḍabbī al-Ṭamhānī al-Naysābūrī al-Shāfi'ī, also known as Ibn al-Bayyi' ﷺ (321-405), the Imām, ḥadīth Master, expert in ḥadīth criticism, and Shaykh of ḥadīth Masters. He took ḥadīth from about two thousand authorities in Khurāsān, Iraq, Transoxiana and elsewhere. Among the most prominent of the Masters who narrated ḥadīth from him are his own teacher al-Dāraquṭnī – who declared him stronger in ḥadīth than Ibn Mandah –, al-Bayhaqī, al-Qushayrī, and others. Abū Ḥāzim said that al-Ḥākim was peerless in his time in Khurāsān, the Ḥijāz, al-Shām, Iraq, Ray, Ṭabaristān, and Transoxiana. His fame became widespread with lightning speed in his own lifetime. Al-Dhahabī said: "I saw an incredible thing – the *muḥaddith* of al-Andalus Abū 'Umar al-Ṭalamankī (d. 429) copied al-Ḥākim's book [*Ma'rifat Anwā'*] *'Ulūm al-Ḥadīth* ("The

706 See the "Salient Fatwās of Imām Aḥmad and his School" in this book.

707 Narrated by Ibn 'Asākir (7:137) with a good chain (*sanad jayyid*) as stated by al-Shawkānī in *Nayl al-Awṭār* (5:180), at the conclusion of *Kitāb al-Manāsik*.

708 In full at http://www.sunnah.org/ibadaat/tawassul.htm.

Sciences of Ḥadīth") in the year 389 from a Shaykh whom he named, from another narrator, from al-Ḥākim."

Al-Ḥākim belongs to the second generation of the Ash'arī school, having taken al-Ash'arī's doctrine at the hands of his students, among them Abū Sahl al-Ṣu'lūkī. He took *taṣawwuf* from al-Sulamī's grandfather and teacher Abū 'Amr ibn Nujayd, Abū al-Ḥasan al-Būshanjī, Abū Sa'īd Aḥmad ibn Ya'qūb al-Thaqafī, Abū Naṣr al-Ṣaffār, Abū Qāsim al-Rāzī, Ja'far ibn Nuṣayr, Abū 'Amr al-Zujājī, Ja'far ibn Ibrāhīm al-Hadhdhā', and Abū 'Uthmān al-Maghribī.

Al-Ḥākim said: "I drank water from Zamzam and asked Allāh for excellence in writing books." He authored the following works among others:

– *Al-Abwāb* ("The Topics")
– *Al-Amālī* ("The Dictations")
– *Amālī al-'Ashiyyāt* ("Night Dictations")
– *Faḍā'il al-Shāfi'ī* ("The Immense Merits of al-Shāfi'ī")
– *Fawā'id al-Nusakh* ("Benefits of the Copies")
– *Fawā'id al-Khurāsāniyyīn* ("Benefits of the People of Khurāsān")
– *Al-Iklīl fī Dalā'il al-Nubuwwa* ("The Diadem: The Marks of Prophethood")
– *Al-'Ilal* ("The Defects of Ḥadīths")
– *Mā Tafarrada bi-Ikhrājihi Kullu Wāḥidin min al-Imāmayn* ("Reports Found Only in al-Bukhārī or Only in Muslim")
– *Al-Madkhal ilā 'Ilm al-Ṣaḥīḥ* ("Introduction to the Science of Sound Reports")
– *Ma'rifat Anwā' 'Ulūm al-Ḥadīth* ("Knowledge of the Different Types of the Ḥadīth Sciences")
– *Al-Mustadrak 'alā al-Ṣaḥīḥayn* ("Supplement for What is Missing From al-Bukhārī and Muslim")
– *Muzakkā al-Akhbār* ("Verified Reports")
– *Al-Ṣaḥīḥān* ("The Two Books of Ṣaḥīḥ Ḥadīths")
– *Al-Talkhīṣ* ("The Summary")
– *Tarājim al-Musnad 'alā Sharṭ al-Ṣaḥīḥayn* ("The Reports of Aḥmad's *Musnad* That Match the Criteria of the Two Books of *Ṣaḥīḥ*.")
– *Tarājim al-Shuyūkh* ("Biographies of the Shaykhs")
– *Tārīkh 'Ulamā' Ahl Naysābūr* ("Biographies of the Scholars of Naysābūr").

It is narrated that a man of letters named Abū al-Faḍl al-Hamadhānī came to Naysābūr where he acquired a following and was named Badī' al-Zamān ("Wonder of the Age"), whereupon he became self-infatuated. If he heard someone recite a hundred verses of poetry but once, he was able to recite them back from memory, starting from the end and back to the beginning. One day he criticised someone for saying: "So-and-so the memoriser of ḥadīth," exclaiming: "Memorising ḥadīth! Is it worthy of mention?" When he heard of this, al-Ḥākim sent him a book of ḥadīth and challenged him to memorise it in a week. Al-Hamadhānī returned the book to him and said: "Who can memorise this? 'Muḥammad son of So-and-So and Ja'far son of So-and-So reported from So-and-So.' It is filled with all sorts of different names and terms!" Al-Ḥākim said: "Therefore know yourself, and understand that to memorise such as this is beyond your sphere."

Al-Ḥākim's *Mustadrak* was criticised by the ḥadīth scholars because of the number of mistakes and inaccuracies found in it. Al-Sakhāwī in *al-I'lān wal-Tawbīkh* and others mention that he declares many forged reports to be rigorously authentic – up to 100 according to some authorities – not to mention weak ones, instead of clinging to his own expressed precondition that only reports with chains of the rank of al-Bukhārī's and Muslim's would be retained. For example, he narrates in the *Mustadrak* from Ibn 'Abbās that Allāh ﷻ revealed to the Prophet ﷺ: "I killed seventy thousand [in punishment] for [the murder of] Yaḥyā ibn Zakariyyā ؑ; and I will kill seventy thousand times seventy thousand [in punishment] for [the murder of] your daughter's son al-Ḥusayn!" Al-Ḥākim said this report has a sound chain but Ibn Ḥibbān said this ḥadīth is untraceable (*lā aṣla lahu*) while al-Dhahabī rejects its text (*matn*) as "disclaimed" (*munkar*) in the *Siyar* and Ibn Kathīr similarly declares it "highly anomalous" (*gharīb jiddan*) in *al-Bidāya*.709

Al-Dhahabī went to excess in regretting that al-Ḥākim had compiled the *Mustadrak* in the first place.710 His classing al-Ḥākim "among those who are lenient, like al-Tirmidhī"711 does not apply to al-Ḥākim

---

709 See Ibn Ḥibbān, *al-Majrūḥīn* (2:215), al-Khaṭīb, *Tārīkh Baghdād* (1:142), al-Ḥākim (1990 ed. 2:319, 2:648, and 3:195), al-Munāwī, *Fayḍ al-Qadīr* (1:205), *Tadhkirat al-Ḥuffāẓ* (1:77 *gharīb*), *Mīzān* (s.v. Qāsim ibn Ibrāhīm al-Hāshimī), and *Siyar* (Risāla ed. 4:342-343).

710 "It would have been better if al-Ḥākim had never compiled it"! Cf. Bashshār 'Awwād Ma'rūf in his book *al-Dhahabī wa-Manhajuhu fī Kitābihi Tārīkh al-Islām*.

711 In *Dhikr Man Yu'tamadu Qawluhu fīl-Jarḥ wal-Ta'dīl* (p. 172).

in absolute terms but only to his grading of narrations in the *Mustadrak*, which the scholars pointed out that he compiled in his old age, intending to revise it, a task left unfinished beyond the first volume.[712] This is proven by the fact that al-Ḥākim's mistakes are fewer in the first volume of the *Mustadrak*, as shown by al-Dhahabī's own minimal corrections there. "Outside of the *Mustadrak*," Shaykh Maḥmūd Mamdūḥ said, "his positions are as strict as those of any of the meticulous Imāms of ḥadīth."[713] In fact, al-Ḥākim often criticises al-Bukhārī and Muslim for narrating ḥadīths from narrators who have been questioned.[714] More accurately, the criterion of soundness (*ṣiḥḥa*) for both al-Ḥākim and al-Dhahabī includes the narrations others classified as merely fair (*ḥasan*).[715]

Al-Kattānī in *al-Risāla al-Mustaṭrafa* described the *Mustadrak* as consisting half of sound narrations per the criteria of al-Bukhārī and Muslim or of either one, a quarter of sound narrations that do not meet their criteria, and a quarter of unsound narrations including forgeries. Among the *takhrīj* commentaries on the *Mustadrak* are al-Dhahabī's *Talkhīṣ al-Mustadrak*, al-Suyūṭī's *Tawḍīḥ al-Madrak fī Taṣḥīḥ al-Mustadrak*, a work by Burhān al-Dīn al-Ḥalabī, and others such as the recent *Tanbīh al-Wāhim* by Ramaḍān 'Alī Muḥammad.

Another criticism is al-Ḥākim's alleged Shī'īsm. Al-Dhahabī one time names him "one of the oceans of knowledge although slightly Shī'ī" (*'alā tashayyu'in qalīlin fīh*), another time "al-Ḥākim the Shī'ī," and another time "a famous Shī'ī" (*shī'iyyun mashhūr*),[716] an echo of Ibn al-Jawzī's barb: "Al-Ḥākim was Shī'ī-leaning (*mutashayyi'*) and this

712 Cf. Mamdūḥ, *Raf' al-Mināra* (p. 153 n. 1).

713 *Ibid.*

714 Shaykh 'Abd Allāh Sirāj al-Dīn said in *Sharḥ al-Manẓūma al-Bayqūniyya* (p. 47): "Al-Suyūṭī said in *al-Tadrīb* [Egyptian ed. p. 72] that Ibn al-Ṣalāḥ excepted the ḥadīths that attracted criticism [from his statement that all that is in the two *Ṣaḥīḥs* is definitely *ṣaḥīḥ*]. These are the ḥadīths which al-Dāraquṭnī and others have criticized, 210 narrations as the *ḥāfiẓ* Ibn Ḥajar said, 32 shared by al-Bukhārī and Muslim, while al-Bukhārī alone has 78 and Muslim alone 100."

715 For a critique of al-Dhahabī's statement about al-Tirmidhī's leniency see 'Itr's masterpiece *al-Imām al-Tirmidhī*.

716 "Al-Dhahabī likes to fuss over whomever he suspects of shī'ism (*tashayyu'*)." Al-Ghumārī, *al-Mudāwī* (5:424). (Al-Ghumārī himself is definitely guilty of it in his book *al-Burhān al-Jalī*.) Al-Dhahabī goes so far – in the *Siyar* (10:627) – as to claim that al-Ḥākim leans to the Karrāmiyya!

is a flagrant trait of his."[717] Ibn al-Subkī rejects the label of Shī'ī as baseless because Ibn 'Asākir includes al-Ḥākim among the Ash'arīs, who consider the Shī'īs innovators.

The first ḥadīth of the Prophet ﷺ al-Ḥākim narrated in his *Ma'rifat Anwā' 'Ulūm al-Ḥadīth* is: "Allāh make radiant the face of one who hears one of my sayings and then carries it to others. It may be one carries understanding without being a person of understanding; it may be one carries understanding to someone who possesses more understanding than he."[718] This is one of the fundamental ḥadīths.

[717] Ibn al-Jawzī, *al-Muntaẓam* (8:269).

[718] A mass-transmitted (*mutawātir*) ḥadīth narrated from the following Companions: (**1**) Zayd ibn Thābit by al-Tirmidhī (*ḥasan* in the printed eds.), Abū Dāwūd, Ibn Mājah, Aḥmad, al-Dārimī, al-Shāfi'ī in his *Risāla* (§1102), al-Ṭabarānī in *al-Kabīr* (§4891-4892, §4925, §4994), Ibn 'Abd al-Barr in *Jāmi' Bayān al-'Ilm* (1:175 §184), al-Rāmahurmuzī in *al-Muḥaddith al-Fāṣil* (p. 64), Ibn Abī 'Āṣim in *al-Sunna* (p. 45 §94), al-Khaṭīb in *Sharaf Aṣḥāb al-Ḥadīth* (p. 24) and *al-Faqīh wal-Mutafaqqih* (2:71), al-Ṭaḥāwī in *Sharḥ Mushkil al-Āthār* (2:232=4:282 §1600), and Ibn Ḥibbān (1:270 §67, 2:454 §680), all with sound chains as stated by al-Arna'ūṭ and others; (**2**) Jubayr ibn Muṭ'im by Ibn Mājah, Aḥmad, al-Dārimī, al-Ṭabarānī in *al-Kabīr* (§1541-1544), Abū Ya'lā (1:347 §7413), al-Ḥākim (1:87= 1990 ed. 1:162), al-Quḍā'ī in *Musnad al-Shihāb* (§1421), al-Ṭaḥāwī in *Sharḥ Mushkil al-Āthār* (2:232= 4:282 §1601), al-Khaṭīb in *Sharaf Aṣḥāb al-Ḥadīth* (p. 18), and Ibn 'Abd al-Barr in *Jāmi' Bayān al-'Ilm* (1:184-187 §195-197), all with weak chains because of Muḥammad ibn Isḥāq who is a concealer in his narrative chains (*mudallis*), cf. al-Haythamī (1:139); (**3**) Anas by Ibn Mājah, Aḥmad, al-Ṭabarānī in *al-Awsaṭ*, and Ibn 'Abd al-Barr in *Jāmi' Bayān al-'Ilm* (1:187-189 §198-199) with weak chains – as stated by al-Haythamī (1:138-139) – the collected force of which raise the ḥadīth to the grade of fair; (**4**) Abū Sa'īd al-Khudrī by al-Bazzār with a chain of trustworthy narrators except for Sa'īd ibn Bāzigh who may be unknown as stated by al-Haythamī (1:137); (**5**) Abū al-Dardā' by al-Dārimī and al-Ṭabarānī in *al-Kabīr* with a very weak chain because of 'Abd al-Raḥmān ibn Zayd ("ibn Zubayd al-Yāmī" in al-Dārimī) as stated by al-Haythamī (1:137); (**6**) 'Umayr ibn Qatāda al-Laythī by al-Ṭabarānī in *al-Kabīr* with a chain containing one narrator whose status is unsure, as mentioned by al-Haythamī (1:138); (**7**) al-Nu'mān ibn Bashīr by al-Ṭabarānī in *al-Kabīr* with a very weak chain because of 'Īsā al-Khabbāṭ and by al-Ḥākim (1:88=1990 ed. 1:164) with a sound chain as indicated by al-Haythamī (1:138); (**8**) Jābir and (**9**) Sa'd ibn Abī Waqqāṣ by al-Ṭabarānī in *al-Awsaṭ* with weak chains as stated by al-Haythamī (1:138-139); (**10**) Ibn Mas'ūd by al-Tirmidhī with two chains (*ḥasan ṣaḥīḥ*), Ibn Mājah, Aḥmad, Abū Ya'lā (§5126, §5296), al-Shāfi'ī in his (1:14), al-Baghawī in *Sharḥ al-Sunna* (1:233-234), al-Khaṭīb in *al-Kifāya* (p. 29, p. 173) and *Sharaf Aṣḥāb al-Ḥadīth* (p. 18-19, p. 26), al-Bayhaqī in *Ma'rifat al-Sunan* (1:15-16, 1:43) and *Dalā'il al-Nubuwwa* (6:540), Abū Nu'aym in *Dhikr Akhbār Aṣbahān* (2:90) and *al-Ḥilya* (7:331) where he graded it *ṣaḥīḥ*, al-Ḥākim in *Ma'rifat Anwā' 'Ulūm al-Ḥadīth* (p. 322), Ibn 'Abd al-Barr in *Jāmi' Bayān al-'Ilm* (1:178-182 §188-191), Ibn Ḥibbān (1:268 §66, 1271-272 §68-69) with

عَنْ أَنَسِ بْنِ مَالِكٍ رَضِيَ اللهُ عَنْهُ قَالَ قَالَ رَسُولُ اللهِ صَلَّى اللهُ عَلَيْهِ وَسَلَّمَ نَضَّرَ اللهُ عَبْدًا سَمِعَ مَقَالَتِي فَوَعَاهَا ثُمَّ بَلَّغَهَا عَنِّي فَرُبَّ حَامِلِ فِقْهٍ غَيْرِ فَقِيهٍ وَرُبَّ حَامِلِ فِقْهٍ إِلَى مَنْ هُوَ أَفْقَهُ مِنْهُ الحديث رواه الترمذي وأبو داود وابن ماجه وهذا لفظه وأحمد وهو متواتر وفي الترمذي عن عبد الله بن مسعود مرفوعا فَوَعَاهَا وَحَفِظَهَا وَبَلَّغَهَا

On the 3rd of Safar 405 al-Ḥākim went into the bath, came out after bathing, said "Āh" and died wearing but a waist-cloth before he had time to put on a shirt. Al-Ḥasan ibn Ashʿath al-Qurashī said: "I saw al-Ḥākim in my dream riding a horse with a handsome appearance and saying: 'Salvation!' I asked him: 'Al-Ḥākim! In what?' He replied: 'Writing the ḥadīth.'"[719]

AL-BAYHAQI[720]

Aḥmad ibn al-Ḥusayn ibn ʿAlī ibn ʿAbd Allāh ibn Mūsā, Abū Bakr al-Bayhaqī al-Naysābūrī al-Khusrawjirdī al-Shāfiʿī al-Ashʿarī ؒ (384-458), was the Seal of the Shāfiʿī *Mujtahids*. "The jurisprudent Imām, ḥadīth Master, authority in the principles (*uṣūlī*), scrupulous and devoted ascetic, defender of the School both in its foundations and its branches, one of the mountains of Islamic knowledge." He is known in the books of the Scholars of Naysābūr and his direct students as "*al-Faqīh* Aḥmad." He took *fiqh*, among others, from Imām Abū al-Fatḥ Nāṣir ibn al-Ḥusayn ibn Muḥammad al-Qurashī al-ʿUmarī al-Marwazī al-Shāfiʿī al-Naysābūrī (d. 444).

---

three fair chains according to al-Arnaʾūṭ, one of them with the wording "Allāh have mercy on someone who hears a ḥadīth from me then conveys it." Kattānī in *Naẓm al-Mutanāthir* adds the following Companion-narrators of this ḥadīth: (11) Bashīr ibn al-Nuʿmān; (12) Muʿādh ibn Jabal; (13) Abū Qirfāṣa; (14) Rabīʿa ibn ʿUthmān al-Taymī; (15) Ibn ʿUmar; (16) Zayd ibn Khālid al-Juhanī; (17) ʿĀʾisha; (18) Abū Hurayra; and (19) Shayba ibn ʿUthmān. Al-Tirmidhī's version does not mention the last sentence while al-Shāfiʿī's adds "and guard them from delusion." This is also the first narration in al-Ājurrī's book *al-Sharīʿa* and others. On the variant wordings of this important ḥadīth also see ʿAbd al-Fattāḥ Abū Ghudda's *al-Rasūl al-Muʿallim* (p. 55-56).

[719] Main Sources: *Tabyīn* (p. 226-229); *Mīzān* (3:608 §7804, 3:551 §7544); *Siyar* (13:97-106 §3714); *Ṭabaqāt al-Shāfiʿiyya al-Kubrā* (4:155-171 §329).

[720] Main Sources: *Tabyīn* (p. 260-262); *Ṭabaqāt al-Shāfiʿiyya al-Kubrā* (4:8-15 §251); *Siyar* (13:529-533 §4159); *al-Bidāya wal-Nihāya*.

[721] This is not the Ṣūfī master Abū ʿAlī Aḥmad ibn Muḥammad ibn al-Qāsim al-

He took *kalām* from the two Ash'arī Imāms Ibn Fūrāk and Abū Manṣūr al-Baghdādī and had more than a hundred Shaykhs. His oldest Shaykh was the Imām and ḥadīth Scholar of Khurāsān al-Sayyid Abū al-Ḥasan Muḥammad ibn al-Ḥusayn ibn Dāwūd al-'Alawī al-Ḥasanī al-Naysābūrī al-Ḥasīb (d. 401) who was also al-Ḥākim's Shaykh.

Al-Bayhaqī's other Shaykhs in ḥadīth include the ḥadīth Master Abū 'Alī al-Ḥusayn ibn Muḥammad ibn Muḥammad al-Rudhbārī al-Ṭūsī (d. 403);[721] the ḥadīth Master al-Ḥākim al-Naysābūrī (d. 405), whose foremost pupil he was; the Ash'arī Imām in the tenets of faith Abū Bakr ibn Fūrāk (d. 406); the Imām, jurist, philologist, and ḥadīth Master of Khurāsān Abū Ṭāhir Muḥammad ibn Muḥammad ibn Maḥmish al-Ziyādī al-Shāfi'ī al-Naysābūrī (d. 410); the Ṣūfī master, Ash'arī Imām, ḥadīth Master, and author of *Ṭabaqāt al-Ṣūfiyya* Muḥammad ibn al-Ḥusayn ibn Muḥammad, Abū 'Abd al-Raḥmān al-Azdī al-Sulamī (d. 411); Muḥammad ibn Hibat Allāh al-Lālikā'ī's teacher, Muḥammad ibn al-Ḥusayn ibn Muḥammad ibn al-Faḍl al-Qaṭṭān al-Baghdādī (d. 415); and the Ash'arī Imām, jurist, and heresiologist Abū Manṣūr 'Abd al-Qāhir al-Baghdādī al-Shāfi'ī (d. 429).

Al-Dhahabī said, "His sphere in ḥadīth is not large" and claimed al-Bayhaqī had no knowledge of al-Tirmidhī, al-Nasā'ī, or Ibn Mājah's *Sunan*. This is incorrect as al-Bayhaqī's *Sunan al-Kubrā* shows extensive knowledge of the first two. His sphere in ḥadīth is so impressively large – about 300 sources – that one scholar exclaimed: "This assessment is very strange indeed, and stranger yet the fact it came from such an accomplished authority as al-Dhahabī!"[722]

Perpetual Fasting

Al-Bayhaqī lived frugally in the manner of the pious scholars. He began fasting perpetually thirty years before his death. Perpetual fast is the practice of several of the Companions and *Salaf* such as 'Umar, his son 'Abd Allāh, 'Uthmān, Abū Ṭalḥa, 'Ā'isha, Abū Umāma, Sa'īd ibn al-Musayyab, Thābit al-Bunānī, Abū Ḥanīfa, Sa'd ibn Ibrāhīm ibn 'Abd al-Raḥmān ibn 'Awf al-Zuhrī, Shu'ba, al-Shāfi'ī, al-Tustarī, Manṣūr Abū 'Attāb al-Sulamī, Wakī', al-Nawawī, and countless others.

Rudhbārī (d. 322).

722 Najm 'Abd al-Raḥmān Khalaf, *Mawārid al-Imām al-Bayhaqī fī Kitābihi al-Sunan al-Kubrā* (p. 52).

723 Cf. Ibn Khuzayma, *Ṣaḥīḥ* (3:312-313); Ibn Ḥibbān, *Ṣaḥīḥ* (8:349-350). See also

Ibn Khuzayma and his student Ibn Ḥibbān each devoted chapters of their *Ṣaḥīḥs* to the subject.[723] Ibn Ḥibbān said, commenting on the ḥadīth of the Prophet ﷺ: "Whoever fasts all his life has neither fasted nor broken his fast"[724]:

> He means: whoever fasts all his life including the days in which one was forbidden to fast, such as the days of *tashrīq*[725] and the two *'Īds*. By the words: "he has neither fasted nor broken his fast" he means that he did not in fact fast all his life in order to reap reward for it. For he did not omit [fasting] the days in which he was forbidden to fast. That is why the Prophet ﷺ said: "Whoever fasts all his life, the Fire shall straiten him for this much," and he counted ninety on his fingers,[726] meaning the days of his life in which he was forbidden to fast. It does not apply to the person who fasts all his life – being strong enough to do so – without the prohibited days.[727]

The above is confirmed by Imām Mālik in his *Muwaṭṭa'*: "There is no harm in perpetual fast (*ṣiyām al-dahr*) provided one breaks one's fast on the days which the Prophet ﷺ forbade fasting."[728] Mālik praised the qāḍī 'Abd Allāh ibn 'Abd al-Raḥmān ibn Ma'mar and said he fasted perpetually.[729] Imām al-Nawawī said:

> Ibn 'Umar fasted permanently, *i.e.* except the days of 'Id and *tashrīq*. This perpetual fast is his way and the way of his father 'Umar ibn al-Khaṭṭāb, 'Ā'isha, Abū Ṭalḥa and others of the *Salaf* as well as al-Shāfi'ī and other scholars. Their position is that perpetual fasting is not offensive.[730]

Ibn Qudāma states something similar in *al-Mughnī* and adds that the same view is related from Aḥmad and Mālik, and that after the Prophet's ﷺ death Abū Ṭalḥa fasted permanently for forty years,

Ibn Ḥajar's notes on the topic in *Fatḥ al-Bārī* (1989 ed. 4:222).

724 Narrated from 'Abd Allāh ibn 'Amr by al-Bukhārī and Muslim, and from 'Abd Allāh ibn al-Shikhkhīr by Aḥmad, al-Nasā'ī, al-Ḥākim, Ibn Ḥibbān, Ibn Abī Shayba, and others.

725 The Days of drying the sacrificial meat after *'Īd al-Aḍḥā*=11, 12, and 13 of Dhūl-Ḥijja.

726 Narrated from Abū Mūsā al-Ash'arī with a sound chain by Aḥmad and Ibn Ḥibbān.

727 Ibn Ḥibbān (8:349-350).

728 *Muwaṭṭa'* (1:300).

729 Cf. Ibn 'Abd al-Barr, *al-Tamhīd* (17:416).

730 *Sharḥ Ṣaḥīḥ Muslim, Kitāb* 37, *Bāb* 2, §10.

731 Ibn Qudāma, *al-Mughnī* (Beirut, 1994 ed. 3:119).

among other Companions.[731] Ibn Ḥajar al-Haytamī in *al-Khayrāt al-Ḥisān* similarly relates that Abū Ḥanīfa was never seen eating except at night.[732] In our time the late *Sharīf* and Moroccan ḥadīth Master of Damascus Badr al-Dīn al-Ḥasanī also used to fast permanently, including on the day of 'Arafa while on pilgrimage.[733]

Al-Bayhaqī's Works

The works of al-Bayhaqī count among the treasures of Islamic knowledge for their meticulousness, reliability, and near-perfection in the estimation of the scholars. He pledged that none of those works contained a single narration he knew was a forgery.[734] Among those published to date are the following:

- *Al-Arba'ūn al-Ṣughrā* ("The Minor Collection of Forty Ḥadīths"), which is devoted to the purification of the self and the acquisition of high manners.
- *Al-Asmā' wal-Ṣifāt* ("The Divine Names and Attributes"), concerning which Ibn al-Subkī said: "I do not know anything that compares to it." This work is the most reliable sourcebook for the doctrine of the *Salaf* concerning the Divine Attributes.
- *Bayān Khaṭa' man Akhṭa'a 'alā al-Shāfi'ī* ("Exposition of the Error of Those Who Attributed Error to al-Shāfi'ī"), which complements the *Sunan* and the *Ma'rifa* in the presentation of the textual evidence of the Shāfi'ī school.
- *Al-Da'awāt al-Kabīr* ("The Major Book of Supplications") in two volumes in which he arranged the narrations related to the subject by circumstance, like al-Nawawī's *al-Adhkār* and similar books by al-Ṭabarānī and al-Jazarī.
- *Dalā'il al-Nubuwwa* ("The Marks of Prophethood") in about seven volumes, the foremost large book exclusively devoted to the person of the Prophet ﷺ, as al-Qāḍī 'Iyāḍ's *al-Shifā fī Ma'rifati Ḥuqūq al-Muṣṭafā* ("The Healing in Knowing the Rights of the Elect Prophet ﷺ") is the foremost condensed book on this noble subject.

732 Al-Haytamī, *al-Khayrāt al-Ḥisān fī Manāqib al-Nu'mān* (Cairo: Ḥalabī, 1326/1908) p. 40.

733 Narrated to the author by Dr. Wahbī al-Zuhaylī.

734 As cited by al-Kattānī in *al-Risāla al-Mustaṭrafa* (chapter on the books of *Sunan*).

735 Narrated from Ibn 'Abbās by Ibn Mājah through Dāwūd ibn 'Aṭā', whose weak-

- *Faḍā'il al-Awqāt* ("Times of Particular Merit" [for worship]).

Among al-Shāfi'ī's legal positions reported by al-Bayhaqī is the following in his book *Faḍā'il al-Awqāt*:

> The ḥadīth of Ibn 'Abbās whereby the Prophet ﷺ forbade the fasting of all of the month of Rajab is not strong.[735] [...] Even if it were authentic, its meaning would be that of dislike only, as al-Shāfi'ī said in the Old School: "I dislike that someone single out the month of Rajab among all other months in order to fast it completely in the way that he completes Ramaḍān." He cited as his evidence the ḥadīth of 'Ā'isha ؓ: "The Messenger of Allāh used to fast until we would say that he would never break it, and he used to break his fast until we would say that he would never fast again. Nor did I ever see the Messenger of Allāh ﷺ fast a complete month except Ramaḍān, and I never saw him fast more than in Sha'bān."[736] He also said: "Likewise, that someone single out a specific day among all other days." He continued: "I only disliked it so that an ignorant person will not emulate the one who fasts, thinking that it is obligatory. Otherwise, to fast it is fine (*wa-in fa'ala fa-ḥasan*)." Thus al-Shāfi'ī gave the reason for the reprehensibility [of fasting Rajab] then he said: "But if one fasts it, then fine and good." This is because part of what is universally known among Muslims is that no fast was made obligatory by the foundation of the Law other than that of Ramaḍān. This eliminates the reprehensible sense, and Allāh knows best.[737]

Ibn al-Subkī comments:

> On the whole, this text of al-Shāfi'ī cited by al-Bayhaqī provides a clear proof that to fast the month of Rajab in its entirety is fine and good, and that if the prohibition of fasting it entirely is inauthentic, then the fast remains desirable in the Law. This supports what Shaykh al-Islām al-'Izz ibn 'Abd al-Salām said: "Whoever forbids the fast of Rajab is ignorant of the methods used for inferring legal rulings."[738] He then expanded on the topic [...] Nor should

ness is agreed upon as stated in the collective *Sharḥ Sunan Ibn Mājah.*

736 Narrated by al-Bukhārī, Muslim, Mālik, Abū Dāwūd, and Aḥmad.

737 Al-Bayhaqī, *Faḍā'il al-Awqāt* (p. 104-109).

738 Ibn 'Abd al-Salām, *Fatāwā Mawṣiliyya* (p. 132).

739 Ibn al-Subkī, *Ṭabaqāt al-Shāfi'iyya al-Kubrā* (4:12).

any proof against al-Bayhaqī be adduced from the ḥadīth of Ibn 'Abbās prohibiting the fast of Rajab in Ibn Mājah's *Sunan* as it has been definitely established to be unsound.[739]

Here is the text of Ibn 'Abd al-Salām's fatwā on the Rajab fast:

Most ḥadīth Scholars are far removed from the knowledge of the foundations of the Law and the methods followed for the derivation of rulings [from the evidence]. Consequently, their actions carry no weight. On the contrary, they should be reproved, for they are not fit to exert *ijtihād*. As for what the preachers mention concerning the merits of certain months, there are true things and false things in it, although the false is probably more than the true. Now, to swear a vow (*nadhr*) that one shall fast the month of Rajab is binding and one seeks nearness to Allāh ﷻ by such fasts. Whoever forbids the fast of Rajab is ignorant of the methods used for inferring legal rulings. How could it be forbidden when none of the scholars who compiled the *Sharī'a* ever mentioned that Rajab was one of the times when it is disliked to fast? Rather, to fast that month is an act of drawing near to Allāh ﷻ because of the sound narrations that came to us concerning fasting such as, 'Every deed of a human being is for himself except fasting,'[740] and 'The very breath of the person who fasts is dearer to Allāh than the scent of musk,'[741] and 'The best fast is the fast of my brother Dāwūd.'[742] Dāwūd ﷺ liked to fast without restricting himself to times other than the month of Rajab. Whoever dignifies the month of Rajab for a purpose other than that current in *Jāhiliyya* is not imitating *Jāhiliyya*![743] Nor does everything that the *Jāhiliyya* did become automatically forbidden except if the

740 Narrated from Abū Hurayra by al-Bukhārī as part of a longer ḥadīth.

741 Part of the ḥadīth just cited.

742 Narrated from 'Abd Allāh ibn 'Amr by al-Bukhārī and Muslim.

743 Cf. 'Umar's punishment of the *mutarajjibūn* – those who fasted the month of Rajab in imitation of the *Jāhiliyya* – by striking their hands until they broke their fast, as they emphasized Rajab over Ramaḍān as the fasting month. This is clearly not feared for later Muslims, as proved by the complete words of 'Umar: "Eat! For this is but a month the people of *Jāhiliyya* used to venerate." Narrated by Ibn Abī Shayba (1:130) and cited by Ibn Qudāma in *al-Mughnī* (3:167).

744 *Fatāwā Mawṣiliyya* (p. 132-134).

Sharī'a forbids it and the Foundations of the *Sharī'a* indicate that it should be avoided. Nor is such [a fast] abandoned just because the perpetrators of falsehood did it. Whoever forbade it among the ḥadīth Scholars is known for being an ignoramus and it is impermissible for any Muslim to imitate him in his religion. It is not allowed to imitate someone except if he has become known to be knowledgeable in the Divine rulings and the methods of inferring them, whereas the one to whom this [*fatwā*] is attributed is far removed from the knowledge of the Religion of Allāh, so he is not to be imitated in it. Whoever imitates him has imperiled his religion.[744]

- *Ḥayāt al-Anbiyā' fī Qubūrihim.* This brief masterpiece gathers many of the ḥadīths that pertain to the life of the Prophets in their graves and received several editions of varying quality to date. Shaykh Muḥammad 'Alawī al-Mālikī used it among his principal sources for the section on *Nubuwwāt* in his *Manhaj al-Salaf fī Fahm al-Nuṣūṣ.*[745]
- *Al-I'tiqād 'alā Madhhab al-Salaf Ahl al-Sunna wal-Jamā'a* ("Islamic Doctrine According to the School of the Predecessors which is the School of the People of the Prophet's ﷺ Way and Congregation of His Companions ﷺ") in about forty brief chapters. In it he states:

The Prophet ﷺ said: "Four types will have excuses on the Day of Resurrection: the deaf one, the simpleton, the senile old man, and the one who died in the inter-Dispensation period (*al-fatra*). The first will say, 'I did not hear anything'; the second, 'Islām came while street-children were throwing dung at me'; the third, 'Islām came and I did not have my wits anymore,' and the fourth, 'My Lord, no Messenger came to me.' Allāh Himself shall take from them their covenant to obey Him. They will be told to enter the fire [as a test]. Those who obey will find it cool and safe, while those who refuse will be dragged to it."[746]

The Prophets – the blessings and peace of Allāh upon them – after they die, their souls are returned back to them and so they

745 Translated by the author under the title *The Life of Prophets in the Grave.*

746 Narrated from al-Aswad ibn Sarī' and Abū Hurayra by Aḥmad.

747 Al-Bayhaqī, *al-I'tiqād* (1981 ed. p. 305).

are ﴿**alive in the presence of their Lord**﴾ (3:169) like the martyrs. Our Prophet ﷺ saw, on the Night of the Ascension, a number of them. We have compiled a monograph establishing the facts of their life in the grave.[747]

- *Al-Khilāfiyyāt* ("The Divergences" [between al-Shāfi'ī and Abū Ḥanīfa]) of which Ibn al-Subkī said: "No one preceded him in writing a book of this kind, nor followed him in writing its like. It is an independent method in ḥadīth science which is appreciated only by experts in both *fiqh* and *ḥadīth.* It is precious for the texts it contains." A refutation of the Ḥanafī School summing up his *Sunan al-Kubrā* on *fiqh* divergences, it was counter-refuted by Imām 'Alī ibn'Uthmān ibn Ibrāhīm 'Ala' al-Dīn al-Mardīnī – known as Ibn al-Turkmānī – (d. 750) with his two-volume *al-Jawhar al-Naqī fil-Radd 'alā Sunan al-Bayhaqī.*[748]
- *Al-Mabsūṭ* ("The Expanded [Reference-Book]"), on Shāfi'ī Law.
- *Al-Madkhal ilā al-Sunan al-Kubrā* ("Introductory to the Major Book of the Sunnas"). This work has received a new edition in two volumes.
- *Manāqib al-Imām Aḥmad* ("The Immense Merits of Imām Aḥmad").
- *Manāqib al-Shāfi'ī* ("The Immense Merits of al-Shāfi'ī") in two volumes, which al-Nawawī said was the most reliable book of merits on the Imām. Ibn al-Subkī said: "Of *al-I'tiqād, Dalā'il al-Nubuwwa, Shu'ab al-Īmān, Manāqib al-Shāfi'ī,* and *al-Da'awāt al-Kabīr,* I swear that none of them has any peer." In the *Manāqib* al-Bayhaqī gives this analysis of the variant wordings and chains of the ḥadīth "Where is Allāh?":

As for the ḥadīth of Mu'āwiya ibn al-Ḥakam then [that of] 'Ubayd Allāh contradicts it in its wording. The latter, even if

748 This work exists in print (Hyderabad 1316/1898) and should be reissued in response to the anti-Ḥanafī campaign being waged in the Indo-Pakistani subcontinent, as part of which al-Bayhaqī's *Khilafiyyāt* has recently been edited and published by two people, one of them the "Salafī" Mashhūr Ḥasan Salmān, the man who authored a book against Imām al-Nawawī. On Ibn al-Turkmānī see al-Lacknawī's *al-Fawā'id al-Bahiyya* (p. 207) and Ibn Ḥajar's *al-Durar al-Kāmina* (3:156-157).

749 Narrated by Mālik in the *Muwaṭṭa'* from al-Zuhrī, from 'Ubayd Allāh; al-Shāfi'ī in

mursal, has narrators who possess more *fiqh*.[749] Further, it is confirmed by [the narration of] al-Sharīd ibn Suwayd al-Thaqafī – also *mursal*.[750] It was also narrated from 'Awn ibn 'Abd Allāh ibn 'Utba, from his father, with both a different text and a different chain.[751] The latter, if sound, is as if the Prophet ﷺ addressed her

al-Za'farānī's narration from him in *al-Kitāb al-Qadīm* cf. al-Bayhaqī, *Manāqib al-Shāfi'ī* (1:395); and Aḥmad in his *Musnad*: "'Abd al-Razzāq narrated to us: Ma'mar narrated to us, from al-Zuhrī, from 'Ubayd Allāh ibn 'Abd Allāh [ibn 'Utba], that a man from the *Anṣār* brought a black slave-girl and said, 'Messenger of Allāh, I am obligated to free a Muslim slave, therefore, if you consider that this girl is a believer, I shall free her.' The Messenger of Allāh ﷺ said to her: 'Do you bear witness that there is no God but Allāh?' She said yes. 'And do you bear witness that I am the Messenger of Allāh?' She said yes. He said: 'Do you believe in Resurrection after death?' She said yes. He said: 'Free her!'" The same is narrated by al-Bayhaqī in *al-Sunan al-Kubrā* (7:388), Ibn Khuzayma in *al-Tawḥīd*, al-Dhahabī in *al-'Ulūw*, and Ibn Kathīr in his *Tafsīr* (2:534-535) where he declared it *ṣaḥīḥ* and said the missing Companion-link does not affect its authenticity.

750 Narrated by Aḥmad in his *Musnad*: "'Abd al-Ṣamad (ibn 'Abd al-Wārith al-'Anbarī) [also Muḥammad ibn 'Abd al-Ḥamīd] narrated to us: Ḥammād ibn Salama narrated to us: Muḥammad ibn 'Amr narrated to us, from Abū Salama, from al-Sharīd, that his mother willed that he free a Muslim slave on her behalf so he asked the Messenger of Allāh ﷺ about it, saying, 'I have a black or Nubian slave-girl, shall I free her?' He said, 'Bring her.' He brought her and [the Prophet ﷺ] asked her, 'Who is your Lord?' She said, 'Allāh.' He asked, 'Who am I?' She replied, 'You are the Messenger of Allāh.' He said: 'Free her, for she is a believer!'" The same is narrated by al-Nasā'ī in *al-Sunan al-Kubrā* (4:110), Ibn Ḥibbān in his *Ṣaḥīḥ* (1:418), and al-Ṭabarānī in *al-Kabīr* (7:320), while al-Dārimī narrates it in part.

751 Narrated from Abū Hurayra by Abū Dāwūd, Aḥmad, and al-Bayhaqī in the *Sunan al-Kubrā* (7:388): "A man brought to the Prophet ﷺ a black slave-girl, saying, 'Messenger of Allāh, I am obligated to free a Muslim slave.' He asked her: 'Where is Allāh?' She pointed to the sky with her index finger. He said to her: 'And who am I?' She pointed to the Prophet ﷺ and to the sky in turn, as if she meant, 'You are the Messenger of Allāh.' The Prophet ﷺ said: 'Free her, for she is a believer!'"

Yet another wording is narrated – with a chain authenticated by al-Dāraquṭnī in his *'Ilal* (5:194) – through Abū 'Āṣim al-Nabīl, from Abū Ma'dān, from 'Awn ibn 'Abd Allāh ibn 'Utba from his father, from his grandfather, by al-Ṭabarānī in *al-Kabīr* (17:136), al-Bayhaqī (7:388), al-Ḥākim (1990 ed. 3:289): "A woman brought to the Prophet ﷺ a black slave-girl, saying, 'Messenger of Allāh, I am obligated to free a Muslim slave. Does this girl fulfill this obligation of mine?' The Messenger of Allāh ﷺ asked her: 'Who is your Lord?' She said, 'Allāh.' He asked, 'And what is your religion?' She said, 'al-Islām.' He asked, 'And who am I?' She replied, 'You are the Messenger of Allāh.' He asked: 'Do you pray the Five [Prayers] and do you accept what I have brought from Allāh?' She said yes. Whereupon the Prophet ﷺ slapped her on the chest and said: 'Free her!'"

752 Al-Bayhaqī, *Manāqib al-Shāfi'ī* (1:396-398).

according to her ability and understanding. For she and her likes, before Islām, used to believe in idols as gods on earth. Accordingly, he wanted to know what she believed and asked her: "Where is Allāh?" Had she pointed to the idols, it would have been known that she was not a believer. When she said, "in the heaven," it became known that she had abandoned idols and that she was a believer in Allāh ﴾**Who in the heaven is God, and in the earth God**﴿ (43:84) or he gestured, as she gestured, to the literal wording of what was mentioned in the Book. Further, the meaning of His saying in the Book, ﴾**who is in the heaven** (*fil-samā'*)﴿ (67:16-17) is, "who is above the heaven" and over the Throne (*fawq al-samā'i 'alā al-'arsh*) as He said, ﴾**the Merciful established Himself over the Throne**﴿ (20:5), and all that is on high is called a heaven (*kullu mā 'alā fahuwa samā'*), and the Throne is atop the heavens (*al-'arshu a'lā al-samāwāt*). Therefore, He is "over the Thone" (*'alā al-'arsh*) just as He said, without how, separate from His creation, without any sort of contact with His creation, ﴾**There is nothing whatsoever like unto Him, and He is the All-Hearing, the All-Seeing**﴿ (42:11).[752]

- *Ma'rifat al-Sunan wal-Āthār* ("The Knowledge of Sunnas and Reports") in about fifteen volumes, also known as *al-Sunan al-Wusṭā*, listing the textual evidence of the Shāfi'ī School under *fiqh* sub-headings. Ibn al-Subkī said: "No Shāfi'ī jurist can do without it," while his father said: "He meant by the title, al-Shāfi'ī's knowledge of the *Sunnas* and reports." Al-Bayhaqī in his introduction unfairly deprecates al-Ṭaḥāwī's *Sharḥ Ma'ānī al-Āthār* as unreliable, a claim refuted and turned against al-Bayhaqī himself by Ibn al-Turkmānī.[753]
- *Al-Qirā'a Warā' al-Imām* ("Reciting [the Fātiḥa] behind the Imām").
- *Al-Risālat al-Ash'ariyya* ("The Ash'arī Letter"). Al-Bayhaqī wrote this short letter to the governor of Naysābūr as a defense and illustration of "our Shaykh, Abū al-Ḥasan al-Ash'arī" and his School of doctrine. Ibn 'Asākir and Ibn al-Subkī cited it in full in their own famous defenses of the School respectively titled *Tabyīn Kadhib al-Muftarī* and *Ṭabaqāt al-Shāfi'iyya al-Kubrā*

[753] See the notice on al-Ṭaḥāwī in Ibn Abī al-Wafā's *al-Jawāhir al-Muḍī'a*.

together with al-Qushayrī's similar letter titled *Shikāyat Ahl al-Sunna.*[754]

In this epistle Imām al-Bayhaqī states: "The Ḥanafīs, Mālikīs, and Shāfi'īs do not go the way of the nullification of meanings (*ta'ṭīl*) as the Mu'tazila do, nor do they go the way of likening [Allāh to creation] (*tashbīh*) the way the anthropomorphists (*mujassima*) do." He goes on to show that the Prophet ﷺ praised the Ash'arīs in numerous narrations that bore not only the external meaning of the tribe of the Companion Abū Mūsā al-Ash'arī but also the additional meaning of the followers of his descendant Abū al-Ḥasan, meaning the entire Ash'arī school. Among these narrations is that of the circumstances surrounding the revelation of the verse, ﴿**O you who believe! Whoever among you turns back from his Religion, know that in his stead Allāh shall bring a people whom He loves and who love Him, humble toward believers, stern toward disbelievers, striving in the way of Allāh, and fearing not the blame of any blamer. Such is the grace of Allāh which He gives to whom He will. Allāh is All-Embracing, All-Knowing**﴾ (5:54).[755] When Allāh revealed this verse, the Prophet ﷺ pointed to Abū Mūsā al-Ash'arī[756] saying: "They are that man's people."[757] Al-Qushayrī said: "Therefore, the followers of Abū al-Ḥasan al-Ash'arī are also among his [Abū

754 In *Tabyīn Kadhib al-Muftarī* (Kawtharī ed. p. 100-108) and *Ṭabaqāt al-Shāfi'iyya al-Kubrā* (3:395-399).

755 Al-Qushayrī said in *Laṭā'if al-Ishārāt* (2:126): "There is in this verse tremendous glad tidings for the believers, as it must be known that whoever does not turn back from the Religion, Allāh loves him."

756 'Abd Allāh ibn Qays ibn Sulaym ibn Ḥaḍḍār ibn Ḥarb ﷺ. Ibn Burayda said: "He was short, of sparse beard / thin side-beard (*athaṭṭ*), and light frame." Ibn Sa'd, *Ṭabaqāt* (4:115), al-Dhahabī, *Siyar* (4:45).

757 Narrated from the Companion 'Iyāḍ ibn 'Amr by Ibn Sa'd (4:107), al-Ṭabarī, *Tafsīr* (6:284), Ibn Abī Shayba (6:387 §32261), Ibn Abī 'Āṣim, *Āḥād wal-Mathānī* (4:460-462 §2515), Abū Nu'aym, *Dhikr Akhbār Aṣbahān* (1:59), al-Khaṭīb, *Tārīkh* (2:39) cf. Aḥdab, *Zawā'id Tārīkh Baghdād* (1:466-470 §127 *ḥadīth ṣaḥīḥ*), al-Ḥākim (with the wording: "They are your people, Abū Mūsā!" 2:313=1990 ed. 2:342 *ṣaḥīḥ* by Muslim's criterion), al-Bayhaqī in the *Dalā'il* (5:351), and al-Ṭabarānī, *al-Kabīr* (17:371) with a chain of *Ṣaḥīḥ* narrators according to al-Haythamī (7:16). It is narrated from 'Alī, al-Ḥasan al-Baṣrī, Qatāda, al-Ḍaḥḥāk, and Ibn Jurayj that it is "Abū Bakr and his friends" who are the "people whom Allāh loves and who love Him" in the verse cf. al-Rāzī, *al-Tafsīr al-Kabīr* (3:427), al-Qurṭubī, and others.

Mūsā's] People. For in every place that a people are affiliated to a Prophet [in the Qur'ān], what is meant is the followers of that Prophet."758 This is also the position of Ibn 'Asākir in the *Tabyīn*, Abū al-Muẓaffar al-Isfarāyīnī in *al-Tabṣīr fīl-Dīn*, al-Qurṭubī in his *Tafsīr*, Ibn al-Subkī in *Ṭabaqāt al-Shāfi'iyya al-Kubrā*, and others of the Ash'arī School.759

Al-Bayhaqī also adduces the following narrations without positively attributing them to the Prophet 🕊:

1. "The sultan is the shadow (*ẓill*) of Allāh on earth." There are several wordings of this ḥadīth which Imām al-Dāraquṭnī averred to be most correctly a saying of Ka'b al-Aḥbār.760 (a) One wording continues: "Therefore, whoever counsels them faithfully and supplicates on their behalf is well-guided and whoever cheats them and supplicates against them is misguided."761 (b) Another wording states: "If you pass by a town that does not have a sultan do not enter it. The sultan is but the shadow of Allāh and his lance on earth." 762 (c) Another wording: "The sultan is the shadow of

---

758 As quoted in al-Qurṭubī's *Tafsīr* (verse 5:54).

759 As cited in the *Tabyīn* and *Ṭabaqāt al-Shāfi'iyya al-Kubrā* (3:362-363, 3:375).

760 Al-Dāraquṭnī in his *'Ilal* according to al-Zarkashī in *al-Tadhkira fīl-Aḥādīth al-Mushtahara* (p. 173) cf. al-Suyūṭī, *al-Durar al-Muntathira* (p. 186 §277).

761 Narrated [1] from Abū Hurayra by Abū Nu'aym in *Faḍīlat al-'Ādilīn min al-Wulāt* (p. 141 §31) with a very weak chain through Yaḥyā ibn Maymūn al-Tammār who is accused of lying; cf. al-Dhahabī, *Mughnī fīl-Ḍu'afā'* (2:414 §7058) and *Mīzān*; [2] from Anas by Abū Nu'aym in *Faḍīlat al-'Ādilīn min al-Wulāt* (p. 142 §32) and al-Daylamī in *Musnad al-Firdaws;* cf. *Kanz* (6:11 §14616) with a very weak chain through Dāwūd ibn al-Muḥabbar who is discarded and accused of lying [cf. al-Bukhārī, *Ḍu'afā' al-Kabīr* (2:35), *Ḍu'afā' al-Ṣaghīr* (§110), Abū Nu'aym, *Ḍu'afā'* (§61), al-'Uqaylī in *al-Ḍu'afā'* (3:353-354 *ḥadīth munkar*)]; [3] *mawqūf* as a saying of Anas himself by al-Bayhaqī in his *Shu'ab* (6:18 §7376) through 'Uqba ibn 'Abd Allāh al-Rifā'ī who is weak and possibly with a missing link between him and Qatāda; [4] *maqṭū'* as a saying of Ka'b al-Aḥbār, *ibid.* (6:18:7377) through al-Ash'ath ibn Barāz who is discarded.

762 Narrated from Anas by al-Bayhaqī in his *Sunan* (8:162) and *Shu'ab* (6:18 §7375) through 'Abbās ibn 'Abd Allāh al-Tarqafī from Sa'īd ibn 'Abd Allāh al-Dimashqī from al-Rabī' ibn Ṣabīḥ who are both weak [cf. al-Dhahabī, *Mughnī fīl-Ḍu'afā'* (1:262) and Ibn Abī Ḥātim, *'Ilal* (2:409 *ḥadīth munkar*)] and with a missing *Tābi'ī* link, possibly Yazīd ibn Abān al-Raqāshī who is also weak. Also narrated from Anas with the previous chain where the missing link is named as al-Ḥasan al-Baṣrī by Abū al-Shaykh in his *Thawāb al-Ṣalāt 'alā al-Nabī* [cf. *Kanz* (6:5) and al-Sakhāwī in his *Takhrīj Aḥādīth al-'Ādilīn min al-Wulāt*] and al-Bayhaqī, *Shu'ab* (6:18 §7375).

Allāh on earth: the weak seeks refuge in him, through him is the oppressed helped, and whoever honors the sultan of Allāh in this world, Allāh will honor him on the Day of Resurrection."[763] (d) Another wording: "The sultan is the shadow of Allāh on earth. Whoever honors him honors Allāh and whoever reviles him reviles Allāh."[764] (e) Another wording: "The sultan is the shadow of Allāh on earth: every oppressed one seeks refuge in him."[765] (f) Another wording: "The just and humble ruler (*wālī*) is the shadow of Allāh and his lance on earth. Whoever shows him sincere faithfulness in himself and among the servants of Allāh, Allāh will raise him in his group the day there will be no shade other than His shade."[766] (g) Another wording: "Do not insult the sultan for he is the shadow (*ẓill*) of Allāh on earth. With him are rights upheld and the religion made to vanquish. With him does Allāh remove injustice and destroy transgressors."[767] (h) Another

[763] Narrated from Abū Hurayra by Ibn al-Najjār in *Dhayl Tārīkh Baghdād* (17:106) with a very weak chain through Aḥmad ibn 'Abd al-Raḥmān ibn Wahb; cf. Ibn 'Adī, *Kāmil* (1:188).

[764] Narrated from Abū Bakrah by Ibn Abī 'Āṣim in *al-Sunna* (p. 478 §1024) with a weak chain through Ziyād ibn Kusayb al-'Adawī who is unknown since only one or two are known to narrate from him [cf. al-Arna'ūṭ, *Musnad* (34:79-80 §20433)], even if Ibn Ḥajar, ranks him as "acceptable" in the *Taqrīb* and al-Tirmidhī even declares his ḥadīth "fair" (*ḥasan*) in the *Sunan*, without the words "The sultan is the shadow of Allāh on earth."

[765] Part of a longer ḥadīth narrated from Ibn 'Umar by al-Quḍā'ī in *Musnad al-Shihāb* (1:201 §304), al-Ḥakīm al-Tirmidhī in *Nawādir al-Uṣūl* (4:153), Tammām al-Rāzī in his *Fawā'id* (1:212-213 §502), and al-Daylamī in *Musnad al-Firdaws* (2:343) through Sa'īd ibn Sinān Abū Mahdī who is discarded and accused of forgery; cf. al-Haythamī (5:196) and Ibn Ḥajar, *Mukhtaṣar Zawā'id al-Bazzār* (1:676 §1241). Al-Ghumārī said in *al-Mudāwī* (4:270) it is "undoutedly forged." Something similar is narrated from 'Umar by Abū Nu'aym in *Faḍīlat al-'Ādilīn* (p. 155-156 §40) through al-Ḥasan ibn 'Amr al-Fuqaymī who is discarded and accused of forgery. Despite all this Ibn Taymiyya declares it sound in *Majmū' al-Fatāwā* (35:45).

[766] Narrated from Abū Bakr al-Ṣiddīq by Abū Nu'aym in *Faḍīlat al-'Ādilīn* (p. 124), al-Jurjānī in *Tārīkh Jurjān* (p. 69) and others with a very weak broken chain through two unknowns: Sulaymān ibn Rajā' and Abū Nuṣayra al-'Abdī cf. Ibn Abī Ḥātim, *al-Jarḥ wal-Ta'dīl* (4:117 §508) and his *'Ilal* (2:427 *ḥadīth munkar*) and Ibn Ḥajar, *al-Amālī al-Muṭlaqa* (p. 116).

[767] Narrated *mawqūf* as a saying of Ḥudhayfa ibn al-Yamān by Abū Nu'aym in *Faḍīlat al-'Ādilīn* (p. 156 §41) with a weak chain because of Muḥammad ibn 'Abd al-Raḥmān ibn Abī Laylā as per al-Sakhāwī.

wording: "Do not insult the sultan for he is the shadow (*fay'*) of Allāh on earth."[768] Al-Khaṭṭābī said: "The meaning of 'the shadow' is power and invincibility (*al-'izzatu wal-man'a*)."[769]

2. "One day in the life of a just leader is better than sixty years of worship."[770] Another version states: "The work of the just [governor] among his charge for a single day is certainly better than the work of the devout worshipper in his family for an hundred – or fifty – years."[771]
3. "Disagreement in my Community is a mercy." This statement has no known chain of transmission to the Prophet ﷺ. However, it is a well-established principle of the authorities in ḥadīth and *fiqh* among the pious *Salaf* that differences in the Community are a mercy (*ikhtilāf al-Umma raḥma*), as stated by al-Shāṭibī.[772] This is illustrated by the following narrations:

   a) 'Umar ibn 'Abd al-'Azīz ؓ used to say: "I would dislike it if the Companions of Muḥammad ﷺ did not differ among themselves, because had they not differed there would be no leeway (for us)."[773]

[768] Narrated *mawqūf* as a saying of Abū 'Ubayda ibn al-Jarrāḥ by al-Quḍā'ī in *Musnad al-Shihāb* (2:79-80 §922), Ibn Abī 'Āṣim in *al-Sunna* (p. 473 §182), al-Bayhaqī in the *Shu'ab* (6:17 §7372), and al-Daylamī in *Musnad al-Firdaws* (5:11 §7291) cf. al-Sakhāwī in his *Takhrīj Aḥādīth al-'Ādilīn* (p. 156-157) through two weak narrators: 'Abd al-A'lā ibn 'Abd Allāh ibn Qays and Ismā'īl Mawlā al-Muzaniyyīn cf. al-'Uqaylī, *Ḍu'afā' al-Kabīr* (3:59-60).

[769] Al-Khaṭṭābī, *Gharīb al-Ḥadīth* (1:707).

[770] Narrated from Ibn 'Abbās by al-Ṭabarānī in *al-Kabīr* (11:337 §11932) and *al-Awsaṭ* (5:92 §4765), al-Bayhaqī in the *Sunan* (8:162) and the *Shu'ab* (6:19 §7379) cf. Abū Nu'aym in *Faḍīlat al-'Ādilīn* (p. 117-119) and *Kanz* (§14623), all through Abū Ghaylān Sa'd al-Shaybānī or Zurayq ibn al-Sakht who are both unknown cf. al-Haythamī (5:197, 6:263) but al-Mundhirī in *al-Targhīb* (1997 ed. 3:117, 3:172) said the chain of the *Kabīr* is fair (*ḥasan*) cf. al-Sha'rānī, *al-'Uhūd al-Muḥammadiyya* (p. 384), and the narration is strengthened by sound ḥadīths cf. Ibn Ḥajar, *Dirāya* (2:167) and al-Sakhāwī, *Takhrīj Aḥādīth al-'Ādilīn* (p. 117-119). As for the wording from Abū Hurayra: "Justice for a moment is better than sixty years of worship" it comes only through Aḥmad ibn 'Isā al-Khashshāb who is accused of forgery.

[771] Narrated from Abū Hurayra by al-Qāsim ibn Sallām in *al-Amwāl* (p. 16) and, through him, Ibn Abī Usāma in his *Musnad* (2:626 §597=Ṭalā'i' ed. p. 187) and Abū Nu'aym in *Faḍīlat al-'Ādilīn* (p. 123 §17) through an unknown *Tābi'ī* narrator.

[772] In *al-I'tiṣām* (3:11=1995 Beirut ed. p. 395). See, for a fanatical defense of the opposite view, al-Ghumārī, *al-Mudāwī* (1:235-236) on the narration "Differences in my Umma are a mercy."

[773] Al-Zarkashī, *al-Tadhkira fil-Aḥādīth al-Mushtahara* (p. 64) and al-'Ajlūnī, *Kashf al-*

b) Imām al-Qāsim ibn Muḥammad ibn Abī Bakr al-Ṣiddīq ﵁ said: "The differences among the Companions of Muḥammad ﷺ are a mercy for the servants of Allāh."[774]

c) Imām Mālik ﵁ said the same.[775]

d) Similarly Abū Yazīd al-Bisṭāmī ﵁ said: "I strove in utmost effort (*mujāhada*) for thirty years and did not find anything more difficult than knowledge and its pursuit. Were it not for the differences of the Ulema, I would have remained stalled. The differences of the Ulema are a mercy except in the absoluteness of monotheism."[776]

e) Al-Layth ibn Sa'd ﵁ said: "The people of knowledge are the people of flexibility (*tawsi'a*). Those who give *fatwas* never cease to differ, and so this one permits something while that one forbids it, without one finding fault with the other when he knows of his position."[777]

f) Al-Khaṭīb related something similar from Sufyān ibn 'Uyayna ﵁ in *al-Faqīh wal-Mutafaqqih*.

g) Imām Aḥmad ﵁ also said something similar.[778]

The above principle is reiterated by Ibn Taymiyya: "The Consensus of the Imāms [of *fiqh*] on a question is a definitive proof and their divergence of opinion is a vast mercy;"[779] "The differences among the wise scholars of knowledge was made a mercy and a leeway for the Community."[780] In all this he is faithfully following his teacher Ibn Qudāma.[781] Al-Bayhaqī quotes al-Qaffāl al-Shāshī's explanation that "this means the difference in their energies and capacities (*ikhtilāfu*

Khafā (1:66).

774 Narrated by Ibn Sa'd (5:189) and Abū Nu'aym, *Ḥilyat al-Awliyā'* (1985 ed. 7:119 =1997 ed. 7:132 §9907). Al-Zarkashī in *al-Tadhkira fil-Aḥādīth al-Mushtahara* (p. 64) and al-'Ajlūnī in *Kashf al-Khafā* (1:66) said that al-Bayhaqī cited it in *al-Madkhal*.

775 See p. 164.

776 Narrated by al-Qushayrī in his *Risāla* (p. 88) and cited by Ibn Taymiyya in *al-Istiqāma* (1:251).

777 Narrated from Yaḥyā ibn Sa'īd by al-Dhahabī in *Tadhkirat al-Ḥuffāẓ* (1:138) and al-Sakhāwī in *al-Maqāṣid al-Ḥasana* (p. 49 §39).

778 See p. 313.

779 Ibn Taymiyya, *Mukhtaṣar al-Fatāwā al-Miṣriyya* (Cairo, 1980) p. 35.

780 Ibn Taymiyya, *Sharḥ al-'Umda* (Riyad: Maktabat al-'Ubaykān, 1993) 4:569.

781 Cf. Ibn Qudāma, concluding words of *Lam'at al-I'tiqād*.

himamihim). That is, one's sagacity might be in *fiqh* while the energy of another might be in *kalām*[...] so that each might say what contains the welfare of people and states." Al-Bayhaqī continues:

> One who has devoted his energy to the knowledge of the evidentiary texts of *fiqh* and its proofs does not contest, in his own mind, the positions adopted by the experts of principles (*ahl al-uṣūl*). More than that, he adopts their own positions in the *Madhhab* and does so with the least evidentiary proof available for such, except that he deems his involvement in his own discipline more beneficial and more appropriate. Conversely, one who has devoted his energies to the knowledge of the evidentiary texts of *uṣūl* and its proofs follows, in the branches, the School of one of the major great Jurist Imāms of the Muslim world, except that he deems his involvement in the principles, at a time when innovations creep up, more beneficial and more pressing. The Ulema of the Sunna are therefore one in this, including the Ash'arīs, because they are one in the science of the foundations and in complete agreement.[782]

- *Shu'ab al-Īmān* ("The Branches of Belief") in about fourteen volumes, in which al-Bayhaqī provides a monumental, comprehensive commentary on the ḥadīth of the Prophet ﷺ, "Faith has seventy-odd branches."[783] Al-Bayhaqī titled the fifteenth Branch of his *Shu'ab*: "The Fifteenth Branch of Faith, Namely, the Chapter on Rendering Honor to the Prophet ﷺ, Declaring His High Rank, and Revering Him (*al-khāmis 'ashar min shu'ab al-īmān wa-huwa bābun fī ta'ẓīmi al-Nabī* ﷺ *wa-ijlālihi wa-tawqīrih*). In it he narrates the following ḥadīth:

> Usāma ibn Sharīk narrates: "I came to see the Prophet ﷺ while his Companions were with him, and they seemed as still as if birds had alighted on top of their heads. I gave him my salaam and I sat down. [Then Bedouins came and asked questions which the Prophet ﷺ answered.] ... The Prophet ﷺ then got up

782 Al-Bayhaqī, *al-Risāla al-Ash'ariyya* in Ibn 'Asākir, *Tabyīn* (Kawtharī ed. p. 106).
783 Narrated from Abū Hurayra by Muslim, Aḥmad, and others.

and the people got up. They began to kiss his hand ﷺ, whereupon I took his hand and placed it on my face. I found it more fragrant than musk and cooler than sweet water."[784]

The *Shu'ab* was abridged into a slim pocketbook by the Damascus Imām and Qāḍī al-Quḍāt Imām al-Dīn Abū al-Ma'ālī 'Umar ibn Sa'd al-Dīn 'Abd al-Raḥmān ibn Imām al-Dīn Abī Ḥafṣ 'Umar al-Tibrīzī al-Qazwīnī al-Shafi'ī (653-699). This epitome was translated by the Cambridge Shaykh 'Abd al-Ḥakīm Murād.

- *Al-Sunan al-Kubrā* ("The Major Book of the Prophet's ﷺ *Sunnas*") in about ten large volumes, concerning which Ibn al-Subkī said: "No such book was ever compiled in the science of ḥadīth with respect to classification, arrangement, and elegance."
- *Tārīkh Ḥukamā' al-Islām* ("History of the Rulers of Islām").
- *Al-Zuhd al-Kabīr* ("The Major Book of Asceticism"), which arranges the relevant narrations of the Companions and early Ṣūfīs by subject-heading.

Al-Bayhaqī is the last of those who comprehensively compiled the textual evidence of the Shāfi'ī School including the ḥadīth, the positions of the Imām, and those of his immediate companions. Imām al-Ḥaramayn said: "There is no Shāfi'ī who does not owe a huge debt to al-Shāfi'ī, except al-Bayhaqī, to whom al-Shāfi'ī owes a huge debt for his works which established al-Shāfi'ī's School and his sayings."[785] Al-Dhahabī comments: "Abū al-Ma'ālī is right! It is as he said, and if al-Bayhaqī had wanted to found a school of Law for himself he would have been able to do so, because of the vastness of his sciences and his thorough knowledge of juridical differences."

AL-QĀḌĪ ḤUSAYN

"The High Authority of the Community" (*Ḥabr al-Umma*), Ḥusayn ibn Muḥammad ibn Aḥmad Abū 'Alī al-Marwazī (d. 462), known as "al-Qāḍī" in the books of the Shāfi'īs, his fatwas and explanations are

[784] Narrated by al-Bayhaqī in the *Shu'ab* (2:200 §1528). In the Nine Books the first part is narrated from Usāma ibn Sharīk by Abū Dāwūd, al-Tirmidhī (*ḥasan ṣaḥīḥ*), Ibn Mājah, al-Ḥākim (4:399), and Aḥmad while the latter part is narrated from Abū Juḥayfa by al-Bukhārī and Aḥmad.

[785] Quoted in *Ṭabaqāt al-Shāfi'iyya al-Kubrā* (4:10-11) and *Siyar* (13:532).

abundantly cited by all that followed, the teacher of Imām al-Ḥaramayn and others.[786] His teacher was al-Qaffāl al-Shāshī, himself a companion of Imām Abū al-Ḥasan al-Ash'arī and like him a former Mu'tazilī. Al-Nawawī said: "Among the Shāfi'īs who hold it obligatory for someone who is sitting when hearing the verse of prostration to rise and stand before prostrating are "Abū Muḥammad al-Juwaynī, al-Qāḍī Ḥusayn, his two companions the authors of *al-Tatimma* and *al-Tahdhīb*,[787] and the verifying Imām Abū al-Qāsim al-Rāfi'ī. Imām al-Ḥaramayn [Ibn al-Juwaynī] relates this from his father Shaykh Abū Muḥammad, then rejects it saying: 'I cannot find any basis nor any previous mention of this.' The statement of Imām al-Ḥaramayn is obvious, for nothing has been established from the Prophet ﷺ to that effect nor from those of the *Salaf* who are our examples. The vast majority of our Scholars did not address it. Allāh knows best."[788]

Biographies of al-Shāfi'ī

Ibn Ḥajar said that the first to write a biography of the Imām titled *Manāqib al-Shāfi'ī* was Dāwūd al-Ẓāhirī (d. 275). Al-Nawawī mentioned that the best biography of al-Shāfi'ī was al-Bayhaqī's *Manāqib al-Shāfi'ī* – used for the present text – for its sound chains of transmission.[789] Ibn Ḥajar summarised it and added to it al-Shāfi'ī's *Musnad* in his

786 The title "al-Qāḍī" refers to Ḥusayn ibn Muḥammad al-Marwazī in the books of the Shāfi'īs; Abū Yūsuf in those of the Ḥanafis; 'Iyāḍ in those of the Mālikīs; and Abū Ya'lā al-Farrā' in those of the Hanbalīs.

787 Respectively the two Shaykhs of Shāfi'īs, the *faqīh* and *uṣūlī* Sharaf al-A'imma Abū Sa'd 'Abd al-Raḥmān ibn Ma'mūn ibn 'Alī al-Ābiwardī known as al-Mutawallī (d. 478) the author of the *Tatimmat al-Ibāna fī Fiqh al-Shāfi'ī* – a completion of the unfinished *Ibāna* of Imām Abū al-Qāsim 'Abd al-Raḥmān ibn al-Furānī (d. 461) – and the Imām, *faqīh*, commentator of Qur'ān, and ḥadīth Master Muḥyī al-Sunna Abū Muḥammad al-Ḥusayn ibn Mas'ūd al-Farrā' al-Baghawī al-Shāfi'ī (d. 516) the author of *al-Tahdhīb fī Fiqh al-Imām al-Shāfi'ī* in four large tomes, an emendation of al-Qāḍī Ḥusayn's *al-Ta'līqa*, from which al-Nawawī frequently quotes in his *Rawḍa*.

788 Al-Nawawī, *al-Tibyān* (p. 96-98). The preference for standing before prostrating seems based – and Allāh knows best – on the literal application of the verb "to fall" (*kharra*) used in some of the verses of prostration such as ﴾**They fall down on their faces, weeping, and it increases humility in them**﴿ (17:109), ﴾**When the revelations of the Beneficent were recited unto them, they fell down, adoring and weeping**﴿ (19:58), and ﴾**Only those believe in Our revelations who, when they are reminded of them, fall down prostrate**﴿ (32:15).

789 In *Tahdhīb al-Asmā' wal-Lughāt* (1:44).

Tawālī al-Ta'nīs fī Ma'ālī Ibn Idrīs.[790] Among many other scholars who wrote the Imām's *Manāqib* were: Ibn Abī Ḥātim, Zakariyyā al-Sājī, Abū Nu'aym al-Aṣbahānī, al-Ḥākim, Abū al-Ḥusayn Muḥammad ibn al-Ḥusayn ibn Ibrāhīm al-Ābirrī al-Sijistānī (d. 363), Ibn Ḥibbān, Ibn al-Muqrī, Abū Manṣūr al-Baghdādī, Fakhr al-Dīn al-Rāzī, Ibn Kathīr, Abū 'Alī al-Ḥasan ibn al-Ḥusayn ibn al-Ḥamakān, Ismā'īl ibn Ibrāhīm al-Qarrāb, and al-Ḥusayn al-Asadī.[791] There are also lengthy chapters on the Imām in Abū Nu'aym's *Ḥilyat al-Awliyā'*, Ibn 'Abd al-Barr, *al-Intiqā' fī Faḍā'il al-A'immat al-Fuqahā'*, al-Nawawī's *Tahdhīb al-Asmā' wal-Lughāt*, al-Dhahabī's *Tārīkh* and *Siyar*, Ibn al-Subkī's *Ṭabaqāt al-Shāfi'iyya al-Kubrā*, and other major works of biographical history.

790 Incorrectly entitled *Tawālī al-Ta'sīs* in the Dār al-Kutub al-'Ilmiyya edition.

791 Cf. Ibn al-Subkī, *Ṭabaqāt* (2:72, 2:100, 2:136, 2:175, 3:147, 3:325-327, 3:147, 4:9, 4:266-270, 7:77).

AḤMAD IBN ḤANBAL[792] ﵁

Allāh Be Well-Pleased with Him

AḤMAD IBN MUḤAMMAD IBN ḤANBAL, Abū 'Abd Allāh al-Dhuhlī al-Shaybānī al-Marwazī al-Baghdādī ﵁ (164-241) was the pious, ascetic, foremost meticulous leader of the ḥadīth Masters, "the true Shaykh of Islām and leader of the Muslims in his time, the ḥadīth Master and proof of the Religion" (*al-Dhahabī*) by whom "Allāh reinforced this Religion at the time of the Ordeal (*al-miḥna*) as He had reinforced it with Abū Bakr al-Ṣiddīq ﵁ on the day of the Great Apostasy (*al-Ridda*)" (Ibn al-Madīnī). He is the last of the *Mujtahid* Imāms whose Schools remain to this day and "probably the most learned in the sciences of ḥadīth of the four great Imāms of Sacred Law." Imām al-Bukhārī narrates two ḥadīths through him in his *Ṣaḥīḥ*, one directly, and one through Abū al-Ḥasan Aḥmad ibn al-Ḥasan ibn Junaydib al-Tirmidhī al-Ḥimṣī.

His Foremost Teachers in Ḥadīth

"He took ḥadīth from Hushaym, Ibrāhīm ibn Sa'd, Sufyān ibn 'Uyayna, 'Abbād ibn 'Abbād, Yaḥyā ibn Abī Zā'ida, Yaḥyā ibn Sa'īd al-Qaṭṭān, and their layer. From him narrated al-Bukhārī [two ḥadīths in the *Ṣaḥīḥ*], Muslim [22], Abū Dāwūd [254], Abū Zur'a, Muṭayyan, 'Abd Allāh ibn Aḥmad, Abū al-Qāsim al-Baghawī, and a huge array of Scholars. His father was a soldier – one of those who called to Islām – and he died young" (al-Dhahabī).

Isḥāq al-Shāhidī narrates:

> I would see Yaḥyā al-Qaṭṭān – Allāh the Exalted have mercy on him! – pray the mid-afternoon prayer, then sit with his back against the base of the minaret of his mosque. Then 'Alī ibn al-Madīnī, al-Shādhakūnī, 'Amr ibn 'Alī, Aḥmad ibn Ḥanbal, Yaḥyā ibn Ma'īn, and others would come before him and ask him questions about ḥadīth standing on their feet until it was time for the

792 Main sources: al-Dhahabī, *Siyar* (9:434-547 §1876), *Tadhkirat al-Ḥuffāẓ* (2:431 §438); Ibn al-Jawzī, *Manāqib Aḥmad* (p. 156, 191, 256); Ibn Abī Ya'lā, *Ṭabaqāt al-Ḥanābila* (1:334).

sunset prayer. He would not say to a single one of them: "Sit" nor would they sit, out of awe and reverence.[793]

Al-Khaṭīb narrates that Yaḥyā ibn Ma'īn said to Aḥmad ibn Ḥanbal: "I want to test Abū Nu'aym [al-Faḍl ibn Dukayn, *Amīr al-Mu'minīn fil-Ḥadīth*]." Aḥmad replied: "Do not, for he is trustworthy (*thiqa*)!" But he insisted, so the two went to Abū Nu'aym in Kūfa and Yaḥyā prepared thirty ḥadīths narrated by Abū Nu'aym into which he inserted three which did not belong to Abū Nu'aym's record. Then he read to Abū Nu'aym the first third containing one of the spurious ḥadīths, at which Abū Nu'aym said: "Strike it out, it is not mine." Then the second third and the second spurious ḥadīth, at which Abū Nu'aym repeated his statement. Upon hearing the third spurious ḥadīth Abū Nu'aym rolled his eyes and said: "As for him – pointing to Aḥmad – he is too fearful of Allāh to do such a thing; and as for him – pointing to 'Alī ibn al-Madīnī – he would never do such a thing; so this is your handiwork, scoundrel!" Then he stretched his leg and, grabbing Ibn Ma'īn, tripped him and threw him on the ground. Aḥmad said to Yaḥyā: "Did I not tell you not to test him? Did I not tell you he was trustworthy?" Yaḥyā replied: "By Allāh, indeed his tripping me is dearer to me than my travelling [to him for ḥadīth]!"[794]

His Teachers in *Fiqh*: al-Shāfi'ī and the Ḥanafī Imāms

The greatest influence on Imām Aḥmad in jurisprudence was probably Imām al-Shāfi'ī, who came to Iraq in the year 195. Al-Za'farānī said: "I never visited al-Shāfi'ī without finding Aḥmad ibn Ḥanbal in his gathering. Aḥmad was more assiduous than I was in attending al-Shāfi'ī."[795] Ibn Khuzayma once rebuked someone who had brought up the Ḥanbalī School with the words: "Is Aḥmad ibn Ḥanbal anything but one of al-Shāfi'ī's pupils?"

Al-Karābīsī said that Aḥmad used to attend the gatherings of the jurists with his face covered.[796]

Aḥmad also took *fiqh* from the Ḥanafī Imāms among others. Yaḥyā

793 Narrated by al-Nawawī in *al-Tarkhīṣ fil-Ikrām bil-Qiyām* (p. 58) cf. the chapter (§26) on getting up out of respect in al-Bayhaqī's *al-Madkhal ilā al-Sunan.*

794 Narrated by al-Khaṭīb in *Tārīkh Baghdād* (12:353-354).

795 Narrated by al-Bayhaqī in *Manāqib al-Shāfi'ī* (1:227).

796 Narrated by al-Bayhaqī in *Manāqib al-Shāfi'ī* (1:227).

ibn Ma'īn narrated in his *Tārīkh* that Imām Aḥmad said: "I frequented Abū Yūsuf, then the scholars that came after him." Al-Khaṭīb narrates with his chain from 'Abd Allāh ibn Aḥmad: "My father took three receptacles' worth of learning from Abū Yūsuf and Muḥammad [ibn al-Ḥasan]."[797] Aḥmad also took knowledge from a third com-panion of Imām Abū Ḥanīfa, Asad ibn 'Amr ibn 'Āmir al-Bajalī al-Kūfī (d. 190). At the same time he, like al-Bukhārī and others, recom-mended against narrating anything from any of them lest juridical opinion (*ra'ī*), in his view, compete with the Qur'ān and Sunna.[798]

His Foremost Leadership in Ḥadīth Memorization

'Abd Allāh ibn Aḥmad said: "I heard Abū Zur'a [al-Rāzī] say: 'Your father memorised a million ḥadīths.' I asked him how he knew and he replied: 'By rehearsing the topical headings with him.'"[799] Ḥanbal said: "I heard Abū 'Abd Allāh say: 'I memorised everything which I heard from Hushaym when he was alive.'"

An Authority in Ḥadīth Rather than *Fiqh*?

Al-Nasā'ī cites Imām Aḥmad among the great Jurisprudents toward the end of his monograph *Tasmiyat Fuqahā' al-Amṣār.* However, many of the authorities preferred to class the Imām among the ḥadīth Masters rather than the Jurisprudents. In his book *Ikhtilāf al-Fuqahā'* ("The Differences of the Jurisprudents"), Imām al-Ṭabarī mentions the differences of opinion between Mālik, al-Awzā'ī, Sufyān al-Thawrī, al-Shāfi'ī, Abū Ḥanīfa, Abū Yūsuf, Muḥammad ibn al-Ḥasan, and Abū Thawr. He mentions some of the Jurists among the Companions, the

797 Al-Khaṭīb, *Tārīkh Baghdād* (3:15). Cf. al-Dhahabī, *Siyar* (7:708).

798 On this fanatic boycott of the Ḥanafīs by early ḥadīth scholars in the name of textualism see Shaykh 'Abd al-Fattah Abū Ghudda's marginalia on Ibn 'Abd al-Barr's *al-Intiqā'* (p. 331-334).

799 By the phrase "a million ḥadīths" are meant the chains of transmission. "The ḥadīth scholars count as a ḥadīth every report or statement from the Prophet ﷺ, or from a Companion or a Successor, or in explanation of a linguistic difficulty or missing word and so forth, if narrated with a chain of transmission." Abū Ghudda in *Qīmat al-Zamān 'Inda al-'Ulamā'* (p. 35) in commentary of Ibn Ma'īn's statement: "I wrote a million ḥadīths with my own hand." " Once it is realised that the *isnad* did, indeed, initiate a chain reaction that resulted in an explosive increase in the number of traditions, the huge numbers that are credited to Ibn Hanbal, Muslim and Bukhārī seem not so fantastic after all," Nabia Abbot, *Studies in Arabic Literary Papyri* (2:72).

Successors, and their followers up to the second century. Asked why he did not mention Imām Aḥmad ibn Ḥanbal in his book, al-Ṭabarī replied that "Aḥmad was not a *Faqīh* but a *Muḥaddith.*" The followers of the Ḥanbalī School took offense and reportedly roused the people against him, preventing visitors and students from visiting him in the daytime, so he died and was buried in his house.

Al-Ṭabarī's reply is neither new nor unique of its kind. Several of those who wrote about the differences among jurists did not mention Imām Aḥmad ﵀. Among them were al-Ṭaḥāwī, al-Dabbūsī, al-Nasafī, 'Alā' al-Dīn al-Samarqandī, al-Firahī al-Ḥanafī (one of the scholars of the seventh century) in his book *Dhāt al-'Uqdayn,* and others among the Ḥanafīs who wrote on the subject, who all omitted him. Ibn al-Farḍī said in his chronicle of the scholars of al-Andalus, upon mentioning Abū Muḥammad 'Abd Allāh ibn Muḥammad al-Aṣīlī al-Mālikī, that the latter wrote a book concerning the differences of Mālik, al-Shāfi'ī, and Abū Ḥanīfa called *al-Dalā'il fī Ummahāt al-Masā'il* ("The Proofs for the Paramount Questions"). He states:

> The author of *Kashf al-Ẓunūn* said that Muḥammad ibn 'Abd al-Raḥmān al-Samarqandī al-Sakhāwī[800] who died in Mardīn in 721 in *'Umdat al-Ṭālib li-Ma'rifat al-Madhāhib* ("The Reliance of the Student of the Knowledge of the Schools") mentioned the differences among jurists and said in the end: "I placed in my book the views of al-Nu'mān [Abū Ḥanīfa], Ya'qūb [Abū Yūsuf], Muḥammad [ibn al-Ḥasan al-Shaybānī] and their excellent companions, also al-Shāfi'ī, Mālik, and all in which they differed with the Shī'as. May Allāh give them life and every reward."

Nor did al-Ghazzālī, who also wrote about *ikhtilāf,* mention Aḥmad in his *Wajīz;* nor did Abū al-Barakat al-Nasafī in his *al-Wāfī.* As for the authors of books of history and geography, Ibn Qutayba did not mention Aḥmad in *al-Ma'ārif*; al-Maqdisī does mention him in *Aḥsan al-Taqāsīm fī Aṣḥāb al-Ḥadīth* but does not include him among the *Aṣḥāb al-Fiqh* while he includes Dāwūd al-Ẓāhirī. Ibn 'Abd al-Barr wrote *al-Intiqā' fī Faḍā'il al-Thalāthat al-Fuqahā'* ("The Hand-Picked Excellent Merits of the Three Great Jurisprudent Imāms: Mālik,

[800] This is not Ibn Ḥajar's student Shams al-Dīn Muḥammad ibn 'Abd al-Raḥmān ibn Muḥammad ibn Abī Bakr al-Sakhāwī al-Shāfi'ī, who died in 902 in Madīna and is buried in al-Baqī' near the grave of Imām Mālik – Allāh be well pleased with them.

al-Shāfi'ī, and Abū Ḥanīfa"),[801] concerning which Shaykh 'Abd al-Fattāḥ Abū Ghudda said: "It appears that Ibn 'Abd al-Barr considered Imām Aḥmad a foremost authority in ḥadīth who chose certain positions in *fiqh*, as was al-Ṭabarī's view of Aḥmad before him." The anonymous *'Umdat al-'Ārifīn* ("Reliance of the Knowers") mentions as the fourth of the Four Imāms not Aḥmad but Sufyān al-Thawrī. Al-Ghazzālī said: "He and Aḥmad were of the most famous Imāms for their strong fear of Allāh, and for the small number of their followers. As for now, the School of Sufyān is abandoned, and the consensus of the Muslims is around the four known schools." However, the School of Sufyān survived long enough for al-Nawawī to cite it among "the five Schools that are followed."[802]

Al-Khaṭīb al-Baghdādī was also taken to task by the Ḥanbalīs for naming Aḥmad "the Master of ḥadīth Scholars" (*sayyid al-muḥaddithīn*) in his biographies of the Scholars of Baghdād while reserving the highest level of jurisprudence for al-Shāfi'ī.

His Flight from Authorship in Jurisprudence

Upon hearing that Isḥāq ibn Manṣūr al-Kawsaj had published a compilation of Aḥmad's juridical views, the latter gathered his companions and declared that he had disclaimed all of them. Al-Kawtharī points out that despite this disclaimer, al-Tirmidhī relies on al-Kawsaj's compilation whenever citing the legal positions of Aḥmad. It is partly because of this scrupulous fear (*wara'*) of seeing his *fiqh* etched in stone that on so many specific issues two, three, or up to ten different positions are related from Imām Aḥmad. Abū Bakr al-Khallāl gathered all these views into a massive, forty-volume Ḥanbalī collection entitled *al-Jāmi' li-'Ulūm Aḥmad ibn Ḥanbal* after the Imām's death. Majd al-Dīn ibn Taymiyya ('Abd al-Salām ibn 'Abd Allāh ibn al-Khaḍir al-Ḥarrānī d. 652) then reduced this unwieldy compilation into a single volume entitled *al-Muḥarrar min al-Fiqh 'alā Madhhab al-Imām Aḥmad ibn Ḥanbal.*

801 The order of sequence reflects the view of the Mālikī school that Madīna is superior to Makka as shown by Ibn 'Abd al-Barr's words in the introduction to *al-Intiqā'* (p. 34): "They are Abū 'Abd Allāh Mālik ibn Anas al-Aṣbaḥī al-Madanī, Abū 'Abd Allāh Muḥammad ibn Idrīs al-Shāfi'ī al-Muṭṭalibī al-Makkī, and Abū Ḥanīfa al-Nu'mān ibn Thābit al-Kūfī."

802 Al-Nawawī, *Irshād* (p. 239-240).

His Godfearing Modesty and Self-Deprecation

To a man who said to him: "May Allāh repay you with goodness on the part of Islām" Aḥmad replied with a distressed countenance: "Rather, may Allāh repay Islām with goodness on my part. Who am I and what am I?" Ṣālīḥ ibn Aḥmad said: "Whenever a man supplicated on behalf of my father the latter would say [the Prophetic ḥadīth]: 'Actions count only according to their conclusions (*innamā al-a'mālu bil-khawātīm*).'"[803] That is, wait until a man dies upon Islām before praising him in his Religion.

عَنْ سَهْلِ بْنِ سَعْدٍ السَّاعِدِي ﵁ قَالَ النَّبِيُّ ﷺ إِنَّ الْعَبْدَ لَيَعْمَلُ عَمَلَ أَهْلِ النَّارِ وَإِنَّهُ مِنْ أَهْلِ الْجَنَّةِ وَيَعْمَلُ عَمَلَ أَهْلِ الْجَنَّةِ وَإِنَّهُ مِنْ أَهْلِ النَّارِ وَإِنَّمَا الأَعْمَالُ بِالْخَوَاتِيمِ خ حم

His Stringent Criterion for *Ijtihād*

Zakariyyā ibn Yaḥyā al-Ḍarīr asked Imām Aḥmad: "How many memorised ḥadīths are sufficient for someone to be a Mufti [meaning a *mujtahid* Jurist]? Are one hundred thousand sufficient?" He said no. "Two hundred thousand?" He said no. "Three?" He said no, until Zakariyyā said: "Five hundred thousand?" Aḥmad said: "I hope that that should be sufficient."[804] At the same time, when Muḥammad ibn Yazīd al-Mustamlī asked Aḥmad about the undisputed ḥadīth Master 'Abd al-Razzāq al-Ṣan'ānī – one of al-Bukhārī's teachers: "Did he ['Abd al-Razzāq] possess *fiqh*?" Aḥmad lamented: "How rare is *fiqh* among those who know ḥadīth!"

The Danger of Misusing Ḥadīth

Aḥmad narrated from Muḥammad ibn Yaḥyā al-Qaṭṭān that the latter said: "If someone were to follow every *rukhṣa* that is in the ḥadīth, he would become a transgressor (*fāsiq*)."[805]

Advice to Would-Be Writers

To 'Ayyāsh al-Qaṭṭān who told Aḥmad of his desire to compile the nar-

803 Narrated by Sahl ibn Sā'd al-Sa'idī by al-Bukhārī and Aḥmad.

804 Al-Dhahabī, *Siyar* (9:469=al-Arna'ūṭ ed. 11:232).

805 Aḥmad, *al-'Ilal* (1:219).

rations of the Prophets, Aḥmad replied: "Not until you are done with the narrations of our Prophet ﷺ!"[806]

Admiration of His Contemporaries

Al-Dhahabī cites the following praises of Imām Aḥmad:

- Ibrāhīm al-Ḥarbī said: "I held Aḥmad as one for whom Allāh had gathered up the combined knowledge of the first and the last."
- Ḥarmala said: "I heard al-Shāfi'ī say: 'I left Baghdād and did not leave behind me anyone more virtuous (*afḍal*), more learned (*a'lam*), nor more perspicuous (*afqah*) than Aḥmad ibn Ḥanbal!'" Shaykh 'Abd al-Fattāḥ Abū Ghudda noted that at the time this statement was made, Baghdād was home to several major jurists of the schools of Abū Ḥanīfa and al-Shāfi'ī and other schools, such as Muḥammad ibn Samā'a, 'Īsā ibn Abān, al-Za'farānī, al-Karābīsī, Abū Thawr, al-Qāsim ibn Sallām, Isḥāq ibn Rāhūyah and others. Yet al-Shāfi'ī ranked Aḥmad ibn Ḥanbal above all of them in virtue, learning, and knowledge. This alone suffices to refute the view held by some, that Imām Aḥmad was not a *faqīh*.
- 'Alī ibn al-Madīnī said: "Truly, Allāh reinforced this Religion with Abū Bakr al-Ṣiddīq ؓ on the day of the Great Apostasy (*al-Ridda*), and He reinforced it with Aḥmad ibn Ḥanbal ؓ at the time of the Ordeal (*al-miḥna*)."
- Abū 'Ubayd said: "The Science at its peak is in the custody of four men, of whom Aḥmad ibn Ḥanbal is the most knowledgeable."
- Ibn Ma'īn said, as related by 'Abbās [al-Dūrī]: "They meant for me to be like Aḥmad, but – by Allāh! – I shall never in my life compare to him."
- Muḥammad ibn Ḥammād al-Ṭaharānī said: "I heard Abū Thawr say: 'Aḥmad is more learned – or knowledgeable – than al-Thawrī.'"

His Insistence on Written Records in Ḥadīth Narration

'Alī ibn al-Madīnī said: "Sayyidī Aḥmad ibn Ḥanbal said to me, 'Do not narrate anything to me except from a written record' (*lā tuḥaddithnī illā min kitāb*)."[807]

[806] Narrated by al-Khaṭīb in *al-Jāmi' li-Akhlāq al-Rāwī* (2:465 §1988).

[807] Narrated by al-Khaṭīb in *al-Jāmi' li-Akhlāq al-Rāwī wa-Ādāb al-Sāmi'* (2:12 §1032) and al-Sam'ānī, *Adab al-Imlā' wal-Istimlā'* (p. 47).

Works Related from the Imām

Among Imām Aḥmad's works listed by Ibn al-Jawzī and al-Dhahabī:

* *Al-Ashriba* in which he declared *nabīdh* fruit mash forbidden, even if made of other than grapes or dates, and any kind of fruit juice after three days.[808]
* *Al-Imāma*. Regarding the first Caliphate Imām Aḥmad said: "When the Prophet ﷺ was ill he ordered Abū Bakr to pray as imām although there were others present who were more proficient in the Qur'ān (*aqra'*), but he ﷺ was pointing to the Caliphate."[809] He took this position from Imām al-Shāfi'ī.
* *Al-Īmān*.
* *Manāqib al-Ṣaḥāba*, with additions by his son 'Abd Allāh ibn Aḥmad and his companion Abū Bakr al-Qaṭī'ī and which contains many weak narrations.[810]
* *Al-Mansak*.
* *Al-Muqaddam wal-Mu'akhkhar fīl-Qur'ān*.
* *Al-Musnad*. This is the first comprehensive collection of ḥadīths that are *musnad* or "related on the authority of the Prophet ﷺ" which Aḥmad arranged in chapter-headings bearing the names of the Companion-narrators and ordered according to the sequence of seniority in Islām, beginning with Abū Bakr ؓ. The total number of its narrations is around 27,000, of which a handful are sayings by the Companions. Ibn al-Sammāk narrated from Ḥanbal (Aḥmad's uncle): "Aḥmad ibn Ḥanbal gathered us – me, Ṣāliḥ, and 'Abd Allāh – and read to us the *Musnad* before anyone else ever heard it. Then he said: 'This book I have gathered together and carefully selected out of a total of 750,000 narrations. Whatever the Muslims differ about concerning a ḥadīth of the Messenger of Allāh ﷺ, refer back to it. If you find it in it, fine – otherwise, such a ḥadīth does not constitute a proof.'"

Al-Dhahabī remarked that the Imām's statement (1) excludes the narrations found in the two *Ṣaḥīḥ*s that are not in

---

[808] Cf. Ibn Taymiyya, *al-Qawā'id al-Nūrāniyya* (al-Fiqqī ed. p. 105).

[809] Narrated from Abū Bakr al-Marwazī by Ibn al-Jawzī in *Manāqib Aḥmad ibn Ḥanbal* (p. 160).

[810] The weak narrations narrated by Aḥmad in the *Musnad* and elsewhere were analyzed by al-Khallāl in *al-'Ilal* among other specialized works.

the *Musnad*, for the Muslims do not differ concerning them; and (2) does not necessitate that everything that is in the *Musnad* is a proof, as it contains a number of weak ḥadīths and very few near-forgeries.[811]

- *Nafy al-Tashbīh* ("The Negation of Anthropomorphism"). It may be on the basis of this work that al-Shahrastānī said:

> Imām Aḥmad and his School abhorred likening Allāh ﷻ to His creation (*tashbīh*) to such an extent that they used to say: "Whoever moves his hand while reciting the verse ﴾**I created with both My Hands**﴿ (38:75) or gestures with his fingers when narrating the ḥadīth "The heart of the believer is between two fingers of the Merciful,"[812] cut their hands or fingers off!"[813]

- *Al-Nāsikh wal-Mansūkh.*
- The spurious *al-Radd 'alā al-Zanādiqa* ("The Refutation of the Heretics"), relied upon by Ibn Taymiyya (who alternately calls it *al-Radd 'alā al-Jahmiyya* and *al-Radd 'alā al-Jahmiyya wal Zanādiqa*)[814] and falsely attributed to Imām Aḥmad as pointed out by al-Dhahabī.[815] It is revealing that certain "Salafīs" continue to attribute it to him and publish it under his name.[816] What is worse than this irresponsible deception is that the book misrepresents Imām Aḥmad as indulging in the worst type of *kalām*, and holding views that border on disbelief, such as the following:

> They [the Jahmīs] say: "Whenever it comes to your mind that Allāh is something which you know, Allāh is other than that."[817] Aḥmad says: We say that He is a thing. They said: "He is

[811] See on this point Ibn Ḥajar's *al-Qawl al-Musaddad fil-Dhabb 'an Musnad al-Imām Aḥmad* published by Shaykh Aḥmad Shākir in his edition of the *Musnad*.

[812] See n. 187.

[813] Al-Shahrastānī, *al-Milal wal-Niḥal* (Cairo, 1317 ed. p. 145, 137-138).

[814] Ibn Taymiyya, *Fatāwā* (5:496, 5:555, 6:153, 7:89, 8:385, 15:284, 16:213, 17:300).

[815] Al-Dhahabī, *Siyar A'lām al-Nubalā'* (9:503).

[816] Cf. "Aḥmad ibn Ḥanbal," *al-Radd 'alā al-Zanādiqa wal-Jahmiyya*, ed. Muḥammad Ḥasan Rashīd (Cairo: al-Maṭba'at al-Salafiyya, 1973) and *al-Radd 'alā al-Jahmiyya lil-Imām Aḥmad ibn Ḥanbal*, ed. Aḥmad Bakir Mahmūd (Beirut: Dār Qutayba, 1990).

[817] A saying not of the *Jahmiyya* but of Dhūl-Nūn al-Miṣrī narrated by al-Qushayrī in the *Risāla* and extolled by 'Iyāḍ in his *al-Shifā*!

> 'something' unlike any other thing."[818] We say: The thing that is unlike any other thing, rational people know to be non-existent. It is therefore clear to everyone that they [the Jahmīs] do not believe in anything.[819]

In this excerpt "the Jahmīs" express the Sunni viewpoint while "Aḥmad" expresses an untenable position that flatly contradicts the Qur'ān – something from which the real Aḥmad was the farthest of people.

- *Al-Risāla fil-Ṣalāt,* also a misattribution according to al-Dhahabī.
- *Al-Tafsīr* according to Ibn al-Jawzī, but "it never existed" according to al-Dhahabī, contrary to Ibn Taymiyya's opinion in his *Muqaddima fī Uṣūl al-Tafsīr* although the latter himself quotes Imām Aḥmad as saying, "Three matters have no [highly verifiable] chain of transmission: *tafsīr,* chronicles of battles (*maghāzī*), and end-of-time battles (*malāḥim*)."[820]
- *Al-Tārīkh.*
- *Uṣūl al-Sunna,* "Principles of the Sunna," translated and published under the title "Foundations of the Sunna"[821]: this is not a book but the creed narrated from 'Abdūs ibn Mālik from the Imām by Ibn Abī Ya'lā in *Ṭabaqāt al-Ḥanābila* and al-Lālikā'ī in *Sharḥ Uṣūl I'tiqād Ahl al-Sunna,* both through Abū Ja'far ibn Sulaymān ibn Dāwūd al-Baṣrī al-Minqarī who is of unknown reliability and whom Ibn al-Jawzī declared weak.[822]

The Persecution (*al-Miḥna*)

Imām Aḥmad lived at a time when the power of the Mu'tazila over the caliphate became such that *Ahl al-Sunna* scholars were routinely perse-

[818] Cf. Ibn Khafīf, *al-'Aqīda al-Ṣaḥīḥa* §5: "He is 'something' yet not like things" (*shay'un lā kal-ashyā'*) [or: "He is an entity but not in the sense of created entities."]

[819] *"Al-Radd 'alā al-Zanādiqa wal-Jahmiyya"* (p. 20-21).

[820] Ibn Taymiyya, *Muqaddima fī Uṣūl al-Tafsīr* (p. 49=*Majmū' al-Fatāwā* 13:346); cf. al-Suyūṭī, *Itqān* (chapter 78) and al-Zarqānī, *Manāhil al-'Irfān* (2:12, 2:19).

[821] Birmingham: Salafi Publications, 1997. This publication is a deception as its cover claims that the author of this 200-page book is Imām Aḥmad whereas it contains only three very brief Ḥanbalī texts from *Ṭabaqāt al-Ḥanābila* covering 60 pages, of which the Creed of the Imām is the first. The rest of the book and its greater part is a long text by an unknown contemporary author, beginning with the life and trial of Imām Aḥmad and ending with a confused defense of anthropomorphism and attacks on the Ash'arī School.

[822] In *al-'Ilal al-Mutanāhiya* (2:619-620).

cuted over issues such as the uncreatedness of the Qur'ān and the vision of Allāh ﷻ in the hereafter. Most of the scholars caved in to the threat of torture except a handful: Aḥmad ibn Ḥanbal who was jailed and lashed, Aḥmad ibn Naṣr al-Khuzā'ī who was decapitated by al-Wāthiq's own hand then crucified for six years for declaring that Allāh ﷻ could be seen in the hereafter, Muḥammad ibn Nūḥ, Nu'aym ibn Ḥammād who died in chains, al-Faḍl ibn Dukayn who replied to his inquisitor, "The Qur'ān is the Speech of Allāh and I fear less for my neck than for my shirt-button," 'Affān ibn Muslim, al-Buwayṭī who died in chains, Ismā'īl ibn Abī Uways, Abū Muṣ'ab al-Zuhrī, Abū Yaḥyā al-Ḥammānī, 'Abd al-A'lā ibn Mus-hir who died in prison, and al-Ḥārith ibn Miskīn al-Ḍibbī. Others simply answered "Yes, it is created" and were released with a gift of two dinars.

At the time of Imām Aḥmad's 28-month[823] detention and lashing by the authorities he was pressed to admit to the creation of the Qur'ān by the following arguments as narrated by his son the ḥadīth Master Abū al-Faḍl Ṣāliḥ ibn Aḥmad in his *Sīrat al-Imām Aḥmad*:

QUESTIONER: What do you say about the Qur'ān?

IMĀM AḤMAD: And you, what do you say about the knowledge of Allāh ﷻ?

ANOTHER QUESTIONER: Did not Allāh say: ﴾**Allāh is the Creator of all things**﴿ (13:16), and is not the Qur'ān a thing?

IMĀM AḤMAD: Allāh also said: ﴾**Destroying all things**﴿ (46:25), then it [the wind] destroyed all except whatever Allāh willed.

ANOTHER QUESTIONER: ﴾**Never comes there unto them a new** (*muḥdath*) **reminder from their Lord**﴿ (21:2). Can something new be anything but created?

IMĀM AḤMAD: Allāh said: ﴾**Ṣād. By the Qur'ān that contains the Reminder**﴿ (38:1). "The" reminder is the Qur'ān, while the other verse does not say "the".[824]

ANOTHER QUESTIONER: But the ḥadīth of 'Imrān ibn Ḥuṣayn states: "Allāh created the Reminder."

823 Shaykh Shu'ayb al-Arna'ūṭ's mention of "ten years" in his introduction to *Ṣaḥīḥ Ibn Ḥibbān* (p. 22) is inaccurate.

824 Another version states that he answered: "It is possible that it is the Qur'ān's revelation to us (*tanzīluhu ilaynā*) that is new; not the *dhikr* itself." Narrated through al-Bayhaqī by Ibn Kathīr in *al-Bidāya* (10:342-343).

IMĀM AḤMAD: That is not correct. Several narrated it to us as: "Allāh wrote the Reminder."[825]

They cited the ḥadīth of Ibn Mas'ūd: "Allāh ﷻ did not create a garden of Paradise nor a fire of Hell nor a heaven nor an earth more tremendous (*a'ẓam*) than the verse of the Throne (2:255)."[826]

IMĀM AḤMAD: The creating here applies to the garden, the fire, the heaven, and the earth. It does not apply to the Qur'ān.

ANOTHER QUESTIONER: The narration of Khabbāb states: "I admonish you to approach Allāh with all that you can; but you can never approach Him with something dearer to Him than His speech."[827]

IMĀM AḤMAD: And that is true.[828]

When he was advised to invoke against his oppressors, Aḥmad replied: "He is not long-suffering (*ṣābir*) who invokes against his oppressor."[829]

Yaḥyā ibn Ma'īn visited Aḥmad during the latter's sickness and bade him salaam but Aḥmad did not answer him as he had sworn an oath not to address anyone who had replied yes during the inquisition on the createdness of the Qur'ān. "Yaḥyā kept apologizing and mentioning the ḥadīth of 'Ammār, 'and Allāh said ﴾**save him who is forced thereto and whose heart is still content with Faith**﴿ (16:106).' But Aḥmad would turn his face the other way. Then Yaḥyā stood up dejected [and walked out] saying: 'He will not accept any excuse from us!' I went out after him as he was sitting at the door. He said: 'What did Aḥmad say after I went out?' I replied: 'He said that you are citing the ḥadīth of 'Ammār, which states: "I passed by as they were insulting

[825] Al-Bukhārī, *Ṣaḥīḥ*, book of the Beginning of Creation: "Allāh was when there was nothing else than Him, and His Throne was upon the water, and He wrote in the Reminder (*al-dhikr*) all things, and He created the heavens and the earth."

[826] Narrated by Sa'īd ibn Manṣūr, Ibn al-Mundhir, Ibn al-Ḍarīs, al-Ṭabarānī, and al-Bayhaqī in *Shu'ab al-Īmān*, as stated by al-Suyūṭī in *al-Durr al-Manthūr*. Al-Tirmidhī in his *Sunan* mentions Sufyān ibn 'Uyayna's explanation whereby this is because the garden, the fire, etc. are created as opposed to the Qur'ān.

[827] Narrated by al-Ḥākim (2:441) who declared it sound and by al-Bayhaqī in *al-Asmā' wal-Ṣifāt* with two sound chains (1:587-588 §513-514).

[828] *Siyar* (9:478), *Ṭabaqāt al-Shāfi'iyya al-Kubrā* (2:46-47). Cf. Ṣāliḥ ibn Aḥmad, *Sīrat al-Imām Aḥmad* (p. 32–47).

[829] Ibn Abī Ya'lā, *Ṭabaqāt al-Ḥanābila* (2:289).

you, so I forbade them and they beat me,"[830] whereas it was only said to you all "We *shall* beat you."' When he heard this, Yaḥyā said: 'It is bitter, *yā* Aḥmad, may Allāh forgive you! By Allāh! I never saw under the sky anyone more discerning than you in the Religion of Allāh.'"[831]

His *Taraḥḥum* of Abū Ḥanīfa Under the Whip

Whenever Abū Ḥanīfa was mentioned to Imām Aḥmad he would speak kindly of him and when, under the whip, he was reminded that Abū Ḥanīfa had suffered the same treatment for refusing a judgeship, he wept and said: *Raḥimahullāh.*[832]

His Respect for Difference of Opinion and Other Schools

Aḥmad is famous for his serene acceptance of juridical divergences among the Imāms. Asked about cupping, he responded that ablution was obligatory after it. The questioner went on, "Should I pray behind an imām who does not renew his ablution in such a case?" Aḥmad replied: "Glory to Allāh! Would you not pray behind Sa'īd ibn al-Musayyab and Mālik ibn Anas?"[833]

According to the Ḥanbalī authorities Ibn 'Aqīl, Abū Bakr al-Dīnawarī, and Ibn Taymiyya, Aḥmad – just like Mālik – **considered every *Madhhab* correct and abhorred that a *Faqīh* insist people follow his even if he considered them wrong and even if the truth is one in any given matter.** To his student Isḥāq ibn Bahlūl al-Anbārī who had compiled a book on juridical differences which he had named "The Core of Divergence" (*Lubāb al-Ikhtilāf*) Imām Aḥmad said, "Name it 'The Book of Leeway' (*Kitāb al-Sa'a*) and not the book of divergence."[834]

Ibn Qudāma cites another example of the above principle. Al-Ḥusayn ibn Bashshār asked Aḥmad something about oaths and

[830] Cited by al-Dhahabī in the *Siyar* (3:262=Risāla ed. 1:420), and he references it to Abū 'Awāna's *Musnad* and Abū Ya'lā.

[831] Narrated from Abū Bakr al-Marwazī by Ibn al-Jawzī in *Manāqib Aḥmad* (p. 389).

[832] Narrated by al-Khaṭīb in *Tārīkh Baghdād* (13:360), al-Dhahabī in *Tārīkh al-Islām* (6:141), and Ibn 'Imād, *Shadharāt al-Dhahab* (1:228).

[833] In Ibn Taymiyya, *Majmū' al-Fatāwā* (20:365).

[834] Ibn Abī Ya'lā, *Ṭabaqāt al-Ḥanābila* (1:111), Ibn Mufliḥ, *al-Maqṣad al-Arshad fī Dhikr Aṣḥāb al-Imām Aḥmad* (1:248), and Ibn Taymiyya, *Sharḥ al-'Umda* (4:567), *Majmū' al-Fatāwā* (14:159), and *Miswaddat Āl Taymiyya* (p. 401).

divorce. The latter said: "In such a case, one has perjured himself." Ibn Bashshār insisted: "What if someone gave me a contrary *fatwa*?" Aḥmad said: "Do you know the circle of the Madīnans in al-Ruṣāfa [Baghdād]?" Bashshār said: "If they give me such a *fatwa*, is it licit to follow it?" Aḥmad said yes.[835]

Some of the Imām's Contemporaries and Colleagues

BISHR AL-ḤĀFĪ[836]

Bishr ibn al-Ḥārith, Abū Naṣr al-Khurāsānī al-Marwazī al-Baghdādī, known as Bishr al-Ḥāfī ﷺ (151-227), was a disciple of Fuḍayl ibn 'Iyāḍ (d. 187) and teacher of Sarī al-Saqaṭī. He took ḥadīth from Imām Mālik, Ibn al-Mubārak, Ḥammād ibn Zayd, Sharīk, Hushaym, and others. Al-Dāraquṭnī called him *zāhid jabal thiqa* – "an ascetic who is a mountain of knowledge and trustworthiness." The Scholars of ḥadīth have rarely used the term *jabal*, which is above *ḥujja* ("Proof in himself"), which is above *thiqa* ("trustworthy"). Among his sayings:

- "I do not know anything better than the pursuit of ḥadīth science for whoever fears Allāh and keeps a good intention in this activity; as for myself, I ask the forgiveness of Allāh from having ever pursued it, and from every single step I took in it." Imām al-Sha'rānī explained that the reason Bishr abandoned the study of ḥadīth is that he considered it a conjectural science in comparison with the certitude in belief imparted by frequenting Fuḍayl ibn 'Iyāḍ.[837] However, the early sources show that this was done out of scrupulous fear of Allāh.[838] Sufyān al-Thawrī similarly said: "Would that all my knowledge were erased from my breast! How can I face being asked, tomorrow, about each single ḥadīth I ever narrated: 'What was your purpose in narrating it?'" He also said: "Would that my hand had been cut off and I never sought after a single ḥadīth!"[839]
- "If talking pleases you, keep silent; and if silence pleases you, then speak."

[835] Ibn Qudāma, *Rawḍat al-Nāẓir* (Azhariyya ed. p. 344=Ryadh ed. p. 386).

[836] Ibn al-Jawzī, *Ṣifat al-Ṣafwa* (2:216-218); al-Dhahabī, *Siyar* (9:170-172 §1691).

[837] Al-Sha'rānī, *al-Ṭabaqāt al-Kubrā* (1:57).

[838] See the chapters on Bishr in al-Sulamī's *Ṭabaqāt al-Ṣūfiyya*, al-Qushayrī's *Risāla*, and Ibn al-Mulaqqin's *Ṭabaqāt al-Awliyā'*.

[839] Both reports cited by al-Dhahabī in the *Siyar* (al-Arna'ūṭ ed. 7:255, 7:274).

- "O Allāh! You know, above Your Throne, that lowliness is more beloved to me than nobility. O Allāh! You know, above Your Throne, that poverty is more beloved to me than wealth. O Allāh! You know, above Your Throne, that I do not put anything before Your love."

Imām al-Nawawī in his monograph entitled *al-Tarkhīṣ fil-Ikrām bil-Qiyām* narrates the following commentary by Bishr on the ḥadīth of Mu'āwiya to ['Abd Allāh] Ibn 'Āmir: "Sit, for I heard the Prophet ﷺ say: 'Whoever likes men to stand up for him, let him take his place in the fire'"[840]:

> The Prophet ﷺ only disliked the standing of others from the perspective of arrogance, but from the perspective of sincere love he did not, since he himself stood up for 'Ikrima ibn Abī Jahl, and he said [concerning Sa'd ibn Mu'ādh]: "Stand for your chief," and he said: "He who likes people to stand for him..." indicating that whoever likes people to stand for him, only then must you not stand for him.

It is also established that the Prophet ﷺ used to stand up for his daughter Fāṭima, take her by the hand, and kiss her, and she used to stand up for him, take his hand, and kiss him.[841]

Also related from Bishr al-Ḥāfī is the statement: "None criticises Abū Ḥanīfa except an envier or an ignoramus."[842] Bishr either followed the School of Abū Ḥanīfa in *fiqh* or that of Sufyān al-Thawrī.

Bishr al-Ḥāfī's grandfather was a Zoroastrian from Khurāsān named Bābūr. Ibn al-Jawzī relates from Zubda, the sister of Bishr:

> One time Bishr entered my house late at night. He placed one of his feet inside the house and the other outside, and remained thus in reflection until dawn. Afterwards I said to him: "What were you thinking about all night?" He said: "I was thinking of Bishr-

[840] Narrated by Abū Dāwūd, al-Tirmidhī who said: *ḥasan* ("fair") and Aḥmad.

[841] Narrated from 'Ā'isha by al-Bayhaqī in *al-Sunan al-Kubrā* (7:101 §13346) and al-Ḥākim (3:154=1990 ed. 3:167, *ṣaḥīḥ*). Cf. 'Abd Allāh al-Ghumārī, *I'lām al-Nabīl bi-Jawāz al-Taqbīl*, 2nd ed. (Cairo: Maktabat al-Qāhira 1994). See also, on this issue, the chapter (§26) on getting up out of respect in al-Bayhaqī's *al-Madkhal ilā al-Sunan*.

[842] Narrated by al-Dhahabī, *Tārīkh al-Islām* (6:142) and *Manāqib Abī Ḥanīfa* (p. 32).

the-Christian, and Bishr-the-Jew, and Bishr-the-Zoroastrian, and about my soul, and about my name of 'Bishr,' and I said to myself: 'What have you done to merit that He single you out [with Islām]?' And I kept thinking of His immense favour towards me, and thanking Him that He has made me one of His special servants and clothed me with the vestment of His beloved ones."

Ibn al-Jawzī also relates from Muḥammad ibn Qudāma: "Bishr ibn al-Ḥārith once met a drunkard on the road who began kissing him and shouting: *'Yā sayyidī! Yā Abā Naṣr!'* and Bishr did not push him away from him. When the drunkard left, Bishr's eyes filled with tears and he said: 'A man who loved another man because he imagined that there was some good in him – yet, perhaps, the lover is saved, while the one who is loved is uncertain about his own condition.'"

Imām Aḥmad was awed by Bishr al-Ḥāfī and considered him one of the *Abdāl* – major Saints of the time – only regretting that he did not complete the Sunna by marrying.

IBN AL-MADĪNĪ

'Alī ibn al-Madīnī, Abū al-Ḥasan 'Alī ibn 'Abd Allāh ibn Ja'far al-Sa'dī al-Baṣrī al-Madīnī ﷺ (d. 234) was the trustworthy Imām and ḥadīth Master and one the most knowledgeable of the ḥadīth Masters of his time. He narrated ḥadīth from his father, from Ḥammād ibn Zayd, and a large number of ḥadīth Masters. From him narrated al-Bukhārī, Abū Dāwūd, al-Baghawī, Abū Ya'lā, and others. He was a student of Yaḥyā ibn Sa'īd al-Qaṭṭān together with al-Shādhakūnī, 'Amr ibn 'Alī, Aḥmad ibn Ḥanbal, and Yaḥyā ibn Ma'īn.

Ibn al-Madīnī once said: "I may find the minute defect (*'illa*) of a ḥadīth narration forty years later." His Shaykh 'Abd al-Raḥmān ibn Mahdī said: "'Alī ibn al-Madīnī is the most knowledgeable of all human beings in the ḥadīth of the Messenger of Allāh ﷺ, especially in what Ibn 'Uyayna narrates. Do you blame me for loving 'Alī ibn al-Madīnī too much? By Allāh! I learn more from him than he does from me." His other Shaykhs Yaḥyā al-Qaṭṭān and Sufyān ibn 'Uyayna said the same about him. Al-Bukhārī said: "I did not think little of myself before anyone except before 'Alī (ibn al-Madīnī)." Al-Nasā'ī said: "It is as if Allāh created him only for this science (ḥadīth)." He died in Sāmarrā. Ibn al-Athīr said that the name of Madīnī is related to the city of the Prophet ﷺ

but al-Jawharī said that the latter would be "Madanī," "Madīnī" referring to the city built by the caliph al-Manṣūr, al-Madā'in (Iraq).[843]

AL-QĀSIM IBN SALLĀM[844]

Al-Qāsim ibn Sallām ibn 'Abd Allāh, Abū 'Ubayd al-Harawī ﵀ (d. 224) was one of the great early ḥadīth Masters and philologists, author of *Gharīb al-Ḥadīth, Faḍā'il al-Qur'ān, al-Nasab, al-Gharīb al-Muṣannaf* – an encyclopedia forty years in the making and his greatest work – among others. A student of al-Shāfi'ī, Hushaym, Ibn 'Uyayna, Ghundar, Ibn al-Mubārak, Wakī', Ibn Mahdī, al-Aṣma'ī, al-Naḍr ibn Shumayl, and others, he was one of 'Abbās al-Dūrī's Shaykhs. Isḥāq ibn Rāhūyah said: "As Allāh loves the truth, Abū 'Ubayd is better versed and more knowledgeable in the Law than I." Ibrāhīm al-Ḥarbī said: "Abū 'Ubayd was like a mountain into which the Spirit was breathed. He excelled in everything, except that ḥadīth was the specialty of Aḥmad [ibn Ḥanbal] and Yaḥyā [ibn Ma'īn]."

'Abbās al-Dūrī said: "I heard Abū 'Ubayd al-Qāsim ibn Sallām mention the vision of Allāh [in the hereafter], the [narration of Ibn 'Abbās on the] *kursī* 'where the two feet are placed,'[845] our Lord's laughter, and where He was [before creation], then he said: 'All these are sound (*ṣaḥīḥ*) narrations transmitted by the scholars of ḥadīth and *fiqh* one from another; we consider them the truth and do not doubt them. But if it were asked: How does He laugh? or how does He place His *qadam*? We reply: We do not explain this; nor did we ever hear anyone explain it.'"

843 Source: al-Khaṭīb, *al-Jāmi'* (2:385 §1841).

844 Sources: Ibn Abī Ya'lā, *Ṭabaqāt al-Ḥanābila* (1:259-262 §369); al-Dhahabī, *Siyar* (9:183-191 §1702, 8:287-289 §1482); Ibn 'Abd al-Barr, *al-Intiqā'* (p. 167).

845 A *mawqūf* statement of Ibn 'Abbās narrated with a sound chain by al-Ṭabarānī in *al-Kabīr* (12:39 §12404) as stated by al-Haythamī (6:323), al-Bayhaqī in *al-Asmā' wal-Ṣifāt* (2:196 §758), Ibn Khuzayma in *al-Tawḥīd* (p. 108), al-Ḥākim (2:282), who declared it *ṣaḥīḥ*, al-Khaṭīb in *Tārīkh Baghdād* (9:251), Ibn Abī Shayba in *Kitāb al-'Arsh* (p. 79 §61), Abū al-Shaykh in *al-'Aẓama* (2:552-553 §196, 2:582 §216); and *marfū'* – erroneously – by al-Dāraquṭnī in *al-Ṣifāt* (p. 49-50 §36) and Ibn Mandah in *al-Radd 'alā al-Jahmiyya* (p. 44-45). Ibn al-Jawzī in *al-'Ilal* (1:22) declared that it should not be considered a *marfū'* Prophetic report. This verdict is confirmed by al-Dhahabī in his *Mīzān* (2:265), Ibn Kathīr in his *Tafsīr* (1:317), and Ibn Ḥajar, *al-Tahdhīb* (4:274) cf. al-Aḥdab, *Zawā'id* (7:37-39 §1383). Al-Bayhaqī said: "He did not attribute the feet [to Allāh ﷻ], nor did Abū Mūsā al-Ash'arī in his own identical statement [*al-Asmā'* (2:296-297 §859) with a weak chain], and this [non-attributive form] seems the soundest version."

Al-Bayhaqī said of the "footstool report":

> Its interpretation among the authorities is that the *kursī* in relation to the Throne is as the footstool is in relation to the couch under which a footstool is placed for the person reclining on it[...] At any rate this is a halted report which is not narrated from the Prophet ﷺ. As for our early companions they did not explain such cases nor did they preoccupy themselves with interpreting them believing, at the same time, that Allāh ﷻ is One without parts nor limbs.[846]

Al-Qurṭubī quoted from Ibn 'Aṭiyya in his *Tafsīr* of the Verse of the Throne that the meaning was that the *kursī* was placed in front of the *'arsh* "just like" the footstool is placed in front of a high chair, indicating that it did not necessitate reference to an actual footstool but referred, for example, to a seat or station. Al-Bayhaqī states the same.[847] The more authentic explanation of the *kursī* according to the *Salaf* such as al-Bukhārī, al-Ṭabarī, Sufyān al-Thawrī, 'Abd al-Raḥmān ibn Mahdī, and Wakī' – as well as al-Bayhaqī himself[848] – is Ibn 'Abbās's report that "The *kursī* means His knowledge."[849] Al-Ṭabarī chooses it as the most correct explanation: "The external wording of the Qur'ān indicates the correctness of the report from Ibn 'Abbās that it [*the kursī*] is His *'ilm* [...] and the original sense of al-*kursī* is *al-'ilm.*"

As for the *qadam*, we have already mentioned that al-Ḥasan al-Baṣrī similarly narrated that it meant something other than its external meaning.

[846] Al-Bayhaqī, *al-Asmā' wal-Ṣifāt* (2:196-197).

[847] In *al-Asmā' wal-Ṣifāt* (2:197, 2:297).

[848] In *al-Asmā' wal-Ṣifāt* (2:272).

[849] Narrated *marfū'* from the Prophet ﷺ by Sufyān al-Thawrī with a sound chain according to Ibn Ḥajar in *Fatḥ al-Bārī* (1959 ed. 8:199) and al-Ṭabarānī in *al-Sunna*; and *mawqūf* from Ibn 'Abbās by al-Ṭabarī with three sound chains in his *Tafsīr* (3:9-11), al-Māwardī in his *Tafsīr* (1:908), al-Suyūṭī in *al-Durr al-Manthūr* (1:327), al-Shawkānī in *Fatḥ al-Qadīr* (1:245), and others. Also narrated in "suspended" form (*mu'allaq*) by al-Bukhārī in his *Ṣaḥīḥ* from Sa'īd ibn Jubayr (Book of *Tafsīr*, chapter on the saying of Allāh ﷻ: ﴾**And if you go in fear, then (pray) standing or on horseback**﴿ (2:239). Its chains are documented by Ibn Ḥajar in *Taghlīq al-Ta'līq* (2/4:185-186) where he shows that Sufyān al-Thawrī, 'Abd al-Raḥmān ibn Mahdī, and Wakī' narrated it *marfū'* from the Prophet ﷺ, although in the *Fatḥ* he declares the *mawqūf* version from Ibn 'Abbās more likely.

Among the sayings of Ibn Sallām:

- "He who follows the Sunna is like one who is grasping a hot coal. A day spent following the Sunna is, to me, preferable to striking sword-blows in the way of Allāh Almighty."
- "I am puzzled by those who leave the principles to study the branches."[850] Shaykh Muḥammad 'Ajāj al-Khaṭīb said that he meant by the principles the foundational books (*al-kutub al-ummahāt*) of proof-texts as opposed to the books of *fiqh*.[851]

Ibn Abī Ya'lā relates from Ibn Abī al-Dunyā (the ḥadīth Master 'Abd Allāh ibn Muḥammad ibn 'Ubayd (208-281)) the following account by Abū 'Ubayd:

> I visited Aḥmad ibn Ḥanbal one day. When I entered his house he got up and embraced me, then he made me sit at the head of his gathering. I said: "Abū 'Abd Allāh! Is it not said that the owner of the house, or chief of the gathering, is the most deserving to sit at the head of his house or gathering?" He replied: "Yes, he sits there, and seats whom he wishes there." I thought to myself: "*Take benefit from what you just heard, Abū 'Ubayd!*" Then I said: "Abū 'Abd Allāh! If I were to come and see you according to what befits you, I would come and see you each and every day." He replied: "Do not say that. I have brothers whom I do not see all year but once, and in whose love I trust more than those I see every day." I said to myself: "*This is another one, Abū 'Ubayd!*" When I got up to leave he got up with me. I said: "Please do not, Abū 'Abd Allāh!" He said: "Al-Sha'bī said: Part of the perfection of the visitor's call is that he be accompanied to the door of the house [when he leaves], and to hold the reins of his mount for him." I said: "Abū 'Abd Allāh! From al-Sha'bī?" He said: "From Ibn Abī Zā'ida, from Mujālid, from al-Sha'bī." I said to myself: "*Abū 'Ubayd, this is the third benefit for you!*"

Ibn Abī Ya'lā continues: "It is narrated from Abū Qilāba, from Ibn 'Abbās, that the Prophet ﷺ said: 'Whoever holds the reins of some-

[850] Narrated by al-Khaṭīb in *al-Jāmi' li-Akhlāq al-Rāwī* (2:270 §1612).

[851] This objection is addressed in depth in the section titled "The Superiority of *Fiqh* over Ḥadīth" in the chapter on al-Shāfi'ī.

one's mount not hoping [for any material benefit] from him nor fearing him, his sins are forgiven.'[852] Al-Sha'bī narrated that Ibn 'Abbās held the reins of Zayd ibn Thābit's mount, so the latter said: 'You are holding them for me, you, the Prophet's ﷺ cousin?' Whereupon Ibn 'Abbās replied: 'This is our practice with the Ulema.'"[853] It is also narrated that Ibn 'Abbās would wait for Zayd to come out outside his door in order to take knowledge from him; and when Zayd died he said: "Thus is knowledge taken away."

(Abū 'Ubayd must not be confused with his contemporary and philologist name-sake Abū 'Ubayda who is Ma'mar ibn al-Muthannā al-Taymī (d. ca. 210). He authored *Majāz al-Qur'ān*[854] and the lost *Gharīb al-Ḥadīth* as well as historical and lexicographical works. He is cited heavily in Qur'ānic commentaries. Al-Baghawī reports in his that he explained *istawā* as "He mounted" (*ṣa'ida*) in the verse ﴿**Then He established Himself over the Throne**﴾ (32:4).[855] Pickthall followed that sense in his translation of the verse as "Then He mounted the Throne.")

IBN ABĪ SHAYBA[856]

'Abd Allāh ibn Muḥammad ibn Abī Shayba Ibrāhīm ibn 'Uthmān ibn Khuwasta, Abū Bakr al-Abas ؓ (d. 235) was described by al-Dhahabī as the brother, father, and uncle of ḥadīth Masters and their most prestigious representative, "the master of ḥadīth Masters," "one of those who have reached the sky, a pinnacle of trustworthiness," "one of the oceans of knowledge," the author of *al-Musnad, al-Aḥkām, al-Muṣannaf,* and *al-Tafsīr,* "one of the peers of Aḥmad ibn Ḥanbal, Isḥāq ibn Rāhūyah, and 'Alī ibn al-Madīnī in age, place of birth, and ḥadīth memorization." Abū Zur'a al-Rāzī said: "I never saw anyone with more mastery of the ḥadīth than Abū Bakr ibn Abī Shayba;"

852 Narrated by Ibn 'Asākir.

853 This ḥadīth is narrated by al-Khaṭīb in *al-Faqīh wal-Mutafaqqih* (2:99), al-Bayhaqī in *al-Madkhal* (p. 137), Ibn Sa'd (2:360) from Abū Nu'aym with a sound (*ṣaḥīḥ*) chain according to Ibn Ḥajar in *al-Iṣāba* (1:561), al-Ṭabarānī with a sound chain as indicated by al-Haythamī in the chapter on Zayd in *Majma' al-Zawā'id*, Ibn al-Muqri' in *al-Rukhṣa fī Taqbīl al-Yad* (p. 95 §30), al-Ṭabarī in his *Tārīkh* (11:57, Sūrat al-Fatḥ), and Ibn 'Asākir in his *Tārīkh* in the biography of Zayd.

854 Published in Cairo in two volumes edited by Fu'ād Sezgīn (1955 and 1962).

855 In his commentary entitled *Ma'ālim al-Tanzīl* (al-Manār ed. 3:488).

856 Main sources: al-Dhahabī, *Siyar* (9:394-396 §1841) and *Tadhkira* (2:432-433).

lavish praise in light of al-Rāzī's familiarity with Aḥmad ibn Ḥanbal and al-Bukhārī. His scholarly relatives were: his brothers 'Uthmān ibn Abī Shayba and al-Qāsim ibn Abī Shayba; his son Ibrāhīm ibn Abī Bakr ibn Abī Shayba; and his nephew Abū Ja'far Muḥammad ibn 'Uthmān ibn Abī Shayba. All are ḥadīth Masters except al-Qāsim, who is weak.

'Abd Allāh ibn Abī Shayba took ḥadīth from Sharīk ibn 'Abd Allāh al-Qāḍī at age fourteen, Ibn al-Mubārak, Sufyān ibn 'Uyayna, Hushaym ibn Bashīr, Wakī' ibn al-Jarrāḥ, Yaḥyā al-Qaṭṭān, Ismā'īl ibn 'Ayyāsh, Ismā'īl ibn 'Ulayya, and other major authorities. From him took al-Bukhārī and Muslim, Abū Dāwūd, Ibn Mājah, Aḥmad ibn Ḥanbal, Abū Zur'a, Ibn Abī 'Āṣim, Baqī ibn Makhlad, al-Bāghandī, Abū Ya'lā al-Mawṣilī, Ṣāliḥ Jazara, 'Abdān, Abū al-Qāsim al-Baghawī, and others.

Ibn Abī Shayba showed hostility to Abū Ḥanīfa ﷺ as he named one of the longest chapters of his *Muṣannaf* "Book of the Refutation of Abū Ḥanīfa" in which he proceeded to list about one hundred and twenty five "Prophetic ḥadīths which Abū Ḥanīfa contradicted."[857] This charge, together with Ibn Abī Shayba's refutation, is refuted in detail in the books of Imām Muḥammad Zāhid al-Kawtharī among others, particularly *al-Nukat al-Ṭarīfa fil-Taḥadduth 'an Rudūd Ibn Abī Shayba 'alā Abī Ḥanīfa* ("The Witty Anecdotes in Discussing Ibn Abī Shayba's Rebuttals of Abū Ḥanīfa"). The *Muṣannaf*, however, remains a precious mine of information on the legal positions of the Companions and Successors.

Ibn Abī Shayba narrates in the chapter entitled: "Touching the grave of the Prophet" with a *ṣaḥīḥ* chain according to Ibn Ḥajar and al-Qāḍī 'Iyāḍ in *al-Shifā* (in the chapter entitled: "Concerning the visit to the Prophet's grave ﷺ, the excellence of those who visit it and how he should be greeted"):

> Yazīd ibn 'Abd al-Mālik ibn Qusayṭ and al-'Utbī narrated that it was the practice of the Companions in the mosque of the Prophet ﷺ to place their hands on the pommel of the hand rail (*rummāna*) of the pulpit (*minbar*) where the Prophet ﷺ used to place his hand. There they would face the *Qibla* and supplicate to Allāh ﷻ hoping He would answer their supplication because they were placing their hands where the Prophet ﷺ placed his

[857] Ibn Abī Shayba (7:277-325).

while making their supplication. Abū Mawdūda said: "And I saw Yazīd ibn 'Abd al-Mālik do the same."[858]

It is also narrated that Ibn 'Umar would place his hand on the seat of the Prophet's *minbar* then wipe his face with it[859] and that Abū Ayyūb was seen resting his face on the Prophet's ﷺ grave.[860] This practice of the Companions clarifies two matters. The first is the permissibility of asking Allāh for things by the Prophet ﷺ after his death since by their act the Companions were truly making *tawassul.* Likewise it is permissible to ask Allāh ﷻ for things by means of other pious Muslims. The second is the permissibility of *tabarruk* or seeking blessing (*baraka*) from objects connected to the Prophet ﷺ.

It is similarly related that in the year of the drought called al-Ramāda (17-18) during the successorship of 'Umar, the Companion Bilāl ibn al-Ḥārith ؓ, while slaughtering a sheep for his kin, noticed that the sheep's bones had turned red because the drying flesh was clinging to them. He cried out *"Yā Muḥammadāh!"* Then he saw the Prophet ﷺ in a dream ordering him to go to 'Umar with the tidings of coming rain on condition that 'Umar show wisdom. Hearing this, 'Umar assembled the people and came out to pray for rain with al-'Abbās, the uncle of the Prophet ﷺ.[861]

The same is related from the *mukhaḍram* (Companion or Successor) Mālik ibn 'Iyāḍ, also known as Mālik al-Dār:[862] A man came to the grave of the Prophet ﷺ and said: "Messenger of Allāh, ask

858 Ibn Abī Shayba (4:121).

859 Ibn Qudāma, *al-Mughnī* (5:468) and al-Buhūtī, *Kashshāf*; (2:517) cf. al-Mardāwī, *Inṣāf* (4:54), Ibn Mufliḥ, *Furū'* (3:523). Ibn Bāz had the effrontery to call this act *shirk.*

860 Narrated by Aḥmad (38:558 §23585 *"isnād ḍa'īf"*) and al-Ḥākim (4:515=1990 ed. 4:560 *ṣaḥīḥ*), both with an inconclusive chain because of Dāwūd ibn Abī Ṣāliḥ who is unknown although no one deemed him weak cf. al-Haythamī (4:2); hence Majd al-Dīn Ibn Taymiyya adduces it in *al-Muntaqā* (2:261) as do Shaykh al-Islām al-Subkī in *Shifā' al-Siqām* (p. 126) and al-Samhūdī in *Wafā al-Wafā'* (4:1359).

861 Narrated by al-Ṭabarī in his *Tārīkh* (2:509).

862 "'Umar ibn al-Khaṭṭāb's freedman. He narrated from Abū Bakr and 'Umar. He was known." Ibn Sa'd (5:12). "He is agreed upon (as trustworthy), the Successors have approved highly of him." Abū Ya'lā al-Khalīl ibn 'Abd Allāh al-Khalīlī al-Qazwīnī, *Kitāb al-Irshād fī Ma'rifat 'Ulama' al-Ḥadīth,* as quoted in 'Abd Allāh al-Ghumārī in *Irghām al-Mubtadi' al-Ghabī bi-Jawāz al-Tawassul bil-Nabī,* ed. Ḥasan al-Saqqāf, 2nd ed. (Amman: Dār al-Imām al-Nawawī, 1992 p. 9). "Mālik ibn 'Iyāḍ: 'Umar's freedman. He is the one named Mālik al-Dār. He saw the Prophet ﷺ and heard narrations from Abū Bakr al-Ṣiddīq. He narrated from Abū Bakr and 'Umar, Mu'ādh, and Abū 'Ubayda ibn al-

for rain for your Community (*istasqi li-ummatik*), for verily they have but perished!" after which the Prophet ﷺ appeared to him in a dream telling him: "Go to 'Umar and give him my greeting, then tell him that they will have water. Tell him: Be clever!" The man went and told 'Umar. The latter wept and said: "My Lord! I spare no effort except in what escapes my power!"[863] Ibn Ḥajar identifies Mālik al-Dār as 'Umar's treasurer and the man who visited and saw the Prophet ﷺ in his dream as the Companion Bilāl ibn al-Ḥārith, counting this ḥadīth among the reasons for al-Bukhārī's naming of the chapter "The people's request to their leader for rain if they suffer drought."

'Abd Allāh ibn Abī Shayba should not be confused with the anthropomorphist forger, his nephew Abū Ja'far Muḥammad ibn 'Uthmān ibn Abī Shayba[864] (d. 297) the teacher of Abū Bakr al-Najjād and author of *Kitāb al-'Arsh* ("Book of the Throne") in which he states:

> All of creation concurs that whenever they supplicate Allāh ﷻ they raise their hands to the sky. If Allāh ﷻ were in the lowest earth they would not have raised up their hands up to the sky since He would be with them on the earth. Furthermore, the reports are mass-narrated that Allāh ﷻ created the Throne then established Himself over it with His Essence (*bi-dhātih*),[865]

Jarrāḥ. From him narrated Abū Ṣāliḥ al-Samān and his (Mālik's) two sons 'Awn and 'Abd Allāh [...]" *Iṣāba* (6:164 §8350 Mālik ibn 'Iyāḍ).

[863] Ibn Kathīr cites it thus from al-Bayhaqī's *Dalā'il al-Nubuwwa* (7:47) in *al-Bidāya* (Ma'ārif ed. 7:91-92=Dār Iḥyā' al-Turāth ed. 7:105) saying: "*isnāduhu ṣaḥīḥ*" and he also declares its chain sound (*isnāduhu jayyidun qawī*) in his *Jāmi' al-Masānīd* (1:223) in *Musnad 'Umar*. Ibn Abī Shayba cites it (6:352= 12:31-32) with a sound (*ṣaḥīḥ*) chain as confirmed by Ibn Ḥajar who says: "*rawā Ibn Abī Shayba bi-isnādin ṣaḥīḥ*" and cites the ḥadīth in *Fatḥ al-Bārī*, Book of *istisqā'*, ch. 3 (1989 ed. 2:629-630= 1959 ed. 2:495) as well as in *al-Iṣāba* (6:164 §8350=3:484) where he says that Ibn Abī Khaythama cited it. It is also narrated by al-Khalīlī in *al-Irshād* (1:313-314) and Ibn 'Abd al-Barr in *al-Istī'āb* (2:464=3:1149). Al-Albānī attempted to weaken this report in his *al-Tawassul* (p. 120) but was refuted in the lengthy analysis given by Mamdūḥ in *Raf' al-Mināra* (p. 262-278), which refutes other similar attempts; cf. Ibn Bāz's marginalia on *Fatḥ al-Bārī*, Abū Bakr al-Jazā'irī's tract *Wa-Jā'ū Yarkuḍūn*, Ḥammād al-Anṣārī's articles "*al-Mafhūm al-Ṣaḥīḥ lil-Tawassul*" also entitled "*Tuḥfat al-Qārī fil-Radd 'alā al-Ghumārī*," and other such literature.

[864] He was declared a liar by 'Abd Allāh ibn Aḥmad ibn Ḥanbal and a forger by 'Abd al-Raḥmān ibn Khirāsh, cf. *Mīzān* (3:642), *Siyar* (11:120 §2532), and *Lisān* (5:317).

[865] See our article, "The Innovated Phrase, 'In Person'." Al-Dhahabī suppressed the phrase when citing this passage in *al-'Ulūw* (p. 494 §103) = *Mukhtaṣar* (p. 220 §103).

following which He created the earth and the heavens, so He turned (*fa-ṣāra*) from the earth to the heaven and from the heaven to the Throne. Therefore, He is above the heavens and above the Throne with His essence, wholly distinct (*mutakhalliṣan*) from His creation and separate (*bā'in*) from them.[866]

IBN RĀHŪYAH[867]

Isḥāq ibn Ibrāhīm ibn Makhlad, known as Isḥāq ibn Rāhūyah ﷺ (per the *Muḥaddithūn*) or Rāhawayh (per the grammarians), Abū Ya'qūb al-Tamīmī al-Marwazī al-Ḥanẓalī (d. 238)was one of the major ḥadīth Masters. Abū Qudāma considered him greater than Imām Aḥmad in memorization of ḥadīth, a remarkable assessment considering Aḥmad's knowledge of 700,000 to a million narrations according to his son 'Abd Allāh's and Abū Zur'a al-Rāzī's estimations. Aḥmad himself named him "Commander of the Believers in Ḥadīth," the highest grade in ḥadīth Mastership, owned by no more than thirty Masters in Islamic history. He once said of himself: "I never wrote anything without memorizing it, and I can now see before me more than 70,000 ḥadīths in my book"; "I know the place of 100,000 ḥadīths as if I were looking at them, and I have memorised 70,000 of them by heart – all sound (*ṣaḥīḥa*) – and 4,000 falsified ones."[868] He did not reach the same stature in *fiqh*. Al-Bayhaqī and others narrate that he debated with al-Shāfi'ī on a legal question, after which the latter disapproved of his title as the "Jurisprudent of Khurāsān."

To a Jahmī scholar who said: "I disbelieve in a Lord that descends from one heaven to another heaven," Ibn Rāhūyah replied: "I believe in a Lord that does what He wishes."[869] Al-Bayhaqī comments: "Isḥāq ibn Ibrāhīm al-Ḥanẓalī made it clear, in this report, that he considers the Descent (*al-nuzūl*) one of the Attributes of Action (*min ṣifāt al-fi'l*). Secondly, he spoke of a descent without 'how'. This proves he did not hold the theory displacement (*al-intiqāl*) and movement from one

[866] Abū Ja'far ibn Abī Shayba, *Kitāb al-'Arsh wa-Mā Ruwiya Fīh*, ed. Muḥammad ibn Ḥamd al-Ḥammūd (Kuwait: Maktabat al-Ma'allā, 1986) p. 51.

[867] Sources: Ibn Abī Ya'lā, *Ṭabaqāt al-Ḥanābila* (1:6, 1:184); al-Bayhaqī, *Manāqib al-Shāfi'ī* (1:213) and *al-Asmā' wal-Ṣifāt* (2:375-376 §951); al-Dhahabī, *Siyar* (9:558 §1877); Ibn al-Subkī, *Ṭabaqāt al-Shāfi'iyya al-Kubrā* (2:89-90, 9:81).

[868] Narrated by al-Khaṭīb in *al-Jāmi' li-Akhlāq al-Rāwī* (2:380-381 §1832-1833).

[869] Narrated by al-Dhahabī who identifies the scholar as Ibrāhīm ibn (Hishām) Abī Ṣāliḥ, cf. *Mukhtaṣar al-'Ulūw* (p. 191 §234).

place to another (*al-zawāl*) concerning it."[870]

Both al-Qāsim ibn Sallām and Ibn Rāhūyah were teachers of Ibn Qutayba.

AL-BUKHĀRĪ[871]

Muḥammad ibn Ismā'īl ibn Ibrāhīm ibn al-Mughīra ibn Bardizbah, Abū 'Abd Allāh al-Ju'fī al-Bukhārī ﵀ (194-256)was "the Imām of the Muslims, the examplar of those who declare the Oneness of God, the Shaykh of the believers, he who is relied upon concerning the sayings of the Master of Messengers, the keeper of the rule of Religion, Abū 'Abd Allāh al-Ju'fī al-Bukhārī, the author of *al-Jāmi' al-Ṣaḥīḥ* ('The Compendium of Sound Narrations')." His ḥadīth-dictation lesson in Baghdād numbered twenty thousand listeners.[872] Towards the end of his life he fell victim to the envy of his enemies and was hounded out of his native Bukhārā, then out of Naysābūr, then out of Samarqand, until he died in loneliness in the small village of Khartenk near Samarqand. Aḥmad ibn Ḥafṣ narrated from him and said: "I went into his house to see him before he died and he said to me: 'I do not know in all my possessions of a single dirham the licitness of which I am unsure about.' When I heard this, I was humbled to my soul."

Al-Bukhārī was born in 194 and was raised an orphan. The beginning of his study of ḥadīth was in 205 at which time he began memorizing the compilations of Ibn al-Mubārak and Wakī' ibn al-Jarrāḥ, probably covering the *fiqh* of Abū Ḥanīfa and Sufyān al-Thawrī in the process. He began to travel in 210 after having studied ḥadīth from many people in his own land of Bukhārā. He travelled to Balkh, Marw, Naysābūr, Rayy, Baghdād, Baṣra, Kūfa, Madīna, and Makka, where he heard from 'Abd Allāh ibn al-Zubayr al-Ḥumaydī – al-Shāfi'ī's student – receiving al-Shāfi'ī's *fiqh* from him as well as from al-Za'farānī, Abū Thawr, and al-Karābīsī. Ibn al-Subkī therefore included him among the scholars of the Shāfi'ī School while Ibn Abī

870 Al-Bayhaqī, *Asmā'* (2:375-376 §951). See our article, "The 'Descent' of Allāh ﷻ" in *Sunna Notes: The Divine Names and Attributes*. Cf. n. 670. See the ḥadīth p. 168.

871 Main sources: al-Nawawī, *Tahdhīb al-Asmā' wal-Lughāt* (1:67-76 §3); Ibn al-Subkī, *Ṭabaqāt al-Shāfi'iyya al-Kubrā* (2:212-241 §50); al-Dhahabī, *Siyar* (10:277-321 §2136).

872 Narrated from Abū 'Alī Ṣāliḥ ibn Muḥammad al-Baghdādī by al-Sam'ānī in *Adab al-Imlā' wal-Istimlā'* (p. 17).

Ya'lā includes him in his *Ṭabaqāt al-Ḥanābila.*

In truth, al-Bukhārī was neither Shāfi'ī nor Ḥanbalī but a *mujtahid muṭlaq* with his own *madhhab* which did not survive him as he was uninterested in other than his *Ṣaḥīḥ* for a school, and the *Ṣaḥīḥ* is a complex and concise *fiqh* manual. Muslim was al-Bukhārī's close student and probably followed his *madhhab* but he was definitely a *mujtahid murajjiḥ* – one with full knowledge of *ijmā'* and *khilāf*, competent to evaluate all the pre-existing juridical conclusions of the Schools of the Companions and *Tābi'īn* and choose the most correct in his view. Al-Tirmidhī was also al-Bukhārī's close student and a *mujtahid murajjiḥ* and comparatist of the first rank whose method and school, like al-Bukhārī's, are developed in his book – the *Jāmi'* – not only in the chapter-titles like al-Bukhārī, but in the bodies of the chapters themselves and in more explicit terms than his teacher, both he and Muslim being hugely indebted to al-Bukhārī in their achievement.[873] Abū Dāwūd was a student of Imām Aḥmad whose *madhhab* he followed. Al-Nasā'ī was without doubt a Shāfi'ī. The Two Shaykhs and the compilers of the Sunan are correctly called *Ahl al-Ḥadīth* because they focussed primarily on ḥadīth and its sciences, whereas their counterpart, *Ahl al-Ra'y* – such as Imāms Mālik, Abū Ḥanīfa and their students – emphasised jurisprudence over ḥadīth narration. Ibn Qutayba in *al-Ma'ārif* also included Ibn Abī Laylā, al-Awzā'ī, Sufyān al-Thawrī, and Rabī'a in the latter category. However, there is no such thing as "The School of *Ahl al-Ḥadīth*" in the singular, nor "The School of *Ahl al-Ra'y*" unless one specifically means the Ḥanafī *madhhab*, as in the phrase *Ahl al-Kūfa.* Imām al-Shāfi'ī, by the grace of Allāh, united with near-perfection the two currents of Ḥadīth and *Ra'y*, and so did his students such as al-Muzanī and Abū Thawr. Hence, Ulema such as 'Abd al-Raḥmān ibn Mahdī could not find enough words to praise his intelligence, and the vast majority of the Imāms of ḥadīth and ḥadīth Masters after his time follow the Shāfi'ī *madhhab* beginning with al-Dāraquṭnī, Ibn Abī Ḥātim and his father, al-Baghawī, Ibn Khuzayma, Ibn Ḥibbān, al-Khaṭīb, and others, while al-Ṭabarī, Dāwūd al-Ẓāhirī, al-Ṭaḥāwī, Ibn Ḥazm, and Ibn 'Ābidīn began as Shāfi'īs.

Al-Bukhārī also took ḥadīth from innumerable transmitters in Damascus, Caesarea, 'Asqalān, and Ḥimṣ. He mentioned that he heard from a thousand shaykhs in all. Ja'far ibn Muḥammad al-Qaṭṭān

[873] See 'Itr, *al-Imām al-Tirmidhī wal-Muwāzana bayna Jāmi'ihi wa-bayn al-Ṣaḥīḥayn.*

said: "I heard Muḥammad ibn Ismā'īl say: 'I wrote ḥadīth from 1,000 shaykhs or more, from each of them 10,000 ḥadīths or more, and I have not taken a single ḥadīth without remembering its chain of transmission.'"

He related ḥadīth to the Scholars of that science in the Ḥijāz, 'Iraq, Khurāsān, and Transoxiana, "with hardly a hair on his face." Among those that related ḥadīth from him were: Abū Zur'a, Abū Ḥātim al-Rāzī, al-Tirmidhī, Muslim (outside his *Ṣaḥīḥ*), Abū Naṣr al-Marwazī, Ṣāliḥ ibn Muḥammad Jazara, and Ibn Khuzayma. Ibn Abī Ḥātim said: "Abū Zur'a and my father [Abū Ḥatim] stopped narrating from him because of the question of the pronunciation of the Qur'ān."[874] Al-Dhahabī said: "Whether they narrated from him or stopped narrating from him he is the Imām of the world in ḥadīth." Ibrāhīm [ibn Aḥmad ibn Ismā'īl] al-Khawwāṣ said: "I saw Abū Zur'a sitting like a boy at the feet of Muḥammad ibn Ismā'īl, asking him questions about what makes a ḥadīth weak." Al-Khaṭīb al-Baghdādī said: "Al-'Abbās ibn al-Faḍl al-Rāzī al-Ṣāyigh was asked: 'Who has memorised more, Abū Zur'a or al-Bukhārī?' He replied: 'I met al-Bukhārī between Ḥulwān and Baghdād and I travelled with him for a while. I tried my best to mention one ḥadīth that he did not know but could not. I can puzzle Abū Zur'a as many times as I have hairs on my body!'"

Ibn 'Adī said: I heard al-Bazzār say: I saw al-Bukhārī in his old age. He was thin, neither tall nor short. He lived sixty-two years less thirteen days. Aḥmad ibn al-Faḍl al-Balkhī said: When he was young he lost his eyesight. His mother saw the Prophet Ibrāhīm ﷺ in her dream, and he said to her: 'Allāh has returned your son his eyesight due to your profuse weeping' or 'due to your many supplications'.

Al-Bukhārī said to Abū Ja'far Muḥammad ibn Abī Ḥātim al-Warrāq: "I learned the books of Ibn al-Mubārak and Wakī' and knew their sayings by heart at age sixteen. When I turned eighteen, I began to compile the deeds of the Companions and Successors and their sayings at the time of 'Ubayd Allāh ibn Mūsā. I compiled *Kitāb al-Tārīkh* ("Biographical History") by the grave of the Prophet ﷺ during moonlit nights. For almost every name in Islamic history I have mentioned a story in connection with it, yet I disliked to make the book too long." Al-Dhahabī said that al-Bukhārī's *Tārīkh* comprises over 40,000 biographical notices, his *al-Ḍu'afā'* under 700, while his *Ṣaḥīḥ* uses the

[874] See Appendix titled, "The Controversy over the Pronunciation of the Qur'ān."

reports of under 2,000 narrators, which al-Dhahabī said showed that the *Ṣaḥīḥ* is abridged in the extreme.

Al-Bukhārī said: "Whoever compiles a book should begin it with the ḥadīth: 'Actions count only according to intentions.'"[875] The same position is related from 'Abd al-Raḥmān ibn Mahdī,[876] while one of 'Abdān's students saw the Prophet ﷺ in his sleep advising that 'Abdān begin his book with the ḥadīth: "Allāh brighten the face of him among His servants who hears my words, remembers them, guards them, and transmits them. Many a transmitter of knowledge does not himself understand it, and many may transmit knowledge to others who are more versed in it than they."[877]

'Umar ibn Ḥafṣ al-Ashqar said: "We were in Baṣra writing ḥadīth. One day we visited him and we found him in a house naked. He had exhausted all his resources. We chipped in and clothed him." Al-Warrāq said: "I heard Muḥammad ibn Ismā'īl say: 'It is not right for a Muslim to face a difficulty and not be granted his supplication if he supplicates.' I heard him say once: 'I travelled to see Ādam ibn Abī Iyās and ran out of money. I began to eat grass without telling anyone. On the third day a stranger came up to me and handed me a purse full of dinars saying: 'Spend this on yourself.'''"

'Abd al-Raḥmān ibn Muḥammad al-Bukhārī said: I heard Muḥammad ibn Ismā'īl say: "I met more than a thousand men from Ḥijāz, Iraq, Shām, Egypt, Khurāsān," and so on until he said: "I never saw a single one of them differ on the following: 'Religion consists in words and deeds, and the Qur'ān is the Speech of Allāh.'" The first half of the statement is directed against the *Murji'a* and the doctrine of Imām Abū Ḥanīfa that deeds are the complement and not the essence of *īmān* – against whom al-Bukhārī directs many of the chapter-headings of his *Ṣaḥīḥ*[878] – while the second half is directed against the Jahmiyya and Mu'tazila.

Al-Warrāq said he heard Ḥāshid ibn Ismā'īl and another say: "Al-Bukhārī used to come with us to the ḥadīth sessions when he was a boy. He would not write anything. After a while we mentioned it to him. He said: 'You pressure me too much; show me what you have

875 See n. 217.

876 Both are narrated by al-Khaṭīb in *al-Jāmi' li-Akhlāq al-Rāwī* (2:463 §1984-1985).

877 In al-Khaṭīb, *al-Jāmi'* (2:464 §1987). On the ḥadīth see n. 718.

878 See the chapter entitled "Sunnī *Irjā*" in the chapter of Abū Ḥanīfa.

written.' We produced what we had, which was more than 15,000 ḥadīths. He recited them all to us from memory, until we took to correcting what we had according to his recital. Then he said: 'Am I studying in vain, or wasting my time?' At that time we realised that no one could better him." They continued: "The people of knowledge used to put him forward in the study of ḥadīth when he was but a young man, even against his will. They would make him sit by the roadside until thousands would gather around him. Most of them would write his narrations. He was still beardless." Al-Warrāq said: I heard Sālim ibn Mujāhid say: I was visiting Muḥammad ibn Salām al-Bīkandī and he said to me: "If you had come earlier you would have seen a boy who has memorised 70,000 ḥadīths." I went out looking for him. When I found him I said: "Are you the one who says: I have memorised 70,000 ḥadīths?" He said: "Yes, and more than that, and I will not cite you a ḥadīth from the Companions or Successors without knowing the date and place of birth of most of them and that of their death, and where they lived. Nor do I narrate any of them save what I know for certain to be based on a principle of the Religion from the book of Allāh or the Sunna of His Messenger."[879]

Al-Bukhārī interpreted the "Face" (*wajh*) of Allāh to mean His dominion or sovereignty (*mulk*) in the verse ﴾**Everything will perish save His countenance**﴿ (28:88), as shown by his statement in the book of *Tafsīr* in his *Ṣaḥīḥ*: "Except His *wajh* means except His *mulk*, and it is also said: Except whatever was for the sake of His countenance."[880]

He also interpreted the laughter of Allāh ﷻ in the ḥadīth "Last night Allāh laughed or was astonished [the narrator hesitated] at what you two did"[881] to mean good pleasure. Ibn Ḥajar states that he did not see this in the manuscripts of al-Bukhārī which have reached him but al-Bayhaqī states that it is narrated from al-Bukhārī by his student al-Firabrī. Ibn al-Jawzī explains the laughter of Allāh as His generosity (*karam*) and favour (*faḍl*) while quoting al-Marwazī's relation from Imām Aḥmad that the latter explained the laughter of Allāh as His abundant generosity (*kathrat al-karam*) and vast good pleasure

879 Meaning he was not merely a memorizer but knew the *fiqh* of each ḥadīth. Ibn Ḥibbān considered weak any ḥadīth Master that did not know the *fiqh* of the ḥadīths he narrated, cf. Ibn Rajab, *Sharḥ 'Ilal al-Tirmidhī, al-riwāya bil-ma'nā.*

880 Cf. al-Bayhaqī's explanations in his section on the *Wajh* in *al-Asmā' wal-Ṣifāt*.

881 Narrated from Abū Hurayra by al-Bukhārī and Muslim.

(*sa'at al-riḍā*). Ibn 'Abd al-Salām states the same in his *Ishāra ilāl-Ījāz fī Ba'ḍ Anwā' al-Majāẓ*. Al-Nawawī in *Sharḥ Ṣaḥīḥ Muslim* cites Qāḍī 'Iyāḍ as explaining it as a metaphor (*isti'āra*) for good pleasure, bestowal of reward (*thawāb*), and love (*maḥabba*). 'Iyāḍ added that another possible meaning is that the laughter here is that of the angels of Allāh in charge of seizing the souls of the two men and leading them to Paradise. This is also the interpretation favoured by Ibn Ḥibbān.[882] Al-Bīkandī said: "Muḥammad ibn Ismā'īl came to see us and we gathered around him. One of us said: 'I heard Isḥāq ibn Rāhūyah say: "I have recorded about 70,000 ḥadīths."' Muḥammad said: 'Does this surprise you? There may be in our own time someone who has recorded 200,000 ḥadīths.' This is what he himself had done." Ibn 'Adī narrated from Muḥammad ibn Ḥamdūyah: "I heard Muḥammad ibn Ismā'īl say: 'I know by memory 100,000 *ṣaḥīḥ* ḥadīths, and 200,000 non-*ṣaḥīḥ* ḥadīths." Someone said: "I was visiting Muḥammad ibn Salām al-Bīkandī, at which time Muḥammad ibn Ismā'īl entered. After he went out again, Muḥammad ibn Salām said: 'Every time this boy comes to see me I become perplexed, and the matter of ḥadīth becomes full of ambiguities for me. I remain afraid (to speak) until he leaves!'"

Aḥmad ibn Ḥanbal said: "The pinnacle of memorization is in four people of Khurāsān: Abū Zur'a, Muḥammad ibn Ismā'īl, ['Abd Allāh ibn 'Abd al-Raḥmān] al-Dārimī, and al-Ḥasan ibn Shujā' al-Balkhī." Ibn Khuzayma said: "I never saw under the sky more knowledgeable a person in ḥadīth than Muḥammad ibn Ismā'īl al-Bukhārī." Al-Ḥākim narrated from Aḥmad ibn Ḥamdūn: "I heard Muslim ibn al-Ḥajjāj say, as he came to see al-Bukhārī, after kissing his forehead: 'Allow me to kiss your feet, Teacher of teachers, rampart of ḥadīth scholars, and physician of the ḥadīth in its minute defects!'"

Ibn 'Adī said: "A number of shaykhs heard that al-Bukhārī was coming to Baghdād. They chose 100 ḥadīths and shuffled their chains of transmission and texts, giving each text a different chain. Each took ten of these ḥadīths and prepared to test al-Bukhārī with them during their gathering. The people assembled, and one of the scholars confronted al-Bukhārī with one of these ḥadīths. He replied: "I do not

[882] Ibn Ḥajar, *Fatḥ al-Bārī* (3:383n.); al-Bayhaqī, *al-Asmā' wal-Ṣifāt* (Kawtharī ed. p. 298; Ḥāshidī ed. 2:72); Ibn al-Jawzī. *Daf' Shubah al-Tashbīh* (1998, al-Kawtharī repr. p. 45-46); al-Nawawī, *Sharḥ Ṣaḥīḥ Muslim* (13:36); Ibn Ḥibbān (10:522).

know it." Then he asked him about another. He replied "I do not know it." Then another: "I do not know it." And so forth until he finished his ten. Those in the know looked at each other saying: "The man understands." The rest thought he knew nothing. Then another scholar read his ten, then another his ten, then another until they read 100 ḥadīths and al-Bukhārī kept saying each time: "I do not know it; I do not know it." When he saw that they had finished, he turned to the first scholar and said: "The correct chain of your first ḥadīth is such-and-such; the correct chain of your second ḥadīth is [...]" then he turned to the second scholar, then the third, and so on with every single one of the one hundred ḥadīths. At that time the people concurred that he was a ḥadīth Master (*ḥāfiẓ*)."

Muḥammad ibn Yūsuf al-Bukhārī said: "I was visiting Muḥammad ibn Ismā'īl in his house that night. I counted that he got up and lit his lamp eighteen times to remind himself or jot down something during the night." Al-Warrāq said: "When I travelled with Abū 'Abd Allāh, if we happened to sleep in the same house, I would see him get up in the same night between fifteen and twenty times. Every time he would light his candle and document narrations. Then he would lay his head down again. Around the time before dawn entered he would pray thirteen *rak'as*. He would never wake me up. I said to him once: "You endure all this yourself. Why do you not wake me up?" He replied: "You are a young man and I dislike to ruin your sleep."[883]

Ibrāhīm ibn Ma'qil said: I heard him (Muḥammad ibn Ismā'īl al-Bukhārī) say: "I was with Isḥāq ibn Rāhūyah when a man said: 'Why do you not compile an epitome (*mukhtaṣar*) of the prophetic ways?' This stayed with me, and was the reason why I compiled this book (the *Ṣaḥīḥ*)."[884] Al-Dhahabī said: "It has been narrated through two firm

[883] Ḍamra ibn Rabī'a said: "We went on pilgrimage with al-Awzā'ī in the year 150, and I never saw him lying down in the camel-top bench (*al-maḥmil*) in the day nor in the night. He would pray, and, if overcome by sleep, would lean back against the pole." Cited by al-Dhahabī in the *Siyar* (1997 ed. 7:94).

[884] M.M. A'ẓamī writes: "Al-Bukhārī did not claim that what he left out were the spurious, nor that there were no authentic traditions outside his collection. On the contrary, he said: 'I only included in my book *al-Jāmi'* those that were authentic, and I left out many more authentic traditions than this to avoid unnecessary length.' He had no intention of collecting all the authentic traditions. He only wanted to compile a manual of ḥadīth according to the wishes of his shaykh Isḥāq ibn Rāhūyah, and his function is quite clear from the title of his book *al-Jāmi' al-Musnad al-Ṣaḥīḥ al-Mukhtaṣar min Umūr Rasūl Allāh wa-*

channels of transmission that al-Bukhārī said: 'I extracted this book from about 600,000 ḥadīths, and I compiled it over sixteen years, and I made it a plea for what lies between myself and Allāh.'"[885] Al-Firabrī said: Muḥammad ibn Ismā'īl said to me: "I never included in the *Ṣaḥīḥ* a ḥadīth without making a major ablution (*ghusl*) and praying two *rak'as* beforehand."

Al-Nawawī said: "The scholars have agreed that the soundest of all ḥadīth compilations are the two *Ṣaḥīḥs* of al-Bukhārī and Muslim, and their vast majority have agreed that the soundest and most beneficial of the two was al-Bukhārī's." He continued: "The totality of its ḥadīths are 7,275 with the repetitions and about 4,000 without."

ARE THE TWO ṢAḤĪḤS 100% ṢAḤĪḤ?

In *Kitāb al-Tatabbu'* al-Dāraquṭnī argues for the weakness of 78 ḥadīths in al-Bukhārī, 100 in Muslim, and 32 in both based mostly on chain (*isnād*) criticism. Yet al-Nawawī said: "The two *Ṣaḥīḥs* differ from all other books only with respect to the fact that what is in them is *ṣaḥīḥ* and does not require investigation."[886] Ibn al-Ṣalāḥ said: "Whatever only al-Bukhārī or only Muslim narrates enters [also] into the category of what is definitely *ṣaḥīḥ* [...] except a few words which some of the expert critics objected to, such as al-Dāraquṭnī and others – and these are known to the specialists."[887] He said this after stating that what they agree upon is "definitely *ṣaḥīḥ*" (*maqṭū'un bi-ṣiḥḥatihi*) for the *Umma*.

Imām al-Nawawī objected to the terms "definitely *ṣaḥīḥ*" while granting all that is in the *Ṣaḥīḥayn* the level of "strongly presumed

---

Sunanihi, wa-Ayyāmih ("The Compendium of Sound Narrations Linked Back With Uninterrupted Chains Epitomizing the Matters of the Messenger of Allāh, His Ways, and His Times"). The word *al-mukhtaṣar*, epitome, itself explains that al-Bukhārī did not make any attempt at a comprehensive collection." *Studies in Early Ḥadīth Literature* (p. 304-305). This should be understood by those who ask: "If ḥadīth x is not in al-Bukhārī nor Muslim then how can it be authentic?"

885 Narrated by al-Khaṭīb, *al-Jāmi' li-Akhlāq al-Rāwī* (2:270-271 §1613).

886 Introduction to his *Sharḥ Ṣaḥīḥ Muslim* (1:20): "*Innamā yaftariqu al-Ṣaḥīḥāni 'an ghayrihimā min al-kutub fī kawni mā fīhimā ṣaḥīḥan lā yuḥtāju ilā al-naẓari fīh.*"

887 Ibn al-Ṣalāḥ, *'Ulūm al-Ḥadīth*, chapter on the *ṣaḥīḥ* ḥadīth (Dār al-Fikr ed. p. 29): "*Mā infarada bihi al-Bukhārī aw Muslimun mundarijun fī qābili mā yuqṭa'u biṣiḥḥatihi... siwā aḥrufin yasīratin takallama 'alayhā ba'ḍu ahli al-naqdi min al-ḥuffāẓ kal-Dāraquṭnī wa-ghayrih, wa-hiya ma'rūfatun 'inda ahli hādha al-sha'n.*"

(*ṣaḥīḥ*) as long as it is not *mutawātir*" (*yufīdu al-ẓanna mā lam yatawātar*) as is the rule with all *ṣaḥīḥ* lone-narrated (*āḥād*) ḥadīths.[888] However, Ibn Kathīr differed: "I am with Ibn al-Ṣalāḥ in his conclusion and directives, and Allāh knows best."[889] Al-Suyūṭī in *Tadrīb al-Rāwī* cites Ibn Kathīr's words verbatim, then states: "And this is also my choice and none other."[890] This is because of the standing of the two *Ṣaḥīḥs* in the *Umma* and because none of the past Imāms in Islām ever declared explicitly and rightly that all they had gathered in their respective books was *ṣaḥīḥ* except al-Bukhārī and Muslim, and the verifying experts have confirmed their claim. Al-Suyūṭī also states:

> Shaykh al-Islām said: "What al-Nawawī mentioned in *Sharḥ Ṣaḥīḥ Muslim* is based on the perspective of the majority (*al-aktharīn*); as for that of the verifying authorities (*al-muḥaqqiqūn*), then no. For the verifying authorities also agree with Ibn al-Ṣalāḥ."[891]

By "Shaykh al-Islām" al-Suyūṭī means the spotless *Ḥāfiz* and immaculate Imām Ibn Ḥajar al-'Asqalānī and his book *al-Nukat 'alā Ibn al-Ṣalāḥ*.[892] Al-Suyūṭī goes on to quote in detail – mostly from *Hady al-Sārī* – the refutations of Ibn Ḥajar of al-Dāraquṭnī's criticism, showing that, in effect, the latter fails to invalidate the view of the *Ṣaḥīḥayn* as 100% ṣaḥīḥ.

The fact is that they are all *ṣaḥīḥ*, but not all of them reach the same

[888] Al-Nawawī, *Taqrīb wal-Taysīr* (p. 70) and *Sharḥ Ṣaḥīḥ Muslim* (1:20).

[889] Ibn Kathīr, chapter on the *ṣaḥīḥ* ḥadīth of his *Ikhtiṣār 'Ulūm al-Ḥadīth* (p. 45).

[890] Al-Suyūṭī, *Tadrīb al-Rāwī* (Dār al-Kalim al-Ṭayyib ed. 1:145).

[891] *Tadrīb al-Rāwī* (1:143).

[892] Cf. Ibn Ḥajar, *al-Nukat 'alā Ibn al-Ṣalāḥ* (1:371). See also his words from his *Sharḥ Nukhbat al-Fikar* (p. 230-231) to the effect that the foremost ḥadīth expert's examination of and familiarity with any given *āḥād* ḥadīth may take him to the conclusion that it is *qaṭ'ī al-thubūt* – categorically established as *ṣaḥīḥ*, i.e. in effect of *mutawātir*-like authenticity – unlike the feel of the rest of the scholars with regard to the same ḥadīth. The knowledge of the expert is named by Dr. 'Itr, after Ibn al-Ṣalāḥ, "non-absolutely-binding inductive knowledge reaching certainty" (*al-'ilm al-naẓarī al-yaqīnī ghayr al-ḍarūrī*) and he places it midway between *al-'ilm al-yaqīnī al-qaṭ'ī al-ḍarūrī* which is absolutely binding, and "knowledge based on compelling assumption (*'ilm ghalabat al-ẓann*), which is relatively binding. From his unpublished inaugural lecture to the Preparatory Class of Abū al-Nūr Institute, Damascus, October 1997.

high degree of *ṣaḥīḥ*.[893] This is in essence what al-Dhahabī concluded concerning the few narrators of the *Ṣaḥīḥayn* whose grading was questioned: "The narration of one such as those, does not go below the rank of *ḥasan* which we might call the lowest rank of the *ṣaḥīḥ*."[894] Shaykh Abū Ghudda comments in the margin: "This is an explicit confirmation that al-Bukhārī and Muslim did not confine themselves, in the narrations of their respective books, only to narrate ḥadīths that have the highest degree of *ṣiḥḥa*." Then again in his appendix (p. 144) he states:

> Our Shaykh, the *'Allāma* Aḥmad Shākir – Allāh have mercy on him – stated: "The truth without doubt among the verifiers of those who have knowledge of the sciences of ḥadīth[...] is that the ḥadīths of the two *Ṣaḥīḥs* are all *ṣaḥīḥ* and there is not in a single one of them a cause for true [technical] disparagement or weakness. What al-Dāraquṭnī and others criticised is only on the basis that it did not reach the high criterion which each of them defined in their respective books. As for the [criterion of] soundness [*ṣiḥḥa*] of the ḥadīths in themselves, then both of them lived up to it.

Dr. Badī' al-Sayyid al-Laḥḥām in his edition of Ibn Kathīr's *Ikhtiṣār 'Ulūm al-Ḥadīth* (p. 44-45) also closes the discussion on the topic of the *Ṣaḥīḥayn* with the same words but without attributing them to Shākir. Abū Ghudda concludes (p. 145): "All these texts show that most of what is in *Ṣaḥīḥ al-Bukhārī* and *Ṣaḥīḥ Muslim* is of the highest degree of the *ṣaḥīḥ*, and that some of what is in them is not of the highest degree of the *ṣaḥīḥ*." More to the point, our teacher Dr. Nūr al-Dīn 'Itr said in his manual *Manhaj al-Naqd fī 'Ulūm al-Ḥadīth*: "The ruling concerning the ḥadīths of the two *Ṣaḥīḥs* is that they are all *ṣaḥīḥ*."[895] All those mentioned above – Ibn al-Ṣalāḥ, al-Nawawī, al-Dhahabī, Ibn Kathīr, Ibn Ḥajar, al-Suyūṭī, Aḥmad Shākir, Abū Ghudda, 'Itr, al-Laḥḥām – agreed on the fact that all of what is in al-Bukhārī and Muslim is *ṣaḥīḥ*, and, apart from al-Nawawī's duly recorded dissent,

[893] Cf. Abū Ghudda, appendix to al-Dhahabī's *Mūqiẓa* (p. 141-145).
[894] Al-Dhahabī, *al-Mūqiẓa* (p. 80).
[895] 'Itr, *Manhaj al-Naqd fī 'Ulūm al-Ḥadīth* (3rd ed. p. 254).

the *muḥaqqiqūn* such as Ibn al-Ṣalāḥ, Ibn Kathīr, Ibn Ḥajar, and al-Suyūṭī consider all the ḥadīths contained in them *maqṭū'un bi-ṣiḥḥatihi, i.e.* of the same probative force as *mutawātir* ḥadīth. Further examination of the positions of the major ḥadīth Masters might add more names to this distinguished list.

The questions are sometimes asked (1) whether all the Ulema of Ḥadīth agree that all the ḥadīths in al-Bukhārī and Muslim are *ṣaḥīḥ*, or (2) if there are any scholars who consider them to contain some weak narrations, and (3) whether one who believes that "the *Ṣaḥīḥayn* are not 100% *ṣaḥīḥ*" is an innovator. As was just shown, some of the greatest ḥadīth authorities such as Ibn al-Ṣalāḥ, Ibn Kathīr, and al-Suyūṭī answered yes to the first question. Imām al-Ḥaramayn (al-Juwaynī) said that if a man swore on pain of divorce that all that is in al-Bukhārī and Muslim is *ṣaḥīḥ* his marriage would be safe.[896] However, Imām al-Dāraquṭnī said a small number may not reach that level, so the answer to the second question has to be yes. Yet the objections were refuted one by one by Ibn Ḥajar at the beginning of *Fatḥ al-Bārī* and Imām al-Nawawī at the beginning of *Sharḥ Ṣaḥīḥ Muslim*. The formula "whether the *Ṣaḥīḥayn* are or not 100% *ṣaḥīḥ*" remains tenuous and misleading, for the *Umma* far and wide – meaning the Consensus of the *Fuqahā'* generation after generation – have been satisfied that they are. The above conclusion excludes the *mursal* or unattributed reports al-Bukhārī sometimes adduces in his chapter-titles or appends to certain narrations. This conclusion is proof that the position that "everything that is found in the two *Ṣaḥīḥs* is rigorously sound" refers only to full-chained reports positively attributed to the Prophet ﷺ, and Allāh knows best.[897]

Khalaf al-Khayyām said: I heard Abū 'Amr Aḥmad ibn Naṣr al-Khaffāf say: Muḥammad ibn Ismā'īl is twenty degrees more knowledgeable in ḥadīth than Aḥmad (ibn Ḥanbal) and Isḥāq (ibn Rāhūyah), and whoever has doubts about it, let him be cursed by me 1,000 times!" Abū 'Īsā al-Tirmidhī said: 'Abd Allāh ibn Munīr said to Muḥammad ibn Ismā'īl when he was about to leave him: "Abū 'Abd Allāh, may Allāh make you the adornment of this Community!" Abū 'Īsā said: His wish has been granted. Ja'far ibn Muḥammad al-

[896] Cf. Shaykh 'Abd Allāh Sirāj al-Dīn, *Sharḥ al-Manẓūmat al-Bayqūniyya* (p. 46).

[897] See more on this issue at http://webpages.marshall.edu/~laher1/bkhr_mslm .html.

Mustaghfirī in *Tārīkh Nasaf* said, mentioning al-Bukhārī: "If I had to choose I would say he is superior to all his Shaykhs, and I would say that he never met his like."

Muḥammad ibn Abī Ḥātim said: I heard Muḥammad ibn Yūsuf say: I was visiting Abū Rajā' – he meant Qutayba – and he was asked about the divorce pronounced by the drunk (*i.e.* is it valid?). He replied: "Here is Aḥmad ibn Ḥanbal, Ibn al-Madīnī, and Ibn Rāhūyah all wrapped in one – Allāh brought him to you!" And he pointed to Muḥammad ibn Ismā'īl.[898]

Aḥmad ibn Ḥanbal said: "Khurāsān did not produce the like of al-Bukhārī." The latter's shaykh, Muḥammad ibn Bashshār said when al-Bukhārī entered Baṣra: "Today the Master of Jurists (*sayyid al-fuqahā'*) came to us."

Al-Firabrī – one of the narrators of the *Ṣaḥīḥ* – said: "I saw the Prophet ﷺ in my sleep and he said to me: 'Where are you going?' I replied: 'To see al-Bukhārī.' He said: 'Give him my *salām*.'" He also narrated from Najm ibn al-Fuḍayl: "I saw the Prophet ﷺ in my sleep as he was coming out of a village with Muḥammad ibn Ismā'īl behind him. Wherever the Prophet ﷺ trod he trod, placing his foot exactly where the Prophet ﷺ placed his, following his traces."

Al-Bukhārī used to recite the entire Qur'ān once every day, and recite one third of it in the period before dawn. Thus his normal daily devotional practice (*wird*) consisted in one *khatma* and a third.

Ibn Abī Ḥātim narrates that al-Bukhārī was invited to a friend's garden in which he led the people in prayer. Afterwards he prayed supererogatory prayers. When he finished he lifted the hem of his shirt at the back and said to his friend: "Look there and tell me if you see anything." They saw that he had been stung by a hornet in sixteen or seventeen places and his body had become swollen. One of them said to him: "Why did you not come out of the prayer the first time it stung you?" He said: "I was in the middle of a Sūra and I wanted to complete it."

Nasj ibn Sa'īd said: "On the first night of every month of Ramaḍān his companions would gather around al-Bukhārī and he would lead them in prayer and recite in every *rak'a* twenty verses, and so on until he finished the Qur'ān. He used to recite one third daily at every pre-

[898] The answer was: divorce does not take effect from one who is deprived of his mental faculties and does not remember what happened to him in his drunkenness. See also above, chapter of Abū Ḥanīfā, section on Zufar.

dawn period, and he would recite the entire Qur'ān daily in the daytime. He would finish it at the time of breaking fast every evening. He used to say: 'At every *khatm* (time of finishing the entire recitation of Qur'ān) there is a supplication that is answered.'"

Bakr ibn Munīr said: I heard al-Bukhārī say: "I hope to meet my Lord without being taken to account for slandering anyone." Al-Dhahabī said: "A witness to this is his manner of speech in the criticism and authentication of ḥadīth. He would say, at most, about the sub-narrator who is abandoned for unreliability: '*Fīhi naẓar* – He is subject to investigation'; or: '*Sakatū 'anh* – The authorities do not mention him.' He would not say 'So-and-so is a liar' nor 'He is a forger.' That was due to his strong fear of Allāh." Al-Subkī said: "The most damning judgment he would give about an unreliable narrator is *munkar al-ḥadīth* – his narrations are disclaimed." Ibn al-Qaṭṭān related that al-Bukhārī said: "Anyone about whom I say: *munkar al-ḥadīth*, it is not permissible to narrate from him."

Al-Bukhārī narrated in his *Ṣaḥīḥ* from al-Ḥasan al-Baṣrī: "If thirty men fast one day on behalf of someone who died without having fasted an entire month of Ramadan, he will get the reward of their fast."[899]

Muḥammad ibn Ya'qūb al-Akhram said: "I heard our companions say that when al-Bukhārī came to Naysābūr he was welcomed by 4,000 men on horseback, not counting those that rode mules or donkeys nor those that were on foot." Al-Ḥasan ibn Muḥammad ibn Jābir said: "Al-Dhuhlī said to us when al-Bukhārī came to Naysābūr: 'Go and see that pious man, and listen to his narrations.' The people went to him and began to take ḥadīth from him, until al-Dhuhlī's circle depleted. At that time the latter began to envy him and speak against him."[900] Al-Ḥākim narrated that Muḥammad ibn Yaḥyā al-Dhuhlī said: "This al-Bukhārī has openly subscribed to the doctrine of 'pronunciationists' (*al-lafẓiyya*), and for me those are worse than the Jahmiyya." Aḥmad ibn Salama then visited al-Bukhārī and told him: "Abū 'Abd Allāh, this is a respected man in Khurāsān, especially in this town

899 This was also mentioned by al-Baghawī in *Sharḥ al-Sunna* (6:326) and is the position of the Shāfi'ī school as specified by al-Nawawī in *al-Majmū'* (6:431) and Taqī al-Dīn al-Subkī in *Sharḥ al-Minhāj*.

900 See Appendix, "The Controversy Over the Pronunciation of the Qur'ān" for what transpired between al-Dhuhlī and al-Bukhārī.

(Naysābūr), and he has thundered with this speech until none of us can say anything to him about it, so what do you think we should do?" Al-Bukhārī grasped his beard and said: ﴾**I confide my cause unto Allāh. Lo! Allāh is Seer of His slaves**﴿ (40:44). He continued: "O Allāh! You know that I did not want for one moment to settle in Naysābūr out of arrogance, nor in quest of leadership, but only because my soul would not let me return to my own land (Bukhārā) because of my opponents; and now this man intends harm for me out of jealousy, only because of what Allāh gave me and for no other reason." Then he said to me: "Aḥmad, tomorrow I shall leave and you will be rid of his talk which I have caused." Then al-Bukhārī went to Samarqand.

Concerning al-Bukhārī's remark about his native Bukhārā, Bakr ibn Munīr ibn Khulayd al-Bukhārī said: "The emir Khālid ibn Aḥmad al-Dhuhlī, governor of Bukhārā, had sent the following message to Muḥammad ibn Ismā'īl: 'Bring the *Jāmi' al-Ṣaḥīḥ* and the *Tārīkh* and other books of yours, and come and read before me.' He replied through the messenger: 'I do not debase learning nor do I carry it to the doors of people. If you need learning from me, come to my mosque or my house. I you do not like this, you are the sultan and you may forbid my stay here so that I will have an excuse before Allāh on the Day of the Rising that I did not conceal knowledge." This is the origin of the enmity between them.

Abū Bakr ibn Abī 'Amr al-Bukhārī said "the reason for al-Bukhārī's estrangement [from Bukhārā] was that Khālid ibn Aḥmad, who represented the Ẓāhirī School (of Dāwūd ibn Khalaf) in Bukhārā, had asked him to come to his house and read the *Jāmi' al-Ṣaḥīḥ* and the *Tārīkh* to his children, but he refused. Then he wrote to him asking him to teach his children privately but he refused again, saying: "I do not give private lessons to anyone." Then Khālid ibn Aḥmad resorted to Ḥurayth ibn Abī al-Warqā' and others against al-Bukhārī; they spread rumors against him concerning his doctrine (*madhhab*), after which the governor expelled him. Ibn Abī 'Amr continued, "then al-Bukhārī supplicated to Allāh against them. Not a month passed before the Ẓāhirīs ordered that Khālid be publicly denounced, and he was jeered out of Bukhārā on a she-ass. As for Ḥurayth he was severely tried in marital matters and saw things that cannot be decently mentioned. As for So-and-so, he was tried in his children." Al-Ḥākim narrated it from Muḥammad ibn al-'Abbās al-Ḍabbī, from Abū Bakr. Ḥurayth ibn Abī al-Warqā' was one of the great Jurists of the school of juridical opinion (*ra'y*) in Bukhārā.

Ibn 'Adī narrates from 'Abd al-Quddūs ibn 'Abd al-Jabbār al-Samarqandī: "Al-Bukhārī came to Khartenk – a village in Samarqand two parsangs from the main town – to see relatives with whom he used to stay. I heard him say in his supplication one night after the late-night prayer: 'O Allāh, the earth and its welcome have become narrow for me, so take me back to You.' The month was not over before Allāh took him back, and his grave is in Khartenk."

Al-Ḥākim narrated from Abū Ḥassān Miḥnāb ibn Sulaym al-Karmānī: "Muḥammad ibn Ismā'īl died in our village – Allāh have mercy on him! – the night of *'Īd al-Fiṭr*, the first night of Shawwāl in the year 256. He had reached the age of 62 years less twelve days. He was born in Shawwāl of 194. He was alone in the house, and we found him the morning after he died."

From 'Abd al-Wāḥid ibn Ādam al-Ṭawāwīsī: "I saw the Prophet ﷺ in my sleep with a group of his Companions. I greeted him and he returned my greeting, then I said: 'What are you waiting for, Messenger of Allāh?' He replied: 'Muḥammad ibn Ismā'īl al-Bukhārī.' After a few days I heard news of the latter's death. He had died on the very hour that I saw the Prophet ﷺ in my dream."

Al-Warrāq narrated from Ghālib ibn Gibrīl, with whom al-Bukhārī spent his last days: "Abū 'Abd Allāh stayed with us for a few days and took ill, then his state worsened, until the messenger came to Samarqand with the order of expulsion. Al-Bukhārī got up and got ready to travel. He wore his two leather socks and his turban. He walked about twenty steps and I was supporting him while another man was bringing the animal for him to ride. Then he said: 'Leave me, I feel too weak.' He began to supplicate to Allāh at length, then he took to his bed and he died – may Allāh have mercy on him. An indescribable amount of perspiration came out of him. When this abated, we shrouded him. We followed his instructions in this as he had said: 'Wrap me in three white cloths, without shirt or turban.' This we did. When we buried him an ineffable scent exuded from the earth of his grave which lasted for days, and facing his grave long white columns (*sawārī*) reaching up to the heaven were seen, so people began to visit his grave in astonishment. People began to take for themselves handfuls of earth from his grave until the grave lay open again. It was impossible to protect it even with the posting of guards. We were overwhelmed, so we built over it a wooden lattice which prevented access to the grave itself. The sweet smell lasted for a long time and was the talk of the people of the region who were amazed at this. Those who had opposed him before realised his status after he died. Some of them came to his grave and showed the marks of repentence and remorse. Ghālib did not live long after this and was buried at al-Bukhārī's side."

The ḥadīth Master Abū 'Alī al-Ghassānī narrated that Abū al-Fatḥ Naṣr ibn al-Ḥasan al-Sakanī al-Samarqandī came to them in 464 and said: "We had a drought in Samarqand some years ago. The people made the *istisqā'* prayer but they did not get rain. A saintly man named al-Ṣalāḥ came to the judge and said to him: 'I have an opinion I would like to tell you. It is that you come out followed by the people and that you all go to the grave of Imām Muḥammad ibn Ismā'īl al-Bukhārī and pray for rain there. Perhaps Allāh will give us rain.' The judge said: 'What a good opinion you have!' He came out and the people followed him, and he prayed for rain in front of them at the grave while people wept and sought the intercession of the one that was in it. Allāh sent such heavy rain that those who were in Khartenk could not reach Samarqand for seven days because of the rain's abundance."

Concerning the derivation of blessings (*tabarruk*) through al-Bukhārī's *Ṣaḥīḥ* Ibn al-Subkī said: "As for the *Jāmi' al-Ṣaḥīḥ* itself and its property as a recourse against difficulties and a proven means for the fulfillment of needs, it is a well-known matter. Should we engage in mentioning its many excellences and what is agreed upon concerning it, it would take us to inordinate lengths."

Al-Ḥākim cites the following lines from the poetry of al-Bukhārī:

Avail yourself in leisure of the benefit of prayer
For it may happen that your death will be sudden.
How many a sound man did I see without ailment
Whose sound soul departed without warning!

and

Like the dumb beasts who see not their ends
Until driven to the slaughterhouse to be sacrificed.

and

If you wish to stay (in the world)
you will soon be bereaved of all your beloved ones
But the annihilation of your soul
— woe to you! — is more distressing yet.

and

He who grows old finds in himself
What he would wish for his enemies.

and

This is the requital of a man
Whose peers departed before him
And who piously wished for a delay in his term of life.

AL-ATHRAM[901]

Abū Bakr Aḥmad ibn Muḥammad ibn Hāni' al-Ṭā'ī (or al-Kalbī) al-Baghdādī al-Iskāfī al-Athram 🕮 (d. 273 or >260) was one of the Imāms and ḥadīth Masters of superlative intelligence among the immediate companions of Imām Aḥmad. He took ḥadīth from him, al-Qaʿnabī, al-Sahmī, al-Faḍl ibn Dukayn, Ibn Abī Shayba, Nuʿaym ibn Ḥammād, Sulaymān ibn Ḥarb, and others. From him took al-Nasā'ī, Ibn Abī al-Dunyā, and others. He authored *al-Nāsikh wal-Mansūkh fīl-Ḥadīth*, a book on *ʿIlal*, and a compilation of Aḥmad's jurisprudence.

Ibrāhīm al-Aṣbahānī said that al-Athram was "stronger in memorization than Abū Zurʿa and more meticulous" while al-Khallāl said "his keenness of mind was truly astonishing" (*kāna maʿahu tayaqquzun ʿajībun jiddan*). He narrated with his chain to Yaḥyā ibn Maʿīn that the latter said one of the two parents of al-Athram was a jinnī. The same is related from Yaḥyā ibn Ayyūb about al-Athram.

Al-Athram was a ḥadīth Master thoroughly versed in *fiqh* and familiar with the differences in the early Schools until he met Aḥmad, after which he left everything he was doing and embraced his *fiqh*, not differing with him on a single point. He deeply loved and revered the

---

[901] Sources: al-Khaṭīb, *Tārīkh Baghdād* (5:316-318), Ibn Abī Yaʿlā, *Ṭabaqāt al-Ḥanābila* (1:66-74), al-Dhahabī, *Siyar* (Risāla ed. 12:623-628).

Imām whom he called "a shield (*sitr*) from Allāh." He compiled his *fiqh* to a point even the latter disliked as is known from his reluctance to write down other than the proof-texts themselves.

Al-Athram said Aḥmad never rose from a gathering without saying *Subḥānak Allāhumma wa-biḥamdik* [...] He once asked the Imām about the gathering of the people in mosques on the Day of 'Arafa, to which Aḥmad replied: "I see no harm in it. Several of the *Salaf* did this: al-Ḥasan [al-Baṣrī], Bakr ibn 'Abd Allāh [al-Muzanī], Thābit [al-Bunānī], and Muḥammad ibn Wāsi' all used to keep to the mosque on the day of 'Arafa." Among the things he narrated from the Imām are the rulings that wiping the head during *wuḍū'* is with both hands, wiping from the front to the back and again to the front in a single movement, without lifting them up, and that *wuḍū'* remains invalid unless one washes the nostrils and mouth, the former being more emphatically stressed than the latter.

Among al-Athram's sayings in his critique of extravagance in the statements of certain Ṣūfīs: "It is better to be a follower in goodness (*tābi' fil-khayr*) than a leader in evil (*ra'sun fil-sharr*) [...]. Al-Qāsim ibn Muḥammad said: 'That a man live ignorant is better for him than to say about Allāh what he knows not."

AL-MARWAZĪ

Aḥmad ibn Muḥammad ibn al-Ḥajjāj, Abū Bakr al-Marwazī or Marwadhī or Marrūdhī ﵀ (d. 275) was a trustworthy ḥadīth Master and the closest companion of Imām Aḥmad whom he washed and laid in his grave. He was celebrated for his piety. He wrote a book on the difficulties of ḥadīth. Ibn Abī Ya'lā relates that al-Marwazī said: "I asked Aḥmad ibn Ḥanbal about the ḥadīths which the Jahmīs reject concerning the Attributes, the vision of Allāh [in the hereafter], the Prophet's ﷺ ascension [body and soul], and the story of the Throne;[902] he declared them sound and said: 'The Community accepted them, and these reports are taken exactly as they come' [*i.e.* without one seeking to explain them]."[903] Among his junior students was al-Ḥasan ibn 'Alī ibn Khalaf, Abū Muḥammad al-Barbahārī (d. 329). He should not be confused with Abū Bakr al-Khallāl, the first

[902] *I.e.* the reports about the seating of the Prophet ﷺ on the Throne on the Day of Resurrection, cf.note 922.

[903] Ibn Abī Ya'lā, *Ṭabaqāt al-Ḥanābila* (1:56).

compiler of the Ḥanbalī School, who probably never met Imām Aḥmad but learned from his students.

ABŪ DĀWŪD[904]

Sulaymān ibn al-Ash'ath ibn Isḥāq[905] ibn Bishr[906] ibn Shaddād ibn 'Amr ibn 'Āmir, Abū Dāwūd al-Azdī al-Sijistānī ﷺ (d. 275) was one of the major Imāms of ḥadīth, the meticulous author of the *Sunan* – one of the motherbooks – and a student of Imām Aḥmad. Al-Dhahabī and others related that he declared having heard 500,000 ḥadīths of the Prophet ﷺ among which he selected 4,800 for his *Sunan.* Abū Sulaymān al-Khaṭṭābī heard Abū Sa'īd ibn al-I'rābī say in a ḥadīth gathering while the *Sunan* was being read: "If all the knowledge a man possesses consists in a volume of the Qur'ān and this book, he will not need anything else at all." The Ṣūfī Master Sahl ibn 'Abd Allāh al-Tustarī once said to Abū Dāwūd: "Bring out for me your tongue with which you narrate the Prophet's ﷺ ḥadīths so that I may kiss it," whereupon Abū Dāwūd drew out his tongue and al-Tustarī kissed it.

Abū Dāwūd in his *Sunan* was more concerned with the jurisprudence of the ḥadīth than with its chains of transmission.[907] In his letter to the Ulema of Makka he writes, "As a rule, any ḥadīth in my book that contains a strong defect, I mention it, as well as those whose chains of transmission are unsound. Anything concerning which I say nothing, is usable (*ṣāliḥ*), some of them being sounder than others." His criterion of soundness is generally stricter than al-Tirmidhī's and similar to al-Nasā'ī's.

Abū Dāwūd said: "The entire Law revolves around four ḥadīths: [1] 'The lawful is as clear as day and the unlawful is as clear as day,'[908]

904 Al-Dhahabī, *Siyar* (10:572-574 §2335; 13:5); al-Khaṭīb, *al-Jāmi'* (2:441-442).

905 According to Ibn Dāsa and Abū 'Ubayd al-Ājurrī.

906 According to some, while others said Bashīr.

907 As stated by Ibn Rajab in *Sharḥ 'Ilal al-Tirmidhī* (1:411).

908 Narrated from al-Nu'mān ibn Bashīr in the Six Books. The complete ḥadīth states: "Verily, the lawful is manifest and the forbidden is manifest, but between them there are dubious matters which many people do not know. Therefore, whoever bewares of dubious matters has made himself exempt [of guilt] for the sake of his religion and his honor, and whoever falls into dubious matters, falls into the forbidden. It is as the shepherd that grazes his flock around guarded grounds: he greatly risks grazing it inside them. Lo! Every king possesses guarded grounds. Lo! Verily, Allāh's guarded grounds are His prohibitions. Lo! Verily, there is in the body a small piece of flesh; if it is good the whole body is

عَنِ النُّعْمَانِ بْنِ بَشِيرٍ ﵄ قَالَ سَمِعْتُ رَسُولَ اللَّهِ ﷺ يَقُولُ وَأَهْوَى النُّعْمَانُ
بِإِصْبَعَيْهِ إِلَى أُذُنَيْهِ إِنَّ الْحَلَالَ بَيِّنٌ وَإِنَّ الْحَرَامَ بَيِّنٌ وَبَيْنَهُمَا مُشْتَبِهَاتٌ لَا يَعْلَمُهُنَّ
كَثِيرٌ مِنَ النَّاسِ فَمَنِ اتَّقَى الشُّبُهَاتِ اسْتَبْرَأَ لِدِينِهِ وَعِرْضِهِ وَمَنْ وَقَعَ فِي
الشُّبُهَاتِ وَقَعَ فِي الْحَرَامِ كَالرَّاعِي يَرْعَى حَوْلَ الْحِمَى يُوشِكُ أَنْ يَرْتَعَ فِيهِ أَلَا
وَإِنَّ لِكُلِّ مَلِكٍ حِمًى أَلَا وَإِنَّ حِمَى اللَّهِ مَحَارِمُهُ أَلَا وَإِنَّ فِي الْجَسَدِ مُضْغَةً
إِذَا صَلَحَتْ صَلَحَ الْجَسَدُ كُلُّهُ وَإِذَا فَسَدَتْ فَسَدَ الْجَسَدُ كُلُّهُ أَلَا وَهِيَ
الْقَلْبُ رواه الستة وهذا لفظ م

[2] 'Actions count only according to intentions,'[909]

عَنْ عُمَرَ رَضِيَ اللهُ تَعَالَى عَنْهُ قَالَ سَمِعْتُ رَسُولَ اللَّهِ صَلَّى اللَّهُ عَلَيْهِ
وَسَلَّمَ يَقُولُ إِنَّمَا الْأَعْمَالُ بِالنِّيَّاتِ وَإِنَّمَا لِكُلِّ امْرِئٍ مَا نَوَى فَمَنْ كَانَتْ هِجْرَتُهُ
إِلَى اللَّهِ وَرَسُولِهِ فَهِجْرَتُهُ إِلَى اللَّهِ وَرَسُولِهِ وَمَنْ كَانَتْ هِجْرَتُهُ لِدُنْيَا يُصِيبُهَا

---

good and if it is corrupted the whole body is corrupted; lo! It is the heart." Also narrated as part of a long saying of Ibn Mas'ūd: "Pass judgment according to what is in the Book of Allāh. If [the basis for judgment is] not in the Book of Allāh, then according to what is in the Sunna of the Messenger of Allāh. If [the basis for judgment is] not in the Sunna of the Messenger of Allāh, then according to what the righteous (*al-ṣāliḥūn*) have judged. <And if something comes up that is not in the Book of Allāh, nor did the Prophet ﷺ pass judgment concerning it, nor did the righteous pass judgment concerning it, then let one exert his own reasoning (*faliyajtahid ra'yahu*).> Let no one say: 'I am afraid, I am afraid [to judge]! The lawful is clear and the unlawful is clear, and between the two are doubtful matters. Therefore, leave what seems dubious to you for what does not seem dubious to you." Narrated *mawqūf* from Ḥurayth ibn Zuhayr by al-Nasā'ī both in the *Sunan* and *al-Sunan al-Kubrā* (3:469 §5911), al-Dārimī (without the bracketed segment), al-Ṭabarānī in *al-Kabīr* (9:187), al-Bayhaqī in *al-Sunan al-Kubrā* (10:115 §20115), and Ibn Abī Shayba with a sound chain according to Ibn Ḥajar in *Fatḥ al-Bārī* (1959 ed. 13:288).

909 See n. 217.

أَوْ امْرَأَةٍ يَنْكِحُهَا فَهِجْرَتُهُ إِلَى مَا هَاجَرَ إِلَيْهِ كذا أورده الإمام النووي رحمه الله وهو

متفق عليه

[3] 'Whatever I forbade you, avoid, and whatever I ordered you to do , do to the extent that you can,'[910]

عَنْ أَبِي هُرَيْرَةَ رَضِيَ اللهُ عَنْهُ سَمِعَ رَسُولَ اللَّهِ صَلَّى اللَّهُ عَلَيْهِ وَسَلَّمَ يَقُولُ

مَا نَهَيْتُكُمْ عَنْهُ فَاجْتَنِبُوهُ وَمَا أَمَرْتُكُمْ بِهِ فَافْعَلُوا مِنْهُ مَا اسْتَطَعْتُمْ الحديث ق

ت ن جه حم

and [4] 'Let there be neither harm done nor harm reciprocated' (*lā ḍarar walā ḍirār*)."[911]

عَنْ ابْنِ عَبَّاسٍ ﷺ قَالَ رَسُولُ اللَّهِ صَلَّى اللَّهُ عَلَيْهِ وَسَلَّمَ لَا ضَرَرَ وَلَا

ضِرَارَ جه حم

Another narration mentions that he added a fifth ḥadīth: "Truly, Religion is nothing but sincere faithfulness (*naṣīḥa*)."[912]

عَنْ تَمِيمٍ الدَّارِيِّ رَضِيَ اللهُ تَعَالَى عَنْهُ قَالَ قَالَ رَسُولُ اللَّهِ صَلَّى اللَّهُ عَلَيْهِ

وَسَلَّمَ إِنَّمَا الدِّينُ النَّصِيحَةُ قَالُوا لِمَنْ يَا رَسُولَ اللَّهِ قَالَ لِلَّهِ وَلِكِتَابِهِ وَلِرَسُولِهِ

وَلِأَئِمَّةِ الْمُسْلِمِينَ وَعَامَّتِهِمْ م د ن وهذا لفظه وفي الباب عن أبي هريرة ت ن حم قال الترمذي

حسن صحيح وعن ابن عمر ز وثوبان خت

[910] Narrated from Abū Hurayra by Muslim, al-Nasā'ī, and Aḥmad. Also narrated with a longer wording by al-Bukhārī, al-Tirmidhī (*ḥasan ṣaḥīḥ*), Ibn Mājah, and Aḥmad.

[911] Narrated from Yaḥyā ibn 'Umāra al-Māzinī and from both Ibn 'Abbās and 'Ubāda ibn al-Ṣāmit by Ibn Mājah and Aḥmad among others.

[912] Narrated from Abū Hurayra by al-Tirmidhī (*ḥasan ṣaḥīḥ*) and Aḥmad, from Tamīm al-Dārī by Abū Dāwūd, Muslim and al-Nasā'ī, from Abū Hurayra by al-Nasā'ī

Among Abū Dāwūd's and 'Abd Allāh ibn Aḥmad's students was Abū Bakr al-Najjād, teacher to Ibn Baṭṭa.

AL-TUSTARĪ[913]

Sahl ibn 'Abd Allāh ibn Yūnus, Abū Muḥammad al-Tustarī ﷺ (d. 283) was named by al-Dhahabī "the master of knowers (*shaykh al-'ārifīn*), the ascetic ṣūfī (*al-ṣūfī al-zāhid*) [...] He has a firm foothold in the path." He related that when he was three years old he would wake up at night to watch his uncle Muḥammad ibn al-Sawwār pray. He spent his early years with his uncle and Dhūl-Nūn al-Miṣrī whom he met during pilgrimage. Al-Qushayrī said: "He had no peer in his time for correctness of transaction and superlative Godwariness, and he was a person of *karāmāt.*" He narrates from 'Umar ibn Wāṣil al-Baṣrī that Sahl said: "My uncle once told me: 'Remember Allāh Who created you.' I said: 'How should I remember him?' He replied: 'Say in your heart, whenever you are alone at night, three times, without moving your tongue: Allāh is with me; Allāh is looking at me; Allāh is watching me.'" This became his lifelong devotion. He memorised the Qur'ān by age seven. He used to practice perpetual fasting and prayed all night. He reached a point where he broke his fast only once every twenty-five nights on one dirham's worth of barley bread for twenty years. Hence, his saying: "Hunger is the secret of Allāh on His earth, He does not confide it to one who divulges it." To a Shaykh who told him that whenever he performed ablution the water that dripped from him changed into sticks of gold he said: "Children are given rattles."

Al-Tustarī considered the audition and study of the ḥadīth of the Prophet ﷺ the highest pursuit as is evident from the following sayings:

- From Ibn Durustūyah: Sahl said to the scholars of ḥadīth: "Endeavor not to meet Allāh without your inkwell in hand."
- Asked until when a man should write down the ḥadīth of the Prophet ﷺ, he replied: "Until death, and the rest of his ink is poured into his grave."

---

and Aḥmad, from Ibn 'Umar by al-Bazzār, and from Thawbān by al-Bukhārī in *al-Tārīkh al-Kabīr*. This ḥadīth is §7 of al-Nawawī's "Forty".

913 Sources: *Risāla Qushayriyya* (p. 16-17); *Ḥilya* (0:198-222 §544, 10:204 §14934); al-Khaṭīb, *Iqtiḍā' al-'Ilm*; *Siyar* (10:647-649 §2369); Ibn Farḥūn, *Dībāj* (p. 345).

- From 'Alī ibn al-Ḥusayn al-Daqīqī: "Whoever desires this world and the next, let him write down the ḥadīth, for it contains the good of this world and the next."

He also said:

- "The ignorant one is dead, the forgetful one is asleep, the sinner is drunk, and the obstinate one is destroyed."
- "People are all drunk except the Ulema, and the Ulema are all confused except those who practice what they know."
- "Whoever rises not believing that he will enter his grave that very evening will be the plaything of devils all day."
- "Knowledge is all *dunyā*, and the hereafter part of it is its practice."
- "This world is ignorance on top of mortality. Knowledge is all evidence that convicts except whatever is put into practice, but practice is all smoke except sincerity, and sincerity remains in the greatest peril until death."
- "We have six principles: Holding fast to the Qur'ān; taking the Sunna as a guide; eating what is licit; quitting harm and avoiding sins; repentence; and fulfillment of obligations."
- "There are three types of eaters: one eats light and faith from the start of his food to the end; one eats nothing but food; and one eats garbage (*sirjīn*). The first one names Allāh at the beginning, remembers Him with every bite, and thanks Him at the end; the second one names Him at the beginning and thanks Him at the end; the third one neither names Him nor thanks Him nor remembers Him."
- "Whoever speaks about what does not concern him will be prohibited from obtaining truthfulness; whoever busies himself with superfluity will be prohibited from obtaining true fear of Allāh; and whoever entertains bad opinions will be prohibited from obtaining certitude. Whoever is prohibited from obtaining these three, is destroyed!"
- "Among the manners of the most truthful and trustful Saints (*al-Ṣiddīqīn*) is that they never swear by Allāh ﷻ, nor commit backbiting, nor does backbiting take place around them, nor do they eat to satiation. If they promise, they are true to their word, and they never speak in jest."

- "None truly knows ignorance except a wise, worshipful, learned Jurisprudent of simple living (*'ālim faqīh zāhid 'ābid ḥakīm*)."
- "Allāh does not open the heart of a servant if it still contains three things: loving to remain [in the world], love of wealth, and concern about tomorrow."
- Asked when the *faqīr* attains relief from his ego he replied: "When he no longer sees any time other than the time he is in."
- "Allāh ﷻ is the *qibla* of intention; intention is the *qibla* of the heart; the heart is the *qibla* of the body; the body is the *qibla* of the limbs; and the limbs are the *qibla* of *dunyā*."
- "When the servant abides in a specific sin, all his good deeds are mixed with his egotism (*hawā*). His good deeds are not purified as long as he abides in a single sin. He will not deliver himself from his egotism until he ousts from himself all that he knows Allāh detests."
- "Lukewarmth is heedlessness; dread is vigilance; hardness is death."
- Asked in what consists the solace of hearts, he replied: "The coming of the revelation: ﴾**Woe unto those whose hearts are hardened against remembrance of Allāh**﴿ (39:22)."
- Asked in what spiritual knowledge consists (*al-ma'rifa*) he said: "None attains it except after a long, hard struggle. After this, one finds pleasure in contradicting his ego more than he finds pleasure in following his ego. At that time, he knows."[914]
- "Whoever argues over reliance upon Allāh (*al-tawakkul*) argues over belief (*īmān*); and whoever argues over earning (*al-takassub*) argues over the Sunna." He defined true *tawakkul* as "Forgetting *tawakkul*."
- "Sit with one whose limbs address you, not his mouth."[915] This is similar to the saying of 'Abd Allāh ibn al-Mu'tazz: "The knowledge of the hypocrite is his speech while the knowledge of the Believer is his actions."[916]
- "No one is given a better knowledge than that by which he increases his utter dependence on Allāh."

914 Narrated by al-Bayhaqī in *al-Zuhd al-Kabīr* (p. 152 §322).

915 *I.e.* one who benefits others not through discourse but through states of being, in action or in repose, in public or in private, in solace and in hardship.

916 Narrated by al-Khaṭīb in *Iqtiḍā' al-'Ilm al-'Amal*.

- "Life is of four kinds. The life of angels consists of obedience. The life of Prophets consists of *'ilm* and the anticipation of revelation. The life of truthful and trustful Saints (*al-Ṣiddīqīn*) consists of following guidance (*al-iqtidā'*). And the life of the remainder of the people – whether knowledgeable, ignorant, ascetic, or devoted to worship – consists of eating and drinking."
- "Good deeds both the righteous (*al-barr*) and the hardened sinner (*al-fājir*) perform; none but the Ṣiddīq avoids disobedience."
- He mentioned the visionary unveiling (*kashf*) of the Saints in the poetic verse:

Qulūbu al-'ārifīna lahā 'uyūnun *Tarā mā lā yarāhu al-nāẓirūna*
The hearts of Knowers have eyes *that see what onlookers cannot see.*

Al-Tustarī was a teacher to the Ḥanbalī anthropomorphist Abū Muḥammad al-Barbahārī who related:

> I heard Sahl say: "Allāh created the world and placed in it those who are ignorant and those who have knowledge. The best knowledge is that which one acts upon. For knowledge is all a proof [against oneself] except what is put into practice. However, what is put into practice is all wind except what is sound and correct. As for what is sound and correct: I do not declare with certainty any act to be so, except what Allāh wills."[917]

Al-Qushayrī related in his *Risāla*: "I heard the Shaykh Abū 'Abd al-Raḥmān al-Sulamī say: I heard Manṣūr ibn 'Abd Allāh say: I heard Abū al-Ḥasan al-'Anbārī say: I heard Sahl ibn 'Abd Allāh al-Tustarī say: 'The believers shall look at Him with their eyesights (*bil-abṣār*) without encompassment (*iḥāṭa*) nor attainment (*idrāk*).'"[918] Al-Qushayrī also said: "Sahl ibn 'Abd Allāh said: 'Letters are the speech of act, not that of essence (*al-ḥurūfu lisānu fi'lin lā lisānu dhāt*). For they are an effect in something effected (*fi'lun fī maf'ūl*).' This is also an explicit affirmation that letters are created."

Al-Tustarī addressed the issue of the establishment of Allāh (*istiwā'*) over the Throne in the manner of Imām al-Ash'arī, by declaring it a

917 In Ibn Abī Ya'lā, *Ṭabaqāt al-Ḥanābila* (2:18).

918 An explicit denial of both limit (*ḥadd*) and direction (*jiha*) on the part of al-Tustarī.

Divine act that is neither qualified nor enquired about: "Reason alone cannot point to One Who is without beginning and without end above a Throne that is brought into being. Allāh erected the Throne as a sign and as tidings for us so that by it the hearts should be guided to Him without trespassing. He did not require the hearts to obtain knowledge of its exact nature. Therefore, His establishment over it is unqualified (*lā kayfa lahu*) and it is impermissible to ask: 'How does *istiwā'* apply to the Creator of *istiwā*?' The believer must only accept and submit in accordance with the saying of the Prophet ﷺ: 'He is over His Throne' (*innahu 'alā 'arshihi*)." The latter is a reference to three weak reports:

(i) The "ḥadīth of the groaning" narrated from Jubayr ibn Muṭ'im from his father from his grandfather: "Allāh is above His Throne, and His Throne is above His Heavens."[919] Al-Dhahabī terms it an "extremely strange" one-chained narration (*gharīb jiddan*) and says: "Allāh knows best if the Prophet ﷺ ever said such a thing or not; Allāh – ﴾**there is nothing whatsoever like unto Him**﴿ (42:11)!"[920] Ibn Kathīr also termed it extremely strange. The ḥadīth is graded weak by the author of *'Awn al-Ma'būd* while its chain of narration is declared weak by the editors of Ibn Abī 'Āṣim's *al-Sunna* and al-Ājurrī's *al-Sharī'a.* This is due to the concealment (*tadlīs*) of the mode of transmission through *'an'ana* or undecisive transmission terminology by one of its narrators, Muḥammad ibn Isḥāq ibn Yasār while another narrator, Jubayr ibn Muhammad ibn Jubayr ibn Muṭ'im, is merely acceptable (*maqbūl*)[921] which makes him unreliable in a narration that is not independently verifiable. There are other problems with the chain and the text, which Ibn 'Asākir addresses in his monograph *Bayān al-Wahm wal-Takhlīṭ fī Ḥadīth al-Aṭīṭ*

[919] Part of a long report narrated by Abū Dāwūd, *Sunan, Kitāb al-Sunna,* ch. 19 (4:232 §4726), al-Bazzār (1:29 §39), al-Ṭabarī in his *Tafsīr* (3:10), Abū Ya'lā as mentioned by al-Haythamī (10:159), Ibn Abī 'Āṣim in *al-Sunna* (p. 252-253 §575-576), al-Ājurrī in *al-Sharī'a* (p. 298 §678), and Ibn Khuzayma in *al-Tawḥīd* (p. 69=1:239-240 §147).

[920] In *al-'Ulūw* (p. 37-39). Al-Dhahabī also says: "There is not a single established text [*i.e.* sound] that has the word "groaning" (*aṭīṭ*) in it." *Mukhtaṣar al-'Ulūw* (p. 124). Al-Albānī reiterates this statement in his *Silsila Ḍa'īfa* (2:307 §906).

[921] As stated by Ibn Ḥajar in his *Taqrīb* (p. 138 §902) and confirmed by Ma'rūf and al-Arna'ūṭ in *Taḥrīr Taqrīb al-Tahdhīb* (1:210 §902).

("The Exposition of Error and Confusion in the Narration of the [Throne's] Groaning"). Ibn al-Qayyim alone insists this narration is authentic.[922]

(ii) The "ḥadīth of the mountain-goats" narrated from al-'Abbās 🙏, which has the wording "the Throne is above all this, and Allāh is above all this."[923]

(iii) The saying of Ibn Mas'ūd 🙏: "Between the heaven and the earth there is a distance of five hundred years' travel, and the thickness of each heaven is a distance of five hundred years' travel, then between the seventh heaven and the Footstool (*al-kursī*) there are five hundred years, then between the Footstool and the water there are five hundred years. The Footstool is above the water, and Allāh is above the Throne – one version states: 'above the Footstool' (*kursī*) – and nothing is hidden to him of all your deeds."[924] This report is weakened by the following aspects: (1) it is a *mawqūf* report halted at a Companion; (2) it has Ḥammād ibn Salama in all its chains;[925] (3) Al-Bayhaqī's similar second-to-next report in the *Asmā'* is narrated from 'Abd Allāh ibn 'Amr ibn al-'Āṣ while al-Dhahabī in *al-'Ulūw* narrates two similar reports from Ka'b al-Aḥbār quoting from the Torah,[926] which raises the likelihood of a common Israelite source through Ka'b or Ibn 'Amr or

---

[922] See full study in the forthcoming fourth volume of our *Sunna Notes: The Divine Names and Attributes*.

[923] Part of a long report narrated from al-'Abbās ibn 'Abd al-Muṭṭalib 🙏 by al-Tirmidhī (*ḥasan gharīb*), Abū Dāwūd, Ibn Mājah, Aḥmad (2:375-376 §1770-1771) and Abū Ya'lā (12:75 §6713), al-Ḥākim (2:288, 2:378, 2:501), Ibn Abī 'Āṣim in *al-Sunna* (p. 253 §577), al-Ājurrī in *al-Sharī'a* (p. 297-298 §674-676), al-Bayhaqī in *al-Asmā' wal-Ṣifāt* (2:285 §847, 2:316 §882), Ibn Khuzayma in *al-Tawḥīd* (p. 102), and Ibn al-Jawzī in *al-'Ilal al-Mutanāhyia* (1:23-25 §5-6) cf. Ibn Taymiyya, *Fatwā Ḥamawiyya* (p. 221-223) = *Majmū' al-Fatāwā* (5:13-14).

[924] Narrated with a fair chain by al-Bayhaqī in *al-Asmā' wal-Ṣifāt* (Kawtharī ed. p. 401; Ḥāshidī ed. 2:291-292 §851), Ibn Khuzayma in *al-Tawḥīd* (p. 105-106=1:242-244), al-Ṭabarānī in *al-Kabīr* (9:228 §8987), Ibn 'Abd al-Barr in *al-Tamhīd* (7:139), al-Dhahabī in *al-'Ulūw* (p. 196-197=*Mukhtaṣar* p. 103-104 §48), al-Lālikā'ī with a weak chain in *Sharḥ Uṣūl I'tiqād Ahl al-Sunna* (1:91 §659) and others.

[925] Al-Dhahabī said of him in *al-Mughnī fīl-Ḍu'afā'* (1:279 §1711): "Ḥammād ibn Salama: a trustworthy Imām who is responsible for some blunders and strange things which he alone narrates. Others are more firmly established than he."

[926] Al-Dhahabī, *al-'Ulūw* (p. 365-366 §280-281=*Mukhtaṣar* p. 128 §97).

both. Their *mawqūf* reports are subject to definite caution on the part of the experts.[927]

Al-Dhahabī in his *Siyar* and in *Mukhtaṣar al-'Ulūw* expresses caution in commentary of a similar statement of Divine aboveness by 'Uthmān ibn Sa'īd al-Dārimī (d. 280):

> In his book *al-Naqd* he ['Uthmān al-Dārimī] said: "The Muslims all agree that Allāh is above His Throne, above His heavens." I say the clearest thing on this topic is the saying of Allāh: ﴾**The Merciful established Himself over the Throne**﴿ (20:5). Therefore, let it pass as it came, just as we learned to do from the school of *Salaf*.[928]
>
> Al-Dārimī's book also contains bizarre findings in which he exaggerates the affirmation [of the Divine Attributes], concerning which silence would have been more in keeping with the way of the *Salaf* both then and now."[929]

On the same subject Ibn Ḥajar said:

> When we say: "Allāh is above the Throne," it does not mean that He is touching it or that He is located on it or bounded by any side of the Throne. Rather, it is a report which is transmitted as is, and so we repeat it while at the same time negating any modality, for ﴾**There is nothing whatsoever like unto Him**﴿ (42:11), and from Him comes all success.[930]

Al-Tustarī authored a renowned Ṣūfī commentary of the Qur'ān which has been translated into English. In it he gives the following explanations:

- ﴾**And give me from Your presence a sustaining Power**﴿ (17:80): "A tongue that speaks on Your behalf, and on behalf of no one else."
- ﴾**Forsake the outwardness of sin and the inwardness thereof**﴿

[927] Cf. Ibn Ḥajar's *Nukat 'alā Ibn al-Ṣalāḥ* (2:532); Ibn Kathīr (on Ka'b al-Aḥbār and Wahb ibn Munabbih) in his *Tafsīr* (3:379 on 27:41-44); al-Qārī, *Sharḥ Sharḥ Nukhbat al-Fikar* (p. 548-549); al-Sakhāwī's *Fatḥ al-Mughīth* (1992 ed. 1:150-151); 'Itr, *Manhaj al-Naqd fī 'Ulūm al-Ḥadīth* (p. 328).

[928] Al-Dhahabī, *Siyar* (10:643).

[929] Al-Dhahabī, *Mukhtaṣar al-'Ulūw* (p. 214).

[930] Ibn Ḥajar, *Fatḥ*, *Tawḥīd*, ch. 22 (1989 ed. 13:508).

(6:120): "The outwardness of sin is its commission; the inwardness, its love."

IBRĀHĪM AL-ḤARBĪ[931]

Abū Isḥāq Ibrāhīm ibn Isḥāq ibn Ibrāhīm al-Ḥarbī ﵀ (198-285) of Merv was a prominent companion and student of Imām Aḥmad. He pursued knowledge from an early age and heard many of the great masters of his time. Al-Khaṭīb said of him: "He was an Imām in learning, a leader in asceticism, an expert in the Law, perspicuous in rulings, a master in the memorization of ḥadīth, thoroughly versed in its defects, accomplished in literature, and an encyclopedia of the Arabic language." He authored *Gharīb al-Ḥadīth* among other books. Al-Ḥākim relates that he was pre-eminent in Baghdād for four traits: his superlative manners, his knowledge of the Law, his knowledge of ḥadīth, and his asceticism (*zuhd*). Al-Dāraquṭnī said he compared to Aḥmad himself in all these respects. However, al-Dhahabī said many of his transmission chains were more those of a student than a master due to their length.

Among his sayings:

- "The stranger is the one who once lived among saintly people who helped him when he ordered good and forbade evil and supplied him when he had some worldly need, then they died and left him alone."
- "I never wasted anything, nor ate twice in the same day."
- "People are four types: a gentle and pleasant person who acts gently and pleasantly (*malīḥ yatamallaḥ*); a gently and pleasant person who acts inimically (*malīḥ yatabaghghaḍ*); an inimical person who acts gently and pleasantly (*baghīḍ yatamallaḥ*); and an inimical person who acts inimically (*baghīḍ yatabaghghaḍ*). The first is grace personified (*munā*); the second is bearable (*yuḥtamal*); the third I pity; and from the fourth I run as fast as I can."
- To a man who asked him about "the name and the named" (*al-ism wal-musammā*): "Do you know everything?" He replied no. Al-Ḥarbī said: "Then make this part of what you do not know."
- "Not every separation is estrangement, nor is every reunion love;

931 Sources: Ibn al-Jawzī, *Ṣifat al-Ṣafwa* (2:410, 2:214); al-Dhahabī, *Siyar* (10:666-676 §2391 and 8:219 §1425).

only the nearness of the hearts is love."

- He disapproved of 'Alī ibn al-Madīnī because he once saw him going to pray behind the Jahmī judge and grand inquisitor against *Ahl al-Sunna*, Aḥmad ibn Abī Du'ād (d. 240). The latter was principally responsible for the 28-month-long jailing and flogging of Imām Aḥmad ibn Ḥanbal who had declared him a disbeliever (*kāfir*) for holding that the Qur'ān was created.[932]

Al-Ḥarbī did not wash his garments more than once every four months. Ibn al-Mukhalliṣ said: "He slipped in mud once. I could see the trace of mud on his clothes until he washed them."

Al-Dhahabī relates that al-Ḥarbī's grave in Baghdād is a place one visits for blessings. Ibn al-Jawzī included himself in the number of those who performed this visitation and relates that al-Ḥarbī himself used to say: "Ma'rūf al-Karkhī's grave is proven medicine." This is also related by al-Dhahabī who comments: "The supplication of those in need is answered at every blessed site."

'ABD ALLĀH IBN AḤMAD[933]

'Abd Allāh ibn Aḥmad (ibn Muḥammad) ibn Ḥanbal ﵀ (d. 290), the Imām's son, compiled and transmitted the *Musnad* of his father and the latter praised his knowledge of ḥadīth. When he died he asked to be buried in al-Qaṭī'a instead of at his father's gravesite in Baghdād, saying: "I have authentic proof that there is a Prophet buried in al-Qaṭī'a and I prefer to be [buried] near a Prophet to being near my father."[934]

Ibn Abī Ya'lā narrates through him the following reports from Imām Aḥmad:

- My father said: "The graves of the great sinners of *Ahl al-Sunna* are a garden, while those of the ascetics (*zuhhād*) among the innovators are a pit; the transgressors (*fussāq*) of *Ahl al-Sunna* are the Friends of Allāh, while the ascetics of the innovators are the enemies of Allāh."

932 Narrated by al-Khaṭīb in *Tārīkh Baghdād* (4:142-153 §1825), al-Dhahabī in the chapter on Imām Aḥmad in the *Siyar*, Ibn al-Subkī in *Ṭabaqāt al-Shāfi'iyya al-Kubrā* (2:37-51), and others.

933 Sources: Ibn Abī Ya'lā, *Ṭabaqāt al-Ḥanābila* (1:29, 1:184-186); al-Dhahabī, *Siyar* (9:512).

934 In Yāqūt al-Ḥamawī's *Mu'jam al-Buldān* (1:306).

- I asked my father about those who said: "When Allāh ﷻ spoke to Mūsā ﷺ He did not speak with a voice." My father said: "Allāh did speak with a voice! We narrate those ḥadīths [which prove it] exactly as they came. The ḥadīth of Ibn Mas'ūd states: 'When Allāh speaks to send a revelation a voice is heard from Him like the dragging of a chain on top of a rock.'[935] The Jahmīs deny this ḥadīth; they are disbelievers." This cannot be authentic from the Imām as he could not have failed to know that the voice that is heard is that of the angels as indicated in the narration and as explained in *Fatḥ al-Bārī*.
- From [Abū] al-Ḥuwayrith 'Abd al-Raḥmān ibn Mu'āwiya (d. 130): "Mūsā remained for forty nights such that no one could look at him without falling dead due to the light from the Lord of the worlds."[936]

'Abd Allāh also narrated: "I asked my father about the man who touches and kisses the pommel of the Prophet's ﷺ *minbar* to obtain blessing, or does the same with the grave of the Prophet ﷺ, or something to that effect, intending thereby to draw closer to Allāh. He replied: 'There is nothing wrong with it.'"[937]

A book entitled *Kitāb al-Sunna* is attributed to 'Abd Allāh ibn Aḥmad. Its first edition was sponsored by King 'Abd al-'Azīz ibn Sa'ūd and a Jedda businessman named Muḥammad Ḥusayn Naṣīf (d. 1971 CE).[938] It was published in Cairo in 1349/1930 by al-Maṭba'at al-Salafiyya. Al-Kawtharī in his *Maqālāt* (p. 355) lambasted it as a

935 The ḥadīth is actually narrated from Ibn 'Abbās by al-Bayhaqī, Ibn Abī Shayba, Ibn Mardūyah, Abū Nu'aym in *Dalā'il al-Nubuwwa*, and from Abū Hurayra by al-Bukhārī, al-Tirmidhī, Ibn Mājah, and others.

936 Suyūṭī cites it in *al-Durr al-Manthūr* and says it is narrated by Abū al-Shaykh, Ibn al-Mundhir, Ibn Abī Ḥātim, and al-Ḥākim, while al-Dhahabī declared its chain "soft" (*layyin*). Al-Sha'rānī in *al-Yawāqīt* (p. 281) mentions that not death but blindness ensued which Mūsā would then cure with a touch of his hand. Allāh knows best.

937 Narrated by 'Abd Allāh ibn Aḥmad ibn Ḥanbal in his *'Ilal* (2:492).

938 This man also financed the attack on Imām al-Kawtharī by 'Abd al-Raḥmān al-Mu'allimī al-Yamānī (d. 1976 CE) entitled *al-Tankīl limā Warada fī Ta'nīb al-Kawtharī min al-Abāṭīl* in which the latter declared: "Allāh has a body unlike bodies" and which Albānī published. The author heard in Damascus from Shaykh Wā'il al-Hanbalī, from 'Abd al-Rahmān ibn Nāsīr al-Albānī, that a dispute over the sales of this books was the reason Albānī and Zuhayr al-Shāwīsh ended their friendship."

collection of anthropomorphist forgeries and renamed it *Kitāb al-Zaygh* ("The Book of Deviation"). He quoted from it the following excerpts:

- "Is establishment (*istiwā'*) other than by sitting (*julūs*)?"[939]
- "Allāh spoke to Mūsā with His lips (*mushāfahatan*)."
- "Allāh did not touch anything with His hand except Ādam."
- "When Allāh sits on the Throne, it squeaks like a new saddle."
- "Allāh sits on the Throne and only four spans remain vacant."
- "Allāh ﷻ showed part of Himself."
- "His ﷻ other hand was empty without anything in it."

Ibn Abī Ya'lā relates something similar from Aḥmad ibn Ja'far ibn Ya'qūb al-Iṣṭakhrī[940] attributed to Imām Aḥmad himself: "Whoever claims that our pronunciation and recitation (*alfāẓunā wa-tilāwatunā*) of the Qur'ān are created, even if they say that the Qur'ān is the word of Allāh, is a Jahmī, and whoever does not declare him a disbeliever is like him, and Allāh spoke to Mūsā from His mouth (*min fīh*), and He handed him the Torah from His hand to his hand." Al-Dhahabī categorically denies the authenticity of its ascription to Aḥmad.[941]

Kitāb al-Sunna received two recent editions: by Muḥammad Basyūnī Zaghlūl who based his work on the 1930 edition; and by Muḥammad al-Qaḥṭānī, an Umm al-Qurā University graduate and author of the dubious *al-Walā' wal-Barā'*.

Shaykh Nūḥ Keller commented on *Kitāb al-Sunna*:

> I looked this book over with our teacher in ḥadīth, Sheikh Shu'ayb al-Arna'ūṭ, who had examined it one day, and said that at least 50 percent of the ḥadīths in it are weak or outright forgeries.

---

939 Al-Qinnawjī wrote in his *Qiṭf al-Thamar* (p. 39): "Whoever believes that His establishment over the Throne is like the establishment of a creature over a chair is an ignorant and misguided innovator."

940 He is unknown.

941 See al-Dhahabī's *Siyar* (9:503), chapter on Imām Aḥmad, section entitled *Ḥāl al-Imām Aḥmad fī Dawlat al-Mutawakkil.* Al-Dhahabī also dismisses the attribution of *al-Radd 'alā al-Jahmiyya* to Imām Aḥmad. Further down (9:512), al-Dhahabī cites most of al-Iṣṭakhrī's narration from Aḥmad and exclaims: "By Allāh! The Imām never said these things. May Allāh destroy the one who forged them!... Look at the ignorance of the ḥadīth scholars, who narrate such nonsense without a peep."

He was dismayed how Muḥammad al-Qaḥṭānī, the editor and commentator, could have been given a Ph.D. in Islamic faith (*'aqīda*) from Umm al-Qurā University in Saudi Arabia for readying for publication a work as sadly wanting in authenticity as this.

Ostensibly a "ḥadīth" work, it contains some of the most hardcore anthropomorphism found anywhere, such as the ḥadīth that "when He Most Blessed and Exalted sits on the *kursī*, a squeak is heard like the squeak of a new leather saddle" (*Kitāb al-Sunna* [Dammam: Dār Ibn al-Qayyim, 1986 / 1406], 1:301), or "Allāh wrote the Torah for Moses with His hand while leaning back on a rock, on tablets of pearl, and the screech of the quill could be heard. There was no veil between Him and him" (*ibid*, 1:294), or "The angels were created from the light of His two elbows and chest" (*ibid*, 2:510), and so on.

The work also puts lies in the mouths of major Ḥanbalī scholars and others, such as Khārija [ibn Muṣ'ab al-Sarakhsī] (d. 168/785), who is quoted as saying on *istiwā'*: "Does *istiwā'* mean anything except sitting?" (*ibid.*, 1:106), with a chain of transmission containing a liar (*kadhdhāb*), an unidentifiable (*majhūl*), plus the text with its contradiction (*mukhālafa*) of Islamic faith (*'aqīda*). Or consider the forty-nine pages of revilement of Abū Ḥanīfa and his school that it mendaciously ascribes to major Imāms, such as that relating that Isḥāq ibn Manṣūr al-Kūsaj (d. 251/865) said, "I asked Aḥmad Ibn Ḥanbal, 'Is a man rewarded by Allāh for loathing Abū Ḥanīfa and his colleagues?' and he said, 'Yes, by Allāh'" (*ibid.*, 1:180). To ascribe things so stupid to a man of Godfearingness (*taqwā*) like Aḥmad, whose respect for other scholars is well attested to by chains of transmission that are rigorously authenticated (*ṣaḥīḥ*), is one of the things by which this counterfeit work overreaches itself, and ends in cancelling any credibility that the name on it may have been intended to give it. Sheikh Shu'ayb told us he doesn't believe it is really from Aḥmad ibn Ḥanbal's son 'Abdullah, since there is an unidentifiable (*majhūl*) transmitter in the book's chain of ascription to 'Abdullah. But the fact that such a work exists may give you an idea of the kinds of things that have been circulated about Aḥmad after his death, and the total lack of scrupulousness among a handful of anthropomorphists who tried literally everything to spread their *bidʻas*.[942]

Later Figures Connected to the Ḥanbalī School

AL-KHALLĀL[943]

Aḥmad ibn Muḥammad ibn Hārūn, Abū Bakr al-Baghdādī al-Khallāl 🕮 (230?-311)was a Ḥanbalī ḥadīth Master who is the most important narrative link between Imām Aḥmad and posterity. Some count him among the junior companions of Imām Aḥmad while al-Dhahabī only states: "It is possible he may have seen him as a boy." He authored *al-Jāmiʻ li-ʻUlūm Aḥmad ibn Ḥanbal* in forty volumes – the first compilation of Imām Aḥmad's teachings in *fiqh*–, *al-ʻIlm*, *al-ʻIlal*, *al-Sunna*, and *Akhlāq Aḥmad ibn Ḥanbal*. A frank anthropomorphist, he states at length in his *Kitāb al-Sunna* that whoever denies that "Allāh sits on the *kursī* and there remains only four spans vacant" is an unbeliever.

AL-BARBAHĀRĪ[944]

Al-Ḥasan ibn ʻAlī ibn Khalaf, Abū Muḥammad al-Barbahārī 🕮 (d. 329)was a ḥadīth Master who accompanied Aḥmad's foremost companion Abū Bakr al-Marwazī, as well as the Ṣūfī Master of his time, Sahl ibn ʻAbd Allāh al-Tustarī. Ibn Abī Yaʻlā reports that al-Barbahārī composed a *Sharḥ Kitāb al-Sunna* in which he said: "Whoever takes up arms against one of the Imāms of the Muslims [i.e. one of the Caliphs] is a *Khārijī* who has split the unity [lit. 'split the staff'] of Muslims and contravened the Prophetic reports, and his death is a death in *Jāhiliyya*." He also said: "Know that the Religion is nothing other than imitation (*iʻlam anna al-dīna innamā huwa al-taqlīd*), and I mean imitation of the Companions of the Prophet 🕮 (*wal-taqlīdu li-aṣḥābi rasūlillah ṣallallāhu ʻalayhi wa-sallam*)." This book was published in Madīna at Maktabat al-Ghurabā' al-Athariyya (1993) and is popular among "Salafīs" although the above excerpts show a clear condemnation of the *lā-madhhabiyya* heresy and cites the rule on which the Ulema based their anathema of the Wahhābīs for rebelling against the Muslim *Dawla*.

---

[942] From the website http://www.masud.co.uk/ISLAM/nuh/masudq5.htm.
[943] See on him the *Siyar* (11:311, 9:530-531) and *Tadhkirat al-Ḥuffāẓ* (3:785).
[944] Sources: Ibn Abī Yaʻlā, *Ṭabaqāt al-Ḥanābila* (2:18-29 §588); Ibn al-Athīr, *al-Kāmil fīl-Tārīkh* (Dār Ṣādir ed. 8:307-309, 8:378); al-Dhahabī, *Siyar* (11:543-45 §2899).

Concerning the Jahmīs, al-Barbahārī declared: "Whoever says that his pronunciation of the Qur'ān is created is a Jahmī, and whoever keeps uncommitted, saying that it is neither created nor uncreated, is a Jahmī. This is what Aḥmad ibn Ḥanbal said." Ibn 'Abd al-Barr in *al-Intiqā'* relates otherwise from Aḥmad. We already mentioned that Imām al-Bukhārī considered the pronunciation of the Qur'ān created and was expelled from Bukhārā by the Ḥanbalīs for it.

The group of Ḥanbalīs led by al-Barbahārī in Baghdād considered themselves reformers and often took to the streets to forcibly redress what they considered unacceptable contraventions of the Religion, injuring or killing those they considered Jahmīs, destroying taverns and musical instruments, striking women singers, etc. In the year 320 in Baghdād, al-Barbahārī was declared wanted by the authorities and the houses of his followers were ransacked. He fled and remained in hiding until his death nine years later.

The worst controversy attached to al-Barbahārī and his group by far was their anthropomorphist teaching on the basis of weak narrations attributing limbs and place to Allāh ﷻ. Ibn Abī Ya'lā relates in his *Ṭabaqāt* that al-Barbahārī never sat to teach without mentioning that the Prophet ﷺ sits "next to Allāh" on the Throne.[945] Ibn al-Athīr relates the Caliph al-Rāḍī's edict against the Ḥanbalīs in the year 323, in which he said: "You mention the 'hand' and the 'fingers' and the 'two feet' and the 'two gilded sandals' and the 'short and curly hair' and the 'climbing' to heaven and the 'descending' to the world – Exalted is Allāh far above what the oppressors and rejecters say of Him! The Commander of the Believers swears an oath before Allāh by which he binds himself, that unless you put an end to your vile belief and crooked way, to destroy you to the last man by sword and by fire inside your very houses!"

AL-NAJJĀD[946]

Aḥmad ibn Salmān ibn al-Ḥasan, Abū Bakr al-Baghdādī al-Ḥanbalī al-Najjād ﷺ (d. 348), eulogised by al-Dhahabī as "the Imām, the ḥadīth scholar, the ḥadīth Master, the jurisprudent, the Mufti, the Shaykh of Iraq," was the Shaykh of al-Dāraquṭnī, al-Ḥākim, al-Khaṭṭābī, Ibn Man-

945 Ibn Abī Ya'lā, *Ṭabaqāt al-Ḥanābila* (2:43). See website cited in n. 902.

946 Main sources: Ibn Abī Ya'lā, *Ṭabaqāt al-Ḥanābila* (2:7-8); al-Dhahabī, *Siyar* (12:137 §3132), *Mīzān* (1:101).

dah, al-Khiraqī, and others. He narrated from 'Abd Allāh ibn Aḥmad ibn Ḥanbal and was the last to narrate from Abū Dāwūd. He was reported to relate narrations which were not kept in his own records, perhaps due to the loss of his sight.

Abū 'Alī ibn al-Ṣawwāf said: "Aḥmad ibn Salmān al-Najjād used to come with us to the ḥadīth scholars such as Bishr ibn Mūsā and others, holding his shoes in his hands because, he said, 'I love to walk barefoot in pursuit of the ḥadīth of the Prophet ﷺ.'" Ibn Abī Ya'lā comments: "He may have done so to conform with the Prophet's ﷺ saying: 'Shall I not inform you of the one who will carry the lightest burden on the Day of Judgment in front of Allāh? It is the one who races towards good deeds, walking barefoot. Gibrīl told me: 'Allāh looks kindly upon a servant of His who walks barefoot in the pursuit of good.''"[947]

Al-Najjād used to fast every day of the year, and he would break his fast every night with a loaf of bread of which he left aside one mouthful. On the night of *Jumu'a* he would give away his loaf as charity, and eat the mouthfuls he had put aside. He relates:

> One time I found myself in difficulty so I went to visit Ibrāhīm al-Ḥarbī. I told him of my condition and he said: "You should know that I too found myself in difficulty, until I only had small change left in my possession. My wife said to me: 'Look among your books, see what you do not need, and sell it!' After I prayed *'ishā* I sat in the lobby of my house (*al-dihlīz*) to write, whereupon someone knocked at the door. I asked who it was and he said: 'Let me

947 Al-Munāwī cited similar narrations in *Fayḍ al-Qadīr*: "If you race with each other towards good, walk barefoot, because Allāh multiplies the reward of those who walk barefoot over those who wear shoes." Al-Munāwī said: "Narrated from Ibn 'Abbās by al-Ṭabarānī in *al-Awsaṭ*, al-Khaṭīb in *Tārīkh Baghdād*, and al-Ḥākim in his *Tārīkh Naysābūr*. Its chain contains 'Īsā ibn Nujayḥ who, al-Dhahabī said, forged narrations. Hence, Ibn al-Jawzī included it among his *Mawḍū'āt* (1:217). It is somewhat strengthened by al-Ṭabarānī's other report whereby 'Whoever walks barefoot in Allāh's obedience, Allāh will not ask him to account for His orders on the Day of Judgment.' However, even the latter report was said to be a fabrication." Ibn al-Jawzī's verdict was confirmed by al-Suyūṭī in *al-La'ālī* (1983 ed. 1:194), Ibn 'Arrāq in *Tanzīh al-Sharī'a* (1:251), al-Ghumārī in *al-Mughīr* (p. 14) and al-Aḥdab in *Zawā'id Tārīkh Baghdād* (8:199-200 §1745). Of note here is Shu'ba's saying: "Those who go in pursuit of the ḥadīth on horseback (*'alā al-dawābb*) cannot succeed." Narrated by Abū Nu'aym in the *Ḥilya* (7:179 §10117).

speak to you.' I opened the door. He said to me: 'Put out the light,' so I put it out. He came into the lobby and put down a food-basket (*karra*). Then he said to me: 'We have prepared food for the children, and we wanted you and your children to have your share of it. This is something else together with it,' and he placed something next to the basket, adding: 'Use it as you wish.' I did not know who that man was. Then he left. I called my wife and told her to light the candles. She lit them and came to see. The basket was wrapped in an expensive scarf and contained fifty different kinds of food. Next to it was a purse containing a thousand dinars." I got up and took my leave of al-Ḥarbī, after which I went to Aḥmad [ibn Ḥanbal]'s grave to visit him. Then I went on my way. As I was walking on the side of the road, an old woman, one of our neighbors, met me and said: "Aḥmad, why do you look so downcast?" I told her of my predicament. She said: "Do you know that your mother gave me three hundred dirhams before she died, and said to me: 'Keep them, and if you see my son in difficulty or downcast one day, give them to him.' Come with me so I can give them to you." I went with her and she gave me the sum.

IBN BAṬṬA[948]

'Ubayd Allāh ibn Muḥammad, Abū 'Abd Allāh al-'Ukbarī, known as Ibn Baṭṭa ⚛ (d. 387), a student of al-Najjād and one of the main authorities in doctrine and law in the Ḥanbalī school, was a pious scholar who never left his house in forty years and fasted permanently, except on the two *'Īds*. Al-Dhahabī declares him "an Imām in the Sunna and an Imām in *fiqh*" but then cites Abū al-Qāsim al-Azharī's verdict that "Ibn Baṭṭa is extremely weak" (*ḍa'īf ḍa'īf*) while al-Khaṭīb declares him a forger and narrates from Abū Dharr al-Harawī and others that al-Dāraquṭnī questioned his truthfulness. Ibn Ḥajar states: "I discovered something in connection with Ibn Baṭṭa which I found scandalous and hideous." He then shows that Ibn Baṭṭa may have added words to a ḥadīth to give it an anthropomorphic slant. The ḥadīth in question is Ibn Mas'ūd's ḥadīth of the Burning Tree narrated by al-Tirmidhī with a weak chain, whereby the Prophet ﷺ

---

[948] Sources: al-Khaṭīb, *Tārīkh Baghdād* (10:371-374, 13:167); al-Dhahabī, *Mīzān al-I'tidāl* (3:15 §5394); Ibn Ḥajar, *Lisān al-Mīzān* (4:113-114 §231).

said: "When Allāh spoke to Mūsā ﷺ, the latter was wearing a robe of wool, a wool cloak, and a pair of sandals made of untanned ox leather." The addition cited by Ibn Ḥajar and apparently forged by Ibn Baṭṭa reads: "He [Mūsā] said: 'Who is that Hebrew (*al-'ibrānī*) speaking from the tree?' Allāh said: 'I am Allāh.'" This addition supports two tenets of anthropomorphism, direction and voice, while the position of *Ahl al-Sunna* is that Mūsā ﷺ heard Allāh without either.[949]

IBN ABĪ YA'LĀ AND HIS FATHER[950]

Muḥammad ibn al-Qāḍī Muḥammad Abī Ya'lā ibn al-Ḥusayn, al-Qāḍī Abū al-Ḥusayn al-Farrā', known as Ibn Abī Ya'lā ﷺ (d. 526) was the author of *Ṭabaqāt al-Ḥanābila* ("Synchronic Layers of the Ḥanbalīs"). Al-Dhahabī said of him: "He exaggerated concerning the Sunna and harped on the Attributes [...]. Al-Silafī said: 'He showed fanaticism for his School and criticised Ash'arīs a lot without fearing any reproach; he composed books pertaining to his School; he was devout, trustworthy, and well-established as a narrator and we took ḥadīth from him.'" Some of what he relates in the *Ṭabaqāt* is from unknown sources or individuals and therefore unverifiable. Al-Bukhārī himself cast doubt on the authenticity of what is related from Imām Aḥmad by the early Ḥanbalīs.[951] However, this biographical compendium is full of valuable information as well as interesting anecdotes about Imām Aḥmad and his school. The ḥadīth Master Ibn Rajab continued the work by providing biographical notices on the layers between his time and that of Ibn Abī Ya'lā.

Ibn Abī Ya'lā's father, al-Qāḍī Abū Ya'lā ibn al-Farrā' – Muḥammad ibn al-Ḥusayn ibn Muḥammad ibn Khalaf – (d. 458) was one of the major jurisprudent scholars of the Ḥanbalī school and the author of *Ibṭāl al-Ta'wīlāt li-Akhbār al-Ṣifāt,* also known as *Ibṭāl al-Ta'wīl* ("The Invalidation of Figurative Interpretation") in which, al-Dhahabī says, "he was verbose and cited worthless narrations inappropriate for use to assert any Divine Attribute whatsoever!"[952] Abū Ya'lā is dismissed as

[949] As narrated from al-Nakha'ī in al-Tha'ālibī's *Tafsīr* (4:117).

[950] Sources: al-Dhahabī, *Siyar* (14:481 §4749); Ibn al-Athīr, *al-Kāmil fil-Tārīkh* (Dār Ṣādir ed. 10:52 [year 458]).

[951] In *Khalq Af'āl al-'Ibād,* cf. al-Kawtharī in his edition of *al-Asmā' wal-Ṣifāt* (p. 266).

[952] Al-Dhahabī, *Mukhtaṣar al-'Ulūw* (p. 271), cf. Ibn Abī Ya'lā, *Ṭabaqāt al-Ḥanābila*

an anthropomorphist (*mujassim*) by his own Ḥanbalī colleagues such as Abū Muḥammad al-Tamīmī and Ibn al-Jawzī throughout the latter's book *Radd Shubah al-Tashbīh.*[953] There might be an oblique reference to him in Ibn Qudāma's closing words in *Dhamm al-Ta'wīl*: "Whoever affirms an attribute for Allāh ﷻ on the basis of any of those forged ḥadīths is in a worse state than those who interpret the sound ḥadīths figuratively!" Abū Ya'lā's *Ibṭāl* was recently resuscitated and reinjected into the book market under the editorship of an Abū 'Abd Allāh al-Najdī.

Imām Aḥmad and *Kalām* Theology

One of the misunderstandings prevalent among the "Salafis" who misrepresent Imām Aḥmad's school today is his position regarding *kalām* or dialectic theology. It is known that he was uncompromisingly opposed to *kalām* as a method, even if used as a means to defend the truth, preferring to stick to the plain narration of textual proofs and abandoning all recourse to dialectical or rational ones. Ibn Abī Ya'lā and Ibn al-Jawzī relate his saying: "Do not sit with the people of *kalām*, even if they defend the Sunna." This attitude is at the root of Aḥmad's ostracism of the Shāfi'ī Ṣūfī and *mutakallim* al-Ḥārith al-Muḥāsibī although the alleged condemnation of al-Muḥāsibī as a Jahmī is excessive. It also explains the disaffection of later Ḥanbalīs towards Imām al-Ash'arī and his school, despite the latter's subsequent standing as the Imām of the Sunni creed *par excellence.* The reasons for this rift are now obsolete although the rift has amplified beyond all recognizable shape, as it is evident, in retrospect, that opposition to Ash'arīs, for various reasons, came out of a major misunderstanding of their real contributions within the Community, whether as individuals or as a whole.

There are several general reasons why the Ḥanbalī-*mutakallim* rift should be considered artificial and obsolete. First, *kalām* in its original form was an innovation in Islām (*bid'a*) against which there was near-unanimous opposition among *Ahl al-Sunna wal-Jamā'a.* Accordingly

---

(2:197) and Ibn al-Athīr, *al-Kāmil* (8:228=8:16). See a modern refutation by Sa'īd Fawda at http://www.al-razi.net/website/pages/m21.htm.

953 Al-Tamīmī said: "He [Abū Ya'lā] has beshat the Ḥanbalīs with filth that water cannot wash away!" Ibn al-Athīr, *al-Kāmil* (8:378=8:104). Cf. Abū Bakr ibn al-'Arabī in his *al-Qawāṣim wal-'Awāṣim* (2:283=p. 209).

there was resistance among the *Salaf* to the use of *kalām* for the purpose of defending the Sunna, exemplified by Imām Aḥmad's position cited above. One reason why they disallowed it was *wara'*: because of extreme scrupulousness against learning and practicing a discipline initiated by the enemies of the Sunna. Thus many of them considered *kalām* reprehensible but not forbidden in absolute terms, as is clear from al-Shāfi'ī's statement narrated by Ibn Abī Ḥātim: "If I wanted to publish books refuting every single opponent [of the Sunna] I could easily do so, but *kalām* is not for me, and I dislike that anything of it be attributed to me."[954] This shows that al-Shāfi'ī left the door open for others to enter a field which he abstained from entering out of strict Godwariness. Others, like Abū Ḥanīfa, felt confident enough to enter *kalām* disputations against non-Sunnis without finding themselves in a moral quandary.

Second, *kalām* is a difficult and delicate science that demands a mind above the norm. The Imāms forbade it as a *sadd al-dharī'a* or precautionary measure. They rightly foresaw that unless one possessed an adequate capacity to practice it, one was courting disaster. This was the case with Aḥmad's student Abū Ṭālib[955] and other early Ḥanbalīs who misinterpreted Aḥmad's doctrinal positions – as al-Bukhārī indicated – and whom Aḥmad himself rebuked for it. Al-Bukhārī, Aḥmad, and others of the *Salaf* thus experienced first hand that one who dabbled in *kalām* could easily lapse into heresy, innovation, or disbelief. This was made abundantly clear in Imām Mālik's answer to the man who asked how the Merciful established Himself over the Throne: "The establishment is known, the 'how' is inconceivable, and to ask about it is an innovation."[956] Mālik's answer is the essence of *kalām* at the same time as it warns against the misuse of *kalām*, as observed by the late Dr. Abū al-Wafā' al-Taftazānī.[957] Mālik's reasoning is echoed by al-Shāfi'ī's advice to his student al-Muzanī: "Take proofs from creation to know about the Creator, and do not burden yourself with the knowledge of what your mind cannot reach." Similarly, Ibn Khuzayma and Ibn Abī Ḥātim

954 Narrated from al-Rabī' by al-Dhahabī in the *Siyar* (8:388).

955 See appendix "The Controversy over the Pronunciation" (n. 1105).

956 See notes 378-380.

957 See the relevant citation in the collection of essays entitled *Al-Duktūr Abū al-Wafā al-Taftazānī ustādhan lil-taṣawwuf wa-mufakkiran Islāmiyyan, 1930-1994: buḥūth 'anhu wa-dirāsāt muhdāt ilayh*, ed. 'Āṭif al-Irāqī (Cairo: Dār al-Hidāya, 1995).

admitted their technical ignorance of the science of *kalām*, at the same time acknowledging its possible good use by qualified experts. As for Ibn Qutayba, he regretted his *kalām* days and preferred to steer completely clear of it.

Third, in the language of the early scholars, *kalām* was synonymous with the doctrines of the Qadariyya, Murji'a, Jahmiyya, Jabriyya, Rawāfiḍ, and Mu'tazila and their multifarious sub-sects. This is shown by the examples Ibn Qutayba gives of *kalām* and *mutakallimūn* in *Mukhtalif al-Ḥadīth*, none of which belongs to *Ahl al-Sunna* except the Sunnī type of Murji'a.[958] Similarly the adherents of *kalām* brought up in the speech of al-Ḥasan al-Baṣrī, Ibn al-Mubārak, Ibn Rāhūyah, Imām al-Shāfi'ī and the rest of the pre-Ḥanbalī scholars of ḥadīth are the innovators of the above-mentioned sects, not those who later opposed them using the same methods of reasoning. The latter cannot be put in the same category. Therefore the early works blaming *kalām* cannot be applied to the Sunni *mutakallimūn* such as Ash'arīs and Māturīdīs in the same breath with the innovators, and only those ignorant of the context of those condemnations fail to see this.

IBN 'ASĀKIR'S *FATWĀ* ON *KALĀM*

The above is the position of all the early Ash'arī Imāms including al-Qushayrī, al-Bayhaqī, al-Ghazzālī, and Ibn 'Asākir. The latter said:

> **The condemned *kalām* is the *kalām* of the people of vain disputation** and whatever positions the rebellious innovators try to promote in the most artful terms. As for the *kalām* that conforms with the Book and the Sunna, articulating the actual positions of the Doctrine at the time dissension rears its head, such a *kalām* is highly praiseworthy among the Ulema as well as those who teach it. Al-Shāfi'ī excelled at it and understood it. He confronted more than one innovator and cited proofs against them until they were defeated [...]. Those of our Imāms that considered it desirable to relinquish probing into *kalām* did so only in relation to that specific context, namely, that the condemned *kalām* is only the *kalām* of the people of innovations which contravenes

[958] Cf. p. 42-44 above.

the Book and the Sunna. As for the *kalām* that conforms to the Book and the Sunna, exposing [the truth] reasonably and eloquently, it is highly praiseworthy and desirable in time of need.[959]

AL-SHĀṬIBĪ'S *FATWĀ* ON *KALĀM*

Al-Shāṭibī said in his *Muwāfaqāt*: "The Congregation of the Muslims follow Imām Mālik's position, unless one is obliged to speak. One must not remain silent if his purpose is to refute falsehood and guide people away from it, or if one fears the spread of misguidance or some similar danger."[960] Imām al-Kawtharī spoke similarly in the introduction to Ibn 'Asākir's *Tabyīn* and so did Shaykh Wahbī Ghāwjī in the introduction to Badr al-Dīn Ibn Jamā'a's *Īḍāḥ al-Dalīl*.[961]

IBN AL-SUBKĪ'S *FATWĀ* ON *KALĀM*

Imām Ibn al-Subkī spoke similarly of the obligatory nature of *kalām* in certain specific circumstances, as opposed to its superfluousness at other times: "The use of *kalām* in case of necessity is a legal obligation (*wājib*), and to keep silent about *kalām* in other cases is a *sunna*."[962]

AL-QUSHAYRĪ'S *FATWĀ* ON *KALĀM*

Ibn al-Subkī gave the above reply following the *fatwā* by Imām Abū al-Qāsim al-Qushayrī in response to those who charged Imām Abū al-Ḥasan al-Ash'arī with innovation:

> Al-Ash'arī and all the Muslim people of accomplished learning (*ahl al-taḥṣīl*) hold that the responsible Muslim has to know the Creator Who is the object of his worship, with the proofs He has established of His oneness and of His absolutely deserving all the attributes of Lordship. They did not require that they know

959 Ibn 'Asākir, *Tabyīn* (al-Kawtharī ed. p. 339 and 351).

960 Al-Shāṭibī, *al-Muwāfaqāt* (2:332). See also page 419 and footnote 1115 *infra*.

961 Ibn 'Asākir, *Tabyīn* (Kawtharī ed. p. 21); Ibn Jamā'a, *Īḍāḥ al-Dalīl* (1990 ed. p. 16). There are three different Ibn Jamā'as: the Qāḍī Badr al-Dīn Muḥammad ibn Ibrāhīm ibn Sa'd Allāh al-Ḥamawī *thumma* al-Miṣrī (639-733) cf. *Bidāya* (14:131), *Durar* (3:367); the ḥadīth Master Qāḍī al-Quḍāt 'Izz al-Dīn 'Abd al-'Azīz ibn Muḥammad ibn Ibrāhīm al-Dimashqī *thumma* al-Miṣrī (694-767) cf. *Durar* (2:489); and the *Mufassir* Qāḍī Burhān al-Dīn Abū Isḥāq Ibrāhīm ibn 'Abd al-Raḥīm ibn Muḥammad al-Miṣrī *thumma* al-Maqdisī al-Dimashqī (725-790) cf. *Durar* (1:39).

962 Ibn al-Subkī, *Ṭabaqāt al-Shāfi'iyya al-Kubrā* (2:230).

the jargon of the theologians such as "substance" and "accident" (*al-jawhar wal-'araḍ*). What they required is that investigation (*al-naẓar*) take place and that conclusions be drawn that lead one to knowledge of Allāh Almighty. The *mutakallimūn* only used such terminology to make [this process] more comprehensible and easier for students. **The pious predecessors, even if they did not use such terms, suffered no gaps in their sciences.** The later generations that used such terms did not do so to part from the way of truth or to innovate in the Religion. Just as the Jurists that came after the time of the Companions and Successors used jurisprudential terminology such as "causation" and "the thing caused" and "analogy" (*al-'illa wal-ma'lūl wal-qiyās*) among others. Their use of these terms was not a *bid'a*. Nor was the lack of their use by the *Salaf* a deficiency on their part. The same applies to the grammarians, the conjugators, the chroniclers, each group using its own specific jargon.

If they say that preoccupation with the science of *kalām* is a *bid'a* and contravenes the way of the *Salaf*, the answer is that al-Ash'arī is not the only one from the people of the *Qibla* at whose feet such a charge can be laid. Furthermore, such a charge is typical of the rabble (*al-Ḥashwiyya*) who possess no learning in the first place. Now, how can the *Salaf* of the Community be thought of as not taking the path of investigation and being content with imitation? Perish the thought – by Allāh! – that such be their description. Rather, the *Salaf* among the Companions were fully independent in their knowledge of the truth. They heard from the Messenger ﷺ the characteristics of the worshipped Deity and pondered them in the light of the proofs forwarded in the Qur'ān and the reports of the Messenger ﷺ in the questions of *tawḥīd*. Exactly so did the Successors and their followers, thanks to their nearness to the time of the Messenger ﷺ. When the people of lusts appeared and the innovators became rife – the Khawārij, Jahmiyya, Mu'tazila, Qadariyya – and produced their false arguments, the Imāms of *Ahl al-Sunna* mobilised to confront them. They rose to defend the Muslims with all that enlightened their path. When they feared for the hearts of the Muslims lest they ferment and seethe in the adversaries' falsehoods, they entered the fray in fighting back and exposing their corruption. They replied to their questions and guarded the Religion of Allāh from them by clarifying its proofs. For Allāh Most High said, ﴾**and reason with them in the better way**﴿ (16:125). Learn from His Manners – exalted is He! Nor did they say, in the questions of *tawḥīd*, other than what Allāh Most High had taught them well in the unambiguous parts of His Revelation.

One wonders at those who say, "There is no science of theology in the Qur'ān" while he finds the verses of juridical rulings and those of jurisprudential principles, although they are quantitatively less by far! In sum, none denies the science of theology except two types. The first type is an ignoramus who resorts to *taqlīd*. He finds it too hard to tread the path of the people of learning and is far from that of the people of investigation. People are the enemies of what they do not know. Seeing himself prevented from achieving any competence in this science, he turns to prohibit others as well, so as to misguide others just as he has been misguided.

The second type is a person who holds corrupt views. He conceals surreptitious innovations of misguidance. He hides from people the shame of his views and keeps them in the dark as to the disgraces of his secret beliefs and his *'aqīda*. He knows very well that the people of accomplished learning and investigation are experts at tearing down the deceptive veils of innovators and exposing the ugliness of their beliefs to all. The swindler hates the mint master! But the fault is in the false coins in the swindler's hand, not in the master money-changer. ﴾**Are those who know equal with those who know not?**﴿ (39:9).[963]

ABŪ ZAHRA'S AND OTHER *FATWĀ* ON *KALĀM*

Similarly, Shaykh Muḥammad Abū Zahra said: "Whenever you hear Abū Yūsuf or Muḥammad [ibn al-Ḥasan] or al-Shāfi'ī or Ibn Ḥanbal and others [among the early Imāms] revile the science of *kalām* and those who take knowledge by following the methods of the *mutakallimūn*, know that they only meant by their criticism the Mu'tazila and the methodology of the Mu'tazila."[964] Among those

963 Al-Qushayrī, *Shikāyat Ahl al-Sunna bi-Ḥikāyat mā Nālahum min al-Miḥna* in Ibn al-Subkī, *Ṭabaqāt al-Shāfi'iyya al-Kubrā* (3:420-421).

964 Abū Zahra, *Abū Ḥanīfa* (p. 133).

infamous *mutakallimūn* were Ibn Abī Du'ād and Abū 'Īsā Barghūth al-Jahmī who both disputed with Imām Aḥmad at the time of his ordeal.

Similarly, Shaykh 'Abd al-Wakīl Durūbī said: "What al-Shāfi'ī meant [by the prohibition of engaging in *kalām*] was the heretical scholastic theology that proliferated in his time and put rationalistic theories ahead of the Qur'ān and Sunna, not the science of theology (*'ilm al-tawḥīd*) by which Ash'arī and Māturīdī Scholars have clarified and detailed the tenets of Sunni Islām, which is an important part of the Islamic sciences."[965]

Similarly, Imām al-Ghazzālī in the *Qawā'id al-'Aqā'id* part of his *Iḥyā'* cites several examples among the Imāms of the Companions and *Salaf* who engaged in *kalām* disputations in response to the need of the moment, such as Ibn 'Abbās with the Khawārij, 'Alī with the philosopher, al-Ḥasan al-Baṣrī with the Qadarī, etc.

What goes for the condemnation of *kalām* also goes for the condemnation of juridical opinion (*ra'ī*). Imām al-Kawtharī said:

> What is found in the words of Ibrāhīm al-Nakha'ī and those of his synchronical layer (*ṭabaqa*) that "the people of *ra'ī* are the enemies of the *Sunan*"[966] is in the sense of the *ra'ī* that contradicts the Sunna that is transmitted concerning doctrine. They meant by it the Khawārij, the Qadariyya, the Mushabbiha, and similar innovators. They did not mean *ra'ī* in the sense of scholarly exertion (*ijtihād*) in the branches of the Law that concern legal rulings. To give this any other sense is to tamper with their wording. How can it be otherwise when al-Nakha'ī himself and Ibn al-Musayyab himself are among those who express personal juridical opinion in the branches, in spite of those who cannot picture them doing so?[967]

965 In *Reliance of the Traveller* (p. 9).

966 Narrated from 'Amr ibn Ḥurayth and others by al-Dāraquṭnī in his *Sunan* (4:146), al-Bayhaqī in *al-Madkhal* (p. 190), Ibn Ḥazm in *al-Iḥkām* (6:213), Ibn 'Abd al-Barr in *Jāmi' Bayān al-'Ilm* (2:1041-1042 §2001-2005) and al-Lālikā'ī in *Sharḥ Uṣūl I'tiqād Ahl al-Sunna* (1:123). Also attributed to al-Zuhrī, cf. Ibn 'Abd al-Barr, *Jāmi'* (2:1052 §2032). See the definition of praiseworthy *ra'ī* by Ibn Ḥajar in *Fatḥ al-Bārī* (1959 ed. 13:189 and 13:287-288) and Ibn al-Qayyim in *I'lām al-Muwaqqi'īn* (1:83) as well as al-Kawtharī's *Fiqh Ahl al-'Iraq* and the introduction to al-Tahānawī's *I'lā' al-Sunan*.

967 Al-Kawtharī, *Fiqh Ahl al-'Iraq* (p. 23-24). Cf. Ibn 'Abd al-Barr, *Jāmi' Bayān al-'Ilm* (2:1052).

In conclusion, any careful reader of Islamic intellectual history can see that if the Ash'arī scholars of *kalām* had not, by the grace of Allāh ﷻ, engaged and defeated the various theological and philosophical sects on their own terrain, the silence of *Ahl al-Sunna* might well have sealed their defeat at the hands of their opponents.

Aḥmad's Positions in *Kalām*: On *Istiwā'*

Abū al-Faḍl al-Tamīmī related that Aḥmad said, concerning *istiwā'*:

> [*Istiwā'*] means height/exaltation (*'ulūw*) and elevation (*irtifā'*). Allāh ﷻ is ever Exalted (*'ālī*) and Elevated (*rafī'*) without beginning, before He created the Throne. He is above everything (*huwa fawqa kulli shay'*), and He is exalted over everything (*huwa al-'ālī 'alā kulli shay'*). He only specified the Throne because of its particular significance which makes it different from everything else, as the Throne is the best of all things and the most elevated of them. Allāh ﷻ therefore praised Himself by saying that He ﴿**established Himself over the Throne**﴾ (20:5, 40:7), that is, He exalted Himself over it (*'alayhi 'alā*). It is impermissible to say that He established Himself with a contact or a meeting with it. Exalted is Allāh above that! Allāh is not subject to change, substitution, nor limits, whether before or after the creation of the Throne.[968]

An identical position is related from Abū Ḥanīfa in the *Waṣiyya* and al-Ash'arī in the *Ibāna*.

On Allāh Not Possessing a Limit *(Ḥadd)*

It is a leitmotiv of anthropomorphists – forwarded by Ibn Taymiyya – that Imām Aḥmad upheld the doctrine that Allāh ﷻ possesses a limit (*ḥadd*), although Aḥmad, like the rest of the *Salaf*, held the position that Allāh ﷻ has no limit.[969] Yet Ibn Taymiyya asserts: "Al-Qāḍī

[968] Ibn Abī Ya'lā, *Ṭabaqāt al-Ḥanābila* (2:296-297).

[969] Ibn Taymiyya, *Bayān Talbīs al-Jahmiyya* (1:445 and 2:162): "The Book and the Sunna definitely show that concept [that Allāh exists and is separate from His creation and firmly established to be real] as already mentioned of Imām Aḥmad's adducing as proof for this what the Qur'ān says, which indicates that Allāh ﷻ has a limit by which He distinguishes Himself from creatures, and that there is a divide (*infiṣāl*) and a separation (*mubāyana*) between Him and creation, so it is true that matters ascend and rise up to Him, and it is true that He comes and arrives." "Al-Khallāl said: Muḥammad ibn 'Alī al-Warrāq narrated to us: Abū Bakr al-Athram narrated to us: Muḥammad ibn

[Abū Ya'lā] said that Aḥmad asserts in absolute terms that Allāh ﷻ had a limit but he negates it in Ḥanbal's narration, saying: 'We believe that Allāh is on the Throne in the manner He wishes and however He wishes, without limit nor description anyone could give or define Him by.' So he negated the limit that pertains to the description he mentioned, meaning the limit known by creatures [...] And that is the meaning of Aḥmad's statement: 'Allāh ﷻ has a limit that only He knows.'"[970] The latter phrase contradicts what is authentically reported from Imām Aḥmad:

- [1] by al-Khallāl: "Allāh ﷻ has a Throne and the Throne has carriers carrying it while Allāh ﷻ is on His Throne although He has no limit, and Allāh ﷻ knows best its limit"[971];
- [2] by Ḥanbal ibn Isḥāq, the Imām's cousin: "Allāh ﷻ is not to be described more than whatever He described Himself with, or His Prophet described Him with, without limit nor delimitation (*bilā ḥaddin walā ghāya*)"[972];
- [3] by Ḥanbal also, as cited above: "We believe that Allāh is on the Throne in the manner He wishes and however He wishes, without limit nor description anyone could give or define Him by."[973]
- [4] by Ḥanbal also, in commentary of the verse ﴿**And He is with you wheresoever you may be**﴾ (57:4): "[I.e.] His knowledge. His knowledge encompasses all, and our Lord is over the Throne without limit (*bilā ḥadd*) or description."[974]
- [5] by Abū al-Faḍl al-Tamīmī: "Allāh ﷻ is not subject to change, substitution, nor limits, whether before or after the creation of the Throne."[975]

Ibrāhīm al-Qaysī narrated to me: I said to Aḥmad ibn Ḥanbal that it is said that Ibn al-Mubārak was asked: How do we know our Lord? and he replied: 'In the seventh heaven on His Throne, with a limit.' Aḥmad said: 'That is what we say too.'"

970 Ibn Taymiyya, *Bayān Talbīs* (2:173). Of the sources of these beliefs is 'Uthmān ibn Sa'īd al-Dārimī, cf. Imām al-Kawtharī in his essay *Taḥdhīr al-Umma min Du'āt al-Wathaniyya* ("Warning the Community about Those Who Call to Idol-Worship").

971 Aḥmad ibn Ḥanbal, *al-'Aqīda Riwayata Abī Bakr al-Khallāl*, ed. 'Abd al-'Azīz 'Izz al-Dīn al-Sayrawān (Damascus: Dār Qutayba, 1988) p. 78.

972 Narrated by Ibn Qudāma in *Dhamm al-Ta'wīl* (p. 20 §32).

973 Narrated by Abū Ya'lā in *Ibṭāl al-Ta'wīl* per Ibn Taymiyya, *Bayān Talbīs* (2:173).

974 Narrated by al-Dhahabī cf. *Mukhtaṣar al-'Ulūw* (p. 190 §229) and by al-Lālikā'ī.

975 Narrated by Ibn Abī Ya'lā, *Ṭabaqāt al-Ḥanābila* (2:296-297).

The same position is narrated from the following:

- ʿAlī ibn Abī Ṭālib ﷺ: "He ﷻ spoke to Mūsā ﷺ directly (*taklīman*) without limbs, without organs, without lips, and without uvula! Glorified is He above the imposition of modality by attributes. Whoever claims that our God has boundaries is ignorant of the Creator Who is worshipped. Whoever says that locations encompass Him is inevitably heading for perplexity and confusion."[976]
- Ibn al-Mājishūn: "As for He Who never changes, never ceases to exist, has always existed without beginning, and like unto Whom there is nothing and no one: no one knows "how" He is except He. How could He be known as He is Who has no beginning, does not die, and does not turn to dust? How can the attribute of anything of His possess a limit (*ḥadd*) or an endpoint (*muntahā*) that anyone might get to know or the extent of which he might define??"[977]
- Al-Tustarī: "I heard the Shaykh Abū ʿAbd al-Raḥmān al-Sulamī say: I heard Manṣūr ibn ʿAbd Allāh say: I heard Abū al-Ḥasan al-ʿAnbārī say: I heard Sahl ibn ʿAbd Allāh al-Tustarī say: 'The believers shall look at Him with their eyesights (*bil-abṣār*) without encompassment (*iḥāṭa*) nor attainment (*idrāk*).'"[978]
- Ibn Kullāb, Abū Ḥātim al-Rāzī, al-Khaṭṭābī, Ibn Ḥibbān: "The position that He is above the Throne but has no limit (*ḥadd*) nor dimension nor body is that of many of the upholders of the Divine Attributes (*al-ṣifātiyya*) among the followers of Ibn Kullāb and the Ashʿarī Imāms including their early authorities and whoever agrees with them among the jurists, [...] the ḥadīth scholars, and the Ṣūfīṣ [...] among them Abū Ḥātim, Ibn Ḥibbān, and Abū Sulaymān al-Khaṭṭābī."[979] On Ibn Ḥibbān see also his biographical notice in the chapter on al-Shāfiʿī.
- Jaʿfar al-Ṣādiq: "Whoever claims that Allāh is in (*fī*) something or from (*min*) something or on (*ʿalā*) something has associated

976 Narrated from Muḥammad ibn Isḥāq, from al-Nuʿmān ibn Saʿd by Abū Nuʿaym in *Ḥilyat al-Awliyā'* (1997 ed. 1:114-115 §227=1985 ed. 1:73). Abū Nuʿaym said: "This narration is single-chained and narrated only by al-Nuʿmān, and Ibn Isḥāq narrated it from him with a missing link (*mursal*).

977 Cf. Ibn Taymiyya, *Fatwā Ḥamawiyya* (p. 311-321)=*Majmūʿ al-Fatāwā* (5:42-46).

978 Narrated by al-Qushayrī in his *Risāla*, section titled "Doctrine of the Sufis" (§59).

979 Ibn Taymiyya, *Bayān Talbīs al-Jahmiyya* (1:548, 1:600, 2:169).

something with Him. For if He were on something He would be carried; and if He were in something He would be limited; and if He were from something He would be created."[980]

- Abū Dāwūd [al-Ṭayālisī] said: "Sufyān al-Thawrī, Shu'ba, Ḥammād ibn Zayd, Ḥammād ibn Salama, Sharīk, and Abū 'Awāna did not hold [that Allāh ﷻ had] a limit or a likeness or a similitude. They would narrate the ḥadīths [of the Attributes] without saying 'how'. If asked, they would answer with whatever was transmitted. And this is also our position."[981]
- Abū al-Ḥasan al-Ash'arī: Al-Subkī said: "Al-Ash'arī and most of the Scholars of *kalām* have declared as disbelievers any innovator whose innovation constitutes or leads to disbelief. For example, if he claims that the object of his worship possesses an image (*ṣūra*) or a limit (*ḥadd*) and boundary (*nihāya*), or that it is permissible to attribute to him movement and stillness."[982]
- Mālik ibn Anas: "He is neither ascribed a limit nor likened with anything" (*lā yuḥaddad walā yushabbah*). Ibn al-'Arabī al-Mālikī said after citing it: "This is a pinnacle of *tawḥīd* in which no Muslim preceded Mālik."[983]
- Al-Ṭaḥāwī in his *'Aqīda* (§38): "He is beyond having limits placed on Him, or being confined, or having parts or limbs. Nor is He contained by the six directions as all created things are" (*wata'ālā 'anil-ḥudūdi wal-ghāyāti wal-arkāni wal-a'ḍā'i wal-adawāt, lā taḥwīhi al-jihātu al-sittu kasā'iri al-mubtada'āt*).
- Ibn Khafīf in his *'Aqīda* (§31): "They will see Him without encompassment (*iḥāṭa*) or delimitation (*taḥdīd*) within any given limit (*ḥadd*), whether from the front, the back, above, below, right, or left."
- Ibn Fūrāk: "The Teacher Abū Bakr ibn Fūrāk also mentioned the above method in interpretation from one of our companions who said: 'He established Himself in the sense of elevated.' Then he said that such elevation is not in the sense of distance, nor boundary, nor place in which He is firmly fixed. Rather, he means by it what Allāh meant when He said: ﴾**Have you taken**

[980] Cited by al-Qushayrī in his *Risāla*, section titled "Doctrine of the Sufis" (§84).

[981] Al-Bayhaqī, *Asmā' wal-Ṣifāt* (Kawtharī ed. p. 426-427; Ḥāshidī ed. 2:334-336).

[982] Cited in al-Kawtharī, *Maqālāt* (p. 374).

[983] In *Aḥkām al-Qur'ān* (4:1740).

security from Him Who is in the heaven...﴿ (67:16-17), that is, above it, together with the preclusion of limit (*ḥadd*) for Him and the fact that He admits neither of being contained by a heavenly stratum nor of being encompassed by an earthly expanse of space. Allāh Almighty was described thus in the evidence transmitted, and so we do not dispute what the evidence said."[984]

- Al-Qushayrī: "﴾**He established Himself over the Throne**﴿ (7:54; 13:2; 20:5; 25:59; 32:4), however, the One without beginning has no limit (*al-qadīm laysa lahu ḥadd*). He 'established Himself over the Throne,' however, it is impermissible to attribute to Him proximity with His Essence or remoteness. He 'established Himself over the Throne,' however, the Throne would be the most needful of all things to an iota of connection (*al-wiṣāl*) [with Him] if it were only alive! But it is a lifeless solid, and when did solids ever possess volition? He 'established Himself over the Throne,' however, He is the Everlasting Sovereign (*al-Ṣamad*) without rival, the Unique without limit!"[985]

Examples of Aḥmad's *Ta'wīl* in the Attributes

Imām Aḥmad interpreted the "coming" of Allāh in the verse ﴾**Wait they for aught else than that Allāh should come unto them in the shadows of the clouds with the angels?**﴿ (2:210) to mean that His order (*amr*) should come, in the light of His saying: ﴾**Wait they for naught else than that the angels should come unto them or your Lord's command should come to pass?**﴿ (16:33).[986] He further interpreted ﴾**Your Lord shall arrive**﴿ (89:22) to mean His reward (*thawāb*) should come.[987] This interpretation is in line with both the view of the early Salaf and that of the early and late Ash'arī School:

- The Tābi'ī Abū al-'Āliya (d. 90) and al-Rabī' (d. 139) said of 2:210: "It means the angels come in the clouds. It is confirmed by His saying: ﴾**A day when the heaven with the clouds will be rent asunder**

[984] Al-Bayhaqī, *Asmā' wal-Ṣifāt* (Kawtharī ed. p. 410-411=Ḥāshidī ed. 2:308-309).

[985] Al-Qushayrī, *Laṭā'if al-Ishārāt* (5:139).

[986] Narrated by Ibn Ḥazm, *al-Fiṣal* (2:173). Al-Kawtharī in his edition of al-Bayhaqī's *al-Asmā' wal-Ṣifāt* (p. 448 cf. p. 292) states that Abū Ya'lā also narrates it from Aḥmad. See also Ibn al-Jawzī's *Daf' Shubah al-Tashbīh* (Saqqāf ed. p. 110 and 141).

[987] Narrated through al-Bayhaqī by Ibn Kathīr in *al-Bidāya* (10:361=10:342-343), al-Bayhaqī in *Manāqib Aḥmad*, and Ibn al-Jawzī in *Daf' Shubah al-Tashbīh* (p. 13).

and the angels will be sent down, a great descent﴿ (25:25)."[988]

- Al-Bayhaqī said: "[Abū al-'Āliya's] commentary rightly establishes that the clouds are a place and vehicle only for the angels, whereas there is neither place nor vehicle for Allāh Almighty."[989]
- Al-Ash'arī said that Allāh Almighty on the Day of Judgment shall bring about a certain act (*fi'l*) which He named "coming" and "arrival."[990]
- Al-Qurṭubī reiterated al-Ash'arī's explanation and said: "It is based on the lexical meaning of *ityān*, which is to proceed to do something (*al-qaṣd ilā al-shay'*). The meaning of the verse is thus: Wait they for naught else than that Allāh should cause to pass a certain act with some of His creatures whereby He shall proceed to requite them and judge them, just as He brought to be a certain act which He called 'descent' and another which He called 'establishment.'"[991]
- The grammarian al-Akhfash (d. 210) said that ﴾**that Allāh should come**﴿ (2:210) is not understood literally concerning Allāh, but means that His order (*amr*) should come.[992]
- The grammarian al-Zajjāj (d. ca 310) said: "It means the promised reckoning and punishment shall come to them in the form of a cloud, as in His saying: ﴾**Allāh visited them from a place whereof they reckoned not**﴿ (59:2), that is: by abasing them."[993]
- Al-Fakhr al-Rāzī reiterated Aḥmad's interpretation of verse 2:210: "It means that His order should come unto them, as proved by His saying: ﴾**Await they aught save that the angels should come unto them or your Lord's command should come to pass?**﴿ (16:33).

988 Narrated from Abū al-'Āliya [al-Riyāḥī the student of Ibn 'Abbās] by al-Bayhaqī in *al-Asmā'* (Kawtharī ed. p. 448; Ḥāshidī ed. 2:370 §943) through al-Ḥākim with a chain containing Abū Ja'far al-Rāzī ('Īsā ibn Abī 'Īsā Māhān) whom al-Khaṭīb and Ibn Ḥajar declared "truthful but poor in memorizing" – although considered trustworthy (*thiqa*) by Ibn al-Madīnī, Ibn Ma'īn, Abū Ḥātim, and al-Ḍiyā' al-Maqdisī – and by al-Ṭabarī, Ibn Abī Ḥātim, al-Qurṭubī, and al-Suyūṭī in their *Tafsīrs* (verse 2:210), also by Abū 'Ubayd ibn Sallām and Ibn al-Mundhir as stated in al-Suyūṭī's *al-Durr al-Manthūr*.

989 Al-Bayhaqī, *Al-Asmā' wal-Ṣifāt* (Kawtharī ed. p. 448; Ḥāshidī ed. 2:370).

990 *Ibid.* (Kawtharī ed. p. 448; Ḥāshidī ed. 2:371).

991 Al-Qurṭubī, *Tafsīr* (verse 2:210).

992 As cited by al-Qurṭubī in his *Tafsīr* (verse 2:210).

993 *Ibid.*

The two verses relate a single event, and one explains the other."[994]

- Al-Rāzī further said that the saying of Allāh ﴿**Wait they**﴾ (2:210, 16:33) is referring to the Jews: "His saying: ﴿**O you who believe! Come, all of you, into submission**﴾ (2:208) was revealed only concerning the Jews.[995] Then His saying ﴿**And if you slide back after the clear proofs have come unto you**﴾ (2:209) addresses the Jews, and therefore His saying ﴿**Wait they**﴾ is referring to them.[996] The meaning is: 'They shall accept your Religion only if Allāh comes to them in the shadows of the clouds so that they can see Him distinctly, for the Jews were anthropomorphists (*mushabbiha*). They considered it possible for Allāh to come and go, and they said that He manifested Himself to Mūsā ﷺ on the Mount in the shadows of the clouds. So they asked for something similar in the time of Muhammad ﷺ."[997]

Concerning the ḥadīth: "On the Day of Resurrection, Allāh shall come to the people in the form (*ṣūra*) that is familiar to them"[998]:

عَنْ أَبِي هُرَيْرَةَ رَضِيَ اللهُ عَنْهُ قَالَ رَسُولُ اللَّهِ صَلَّى اللَّهُ عَلَيْهِ وَسَلَّمَ يَجْمَعُ اللَّهُ النَّاسَ يَوْمَ الْقِيَامَةِ فَيَقُولُ مَنْ كَانَ يَعْبُدُ شَيْئًا فَلْيَتَّبِعْهُ فَيَتَّبِعُ مَنْ كَانَ يَعْبُدُ الشَّمْسَ الشَّمْسَ وَيَتَّبِعُ مَنْ كَانَ يَعْبُدُ الْقَمَرَ الْقَمَرَ وَيَتَّبِعُ مَنْ كَانَ يَعْبُدُ الطَّوَاغِيتَ الطَّوَاغِيتَ وَتَبْقَى هَذِهِ الأُمَّةُ فِيهَا مُنَافِقُوهَا فَيَأْتِيهِمُ اللَّهُ تَبَارَكَ وَتَعَالَى فِي صُورَةٍ غَيْرِ صُورَتِهِ الَّتِي يَعْرِفُونَ فَيَقُولُ أَنَا رَبُّكُمْ فَيَقُولُونَ نَعُوذُ بِاللَّهِ مِنْكَ هَذَا مَكَانُنَا حَتَّى يَأْتِيَنَا رَبُّنَا فَإِذَا جَاءَ رَبُّنَا عَرَفْنَاهُ فَيَأْتِيهِمُ اللَّهُ تَعَالَى فِي صُورَتِهِ الَّتِي يَعْرِفُونَ فَيَقُولُ أَنَا رَبُّكُمْ فَيَقُولُونَ أَنْتَ رَبُّنَا الحديث ق

وفي الباب عن أبي سعيد الخدري رضي الله عنه

994 As cited by al-Kawtharī, *Al-Asmā' wal-Ṣifāt* (Kawtharī ed. p. 447).

995 As established in al-Wāḥidī's *Asbāb al-Nuzūl* and al-Suyūṭī's *Asbāb al-Nuzūl*.

996 This is also the position of Ibn Kathīr, al-Qurṭubī, and others on verse 2:210.

997 As cited by al-Kawtharī, *Al-Asmā' wal-Ṣifāt* (Kawtharī ed. p. 448).

998 Narrated in a long ḥadīth from Abū Hurayra and Abū Sa'īd by al-Bukhārī and Muslim.

Imām al-Bayhaqī said:

This can be interpreted to mean that He shall come to them in the Attribute (*ṣifa*) that is familiar to them [...] What confirms this interpretation is the Prophet's ﷺ saying in the narration of 'Aṭā' ibn Yasār from Abū Sa'īd al-Khudrī: "Then Allāh will come to them in a form lower [or more suitable] (*adnā*) than the one wherein they had seen Him,"[999] whereas they had not seen Him at all prior to this. One understands therefore that the meaning of "form" here is "Attribute."[1000]

Similarly, Imām Abū Sulaymān al-Khaṭṭābī said:

The meaning of "Allāh shall come to the people etc." is He shall lift the veil for them so that they shall see Him with the eyes (*ḥattā yarawnahu 'iyānan*) just as they used to know Him in the world through proofs (*kamā kānū 'arafūhu fil-dunyā istidlālan*). And the sight of Him after they used not to see Him is equivalent to the coming of someone never seen heretofore.[1001]

Similarly, Sulṭān al-'Ulamā' said:

His coming (*majī'uhu*) is a figure of speech (*majāz*) for His being present (*ḥuḍūr*) and His appearing for the eyes to see following invisibility, as in the verse ﴾**And your Lord shall arrive with angels, rank on rank**﴿ (89:22)."[1002]

Similarly, Shaykh al-Islām said:

Know that there are two positions among the people of learning on the narrations and verses of the Divine Attributes. The first one – and this is the school of the majority of the *Salaf* or rather all of them – states that one does not address their meaning but says:

999 Narrated by al-Bukhārī.

1000 *Al-Asmā' wal-Ṣifāt* (Kawtharī ed. p. 296; Ḥāshidī ed. 2:70).

1001 In Ibn al-Jawzī, *Daf' Shubah al-Tashbīh* (1998 al-Kawtharī repr. p. 35).

1002 Ibn 'Abd al-Salām, *al-Ishāra ilā al-Ījāz* (p. 106-107).

We are obliged to believe in them and we hold, concerning them, whatever befits the majesty of Allāh ﷻ and His magnificence, at the same time categorically believing of Allāh ﷻ that ﴾**Nothing whatsoever is like unto Him**﴿ (42:11) and that He is declared transcendent (*munazzah*) beyond corporeality (*al-tajsīm*), displacement (*al-intiqāl*), dimensionality (*al-taḥayyuz*) in any given direction (*jiha*), and all the rest of the attributes of creatures. And this position is that of a group of the scholars of *kalām* and a group of their verifying scholars have preferred it. And it is the safest position (*wa-huwa al-aslam*). The second position – and it is that of most of the *mutakallimūn* – is that such texts be interpreted (*tata'awwal*) according to what befits them in their respective contexts, and that this is permissible only to those who are qualified to interpret them. Namely, one thoroughly versed in the language of the Arabs, the principles of jurisprudence, and the branches of the Law, with mastery in learning. According to this position one says, about the words "Then Allāh shall come to them": the "coming" (*al-ityān*) is an expression for their seeing Him. For custom dictates that whoever is absent from someone else cannot be seen by the latter except by coming to him. So the "coming" and "arrival" (*majī'*) here express the vision metaphorically (*majāzan*). It was also said that the "coming" is an act among the acts of Allāh ﷻ which He named "coming." It was also said that by the coming of Allāh is meant that one of the angels of Allāh comes to them. Al-Qāḍī 'Iyāḍ said: "This latter meaning is the most correct for the ḥadīth in my view."[1003]

The above suffices to refute any claim of a supposed consensus of the *Salaf* whereby they did not interpret the "coming" of Allāh ﷻ as His order.[1004]

[1003] Al-Nawawī, *Sharḥ Ṣaḥīḥ Muslim* (Turāth ed. 3:19).

[1004] "To explain these verses as a reference to the coming or arrival of the order of Allāh is unsound because it contravenes the literal meaning (*ẓāhir al-lafẓ*) of the verse and the consensus of the *salaf*, and there is no proof for it" Muḥammad ibn Ṣāliḥ al-'Uthaymīn, Commentary on Ibn Taymiyya's *'Aqīda Wāsiṭiyya* (Cairo: Maktabat al-'Ilm, p. 23). In reality, such interpretation is in strict conformity with the principles of Qur'anic commentary nor is there any consensus to its contrary, as shown by the above quotes. As for its proof, it is given in the verse (16:33) adduced by Imām Aḥmad.

Aḥmad's *'Aqīda* and Pseudo-Ḥanbalī *'Aqīda*

The Shāfi'ī *faqīh,* Shaykh al-Islām al-Haytamī was asked: "Was the belief of Imām Aḥmad ibn Ḥanbal the same as [certain] present-day Ḥanbalīs claim?" He replied:

> Concerning the doctrine of the Imām of *Ahl al-Sunna,* Aḥmad ibn Ḥanbal ﷺ – may Allāh ﷻ grant him the loftiest of gardens as his resting-place and destination, bestow upon us and him His bounties, and grant him a dwelling in the loftiest *firdaws* – his doctrine was in absolute conformity with the belief of *Ahl al-Sunna,* and completely concordant. It included the belief that Allāh ﷻ is exalted beyond those matters that the oppressors and dissenters attribute to Him. That is, Allāh ﷻ is exalted from possessing direction, parts, corporeality, and so forth among the various Attributes of imperfection.
>
> The truth of the matter is that Allāh is free from all the Attributes that are not characterised by absolute perfection; and all those things that are being circulated and publicised among the ignoramuses as being said by this great *mujtahid* Imām are a slander. It is an outright lie that this Imām ever claimed direction or the like in describing the Attributes of Allāh ﷻ. May Allāh lead to perdition those who attribute such positions to the Imām who is entirely exonerated of having said such things!
>
> All these matters have been explained by the ḥadīth Master, Imām Abū al-Faraj Ibn al-Jawzī, who belongs to his [Imām Aḥmad's] School. He has cleared the Imām's name of such foul slanders and has provided explicit proofs exposing the lies of the slanderers.
>
> And beware of what Ibn Taymiyya, his student Ibn Qayyim al-Jawziyya and others wrote; he [Ibn Taymiyya] is a man who took his lusts for his lord, for which Allāh led him astray despite his learning, sealed upon his hearing and heart, and put a veil upon his sight; and who can guide him after Allāh let him be misguided? Why should He not, when these heretics have gone past the boundaries set by the *Sharī'a* and trampled on them? Yet they imagine that they are the guided ones, that they are guided by their Lord Almighty when the truth is that they are not. Rather, they are on the wrong path, the most heinous, misleading way

and most abominable traits. They are afflicted by vices and have incurred a great loss. May Allāh humble their followers and wipe the earth clean from their like![1005]

A CONTEMPORARY EXAMPLE OF THIS DIFFERENCE

A contemporary example of the disparity between Ḥanbalī *'aqīda* and puristic Taymiyyan views is the recent edition of the Ḥanbalī Shaykh al-Islām, the Imām and *Musnid* Shams al-Dīn Muḥammad ibn Badr al-Dīn ibn Balbān al-Dimashqī al-Ṣāliḥī's (1006-1083) compendium of *fiqh, adab* and *'aqīda* titled *Mukhtaṣar al-Ifādāt fī Rub' al-'Ibādāt wal-Ādāb wal-Ziyādāt* by a "Salafī" student and his teacher Muḥammad Sulaymān al-Ashqar who injected into the work the following aberrations:[1006]

IBN BALBĀN'S TEXT	"SALAFĪ" FOOTNOTE	REBUTTAL
Conclusion: On knowledge of Allāh ﷻ and what pertains thereto and what the legally qualified person must believe [p.485]	The author was not blessed with success – Allāh forgive him! – in reporting the *'Aqīda* of the *Salaf* that Imām Aḥmad ibn Ḥanbal and the expert authorities of the *Madhhab* held.	Ibn Balbān – Allāh reward him! – shows mastery of the *'Aqīda* of the Sunni *Salaf* including Abū Ḥanīfa, Aḥmad, and al-Ash'arī with a view to confront innovations current in his time in and outside his own School, including *tajsīm* and *i'tizāl.*
It is obligatory to categorically affirm (*al-jazm*) that He ﷻ is one, indivisible and not made of parts, single not in the sense of number... [p.487]	Shaykh al-Islām [Aḥmad] Ibn Taymiyya warned against such newfangled terms and cites the very same terms used by the author as examples of what not to say.	Ibn Balbān echoes Ash'arī (Ibn Khafīf) and Māturīdī (*Fiqh al-Akbar*) *'aqīda* while Ibn Taymiyya innovated triple-*tawḥīd* terminology never used by Imām Aḥmad and claims that Aḥmad believed Allāh has a limit whereas it is established he held the opposite.
It is obligatory to categorically affirm that He ﷻ is neither a substance (*jawhar*) nor a body (*jism*) nor an atom (*'araḍ*).	Shaykh al-Islām IT said...: "the terms *jism, jawhar* and the like are neither in the Book of Allāh nor the Sunna of His Prophet, nor the words of any of the Companions and their pious Successors to the Day of Judgment [*sic*] and the rest of the Imāms of the Muslims, whether to affirm or deny."	Al-Ash'arī uses the very same terms in his *Risāla ilā Ahl al-Thughar.* Further, the term "uncreated" (*ghayr makhlūq*) is not found in the Qur'ān, the Sunna or the language of the Companions and Successors yet Aḥmad used it against those who affirmed the createdness of the Qur'ān.

1005 Al-Haytamī, *Fatāwā Ḥadīthiyya* (p. 203).

1006 Ibn Balbān, *Mukhtaṣar al-Ifādāt,* ed. Muḥammad Nāṣir al-'Ajmī (Beirut: Dār al-Bashā'ir al-Islāmiyya, 1998).

Contingencies never indwell Him (*lā taḥulluhu al-ḥawādith*) nor does He indwell any of them, nor can any of them encompass Him.	Our shaykh Muḥammad [Sulaymān] al-Ashqar said: "This is innovated speech that misses the mark, which no legal proof affirms nor denies therefore it can neither be confirmed nor denied. And even if it were confirmed it could suggest what is untrue, as it would if it were denied."	This naysaying aims to justify the heresy of "pre-existent contingencies indwelling the Deity" (*ḥawādith lā awwala lahā ḥālla fī dhāt Allāh*) for which al-Ikhmaymī (d.764) suspected Ibn Taymiyya of *dahriyya* or Aristotelian freethinking as did al-Ṣan'ānī in *Risāla fīmā Yata'allaqu bikam al-Bāqī min 'Umr al-Dunyā?* ("Concerning the Remaining Age of the World") and al-Būṭī in *al-Salafiyya* (p. 164-175).
So whoever believes or says that Allāh is, in His essence (*bi-dhātih*), in every place or in a place, is a *kāfir*. It is obligatory to categorically affirm that He ﷻ is separate (*bā'in*) from His creation. Allāh ﷻ was when there was no place then He created place and He is now as He was before He created place. [p. 489]	The denial of place is an imprecise term (*lafẓ mujmal*) [!] and innovated speech while Allāh ﷻ has said that He is established (*mustawin*) over His Throne above His heavens in absolute height (*fil-'ulūw al-muṭlaq*). So the words of the author – Allāh forgive him! – are novel in meaning as they are novel in wording.	The commentator defends *kufr* by crying *bid'a* while Ibn Balbān's words are reiterated verbatim by Sulaymān ibn 'Abd Allāh ibn Muḥammad ibn 'Abd al-Wahhāb in his letter on *'aqīda* entitled *al-Tawḍīḥ 'an Tawḥīd al-Khallāq fī Jawāb Ahl al-'Irāq* (1319/1901, p. 34, and Riyadh: Dār Ṭaybah, 1984).
Whoever likens Him to anything in His creation has definitely committed *kufr*, for example, he who says "He is a body" or says "He is a body unlike bodies" (*jismun lā kal-ajsām*).	This is innovated speech that misses the mark, which no legal proof affirms nor denies therefore it can neither be confirmed nor denied. And even if it were confirmed it could suggest what is untrue, as it would if it were denied.	No comment needed.
In any case, whatever occurs in the mind and dawns upon the imagination, such is other than the Owner of Generosity and Majesty. [p. 490]	The author did not broach the *tawḥīd* of Godhead which is the root of the Religion but instead comes up with those newfangled expressions that are not found in the Book nor in the Sunna and are unknown by the *Salaf*.	Ibn Balbān defined the creed of Oneness of Godhead at length in the very passage rejected by the commentator as unspeakable. The statement "whatever occurs in the mind" is established from Dhūl-Nūn al-Miṣrī ﵀. Al-Shāfi'ī said something similar.
The authentically transmitted Divine Names and Attributes must be accepted, believed, and conveyed just as they came even if the meaning cannot be conceived (*wa'in lam yu'qal ma'nāh*). [p. 491]	No, the meaning is known!	Mālik said of *istiwā'* "its 'how' is **inconceivable**" while al-Shāfi'ī said, "I believe in what came from Allāh **in the meaning meant** (*murād*) **by Allāh** and I believe in what came from the Messenger of Allāh **in the meaning meant by the Messenger** of Allāh ﷺ."

My ailment left me through the blessing of seeing [Imām Aḥmad] in dream, Allāh be well-pleased with him! [p.493]	It only left him through the Divine decree.	First, the *Jumhūr* said one may attribute effects to other than the Causator metaphorically. Second, the denial of causes and effects in the world of causes and effects is the doctrine of the fatalists (Jabriyya).
We ask Him ﷻ to make us firm upon Sunni *'Aqīda* with the *baraka* of our Prophet, the Leader of creation. [p.493]	This is part of the forbidden and illicit *tawassul* as was assessed by Ibn Tamiyya.	Imām Aḥmad assessed that *Tawassul* through the Prophet ﷺ be part of every Muslim's *du'ā'* as admitted by IT himself.
The *Madhhab* of *Ahl al-Sunna* is the affirmation (*ithbāt*) of the Names and Attributes together with the negation of likeness (*tashbīh*) and organs (*adawāt*). [p.494]	If he means by organs, such as Allāh ﷻ has affirmed for Himself of the two hands, the eye, and others of His lofty Attributes, then his words are incorrect because they contradict the text of the Qur'ān.	Al-Ṭaḥāwī said in his *'Aqīda* (§38): "He is beyond having limits placed on Him, or being bounded, or having parts or limbs or organs (*ta'ālā 'anil-ḥudūdi wal-ghāyāti wal-arkāni wal-a'ḍā'i wal-adawāt*)."
Know that everything other than Allāh and His Attributes is contingent and that He has created it, brought it into being, and originated it from nothing, by no prior cause (*'illa*) nor driving purpose (*gharaḍ*) nor motive (*dā'in*) nor need (*ḥāja*) nor necessity (*mūjib*), nor is consideration of any of the above incumbent upon Him whatsoever in His acts, yet He does nothing in vain. [p.496]	This cannot be correct, Allāh ﷻ does what He wishes to Whom He wishes, the noble Qur'ān is full of the causality (*ta'līl*) of His acts as in His saying, ﴾**For that cause We decreed for the Children of Israel**﴿ (5:32), ﴾**and for that He did create them**﴿ (11:119); and this talk is incoherent, because the last of it ('in vain') contradicts the statement 'by no prior cause nor driving purpose.'	Al-Ashqar is unaware that *Ahl al-Sunna* never attribute cause to the Divine decrees and acts but wisdom (*ḥikma*) while the Mu'tazila cite the Qur'ān claiming that Allāh is driven by cause and that His acts are motivated by good. Al-Māturīdī in *al-Tawḥīd* (p. 215-216) ranks the attribution of *'illa* to the Divine acts among the aberrations of the Mu'tazila who pretexted that, otherwise, Allāh would be acting in vain. Ibn Khafīf: "He brings near Him whomever He will without [need for] cause and removes far from Him whomever He will without [need for] cause."
He ﷻ is free to torture and punish creatures without prior offense nor subsequent recompense nor fitting regard. He can do what He likes and decree freely over them in any terms He wishes, yet all this is excellent (*ḥasan*) on His part because they are His dominion and He owns them and cannot be taken to account. Rather, they are taken to account. [p.497]	He ﷻ said: ﴾**Your Lord wrongs no one**﴿ (18:49) and injustice is evil and prohibited. How then could He possibly punish them without prior offense, yet this be *ḥasan*?	Al-Ashqar's objection is the Mu'tazilī doctrine in a nutshell as phrased by al-Jubbā'ī to al-Ash'arī after which the latter left them. Ibn Khafīf said: "Allāh is doer of what He will ﴾**Know you not that unto Allāh belongs the Sovereignty of the heavens and the earth? He punishes whom He will, and forgives whom He will. Allāh is Able to do all things**﴿ (5:40)]:

We add: Injustice is not attributed to Him, He rules over His dominion just as He will, without [anyone's entitlement to] objection whatsoever [﴾**Say: Who then can do aught against Allāh, if He had willed to destroy the Messiah son of Mary, and his mother and everyone on earth? To Allāh belongs the Sovereignty of the heavens and the earth and all that is between them. He creates what He will. And Allāh is Able to do all things**﴿ (5:17); ﴾**The sentence that comes from Me cannot be changed, and I am in no wise a tyrant unto the slaves**﴿ (50:29)]." At the same time it is obligatorily known that Allāh does not take back His promise to reward those who believe and do good and punish evil-doers: ﴾**But as for those who believe and do good works We shall bring them into gardens underneath which rivers flow, wherein they will abide for ever. It is a promise from Allāh in truth; and who can be more truthful than Allāh in utterance?**﴿ (4:122). The scholars have described the former evidence as "based on reason" (*dalīl 'aqlī*) and the latter as "based on law" (*dalīl sharʿī*), noting that it is the latter which takes precedence over the former. Cf. al-Būṭī, *Kubrā al-Yaqīnāt* (p. 149).

Aḥmad and al-Ḥārith al-Muḥāsibī

Al-Ḥārith ibn Asad ibn al-Layth, Abū Abd Allāh al-Muḥāsibī al-Baghdādī (d. 243) was the Shāfiʿī *faqīh*, expert in *kalām*, and Ṣūfī master whose words moved Imām Aḥmad to tears although the latter's opposition to him resulted in the people's desertion of al-Muḥāsibī who died in isolation. His name means "he who calculates his actions" or "he who excels in the examination of his conscience." He was one of the earliest authors of Ṣūfī treatises and the teacher of al-Junayd.

There are three reasons for the rift between al-Muḥāsibī and his opponents: the aberrant charge of Jahmism reportedly made by Imām Aḥmad or Abū Zurʿa; his use of *kalām*, which is probably the main reason why he was boycotted by Aḥmad's circle, as diagnosed by al-Dhahabī; and his *taṣawwuf*, which irked Abū Zurʿa and other scholars of ḥadīth who found it overly strict, according to Ibn Kathīr. Shaykh 'Abd al-Fattāḥ Abū Ghudda said:

> Among the innovations are (1) the compilation of ḥadīth; (2) the commentaries on the Qur'ān; (3) the compilation of juridical questions stemming from pure opinion; (4) compilations connected with the works of the heart. As for the first, it was castigated by 'Umar and Abū Mūsā al-Ashʿarī and others, while the majority [of the Companions] allowed it; the second was castigated by a number of Successors such as al-Shaʿbī; the third was castigated by Imām Aḥmad and a small group; Imām Aḥmad also castigated the fourth.[1007]

[1007] Abū Ghudda, introduction to al-Muḥāsibī's *Risālat al-Mustarshidīn* (p. 48).

Doctrinally, al-Muḥāsibī differed little with Aḥmad. Ibn al-Jawzī related that he had praised him with the words: "Aḥmad ibn Ḥanbal was tested as were never tested Sufyān al-Thawrī and al-Awzā'ī."[1008] The same Ibn al-Jawzī narrated that al-Muḥāsibī was reportedly accused of "converting people to Jahm's opinion,"[1009] an unfortunate mistake in light of al-Muḥāsibī's intense opposition to the *Jahmiyya*: he publicly disavowed his father for stopping short of declaring the Qur'ān uncreated, exhorted him to divorce his mother on grounds of separate religions, and turned down his huge inheritance despite his poverty on the basis of the Prophet's ﷺ ḥadīth: "[The adherents of] two different religious communities do not inherit from one another."[1010] His book on the afterlife titled *al-Tawahhum* shows that he understood the sight of Allāh in the hereafter and the rewards of Paradise and punishments of Hell literally, as his book *Fahm al-Qur'ān* held that the Qur'ān was uncreated, in conformity with *Ahl al-Sunna* and contrary to the position of the *Jahmiyya* on the two topics. The *Jahmiyya* further believed that the Divine Attributes were purely allegorical, even denying that Attributes which could lexically be applied to human beings belonged to Allāh, whereas 'Abd al-Qāhir al-Baghdādī defines al-Muḥāsibī as one of *al-mutakallimūn al-ṣifātiyya* that affirm all the Divine Attributes without anthropomorphism (*tashbīh*) nor nullification (*ta'ṭīl*).[1011]

Al-Muḥāsibī's teachings are held in the highest esteem by subsequent Scholars. He is frequently quoted by al-Nawawī. Ibn Taymiyya cites him at length in *al-Risāla al-Tadmuriyya* and *al-Fatwā al-Ḥamawiyya al-Kubrā*. 'Abd al-Qāhir al-Baghdādī, Tāj al-Dīn Ibn al-Subkī, and Jamāl al-Dīn al-Isnawī all reiterate the statement whereby "Upon the books of al-Ḥārith ibn Asad al-Muḥāsibī on *kalām*, *fiqh*, and ḥadīth rest those among us who are *mutakallim*, *faqīh*, and ṣūfī."[1012] Al-Baghdādī said:

[1008] Ibn al-Jawzī, *Manāqib al-Imām Aḥmad ibn Ḥanbal* (p. 121).

[1009] As reported from Imām Aḥmad by Ibn al-Jawzī in his *Talbīs Iblīs*.

[1010] A fair narration from several Companions in al-Tirmidhī, Abū Dāwūd, Ibn Mājah, al-Dārimī, and Aḥmad. This is the position of the vast majority of the Scholars including the Four Imāms, although Ibn Kathīr in *al-Bidāya* (5:103) reports another position from Mu'ādh, Ibn Burayda, Mu'āwiya, Yaḥyā ibn Ma'mar, and Isḥāq ibn Rāhūyah.

[1011] In *al-Farq Bayn al-Firaq* (p. 217).

[1012] 'Abd al-Qāhir al-Baghdādī, *Uṣūl al-Dīn* (p. 308-309); Tāj al-Dīn Subkī, *Ṭabaqāt al-Shāfi'iyya*; Jamal al-Dīn al-Isnawī, *Ṭabaqāt al-Shāfi'iyya* (1:26-27 §9).

"He authored many books on *taṣawwuf*, the foundations of belief, and the refutation of the Mu'tazila and Rāfiḍa."[1013]

Among al-Muḥasibī's sayings:

> Al-Junayd said: "Al-Ḥārith said to me: 'How often do you exclaim: "My seclusion is my familiarity!" If half of creation came close to me I would not experience any familiarity with them, and if the other half deserted me, I would not feel lonely.'" "The renunciation of the world together with its remembrance is the attribute of ascetics (*zāhidīn*), while the renunciation of the world together with its forgetfulness is the attribute of knowers (*'ārifīn*)."[1014]

Al-Khaṭīb al-Baghdādī narrates in his biographical dictionary of Baghdād:

> Aḥmad ibn Ḥanbal disliked al-Ḥārith's speculations in *kalām* and the fact that the latter wrote books about it. He used to warn people against al-Ḥārith. Muḥammad ibn Aḥmad ibn Ya'qūb was told by Muḥammad ibn Nu'aym al-Ḍibbī: I heard Imām Abū Bakr Aḥmad ibn Isḥāq – al-Ṣibjī – say: I heard Isma'īl ibn Isḥāq al-Sarrāj say: "Aḥmad ibn Ḥanbal told me one day: 'I hear that this Ḥārith is often at your house. Could you invite him and place me somewhere so that I could hear him without being seen?' I answered him: 'Certainly, Abū 'Abd Allāh!' and I was happy with this first step on his part. I went and asked al-Ḥārith to come to us that very night, and to do so as his companions would be present also. 'Ismā'īl, they are many, so serve them nothing other than butter and dates, and only as much as you can afford.' I followed his instructions and went to Abū 'Abd Allāh to inform him. He came after *maghrib*, went up to a small room and began to recite his usual devotions (*wird*). Al-Ḥārith and his companions arrived, ate, and stood for *ṣalāt al-'ishā*, and they did not pray after it. Then they sat silently in front of al-Ḥārith and remained speechless until the middle of the night. One of them asked al-Ḥārith a question and he began to speak. His companions

1013 His works are listed in his entry in the *Encyclopedia of Islamic Doctrine*.

1014 Abū Nu'aym, *Ḥilyat al-Awliyā* (10:75); al-Khaṭīb, *Tārīkh Baghdād* (8:214); al-Dhahabī, *Siyar* (10:100 §2000), *Mīzān* (1:430); Ibn Kathīr, *Bidāya* (10:363).

listened to him as if afraid to scare a bird away. Some wept. Others muffled cries as he spoke. Then I went to the room to enquire about Abū 'Abd Allāh and found that he had passed out after weeping much. I went back down. They continued thus until the morning at which time they got up and went their way. I went back up to see Abū 'Abd Allāh. He was a changed man. 'What do you think of these people now, Abū 'Abd Allāh?' I asked. He said: 'As far as I know, I have never seen their like nor heard, on the Science of Realities (*'ilm al-ḥaqā'iq*), words such as those uttered by that man. However, despite what I have just said, in truth, I do not see fit for you to keep their company.' Then he got up and left."[1015]

Ibn al-Subkī explained Imām Aḥmad's ambiguous reaction thus: Ponder this account carefully and know that Aḥmad ibn Ḥanbal did not consider it wise for this man (al-Sarrāj) to join their company because he was not one to raise himself to their state. In truth they were in a difficult path which all cannot equally undertake and which makes one fear for one who undertakes it. Otherwise, would Aḥmad have wept and praised al-Ḥārith the way he praised him?[1016]

Imām Aḥmad's *Taṣawwuf* and Fond Love of Ṣūfīs

Ṣāliḥ ibn Aḥmad ibn Ḥanbal said: "My father would send for me whenever a self-denier or ascetic (*zāhid aw mutaqashshif*) visited him so I could look at him. He loved for me to become like this."[1017] Ibn Abī Ya'lā in his *Ṭabaqāt al-Ḥanābila* narrates from Imām Abū Muḥammad Rizq Allāh 'Abd al-Wahhāb ibn 'Abd al-'Azīz al-Tamīmī (400-488) that Imām Aḥmad was once asked about the meaning of the "seeker"

[1015] As narrated with a sound chain by al-Khaṭīb in his *Tārīkh Baghdād* (8:214), al-Dhahabī in the *Siyar* and *Mīzān al-I'tidāl* (1:430), and Ibn al-Jawzī in *Manāqib Aḥmad* (p. 185-186) cf. Ibn Mufliḥ, *al-Furū'* (5:238) and Ibn Badrān, *al-Madkhal* (p. 101). Al-Dhahabī said: "The chain is sound, but I cannot believe this on the part of Imām Aḥmad!" The best internal proof that the incident took place – and Allāh knows best – is the unyielding position of the Imām in his parting words.

[1016] Ibn al-Subkī, *Ṭabaqāt al-Shāfi'iyya al-Kubrā* (2:279). As for why or how Aḥmad did not join the *'ishā* prayer although the known Ḥanbalī position is that joining the group prayer is obligatory, the answer is that the text nowhere says that he did not join it – without exposing his presence.

[1017] Al-Dhahabī, *Siyar* (10:361)

(*murīd*) to which he replied, "It is to be with Allāh as Allāh wants him, and to abandon what he seeks in exchange for what He seeks." Al-Tamīmī continues: "And he [Aḥmad] used to greatly respect the Ṣūfīs and show them kindness and generosity. He was asked about them and was told that they sat in mosques constantly to which he replied, 'Knowledge made them sit.'"[1018]

The full text of the latter report was narrated by al-Silafī in his *Ṭuyūriyyāt,* a book of narrations by the Ḥanbalī Abū al-Khayr al-Ṣayrafī al-Ṭuyūrī: from al-'Utayqī, from Abū al-Ḥasan 'Alī ibn al-Ḥasan ibn Ḥamdān al-Ṭarasūsī, from al-Ṭabarānī, from 'Abd Allāh ibn Aḥmad ibn Ḥanbal: "They said, 'Those Ṣūfīs sit in the mosques practicing reliance without knowledge.' I heard my father reply, 'Knowledge made them sit.' They said, 'Their whole energy is towards defeat (*kasra*) and ineptitude (*khurqa*).' He replied, 'I know of no people worthier than those whose energy for the world is defeat and ineptitude.' They said, 'When they hear the recital they get up and dance!' He replied, 'Allāh have mercy on them! Leave them enjoy their Lord for a time.'" This report is forged.[1019]

Among Imām Aḥmad's Ṣūfī students were Aḥmad ibn al-Ḥasan ibn 'Abd al-Jabbār ibn Rāshid, Abū 'Abd Allāh al-Ṣūfī; Aḥmad ibn Abī Badr al-Mundhir, Abū Bakr al-Maghāzilī, nicknamed Badr, held by his contemporaries to be a *walī*; Aḥmad ibn Abī al-Ḥawārī and whom al-Junayd nicknamed "the ambrosia (*rayḥāna*) of al-Shām"; Abū Ḥamza al-Baghdādī al-Bazzāz; and others.[1020] Of Ma'rūf al-Karkhī Imām Aḥmad said: "He is one of the Substitute-Saints (*al-Abdāl*), and his supplication is answered."[1021] Someone remarked of Ma'rūf one time, "He is not very knowledgeable." Imām Aḥmad said: "*Bah!* Allāh forgive you! Is anything meant by Knowledge other than what Ma'rūf has attained?"[1022] Whenever the Ṣufīs or some of their sayings were

[1018] Ibn Abī Ya'lā, *Ṭabaqāt al-Ḥanābila* (2:279) cf. Ibn Mufliḥ, *Furū'* (5:238).

[1019] Forged by al-Ṭarasūsī according to al-Dhahabī in the *Mīzān* (5:150) and Ibn Ḥajar in *Lisān al-Mīzān* (4:220 misnaming al-Ṭabarī instead of al-Ṭabarānī). Cited in al-Munāwī's *Ṭabaqāt al-Ṣūfiyya al-Kubrā* (1:520-521), al-Saffarīnī's *Ghidhā' al-Albāb* (1:120), al-Nābulusī's *Jam' al-Asrār* (p. 123), and Shaykh 'Abd al-Qādir 'Īsā in *Ḥaqā'iq 'an al-Taṣawwuf.* On al-Ṭarasūsī see *Tārīkh Jurjān* (p. 312 §543).

[1020] Cf. 'Abd al-Ḥafīẓ al-Makkī, *Mawqif A'immat al-Ḥaraka al-Salafiyya min al-Taṣawwuf wal-Ṣūfiyya* (p. 255-287).

[1021] In Ibn Abī Ya'lā, *Ṭabaqāt al-Ḥanābila* (1:382).

[1022] Narrated by al-Khaṭīb, *Tārīkh* (13:200), Ibn Mufliḥ, *al-Maqṣad al-Arshad* (3:36),

mentioned in Aḥmad's gathering, he would turn to Abū Ḥamza al-Baghdādī al-Bazzāz and say, "What do you say about it, Ṣūfī?"[1023]

Abū Ja'far Muḥammad ibn Aḥmad ibn al-Muthannā al-Ṣūfī waited one day at Aḥmad's door for him to come out. When he did, he stood and stood by him. Imām Aḥmad said: "Do you not know that the Prophet ﷺ said: 'Whoever likes for people to stand for him, let him prepare for his seat in the Fire'?" Abū Ja'far replied: "I stood *coming to* you (*ilayka*), not *for* you (*laka*)." Aḥmad liked this answer. Another time, Abū Ja'far asked the Imām about Bishr ibn al-Ḥārith (Bishr al-Ḥāfī) and he replied: "You have asked me about the fourth of seven Substitute-Saints (*Abdāl*) – either he or 'Āmir ibn 'Abd Qays! I do not consider him other than a man who fixed his spear in the ground and stood his ground fighting. Do you think he left such a spot for anyone else?"[1024]

Another time, Imām Aḥmad joked with one of his Ṣūfī visitors – a friend of Dhūl-Nūn al-Miṣrī – then narrated to him a moving Prophetic ḥadīth about utter reliance on Allāh (*tawakkul*). Yūsuf ibn al-Ḥusayn al-Rāzī said: "I came to Aḥmad ibn Ḥanbal in the early days of al-Mutawakkil's rule and said, 'Narrate a ḥadīth to me.' He replied, 'Do you not know that I stopped narrating ḥadīth?' Another version has: 'And what will you do with ḥadīth, Ṣūfī?' I said, 'Narrate something to me by which I shall remember you and invoke mercy upon you.' He said, 'Marwān al-Fazārī narrated to us, from Hilāl Abū al-'Alā', from Anas: Two birds were offered to the Prophet ﷺ and one of them was brought to him. The next morning, he said: Do you have anything to eat? Whereupon the other bird was brought. He said: From where is this? Bilāl said, I put it aside for you, Messenger of Allāh. He said: Bilāl, do not fear parsimony (*al-iqlāl*) from the Owner of the Throne. Allāh provides the livelihood for each morning.'" Then Aḥmad said: "This is very suited to you, Ṣūfī!" (*hādhā min bābatik yā ṣūfī*).[1025]

Ibn Abī Ya'lā, *Ṭabaqāt al-Ḥanābila* (1:382), al-Dhahabī, *Siyar* (Risala ed. 9:340).

[1023] Narrated by al-Khaṭīb, *Tārīkh* (1:390), Ibn Abī Ya'lā, *Ṭabaqāt al-Ḥanābila* (1:268), al-Sulamī in *Ṭabaqāt al-Ṣūfiyya* (p. 295), Ibn al-Jawzī in *Muntaẓam* (5:69).

[1024] In Ibn Abī Ya'lā, *Ṭabaqāt* (1:263) and Ibn Ḥajar, *Tahdhīb* (1:445). 'Āmir ibn 'Abd Qays al-Tamīmī al-Baṣrī was a celibate *Tābi'ī* famous for his piety and simple living. He prayed from sunrise to *'aṣr* until his feet swelled and he would tell himself: "Evil counselor! You were created for worship." Ka'b al-Aḥbār met him and named him the monk of this *Umma*; cf. Ibn Sa'd (7:77), Ibn al-Athīr, *Usd al-Ghāba* (3:132), *Siyar* (5:66).

[1025] In Ibn Abī Ya'lā, *Ṭabaqāt al-Ḥanābila* (1:418-419) cf. Ibn Mufliḥ, *al-Maqṣad al-*

When Aḥmad narrated similar "Ṣūfī" ḥadīths he would say, "Where is Badr [Abū Bakr al-Maghāzilī]? This is just right for him."[1026]

Aḥmad Recommended *Tawassul* in Every *Du'ā'*

Abū Bakr al-Marwazī narrated in his *Mansak* that Imām Aḥmad preferred one to make *tawassul* through the Prophet ﷺ in every supplication with the wording: "O Allāh! I am turning to You with Your Prophet, the Prophet of mercy. O Muḥammad! I am turning with you to my Lord for the fulfillment of my need." The report is mentioned in the books of the Ḥanbalī *madhhab* as it bears on the *adab* of *du'ā* as a *fiqh* issue.[1027] Ibn Qudāma recommends it for the obtainment of need in his *Waṣiyya*.[1028] Ibn Taymiyya cites the Ḥanbalī fatwa on the desirability of *tawassul* in every *du'ā* in his *Qā'ida fil-Tawassul wal-Wasīla* where he attributes it to "Imām Aḥmad and a group of the *Salaf*" from *Mansak al-Marwazī* as his source, and in his *Radd 'alā al-Akhnā'ī* where he cites the text of the *du'ā* in full, similar to the *du'ā* of the blind man in al-Tirmidhī and elsewhere and with the wording *Yā Muḥammad*. The practice of *tawassul* is also related from Imām al-Shāfi'ī and Imām Mālik.[1029]

Arshad fī Dhikr Aṣḥāb al-Imām Aḥmad (3:132). Shaykh 'Abd al-Ḥafīẓ ibn Malik 'Abd al-Ḥaqq al-Makkī mentions this report in his book *Mawqif A'immat al-Ḥaraka al-Salafiyya min al-Taṣawwuf wal-Ṣūfiyya* (p. 274-275) then comments: "Imām Aḥmad ibn Ḥanbal did not know that at the end of time a certain people would come and claim that all *taṣawwuf* is but falsehood and that the Ṣūfīs are a group that have nothing to do with Islām; otherwise, he would have never treated this Ṣūfī with such love and overindulgence!" The ḥadīth is narrated by Aḥmad (20:339 §13043 *isnād ḍa'īf* per al-Arna'ūṭ, *ḥasan* per al-Haythamī 10:303), Abū Ya'lā (7:224 §4223), Ibn Abī 'Āṣim in *al-Zuhd* (p. 8), al-Dūlābī in *al-Kunā* (2:124), Abū Nu'aym in the *Ḥilya* (1985 ed. 10:243), al-Khaṭīb in the *Tārīkh* (14:314-315), al-Bayhaqī in the *Shu'ab* (2:119 §1347-1348), all through Hilāl, whose correct full name is Abū al-Mu'allā Hilāl ibn Suwayd al-Aḥmarī, a weak narrator; cf. *Lisān* (6:201). Also narrated from Anas by Ibn Abī Shayba (13:249) with another weak chain through an unnamed narrator. The narration is raised to the grade of "fair" (*ḥasan*) through many other stronger witness-chains: from Abū Hurayra by al-Bazzār (§3654) and al-Ṭabarānī in *al-Kabīr* (1:34) as well as Bilāl, Abū Sa'īd al-Khudrī, 'Ā'isha, and Ibn Mas'ūd cf. notes to al-Mālīnī's *Arba'īn fī Shuyūkh al-Ṣūfiyya* (p. 186-187), al-Quṭay'ī's *Juz' al-Alf Dīnār* (p. 485), Ibn al-Sunnī's *al-Qanā'a* (p. 81).

[1026] In Ibn Abī Ya'lā, *Ṭabaqāt al-Ḥanābila* (1:78).

[1027] Cf. al-Mardāwī's *Inṣāf* (2:456); Ibn 'Aqīl's *Tadhkira*; al-Buhūtī, *Kashshāf al-Qinā'* (2:68); Shams al-Dīn ibn Mufliḥ, *al-Furū'* (2:159, 1:595=2:204); al-Ḥajjāwī, *al-Iqnā'* (1:208).

[1028] *Waṣiyyat al-Muwaffaq Ibn Qudāma al-Maqdisī* (p. 93).

[1029] Cf. above, respectively notes 206 and 181. Cf. Ibn Taymiyya, *Qā'ida fil-Tawassul*

Aḥmad Practiced *Tabarruk* or Blessing from Relics

Al-Dhahabī relates that Imām Aḥmad used to seek blessings from the relics of the Prophet ﷺ. Al-Dhahabī then lambasts whoever would fault the practice of *tabarruk* or seeking blessings from blessed objects:

'Abd Allāh ibn Aḥmad said: "I saw my father take a hair that belonged to the Prophet ﷺ, put it on his mouth, and kiss it. I think I saw him put it on his eyes. He also dipped it in water and drank the water to obtain a cure. I saw him take the Prophet's ﷺ bowl (*qaṣ'a*), wash it in water, and drink from it. I saw him drink Zamzam water in order to seek cure with it, and he wiped his hands and face with it." I say: Where is the quibbling critic of Imām Aḥmad now? It is also authentically established that 'Abd Allāh asked his father about those who touch the pommel of the Prophet's ﷺ pulpit and touch the wall of the Prophet's ﷺ room, and he said: "I do not see any harm in it." May Allāh protect us and you from the opinion of the *Khawārij* and from innovations![1030]

The above is a proof from Imām al-Dhahabī that he considers those who object to *tawassul* and *tabarruk* to be innovators and *Khawārij*. In the entry of his *Mu'jam al-Shuyūkh* devoted to his Shaykh Aḥmad ibn 'Abd al-Mun'im al-Qazwīnī, al-Dhahabī writes the following lines:

> Aḥmad ibn al-Mun'im related to us... [with his chain of transmission] from Ibn 'Umar that the latter disliked to touch the Prophet's ﷺ grave. I say: He disliked it because he considered it disrespect. Aḥmad ibn Ḥanbal was asked about touching the Prophet's ﷺ grave and kissing it and he saw nothing wrong with it. His son 'Abd Allāh related this from him. If it is asked: "Why did the Companions not do this?" We reply: "Because they saw him with their very eyes when he was alive, enjoyed his presence directly, kissed his very hand, nearly fought each other over the remnants of his ablution water, shared his purified hair on the day of the greater Pilgrimage, and even if he spat it would virtually not fall except into someone's hand so that he could pass it over his face. Since we have not had the tremendous fortune of sharing in this, we throw ourselves on his grave as a mark of commitment, reverence, and acceptance, even to kiss it. Do you not see what

---

wal-Wasīla (p. 98 and 155) and *al-Radd 'alā al-Akhnā'ī* (p. 168).

1030 Al-Dhahabī, *Siyar* (9:457). Ch. on Imām Aḥmad, section entitled *Min ādābih.*

Thābit al-Bunānī did when he kissed the hand of Anas ibn Mālik and placed it on his face saying: "This is the hand that touched the hand of the Messenger of Allāh ﷺ"? Muslims are not moved to these matters except by their excessive love for the Prophet ﷺ, as they are ordered to love Allāh and the Prophet ﷺ more than their own lives, their children, all human beings, their property, and Paradise and its maidens. There are even some believers that love Abū Bakr and 'Umar more than themselves [...].

Do you not you see that the Companions, in the excess of their love for the Prophet ﷺ, asked him: "Should we not prostrate to you?" and he replied no, and if he had allowed them, they would have prostrated to him as a mark of utter veneration and respect, not as a mark of worship, just as the brothers of the Prophet Yūsuf ﷺ prostrated to him. Similarly the prostration of the Muslim to the grave of the Prophet ﷺ is for the intention of magnification and reverence. One is not to be accused of disbelief because of it whatsoever (*lā yukaffaru aṣlan*), but he is being disobedient [to the Prophet's injunction to the Companions]. Let him, therefore, be informed that this is forbidden (*ḥarām*). It is likewise in the case of one who prays towards the grave.[1031]

The son of Imām Aḥmad, like his brother 'Abd Allāh a trustworthy ḥadīth Master, Ṣāliḥ ibn Aḥmad, narrates in his biography of his father in the chapter of Aḥmad's torture by the authorities:

My father [Aḥmad ibn Ḥanbal] said: "I had in my possession one or two hairs of the Prophet ﷺ which I had sewn in a pouch in my shirt-sleeve. Isḥāq ibn Ibrāhīm [ibn Muṣ'ab the deputy governor of Baghdād] saw the pouch in my shirt-sleeve. He turned and asked me: 'What is this pouch in your [chest] sleeve?' I said: 'Some of the hair of the Prophet ﷺ.' Some of them grabbed it to tear it open as I was being positioned between the two wood-planks [for lashing]. He said to them: 'Do not tear it up; just remove it from him.' I believe the shirt was spared from being rent because of the hair that was in it. Then I was positioned between the two planks with my hands tied up and a chair was

[1031] Al-Dhahabī, *Mu'jam al-Shuyūkh* (1:73 §58). See on the prohibition of the prostration of respect the fatwa of the Ḥanafī *Mujaddid* Imām Aḥmad Riḍā Khān, entitled *al-Zubdat al-Zakiyya li-Taḥrīm Sujūd al-Taḥiyya.*

brought for al-Mu'taṣim, Ibn Abī Du'ād [the Mu'tazilī] standing next to him, as was everyone else present...."[1032]

His Marriages

Imām Aḥmad married Umm Abī 'Abbāsa who gave birth to Ṣāliḥ, then married an Arab woman named Rayḥāna, after the death of his first wife – who gave him 'Abd Allāh. Al-Khallāl heard Abū Bakr al-Marwazī say: "I heard Abū 'Abd Allāh invoke Divine mercy upon his [late second] wife and say: 'We lived together twenty years and never quarrelled once.'" He did not marry a third time but Zuhayr ibn Ṣāliḥ ibn Aḥmad narrated that he bought a bondwoman (*jāriya*) named Ḥusn who bore him several children, one of them named Ḥasan. When Ḥasan was born, Imām Aḥmad gave her a dirham and told her to buy a sheep upon which they feasted. Then he said to her: "Ḥusn! This was my last dirham." Ḥusn later said: "Whenever he found himself owning nothing, he was happy that day."

His Turban and Dress

'Abd al-Mālik al-Maymūnī said: "I never saw Abū 'Abd Allāh wearing his turban (*'imāma*) without passing it under his chin (*taḥannak*). He disliked any other manner of wearing it." The same is reported from the Imām of the Prophet's ﷺ city, Mālik ibn Anas. A report mentions that 'Umar saw a man wearing his turban without anything under his chin whereupon he exclaimed, "Degenerate fashion? (*hādhihi al-fāsiqiyya?*)" and passed one of its coils under his chin.[1033] *Taḥnīk* originated in order to keep the turban from falling in the course of jihād and riding. "The *Salaf* used to tie the turban under the chin for they rode horses and fought in the way of Allāh and, if they did not tie their turbans under the chin, they would fall [...] hence Aḥmad mentioned that the people of al-Shām had preserved this Sunna. For they were the *mujāhidūn* in their time. Isḥāq ibn Rāhūya mentioned with his chain that the sons of the *Muhājirūn* and *Anṣār* wore the turbans without *taḥnīk* because, in the time of the *Tābi'īn* in the Ḥijāz, they did not make jihād. Isḥāq and others therefore permitted wearing the turban without it."[1034] If this is correct, it shows that wearing the turban with and without *taḥnīk* is indifferently permitted but the first is superior,

[1032] Ṣāliḥ ibn Aḥmad, *Sīrat al-Imām Aḥmad* (p. 43).

[1033] Cited by Ibn Qudāma in *al-Mughnī* (1:381).

[1034] Ibn Taymiyya, *Majmū' al-Fatāwā* (21:187).

just as the Prophet ﷺ wore the back-hanging turban-end (*'adhaba*) and commended it.[1035]

عَنْ ابْنِ عُمَرَ رَضِيَ اللهُ عَنْهُمَا قَالَ كَانَ النَّبِيُّ صَلَّى اللَّهُ عَلَيْهِ وَسَلَّمَ إِذَا اعْتَمَّ سَدَلَ عِمَامَتَهُ بَيْنَ كَتِفَيْهِ قَالَ نَافِعٌ وَكَانَ ابْنُ عُمَرَ يَسْدِلُ عِمَامَتَهُ بَيْنَ كَتِفَيْهِ قَالَ عُبَيْدُ اللَّهِ وَرَأَيْتُ الْقَاسِمَ وَسَالِمًا يَفْعَلَانِ ذَلِكَ ت وقال حَدِيثٌ حَسَنٌ غَرِيبٌ

Al-Maymūnī also said: "I never saw anyone more immaculate nor whiter in his clothing than Aḥmad." Al-Khallāl narrated with his chain from Ṣāliḥ ibn Aḥmad: "My father owned a headcover (*qalansuwa*) which he had sewn himself, partly made of cotton. When he rose up to pray at night he would wear it."

A Reply to Ibn Abī al-Dunyā

To Ibn Abī al-Dunyā who asked him: "What should I say between each two *takbīrs* during the *'Īd* prayer?" Imām Aḥmad replied: "Glorify Allāh and invoke blessings on the Prophet ﷺ."[1036]

On *Tahajjud* for the Student of Knowledge

'Āṣim ibn 'Iṣām al-Bayhaqī said: "I spent one night at Aḥmad ibn Ḥanbal's house. He brought me a container of water. The next morning he saw the water left untouched and said: "Allāh be exalted! A man who pursues the Science, yet does not have a nightly habitual devotion (*wird*)?" He said the same thing to 'Abd al-Ṣamad ibn Sulaymān ibn Abī Maṭar who replied: "I am travelling." The Imām said: "Even if you are

[1035] Narrated from Ibn 'Umar by al-Ṭabarānī in *Musnad al-Shāmiyyīn* (2:391 §1558), al-Ḥākim (1990 ed. 4:583=4:540 *isnād ṣaḥīḥ*), with a fair chain per al-Suyūṭī cf. al-Mubārakfūrī, *Tuḥfat al-Aḥwadhī* (5:338), 'Aẓīm Ābādī, *'Awn al-Ma'būd* (11:89), and al-Shawkānī, *Nayl* (2:107). The first half is narrated from Ibn 'Umar by al-Tirmidhī (*ḥasan gharīb*). See also the *Shamā'il* of al-Tirmidhī and its commentaries by al-Baghawī, al-Munāwī, and al-Qārī as well as al-Laḥjī's (d. 1410) *Muntahā al-Sūl 'alā Wasā'il al-Wuṣūl* (1:510-514), a two-thousand page commentary on al-Nabhānī's compilation of the Prophetic Attributes titled *Wasā'il al-Wuṣūl ilā Shāmā'il al-Rasūl* ﷺ.

[1036] Narrated by Ibn Abī Ya'lā in *Ṭabaqāt al-Ḥanābila* (1:195).

travelling! Masrūq went on pilgrimage and he did not go to sleep without being in prostration."[1037] Imām Aḥmad himself prayed three hundred supererogatory *rak'as* daily until he fell sick from this, after which he prayed a hundred and fifty *rak'as* daily.[1038]

His Prohibition of Cursing Yazīd ibn Mu'āwiya

Ibn al-Jawzī in *al-Radd 'alā al-Muta'aṣṣib al-'Anīd al-Māni' min Dhammi Yazīd* ("Refutation of the Obdurate Sectarian who Forbids the Blame of Yazīd") asserts that the Ulema deemed it permissible to curse Yazīd ibn Mu'āwiya – together with al-Ḥajjāj – as did the Ḥanafīs Ḥāfiẓ al-Dīn al-Kurdī (who said it was preferable not to) and Sa'd al-Dīn al-Taftazānī.[1039] Al-Haytamī in *al-Ṣawā'iq al-Muḥriqa* cites Ibn al-Jawzī's attribution of this position to Imām Aḥmad via Abū Ya'lā in his *Mu'tamad fil-Uṣūl*, the latter narrating it from Ṣāliḥ ibn Aḥmad, from the Imām. However, Abū Muḥammad al-Tamīmī in his *'Aqīdat al-Imām Aḥmad* relates a contrary position from Imām Aḥmad as does Abū Ṭālib al-'Ukbarī, as narrated by Abū Ya'lā's son in *Ṭabaqāt al-Ḥanābila* and Ibn Mufliḥ in *al-Maqṣad al-Arshad*:

> He [Imām Ahmad] withheld saying anything about Yazīd ibn Mu'āwiya but rather committed his matter to Allāh. He would refrain from speaking against anyone from the first century. But our [Ḥanbalī] colleagues differ concerning him [Yazīd]. Some declared it permissible to blame him because he terrified al-Madīna and the Prophet ﷺ cursed whoever terrified al-Madīna. Others withheld from taking any position. Imām Aḥmad was asked about it and he said: "People prayed behind him and took his alms." Others considered him among the Muslims that sinned and it is better to refrain from taking any position in what is not obligatory. It was impermissible to curse any Muslim unless the Law provided a proof-text to that effect. For it is narrated and transmitted that to curse a Muslim is like killing him and that the Believer is not one given to cursing.[1040]

[1037] Ibn al-Jawzī, *Manāqib al-Imām Aḥmad* (p. 199).

[1038] Cited by al-Dhahabī in his chapter on the Imām in the *Siyar.*

[1039] Cited by al-Munāwī in *Fayḍ al-Qadīr* (§281); cf. al-Taftazānī, *Sharḥ al-'Aqā'id al-Nasafiyya* (p. 117).

[1040] Ibn Abī Ya'lā, *Ṭabaqāt* (1:246, 2:273), al-Haytamī, *al-Ṣawā'iq* (2:635), Ibn Mufliḥ, *al-Maqṣad al-Arshad* (2:283).

From the above it can be seen that the claim that "Imām Aḥmad ibn Ḥanbal permits that curses be pronounced against Yazīd"[1041] is not correct even though he forbade narrating from him.[1042] Imām al-Ghazzālī also forbade the cursing of Yazīd, as did many early and late Ulema.[1043] The rightly-guided Caliph 'Umar ibn 'Abd al-'Azīz ﷺ reportedly would say *raḥimahullāh* after the name of Yazīd but when he heard a man call him *"Amīr al-Mu'minīn"* he had him lashed twenty times.[1044]

On the Term *Ummat Muḥammad* ﷺ

Al-Khallāl opens his book *Aḥkām Ahl al-Milal* with the report of Abū Bakr al-Marwazī: "I asked Abū 'Abd Allāh [Imām Aḥmad] about the Jews and the Christians: Are they from the *Umma* of Muḥammad ﷺ or not?" He became very angry and said: "What a disgusting question! Unmentionable!" Another report states he replied: "Can a Muslim say such a thing?"[1045]

On Obligatory Imitation *(Taqlīd)* in the Religion

Like Ibrāhīm al-Nakha'ī, Abū Ḥanīfa, Mālik, and al-Shāfi'ī before him, Aḥmad emphasised the duty of imitating the Companions: "Know that the Religion is nothing but imitation itself (*al-dīnu innamā huwa al-taqlīd*). This imitation is of the Companions of the Messenger of Allāh ﷺ."[1046] He also said: "Allāh, Allāh! [Remember Him] concerning your soul. Cling to the transmitted reports, those who transmit them, and imitation. For Religion is nothing other than imitation itself. That is, imitation of the Prophet ﷺ, his Companions ﷺ, and those who came before us and did not induce us into error – imitate those with-

[1041] Claimed by al-Barzanjī in *al-Ishā'a fī Ashrāṭ al-Sā'a* (Shukrī ed. p. 77 and 144).

[1042] Cf. *Ṭabaqāt al-Ḥanābila* (1:347) from Muhannā ibn Yaḥyā al-Shāmī.

[1043] Cf. *Iḥyā' 'Ulūm al-Dīn* (3:108); al-Zabīdī, *Itḥāf al-Sādat al-Muttaqīn* (7:488); al-Damīrī's *Ḥayāt al-Ḥayawān*, section on the Caliphs (2:186); Ibn 'Ābidīn's *Ḥāshiya* (2:587); Gangohī's *Fatāwā Rashīdiyya* (1:3/26); 'Abd al-Ḥayy al-Lacknawī's *Fatāwā* (1:36); al-Haytamī's *Fatāwā Ḥadīthiyya* (p. 270), etc.

[1044] Narrated by Ibn Ḥajar in *Lisān al-Mīzān* (6:294).

[1045] Shaykh Muḥammad Sa'īd Ramaḍān al-Būṭī has argued that the Jews and Christians are indeed included in the *Umma* of the Prophet Muḥammad ﷺ and that they are among the seventy-two sects that are cast into the Fire in the well-known ḥadīth of the sects.

[1046] Narrated from Abū Muḥammad al-Barbahārī by Ibn Abī Ya'lā in *Ṭabaqāt al-Ḥanābila* (1:29).

out fear."[1047]

Similarly, al-Nakha'ī said: "If the Companions made ablution to the wrists I swear I would have done the same, even as I read the verse of ablution as stating ﴾ **to the elbows** ﴿ (5:6)."[1048] Abū Ḥanīfa said: "As for the Companions of the Messenger of Allāh, I follow the position of whomever I wish among them nor do I differ from the position of all of them. I only need investigate the positions of those who come after them – the *Tābi'īn* and subsequent generations."[1049]

To al-Ṣayrafī who was asking him whether it is permissible to examine the variant positions of the Companions "to know which is correct so that we may follow it," Aḥmad replied: "It is not permissible to examine [the differences] among the Companions of the Messenger of Allāh." Al-Ṣayrafī said: "Then what do we do?" He replied: "You imitate whomever of them you like!" (*tuqallidu ayyahum aḥbabt*).[1050] This is an explicit stipulation (*naṣṣ*) from Imām Aḥmad that by *taqlīd* he means *taqlīd*, not "following the proof" or "*ittibā'*" or some such invented distinctions aimed at diluting or nullifying the meaning of *taqlīd*. Abū Bakr said to a desert Arab who had objected to the allotment for him agreed upon by the Muslims: "If the Emigrants are satisfied, you are but followers!"[1051] – using the word "followers" (*taba'un*) to mean 'without any prerogative to consider, question, or discuss.'" Similar to this is the word of Allāh: ﴾ **When those who were followed** (*uttubi'ū*) **disown those who followed** (*ittaba'ū*) ﴿ (2:166), which uses (*ittibā'*) to denote the most basic blind imitation. More on this below.

Aḥmad said to al-Maymūnī: "Abū al-Ḥasan! Never speak over any matter in which you do not have an Imām [to imitate]."[1052]

One of the Imām's devoted followers, 'Abd al-Wahhāb ibn 'Abd al-Ḥakam al-Warrāq (d. 251), said: "Abū 'Abd Allāh [Imām Aḥmad] is our Imām. He is one of ﴾ **those who are firmly grounded in knowl-**

[1047] *Op. cit.* (1:39). Cf. al-Barbahārī's definition of Islām in his *Sharḥ Kitāb al-Sunna* as "nothing other than imitation (*i'lam annal-dīna innamā huwal-taqlīd*), and I mean imitation of the Companions of the Prophet (*wal-taqlīdu li-aṣḥābi rasūlillah ṣallallāhu 'alayhi wa-sallam*)."

[1048] In Ibn Abī Zayd al-Qayrawānī, *al-Jāmi' fil-Sunan* (p. 150 §18).

[1049] Cited by Ibn 'Abd al-Barr in his *Jāmi' Bayān al-'Ilm* (2:908).

[1050] Narrated by Ibn 'Abd al-Barr in *Jāmi' Bayān al-'Ilm* (2:909 §1705).

[1051] Narrated by al-Muḥibb al-Ṭabarī in *al-Riyāḍ al-Naḍira* (2:235-236).

[1052] Narrated by Ibn al-Jawzī in *Manāqib Aḥmad* (p. 178).

edge﴿ (3:7, 4:162). If I were to stand tomorrow before Allāh and He asked me: 'Who did you follow?' I would say: 'Aḥmad ibn Ḥanbal.'" Al-Warrāq also said "When the Prophet ﷺ said: 'Defer the question [about the Qur'ān] to the one who has knowledge of it,'[1053] we deferred it to Aḥmad ibn Ḥanbal."[1054] Abū Bakr al-Marwazī narrated in his book *al-Wara'*[1055] that when Aḥmad was asked on his deathbed who would succeed him as the Imām of the School, he said: "Put all your questions to 'Abd al-Wahhāb [al-Warrāq]." One of those present, Fatḥ ibn Abī al-Fatḥ, said: "But he does not have much learning!" Aḥmad replied: "He is a saintly man (*rajul ṣāliḥ*): one such as him is granted success in speaking the truth."[1056]

Ṣāliḥ ibn Aḥmad ibn Ḥanbal related that his father said: "The people [of knowledge] (*al-nās*) are none other than those who say: "X narrated to us and Y told us" (*ḥaddathanā wa-akhbaranā*). The rest are no good."[1057] He took this from al-Shāfi'ī who said: "Knowledge is what contains the words: 'Narrated to us.' All else is satanic whisperings."[1058] This is identical to Imām al-Awzā'ī's recommendation to Baqiyya ibn al-Walīd: "Baqiyya! Knowledge (*al-'ilm*) is whatever came to us from the Companions of Muḥammad ﷺ. Whatever did not come to us from them is not knowledge."[1059] However, as shown by Aḥmad's remarks on Ma'rūf al-Karkhī and 'Abd al-Wahhāb al-Warrāq, it is not enough to say *ḥaddathanā wa-akhbaranā*. Nor are the persons who make a loud show of calling themselves "followers of reports" (*atharī*) and "followers of the *Salaf*" (*salafī*) nowadays considered people of knowledge, since their circles are characterised not only by innovation but by narrative untrustworthiness and ignorance.

[1053] A reference to the ḥadīth: "The Qur'ān was revealed in seven dialects, and speculative wrangling (*al-mirā'*) about it is disbelief" – he said it three times – "therefore whatever you understand of it, put it into practice, and whatever you do not understand, defer it to the one who has knowledge of it." Narrated from Abū Hurayra by Imām Aḥmad with a sound chain as stated by al-Haythamī (7:151) and by Shākir and al-Zayn in their edition of the *Musnad* (8:107 §7976).

[1054] Ibn Abī Ya'lā, *Ṭabaqāt al-Ḥanābila* (1:211).

[1055] Published under the name of Imām Aḥmad (p. 10).

[1056] Cf. Ibn Abī Ya'lā, chapter on al-Warrāq in *Ṭabaqāt al-Ḥanābila* (1:210-212).

[1057] Cited by al-Qāḍī 'Iyāḍ in *al-Ilmā'* (p. 28) and his student Ibn Bashkuwāl in *al-Ṣila* (1:255) as mentioned by 'Awwāma in *Adab al-Ikhtilāf* (p. 144).

[1058] Al-Shāfi'ī, *Dīwān* per al-Qārī in his introduction to *Sharḥ al-Fiqh al-Akbar.*

[1059] In al-Dhahabī, *Siyar* (1997 ed. 7:95), Ibn Ḥajar, *Fatḥ al-Bārī* (1959 ed. 13:291).

As Munīr 'Abduh Aghā said:

> It can be firmly verified that the troublemakers (*al-mushāghibūn*) in our time who claim that they belong to the school of the *Salaf*, outwardly making a show of such affiliation, do not in any way whatsoever belong to it, neither in knowledge nor in practice. They are propagators of falsehood, deception, and misguidance devoid of all guidance. They claim that the school of the pious *Salaf* consists in instilling doubt in people concerning their Religion and inciting the general public to embrace false beliefs, all the while embellishing this activity by attributing it to our masters the *Salaf* who are completely innocent of it![1060]

Those Who Are Imitated in Islām *(al-Muqalladūn)*

Imām Mālik preceded Imām Aḥmad in upholding imitation as the basis of the Religion by founding his School on the principle of imitation of the learned authorities of Madīna the Radiant. Mālik considered that they were the closest of all people on earth to represent the practice of the Prophet ﷺ accurately. The *Muwaṭṭa'* therefore abounds with the remark: "This what I have seen the knowledgeable people of Madīna do." Imām Abū Manṣūr al-Baghdādī relates in *Naqd Abī 'Abd Allāh al-Jurjānī fī Tarjīḥ Madhhab Abī Ḥanīfa* that Mālik also said that when the Seven Jurists of Madīna concur on a ruling, they constitute Consensus in Islām which becomes binding upon all and forbidden to contravene.[1061] These seven are Sa'īd ibn al-Musayyab, Khārija ibn Zayd, 'Urwa ibn al-Zubayr, Sulaymān ibn Yasār, al-Qāsim ibn Muḥammad ibn Abī Bakr, Abū Salama ibn 'Abd al-Raḥmān, and Muḥammad ibn 'Amr ibn Ḥazm or, alternately, Sālim ibn 'Abd Allāh ibn 'Umar ﷺ.

Ibn al-Qayyim said: "There is an obligatory imitation (*taqlīd wājib*), a forbidden imitation, and a permitted imitation [...]. The obligatory one is the imitation of those who know better than us, as when a person has not obtained knowledge of a proof from the Qur'ān or the Sunna concerning something. Such an imitation has been reported from Imām al-Shāfi'ī ﷺ in many places, where he would say: 'I said

[1060] Munīr 'Abduh Aghā, *Namūdhaj min al-A'māl al-Khayriyya fil-Maṭba'at al-Munīriyya* (p. 131-134).

[1061] In Ibn al-Subkī, *Ṭabaqāt al-Shāfi'iyya al-Wusṭā*, as cited in the 1992 ed. of his *Ṭabaqāt al-Shāfi'iyya al-Kubrā* (5:147).

this in *taqlīd* of 'Umar ﷺ' or 'I said that in *taqlīd* of 'Uthmān ﷺ' or 'I said that in *taqlīd* of 'Aṭā' ﷺ.' As al-Shāfi'ī said concerning the Companions: 'Their opinion for us is better than our opinion for ourselves.'"[1062]

A similar, though more strictly imitative path is reported from Imām Aḥmad as already mentioned. Thus we see that all the four Sunni Imāms put in practice the ḥadīth "My Companions are like the stars, whoever among them you use for guidance, you will be rightly guided."[1063]

Al-Dhahabī said:

[1062] Ibn al-Qayyim, *I'lām al-Muwaqqi'īn 'an Rabb al-'Ālamīn* (2:186-187).

[1063] Narrated from **[1]** Ibn 'Umar by 'Abd ibn Ḥumayd in his *Musnad* (*Muntakhab* Kuwait ed. 2:28=Cairo ed. p. 250), Ibn 'Abd al-Barr in *Jāmi' Bayān al-'Ilm* (2:924 §1759), and Ibn 'Adī in *al-Kāmil* (2:785-786), all with very weak chains through the forger Ḥamza ibn Abī Ḥamza al-Ju'fī al-Jazīrī; cf. al-Suyūṭī in *Manāhil al-Ṣafā* (p. 193 §1027), Ibn 'Adī in *al-Kāmil*, and *Talkhīṣ al-Ḥabīr* (4:190); **[2]** Jābir by al-Dāraquṭnī in *Faḍā'il al-Ṣaḥāba* and *al-Mu'talif wal-Mukhtalif* (4:1778), Ibn 'Abd al-Barr in *Jāmi' Bayān al-'Ilm* (2:925 §1760=2:110-111 *ḍa'īf*), and Ibn Ḥazm in *al-Iḥkām* (6:244 *mawḍū'*) with a weak chain because of Sallām ibn al-Ḥārith although this is the best chain in this chapter and al-Bayhaqī declares it strong in *al-I'tiqād* (p. 319); Ibn Ḥazm narrates it through Sallām ibn Sulaymān (ibn Sawwār) who is also weak; **[2a]** Jābir by al-Dāraquṭnī in *Gharā'ib Mālik* through an unknown from Imām Mālik; cf. *Talkhīṣ al-Ḥabīr*, **[3]** Abū Hurayra by al-Quḍā'ī in *Musnad al-Shihāb* (2:275 §1346) with a very weak chain because of Ja'far ibn 'Abd al-Wāḥid al-Hāshimī who was declared a liar as stated by Ibn Ḥajar; **[4]** 'Umar (a *ḥadīth qudsī*) by al-Bayhaqī in *al-Madkhal* (p. 162=1:145-146 §151), al-Khaṭīb in *al-Kifāya* (p. 48=p. 66=p. 95), al-Bazzār who graded it *ḍa'īf munkar* as quoted by Ibn 'Abd al-Barr in *Jāmi' Bayān al-'Ilm* (2:924), Niẓām al-Mulk (408-485) in *Majlisān min Amālī Niẓām al-Mulk* (p. 52), al-Sijzī in *al-Ibāna*, and Ibn 'Asākir, all with a very weak chain because of 'Abd al-Raḥīm ibn Zayd al-'Ammī who is discarded; cf. Ibn al-Jawzī, *'Ilal* (1:282), al-Dhahabī, *Mīzān* (*bāṭil*), al-Suyūṭī, *Jāmi' Ṣaghīr* (§4603 *ḍa'īf*), al-Ṣan'ānī, *Tawḍīḥ al-Afkār* (p. 264), al-Munāwī, *Fayḍ al-Qadīr* (4:76 *bāṭil*), and al-Ghumārī, *al-Mughīr* (p. 56 *mawḍū'*); **[5]** Ibn 'Abbās *munqaṭi'* by al-Khaṭīb in *al-Kifāya* (p. 48=p. 65-66=p. 95), al-Bayhaqī in *al-Madkhal* (p. 163-164=1:147-148), and Ibn 'Asākir; cf. al-Suyūṭī, *Miftāḥ al-Janna* (p. 45=p. 93-94 §180), all with a very weak chain because of Juwaybir ibn Sa'īd al-Azdī (cf. *Taqrīb*) in addition to its being broken between al-Ḍaḥḥāk and Ibn 'Abbās; **[6]** Anas through al-Bazzār; cf. Ibn Ḥajar in *Talkhīṣ al-Ḥabīr* (4:191 *isnād wāhin*) and *al-Maṭālib al-'Āliya* (4:146 *isnād ḍa'īf*). **[7]** Jawwāb ibn 'Ubayd Allāh the Tābi'ī *mursal* by al-Bayhaqī in *al-Madkhal* (p. 163=1:148 §153) through Juwaybir. Qāḍī 'Iyāḍ attributes it positively to the Prophet ﷺ in *al-Shifā* (p. 535 §1302). Al-Bajawī said in his commentary of the *Shifā* (2:613): "The ḥadīth Master al-'Irāqī said: The author ('Iyāḍ) should not have cited it as if it were definitely a ḥadīth of the Prophet." Al-Ḥalabī said: "The author should not have cited it as if it were definitely a ḥadīth of the Prophet ﷺ because of what is known about it among the scholars of this science, and he has done the same thing

Those who are imitated (*al-muqalladūn*) in Islām are

- The Prophet's Companions ☙ provided the chain of transmission back to them is firmly established.
- Then the [senior] Imāms of the Successors such as

–'Alqama [ibn Qays] (d. 62);
–Masrūq [ibn al-Ajda'] (d. 63);
–'Abīdat al-Salmānī (d. 74);

several times before." Al-Qārī replies in his *Sharḥ al-Shifā'* (2:91): "It is possible that he ['Iyāḍ] had established a chain for it, or that he considered the multiplicity of its chains to raise its grade from *ḍa'īf* to that of *ḥasan*, due to his good opinion of it, not to mention the fact that even the weak ḥadīth may be put into practice for meritorious acts (*faḍā'il al-a'māl*), and Allāh knows best." See also Ibn al-Athīr, *Jāmi' al-Uṣūl* (8:556-557). Al-Bayhaqī in *al-Madkhal* concludes, "Its *matn* is well-known and its chains are weak, not one of them being sound" but he declares one of its chains strong and adduces it in *al-I'tiqād* (p. 319), confirming its meaning while Ibn Ḥajar supports him in *Talkhīṣ al-Ḥabīr* (4:191); cf. al-Mubārakfūrī, *Tuḥfat al-Aḥwadhī* (10:156). Al-Ḥakīm al-Tirmidhī in *Nawādir al-Uṣūl* (3:62) considers its meaning true. Ibn 'Abd al-Barr rejects al-Bazzār's grading of *munkar* and also tends to strengthen it; cf. Ibn Ḥajar in his *Takhrīj Aḥādīth Mukhtaṣar Ibn al-Ḥājib* (*i.e.* Ibn al-Ḥājib's abridgment of his own *Muntahā al-Sūl wal-Amal fī 'Ilmay al-Uṣūli wal-Jadal*) as cited in al-Ṣan'ānī's *Tawḍīḥ al-Afkār* (p. 264). Al-Ṣāghānī declared it fair (*ḥasan*) as stated by Ḥasan al-Ṭībī and al-Sayyid's respective commentaries on the *Mishkāt*. Shaykh 'Abd al-Fattāḥ Abū Ghudda in his commentary on al-Qārī's *Fatḥ Bāb al-'Ināya* (1:13) and his *al-Maṣnū' fī Ma'rifat al-Ḥadīth al-Mawḍū'* (p. 273) rejects the grading of *mawḍū'* and equally rejects al-Lacknawī's grading of *ṣaḥīḥ*, in his marginalia on the latter's *Tuḥfat al-Akhyār* entitled *Nukhbat al-Anẓār* (p. 53) and the introduction to his *al-Āthār al-Marfū'a fil-Akhbār al-Mawḍū'a* – for which the latter cited al-Sha'rānī's phrase in the *Mīzān al-Kubrā*: "Even if the authenticity of this ḥadīth is questioned among the scholars of ḥadīth, nevertheless it is sound among the people of spiritual unveiling (*kashf*)." See also the Tamīm brothers' marginalia on al-Qārī's *Sharḥ Sharḥ Nukhbat al-Fikar* (p. 557). The "Salafī" Sa'īd Ma'shāsha in his tract *al-Muqallidūn wal-A'immat al-Arba'a* (Beirut: al-Maktab al-Islāmī and Dār Ibn Ḥazm, 1999) (p. 102) said, "this ḥadīth is forged (*mawḍū'*) as Ibn Ḥazm said in *[al-Iḥkām fī] Uṣūl al-Aḥkām* (§810), al-Shawkānī in *al-Qawl al-Mufīd* (p. 30), and al-Albānī in *al-Silsila al-Ḍa'īfa* (§58-61) and a number of the scholars." This statement is a flat untruth as al-Shawkānī adduces this narration in *Irshād al-Fuḥūl* (1:337, 1:394) and all he said in *al-Qawl al-Mufīd fī Adillat al-Ijtihād wal-Taqlīd* on page 9 of its original 1347/1929 edition is: "This ḥadīth was narrated through different routes from Jābir and Ibn 'Umar, and the Imāms of narrator-criticism have explicitly said that none of them are sound (*lā yaṣiḥḥu minhā shay'*) and that this ḥadīth is not firmly established as a Prophetic narration [...]. In sum, this ḥadīth forms no proof." This is the same opinion as those we have quoted from the majority of the scholars, but it is a far cry from saying the ḥadīth is forged. Furthermore, it is untrue that "a number of the scholars" have declared it forged, as the only scholar

–Sa'īd ibn al-Musayyab or al-Musayyib (d. 93);
–Abū al-Sha'thā' [Jābir ibn Zayd al-Azdī] (d. 93);
–Sa'īd ibn Jubayr (d. 94);
–'Ubayd Allāh ibn 'Abd Allāh (d. 98 or 99);
–'Urwa [ibn al-Zubayr] (d. 93-101?);
–al-Qāsim [ibn Muḥammad] (d. 106);
–al-Sha'bī (d. 104 or 105 or 106);[1064]
–al-Ḥasan [al-Baṣrī] (d. 110);
–Ibn Sīrīn (d. 110);
–and Ibrāhīm al-Nakha'ī (d. 96) ﷺ.

❖ Then [the junior Imāms of the Successors] such as
–al-Zuhrī (d. 124),
–Abū al-Zinād (d. 130),
–Ayyūb al-Sikhtiyānī (d. 131),
–Rabī'a (d. 136), and their synchronic layer ﷺ.

❖ Then such as
–Abū Ḥanīfa (d. 150),
–Mālik (d. 179),
–al-Awzā'ī (d. 157),
–Ibn Jurayj (d. 150),
–Ma'mar [ibn Rāshid] (d. 154),
–[Sa'īd] Ibn Abī 'Arūba (d. 156),
–Sufyān al-Thawrī (d. 161),
–the two Ḥammāds [ibn Salama (d.167) and ibn Zayd]
–Shu'ba [ibn al-Ḥajjāj] (d.160),
–al-Layth [ibn Sa'd] (d. 175),
–Ibn al-Mājishūn (d. 164),
–and Ibn Abī Dhi'b (d. 158) ﷺ.

❖ Then such as
–Ibn al-Mubārak (d. 181),
–Muslim [ibn Khālid] al-Zanjī (d. 180),
–al-Qāḍī Abū Yūsuf (d. 208),
–al-Hiql ibn Ziyād (d. 179),
–Wakī' (d. 196),

---

who did so was Ibn Ḥazm, imitated in our time by various semi-Ulema. One of the ironies of Ma'shāsha's book is that he attacks *taqlīd* in every page, yet relies blindly on Albānī for ḥadīth authentication, without any reference to the ḥadīth Masters!

[1064] He had a photographic memory: "I never wrote anything black on white with-

–al-Walīd ibn Muslim (d. 195), and their layer ﷺ.

- Then such as

  –al-Shāfi'ī (d. 204),
  –Abū 'Ubayd [al-Qāsim ibn Sallām] (d. 224),
  –Aḥmad [ibn Ḥanbal] (d. 241),
  –Isḥāq [ibn Rāhūyah] (d. 238),[1065]
  –Abū Thawr (d. 240),
  –al-Buwayṭī (d. 231),
  –and Abū Bakr ibn Abī Shayba (d. 235) ﷺ.

- Then such as

  –al-Muzanī (d. 264),
  –Abū Bakr al-Athram (d. 260),
  –al-Bukhārī (d. 256),
  –Dāwūd ibn 'Alī [al-Ẓāhirī] (d. 275),[1066]
  –Muḥammad ibn Naṣr al-Marwazī (d. 294),
  –Ibrāhīm al-Ḥarbī (d. 285),
  –and Ismā'īl [ibn Isḥāq ibn Ismā'īl] al-Qāḍī (d. 282) ﷺ.

- Then such as

  –Muḥammad ibn Jarīr al-Ṭabarī (d. 310),
  –Abū Bakr ibn Khuzayma (d. 311),
  –Abū al-'Abbās [Aḥmad ibn 'Umar] ibn Surayj (d. 303),
  –Abū Bakr [Muḥammad ibn Ibrāhīm] ibn al-Mundhir (d. 318),
  –Abū Ja'far al-Ṭaḥāwī (d. 321),
  –and Abū Bakr al-Khallāl (d. 311) ﷺ.[1067]

Some people invoke a distinction between "following the proof" – which they call *ittibā'* by the *muttabi'* – and "following the imām with-

out having memorized it, nor heard any man's discourse and then needed to have it repeated back to me." Narrated by al-Khaṭīb in *al-Jāmi' li-Akhlāq al-Rāwī* (2:380 §1831-1832).

[1065] He also had a photographic memory: "Do you find this [al-Sha'bī's prodigious memory] extraordinary, O Abū Ḥasan? I shall only mention to you my own example. I never wrote anything without memorizing it, and I can now see before me more than 70,000 ḥadīths in my book." Narrated by al-Khaṭīb in *al-Jāmi' li-Akhlāq al-Rāwī* (2:380-381 §1832).

[1066] Al-Dhahabī openly expresses his approval of Dāwūd al-Ẓāhirī's rigid adherence to the texts in the *Siyar* (cf. 7:411).

[1067] Al-Dhahabī, *Siyar A'lām al-Nubalā'* (Fikr ed. 7:410).

out knowing the proof" – which they call *taqlīd* by the *muqallid* and arbitrarily declare forbidden.[1068] This distinction has no basis in the Qur'ān and Sunna and none of the *Salaf* – especially not Imām Aḥmad, who only spoke of *taqlīd* – nor the established scholars of the *Khalaf* used it. Furthermore, Qur'ānic usage shows that the term "follow" can be meant in both the good and the bad sense of following either the Prophet ﷺ or false deities:

> ﴿ **Say, (O Muḥammad, to mankind): If you love Allāh, follow me; Allāh will love you and forgive you your sins. Allāh is Forgiving, Merciful** ﴾ (3:31).
> ﴿ **(On the day) when those who were followed disown those who followed (them), and they behold the doom, and all their aims collapse with them** ﴾ (2:166).

In both examples the term "to follow" neither specifies nor implies a distinction between followership and pure imitation but in fact means both, as shown by the Imāms' definition of Islām as consisting in right imitation (*taqlīd*) in all the excerpts cited above.

Those Who Wrote Imām Aḥmad's Biography

Al-Dhahabī said: "Al-Bayhaqī wrote Aḥmad's biography (*sīra*) in one volume, so did Ibn al-Jawzī, and also Shaykh al-Islām[1069] ['Abd Allāh al-Harawī] al-Anṣārī in a brief volume. He passed on to the good pleasure of Allāh on the day of *Jumu'a*, the twelfth of *Rabī' al-Awwal* in the year 241, at the age of seventy-seven. I have two of his short-chained narrations (*'awālīh*), and a licence (*ijāza*) for the entire *Musnad.*" Al-Dhahabī's chapter on Imām Aḥmad in *Siyar A'lām al-Nubalā'* consists of no less than 113 pages.

From the *Reliance of the Traveller*

The biographical notice on Imām Aḥmad in the *Reliance of the Traveller* reads:

> Out of piety, Imām Aḥmad never gave a formal legal *opinion* (fatwā) while Shāfi'ī was in Iraq, and when he later formulated his school of jurisprudence, he mainly drew on explicit texts from

[1068] Cf. the "Salafī" student thrashed by al-Būṭī in the debate reported in *al-Salafiyya.*
[1069] See Appendix, "The Title: *Shaykh al-Islām.*"

the [Qur'ān], ḥadīth, and scholarly consensus, with relatively little expansion from analogical reasoning (*qiyās*). He was probably the most learned in the sciences of ḥadīth of the four great Imāms of Sacred Law, and his students included many of the foremost Scholars of ḥadīth. [...] He said, 'I saw the Lord of Power in my sleep, and said, "O Lord, what is the best act through which those near to You draw nearer?" and He answered, "Through [reciting] My word, O Aḥmad." I asked, "With understanding, or without?" and He answered, "With understanding and without."' [...] Aḥmad was imprisoned and tortured for twenty-eight months under the Abbāsid caliph al-Mu'taṣim in an effort to force him to publicly espouse the [Mu'tazila] position that the Holy [Qur'ān] was created, but the Imām bore up unflinchingly under the persecution and refused to renounce the belief of *Ahl al-Sunna* that the [Qur'ān] is the uncreated word of Allāh,[1070] after which Allāh delivered and vindicated him. When Aḥmad died in 241/855, he was accompanied to his resting place by a funeral procession of eight hundred thousand men and sixty thousand women, marking the departure of the last of the four great *mujtahid* Imāms of Islām.

His Meeting with the Prophet ﷺ in Dream

In another dream reported from Imām Aḥmad he saw the Prophet ﷺ and asked him: "Messenger of Allāh, is all that Abū Hurayra narrated from you true?" He replied yes.[1071]

A *Ṣiddīq*

Ibn al-Jawzī narrates with his chain from Bilāl al-Khawwās. that the latter met al-Khaḍir and asked him: "What do you say of al-Shāfi'ī?" He replied: "He is one of the Pillar-Saints *(al-awtād)*." "And Aḥmad ibn Ḥanbal?" He said: "He is a *Ṣiddīq*."[1072]

[1070] *Ahl al-Sunna* agree one and all that the Qur'ān is the pre-existent, pre-eternal, uncreated Speech of Allāh ﷻ. See the Appendix entitled "The Controversy over the Pronunciation of the Qur'ān."

[1071] In Ibn Abī Ya'lā, *Ṭabaqāt al-Ḥanābila* (1:268). See al-Nawawī's important remarks on the pre-conditions and limitations of ḥadīth gradings or any other rulings seen or mentioned in dreams in his *Sharḥ Ṣaḥīḥ Muslim,* discussion on Abān ibn Abī 'Iyāsh and our article on *kashf* in *Sunna Notes I.*

[1072] Ibn al-Jawzī, *Manāqib al-Imām Aḥmad* (p. 144); cf. *Ḥilya* (9:187).

Major Figures of the Late *Madhhab*

The later Ḥanbalī School begins with the Ash'arī-leaning polymath Abū al-Wafā' **Ibn 'Aqīl** whose full name was 'Alī ibn 'Aqīl ibn Muḥammad ibn 'Aqīl ibn Aḥmad al-Baghdādī al-Ẓafar (431-513), author of a 200-volume encyclopedia of the sciences titled *Kitāb al-Funūn* of which, unfortunately, little survives, and of *al-Wāḍiḥ fī Uṣūl al-Fiqh*, preserved in full.[1073] The Ḥanbalī jurist and ḥadīth Master Abū al-Khaṭṭāb Maḥfūẓ ibn Aḥmad **al-Kalwadhānī** (432-510) was an exact contemporary of Ibn 'Aqīl and teacher to Ibn Nāṣir, Ibn al-Jawzī's teacher. Al-Kiyā would say at the approach of al-Kalwadhānī: "Here is *Fiqh* itself coming our way!"[1074] He is followed in the School by the learned vizir 'Awn al-Dīn Abū al-Muẓaffar Yaḥyā ibn Muḥammad **ibn Hubayra** (d. 560).

Abū al-Faraj **Ibn al-Jawzī**: 'Abd al-Raḥmān ibn 'Alī ibn Muḥammad al-Qurashī al-Taymī al-Bakrī al-Baghdādī (509/510-597) was a descendent of Abū Bakr al-Ṣiddīq. With his Ḥanbalī colleague Shaykh 'Abd al-Qādir al-Gīlānī, forty years his senior, Ibn al-Jawzī was the Imām of the School and foremost orator of kings and princes in his time, whose gatherings reportedly reached one hundred thousand, a ḥadīth Master, philologist, commentator of Qur'ān, expert jurist, physician, and historian of superb character and exquisite manners. Orphaned of his father at age three, Ibn al-Jawzī was raised by his aunt who later brought him to the ḥadīth scholar Ibn Nāṣir, his first Shaykh. He took ḥadīth from him as well as over eighty Shaykhs and was teacher to his grandson Abū al-Muẓaffar Shams al-Dīn Yūsuf ibn Farghal ibn 'Abd Allāh al-Baghdādī al-Ḥanafī – Sibt Ibn al-Jawzī – as well as some of the greatest Ḥanbalī ḥadīth Masters and jurists such as Muwaffaq al-Dīn Ibn Qudāma, Ibn al-Najjār, and Ḍiyā' al-Dīn al-Maqdisī. He courageously denounced the anthropomorphism of some of his School in the interpretation of the Divine Attributes in his visionary landmark *Daf' Shubah al-Tashbīh bi-Akuff al-Tanzīh* ("Rebuttal of the Insinuations of Anthropomorphism at the Hands of Divine

[1073] Ibn 'Aqīl and his time have been studied in depth by George Makdisī, the foremost student of the French orientalists Louis Massignon and the Ḥanbalī specialist Henri Laoust, both of whom he surpassed in his technique; cf. Makdisī's bio-bibliographical 600-page study *Ibn 'Aqīl et la résurgence de l'Islam traditionaliste au XIe siècle* (*Ve siècle de l'Hégire*) (Damascus: Institut Français de Damas, 1963).

[1074] Ibn Rajab, *Dhayl Ṭabaqāt al-Ḥanābila* (1:144).

Transcendence") which he began with the words:

> I have seen among the followers of our School some who hold unsound discourses on doctrine. Three in particular have applied themselves to write books in which they distort the Ḥanbalī *madhhab*: Abū 'Abd Allāh ibn Ḥāmid,[1075] his friend al-Qāḍī (Abū Ya'lā),[1076] and Ibn al-Zāghūnī.[1077] I have seen them descend to the level of popular belief, construing the Divine Attributes according to the requirements of what the human senses know. They have heard that Allāh created Ādam in H/his likeness and form (*'alā ṣūrātihi*), so they affirm that Allāh has a form and face in addition to His Essence, as well as two eyes, a mouth, an uvula, molar teeth, a physiognomy, two hands, fingers, a palm, a little finger, a thumb, a chest, thighs, two legs, two feet! [...] Then they placate the common people by adding: "But not as we think!" [...] Then they become offended when imputed with likening Allāh to His creation (*tashbīh*) and express scorn at such an attribution to themselves, clamoring: "We are *Ahl al-Sunna*!" Yet their discourse is clearly couched in terms of *tashbīh*. And some of the masses follow them.

Some later Ḥanbalīs never quite forgave Ibn al-Jawzī because of this book.[1078]

The later School is dominated by the towering figure of the saintly, erudite student of Shaykh **'Abd al-Qādir al-Gīlānī** ﵁ (470-561) known as **Ibn Qudāma**, the author of *al-Mughnī*, which ranks with or surpasses al-Nawawī's *Majmū'* as a general comparative reference work of *fiqh* even if designed to serve a single School. Ibn Qudāma's full name is Muwaffaq al-Dīn Abū Muḥammad 'Abd Allāh ibn Aḥmad ibn Muḥammad ibn Qudāma al-Maqdisī al-Dimashqī ﵁ (d. 620). He belongs to a large family of Palestinian Jurists who fled the Frankish onslaught on Jerusalem and came to the Qāsyūn Ṣāliḥiyya district of Damascus where they founded schools and mosques. In addition to

[1075] Abū 'Abd Allāh al-Ḥasan ibn Ḥāmid al-Baghdādī al-Warrāq al-Ḥanbalī (d. 403), Abū Ya'lā's teacher, author of *Sharḥ Uṣūl al-Dīn.*

[1076] The father of the author of *Ṭabaqāt al-Ḥanābila*, al-Qāḍī Abū Ya'lā Muḥammad ibn al-Ḥusayn ibn al-Farrā' al-Ḥanbalī (d. 458).

[1077] Abū al-Ḥasan 'Alīy ibn 'Ubayd Allāh al-Zāghūnī al-Ḥanbalī (d. 527), author of *al-Īḍāḥ fī Uṣūl al-Dīn* and one of Ibn al-Jawzī's teachers; cf. *Muntaẓam* (10:30).

[1078] See notice on Ibn al-Jawzī – *in shā' Allāh* – in our *Ash'arī School*.

his contributions in jurisprudence, Ibn Qudāma also wrote several brief statements of doctrine and refutations of the Ash'arī School such as *Lam'at al-I'tiqād al-Hādī ilā Sabīl al-Rashād* ("The Spark of the Belief that Leads to the Paths of Uprightness"), *Dhamm al-Ta'wīl* ("The Blame of Figurative Interpretation"), and *Taḥrīm al-Naẓar fī Kutub Ahl al-Kalām* ("The Prohibition of Looking into the Books of the Theologians"), the latter also titled *al-Radd 'alā Ibn 'Aqīl* in reference to Ibn Qudāma's own distinguished colleague. Ibn Qudāma's *Lam'a* ends with the statement:

> As for affiliation to an Imām in the branches of the Religion such as the four Schools, such affiliation is never a bad thing. The differences in the branches is a mercy. Those that differ in them are thanked and congratulated in addition to being rewarded for their effort. Their divergence is a vast mercy and their agreement is a decisive argument (*ikhtilāfuhum raḥmatun wāsi'a wa-ittifāquhum ḥujjatun qāṭi'a*).

Other prominent figures of the School are **Majd al-Dīn Ibn Taymiyya** the grandfather; Shams al-Dīn Muḥammad **ibn Mufliḥ** al-Maqdisī (d. 763) who reconciled the positions of Taqī al-Dīn Ibn Taymiyya with the School; Shams al-Dīn Muḥammad ibn 'Abd Allāh ibn Muḥammad **al-Zarkashī** (d. 772) whose *Sharḥ al-Khiraqī* is considered superior even to the *Mughnī*; the peerless Master Abū al-Faraj Zayn al-Dīn 'Abd al-Raḥmān ibn Aḥmad **ibn Rajab** al-Dimashqī (d. 795) whose *Qawā'id Fiqhiyya* are a masterpiece of the genre; 'Alā' al-Dīn Abū al-Ḥasan 'Alī ibn Sulaymān ibn Aḥmad **al-Mardāwī** (d. 885); "the Shaykh of the *Madhhab*, its reexaminer and amender"; Sharaf al-Dīn Abū al-Najā Mūsā ibn Aḥmad ibn Mūsā **al-Ḥajjāwī** al-Dimashqī (d. 968); Taqī al-Dīn Abū Bakr Muḥammad ibn Aḥmad ibn 'Abd al-'Azīz, known as **Ibn Najjār** and **al-Futūḥī** (d. 972); the great Egyptian Ṣūfī Jurist **Mar'ī** ibn Yūsuf ibn Abī Bakr al-Karmī al-Maqdisī (d. 1033), author of countless valuable works still extant, among them *Tanwīh Baṣā'ir al-Muqallidīn fī Manāqib al-A'immat al-Mujtahidīn*; "the Shaykh of the *Madhhab* and Seal of the Verifying Authorities" Abū al-Sa'ādāt Manṣūr ibn Yūnus **al-Buhūtī** (d. 1051); Shihāb al-Dīn Abū al-'Abbās Aḥmad ibn 'Abd Allāh ibn Aḥmad **al-Ba'lī** al-Dimashqī (d. 1189); and Zayn al-Dīn 'Abd al-Raḥmān ibn 'Abd Allāh ibn Aḥmad **al-Ba'lī** al-Ḥalabī (d.1192). One of the last great Ḥanbalī Jurists was the

Damascene Shaykh 'Abd al-Qādir ibn Aḥmad ibn Muṣṭafā, known as **Ibn Badrān** (d. 1346) – Allāh have mercy on all of them.

Salient Fatwās of Imām Aḥmad and his School

DESIRABILITY OF VISITING THE PROPHET ﷺ IN MADĪNA

Al-Mardāwī, Ibn Hubayra, and others stated that the entirety of the early and late authorities in the Ḥanbalī Madhhab stipulate the desirability (*istiḥbāb*) of visiting the grave of the Prophet ﷺ in Madīna, most especially after Ḥajj, and/or travelling to do so.[1079] Ibn Mufliḥ, al-Mardāwī, and Mar'ī ibn Yūsuf in *Ghāyat al-Muntahā* stated the Sunnī character of visiting the graves of the Muslims and the permissibility (*ibāḥa*) of travelling to do so. Mar'ī reiterates this ruling in his unpublished monograph on the ethics of graves and visitation, *Shifā' al-Ṣudūr fī Ziyārat al-Mashāhid wal-Qubūr.*[1080]

DESIRABILITY OF SEEKING BLESSING FROM THE RELICS OF THE PROPHET ﷺ AND THE SAINTS

We mentioned the position of Imām Aḥmad, related by his son 'Abd Allāh, that touching the hair, bowl, grave, chamber walls, and pulpit of the Prophet ﷺ for the intention of deriving blessing (*tabarruk*) is permissible.[1081] Ibn Qudāma further narrates from Ibrāhīm ibn 'Abd al-Raḥmān ibn 'Abd al-Qārī that the latter saw Ibn 'Umar place his hand on the seat of the Prophet's ﷺ *minbar,* then wipe his face with it. He then states the ruling that such an act is desirable for every visitor of the Prophetic Mosque, as do others.[1082] A report from

[1079] Ibn Qudāma, *al-Mughnī* (3:117, 3:297, 5:465), *al-Muqni'* (1:466), *al-Kāfī* (1:619); Ibn Mufliḥ, *al-Mubdi' fī Sharḥ al-Muqni'* (3:259); al-Buhūtī, *Kashshāf al-Qinā'* (2:514-515; 5:36), *al-Rawḍ al-Murba'* (1:522); Ibn Dawyān, *Manār al-Sabīl* (1:256); Shams al-Dīn ibn Mufliḥ, *Furū'* (3:523); al-Ḥajjāwī, *Iqnā'* (1:395); 'Abd al-Raḥmān al-Ba'lī, *Kashf al-Mukhaddarāt* (p. 193); Mar'ī, *Ghāyat al-Muntahā* (1:418), *Dalīl al-Ṭālib* (p. 88); Aḥmad al-Ba'lī, *al-Rawḍ al-Nadī* (p. 190); Bahā' al-Dīn al-Maqdisī (p. 209); Ibn al-Najjār, *Muntahā al-Irādāt* (1:286); Ibn al-Jawzī, *al-Madhhab al-Aḥmad* (p. 68); Shams al-Dīn Ibn Qudāma, *al-Sharḥ al-Kabīr* (3:494); Ibn Hubayra, *Ifṣāḥ* (1:297); al-Kawladhānī, *Hidāya* (p. 105); al-Mardāwī, *Inṣāf* (4:53).

[1080] Ẓāhiriyya ms. cf. Ibn Mufliḥ, *Mubdi'* (2:107), Mar'ī, *Ghāya* (1:258), al-Mardāwī, *Inṣāf* (2:317).

[1081] Cf. above (p. 355).

[1082] Ibn Qudāma, *Mughnī* (5:468), al-Buhūtī, *Kashshāf* (2:517), al-Mardāwī, *Inṣāf* (4:54), Ibn Mufliḥ, *Furū'* (3:523).

Aḥmad states, "it is desirable (*mustaḥabb*) to touch the visited grave – Abū al-Ḥusayn [Ibn Abī Ya'lā] said it is *ṣaḥīḥ* [from Aḥmad] – because it resembles the handshake of the living; especially from one whose blessing is sought (*lā siyyamā mimman turjā barakatuh*)." The *Madhhab* similarly permits the touching of a grave by the hand, especially if *baraka* is sought from its pious dweller.[1083] Ibn Qudāma began his *Mughnī* by stating that he will mention the position of every Imām to obtain the *baraka* of his name, and that "we obtain blessing from the great Imām al-Khiraqī's book."[1084] The School also stipulates the desirability of burial near the graves of pious persons or in honored spots (*al-biqā' al-sharīfa*).[1085] We mentioned that the son of Imām Aḥmad – Imām 'Abd Allāh – preferred to be buried in a spot rumoured to be near a Prophet ﷺ rather than to be near his father.

TAKBĪR UPON TERMINATING RECITATION OF THE QUR'ĀN

Ibn Qudāma said Imām Aḥmad considered it desirable to recite *Allāhu akbar* at the conclusion of every Sūra from *al-Ḍuḥā* to the end of the Qur'ān on the basis of the narration from Ubay ibn Ka'b that such was the command of the Prophet ﷺ to him, as narrated by al-Qāḍī Abū Ya'lā in his *Jāmi'*.[1086]

OBLIGATORINESS OF PRAYING *ẒUHR* AFTER *JUMU'A*

The entirety of the Ḥanbalī authorities stipulated that, short of need, it is impermissible to hold more than a single *Jumu'a* in a single region; otherwise it is permissible. If more than one *Jumu'a* is held without need, all congregations other than that of the Muslim leader – or, in his absence, the first *Jumu'a* – have also to pray the *Ẓuhr* prayer.[1087]

[1083] Ibn Mufliḥ, *Mubdi'* (2:281), Shams al-Dīn, *Furū'* (2:300), Mar'ī, *Ghāya* (1:259).

[1084] Ibn Qudāma, *Mughnī* (1:5).

[1085] Ibn Qudāma, *Mughnī* (3:442), Shams al-Dīn Ibn Qudāma, *al-Sharḥ al-Kabīr* (2:389), Ibn Rajab, *Ahwāl al-Qubūr* (p. 96).

[1086] Ibn Qudāma, *Mughnī* (2:610).

[1087] Ibn Qudāma, *Mughnī* (3:212), *Kāfī* (1:294), *Muqni'* (1:250); Ibn Mufliḥ, *Mubdi'* (2:166); al-Buhūtī, *Kashshāf* (2:39), *Rawḍ* (1:296); Shams al-Dīn ibn Mufliḥ, *Furū'* (2:102); al-Ba'lī, *Rawḍ* (p. 117); al-Ḥajjāwī, *Iqnā'* (1:196); Ibn al-Najjār, *Muntahā* (1:137); Mar'ī, *Ghāya* (1:212), *Dalīl* (p. 55); 'Abd al-Raḥmān al-Ba'lī, *Kashf al-Mukhaddarāt* (p. 110); Bahā' al-Dīn al-Maqdisī, *'Idda* (p. 109).

DESIRABILITY OF PRONOUNCING INTENTION BEFORE PRAYER AND ACTS OF WORSHIP

Ibn Qudāma, the two Ibn Mufliḥ, al-Buhūtī, al-Baʿlī, and Ibn Hubayra state that it is desirable and more perfect to pronounce intention (*niyya*) before initiating an act of worship, while the seat of the intention is the heart.[1088]

TARĀWĪḤ PRAYER IS TWENTY *RAKʿAS*

Like the other Sunni Schools, Imām Aḥmad and his School consider that the desirable number of *rakʿas* and its *Sunna* in the prayer of *Tarāwīḥ* is twenty, except for the Mālikīs who put them at thirty-three or more.[1089]

INSTRUCTING THE DEAD FOLLOWING BURIAL

The vast majority of the Ḥanbalī authorities stipulated that it is desirable (*mustaḥabb*) to instruct the dead (*talqīn al-mayyit*) directly following burial while Imām Aḥmad deems it merely permissible as reported by Ibn Qudāma and Ibn Mufliḥ.[1090] Part of their evidence for this is the ḥadīth of Abū Umāma that

> the Prophet ﷺ said: "When one of you dies and you have settled the earth over him, let one of you stand at the head of his grave and then say: O So-and-so, son of So-and-so [name of the mother]! for he will hear him even if he does not reply. Then let him say a second time: O So-and-so, son of So-and-so [name of

[1088] Ibn Qudāma, *Mughnī* (2:132), *Kāfī* (1:28); Ibn Mufliḥ, *Mubdiʿ* (1:414); al-Buhūtī, *Kashshāf* (1:314); Ibn Mufliḥ, *Furūʿ* (1:139); Baʿlī, *Rawḍ* (p. 35); Ibn Hubayra, *Ifṣāḥ* (1:70).

[1089] Ibn Qudāma, *Mughnī* (2:604), *Kāfī* (1:198), *Muqniʿ* (1:187); Ibn Mufliḥ, *Mubdiʿ* (2:17); al-Buhūtī, *Kashshāf* (1:425), *al-Rawḍ al-Murbaʿ* (1:220); Shams al-Dīn ibn Mufliḥ, *Furūʿ* (1:546); al-Baʿlī, *Rawḍ* (p. 92); al-Ḥajjāwī, *Iqnāʿ* (1:147); Ibn al-Najjār, *Muntahā* (1:100); Marʿī, *Ghāya* (1:156), *Dalīl* (p. 43); ʿAbd al-Raḥmān al-Baʿlī, *Kashf al-Mukhaddarāt* (p. 85); Bahāʾ al-Dīn al-Maqdisī, *ʿIdda* (p. 90); al-Zarkashī, *Sharḥ Mukhtaṣar al-Khiraqī* (2:78); Shams al-Dīn Ibn Qudāma, *al-Sharḥ al-Kabīr* (1:745); al-Kawladhānī, *Hidāya* (p. 38).

[1090] Ibn Qudāma, *Mughnī* (2:319), *Kāfī* (1:362); Shams al-Dīn Ibn Qudāma, *al-Sharḥ al-Kabīr* (2:385); Ibn Mufliḥ, *Mubdiʿ* (2:272); Shams al-Dīn ibn Mufliḥ, *Furūʿ* (2:274); al-Ḥajjāwī, *Iqnāʿ* (1:232); Marʿī, *Ghāya* (1:249); Ibn al-Najjār, *Muntahā* (1:166); ʿAbd al-Raḥmān al-Baʿlī, *Kashf al-Mukhaddarāt* (p. 134); al-Buhūtī, *Rawḍ* (1:351); al-Baʿlī, *Rawḍ* (p. 139); al-Kawladhānī, *Hidāya* (p. 62).

the mother]! whereupon he will sit up [in his grave]. Then let him say: O So-and-so, son of So-and-so [name of the mother]! At this the other will say: Instruct me, and may Allāh grant you mercy! even if you cannot hear it – or: even if you cannot notice it. Then let him say: Remember the state in which you left this world, which is your witnessing that there is no god except Allāh, and that Muḥammad is His Servant and Messenger; that you are pleased with Allāh as your Lord, Islām as your religion, Muḥammad as your Prophet, and the Qur'ān as your Book. At that Munkar and Nakīr [the angels of the questioning in the grave] hold each other back, saying: Let us go; there is no need for us to tarry here, for he has been instructed correctly what to say. [In al-Ṭabarāni's and Ibn Qudāma's narration:] And Allāh will accept his argument without the two of them." A man said: Messenger of Allāh, what if his mother's name is not known?" He replied: "Let him say: Son of Ḥawwā' [Eve]."[1091]

The deciding factor in accepting this ḥadīth is that Imām Aḥmad relates its use by the trustworthy *Tābi'īn* of Shām. The rule is that wide-spread practice by the early generations in the *Umma* forms applicable evidence in the Law as stated by Ibn al-Qayyim in *al-Rūḥ*.[1092]

RECITING THE QUR'ĀN OVER THE GRAVES

The *Madhhab* stipulates the desirability (*istiḥbāb*) of reciting the Qur'ān over the dead and in the graveyard without any offensiveness.

[1091] Narrated through unknowns by al-Raba'ī in *Waṣāyā al-'Ulamā' 'inda Ḥuḍūr al-Mawt* (p. 61-63 §31), al-Ṭabarānī in *al-Kabīr* (8:249), Ibn Mandah, and Ibn 'Asākir (6:424) cf. al-Haythamī (2:324, 3:45) and al-Suyūṭī, *Sharḥ al-Ṣudūr* (p. 154). Ibn Qudāma, *Mughnī* (1994 ed. 2:319) mentions that Ibn Shāhīn narrates it in *Dhikr al-Mawt* with his chain. Ibn Ḥajar in *Talkhīṣ al-Ḥabīr* (2:143) said that al-Ṭabarānī narrates it with a usable chain (*isnaduhu ṣāliḥ*) which, despite its weakness, is consolidated by corroborative sound ḥadīths, and that Ḍiyā' al-Dīn al-Maqdisī declared it strong (*qawwāh*) in his *Aḥkām* cf. Ibn al-Mulaqqin in *Khulāṣat al-Badr al-Munīr* (1:275). Al-Shawkānī also narrates it in *Nayl al-Awṭār* (4:89-90) from the narration of Sa'īd ibn Manṣūr in his *Sunan* from Rāshid ibn Sa'd and Ḍamura ibn Ḥabīb, and he mentions that 'Abd al-'Azīz al-Ḥanbalī also narrated it in *al-Shāfī*. Al-Shawkāni's citation of Sa'īd's narration is not traced back to the Prophet ﷺ and its wording is: "They used to like (*kānū yastaḥibbūn*) that it be said to the dead…", "they" referring to the Companions, and al-Shawkānī added that al-Shāfi'ī's companions also considered it *mustaḥabb*, desirable. Muḥammad ibn 'Abd al-Wahhāb cites this in his *Aḥkām Tamannī al-Mawt* (p. 19).

[1092] Ibn al-Qayyim, *al-Rūḥ* (p. 70-71).

Furthermore, Ibn Qudāma stated that the permissibility of donating its reward to the dead is a matter of Consensus in Islām.[1093]

Allāh knows best.

[1093] Ibn Qudāma, *Mughnī* (3:518-520); Ibrāhīm ibn Mufliḥ, *Mubdi'* (2:278); al-Ḥajjāwī, *Iqnā'* (1:236); Shams al-Dīn Ibn Qudāma, *al-Sharḥ al-Kabīr* (2:424); Shams al-Dīn ibn Mufliḥ, *Furū'* (2:305); Mar'ī, *Ghāya* (1:259); Ibn al-Najjār, *Muntahā* (1:171); 'Abd al-Raḥmān al-Ba'lī, *Kashf al-Mukhaddarāt* (p. 135); al-Buhūtī, *Rawḍ* (1:353), *Kashshāf* (2:147); al-Ba'lī, *Rawḍ* (p. 141); al-Kalwadhānī, *Hidāya* (p. 63); al-Mardāwī, *Inṣāf* (2:559).

The Controversy Over the Pronunciation of the Qur'ān[1094]

"Learn from me my urgent recommendation: Do not speak about this nor ask about this ever. Stop at the fact that it is the Speech of Allāh and add not one word more. I do not believe this matter will end before it causes the people of Islām an insoluble problem. Allāh protect you and us from Satan the accursed!"

ABŪ ḤANĪFA[1095]

"Whoever claims that the letter *s* in *bismillāh,* which comes after the letter *b,* and the letter *m* which comes after the letter *s,* have no beginning, he has taken leave of his sense of reason, denied what is obligatorily known, and contradicted the obvious [...] And how can we hope to direct through proofs someone mulish enough to deny what is necessarily known?"

IBN AL-BĀQILLĀNĪ[1096]

A*hl al-Sunna* agree one and all that the Qur'ān is the pre-existent, pre-eternal, uncreated Speech of Allāh ﷻ. The Mu'tazila – and the Shī'a in their wake – held that the Attributes are none other than the Essence, otherwise, they claimed, there would be a multiplicity of Pre-eternal Entities (*qudamā'*); therefore, to them, the Qur'ān is created and both they and the Shī'īs deny the reality and pre-existence of the Attribute of Divine Speech. The vast majority of the early Muslims including *Ahl al-Bayt* rejected this reasoning as fallacious, as summed up by Imām Mālik's statement quoted below and al-Ṭaḥāwī in his *'Aqīda Ṭaḥāwiyya*: "It [the Qur'ān] is not created like the speech of creatures."This is the position of the totality of the *Salaf* including the Four Imāms and their immediate colleagues, in addition to Sufyān al-Thawrī, 'Abd Allāh ibn al-

[1094] See al-Būṭī, *Kubrā al-Yaqīnāt* (p. 126-127). Also see in Ibn Khafīf's *'Aqīda* and al-Bayhaqī's *al-Asmā' wal-Ṣifāt,* sections entitled "The Speech of Allāh" and "The Recitation of the Qur'ān" as well as Ibn 'Abd al-Salām's extensive explanations in the sections of his *Mulḥa* titled "His Speech Does Not Materialize", "Proofs Against the Pre-eternality of Recitation and Writing" etc. in our *Ash'arī School.*

[1095] Narrated by Ibn al-Dakhīl in *Manāqib Abī Ḥanīfa* as cited by Ibn 'Abd al-Barr in *al-Intiqā'* (p. 317-318).

[1096] Cited by al-Kawtharī in his marginalia on Imām al-Ḥaramayn's *Niẓāmiyya* (p. 21).

Mubārak, al-Awzāʿī, Jaʿfar ibn Muḥammad, Abū Jaʿfar al-Ṭabarī, Dāwūd ibn Khalaf, Zayd ibn ʿAlī and others of *Ahl al-Bayt*, Isḥāq ibn Rāhūyah, al-Bukhārī and his 1,000 shaykhs by his own report in *Khalq Afʿāl al-ʿIbād*, and countless others of the pious Predecessors.

In a demonstration of classic *kalām* reasoning, Imām Mālik gave the most succinct statement of this doctrine: "The Qur'ān is the Speech of Allāh, the Speech of Allāh is part of Him (*kalāmullāhi minh*), and nothing created can be part of Allāh ﷻ."[1097] Where the Imāms differed was over the pronunciation of the Qur'ān. Some, like Abū Ḥanīfa and his colleagues, al-Shāfiʿī, al-Bukhārī, Muslim, and the entire Ashʿarī and Māturīdī Schools, considered the pronunciation created, while others, like the Ḥanbalīs, insisted that the pronunciation was governed by the same belief in uncreatedness as the Qur'ān itself.

In the chapter of *Manāqib al-Shāfiʿī* on the Speech of Allāh and His other Essential Attributes, al-Bayhaqī narrates that al-Shāfiʿī said: "The Qur'ān is the Speech of Allāh, uncreated."[1098] In the same chapter he also narrates from the Imām the statement: "I prefer [Qur'anic] recitation (*al-qirā'a*) during circumambulation. Recitation is the best of what a human being can speak."

Al-Bayhaqī comments:

> Al-Shāfiʿī thus considered recitation as part of the earning (*kasb*) of the reciter since he linked it to the fact that the reciter "speaks it." Since we related previously that he said "The Qur'ān is the Speech of Allāh," this shows that he differentiated between recitation and the thing recited (*al-maqrū'*). He considered recitation part of the earning of the reciter [*i.e.* a created act], and he believed that the thing recited was the uncreated Speech of Allāh ﷻ.[1099]

Ibn Abī Yaʿlā narrates in his *Ṭabaqāt al-Ḥanābila* that Muḥammad ibn Ismāʿīl al-Sulamī heard Imām Aḥmad say: "The 'pronunciationists' – those who say that their pronunciation of the Qur'ān is created – are Jahmīs (*al-lafẓiyya jahmiyya*). Allāh said: ﴾**Until he hears the Speech of Allāh**﴿ (9:6). From whom does he hear it?"[1100] This is simi-

[1097] Al-Dhahabī, *Siyar* (7:416). Cf. Ibn Khafīf, *al-ʿAqīda al-Ṣaḥīḥa* §26.

[1098] Narrated from Abū Saʿīd al-Miṣrī by al-Bayhaqī in *Manāqib al-Shāfiʿī* (1:407).

[1099] Al-Bayhaqī in *Manāqib al-Shāfiʿī* (1:407, 1:411).

lar to Ibn Abī Ya'lā's report from the ḥadīth Master Musaddad ibn Musarhad al-Asadī's (d. 228) narration from Aḥmad with a weak chain:

> Whatever is in the volumes of Qur'ān (*maṣāḥif*), whatever recitation is performed by the people, whatever way it is recited, and whatever way it is described: all this is the Speech of Allāh, uncreated. Whoever says it is created is a disbeliever in Allāh Almighty; and whoever does not declare him so, is himself a disbeliever! ... Some of the Jahmīs said: "Our pronunciation of the Qur'ān is created." All these are disbelievers.[1101]

Similar sweeping utterances are attributed to Imām Aḥmad himself in the spurious *Radd 'alā al-Zanādiqa*,[1102] prompting Dr. al-Būṭī to conclude inaccurately that "Aḥmad ibn Ḥanbal and some of his followers held that these letters and sounds were also without beginning in their essence."[1103] Besides the inauthenticity of the *Radd*, there is no proof that Imām Aḥmad ever held such a creed. Further, it is disavowed by the following reports:

Something Ibn Shaddād had written was handed to Abū Bakr al-Marwazī which contained the phrase: "My pronunciation of the Qur'ān is uncreated" and the latter was asked to show it to Aḥmad ibn Ḥanbal for corroboration. The latter crossed out the phrase and wrote instead: "The Qur'ān, however disposed (*haythu yuṣraf*), is uncreated."[1104]

In another sound narration, Abū Bakr al-Marwazī, Abū Muḥammad

1100 Narrated through reliable narrators by Ibn Abī Ya'lā, *Ṭabaqāt* (1:280 §388).

1101 In *Ṭabaqāt al-Ḥanābila* (1:342 §494).

1102 On this book and its false attribution to Imām Aḥmad see his biography.

1103 Al-Būṭī, *Kubrā al-Yaqīnāt al-Kawniyya* (p. 126), citing *al-Radd 'alā al-Zanādiqa*.

1104 *Al-Asmā' wal-Ṣifāt* (Kawtharī ed. p. 265; Ḥāshidī ed. 2:18). Narrated with a sound chain by al-Bayhaqī. Al-Kawtharī commented on this and the next narration as follows: "Due to such equivocal expressions, many of Aḥmad's companions erroneously thought that anything remotely connected with the Qur'ān is pre-eternal (*qadīm*). Al-Bukhārī said in *Khalq Af'āl al-'Ibād*: 'As for what the two parties from the School of Aḥmad have claimed as proof, each for his own position, much of what they relate is not established as authentic.' It is probable they did not comprehend the subtleness of his position. What is known from Aḥmad and the people of knowledge is that the Speech of Allāh is uncreated and all else is created. But they hated to discuss and explore obscure matters, avoiding dialectic theologians and their queries and disputations except in what was a matter of knowledge and which the Prophet ﷺ had clarified."

Fawrān [or Fawzān], and Ṣāliḥ ibn Aḥmad ibn Ḥanbal witnessed Aḥmad rebuking one of his students named Abū Ṭālib[1105] with the words: "Are you telling people that I said, 'My pronunciation of the Qur'ān is uncreated'?" Abū Ṭālib replied: "I only said this from my own." Aḥmad said: "Do not say this – neither from me, nor from you! I never heard any person of knowledge say it. The Qur'ān is the Speech of Allāh uncreated, whichever way it is used." Ṣāliḥ said to Abū Ṭālib: "If you told people what you said, now go and tell the same people that Abū 'Abd Allāh [Imām Aḥmad] forbade them to say it!"[1106]

The sum of these reports shows that Imām Aḥmad condemned the statement that the pronunciation was created but did not hold the opposite. Al-Bukhārī said in *Khalq Af'āl al-'Ibād*: "As for what the two parties from the school of Aḥmad have claimed as proof, each for his own position: Much of what they relate is not established as authentic."[1107] Ibn al-Subkī said that what was [authentically] related from Imām Aḥmad is that he declared as an innovation, not disbelief, al-Karābīsī's statement that one's pronunciation of the Qur'ān was created (*lafẓuka bihi makhlūq*).[1108] What reconciles the two views reported from Aḥmad is that some may have given his words the most severe meaning possible, namely the sense of a *bid'a mukaffira* or innovation that constitutes disbelief. Note that it was also al-Karābīsī's view that whoever contradicts his statement that one's pronunciation of the Qur'ān was created commits disbelief, and so Aḥmad did not contradict it, but declared it an innovation instead. As for Shaykh 'Īsā al-Ḥimyarī's claim in his book *al-Ijhāz 'alā Munkirī al-Majāz* (p. 132) that "Aḥmad ibn Ḥanbal said: The pronunciation of the Qur'ān is created (*lafẓ al-Qur'ān muḥdath*)," this is only al-Ḥimyarī's imprudent paraphrase of the Imām's reply to his inquisitor.[1109]

The debate is largely a reaction explained by the charged climate prevalent in Aḥmad's time and the sway the Mu'tazila and Jahmiyya

[1105] This is either Aḥmad ibn Ḥumayd al-Mishkānī, cf. Ibn Abī Ya'lā, *Ṭabaqāt al-Ḥanābila* (1:39-40) or 'Iṣma ibn Abī 'Iṣmat al-'Ukbarī cf. *Ṭabaqāt* (1:246).

[1106] *Al-Asmā' wal-Ṣifāt* (Kawtharī ed. p. 265-266; Ḥāshidī ed. 2:18). This is a sound narration also found in Ṣāliḥ ibn Aḥmad's book *al-Miḥna* (p. 70-71), Ibn 'Asākir's *Tabyīn* (p. 376=p. 407-408), Ibn al-Jawzī's *Manāqib al-Imām Aḥmad* (p. 155), and Ibn Taymiyya in *Majmū' al-Fatāwā* (12:360, 12:425).

[1107] As quoted by al-Kawtharī in his notes on *al-Asmā' wal-Ṣifāt* (p. 266) cf. n. 1104.

[1108] Ibn al-Subkī, *Ṭabaqāt al-Shāfi'iyya* (2:118-119).

[1109] Cf. above, p. 311.

held over the caliphate which culminated in the persecution of *Ahl al-Sunna* Scholars including Imām Aḥmad who was detained and lashed for twenty-eight months for refusing to say that the Qur'ān was created. Three successive caliphs were responsible for this persecution: Hārūn al-Rashīd's sons al-Ma'mūn the scholar (198-218) and the near-analphabet al-Mu'taṣim (218-227), and the latter's profligate son al-Wāthiq (227-232), abetted by his vizier Ibn Abī Du'ād.[1110] It was not until the time of al-Wāthiq's brother, al-Mutawakkil (232-247) that a general amnesty was declared for the Sunnis who were still in jail at the time. After Imām Aḥmad's release, he refused to have anything to do with the numerous scholars who had caved in to the threat of punishment and spoken the words that were required of them, such as Yaḥyā ibn Ma'īn, 'Alī ibn al-Madīnī, Abū Khaythama, Abū Naṣr al-Tammār, and others.

The Ḥanbalīs sometimes went too far in their reaction, as shown by the boycott of Imām al-Bukhārī led by the *Amīr al-Mu'minīn fil-Ḥadīth* ("Commander of the Faithful in the Science of Ḥadīth") of Khurāsān, Muḥammad ibn Yaḥyā al-Dhuhlī (d. 258), whom Abū Zur'a ranked above Muslim and who once said: "I have made Aḥmad ibn Ḥanbal an Imām in all that stands between me and my Lord."[1111] Al-Dhuhlī's boycott led to al-Bukhārī's ultimate expulsion from Naysābūr for saying something that aroused their suspicion that he was a *Jahmī*![1112]

Imām Ibn al-Subkī wrote in his *Ṭabaqāt al-Shāfi'iyya al-Kubrā*:

> Abū Muḥammad ibn 'Adī said: "Many shaykhs mentioned to me that from the time Muḥammad ibn Ismā'īl (al-Bukhārī) came to Naysābūr and was surrounded by the throngs, some of the shaykhs began to feel jealous of him and said to the authorities in ḥadīth: 'Muḥammad ibn Ismā'īl says: "The pronouncing of the Qur'ān is created," so investigate him.' When the people gathered, one man got up and asked him: 'Abū 'Abd Allāh, what do you say about pronouncing the Qur'ān, is it created or uncre-

[1110] In the year 231, 1,600 Muslim prisoners were released by the Byzantines, whereupon Ibn Abī Du'ād said: "Whoever of the prisoners says: 'the Qur'ān is created,' set him free and give him two dinars, and whoever refuses, leave him in prison." Narrated by al-Suyūṭī in *Tārīkh al-Khulafā'*.

[1111] Narrated by al-Dhahabī in the *Siyar* (10:205). On the title *Amīr al-Mu'minīn fil-Ḥadīth* see next appendix.

[1112] Cf. al-Dhahabī, *Siyar* (10:207, 10:311-316).

ated?' He ignored him and did not reply, so the man repeated the question, so he ignored him again, so he repeated it again, at which point al-Bukhārī turned to him and said: 'The Qur'ān is the Speech of Allāh and is uncreated; the actions of servants are created; and investigating someone is an innovation.' At this the man cried out, there was a general uproar, the crowd dispersed, and al-Bukhārī sat alone in his house."

Muḥammad ibn Yūsuf al-Firabrī said:

I heard Muḥammad ibn Ismā'īl say: "As for the actions of servants, they are created: 'Alī ibn 'Abd Allāh narrated to us: Marwān ibn Mu'āwiya narrated to us: Abū Mālik narrated to us from Rib'ī from Ḥudhayfa who said that the Prophet ﷺ said: 'Truly, Allāh makes every maker and what he makes' (*innallāha yaṣna'u kulla ṣāni'in wa-ṣan'atahu*).[1113] And I heard 'Ubayd Allāh ibn Sa'īd [Abū Qudāma al-Sarkhasī] say: I heard Yaḥyā ibn Sa'īd [al-Qaṭṭān] say: I can still hear our companions saying: 'Truly, the actions of servants are created.'"

Al-Bukhārī continued:

Their motions (*ḥarakāt*), voices (*aṣwāt*), earning (*iktisāb*), and writing (*kitāba*) are created. As for the Qur'ān that is declaimed (*matlū*), consigned (*muthbat*) in the volumes, inscribed (*masṭūr*), written (*maktūb*), contained (*mū'ā*) in the hearts: that is the Speech of Allāh, uncreated. Allāh said: ﴾**But it is clear revelations in the hearts of those who have been given knowledge**﴿ (29:49). [Al-Bayhaqī's narration in *al-Asmā' wal-Ṣifāt* adds al-Bukhārī said: Isḥāq ibn Ibrāhīm [Ibn Rāhūyah] said: "As for the containers, who doubts that they are created?"[1114]] It is said: 'So-and-so's recitation is excellent,' and 'So-and-so's recitation is bad.' It is not said: 'His Qur'ān is excellent' or 'His Qur'ān is bad.' And to the servants is the recitation attributed, for the Qur'ān is the Speech of Allāh, while the recitation is the act of the servant, and no one can legislate concerning Allāh without knowledge unlike some

[1113] Narrated by al-Bukhārī in *Khalq Af'āl al-'Ibād*, al-Bayhaqī in *al-Asmā' wal-Ṣifāt* with three sound chains and in the *Shu'ab*, and al-Ḥākim with a sound (*ṣaḥīḥ*) chain.

[1114] Al-Bayhaqī, *al-Asmā' wal-Ṣifāt* (Ḥāshidī ed. 2:7 §570).

have claimed when they said that the Qur'ān is one with our pronouncing it, that our pronouncing it is one thing together with it, that declamation (*al-tilāwa*) is itself the thing declaimed (*al-matlū*), and recitation (*al-qirā'a*) is itself the thing recited (*al-maqrū'*). Such a person must be told that declamation is the act of the reciter and the deed of the one declaiming.

Abū Ḥāmid al-A'mashī said:

I saw al-Bukhārī at the funeral of Sa'īd ibn Marwān, at which time al-Dhuhlī was asking him about the names and patronyms [of narrators] and the defects [of narrations], and al-Bukhārī was going through them like an arrow. Less than a month later, al-Dhuhlī told us: "Whoever goes to his gathering, let him not come to ours. They wrote to us from Baghdād that he spoke about pronunciation [of the Qur'ān], and we ordered him to stop, which he did not, therefore do not go near him." It had been related from al-Bukhārī that he had said: "My pronunciation of the Qur'ān is created," while al-Dhuhlī had said: "Whoever claims that his pronunciation of the Qur'ān is created, he is an innovator whose company must be shunned, and whoever claims that the Qur'ān is created has committed disbelief."

Muḥammad ibn Yaḥyā only meant – and Allāh knows best – what Aḥmad ibn Ḥanbal meant, namely to forbid from entering into that subject. He did not mean to contradict al-Bukhārī. If he did mean to contradict him and to claim that the pronunciation which comes out of his own created lips is pre-eternal, that would be an enormity. One would like to believe that he meant other than that and that both he, Aḥmad ibn Ḥanbal, and other Imāms only meant to prohibit people from entering into problems of *kalām*! For us, al-Bukhārī's words are to be understood as a permission to mention *kalām* if needed, since **the use of *kalām* out of necessity is an obligation (*wājib*), while keeping silence about *kalām* in other than necessity is a *sunna*.**[1115]

Understand this well! So leave the rantings of historians and

[1115] This position is reiterated by Ibn al-Subkī's younger contemporary al-Shāṭibī (d. 790) in his book *al-Muwāfaqāt* (2:332): "Mālik ibn Anas used to say: 'I detest talking about Religion, just as the people of our country [al-Madīna] detest and prohibit it, in the sense of Jahm's doctrine, *qadar*, and the like. I do not like to speak except about

ignore once and for all the distortions of the misguided who think that they are Scholars of ḥadīth and that they are acting on the Sunna when in fact they could not be further from it. How could anyone possibly think that al-Bukhārī has anything in common with the position of the Mu'tazila when it has been authentically reported from him by al-Firabrī and others that he said: "I consider as ignorant whoever does not declare the Jahmīs to be disbelievers"? The impartial observer will not doubt that Muḥammad ibn Yaḥyā al-Dhuhlī suffered from envy, from which none is safe except those who are immune to sin. Some even asked al-Bukhārī about him and he said: "How can envy concerning learning possess Muḥammad ibn Yaḥyā, when learning is the wealth of Allāh ﷻ which He gives to whomever He pleases?"

Al-Bukhārī gave a sample of his great intelligence when in reply to Abū 'Amr al-Khaffāf who said to him, "People are questioning your words, 'My pronunciation of the Qur'ān is created,' al-Bukhārī said: "Abū 'Amr, remember what I say to you: Whoever claims, among the people of Naysābūr, Qāmūs, Ray, Hamadhān, Baghdād, Kūfa, Baṣra, Makka, and Madīna, that I ever said: 'My pronunciation of the Qur'ān is created,' he is a liar; truly I never said it. All I said is that the actions of servants are created."

Observe his words well and see how intelligent he is! Its meaning is – and Allāh knows best: "I did not say that my pronunciation of the Qur'ān is created for to say such would constitute entering into problematics of dialectical theology and of the Attributes of Allāh wherein it is unfitting to enter except due to necessity; what I said is: the actions of servants are created, and it is a general foundation which exempts one from mentioning the problematics specifically. For every rational person understands that our pronunciation is part of our actions, and our actions are created, therefore our pronunciation is created."

He has made this meaning explicit in another sound narration reported from him by Ḥātim ibn Aḥmad ibn al-Kindī who said: I

what relates to practice. As for talk about the Religion, I prefer to keep silent about it.' [Narrated by al-Lālikā'ī in *Sharḥ I'tiqād Ahl al-Sunna* (1:148).] The Congregation of [Sunni] Muslims follow Imām Mālik's position, except if one is obliged to speak. One must not remain silent if his purpose is to refute falsehood and guide people away from it, or if one fears the spread of misguidance or some similar danger."

heard Muslim ibn al-Ḥajjāj say – and he recounted the narration in which is the following: "A man stood before al-Bukhārī and asked him about the pronunciation of the Qur'ān, and he replied: 'Our actions are created, and our pronunciation is part of our actions.'" The story also mentions that the people at that time differed concerning al-Bukhārī, some saying that he had said: My pronunciation of the Qur'ān is created, others denying it. I say that the only ones to blame are those who indulge in discourse concerning the Qur'ān.

In conclusion we repeat what we said in the biography of al-Karābīsī:[1116] Aḥmad ibn Ḥanbal, and others of the masters of learning to whom Allāh has granted success, forbade people from discourse concerning the Qur'ān although they did not differ (with al-Bukhārī) on the question of pronunciation. This is what we believe about them with due respect to them, based on their sayings in other narrations, and to exonerate them from saying something which neither reason nor transmitted evidence supports. Furthermore, al-Karābīsī, al-Bukhārī, and others of the Imāms to whom Allāh has granted success have made it explicit that their pronunciation is created when they felt the necessity to make it explicit, if it is established that they actually took such an explicit position.[1117] We have otherwise brought to the reader's attention al-Bukhārī's saying that whoever relates that he said such a thing, he has reported something false from him.

The reader may ask: If it is the truth then why did he not say it explicitly? I answer: Glory to Allāh! We have told you that the gist of this matter is their insistence on prohibiting discussions of dialectical theology lest such discussions take them to unseemly consequences. Not every science can be made explicit, therefore remember what we impart to you and hold on to it tightly.

I like what al-Ghazzālī quotes in *Minhāj al-'Ābidīn* attributing it to a member of the Prophet's ﷺ House, [Zayn al-'Ābidīn 'Alī ibn al-Ḥusayn ibn 'Alī]:

[1116] In *Ṭabaqāt al-Shāfi'iyya al-Kubrā* (2:118-120).

[1117] Such as al-Ḥārith al-Muḥāsibī, Muḥammad ibn Naṣr al-Marwazī, Muslim ibn al-Ḥajjāj, and Aḥmad ibn Salama.

I keep the jewels of my knowledge concealed
Lest the ignorant see Truth and turn away.
How many an essential knowledge, if I divulged it,
I would be told for it: You are of the idol-worshippers;
And righteous men would deem licit my blood
And think well of the ugly deed they would commit
This is what Abū al-Ḥasan ('Alī) had already
Advised al-Ḥusayn and, before him, al-Ḥasan.[1118]

The final position of the Ḥanbalī School on the question is moderation, as shown by Ibn Qudāma's statement on the subject:

> Part of the Speech of Allāh is the noble Qur'ān, the book of Allāh that clarifies all, His firm rope, His straight path, the revelation of the Lord of the worlds. The faithful Spirit brought it down to the heart of the master of Messengers in a clear Arabic tongue. It is revealed, not created, from Him [Allāh] did it issue and to Him it shall return. It consists in precise sūras, clear verses, letters and words. Whoever recites it (*qara'ahu*) and pronounces it clearly and distinctly (*a'rabahu*) shall receive ten blessings for every letter. It has a beginning and an end, sections and parts. It is recited (*matluwwun*) with the tongues, preserved in the breasts, heard with the ears, written in the volumes. It comprises the precise and the ambiguous, the abrogating and the abrogated, the specific and the general, the command and the prohibition. ﴾**No falsehood can approach it from before or behind it: it is sent down, by One Full of Wisdom, worthy of all Praise**﴿ (41:42). ﴾**Say: if the whole of mankind and Jinns should assemble to produce the like of this Qur'ān, they could not produce the like thereof, even if they backed up each other with help and support**﴿ (17:88).[1119]

Another authoritative statement of doctrine on this topic is given by Ibn al-Subkī himself:

> The Qur'ān itself is really written in the volumes (*al-maṣāḥif*), preserved in the hearts of the believers, read and recited in reality with the tongues of the reciters among the Muslims, just as Allāh Almighty is really, and not metaphorically, worshipped in our

[1118] *Ibn al-Subkī, Ṭabaqāt al-Shāfi'iyya al-Kubrā* (2:228-231) cf. *Tārikh Baghdad* (12:489).
[1119] Ibn Qudāma, *Lam'at al-I'tiqād* (p. 17 §13).

mosques, known in our hearts, and mentioned with our tongues. This is clear, with the grace of Allāh and thanks to Him. Whoever deviates from this path is an "isolationist" proponent of absolute free will (*qadarī mu'tazilī*).[1120]

Of note is Ibn al-Subkī's sharp contradiction of the image given by Ibn Abī Ya'lā of Imām Aḥmad, and Ibn al-Subkī's twofold denial, first, that Imām Aḥmad ever considered as disbelief the doctrine that pronunciation is created; second, that he ever held that the pronunciation of the Qur'ān was uncreated.[1121] Al-Dhahabī's position, on the other hand, is to ascribe both views to Imām Aḥmad.[1122] At the same time he admits, in circuitous fashion, the difference between pronunciation (*al-talaffuẓ*) and its content (*al-malfūẓ*), recitation (*qirā'a*) and its content (*al-maqrū'*), and the contingent (*muḥdath*) nature of pronunciation, voice (*al-ṣawt*), movement (*al-ḥaraka*), and utterance (*al-naṭq*), although reluctant to admit verbatim that they are created.[1123] Al-Dhahabī does open up in his notice on al-Ash'arī's companion, the Shāfi'ī Imām al-Karābīsī.[1124] When al-Karābīsī heard that Imām Aḥmad had declared his statement an innovation whereby the pronunciation of the Qur'ān was created, he said: "Pronunciation means other than the thing pronounced" (*talaffuẓuka ya'nī ghayra al-malfūẓ*). Then he said of Aḥmad: "What shall we do with this boy? If we say 'created' he says *bid'a,* and if we say 'not created' he says *bid'a.*"[1125] Al-Dhahabī comments: "There is no doubt that what al-Karābīsī innovated and explained in the question of the pronunciation is the truth, but Imām Aḥmad refused it in order to preclude the extension of the question to the Qur'ān itself, since one cannot distinguish the pronunciation from the pronounced, which is the Speech of Allāh, except in the mind."

Al-Dhahabī considers that at the root of the disagreement lies a rigid refusal, on the part of Imām Aḥmad's circle, to countenance any concession to what they considered dialectic theology (*kalām*) and

1120 Ibn al-Subkī, *Ṭabaqāt al-Shāfi'iyya al-Kubrā* (3:418).
1121 In the *Ṭabaqāt* (2:118-120).
1122 *Siyar* (9:503-505).
1123 *Siyar* (9:505).
1124 Al-Dhahabī, *Siyar* (10:81-82 §1988).
1125 Narrated by al-Khaṭīb in *Tārīkh Baghdād* (8:65) and cited by al-Dhahabī.

therefore innovation. This attitude was not shared by al-Bukhārī and Muslim among others:

> Al-Dhuhlī was fierce (*shadīd*) in his adhesion to the Sunna. He confronted Muḥammad ibn Ismā'īl [al-Bukhārī] because the latter had alluded, in his *Khalq Af'āl al-'Ibād*, to the fact that the reader's utterance of the Qur'ān was created. Al-Bukhārī made it understood without explicitly saying it, but he certainly made it clear. On the other hand Aḥmad ibn Ḥanbal flatly refused to explore the question, as well as Abū Zur'a and al-Dhuhlī, or indulge in the conventions of dialectic theologians (*mutakallimūn*), and they did well – may Allāh reward them excellently. Ibn Ismā'īl had to travel from Naysābūr under cover, and was pained by what Muḥammad ibn Yaḥyā [al-Dhuhlī] had done to him.[1126]
>
> Among those who narrated from al-Dhuhlī is Muḥammad ibn Ismā'īl al-Bukhārī,[1127] but he conceals his name a lot (*yudallisuhu kathīran*). He does not name him "Muḥammad ibn Yaḥyā" but only "Muḥammad," or "Muḥammad ibn Khālid," or "Muḥammad ibn 'Abd Allāh," linking him to his great-grandfather [and grandfather respectively] and obscuring his name because of the incident that took place between them.[1128]
>
> Al-Ḥākim [narrated with his chains]: Muḥammad ibn Yaḥyā [al-Dhuhlī] said: "This Bukhārī has openly subscribed to the doctrine of 'pronunciationists' (*al-lafẓiyya*), and for me those are worse than the *Jahmiyya*." [...] Aḥmad ibn Salama visited al-Bukhārī and told him: "Abū 'Abd Allāh, this is a respected man [*i.e.* al-Dhuhlī] in Khurāsān, especially in this town [Naysābūr], and he has thundered with this speech until none of us can say anything to him about it, so what do you think we should do?"Al-Bukhārī grasped his beard then he said: ﴾**I confide my cause unto Allāh. Lo! Allāh is Seer of His slaves**﴿ (40:44). He continued: "O Allāh! You know that I did not want for one moment to settle in Naysābūr out of arrogance, nor in quest of leadership,

[1126] Al-Dhahabī, *Siyar* (10:207).

[1127] Thirty-four ḥadīths according to Ibn Ḥajar in *Tahdhīb al-Tahdhīb* (9:516).

[1128] Al-Dhahabī, *Siyar* (10:201). This kind of concealment is called *tadlīs al-shuyūkh* cf. Glossary (p. 464-465)

but only because my soul would not let me return to my own country [Bukhārā] because of my opponents; and now this man intends harm for me out of jealousy, only because of what Allāh gave me and for no other reason." Then he said to me: "Aḥmad, tomorrow I shall leave and you will be rid of his talk which I caused." [...] The ḥadīth Master Muḥammad ibn Ya'qūb said: "When al-Bukhārī settled in Naysābūr Muslim ibn al-Ḥajjāj took to visiting him frequently. When the affair of the pronunciation of Qur'ān took place between al-Bukhārī and [al-Dhuhlī] and the latter roused people against him and forbade them to visit him, most people stopped visiting him, but not Muslim.[1129] Then al-Dhuhlī said: 'Anyone that subscribes to the pronunciation [being created], it is not permitted for them to attend our gathering.' Whereupon Muslim placed a cloak on top of his turban, stood up, and walked out, sending back to al-Dhuhlī a camel-load of what he had written from him. For Muslim openly subscribed to the pronunciation and made no attempt to conceal it." [...] Aḥmad ibn Manṣūr al-Shīrāzī also narrated this from Muḥammad ibn Ya'qūb, adding: "And Aḥmad ibn Salama stood up and followed him."[1130]

The Ash'arī view concerning the *maktūb* or content of writing is the same as al-Bukhārī's, as shown by al-Bayhaqī's expression: "The *maktūb* is the Speech of Allāh and one of His Attributes inseparable from Him."[1131]

What reconciles the different views on this subject somewhat is that *lafẓ* is used by some to mean the revealed, uncreated words and contents of recitation, while others mean thereby the mere act of pronunciation, which is created; hence the extreme caution shown by some, such as Imām al-Bukhārī, who fell short of saying: "My *lafẓ* is created" even though he used it in the second sense, since he said: "*Lafẓ* is an act of human beings, and our acts are created." This lexical ambiguity is a proof of sorts that the differences on this particular question were largely in terminology rather than essence. Added to this is a fun-

1129 Nor the Imām and ḥadīth Master of Khurāsān, al-Ḥusayn ibn Muḥammad ibn Ziyād, Abū 'Alī al-Naysābūrī al-Qabbānī (d. 289), whom al-Ḥākim described as "One of the pillars of ḥadīth and ḥadīth Masters in the world." *Siyar* (11:51-54).

1130 Al-Dhahabī, *Siyar* (10:314-315). Cf. al-Bayhaqī's *Asmā'* (2:20-21 §591).

1131 In *al-Asmā' wal-Ṣifāt* (1:478, 2:125).

damental difference in method around the appropriateness of such dialectic, which poisoned the air with unnecessary condemnations on the part of Imām Aḥmad's followers – and Allāh knows best.

In some of these questions it is obvious that many originally justifiable positions from Imām Aḥmad seemingly acquired a life of their own to end up in the form of extreme statements and even grave errors at the hands of his epigones. These errors generally bear the stamp of literalism, and are being propagated in one form or another today by certain parties far less knowledgeable and Godfearing than the Scholars of the past.[1132]

[1132] See also Shaykh ʿAbd al-Fattāḥ Abū Ghudda's monograph entitled *Mas'alat Khalq al-Qur'ān wa-Atharuhā fī Ṣufūf al-Ruwāt wal-Muḥaddithīn wa-Kutub al-Jarḥ wal-Taʿdīl* ("The Question of the Createdness of the Qur'ān and its Scathing Effect on the Ranks of the Narrators and Ḥadīth Scholars as Well as on the Books of Narrator-Authentication").

The Titles "Elder of Islām" (*Shaykh al-Islām*), "Ḥadīth Auhority" (*Muḥaddith*), "Person of Learning" (*'Ālim*),

(by Shams al-Dīn al-Sakhāwī)[1133]

and "Commander of the Believers in Ḥadīth" (*Amīr al-Mu'minīn fil-Ḥadīth*)

(by al-Shinqīṭī and Abū Ghudda)[1134]

"He is not an Imām in *'ilm* who follows anomalous positions (*al-shādhdh*).
He is not an Imām in *'ilm* who narrates from each and everyone.
He is not an Imām in *'ilm* who narrates all that he hears.
Memorization (*al-ḥifẓ*) means precise mastery (*al-itqān*)."

'ABD AL-RAḤMĀN IBN MAHDĪ[1135]

[AL-SAKHĀWĪ:] "*Shaykh al-Islām,*" as inferred from its use as a term among the authorities, is a title attributed to the follower of the Book of Allāh ﷻ and the example of His Messenger ﷺ who possesses the knowledge of the principles of the Science [of Religion], has plunged deep into the different views of the Scholars, has become able to extract the legal evidences from the texts, and has understood the rational and the transmitted proofs to a satisfactory level.

At times, this title is given to those who have attained the level of friendship with Allāh (*wilāya*), and from whom people derive blessings both when they are alive and when they are dead. Similarly, whoever has trod the true path of the People of Islām and has come out unscathed from the folly and ignorance of youth; and whoever has become a living apparatus for others in solving difficulties or winning a struggle, and a refuge in every difficulty: these are the meanings of the

[1133] Al-Sakhāwī, *al-Jawāhir wal-Durar* (p. 14-23). It is the author's belief that Dr. Nūr al-Dīn 'Itr was given the attributes of imāmate and mastership here described and that he is the closest thing to Imām Aḥmad in our time, *wal-Ḥamdu lillāh.*

[1134] Muḥammad Ḥabīb Allāh al-Shinqīṭī, *Hadiyyat al-Mughīth* (p. 21-31) and Abū Ghudda, *Umarā' al-Mu'minīn fil-Ḥadīth* in *Jawāb al-Ḥāfiẓ al-Mundhirī* (p. 109-121).

[1135] Narrated by al-'Uqaylī in the introduction to *al-Ḍu'afā'* (1:9) and Ibn 'Abd al-Barr in *al-Intiqā'* (p. 62).

word as used by the general public.

At times, this title is also given to those who grow old in the fold of Islām and become outstanding among their peers for long life, entering into the meaning of the ḥadīth, "There will be a light for those who grow old in the fold of Islām."[1136]

This title was not common among the earlier generations after the two Shaykhs, al-Ṣiddīq and al-Fārūq, and we know that 'Alī applied it to them ﷺ. Al-Muḥibb al-Ṭabarī (d. 694) related in his book *al-Riyāḍ al-Naḍira* ["The Resplendent Groves"], without providing a chain of authorities, that Anas ﷺ said that a man came to 'Alī ibn Abī Ṭālib ﷺ and said: "Commander of the Believers, I heard you saying on the pulpit, 'O Allāh, help me as you helped the rightly-guided and enlightened caliphs.' Who are they?" Anas said: Tears welled up in 'Alī's eyes and began to pour down, then he replied: "Abū Bakr and 'Umar, Allāh be well-pleased with them, the two leaders of rightful guidance and the two Shaykhs of Islām, the two men of Quraysh, the two who are followed after the Messenger of Allāh ﷺ. Whoever follows these two gains respect; whoever lives up to the legacy of these two is guided to a straight path; whoever sticks with these two is from the party of Allāh, ﴾**and the party of Allāh – these are the successful**﴿ (5:56)!"[1137]

Al-Dhahabī reported in *al-Kāshif* on the authority of Ibn al-Mubārak (d. 181) – mark him, Reader, as one who was a *Shaykh al-Islām*: "The only one to carry the title *Shaykh al-Islām* is Abū Bakr al-Ṣiddīq ﷺ, who preserved the *zakāt* and fought against the apostates.

[1136] Narrated from 'Amr ibn Abasa by al-Tirmidhī (*ḥaṣan ṣaḥīḥ gharīb*), al-Nasā'ī, and Aḥmad; from Ka'b ibn Murra by al-Tirmidhī (*ḥasan*), al-Nasā'ī, Aḥmad, and al-Dāraquṭnī in his *Sunan*; from 'Abd Allāh ibn 'Amr by Abū Dāwūd; from 'Umar by Ibn Ḥibbān with a strong chain (7:251 §2983), al-Ṭabarānī in *al-Kabīr* (1:58), Ibn Rāhūyah, and Abū Nu'aym in *Ma'rifat al-Ṣaḥāba*; from Mu'ādh ibn Jabal by al-Ṭabarānī in *al-Kabīr*; from Abū Nujayḥ al-Sulamī by Ibn Ḥibbān with a sound chain (7:252 §2984), al-Bayhaqī in the *Sunan* (9:161), and, as part of a longer ḥadīth, by Aḥmad with a sound chain; from Abū al-Dardā' by Abū al-Shaykh; from Jābir by Ibn 'Asākir; from Abū Hurayra by al-Quḍā'ī in *Musnad al-Shihāb* (p. 457); from Faḍāla ibn 'Ubayd by al-Ṭabarānī in *al-Kabīr* (18:782-783), Aḥmad, and al-Bazzār; and from Umm Sulaym by al-Ḥākim in *al-Kunā*; also from 'Amr ibn 'Abasa but as part of a longer ḥadīth, by Aḥmad with a sound chain, and al-Bayhaqī in the *Sunan* (9:272).

[1137] Muḥibb al-Dīn al-Ṭabarī, *al-Riyāḍ al-Naḍira* (1:379 §276); al-Zamakhsharī, *Mukhtaṣar al-Muwāfaqa* fol. 23; al-Sakhāwī, *al-Jawāhir wal-Durar*, Introduction.

Know this very well." The report ends here.

Abū Ismā'īl al-Harawī (d. 481) came to be known by this title. His full name was 'Abd Allāh ibn Muḥammad [ibn 'Alī ibn Matt] al-Anṣārī, a Ḥanbalī scholar and the author of *Manāzil al-Sā'irin* and *Dhamm al-Kalām*. Abū 'Alī Ḥassān ibn Sa'īd al-Mānī'ī al-Shāfi'ī and Abū al-Ḥasan al-Hakkārī[1138] were also known by this title. Ibn al-Sam'ānī said about the latter that he was called *Shaykh al-Islām*. He also was a Shāfi'ī.

Among the scholars of the Ḥanafī school, the following carried this title:

–Abū Sa'īd al-Khalīl ibn Aḥmad ibn Muḥammad ibn al-Khalīl al-Sijzī, who died after 370;
–Abū al-Qāsim Yūnus ibn Ṭāhir ibn Muḥammad ibn Yūnus al-Baṣrī – Ibn Mandah mentions him – who died in 411;
–The judge Abū al-Ḥasan Alī ibn al-Ḥusayn ibn Muḥammad al-Sughdī who died in 461 – also called *Rukn al-Islām*;
–Abū Naṣr Aḥmad ibn Muḥammad ibn Ṣā'id al-Ṣā'idī. Al-Dhahabī said about him: "He is one of those who are called *Shaykh al-Islām*." He died in 482;
–Alī ibn Muḥammad ibn Ismā'īl ibn Alī al-Isbijābī, who died in 535;
–His student, the author of *al-Hidāya*, Burhān al-Dīn Alī ibn Abī Bakr 'Abd al-Jalīl al-Farghānī, who died in 593;
–Muḥammad ibn Muḥammad ibn Muḥammad al-Ḥalabī [d. 817];
–Al-'Imād Mas'ūd ibn Shayba ibn al-Ḥusayn al-Sindī;
–Abū Sa'd al-Muṭahhar ibn Sulaymān al-Zanjānī;
–Sadīd ibn Muḥammad al-Ḥannāṭī.

The Master Abū 'Uthmān Ismā'īl ibn 'Abd al-Raḥmān ibn Aḥmad al-Ṣābūnī al-Shāfi'ī (d. 449) was also known by this title. Ibn al-Sam'ānī gave it to him in *al-Dhayl*. Also known by this title was Tāj al-Dīn al-Firkah, who was a Shāfi'ī. Ibn Daqīq al-'Īd (d. 702) gave this title to his master Ibn 'Abd al-Salām. He said: He is *Shaykh al-Islām*. Also known by this title were Abū al-Faraj [Shams al-Dīn] ibn Abī 'Umar the Ḥanbalī – the first who held the judgeship for the Ḥanbalīs [in Makka] – Ibn Daqīq al-'Īd himself, and Ibn Taymiyya. Abū al-Ḥajjāj al-Mizzī (d. 742) did not give this title to anyone else among his

1138 See n. 1140.

contemporaries besides Ibn Taymiyya, Ibn Abī 'Umar, and Taqī al-Dīn al-Subkī.[1139] In the latter's time and in his son's time the use of this title increased, especially in Damascus. Later, Sirāj al-Dīn al-Bulqīnī [Ibn Ḥajar's Shaykh] was given this title. I read in Ibn 'Ammār's own hand that it was used exclusively for him...

Since the beginning of the Eighth Century innumerable people have been given this title, to the extent that even the chief judges came to be called it even if they lacked the knowledge and the age. Indeed, ignorant writers and others took to attributing to individuals all manners of qualities which nowadays exist only among selected persons. Those who confirm them in this abuse are the strangest of all. Verily we belong to Allāh and to Him do we return.

Ibn Ḥajar – Allāh have mercy on him! – entirely merits being called by this title because he had most of the qualities that are mentioned above, and when that title was used by the authorities in his time he was meant and no one else. Even if he was not an authority in everything, in the field of the ḥadīth of the Prophet ﷺ he was, beyond question, *Shaykh al-Islām*. Aḥmad ibn Ḥanbal, whose piety is beyond question, called Abū al-Walīd al-Ṭayālisī and Aḥmad ibn Yūnus *Shaykh al-Islām* although they had only the knowledge of ḥadīth, whereas Ibn Ḥajar's authority was not limited to this one field only. May Allāh have mercy on them and us![1140]

As for the ḥadīth scholar (*al-muḥaddith*), he is the one who [1] knows the masters of ḥadīth in his homeland as well as other lands; [2] has a precise knowledge of their date and place of birth and death, their ranking in the Sciences, and the various types of narratives they have in their possession; [3] differentiates those with longer chains of transmission from those with shorter ones; [4] is able to spot

[1139] Cf. Ibn al-Subkī, *Ṭabaqāt al-Shāfi'iyya al-Kubrā* (10:195).

[1140] Ibn Ḥajar himself applies the title *Shaykh al-Islām* to his teacher, the ḥadīth Master Zayn al-Dīn al-'Irāqī, unless he names someone else. Cf. "Our shaykh, *Shaykh al-Islām*, said..." *Fatḥ al-Bārī* (1959 ed. 1:18 §1; 1:27 §3; 1:33 §7; 1:192 §97; 1:458; 3:361 §1425; 8:223 §4278 etc.), but "Our shaykh, *Shaykh al-Islām* al-Bulqīnī said..." *Ibid.* (1:22 §2; 13:547 §7124; cf. 1:45). Like al-Sakhāwī, al-Suyūṭī applies the title to Ibn Ḥajar, while both al-Haytamī and al-Sha'rānī apply it to their Shaykh, Zakariyyā al-Anṣārī. Al-Dhahabī in his monograph on titles and nicknames entitled *al-Muqaddima Dhāt al-Niqāb fil-Alqāb* (p. 74 §319-320) typically reserves the title to two Ḥanbalīs: the anthropomorphist Abū Ismā'īl 'Abd Allāh ibn Muḥammad al-Anṣārī of Herat and the forger Abū al-Ḥasan 'Alī ibn Aḥmad al-Hakkārī.

the ḥadīth Masters (*al-ḥuffāẓ*) in the layers and the chains; [5] records them in writing; [6] recognises the handwritings of the masters even if the same person's handwriting varies; [7] examines critically the narratives of the masters and extracts what he considers good from their narratives as well as his own, keeping aware of such qualities of chains as *badal, muwāfaqāt, musāwāt,* and the like (of chain variants); [8] keeps a record of the names of his auditors even if their number is one thousand; [9] is an expert in the names of narrators, particularly those apt to be confused with one another, and obtains this discernment from the leaders in the discipline; [10] knows with precision the unusual words or names one comes across within the texts of ḥadīth, or at least most of them, to avoid misspelling; [11] knows enough Arabic grammar to protect himself from language mistakes in most cases; [12] masters the terminology of experts in such a way as is sufficient for teaching and explanation, and [13] keeps the proper terminology with respect to this and other disciplines.

The general practice is in accordance with this approach, although some were called *muḥaddith* without actually having all of these qualifications.

There is a code of conduct for the *muḥaddith.* Our masters have written about it and the most remarkable book on this is *al-Jāmi' li-Akhlāq al-Rāwī wa-Ādāb al-Sāmi'* ("Compendium of the Desirable Manners of the Ḥadīth Narrator and Inveterate Practices of the Auditor") by al-Khaṭīb. I read it and heard Ibn Ḥajar say – apparently reporting it from someone else: "And he must be fast in writing, reading, eating and walking." His words end here.

The ḥadīth Master Abū al-Fatḥ ibn Sayyid al-Nās (671-734) – may Allāh have mercy on him! – gave this definition of the *muḥaddith*: "The *muḥaddith* in our time is he who busies himself with the oral narration of ḥadīth and its writing, collecting information about the narrators, and getting to know many of the narrators and narrations in his time. He gains expertise in these matters to the extent that his handwriting becomes known and he becomes reputed for accuracy."

This is easier than what the savant and judge Tāj al-Dīn Abū Naṣr [Ibn] al-Subkī (727-771) said in his book *Mu'īd al-Ni'am wa-Mubīd al-Niqam* ("The Renewer of Favours and Allayer of Trials"), as the Master al-'Izz Abū Muḥammad al-Qāḍī [Ibn 'Abd al-Salām], the last of the narrators of chains, reported from him:

The *muḥaddith* is the one who knows the chains, their defects, the names of the narrators, the short and long chains, and, in addition, has memorised an abundant amount of the ḥadīth texts [as distinct from the chains], and heard [directly from a teacher] the Six Books, the *Musnad* of Imām Aḥmad ibn Ḥanbal, the *Sunan* of al-Bayhaqī, the *Mu'jam* of al-Ṭabarānī, and at least a thousand more monographs on ḥadīth. After he has heard what we have mentioned, and written on all the layers of the narrators, and travelled far and wide to see the masters, and lectured about ḥadīth defects, dates of birth and death, and chains of transmission – at that time he attains to the beginning level of ḥadīth narrators. After that Allāh increases those He wants with what He wants.

The opinion of the Savant [and ḥadīth Master Abū 'Abd Allāh 'Alā' al-Dīn Ibn Qalīj al-Bakjarī al-Turkī al-Miṣrī al-Ḥanafī] Mughalṭāy[1141] (689-762) resembles [Ibn] al-Subkī's view: "In the usage of ḥadīth narrators those who are given the title of *muḥaddith* must have written, read, heard, memorised, travelled to cities and villages, inferred from the sources, and expanded the branches from the books of ḥadīth compilations and manuals on ḥadīth defects and histories, from about a thousand books."

The one who focuses exclusively on audition of ḥadīth is not called a *muḥaddith*. Imām Tāj al-Dīn Ibn Yūnus [al-Mawṣilī 598-670] said in the commentary on *al-Ta'jīz fī Ikhtiṣār al-Wajīz* ("The Inimitable Discourse On the Abridgment of al-Ghazzālī's "Synopsis of the Jurisprudence of the Shāfi'ī School" [*al-Wajīz fī Fiqh Madhhab al-Imām al-Shāfi'ī*]): "If someone bequeaths something 'for the *Muḥaddiths*,' the will concerns those who know the various chains by which a ḥadīth is established and the integrity of its narrators known, for whoever exclusively focuses on listening is not a ḥadīth Scholar."

This is supported by al-Rāfi'ī's (557-623) opinion in keeping with that of the companions [of al-Shāfi'ī] regarding the person who made a will "for the Scholars (*al-'ulamā'*)": Those who merely listen to ḥadīth without knowledge of the chains nor of the details pertaining to the narrators and the texts are not included here, for listening

[1141] Al-'Irāqī considered him stronger than Ibn Kathīr, Ibn Rāfi', and al-Sharīf al-Ḥusaynī; cf. al-Suyūṭī, *Ṭabaqāt al-Ḥuffāẓ* (p. 537).

alone is not scholarship.

Similar to this is the view of [Ibn] al-Subkī: "Those who focus exclusively on listening do not enter the community of ḥadīth. This is also what some of the later scholars said: for the Jurists (*al-fuqahā'*), the word *muḥaddith* can be used only for those who memorise texts of ḥadīths and those who know the reliability or unreliability of the different narrators. Those who focus exclusively on listening fall into neither category."

Al-Fāriqī said: "The term should not be used for those who know chains of ḥadīth but not the legal rulings derived from them. For one cannot be counted among the scholars of the law with only the former amount of knowledge." His student [Sharaf al-Dīn 'Abd Allāh ibn Muḥammad] Ibn Abī 'Aṣrūn [al-Tamīmī al-Shāfi'ī 492-585] also followed him in his book *al-Intiṣār* ("The Victory"). Ibn Ḥajar stopped short of this view and said: "This is an overemphasis because the divisions [of ḥadīth sciences] are fourfold, the highest of which being the abundance in audition (*samā'*) and the knowledge of chains and their defects." I say that perhaps the first two refused to call such a person a *muḥaddith* only because, literally speaking, he is a *musnid*, *i.e.* one who simply conveys chains of authorities [without critiquing them]. The rest, however, use the term *muḥaddith* figuratively.

What are the "ways or paths of the ḥadīth" (*ṭuruq al-ḥadīth*)? The author of *al-Dhakhā'ir* states that this is the knowledge of the rulings comprised in the ḥadīths along with the knowledge of their narrators. This view is inconsistent with the terminology of the experts because what they mean by "the ways of ḥadīth" is the mere enumeration of its chains of transmission, and the various aspects in which a ḥadīth is transmitted. The author of *al-Wāfī* said: "What is meant by "the ways of ḥadīth" is the sound ḥadīth (*ṣaḥīḥ*), the weak (*ḍa'īf*), the rare (*gharīb*), knowledge of the names of narrators, their reliability and unreliability, and knowledge of its meanings. Then he becomes a scholar (*'ālim*) unlike the reciter of the Qur'ān, for it is not a science but a transmission." Towards the end of his words, the author of *al-Wāfī* points to al-Māwardī's view in *al-Waqf*: "It [the word 'scholar'] should not be used for the reciters of the Qur'ān nor the community of ḥadīth, because knowledge resides in meaning, not in what is memorised for recitation."

What we report from the ḥadīth Master al-Silafī should be understood in this context. He said: "I enquired from our master al-Imām Abū al-Ḥasan al-Ṭabarī, also known as al-Kiyā (450-504), about someone who made a will stipulating that one third of his wealth be distributed to the Ulema and *Fuqahā'*: are the scribes of ḥadīth included in this stipulation? He said: Yes, how can it be otherwise? The Prophet ﷺ said: "Whoever in my Community memorises forty ḥadīths pertinent to his religious life, Allāh will resurrect him in the Day of Judgement as a wise man (*faqīh*) of learning (*'ālim*)."[1142]

The following is reported from Mālik: "The Science cannot be taken from him who exclusively focuses on audition (*samā'*)." The exact wording of his view as reported by the Qāḍī 'Abd al-Wahhāb [ibn 'Alī al-Tha'labī al-Baghdādī 362-422] in *al-Mulakhkhaṣ* ("The Summary") through 'Īsā ibn Abān is: "There are four from whom the Science cannot be taken," and he counted them and continued: "Nor from him who does not know this matter." The Qāḍī explained that what he meant by this is one who neither knows narrators nor if anything was added in or abstracted from the narrative.

The practice in our time contradicts this view. In our time, the reliance is for the most part on the reader-reciter (*qāri'*). For this reason I advocate preventing students from doing a lot of reading and reciting when they do not first master texts and chains, nor have any idea who among the narrators has no analytical thinking or whose ḥadīth can be accepted as reliable in the first place.

How well did the ḥadīth Master Abū 'Abdullah al-Dhahabī (d. 748) speak in what I read by his own handwriting about the above – even if he exaggerated, nevertheless he is excused:

> Most of the ḥadīth scholars have no understanding, no diligence in the actual knowledge of ḥadīth, and no fear of Allāh regarding it. Worse, the sound and the forged look alike to them. The narrators do not correct their manners according to the ethics of ḥadīth, and never wake up from the stupor of audition. At one and the same time a scholar hears a book and his ego entertains the prospect of teaching it, in fifty years perhaps? Woe to you! How long is your hope, how evil your works! Verily Sufyān al-Thawrī is excused for saying according to the narration of

[1142] Narrated from Abū Sa'īd al-Khudrī by Ibn al-Najjār and al-Nawawī who declared it weak in the introduction to his famous compilation of forty ḥadīths. This is one of the famous weak ḥadīths the *Umma* put in practice since the earliest times.

Aḥmad ibn Yūsuf al-Taghlabī: Khālid ibn Khidāsh narrated to us that Ḥammād ibn Zayd narrated to us that Sufyān al-Thawrī said: "If ḥadīth were a good it would have vanished just as goodness has vanished."

By Allāh! he has spoken the truth. What good is there in ḥadīth where the sound is mixed with the unreliable, while you do nothing to sift one from the other, or to research its narrators, and you do not practice it nor fear Allāh concerning it? Today, in our time, the quest for knowledge and ḥadīth audition no longer means for the *muḥaddith* the obligation of living up to it, which is the goal of ḥadīth. The basis of ḥadīth audition has become the prestige of narrating ḥadīth. This, by Allāh, is not for the sake of Allāh! I am only addressing you, O ḥadīth narrator – not those who do not listen, think, keep the five daily prayers, shun corruption and intoxicants, and strive for perfection in speaking the truth: O listener! Do not become a criminal like me [says the corrupt man], for we feel the worst afflictions.

Today, the student of ḥadīth should first copy by hand *al-Jam' Bayn al-Ṣaḥīḥayn* ("The Convergence of the Two Sound Books" *i.e.* al-Bukhārī and Muslim's *Ṣaḥīḥs*), 'Abd al-Ḥaqq's [ibn al-Kharrāṭ al-Ishbīlī 509-580] *al-Aḥkām al-Shar'iyya* ("The Legal Rulings"), and *al-Ḍiyā'* ("The Illumination"). He should master these books. Also, he should frequently study the works of al-Bayhaqī, for they are beneficial. He should also study no less than a concise book like [Ibn Daqīq al-'Īd's] *al-Ilmām fī Aḥādīth al-Aḥkām* ("The Acquaintance with the Prophetic Narrations that Serve as a Basis for Legal Rulings"), and teach it.

What good is there in ḥadīth audition under ignorant teachers who sleep while children play and young men prate, making jokes while reporting ḥadīth, soon feeling sleepy, debating haughtily while their readers make spelling mistakes? They repeat meaningless words such as *aw kamā qāl* ("or as he [the Prophet ﷺ] said") and yawn.[1143] For the sake of Allāh, leave us alone, for we have become the laughingstock of sensible people! They look at us and say: "Are these the People of Ḥadīth?"

He also said in another place:

[1143] Nevertheless the phrase *aw kamā qāl* should always be spoken after citing a ḥadīth if one is at all uncertain of its definite phrasing cf. above, n.309.

It is reported from Sufyān al-Thawrī that he said: "Pursuing the study of ḥadīth is not part of the preparation for death, but a disease that preoccupies people."[1144] He said this verbatim. He is right in what he said because pursuing the study of ḥadīth is other than the ḥadīth itself. Pursuing ḥadīth is a conventional name comprising matters that are additional to learning the meaning of ḥadīth. Many of these matters lead to knowledge, but most are a source of pride for the narrators, such as obtaining ornamented copies of a book, or trying to find the shortest chain for a ḥadīth, or increasing the number of one's teachers, or pleasure with titles, or hope for a long life so that he can narrate ḥadīth (to subsequent students), or desire to become unique (*infirād, i.e.* by outliving his generation-layer of narrators), and many other similar matters required for egotistic purposes but not for deeds aimed at gaining the blessing of Allāh.

If your quest for ḥadīth is surrounded by these disasters, when will be you be freed from them to gain sincerity? If the sciences of transmission (*'ulūm al-athar*) have become diseased, what do you think about the rational sciences which divert from faith and instill doubts that did not exist in the age of the Companions and the Successors? Their Sciences were the Qur'ān, the Ḥadīth, and Jurisprudence!

Imām Abū Shāma (595-665) said:

Today the sciences of ḥadīth are three. The most honorable one is the memorization of the texts, the knowledge of rare ḥadīth, and its relation to jurisprudence. The second [science of ḥadīth] consists in memorizing the chains of transmission, knowing the narrators, and discerning the reliable chains from the problematic ones. This used to be paramount, but now it suffices for the student of the Science to know what is compiled and written in this branch, and there is no benefit in redoing what is already done. The third [science of ḥadīth] consists in collecting, writing, hearing, and learning the various chains through

1144 Shaykh 'Abd al-Qādir al-Gīlānī similarly told his student Shaykh al-Islām Abū Ḥafṣ 'Umar al-Suhrawardī that pursuing the study of *tawḥīd* is not part of the preparation for the grave; cf. Ibn Rajab, *Dhayl Ṭabaqāt al-Ḥanābila* (1:296-297).

which a ḥadīth has been narrated, searching for the shortest chains and traveling for this purpose. However, the one who focusses on this is diverted from the most important of the useful sciences [*i.e.* the first], in addition to being distracted from the actions which are the primary purpose. Allāh Most High says ﴿**I created the jinn and humankind only that they might worship me**﴾ (51:56). However, it is acceptable for those who have freed themselves from distractions to spend time in this third branch because it helps perpetuate the unbroken "from" chains (*silsilat al-'an'ana al-muttaṣila*) back to the most honorable of mankind – the blessings and peace of Allāh upon him! These chains are one of the peculiarities of this Community.

He also said: "One should stay away from that which is commonly shared by the young and the old, the mediocre and the intelligent, the ignorant and the scholar."

Al-A'mash [Abū Muḥammad Sulaymān ibn Mahrān al-Asadī the *Tābi'ī* 61-148] said: "The ḥadīth that jurists circulate among themselves is better than that which ḥadīth narrators circulate among themselves." Someone criticised Imām Aḥmad ibn Ḥanbal, Allāh have mercy upon him, for attending the circle of Imām al-Shāfi'ī and leaving the circle of Sufyān ibn 'Uyayna. Aḥmad told him: "Hush! If you miss a ḥadīth with a shorter chain you can find it with a longer chain and it will not harm you. However, if you do not have the reasoning of this man [al-Shāfi'ī] I am afraid you will not be able to find it."

Ibn Ḥajar said:

There is some disagreement in some of the above doctrine. Abū Shāma's view that "it suffices for the student of the Science to know what is compiled and written in this branch" was rejected by the savant Abū Ja'far ibn al-Zubayr and others. The argument can be made against him in the following way. If the amount of compilations that have been written in the first branch makes reliance upon them necessary without need for pursuing its sources, then the same can be said about the first branch which Abū Shāma says about the second (*i.e.* that "it suffices for the student of the Science to know what is compiled and written in this branch"), for the books written on the jurisprudence of ḥadīth and the rare ḥadīth cannot be counted. Indeed, if someone were to claim that the works in the latter fields are more numerous than the works about narrator-criticism and the works that distinguish the sound ḥadīth from the unsound, he would not be far from the truth. To be sure this is the reality. If studying the first branch is important, then the study of the second branch becomes even more important, for it is the staircase that leads to the first. Therefore, whoever neglects the second science [according to Abū Shāma's classification] is bound to mix unwittingly the unsound ḥadīth with the sound and the narrator who is considered trustworthy with the unreliable. That is enough discredit for such a method.

The truth is, both the first and the second science are important in the science of ḥadīth. There is no doubt that whoever can master both will attain the highest station, even if he is remiss in the third, while he who neglects the first and second can have no part in being called a ḥadīth Master (*ḥāfiẓ*). As for he who masters the first but neglects the second, he remains far from the definition of ḥadīth scholar (*muḥaddith*), while he who masters the second and neglects the first may still be called a *muḥaddith*, although there is a deficiency in him with regard to the first science.

[AL-SHINQĪṬĪ AND ABŪ GHUDDA:] The Commanders of the Believers in Ḥadīth (*Umarā' al-Mu'minīn fil-ḥadīth*) thus named by the *Salaf* are:

1. Imām Mālik ibn Anas al-Aṣbaḥī al-Madanī (93-179). (Per al-Shāfi'ī, Wuhayb ibn al-Ward, and Yaḥyā ibn al-Madīnī.) §7 in Abū Ghudda's list.
2. Imām Abū al-Zinād 'Abd Allāh ibn Dhakwān al-Tābi'ī (64-130) the Jurist of al-Madīna and Shaykh of Imām Mālik. (Per Sufyān al-Thawrī and Aḥmad ibn Ḥanbal.) §1 in Abū Ghudda's list.
3. Imām Sufyān ibn Sa'īd al-Thawrī al-Kūfī (97-161). (Per Shu'ba, Sufyān ibn 'Uyayna, Abū 'Āṣim, Yaḥyā ibn Ma'īn, Yaḥyā ibn Yamān, and others) §5 in Abū Ghudda's list.
4. Imām Abū Bisṭam Shu'ba ibn al-Ḥajjāj al-Wāsiṭī al-Baṣrī (82-

160) the Shaykh of *Ahl al-Ḥadīth* in Iraq. (Per Sufyān al-Thawrī and Abū Zayd al-Anṣārī.) §4 in Abū Ghudda's list.

5. Imām Abū Ya'qūb Isḥāq ibn Rāhūyah al-Ḥanẓalī al-Marwazī (166-235). (Per Aḥmad ibn Ḥanbal.) §16 in Abū Ghudda's list.
6. Imām Abū Bakr Hishām ibn 'Abd Allāh al-Dastawā'ī[1145] al-Baṣrī (d. 153). (Per Abū Dāwūd al-Ṭayālisī.) §3 in Abū Ghudda's list.
7. Imām Abū Nu'aym al-Faḍl ibn Dukayn al-Taymī al-Mulā'ī al-Kūfī (130-210), the student of Abū Ḥanīfa. (Per Abū Aḥmad al-Farrā'.) §13 in Abū Ghudda's list.
8. Imām Abū 'Abd Allāh Muḥammad ibn Yaḥyā al-Dhuhlī al-Naysābūrī (ca. 170-258), Shaykh al-Islām. (Per Ibn Abī Dāwūd and Abū Bakr ibn Ziyād) §18 in Abū Ghudda's list.
9. The Shaykh of the Shaykhs of Islām and Mountain of Memorization and Ḥadīth Science, Imām Abū 'Abd Allāh Muḥammad ibn Ismā'īl ibn Ibrāhīm al-Ju'fī al-Bukhārī (196-256). (Per al-Khazrajī but "He is beyond evaluation.") §17 in Abū Ghudda's list.
10. Imām Abū al-Ḥasan 'Alī ibn 'Umar al-Dāraquṭnī al-Baghdādī (306-358). (Per Abū al-Ṭayyib al-Ṭabarī.) §20 in Abū Ghudda's list.
11. Imām Abū Bakr Muḥammad ibn Isḥāq ibn Yasār al-Akhbarī al-Muṭṭalibī al-Madanī (80-152), the author of the most famous *Sīra*. (Per Shu'ba, Sufyān al-Thawrī, Yazīd ibn Hārūn, 'Abd al-Raḥmān ibn Mahdī, Ibn Sayyid al-Nās, al-Dhahabī, and Ibn Khallikān.) §2 in Abū Ghudda's list.
12. Imām Abū 'Abd Allāh Muḥammad ibn 'Umar ibn Wāqid al-Sahmī al-Madanī al-Wāqidī (130-207) the author of the first *Sīra*. (Per al-Darāwardī, but al-Dhahabī said in *Mīzān al-I'tidāl*: "Consensus has formed on holding al-Wāqidī unreliable.") §12 in Abū Ghudda's list.
13. Shaykh al-Islām, Imām Abū Salama Ḥammād ibn Salama al-Baṣrī (ca. 90-167). (Per 'Affān ibn Muslim al-Baṣrī.) §6 in Abū Ghudda's list.
14. Shaykh al-Islām, Imām Abū 'Abd al-Raḥmān 'Abd Allāh ibn al-Mubārak al-Marwazī (118-181). (Per Yaḥyā ibn Ma'īn and Abū Usāma Zayd ibn Abī Unaysa al-Ruhawi.) §8 in Abū Ghudda's list.

[1145] Also spelled al-Dastuwā'ī.

15. Imām Abū Muḥammad 'Abd al-'Azīz ibn Muḥammad al-Darāwardī al-Madanī (d. 187). (Per Ma'n ibn 'Īsā al-Mufliḥ.) §9 in Abū Ghudda's list.
16. Imām Shihāb al-Dīn Abū al-Faḍl Aḥmad ibn 'Alī ibn Muḥammad ibn Ḥajar al-'Asqalānī al-Kinānī al-Miṣrī (773-852). (Per Burhān al-Dīn al-Laqānī, Ridwān ibn Muḥammad al-'Uqbī, al-Sakhāwī, 'Abd al-Karīm al-Qalqashandī, and Ibn 'Allān: Muḥammad 'Alī ibn Muḥammad 'Allān ibn Ibrāhīm al-Bakrī al-Ṣiddīqī.) §23 in Abū Ghudda's list.

[ABŪ GHUDDA:] Also thus named are:

17. Imām Abū 'Abd Allāh al-Faḍl ibn Mūsā al-Sinānī al-Marwazī (115-192). (Per al-Sam'ānī.) §10 in Abū Ghudda's list.
18. Imām Abū Sa'īd Yaḥyā ibn Sa'īd al-Qaṭṭān al-Baṣrī (120-198). (Per al-Dhahabī.) §11 in Abū Ghudda's list.
19. Imām Abū al-Walīd Hishām ibn 'Abd al-Mālik al-Ṭayālisī al-Baṣrī (133-227). (Per Aḥmad ibn Sinān al-Wāsiṭī.) §14 in Abū Ghudda's list.
20. Imām Abū al-Ḥasan 'Alī ibn 'Abd Allāh ibn Ja'far al-Baṣrī, known as Ibn al-Madīnī (161-224). (Per al-Dhahabī.) §15 in Abū Ghudda's list.
21. Imām Abū Ḥātim al-Rāzī, Muḥammad ibn Idrīs al-Ḥanẓalī al-Rāzī (195-277). (Per Ibn Dīzīl.) §19 in Abū Ghudda's list.
22. Abū Muḥammad Taqī al-Dīn 'Abd al-Ghanī ibn 'Abd al-Wāḥid al-Maqdisī al-Jammā'ilī al-Dimashqī (541-600). (Per Ḍiyā' al-Dīn al-Maqdisī.) §21 in Abū Ghudda's list.
23. Imām Burhān al-Dīn Abū al-Wafā' Abū Isḥāq Ibrāhīm ibn Muḥammad ibn Khalīl, Sibṭ Ibn al-'Ajamī al-Ḥalabī (753-841). (Per Abū al-Barakāt Muḥammad ibn Muḥammad ibn Muḥammad al-Farrāqī.) §22 in Abū Ghudda's list.
24. Imām Wajīh al-Dīn Abū Muḥammad 'Abd al-Raḥmān ibn 'Alī ibn al-Dayba' al-Shaybānī al-Yamānī al-Zabīdī (866-944). (Per 'Abd al-Qādir ibn 'Abd Allāh al-'Aydarūsī.) §24 in Abū Ghudda's list.
25. Imām 'Abd Allāh ibn Sālim ibn Muḥammad al-Baṣrī al-Makkī (1048-1124). (Per Ismā'īl ibn Muḥammad Sa'īd Safar.) §25 in Abū Ghudda.

26. Imām Muḥammad ibn Ismā'īl al-Amīr al-Ṣan'ānī (1099-1182), the author of *Subul al-Salām.* (Per Wajīh al-Dīn 'Abd al-Raḥmān ibn Sulaymān al-Ahdal al-Zabīdī.) §26 in Abū Ghudda's list.

[AL-SHINQĪṬĪ:] And among those who could also be thus categorised are:

27. Imām Abū Zakariyyā Yaḥyā ibn Ma'īn al-Murrī al-Baghdādī (158-233). (Per Nu'aym ibn Ḥammād.) Page 121 after Abū Ghudda's list.
28. Imām Aḥmad ibn Ḥanbal.
29. Imām Muslim ibn al-Ḥajjāj.
30. Imām Jalāl al-Dīn al-Suyūṭī.

The Title *Ahl al-Ḥadīth*

The name *Ahl al-Ḥadīth* designated, in the early centuries, those Scholars of *Ahl al-Sunna* that focussed on ḥadīth audition, analysis, criticism, compilation, narration, and transmission until they became like reflections of the pure speech of the Prophet ﷺ – the Divine revelation which is not obligatory to recite (*waḥī ghayr matlū*) – so that "whenever I meet one of the *Ahl al-Ḥadīth,* it is as if I saw the Messenger of Allāh ﷺ" (al-Shāfi'ī). By synecdoche, the term denoted all *Ahl al-Sunna.*

In his book *Sharaf Aṣḥāb al-Ḥadīth* ("The Eminence of the Masters of Ḥadīth"), the great ḥadīth Master al-Khaṭīb al-Baghdādī narrated Abū Dāwūd's saying: "Were it not for this band of people we would not be studying Islām."[1146] The narrations al-Khaṭīb gathered in this precious book list the titles conferred by the Imāms of ḥadīth on the scholars of the Prophetic narrations:

"Those Who Command Good and Forbid Evil" [Ibrāhīm ibn Mūsā]

"The Substitute-Saints" [Sufyān al-Thawrī, Yazīd ibn Hārūn, Aḥmad ibn Ḥanbal]

[1146] Al-Khaṭīb, *Sharaf Aṣḥāb al-Ḥadīth* (p. 52 §106).

"The Pillars of the *Sharī'a*" [al-Khaṭīb]

"The Nearest of People to the Prophet ﷺ" [because of the ḥadīth: "Truly the nearest of people to me on the Day of Resurrection are those who invoked the most blessings upon me"[1147]].

"The Owners of Transmission Chains [to the Prophet ﷺ]" [Yazīd ibn Zuray']

"The Owners of Frayed Garments and Inkwells" [Caliph al-Ma'mūn]

"The Best of All Scholars" [al-Khaṭīb]

"The Best of All People" [al-Awzā'ī]

"The Best of Those Who Spoke About Knowledge" [Aḥmad]

"The Trustees of Allāh Over His Religion" [Abū Ḥatim al-Rāzī]

"The Trustees of the Messenger ﷺ" [al-Khaṭīb]

"The People of Belief" [because of the ḥadīth: "Do you know who of those who possess belief is the best in belief?" They said the angels. He replied: "This is true, and it is right that they should be so, but nothing stands in their way because of the position in which Allāh ﷻ has placed them. I mean others." They said: "The Prophets whom Allāh honoured with Prophetship and Messengership." He replied in the same way. They said the martyrs. He replied: "This is true, and it is right that they should be so, but nothing stands in their way because of the honour Allāh bestowed upon them with martyrdom. I mean oth-

1147 Narrated from Ibn Mas'ūd by al-Tirmidhī (*ḥasan gharīb*), Abū Ya'lā in his *Musnad* (8:428, 9:15), al-Bukhārī in *al-Tārīkh al-Kabīr* (5:177), Ibn Abī Shayba (11:505), al-Baghawī in *Sharḥ al-Sunna* (§686), al-Bayhaqī in *Shu'ab al-Īmān* (2:212), al-Haythamī in *Mawārid al-Ẓam'ān* (p. 594), al-Khaṭīb in *al-Faṣl lil-Waṣl* (2:770-773) and *Sharaf* (p. 34-35 §63) and Ibn Ḥibbān all with weak chains according to al-Arna'ūṭ (3:192 §911) because of Mūsā ibn Ya'qūb al-Zam'ī and 'Abd Allāh ibn Kaysān (cf. al-Mizzī, *Tahdhīb al-Kamāl* [15:482], Ibn 'Adī, *al-Kāmil* [6:2342], al-Dāraquṭnī, *al-'Ilal* [5:112], Ibn Ḥajar, *Tahdhīb al-Tahdhīb* [5:326]). However, it has a witnessing narration whereby the Prophet ﷺ said: "Invoke abundant blessings upon me on the day of *Jumu'a* for my Community's *ṣalāt* is shown to me [especially] on every *Jumu'a*, therefore, whoever among them invokes blessings upon me the most, is nearest to me in station." Narrated from Abū Umāma by al-Bayhaqī in his *Sunan* (3:249 §5785) and *Ḥayāt al-Anbiyā'* (p. 11) with a fair chain according to al-Mundhirī in *al-Targhīb* (1994 ed. 2:390 §2519=1997 ed. 2:328= 3:303) "except that it is said Makḥūl did not hear from Abū Umāma directly," while Ibn Ḥajar said in *Fatḥ al-Bārī* (1959 ed. 11:167): "There is no harm in its chain." Ibn al-Sakan included Ibn Mas'ūd's ḥadīth among the sound narrations in his *Ṣiḥāḥ* according to Ibn al-Mulaqqin in *Tuḥfat al-Muḥtāj* (1:527). Ibn Ḥajar assembled a full documentation of the paths of this noble narration.

ers." They asked: "Who then, Messenger of Allāh?" He said: "Generations yet in the loins of men who shall come after me; they shall believe in me without seeing me and confirm me without seeing me. They shall see the suspended leaves [of the Law] and put them into practice."[1148]

"The People of Truth" [al-Khaṭīb]

"The People of Righteousness" ['Umar ibn 'Abd al-'Azīz]

"The Vessels of Knowledge" [al-Khaṭīb]

"The People Most Meritorious of Salvation in the Hereafter" [because of the ḥadīth: "Truly the safest of you against the disasters of the Day of Resurrection on that day are those of you who invoked the most blessings on me in the world"[1149]].

"The Friends of Allāh" [al-Khalīl ibn Aḥmad]

"The Massive Throng" [al-Khaṭīb]

"The Guardians of the Earth" [Sufyān al-Thawrī]

"The Guardians of the Religion" [al-A'mash]

"The Implanters of the Religion" [Ibn al-Mubārak]

"The Party of Allāh" [al-Khaṭīb]

"The Preservers of the Pillars of the Law" [al-Khaṭīb]

"The Preservers of the Prophet's Sunna" [al-Khuraybī]

"The Custodians of the Faith" [Kahmas]

"The Protectors of the Faith" [al-Khaṭīb]

"The Repellers of False Imputations to the Prophet" [Ibn Ma'īn]

"The Carriers of Knowledge" [al-Khuraybī]

"The Storehouses of the Religion" [al-Khaṭīb]

"The Successors of the Messenger ﷺ" [al-Khaṭīb]

"The Elect Among Tribes" [Ḥafṣ ibn Ghiyāth]

"The Elect Among People" [Abū Bakr ibn 'Ayyāsh]

"The Elect Among Worshippers" [Abū Muzāḥim al-Khāqānī]

"The Virile Among Men" [al-Zuhrī][1150]

[1148] Narrated from 'Umar by al-Bazzār (1:413) with a fair chain as stated by al-Haythamī (10:65), al-Khaṭīb, *Sharaf* (p. 33-34 §62), al-Ḥākim (4:85-86) with a weak chain because of Muḥammad ibn Abī Ḥumayd as indicated by al-Dhahabī, Abū Ya'lā (1:147) with a weak chain according to Shaykh Ḥusayn Asad, and from Ibn 'Abbās by al-Ṭabarānī in *al-Kabīr* (12:87) and al-Ṭaḥāwī in *Sharḥ Mushkil al-Āthār* (6:269-270 §2472) with the statement "Those are my brothers" instead of the last sentence, with a chain of sound narrators except for 'Aṭā' ibn al-Sā'ib whose narrations are confused.

[1149] Narrated from Anas by al-Khaṭīb in *Sharaf* (p. 56-57 §113).

[1150] Al-Hudhalī narrated that al-Zuhrī asked him: "O Hudhalī! Does ḥadīth please

"The Trustees Who Preserve the Reports of the Messengers" [Abū Ḥātim al-Rāzī]

"The Strangers" ['Abdān]

"The Knights of this Religion" [Yazīd ibn Zuray']

"The Caretakers of the Matter of *Sharī'a*" [al-Khaṭīb]

"The Strivers In the Preservation of the Faith" [al-Khaṭīb]

"Mankind" (*al-nās*) [Aḥmad ibn Ḥanbal]

"Those Who Belong to No Tribe" ['Abdān]

"The Intermediaries Between the Prophet ﷺ and His Community" [al-Khaṭīb]

"Muḥammad's Inheritors" [Ibn Mas'ūd]

"The Inheritors of the Prophets" [al-Fuḍayl ibn 'Iyāḍ]

"The Beneficiaries of the Messenger of Allāh" [Abū Sa'īd al-Khudrī, according to the ḥadīth of the Prophet ﷺ: "There shall come after me a people <from the East[1151]/from the regions of the world[1152]> who will ask you about me. When they come to you, treat them kindly and narrate to them <, make them memorise the ḥadīth and make room for them in gatherings[1153]>"[1154]].

---

you?" Al-Hudhalī said yes. Al-Zuhrī continued: "Truly, it pleases the virile among men, while the effeminate among them hate it." Al-Khaṭīb, *Sharaf* (p. 70 §150).

[1151] In al-Tirmidhī.

[1152] In Ibn Mājah.

[1153] In al-Dārimī's *Sunan*, Ibn Abī Ḥātim al-Rāzī, *al-Jarḥ wal-Ta'dīl* (2:12), and others: Abū Sa'īd used to say, whenever he saw the young *Tābi'ī* students of ḥadīth: "Welcome to the beneficiaries (*waṣiyya*) of the Messenger of Allāh ﷺ," while the ḥadīth Master Abū Muḥammad al-Rāmahurmuzī's (d. 362) narration in *al-Muḥaddith al-Fāṣil Bayn al-Rāwī wal-Wā'ī* ("The Ḥadīth Scholar That Differentiates Between Narrators and Containers") (p. 175) adds: "who ordered us to make you memorize the ḥadīth and make room for you in gatherings." Al-Dhahabī lauds al-Rāmahurmuzī's book in his *Siyar* (1996 ed. 12:233) and relates that al-Silafī carried it wherever he went. Dr. Nūr al-Dīn 'Itr pointed out in a class communication that it was the first comprehensive book on ḥadīth science ever, after which came the works of al-Ḥākim, al-Khaṭīb, and Ibn al-Ṣalāḥ.

[1154] Narrated from Abū Sa'īd al-Khudrī by al-Ḥākim (1:88=1990 ed. 1:164) who declared it sound. The ḥadīth Master Mughalṭāy also declared it sound according to al-Munāwī (2:400) while it remains a fair (*ḥasan*) narration according to al-Suyūṭī and others. Also narrated from Abū Sa'īd by Ibn 'Abd al-Barr in his *Jāmi'* (1:578 §991), al-Khaṭīb in his (1991 ed. 1:305-306 §360 = 1983 ed. 1:202), Ibn Wahb in his *Musnad* (8:167), and 'Abd al-Ghanī al-Maqdisī in *al-'Ilm* (1:50), all with weak chains because of Layth ibn Abī Sulaym; and by al-Tirmidhī, Ibn Mājah, 'Abd al-Razzāq (11:252), Tammām al-Rāzī in his *Fawā'id* (1:64, 1:69), al-Baghawī in *Sharḥ al-Sunna* (1:286), and

The term *Ahl al-Ḥadīth*, therefore, refers to that superb reality and early examplar in Islamic history, not to the modern sect that arose in India and proclaimed rejection of *taqlīd* in the name of direct following of the mother sources – as if the Sunni Schools of Law were anything other than a direct following of the mother sources! – thus causing division and *fitna* in the *Umma*. Indo-Pakistani Muslims, in particular, should be aware of that distinction and know the difference between that noble, large, early group over whose high esteem there is Consensus and that small, late group characterised by controversy who are Ẓāhirī from certain angles and Mu'tazilī from others. Such a dubious group should never be referred to as *Ahl al-Ḥadīth* even if that is the practice in India. There is a huge difference between the *Ṣiddīq* and the *Zindīq*. Our terminology must reflect this distinction, and Allāh knows best.

---

al-Rāmahurmuzī in *al-Muḥaddith al-Fāṣil* (p. 176), all with very weak chains because of Abū Hārūn al-'Abdī ('Amāra ibn Juwayn) who is discarded as a narrator (cf. Ibn 'Adī, *al-Kāmil* [5:77] and Ibn Ḥajar's *Taqrīb*).

A Concise Sunni Glossary of *Fiqh*, Ḥadīth, *Kalām*, and *Taṣawwuf*

Abdāl, sing. ***Badal:*** "Substitutes." Spiritually accomplished human beings by means of whom goodness remains in the world. Cf. documentation under ḥadīth §8 of our *Forty Ḥadīths on the Excellence of Syro-Palestine and Its People.*

adhān: The call to prayer raised by the *mu'adhdhin.*

aḥad, pl. ***āḥād:*** "Solitary." A lone-narrator, non-***mutawātir*** ḥadīth that is either ***gharīb***, ***'azīz***, or ***mashhūr***. "That which [if ***ṣaḥīḥ***] necessarily leads to action (*'amal*) but does not necessarily lead to positive knowledge (*'ilm*) because of the possibility of it being a mistake." (Ibn al-Juwaynī)

Ahl al-Bid'a: "People of Innovation." Muslims who deviate from the doctrines and practices of *Ahl al-Sunna.* A common name synonymous with *Ahl al-ahwā'* or the "people of vain lusts."

Ahl al-Ḥaqq: "The People of Truth." The term denotes *Ahl al-Sunna wal-Jamā'a* as opposed to the sects and is identical with "The Saved Group" (*al-firqat al-nājiya*) mentioned in the ḥadīth of the Prophet ﷺ. "*Ahl al-Sunna* consist of three groups: the textualists (*al-Athariyya*), whose Imām is Aḥmad ibn Ḥanbal; the Ash'arīs, whose Imām is Abū al-Ḥasan al-Ash'arī; and the Māturīdīs, whose Imām is Abū Manṣūr al-Māturīdī [...]. They are all one sect, the saved sect, and they are *Ahl al-Ḥadīth*" (Al-Saffarīnī). Anyone that deviates from this meaning is an ***innovator***.

Ahl al-Sunna wal-Jamā'a: "People of the Way of the Prophet ﷺ and the Congregation [of the Muslims]," also known as Sunni Muslims.

ākhira: The hereafter.

'ālim, pl. ***'ulamā':*** Possessor of knowledge in Islam or ***'ilm*** in contrast to the ***'āmmī*** and subject to peer recognition.

'āmmī, pl. ***'awāmm:*** One who lacks Islamic scholarly training and learning: layman; the common people; the general public. One may be a *'ālim* in one discipline and a *'āmmī* in others.

'an'ana: Indecisive ḥadīth transmission terminology through the use of the phrase "from X" (*'an fulān*) instead of the phrase "X narrated to us" (*ḥaddathanā fulān*). *'An'ana* may denote ***tadlīs*** and ***irsāl.***

'araḍ, pl. ***a'rāḍ:*** "Accident."

'ārif: Knower of Allāh. One who possesses ***ma'rifa.***

Ash'arīs: Adherents to the doctrinal tenets of Abū al-Ḥasan al-Ash'arī, mostly from the Shāfi'ī and Mālikī Schools of Law, and forming the massive majority of the Ulema of ***Ahl al-Sunna wal-Jamā'a.***

azal, adj. ***azalī:*** Pre-eternity without beginning, applying both to the existent (*mawjūd*) and the non-existent (*ma'dūm*). In the latter sense the inexistence of creatures has no beginning and so is pre-eternally inexistent (*ma'dūmun azalī*) (but it has an end coinciding with the beginning of their existence). *Azal* is thus distinct from the beginninglessness of ***qidam,*** "pre-existence," which applies only to the pre-eternally existent. *Qidam,* unlike *azal,* is also necessarily everlasting.

'azīz: "Rare." Applied to a ḥadīth, it refers to a type of *aḥad* narration that has only two narrators in each link of its chain and is thus between the level of *gharīb* and that of *mashhūr.* A *'azīz* ḥadīth may be either *ṣaḥīḥ, ḥasan,* or *ḍa'īf.*

bid'a, pl. ***bida':*** "Innovation," classed by al-Shāfi'ī as either good (*ḥasana*) or bad (*sayyi'a*), the latter being in doctrine, practice, or both, and unsupported by the principles of the Law. "*Bid'a* is two types. There is the minor *bid'a* such as the mild **Shī'ism** of many of the Successors and their successors, together with religion, scrupulous fear of Allāh and truthfulness. And there is the major *bid'a* of complete ***Rafḍ*** and ***ghulūw*** in it."[1155] Examples of good innovations are those begun by the first Four Caliphs of Islam ﷺ. Examples of misguided innovations include anthropomorphism of the Deity; questioning established rulings of *'aqīda* or *fiqh* such as intercession (*shafā'a, tawassul*), the delight or torture of the grave, the finality of Paradise and Hell; rejecting agreed-upon ḥadīths or ḥadīth as a whole; do-it-yourself *ijtihād;* manipulating the principles of the Law with concepts like "moratorium" on criminal penalties or polygamy; altering the principles of

[1155] Al-Dhahabī, *Mīzān al-I'tidāl* (§2).

jurisprudence, for example in saying that there is no such thing as a good innovation; devising new principles in the authentication and disauthentication of ḥadīth; dispensations for bank interest or removing the *ḥijāb* partly or completely; rabid feminism; rampant imitation of non-Muslims in dress, speech, keeping dogs as pets, keeping mixed company and encouraging others to do so, etc. An innovator is a *bid'ī* or *mubtadi'*, collectively named ***Ahl al-Bid'a***.

"The Companions": Those who encountered the Prophet ﷺ in his lifetime even for a moment, believing in him, and died as Muslims ﷺ. Ar. *ṣaḥābī*, pl. *ṣaḥāba, aṣḥāb*; fem. *ṣahābiyya*, pl. *ṣahābiyyāt*. A group of scholars restrict the name to those who accompanied the Prophet ﷺ for some time.

ḍa'īf, pl. ***ḍu'afā'***, ***ḍi'āf***: "Weak." Low grading of a ḥadīth or of its chain of transmission as opposed to *ṣaḥīḥ* or *ḥasan* which are high gradings, or of a ḥadīth narrator as opposed to *ṣadūq* or *thiqa*; one of the lowest gradings in the terminology of narrator-discreditation. Ahmad and Abū Dāwūd made use of weak ḥadīths for lack of strong ones in the inference of legal rulings, preferring them to conjecture. The majority of scholars infer legal rulings from ḥadīths of either sound or fair grade exclusively, and make use of weak ones in other than legal rulings.

dhāt: Essence, Entity, Self, Person. *Al-Dhāt wal-Ṣifāt*, the (divine) Essence and the Attributes. *Al-Dhāt al-Qudsiyya*, the divine Entity. *Bi-dhātihi*, in person.

dhikr: Silent remembrance or spoken invocation. Mention, especially of Allāh. The Qur'an is named *al-Dhikr*. It is also a name for prayer and the Jumu'a *khuṭba*.

du'ā': Invocation or supplication to Allāh.

dunyā: The world, as opposed to the hereafter or ***ākhira***.

faqīh, pl. ***fuqahā'***: Person of superior understanding; Jurisprudent.

farḍ: Categorically obligatory. One of the five legal rulings that apply to all acts in *fiqh*, the other four being ***mustaḥabb*** (synonymous with ***mandūb*** and also, sometimes, with ***sunna***), ***mubāḥ*** ("indifferent"), ***makrūh*** ("offensive"), ***ḥarām*** ("prohibited") – and applying in the usage of Jurists from the second Hijrī century.

fatwā, pl. ***fatāwā***: Pronouncement. A qualified legal response to a specific question.

fiqh: Superlative understanding; Islamic Jurisprudence and Law; thorough knowledge of the Law. ***Al-fiqh al-akbar*** = ***uṣūl al-dīn.***

firāsa: keen discernment and intuition, similar to ***kashf.*** The Prophet ﷺ said: "Beware the *firāsa* of the Believer for he sees with the light of Allāh."[1156]

"The Four Imāms": Abū Ḥanīfa, Mālik, al-Shāfi'ī, and Aḥmad ibn Ḥanbal.

"The Four Rightly-Guided Caliphs": Abū Bakr al-Ṣiddīq, 'Umar al-Fārūq, 'Uthmān ibn 'Affān, and 'Alī ibn Abī Ṭālib.

"The Four Schools": The Ḥanafī School, the Malikī School, the Shāfi'ī School, and the Ḥanbalī School.

"The Four *Sunan*": al-Tirmidhī's *Sunan* = *al-Jāmi' al-Ṣaḥīḥ,* al-Nasā'ī's *Sunan,* Abū Dāwūd's *Sunan,* and Ibn Mājah's *Sunan.*

gharīb: Singular, obscure; applied to a ḥadīth chain (e.g. by al-Tirmidhī in his *Sunan*), it refers to a type of *aḥad* narration and means "with a single-narrator chain," *i.e.* with only one narrator among the Companions and the subsequent links. Applied to the ḥadīth content, it refers to something not narrated anywhere else. This is not an index of its authenticity, as a *gharīb* ḥadīth may be either *ṣaḥīḥ, ḥasan,* or *ḍa'īf.*[1157] A famous authentic *gharīb* ḥadīth is, "Actions are only according to intentions."[1158] Applied to lexical terms, *gharīb* denotes cruxes or difficulties. There are manuals devoted to the *gharīb* of the Qur'an and ḥadīth.

Ghulāt: "Extremists," especially among the Shī'ī offshoots such as the "gnostic" (*Bāṭinī*) sects including the permissive and/or incarnationist Ismā'īlīs and pseudo-Ṣūfīs such as the Baktāshīs and Qalandarīs; and any of the modern ***Khawārij*** that indulge in declaring apostate (*takfīr*) other Muslims in addition to holding heretical views in doctrine and Law. See also ***bid'a.***

Ghulūw: "Extremism." The attribute of the ***Ghulāt.*** "Shī'ī *Ghulūw* in the time of the *Salaf* and their usage consisted in criticizing and

[1156] See note 638.

[1157] Al-Dhahabī, *Mūqiẓa* (p. 43). For *gharīb* in al-Tirmidhī's usage see Nūr al-Dīn 'Itr's comments in *al-Imām al-Tirmidhī* (p. 185-199) and his notes on Ibn al-Ṣalāḥ's *Ulūm al-Ḥadīth* (p. 39-40) and Ibn Rajab's *Sharḥ 'Ilal al-Tirmidhī* (1:385-393). When al-Tirmidhī says of a ḥadīth "*gharīb*" without any further grading, the ḥadīth is weak in his view.

[1158] Narrated from 'Umar ibn al-Khaṭṭāb alone by al-Bukhārī and Muslim.

possibly insulting 'Uthmān, al-Zubayr, Ṭalḥa, Mu'āwiya, and some of those who fought 'Alī ﷺ. *Ghulūw* in our time and usage is for one to declare those noble leaders apostates and also wash one's hands of the **Two Shaykhs.** Such a person is a miserable misguided heretic."[1159]

ghusl: Major ablution lifting the state of *janāba* from one who is ***junub*** or renewing the state of purity as a Sunna before going to *Jumu'a*, before *'Īd*, and before entering Madīna or Makka.

ḥadath: The quality of things originated and created. Anything other than Allāh ﷻ and His Attributes. In Law, whatever state or act that necessitates the ablution (***wuḍū'***) or greater ablution (***ghusl***).

ḥādith, pl. ***aḥdāth:*** Originated; brought into being; contingent; created. Possessing the quality of ***ḥudūth*** and ***ḥadath*** as opposed to what is without beginning or pre-existent (***qadīm***).

ḥadīth, pl. ***aḥādīth:*** Saying. Narration of the Prophet's ﷺ speech, deed, and approval or disapproval, whether spoken or tacit, about something as well as his ways, dress, and attributes. Most Scholars extend this nomenclature to the sayings of the Companions, and some to those of the Successors, although many reserve the term for Prophetic narrations and call everything else *athar*, pl. *āthār*, or *khabar*, pl. *akhbār*. See also ***Sunna***.

ḥāfiẓ, pl. ***ḥuffāẓ:*** "Memoriser." A ḥadīth Master who possesses memorization of the texts, knowledge of rare ḥadīth, knowledge of its relation to jurisprudence, knowledge of the chains of transmission and narrators, and discerns the reliable chains from the problematic ones. (Abū Shāma and Ibn Ḥajar) See also ***muḥaddith.*** In absolute usage (*al-Ḥāfiẓ*), the term refers to Ibn Ḥajar al-'Asqalānī.

ḥāl, pl. ***aḥwāl:*** State. In *taṣawwuf*, an overwhelming but transitory spiritual state. Often used in contradistinction with "station" or ***maqām***, pl. ***maqāmāt.***

ḥaqīqa: Truth, reality. Lexically, the real sense as opposed to the figurative.

ḥaqīqī: Real. Distinguished from ***ẓāhir***, "literal," and *majāzī*, "figurative."

ḥarām: Strictly prohibited and the commission of which constitutes a sin. One of the five legal rulings that apply to all acts in *fiqh*, the

[1159] Al-Dhahabī, *Mīzān al-I'tidāl* (§2).

other four being ***farḍ*** ("categorically obligatory"), ***mustaḥabb*** (synonymous with ***mandūb*** and also, sometimes, with ***sunna***), ***makrūh*** ("offensive"), and ***mubāḥ*** ("indifferent") in the usage of Jurists from the second Hijrī century.

ḥasan: Fair, authentic. The next to highest grading of a ḥadīth or of its chain of transmission. The chain alone can be fair but not necessarily the ḥadīth itself, or vice versa: a fair ḥadīth can be found narrated through a defective chain.

Ḥashwiyya: Gross anthropomorphists. Literally, "Visceralists." Those who interpret corporal attributions literally in the verses and narrations of the Divine Attributes.

ḥudūth: Contingency. Originated or created nature of all other than Allāh.

ḥujja: "Proof." See ***thiqa***.

ḥulūl: The heresy holding the indwelling or incarnation of the Divine into a created being, place, or quality.

Ibāḍīs: A sub-sect of the *Khawārij* that survives in Oman and parts of North Africa. Ibāḍī doctrine adopts the positions of the ***Mu'tazila***, denying the possibility of seeing Allāh in this life or the afterlife, rejecting the existence of the Attributes that are distinct from the Essence, and upholding the doctrine of the creation of the Qur'ān. They also part ways with Sunni Muslims in disparaging 'Uthmān, 'Alī and Mu'āwiya ﷺ and rejecting the Prophet's ﷺ intercession on behalf of grave sinners. They reject all possibility of rescue from hellfire and hold that punishment in hellfire is eternal for all who enter it including Muslims. On the question of *qadar* the Ibāḍī position is virtually identical to that of al-Ash'arī: Allāh ﷻ is the creator of all human acts, which are termed "acquisitions" (*kasb*).

iḥsān: Excellence; perfection; to worship Allāh as if one saw Him.

ijāza: "Permission," license or certificate of transmission bestowed by a teacher to a student and allowing the *mujāz* or certified person to convey knowledge received from the *mujīz* or certifying authority.

Ijmā': Scholarly Consensus in Islam. ***Ijmā'*** disregards the opinions of the non-Sunnī schools and sects such as the Ẓāhirīs, Shī'īs, Mu'tazilīs, etc.

ijtihād: Striving; scholarly endeavour; competence to infer expert legal rulings from foundational proofs within or without a particular School. The attribute of the ***mujtahid.*** A person can have *ijtihād* in particular issues and be a ***muqallid*** in others.

ikhtilāf: Divergence, difference in the positions of the Scholars also named *khilāf.* Shaykh Muḥammad 'Awwāma forwards the view that these are not synonymous but that one refers to differences that can coexist while the latter refers to disagreement that cannot coexist.

'illa, pl. ***ilal:*** In ***uṣūl al-fiqh,*** the rational reason for a given ruling that is a basis for analogical reasoning (***qiyās***). In **ḥadīth**, a defect or defects hidden within the chain or text of an ostensively sound ḥadīth. Knowledge of the *'ilal* is an integral part of ḥadīth expertise. Among those who authored works focussing on the *'ilal* are Imām Aḥmad, Abū Ḥātim al-Rāzī, al-Athram, al-Tirmidhī, al-Dāraquṭnī, Ibn Ḥibbān, al-Ḥākim, Ibn al-Jawzī, and Ibn Ḥazm. One of its greatest experts was Imām al-Bukhārī.

'ilm: Knowledge, esp. in the Religion; pl. ***'ulūm:*** the Islamic sciences. The attribute of the *'ālim.*

'ilm al-tawḥīd: Science of the affirmation of monotheism. See ***uṣūl.***

imām: "Leader." This applies to the overall leader of the Muslims or Caliph (*al-imām al-a'ẓam/al-akbar*), or the political leader in a more local sense, or the leader of group prayer or a mosque, or – with a capital initial – a major authority among those who are imitated in the Religion. The term also refers to the Qur'ān, a book, or a reference or precedent.

Īmān: Belief, faith in Allāh, His angels, His Books, His Apostles, the Last Day, the Foreordained Decree (both the good and the bad as ordained by Allāh ﷻ) and Resurrection after death. The attribute of the ***mu'min.*** In the above sense *īmān* is different from ***islām,*** otherwise they are synonyms.

innovators: Also known as ***Ahl al-Bid'a,*** deviant Muslims who follow other than the doctrines and beliefs of ***Ahl al-Sunna*** = ***Ahl al-Ḥaqq.***

irsāl: See ***mursal.***

islām: "Submission," "surrender"; to declare "There is no God but Allāh, and Muḥammad is the Messenger of Allāh," perform *ṣalāt,* pay *zakāt,* fast the month of Ramaḍān, and perform the *Ḥajj* if one is able. The attribute of the Muslim. See ***īmān.***

iṣṭilāḥ = ***muṣṭalaḥ.***

jabal: "Mountain." See ***thiqa***.

Jabriyya: Those who held that a human being's acts are all predetermined and that human beings are legally helpless and thus unaccountable.

jahl: Ignorance, either "basic" (*basīṭ*), such as in the commonality of people, or "compound" (*murakkab*), such as in the leaders of innovation. Basic ignorance is when someone knows he does not know. Compound ignorance is when someone thinks he knows but knows wrong, incompletely, or not at all.

Jahmiyya: Followers of Jahm ibn Ṣafwān (d. 128) who believed that Allāh was "the wind and everything else," considered the Qur'ān created and upheld the finiteness in time of Heaven and Hell. The **Mu'tazila** and **Shī'is** adopted his denial or over-interpretation of the Divine Attributes and his view that the Qur'ān is created while Ibn Taymiyya alternately adopted his view that Hell would come to an end and alternately denied it.

Jamā'a: Congregation.

jarḥ: Narrator-discreditation, by which a narrator is declared untrustworthy.

jāriḥa, pl. ***jawāriḥ:*** "Limbs." That which is precluded from the Deity whenever the Attributes that connote corporality are mentioned, such as the face (*wajh*), hand (*yad*), eye (*'ayn*), foot (*qadam*), and so forth. Abū Bakr al-Ismā'īlī said in *I'tiqād A'immat al-Ḥadīth*: "One must not attribute organs (*a'ḍā'*) or limbs (*jawāriḥ*) to Allāh ﷻ nor length nor breadth nor density nor thinness (*wa-lā al-ṭūl wal-'arḍ wal-ghilẓa wal-diqqa*) nor any such characteristic the like of which applies to created beings."[1160] This never means that we negate the Qur'anic attribution of *yad*, *'ayn*, and other to the Deity. However, we let such verses pass without comment.

jawāz: Possibility or permissibility, whether rational possibility and conceivability of something or its licitness in the Religion.

jawhar: "Substance." That which is precluded from the Deity. "Allāh is neither a body (*jism*), nor an accident (*'araḍ*) [in the sense of an attribute characterizing, like "substance," created things] nor an indivisible substance (*jawhar*)" (Ibn Khafīf).[1161]

[1160] Al-Ismā'īlī, *I'tiqād A'immat al-Ḥadīth* (p. 51-52) cf. Ibn Ḥajar, *Fatḥ* (8:664).

jihād: Struggle; fighting by the *mujāhid* (pl. *mujāhidūn, mujāhidīn*) for the sake of Allāh against the enemies of the Religion. "The most obligatory of all jihads (*afrad al-jihād*) are the jihād against the ego, the jihād against lusts, the jihād against the devil, and the jihād against the lower world." (Ibn al-Qayyim).[1162] See ***ribāṭ***.

jism: See ***Mujassima***.

junub: One who is in a state of *janāba* or major ritual impurity necessitating ***ghusl***.

kalām: Lit. "Discourse," "discussion," "speech"; dialectic, speculative, or systematic theology; theological discourse and the science of ***tawḥīd*** in general, also called ***uṣūl al-dīn*** and *al-fiqh al-akbar*. In the terminology of the **Four Imāms** it refers to the doctrines and methods of the ***Mu'tazila*** and their ***Qadarī*** and ***Jahmī*** subsects. Later, "a science consisting in the proofs of the credal doctrines through rational evidence and the rebuttal of the heretics who strayed from the way of the ***Salaf*** and ***Ahl al-Sunna***" (Ibn Khaldūn, *Muqaddima*). The latter definition clearly differentiates between blameworthy and praiseworthy *kalām*. "*Al-Kalām*" also refers to the Qur'an.

karāma, pl. ***karāmāt***: Miraculous gift such as are granted to a ***walī***.

Karrāmiyya: Followers of Muḥammad ibn Karrām (d. 255) who considered it impossible for anything to exist without a body and thus said: "Allāh is a body unlike bodies."

kashf: Disclosure, unveiling. Insight into the unseen through ***karāma***.

Khalaf: "Those that followed." A name used for Muslims that came after the ***Salaf***.

Khawārij, sing. ***Khārijī***: "Separatists." Those of ***Ahl al-Bid'a*** who, in any day and age, fight against the caliph and/or against the mainstream Ulema of the Muslims and their commonality by force of arms and/or recourse to anathema which includes falsely declaring others "disbelievers" (*takfīr*), "pagans" (*tashrīk*), "misguided"

[1161] Cf. also Shāh Walī Allāh al-Dihlawī in *al-I'tiqād al-Ṣaḥīḥ*, printed with Ṣiddīq Ḥasan Khān al-Qinnawjī's commentary on the margins of his friend Nu'mān al-Alūsī's *Jalā' al-'Aynayn fī Muḥākamat al-Aḥmadayn*: "He is neither an indivisible substance, nor an accident, nor a body, nor is He spatially bounded, nor does He possess direction."

[1162] In *al-Fawā'id* (p. 50).

(*taḍlīl*), "innovators" (*tabdī'*), "pantheists" (*ittiḥādī, ḥulūlī*), "grave-worshippers" (*qubūrī*), "cultists" (*ṭuruqī*), and so forth. Modern *Khawārij* include [1] the ***Wahhābiyya*** (as stated by Ibn 'Ābidīn, al-Ṣāwī, 'Abd Allāh ibn Ḥasan ibn Faḍl Bā 'Alawī, 'Alawī ibn Aḥmad al-Ḥaddād, Abū Zahra, etc.) and their myriad modernist offshoots and hybrid grouplets and parties East and West – many purportedly Sunni – including certain professed Ṣūfis, reformists such as the Quṭb brothers, Taqī al-Dīn al-Nabhānī, Bannā', and [2] the ***Rāfiḍa***. Modern *Khawārij*, unlike the early ones, mostly permit lying, forgery, and book-tampering in the furtherance of their causes.

kufr: Disbelief in any part of the creed of Islam, apostasy, blasphemy. May refer to a statement that amounts to *kufr* without causing *kufr* in its speaker, such as saying: "This medicine saved my life" or "Country X. is a superpower," unless meant literally. One convicted of *kufr* is a *kāfir.*

lā ilāha illallāh: "There is no God except Allāh." With the affirmation that Muḥammad ﷺ is the Messenger of Allāh (*Muḥammadun Rasūlullāh*), this phrase brings one into Islam. "The people of *lā ilāha illallāh*" are the Muslims.

layyin: "Soft," said of a ḥadīth narrator or chain that is somewhat weak.

madhhab: "Path." A School of Law (*madhhab fiqhī*) in Islām, varying in number from a single ***Mujtahid*** over a single position – such as the *Madhhab* of Abū Hurayra in considering the wearing of gold prohibited even for women – to an Imām of ***fiqh*** and his entire School down to our time, such as the four *Madhāhib* of Abū Ḥanīfa, Mālik, al-Shāfi'ī, and Aḥmad whose Jurisprudence encompass all aspects of public and private life. Al-Nawawī in his time spoke of "the five *Madhāhib*," including that of Sufyān al-Thawrī. Other defunct Schools include those of al-Awzā'ī, al-Ṭabarī, Abū Thawr, Dāwūd ibn 'Alī, and al-Layth. Among the multifarious non-Sunnī Schools some survive to our time, such as the Ja'farī ("Twelver" or "Duodeciman") **Shī'īs** – nowadays mostly **Rāfiḍa**; the moderate Zaydīs in Yemen; the moderate Khārijī **Ibāḍīs** in Oman and North Africa; and others.

majhūl: "Unidentifiable." Said of a narrator whose reliability is unknown and from whom only one person narrates. Of slightly stronger status is the ***majhūl al-ḥāl*** or "unknown in status," also called ***mastūr*** or "out of view," a narrator concerning whom neither commendation nor discreditation is available. The status of unknown maybe lifted if two or more trustworthy sources narrate from them, or even a single Imām known to narrate only from those who are trustworthy.

makrūh: Offensive, abominable, disliked. One of the five legal rulings that apply to all acts in *fiqh*, the other four being ***mustaḥabb*** ("desirable," synonymous with ***mandūb*** and also, sometimes, with ***sunna***), ***mubāḥ*** "indifferent"), ***farḍ*** ("categorically obligatory"), ***ḥarām*** ("prohibited"), in the usage of Jurists from the second Hijrī century.

mansūkh: Abrogated text in the Qur'an or ḥadīth, as opposed to ***nāsikh.*** The verse ﴿**whether you make known what is in your minds or hide it, Allāh will bring you to account for it**﴾ (2:284) is abrogated by the verse ﴿**Allāh tasks not a soul beyond its scope. For it (is only) that which it has earned, and against it (only) that which it has deserved**﴾ (2:286). Abrogation is restricted to legal texts and excludes texts that concern beliefs.

maqām, pl. ***maqāmāt***, see ***ḥāl.***

maqṭū': "Severed." Said of a ḥadīth that is linked only up to a Successor.

marfū': "Raised." A ḥadīth linked back to the Prophet ﷺ.

ma'rifa: Knowledge of Allāh. The attribute of the ***'ārif.***

mashhūr: "Famous." Applied to a ḥadīth, it refers to a well-known ḥadīth that may be either *ṣaḥīḥ* (even *mutawātir*) or not, or to a type of *aḥad* narration that has three or more narrators at each link of its chain. The label of *mashhūr* is sometimes given to merely famous narrations which are well-known to people, whether or not they meet the criteria of the ḥadīth Scholars. The *mashhūr* is also called *mustafīḍ.*

mastūr: See ***majhūl al-ḥāl.***

Māturīdīs: Adherents of the Sunni doctrinal school of Abū Manṣūr al-Māturīdī, mostly from the Ḥanafī School of Law. They differ with Ash'arīs on a small number of issues.

mawḍū': Forged, forgery. Knowledge of forged narrations is an integral part of the ḥadīth sciences. The most famous index of forgeries is Ibn al-Jawzī's *Mawḍū'āt.* The most reliable such compilation is Ibn 'Arrāq's *Tanzīh al-Sharī'at al-Marfū'a,* followed by al-Suyūṭī's *al-La'āli' al-Maṣnū'a,* al-Qārī's *al-Asrār al-Marfū'a,* and al-Shawkānī's *al-Fawā'id al-Mawḍū'a.*

mawqūf: "Halted." A ḥadīth linked only up to a Companion.

mu'adhdhin: One who calls out the *adhān* or call to prayer.

mu'allaq: "Suspended." Said of a report whose chain is suppressed except for its last link or two, as found in the chapter-titles of al-Bukhārī's *Ṣaḥīḥ.*

Mu'aṭṭila: Those who nullify meanings. The *Mu'aṭṭila* of the Divine Attributes divest them of reality or over-interpret them, at the opposite extreme of the ***Ḥashwiyya***. The *Mu'aṭṭila* of the Hereafter (such as the ***Mu'tazila***, ***Shī'a***, and those who follow them) deny the reality of the life of the grave, the torture of the Fire, the delights of Paradise, and the beatific vision. The *Mu'aṭṭila* of the *Sharī'a* deny its binding character and manipulate it at their convenience and according to their needs. The latter category includes pseudo-Ṣūfīs; modernists; extremists; others of the Islamically illiterate mass that deny Ḥadīth in part or in whole; and all the reformers and exploiters of Islam for worldly purposes who claim to speak for it.

mubāḥ: Indifferent, permissible. One of the five legal rulings that apply to all acts in *fiqh,* the other four being ***farḍ*** ("categorically obligatory"), ***mustaḥabb*** (synonymous with ***mandūb*** and also, sometimes, with ***sunna***), ***makrūh*** ("offensive"), ***ḥarām*** ("prohibited") in the usage of Jurists from the second Hijrī century.

mu'ḍal: "Problematic." A ḥadīth of the Prophet ﷺ narrated with a chain missing at least two successive links.

mudallis: "Concealer." A narrator that omits one or more links in his chain of transmission by using ***'an'ana*** or indecisive transmission terminology or deliberately misnaming a link. There are different types of ***tadlīs.***

muḍṭarib: "Muddled, discrepant." Said of a chain of transmission or textual content that present implausible variations, strongly suggesting error on the part of one or more of the narrators.

muftī: One who issues legal opinions and responses rightly or wrongly.

muḥaddith, pl. ***muḥaddithūn:*** Scholar of ḥadīth. One who has memorised the chains of transmission, knows the narrators, and discerns the reliable chains from the problematic ones without necessarily memorizing the texts, nor their relation to Jurisprudence, nor having knowledge of rare ḥadīth. (Ibn Ḥajar). See also ***ḥāfiẓ***.

muḥdath: "Contingent, originated." Said of all created things, which are *mumkin al-wujūd*, "of non-necessary existence" as opposed to Allāh Most High, the One and only Incontingent Who is *wājib al-wujūd*, "of necessary existence."

mujāhid: See ***jihād***.

Mujassima: Those who attribute a body (*jism*) to Allāh.

mu'jiza, pl. ***mu'jizāt:*** "Staggering" evidentiary miracle performed by a Prophet.

mujtahid: Qualified to exercise ***ijtihād***. A *mujtahid muṭlaq* or "absolute *mujtahid*" is one that attained the rank of the Four Imams in knowledge of Arabic, qualification to apply legal reasoning, draw analogies, and infer rulings from the evidence independently of the methodology and findings of the Sunni Schools, through his own linguistic and juridical perspicuity and extensive knowledge of the texts, both the primary and those dealing with Jurisprudential *khilāf* from the *Ṣaḥāba* to his time.

mu'min, pl. ***mu'minūn:*** Believer. One who possesses ***īmān***. A Muslim generally speaking. "The *mu'min* is he who watches his Lord, takes account from himself, and prepares for his return" (al-Tustarī).

munkar: Condemned, detested, disclaimed. Any act (pl. ***munkarāt***) the Law prohibits or abhors. Applied to a ḥadīth (pl. ***manākīr***), a usually very weak chain or ḥadīth contradicted by established narrations. Applied to a narrator by association: "Anyone about whom I say: *munkar al-ḥadīth*, it is not permissible to narrate from him" (al-Bukhārī).

munqaṭi': "Cut up." The chain of a Prophetic ḥadīth that is missing one or more links anywhere in the chain as per the majority of the Masters, while Ibn Hajar and others specified that they be at or "lower," i.e. more recent than the Successor-link, and non-successive.

muqallid: "Imitator, follower" of a ***Mujtahid*** or a School of Law. See ***taqlīd***.

murābiṭ: See ***ribāṭ***.

Murji'a: Those who dissociate acts from the sphere of basic belief, as does the entire Sunni Māturīdī School, deeming deeds an "additional pillar" (*rukn zā'id*). The non-Sunni *Murji'a* add the stipulation that sins do not harm one's belief, whereas Abū Ḥanīfa said in *al-Fiqh al-Akbar*: "We do not say that sins do not harm the believer."

mursal: "Dispatched." A ḥadīth of the Prophet narrated with a chain missing the Companion-link or, sometimes, a lower link through *irsāl*.

Mushabbiha: Those who liken Allāh to creation and to created beings.

mushrik, pl. ***mushrikūn:*** Idolater. One who practices ***shirk*** by believing in and obeying other than Allāh and His Prophet ﷺ.

musnad: "Founded." A narration or compilation of narrations that are supported by an unbroken narrative chain going back to the Prophet ﷺ.

mustafīḍ: See ***mashhūr***.

mustaḥabb: "Desirable." Synonymous with ***mandūb*** and also, sometimes, with ***sunna*** among the five legal rulings that apply to all acts in ***fiqh***, the other four being ***farḍ*** ("categorically obligatory), ***mubāḥ*** ("indifferent"), ***makrūh*** ("offensive"), and ***ḥarām*** ("prohibited") in the usage of Jurists from the second Hijrī century.

muṣṭalaḥ: Nomenclature, convention, usage, terminology, especially in ḥadīth science.

mutakallim, pl. ***mutakallimūn:*** Expert in *kalām*.

Mu'tazila: "Isolationists." A sect that made reason the ultimate criterion of truth, forged a political alliance with the **Shī'a** and, like them, held the Qur'an to be created and the Attributes to be null in themselves and to mean none other than the Essence. They also deny intercession (*shafā'a*) and the ***karāmāt*** of the *Awliyā'*. "All *Mu'tazilīs* are ***Qadarīs*** but not vice-versa" (al-Maghnīsāwī). Modernists are fond of Mu'tazilism as [1] it affords them a historical antecedent without which their novelty shows too plainly, [2] it provides them with language against the Ulema of *Ahl al-Sunna*, [3] it allows them to remould their ignorance or dislike of the Sunna and even their atheism into a methodological posture.

mutawātir: Mass-narrated. "That which necessarily leads to positive knowledge (*'ilm*)" (Ibn al-Juwaynī). Applies to a narration or conveyance that has, at each link of its transmission chain, a number of narrators such that it precludes collusion and collective fabrication on their part, forming *tawātur*. The determination of that number varies among the scholars of ḥadīth. Al-Suyūṭī considers they must be at least ten at each link of the chain. The *mutawātir* must report something that is directly observed, such as wiping on the *khuffs* in ***wuḍū'***, the insistence on brushing one's teeth before every *Ṣalāt*, the immense merit of *lā ilāha illā-llāh*, the prohibition on lying concerning the Prophet ﷺ, the narrations of the seven canonical readings of the Qur'ān and others, denying or disbelieving any of which constitutes *kufr*.

muttaqī: See ***taqwā.***

nafl: Superogatory worship.

naḥw: Arabic grammar and related disciplines.

nāsikh: Abrogating text, as opposed to ***mansūkh.***

"The Nine Books": Al-Bukhārī's *Ṣaḥīḥ*, Muslim's *Ṣaḥīḥ*, Mālik's *Muwaṭṭa'*, Abū Dāwūd's *Sunan*, al-Tirmidhī's *Sunan*, al-Nasā'i's *Sunan*, Ibn Mājah's *Sunan*, al-Dārimī's *Sunan*, and Aḥmad's *Musnad*.

qaḍā': Divine foreordainment. "When ***qaḍā'*** comes to pass, it is called ***qadar***." (Al-Buṭī)

qadar: Divinely foreordained destiny, in the sense of each and every event that takes place in creation. *Ahl al-Sunna* hold that Allāh creates *qadar* while human beings bear responsibility and earn credit for their acts or, more specifically, for their intentions.

qāḍī: Judge.

Qadarīs, Qadariyya: A sect that held (like most Christians) that a human being creates his own destiny and that Allāh finds out man's acts after enactment. Like the ***Mu'tazila*** and most Christians, they also believe that Allāh only creates good, while evil has other creators. Al-Maghnīsāwī considers the ***Shī'a*** and the ***Mu'tazila*** doctrinal subsects of the *Qadariyya*.

Qarāmiṭa: pl. of *Qarmaṭī*, a heretical "gnostic" (*bāṭinī*) sect also known as Ismā'īlīs (al-Shahrastānī). They stole the Black Stone and returned it by catapult, breaking it in the process. They still exist today and are known for their extreme syncretism.

qāṣṣ, pl. ***quṣṣāṣ:*** "Storyteller." A pejorative name for an admonisher who mostly does not differentiate between sound reports and forgeries.

Qibla: The direction of prayer, i.e. the Ka'ba in Makka the Magnificent.

qidam, adj. ***qadīm:*** Pre-existence without beginning in addition to everlastingness. "The Pre-Existent without end" (*al-Qadīm*) is one of the exclusive Attributes of Allāh Most High, applicable also to His Attributes including his Attribute of Speech, hence to the Glorious Qur'ān and the other revealed Books.

Qiyās: Analogical reasoning in the principles of jurisprudence (***uṣūl al-fiqh***), the fourth source of the Law after the Qur'ān, the **Sunna**, and ***Ijmā'***.

quṭb: "Pole." One or more human beings who occupy a pivotal spiritual position in the world. Synonymous with ***ghawth*** according to al-Shāfi'ī.[1163]

rak'a: Cycle of prayer within ***Ṣalāt.***

Rafḍ: The heresy of the ***Rawāfiḍ.***

Rawāfiḍ or ***Rāfiḍa***, sing. ***Rāfiḍī:*** "Rejecters." The Shī'a who disrespect Abū Bakr and 'Umar ﷺ and deny the validity of their imamate and 'Uthmān's ﷺ, declaring apostate the majority of the Companions and of the *Umma* to our time, including the Mothers of the Believers .

ribāṭ: Garrison or being stationed in one for the purpose of the military **jihād** by the *murābiṭ* (pl. *murābiṭūn*) but also used in the spiritual sense. The Prophet ﷺ said: "To wait for the next prayer after finishing praying is the greatest soldiery (*al-ribāṭ al-akbar*)"[1164] and "Perfect ablution in rough conditions, walking to the mosques, and waiting for the next prayer after finishing praying: this is the true fort (*dhālikum al-ribāṭ*)!"[1165]

ṣaḥābī, pl. ***ṣaḥāba,*** see Companions ﷺ.

ṣadūq: "Truthful." One of the ranks of narrator-commendation, applied to a narrator whose rank falls short of "trustworthy" (***thiqa***). A *ṣadūq*'s narrations reach the rank of "fair" (***ḥasan***).

ṣaḥīḥ: Sound, rigorously authentic. The highest grading of a ḥadīth

[1163] As cited in Ibn 'Ābidīn, *Rasā'il* (2:276). Cf. also al-Haythamī, *Fatāwā Ḥadīthiyya* (p. 322-325).

[1164] Narrated from Abū Hurayra by Aḥmad with a fair chain.

[1165] Narrated from Abū Hurayra by Muslim, Mālik, and Aḥmad.

or of its chain of transmission. Note that the chain alone can be sound but not the ḥadīth itself, or vice versa, as a sound ḥadīth can also be narrated through a defective chain.

Salaf: "The Predecessors"; a name applied specifically to the righteous Muslims of the first three centuries of Islam.

"Salafī"*:* Properly, a strict imitator of the *Salaf* such as the adherents of the Four Sunnī Schools, but the *Salafiyya* today is a misnomer referring to an anti-traditional free-thinking would-be-salafī (*mutasallif*) current generated by the ***Wahhābiyya***, both patching together views from modernism, the ***Mu'tazila***, the ***Ẓāhiriyya***, and the ***Karrāmiyya***, and both claiming to represent ***Ahl al-Sunna*** in vociferous opposition to the Four Schools and to **Ash'arīs** and **Māturīdīs**. The "Salafīs" give themselves the names of *Ahl al-Ḥadīth* (in India and Pakistan) and *Atharī* (in the Gulf) while their opponents name them ***Ḥashwiyya, Mujassima, Lā-Madhhabiyya*** and ***Khawārij***.

Ṣalāt: Prayer. Lexically: "supplication." Defined by the Holy Prophet ﷺ as the pillar of the Religion and as the first thing a human being is asked about in the hereafter.

shādhdh: "Wayward," anomalous. Said of an ostensibly authentic ḥadīth or chain by which a trustworthy narrator singled himself out in contradiction to firmly established narrations. Also applied to aberrant fatwas and/or beliefs.

Shī'a: "Faction." Originally, those who sided with 'Alī against his foes. After 'Alī's time: those that hold 'Alī to be better than Abū Bakr and 'Umar, rejecting the Prophetic narrations in praise of the latter two and a host of other principles. What originally started as a movement focussing on political precedence turned into a full-fledged Perso-centric sect with its own *'aqīda, uṣūl,* sources, and *fiqh*. The Shī'a are the first sect in Islām and have split into multifarious groups, the most important of which are the Zaydīs and the Ja'farīs, although there are no such schools in the *mutawātir* sense that prevails in the Four Schools. The Shī'īs share many doctrinal positions with the ***Qadariyya*** and ***Mu'tazila***, and these including the denial of the vision of Allāh ﷻ in the hereafter and the belief that the Qur'ān is created.

shirk: Idolatry; polytheism; belief in more than one God, such as paganism and animism; or in incarnation of the Divine, as in the

Greek, Roman, Christian, and Hindu creeds; or in a many-personed Divine Substance such as Trinitarianism and Vedantism.

ṣiddīq: Most truthful and trustful. The title of Abū Bakr. The highest level of sainthood after Prophethood.

"The Six Books": Al-Bukhārī's *Ṣaḥīḥ,* Muslim's *Ṣaḥīḥ,* and the *Sunan* of al-Tirmidhī, al-Nasā'ī, Abū Dāwūd, and Ibn Mājah.

"The Successors": Those Muslims that met at least one Companion, even for a moment, and died as Muslims. Ar. *Tābi'ī,* pl. *Tābi'ūn.*

Ṣūfī, pl. ***Ṣūfiyya:*** One who follows a path of ***taṣawwuf,*** "He who gazes at the Real in proportion to the state in which He maintains him" (Bundar). They wore wool (*ṣūf*): "I found the redress of my heart between Makka and Madīna with a group of strangers – people of wool and cloaks" (*aṣḥāb ṣūf wa-'abā'*).[1166] However, the correctness of the etymology of the word is an irrelevance as there is no claim that the Ṣūfīs who used the term were concerned with literary precision.

Sunna, pl. ***sunan:*** "Road" or "practice(s)." Standard practice, primarily of the Prophet ﷺ, including his sayings, deeds, tacit approvals or disapprovals. Ḥadīth Scholars add his personal traits – including physical features – to this definition. The "sciences of the Sunna" (*'ulūm al-Sunna*) refer to the biography of the Prophet ﷺ (*sīra*), the chronicle of his battles (*maghāzī*), his everyday sayings and acts or "ways" (*sunan*) including his personal and moral qualities (*shamā'il*), and the host of the ancillary ḥadīth sciences such as the circumstances of occurrence (*asbāb al-wurūd*), knowledge of the abrogating and abrogated ḥadīth, difficult words (*gharīb al-ḥadīth*), narrator criticism (*al-jarḥ wal-ta'dīl*), narrator-biographies (*al-rijāl*), etc. This meaning is used in contradistinction to the Qur'ān in expressions such as "Qur'ān and Sunna" and applies in the usage of ḥadīth Scholars. "The Sunna in our definition consists of the reports transmitted from the Messenger of Allāh ﷺ, and the Sunna is the commentary (*tafsīr*) of the Qur'ān and contains its directives (*dalā'il*)" (Aḥmad). The early Sunnī ḥadīth Masters such as al-Ḥumaydī, Abū Dāwūd, and Abū Naṣr al-Marwazī also used the term "the Sunna" in the narrow sense to refer to Sunnī

[1166] Sufyān al-Thawrī as cited from Khalaf ibn Tamīm by al-Dhahabī, *Siyar* (7:203).

Doctrine as opposed to the creeds of non-Sunnī sects. In the terminology of *uṣūl al-fiqh* or principles of jurisprudence, *sunna* denotes a saying (*qawl*), action (*fi'l*) or approval (*taqrīr*) related from (*nuqila 'an*) the Prophet ﷺ or issuing (*ṣadara*) from him other than the Qur'ān. In the terminology of *fiqh* or jurisprudence, *sunna* denotes whatever is firmly established (*thabata*) as called for (*maṭlūb*) in the Religion on the basis of a legal proof (*dalīl shar'ī*) but without being obligatory, the continued abandonment of which constitutes disregard (*istikhfāf*) of the Religion and sin, and incurs blame (*lawm, 'itāb, taḍlīl*) (also punishment (*'uqūba*) according to some jurists). Some made a distinction between what they called "Emphasised Sunna" (*sunna mu'akkada*) or "Sunna of Guidance" (*sunnat al-hudā*), such as what the Prophet ﷺ ordered or emphasised in word or in deed, and other types of Sunna considered less binding in their legal status, such as what they called "Non-Emphasised Sunna" (*sunna ghayr mu'akkada*) and "Sunna of Habit" (*sunnat al-'āda*). The above jurisprudential meanings of Sunna are used in contradistinction to the other four of the five legal categories for human actions : ***farḍ*** ("obligatory"), ***mubāḥ*** ("indifferent"), ***makrūh*** ("offensive"), ***ḥarām*** ("prohibited"), and apply in the usage of jurists from the second Hijrī century.

tābi'ī, pl. ***tābi'ūn, tābi'īn***: see **Successors**.

ta'dīl Narrator-commendation whereby a narrator is declared reliable. Ibn Ḥajar concludes in *Ta'jīl al-Manfa'a* that al-Bukhārī's and Ibn Abī Ḥātim's silence concerning a narrator they mention in *al-Tārīkh al-Kabīr* and *al-Jarḥ wal-Ta'dīl* respectively, is a *ta'dīl* on their part.

tadlīs: Concealment of one's source by a ***mudallis*** narrator of ḥadīth, often accompanied by ***'an'ana*** or undecisive transmission terminology. There are three types of *tadlīs*: *tadlīs al-shuyūkh, tadlīs al-taswiya,* and *tadlīs al-isnād.* In the first case all links are present and none is omitted, except that the *mudallis* deliberately names his link as other than the commonly known name due to one reason or another such as (a) wanting to give the impression that the link is someone else or that one narrates from more people than what is actually the case; (b) wanting one's source not to be recognised easily for reasons of political or personal safety, as in the case of narrations from *Ahl al-Bayt* under the Umawī regimes; (c) disliking to acknowledge one's source because of some personal enmity, as happened between al-Bukhārī and al-Dhuhlī. The second type of *tadlīs* is the worst type, as there is actually one or more omitted links and the *mudallis* is often trying to hide the weakness in his chain by only citing the strong links. The third type of *tadlīs,* called *tadlīs al-isnād,* is the most difficult to detect: A not only omits mentioning B, but is on top of it contemporary with C. So the concealment here is harder to detect because it is historically plausible that A actually heard C when in fact he did not.

tafwīḍ: Committal. The resignation of knowledge to Allāh ﷻ exemplified in al-Shafi'i's saying: "We believe in what came from Allāh in the meaning meant by Allāh and we believe in what came from the Messenger of Allāh in the meaning meant by the Messenger of Allāh ﷺ" (al-Shāfi'ī).

tanzīh: Divine transcendence beyond the attributes of things created, such as lying or taking a mate and son. The affirmation of transcendence is required of every true monotheist (*Muwaḥḥid*) and is expressed in *tasbīḥ, taḥmīd, takbīr,* and *tahlīl*: respectively saying that Allāh is beyond all imperfections (*"subḥān Allāh"*), praising and glorifying Him (*"al-ḥamdu lillāh"*), magnifying Him above all things (*"Allāhu akbar"*), and declaring His absolute oneness (*"lā ilāha illā Allāh"*). Synonymous with ***taqdīs.***

taqdīs: The affirmation of Divine transcendence beyond any defect or other attributes of things created such as corporeality, as in Fakhr al-Dīn al-Rāzī's *Asās al-Taqdīs* ("Foundation of Transcendence"). Synonymous with ***tanzīh.***

taqlīd: Imitation. Following a ***Mujtahid*** Imām or School of Law. The attribute of the ***muqallid*** and of all those unqualified to exert ***ijtihād,*** including the overwhelming mass of Muslims.

taqwā: Godwariness. The attribute of the *muttaqī* (pl. *muttaqūn*), "To keep clear of what Allāh has forbidden" (Abū 'Uthmān al-Maghribī).

ṭarīqa: Path, specifically Ṣūfī path.

taṣawwuf: Purification of the self from everything other than the remembrance and obedience of Allāh; the realization of ***iḥsān***; ***zuhd*** combined with ***ma'rifa***; the attribute of the **Ṣūfī**. "Ceasing objection" (Ṣu'lūkī); "Renouncing the world and its people" (Ibn Sam'ūn). "Knowing the excuses of God's servants" (*Risāla Qushayriyya*). "*Taṣawwuf* is neither knowledge nor deeds but an attribute with which the essence of the Ṣūfī adorns itself, possessing knowledge and deeds, and consisting in the balance in which these two are weighed" (Ibn Khafīf).

tawātur: Mass transmission. See ***mutawātir.***

tawḥīd: The affirmation of Oneness. Islamic belief and doctrine. Another name for Sūrat al-Ikhlāṣ (§112).

ta'wīl: Explanation, particularly of the Qur'ān, as in the *ṣaḥīḥ* invocation of the Prophet ﷺ for Ibn 'Abbās ؓ in the *Musnad* and others: "O Allāh! Grant him ***fiqh*** in the Religion and teach him *ta'wīl.*" Later, it tends to refer specifically to figurative interpretation and metaphorical reading. In the latter senses *ta'wīl* is defined as "the diversion of meaning away from the patent sense of the word."

thabat: In the Muslim East, a Scholar's collected chains of transmission (*e.g. Thabat Ibn 'Ābidīn*), synonymous with *barnāmij* and *fahrasa* in the Maghreb (*e.g.* Imām Muḥammad 'Abdal Ḥayy al-Kattānī's *Fahras al-Fahāris*). Another synonym is *mashyakha.*

thabt: Firmly established as a reliable and trustworthy ***thiqa*** narrator.

thiqa, pl. ***thiqāt:*** "Trustworthy." Top ranking in narrator-commendation. A *thiqa*'s narrations reach the rank of "sound" ***(ṣaḥīḥ).*** The *thiqa* is both morally upright (*'adl*) and accurate (*ḍābiṭ*) by definition. The ***Muḥaddithūn*** have also used the term *jabal* ("Mountain") and *ḥujja* ("Proof in himself"), both beyond *thiqa.* Also used are the compounds *thiqa thiqa, thiqa* **thabt**, *thiqa ma'mūn, thiqa imām.* Rarest of superlatives is the title *ḥākim* ("Wise man").

"The Two *Ṣaḥīḥs*": Al-Bukhārī's *Ṣaḥīḥ* and Muslim's *Ṣaḥīḥ.*

"The Two Shaykhs": in Islām, Abū Bakr al-Ṣiddīq and 'Umar al-Fārūq; in ḥadīth terminology, al-Bukhārī and Muslim; in Ḥanafī *fiqh*, Abū Ḥanīfa and Abū Yūsuf; in Shāfi'ī *fiqh*, al-Rāfi'ī and al-Nawawī; in the canonical readings (*qirā'āt*), Ḥamza and al-Kisā'ī; in the Qur'anic script (*rasm*), Abū 'Amr al-Dānī and Abū Dāwūd Sulaymān ibn Najāḥ.

'ulūw: Elevation, height; applied to Allāh: exalted rank, loftiness.

"Allāh has made Himself exalted over the heaven with the *'ulūw* of sovereignty and authority, not that of movement or displacement." (Al-Ṭabarī)

uṣūl, sing. ***aṣl:*** Bases; the tenets of Faith and principles of Islamic belief; Islamic doctrine. Also known as *uṣūl al-dīn, 'ilm al-tawḥīd,* and *al-fiqh al-akbar.* Applied to jurisprudence (*uṣūl al-fiqh*), the principles and methodology of the Law. The term *uṣūl* is also used in conjunction with *tafsīr* and *ḥadīth* to refer to their respective methodologies.

Wahhābiyya: The most important sect in latter-day Islām. Abū Zahra said in his book on the history of the *madhāhib* in Islām: "The Wahhābīs appeared in the Arabian desert [...] and revived the School of Ibn Taymiyya. The founder of the Wahhābiyya is Muḥammad ibn 'Abd al-Wahhāb who died in 1786. He had studied the books of Ibn Taymiyya which became inestimable in his sight, deepening his involvement in them until he brought them out from the realm of opinion into the realm of practice. [...] The Wahhābīs exaggerated [and bowdlerised] Ibn Taymiyya's positions and instituted practical matters that can be summarised thus: **I.** They did not restrain themselves to view worship (*'ibāda*) in the same way that Islām had stipulated in the Qur'ān and Sunna and as Ibn Taymiyya had mentioned, but they wished to include customs (*'ādāt*) also into the province of Islām so that Muslims would be bound by them. Thus they declared cigarette smoking ***ḥarām*** and exaggerated this ruling to the point that their general public considered the smoker a ***mushrik.*** As a result they resembled the ***Khawārij*** who used to declare apostate whoever committed a sin. **II.** In the beginning of their sway they would also declare coffee and whatever resembled it as *ḥarām* to themselves but it seems that they became more lenient on this point as time went by. **III.** The Wahhābis did not restrain themselves to proselytism only, but resorted to warmongering against whoever disagreed with them on the grounds that they were fighting innovations, and innovations are an evil that must be fought, and it is obligatory to command good and forbid evil.[1167] [...] The leader of Wahhābī thought in the field of war and battle was Muḥammad ibn Sa'ūd, the ancestor of the ruling Sa'ūdī family in the Arabian lands. He was a brother-in-law to Shaykh Muḥammad ibn 'Abd al-Wahhāb and embraced his ***madhhab***, defending it fervently and calling unto it by force of arms. He announced that he was doing this so as to uphold the Sunna and eradicate ***bid'a***. Perhaps, this religious mission that took a violent turn was carrying with itself a rebellion against Ottoman rule. [...] until the governor of Egypt, Muḥammad 'Alī Bāshā al-Albānī, faced them and pounced on the Wahhābīs with his strong army, routing them in the course of several battles. At that time their military force was reduced and confined to the Arabian tribes. Riyadh and its vicinity was the center for this permanent *da'wa* that would turn violent whenever they found the strength and then lie still whenever they found violent opposition. **IV.** Whenever they were able to seize a town or city they would come to the tombs and turn them into ruins and destruction [...] and they would destroy whatever mosques were with the tombs also. [...] **V.** Their brutality did not stop there but they also came to whatever graves were visible and destroyed them also. And when the ruler of the Ḥijāz regions caved in to them they destroyed all the graves of the **Companions** and razed them to the ground. [...] **VI.** They would cling to small matters which they condemned although they had nothing to do with idolatry nor with whatever leads to idolatry, such as photography. We found this in their fatwas and treatises at the hands of their Ulema, although their rulers ignore this saying of theirs completely and cast it by the wayside. **VII.** They expanded the meaning of *bid'a* to strange proportions, to the point that they actually claimed that draping the walls of the noble *Rawḍa* is an innovated matter. Hence they forbade the renewal of the drapes that were in it, until they fell in tatters and became unsightly, were it not for the light that pours out to all that are in the presence of the Prophet ﷺ or feels that in this place was the abode of Revelation on the Master of Messengers. In fact, we find among them, on top of this, those who consider that the Muslim's expression "our Master Muḥammad" (*sayyidunā Muḥammad*) is an impermissible *bid'a* and they show true extremism about this and, for the sake of

[1167] To this day, the *Khawārij* include *al-amr bil-ma'rūf wal-nahy 'an al-munkar* in their books of *fiqh*. The *Mu'tazila* also included it in their "five pillars."

their mission, use foul and furious language until most people actually flee from them as fast as they can. **VIII.** In truth, the Wahhābīs have actualised the opinions of Ibn Taymiyya and are extremely zealous followers and supporters of those views. They adopted the positions of Ibn Taymiyya that we explained in our discussion of those who call themselves ***Salafiyya***. However, they expanded the meaning of *bid'a* and construed as innovations things that have no relation to worship. [...] In fact, it has been noticed that the Ulema of the Wahhābīs consider their own opinions correct and not possibly wrong, while they consider the opinions of others wrong and not possibly correct. Moreover, they consider what others than themselves do in the way of erecting tombs and circumambulating them, as near to idolatry.[1168] In this respect they are near the ***Khawārij*** who used to declare those who dissented with them apostate and fight them as we already mentioned. This was a relatively harmless matter in the days when they were cloistered in the desert and not trespassing its boundaries; but when they mixed with others until the Ḥijāz country was in the hand of the Sa'ūd family,[1169] the matter became of the utmost gravity. This is why the late King 'Abd al-'Azīz of the Sa'ūd family opposed them, and treated their opinions as confined to themselves and irrelevant to others."[1170] Among the titles Wahhābīs gave themselves are the names *Muwaḥḥidūn, Iṣlāḥiyyūn,* and *Salafiyyūn* while their opponents name them ***Ḥashwiyya, Mujassima*** and ***Khawārij***. They name Muḥammad ibn 'Abd al-Wahhāb *Shaykh al-Islām* and name his descendants *Āl al-Shaykh* while his brother Sulaymān declares him a heretic in his fatwā printed under the title *Faṣl al-Khiṭāb min Kitāb Allāh wa-Ḥadīth al-Rasūl* ﷺ *wa-Kalām Ulī al-Albāb fī Madhhab Ibni 'Abd al-Wahhāb* ("The Final Word from the Qur'ān, the Ḥadīth, and the Sayings of the Scholars Concerning the School of Ibn 'Abd al-Wahhāb"), also known as *al-Ṣawā'iq al-Ilāhiyya fī Madhhab al-Wahhābiyya* ("The Divine Thunderbolts Concerning the Wahhābī School"). This book is the earliest

[1168] Ironically, the Wahhābīs do not consider it idolatry to plaster up pictures of their kings and celebrate anniversaries and jubilees of their State.

[1169] Through non-Muslim money and arms.

[1170] Abū Zahra, *Tārīkh al-Madhāhib al-Islamiyya* (p. 235-238).

refutation of the Wahhābī sect in print, consisting in over forty-five concise chapters spanning 120 pages that show beyond doubt the fundamental divergence of the Wahhābī school, not only from the Consensus and *uṣūl* of *Ahl al-Sunna wal-Jamā'a* and the *fiqh* of the Ḥanbalī *madhhab*, but also from their putative Imāms, Ibn Taymiyya and Ibn al-Qayyim on most or all the issues reviewed.[1171] The last point shows the fundamental dishonesty of Salafism toward the very Imāms they claim as their true link to the *Salaf*. Other literature on that sect includes Sayyid 'Alawī ibn Aḥmad ibn al-Ḥasan ibn al-Quṭb 'Abd Allāh al-Ḥaddād's *Miṣbāḥ al-Anām fī Radd Shubuhāt al-Bid'ī al-Najdī al-Latī Aḍalla bihā al-'Awāmm* ("The Lamp of Mankind in Refuting the Insinuations Used by the Innovator from Najd to Misguide the Public" [1216]); Sayyid 'Abd Allāh ibn Ḥasan ibn Faḍl Bā 'Alawī's *Ṣidq al-Khabar fī Khawārij al-Qarn al-Thānī 'Ashar* ("The Truthful News Concerning the Khārijīs of the Twelfth Century"); Ḥasan ibn 'Umar ibn Ma'rūf al-Shaṭṭī al-Ḥanbalī's (1205-1274) *al-Nuqūl al-Shar'iyya fil-Radd 'alāl-Wahhābiyya* ("The Legal Texts that Refute the Wahhābīs"); Sayyid Aḥmad ibn Zaynī Daḥlān's (d. 1304) *al-Durar al-Saniyya fil-Radd 'alā al-Wahhābiyya* ("The Resplendent Pearls in Refuting the Wahhābīs"); Ibrāhīm al-Samannūdī al-Manṣūrī's (d. 1314) *Sa'ādat al-Dārayn fil-Radd 'alā al-Firqatayn al-Wahhābiyya wal-Ẓāhiriyya* ("The Bliss of the Two Abodes in the Refutation of the Two Sects: Wahhābīs and Ẓāhirīs"); Shaykh Salāmat al-'Azzāmī's (d. 1376) *al-Barāhīn al-Sāṭi'a fī Radd Ba'ḍ al-Bida' al-Shā'i'a* ("The Radiant Proofs in Refuting Certain Widespread Innovations"); and al-Ḥabīb Zayn al-'Ābidīn Āl Sumayṭ al-'Alawī's *al-Ajwiba al-Ghāliya fī 'Aqīdat al-Firqat al-Nājiya* ("The Precious Replies Concerning the Doctrine of the Saved Group").

***walī*, pl. *awliyā'*:** Friend of Allāh; Saint.

***wuḍū'*:** Minor ablution resulting in ritual purity that allows one to pray, read from or touch the *muṣḥaf* or volume of the Qur'ān, circumambulate the Ka'ba, and is recommended for raising

[1171] The *Faṣl/Ṣawā'iq* received the following editions: [1] Bombay: Maṭba'a Nukhbat al-Akhbār, 1306/1889; [2] Cairo; [3] Istanbul: Ishik reprints at Wakf Ihlas, 1399/1979; [4] (Unannotated) Damascus, 1418/1997 (*al-Ṣawā'iq*); [5] (Annotated) Damascus, 1420/1999 (*Faṣl*).

adhān and other devotional acts, all provided one is not ***junub***.

zāhid, pl. ***zuhhād:*** Ascetic; Ṣūfī. See ***zuhd.***

ẓāhir, pl. ***ẓawāhir:*** Outward, external, plain, literal, obvious, patent. Sometimes opposed to and sometimes identical with ***ḥaqīqī***, "real," "literal" as opposed to *majāzī*, "metaphorical." "The external wording (*ẓāhir al-lafẓ*) is whatever jumps to mind, whether literal or metaphorical." (Ibn Qudāma, *Dhamm al-Ta'wīl*). *Al-Ẓāhir*: the All-Victorious; the Manifest.

Ẓāhiriyya: Name of a defunct ***Madhhab*** founded by the former Shāfi'ī Dāwūd ibn Khalaf, notorious for taking the outward understanding of the Qur'ān and Sunna to extremes and rejecting the validity of analogy (*qiyās*). Its most brilliant adherent was the erudite, acerbic Andalusian Ibn Ḥazm, formerly a Mālikī then a Shāfi'ī, among whose many contradictions is his rabid anti-Ash'arism and anti-Madhhabism although he is an Ash'arī in his interpretation of the Divine Attributes and he ridicules *lā-madhhabīs* in his *Risāla fil-Imāma.*

zindīq, pl. zanādiqa: Lit. Mazdean. Free-thinker, atheist, heretic guilty of *zandaqa* such as most of the ***Ghulāt*** and the manufactured modern sects and movements of the Qādiyānīs, Babis and Bahais, "Qur'ān-onlys," "Progressives" and others.

zuhd: Simple living; detachment from the world; "doing-without"; asceticism. The attribute of the ***zāhid.*** "Freedom of the heart from whatever the hand does not possess" (al-Junayd).

رَبِّ أَوْزِعْنِيٓ أَنْ أَشْكُرَ نِعْمَتَكَ ٱلَّتِيٓ أَنْعَمْتَ
عَلَيَّ وَعَلَىٰ وَٰلِدَيَّ وَأَنْ أَعْمَلَ صَٰلِحًا تَرْضَىٰهُ وَأَصْلِحْ لِي فِي
ذُرِّيَّتِيٓ ۖ إِنِّي تُبْتُ إِلَيْكَ وَإِنِّي مِنَ ٱلْمُسْلِمِينَ

O my Lord, arouse me to be thankful for Your favour
with which You have favoured me
and my parents,
and to do good that shall be pleasing unto You,
and be gracious unto me in my children.
Lo! I repent ever unto you.
Lo! I am of those who surrender unto You.
(46:15)

أَنتَ وَلِيِّۦ فِي ٱلدُّنْيَا وَٱلْءَاخِرَةِ ۖ تَوَفَّنِي
مُسْلِمًا وَأَلْحِقْنِي بِٱلصَّٰلِحِينَ

You are my Protecting Friend
in the world and the Hereafter.
Make me to die submissive (*unto You*),
and join me to the righteous.
(12:101)

This is the end of the book *The Four Imāms and Their Schools: Abū Ḥanīfa, Mālik, al-Shāfiʿī, Aḥmad* – Allāh be well-pleased with them and grant them the highest ranks in Paradise! – by the weak servant in need of His Lord's forgiveness, al-Ḥājj Gibrīl ibn Fouād Ḥaddād. The final text was completed on al-Khamīs 27 Dhūl-Qiʿda 1423, Thursday 30 January 2003 on Mount Qāsyūn, Damascus – Allāh protect her! There is no change nor might except by Allāh, Exalted, Almighty. May Allāh send the most abundant and fragrant blessings and greetings of peace upon His Messenger, our Master Muḥammad, and upon his Family and Companions. Praise belongs to Allāh, first and last, inwardly and outwardly, the Lord of the Worlds!

INDICES

Index Of Qur'ānic Verses 476
Index of Ḥadīths 477
Index Nominum 483
Index Operum 509
Index of Topics and Arabic Terms 525
Index of Groups, Sects, and Tribes 532
Index of Places 533
Index of Poetry 535
Bibliography 537

I. Index of Qur'ānic Verses

20:5, 82-83, 153, 167, 219, 263, 291, 352, 370, 374
1:1, 214
1:2, 82
2:107, 82
2:115, 217
2:117, 233
2:129, 174
2:133, 60
2:166, 396, 403
2:107, 82
2:208, 376
2:209, 376
2:210, 374-376
2:237, 88
2:255, 312
2:269, 197
2:282, 71
3:7, 1, 397
3:31, 90, 403
3:48, 174
3:73, 170
3:85, 50
3:169, 289
3:189, 82
4:43, 215
4:58, 263
4:59, vi
4:122, 383
4:162, 397
4:176, 71
5:3, 50
5:6, vi
5:17-18, 82, 383
5:28, 82
5:32, 382
5:40, 82, 382
5:56, 428
5:64, 170, 219
6:45, 82
6:120, 352-353
6:162, 82
7:21, 131
7:54, 82-83, 374
7:73, 83
7:182, 108
7:195, 263
8:70, 88
9:6, 414
9:24, 254
9:100, 156
10:2, 89-90
10:3, 83
11:37, 170
11:64, 83
11:119, 382
12:95, 72
12:101, 472
13:2, 374
13:8, 121
13:16, 82, 311
14:7, 96
15:75, 96, 248
16:33, 374-375
16:43, vi
16:69, 90
16:106, 312
16:125, 368
16:128, 82-83
17:79, 258
17:80, 352
17:88, 422
17:102, 82
18:14, 82
18:49, 382
19:12, 103, 174
19:65, 82
20:5, see top line
20:39, 170
21:2, 311
21:7, vi
21:56, 83
21:79, 171
23:27, 170

25:25, 375
25:59, 374
26:20, 71
28:88, 329
29:49, 418
29:96, 251
30:47, 38
32:4, 320, 374
33:21, 250
33:34, 174
33:57, 61
35:28, 1
37:61, 112
38:1, 311
38:75, 309
38:86, 126
39:9, vi, 368
39:17-18, 156
39:22, 348
39:67, 219
39:74, 112
39:75, 81
40:7, 81-82, 153, 370
40:44, 338, 424
41:42, 422
42:11, 268, 291, 350, 352, 378
42:13, 71
43:63, 174
43:84, 82, 291
46:15, 472
46:25, 311
48:10, 75, 170
48:29, 175
49:2, 194
49:12, 66
50:16, 82
50:29, 383
51:56, 437
52:48, 170
53:32, 271
54:14, 170
56:85, 82
57:4, 82, 371
57:29, 170
58:7, 82
58:11, 1
59:2, 375
59:8-10, 218-219
59:10, 2, 218
62:2, 174
67:1, 88
67:4, 149
67:16-17, 291, 374
68:1, 272
68:44, 108
69:17, 81
71:10-12, 96
72:18, 83
74:48, 64
75:22-23, 181
80:16, 111
83:15, 181
89:22, 374, 377
91:13, 83
(*) 100, 235, 328, 344, 449

II. Index of Ḥadīths

'Abbās is part of me, I of him, 61
Abū Ayyūb was seen resting his face on the grave, 322
Abū Bakr and 'Umar, the two Shaykhs of Islm! ('Alī), 428
Actions count only according to intentions, 100, 235, 328, 344, 349
Actions count only according to their conclusions, 306
'Alī delayed praying *'aṣr*, 36
'Alī is the most knowledgeable about the Sunna ('Ā'isha), 94
Allāh brighten the face..., 328
Allāh created Ādam in his image, 170, 211f., 262, 406

Allāh created Ādam in the image of the Merciful, 213
Allāh ﷻ did not create anything greater than the verse of the Throne, 312
Allāh has servants who know signs, 248
Allāh have mercy on someone who prays, 36
Allāh is above His/the Throne, 350-352
Allāh make radiant the face of one…, 281
Allāh make your grandfather happy!, 11
Allāh makes every maker and his making, 418
Allāh multiplies reward for the barefoot, 360
Allāh sends at the onset of every 100 years, 188
Allāh was when there was nothing else, 312
Allāh wrote the Reminder, 312
And I bear witness to the same, 221
As long as one adduces the meaning, let him narrate it, 138
As long as you do not make licit the illicit, 137
Ask me, ask me! ('Alī), 94
Balance is in the hand of the Merciful, 88
Banū Hāshim and Banū 'Abd al-Muṭṭalib are but one, 186
Be content with what Allāh allotted you, 85
Beautify your manners…, 144
Believer is easy and lenient, 173
Believer is guileless and noble, 173
Believer is not given to cursing, 394
Best fast is that of my brother Dāwūd, 287
Best of you is the one who learnt the Qur'ān, 107
Between heaven and earth is a distance, 351
Beware the vision of the believer, 248
Bilāl, do not fear parsimony, 388
Companions used to place their hands on the pommel, 177, 321, 355, 390
Could they not ask if they knew not?, vii
Cursing a Muslim is like killing him, 394
Degenerate fashion? ('Umar ﵁), 392
Differences are a mercy, 164, 295-296
Divorce of the coerced is void, 159-160
Do not harm the living by insulting the dead, 61
Do not insult our dead, 61
Do not insult the sultan for he is the shadow of Allāh, 293-294
Do not laugh much, 85
Do not lie about the Messenger of Allāh! (Ibn'Umar), 130
Do not swear!, 241
Do you bear witness there is no God but Allāh?, 290
Do you know the right owed to Allāh, 40
Do you know who is the best in belief?, 442
Do you pray the Five Prayers? 290
Draw near, Banū Farrūkh! (Abū Hurayra), 7
Earth will never lack forty men…, 85
Energy of the Ulema is care and help, 201
Every deed of a human being is for himself, 287
Faith has seventy-odd branches,

265, 297
Forbidden to the Fire is every gentle..., 172
Four types will have excuses on the Day of
Resurrection, 288
Free her, for she is a believer, 48, 237, 290
Generations yet in the loins of men shall come after me, 443
Gibrīl ﷺ was seen in the image..., 178
Go make pilgrimage with your wife, 270
Go to 'Umar and give him my greeting, 323
Guard yourself from prohibited matters, 85
Has any of you ever recited anything (Wāthila), 138
Has any of you stood in prayer at length
(Makḥūl), 139
He ﷻ spoke to Mūsā directly ('Alī), 372
He came to teach you your religion, 50
He for whom Allāh desires immense good, 91, 197
He is trying to teach us the Sunna! ('Alī), 36
He repented with a repentence such..., 13
He who starts something good in Islām..., 27
Heart of the believer lies between two fingers, 88, 309
Hellfire will keep asking: "Is there more?", 89
His father is not alive (Baḥīrā), 60
I admonish you to approach Allāh, 312
I am the Prophet, this is no lie..., 60
I came to see the Prophet ﷺ while his Companions, 297
I can almost see Mūsā placing his fingers in his ears, 270
I did not mean to prohibit that one not narrate verbatim, 138
I fear for you that you will speak in gatherings... ('Umar), 128
I found his hand ﷺ more fragrant than musk, 298
I hope for everything good, 64
I make glorification according to my ransom (Abū Hurayra), 92
I never ate to satiation (Ibn 'Umar), 241
I passed by as they were insulting you ('Ammār), 312-313
I prayed behind the Messenger ﷺ (Ibn 'Umar), 131
I saw someone the Day of the Trench... ('Ā'isha), 26
I seek refuge in Allāh from a problem... ('Umar), 94
I shall take out of the fire whoever said..., 93
I was ordered to fight people until..., 221
I would dislike it if the Companions did not differ ('Umar ibn 'Abd al-'Azīz), 295
Ibn Mas'ūd delayed praying *'aṣr*, 36
Ibn 'Umar would place his hand on the *minbar*, 322, 408
If a trustworthy source tells us of a *fatwā*... (Ibn 'Abbās), 94
If clouds appear towards the sea, 144
If I did not fear Quraysh's tyranny..., 187-188
If the Emigrants are satisfied..., 396
If you fight your brother, avoid..., 262
If you hear a ḥadīth reported from me which your hearts

recognise, 194
If you pass by a town that does not have a sultan, 293
If you race with each other, 360
If you were to dangle a man with a rope, 85
In truth I do not forget, 143
Invoke abundant blessings upon me, 442
Is he at all insane? 13
Islām is built upon five [pillars], 219
It may be one carries understanding without... 197-198, 281
Justice for a moment is better than sixty years of worship, 295
Killing a Muslim is forbidden except..., 100
Kursī is where the two feet are placed (Ibn 'Abbās), 317
Lawful is clear as day, 344
Let no-one speak publicly except..., 127
Let there be neither harm done nor reciprocated, 345
Let your reliance be upon transmitted reports (Ibn al-Mubārak), 113
Likeness of my Companions is like salt, 87
Love for people whatever you love for yourself, 85
Make them memorize the ḥadīth and make room for them, 444
Man does the deeds of the people of Paradise, 46
Messenger of Allāh ﷺ cursed the men who imitate women, 221
Messenger of Allāh, ask for rain! (Bilāl ibn al-Ḥārith), 322-323
Most of the people of Paradise are the naïve, 172
Most trusting of people is the most truthful(Abū Umāma), 131-132
Mūsā remained for forty nights, 355
My Companions are like the stars, 399
My father and your father are both in the Fire, 56-59
Nearest of people to me on the Day of Resurrection, 442
None dedicates to Allāh forty days except, 249
O Allāh! Do not make any loss of ours..., 171
O Allāh! Guide Quraysh, 186
O Allāh! I am turning to You with Your Prophet, 389
O Allāh, I ask You by the joints of power, 39-40
O Allāh, I ask You by the right of those who ask You, 39
O Transformer of hearts! Make firm our hearts, 88
One day in the life of a just leader is better than sixty years of worship, 295
One waiting for the next prayer is in the greatest soldiery (*al-ribāṭ al-akbar*), 461
One who will carry the lightest burden, 360
Only cure to ignorance is to ask, vii
Our Lord ﷻ descends every night, 168
Our Lord descends to the nearest heaven, 267
Paradise says none enters me but the weak, 173
People of Paradise shall enter Paradise naked, 213
People shall set forth from East and West..., 122
Prophetﷺ circumambulated mounted, 122
Prophet ﷺ commanded the sun which lagged, 25

Prophet ﷺ forbade the fasting of all of Rajab, 286
Prophet ﷺ forbade the two self-displays, 177
Prophet ﷺ hastened to pray *ẓuhr* and delayed, 35
Prophet ﷺ prohibited the sale of surplus water, 122
Prophet ﷺ slaughtered a cow on behalf of 'Ā'isha, 122
Allah have mercy on someone who hears a ḥadīth, 282
Prophet ﷺ supplicated until the sun moved back, 24
Prophet ﷺ used to stand up for his daughter, 315
Prophet ﷺ was shown the lifespans..., 143
Prophet ﷺ wore the back-hanging turban-end, 393
Qur'ān was revealed in seven dialects, 138, 397
Recite *Allāhu Akbar* from al-Ḍuḥā to the end, 409
Recite the Qur'ān and ask Allāh with it, 128
Religion is nothing but sincere faithfulness, 345
Safest of you against the disasters of the Day, 443
Seek knowledge even as far as China, 256
Seeking knowledge is an obligation, 256
Should we not prostrate to you? 391
Similitude of the hypocrite..., 129
Stand for your chief, 315
Subḥānak Allāhumma wa-bi-ḥamdik, 342
Sultan is the shadow of Allāh on earth, 293-294
Take care of what you say, 47
There is no harm as long as he adduces the meaning, 138
There shall come after me a people, 444
There will be a light for those who grow old, 428
They began to kiss his hand ﷺ, 298
They both have immense goodness, 238
They shall believe in me without seeing me, 443
Thigh is nakedness, 102
This is Gibrīl ﷺ, he ordered me, 26
This is our practice with the *Ulema* (Ibn'Abbās), 320
This is the hand that touched the hand(Thābit), 391
This is true *ribāṭ!* 461
This son of mine shall achieve..., 60
Thus is knowledge taken away (Ibn 'Abbās), 320
Time shall grow short and knowledge decrease, 269
Treat your neighbour with utmost kindness, 85
Tree-stump ḥadīth, 234
Two different religious communities do not inherit, 384
'Umar assembled the people to pray for rain, 322
Use, for personal opinion, what the ḥadīth expounds to you (Ibn al-Mubārak), 113
Very breath of the person who fasts..., 287
Very soon will people beat the flanks of camels..., 121
We [Banū Hāshim] and they [Banū 'Abd al-Muṭṭalib] are but one, 186
We are Bedouin Arabs (Ḥudhayfa), 139
We hail from the water, 59
Welcome to the beneficiaries of the Prophet! (Abū Sa'īd al-

Khudrī), 444
Were belief to be found at the Pleiades..., 7
Were knowledge hanging at the Pleiades..., 7
What about my lineage? 62
What is the reality of your belief? 47
Whatever I forbade you, avoid, 345
When Allāh speaks to send a revelation, 355
When Allāh spoke to Mūsā ?, 362
When one of you dies and you have settled the earth, 410
When one of you fights, avoid..., 213
Where is Allāh? 75, 289-291
Who am I? 290
Who among the dwellers of the earth, 61
Who is your Lord? What is your religion? 290
Who shall take from me these words and put them into practice? 85
Whoever begs people for money..., 257
Whoever does not know, let him say, 'Allāh knows best!' (Ibn Mas'ūd), 126
Whoever harms my relatives harms me, 62
Whoever holds the reins of someone's mount, 319
Whoever honors the sultan, 294
Whoever in my Community memorises forty, 434
Whoever invokes blessings upon me..., 110, 442
Whoever laughs [during prayer]..., 40
Whoever lies about me willfully..., 132
Whoever likes for men to stand up, 315
Whoever likes for people to stand for him, 315, 388
Whoever makes pilgrimage and does not visit me, 274
Whoever makes pilgrimage then visits me, 274
Whoever says I said something which I did not say, 138
Whoever visits me in al-Madīna, 274
Whoever visits me without any avowed purpose, 273-274
Whoever visits my grave, 273-274
Whoever walks barefoot in Allāh's obedience, 360
Wrestling ḥadīth, 185
Yā Muḥammad! (Blind man ḥadīth), 389
Yā Muḥammadāh! (Bilāl ibn al-Ḥārith), 322
You might see among them men with deeds, 186-187
Your life in comparison to past nations, 34
Your menses are not in your hand, 203
Your mother is in the Fire..., 63
Zamzam water makes true whatever it is drunk for, 259-260

III. Index Nominum

Abān ibn 'Uthmān ibn 'Affān, 142
Abarqūhī, 13
'Abbād ibn 'Abbād, 301
'Abbād ibn Hishām, 87
'Abbād ibn Kathīr, 159
'Abbās al-Dūrī, 307, 317
'Abbās ibn 'Abd Allāh al-Tarqafī, 293
'Abbās ibn 'Abd al-Muṭṭalib, 61, 64, 322, 351
'Abbās ibn al-Faḍl, 327
'Abbās ibn al-Walīd, 99
'Abd Allāh al-Būsnawī, 54
'Abd Allāh ibn 'Abd al-'Azīz al-'Umarī, 123
'Abd Allāh ibn 'Abd al-Ḥākim, 77
'Abd Allāh ibn 'Abd al-Muṭṭalib, 59
'Abd Allāh ibn Aḥmad ibn Ḥanbal, 87, 101-102, 209, 301-303, 308, 323, 346, *354-358*, 360, 387, 390, 392
'Abd Allāh ibn 'Alawī al-Ḥaddād, 80
'Abd Allāh ibn 'Alī, 100
'Abd Allāh ibn 'Āmir ibn Rabī'a, 111
'Abd Allāh ibn 'Āmir ibn Yazīd, 315
'Abd Allāh ibn 'Amr, 88, 238, 259, 284, 287, 351, 428
'Abd Allāh ibn al-Ḥārith, 9
'Abd Allāh ibn Ḥasan Bā 'Alawī, 455, 470
'Abd Allāh ibn Ḥasan ibn al-Ḥasan, 159
'Abd Allāh ibn Ibrāhīm al-Ghifārī, 273
'Abd Allāh ibn Kaysān, 442
'Abd Allāh ibn Munīr, 335
'Abd Allāh ibn al-Mu'tazz (Caliph), 201, 348
'Abd Allāh ibn Nāfi', 169
'Abd Allāh ibn Rāfi' al-Tannūkhī, 239
'Abd Allāh ibn Ṣafwān, 130
'Abd Allāh ibn Ṣāliḥ al-Juhanī, 150, 248
'Abd Allāh ibn Sālim ibn Muḥammad, 440
'Abd Allāh ibn al-Shikhkhīr, 284
'Abd Allāh ibn 'Umar al-'Umarī, 276
'Abd Allāh ibn 'Umar ibn Ḥafṣ, 26
'Abd Allāh ibn Unays, 9
'Abd Allāh ibn 'Utba, 175
'Abd Allāh ibn Wahb, *see* Ibn Wahb
'Abd Allāh ibn al-Zubayr al-'Awwām, 60, 161
'Abd Allāh ibn al-Zubayr al-Ḥumaydī, 209, 325
'Abd al-'Azīz al-Dihlawī, 23
'Abd al-'Azīz al-Uwaysī, 178, 179
'Abd al-'Azīz ibn 'Alī, 13
'Abd al-'Azīz ibn al-Muṭṭalib, 178
'Abd al-A'lā ibn 'Abd Allāh ibn Qays, 295
'Abd al-A'lā ibn Mus-hir, 311
'Abd al-Ḥafīẓ al-Makkī, 387, 389
'Abd al-Ḥamīd al-Ḥimmānī, 107, 119
'Abd al-Ḥamīd ibn Ja'far, 159
'Abd al-Ḥaqq al-Ishbīlī, 275, 435
'Abd al-Karīm Abū Umayya, 9
'Abd al-Karīm ibn Mālik, 73
'Abd al-Majīd ibn Abī Rawād, 9
'Abd al-Mālik al-Maymūnī, 392, 393, 396
'Abd al-Mālik ibn Ziyād, 181
'Abd al-Muṭṭalib, 59-60, 185, 186
'Abd al-Qādir al-Gīlānī, 253, 405, 406, 436
'Abd al-Qādir 'Īsā, 387
'Abd al-Qādir al-Qurashī, 23
'Abd al-Qāhir al-Baghdādī, 65, 76,

79, 155, 189, 283, 300, 384, 398
'Abd al-Qays, 48, 51
'Abd al-Quddūs ibn 'Abd al-Jabbār, 339
'Abd al-Raḥīm ibn Zayd al-'Ammī, 399
'Abd al-Raḥmān ibn Khāqān, 212
'Abd al-Raḥmān ibn Khirāsh, 323
'Abd al-Raḥmān ibn Mahdī. *See* Ibn Mahdī
'Abd al-Raḥmān ibn Mālik, 17
'Abd al-Raḥmān ibn Muḥammad al-Bukhārī, 328
'Abd al-Raḥmān ibn al-Qāsim, 26, 99, 146-148, 150-152, 158, 161, 171,
'Abd al-Raḥmān ibn Ya'mar, 267
'Abd al-Raḥmān ibn Zayd, 281
'Abd al-Raḥmān ibn Ziyād ibn An'um, 238
'Abd al-Razzāq, xx, 9, 31, 36, 41, 48, 86, 87, 110, 111, 122, 125, 173, 204, 205, 290, 306
'Abd al-Ṣamad ibn 'Abd al-Wārith al-'Anbarī, 290
'Abd al-Ṣamad ibn Sulaymān ibn Abī Maṭar, 393
'Abd al-Wāḥid ibn Ādam, 339
'Abd al-Wāḥid ibn Zayd, 86
'Abd ibn Ḥumayd, 47, 399
'Abdān, 28, 137, 139, 321, 328, 444
'Abdān ibn 'Uthmān, 113
'Abdarī, 182, 246
'Abdūs ibn Mālik, 310
'Abīdat al-Salmānī, 400
'Ābidīn ('Abd al-Ghanī), 12
'Ābidīn (Abū al-Yusr), 12, 55
'Ābidīn (Muḥammad, Ibn), 9, 26, 37, 38, 40, 54, 55, 226, 232, 233, 252, 252, 326, 395, 455, 461
Ābirrī, 300
Ābiwardī al-Mutawallī, 299
Abū al-'Abbās al-Aṣamm, 25
Abū 'Abd Allāh al-Ṣūfī, 387
Abū 'Abd al-Raḥmān al-Muqrī, 9
Abū Aḥmad al-Farrā', 439
Abū 'Alī al-Ghassānī, 340
Abū 'Alī al-Naysābūrī, 203, 425
Abū al-'Āliya, 40, 374, 375
Abū 'Amr al-Zujājī, 278
Abū 'Amr ibn 'Alwān, 249
Abū 'Āṣim, 9, 16, 34, 290, 438
Abū 'Ātika al-Baṣrī, 256
Abū 'Awāna, 49, 269, 313
Abū Ayyūb, 249, 277, 322
Abū Bakr al-A'yān, 212
Abū Bakr al-A ṣamm, 78
Abū Bakr al-Marwadhī, 104
Abū Bakr al-Ṣiddīq, 40, 41, 44, 62, 64, 95, 104, 108, 113, 119, 129, 131, 153, 163, 210, 233, 241, 242, 255, 272, 294, 301, 307, 308, 322, 339, 391, 396, 405, 428, 449, 461, 463, 466
Abū Bakr al-Wāsiṭī, 46
Abū Bakr ibn 'Abd al-Ra ḥmān ibn al- Ḥārith, 155
Abū Bakr ibn Abī 'Amr, 338
Abū Bakr ibn Muḥammad ibn 'Āṣim, 183
Abū Bakr ibn Ziyād, 439
Abū Bakrah, 294
Abū al-Dardā', 134, 136, 157, 201, 281, 428
Abū Dāwūd, vii, xvii, xx, 7, 21, 26, 35, 60, 100, 102, 107, 127, 168, 173, 185, 188, 198, 202, 208, 211, 214, 221, 253, 263, 281, 286, 290, 298, 301, 315, 316, 321, 326, *343-346*, 350, 351, 360, 384, 428, 441, 448, 449, 460, 463, 464, 467
Abū Dharr, 85, 144, 157, 249,
Abū Dharr al-Harawī, 271, 361
Abū al-Fatḥ al-Qawāsī, 271
Abū al-Fatḥ ibn Abī al-Fawāris, 271
Abū Ghaylān Sa'd al-Shaybānī, 295
Abū Ghudda ('Abd al-Fattāḥ), 9, 42, 44, 45, 74, 123-125, 140, 145, 157,

159, 169, 179, 181, 188, 192, 199, 204, 205, 256, 273-275, 282, 303, 305, 307, 334, 383, 400, 426, 427, 438-441
Abū Ḥafṣ al-Muṭawwi'ī, 253
Abū Ḥafṣ al-Ṣaghīr, 65
Abū Ḥāmid al-A'mashī, 419
Abū Ḥamza al-Ṣūfī, 387-388
Abū Ḥātim, 39, 94, 169, 208, 248, 274, 372, 375
Abū Ḥayyān al-Ziyādī, 33
Abū Ḥāzim, 15, 277
Abū Ḥumayd al-Anṣārī, 194
Abū Hurayra, 7-8, 25, 40, 62, 85, 92, 121, 122, 129, 134, 137, 168, 173, 177, 186, 188, 201, 211, 213, 248, 257, 262, 269, 282, 287, 288, 290, 293, 295, 297, 329, 345, 355, 376, 389, 397, 399, 404, 428, 455, 461
Abū Isḥāq al-Sabī?ī, 103
Abū Isḥāq al-Shaybānī, 11
Abū Ja'far ibn al-Zubayr, 437
Abū Ja'far ibn Sulaymān al-Minqarī, 310
Abū Jahm, 189-190
Abū Juḥayfa, 298
Abū Khālid al-Aḥmar, 20
Abū Khaythama, 8, 203, 417
Abū Khāzim, 21
Abū Lahab, 59, 62
Abū al-Layth al-Samarqandī, 37, 38, 75, 110
Abū Ma'dān, 290
Abū Mālik, 418
Abū Manṣūr al-Baghdādī. See 'Abd al-Qāhir al-Baghdādī
Abū Mawdūda, 322
Abū Miljaz, 210
Abū Mu'āwiya, 7, 11, 85
Abū Muḥammad al-Juwaynī, 299
Abū Muḥammad Fawrān, 415-416
Abū Muqātil, 68, 75
Abū Muṣ'ab al-Yasārī al-Hilālī. See Muṭarrif
Abū Muṣ'ab al-Zuhrī, 145, 147, 159, 160, 170, 311
Abū Mūsā al-Aṣbahānī, 137
Abū Mūsā al-Ash'arī, 122, 284, 292, 317, 383
Abū Muṭī' al-Balkhī, 18, 56, 75
Abū Muzāḥim al-Khāqānī, 443
Abū Naṣr, 85
Abū Naṣr al-'Ayādī, 79
Abū Naṣr al-Marwazī, 327, 464
Abū Naṣr al-Ṣaffār, 278
Abū Naṣr al-Tammār, 417
Abū Nu'aym al-Aṣfahānī, 7, 31, 39, 40, 47, 62, 86, 87, 92, 93, 109, 121, 133, 159, 164, 165, 167, 173-176, 183, 186, 188, 192, 204, 205, 230, 231, 241, 248-250, 281, 292-296, 300, 302, 320, 355, 360, 372, 385, 428, 439
Abū Nu'aym al-Kūfī, see al-Faḍl ibn Dukayn
Abū Nu'aym al-Taymī, see al-Taymī
Abū Nujayḥ al-Sulamī, 428
Abū Nuṣayra al-'Abdī, 294
Abū Qaḥdham ibn Ma'bad, 186
Abū al-Qāsim al-Azharī, 361
Abū Qāsim al-Rāzī, 278
Abū Qays, 210
Abū Qilāba, 188, 201, 319
Abū Qudāma, 259, 324, 418
Abū Quḥāfa, 64
Abū Ṣāliḥ al-Samān, 323
Abū Sa'īd al-Khudrī, 39, 113, 234, 248, 256, 281, 377, 389, 434, 444
Abū Sa'īd al-Miṣrī, 224, 414
Abū Salama ibn 'Abd al-Raḥmān, 155, 189 290, 398
Abū al-Salṭ al-Harawī, 43
Abū Shāma, 233, 436-438, 450
Abū al-Sha'thā', 401
Abū al-Shaykh, 63, 83, 144, 248, 273, 293, 317, 355, 428

Abū Shujā', 22
Abū Sufyān al-Sa'dī, 9
Abū Sufyān ibn Ḥarb ibn Umayya, 44
Abū Ṭāhir al-Mukhliṣ, 13
Abū Ṭalḥa, 283, 284
Abū Ṭālib ibn 'Abd al-Mu ṭ ṭalib, 52, 56-60, 63, 64
Abū Ṭālib al-Ḥanbalī, 198, 364, 416
Abū Ṭāriq, 85
Abū Tamīma al-Hujaymī, 130-131
Abū al-Ṭayyib al-Ṭabarī, 439
Abū Thawr, 158, 203, 207, 209, 210, *211-213*, 220, 222, 246, 253, 257-258, 262, 307, 325-326, 402, 455
Abū al-Ṭufayl, 9
Abū 'Ubayda ibn al-Jarrāḥ, 295, 322
Abū Umāma, 131, 248, 283, 410, 442
Abū 'Umar al-Kindī, 33
Abū 'Urwa al-Zubayrī, 175
Abū Usayd al-Sā'idī, 194
Abū 'Uthmān al-Maghribī, 174, 278, 465
Abū al-Wafā' al-Afghānī, 13, 15,
Abū Yaḥyā al-Ḥammānī, 9, 311
Abū Ya'lā, xx, 42, 67, 86, 102, 137, 204, 212, 234, 264, 281, 313, 316, 321, 322, 350, 351, *362-363*, 371, 374, 389, 394, 406, 442, 443
Abū Yazīd al-Bisṭāmī, 296
Abū Yūsuf, *10-13*, 14-18, 20, 32, 36, 40, 67, 69, 76, 101, 116, 118, 150, 192, 257, 299, 303, 304, 368, 466
Abū Zahra (Muḥammad), 76, 132, 368, 455, 467, 469
Abū Zayd al-Anṣārī, 439
Abū al-Zinād, 155, 401, 438
Abū al-Zubayr. *See* Muḥammad ibn Muslim al-Azdī
Abū Zur'a, 150, 169, 200, 208, 248, 301, 303, 320, 324, 327, 330, 341, 383, 417, 424
Ādam ﷺ, 60, 211-213, 262,,356, 406
Ādam ﷺ and Eve ﷺ, 131
Ādam ibn Abī Iyās, 328
'Adawī, 180
Adhra'ī, 23
'Adī ibn Thābit, 9
'Affān ibn Muslim, 54, 311
'Āfiyat al-Awdī, 18
Aḥdab (Khaldūn), 186, 248, 292, 317
Aḥmad ibn 'Abd al-Jabbār, 85
Aḥmad ibn 'Abd al-Raḥmān ibn Wahb, 294
Aḥmad ibn 'Abda, 29
Aḥmad ibn Abī Badr, 387
Aḥmad ibn Abī Ghālib, 13
Aḥmad ibn Abī 'Imrān, 15, 21, 208
Aḥmad ibn Abī Rajā', 15
Aḥmad ibn 'Alī ibn Sa'īd, 30
Aḥmad ibn al-Faḍl, 327
Aḥmad ibn Ḥafṣ, 325
Aḥmad ibn Ḥamdūn, 330
Aḥmad ibn al-Ḥasan al-Tirmidhī, 310
Aḥmad ibn al-Ḥasan ibn 'Abd al-Jabbār, 387
Aḥmad ibn Ḥumayd, 416
Aḥmad ibn 'Īsā al-Khashshāb, 295
Aḥmad ibn Isḥāq al-Abarqūhī, 13
Aḥmad ibn Isḥāq al-Ṣibjī, 385
Aḥmad ibn Manṣūr al-Shīrāzī, 425
Aḥmad ibn Mas'ūd al-, 67
Aḥmad ibn Muḥammad ibn Hārūn. *See* al-Khallāl
Aḥmad ibn al-Mun'im, 390
Aḥmad ibn Muṣṭafā al-'Umarī, 56
Aḥmad ibn Naṣr, 311, 335
Aḥmad ibn Qāsim al-'Abbādī, 258
Aḥmad ibn Ṣāliḥ, 25, 147, 199, 235
Aḥmad ibn Salama, 337, 421, 424, 425

Aḥmad ibn Salmān ibn al-Ḥasan. *See* al-Najjād
Aḥmad ibn Sinān, 440
Aḥmad ibn Ya'qūb al-Thaqafī, 278
Aḥmad ibn Yūnus, 109, 111, 430
Aḥmad Riḍā Khān, 391
Aḥnaf ibn Qays, 86
Ā'isha bint 'Ajrad, 9
Ā'isha bint al-Ṣiddīq, 26, 53, 60, 64, 94, 100. 115, 122, 134, 140, 155, 203, 277, 282-284, 286, 315, 389
Ā'isha bint Yūnus, 274
A'mash, 16, 85, 198, 202, 210, 437, 443
Ahdal, 360, 441
'Ajāj al-Khaṭīb (Muḥammad), 116, 256, 319
'Ajlūnī, 26, 87, 91, 109, 164, 172, 188, 249, 256, 274, 295, 296
Ājurrī, 169, 231, 282, 343, 350, 351
Akhfash, 375
'Alā'ī, 125, 268
'Alawī ibn 'Abbās al-Mālikī, 115
'Alawī ibn Aḥmad al-Ḥaddād, 470
Albānī (Nāṣir), 39-40, 63, 92, 102, 169, 205, 224, 276, 323, 350, 355, 400, 401, 468
'Alī al-Ḥajjār, 178
'Alī ibn 'Abd Allāh al-Baṣrī, 316, 418, 440
'Alī ibn 'Ubayd Allāh al-Lughawī, 255
'Alī ibn Abī Ṭālib, 9, 24, 36, 41, 44, 64, 72, 74, 77, 86, 93, 94, 100, 102, 107, 108, 157, 159, 185, 186, 195, 272, 369, 372, 428, 449, 450, 451, 462
'Alī ibn Aḥmad al-Fārisī, 68
'Alī ibn al-Aqmar, 9
'Alī ibn al-Ḥasan ibn Shaqīq, 113
'Alī ibn al-Ḥusayn al-Daqīqī, 347
'Alī ibn al-Ḥusayn ibn 'Alī, 421
'Alī ibn al-Ḥusayn ibn Shaqīq,
'Alī ibn al-Ja'd, 11
'Alī ibn al-Madīnī. *See* Ibn al-Madīnī
'Alī ibn Bakkār, 100
'Alī ibn Ḥarmala, 12
'Alī ibn Ma'bad, 33
'Alī ibn Maymūn, 206
'Alī ibn Mus-hir. 9, 18
'Alī ibn Muslim, 11
'Alī ibn Shaybān, 35
'Alī ibn Zayd, 85
'Alī ibn Ziyād, 150
'Allūsh ('Abd al-Salām), 157
Alma'ī, 75
'Alqama ibn Abī 'Alqama, 125
'Alqama ibn Marthad, 9, 13, 87, 99, 104, 118
'Alqama ibn Qays, 400
Alūsī (Nu'mān), 59, 454
Amāra ibn Juwayn, 455
Āmina bint Wahb, 63
Amīr al-Kabīr, 183
'Āmir ibn 'Abd Allāh ibn al-Zubayr, 161
'Āmir ibn 'Abd Qays, 388
'Āmir ibn Rabī'a al-'Anzī, 111
'Āmir ibn Wāthila, 9
'Ammār ibn Yāsir, 62, 312
'Amr ibn 'Alī, 30, 301, 316
'Amr ibn Abasa, 428
'Amr ibn Abī 'Amr, 11
'Amr ibn Abī al-Miqdām, 94
'Amr ibn Abī Salama, 102
'Amr ibn al-'Āṣ, 157
'Amr ibn al-Ḥārith, 199
'Amr ibn Dīnār, 134, 139
'Amr ibn Murra, 134
'Amr ibn Sawwād, 234
'Amr ibn Shu'ayb, 99
'Amrāwī and Murād, 55
Anas ibn Mālik, 8-9, 39, 42, 50, 83, 85, 87, 88, 89, 93, 134, 136, 172, 234, 248, 249, 256, 274, 281, 293, 388, 389, 391, 399, 428, 443
Anas ibn Sīrīn, 204

Anbārī (Abū al-Ḥasan Muthannā ibn Jāmi'), 349, 372
Anbārī (Abū Ya'qūb Isḥāq ibn Bahlūl), 313
Anmāṭī (Abu al-Qāsim), 253
'Ārif Ḥikmat, 57, 68
Arna'ūṭ, 21, 24, 39, 56, 59, 60, 78, 86, 102, 121, 150, 169, 170, 194, 201, 202, 230, 248, 264, 264, 266, 281, 282, 294, 306, 311, 350, 356, 389, 442
Asad (Ḥusayn), 87, 443
Asad ibn 'Amr, 9, 17, 150, 303
Asad ibn al-Furāt, 145, *150*
Aṣbagh, 147, *151*
Ash'arī (Abū al- Ḥasan), 45-47, 53, 58, 64, 65, 67-69, 76-80, 84, 209, 221, 254, 267, 270, 271, 278, 281, 283, 284, 291-293, 310, 349, 362, 262, 365-367, 369, 370, 372-375, 380, 382, 383, 405-407, 414, 423, 425, 446, 447, 451, 462, 471
Ash'ath ibn Barāz, 293
Ashhab, 146-*148*, 150-152, 178
Ashja'ī, 106
Ashqar ('Umar ibn Ḥafṣ), 328
Ashqar (Muḥammad Sulaymān), 380-382
Aṣīlī, 304
'Āṣim ibn 'Iṣām al-Bayhaqī, 393
'Āṣim ibn 'Ubayd Allāh, 111
'Āṣim ibn 'Umar ibn Qatāda, 142
'Āṣim ibn Abī al-Nujūd, 9
'Āṣim ibn Sulaymān al-Aḥwal, 132
'Askarī, 48, 91
Asmā' bint 'Abd al-Raḥmān, 93
Asmā' bint 'Umays, 24, 25
Aṣma'ī, 317
Aswad, 104, 118
Aswad ibn Sarī', 288
'Aṭā' al-Khaffāf, 108
'Aṭā' al-Khurāsānī, 99, 125, 133
'Aṭā' ibn Abī Rabāḥ, 9, 32, 73, 93, 99, 177, 195, 399
'Aṭā' ibn al-Sā'ib, 11, 443
'Aṭā' ibn Yasār, 377
Athram, 150, 176, *341-342*, 370, 402, 452
'Aṭiyya ibn Sa'd al-'Awfī, 248
'Aṭiyya ibn Sa'īd, 9
'Awn ibn 'Abd Allāh ibn 'Utba, 290
'Awwāma (Muḥammad), 116, 165, 192, 199, 200, 205, 397, 452
Awzā'ī, 12, 14, 29, 30-32, 41, 78, *98-103*, 104, 125, 146, 161, 164, 174, 215, 257, 303, 326, 331, 384, 397, 401, 414, 442, 455
Ayādī. *See* Abū Naṣr al-'Ayādī
'Aydarūsī, 440
'Aynī, 21, 23, 37, 91
'Ayyāsh al-Qaṭṭān, 306
A'ẓamī (Ḥabīb al-Raḥmān), 218
A'ẓamī (Muḥammad Muṣṭafā), 331
'Aẓīm Ābādī, 12, 51, 53, 188, 393
Āzar, 59
Azdī, 87, 181, 189
'Azzāmī (Salāmat), 470
Bā 'Alawī ('Abd Allāh), 455
Ba'lī, 407-410, 412
Bābartī, 22
Bābūr, 315
Badī' al-Zamān al-Hamadhānī, 279
Badr al-Dīn al-Ḥasanī, 285
Bāghandī, 321
Baghawī, 39, 50, 86, 87, 91, 102, 167, 168, 208, 211, 259, 270, 281, 299, 301, 316, 320, 321, 326, 337, 393, 442, 444
Baḥīrā, 60
Bāhilī, 81
Bajawī, 399
Bājī (Abū al-Walīd), 147, 170, 271
Bājūrī, 54, 55, 221, 256
Bakkār ibn Qutayba
Bakr al-'Ammī, 15
Bakr ibn 'Abd Allāh al-Muzanī, 342
Bakr ibn al-Ḥasan, 249
Bakr ibn Khunays, 239

Bakr ibn Munīr, 337, 338
Bālī al-Madanī, 54
Bānī, 192
Baqī ibn Makhlad, 321
Bāqir. *See* Muḥammad ibn 'Alī
Baqiyya ibn al-Walīd, 99, 397
Barbahārī, 342, 349, *358-359*, 395, 396
Bardha'ī, 150, 182
Barghūth, 78, 369
Bāriqī, 33
Barzanjī, 54, 63, 395
Baṣīr (Muṣṭafā), 45
Bashīr ibn al-Nu'mān, 282
Battī, 16, 42, 45, 69, 74
Bayāḍī, 65, 67, 68, 76, 76, 79
Bayḍāwī, 60, 80
Bayhaqī-, 7, 22, 39, 40, 48, 59, 64, 78, 85, 90, 92, 98, 100-102, 113-115, 121, 138, 143, 144, 159, 167-169, 172-175, 177, 179, 186, 188, 189, 192, 197, 199, 209, 213 214, 216, 217, 220-224, 229235, 237, 238, 248, 253, 256, 259, 262, 273-275, 277, 281-283, 285-287, 289-293, 295-299, 302, 311, 312, 315, 317, 318, 320, 323-325, 329, 330, 344, 348, 351, 355, 369, 373-375, 377, 389, 393, 399, 400, 403, 413-415, 418, 425, 428, 432, 435, 442
Bazzār, 25, 42, 47, 58, 86, 87, 100, 172, 194, 214, 248, 273, 281, 327, 346, 350, 389, 399, 400, 428, 443
Bewley ('Ā'isha), 123
Bīkandī, 329, 330
Bilāl al-Ḥabashī. *See* Bilāl ibn Rabāḥ
Bilāl al-Khawwāṣ, 404
Bilāl ibn al-Ḥārith, 277, 322-323
Bilāl ibn Rabāḥ, 157, 277, 388-389
Bilāl ibn Sa'd, 99
Bishr al-Ḥāfī, 104, *314-316*, 388
Bishr al-Marīsī, 78
Bishr ibn al-Walīd, 11
Buhlūl ibn Rāshid, 150
Buhūtī, 182, 277, 322, 389, 407-410, 412
Bukayr ibn Ma'rūf, 119
Bukhārī, 7, 26, 31, 33, 35, 42, 44-46, 48, 49, 59, 60, 62, 64, 69, 78, 89, 93, 100, 107, 112, 114, 124, 126, 132, 138, 140, 142, 145, 159, 168, 169, 186, 190, 196, 197, 202, 203, 211, 213, 219, 221, 231, 234 237, 239, 244, 246, 248, 257-260, 262, 269, 270, 273, 278-280, 284, 286, 287, 293, 298, 301, 303, 306, 312, 316, 318, 321, 323, *325-340*, 345, 346, 355, 359, 362, 364, 376, 377, 402, 414-421, 424, 425, 435, 439, 442, 449, 452, 457, 458, 460, 463, 464-466
Bulqīnī, 430
Bundar, 463
Burayda, 13, 234
Burhān al-Dīn al-Ḥalabī, 25, 280
Būṣīrī (Shihāb al-Dīn), 39, 239, 259
Būshanjī, 278
Būṭī, 381, 383, 395, 403, 413, 415
Buwayṭī, 179, *207*, 209, 223, 242, 253, 311, 402
Ḍaḥḥāk, 16, 121, 230, 292, 399
Ḍaḥḥāk ibn Qays al-Shaybānī, 66
Ḍamra ibn Rabī'a, 331
Ḍamura ibn Ḥabīb, 411
Ḍiyā' al-Dīn al-Khaṭīb, 254
Dabbūsī, 16, 304
Daḥlān (Aḥmad ibn Zaynī), 53, 64, 470
Damīrī, 395
Dānī (Abū 'Amr), 467
Dāraquṭnī, 8, 9, 15, 31, 36, 39, 40, 125, 147, 168, 253, 259, *270-277*, 280, 290. 293, 314, 317, 326, 332-335, 353, 359, 361,

369, 399, 428, 439, 442, 452
Darāwardī, 94, 124, 151, 154, 193, 439, 440
Dārimī, vii, 63, 100, 101, 127, 133, 144, 168, 234, 238, 263, 267, 273, 281, 290, 330, 344, 352, 371, 384, 444, 460
Dastawā'ī, 439
Dāwūd ﷺ, 287
Dāwūd al-Jawāribī, 67
Dāwūd al-Ṭā'ī, *18-20*, 116
Dāwūd al-Ẓāhirī, 158, 211, 214, *245-246*, 299, 304, 326, 338, 402, 414, 455, 471
Dāwūd ibn 'Aṭā', 286
Dāwūd ibn Abī Ṣāliḥ, 322
Dāwūd ibn al-Muḥabbar, 293
Dāwūd ibn al-Zibriqān, 239
Dāwūd ibn Khalaf. *See* Dāwūd al-Ẓāhirī
Daylamī, 249, 293-295
Dhahabī, 7, 10-13, 15, 21, 25, 28, 31, 32, 36, 41, 44, 48, 56, 59, 60, 63, 75, 78, 84-88, 92-96, 98, 103, 105-107, 114, 121-123, 132, 135, 140-142, 145, 147, 149, 150, 152-154, 158-161, 164, 165, 167-171, 173, 174, 183, 185, 186, 193, 196, 198-204, 206-208, 210, 212, 214, 220-224, 230,235, 241, 246, 249-251, 253-257, 259, 260, 262-264, 267-272, 274, 276, 277, 279-281, 283, 290, 292, 293, 296, 298, 301,303, 306-310, 312-315, 317, 320, 324, 325, 327, 328, 331, 334, 337, 341, 343, 346, 350-356, 358-362, 364, 371, 383, 385-388, 390, 391, 394, 397, 399, 402, 403, 414, 417, 418, 423-425, 428-430, 434, 439, 440, 443, 444, 447, 449, 450, 463
Dhu'ayb ibn 'Imāma, 122
Dhuhlī, 200, 204, 337, 417, 419, 420, 424, 425, 439, 465
Dhūl-Nūn al-Miṣrī, 145, 309, 346, 381, 388
Diḥya al-Kalbī, 26, 178
Dimyāṭī, 22, 39, 260
Dīnawarī, 253, 260, 313
Dirdīr, 55
Dūlābī, 25, 273, 389
Durra bint Abī Lahab, 62
Durūbī ('Abd al-Wakīl), 369
Faḍāla ibn 'Ubayd, 428
Faḍl ibn al-Rabī', 96
Faḍl ibn Dukayn (Abū Nuʿaym al-Kūfī), 9, 16, 17, 20, 31, 118, 208, 302, 311, 341, 439
Faḍl ibn Mūsā, 440
Fādānī, 238
Fakhr al-Dīn al-Rāzī, 59, 78, 188, 225, 254, 262, 268, 292, 300, 321, 375, 376, 465
Fākihī, 259
Farghānī, 257, 429
Farrāqī, 440
Fārūqī (Shaykh Aḥmad al-Sirhindī), 114
Fasawī, 39
Fāṭima, 93, 277, 315
Fāṭima bint Asad, 39, 185
Fāṭima bint al-Mundhir, 140
Fāṭima bint Qays, 189
Fattanī, 172, 256, 274
Fayrūzābādī, 38, 190, 270
Fazārī, 75, 100, 388
Firabrī, 329, 332, 336, 418, 420
Firahī, 304
Firkah, 429
Firyābī, 112, 210
Fu'ād 'Abd al-Bāqī, 121
Fuḍayl ibn 'Iyāḍ, 104, 112, 148, 230, 314, 444
Fulānī, 145
Funaysān (Sa'ūd), 164
Furānī, 299
Furber (Mūsā), 229
Futūḥī, 407

Gangohī, 395
Ghālib ibn Gibrīl, 339-340
Gharnāṭī, 123
Ghassāni, 275, 340
Ghāwjī, Wahbī Sulaymān, 33, 51-53, 55, 57, 66, 68, 75, 366
Ghawwāṣṣ, 55
Ghaznawī, 22, 206
Ghazzālī, 77, 88, 89, 134, 174, 177, 204, 304, 305, 365, 369, 395, 421, 432
Ghazzī, 12
Ghumārī ('Abd Allāh), 8, 53, 58, 145, 235, 315, 322
Ghumārī (Aḥmad), 8, 41, 86, 94, 249, 256, 272, 275, 294, 295, 360, 399
Ghunaymī, 22
Ghundar, 317
Gibrīl, 26, 48, 51, 83, 133, 178, 360
Ḥabīb al-'Ajamī, 85
Ḥabīb ibn Abī Ḥabīb, 168
Ḥabīb ibn Abī Thābit, 33
Ḥaddād ('Abd Allāh ibn 'Alawī), 80
Ḥaddād ('Alawī ibn Aḥmad), 455, 470
Hādī (Caliph), 12, 163
Ḥāfiẓ (Muḥammad Muṭī?), xix, 26
Ḥāfiẓ al-Dīn al-Kurdī, 394
Ḥafṣ al-Fard, 77, 224
Ḥāfṣ ibn 'Umar, 20
Ḥafṣ ibn Abī Dāwūd al-Qārī, 274
Ḥafṣ ibn Ghyāth, 94, 443
Ḥafṣ ibn Salm, 75
Ḥajjāj, 394
Ḥajjāwī, 389, 407-410, 410
Ḥajjī Khalīfa, 65, 68, 81, 304
Ḥakam ibn 'Utayba, 9
Ḥākim al-Naysābūrī, 36, 39, 60, 63, 75, 85, 88, 100. 102, 117, 121, 171, 173, 188, 193, 214, 217, 221, 223, 230, 234, 243, 256, 259, 260, 262-264, 270, *277-282*, 283-284, 290, 292, 298, 300, 312, 315, 317, 322, 330, 337-340, 351, 353, 359, 360, 375, 393, 418, 424, 425, 428, 443, 444, 452
Ḥakīm al-Tirmidhī, 101, 138-139, 248, 273, 294, 400
Ḥakkām ibn Ya'lā, 7
Hakkārī, 224, 429. 430
Hārūn ibn 'Abd al-'Azīz, 257
Ḥalabī, 399
Ḥalīmī, 221, 270
Ḥamdīs, 152
Ḥāmid ibn Ādam, 28
Ḥāmid Mirzā Khān al-Firghānī al-Namnakānī, 92
Ḥammād al-Anṣārī, 40, 323
Ḥammād ibn Abī Ḥanīfa, 9, 15, 32, 56, 67, 68, 125
Ḥammād ibn Abī Sulaymān, 9, 42, 65
Ḥammād ibn Salama, 30, 59, 64, 269, 290, 373, 401, 439
Ḥammād ibn Zayd, 28, 99, 106, 139, 194, 267, 269, 314, 316, 373, 401, 435
Ḥammāmī (Muṣṭafā), 51, 53, 55
Ḥamza, 466
Ḥamza ibn Abī Ḥamza, 399
Ḥamza ibn Ḥabīb, 9
Ḥamza Yūsuf Hanson, 22, 154
Ḥanbal ibn Isḥāq, 303, 371
Hannād, 249
Ḥannāṭī, 429
Haram ibn Ḥayyān, 121
Harawī al-Anṣārī, 76, 106, 159, 202, 220, 229, 233, 245, 262, 267, 403, 429
Ḥarbī, 24, 307, 317, *353-354*, 360, 361, 402
Ḥarīrī, 65
Ḥārith al-Muḥāsibī, 66, 246, 363, 383-386, 421
Ḥārith ibn Idrīs, 20
Ḥārith ibn Miskīn, 311

Ḥārith ibn Mu'āwiya al-Kindī, 128
Ḥāritha ibn al-Na'mān, 47
Ḥāritha ibn Mālik, 47
Ḥarmala, 147, 231, 233, 307
Ḥasan al-Baṣrī, 9, *84-93*, 134-135, 138-139, 171, 292, 293, 318, 337-338, 365, 369, 401
Ḥasan ibn 'Abd al-'Azīz, 102
Ḥasan ibn 'Alī ibn Abī Ṭālib, 60, 159
Ḥasan ibn 'Alī ibn Khalaf, 342, 358
Ḥasan ibn 'Amāra, 32
Ḥasan ibn 'Amr al-Fuqaymī, 294
Ḥasan ibn 'Umar al-Shaṭṭī, 470
Ḥasan ibn Aḥmad ibn Ḥanbal, 392
Ḥasan ibn Ash'ath, 282
Ḥasan ibn Muḥammad ibn Jābir, 337
Ḥasan ibn Ziyād al-Lu'lu'ī, 16, 18, 41, 65, 117,
Ḥāshid ibn Ismā'īl, 328
Ḥasīb, 257
Ḥaskafī, 37
Ḥaskānī, 25
Ḥassān ibn Thābit, 62
Ḥāṭib ibn Balta'a, 274
Ḥaṭṭāb, 182
Ḥātim ibn Aḥmad, 420
Haytamī, 7, 53, 55, 63, 80, 114, 199, 203, 206, 213, 231, 236, 237, 272, 275, 285, 379, 380, 394, 395, 430
Haytham, 161
Haytham ibn Jamīl, 176
Haythamī, 7, 24, 25, 39, 40, 42, 47, 63, 85, 87, 137, 144, 195, 221, 248, 249, 273, 281, 292, 294, 295, 317, 320, 322, 350, 389, 397, 411, 442, 443
Ḥāzimī, 202
Ḥazm ibn Abī Ḥazm, 87
Heraclius, 49
Hilāl Abū al-'Alā', 388
Hilāl ibn Suwayd, 389
Ḥimyarī ('Īsā), 416
Hiql ibn Ziyād, 99, 401
Hishām ibn 'Abd al-Malik, 78
Hishām ibn 'Urwa, 9, 11, 140-141
Ḥudhayfa ibn al-Yamān, 139, 157, 294, 418
Ḥumayd al-Ṭawīl, 91
Ḥumayd ibn 'Abd al-Raḥmān, 133
Ḥumayd ibn Zanjūyah, 198
Ḥumaydī, 190, 209, 217-218, 325, 464
Ḥurayth ibn Abī al-Warqā', 338-339
Ḥusayn al-Asadī, 300
Ḥusayn al-'Ubaydī, 179
Ḥusayn ibn Aḥmad, 33
Ḥusayn ibn 'Alī ibn Abī Ṭālib, 422
Ḥusayn ibn 'Alī al-Ṣaymarī, 205
Ḥusayn ibn Bashshār, 313
Ḥusayn ibn Muḥammad ibn Aḥmad (Qāḍī Ḥusayn), 270, *298*
Ḥusayn ibn Muḥammad ibn Ziyād, 425
Ḥusayn ibn al-Walīd, 16
Ḥusaynak, 256
Ḥusaynī, 137, 196
Hushaym, 31, 135, 301, 303, 314, 317, 321
Ḥuwayrith 'Abd al-Raḥmān ibn Mu'āwiya, 355
Ibn 'Abbās, 39, 48, 61, 74, 77, 83, 85, 94, 132, 134, 138, 159, 160, 176, 186, 214, 221, 234, 241, 249, 256, 259, 270, 279, 286, 287, 295, 317, 318-320, 345, 355, 360, 369, 375, 399, 443, 466
Ibn 'Abd al-Barr, 10-12, 15, 16, 21, 32, 39, 41, 45, 51, 66, 67, 87, 91, 94, 101, 113, 115, 118, 121, 122, 124, 125, 137, 143-145, 154, 158, 159, 164, 166, 168, 169, 174-177, 179, 181, 182, 185, 188, 192, 195, 197, 199-201, 203, 205, 211, 220, 238,

239, 242, 256, 281, 284, 300, 303-305, 317, 323, 351, 359, 369, 396, 399, 400, 413, 444
Ibn 'Abd al-Ḥakam, 146, 147, *150-151*, 164, 193, 218
Ibn 'Abd al-Hādī (Muḥammad), 182, 275-276
Ibn 'Abd al-Hādī (Yūsuf), 9
Ibn 'Abd al-Qārī, 408
Ibn 'Abd al-Salām, xxiii, 40, 46, 49, 80, 88, 89, 101, 196, 204, 225, 232, 233, 286, 287, 330, 377, 413, 429, 431
Ibn 'Abd al-Wahhāb (Muḥammad), 467-470
Ibn Abī 'Arūba, 16, 30, 401
Ibn Abī 'Āṣim, 16, 24, 62, 175, 186, 246, 281, 292, 294, 295, 321, 350, 351, 389
Ibn Abī 'Aṣrūn, 204, 433
Ibn Abī Awfā, 8, 41
Ibn Abī al-'Awwām, 124
Ibn Abī Dāwūd, 19, 29, 33, 259, 274, 439
Ibn Abī Dhi'b, 104, 401
Ibn Abī Du'ād, 132, 354, 369, 392, 417
Ibn Abī al-Dunyā, 273, 274, 319, 341, 393
Ibn Abī al-Fatḥ, 397
Ibn Abī al-Fawāris, 271
Ibn Abī Ḥātim, 39, 85, 102, 113, 114, 163, 165, 189, 192, 199, 202, 207, 222, 223, 234, 248, 293, 294, 300, 327, 336, 355, 364, 375, 444, 464
Ibn Abī al-Ḥawārī, 387
Ibn Abī al-Hind, 20
Ibn Abī al-'Izz, 23, 38, 42, 269
Ibn Abī Khaythama, 32, 41, 94, 204, 323
Ibn Abī Laylā, 11, 205, 294, 326
Ibn Abī Nujayḥ,, 134
Ibn Abī Sharīf, 54
Ibn Abī Shayba (Abū Bakr), 36, 39, 42, 48, 60, 132, 159, 179, 194, 249, 259, 284, 287, 292, 317, *320-324*, 341, 344, 355, 389, 402, 442
Ibn Abī Shayba (Abū Ja'far), 321, 324
Ibn Abī 'Umar al-'Adanī, 95
Ibn Abī 'Umar al-Ḥanbalī, 430
Ibn Abī Usāma, 295
Ibn Abī Uways, 125, 141, 161, 311
Ibn Abī al-Wafā, 79, 81, 200. 206, 291
Ibn Abī Ya'lā, 45, 78, 86, 176, 211-212, 235, 258, 301, 310, 312, 313, 317, 319, 324, 325, 341, 341, 342, 349, 354, 356, 358-360, *362-363*, 370, 371, 386-389. 393-395, 397, 404, 409, 414-416, 423
Ibn Abī Zā'ida, 18, 31, 301, 319
Ibn Abī Zayd, 159, 170, 178-180, 182, 198, 199, 396
Ibn Abī al-Zubayr, 177
Ibn 'Ābidīn, see 'Ābidīn (Muḥammad)
Ibn 'Adī, 39, 41, 59, 94, 142, 168, 169, 172, 188, 248, 273, 294, 327, 330, 339, 399, 417, 442, 445
Ibn 'Ā'isha, 29
Ibn 'Ajība, 180
Ibn 'Ajlān, 152, 159
Ibn 'Allān, 440
Ibn Amīr al-Ḥajj, 40
Ibn 'Ammār, 430
Ibn 'Aqīl, 313, 389, 405, 407
Ibn 'Arabī (Shaykh Muḥyī al-Dīn), 26, 46, 49, 55, 246
Ibn al-'Arabī al-Mālikī, 61, 115-116, 124, 158, 168, 170, 217, 232, 363, 373
Ibn 'Arrāq, 40, 116, 360, 457
Ibn 'Asākir, 26,40, 63, 78, 94, 98,121, 137, 176, 199, 201, 206, 223, 224, 246, 270, 274, 277,

281, 291, 293, 297, 320, 350, 365, 366, 399, 411, 416, 428
Ibn 'Āshir, 183
Ibn 'Āṣim al-Muqri', 25
Ibn Aṣram, 48
Ibn 'Aṭā' Allāh, 48, 201,
Ibn al-Athīr, 24, 164, 174, 257, 358, 359, 362, 363, 400
Ibn 'Ayyāsh, 104, 443
Ibn Badrān, 386, 408
Ibn Baḥr, 230
Ibn Balbān, 380-381
Ibn al-Bāqillānī, 46, 271, 413
Ibn Bashkuwāl, 182, 397
Ibn Bashshār al-Aḥwal, 257
Ibn Baṭṭa, 150, 267, 346, 361-362
Ibn al-Bayyi'. See al-Hākim
Ibn Bāz ('Abd al-'Azīz), 276, 322-323
Ibn Burayda, 13, 292, 384
Ibn Daqīq al-'Īd, 115, 178, 225, 429, 435
Ibn al-Ḍarīs, 32, 312
Ibn al-Dakhīl, 413
Ibn Dāsa, 343
Ibn Dawyān, 277, 408
Ibn al-Dayba', 440
Ibn Diḥya, 53
Ibn Dīzīl, 440
Ibn al-Dubaythī, 273
Ibn Durustūyah, 346
Ibn Fahd, 196
Ibn Farḥūn, 146, 169, 183, 193, 346
Ibn al-Fatḥ al-'Ishārī, 224
Ibn Fihr, 182
Ibn Fūrāk, 24, 283, 373
Ibn al-Ghiṭrīf, 7
Ibn Ḥabīb, 116, 148, 150, 151
Ibn al-Ḥadhdhā', 25
Ibn Ḥajar al-'Asqalānī, xxiii, 7-10, 13, 21-23, 28, 30, 32, 39, 42, 48, 50, 59, 60, 62, 75, 85-87, 92, 98, 105, 113, 115, 125, 136, 137, 139, 144, 145, 167-169, 172, 173, 185, 186, 188, 193, 200, 201, 204, 224, 233, 235, 237, 238, 248, 249, 255, 259, 260, 263, 264, 266, 268, 269, 273-276, 280, 284, 285, 289, 294, 295, 299, 304, 309, 317, 318, 320, 321, 323, 329, 330, 333-335, 344, 350, 352, 361, 362, 369, 375, 387, 388, 395, 397, 399, 400, 411, 424, 430, 431, 433, 437, 440, 442, 445, 450, 453, 458, 464
Ibn al-Ḥājib, 182, 234, 400
Ibn al-Ḥājj, 233
Ibn al-Ḥamakān, 300
Ibn Ḥāmid, 406
Ibn al-Ḥanbalī, 122
Ibn Ḥārith, 152
Ibn al-Ḥawārī, 241
Ibn Ḥazm, 7, 12, 76, 87, 92, 115, 116, 122, 123, 147, 186, 246, 272, 326, 369, 374, 398-401, 452, 471
Ibn Ḥibbān, 7, 15, 22, 39, 44, 88, 90, 91, 102, 121, 123, 137, 171, 172, 181, 194, 198, 199, 256, 259, 260, *264-269*, 274, 279, 281, 284, 290, 300, 311, 326, 329, 330, 372, 428, 442, 452
Ibn Ḥamdūyah, 277, 330
Ibn Hishām, 59, 60, 216
Ibn Hubayra, 33, 405, 408, 410
Ibn al-Humām, 37, 38, 54
Ibn Hurmuz, 131, 154, 161, 176, 178
Ibn 'Imād, 13, 23, 193, 195, 246, 252, 254, 313
Ibn al-I'rābī, 343
Ibn Isḥāq, 16, 30, 62, 94, 137, 140-142, 350 372, 439
Ibn al-Ja'd, 11, 12
Ibn Jahbal, 92, 93
Ibn al-Jallāb, 182
Ibn Jamā'a (Badr al-Dīn), 366
Ibn Jamā'a (Burhān al-Dīn), 366

Ibn Jamā'a ('Izz al-Dīn), 182, 366
Ibn al-Jārūd, 224
Ibn al-Jawzī, 18, 20, 24, 25, 39, 40, 60, 64, 75, 85, 89-92, 103, 106, 133, 134, 137, 159, 170, 172, 174, 181, 202, 212, 230, 238, 248-251, 256, 263, 264, 270, 271, 274, 280, 281, 301, 308, 310, 313-317, 329, 330, 351, 353, 354, 360, 363, 374, 377, 379, 384, 386, 388, 394, 396, 399, 403-406, 408, 416, 452, 457
Ibn Jurayj, 28, 30, 94, 98, 121, 122, 125, 292, 401
Ibn al-Juwaynī. *See* Imām al-Ḥaramayn
Ibn Juzayy, 182
Ibn Karrām, 76, 454
Ibn Kathīr, 7, 12, 21, 22, 25, 34, 48, 50, 99, 102, 151, 159, 174, 190, 193, 195, 196, 224, 233-235, 248, 249, 253, 255, 257, 259, 263, 279, 290, 300, 311, 317, 323, 333-335, 350, 352, 374, 376, 383-385, 432
Ibn al-Kātib, 33
Ibn Khafīf, 33, 46, 237, 238, 244, 254, 310, 373, 380, 382, 413, 414, 454, 466
Ibn Khallikān, 13, 30, 249, 253, 439
Ibn Khuzayma, 22, 39, 207, 211, 213, 223, 224, 253, 256, *259-264*, 270, 275, 284, 290, 302, 317, 326, 327, 330, 350, 351, 364, 402
Ibn al-Kīzānī, 245
Ibn Kullāb, 211, 246-247, 372
Ibn al-Madīnī, 30, 114, 122, 125, 140, 194, 210, 301, 302, 307, 316, 320, 336, 354, 375, 440
Ibn Maḥmish, 283
Ibn Mahdī, 12, 99, 101, 104, 106, 108, 109, 111-112, 114, 122, 125, 146, 193-195, 203, 205, 317, 318, 326, 328, 439
Ibn Mahdī al-Ṭabarī, 24
Ibn Mahrān. *See* Ibn Abī 'Arūba
Ibn Ma'īn, 10-11, 15, 30-32, 86, 94, 114, 116, 122, 142, 151, 194, 197, 202-205, 248, 301-303, 307, 312, 316, 317, 341, 375, 417, 438, 439, 441, 443
Ibn Mājah, vii, 21, 39, 88, 100, 102, 107, 127, 198, 202, 208, 211, 221, 234, 238, 239, 250, 256, 259, 260, 267, 269, 270, 275, 281, 283, 286, 287, 298, 321, 345, 351, 355, 384, 444, 449, 460, 463
Ibn al-Mājishūn, 147-149, 151-152, 158, 194, 372, 401
Ibn Mākūlā, 39
Ibn Ma'mar, 284
Ibn Mandah, 25, 48, 62, 136-137, 270, 277, 317, 411, 429
Ibn Mardūyah, 25, 137, 355
Ibn Mas'ūd, 8, 36, 40, 63, 85, 100, 126, 134, 136, 138, 157, 172, 176, 186, 201, 215, 256, 281, 312, 344, 351, 355, 361, 389, 442, 444
Ibn al-Mibraḍ See Ibn 'Abd al-Hādī (Yūsuf)
Ibn al-Mu'adhdhal, 148
Ibn al-Mubārak, 16, 28-29, 31, 34, 38, 87, 100, 103, 104, 106, *112-114*, 119, 125, 155, 193, 200, 238, 249, 267, 314, 317, 321, 325, 327, 365, 401, 443
Ibn Mufliḥ, 91, 277, 313, 322, 386-389, 394, 407-410, 412
Ibn al-Mukhalliṣ, 354
Ibn al-Mulaqqin, 85, 164, 314, 411, 442
Ibn al-Mundhir, 63, 312, 355, 375, 402
Ibn al-Munkadir, 93, 125
Ibn al-Muqrī, 300

Ibn al-Musayyab, 86, 94, 137, 155, 162, 283, 313, 369, 398, 401
Ibn al-Muthannā (Aḥmad), 388
Ibn al-Muthannā (Ma'mar), 320
Ibn al-Muthannā (Mu'ādh), 235
Ibn Muzāḥim, 28
Ibn al-Nadīm, 77
Ibn Nāfi', 158
Ibn Nāfi' al-Ṣā'igh, *146*, 152, 169
Ibn al-Najjār, 48, 224, 294, 405, 407-410, 412, 434
Ibn Nāṣir, 405
Ibn Nujayd, 278
Ibn Nujaym, 37
Ibn Numayr, 141
Ibn al-Qāḍī Shuhba, 253
Ibn Qāni', 137
Ibn al-Qaṣṣār, 153
Ibn al-Qāsim, 145, *146-148*, 150-152, 158, 171, 176, 182
Ibn al-Qaṭṭān al-Maghribī, 225 337
Ibn al-Qattāt, 230
Ibn al-Qaysarānī, 256
Ibn al-Qayyim=Ibn Qayyim al-Jawziyya, 92, 102, 106, 111, 114, 115, 141, 195, 209, 229, 243, 250, 251, 259, 351, 357, 369, 398, 399, 411, 454, 470
Ibn Qudāma, 40, 122, 204, 217, 225, 259, 277, 284, 285, 287, 296, 313, 314, 322, 363, 371, 389, 392, 405-412, 422, 471
Ibn Qudāma (Muḥammad), 316
Ibn Qunfudh, 161, 182
Ibn Qutayba, 24, 174, 213, 304, 325-326, 365
Ibn Rāfi', 21-22, 432
Ibn Rāhūyah, 113, 158, 197, 202-294, 208-209, 214, 244, 307, 317, 320, *324-325*, 330-331, 335, 336, 365, 384, 392, 402, 414, 418, 428, 439
Ibn Rajab, 26, 49, 59, 92, 106, 114-115, 131, 136, 199, 202-205, 210, 227, 233, 266, 329, 343, 362, 405, 407, 436, 449
Ibn Rushd, 158, 168, 180, 182
Ibn Sa'd, 60, 64, 92, 94, 141, 144, 160, 164, 292, 296, 320, 322, 388
Ibn al-Sakan, 274, 275, 442
Ibn al-Ṣalāḥ, 98, 115, 124, 139, 145, 166, 225-226, 232, 265, 280, 332-335, 340, 352, 449
Ibn Salām, 330
Ibn Sallām, 14, 24, 91, 190, 194, 244, 258, 295, 307, 317, 319, 325, 375, 402
Ibn Samā'a, 15, 69, 307
Ibn al-Sam'ānī, 51, 429
Ibn Sam'ūn, 466
Ibn Sa'ūd (King), 276, 355, 468-469
Ibn al-Ṣawwāf, 360
Ibn Sayyid al-Nās, 116, 164, 431, 439
Ibn Shaddād, 415
Ibn Shāhīn, 25, 98, 411
Ibn Shujā', 18, 330
Ibn Sīrīn, 32, 99, 125, 132, 134, 136, 204, 401
Ibn al-Subkī, 46, 47, 64-65, 80, 98, 155, 164, 178, 185, 190, 199, 203, 206, 208, 225, 232, 234, 238, 246, 248, 253-254, 258, 259, 263, 264, 268, 281, 285-287, 289, 291, 293, 298, 300, 322, 324, 325, 340, 354, 366, 384, 386, 398, 416, 417, 419, 422-423, 430-433
Ibn al-Sunnī, 39, 249, 389
Ibn Surayj, *252-254*, 257, 259, 402
Ibn Ṭāwūs, 136
Ibn Taymiyya (Taqī al-Dīn), 25, 86, 102, 150, 164, 168, 182, 206, 217, 231, 233, 267, 268, 274-276, 294, 309, 370, 380-381, 384, 389, 407, 416, 453, 467
Ibn Taymiyya (Majd al-Dīn), 305, 322, 407

Ibn Tughrīburdā, 41
Ibn al-Turkmānī (ʿAlī ibn ʿUthmān), 23, 41, 289, 291
Ibn Ukayma, 137
Ibn 'Ulayya, 78, 321
Ibn 'Umar, 35-37, 62, 73, 99, 124, 125, 129-131, 135, 136, 155, 171, 176, 215, 219, 234, 241, 248, 256, 257, 270, 273, 274, 276, 277, 282-284, 294, 322, 346, 390, 393, 398-400, 402, 408
Ibn 'Uqda, 41, 199
Ibn 'Uyayna, 16, 31, 95, 104, 106, 111, 112, 114, 122, 123, 125, 134,158, 197, 198, 201, 205, 209, 211, 218, 219, 260, 265, 296, 301, 312, 316, 317, 437, 438
Ibn Waḍḍāḥ, 151, 152
Ibn Wahb, 26, 31, 78, 104, 125, 145, *147-148*, 151, 158, 166, 167, 170, 174-177, 194, 199, 208, 250, 444
Ibn Yūnus, 21, 432
Ibn al-Zāghūnī, 406
Ibn al-Zamalkānī, 25
Ibn Zubar, 198
Ibrāhīm ﷺ, 59, 85, 327
Ibrāhīm al-Aṣbahānī, 341
Ibrāhīm al-Ḥarbī, 24, 307, 317, *353-354*, 402
Ibrāhīm al-Khawwāṣ, 174, 327
Ibrāhīm ibn Abbān, 211
Ibrāhīm ibn Abī Ṣāliḥ, , 322
Ibrāhīm ibn A'yan, 111
Ibrāhīm ibn Ḥammād, 160
Ibrāhīm ibn Ma'qil, 331
Ibrāhīm ibn Maysara, 136
Ibrāhīm ibn al-Mundhir, 141
Ibrāhīm ibn Mūsā, 441
Ibrāhīm ibn Rustum, 33
Ibrāhīm ibn Sa'd, 301
Ibrāhīm ibn Suwayd, 119
Ibrāhīm ibn Ṭahmān, 9
Ījī, 45, 79, 80
'Ikrima, 91, 99, 134
'Ikrima ibn Abī Jahl, 315
'Illīsh (Muḥammad), 229
Imām al-Ḥaramayn (Ibn al-Juwaynī), 192, 298-299, 335, 413
'Imrān ibn Ḥuṣayn, 128, 157, 311
'Imrān ibn Muslim, 135
'Irāqī (Walī al-Dīn), 8, 86
'Irāqī (Zayn al-Dīn), 22, 39, 61, 115, 116, 134, 145, 172, 188, 206, 214, 234, 256, 269, 399, 430, 432
'Iṣām ibn Yūsuf ibn Maymūn, 68
'Iṣma ibn Abī 'Iṣmat, 416
Iṣṭakhrī, 45, 356
'Īsā ﷺ, 234
'Īsā ibn Abān, 15, 307, 434
'Īsā ibn Abī 'Īsā Māhān, 307
'Isā ibn Miskīn, 152
'Īsā ibn Muḥammad ibn 'Alī, 86
'Īsā ibn Nujayḥ, 360
'Īsā ibn Yūnus, 9
Isbijābī, 429
Isfarāyīnī (Abū 'Awāna), 49
Isfarāyīnī (Abū Ḥāmid), 253, 255-256
Isfarāyīnī (Abū Isḥāq), 238
Isfarāyīnī (Abū al-Muẓaffar), 67-68, 75, 79, 293
Isḥāq al-Shāhidī, 30, 301
Isḥāq ibn 'Abd Allāh ibn al-Ḥārith, 64
Isḥāq ibn Abī Isrā'īl, 13
Isḥāq ibn Ibrāhīm ibn Muṣ'ab, 391
Isḥāq ibn Ja'far al-Ṣādiq, 196
Isḥāq ibn Manṣūr al-Kusaj, 305, 357
Isḥāq ibn Muḥammad al-Ḥākim, 79
Ishāq ibn Rāhūyah, 158
Ismā'īl al-Anṣārī, 200
Ismā'īl al-Qāḍī, 148. 265, 402
Ismā'īl al-Saffār, 271

Ismā'īl ibn Abī Uways, 141, 161, 311
Ismā'īl ibn 'Ayyāsh, 99, 321
Ismā'īl ibn Ḥammād, 9, 15, 18, 32
Ismā'īl ibn Ibrāhīm al-Qarrāb, 300
Isma'īl ibn Isḥāq al-Sarrāj, 385-386
Ismā'īl ibn Muḥammad Sa'īd Safar, 440
Ismā'īl ibn Muslim, 87
Ismā'īl ibn 'Ulayya, see Ibn 'Ulayya
Ismā'īl ibn Umayya, 135
Ismā'īl Mawlā al-Muzaniyyīn, 295
Ismā'īlī (Abū Bakr), 51, 453
Isnawī, 253, 258, 384
'Itr (Nūr al-Dīn), 115, 131, 132, 139, 144, 169, 214, 256, 280, 326, 333-334, 352, 427, 444, 449
'Iyāḍ, *See* Qāḍī 'Iyāḍ
'Iyāḍ ibn 'Amr, 292
Ja'far al-Khuldī, 247, 252
Ja'far al-Ṣādiq. *See* Ja'far ibn Muḥammad ibn 'Alī
Ja'far ibn 'Abd al-Wāḥid, 399
Ja'far ibn Ibrāhīm al-Hadhdhā', 278
Ja'far ibn Muḥammad al-Qaṭṭān, 326
Ja'far ibn Muḥammad ibn 'Alī 41, *93-98*, 125, 134, 161, 196, 414
Ja'far ibn Muḥammad ibn al-Ḥārith, 230
Ja'far ibn Muḥammad ibn Ḥāzim, 65
Ja'far ibn Nuṣayr, 278
Ja'far ibn Sulaymān, 160
Jābir, vii, 25, 39, 122, 138, 172, 234, 256, 281, 399, 400, 428
Jahm ibn Ṣafwān, 453
Jāmi' ibn Sawāda, 168
Jarhad al-Aslamī, 102
Jarīr ibn 'Abd Allāh, 27
Jarīr ibn 'Abd al-Ḥamīd, 31
Jarīrī, 252
Jaṣṣāṣ, 23, 136
Jawharī, 13, 150, 317
Jawraqānī, 137
Jawwāb ibn 'Ubayd Allāh, 399
Jazā'irī (Abū Bakr), 55, 63, 323
Jazā'irī (Ṭāhir), 139
Jazarī, 73, 285
Jazīrī, 59, 178
Jazūlī, 54
Jū'ī, 241
Jubayr ibn Muhammad ibn Jubayr ibn Muṭ'im, 350
Jubayr ibn Muṭ'im, 281, 350
Jubbā'ī, 382
Junayd al-Baghdādī, vii, *246-252*, 383, 385, 387, 471
Jundī, 182, 274
Jurjānī, 65, 155, 189, 274, 294, 387, 398
Juwaybir ibn Sa'īd al-Azdī, 399
Jūzjānī, 15, 79
Ka'b al-Aḥbār, 127, 293, 351, 352, 388
Ka'b ibn Murra, 428
Ka'bī, 81, 247
Kahmas, 443
Kalwadhānī, 405, 412
Karābīsī, 23, 207, 209, *210-211*, 220, 233, 244, 302, 307, 325, 416, 421, 423
Kardarī al-Bazzāzī, 65, 67
Kāsānī, 38, 40
Kattānī (Muḥammad ibn Ja'far), 102, 109, 168, 221, 234, 244, 280, 282, 285, 466
Kawladhānī, 408, 410
Kawsaj, 305
Kawtharī, 7, 12, 18, 21-23, 30, 39, 43-45, 54-58, 65, 67-69, 75, 76, 79, 84, 102, 115, 169, 192, 195, 202, 206, 213, 263, 268, 305, 321, 355, 362, 369, 371, 373-376, 413, 415, 416
Keller (Nūḥ), 133, 356
Khabūshānī, 245
Khaḍir, 404

Khafājī, 182
Khalaf al-Khayyām, 335
Khalaf ibn Khalīfa, 154
Khalaf ibn Sālim, 203
Khalaf ibn Tamīm, 463
Khālid ibn Aḥmad al-Dhuhlī, 338
Khālid ibn Aḥmad al-Ẓāhirī, 246
Khālid ibn al-Walīd, 157
Khālid ibn Zayd, 67
Khālid ibn Khidāsh, 176, 435
Khālida bint Asad, 185
Khalīl ibn Aḥmad, 429, 443
Khalīlī, 75, 192, 208, 322, 323
Khallāl, 65, 132, 176, 181, 201, 209, 305, 341, 342, 358, 370-371, 392, 393, 395, 402
Khārija ibn Zayd, 155, 398
Khārija ibn Mu ṣ'ab, 9, 357
Kharsa ('Abd al-Hādī), 64
Khaṭīb, 7-9, 13, 18, 29-31, 65, 67, 91, 99, 101, 113-114, 116, 121, 134-139, 141, 161, 164, 174, 175, 178, 179, 186, 188, 193, 198, 200-201, 205, 206, 235, 243, 245-246, 248, 250, 254-257, 259, 260, 265, 273, 279, 281, 292, 296, 302-303, 307, 313, 317, 319-320, 324, 326-328, 341, 343, 346, 348, 353, 354, 360-361, 375, 385-389, 399, 402, 423, 431, 441-444
Khaṭṭābī, 24, 49, 50, 89, 90, 127, 143, 295, 343, 359, 372
Khazrajī, 439
Khiraqī, 360, 407, 409, 410
Khuraybī, 29, 443
Khushanī, 182
Khwārizmī (Muwaffaq al-Dīn), 65
Kirmānī, 37, 237
Kisā'ī, 466
Kiyā, 405, 434
Kumushkhānawī, 37
Kuzbarī, 12
Lacknawī, 9, 37, 41, 45, 78, 79, 115, 159, 199, 231, 275, 289, 395, 400
Laḥḥām (Badī'), 334
Laḥjī, 393
Laḥmar (Ḥamīd), 171
Lakhmī,, 158
Lālikā'ī, 41, 51, 64, 78, 150, 167, 171, 283, 310, 351, 369, 371, 420
Laoust (Henri), 405
Laqānī, vii, 440
Layth ibn Abī Sulaym, 444
Layth ibn Sa'd, 29-31, 123, 147-148, 150-151, 156-157, 159, 193, 199, 296, 401, 455
Maghāzilī, 387, 389
Maghnīsāwī, 68-69, 459, 460
Maḥmūyah, 15
Mahdawī, 171
Mahdī (Caliph), 12, 162-165
Mā'iz ibn Mālik, 13
Makdisī (George), 405
Makḥūl, 32, 99, 138, 139, 249, 442
Makhzūmī (Muḥammad Taysīr), xix
Makram ibn Aḥmad, 206
Mālik al-Dār = Mālik ibn 'Iyāḍ
Mālik ibn 'Iyāḍ, 322-323
Mālik ibn Mighwal, 14, 17
Ma'mar, 30, 31, 87, 290, 401
Mamdūḥ (Maḥmūd Sa'īd), 39, 40, 92, 248, 249, 266, 274-276, 280, 323
Ma'mūn (Caliph), 165, 191, 417, 442
Ma'n, 125, 170
Ma'n ibn 'Īsā al-Mufliḥ, 440
Māni'ī, 429
Manṣūr (Caliph), 33, 94-96, 116-117, 159-160, 163-164, 181, 317
Manṣūr ibn Zādhān, 33
Maqarrī, 118
Maqbalī, 43
Maqdisī ('Abd al-Ghanī Taqī al-Dīn), 254, 440, 444
Maqdisī (Abū al-Ḥasan), 36

Maqdisī (Bahā' al-Dīn), 408-410
Maqdisī (Ḍiyā' al-Dīn), 225, 274, 275, 375, 411 405, 440
Maqdisī (Shams al-Dīn al-Ḥanafī), 304
Mardāwī, 322, 389, 407-408, 412
Mar'ī, 407-410, 412
Ma'rūf (Bashshār), 59, 102, 279, 350
Ma'rūf al-Karkhī, 354, 387, 397
Marwān al-Tātarī, 100
Marwān ibn Mu'āwiya, 418
Marwazī (Abū Bakr), 45, 308, 313, 329 *342*, 358, 389, 392, 395, 397, 415
Ma'shāsha (Sa'īd), 400-401
Maslama ibn Ja'far, 95
Masrūq, 126, 394, 400
Massignon (Louis), 405
Mas'ūd ibn Shayba, 429
Mas'ūdī (Muḥammad Radīd), 207
Māturīdī, 41, 65, 69, 75, *79-82*, 84, 380, 382, 446, 456
Mawāhibī, 217
Māwardī, 318, 433
Maydānī, 22, 37
Maymūn ibn Ḥamza, 25
Maymūnī. *See* 'Abd al-Mālik al-Maymūnī
Māzarī, 213
Miḥnāb ibn Sulaym, 339
Mindal, 18
Mirghānī, 64
Mis'ar ibn Kidām, 14, 34, 116-117, 200
Miṣṣīṣī, 102
Mizzī, 25, 41, 43, 64, 122, 169, 172, 188, 193, 234, 256, 429, 442
Mu'ādh ibn Jabal, 144, 157, 282, 428
Mu'āfā, 108
Mu'allimī ('Abd al-Raḥmān), 249, 355
Mu'āwiya ibn Abī Sufyān, 33, 66, 114, 189-190, 197, 210, 259, 315, 384, 450, 451
Mu'āwiya ibn 'Ammār, 94
Mu'āwiya ibn al-Ḥakam, 289
Mu'āwiya ibn Ḥudayj, 95
Mubārak ibn Abī al-Jawād, 13
Mubārakfūrī, 393, 400
Mughalṭāy, 432, 444
Mughīra ibn Shu'ba, 61
Muḥammad 'Ābid al-Sindī, 10
Muḥammad 'Alī Bāshā, 468
Muḥammad ibn al-'Abbās al-Ḍabbī, 339
Muḥammad ibn 'Abd al-Ḥamīd, 263
Muḥammad ibn 'Abd al-Raḥmān al-Sulamī, 103
Muḥammad ibn 'Abd al-Raḥmān ibn Abī Laylā, 11, 205, 294, 326
Muḥammad ibn 'Abd al-Raḥmān ibn al-Faḍl, 230
Muḥammad ibn 'Abd al-Wahhāb (al-Kūfī), 109
Muḥammad ibn 'Abd al-Wahhāb (al-Najdī), 381, 467-470
Muḥammad ibn Abī Bakr al-Rāzī, 174
Muḥammad ibn Abī Ḥumayd, 443
Muḥammad ibn Abī Yaḥyā, 230
Muḥammad ibn Aḥmad ibn Ya'qūb, 385
Muḥammad ibn 'Ajlān, 73
Muḥammad ibn 'Alawī al-Mālikī, xix, 39, 288
Muḥammad ibn 'Alī (al-Bāqir), 9, 93, 99, 130
Muḥammad ibn 'Amāra, 17
Muḥammad ibn 'Amr ibn Ḥazm, 155, 290, 398
Muḥammad ibn 'Awf al-Himṣī, 248
Muḥammad ibn Bashshār, 336
Muḥammad ibn Bishr, 9
Muḥammad ibn Fuḍayl, 31
Mu ḥammad ibn Fulayḥ, 141
Muḥammad ibn Hārūn al-Ḥaḍramī, 13

Muḥammad ibn Hārūn al-Rūyānī, 260
Muḥammad ibn al-Ḥasan al-Shaybānī, 9-11, *13-15*, 16-17, 36, 40, 67, 76, 124-125, 146, 150, 190-192, 209, 253, 257, 275, 303, 304, 368
Muḥammad ibn al-Haytham, 135
Muḥammad ibn al-Ḥusayn ibn Muḥammad al-Qaṭṭān, 283
Muḥammad ibn Ibrāhīm al-Qaysī, 370-371
Muḥammad ibn Isḥāq ibn 'Abd Allāh, 137
Muḥammad ibn Ismā'īl al-Sulamī, 414
Muḥammad ibn Jaḥsh, 102
Muḥammad ibn Kathīr al-Miṣṣīṣī, 102
Muḥammad ibn Maslama, 176
Muḥammad ibn Muḥammad ibn Idrīs, 229
Muḥammad ibn Muḥammad ibn Muḥammad al-Ḥalabī, 429
Muḥammad ibn Muslim al-Azdī, 122
Muḥammad ibn Naṣr al-Marwazī, 51, 260-261, 402, 421
Muḥammad ibn Nu'aym al-Ḍibbī, 385
Muḥammad ibn Nūḥ,, 311
Muḥammad ibn Sa'd al-'Awfī, 10
Muḥammad ibn Ṣāliḥ ibn Hāni', 263
Muḥammad ibn Salīm al-Bīkandī, 329-330
Muḥammad ibn Samā'a, see Ibn Samā'a
Muḥammad ibn al-Sawwār, 346
Muḥammad ibn Sūqa, 140
Muḥammad ibn 'Uthmān al-Ṣayrafī. *See* al-Ṣayrafī
Muḥammad ibn 'Uthmān ibn Abī Shayba, 321
Muḥammad ibn Wāsi', 342
Muḥammad ibn Yaḥyā al-Dhuhlī, 200, 204, 337, 417-420, 424-425, 439, 465
Muḥammad ibn Yaḥyā al-Qaṭṭān, 198
Muḥammad ibn Ya'qūb, 337, 425
Muḥammad ibn Yazīd, 204
Muḥammad ibn Yazīd al-Mustamlī, 204, 306
Muḥammad ibn Yūsuf al-Bukhārī, 331, 336
Muhannā ibn Yaḥyā al-Shāmī, 395
Muḥāsibī. *See* Ḥārith al-Muḥāsibī
Muḥibb al-Ṭabarī, 62, 64, 396, 428
Mujāhid, 33, 104, 134, 217, 258, 259, 329,
Mujālid, 319
Muktafī (Caliph), 257
Munāwī, 40, 42, 174, 188, 206, 212, 234, 249, 256, 260, 274, 279, 360, 387, 393, 394, 399, 444
Mundhirī, 39, 140, 141, 225, 260, 295, 427, 442
Munīr 'Abduh Aghā, Munīriyya Press, 79, 398
Munkar and Nakīr, 411
Muqātil, 30
Muqri', 263, 320
Murād (Abd al-Ḥakīm), 298
Murād and 'Amrāwī, 63
Murtaḍā al-Zabīdī, 54, 56, 58, 134, 256
Muṣ'ab ibn al-Miqdām, 9, 111
Muṣṭafā al-Ḥammāmī, 51, 53, 55
Mūsā ﷺ, 96, 355, 362, 372, 376,
Mūsā al-Kāẓim, 93
Mūsā ibn 'Abd al-Raḥmān ibn Mahdī, 193
Mūsā ibn 'Uqba, 142
Mūsā ibn Murdī, 91
Mūsā ibn Ṭāriq, 31
Mūsā ibn Ya'qūb al-Zam'ī, 442
Musaddad ibn Musarhad, 415
Muslim, 7, 8, 21, 26, 27, 45, 46, 49,

58, 59, 61, 62, 64, 89, 100, 106, 113, 115, 121, 122, 124-126, 132, 137, 138, 140, 142, 146, 168, 173, 174, 190, 194, 197, 200, 202, 203, 211-213, 219-221, 234, 237, 257, 259, 260, 262, 269, 270, 272, 273, 278, 280, 284, 287, 292, 297, 301, 321, 326, 327, 329, 330, 332-335, 345, 376, 378, 404, 414, 417, 421, 424, 425, 435, 441, 449, 460, 461, 463, 466
Muslim ibn Khālid al-Zanjī, 94, 147, 190, 401
Mustaghfirī, 336
Muṭarrif, 126, *151*, 168-169, 179
Mu'taṣim (Caliph), 223, 392, 404, 417
Muṭayyan, 301
Mutawakkil (Caliph), 356, 388, 417
Muthannā ibn al-Ṣabbāḥ, 104
Muwaffaq al-Makkī, 33, 65-67, 119
Muzanī, 21, 25, 49-50, 192, *207-208*, 209, 216, 217, 221-223, 233, 243, 244, 253, 254, 259, 261, 277, 326, 364
Nabhānī, (Qāḍī Yūsuf), xix, 25, 54, 87, 182, 393
Nabhānī (Taqī al-Dīn), 455
Nābulusī ('Abd al-Ghanī), 12, 387
Naḍr ibn Ḥumayd, 186
Naḍr ibn Shumayl, 89, 135, 317
Nāfi' ibn Mālik, 125
Nāfi' Mawlā Ibn 'Umar, 73, 93, 99, 125, 135, 162
Nafīsa bint al-Ḥasan, 195-196
Najjād, 323, 346, *359-361*
Najm al-Rāzī, 91
Najm ibn al-Fuḍayl, 336
Nakha'ī, vii, 32, 36, 65, 104, 116, 119, 134, 139, 177, 204, 215, 362, 369, 395, 396, 401
Naṣīf (Muḥammad Ḥusayn), 355
Nāṣir al-Jadya', 276
Nāṣir ibn al-Ḥusayn, 282
Naṣīr ibn Yaḥyā al-Balkhī, 68
Naṣr ibn 'Alī, 29,
Naṣr ibn al-Ḥasan, 340
Naṣṣ (Sāmir), 55
Nasā'ī, 15, 21, 40, 60, 61, 88, 100, 121, 154, 202, 208, 219, 254, 267, 283, 284, 290, 303, 316, 326, 341, 343-345, 428, 449, 463
Nasafī, 16, 69, 304
Nasj ibn Sa'īd, 336
Nawawī, xxiii, 2, 13, 26, 30, 33, 34, 64, 107, 115, 118, 125, 136, 155, 166, 174, 185, 186, 190, 212, 213, 225, 226, 230, 232, 233, 237, 240, 242, 245, 256, 258, 259, 270, 272, 283-285, 289, 299, 300, 302, 305, 315, 322, 325, 330, 332-335, 337, 346, 378, 384, 404, 406, 434, 455
Nawwās ibn Sam'ān, 88
Niẓām al-Mulk, 399
Nu'aym ibn Ḥammād, 31, 311, 341, 441
Nu'mān ibn Bashīr, 281, 343
Nu'mān ibn Sa'd, 372
Nūḥ ﷺ, 175
Nūḥ ibn Abī Maryam, 9
Nuṣayr ibn Dhu'lūq, 272
Palmer, 181
Pazdawī, 69, 79
Pickthall, 181, 320
Qabīṣa, 106, 108, 109
Qābisī, 182
Qāḍī 'Abd al-Wahhāb, 147
Qāḍī Ḥusayn. *See* Ḥusayn ibn Muḥammad ibn Aḥmad
Qāḍī 'Iyāḍ, 25, 30, 45, 78, 118, 121-123, 131, 136, 154, 158, 159, 164, 165, 168, 174, 176, 179, 180-183, 194, 196, 199, 201, 234, 245, 272, 285, 299, 321, 330, 378, 397, 399-400

Qaffāl al-Shāshī, 208, *270*, 296, 299
Qaḥṭānī (Muḥammad), 356
Qal'ajī, 86
Qalqashandī, 440
Qa'nabī, 150, 341
Qarāfī, 183, 229, 233
Qārī, 7-10, 25, 37-38, 40, 41, 43, 44, 51-55, 57, 63, 66, 68, 84, 90, 108, 115, 136, 137, 173, 174, 180, 198, 237, 272, 352, 393, 397, 400
Qāsim ibn Ibrāhīm al-Hāshimī, 279
Qāsim ibn Ma'n, 18
Qāsim ibn Muḥammad ibn Abī Bakr, 26, 93, 123, 136, 155, 162, 203, 296, 342, 398, 401
Qāsim ibn Sallām, *see* Ibn Sallām
Qāsimī, 116, 138, 139
Qasṭallānī, 53
Qaṭī'ī, 308
Qatāda, 85, 99, 292, 293
Qatāda ibn al-Nu'mān, 186
Qāwuqjī, 256
Qayla bint Makhrama, 40
Qazwīnī (Abū al-Ḥasan), 132
Qazwīnī ('Umar), 298
Qinnawjī, 356, 454
Quḍā'ī, 47, 61, 87, 172, 186, 248-249, 281, 294, 399, 428
Qudūrī, 38
Qūnawī, 22
Quraysh, 186-188, 216, 428
Qurṭubī, 64, 90, 121, 172, 209, 211-214, 225, 248, 292-293, 318, 375-376
Qushayrī, 46, 237, 246-249, 251, 277, 292, 296, 309, 314, 346, 349, 365, 366, 368, 372-374
Qutayba, 138, 162, 336
Quṭay'ī, 389
Quṭb brothers (Sayyid and Muḥammad), 455
Qūtlāy, Khalīl Ibrāhīm, 51-53
Raba'ī, 411
Rabbānī (Farāz), 37, 226
Rabī' ibn Anas al-Bakrī,
Rabī' ibn Ṣabīḥ, 293
Rabī' ibn Ṣubayḥ, 30
Rabī' ibn Sulaymān, 25, 150, 198, 206-207, *208-209*, 216, 217, 222, 224, 231, 232, 235, 244, 259, 364
Rabī'a, 154, 157, 167, 168, 178, 193, 326, 401
Rabī'a ibn 'Uthmān al-Taymī, 282
Rabī'a ibn Yazīd, 99
Rāḍī (Caliph), 359
Rāfi'ī, 258, 299, 432, 466
Rāghib al-Aṣfahānī, 213
Raḥmat Allāh al-Sindī, 37
Raḥmatī, 12
Rajā' al-Harawī, 118
Rajā' ibn Ḥaywa, 136
Rajā' ibn Muḥammad al-Mu'addil, 271
Ramaḍān, 33, 48, 219, 232, 244, 286, 287, 336, 295, 452
Ramaḍān 'Alī Muḥammad, 280
Rāmahurmuzī, 179, 204, 281, 444
Rashīd (Caliph), 11-12, 14, 158, 162-165, 190-191, 417
Rāshid ibn Sa'd, 411
Rawḥ ibn 'Ubāda, 28, 31
Rawḥ ibn Ṣalāḥ, 39
Rayḥāna, 392
Rāzī (Abū Bakr). *See* al-Ja ṣṣāṣ
Rāzī (Abū Ḥātim). *See* Abū Ḥātim al-Rāzī
Rāzī (Abū Ja'far). *See* 'Īsā ibn Abī 'Īsā Māhān
Rāzī (Abū Zur'a). *See* Abū Zur'a al-Rāzī
Rāzī (Fakhr al-Dīn). *See* Fakhr al-Dīn al-Rāzī
Rāzī (Ibn Abī Ḥātim). *See* Ibn Abī Ḥātim al-Rāzī
Rāzī (Tammām). *See* Tammām al-Rāzī

Rib'ī ibn Ḥirāsh, 418
Rifā'ī (Yūsuf ibn Sayyid Hāshim), xxii, 63
Riyāḍ (Muḥammad), 158, 182
Rudhbārī, 283
Rukāna, 185-186
Rustughfānī, 79
Ruwaym, 246
Rūyānī, 260
Ṣābūnī (Abū 'Uthmān), 429
Sa'd ibn Abī Waqqāṣ, , 157, 281
Sa'd ibn Ibrāhīm, 33, 283
Sa'd ibn Mu'ādh, 315
Sa'dī, 7, 259
Ṣafadī, 9, 21
Saffarīnī, 80, 387, 446
Ṣafwān ibn Sulaym, 249
Ṣāghānī, 32, 248, 400
Saharanfūrī, 80
Sahl ibn Sa'd, 9, 46, 93, 234, 306
Sahmī, 341
Sā'ib ibn Yazīd,
Sa'īd ibn 'Abd Allāh al-Dimashqī, 293
Sa'īd ibn 'Abd al-'Azīz, 99
Sa'īd ibn Abī Ayyūb, 193
Sa'īd ibn Bāzigh, 281
Sa'īd ibn Ismā'īl al-Ḥayrī, 260
Sa'īd ibn Jubayr, 33, 73, 104, 318, 401
Sa'īd ibn Manṣūr, 234, 273, 312, 411
Sa'īd ibn Marwān, 419
Sa'īd ibn Masrūq, 9
Sa'īd ibn Sinān Abū Mahdī, 294
Sa'īd ibn 'Umayr al-Anṣārī, 110
Ṣā'idī, 429
Ṣā'ib ibn 'Ubayd, 185
Sājī, 209, 300
Sājiqlī Zādah, 54
Sakhāwī, 8,86, 105, 114-116, 118, 137, 172, 179, 188, 191, 197, 202-204, 248, 249, 256, 266, 275-276, 279, 293-296, 352, 427, 428, 430
Sakhāwī al-Samarqandī, 304
Sakhtiyānī, Sikhtiyānī, 16, 38, 125, 401
Saksakī, 263
Salama ibn al-Akwa', 137-138
Salama ibn Kuhayl, 9
Salama ibn Rawḥ, , 172
Ṣāliḥ ibn Abī al-Aswad, 94
Ṣāliḥ ibn Aḥmad ibn Ḥanbal, 277, 311, 312, 386, 391-394, 397, 416
Ṣāliḥ ibn Ayyūb, 168
Ṣāliḥ ibn Muḥammad al-Asadī, 10
Ṣāliḥ ibn Muḥammad Jazara, 327
Ṣāliḥī, 7, 10, 116, 119, 198, 380
Sālim ibn 'Abd Allāh, 155, 398
Sālim ibn 'Ajlān, 73
Sallām ibn al-Ḥārith, 399
Sallām ibn Sulaymān, 399
Salmān (Mashhūr Ḥasan), 63, 289
Salmān al-Fārisī, 7
Sam'ānī, 21, 325, 440
Samannūdī, 470
Samhūdī, 275, 322
Ṣan'ānī, 141, 204, 306, 381, 399, 400
Saqqāf, 51, 53, 55, 59, 89, 90, 149, 169, 263, 322, 374
Sarī al-Saqaṭī, 246, 314
Sarrūjī, 37
Ṣāwī, 455
Ṣayrafī, 19, 210, 396
Sayyārī, 46
Sells (Michael), 252
Seven Jurists, 155, 398
Sha'bī, 32, 134, 139, 176, 215, 319-320, 401-402
Sha'rānī, 53, 64, 295, 314, 355, 400, 430
Shaddād ibn Ḥakīm, 17-18
Shaddād ibn Sa'īd Abū Ṭalḥā al-Rāsibī, 116
Shādhakūnī, 30, 140, 210, 301, 316
Shāh Walī Allāh, 124, 454

Shahafūr. See al-Isfarāyīnī (Abū al-Muẓaffar)
Shahr ibn Ḥawshab, 7
Shahrastānī, 76, 309, 460
Shākir (Aḥmad), 63, 122, 145, 309, 334, 397
Shakūr (Lumumba), 158
Shams al-Dīn Ibn Qudāma, 408-410, 412
Sharīd ibn Suwayd al-Thaqafī, 290
Sharīf al-Ḥusaynī, 432
Sharīk ibn 'Abd Allāh, 17, 116-117, 194, 269, 314, 321, 373
Sharīṭī, 24
Sharqāwī, 258
Shāṭibī, 101, 171, 174, 201, 245, 295, 295, 366, 419
Shaṭṭī, 12, 470
Shāwīsh (Zuhayr), 224, 355
Shawkānī, 63, 92, 98, 115, 116, 182, 182, 206, 248, 249, 260-262, 275, 277, 318, 393, 400, 411, 457
Shayba ibn 'Uthmān, 282
Shaybān al-Rā'ī, 230
Shayrajī, 253
Shīdūyah, 19
Shifā' bint al-Arqam, 185
Shinqīṭī, 145, 427, 438, 441
Shīrāzī, 13, 33, 254
Shīrāzī (Abū Isḥāq), 258, 270
Shirbīnī, 274
Shirwānī, 182
Shīth ibn Ibrāhīm, 78
Shu'ayb ibn al-Ḥajjāb, 139
Shu'ayb ibn Ḥarb, 107
Shu'ba, 30-31, 94, 99, 104, 125, 142, 194, 269, 283, 360, 373, 401, 438-439
Shumayṭ, , 87
Shura ḥbīl ibn Ḥasana, 157
Shurayḥ, 169, 210
Shurayḥ ibn al-Nu'mān, 169
Sibṭ Ibn al-'Ajamī, 440
Sibt Ibn al-Jawzī, 405
Ṣiddīq Ḥasan Khān. *See* al-Qinnawjī
Sijzī, 399, 429
Sikhtyānī, 16, 59, 125, 401
Silafī, 362, 387, 433, 444
Sindī ('Imād al-Dīn Mas'ūd ibn Shayba), 429
Sindī (Muḥammad 'Ābid), 10
Sindī (Raḥmat Allāh), 37
Sindī (Abū al-Ḥasan Ibn 'Abd al-Hādī), 256, 260, 275
Sirāj al-Dīn ('Abd Allāh), 214, 280, 335
Subay'a bint Abī Lahab, 62
Subkī, 40, 64, 168, 225, 273, 275, 322, 337, 373, 430
Ṣufūrī, 119
Sufyān al-Thawrī. *See* al-Thawrī
Sufyān ibn 'Uyayna. *See* Ibn 'Uyayna
Sughdī, 429
Suhaylī, 11, 61
Suhaymī, 64
Suḥnūn, 146-148, 150, *152-153*
Suhrawardī, 436
Sukayna bint al-Ḥusayn, 148
Sulamī, 103, 114, 221, 248, 250, 251, 270, 278, 283, 314, 349, 372, 388
Sulaym ibn 'Itr, 33
Sulaymān ibn 'Abd Allāh ibn Muḥammad ibn 'Abd al-Wahhāb, 182, 469
Sulaymān ibn Abī Shaykh, 32
Sulaymān ibn Burayda, 13
Sulaymān ibn Ḥarb, 341
Sulaymān ibn Mahrān, 16, 437
Sulaymān ibn Najāḥ, 467
Sulaymān ibn Rajā', 294
Sulaymān ibn Yasār, 155, 398
Sulaymān ibn Yazīd, 274
Ṣu'lūkī, 246, 259, 278, 466
Sumayr ibn 'Abd al-Raḥmān, 133
Sumayṭ (Zayn al-'Ābidīn), 470
Surayj ibn al-Nu'mān, 169
Suwayd ibn Sa'īd, 87

Suyūṭī, 7, 9, 21, 25, 26, 34, 40, 52-53, 59, 61, 63, 83, 86, 91-92, 94, 115-116, 132, 134, 136, 143, 144, 159, 172-175, 177, 183, 188, 196, 209, 229, 233, 234, 248, 251, 254, 256, 258-260, 266, 274-275, 280, 293, 310, 312, 318, 333-335, 355, 360, 375-376, 393, 399, 411, 417, 430, 432, 441, 444, 457, 460
Ṭabarānī, 8, 24, 25, 39-40, 47, 53, 60, 62, 85, 136-137, 144, 172-173, 214, 221, 248, 274, 281, 285, 290, 292, 295, 2312, 317, 318, 320, 344, 351, 360, 387, 389, 393, 411, 428, 432, 443
Ṭabarī (Ibn Jarīr), 11, 60, 63, 98, 158, 171, 177, 190, 207, 214, 248, 253, 255-260, 270, 292, 303-305, 318, 320, 322, 375, 387, 402, 414, 455, 467
Ṭabarī (Abd al-Qādir), 51
Ṭabarī (Ibn Mahdī), 24
Ṭabarī (Muḥibb al-Dīn), 62, 64, 396, 428
Taftazānī (Abū al-Wafā'), 364
Taftazānī. (Sa'd al-Dīn), 394
Tahānawī, 36-37, 40, 45, 226, 233, 369
Ṭaḥāwī, 14, *21-26*, 41, 42, 64, 67, 68, 75, 80, 102, 121-123, 192, 207-208, 210, 214, 272, 281, 291, 304, 326, 373, 382, 402, 413, 443
Ṭaḥṭāwī, 54
Ṭaharānī, 307
Ṭalamankī, 277
Tamīm al-Dārī, 33, 129, 345
Tamīm brothers, 400
Tamīmī (Abū al-Faḍl), 370
Tamīmī (Rizq Allāh), 46, 363, 386-387
Tammām al-Rāzī, 294, 444
Ṭarasūsī, 387
Tatā'ī, 180
Ṭāwūs ibn Kaysān, 74
Ṭayālisī, 105, 125, 186, 238, 269, 273, 373, 430, 439, 440
Taymī (Abū Nuʿaym), 60
Taymī, (Sulaymān), 12, 34, 101, 112
Thābit al-Bunānī, 59, 64, 283, 342, 391
Tha'lab, 136
Tha'ālibī, 103, 362
Thawbān, 248, 346
Thawrī, 12, 14, 17, 20, 28, 30-32, 36, 41, 96, 98-99, 101, *103-112*, 113-114, 116, 119 125, 135, 141, 142, 150, 159, 194, 200, 202, 212, 229, 230, 246, 257, 303, 305, 307, 314, 315, 318, 325, 326, 373, 384, 401, 413, 434-436, 438-439, 441, 443, 455, 463
Tilimsānī, 52
Tinnīsī, 145, 180, 208
Tirmidhī, 7, 35-36, 60, 61, 85-86, 88, 100, 107, 113-115, 121, 122, 124-126, 128, 131, 132, 136, 137-139. 142, 144, 168, 170, 171, 173, 185, 186, 190, 198, 202-203, 205, 210, 219, 221, 234, 248, 266, 267, 274, 279-283, 298, 305, 312, 315, 326, 327, 329, 335, 343
Tujībī, 183
Turkmānī (Idrīs ibn Baydakīn), 233
Ṭurṭūshī, 233
Tustarī, 91, 93, 171, 201, 241, 283, 343, *346-353*, 358, 372, 458
Tuwayjirī, 102
Ṭuyūrī, 233
Two Shaykhṣ *See also* al-Bukhārī, Muslim, 8, 41, 99, 119, 272, 299, 326, 428, 450, 466
'Ubāda ibn al-Ṣāmit, 345
Ubay ibn Ka'b, 113, 138, 234, 409
'Ubayd Allāh ibn 'Abd Allāh, 290,

401
'Ubayd Allāh ibn Abī Rāfi',
'Ubayd Allāh ibn 'Amr al-Rāqī, 93
'Ubayd Allāh ibn Mūsā, 327
'Ubayd Allāh ibn 'Umar al-'Umarī,
'Ubayd Allāh ibn 'Utba, 155
'Ubayd ibn 'Abd Yazīd, 185
'Ubayd ibn Abī Qurra, 32
'Ubayda ibn al-Jarrāḥ, 157
'Ubayd ibn 'Umayr, 129-130, 136
'Ujayr, 185
'Ukbarī
  Abū Ṭālib, 394
  Ibn Baṭṭa, *q.v.*
  Ibn Kādish, 224
  'Iṣma ibn Abī 'Iṣma, 416
'Ulaymī, 203
'Umar ibn 'Abd al-'Azīz, 63, 74, 114, 188, 233, 295, 395, 443
'Umar ibn al-Khaṭṭāb, 41, 44, 72, 84, 94, 95, 100, 104, 108, 113, 114, 119, 128-131, 138, 153, 155, 163, 231-235, 242, 255, 272, 283, 284, 287, 294, 322-323, 346, 383, 391, 392, 395, 399, 405, 428, 443, 449, 461, 462, 466
'Umar ibn Ḥafṣ, 328
'Umar ibn Ibrāhīm, 137
'Umar ibn Ibrāhīm al-Muqrī, 206
'Umar ibn Isḥāq ibn Ibrāhīm, 206
'Umar ibn Wāṣil, 346
'Umayr ibn Qatāda al-Laythī, 281
Umm Abī 'Abbāsa, 392
Umm Farwa, 93
Umm al-Khayr, 64
Umm Salama, 35, 84, 189, 210, 234
Umm Sulaym, 428
'Uqaylī, 48, 169, 170, 214, 248, 273, 293, 295, 427
'Uqba ibn 'Abd Allāh al-Rifā'ī, 293
'Uqbī, 440
'Urwa ibn al-Zubayr, 93, 155, 162, 398, 401
Usāma ibn Sharīk, 297, 298
'Usayrān (Ḥusayn Aḥmad), xix
'Utayqī, 387
'Utba ibn Ḥammād, 163
'Utbī, 169, 182, 321
'Uthaymīn (Muḥammad ibn Ṣāliḥ), 378
'Uthmān ibn 'Affān, 33, 41, 43-44, 107, 108, 131, 165, 186, 195, 233, 272, 283, 449-451, 461
'Uthmān ibn Sa'īd al-Dārimī, 263, 352, 371
'Uthmān ibn 'Umayr, 63
Uways al-Qaranī, 90
Wāḥidī, 376
Wahb ibn Munabbih, 352
Wakī' ibn al-Jarrāḥ,, 9, 15, 16, 18, 31, 125, 134, 139, 201, 239, 283, 317, 318, 321, 325, 327, 401
Walīd ibn Abī Walīd, 116
Walīd ibn Ḥammād, 65
Walīd ibn Hishām, 99
Walīd ibn Mazyad, 100, 101
Walīd ibn Muslim, 31, 100, 402
Walīd ibn Salama, 137
Wāqidī, 144, 160, 162, 164, 439
Warrāq ('Abd Allāh ibn Ḥāmid), 406
Warrāq ('Abd al-Wahhāb), 211, 396-397
Warrāq (Abū Ja'far Muḥammad ibn Abī Ḥātim), 327-329, 331, 339, 370
Wāthila ibn al-Asqa', 134, 138
Wāthiq (Caliph), 223, 311, 417
Winter, T.J., 89
Wuhayb ibn al-Ward, 40, 111, 438
Yāfi'ī, 78
Yaḥyā ibn 'Abd al-Malik, 109
Yaḥyā ibn Abī Kathīr, 99
Yaḥyā ibn 'Ammār, 267-268
Yaḥyā ibn Ayyūb, 341
Yaḥyā ibn Bukayr, 168, 193
Yaḥyā ibn Ma'īn,. *See* Ibn Ma'īn

Yaḥyā ibn Ma'mar, 384
Yaḥyā ibn Maymūn al-Tammār, 293
Yaḥyā ibn Sa'īd al-Anṣārī, 9, 16, 93, 144
Yaḥyā ibn Sa'īd al-Qaṭṭān, 30, 94, 99, 104, 106, 125, 132, 134, 135, 196, 198, 200, 201, 205, 225, 283, 301, 306, 316, 321, 418, 440
Yaḥyā ibn Sulayman, 199
Yaḥyā ibn 'Umāra al-Māzinī, 345
Yaḥyā ibn Yaḥyā al-Laythī, 124, 146, *151*
Yaḥyā ibn Yamān, 438
Yaḥyā ibn Zakariyya ??, 279
Yaḥyā ibn Zakariyyā ﷺ. See Ibn Abī Zā'ida
Ya'qūb ﷺ, 72
Ya'qūb ibn Isḥāq al-Ḥaḍramī, 116
Ya'qūb ibn Shayba, 140
Ya'qūbī (Muhammad ibn Sayyid Ibrāhīm), xix, 12
Yāqūt al-Ḥamawī, 354
Yazīd ibn Abān al-Raqāshī, 293
Yazīd ibn 'Abd Allāh, 93
Yazīd ibn 'Abd al-Mālik ibn Qusayṭ, 321
Yazīd ibn Hārūn, 439, 441
Yazīd ibn al-Kumayt, 118
Yazīd ibn Madh'ūr, 103
Yazīd ibn Mu'āwiya, 394
Yazīd ibn Zuray', 9, 442, 444
Yūnus ibn 'Abd al-A'lā, 14, 26, 152, *214*, 220, 230, 235, 244, 257
Yūnus ibn Ṭāhir, 429
Yūnus ibn 'Ubayd, 85, 103
Yūsuf ﷺ, 391
Yūsuf 'Alī, 181
Yūsuf ibn 'Amr ibn Yazīd, 77
Yūsuf ibn al-Ḥusayn al-Rāzī, 388
Yūsuf ibn Asbaṭ, 109
Zabīdī, 10, 38, 54-58, 134, 137-139, 256, 395
Za'farānī, 48, 207, *209*, 216, 220, 237, 244, 245, 253, 290, 302, 307, 325
Zaghlūl (Muḥammad Basyūnī), 356
Zāghūnī, 406
Zā'ida, 104
Zajjāj, 375
Zakariyyā al-Anṣārī, 13, 26, 30, 430
Zakariyyā al-Kandihlawī, 92
Zakariyyā ibn Yaḥyā al-Ḍarīr, 306
Zamakhsharī, 24, 428
Zanjānī, 429
Zaranjārī, 66
Zarkashī, 172, 293, 295, 296, 407, 410
Zarqānī, 53, 143, 145, 182, 223, 310
Zarrūq, 180
Zayd ibn Abī al-Zarqā', 202
Zayd ibn 'Alī, 414
Zayd ibn Aslam, 125, 171
Zayd ibn Khālid al-Juhanī, 282
Zayd ibn Thābit, 84, 177, 281, 320
Zayla'ī, 40, 41, 44, 86, 198
Zayn (Ḥamza), 39
Zayn al-'Ābidīn 'Alī ibn al-Ḥusayn, 421
Ziriklī, 51
Ziyād ibn 'Abd Allāh al-Nakha'ī, 36
Ziyād ibn 'Abd al-Raḥmān al-Nakha'ī, 36
Ziyād ibn 'Alaqa, 9
Ziyād ibn Kusayb al-'Adawī, 294
Zubayr ibn al-'Awwām, 157
Zubayr ibn Bakkār, 164
Zubda the sister of Bishr, 315
Zufar, 9-10, *15-18*, 26, 65, 67, 336
Zuhaylī (Wahbī), 285
Zuhayr ibn Ṣāliḥ ibn Aḥmad, 392
Zuhayrī, 113, 248, 256
Zuhrī, 33, 93, 99, 106, 125-126, 135, 139, 142, 161, 162, 189, 201, 215, 283, 290, 369, 401, 443, 444
Zurāra, 210
Zurayq ibn al-Sakht, 295

IV. Index Operum

Abāṭīl, 137
Abḥāth, 43
Abū Ḥanīfa al-Nu'mān, 57, 66
Abū Ḥanīfa wa-Aṣḥābuhu al-Muḥaddithūn, 45
Abwāb, 278
Adab al-Ikhtilāf, 165, 192, 397
Adab al-Imlā' wal-Istimlā', 307, 325
Adab al-Muftī wal-Mustaftī, 166, 225
Adab al-Qaḍā', 270
Ādāb al-Shāfi'ī, 192
Ādāb al-Shar'iyya, 91
Adab al-Shaykh al-Ḥasan ibn Abī al-Ḥasan al-Baṣrī, 91
Adab al-Ṭalab, 262
Adhkār, 115, 233, 285
Advice to Our Brethren the Ulema of Najd, 63
Āḥād wal-Mathānī, 60, 62, 292
Aḥādīth al-Quṣṣāṣ, 134
Aḥādīth al-Shāmūkhī, 7
Aḥkām 'Abd al-Ḥaqq al-Ishbīlī, 275
Aḥkām Ahl al-Milal, 395
Aḥkām al-Qur'ān, 22, 170, 373
Aḥkām al-Shar'iyya, 255, 435
Aḥkām Ḍiyā' al-Dīn al-Maqdisī, 411
Aḥkām Ibn Abī Shayba, 320
Aḥkām Tamannī al-Mawt, 411
Aḥsan al-Taqāsīm fī Aṣḥāb al-Ḥadīth, 304
Ahwāl al-Qubūr, 409
Ajwiba 'alā al-Qazwīnī, 173
Ajwiba al-Ghāliya fī 'Aqīdat al-Firqat al-Nājiya, 470
Ajwibat al-Fāḍila, 115, 275
Akhbār Abī Ḥanīfa, 22
Akhbār Makka, 259
Akhlāq Aḥmad ibn Ḥanbal, 358
A'lām, 51
Albānī and His Friends, 63
'Ālim wal-Muta'allim, 56-57, 75-76
'Amal al-Yawm wal-Layla, 39
Amālī al-Adhkār, 39
Amālī al-'Ashiyyāt, 278
Amālī al-Ḥākim, 278
Amālī al-Muṭlaqa, 294
Amālī al-Qazwīnī, 132
Amr bil-Ma'rūf, 209
Amthāl, 48, 248
Amwāl, 295
A'yān Dimashq, 12
Aqāwīl al-Thiqāt, 56
'Aqd al-Thamīn fī Ḥadīth Uṭlubū al-'Ilma walaw bil-Ṣīn, 256
'Aqīda al-Aṣfahāniyya, 217
'Aqīda al-Ṣaḥīḥa, 46, 237-238, 310, 413-414
'Aqīdat Aḥmad Riwayata Abī Bakr al-Khallāl, 371
'Aqīda Ṭaḥāwiyya. See Bayān I'tiqād Ahl al-Sunna wal-Jamā'a
'Aqīda Wāsiṭiyya, 378
'Aqīdat al-Imām Aḥmad, 394
'Aqīdat al-Shāfi'ī, pseudo-, 224
Arba'īn 'alā Madhhab al-Mutaḥaqqiqīn min al-Ṣūfiyya, 248
Arba'īn al-Ṣūfiyya, 248
Arba'īn fī Shuyūkh al-Ṣūfiyya, 248, 389
Arba'īn min Amthāl Afṣaḥ al-'Ālamīn, 87
Arba'ūn al-Ṣughrā, 285
'Arḍ 'alā al-Muḥaddith, 265
'Āriḍat al-Aḥwadhī, 116, 168, 232
Arkān al-Īmān, 51, 55
'Arsh wamā Ruwiya Fīh, 324
Asadiyya, 150
Asāmī al-Shādhdha, 265
Asāmī wal-Kunā, 265
Asās al-Taqdīs, 268, 465
Asbāb al-Nuzūl, 376
Ash'arī School, 406, 413
Ashriba, 265, 308
Asmā' wal-Ṣifāt, 90, 102, 114, 167-

169, 213, 221, 223, 264, 285, 312, 317-318, 324, 330, 351, 362, 373-377, 413, 415-416, 418, 425
Asnā al-Maṭālib fī Najāt Abī Ṭālib, 64
Asnā fī Sharḥ Asmā' Allāh al-Ḥusnā, 211-213
Asrār al-Marfū'a, 174, 457
Āthār, 13, 15, 38, 40
Athar al-Ḥadīth al-Sharīf fī Ikhtilāf al-A'immat al-Fuqahā', 205
Āthār al-Marfū'a fil-Akhbār al-Mawḍū'a, 400
Awā'il al-Adilla, 81
Awjaz al-Masālik, 37
Awliyā', 118, 459
'Awn al-Ma'būd, 12, 51, 53, 173, 188, 350, 393
Awsaṭ, 25, 39, 85, 144, 151, 172, 173, 221, 248, 274, 281, 295, 360
Awwal Man Naẓara fil-Rijāl wa-Faḥaṣa 'anhum, 265
'Ayn wal-Athar, 217
'Aẓama, 63, 83, 114, 317
Azhār al-Mutanāthira, 234
Azhār al-Riyāḍ, 118
Bā'ith 'alā al-Khalāṣ min Ḥawādīth al-Quṣṣāṣ, 134
Bā'ith 'alā Inkār al-Bida' wal-Ḥawādith, 233
Badā'i' al-Ṣanā'i', 38, 40
Badhl al-Majhūd, 37
Badr al-Ṭāli', 63, 262
Barāhin al-Sāṭi'a fī Radd Ba'ḍ al-Bida' al-Shā'i'a, 470
Basmala, 193, 214
Bayān al-I'tiqād, 237
Bayān al-Wahm wal-Takhlīṭ fī Ḥadīth al-Aṭīṭ, 350
Bayān Awhām al-Mu'tazila, 80
Bayān I'tiqād Ahl al-Sunna wal-Jamā'a 'alā Madhhab Fuqahā' al-Milla Abī Ḥanīfa wa-Abī Yūsuf al-Anṣārī wa-Muḥammad ['Aqīda Ṭaḥāwiyya], 22, 38, 42, 269, 373, 382, 413
Bayān Khaṭa' man Akhṭa'a 'alā al-Shāfi'ī, 285
Bayān Mushkil Aḥādīth Rasūlillāh ﷺ, 24
Bayān Talbīs al-Jahmiyya, 78, 370-372
Bayān wal-Ta'rif, 137
Bayān wal-Taḥṣīl limā fil Mustakhraja min al-Tawjīh wal-Ta'līl, 182
Bida' al-Tafāsīr, 8
Bidāya wal-Nihāya, 7, 12, 25, 34, 193, 195, 196, 224, 235, 257, 259, 263, 279, 282, 311, 323, 366, 374, 384, 385
Bishārat al-Mu'min bi-Taṣḥīḥ Ḥadīth Ittaqū Firāsat al-Mu'min, 248
Book of Assistance, 80
Bughyat al-Multamis, 125
Burhān al-Jalī, 41, 86, 94, 272, 280
Burhān fī Ma'rifat 'Aqā'id Ahl al-Adyān, 263
Bustān al-'Ārifīn fil-Zuhd wal-Taṣawwuf, 230
Bustān al-Muḥaddithīn, 23
Ḍu'afā', 48, 169, 170, 214, 248, 273, 274, 293, 427
Ḍu'afā' al-Kabīr, 293, 295
Ḍu'afā' al-Ṣaghīr, 293
Ḍu'afā' wal-Matrūkīn, 75, 181
Da'awāt al-Kabīr, 39, 40, 285, 289
Daf' Shubah al-Tashbīh bi-Akuff al-Tanzīh, 89, 90, 170, 212, 264, 330, 374, 377, 405
Dalā'il al-Khayrāt, 54
Dalā'il al-Nubuwwa, 60, 115, 234, 235, 270, 278, 281, 285, 289, 292, 323, 355
Dalā'il fī Gharīb al-Ḥadīth, 24
Dalā'il fī Ummahāt al-Masā'il, 304
Dalīl al-Ṭalib, 408
Dar' Ta'āruḍ al-'Aql wal-Naql, 168, 231

Dhahabī wa Manhajuhu fī Kitābihi Tārīkh al-Islām, 279
Dhakhā'ir, 433
Dhakhā'ir al-'Uqbā fī Manāqib Dhawī al-Qurbā, 62
Dhakhīra, 183
Dhamm al-Kalām, 159, 202, 220, 233, 245, 262, 429
Dhamm al-Ta'wīl, 217, 363, 371, 407, 471
Dhāt al-'Uqdayn, 304
Dhayl Ma'rifat al-Ṣaḥāba, 137
Dhayl 'alā al-Tārīkh, 273
Dhayl Ṭabaqāt al-Ḥanābila, 203, 405, 436
Dhikr Man Yu'tamadu Qawluhu fil-Jarḥ wal-Ta'dīl, 279
Dhurriyyat al-Ṭāhira, 25
Dībāj al-Mudhahhab fī Ma'rifat A'yān 'Ulamā' al-Madhhab, 146, 169, 174, 193, 346
Dirāya fī Takhrīj Aḥādīth al-Hidāya, 295
Dīwān al-Shāfi'ī, 185, 216, 229, 233, 239, 397
Duktūr Abū al-Wafā al-Taftazānī ustādhan lil-taṣawwuf wa-mufakkiran Islāmiyyan: buḥūth 'anhu wa-dirāsāt muhdāt, 364
Durar al-Kāmina, 289, 366
Durar al-Muntathira, 25, 172, 260, 274, 293
Durar al-Saniyya fil-Radd 'alā al-Wahhābiyya, 470
Durr al-Manthūr, 312, 318, 355, 375
Durr al-Mukhtār, 54
Durr al-Naḍīḍ, 206
Durr al-Saḥāba fīman Dakhala Miṣr min al-Ṣaḥāba, 157
Durūj al-Munīfa, 53
Encyclopedia of Islamic Doctrine, 10, 53, 86, 277, 385
Faḍā'il al-A'māl, 274, 275
Faḍā'il al-Awqāt, 143, 286
Faḍā'il al-Qur'ān, 91, 244, 317
Faḍā'il al-Ṣaḥāba, 87, 255, 399
Faḍā'il Mālik, 182
Faḍīlat al-'Ādilīn min al-Wulāt, 293-295
Fahm al-Qur'ān, 384
Fahras al-Fahāris, 446
Fā'iq, 24
Fanā', 252
Faqīh wal-Mutafaqqih, 200, 238, 250, 253, 281, 296, 320
Faraḥ wal-Surūr fī Wāliday al-Rasūl ﷺ, 54
Farq bayn al-Firaq, 76, 384
Faṣl al-Khiṭāb fī Madhhab Ibni 'Abd al-Wahhāb, 469-470
Faṣl lil-Waṣl, 442
Fatāwā Bazzāziyya, 37, 67
Fatāwā Ḥadīthiyya, 53, 55, 199, 203, 213, 272, 380, 395, 461
Fatāwā Hindiyya, 38
Fatāwā al-Lacknawī, 395
Fatāwā wa Masā'il, 226
Fatāwā al-Mawṣiliyya, 40, 89, 204, 286, 288
Fatāwā al-Nawawī, 256
Fatāwā Rashīdiyya, 395
Fatḥ al-Bārī bi-Sharḥ Ṣaḥī ḥ al-Bukhārī, 25, 48, 49, 51, 59, 98, 116, 143, 167-169, 233, 235, 237, 238 248, 264, 276, 284, 318, 323, 330, 335, 344, 352, 355, 369, 397, 430, 442, 453
Fatḥ al-Mughīth, 137, 266, 352
Fatḥ al-Muta'āl, 206
Fatḥ al-Qadīr, 37, 38
Fatḥ al-Wahhāb, 249
Fatḥ Bāb al-'Ināya, 400
Fatwā Ḥamawiyya, 102, 150, 168, 351, 372, 384
Fawā'id, 251, 454, 457
Fawā'id al-Bahiyya fī Tarājim al-Ḥanafiyya, 78, 79, 289
Fawā'id al-Khurāsāniyyīn, 278
Fawā'id al-Majmū'a, 248, 249

Fawā'id al-Maqṣūda fī Bayān al-Aḥādīth al-Shādhdha al-Mardūda, 53, 58
Fawā'id al-Nusakh, 278
Fawā'id Tammām al-Rāzī, 294, 444
Fayḍ al-Qadīr, 25, 42, 174, 188, 212, 250, 256, 279, 360, 394, 399
Fī Tafsīr al-Qur'ān wa Uslūbihi al-Mu'jiz 'Ilmiyyan wa Bayāniyyan, 214
Fihrist, 77
Fiqh 'alā al-Madhāhib al-Arba'a, 59, 178
Fiqh Ahl al-'Iraq, 369
Fiqh al-Absaṭ, 56, 63, 69, 75-76
Fiqh al-Akbar, 44, 47, 48, 51, 55-58, 68, 69, 75, 84, 272, 380, 459
Fiqh al-Akbar, pseudo-, 224
Firaq al-Fuqahā',
Fiṣal fil-Milal wal-Niḥal, 76, 116, 272, 374
Forty Ḥadīths on the Excellence of Syro-Palestine, 85
Funūn, 405
Furū', 322, 386, 387, 408-410, 412
Furūq fi Furū' al-Shāfi'iyya, 254
Futūḥāt al-Rabbāniyya, 115
Gharā'ib Mālik, 399
Gharīb al-Ḥadīth, 24, 127, 295, 317, 320, 353
Gharīb al-Muṣannaf, 317
Ghāyat al-Marām, 254
Ghāyat al-Muntahā, 408-410, 412
Ghidhā' al-Albāb Sharḥ Alfiyyat al-Ādāb, 387
Hadī al-Sārī, 43, 248
Ḥadīth Ikhtilāf Ummatī Raḥma Riwāya wa-Dirāya, 164
Hadiyyat al-Mughīth, 427
Ḥaqā'iq 'an al-Taṣawwuf, 387
Ḥashḥāsa bi-Naqḍ Wuḍū' al-Qahqaha, 41
Ḥāshiyat Ibn 'Ābidīn. See Radd al-Muḥtār,
Ḥāshyat Sunan Ibn Mājah, 256
Ḥathth 'alā al-Tijāra wal-Ṣinā'a wal-'Amal, 181
Ḥawādith wal-Bida', 233
Ḥawāshī Tuḥfat al-Muḥtāj, 182
Ḥāwī fī Sīrat al-Imām al-Ṭaḥāwī, 21, 23
Ḥāwī fī Takhrīj Aḥādīth al-Ṭāḥāwī, 23
Ḥāwī lil-Fatāwā, 61, 63, 92, 233
Ḥāwī min Sīrat al-Ṭaḥāwī, 192
Ḥayāt al-Anbiyā' fī Qubūrihim, 288, 442
Ḥayāt al-Ḥayawān, 395
Ḥayāt al-Ṣaḥāba, 92
Ḥay'at al-Saniyya fil-Hay'at al Suniyya, 83
Ḥazz al-Ghalāṣim, 78
Ḥikam, 201
Ḥilyat al-Awliyā' wa-Ṭabaqāt al-Aṣfiyā', 86, 231, 248, 296, 300, 372, 385
Ḥiyal, 15
Hidāya, 408, 410, 412, 429
Hidāyat al-Sālik ilā Ma'rifat al-Manāsik, 182
Ḥujja, 207
Ḥujjat Allāh 'alā al-'Ālamīn, 25, 54
Ḥusn al-Maqṣid fī 'Amal al-Mawlid, 233
Ibāna 'alā Uṣūl al-Sunna wal-Diyāna, 150
Ibāna 'an Uṣūl al-Diyāna, 370
Ibāna of al-Sijzī, 399
Ibn 'Aqīl et la résurgence de l'Islam traditionaliste au XIe siècle, 405
Ibṭāl al-Ta'wīl, 362, 371
Ibtihāj bi-Takhrīj Aḥādīth al-Minhāj, 235
Īḍāḥ al-Dalīl fī Qaṭ'i Ḥujaji Ahl al-Ta'ṭīl, 366
Īḍāḥ fī Uṣūl al-Dīn, 406
'Idda, 409-410
Ifṣāḥ fī Tafsīr al-Ṣiḥāḥ, 408, 410
Iḥkām fī Uṣūl al-Aḥkām, 7, 12, 116, 186, 369, 399-400

Iḥqāq al-Ḥaqq, 7, 192
Iḥyā' 'Ulūm al-Dīn, 77, 88, 90, 105, 134, 174, 177, 369, 395
Ijhāz 'alā Munkirī al-Majāz, 416
Ijtimā' al-Juyūsh al-Islāmiyya, 102
Ikhtilāf al-Fuqahā', 23, 255, 257-258, 303
Ikhtilāf al-Ḥadīth, 24, 265
Ikhtilāf 'Ulamā' al-Amṣār fī Aḥkām Sharā'i' al-Islām, 255
Ikhwa wal-Akhawāt, 265
Iklīl fī Dalā'il al-Nubuwwa, 278
Ikmāl fī Raf' al-Irtiyāb 'an al-Mu'talif wal-Mukhtalif fīl-Asmā' wal-Kunā wal-Ansāb, 39
Ikmāl fī Sharḥ Muslim, 158
Ikmāl li-Rijāl Aḥmad, 137
I'lā' al-Sunan, 26, 35-37, 40, 45, 226, 369
'Ilal, (*Aḥmad*), 198, 306, 308, 341, 358
'Ilal al-Dāraquṭnī, 273, 290, 293, 442
'Ilal al-Ḥadīth, 265
'Ilal li-Ismā'īl al-Qāḍī, 265
'Ilal al-Kabīr, 136
'Ilal al-Musnad, 265
'Ilal al-Mutanāhiya, 39, 85, 172, 310, 317, 351, 399
'Ilal fī Ma'rifat al-Rijāl, 355
'Ilal Ḥadīth Ibn 'Uyayna, 265
I'lām al-Muwaqqi'īn 'an Rabb al-'Ālamīn, 115, 195, 243, 369, 399
I'lām al-Nabīl bi-Jawāz al-Taqbīl, 315
I'lān wal-Tawbīkh, 118, 179, 191, 279
'Ilm (*Abū Khaythama*), 8
'Ilm (*Ibn Mardūyah*), 137
Ilmā', 136, 397
Ilmām fī Aḥādīth al-Aḥkām, 435
Ilqām al-Ḥajar lil-Mutaṭāwil 'alā al-Ashā'irati min al-Bashar, 51, 53, 55, 59
Imām Abū Ḥanīfa, 57
Imām al-Tirmidhī wal-Muwāzana bayna Jāmi'ihi wa-bayn al-Ṣaḥīḥayn, 326
Imām Mālik Mufassiran, 171
Imāma, 308
Īmān, 308
Imdād al-Fatāwā, 37
Imtā' bi-Sīrat al-Imāmayn al-Ḥasan ibn Ziyād wa Ṣāḥibihi Muḥammad ibn Shujā', 18
Inbā' al-Ghumr, 22, 23
Inṣāf fī Taṣḥīḥ Mā Aṭlaq al-Shaykh al-Muwaffaq min al-Khilāf, 322, 389, 408, 412
Intiqā' fī Faḍā'il al-A'immat al-Thalāthat al-Fuqahā', 10, 11, 17, 33, 41, 45, 66, 67, 121-125, 145, 159, 164, 169, 176, 177, 179, 181, 185, 188, 192, 195, 197, 199, 200, 211, 220, 238, 242, 300, 303-305, 317, 359, 413, 427
Intiṣār al-Faqīr al-Sālik lil-Imām al-Kabīr Mālik, 123
Intiṣār li-A'immat al-Amṣār, 204, 433
Intiṣār li-Wāliday al-Nabī al-Mukhtār ﷺ, 54, 56, 58,
Iqāmat al-Ḥujja 'alā anna al-Ikthār min al-Ta'abbudi Laysa bi-Bid'a, 9, 231
Īqāẓ al-Himam fī Sharḥ al-Ḥikam, 180
Iqnā' li-Ṭālib al-Intifā', 389, 408-410, 412
Iqtiḍā' al-'Ilm al-'Amal, 201, 346, 348
Iqtiḍā' al-Ṣirāṭ al-Mustaqīm Mukhālafat Aṣḥāb al-Jaḥīm, 233
Irghām al-Mubtadi' al-Ghabī bi-Jawāz al-Tawassul bil-Nabī ﷺ, 322
Irshād al-Fuḥūl ilā Taḥqīq al-Ḥaqq min 'Ilm al-Uṣūl, 400
Irshād fī Ma'rifati 'Ulama' al-Ḥadīth, 75, 192, 208, 323
Irshād Ṭullāb al-Ḥaqā'iq ilā Ma'rifati Sunan Khayri al-Khalā'iq, 115, 305

Irwā' al-Ghalīl, 276
Iṣāba fī Tamyīz al-Ṣaḥāba, 48, 60, 62, 92, 137, 185, 320, 323
Ishā'a fī Ashrāṭ al-Sā'a, 395
Ishāra ilā al-Ījāz fī Ba'ḍ Anwā' al-Majāz, 330, 377
Ishārāt al-Marām min 'Ibārāt al-Imām, 65, 67, 68, 75, 76, 79
Iṣlāḥ Ghalaṭ al-Muḥaddithīn, 143
Isnād min al-Dīn, 204, 205
Istī'āb fī Ma'rifat al-Aṣḥāb, 11, 64, 87, 94, 323
Istiqāma (Ibn Aṣram), 48
Istiqāma (Ibn Taymiyya), 230, 296
Itḥāf al-Sādat al-Muttaqīn bi-Sharḥ Asrār Iḥyā' 'Ulūm al-Dīn, 38, 139, 395
I'tiqād 'alā Madhhab al-Salaf Ahl al-Sunna wal-Jamā'a, 237, 288, 289, 399, 400
I'tiqād A'immat al-Ḥadīth, 453
I'tiqād al-Ṣaḥīḥ, 454
I'tiqādāt Firaq al-Muslimīn, 78
I'tiṣām, 295
Itqān fī 'Ulūm al-Qur'ān, 310
Jadal fī Uṣūl al-Fiqh, 80
Ja'diyyāt, 39
Jalā' al-'Aynayn fī Muḥākamat al-Aḥmadayn, 454
Jam' al-Asrār, 387
Jam' Bayn al-Ṣaḥīḥayn, 435
Jāmi' li-Akhlāq al-Rāwī wa Ādāb al-Sāmi', 30, 91, 113, 134, 135, 174, 178, 179, 193, 201, 205, 235, 256, 307, 317, 319, 324, 328, 332, 343, 358, 402, 431
Jāmi' al-Azdī, 87
Jāmi' Bayān al-'Ilm wa-Faḍlih, 12, 32, 91, 101, 113, 118, 154, 166, 174, 201, 203, 205, 239, 248, 256, 281, 369, 396, 399, 444
Jāmi' al-Kabīr, 207
Jamī' al-Manāsik, 37
Jāmi' al-Masānīd, 323
Jāmi' al-Musnad al-Ṣaḥīḥ al-Mukhtaṣar min Umūr Rasūl Allāh wa Sunanihi, wa-Ayyāmih [=*Ṣaḥīḥ al-Bukhārī*] *see* al-Bukhārī
Jāmi' al-Ṣaghīr (Muḥammad ibn al-Ḥasan al-Shaybānī), 15
Jāmi' al-Ṣaghīr (Suyūṭī), 132, 177, 201, 274, 399
Jāmi' fil-Sunan, 159, 167, 170, 178, 179, 199, 396
Jāmi' li-'Ulūm Aḥmad ibn Ḥanbal, 305, 358
Jāmi' al-'Ulūm wal-Ḥikam, 49, 92, 233
Jāmi' al-Uṣūl fī Aḥādīth al-Rasūl, 164
Jāmi' al-Uṣūl min Aḥādīth al-Rasūl, 400
Jāmi' Sufyān, 103
Jarḥ wal-Ta'dīl, 102, 113-114, 163, 169, 199, 202, 294, 444, 464
Jawāb 'an As'ilatin fil-Jarḥ wal-Ta'dīl, 141
Jawāb al-Ḥāfiẓ al-Mundhirī, 140, 427
Jawāb al-Kāfī, 229
Jawāhir al-Muḍiyya fī Tabaqāt al-Ḥanafiyya, 79, 81, 200, 291
Jawāhir wal-Durar fī Tarjamat Shaykh al-Islām Ibn Ḥajar, 105, 114, 197, 202-204, 427, 428
Jawhar al-Munaẓẓam fī Ziyārat al-Qabr al-Mukarram, 275
Jawhar al-Naqī fil-Radd 'alāl-Bayhaqī, 41, 289
Jawharat al-Tawḥīd, vii
Juz' al-Alf Dīnār, 389
Kāfī fī Fiqh Ahl al-Madīna, 182
Kāfī Sharḥ al-Khiraqī fī Fiqh Aḥmad ibn Ḥanbal al-Shaybānī, 277, 408-410
Kāmil fil-Ḍu'afā', 39, 41, 168, 172, 188, 239, 248, 294, 399, 442, 445
Kāmil fil-Tārīkh, 257, 358, 362, 363
Kanz al-'Ummāl, 132, 201, 293, 295
Karāmāt al-Awliyā', 64

Kashf al-Astār, 58
Kashf al-Khafā, 26, 87, 91, 109, 164, 172, 174, 188, 249, 250, 259, 274, 296
Kashf al-Mukhaddarāt, 408-410, 412
Kashf al-Ẓunūn, 65, 68, 81, 304
Kāshif fī Ma'rifat Man Lahu Riwāyatun fil-Kutub al-Sitta, 428
Kashshāf al-Qinā', 182, 277, 322, 389, 408-410, 412
Kashshāf Iṣṭilāḥat al-Funūn, 233
Kawākib al-Darārī Sharḥ Ṣaḥīḥ al-Bukhārī, 237
Khalq Af'āl al-'Ibād, 78, 362, 414-416, 418, 424
Khams Rasā'il fī 'Ulūm al-Ḥadīth, 145, 256
Khayrāt al-Ḥisān fī Manāqib al-Nu'mān, 7, 206, 285
Khilāfiyyāt, 40, 289
Khulāṣat al-Athar, 51
Khulāṣat al-Badr al-Munīr, 411
Kifāya fī 'Ilm al-Riwāya, 114, 134-139, 281, 399
Kitāb Yaḥyā wa-'Abd al-Raḥmān fil-Rijāl, 265
Kubrā al-Yaqīnāt al-Kawniyya, 383, 413, 415
Kunā, 428
Kunā wal-Asmā', 273, 389
La'āli' al-Maṣnū'a, 40, 248, 256, 360, 457
Lam'at al-I'tiqād al-Hādī ilā Sabīl al-Rashād, 217, 296, 407, 422
Lāmiyyat al-Zaqqāq, 183
Laṭā'if al-Ishārāt, 292, 374
Laṭā'if al-Minan, 48
Laṭīf al-Qawl fī Aḥkām Sharā'i' al-Islām, 255
Lawā'iḥ al-Anwār al-Saniyya wa-Lawāqiḥ al-Afkār al-Sunniyya, 80
Letter on the 'Amal of the People of Madīna, 156
Life of Prophets in the Grave, 288
Lisān al-Aḥkām, 41
Lisān al-Mīzān, 39, 75, 168, 172, 224, 245, 255, 263, 268, 269, 274, 323, 361, 387, 389, 395
Lubāb al-Ikhtilāf, 313
Lubāb fī Sharḥ al-Kitāb, 37
Lu'lu' al-Marṣū', 256
Luma' fil-Ḥawādith wal-Bida', 233
Mā Tafarrada bi-Ikhrājihi Kullu Wāḥidin min al-Imāmayn, 278
Ma'ākhidh al-Sharā'i', 80
Ma'ālim al-Hudā, 255
Ma'ālim al-Sunan, 90, 127
Ma'ālim al-Tanzīl, 320
Ma'ārif, 304, 326
Mabānī al-Akhbār fī Sharḥ Ma'ānī al-Āthār, 24
Mabsūṭ, 289
Madārij al-Sālikīn, 106, 229, 250
Madhāhib al-Muḥaddithīn, 265
Madhhab al-Aḥmad, 408
Madīnan Way, 154
Madkhal al-Shar' al-Sharīf, 233
Madkhal ilā 'Ilm al-Ṣaḥīḥ, 278
Madkhal ilā al-Ṣaḥīḥ, 75
Madkhal ilā al-Sunan al-Kubrā, 101, 139, 231, 238, 256, 289, 296, 302, 315, 320, 369, 399-400
Madkhal ilā Ma'rifati Kitāb al-Iklīl, 117
Madkhal ilāl Madhhab al-Imām Aḥmad ibn Ḥanbal, 386
Mafāhīm Yajib an Tuṣaḥḥaḥ, 39
Maghāzī, 16, 142
Maḥāsin al-Sharī'a, 270
Maḥṣūl fil-Uṣūl, 116
Majāz al-Qur'ān, 320
Majlisān min Amālī Niẓām al-Mulk, 399
Majma' al-Zawā'id,. *See* al-Haythamī
Majmū' al-Fatāwā, 38, 86, 102, 115, 150, 164, 178, 217, 267, 294, 310, 313, 351, 372, 392, 416
Majmū' fil-Fiqh al-Mālikī, 183
Majmū' Sharḥ al-Muhadhdhab, 34,

115, 166, 225, 226, 240, 245, 337, 406
Majmū' Tis' Rasā'il, 53
Majrūḥīn, 199, 279
Maktūbāt al-Imām al-Rabbānī, 114
Malābis al-'Arabiyya al-Islāmiyya fil-'Aṣr al-'Abbāsī, 179
Man Ḥaddatha Thumma Raji'a 'anh, 265
Man lā Yuḥtajju bi-Ḥadīthihi wa-lā Yasquṭ, 265
Man Nazala min al-Ṣaḥāba Sā'ir al-Buldān, 265
Man Rawā 'an Rajulin lam Yarah, 265
Man Yu'raf bi-Ismin Dūna Ismi Abīh, 265
Man Yu'raf bil-Laqab wal-'Ilal al-Mutafarriqa, 265
Ma'nā al-Īmān wal-Islām, 46, 49
Ma'nā Qawl al-Imām al-Muṭṭalibī Idhā Ṣaḥḥa al-Ḥadīthu Fahuwa Madhhabī, 225
Manāhil al-'Irfān, 310
Manāhil al-Ṣafā, 399
Manāqib Abī Ḥanīfa, 7, 28, 33, 65-67, 119, 200, 265, 315, 413
Manāqib Aḥmad ibn Ḥanbal, 202, 289, 301, 308, 313, 374, 384, 386, 394, 396, 404, 416
Manāqib al-Ḥasan al-Baṣrī, 91
Manāqib Mālik, 183
Manāqib al-Ṣaḥāba, 142, 308
Manāqib al-Shāfi'ī, 48, 78, 186, 188, 189, 192, 197, 201, 209, 216, 220, 221, 223, 224, 229, 230-233, 237, 245, 265, 289-291, 299, 300, 302, 324, 414
Manāqib al-Shāfi'ī wa-Ādābuh, 189
Manāqib Sufyān al-Thawrī, 103
Manār al-Sabīl, 277, 408
Manāsik, 255, 260, 277
Manāzil al-Sā'irin, 429
Manhaj al-Aḥmad, 203
Manhaj al-Naqd fī 'Ulūm al-Ḥadīth, 115, 139, 334, 352
Manhaj al-Salaf fī Fahm al-Nuṣūṣ, 288
Manhal al-Laṭīf fī 'Ulūm al-Ḥadīth, 115
Mansak al-Marwazī, 308, 389
Mansak Khalīl, 182
Manthūr, 207
Maqālāt al-Kawtharī, 39, 115, 206, 263, 268, 355, 373
Maqālāt al-Māturīdī, 80
Maqālāt al-Islāmiyyīn, 76
Maqāṣid al-Ḥasana, 86, 172, 188, 248-250, 256, 276, 296
Maqṣad al-Arshad fī Dhikr Aṣḥāb al-Imām Aḥmad, 313, 387-388, 394
Marāqī al-Zulaf, 116
Marham al-'Ilal al-Mu'ḍila fī Daf' al-Shubah wal-Radd 'alā al-Mu'tazila, 78
Ma'rifat al-Ṣaḥāba, 136, 137, 428
Ma'rifat al-Sunan wal-Āthār, 100, 113, 121, 186, 214, 281, 291
Ma'rifat al-Tadhkira,
Ma'rifat Anwā' 'Ulūm al-ḤadīthMaṣnū' fī Ma'rifat al-Ḥadīth al-Mawḍū', 25, 400
Masā'il al-Mu'tabara, 207
Masā'il al-Tis', 92
Mas'alat Khalq al-Qur'ān wa-Atharuhā fī Ṣufūf al-Ruwāt wal-Muḥaddithīn wa-Kutub al-Jarḥ wal-Ta'dīl, 426
Masālik al-Ḥunafā' fī Waliday al-Muṣṭafā, 53, 62
Maslak al-Mutaqassi ṭ, 37, 38
Maṭāli' al-Nūr al-Sanī al-Munabbi' 'an Ṭahārati Nasab al-Nabī al-'Arabī ﷺ, 54
Maṭālib al-'Āliya, 87, 399
Matn al-Manār fī Uṣūl al-Fiqh, 69
Mawāhib al-Jalīl, 182
Mawāhib al-Lāduniyya, 53, 182
Mawāhib al-Laṭīfa 'alā Musnad Abī Ḥanīfa, 10

Mawāqif, 45, 80
Mawārid al-Ẓam'ān, 442
Mawḍū'āt, 40, 248, 256, 360, 457
Mawlid al-Dirdīr, 55
Mawqif A'immat al-Ḥaraka al-Salafiyya min al-Taṣawwuf wal-Ṣūfiyya, 387
Mawsū'at Fiqh al-Ḥasan al-Baṣrī, 86
Miftāḥ al-Janna fil-Iḥtijāj bil-Sunna, 175, 251, 399
Minḥa fil-Sibḥa, 91
Minhāj al-'Ābidīn, 421
Minhāj al-Qawīm, 236
Minhāj al-Sunna al-Nabawiyya, 25, 276
Milal wal-Niḥal, 76, 309
Minaḥ al-Rawḍ al-Azhar, 51
Mirqāt al-Mafātīḥ Sharḥ Mishkāt al-Maṣābīḥ, 115, 173-174, 180, 237
Mirqāt al-Su'ūd ilā Sunan Abī Dāwūd, 188
Miṣbāḥ al-Anām fī Radd Shubuhāt al-Bid'ī al-Najdī al-Ladhī Aḍalla bihā al-'Awāmm, 470
Miṣbāḥ al-Zujāja fī Zawā'id Ibn Mājah, 239
Miswaddat Āl Taymiyya, 115, 313
Mīzān al-I'tidāl, 25, 48, 59, 75, 85, 142, 150, 168-170, 186, 224, 239, 245, 248, 249, 268, 269, 279, 282, 293, 317, 323, 361, 385, 399, 439, 447, 450
Mīzān al-Kubrā, 53, 400
Mubāḥathat al-Sā'irīn bi-Ḥadīth Allāhumma Innī As'aluka bi-Ḥaqqi al-Sā'ilīn, 39
Mubdi' fī Sharḥ al-Muqni', 277, 408-410, 412
Mūḍiḥ Awhām al-Jam' wal-Tafrīq, 243
Mudallisīn, 210, 281
Mudāwī li-'Ilal al-Jāmi' al-Ṣaghīr wa Sharḥay al-Munāwī, 249, 250, 275, 280, 294, 295
Mudawwana, 146, 147, 150, 152, 158, 182, 183
Mufradāt Alfāẓ al-Qur'ān, 213
Mughīr, 360, 399
Mughīth al-Khalq, 192
Mughnī 'an Ḥaml al-Asfār, 172, 256
Mughnī al-Muḥtāj, 53, 274
Mughnī fī Fiqh al-Imām Aḥmad ibn Ḥanbal al-Shaybānī, 40, 277, 284, 285, 287, 322, 392, 406, 407-412
Mughnī fil-Ḍu'afā', 87, 169, 239, 293, 351
Muḥaddith al-Fāṣil Bayn al-Rāwī wal-Wā'ī, 179, 204, 281, 444, 445
Muḥallā, 92, 272
Muḥarrar fī Furū' al-Shāfi'iyya, 258
Muḥarrar min al-Fiqh 'alā Madhhab al-Imām Aḥmad ibn Ḥanbal, 305
Mu'īd al-Ni'am wa Mubīd al-Niqam, 431
Mu'jam al-Buldān, 354
Mu'jam al-Kabīr, 248
Mu'jam al-Ṣaghīr, 172
Mu'jam al-Ṣaḥāba, 137
Mu'jam al-Shuyūkh, 390. 391
Mukhtalif al-Ḥadīth, 213, 365
Mukhtār al-Siḥāḥ, 174
Mukhtaṣar al-Fatāwā al-Miṣriyya, 296
Mukhtaṣar al-Ifādāt fī Rub' al-'Ibādāt wal-Ādāb wal-Ziyādāt, 380
Mukhtaṣar Ibn 'Abd al-Ḥakam, 151
Mukhtaṣar Khalīl, 243
Mukhtaṣar al-Muwāfaqa, 428
Mukhtaṣar al-Muzanī, 21, 207, 254
Mukhtaṣar al-Shaykh Khalīl, 182
Mukhtaṣar al-Ṭaḥāwī, 23
Mukhtaṣar al-'Ulūw, 102, 149, 169, 263, 323, 324, 350-352, 362, 371,
Mukhtaṣar Zawā'id Musnad al-Bazzār, 87, 194, 249, 273, 294
Mulakhkhaṣ fil-Fiqh al-Mālikī, 434
Mu'lim bi-Fawā'id Muslim, 213

Mulḥa fī I'tiqād Ahl al-Ḥaqq, 413
Mu'min wal-Muslim wal-Muḥsin, 49
Muntahā al-Irādāt, 408-410, 412
Muntahā al-Sūl 'alā Wasā'il al-Wuṣūl, 393
Muntahā al-Sūl wal-Amal fī 'Ilmay al-Uṣūli wal-Jadal, 400
Muntakhab fil-Fiqh, 122
Muntakhab min Musnad 'Abd ibn Ḥumayd, 399
Muntaqā al-Bājī, 170,
Muntaqā al-Majd Ibn Taymiyya, 322
Muntaẓam fī Tārīkh al-Mulūk wal-Umam, 281, 388, 406
Muqaddam wal-Mu'akhkhar fil-Qur'ān, 308
Muqaddima Dhāt al-Niqāb fil-Alqāb, 430
Muqaddima fī 'Ulūm al-Ḥadīth, 139
Muqaddima fī Uṣūl al-Tafsīr, 78, 310
Muqaddima Ḥaḍramiyya, 236
Muqaddimāt, 158
Muqaddimat al-Jarḥ wal-Ta'dīl, 114
Muqaddimāt al-Mumahhidāt, 182
Muqaddimat Ibn Khaldūn, 454
Muqaddimat Ibn Rushd, 158, 180
Muqallidūn wal-A'immat al-Arba'a, 400
Mūqiẓa, 334, 449
Muqni', 277, 408-410
Murshid al-Mu'īn 'alā al-Ḍarūrī min 'Ulūm al-Dīn, 183
Muṣannaf. See 'Abd al-Razzāq or Ibn Abī Shayba
Muṣtaṣfā, 204
Musāyara, 54
Mus-him fī Ṭuruqi Ḥadīthi Ṭalabu al-'Ilmi Farīḍatun 'alā Kulli Muslim, 256
Mushkil al-Ḥadīth, 24
Musnad 'Abd ibn Ḥumayd, 399
Musnad Abī 'Awāna, 313
Musnad Abī Ḥanīfa, 10, 37, 41
Musnad Abī Ya'lā, 264, 313, 442
Musnad Aḥmad, 63, 85, 121-122, 129, 213, 265, 278, 290, 294, 308-309, 354, 397, 403, 432, 460, 466. See also Aḥmad ibn Ḥanbal
Musnad al-Bazzār, 86-87, 100, 248, 294, See also *Mukhtaṣar al-Zawā'id*
Musnad al-Firdaws, 249, 293, 295
Musnad al-Ḥārith, 295
Musnad al-Ḥumaydī, 218
Musnad Ibn Abī Shayba, 320
Musnad Ibn al-Ja'd, 12, 39
Musnad Ibn Wahb, 444
Musnad Nu'aym ibn Ḥammād, 31
Musnad al-Shāfi'ī, 10, 25, 100, 192, 264, 299
Musnad al-Shāmiyyīn, 248, 393
Musnad al-Shāshī, 186
Musnad al-Shihāb, 47, 61, 87, 172, 248, 249, 281, 294-295, 399, 428
Musnad al-Ṭabarī, 255
Musnad al-Ṭayālisī, 238
Musnad Zayd ibn 'Alī, 250
Mustadrak 'alā al-Ṣaḥīḥayn. See al-Hākim
Mustakhraja, 182
Mu'talif wal-Mukhtalif, 39, 399
Mu'tamad fil-Uṣūl, 394
Mu'tamad min Qadīmi Qawl al-Shāfi'ī, 207
Mu'taqad Abī Ḥanīfata al-Imām fī Abaway al-Rasūl 'Alayhi al-Ṣalāt wal-Salām, 51-52, 63, 198
Muttajir al-Rābiḥ fī Thawāb al-'Amal al-Ṣāliḥ, 39
Muwāfaqāt, 101, 171, 174, 201, 245, 366, 419
Muwaṭṭa, 14, 41, 64, 121, 124-125, 137, 143, 145.147, 150, 151, 154, 155, 162, 165, 177, 182, 189, 204, 215, 231, 273, 275, 284, 290, 398, 460
Muzakkā al-Akhbār, 278
Nafy al-Tashbīh, 309

Naghm al-Akhyār fī Rijāl Ma'ānī al-Āthār, 24
Nahḍat al-Iṣlāḥiyya, 51, 55
Nakhb al-Afkār fī Sharḥ Ma'ānī al-Āthār, 24
Nakhl, 23
Namādhij min Rasā'il al-A'immat al-Salaf wa-Adabihim al-'Ilmī, 42, 44, 157
Namūdhaj min al-A'māl al-Khayriyya fil-Maṭba'at al-Munīriyya, 79, 398
Naqd Abī 'Abd Allāh al-Jurjānī fī Tarjīḥ Madhhab Abī Ḥanīfa, 65, 155, 189, 398
Naqd al-Jahmiyya, 352
Naqd Kitāb al-Mudallisīn, 23
Naṣb al-Rāya, 40, 41, 44, 64, 86, 198
Naṣīḥat Ahl al-Ḥadīth, 198, 235
Nasab, 317
Nāsikh wal-Mansūkh, 309, 341
Nasīm al-Riyāḍ, 87, 182
Nawādir al-Uṣūl, 101, 138, 139, 248, 273, 294, 400
Nawādir wal-Ziyādāt, 182
Nayl al-Awṭār, 92, 98, 116, 182, 260, 275, 277, 393, 411
Naẓm al-Mutanāthir, 102, 168, 221, 234, 282
Nihāya fī Gharīb al-Ḥadīth wal-Athar, 24, 174
Nujūm al-Zāhira, 41
Nukat 'alā Ibn al-Ṣalāḥ, 115, 333, 352
Nukat al-Ṭarīfa fil-Taḥadduth 'an Rudūd Ibn Abī Shayba 'alā Abī Ḥanīfa, 321
Nukhbat al-Anẓār, 400
Nūniyya, 246
Nuqūl al-Shar'iyya fil-Radd 'alāl-Wahhābiyya, 470
Nuzhat al-Majālis, 32, 119
Qā'ida fil-Jarḥ wal-Ta'dīl, 98, 268
Qā'ida fil-Tawassul wal-Wasīla, 389
Qāmūs al-Muḥīṭ, 58, 420
Qanā'a, 389
Qārī wa-Atharuhu fil-Ḥadīth, 52
Qawā'id al-'Aqā'id, 369
Qawā'id Fiqhiyya, 407
Qawā'id al-Kubrā, 232
Qawā'id al-Nūrāniyya, 308
Qawā'id al-Taḥdīth, 116, 138, 139
Qawā'id al-Taṣawwuf, 180
Qawānīn al-Fiqhiyya, 182
Qawāṣim wal-'Awāṣim, 363
Qawl al-Badī' fil-Ṣalāt 'alāl-Ḥabīb al-Shafī', 115116, 275, 276
Qawl al-Mufīd fī Adillat al-Ijtihād wa al-Taqlīd, 400
Qawl al-Musaddad fil-Dhabb 'an Musnad al-Imām Aḥmad, 309
Qīmat al-Zaman 'Inda al-'Ulamā', 303
Qirā'a Warā' al-Imām, 291
Qirā'āt wal-Tanzīl wal-'Adad, 255
Qiṭf al-Thamar, 356
Qubūr, 273
Quṣṣāṣ wal-Mudhakkirīn, 134
Rā'iyya, 246
Radd 'alā al-Akhnā'ī, 389, 390
Radd 'alā al-Jahmiyya, 309, 317, 356
Radd 'alā al-Jahmiyya wal-Zanādiqa, 78, 309, 310, 415
Radd 'alā al-Muta'aṣṣib al-'Anīd al-Māni' min Dhammi Yazīd, 394
Radd 'alā Ibn 'Aqīl, 407
Radd 'alā Ibn Taymiyya, 93
Radd 'alā Man Akhlada ilāl-Arḍ wa-Jahila annal-Ijtihāda fī Kulli 'Aṣrin Farḍ, 258
Radd 'alā Man Ittaba'a Ghayr al-Madhāhib al-Arba'a, 227
Radd 'alā Uṣūl al-Qarāmiṭa, 81
Radd al-Imāma, 81
Radd al-Muḥtār, 9, 37, 40, 54, 55, 233, 395
Radd al-Tahdhīb fil-Jadal, 81
Radd al-Uṣūl al-Khamsa, 81
Radd Awā'il al-Adilla, 81
Radd Shubah al-Tashbīh, 363
Radd Wa'īd al-Fussāq, 81

Raf' al-Mināra li-Takhrīj A ḥādīth al-Tawassul wal-Ziyāra, 39, 266, 275, 276, 280, 323
Raf' wal-Takmīl, 9, 45, 159, 199
Rasā'il al-Qushayriyya, 247
Rasā'il Ibn 'Ābidīn, 226, 252, 461
Rasūl al-Mu'allim, 282
Rawḍ al-Murba', 408-410, 412
Rawḍ al-Nadī, 408-410, 412
Rawḍ al-Unuf, 11, 61
Rawḍat al-Muḥibbīn wa Nuzhat al-Mushtāqīn, 92, 114
Rawḍat al-Nāẓir, 204, 314
Rawḍat al-Ṭālibīn wa-'Umdat al-Muttaqīn, 270, 299
Reliance of the Traveller, 257, 369, 403
Remembrance of Death, 89
Riḥla fī Ṭalab al-Ḥadīth, 256
Risālat Abī Ḥanīfa ilā 'Uthmān al-Battī, 42, 69, 74
Risālat Ahl al-Thughar, 380
Risālat al-Ash'ariyya, 291, 297
Risālat al-Bāhira, 123
Risālat Ibn Abī Zayd, 180, 182
Risālat al-Madaniyya, 123, 217
Risālat Mālik ilāl-Layth fī Faḍli 'Ilmi Ahl al-Madīna wa-Tarjīḥih 'alā 'Ilmi Ghayrihim, 157
Risālat al-Mustarshidīn, 383
Risālat al-Mustaṭrafa, 244, 280, 285
Risāla Niẓāmiyya,
Risāla Qushayriyya, 46, 237, 246, 248, 249, 251, 296, 309, 314, 346, 349, 372, 373, 466
Risālat al-Ṣalāt, 310
Risālat al-Shāfi'ī, 135, 138, 185, 193, 195, 243, 270, 281
Risālat al-Tadmuriyya, 384
Risālat Waṣl al-Balāghāt fil-Muwaṭṭa', 145
Riyāḍ al-Naḍira, 64, 396, 428
Rūḥ, 111, 209, 411
Rūḥ al-Ma'ānī, 59
Rukhṣa fī Taqbīl al-Yad, 320
Ruwāt 'an Mālik, 164
Sa'a, 313
Sa'ādat al-Dārayn, 275
Sa'ādat al-Dārayn fil-Radd 'alā al-Firqatayn al-Wahhābiyya wal-Ẓāhiriyya, 470
Sadād al-Dīn wa-Sidād al-Dayn fī Najāt al-Abawayn al-Sharīfayn, 54, 63
Ṣaḥīḥān lil-Ḥākim, 278
Salafiyya Marḥalatun Mubārakatun lā Madhhab Islāmī, 381, 403
Samā', 247
Sanad al-Anām Sharḥ Musnad al-Imām, 9
Ṣarīḥ al-Sunna, 255
Ṣārim al-Munkī, 182, 275, 276
Ṣawā'iq al-Ilāhiyya fī Madhhab al-Wahhābiyya, 470
Ṣawā'iq al-Muḥriqa 'alā Ahl al-Rafḍ wal-Zandaqa, 394
Ṣawā'iq al-Mursala, 102
Ṣayd al-Khāṭir, 238
Sayf al-Ṣaqīl, 168
Shadharāt al-Dhahab, 13, 23, 193, 196, 246, 254, 313
Shamā'il al-Tirmidhī, 125, 393
Sharaf Aṣḥāb al-Ḥadīth 99, 235, 281, 441-444
Sharḥ Alfiyyat al-Siyar, 234
Sharḥ al-'Aqā'id al-Nasafiyya, 394
Sharḥ al-'Aqīda al-Ṭaḥāwiyya, 38, 42, 269
Sharḥ 'Ayn al-'Ilm, 7, 90, 180
Sharḥ al-Bukhārī, 30
Sharḥ al-Fiqh al-Akbar, 41, 43-45, 51, 52, 55, 68, 84, 397
Sharḥ 'Ilal al-Tirmidhī, 106, 114, 115, 136, 202, 203, 205, 210, 266, 329, 343, 449
Sharḥ Jawharat al-Tawḥīd, 54, 221
Sharḥ al-Kabīr, 408-410, 412
Sharḥ al-Khiraqī, 407
Sharḥ Kitāb al-Sunna, 358, 396
Sharḥ Ma'ānī al-Āthār, 21, 23, 24,

64, 102, 291
Sharḥ al-Manẓūmat al-Bayqūniyya, 280, 335
Sharḥ al-Mawāhib al-Lāduniyya, 182
Sharḥ al-Minhāj, 337
Sharḥ Mukhtaṣar al-Karhkī, 38
Sharḥ Mukhtaṣar al-Khiraqī, 407
Sharḥ Mukhtaṣar Ibn al-Ḥājib, 234
Sharḥ al-Munya, 40
Sharḥ Mushkil al-Āthār, 21, 24, 26, 102, 121, 123, 281, 443
Sharḥ Musnad Abī Ḥanīfa, 9
Sharḥ al-Niqāya, 40
Sharḥ Nukhbat al-Fikar, 139, 333
Sharḥ Ṣaḥīḥ Muslim, 115, 174, 212, 213, 237, 272, 284, 330, 332, 333, 335, 378, 404
Sharḥ Sharḥ Nukhbat al-Fikar fī Muṣṭalaḥāt Ahl al-Athar, 136, 137, 352, 400
Sharḥ al-Shifā', 51, 52, 115, 182, 272, 400
Sharḥ al-Ṣudūr, 209, 411
Sharḥ Sunan Ibn Mājah, 250, 286
Sharḥ al-Sunna, 87, 91, 102, 167-168, 281, 337, 442
Sharḥ al-'Umda, 115, 296, 313
Sharḥ 'Uqūd Rasm al-Muftī, 226
Sharḥ Uṣūl Ahl al-Sunna, 78
Sharḥ Uṣūl al-Dīn, 406
Sharḥ Uṣūl al-Pazdawī, 69
Sharḥ Uṣūl I'tiqād Ahl al-Sunna, 167, 310, 351, 369
Sharḥ al-'Utbiyya, 168-169
Sharī'a, 169, 282, 350
Shawāhid al-Ḥaqq, 182
Shifā fī Ma'rifati Ḥuqūq al-Muṣṭafā, 25, 176, 181, 182, 194, 234, 285, 309, 321, 399
Shifā' al-'Alīl wa-Ball al-Ghalīl fī Ḥukm al-Waṣiyya bil-Khatamāt wal-Tahālīl, 252
Shifā' al-Ṣudūr fī Ziyārat al-Mashāhid wal-Qubūr, 408
*Shifā' al-Siqām fī Ziyārati Khayr al-Anām*ﷺ, 273, 275, 276, 322
Shikāyat Ahl al-Sunna bi-Ḥikāyat mā Nālahum min al-Miḥna, 292, 368
Shu'ab al-Īmān, 7, 48, 143, 144, 172-173, 175, 177, 179, 221, 256, 265, 273, 274, 289, 293, 295, 297-298, 312, 389, 418, 442
Shurūṭ, 25
Shurūṭ al-A'immat al-Khamsa, 202
Ṣidq al-Khabar fī Khawārij al-Qarn al-Thānī 'Ashar, 470
Ṣifat al-Ṣafwa, 18, 60, 64, 91, 92, 133, 159, 174, 230, 250, 251, 270, 314, 353
Ṣila, 397
Silsila Ḍa'īfa, 39, 169, 350, 400
Sīra, 53, 60, 141-142, 439
Sīrat al-Imām Aḥmad, 311, 312, 392
Six Books, 343, 432, 463
Siyar A'lām al-Nubalā', 7, 12, 25, 31, 32, 41, 78, 84, 86, 92, 93, 98, 101, 103, 106, 112, 114, 121,, 132, 133, 135, 140-142, 145, 149, 150, 153, 154, 159-161, 164, 165, 167, 168, 170, 174, 183, 185, 186, 193, 196, 198, 200-202, 206-208, 211-212, 214, 220-221, 223, 224, 230, 232, 234, 235, 245-246, 250, 253, 255, 257, 259, 260, 262-264, 267-268, 270, 279, 280, 282, 292, 298, 300, 301, 303, 306, 309, 312-314, 317, 320, 323-325, 331, 341, 343, 346, 352-354, 356, 358-359, 362, 364, 385-386, 388, 390, 394, 397, 402, 403, 414, 417, 423-425, 444, 463
Siyar al-Kabīr, 15
Studies in Early Ḥadīth Literature, 332
Su'ālāt al-Bardha'ī, 150
Su'ālātuhu Yaḥyā, 266
Subul al-Salām fī Ḥukmi Ābā'i Sayyid

*al-Anām*ﷺ, 54
Ṣūfiyya wal-Fuqarā', 86
Sunan al-Kubrā, 64, 121, 238, 259, 274, 283, 289-290, 298, 315, 344
Sunan al-Shāfi'ī, 10, 25
Sunan al-Ṣiḥāḥ, 274, 275,
Sunan al-Wusṭā, 291
Sunna ('Abd Allāh ibn Aḥmad?), 355-357
Sunna (al-Ṭabarānī), 318
Sunna al-Nabawiyya wa Bayān Madlūlihā al-Shar'ī wa-Ta'rīf Ḥāl Sunan al-Dāraquṭnī, 273
Sunna Notes, 164, 325
Ṭabaqāt al-Awliyā', 85, 314
Ṭabaqāt al-Fuqahā', 13, 190, 270
Ṭabaqāt al-Ḥanābila, 45, 46, 78, 86, c76, 204, 211, 235, 258, 301, 310, 312, 313, 317, 324, 326, 341, 342, 349, 354, 358, 359, 362, 370, 371, 386-389, 393-395, 397, 398, 404-406, 414-416
Ṭabaqāt al-Ḥanafiyya, 13, 41, 79, 206
Ṭabaqāt al-Ḥuffāẓ, 432
Ṭabaqāt Ibn Ḥibbān, 266
Ṭabaqāt al-Kubrā (Ibn Sa'd), 64, 92, 164, 292
Ṭabaqāt al-Kubrā (al-Sha'rānī), 314
Ṭabaqāt al-Mālikiyya, see *al-Dībāj al-Mudhahhab* and *Shajarat al-Nūr al-Zakiyya*
Ṭabaqāt al-Shāfi'īyya (Abū Isḥāq al-Shirāzī), 253
Ṭabaqāt al-Shāfi'īyya (Ibn al-Ṣalāḥ), 265
Ṭabaqāt al-Shāfi'iyya (al-Isnawī), 253
Ṭabaqāt al-Shāfi'iyya al-Kubrā, 47, 64, 65, 80, 98, 155, 164, 178, 185, 190, 199, 203, 206, 211, 212, 245, 246, 248, 251, 253, 254, 258, 259, 263-265, 268, 282, 287, 291-293, 298, 300, 312, 324, 325, 354, 366, 368, 384, 386, 398, 416, 417, 421-423, 430
Ṭabaqāt al-Shāfi'iyya al-Wusṭā, 65, 155, 398
Ṭabaqāt al-Ṣūfiyya (*Harawī*), 106, 229
Ṭabaqāt al-Ṣūfiyya (*Sulamī*), 114, 248, 283, 314, 388
Ṭabaqāt al-Ṣūfiyya al-Kubrā, 206, 387
Tabarruk, 276
Tabṣīr fil-Dīn wa-Tamyīz al-Firqat al-Nājiya min Firaq al-Hālikīn, 68, 75, 79, 293
Tabṣīr Ulī al-Nahī, 255
Tabṣirat al-Ḥukkām fī Uṣūl al-Aqḍiya wa-Manāhij al-Ḥukkām, 183
Tabyīḍ al-Ṣaḥīfa fī Manāqib Abī Ḥanīfa, 7, 9, 34
Tabyīn Kadhib al-Muftarī, 78, 98, 176, 223, 2270, 271, 282, 291-293, 297, 366, 416
Tadhkira fil-Aḥādīth al-Mushtahara, 293, 295, 296
Tadhkirat al-'Ālim wal-Muta'allim, 254
Tadhkirat al-Ḥuffāẓ, , 7, 10, 11, 92, 105, 106, 147, 168, 196, 198, 203, 221, 264, 268, 271, 279, 296, 301, 358
Tadhkirat Ibn 'Aqīl, 389
Tadhkirat al-Mawḍū'āt, 256, 274
Tadhkirat al-Mu'aẓẓamiyya, 117
Tadrīb al-Rāwī fī Sharḥ Taqrīb al-Nawāwī, 115, 136, 260, 266, 280, 333
Tadwīn li-Akhbār Qazwīn, 40
Tafrī' fī Furū' al-Mālikiyya, 182
Tafsīr Gharīb al-Ḥadīth, 266
Tafsīr Ibn Kathīr. *See* Ibn Kathīr
Tafsīr al-Kabīr, 262, 292
Tafsīr al-Māwardī, 318
Tafsīr Mutashābih al-Akhbār, 26

Tafsīr al-Qurṭubī, 64, 121, 172, 212, 214, 293, 375
Tafsīr al-Ṭabarī. See al-Ṭabarī
Tafsīr al-Tha'ālibī, 362
Taghlīq al-Ta'līq,
Ṭaḥāwiyya. See *Bayān I'tiqād Ahl al-Sunna wal-Jamā'a*
Tahdhīb al-Asmā' wal-Lughāt, 43, 64, 185, 233, 242, 258, 299, 300, 325
Tahdhīb al-Āthār, 255
Tahdhīb al-Kamāl, 13, 41, 43, 64, 169, 172, 188, 193, 442
Tahdhīb al-Tahdhīb, 7, 9, 10, 28, 30, 32, 85, 86, 113, 169, 200-201, 274, 317, 388, 424, 442
Tahdhīb fī Fiqh al-Imām al-Shāfi'ī, 299
Taḥdhīr al-Khawāṣṣ min Akādhīb al-Quṣṣāṣ, 134, 258
Taḥdhīr al-Umma min Du'āt al-Wathaniyya, 371
Taḥrīm al-Naẓar fī Kutub Ahl al-Kalām, 407
Taḥrīr Taqrīb al-Tahdhīb, 59, 102, 150, 169, 248, 350
Taḥṣīl, 171
Tāj al-Tarājim fī Tafsīr al-Qur'ān lil-A'ājim, 68
Tāj wal-Iklīl, 182
Ta'jīl al-Manfa'a, 137, 464
Ta'jīz fī Ikhtiṣār al-Wajīz, 432
Takhrīj Aḥādīth al-'Ādilīn min al-Wulāt, 293, 295
Takhrīj al-Ahādīth al-Ḍi'āf min Sunan al-Dāraquṭnī, 275
Takhrīj Aḥādīth al-Iḥyā', 39, 61
Takhrīj Aḥādīth Mukhtaṣar Ibn al-Ḥājib, 400
Talbīs al-Jahmiyya, 78, 268, 370
Talbīs Iblīs, 230, 251, 384
Ta'līqa, 299
Talkhīs Aḥkām al-Janā'iz, 276
Talkhīṣ al-Ḥabīr, 260, 273, 275, 399, 400, 411
Talkhīṣ al-Mustadrak, 280
Talkhīṣ al-Mutashābih fil-Rasm, 273
Talkhīṣ al-Wāhiyāt, 173, 256
Talkhīṣ lil-Ḥākim, 278
Tamhīd, 115, 137, 143-144, 168-169, 175, 195, 284, 351
Tamhīd al-Awā'il, 46
Tanbīh al-Ghāfilīn, 110, 111
Tanbīh al-Wāhim, 280
Tankīl limā Warada fī Ta'nīb al-Kawtharī min al-Abāṭīl, 355
Tanqīḥ, 276
Tanwīh Baṣā'ir al-Muqallidīn fī Manāqib al-A'immat al-Mujtahidīn, 407
Tanwīr al-Ṣaḥīfa bi-Manāqib al-Imām Abī Ḥanīfa, 9
Tanzīh al-Anbiyā' 'an Tasfīh al-Aghbiyā', 63
Tanzīh al-Sharī'at al-Marfū'a, 40, 116, 360, 457
Taqaṣṣī, 144
Taqrīb al-Madārik bi-Sharḥ Risālatay al-Layth ibn Sa'd wa-Mālik, 157
Taqrīb al-Tahdhīb, 59, 87, 169, 239, 248, 294, 350, 399, 445
Taqrīb wal-Taysīr, 136, 155, 333
Taqyīd al-'Ilm, 101
Tarājim al-Musnad 'alā Sharṭ al-Ṣaḥīḥayn, 278
Tarājim al-Shuyūkh, 278
Ṭarb al-Amāthil, 51
Targhīb fil-'Ilm, 207
Targhīb wal-Tarhīb, 40, 295, 442
Ṭarḥ al-Tathrīb, 214, 269
Ta'rif Ahl al-Taqdīs, 86
Tārīkh Aṣbahān
Tārīkh Baghdād, 7-9, 13, 18, 29, 65, 109, 113, 121, 141, 175, 186, 188, 195, 205, 206, 246, 248, 257, 259, 279, 292, 302-303, 313, 317, 341
Tārīkh Dimashq. *See* Ibn 'Asākir
Tārīkh Ḥukamā' al-Islām, 298
Tārīkh Ibn Ḥibbān, 266

Tārīkh Ibn Maʿīn, 303
Tārīkh al-Imām Aḥmad, 310
Tārīkh al-Islām, 13, 44, 84, 202, 300, 313, 315, 354, 360, 361, 385-389, 423
Tārīkh Jurjān, 274, 294
Tārīkh al-Kabīr, 322, 327, 338, 346, 442, 464
Tārīkh al-Khulafā', 94, 159, 417
Tārīkh al-Madhāhib al-Islamiyya, 469
Tārīkh Nasaf, 336
Tārīkh Naysābūr, 223, 264, 278, 360
Tārīkh al-Rijāl, 255
Tārīkh al-Ṭabarī. *See* al-Ṭabarī
Tarkhīṣ fil-Ikrām bil-Qiyām li-Dhawī al-Faḍl min Ahl al-Islām, 30, 302, 315
Tarīqa Notes, 133
Tartīb al-Madārik, 30, 45, 78, 118, 121, 123, 131, 154, 159, 164-165, 168, 174, 179-181, 196, 199, 201
Tartīb al-Mawḍūʿāt, 25
Tartīb al-ʿUlamā', 255
Ta'sīs al-Naẓar, 16
Ta'sīs fī Radd Asās al-Taqdīs, 78, 268
Tasmiyat Fuqahā' al-Amṣār, 154, 303
Taswiya bayn Ḥaddathanā wa Akhbaranā, 26
Tatabbuʿ, 273, 332
Tatārkhāniyya, 40
Tatimmat al-Ibāna fī Fiqh al-Shāfiʿī, 299
Tawahhum, 384
Tawālī al-Ta'nīs fī Maʿālī Ibn Idrīs, 185-186, 188, 193, 300
Tawḍīḥ al-Afkār li-Maʿānī Tanqīḥ al-Anẓār, 399, 400
Tawḍīḥ al-Madrak fī Taṣḥīḥ al-Mustadrak, 280
Tawḍīḥ ʿan Tawḥīd al-Khallāq fī Jawāb Ahl al-ʿIrāq, 381
Tawḥīd, 39, 69, 81, 84, 211, 214, 262-264, 290, 317, 350-352, 382
Ta'wīl al-Aḥādīth al-Mushkalāt al-Wāridāt fil-Ṣifāt, 24
Ta'wīl Mukhtalif al-Ḥadīth, 24, 174
Ta'wilāt Ahl al-Sunna, 81
Ta'wilāt al-Qur'ān, 81
Tawjīh al-Naẓar, 139
Ta'yīd al-Ḥaqīqat al-ʿAliyya wa-Tashyīd al-Ṭarīqat al-Shādhiliyya, 86, 229
Taysīr al-ʿAzīz al-Ḥamīd fī Sharḥ Kitāb al-Tawḥīd, 182
Taʿẓīm wal-Minna, 53
Thawāb al-Ṣalāt ʿalā al-Nabī, 293
Thimār al-Janiyya, 66
Thiqāt, 39, 181, 198, 266, 267
Ṭibb al-Nabawī, 249
Tibyān fī Ādāb Ḥamalat al-Qur'ān, 33, 107, 118, 125, 299
Tuḥfat al-Aḥwadhī, 393, 400
Tuḥfat al-Akhyār, 400
Tuḥfat al-Ashrāf, 122
Tuḥfat al-Ḥukkām fī Nukat al-ʿUqūd wal-Aḥkām, 183
Tuḥfat al-Muḥtāj ilā Adillat al-Minhāj, 164, 182, 442
Tuḥfat al-Mujtahidīn bi-Asmā' al-Mujaddidīn, 254
Tuḥfat al-Taḥṣīl, 86
Turban in Islām, 179
Ṭuyūriyyāt, 387
ʿUhūd al-Muḥammadiyya, 295
ʿUjāla fil-Aḥādith al-Musalsala, 238
ʿUjālat al-Rākib fī Dhikri Ashraf al-Manāqib, 25
ʿUlūm al-Ḥadīth, 115, 139, 332
ʿUlūw, 56, 103, 149, 150, 169, 262-263, 267, 290, 323, 324, 350-352
Umarā' al-Mu'minīn fil-Ḥadīth, 31, 427, 438
ʿUmdat al-ʿĀrifīn, 305
ʿUmdat al-Qārī, 91
ʿUmdat al-Ṭālib li Maʿrifat al-Madhāhib, 304
ʿUmdat al-Taḥqīq fil-Taqlīd wal-

Talfiq, 192
Umm, 25, 144, 192, 207, 235, 254
'Uqalā' al-Majānīn, 116
'Uqūd al-Jawāhir al-Munīfa, 10
'Uqūd al-Jumān fī Manāqib al-Nu'mān, 7, 10, 116, 119, 198
Uṣūl Ahl al-Sunna, 78
Uṣūl al-Bid'at al-Ḥasana fil-Qur'ān wal-Ḥadīth,
Uṣūl al-Dīn, 65, 254, 384
Uṣūl al-Fatwā wal-Qaḍā' fil-Madhhab al-Mālikī, 158
Uṣūl al-Futyā fil-Fiqh, 182
Uṣūl al-Ḥadīth, 116
Uṣūl al-Jarḥ wal-Ta'dīl, 115, 131
Uṣūl al-Pazdawī, 69
Uṣūl al-Sunna, 310
Usd al-Ghāba, 388
'Utbiyya, 169
'Uyūn al-Athar, 164
Wā'iẓun Ghayru Mutta'iẓ, , 55, 63
Wāḍiḥ fī Uṣūl al-Fiqh, 405
Wāḍiḥa, 158
Wafā al-Wafā', 322
Wafayāt, 13, 30, 249
Wāfī bil-Wafayāt, 9
Wāfī fil-Furū', 304, 433
Wajīz fī Fiqh Madhhab al-Imām al-Shāfi'ī, 304, 432
Waqf, 433
Wara', 175, 397
Waṣāyā al-'Ulamā' 'inda Ḥuḍūr al-Mawt, 411
Wasīlat al-Islām bil-Nabī 'alayhi al-Ṣalātu wal-Salām, 161, 182
Waṣiyyat Abī Ḥanīfa, 69, 370
Waṣiyyat Ibn Mandah, 137
Waṣiyyat al-Muwaffaq Ibn Qudāma al-Maqdisī, 389
Waṣiyyat al-Shāfi'ī, pseudo-, 224
Wathā'iq, 207
Wuṣūl al-Tahānī bi-Ithbāt Sunniyyat al-Sibḥa wal-Radd 'alā al-Albānī, 92
Yawāqīt wal-Jawāhir, 53, 355
Ẓafar al-Amānī, 275
Zād al-Ma'ād, 251
Zawā'id ibn Mājah, 259
Zawā'id Tārīkh Baghdād, 186, 248, 292, 317, 360
Ziyādāt al-Jāmi' al-Ṣaghīr, 260
Zubdat al-Zakiyya li-Taḥrīm al-Sujūd al-Taḥiyya, 391
Zuhd (Aḥmad), 90, 249
Zuhd (Hannād), 249
Zuhd (Ibn Abī 'Āṣim), 175, 389
Zuhd (Ibn al-Mubārak), 48, 87, 113, 238, 249
Zuhd al-Kabīr (al-Bayhaqī), 48, 248, 298, 348

V. Index of Topics and Arabic Terms

adawāt, 373, 382
'adhaba, 103, 178, 393
adhān, 29, 113, 277, 446, 457, 471
aḥad, āḥād, 333, 446, 447, 449, 456
aḥdāth, 450
aḥwāl. See *ḥāl*
ākhira, 96, 111, 446, 448
'an'ana, 87, 122, 350, 437, 447, 457, 464
'araḍ, 68, 367, 380, 447, 453
'ālim, 12, 25, 104, 105, 122, 123, 176, 204, 226, 348, 433, 434, 446, 446, 452
'āmmī, 'awāmm, 225, 228, 446
amr, 188, 374, 375
angels, 45, 81, 89, 102, 221, 330, 349, 355, 357, 374-375, 377, 378, 442, 452
apostasy, 100, 219, 301, 307, 455
'aql, 171, 222, 240, 383
'ārif, 249, 346, 385, 447, 456
'arsh *See* Throne

asbāb al-wurūd, 463
astronomy, 261
awliyā', 22, 206, 459, 470
'awra, 102
azal, 447
'azīz, 447
bā'in, 262, 267, 324, 381
balāghāt, 143
beard, 76, 112, 161, 177, 213, 244, 292, 329, 338, 424
beatific vision, 181, 219, 311, 317, 342, 457, 462
bid'a. *See* innovations
bid'a ḥasana, 88, 447
bi-dhātih, 323, 448
Black Stone, 122, 460
Burning Tree, 361
congregational prayer, 111, 160, 231, 261
Consensus, 115, 155, 195, 214, 220, 228, 231, 233, 268, 296, 305, 335, 378, 398, 404, 412, 439, 445, 451, 470
contingencies. *See ḥawādith*
ḍa'īf, 39, 87, 115, 121, 132, 169, 183, 256, 274, 322, 361, 389, 399-400, 433, 447-449
ḥadīth in *faḍā'il*
dalīl 'aqlī, 383
dalīl shar'ī, 383, 464
descent, 156, 168, 324-325, 375
dhāt, 76, 323, 381, 448
dhikr, 113, 132-133, 178, 180, 181, 207, 238, 251, 311, 312, 448
dhikr-beads, 91-92, 152
divorce, 17, 95, 133, 157, 159-160, 189, 314, 335-336, 384
dogs as pets, 448
dreams: ḥadīths and rulings in them, 404
du'ā, 39, 133, 182, 206, 238, 382, 389, 448
dunyā, 96, 153, 347, 348, 448
faḍā'il al-a'māl, 114, 115, 400
fahrasa, 466
faqīr, 348
faqīh, 7, 14, 15, 21, 30, 51, 84, 91, 108, 118, 123, 145, 147, 171, 190, 198, 200, 214, 223, 225, 253, 256, 257, 261, 299, 304, 313, 348, 379, 383, 434, 448
farḍ, 236-237, 254, 261, 448, 456, 457, 459, 464
fasting, 48, 155, 247, 250, 287; month of Rajab, 286-287; perpetual, 20, 283-284, 346
fatra, 288
fatwā, 94, 113, 127, 153, 158, 161, 166, 168, 182, 183, 190, 220, 229, 251, 277, 287, 288, 351, 366, 403, 408, 448, 469
fay', 218, 295
fi'l, 324, 464
fiqh al-akbar, 449, 454, 467
firāsa, 116, 248, 449
fisq, 228
fiṭra, 56-57
food, 87, 107, 153, 260, 261, 347, 361
fuqahā', 22, 37, 45, 199, 201, 251, 335, 336, 433, 434, 448
ghāliya perfume, 96
gharaḍ, 382
gharīb, 36, 85, 113, 171, 173, 186, 205, 234, 248, 279, 350, 351, 393, 428, 433, 442, 446, 447, 449
gharīb al-ḥadīth, 449
ghawth, 417
ghība (slander), 109, 113, 148, 337, 379
ghusl, 215, 332, 450, 454
gnostic, 449, 460
grave, graves
  Abū al-Fatḥ al-Qawāsī's, 271
  Abū Ḥanīfa's, 205-206
  Aḥmad's, 342, 354, 361
  al-Bukhārī's, 339-340
  Ibn Surayj's, 253
  Ibrāhīm al-Ḥarbī's, 354

innovator's, 354
Ma'rūf al-Karkhī's, 354
Mālik's, 304
Prophet's ﷺ, 273-277, 288-289, 321-322, 327, 355, 390-391, 408-409
Prophet's ﷺ, facing during supplication, 37, 182
reciting Qur'ān over, 209, 411
the Scholar's, 346
al-Sakhāwī's,
ḥadath, 246, 450
ḥadd, 68, 149, 267, 349, 370-374
ḥādith, 450
ḥāfiẓ, 57, 280, 331, 438, 450, 458
hair (Prophet's ﷺ), 203, 390-391, 408
ḥāja, 236, 382
Ḥajj, 408, 453
ḥāl, 247, 450
ḥaqīqī, 450, 471
ḥarām, 104, 114, 208, 243, 391, 448, 451, 456, 457, 459, 464, 467
hawā, 89, 201, 348
ḥawādith, 381
henna, 103, 244
ḥijāb, 101, 448
ḥikma, 171, 382
ḥudūth, 450, 451
ḥujja, 99, 212, 314, 407, 466
ḥulūl, 451, 455
hunger, 241, 251, 346
i'tijār, 178
ibāḥa, 158, 208, 408
'Īd, 92, 107, 236, 237, 284, 339, 361, 450
iḥāṭa, 349, 372, 373
iḥsān, 451, 466
ijāza, 12, 26, 403, 451
ijmā', 183, 220, 231, 233, 326, 451, 461
ijtihād, 23, 32, 79, 166, 183, 205, 220, 225-226, 228, 258, 273, 287, 306, 369, 400, 447, 452, 458, 465
ikhtilāf, 157, 220, 304, 407, 452
iktisāb, 418
ilhām, 194
'illa, 248, 316, 382, 452
'ilm, 7, 91, 138, 142, 153, 167, 201, 247, 318, 349, 358, 397, 427, 446, 452, 460
'ilm al-ḥaqā'iq, 386
'ilm al-naẓarī al-yaqīnī ghayr al-ḍarūrī, 333
'ilm al-yaqīnī al-qaṭ'ī al-ḍarūrī, 333
'ilm ghalabat al-ẓann, 333
īmān, 41, 44-46, 48-51, 237, 452
innovations, innovators, *bid'a*, xxiii, 28, 29, 65, 70, 72-74, 76, 77, 84, 88, 125, 141, 151, 163, 164, 167, 177, 200, 201, 210, 223, 231-233, 237, 242, 243, 245, 255, 267-268, 272, 276, 281, 335, 354, 356, 358, 363-368, 373, 381, 383, 397, 416, 418, 419, 423-424, 446-448, 452-455, 467-470
intellect *See 'aql*
intercession, 43, 63-64, 90,95, 273, 276, 340, 447, 451, 459
intiqāl, 324, 378
Irjā', 42-44, 328
Irsāl, 447, 452, 459
iṣṭilāḥ. See muṣṭalaḥ
isnād, 13, 106, 113, 124, 125, 194, 322, 323, 332, 389, 393, 464, 465
isti'āra, 330
istiḥbāb, 408, 411
istikhāra, 236, 261
istīlā', 88
istisqā', 144, 157, 236, 323, 340
istiwā', 69, 75, 81-83, 102-103, 153, 167-170, 219, 236, 258, 262-263, 267, 291, 320, 323-324, 349-352, 356-357, 364, 370-372, 374 381
ithbāt, 382

ittibāʿ, 183, 201, 396, 402. *See taqlīd*
ityān, 375, 378
jabal, 314, 453, 466
Jāhiliyya, 208, 287, 358
jahl, 453
jarḥ wal-taʿdīl, 39, 98, 113-115, 200, 264, 453, 463
jāriḥa, jawāriḥ, 75, 453
jawāz, 453
jawhar, 68, 367, 380, 453-454
jazm, 380
jidāl, 170
jiha, 349, 373, 454
jihād, 15, 79, 88, 107, 112, 113, 251, 269, 392, 454, 458, 461
jism, 68, 213, 380, 453, 454, 458
jizya, 70, 152
Jumuʿa, 107, 155, 160, 236, 257, 360, 403, 409, 442, 448, 450
kabāʾir, 272
kalām, xxii, 12, 65-67, 76-78, 80, 210, 220-224, 232, 233, 245, 247, 254, 261, 283, 297, 309, 363-370, 373, 378, 383-385, 407, 414, 419, 423, 446, 454, 459
karāmāt, 230, 346, 454, 459
kasb, 414, 451
kashf, 249, 349, 400, 449, 454
kayf (modality), 68, 69, 93, 168, 170, 213, 372
khatma, 33, 145, 147, 252, 336
khilāf, 16, 215, 326, 453, 458
khuff, 41, 107, 244, 460
khushūʿ, 101, 161
kissing
  the grave of the Prophet ﷺ, 355, 390
  the hand of the *ʿĀlim*, 91, 106, 391
  the hand of the Prophet ﷺ, 298, 315
kufr, 56-57, 66, 72, 163, 219, 242, 272, 381, 455, 460
kunh, 68
kursī, 317-318, 351, 357-358
lafẓ, , 134, 139, 183, 337, 378, 381, 414, 416, 424-425, 471
laughter, 40, 85, 317, 322, 329-330
layyin, 87, 172, 173, 274, 276, 355, 455
lubān, 117
madhhab, 16, 21, 23, 24, 37, 157-158, 162, 165, 192, 193, 196, 222, 225-226, 228, 232, 246, 248, 253, 255, 258, 261, 297, 305, 313, 326, 338, 358, 380, 382, 389, 405-409, 411, 432, 455, 462, 468, 470, 471
maghāzī, 310, 463
maḥabba, 330
majāz, 50, 377, 378, 450, 471
majhūl, 168, 263, 357, 455-456
majhūl al-ḥāl, 266
makrūh, 448, 451, 456, 457, 459, 464
makrūhāt, 178
maktūb, 418, 425
manākīr, 458
mandūb, 448, 451, 456, 457, 459
mansūkh, 456, 460
maqām, 64, 450, 456
maqṭūʿ, 40, 125, 293, 332, 335, 456
marfūʿ, 39, 144, 317-318, 456
maʿrifa, 348, 447, 456, 466
masḥ ʿalāl-khuffayn, 41
mashhūr, 158, 183, 198, 280, 446, 447, 456, 459
mashīʾa, 43
mastūr, 266, 456
mawḍūʿ, 248, 274, 399, 400, 456
mawqūf, 39, 122, 159, 293-295, 317-318, 351, 352, 45; and Israelite reports, 351
Miḥna, 301, 307, 310
Minbar (Prophet's ﷺ), 159, 321, 322, 3555, 408
money, 29, 104, 105, 107, 257, 328, 368, 469
moustache, 177

mu'adhdhin, 29, 36, 208, 446, 457
mu'allaq, 318, 457
mubāḥ, 39, 448, 451, 456, 457, 464
mu'ḍal, 48, 143, 457
mudallis, 85, 122, 281, 457, 464, 465
mudṭarib, 457
muftī, 12, 14, 56, 146, 148, 153, 457
mughāyara, 215
muḥaddith, 12, 23, 103, 106, 159, 168, 198, 208, 241, 256, 257, 277, 305, 324, 427, 430-433, 435, 438, 450, 457
Muhājirūn, 108, 392
muḥdath, 231, 232, 245, 311, 416, 423, 458
Mujaddid, 253-254, 391
mujāhada, 296
mujāhid, 392, 454, 458
mujassim, mujassima. See anthropomorphists
mu'jiza, 234, 458
mujtahid, 7, 8, 14, 15, 21, 23, 63, 69, 77, 79, 98, 103, 121, 148, 175, 183, 185, 211, 226, 228, 255, 258-259, 282, 301, 306, 326, 379, 404, 452, 455, 458, 465
mujtahid muṭlaq, 23, 226, 258-259, 326, 458
*Mujtahid muṭlaq*s (al-Dhahabī's list), 400
mu'min, 45-47, 49-50, 67, 70-74, 173, 452, 458
mumkin al-wujūd, 458
munkar, 48, 63, 169, 172, 174, 180, 181, 205, 249, 279, 293-294, 399, 400, 411, 458, 468
munkar al-ḥadīth, 337, 458
munqaṭi', 143, 144, 196, 399, 458
murābiṭ, 459, 461
murīd, 217, 381
mursal, 40, 87, 93, 124, 143, 144, 174, 196, 201, 249, 259, 290, 335, 372, 399, 453, 459
mushabbih, mushabbiha, 212, 369, 376, 459
mushrik, 459, 467
musnad, 459
musnid, 12, 380, 433
mustaḥabb, 236, 237, 243, 409-411, 448, 451, 456, 457, 459
muṣṭalaḥ, 136, 453, 459
mut'a, 98
mutāba'āt, 142, 150, 248
mutakallimūn, 76, 79, 238, 365, 367-369, 378, 424, 459
mutarajjibūn, 287
mutashābihāt, 68, 69
mutawātir, 13, 95, 132, 154, 155, 168, 221, 234, 281, 333, 335, 446, 456, 460, 462, 466
muttaqī. See taqwā
nabīdh, 17, 208, 308
nadhr, 287
nafs, 88-89, 251
naïveness, 101
namīma (backbiting), 241, 347
nāsikh, 58, 456, 460
naẓar, 337, 367
Nine Books, 85, 100, 298, 460
niyya, 236, 410
nuzūl, 324
qaḍā', 153, 218, 460
Qāḍī as a definite title in each School, 299
qadam, 89-90, 317-318, 453
qadar, 67, 107, 141, 171, 218, 232, 419, 451, 460,
qadīm, 72, 206, 374, 415, 450, 461
Qadīm, 290, 461
qalansuwa, 17, 244, 393
qāṣṣ, 126, 128, 129, 461
qawl, 177, 183, 193, 464
photographic memory, 105, 152, 401, 402
physiognomy, 117, 406
pilgrimage, 110, 119, 122, 123,

153, 219, 230, 252, 255, 267, 269, 270, 274, 285, 331, 346, 390, 304
poverty, 152, 166, 218, 240, 242, 315, 384
pronunciation, 210-211, 337, 356, 359, 364, 404, 413-416, 419-421, 423-425
prostration to the grave of the Prophet ﷺ, 391
qibla, 2, 37, 73, 177, 181, 217, 321, 348, 367, 461
qidam, 447, 461
qirā'āt, 466
qiyās, 24, 220, 231, 245, 367, 404, 452, 461, 471
qurrā', 250
quṣṣāṣ, 132, 134, 461
quṭb, 461
rak'a, rak'as, 12, 33, 36, 113, 206, 236-237, 244, 246, 260, 331, 332, 336, 394, 410, 461
rasm, 467
ribā, 448
ribāṭ, , 454, 459, 461
rukhṣa, 12, 198, 228, 306
rummāna, 321
ṣadūq, 39, 150, 169, 205, 248, 249, 448, 461, 462
saḥābī, 448, 461
sadd al-dharī'a, 364
samā', 162, 433, 434
shādhdh, 168, 169, 183, 205, 427, 462
shafā'a, 273, 447, 459
shamā'il, 463
Shaykh al-Islām, 13, 26, 30, 57, 68, 79, 98, 103, 105, 112, 113, 168, 214, 225, 232, 271, 275, 286, 322, 333, 377, 379, 380, 403, 427-430, 436, 439, 469
shayṭān, 89
shirk, 38, 221, 238, 262, 322, 459, 463
shukr, 246
Ṣiddīq, 241, 245, 347, 349, 404, 445
sīra, 403, 463
staff, 190, 245, 358
standing for others, 30, 315
sunna mu'akkada, 237, 464
Sunna prayers, 235, 236
ṣūra, 211, 213, 262, 373, 376
swearing oaths, 38, 45, 70, 74, 87, 140, 164, 178, 206, 210, 241, 261, 287, 289, 312, 313, 347, 359, 396
tabarruk, 177, 206, 253, 276, 322, 340, 390
ta'dīl. See jarḥ wal-ta'dīl
tadlīs, 121, 350, 424, 447, 457, 464-465
tafwīḍ, 216, 217, 465
taḥannuk, taḥnīk, 178, 392
taḥayyuz, 378
tajsīm See anthropomorphism
takfīr, 449, 455
talaffuẓ, 210, 423
talqīn al-mayyit, 410
tanzīh, 170, 465
taqdīs, 465
taqlīd, ittibā', vii, 30, 31, 165, 183, 195, 201, 226-229, 358, 368, 395-396, 398-401, 402, 403, 445, 458, 465, 450,
taqrīr, 464
taqwā, 111, 357, 460, 465
tarāwīḥ, 113, 231, 236, 237, 410
ṭarīqa, 465
taṣawwuf, vii, 86, 106, 179-180, 229-230, 241, 246-247, 251, 278, 383, 385-387, 389, 446, 463, 466. See also Ṣūfīṣ
taṣdīq, 50, 70, 238
tashbīh, 76, 292, 309, 382, 406
ta'ṭīl, 68, 219, 292, 384, 457
tawakkul, 348, 388
tawassul, 38-40, 181, 205, 277, 322-323. 382, 389-390, 447
tawassum, 248

tawātur, 228, 460, 466
tawḥīd, xxii, 38, 39, 65, 92, 221-222, 247, 262,-264, 367-369, 373, 381, 436, 453, 454, 466; triple, 380
ta'wīl, 48, 81, 466
  Abū al-'Āliya's, 374
  Aḥmad ibn Ḥanbal's, 329, 374
  al-Akhfash's, 375
  al-Bayhaqī's, 318, 377
  al-Bukhārī's, 48, 318, 329
  al-Ḥasan al-Basrī's, 89
  Ibn 'Abbās's, 318
  Ibn 'Abd al-Salām's, 88, 330, 377
  Ibn Ḥibbān's, 330
  Ibn al-Jawzī's, 329
  Ibn Khuzayma's, 262
  al-Khaṭṭābī's, 377
  Mālik's, 169
  al-Māturīdī's, 82-83
  al-Nawawī's, 377-378
  of the *Salaf* in ḥadīth of the creation of Ādam ﷺ, 212-213
  of the *Salaf* on the verse "if you have touched women", 215
  Qāḍī 'Iyāḍ's, 330
  al-Rabī' ibn Anas's, 374
  al-Shāfi'ī's, 216
  al-Ṭabarī's, 318
  al-Zajjāj's, 375
ṭawīla, 179
tawriya, 59
tayammum, 215
thabat, 466
thabt, 248, 466
thawāb, 330, 374
thiqa, 10, 39, 142, 169, 181, 206, 230 249, 263, 302, 314, 375, 448, 451, 453, 462, 466
Throne, 38, 40, 47, 69, 75, 76, 81-83, 102, 103, 153, 167, 169, 219, 258, 262-263, 267, 291, 312, 315, 318, 320, 323-324, 350-352m 356, 359, 370-372, 374, 381, 388
Torah, 175, 351, 356, 357
transcendent, transcendence, 69, 76, 170, 237, 268, 378, 406, 465
Trinitarianism, 463
turban, 26, 92, 103, 178-179, 244-245, 339, 392-393
ṭuruq al-ḥadīth, 433
Vedantism, 463
Ummat Muḥammad ﷺ, 395
'ulūw, 82, 370, 381, 467
uncreated Qur'ān, 153, 224, 311, 359, 380, 384, 404, 413-416, 423, 425
uṣūl, 136, 143, 452, 454, 462, 467, 470
uṣūl al-dīn, xxii, 220, 282, 297, 449, 467
uṣūl al-fiqh, 452, 461, 464, 467
visitation. *See ziyāra*
voice, 133, 234, 270, 355, 362, 423
wajd, 251
wajh, 217, 329, 453
wājib al-wujūd, 458
walī, 241, 387, 454, 470
wara', 28, 89, 112, 215, 305, 364
weeping, 15, 99, 299, 327, 340 386
  'Alī ibn Abī Ṭālib's, 428
  'Āmir ibn 'Abd Allāh's, 161
  'Umar's, 323
  Aḥmad's, 206, 313, 383, 386
  Bilāl's, 277
  Bishr al-Ḥāfī's, 316
  Ibn al-Mubārak's,
  Ibn Hurmuz's, 161
  Mālik's, 159
  Sufyān al-Thawrī's, 108, 112
wilāya, 34, 427
wird, 15, 145, 147, 336, 385, 393
Witr, 235-237
written record, 248, 307
wuḍū', 107, 215, 236, 342, 450, 460, 471
yad, 69, 453
zāhid, zuhd, 20, 84, 106, 114, 346,

348, 353, 385, 386, 466, 471
ẓāhir, 46, 254, 450, 471
ẓāhir al-lafẓ, 378, 471
Zamzam, 259-260, 278, 390
zawāl, 325
zindīq, 220, 245, 445, 471
ziyāra (visitation), 276-277, 354, 408

VI. Index of Groups, Sects, and Tribes

Abdāl, 15, 85, 316, 387, 388, 446
Ahl al-Bayt, 413, 414, 465
Ahl al-Bid'a, 446, 448, 452, 454
Ahl al-Ḥadīth, xxii, 80, 235, 326, 439, 441, 445-446
Ahl al-Ḥaqq,
Ahl al-Ra'ī, 326
Ahl al-Sunna, xix, xxii, 43, 45, 46, 53, 65, 76, 79-81, 84, 92, 107, 110, 164, 212, 223, 272, 310, 354, 362, 365, 367, 370, 379, 382, 384, 404, 406, 417, 441, 446, 452, 454, 459, 460, 462; *Ahl al-Sunna wal-Jamā'a*, 41, 47, 51, 68, 75, 78-80, 277, 363, 446-447, 470
  and the phrase "I am a *mu'min*", 45
  and the terms *īmān* and *islām*, 45-51
  and use of *kalām*, xxii, 76-79
  defined as Ash'arīs and Māturīdīs, 68, 79
  defined by Sufyān al-Thawrī, 107
  definition, 79
  definition by Abū Ḥanīfa, 41
  distinct from Shī'ism, 272
Imām Aḥmad and Sunnī doctrines, 379
  on direction and voice, 362
  on grave sins not constituting disbelief, 45
  on place inapplicable to Allāh ﷻ, 81-82
  on *Tarāwīḥ* being twenty *rak'as*, 410
  on the ḥadīth of Ādam's ﷺ creation, 212-213
  on the parents of the Prophet ﷺ, 51-64
  on uncreatedness of the Qur'ān, 413-426
  one prays only behind them, 107
  pseudo-, 398, 406
  synonymous with *Ahl al-Ḥadīth*, 441
  the *Murji'a* among them, 42-44
  their persecution by the Mu'tazilīs, 207, 311, 354, 417
  their sinners better than pious innovators, 354
Anṣār, 61, 108, 290, 392
anthropomorphists, anthropomorphism, 23, 38, 76, 77, 98, 149, 170, 212, 213, 237, 243, 245, 246, 262, 267, 269, 292, 309, 310, 323, 356-359, 362, 363, 370, 384, 405, 430, 447, 451
Ash'arīs, xxii, 45-47, 53, 58, 64, 65, 67-69, 76-80, 84, 221, 267, 270, 271, 278, 281, 283, 291-293, 297, 310, 349, 363, 365-367, 369-370, 372-375, 380, 407, 414, 425, 446-447, 456, 462, 471
Athariyya, 80, 446
Bahais, 471
Bakhtāshīs, 449
Banū 'Abd al-Muṭṭalib, 185-186
Banū 'Abd Manāf, 192
Banū Hāshim, 93, 185-186
Bāṭinīs, 449, 460

Christians, 34-35, 103, 247, 395, 460, 463
Copts, 103
Ghulāt, 262, 449, 471
ḥarūriyya, 243
Ḥashwiyya, 66, 77, 367, 451, 457, 462, 469. *See also* Anthropomorphists
Hindus, 463
Hudhayl, 148
Ibāḍīs, *Ibāḍiyya*, 66, 451, 455
Ismā'īlīs, 449, 453, 460
Jabriyya, xxii, 77, 365, 382, 453
Ja'farīs, 455, 462
Jahmīs, *Jahmiyya*, 77-78, 149, 171, 211, 219, 267, 309-310, 324, 328, 337, 342, 354-356, 359, 363, 365, 367, 369, 383-384, 414-417, 419, 420, 424, 453, 454
Jews, 34-35, 103, 219, 376, 395
Kalb, 148
Karrāmiyya, 76, 280, 454, 462
Khārijīs, *Khawārij*, 33, 45, 66, 77, 81, 219, 358, 367, 369, 390, 449, 451, 454, 455, 462, 467-469, 470
Kinda, 126
lā-madhhabiyya, 358, 462
Māturīdīs, xxii, 22m 43-44, 51, 65, 68, 69, 77, 79-82, 84, 238, 365, 369 414, 446, 456, 459, 462
Mazdean, Zoroastrian, 315, 471
Mu'aṭṭila, 219, 457
Murji', *Murji'a*, 42-44, 69-70, 74, 242, 328, 365, 459
Mu'tazilīs, *Mu'tazila*, xxii, 43, 68, 76-81, 132, 221, 223, 226, 247, 270, 292, 310, 328, 365, 367-368, 382, 385, 392, 404, 413, 416, 420, 423, 445, 452-454, 457. 459.460, 462, 468
Pseudo-
Ahl al-Sunna, 398, 406
Ḥanbalī *'Aqīda*, 379-383
Ṣūfīs, 449, 457
Qadarī, *Qadariyya*, xxii, 30, 45, 65, 67-68, 78, 88, 92, 107, 141, 171, 218, 323, 242, 365, 367, 369, 423, 454, 459, 460, 462
Qādiyānīs, 471
Qalandarīs, 449
Qarāmiṭa, 81, 460
Rāfiḍa, *Rāfiḍīs*, *Rawāfiḍ*, 94, 98, 119, 242, 259, 272, 365, 385, 455, 461
Salafī, *Salafiyya*, 55, 63, 174, 225, 262, 269, 289, 309, 358, 380, 397, 400, 403, 462, 469
Shī'a, *Shī'ī*, Shī'ism, 81, 98, 107, 141, 272, 280-281, 304, 413, 447, 449, 451, 453, 455, 457, 459-462
ṣifātiyya, 372, 384
Ṣūfīs, 79, 84, 86, 92, 180-181, 229, 241, 246, 251, 255, 298, 342, 386-389, 463. See also *Taṣawwuf*
Wahhābīs, Wahhābiyya, 63, 92, 358, 455, 462, 467-470
Ẓāhirī School, *Ẓāhiriyya*, 211, 214, 246, 304, 338, 402, 445, 451, 462, 470, 471

VII. Index of Places

Zaydīs, 455, 462
Zoroastrians, Mazdeans 286, 425
Abadān, 86
Aleppo, 63, 214
Andalus, 146, 277
'Arafa, 267, 285, 342
'Asqalān, 189
Badr, 59, 87, 110
Baghdād, 10, 21, 34, 79, 141, 191-192, 195, 209, 218, 244, 250,

253, 257-259, 272, 305, 307, 314, 325, 327, 330, 353, 354, 359, 385, 391, 419, 420
Ba'labak, 98
Balkh, 325
Baqī', 304
Başra, 8, 16, 30, 31, 66, 69, 77, 79, 84, 86, 99, 193, 209, 325, 328, 336, 420
Beirut, 29, 98, 103,
Biqā', 98
Bukhārā, 246, 325, 338-339, 359, 425
Caesarea, 326
Cairo, 23, 33, 51-53, 218, 245, 253
China, 256
Damascus, xix, xxiii, 2, 23, 31, 53, 55, 98, 277, 285, 298, 326, 333, 355, 406, 430, 473
Diyār Bakr, 150
Egypt, 21, 31, 42, 121, 145, 147-148, 151, 157, 168, 195, 206-207, 260, 261, 328, 468
Euphrates, 253
Fusṭāṭ, 208
Ḥimṣ, 49, 152, 157, 326
Heart, 267, 271, 430
Ḥijāz, 42, 62, 99, 124, 158, 189, 277, 327, 328, 392, 468, 469
Ḥulwān, 327
India, 23, 445, 462
Iran, 86, 264
Iraq, 12, 29, 42, 59, 86, 121, 146, 157, 164, 176, 195, 202, 207, 210, 211, 264, 277, 302, 317, 327, 328, 359, 403, 439
Khartenk, 325, 339, 340
Khurāsān, 31, 42, 200, 267, 277, 283, 315, 324, 327, 328, 330, 336, 337, 417, 424, 425
Kūfa, 8, 21, 29-31, 33, 66, 67, 86, 94, 99, 117, 204, 302, 325, 326, 420
Kuwait, xxii
Lebanon, xxii
Madā'in, 317
Madīna, 9, 30, 57, 68, 86, 92, 93, 96, 106, 113, 116, 121-124, 126, 129, 131, 135-142, 145, 146, 148, 149, 154-157, 159, 160, 162, 163, 170, 182, 189, 190-192, 195, 274, 275, 277, 304, 314, 325, 358, 394, 398, 408, 419, 420, 438, 450, 463
Maghreb, 164, 466
Makka, 9, 31, 51, 64, 96, 99, 106, 145, 186, 189, 190, 195, 215, 216, 230, 244, 259, 305, 325, 343, 420, 429, 450, 461, 463
Marw, Merv, 197, 325, 353
Māturīd, 79
Nasā, 265
Naysābūr, 78, 150, 260, 279, 282, 291, 325, 337, 338, 417, 420, 424, 425
Qarāfa, 245
Qāsyūn, 406, 473
Qaṭī'a, 354
Qayrawān, 146, 152
Ray, 29, 31, 325
Ruḥba, 249, 250
Ruṣāfa, 314
Ṣāliḥiyya, 406
Samarqand, 79, 265, 325, 338-340
Sāmarrā, 316
Shām, Syro-Palestine, xix, 12, 21, 72, 98, 121, 146, 152, 157, 164, 189, 246, 277, 328, 387, 392, 411
Sudan, 121
Tārān, 222
Tashkent, 270
Tigris, 253
Transoxiana, 79, 221, 270, 277, 327
Tunis, 146

VIII. Index of Poetry

Yemen, 30, 31, 62, 121, 181, 188-191, 195, 455
Avail yourself in leasure of the benefit of prayer, 340
Be both a jurisprudent and a ṣūfī, 229
Curse them much or not, I care little, 29
Family of the Messenger of Allāh! To love you is an obligation, 234
Family of the Prophet are my intermediary, 234
Glory to Him Who has no comrade nor sitting-companion, 258
He who grows old finds in himself what he would wish for his enemies, 341
Hearts of Knowers have eyes, 349
I complained to Wakī' of my poor memory, 239
I keep the jewels of my knowledge concealed, 422
If you wish to stay you will soon be bereaved, 341
Like the dumb beasts who see not their ends, 340
O worshipper in the Two Sanctuaries, if you could only behold us, 112
This is the requital of a man whose peers departed before him, 341

Bibliography

'Abd ibn Ḥumayd. *Musnad*. Eds. Subḥī al-Badrī al-Sāmirā'i and Maḥmūd al-Sa'īdī. Cairo: Maktabat al-Sunna, 1988.

'Abd al-Razzāq. *Al-Muṣannaf*. 11 vols. Ed. Ḥabīb al-Raḥmān al-A'ẓamī. Beirut: al-Maktab al-Islāmī, 1983. With Ma'mar ibn Rāshid's *Kitāb al-Jāmi'* as the last two volumes.

Al-ʿAbdarī. *Al-Tāj wal-Iklīl*. With al-Ḥaṭṭāb's *Mawāhib al-Jalīl*. 6 vols. 2nd ed. Beirut: Dār al-Fikr, 1978.

Abū Dāwūd. *Al-Marāsīl*. Ed. Shu'ayb al-Arna'ūṭ. Beirut: Mu'assasat al-Risāla, 1988.

———. *Sunan*. 3 vols. Ed. Muḥammad Fu'ād 'Abd al-Bāqī. Beirut: Dār al-Kutub al-'Ilmiyya, 1996. See also al-'Aẓīm Ābādī, *'Awn al-Ma'būd*.

Abū Ghudda, 'Abd al-Fattāḥ. *Al-Isnād min al-Dīn*. With *Ṣafḥatun Mushriqatun min Tārīkh Samāʿ al-Ḥadīth ʿind al-Muḥaddithīn*. Aleppo: Maktab al-Maṭbū'āt al-Islāmiyya, 1992.

———. *Jawāb al-Ḥāfiẓ Abī Muḥammad 'Abd al-'Aẓīm al-Mundhirī al-Miṣrī 'alā As'ilatin fil-Jarḥ wal-Ta'dīl*. With *Umarā' al-Mu'minīn fil-Ḥadīth* and *Kalimāt fī Kashf Abāṭīl wa-Iftirā'āt*. Aleppo: Maktab al-Maṭbū'āt al-Islāmiyya, 1991.

——— and Salmān Abū Ghudda. *Khams Rasā'il fī 'Ulūm al-Ḥadīth:* Ibn 'Abd al-Barr, *Muqaddimat al-Tamhīd*; Ibn al-Ṣalāḥ, *Risāla fī Waṣl al-Balāghāt al-Arba'a fil-Muwaṭṭa'*; al-Mayyānishī, *Mā lā Yasa' al-Muḥaddith Jahlūh*; al-Ṭaḥāwī, *al-Taswiya bayna Ḥaddathanā wa-Akhbaranā*; and Aḥmad Banīs al-Fāsī, *Risāla fī Jawāz Ḥadhfi Qāla 'inda Qawlihim Ḥaddathanā*. Beirut: Dār al-Bashā'ir al-Islāmiyya, 2002.

———, 'Abd al-Fattāḥ. *Namādhij min Rasā'il al-A'immat al-Salaf wa-Adabihim al-'Ilmī*. Aleppo: Maktab al-Maṭbū'āt al-Islāmiyya, 1996. [Abū Ḥanīfa's *Risālat ilā 'Uthmān al-Battī* and Mālik's *Risālatān ilā al-Layth ibn Sa'd* with commentary.]

Abū Ḥanīfa. *Al-'Ālim wal-Muta'allim*. *Al-Fiqh al-Absaṭ*. *Al-Fiqh al-Akbar*. *Risāla ilā 'Uthmān al-Battī*. *Al-Waṣiyya*. Ed. al-Kawtharī. Repr. Cairo: al-Maktabat al-Azhariyya, 2001.

———. *Al-Fiqh al-Akbar*. See al-Qārī, *Sharḥ al-Fiqh al-Akbar*.

———. *Risālat Abī Ḥanīfa ilā 'Uthmān al-Battī*. See Abū Ghudda,

Namādhij.

———. *Waṣiyyat al-Imām al-A'ẓam Abī Ḥanīfa.* Istanbul: Dār al-Sa'āda, 1326/1908.

———. *Waṣiyyat al-Imām al-A'ẓam Abī Ḥanīfa.* Ed. Fu'ād 'Alī Riḍā. Beirut: Maktabat al-Jamāhīr, 1970.

———. *Waṣiyyat al-Imām al-A'ẓam Abī Ḥanīfa li-Tilmīdhihi Yūsuf al-Samtī.* With al-Zarnūjī's [7th c.] *Ta'līm al-Muta'allim.* Ed. 'Abd al-Jalīl al-'Aṭā al-Bakrī. Damascus: Dār al-Nu'mān, 1998.

Abū Khaythama. *Al-ʿIlm.* Ed. Nāṣir al-Albānī. Beirut: al-Maktab al-Islāmī, 1983.

Abū Nu'aym al-Aṣfahānī. [*Al-Muntakhab min*] *Dalā'il al-Nubuwwa.* Eds. Muḥammad Rawwās Qal'ajī and 'Abd al-Barr 'Abbās. Beirut: Dār al-Nafā'is, 1999[4].

———. *Faḍīlat al-'Ādilīn min al-Wulāt.* With al-Sakhāwī's *Takhrīj Aḥādīth al-'Ādilīn min al-Wulāt.* Ed. Mashhūr Ḥasan Salmān. Riyad: Dār al-Waṭan, 1998.

———. *Ḥilyat al-Awliyā' wa-Ṭabaqāt al-Aṣfiyā'.* 12 vols. Ed. Muṣṭafā 'Abd al-Qādir 'Aṭā. Beirut: Dār al-Kutub al-'Ilmiyya, 1997.

———. *Tasmiyatu mā Intahā ilaynā min Ruwāt Sa'īd ibn Manṣūr.* Ed. 'Abd Allāh Yūsuf al-Jadya'. Ryadh: Dār al-'Āṣima, 1989.

Abū al-Shaykh [Ibn Ḥayyān al-Aṣbahānī]. *Al-'Aẓama.* 5 vols. Ed. Riḍā' Allāh al-Mubārakfūrī. Ryad: Dār al-'Āṣima, 1988.

Abū Ṭālib al-Qāḍī. *'Ilal al-Tirmidhī al-Kabīr.* Ed. Ṣubḥī al-Sāmirā'ī, Abū al-Ma'āṭī al-Nūrī, and Maḥmūd al-Sa'īdī. Beirut: 'Ālam al-Kutub, 1989.

Abū Ya'lā al-Mawṣilī. *Musnad.* 13 vols. Ed. Ḥusayn Salīm Asad. Damascus: Dār al-Ma'mūn lil-Turāth, 1984.

Abū Yūsuf. *Al-Āthār.* Ed. Abū al-Wafā al-Afghānī. Hyderabad al-Dakn: Iḥyā' al-Maʿārif al-ʿUthmāniyya, 1355/1936.

Abū Zahra. *Abū Ḥanīfa: Ḥayātuhu wa-'Aṣruhu, Ārā'uhu wa-Fiqhuh.* Cairo: Dār al-Fikr al-'Arabī, 1997. [Repr. of the 1947 ed. with bibl. revisions.]

———. *Ibn Ḥanbal: Ḥayātuhu wa-'Aṣruhu, Ārā'uhu wa-Fiqhuh.* Cairo: Dār al-Fikr al-'Arabī, n.d. [Repr. of the 1947 ed.]

Aghā, Munīr 'Abduh. *Namūdhaj min al-A'māl al-Khayriyya fil-Maṭba'at al-Munīriyya.* Ryadh: Maktabat al-Imām al-Shāfi'ī, 1988.

Al-Aḥdab, Khaldūn. *Zawā'id Tārīkh Baghdād 'alā al-Kutub al-Sitta.* 10 vols. Damascus: Dār al-Qalam, 1996.

Aḥmad ibn Ḥanbal. *Faḍā'il al-Ṣaḥāba.* 2 vols. Ed. Waṣī Allāh Muḥammad 'Abbās. Beirut: Mu'assasat al-Risāla, 1983.

———. *Al-'Ilal wa-Ma'rifat al-Rijāl.* 4 vols. Ed. Waṣī Allāh ibn Muḥammad 'Abbās. Beirut and Ryadh: al-Maktab al-Islāmī, 1988.

———. *Al-Musnad.* 20 vols. Ed. Aḥmad Shākir and Ḥamza Aḥmad al-Zayn. Cairo: Dār al-Ḥadīth, 1995.

———. *Al-Musnad.* 50 vols. Ed. Shu'ayb al-Arna'ūṭ. Beirut: Mu'assasat al-Risāla, 2000-2001.

———. *Al-Waraʿ*. Ed. Muḥammad al-Ḥamūd. Kuwait: al-Dār al-Salafiyya, 1988.

———. *Al-Zuhd.* Beirut: Dār al-Kutub al-'Ilmiyya, 1978.

'Ajāj al-Khaṭīb. See al-Khaṭīb, Muḥammad 'Ajāj.

Al-'Ajlūnī. *Kashf al-Khafā.* 4th ed. 2 vols. Ed. Aḥmad al-Qallāsh. Beirut: Mu'assasat al-Risāla, 1985.

Al-Ājurrī. *Al-Sharī'a.* Ed. 'Abd al-Razzāq al-Mahdī. Beirut: Dār al-Kitāb al-'Arabī, 1996.

Arna'ūṭ, Shuʿayb and Bashshār ʿAwwād Maʿrūf. *Taḥrīr Taqrīb al-Tahdhīb.* 4 vols. Beirut: Mu'assasat al-Risāla, 1997.

Al-Ash'arī. *Risāla ilā Ahl al-Thughar.* 2nd ed. Ed. 'Abd Allāh Shākir al-Junaydī. Madīna: Maktabat al-'Ulūm wal-Ḥikam, 2002.

———. *Uṣūl Ahl al-Sunna wal-Jamā'a al-Musammāt bi-Risālati Ahl al-Thughar.* Ed. Muḥammad al-Sayyid al-Julaynid. Cairo: al-Maktabat al-Azhariyya, 1997.

'Awwāma, Muḥammad. *Adab al-Ikhtilāf.* 2nd ed. Beirut: Dār al-Bashā'ir, 1997.

———. *Athar al-Ḥadīth al-Sharīf fī Ikhtilāf al-A'immat al-Fuqahā' RaḍyAllāhu 'Anhum.* 4th ed. Beirut: Dār al-Bashā'ir al-Islāmiyya, 1997.

Al-ʿAynī. *Bughyat al-Multamas fī Subāʿiyyāt Ḥadīthi Mālik ibn Anas.* Ed. Ḥamdī ʿAbd al-Majīd al-Salafī. Beirut: ʿĀlam al-Kutub, 1985.

———. *ʿUmdat al-Qārī fī Sharḥ Ṣaḥīḥ al-Bukhārī.* 11 vols. <Istanbul:> Dār al-Ṭibāʿat al-ʿĀmira, 1308/1890.

Al-Aẓamī, Muḥammad Muṣṭafā. *Studies in Early Ḥadīth Literature: with a Critical Edition of Some Early Texts.* 2nd ed. Indianapolis: American Trust Publications, 1978.

Al-'Aẓīm Ābādī, Muḥammad Shams al-Ḥaqq. *'Awn al-Ma'būd Sharḥ Sunan Abī Dāwūd.* 14 vols. in 7. Beirut: Dār al-Kutub al-'Ilmiyya, n.d. Includes Abū Dāwūd's *Sunan.*

Al-Baghawī. *Sharḥ al-Sunna.* 8 vols. Eds. Shu'ayb al-Arna'ūṭ and Zuhayr al-Shāwīsh. Beirut: al-Maktab al-Islāmī, 1971.

Al-Bājī. *Al-Muntaqā Sharḥ al-Muwaṭṭa'.* 2 vols. Beirut: Dār al-Kitāb al-Gharbī. Reprint of 1331/1914 edition.

Al-Bājūrī. *Sharḥ Jawharat al-Tawḥīd.* Abridgement by 'Abd al-Karīm al-Rifā'ī. Beirut: Mu'assasat Anas ibn Mālik, 1971-1972.

Al-Bānī al-Ḥusaynī, Muḥammad Saʿīd. *ʿUmdat al-Taḥqīq fil-Taqlīd wal-Talfīq.* Ed. Ḥasan Suwaydān. Damascus: Dār al-Qādirī, 1997.

Al-Bardhaʿī. *Su'ālāt al-Bardhaʿī li-Abī Zurʿata wa-Abī Ḥātim al-Rāziyyayn.* Ed. Saʿdī al-Hāshimī. Al-Manṣūra: Dār al-Wafā', 1989.

Al-Bayāḍī, Kamāl al-Dīn Aḥmad. *Ishārāt al-Marām min 'Ibārāt al-Imām.* Ed.

Yūsuf 'Abd al-Razzāq. Preface by Imām al-Kawtharī. Cairo: Muṣṭafā al-Bābā al-Ḥalabī, 1949.

Al-Bayhaqī. *Al-Asmā' wal-Ṣifāt.* Ed. Muḥammad Zāhid al-Kawtharī. Beirut: Dār Iḥyā' al-Turāth al-'Arabī, n.d. Reprint of the 1358/1939 Cairo edition.

———. *Al-Asmā' wal-Ṣifāt.* 2 vols. Ed. 'Abd Allāh al-Ḥāshidī. Riyad: Maktabat al-Sawādī, 1993.

———. *Al-Da'awāt al-Kabīr.* 2 vols. Ed. Badr ibn 'Abd Allāh al-Badr. Kuwait: Markaz al-Makhṭūṭāt wal-Turāth, 1989.

———. *Dalā'il al-Nubuwwa wa-Ma'rifat Aḥwāl Ṣāḥib al-Sharī'a.* 7 vols. Ed. 'Abd al-Mu'ṭī Amīn Qal'ajī. Beirut: Dār al-Kutub al-'Ilmiyya, 1985.

———. *Faḍā'il al-Awqāt.* Ed. 'Adnān 'Abd al-Raḥmān Mājid al-Qaysī. Makka: Maktabat al-Manāra, 1990.

———. *Al-I'tiqād 'alā Madhhab al-Salaf Ahl al-Sunna wal-Jamā'a.* Beirut: Dār al-Afāq al-Jadīda, 1981; Dār al-Kutub al-'Ilmiyya, 1986².

———. *Al-Madkhal ilā al-Sunan al-Kubrā.* Ed. Muḥammad Ḍiyā' al-Raḥmān al-A'ẓamī. Al-Kuwait: Dār al-Khulafā' līl-Kitāb al-Islāmī, 1984. 2nd ed. 2 vols. Riyadh: Maktabat Aḍwā' al-Salaf, 1990.

———. *Manāqib al-Shāfi'ī.* 2 vols. Ed. Aḥmad Saqr. Cairo: Dār al-Turāth, n. d.

———. *Ma'rifat al-Sunan wal-Āthār.* 15 vols. Ed. 'Abd al-Mu'ṭī Amīn Qal'ajī. Aleppo and Cairo: Dār al-Wa'ī, 1991.

———. *Shu'ab al-Īmān.* 8 vols. Ed. Muḥammad Zaghlūl. Beirut: Dār al-Kutub al-'Ilmiyya, 1990.

———. *Al-Sunan al-Kubrā.* 10 vols. Ed. Muḥammad 'Abd al-Qādir 'Ata. Makka: Maktaba Dār al-Baz, 1994.

———. *Al-Zuhd al-Kabīr.* Ed. 'Āmir Aḥmad Ḥaydar. 3rd ed. Beirut: Mu'assasat al-Kutub al-Thaqāfiyya, 1996.

Al-Bazzār. *Al-Musnad.* [*Al-Baḥr al-Zakhkhār.*] 9 vols. Ed. Maḥfūẓ al-Raḥmān Zayn Allāh. Beirut and Madīna: Mu'assasat 'Ulūm al-Qur'ān & Maktabat al-'Ulūm wal-Ḥikam, 1989.

———. *Mukhtaṣar al-Musnad.* See Ibn Ḥajar, *Mukhtaṣar Zawā'id Musnad al-Bazzār.*

Al-Bukhārī. *Khalq Af'āl al-'Ibād.* Ed. 'Abd al-Raḥmān 'Umayra. Beirut: Mu'assasat al-Risāla, 1990. Ryad: Dār al-Ma'ārif al-Sa'ūdiyya, 1978.

———. *Ṣaḥīḥ.* 8 vols. in 3. Ed. Muḥammad al-Zuhrī al-Ghamrāwī. Bulāq: al-Maṭba'at al-Kubrā al-Amīriyya, 1314/1896. Repr. Cairo: al-Maṭba'at al-Maymūniyya [Muṣṭafā Bābā al-Ḥalabī *et al.*], 1323/1905.

———. *Ṣaḥīḥ.* See Ibn Ḥajar, *Fatḥ al-Bārī.*

———. *Al-Tārīkh al-Kabīr.* 8 vols. Ed. al-Sayyid Hāshim al-Nadwī. Beirut: Dār al-Fikr, n.d.

Al-Būṣīrī. *Miṣbāḥ al-Zujāja fī Zawā'id Ibn Mājah.* 2nd ed. 4 vols. Ed. Muḥammad al-Muntaqā al-Kashnawī. Beirut: Dār al-'Arabiyya, 1983.

Daḥlān. *Al-Sīra al-Nabawiyya wal-Āthār al-Muḥammadiyya.* With *al-Fatḥ al-Mubīn fī Faḍā'il al-Khulafā' al-Rāshidīn wa-Ahl al-Bayt al-Ṭāhirīn.* 2 vols. Miṣr: al-Maṭbaʿat al-Maymuniyya, 1310/1892.

Al-Dāraquṭnī. *Aḥādīth al-Muwaṭṭa' wa-Ittifāq al-Ruwāti 'an Mālikin wa-Ikhtilāfuhum fīhā Ziyādatan wa-Naqṣan.* With Ibn 'Asākir's *Kashf al-Mughaṭṭā fī Faḍl al-Muwaṭṭā.* Ed. Muḥammad Zāhid al-Kawtharī. Reprint Cairo: al-Maktabat al-Azhariyya lil-Turāth, 1996.

———. *Al-'Ilal.* 9 vols. Ed. Maḥfūẓ al-Raḥmān Zayn Allāh al-Salafī. Ryad: Dār Tiba, 1985.

———. *Sunan.* 4 vols. in 2. Together with Muḥammad Shams al-Ḥaqq al-'Aẓīm Ābādī's *al-Ta'līq al-Mughnī.* Ed. Al-Sayyid 'Abd Allāh Hashim Yamānī al-Madanī. Beirut: Dār al-Ma'rifa, 1966. Repr. Beirut: Dār Ihyā al-Turāth al-'Arabī, 1993.

Al-Dārimī. [*Al-Musnad al-Jāmi'.*] *Fatḥ al-Mannān Sharḥ wa-Taḥqīq Kitāb al-Dārimī al-Musammā bil-Musnad al-Jāmi'.* 10 vols. Ed. Abū 'Āṣim Nabīl Hāshim al-Ghamrī. Makka and Beirut: al-Maktba al-Makkiyya and Dār al-Bashā'ir al-Islāmiyya, 1999.

———. *Musnad* [*Sunan*]. 2 vols. Ed. Fu'ād Aḥmad Zamarlī and Khālid al-Sab' al-'Ilmī. Beirut: Dār al-Kitāb al-'Arabī, 1987.

Al-Daylamī, Shīrūyah ibn Shahradār. *Firdaws al-Akhbār bi Ma'thūr al-Khiṭāb 'alā Kitāb al-Shihāb.* Ed. Fawwāz Aḥmad al-Zayralī and Muḥammad al-Mu'taṣim Billāh al-Baghdādī. Beirut: Dār al-Kitāb al-'Arabī, 1987.

Al-Dhahabī. *Manāqib al-Imām Abī Ḥanīfata wa-Ṣaḥibayhi Abī Yūsuf wa-Muḥammad ibn al-Ḥasan.* Beirut: Dār al-Bashā'ir al-Islāmiyya, 1996.

———. *Mīzān al-I'tidāl.* 4 vols. Ed. 'Alī Muḥammad al-Bajawī. Beirut: Dār al-Ma'rifa, 1963.

———. *Mīzān al-I'tidāl.* 8 vols. Eds. 'Alī Muḥammad Mu'awwaḍ and 'Ādil Aḥmad 'Abd al-Mawjūd. Beirut: Dār al-Kutub al-'Ilmiyya, 1995.

———. *Al-Mughnī fil-Ḍu'afā'.* 2 vols. Ed. Nūr al-Dīn 'Itr. Qatar: Idara Iḥyā' al-Turāth al-Islāmī, 1987.

———. *Al-Mūqiẓa fī 'Ilm Muṣṭalaḥ al-Ḥadīth.* 3rd ed. Ed. 'Abd al-Fattāḥ Abū Ghudda. Aleppo: Maktab al-Maṭbū'āt al-Islāmiyya, 1998.

———. *Siyar A'lām al-Nubalā'.* 19 vols. Ed. Muḥibb al-Dīn al-'Amrāwī. Beirut: Dār al-Fikr, 1996.

———. *Siyar A'lām al-Nubalā'.* 23 vols. Ed. Shu'ayb al-Arna'ūṭ and Muḥammad Na'īm al-'Araqsūsī. Beirut: Mu'assasat al-Risāla, 1992-1993.

———. *Tadhkirat al-Ḥuffāẓ.* 4 vols. in 2. Ed. 'Abd al-Raḥmān ibn Yaḥyā al-Mu'allimī. A fifth volume, titled *Dhayl Tadhkirat al-Ḥuffāẓ,* consists in al-Ḥusaynī's *Dhayl Tadhkirat al-Ḥuffāẓ,* Muḥammad ibn Fahd al-Makkī's *Lahẓ al-Alḥāẓ bi Dhayl Tadhkirat al-Ḥuffāẓ,* and al-Suyūṭī's *Dhayl Ṭabaqāt al-Ḥuffāẓ.* Ed. Muḥammad Zāhid al-Kawtharī. Beirut: Dār Iḥyā' al-Turāth al-'Arabī and Dār al-Kutub al-'Ilmiyya, n.d.

Reprint of the 1968 Hyderabad edition.
———. *Tārīkh al-Islām wa-Wafayāt al-Mashāhīr wal-A'lām.* 52 vols. Ed. 'Umar 'Abd al-Salām Tadmurī. Beirut: Dār al-Kitāb al-'Arabī, 1989-2000.
———. *Tartīb al-Mawḍū'āt li-Ibn al-Jawzī.* Ed. Kamāl Basyūnī Zaghlūl. Beirut: Dār al-Kutub al-'Ilmiyya, 1994.
———. *Al-'Uluw lil-'Alī al-Ghaffār.* Ed. 'Abd al-Raḥmān Muḥammad 'Uthmān. Al-Madīna al-Munawwara: al-Maktabat al-Salafiyya, 1968.
———. *Al-'Uluw lil-'Alī al-Ghaffār.* Ed. Ḥasan 'Alī al-Saqqāf. Amman: Dār al-Imām al-Nawawī, 1998.
Encyclopedia of Islamic Doctrine. 7 vols. Moutain View: Al-Sunna Foundation of America, 1998.
Al-Fādānī. *Al-'Ujāla fil-Aḥādith al-Musalsala.* 2nd ed. Damascus: Dār al-Baṣā'ir, 1985.
Ghāwjī, Wahbī Sulaymān. *Abū Ḥanīfa al-Nu'mān Imām al-A'immat al-Fuqahā'.* 6th ed. Damascus: Dār al-Qalam, 1999.
Al-Ghazzālī. *Iḥyā' 'Ulūm al-Dīn.* 4 vols. 1374/1929. Repr. Beirut: 'Ālam al-Kutub, n.d.
Al-Ghumārī, 'Abd Allāh ibn Muḥammad ibn al-Ṣiddīq. *Bida' al-Tafāsīr.* 2nd ed. Cairo: Maktabat al-Qāhira, 1994.
———. *Al-Ibtihāj bi-Takhrīj Aḥādīth al-Minhāj.* With al-Bayḍāwī's *Minhāj al-Wuṣūl fī Ma'rifat 'Ilm al-Uṣūl.* Ed. Samīr Ṭaha al-Majdhūb. Beirut: 'Ālam al-Kutub, 1985.
———. *Irghām al-Mubtadi' al-Ghabī bi-Jawāz al-Tawassul bil-Nabī.* Ed. Ḥasan 'Alī al-Saqqāf. 2nd ed. Amman: Dār al-Imām al-Nawawī, 1992.
———, ed. Ibn al-Ṣalāḥ, *Risāla fī Waṣl al-Balāghāt al-Arba'a fil-Muwaṭṭa'.* In 'Abd al-Fattāḥ and Salmān Abū Ghudda. *Khams Rasā'il fī 'Ulūm al-Ḥadīth.* Beirut: Dār al-Bashā'ir al-Islāmiyya, 2002.
Al-Ghumārī, Aḥmad ibn Muḥammad ibn al-Ṣiddīq. *Al-Burhān al-Jalī fī Taḥqīq Intisāb al-Ṣūfiyya ilā 'Alī.* With *Fatḥ al-Malik al-'Alī bi-Ṣiḥḥat Ḥadīth Bāb Madīnat al-'Ilmi 'Alī.* Ed. Aḥmad Muḥammad Mursī al-Naqshbandī. Cairo: Maṭba'at al-Sa'āda, 1969.
———. *Fatḥ al-Wahhāb bi-Takhrīj Aḥādīth al-Shihāb.* 2 vols. Ed. Ḥamdī 'Abd al-Majīd al-Salafī. Beirut: 'Ālam al-Kutub, 1988.
———. *Al-Mudāwī li-'Ilal al-Jāmi' al-Ṣaghīr wa-Sharḥay al-Munāwī.* 6 vols. Ed. Muṣṭafā Ṣabrī. Cairo al-Maktaba al-Makkiyya, 1996.
———. *Al-Mughīr 'alā al-Aḥādīth al-Mawḍū'a fil-Jāmi' al-Ṣaghīr.* Cairo: Maktabat al-Qāhira, 1998. Reprint.
Ḥaddād, Gibrīl Fouād. *Albānī and His Friends: A Concise Guide to the "Salafī" Movement.* Birmingham: AQSA Publications, 2004.
———. *Al-Arba'ūn fī Faḍli al-Shāmi wa-Ahlih wal-Hijrati ilā Allāhi wa-Rasūlih. The Excellence of Syro-Palestine and Its People in Emigrating to Allāh and His Prophet : Forty Ḥadīths.* Forewords by Shaykh Adīb

Kallās, Shaykh Muṣṭafā al-Turkmānī, and Shaykh Ṣalāḥ Fakhrī. Damascus: Maktabat al-Aḥbāb, 2002.

Ḥajjī Khalīfa. *Kashf al-Ẓunūn 'an Asāmī al-Kutub wal-Funūn.* 2 vols. Beirut: Dār al-Kutub al-'Ilmiyya, 1992.

Al-Ḥākim. *Al-Madkhal ilā Ma'rifati Kitāb al-Iklīl.* Ed. Mu'tazz 'Abd al-Laṭīf al-Khaṭīb. Damascus: Dār al-Fayḥā', 2000.

———. *Al-Madkhal ilā al-Ṣaḥīḥ.* Ed. Rabī' Hādī al-Madkhalī. Beirut: Mu'assasat al-Risāla, 1984.

———. *Ma'rifat 'Ulūm al-Ḥadīth*, ed. Sayyid Mu'aẓẓam Ḥusayn. Dacca: n.p. 1935. Reprint Beirut: Dār al-Kutub al-'Ilmiyya, 1977.

———. *Al-Mustadrak 'alā al-Ṣaḥīḥayn.* With al-Dhahabī's *Talkhīṣ al-Mustadrak.* 5 vols. Indexes by Yūsuf 'Abd al-Raḥmān al-Mar'ashlī. Beirut: Dār al-Ma'rifa, 1986. Reprint of the 1334/1916 Hyderabad edition.

———. *Al-Mustadrak 'Ala al-Ṣaḥīḥayn.* With al-Dhahabī's *Talkhīṣ al-Mustadrak.* 4 vols. Annotations by Muṣṭafā 'Abd al-Qādir 'Aṭā'. Beirut: Dār al-Kutub al-'Ilmiyya, 1990.

Al-Ḥakīm al-Tirmidhī. *Nawādir al-Uṣūl.* Beirut: Dār Sadir, n.d. Repr. of Istanbul ed.

Al-Harawī al-Anṣārī. *Dhamm al-Kalām wa-Ahlih.* 5 vols. Ed. 'Abd Allāh ibn Muḥammad al-Anṣārī. Madīna: Maktabat al-Ghurabā', 1998.

Al-Ḥārith ibn Abī Usāma. *Musnad.* [*Bughyat al-Bāḥith 'an Zawā'id Musnad al-Ḥārith*]. 2 vols. Ed. Ḥusayn Aḥmad Ṣāliḥ al-Bakirī. Madīna: Markaz Khidmat al-Sunna wal-Sīra al-Nabawiyya, 1992.

———. *Musnad.* [*Bughyat al-Bāḥith 'an Zawā'id Musnad al-Ḥārith*]. Ed. Mus'ad 'Abd al-Ḥamīd Muḥammad al-Sa'dānī. Beirut: Dār al-Ṭalā'i', n.d.

Al-Ḥaṭṭāb. *Mawāhib al-Jalīl.* With al-ʿAbdarī's *al-Tāj wal-Iklīl.* 6 vols. 2nd ed. Beirut: Dār al-Fikr, 1978.

Al-Haytamī, Aḥmad. *Al-Fatāwā al-Ḥadīthiyya.* Cairo: Muṣṭafā al-Bābā al-Ḥalabī, Repr. 1970, 1989.

———. *Al-Khayrāt al-Ḥisān fī Manāqib Abī Ḥanīfa al-Nu'mān.* Cairo: Ḥalabī, 1326/1908.

Al-Haythamī, Nūr al-Dīn. *Kashf al-Astār ʿan Zawā'id al-Bazzār ʿalā al-Kutub al-Sitta.* 2 vols. Ed. Ḥabīb al-Raḥmān al-Aʿẓamī. Beirut: Mu'assasat al-Risāla, 1980.

———. *Majma' al-Zawā'id wa-Manba' al-Fawā'id.* 10 vols. in 5. Cairo: Maktabat al-Qudsī, 1932-1934. Repr. Beirut: Dār al-Kitāb al-'Arabī, 1967, 1982, and 1987.

Al-Ḥāzimī. *Shurūṭ al-A'immat al-Khamsa.* With Ibn Ṭāhir al-Maqdisī's *Shurūṭ al-A'immat al-Sitta.* Ed. Muḥammad Zāhid al-Kawtharī. Cairo: Maktabat 'Āṭif, n.d.

Al-Ḥumaydī. *Musnad.* 2 vols. Ed. Ḥabīb al-Raḥmān al-Aʿẓamī. Beirut: Dār al-Kutub al-ʿIlmiyya, n.d.

Ibn ʿAbd al-Barr. *Al-Intiqāʾ fī Faḍāʾil al-Aʾimmati al-Thalāthati al-Fuqahāʾ: Mālik wal-Shāfiʿī wa-Abī Ḥanīfa.* Ed. ʿAbd al-Fattāḥ Abū Ghudda. Beirut: Dār al-Bashāʾir al-Islāmiyya, 1997.

———. *Al-Istīʿab fī Maʿrifat al-Aṣḥāb.* 8 vols. in 4. Ed. ʿAlī Muḥammad al-Bajawī. Beirut: Dār al-Jil, 1992.

———. *Jāmiʿ Bayān al-ʿIlm wa-Faḍlih.* 2 vols. Ed. Abū al-Ashbal al-Zuhayrī. Dammam: Dār Ibn al-Jawzī, 1994.

———. *Al-Tamhīd limā fil-Muwaṭṭaʾ min al-Maʿānī wal-Asānīd.* 22 vols. Eds. Muṣṭafā ibn Aḥmad al-ʿAlawī, Muḥammad ʿAbd al-Kabīr al-Bakrī. Morocco: Wizārat ʿUmūm al-Awqāf wal-Shuʾūn al-Islāmiyya, 1967-1968.

Ibn ʿAbd al-Salām. *Fatāwā.* Ed. ʿAbd al-Raḥmān ibn ʿAbd al-Fattāḥ. Beirut: Dār al-Maʿrifa, 1986.

———. *Al-Fatāwā al-Mawṣiliyya.* Ed. Iyād Khālid al-Ṭabbāʿ. Beirut and Damascus: Dār al-Fikr, 1999.

———. *Fatāwā Shaykh al-Islām ʿIzz al-Dīn Ibn ʿAbd al-Salām.* Ed. Muḥammad Jumuʿa Kurdī. Beirut: Muʾassasat al-Risāla, 1996.

———. *Al-Ishāra ilā al-Ijāz fī Baʿḍ Anwāʿ al-Majāz* Ed. ʿUthmān Ḥilmī. Cairo: al-Maṭbaʿat al-ʿĀmira, 1313/1895.

———. *Maʿna al-Īmān wal-Islām aw al-Farq Bayn al-Īmān wal-Islām.* Ed. Iyād Khālid al-Ṭabbāʿ. Beirut and Damascus: Dār al-Fikr, 1995[2].

———. *Mulḥat al-Iʿtiqād.* Ed. Ḥasan al-Samāḥī Swaydān. Beirut and Damascus, 1993.

———. *Al-Mulḥa fī Iʿtiqād Ahl al-Ḥaqq.* In *Rasāʾil al-Tawḥīd.* Ed. Iyād Khālid al-Ṭabbāʿ. Beirut and Damascus: Dār al-Fikr, 1995.

———. *Al-Mulḥa fī Iʿtiqād Ahl al-Ḥaqq.* In Ibn al-Subkī, *Ṭabaqāt al-Shāfiʿiyya al-Kubrā,* vol. 8 p. 219-229.

Ibn Abī ʿĀṣim. *Al-Āḥād wal-Mathānī fī Faḍāʾil al-Ṣaḥāba.* 6 vols. Ed. Bāsim Fayṣal al-Jawābira. Ryad: Dār al-Raya, 1991.

———. *Al-Sunna.* Ed. Nāṣir al-Albānī. Beirut and Damascus: Al-Maktab al-Islāmī, 1993.

———. *Al-Zuhd.* 2nd ed. Ed. ʿAbd al-ʿAlī Ḥāmid. Cairo: Dār al-Rayyān lil-Turāth, 1988.

Ibn Abī Ḥātim. *Ādāb al-Shāfiʿī wa-Manāqibuh.* Ed. ʿAbd al-Ghanī ʿAbd al-Khāliq. Cairo: s.n., 1953.

———. *Al-Jarḥ wal-Taʿdīl.* 9 vols. Beirut: Dār Iḥyāʾ al-Turāth al-ʿArabī, 1952.

Ibn Abī al-ʿIzz. *Sharḥ al-ʿAqīda al-Ṭaḥāwiyya.* Ed. Muḥammad Nāṣir al-Albānī *et al.* Beirut: al-Maktab al-Islāmī, 1971[4], 1988[9].

Ibn Abī Shayba. *Al-Muṣannaf.* 7 vols. Ed. Kamāl al-Ḥūt. Ryadh: Maktabat al-Rushd, 1989.

Ibn Abī al-Wafāʾ. *Al-Jawāhir al-Muḍiyya fī Ṭabaqāt al-Ḥanafiyya.* Karashi: Mir

Muḥammad Kutub Khana, n.d.
Ibn Abī Ya'lā. *Ṭabaqāt al-Ḥanābila.* 2 vols. Ed. Muḥammad Ḥāmid al-Fiqqī. Cairo: Dār Iḥyā' al-Kutub al-'Arabiyya, n.d.
Ibn Abī Zayd al-Qayrawānī. *Al-Jāmi' fil-Sunan wal-Adab wal-Maghazi wal-Tārīkh.* Ed. M. Abū al-Ajfān and 'Uthmān Baṭṭīkh. Beirut: Mu'assasat al-Risāla; Tunis: al-Maktabat al-'Atīqa, 1982.
Ibn 'Ābidīn. *Radd al-Muḥtār Ḥāshiyat al-Durr al-Mukhtār Sharḥ Tanwīr al-Abṣār.* 6 vols. Bulāq: al-Maṭba'at al-Amīriyya, 1326.
———. *Rasā'il.* 2 vols. Reprint Beirut: 'Alam al-Kutub, n.d.
Ibn 'Adī. *Al-Kāmil fī Ḍu'afā' al-Rijāl.* 7 vols. Ed. Yaḥyā Mukhtār Ghazawī. Beirut: Dār al-Fikr, 1988.
Ibn al-'Arabī, Abū Bakr. *Aḥkām al-Qur'ān.* 4 vols. Cairo: ʿĪsā al-Bābī al-Ḥalabī, 1967-1968.
———. *'Āriḍat al-Aḥwadhī Sharḥ Sunan al-Tirmidhī.* 13 vols. Beirut, Dār al-Kutub al-'Ilmiyya, n.d.
———. *Al-'Awāṣim min al-Qawāṣim fī Taḥqīq Mawāqif al-Ṣaḥāba ba'da Wafāt al-Nabī* ﷺ. Ed. Muḥibb al-Dīn al-Khaṭīb. Cairo: al-Maṭba'at al-Salafiyya, 1952.
———. *Al-Maḥṣūl fī Uṣūl al-Fiqh.* Ed. Ḥusayn ʿAlī al-Yadarī and Saʿīd ʿAbd al-Laṭīf Fawda. Amman and Beirut: Dar al-Bayāriq, 1999.
Ibn 'Arrāq. *Tanzīh al-Sharī'at al-Marfū'a.* 2 vols. 2nd ed. Ed. ʿAbd Allāh al-Ghumārī. Beirut: Dār al-Kutub al-ʿIlmiyya, 1981.
Ibn 'Asākir. *Kashf al-Mughaṭṭā fī Faḍl al-Muwaṭṭa.* See al-Dāraquṭnī, *Aḥādīth al-Muwaṭṭa'.*
———. *Tabyīn Kadhib al-Muftarī fīmā Nasaba ilā al-Imām Abī al-Ḥasan al-Ash'arī.* Ed. Aḥmad Ḥijāzī al-Saqqā. Beirut: Dār al-Jil, 1995.
———. *Ibid.* Ed. Muḥammad Zāhid al-Kawtharī. Damascus: al-Qudsī, 1347/1929. Repr. Dār al-Fikr, 1979.
———. *Tārīkh Dimashq.* 70 vols. Damascus: Dār al-Fikr, 2000.
Ibn al-Athīr al-Jazarī (d. 630). *Jāmi' al-Uṣūl fī Ahādīth al-Rasūl.* 2nd ed. 12 vols. Ed. Muḥammad Ḥāmid al-Fiqqī. Beirut: Dār Iḥyā' al-Turāth al-ʿArabī, 1980.
———. *Jāmi' al-Uṣūl fī Ahādīth al-Rasūl.* 11 vols. Ed. ʿAbd al-Qādir al-Arna'ūṭ. Damascus: Ḥalwānī, 1973.
———. *Al-Kāmil fil-Tārīkh.* 20 vols. Beirut: Dār Ṣādir, 1979.
———. *Al-Kāmil fil-Tārīkh.* 10 vols. Ed. Abū al-Fidā' 'Abd Allāh al-Qāḍī. Beirut: Dār al-Kutub al-'Ilmiyya, 1995.
———. *Al-Nihāya fī Gharīb al-Athar.* 5 vols. Eds. Ṭāhir Aḥmad al-Zāwī and Maḥmūd Muḥammad al-Ṭabbākhī. Beirut: Dār al-Fikr, 1979.
———. *Usd al-Ghāba fī Maʿrifat al-Ṣaḥāba..* 7 vols. Ed. Muḥammad ʿĀshūr, Muḥammad al-Bannā, and Aḥmad Fāyid. Beirut: Maktabat al-Shaʿb, 1970.
Ibn Balbān. *Mukhtaṣar al-Ifādāt fī Rub' al-'Ibādāt wal-Ādāb wal-Ziyādātar al-*

*Ifādāt fī Rub' al-'Ibādāt wal-Ādāb wal-Ziyādāt*ḥammad Nāṣir al-ʿAjamī. Beirut: Dār al-Bashā'ir al-Islāmiyya, 1998.

Ibn al-Bazzāzī al-Kardarī. *Manāqib al-Imām Abī Ḥanīfa (al-Manāqib al-Kardariyya).* With al-Khwārizmī al-Muwaffaq's *Manāqib al-Imām Abī Ḥanīfa.* Hyderabād al-Dakn: Dā'irat al-Maʿārif al-Niẓāmiyya, 1321/1903.

Ibn Farḥūn. *Al-Dībāj al-Mudhahhab fī Ma'rifat 'Ulamā' al-Madhhab.* Ed. Ma'mūn ibn Muḥyī al-Dīn al-Jannān. Beirut: Dār al-Kutub al-'Ilmiyya, 1996.

Ibn Ḥajar. *Amālī al-Adhkār.* See *Natā'ij al-Afkār.*

———. *Al-Durar al-Kāmina fī A'yān al-Mi'ati al-Thāmina.* 4 vols. Hyderabad: Dā'irat al-Ma'ārif al-'Uthmāniyya, 1384/1964.

———. *Fatḥ al-Bārī Sharḥ Ṣaḥīḥ al-Bukhārī.* 13 vols. Ed. Muḥammad Fu'ād 'Abd al-Bāqī and Muḥibb al-Dīn al-Khaṭīb. Beirut: Dār al-Ma'rifa, 1959-1960.

———. *Ibidem.* Cairo: al-Maṭba'at al-Bahiyya, 1348/1929-1930.

———. *Hadī al-Sārī Muqaddimat Fatḥ al-Bārī.* Ed. Muḥammad Fu'ād 'Abd al-Bāqī and Muḥibb al-Dīn al-Khaṭīb. Beirut: Dār al-Ma'rifa, 1959-1960. [1st vol. of *Fatḥ al-Bārī*].

———. *Inbā' al-Ghumr bi-A'mār al-'Umr.* 4 vols. Ed. Ḥasan Ḥabash. Cairo: Lajnat Iḥyā' al-Turāth al-Islāmī, Wizārat al-Awqāf, 1994.

———. *Al-Iṣāba fī Tamyīz al-Ṣaḥāba.* 8 vols in 4. Ed. 'Alī Muḥammad al-Bijāwī. Beirut: Dār al-Jīl, 1992.

———. *Lisān al-Mīzān.* 7 vols. Hyderabad: Dā'irat al-Ma'ārif al-Niẓāmiyya, 1329/1911. Repr. Beirut: Mu'assassat al-A'lamī, 1986.

———. *Al-Maṭālib al-'Āliya.* 4 vols. Kuwait, 1973.

———. *Mukhtaṣar Zawā'id Musnad al-Bazzār.* 2 vols. Ed. Ṣabrī 'Abd al-Khāliq Abū Dharr. Beirut: Mu'assasat al-Kutub al-Thaqāfiyya, 1993.

———. *Natā'ij al-Afkār fī Takhrīj Aḥādīth al-Adhkār.* 3 vols. Ed. Ḥamdī 'Abd al-Majīd al-Salafī. Damascus and Beirut: Dār Ibn Kathīr, 2000.

———. *Al-Nukat 'alā Kitāb Ibn al-Ṣalāḥ.* 2 vols. Ed. Rabī' ibn Hādī 'Umayr. Ryadh: Dār al-Raya, 1997.

———. *Sharḥ Nukhbat al-Fikar.* With 'Alī al-Qārī's commentary, *Sharḥ Sharḥ Nukhbat al-Fikar.* Ed. Muḥammad and Haytham Nizār Tamīm. Beirut: Dār al-Arqam, n.d.

———. *Sharḥ al-Nukhba Nuzhat al-Naẓar fī Tawḍīḥ Nukhbat al-Fikar.* Ed. Nūr al-Dīn 'Itr. Beirut and Damascus: Dār al-Khayr, 1993[2].

———. *Taghlīq al-Ta'līq 'alā Ṣaḥīḥ al-Bukhārī.* 2nd ed. 5 vols. Ed. Sa'īd 'Abd al-Raḥmān Mūsā al-Qizqī. Beirut and Amman: al-Maktab al-Islāmī and Dār 'Ammār, 1989.

———. *Tahdhīb al-Tahdhīb.* 14 vols. Hyderabad: Dā'irat al-Ma'ārif al-Niẓāmiyya, 1327/1909. Repr. Beirut: Dār al-Fikr, 1984.

———. *Ta'jīl al-Manfa'a bi-Zawā'id Rijāl al-A'immat al-Arba'a.* Ed. Ikrām

Allāh Imdād al-Ḥaqq. Beirut: Dār al-Kitāb al-'Arabī, n.d.
———. *Talkhīṣ al-Ḥabīr.* 4 vols. Ed. Sayyid 'Abd Allāh Hashim al-Yamānī. Madīna, 1964. Repr. 4 vols. in 2, Cairo: Maktabat al-Kulliya al-Azhariyya, 1979.
———. *Taqrīb al-Tahdhīb.* Ed. Muḥammad 'Awwāma. Aleppo: Dār al-Rashid, 1997.
———. *Ta'rīf Ahl al-Taqdīs bi-Marātib al-Mawṣūfīn bil-Tadlīs.* 2nd ed. Ed. 'Abd al-Ghaffār al-Bandarī and Muḥammad 'Abd al-'Azīẓ Beirut: Dār al-Kutub al-'Ilmiyya, 1987.
———. [*Tawālī al-Ta'nīs*] *li-Ma'ālī Muḥammad ibn Idrīs.* Ed. 'Abd Allāh al-Qāḍī. Beirut: Dār al-Kutub al-'Ilmiyya, 1986. Incorrectly titled *Tawālī al-Ta'sīs.*
Ibn Ḥazm. *Al-Fiṣal fil-Milal.* 5 vols. Cairo: Maktabat al-Khānjī, repr. of the 1271 ed.
———. *Al-Iḥkām fī Uṣūl al-Aḥkām.* 8 vols. Cairo: Dār al-Ḥadīth, 1984.
———. *Al-Muḥallā.* 11 vols. Beirut: Dār al-Āfāq al-Jadīda, n.d.
———. *Al-Risālat al-Bāhira.* Trans. Muḥammad Ṣaghīr Ḥasan al-Ma'ṣūmī. Kuala Lumpur: International Institute of Islamic Thought and Civilization, 1996.
Ibn Ḥibbān. *Al-Majrūḥīn.* 3 vols. Ed. Maḥmūd Ibrāhīm Zāyid. Aleppo: Dār al-Wa'ī, n.d.
———. *Ṣaḥīḥ Ibn Ḥibbān bi-Tartīb Ibn Balbān.* 18 vols. Ed. Shu'ayb al-Arna'ūṭ. Beirut: Mu'assasat al-Risāla, 1993.
———. *Al-Thiqāt.* Also known as *Tārīkh al-Thiqāt.* 9 vols. Ed. Sayyid Sharaf al-Dīn Aḥmad. N.p.: Dār al-Fikr, 1975.
Ibn Hishām. *Al-Sīrat al-Nabawiyya.* 6 vols. Ed. Ṭāha 'Abd al-Ra'ūf Sa'd. Beirut: Dār al-Jil, 1991.
Ibn 'Imād. *Shadharāt al-Dhahab fī Akhbār Man Dhahab.* 8 vols. Beirut: Dār Iḥyā' al-Turāth al-'Arabī, n.d.
Ibn al-Ja'd. *Musnad.* Ed. 'Āmir Aḥmad Ḥaydar. Beirut: Mu'assasat Nādir, 1990.
Ibn Jamā'a. *Hidāyat al-Sālik ilā Ma'rifat al-Manāsik.* 4 vols. Ed. Nūr al-Dīn 'Itr. Beirut: Dār al-Bashā'ir al-Islāmiyya, 1994.
———. *Īḍāḥ al-Dalīl fī Qaṭ'i Ḥujaji Ahl al-Ta'ṭīl.* Ed. Wahbī Sulaymān al-Ghāwijī. Madīna: Dār al-Salām, 1990.
Ibn al-Jawzī. *Daf' Shubah al-Tashbīh bi-Akuff al-Tanzīh.* Ed. Muḥammad Zāhid al-Kawtharī. Reprint Cairo: al-Maktabat al-Azhariyya līl-Turāth, 1998.
———. *Daf' Shubah al-Tashbīh bi-Akuff al-Tanzīh.* Ed. Ḥasan 'Alī al-Saqqāf. Amman: Dār al-Imām Nawawī, 1991.
———. *Al-Ḍu'afā' wal-Matrūkīn.* 2 vols. Ed. 'Abd Allāh al-Qāḍī. Beirut: Dār al-Kutub al-'Ilmiyya, 1986.
———. *Al-'Ilal al-Mutanāhiya fil-Aḥādīth al-Wāhiya.* 2 vols. Ed. Shaykh

Khalīl al-Mays. Beirut: Dār al-Kutub al-'Ilmiyya, 1983.

———. *Manāqib al-Imām Aḥmad.* 2nd ed. Ed. Muḥammad Amīn al-Khanjī al-Kutbī. Beirut: Khanjī wa-Ḥamdān, 1349/1930-1931.

———. *Al-Mawḍū'āt.* 3 vols. Ed. 'Abd al-Raḥmān Muḥammad 'Uthmān. Madīna: al-Maktabat al-Salafiyya, 1967. See also al-Dhahabī's *Tartīb al-Mawdū'āt.*

———. *Al-Muntaẓam fī Tārīkh al-Mulūk wal-Umam.* 6 vols. Beirut: Dār Ṣādir, 1358/1939.

———. *Ṣayd al-Khāṭir.* Ed. "Board of Editors." Beirut: Dār al-Arqam, 1993.

———. *Ṣifat al-Ṣafwa.* 4 vols. 2nd ed. Eds. Maḥmūd Fākhūrī and Muḥammad Rawwās Qal'ajī. Beirut: Dār al-Ma'rifa, 1979.

Ibn al-Juwaynī. *Al-'Aqīda al-Niẓāmiyya.* Ed. Muḥammad Zāhid al-Kawtharī. Cairo: Maṭba'at al-Anwār, 1367/1948.

———. *Mughīth al-Khalq fī Tarjīḥ al-Qawl al-Ḥaqq.* Cairo: al-Maṭba'at al-Miṣriyya, 1934.

Ibn Kathīr. *Al-Bidāya wal-Nihāya.* 15 vols. Ed. Editing Board of al-Turāth. Beirut: Dār Iḥyā' al-Turāth al-'Arabī, 1993.

———. *Ibid.* 14 vols. Beirut: Maktabat al-Ma'ārif, n.d.

———. *Ikhtiṣār 'Ulūm al-Ḥadīth.* In Aḥmad Shākir, *al-Bā'ith al-Ḥathīth Sharḥ Ikhtiṣār 'Ulūm al-Ḥadīth.* Ed. Badī' al-Sayyid Laḥḥām. Damascus. Dār al-Fayḥā', 1994.

———. *Tafsīr al-Qur'ān al-'Aẓīm.* 4 vols. Beirut: Dār al-Fikr, 1981.

Ibn Khuzayma. *Al-Ṣaḥīḥ.* 4 vols. Ed. Muḥammad Muṣṭafā al-A'ẓamī. Beirut: Al-Maktab al-Islāmī, 1970.

———. *Al-Tawḥīd.* 5th ed. 2 vols. Ed. 'Abd al-'Azīz Ibrāhīm al-Shahwān. Ryadh: Maktabat al-Rushd, 1994.

———. *Al-Tawḥīd.* Ed. Muḥammad Khalīl Harrās. Beirut: Dār al-Kutub al-'Ilmiyya, 1992. Reprint of the Cairo 1388/1968-1969. edition.

Ibn Mājah. *Sunan.* See al-Suyūṭī *et al.*, *Sharḥ Sunan Ibn Mājah.*

Ibn al-Mubārak. *Al-Zuhd.* Ed. Habib al-Raḥmān al-A'zami. Beirut: Dār al-Kutub al-'Ilmiyya, n.d.

Ibn Mufliḥ, Ibrāhīm. *Al-Mubdi' fī Sharḥ al-Muqni'.* 10 vols. Beirut: al-Maktab al-Islāmī, 1980.

———. *Al-Maqṣad al-Arshad fī Dhikri Aṣḥāb al-Imām Aḥmad.* 3 vols. Ed. 'Abd al-Raḥmān Sulaymān al-'Uthaymīn. Riyadh: Maktabat al-Rushd, 1990.

Ibn Mufliḥ, Muḥammad. *Al-Ādāb al-Shar'iyya wal-Minaḥ al-Mar'iyya.* 3 vols. Ed. Muḥammad Rashīd Riḍā. Cairo: Maṭba'at al-Manār, 1929-1931.

Ibn al-Mulaqqin. *Khulāṣat al-Badr al-Munīr fī Takhrīj Kitāb al-Sharḥ al-Kabīr lil-Rāfi'ī.* 2 vols. Ed. Ḥamdī 'Abd al-Majīd al-Salafī. Ryad: Maktabat al-Rushd, 1990.

———. *Ṭabaqāt al-Awliyā'.* Ed. Nūr al-Dīn Shurayba. Cairo: Maktabat al-

Khānjī, 1994[2].
Ibn al-Muqri'. *Al-Rukhṣa fī Taqbīl al-Yad*. Ed. Maḥmūd Muḥammad al-Ḥaddād. Ryad: Dār al-'Asima, 1988.
Ibn Qāni'. *Mu'jam al-Ṣaḥāba*. 3 vols. Ed. Ṣalāḥ ibn Sālim al-Miṣrātī. Madīna: Maktabat al-Ghurabā' al-Athariyya, 1998.
Ibn Qayyim al-Jawziyya. *Al-Fawā'id*. Ed. Muḥammad 'Alī Quṭb. Iskandariyya: Dār al-Da'wa, 1992.
———. *I'lām al-Muwaqqi'īn 'an Rabb al-'Alamīn*. 3 vols. Eds. Yūsuf Aḥmad al-Bakrī, Shākir Tawfīq al-'Arūrī. Beirut: Dār Ibn Ḥazm, 1997.
———. *I'lām al-Muwaqqi'īn 'an Rabb al-'Alamīn*. 4 vols. Ed. Ṭaha 'Abd al-Ra'ūf Sa'd. Beirut: Dār al-Jīl, 1973.
———. *Madārij al-Sālikīn*. 3 vols. Beirut: Dār al-Kitāb al-'Arabī, n.d.
———. *Al-Rūḥ*. 3rd ed. Ed. Yūsuf 'Alī Badyawī. Damascus and Beirut: Dār Ibn Kathīr, 1998.
———. *Al-Rūḥ*. Beirut: Dār al-Kutub al-'Ilmiyya, 1975.
———. *Zād al-Ma'ād fī Hadī Khayr al-'Ibād*. 6 vols. 30th ed. Eds. 'Abd al-Qādir al-Arna'ūṭ and Shu'ayb al-Arna'ūṭ. Beirut: Mu'assasat al-Risāla, 1997.
Ibn Qudāma, Muwaffaq al-Dīn. *Dhamm al-Ta'wīl*. Ed. Badr ibn 'Abd Allāh al-Badr. Sharjah: Dār al-Fatḥ, 1994.
———. *Ithbāt Ṣifat al-'Uluw*. Ed. Badr 'Abd Allāh al-Badr. Kuwait: Dār al-Salafiyya, 1986.
———. *Lam'at al-I'tiqād*. Ed. 'Abd al-Qādir Badran and Bashir Muḥammad 'Uyūn. Damascus: Dār al-Bayān, 1992.
———. *Al-Mughnī fī Fiqh al-Imām Aḥmad ibn Ḥanbal al-Shaybānī*. 10 vols. Beirut: Dār al-Fikr, 1985; Dār al-Kitāb al-'Arabī, 1994.
———. *Rawḍat al-Nāẓir wa-Jannat al-Munāẓir*. With its commentary by 'Abd al-Qādir Badrān, *Nuzhat al-Khāṭir*. 2 vols. Cairo: Maktabat al-Kulliyyāt al-Azhariyya, 1991.
———. *Waṣiyyat al-Muwaffaq Ibn Qudāma al-Maqdisī*. Ed. Muḥammad Anīs Mahrāt. Damascus: Dār al-A'lām, 1994.
Ibn Qunfudh. *Wasīlat al-Islām bil-Nabī 'Alayhi al-Ṣalāt wal-Salām*. Beirut: Dār al-Gharb al-Islāmī, 1984.
Ibn Qutayba. *Al-Ma'ārif*. Beirut: Dār al-Kutub al-'Ilmiyya, 1987.
———. *Ta'wīl Mukhtalif al-Ḥadīth* Ed. Muḥammad Zuhrī al-Najjār. Beirut: Dār al-Jīl, 1972.
———. *Ta'wīl Mukhtalif al-Ḥadīth*. Ed. Muḥammad 'Abd al-Raḥīm. Beirut: Dār al-Fikr, 1995.
Ibn Rajab. *Jāmi' al-'Ulūm wal-Ḥikam*. 2 vols. Ed. Wahba al-Zuḥaylī. Beirut: Dār al-Khayr, 1996[2]. Ed. Shu'ayb al-Arna'ūṭ. Beirut: Mu'assasat al-Risāla, 1998[7].
———. *Sharḥ 'Ilal al-Tirmidhī*. 2 vols. Ed. Nūr al-Dīn 'Itr. Damascus: Dār al-Mallāḥ, 1978.

Ibn Sa'd. *Al-Ṭabaqāt al-Kubrā.* 8 vols. Beirut: Dār Sadir, n.d.

Ibn al-Ṣalāḥ. *Fatāwā wa-Masā'il Ibn al-Ṣalāḥ fil-Tafsīr wal-Ḥadīth wal-Uṣūl wal-Fiqh Wa-ma'ahu Adab al-Muftī wal-Mustaftī.* 2 vols. Ed. 'Abd al-Mu'ṭī Amīn Qal'aji. Beirut: Dār al-Ma'rifa, 1986.

———. *'Ulūm al-Ḥadīth.* Ed. Nūr al-Dīn 'Itr. 3rd ed. Damascus: Dār al-Fikr, 1984.

Ibn Sallām. *Faḍā'il al-Qur'ān.* Beirut: Dār al-Kutub al-'Ilmiyya.

Ibn Sayyid al-Nās. *ʿUyūn al-Athar fī Funūn al-Maghāzī wal-Shamā'il wal-Siyar.* 2 vols. Ed. Ibrāhīm Muḥammad Ramaḍān. Beirut: Dār al-Qalam, 1993.

Ibn al-Subkī, Tāj al-Dīn. *Qā'ida fil-Jarḥ wal-Ta'dīl.* Ed. 'Abd al-Fattāḥ Abū Ghudda. 2nd ed. Cairo, 1978. 5th ed. Aleppo and Beirut: Maktab al-Maṭbū'āt al-Islāmiyya, 1984.

———. *Ṭabaqāt al-Shāfi'iyya al-Kubrā.* 10 vols. Ed. Maḥmūd al-Ṭannāḥī and 'Abd al-Fattāḥ al-Ḥilw. 2nd. ed. Jiza: Dār Hijr, 1992.

Ibn Taymiyya, Aḥmad. *Al-Fatwā al-Ḥamawiyya al-Kubrā.* Ed. Ḥamd ibn 'Abd al-Muḥsin al-Tuwayjirī. Ryad: Dār al-Ṣumay'ī, 1998 = *al-Fatwā al-Ḥamawiyya* in *Majmū' Fatāwā Ibn Taymiyya,* 5:5-120.

———. *Majmū' Fatāwā Ibn Taymiyya.* 36 vols. Cairo, 1984.

Ibn al-Turkmānī. *Al-Jawhar al-Naqī fil-Radd 'alā al-Bayhaqī.* 2 vols. Dā'irat al-Ma'ārif al-Niẓamiyya, 1316/1898.

Ibn al-Zamalkānī. *Ujālat al-Rākib fī Dhikri Ashraf al-Manāqib.* Ed. Khayr Allāh al-Sharīf. Damascus: Dār al-Ṭabbā', 1993.

Al-Ījī. *Al-Mawāqif.* Eds. Ibrāhīm al-Dusūqī 'Aṭiyya and Aḥmad Muḥammad al-Ḥanbūlī. Cairo: Maṭba'at al-'Ulūm, 1357/1938.

Imām al-Ḥaramayn. See Ibn al-Juwaynī.

Al-'Irāqī, Walī al-Dīn. *Tuḥfat al-Taḥṣīl fī Dhikri Ruwāt al-Marāsīl.* Ed. 'Abd Allāh Nawwāra. Ryādh: Maktabat al-Rushd, 1999.

Al-'Irāqī, Zayn al-Dīn. *Al-Bā'ith 'alā al-Khalāṣ min Ḥawādith al-Quṣṣāṣ.* Ed. Muḥammad Luṭfī al-Ṣabbāgh. Damascus: Dār al-Warrāq and Dār al-Nayrabayn, 2001.

———. *Ṭarḥ al-Tathrīb fī Sharḥ al-Taqrīb.* 8 vols. in 4. Ed. Maḥmūd Ḥasan Rabī'. Beirut: Dār Iḥyā' al-Turāth al-'Arabī, 1992. Repr. of the Cairo edition.

'Itr, Nūr al-Dīn. Inaugural lecture to the Preparatory Class of Abū al-Nūr Institute, Damascus. October 1997. Unpublished.

———. *Al-Imām al-Tirmidhī wal-Muwāzana bayna Jāmi'ihi wa-bayn al-Ṣaḥīḥayn.* Beirut: Mu'assasat al-Risāla, 1988.

———. *Manhaj al-Naqd fī 'Ulūm al-Ḥadīth.* Beirut: Dār al-Fikr, 1996.

———. *Uṣūl al-Jarḥ wal-Ta'dīl.* Damascus: n. p., 1998.

'Iyāḍ. *Al-Ilmāʿ ilā Maʿrifati Uṣūl al-Riwāyati wa-Taqyīd al-Samāʿ.* Ed. Sayyid Aḥmad Ṣaqr. Cairo and Tunis: Dār al-Turāth and al-Maktabat al-ʿAtīqa, 1970.

———. *Al-Shifā bi-Ta'rīf Ḥuqūq al-Muṣṭafā.* Ed. 'Abduh 'Alī Kawshak. Damascus and Beirut: Maktabat al-Ghazālī and Dār al-Fayḥā', 2000. Abridged by 'Abd Allāh al-Talīdī, *Itḥāf Ahl al-Wafā bi-Tahdhīb Kitāb al-Shifā.* Beirut: Dār al-Bashā'ir al-Islāmiyya, 2000. See also al-Qārī's *Sharḥ al-Shifā'.*

———. *Tartīb al-Madārik li-Ma'rifati A'lāmi Madhhabi Mālik.* 8 vols. Ed. Sa'īd Aḥmad A'rab. Al-Muḥammadiyya (Morocco): Ministry of *Awqāf* and Religious Affairs of the Kingdom of Maghreb, 1981-1983. Vols. 1-2: 2nd ed.

Al-Jazā'irī, Ṭāhir. *Tawjīh al-Naẓar ilā Uṣūl al-Athar.* 2 vols. Ed. 'Abd al-Fattāḥ Abū Ghudda. Aleppo: Maktab al-Maṭbū'āt al-Islāmiyya, 1995.

Al-Kāsānī. *Badā'i' al-Ṣanā'i'.* 7 vols. Beirut: Dār al-Kitāb al-'Arabī, 1982[2].

Al-Kattānī, Muḥammad ibn Ja'far. *Naẓm al-Mutanāthir fil-Ḥadīth al-Mutawātir.* Ed. Sharaf Ḥijāzī. Cairo: Dār al-Kutub al-Salafiyya, n.d. and Beirut: Dār al-Kutub al-'Ilmiyya, 1980.

———. *Al-Risāla al-Mustaṭrafa li-Bayān Mashhūr Kutub al-Sunna al-Musharrafa.* 4th ed. Ed. Muḥammad al-Muntaṣir ibn Muḥammad al-Zamzamī al-Kattānī. Beirut: Dār al-Bashā'ir al-Islāmiyya, 1986.

Al-Kawtharī, Muḥammad Zāhid. *Fiqh Ahl al-'Iraq.* Ed. 'Abd al-Fattah Abū Ghudda. Aleppo: Maktab al-Maṭbū'āt al-Islāmiyya, 1970.

———. *Al-Ḥāwī fī Sīrat al-Imām Abī Ja'far al-Ṭaḥāwī.* Reprint Cairo: al-Maktabat al-Azhariyya līl-Turāth, 1995.

———. *Iḥqāq al-Ḥaqq bi-Ibṭāl al-Bāṭil fī Mughīth al-Khalq.* Repr. Cairo: al-Maktabat al-Athariyya lil-Turāth, 1998.

———. *Maqālāt.* Ryad and Beirut: Dār al-Aḥnāf, 1993.

———. *Maqālāt.* 2nd ed. Cairo: al-Maktabat al-Azhariyya līl-Turāth, 1994.

———. *Al-Nukat al-Ṭarīfa fīl-Taḥadduth 'an Rudūd Ibn Abī Shayba 'alā Abī Ḥanīfa.* Repr. Cairo: al-Maktabat al-Azhariyya līl-Turāth, 2000.

———. *Ta'nīb al-Khaṭīb 'alā Mā Sāqahu fī Tarjamat Abī Ḥanīfata min al-Akādhīb.* With *al-Tarhīb bi-Naqd al-Ta'nīb.* 5th ed. S.n.: n.p., 1990.

Keller, Noah Ha Mim, ed. and trans. *The Reliance of the Traveller.* Dubai: Modern Printing Press, 1991. Translation of Aḥmad ibn Naqīb al-Miṣrī's *'Umdat al-Salik.*

Khalaf, Najm 'Abd al-Raḥmān. *Mawārid al-Imām al-Bayhaqī fī Kitābihi al-Sunan al-Kubrā.* Ryadh: Maktabat al-Rushd, 1990.

Al-Khalīlī. *Al-Irshād fī Ma'rifati 'Ulama' al-Ḥadīth.* 3 vols. Ed. Muḥammad Sa'īd 'Umar Idrīs. Ryad: Maktabat al-Rushd, 1989.

Al-Khallāl. *Al-Sunna.* 3 vols. Ed. 'Aṭiyya al-Zahrānī. Ryad: Dār al-Rāya, 1990.

Al-Khaṭīb al-Baghdādī. *Al-Faqīh wal-Mutafaqqih.* 2 vols. Ed. 'Ādil al-'Azāzī. Dammām: Dār Ibn al-Jawzī, 1997.

———. *Al-Faqīh wal-Mutafaqqih.* Ed. Ismā'īl al-Anṣārī. Beirut: Dār al-

Kutub al-'Ilmiyya, 1980.
———. *Iqtiḍā' al-'Ilm al-'Amal.* Ed. M. Nāṣir al-Albānī. Beirut: al-Maktab al-Islāmī, 1984[5].
———. *Al-Jāmi' li-Akhlāq al-Rāwī wa-Adab al-Sāmi'.* 2 vols. Ed. Muḥammad 'Ajāj al-Khaṭīb. Beirut: Mu'assasat al-Risāla, 1991.
———. *Al-Jāmi' li-Akhlāq al-Rāwī wa-Adab al-Sāmi'.* 2 vols. Ed. Maḥmūd al-Ṭaḥḥān. Ryad: Maktabat al-Ma'ārif, 1983.
———. *Al-Kifāya fī 'Ilm al-Riwāya.* 2nd ed. Ed. Aḥmad 'Umar Hāshim. Beirut: Dār al-Kitāb al-'Arabī, 1986.
———. *Al-Kifāya fī 'Ilm al-Riwāya.* Eds. Abū 'Abd Allāh al-Ṣawraqī and Ibrāhīm Ḥamdī al-Madanī. Madīna: al-Maktabat al-'Ilmiyya, n.d.
———. *Mūḍiḥ Awhām al-Jam' wal-Tafrīq.* 2 vols. Ed. 'Abd al-Mu'ṭī Qal'ajī. Beirut: Dār al-Ma'rifa, 1987.
———. *Naṣīḥat Ahl al-Ḥadīth.* Ed. 'Abd al-Karīm Aḥmad al-Wiraykat. Al-Zarqā': Maktabat al-Manār, 1988.
———. *Al-Riḥla fī Ṭalab al-Ḥadīth.* Ed. Nūr al-Dīn 'Itr. Beirut: Dār al-Kutub al-'Ilmiyya, 1975.
———. *Al-Riḥla fī Ṭalab al-Ḥadīth.* Ed. Naṣr Abū 'Aṭāyā. See al-Nasā'ī's *Majmū'a Rasā'il fī 'Ulūm al-Ḥadīth.*
———. *Sharaf Aṣḥab al-Ḥadīth.* Ed. Muḥammad Sa'īd Hatīboğlu. Ankara: University Publications, 1972. Repr. Dār Iḥyā' al-Sunna al-Nabawiyya.
———. *Tārīkh Baghdād.* 14 vols. Madīna: al-Maktabat al-Salafiyya, n.d. See also al-Aḥdab, *Zawā'id Tārīkh Baghdād.*
Al-Khaṭīb, Muḥammad 'Ajāj. *Uṣūl al-Ḥadīth.* Damascus: Dār al-Fikr, 1998.
Al-Khaṭṭābī. *Gharīb al-Ḥadīth.* 3 vols. Ed. ʿAbd al-Karīm Ibrāhīm al-Ḥazbāwī. Makka: Jāmiʿat Umm al-Qurā, 1982.
———. *Iṣlāḥ Ghalaṭ al-Muḥaddithīn.* Ed. Muḥammad 'Alī 'Abd al-Karīm al-Radīnī. Damascus: Dār al-Ma'mūn lil-Turāth, 1987.
———. *Ma'ālim al-Sunan Sharḥ Sunan Abī Dāwūd.* 4 vols. in 2. Ed. 'Abd al-Salām 'Abd al-Shafi Muḥammad. Beirut: Dār al-Kutub al-'Ilmiyya, 1996.
Al-Khwārizmī al-Muwaffaq. *Manāqib al-Imām Abī Ḥanīfa.* With Ibn al-Bazzāzī al-Kardarī. *Manāqib al-Imām Abī Ḥanīfa (al-Manāqib al-Kardariyya).* Hyderabād al-Dakn: Dā'irat al-Maʿārif al-Niẓāmiyya, 1321/1903.
Al-Lacknawī. *Al-Ajwibat al-Fāḍila lil-As'ilat al-ʿAshrat al-Kāmila.* Ed. ʿAbd al-Fattāḥ Abū Ghudda. Followed by *al-Taʿlīqāt al-Ḥāfila ʿalā al-Ajwibat al-ʿAshra* by Abū Ghudda. 3rd ed. Aleppo: Maktab al-Maṭbūʿāt al-Islāmiyya, 1994.
———. *Al-Āthār al-Marfūʿa fil-Akhbār al-Mawḍūʿa.* Ed. Muḥammad ibn Basyūnī Zaghlūl. Beirut: Dār al-Kutub al-ʿIlmiyya, 1984.
———. *Al-Fawā'id al-Bahiyya fī Tarājim al-Ḥanafiyya.* With *al-Taʿlīqāt al-*

Saniyya ʿalā al-Fawā'id al-Bahiyya and *Ṭarb al-Amāthil bi-Tarājim al-Afāḍil.* Ed. Aḥmad al-Zuʿbī. Beirut: Dār al-Arqam, 1998.
———. *Iqāmat al-Ḥujja 'alā anna al-Ikthār min al-Ta'abbudi Laysa bi-Bid'a.* Ed. 'Abd al-Fattāḥ Abū Ghudda. Aleppo: Maktab al-Maṭbū'āt al-Islāmiyya, 1966. Repr. Beirut, 1992 and 1998.
———. *Al-Raf wal-Takmīl fil-Jarḥ wal-Taʿdīl.* Ed. ʿAbd al-Fattāḥ Abū Ghudda. 3rd ed. Beirut: Dār al-Bashā'ir al-Islāmiyya, 1987.
———. *Tuḥfat al-Akhyār bi-Iḥyā' Sunnati Sayyid al-Abrār* ﷺ with its commentary *Nukhbat al-Anẓār 'alā Tuḥfat al-Akhyār.* Ed. 'Abd al-Fattāḥ Abū Ghudda. Contains the latter's *Bayān Madlūl Lafẓ al-Sunna* and *Bayān Ḥāl Sunan al-Dāraquṭnī.* Aleppo: Maktab al-Maṭbū'āt al-Islāmiyya, 1992.
———. *Ẓafar al-Amānī.* Ed. 'Abd al-Fattāḥ Abū Ghudda. Aleppo and Beirut: Maktab al-Maṭbū'āt al-Islāmiyya, 3rd ed. 1995.
Laḥmar, Ḥāmid. *Al-Imām Mālik Mufassiran.* Beirut: Dār al-Fikr, 1995.
Al-Lālikā'ī. *Karāmāt al-Awliyā'.* Ed. Aḥmad Saʿd al-Ḥamdān. Ryadh: Dār Ṭayba, 1992.
———. *Sharḥ Uṣūl I'tiqād Ahl al-Sunna.* 4 vols. Ed. Aḥmad Sa'd Ḥamdān. Ryadh: Dār Ṭayba, 1982.
Al-Laqānī, 'Abd al-Salām. *Sharḥ Jawharat al-Tawḥīd al-Musammat* [*sic*] *Itḥāf al-Murīd bi-Jawharat al-Tawḥīd.* Ed. Muḥammad Muḥyī al-Dīn 'Abd al-Ḥamīd. Aleppo: Dār al-Qalam al-'Arabī, 1990.
Mālik ibn Anas. *Al-Muwaṭṭa'.* 2 vols. Ed. Muḥammad Fouad 'Abd al-Bāqī. Beirut: Dār al-Kutub al-'Ilmiyya, n.d.
Al-Malīnī. *Al-Arba'īn fī Shuyūkh al-Ṣūfiyya.* Ed. 'Āmir Ḥasan Ṣabrī. Beirut: Dār al-Bashā'ir al-Islāmiyya, 1997.
Mamdūḥ, Maḥmūd Sa'īd. *Bishārat al-Mu'min bi-Taṣḥīḥ Ḥadīth Ittaqū Firāsat al-Mu'min.* N. p.: 1995.
———. *Mubāḥathat al-Sā'irīn bi-Ḥadīth Allāhumma Innī As'aluka bi-Ḥaqq al-Sā'ilīn.* N. p.: 1995.
———. *Raf' al-Mināra li-Takhrīj Aḥādīth al-Tawassul wal-Ziyāra.* 3rd ed. Cairo: Dār al-Imām al-Tirmidhī, 1997.
———. *Wuṣūl al-Tahānī bi-Ithbāt Sunniyyat al-Sibḥa wal-Radd ʿalā al-Albānī.* 3rd ed. Yemen, Cairo, and Dubai: Dār al-Imām al-Tirmidhī and Maktabat Dār al-Ghannā', 1995.
Al-Maqdisī. *Al-Aḥādīth al-Mukhtāra.* 10 vols. Ed. 'Abd al-Mālik ibn 'Abd Allāh ibn Duhaysh. Makka: Maktabat al-Nahḍat al-Ḥadītha, 1990.
———. *Faḍā'il al-Aʿmāl.* Ed. ʿĀmir Aḥmad Ḥaydar. 3rd. ed. Beirut: Mu'assasat al-Kutub al-Thaqāfiyya, 1987.
Al-Mardāwī. *Al-Inṣāf fī Maʿrifat al-Rājiḥ min al-Khilāf ʿalā Madhhab al-Imām Aḥmad ibn Ḥanbal.* 10 vols. Ed. Muḥammad Ḥāmid al-Fiqqī. Beirut: Dār Iḥyā' al-Turāth al-ʿArabī, n.d.
Maʿrūf, Bashshār ʿAwwād and Shuʿayb al-Arna'ūṭ. *Taḥrīr Taqrīb al-Tahdhīb.*

4 vols. Beirut: Mu'assasat al-Risāla, 1997.

Al-Mas'ūdī, Muḥammad Radīd. *Al-Mu'tamad min Qadīmi Qawl al-Shāfi'ī 'alāl-Jadīd* Riyadh: Dār 'Ālam al-Kutub, 1996.

Al-Māturīdī. *Kitāb al-Tawḥīd.* Ed. Fatḥ Allāh Khalīl. Alexandria: Dār al-Jāmi'at al-Miṣriyya, n.d.

Al-Mizzī. *Tahdhīb al-Kamāl.* 35 vols. Ed. Bashshār 'Awwād Ma'rūf. Beirut: Mu'assasat al-Risāla, 1980.

Al-Mubārakfūrī. *Tuḥfat al-Aḥwadhī bi-Sharḥ Jāmi' al-Tirmidhī.* 10 vols. Beirut: Dār al-Kutub al-'Ilmiyya, 1990. Includes al-Tirmidhī's *Sunan.*

Al-Munāwī. *Fayḍ al-Qadīr Sharḥ al-Jāmi' al-Ṣaghīr.* 6 vols. Cairo: al-Maktaba al-Tijāriyya al-Kubrā, 1356/1937. Repr. Beirut: Dār al Ma'rifa, 1972.

Al-Mundhirī. *Jawāb al-Ḥāfiẓ al-Mundhirī 'an As'ilatin fil-Jarḥ wal-Ta'dīl.* Ed. 'Abd al-Fattāḥ Abū Ghudda. Aleppo: Maktab al-Manshūrāt al-Islāmiyya, 1991.

———. *Al-Targhīb wal-Tarhīb.* 4 vols. Ed. Ibrāhīm Shams al-Dīn. Beirut: Dār al-Kutub al-'Ilmiyya, 1997.

Muslim. *Ṣaḥīḥ.* 5 vols. Ed. M. Fu'ād 'Abd al-Bāqī. Beirut: Dār Iḥyā' al-Turāth al-'Arabī, 1954. Also see al-Nawawī, *Sharḥ Ṣaḥīḥ Muslim.*

Al-Nabhānī, Yūsuf. *Al-Arba'īn min Amthāl Afṣaḥ al-'Ālamīn.* Ed. Maḥmūd al-Arna'ūṭ and Ṣalāḥ al-Sha'al. Kuwait: Dār al-'Urūba, 1988.

———. *Ḥujjat Allāh 'alā al-'Ālamīn bi-Mu'jizāt Sayyid al-Mursalīn.* N.p.: s.n., 1317/1899.

———. *Shawāhid al-Ḥaqq fil-Istighātha bi-Sayyid al-Khalq* ﷺ. N.p.: s.n., 1323/1905.

Al-Nasā'ī. *'Amal al-Yawm wal-Layla.* 2nd ed. Ed. Fārūq Ḥammāda. Beirut: Mu'assasat al-Risāla, 1986.

———. *Sunan.* See al-Suyūṭī, *Sharḥ Sunan al-Nasā'ī.*

———. *Al-Sunan al-Kubrā.* 6 vols. Eds. 'Abd al-Ghaffār Sulaymān al-Bandarī and Sayyid Kisrawī Ḥasan. Beirut: Dār al-Kutub al-'Ilmiyya, 1991.

Al-Nawawī. *Al-Adhkār al-Muntakhaba min Kalām Sayyid al-Abrār.* Cairo: al-Ḥalabī 1348/1929.

———. *Bustān al-'Ārifīn fil-Zuhd wal-Taṣawwuf.* Ed. 'Abd al-Ḥamīd Darwīsh. Damascus: Published by editor, 1999-2000. Also: Beirut: Dār al-Kitāb al-'Arabī, 1985.

———. *Fatāwā.* Ed. Muḥammad al-Ḥajjār. Ḥalab: al-Maṭba'at al-'Arabiyya, 1971.

———. *Irshād Ṭullāb al-Ḥaqā'iq ilā Ma'rifati Sunan Khayri al-Khalā'iq.* 3rd ed. Ed. Nūr al-Dīn 'Itr. Beirut: Dār al-Bashā'ir al-Islāmiyya, 1992.

———. *Al-Majmū' Sharḥ al-Muhadhdhab.* 18 vols. Ed. Zakariyyā 'Alī Yūsuf. Cairo: Maṭba'at al-'Āṣima, 1963-1970.

———. *Tahdhīb al-Asmā' wal-Lughāt.* 3 vols. Cairo: Idārat al-Ṭibā'at al-Munīriyya, [1927?].

———. *Al-Taqrīb wal-Taysīr li-Ma'rifat Sunan al-Bashīr al-Nadhīr.* Beirut: Dār al-Kutub al-'Ilmiyya, 1987. Also in al-Suyūṭī's *Tadrīb al-Rāwī.*

———. *Al-Tarkhīṣ fil-Ikrām bil-Qiyām li-Dhawī al-Faḍli wal-Maziyyati min Ahli al-Islām 'alā Jihat al-Birr wal-Tawqīr wal-Iḥtirām la 'alā Jihat al-Riyā' wal-I'ẓām.* Ed. Kīlānī Muḥammad Khalīfa. Beirut: Dār al-Bashā'ir al-Islāmiyya, 1988.

———. *Al-Tibyān fī Ādāb Ḥamalat al-Qur'ān.* Ed. 'Abd al-'Azīz 'Izz al-Dīn al-Sayrawān. Beirut: Dār al-Nafā'is, 1992[3].

———. *Al-Tibyān fī Ādāb Ḥamalat al-Qur'ān.* Ed. Bashīr Muḥammad 'Uyūn. 2nd ed. Al-Ṭā'if and Damascus: Maktabat al-Mu'ayyad and Maktabat Dār al-Bayān, 1993.

Al-Qārī. *Adillat Mu^ctaqad Abī Ḥanīfat al-Imām al-A^cẓam fī Abaway al-Rasūl Ṣalla Allāhu ^cayahi wa-Sallam.* Ed. Mashhūr ibn Ḥasan ibn Salmān. Madīna: Maktabat al-Ghurabā' al-Athariyya, 1993.

———. *Al-Asrār al-Marfū'a fil-Akhbār al-Mawḍū'a. (Al-Mawḍū'āt al-Kubrā).* 2nd ed. Ed. Muḥammad ibn Luṭfī al-Ṣabbāgh. Beirut and Damascus: al-Maktab al-Islāmī, 1986.

———. *Al-Maslak al-Mutaqassiṭ fil-Mansak al-Mutawassiṭ ^calā Lubāb al-Manāsik Mukhtaṣar Naf al-Nāsik lil-Sindī.* Cairo: al-Maṭba^cat al-^cĀmira, 1303/1886.

———. *Al-Maṣnū^c fī Ma^crifat al-Ḥadīth al-Mawḍū^c.* 5th ed. Ed. ^cAbd al-Fattāḥ Abū Ghudda. Beirut: Dār al-Bashā'ir al-Islāmiyya, 1994.

———. *Minaḥ al-Rawḍ al-Azhar fī Sharḥ al-Fiqh al-Akbar.* Ed. Wahbī Sulaymān Ghāwjī. Beirut: Dār al-Bashā'ir al-Islāmiyya, 1998.

———. *Mirqāt al-Mafātīḥ Sharḥ Mishkāt al-Maṣābīḥ.* 5 vols. Ed. Muḥammad al-Zuhrī al-Ghamrawi. Cairo: al-Maṭba'at al-Maymuniyya, 1309/1892. Reprint Beirut: Dār Iḥyā' al-Turāth al-'Arabī, n.d.

———. *Mirqāt al-Mafātīḥ Sharḥ Mishkāt al-Maṣābīḥ.* With Ibn Ḥajar's *Ajwiba 'alā Risālat al-Qazwīnī Ḥawla Ba'ḍ Aḥādīth al-Maṣābīḥ.* 11 vols. Ed. Ṣidqī Muḥammad Jamīl al-'Aṭṭār. Damascus: Dār al-Fikr, 1994.

———. *Sharḥ 'Ayn al-'Ilm wa-Zayn al-Ḥilm.* 2 vols. in 1. Cairo: al-Maṭba'at al-'Āmira, 1291/1874.

———. *Sharḥ 'Ayn al-'Ilm wa-Zayn al-Ḥilm.* 2 vols. Cairo: Maktabat al-Thaqāfa al-Dīniyya, 1989.

———. *Sharḥ al-Fiqh al-Akbar.* A commentary on Abū Ḥanīfa's *al-Fiqh al-Akbar.* Ed. Shaykh Marwān Muḥammad al-Sha''ār. Beirut: Dār al-Nafā'is, 1997.

———. *Sharḥ Sharḥ Nukhbat al-Fikar.* A supercommentary on Ibn Ḥajar's *Sharḥ Nukhbat al-Fikar.* Ed. Muḥammad and Haytham Nizār Tamīm. Beirut: Dār al-Arqam, n.d.

———. *Sharḥ al-Shifā.* 2 vols. Bulāq: 1275/1858. Repr. Maṭba'at al-Ḥajj al-Busnawī, 1285/ 1868. Repr. Āstāna [Istanbul]: 1290/1873. Repr.

Āstāna: al-Maṭba'at al-'Uthmāniyya, 1316/1898. Repr. Cairo: 1312/1894. Repr. Beirut: Dār al-Kutub al-'Ilmiyya, n.d.

Al-Qāsimī. *Qawā'id al-Taḥdīth.* Beirut: Dār al-Kutub al-'Ilmiyya and Dār Iḥyā' al-Sunna al-Nabawiyya, n.d.

Al-Qinnawjī [Ṣiddīq Ḥasan Khān]. *Qiṭf al-Thamar fī Bayān 'Aqīdat Ahl al-Athar.* Ed. 'Āṣim 'Abd Allāh al-Qaryūṭī. Jordan: Sharikat al-Sharq al-Awsaṭ līl-Ṭibā'a, 1984.

Al-Quḍā'ī. *Musnad al-Shihāb.* 2 vols. Ed. Ḥamdī ibn 'Abd al-Majīd al-Salafī. Beirut: Mu'assasat al-Risāla, 1986.

Al-Qurṭubī. *Al-Asnā fī Sharḥ Asmā' Allāh al-Ḥusnā.* 2 vols. Ed. Muḥammad Ḥasan Jabal, Ṭāriq Aḥmad Muḥammad, and Majdī Fatḥī al-Sayyid. Ṭanṭā: Dār al-Ṣaḥāba līl-Turāth, 1995.

———. [*Tafsīr.*] *Al-Jāmi' li-Aḥkām al-Qur'ān.* 2nd ed. 20 vols. Ed. Aḥmad 'Abd al-'Alīm al-Bardūnī. Cairo: Dār al-Sha'b and Beirut: Dār Iḥyā' al-Turāth al-'Arabī, 1952-1953. Reprint.

———. *Al-Tadhkira bi-Aḥwāl al-Mawt wal-Ākhira.* 3 vols. Ed. Yūsuf 'Alī Badyawī. Damascus and Beirut: Dār Ibn Kathīr, 1999.

Al-Qushayrī. *[Tafsīr] Laṭā'if al-Ishārāt.* 6 vols. Ed. Ibrāhīm Basyūnī. Cairo: Dār al-Kitāb al-'Arabī, 1969.

———. *Al-Risāla.* Cairo: Dār al-Ṭibā'a al-'Āmira, 1287/1870. With Zakariyyā al-Anṣārī's commentary in the margins.

———. *Al-Risāla.* Eds. 'Abd al-Halīm Maḥmūd and Maḥmūd ibn al-Sharīf. Cairo: Rida Tawfīq 'Afīfī, 1974.

———. *Al-Rasā'il al-Qushayriyya.* Ed. Pīr Muḥammad Ḥasan. Sidon and Beirut: al-Maktabat al-'Aṣriyya, 1970.

Qūtlāy, Khalīl Ibrāhīm. *Al-Imām ʿAlī al-Qārī wa-Atharuhu fī ʿIlm al-Ḥadīth.* Beirut: Dār al-Bashā'ir al-Islāmiyya, 1987.

Al-Rāmahurmuzī. *Al-Muḥaddith al-Fāṣil.* Ed. Muḥammad al-Khaṭīb. Beirut: Dār al-Fikr, 1984[3].

Al-Rāzī, Fakhr al-Dīn. *I'tiqādāt Firaq al-Muslimīn wal-Mushrikīn.* Ed. 'Alī Sāmī al-Nashshār. Beirut: Dār al-Kutub al-'Ilmiyya, 1982.

———. *Mafātiḥ al-Ghayb* [*al-Tafsīr al-Kabīr*] with Abū al-Su'ūd's *Tafsīr.* 7 vols. Cairo: al-Maṭba'at al-'Āmira, 1308/1891.

———. *Manāqib al-Imām al-Shāfiʿī.* Ed. Aḥmad Ḥijāzī al-Saqqā. Cairo: Maktabat al-Kulliyyāt al-Azhariyya, 1986.

Al-Rāzī, Tammām. *Al-Fawā'id.* 2 vols. Ed. Ḥamdī ʿAbd al-Majīd al-Salafī. Ryadh: Maktabat al-Rushd, 1992.

Al-Rifā'ī, Yūsuf ibn al-Sayyid Hāshim. *Naṣīḥa li Ikhwāninā 'Ulamā' Najd.* Damascus: Iqra', 2000. *Advice to Our Brothers the Scholars of Najd,* followed by 'Alawī ibn Aḥmad al-Ḥaddād, *Refutation of the Innovator from Najd* (Introduction). Trans. Gibrīl F. Ḥaddād. Damascus, 2000 and 2002.

Riyāḍ, Muḥammad. *Uṣūl al-Fatwā wal-Qaḍā' fil-Madhhab al-Mālikī.* Dār al-

Bayḍā': s.n., 1996.

Sa'īd ibn Manṣūr. *Sunan.* 2 vols. Ed. Ḥabīb al-Raḥmān al-A'ẓamī. India: al-Dār al-Salafiyya, 1982.

Al-Sakhāwī, Muḥammad ibn 'Abd al-Raḥmān. *Fatḥ al-Mughīth bi-Sharḥ Alfiyyat al-Ḥadīth lil-ʿIrāqī.* 5 vols. Ed. ʿAlī Ḥusayn ʿAlī. Cairo: Maktabat al-Sunna, 1995.

———. *Al-I'lān wal-Tawbīkh li-Man Dhamma al-Tārīkh.* Beirut: Dār al-Kitāb al-'Arabī, 1979.

———. *Al-Jawāhir wal-Durar fī Manāqib Shaykh al-Islām Ibn Ḥajar.* Ed. Ḥāmid 'Abd al-Majīd and Ṭaha al-Zaynī. Cairo: Lajnat Iḥyā' al-Turāth al-Islāmī, 1986.

———. *Al-Maqāṣid al-Ḥasana.* Ed. Muḥammad 'Uthmān al-Khisht. Beirut: Dār al-Kitāb al-'Arabī, 1985.

———. *Al-Qawl al-Badī' fil-Ṣalāt 'alā al-Ḥabīb al-Shafī'.* Ed. Muḥammad 'Awwāma. Beirut: Mu'assasat al-Rayyān, 2002. Unedited: Beirut: Dār al-Kutub al-'Ilmiyya, 1987.

Ṣāliḥ ibn Aḥmad ibn Ḥanbal. *Sīrat al-Imām Aḥmad.* Ed. Muḥammad al-Zughlī. Beirut: al-Maktab al-Islāmī, 1997.

Al-Ṣāliḥī. *'Uqūd al-Jumān fī Manāqib al-Imām al-A'ẓam Abī Ḥanīfata al-Nu'mān.* Madīna: Maktabat al-Īmān, <1394/1974?>.

Al-Shāfi'ī. *Dīwān.* Ed. Muḥammad 'Abd al-Raḥīm. Beirut: Dār al-Fikr, 1995.

———. [*Musnad.*] *Tartīb Musnad al-Imām al-Aʿẓam wal-Mujtahid al-Muqaddam Abī ʿAbd Allāh Muḥammad ibn Idrīs al-Shāfiʿī.* 2 vols. Eds. Yūsuf ʿAlī al-Zawlawī al-Ḥasanī and ʿIzzat ʿAṭṭār al-Ḥusaynī. Cairo: n.p., 1951. Repr. Beirut: Dār al-Kutub al-ʿIlmiyya, n.d.

———. *Al-Risāla.* Ed. Aḥmad Muḥammad Shākir. Cairo: n.p., 1939.

———. *Al-Umm.* 8 vols. Ed. Muḥammad Zahrī al-Najjār. Beirut: Dār al-Ma'rifa, 1973.

Al-Shahrastānī. *Al-Milal wal-Niḥal.* 2 vols. Ed. Muḥammad Sayyid Kīlānī. Beirut: Dār al-Ma'rifa, 1984.

Al-Shaʿrānī. *Al-Yawāqīt wal-Jawāhir fī Bayān ʿAqā'id al-Akābir.* With *al-Kibrīt al-Aḥmar fī Bayān ʿUlūm al-Shaykh al-Akbar al-Muntakhab min Kitāb Lawāqiḥ al-Anwār al-Qudsiyya al-Mukhtaṣar min al-Futūḥāt al-Makkiyya.* 2 vols. in 1. Beirut: Dār Iḥyā' al-Turāth al-ʿArabī and Mu'assasat al-Tārīkh al-ʿArabī, 1997.

Shaṭṭā, Ibrāhīm al-Dusūqī. *Sīrat al-Shaykh al-Kabīr Abī 'Abd Allāh Muḥammad Ibn Khafīf al-Shīrāzī.* Cairo: al-Hay'at al-'Āmma li-Shu'ūn al-Maṭābi' al-Amīriyya, 1977.

Al-Shaṭṭī, Muḥammad Jamīl. *Aʿyān Dimashq fil-Qarn al-Thālith ʿAshar wa-Niṣf al-Qarn al-Rābiʿ Ashar.* Damascus: Dār al-Bashā'ir, 1994.

Al-Shawkānī. *Al-Badr al-Ṭāli' bi-Maḥāsin man Ba'd al-Qarn al-Sābi'.* Ed. Ḥusayn 'Abd Allāh al-'Umarī. Beirut: Dār al-Fikr, 1998.

———. *Nayl al-Awṭār.* 9 vols. Beirut: Dār al-Jīl, 1973.
Al-Shīrāzī, Abū Isḥāq. *Al-Ishāra ilā Madhhab Ahl al-Ḥaqq.* Ed. Muḥammad al-Zabīdī. Beirut: Dār al-Kitāb al-ʿArabī, 1999.
———. *Ṭabaqāt al-Fuqahā'.* With *Ṭabaqāt al-Shāfiʿiyya* by Ibn Hidāyat Allāh al-Muṣannif. Beirut: Dār al-Qalam, n.d.
Al-Sindī. *Sharḥ Sunan Ibn Mājah.* See under al-Suyūṭī.
Sirāj al-Dīn, ʿAbd Allāh *Sharḥ al-Bayqūniyya.* Aleppo: Maktabat Dār al-Falāḥ, n.d.
Al-Subkī, Taqī al-Dīn. *Al-Sayf al-Ṣaqīl fīl-Radd ʿalā Ibn Zafīl.* Ed. al-Kawtharī. Cairo: Maṭbaʿat al-Saʿāda, 1937.
———. *Shifāʾ al-Siqām bi-Ziyārati Khayri al-Anām.* Beirut: Lajnat al-Turāth al-ʿArabī, 1971.
Al-Suhaylī. *Al-Rawḍ al-Unuf.* 4 vols. Ed. Majdī Manṣūr al-Shūrī. Beirut: Dār al-Kutub al-ʿIlmiyya, 1997.
Al-Suyūṭī, Jalāl al-Dīn. *Al-Durar al-Muntathira fīl-Aḥādīth al-Mushtahara.* Ed. Muḥammad ʿAbd al-Raḥīm. Beirut: Dār al-Fikr, 1995.
———. *Al-Durr al-Manthūr fīl-Tafsīr al-Maʾthūr.* 8 vols. Beirut: Dār al-Fikr, 1994.
———. *Al-Ḥāwī lil-Fatāwī.* 2 vols. 3rd ed. Ed. Muḥammad Muḥyī al-Dīn ʿAbd al-Ḥamīd. Cairo: al-Maktabat al-Tijāriyyat al-Kubrā, 1959.
———. *Al-Itqān fī ʿUlūm al-Qurʾān.* 2 vols. Ed. Muṣṭafā Dīb al-Bughā. Damascus: Dār Ibn Kathīr, 1993.
———. *Al-Jāmiʿ al-Ṣaghīr min Ḥadīth al-Bashīr al-Nadhīr* ﷺ. 2 vols. Ed. Muḥammad Muḥyī al-Dīn ʿAbd al-Ḥamīd. Damascus: Maktabat al-Ḥalbūnī, 1983.
———. *Al-Laʾāliʾ al-Maṣnūʿa fīl-Aḥādīth al-Mawḍūʿa.* 2 vols. Beirut: Dār al-Maʿrifa, 1983.
———. *Miftāḥ al-Janna fīl-Iʿtiṣām bil-Sunna.* Ed. Badr ibn ʿAbd Allāh al-Badr. Beirut and Kuwait: Muʾassasat al-Rayyān and Dār al-Nafāʾis, 1993.
———. *Sharḥ al-Ṣudūr bi-Sharḥ Ḥāl al-Mawtā wal-Qubūr.* 3rd ed. Ed. Yūsuf ʿAlī Badyawī. Damascus and Beirut: Dār Ibn Kathīr, 1999.
———. *Sharḥ Sunan Ibn Mājah.* With Raḥmat Allāh al-Sindī, ʿAbd al-Ghanī al-Dihlawī, and Fakhr al-Ḥasan al-Gangohi. Karachi: Qadimi Kutub Khana, n.d. Includes Ibn Mājah's *Sunan.*
———. *Sharḥ Sunan al-Nasāʾī.* 9 vols. Ed. ʿAbd al-Fattāḥ Abū Ghudda. Aleppo & Beirut: Maktab al-Maṭbūʿāt al-Islāmiyya, 1986. Includes al-Nasāʾīs' *Sunan.*
———. *Ṭabaqāt al-Ḥuffāẓ.* Ed. ʿAlī ʿUmar. Cairo: Maktabat Wahba, 1973.
———. *Tadrīb al-Rāwī fī Sharḥ Taqrīb al-Nawawī.* 2 vols. Ed. Abū Qutayba al-Firyābī. 3rd ed. Damascus and Beirut: Dār al-Kalim al-Ṭayyib, 1996.
———. *Tadrīb al-Rāwī fī Sharḥ Taqrīb al-Nawawī.* 2 vols. Ed. ʿAbd al-

Wahhāb 'Abd al-Laṭīf. Riyadh: Maktabat al-Riyadh al-Ḥadītha, n.d.
———. *Taḥdhīr al-Khawāṣṣ min Akādhīb al-Quṣṣāṣ*. 2nd ed. Ed. Muḥammad Luṭfī al-Ṣabbāgh. Beirut: al-Maktab al-Islāmī, 1984.
———. *Tanwīr al-Ḥawālik bi-Sharḥ Muwaṭṭa' Mālik*. 2 vols. Cairo: al-Maktabat al-Tijāriyya al-Kubrā, 1969.
———. *Tārīkh al-Khulafā'*. Ed. Raḥāb Khiḍr 'Akkāwī. Beirut: Mu'assasat 'Izz al-Dīn, 1992.
Al-Ṭabarānī. *Al-Mu'jam al-Awsaṭ*. 10 vols. Eds. Ṭāriq ibn 'Awaḍ Allāh and 'Abd al-Muḥsin ibn Ibrāhīm al-Ḥusaynī. Cairo: Dār al-Ḥaramayn, 1995.
———. *Al-Mu'jam al-Kabīr*. 20 vols. Ed. Ḥamdī ibn 'Abd al-Majīd al-Salafī. Mosul: Maktabat al-'Ulūm wal-Ḥikam, 1983.
———. *Al-Mu'jam al-Saghīr*. 2 vols. Ed. Muḥammad Shakūr Maḥmūd. Beirut and Amman: Al-Maktab al-Islāmī, Dār 'Ammār, 1985.
———. *Musnad al-Shāmiyyīn*. 2 vols. Ed. Ḥamdī ibn 'Abd al-Majīd al-Salafī. Beirut: Mu'assasat al-Risāla, 1984.
Al-Ṭabarī, Muḥammad ibn Jarīr. *Jāmi' al-Bayān fī Tafsīr al-Qur'ān*. 30 vols. Beirut: Dār al-Ma'ārif, 1980; Dār al-Fikr, 1985.
———. *Tārīkh al-Umam wal-Mulūk*. 13 vols. in 6. Beirut: Dār al-Qāmūs al-Ḥadīth, n.d.
Al-Ṭabarī, Muḥibb al-Dīn. *Dhakhā'ir al-'Uqbā fī Manāqib Dhawī al-Qurbā*. Cairo: Dar al-Kutub al-Miṣriyya, n.d.
———. *Al-Riyāḍ al-Naḍira fī Manāqib al-'Ashara*. 2 vols. Ed. 'Īsā al-Ḥimayrī. Beirut: Dār al-Gharb al-Islāmī, 1996.
———. *Al-Samṭ al-Thamīn fī Manāqib Ummahāt al-Mu'minīn*. Ed. 'Abd al-Majīd Ṭu'ma Ḥalabī. Beirut: Dār al-Ma'rifa, 1997.
Al-Tahānawī. *I'lā' al-Sunan*. 21 vols. Ed. Muḥammad Taqī 'Uthmānī. Karachi: Idārat al-Qur'ān wal-'Ulūm al-Islamiyya, 1995. First two introductory volumes contain [1] al-Tahānawī's *Qawā'id fī 'Ulūm al-Ḥadīth*, ed. 'Abd al-Fattāḥ Abū Ghudda; [2] al-Kirānawī's *Fawā'id fī 'Ulūm al-Fiqh* and al-Tahānawī's *Abū Ḥanīfa wa-Aṣḥābuhu al-Muḥaddithūn*.
Al-Ṭaḥāwī. *Al-ʿAqīda al-Ṭaḥāwiyya*. Ed. Bassām ʿAbd al-Wahhāb al-Jābī. Damascus: Dār al-Bashā'ir, 1992.
———. *Al-ʿAqīda al-Ṭaḥāwiyya*. Ed. Muḥammad Nāṣir al-Albānī. 2nd ed. Beirut: al-Maktab al-Islāmī, 1993.
———. *Mushkil al-Āthār*. 4 vols. Hyderabad: Dā'irat al-Ma'ārif al-'Uthmāniyya, 1915. Repr. Beirut: Dār Sadir, n.d.
———. *Sharḥ Ma'ānī al-Āthār*. 4 vols. Ed. Muḥammad Zuhrī al-Najjār. Beirut: Dār al-Kutub al-'Ilmiyya, 1979.
———. *Sharḥ Mushkil al-Āthār*. 16 vols. Ed. Shu'ayb al-Arna'ūṭ. Beirut: Mu'assasat al-Risāla, 1994.
Al-Ṭayālisī, Abū Dāwūd. *Musnad*. Beirut: Dār al-Kitāb al-Lubnānī; Dār al-

Ma'rifa; Dār al-Tawfīq, n.d. All three are offset reprints of the 1321/1903 edition of Dā'irat al-Ma'ārif al-'Uthmāniyya in Hyderabad.

Al-Taymī, Ismā'īl. *Dalā'il al-Nubuwwa*. Ed. Muḥammad Muḥammad al-Ḥaddād. Riyadh: Dār Ṭayba, 1989.

Al-Tirmidhī. *Al-'Ilal*. See Abū Ṭālib al-Qāḍī's *'Ilal al-Tirmidhī al-Kabīr*.

———. *Al-Sunan*. See al-Mubārakfūrī, *Tuḥfat al-Aḥwadhī*.

Al-Turkmānī, Idrīs ibn Baydakīn. *Al-Luma' fil-Ḥawādith wal-Bida'*. 2 vols Ed. Subḥī Labīb. Cairo: al-Ma'had al-Almānī and Wiesbaden: Franz Steiner Verlag, 1986.

Al-'Uqaylī, *al-Ḍu'afā' min al-Ruwāt*. 4 vols. Ed. 'Abd al-Mu'ṭī Amīn Qal'ajī. Beirut: Dār al-Kutub al-'Ilmiyya, 1984.

Al-Yāfi'ī. *Marham al-'Ilal al-Mu'ḍila fī Daf' al-Shubah wal-Radd 'alā al-Mu'tazila*. Ed. E. Denison Ross. Calcutta: Asiatic Society of Bengal, 1910.

———. *Marham al-'Ilal al-Mu'ḍila fī Daf' al-Shubah wal-Radd 'alā al-Mu'tazila*. Ed. Maḥmūd Muḥammad Naṣṣār. Beirut: Dār al-Jīl, 1992.

Yāqūt al-Ḥamawī. *Mu'jam al-Buldān*. 5 vols. Beirut: Dār al-Fikr, n.d.

Al-Zabīdī, *Itḥāf al-Sādat al-Muttaqīn bi-Sharḥ Asrār Iḥyā' 'Ulūm al-Dīn*. Printed together with the text of the *Iḥyā'* in the margins. Also with 'Abd al-Qādir ibn 'Abd Allāh al-'Aydarūs Bā 'Alawī's *Ta'rīf al-Aḥyā' bi-Faḍā'il al-Iḥyā'* and al-Ghazzālī's *al-Imlā 'an Ishkālāt al-Iḥyā*. 10 vols. Cairo: al-Maṭba'at al-Maymuniyya, 1311/1893.

Al-Zarkashī. *Al-Tadhkira fil-Aḥādīth al-Mushtahara*. Ed. Muṣṭafā 'Abd al-Qādir 'Aṭā. Beirut: Dār al-Kutub al-'Ilmiyya, 1986.

Al-Zayla'ī. *Naṣb al-Rāya li-Aḥādīth al-Hidāya*. 4 vols. Ed. Muḥammad Yūsuf al-Binūrī. Cairo: Dār al-Ḥadīth, 1357/1938.

Al-Zarqānī. *Manāhil al-'Irfān fī 'Ulūm al-Qur'ān*. 2 vols. Beirut: Dār al-Fikr, 1996.

———. *Sharḥ al-Muwaṭṭa'*. 4 vols. Beirut: Dār al-Kutub al-'Ilmiyya, 1981.

Al-Ziriklī. *Al-A'lām*. 8 vols. Beirut: Dār al-'Ilm lil-Malāyīn, 1984.

www.ingramcontent.com/pod-product-compliance
Lightning Source LLC
Chambersburg PA
CBHW030507080526
44586CB00011B/99